Elements of Language

Fourth Course

TEXAS ANNOTATED TEACHER'S EDITION

Lee Odell

Richard Vacca

Renée Hobbs

Grammar, Usage, and Mechanics
Instructional Framework by

John E. Warriner

 HOLT, RINEHART AND WINSTON

A Harcourt Classroom Education Company

Austin • New York • Orlando • Atlanta • San Francisco • Boston • Dallas • Toronto • London

STAFF CREDITS

EDITORIAL

Director
Mescal Evler

Manager of Editorial Operations
Bill Wahlgren

Executive Editor
Kristine E. Marshall

Project Editors
Marcia L. Kelley
Suzanne Thompson

Annotated Teacher's Edition Editors
Eileen Joyce
Susan Lynch

Writing and Editing
Roger Boylan, David Bradford, Susan Britt, Karen Kolar, Barbara Knaggs, David Knaggs, Kevin Lemoine, Chi Nguyen, Kathryn Rogers, Jennifer Schwan, Mary Shaw

Copyediting
Michael Neibergall, *Copyediting Manager;* Mary Malone, *Senior Copyeditor;* Joel Bourgeois, Gabrielle Field, Suzi A. Hunn, Jane Kominek, Millicent Ondras, Theresa Reding, Désirée Reid, Kathleen Scheiner, Sarah Searcy, *Copyeditors*

Project Administration
Marie Price, *Managing Editor;* Lori De La Garza, *Editorial Operations Coordinator;* Tracy DeMont, Heather Cheyne, Mark Holland, Marcus Johnson, Jill O'Neal, Joyce Rector, Janet Riley, Kelly Tankersley, *Project Administration;* Gail Coupland, Elizabeth Dickson, Ruth Hooker, Margaret Sanchez, *Word Processing*

Editorial Permissions
Janet Harrington

ART, DESIGN AND PHOTO

Book Design
Senior Design Director
Diane Motz

Teresa Carrera-Paprota, *Designer*
Tim Hovde, *Design Associate*

Cover Design
Joe Melomo, *Design Director*

Graphic Services
Kristen Darby, *Manager*

PRODUCTION
Beth Prevelige, *Prepress Manager*
Simira Davis, *Supervisor*
Joan Lindsay, *Production Coordinator*

MANUFACTURING
Belinda Lopez, *Senior Production Coordinator*
Ben Saffer, *Production Assistant*

Texas Photo Credit
© 2000 Laurence Parent Photography

Copyright © 2001 by Holt, Rinehart and Winston

All rights reserved. No part of this publication may be reproduced or transmitted in any form or by any means, electronic or mechanical, including photocopy, recording, or any information storage and retrieval system, without permission in writing from the publisher.

Requests for permission to make copies of any part of the work should be mailed to the following address: Permissions Department, Holt, Rinehart and Winston, 1120 South Capital of Texas Highway, Austin, Texas 78746-6487.

Acknowledgments and other credits appear on pages 1032–1033 and 1034–1035, which are extensions of the copyright page.

Printed in the United States of America
ISBN 0-03-056681-9
1 2 3 4   048   03 02 01 00

How to Build a Bigger Texas

Holt, Rinehart and Winston has created *Elements of Language* with your Texas classroom in mind. We recognize that you want your students to be prepared for any reading and writing situation they encounter. With the adoption of the new TEKS, there are more and bigger challenges ahead, including increased emphasis on research and inquiry, viewing and representing, and error-free final drafts. *Elements of Language* can help you give your students the competence and confidence that result from solid language arts instruction.

Elements of Language gives you the tools to help students become more active readers and writers. In **Part 1: Communications**, the Reading Workshops demonstrate specific strategies for tackling the nonfiction texts students will encounter on the TAAS and other tests. The Writing Workshops provide a visual framework for writing, as well as extensive suggestions for prewriting and revising—helping you integrate test preparation into engaging, meaningful writing instruction.

Part 2: Sentences and Paragraphs provides practice in writing sentences and paragraphs and shows students how to identify areas in their drafts that need revision. These practice exercises allow you to improve student performance on TAAS writing tests by teaching specific strategies for revising and editing.

Each chapter in **Part 3: Grammar, Usage, and Mechanics** is based on Warriner's time-tested model for grammar instruction—rule, example, exercise. Writing Application exercises show students how to apply a rule or skill, creating a compelling context for grammar instruction and forging a solid connection between practice exercises and the editing process.

The speed and complexity of communication in the twenty-first century suggest a need for broadening language arts instruction. To help you prepare Texas students for a technological age, *Elements of Language* includes activities that ask students to access, view, critique, and create a range of media representations. Participation in the wider world requires new uses of language. With *Elements of Language* as a resource, you can build a better curriculum and a bigger world for your students.

Texas Teaching Resources

TAAS Tool Kit for Reading and Writing

Designed specifically for Texas classrooms, the tool kit addresses TAAS objectives for both reading and writing. These high-interest activities keep your students involved and challenged and allow them to monitor their own performance as they work to master TAAS objectives.

(Grades 6–8)

Preparation for TAAS

This resource helps you effectively integrate TAAS test preparation with the language arts instruction in *Elements of Language*. The booklet includes practice tests for reading in standardized formats, graphic organizers for writing, tips for test success, practice TAAS tests, and an answer key.

(Grades 6–10)

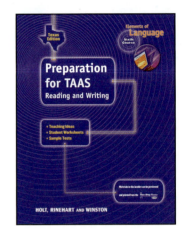

Preparing for English II End-of-Course Examination

This helpful booklet includes reading and writing practice tests, test-taking strategies, and writing models to prepare students for the English II End-of-Course Examination.

(Grades 9–10)

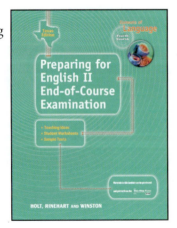

Lesson Planner Including Strategies for English-Language Learners, Texas Edition

Besides correlating instruction to the TEKS, TAAS, and EOCE, this invaluable planner focuses on how to plan instruction for the reading, writing, speaking, listening, viewing, and representing lessons in the *Pupil's Editions*. These lesson plans give suggestions for integrating composition instruction with grammar and with literature.

(Grades 6–12)

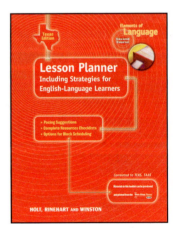

Texas Technology Resources

Media Literacy and Communication Skills, Texas Edition

The new opportunities and challenges of the technological age demand that students learn viewing and representing skills. In Texas, students must learn how to interpret a variety of media messages and performances and to produce visual media themselves. This package is designed to support the TEKS and the lessons in *Elements of Language* by addressing speaking, listening, viewing, and representing skills.

- **Videocassettes** provide video segments that demonstrate oral, visual, and media activities such as how to give speeches and make documentaries. Lessons on camera angles, visual effects, and strategies for media analysis are also included.

- *A How-to Handbook* guides students step-by-step through speaking, listening, and media-based activities.

- *Support and Practice* contains viewing guides, planning checklists, and transparencies to support each speaking, listening, viewing, and representing lesson in the *Pupil's Edition*.

- *A Teacher's Guide* includes annotations to the TEKS and options for teaching the oral-visual literacy lessons, including ideas for using the video segments.

(**Grades 6–12**)

One-Stop Planner CD-ROM with Test Generator for Macintosh® and Windows®, Texas Edition

Planning and managing lessons has never been easier than with the *One-Stop Planner CD-ROM*. This convenient, all-in-one planning software program includes teaching resources for *Elements of Language, Texas Edition,* plus valuable planning and assessment tools. The *One-Stop Planner* provides

- editable lesson plans
- previews of teaching resources
- an easy-to-use test generator

To preview a video segment or transparency, or to print out tests and worksheets for students, simply select and click.

(**Grades 6–12**)

Alignment with the Texas Essential Knowledge and Skills

 For your convenience, TAAS/TEKS alignments are also noted on the pages of the *Annotated Teacher's Edition* and on the *Texas Lesson Plans*.

 Watch the HRW Internet site (http://www.hrw.com/eol/tx) for updates on changes in the state assessment programs.

Required Language and Composition TEKS

This section of the Alignment covers those TEKS required by the Texas Proclamation for language and composition textbooks.

10.1 Writing/Purposes. The student writes in a variety of forms, including business, personal, literary, and persuasive texts, for various audiences and purposes. The student is expected to:

(A) write in a variety of forms with an emphasis on persuasive forms such as logical argument and expression of opinion, personal forms such as response to literature, reflective essay, and autobiographical narrative, and literary forms such as poems, plays, and stories;

Intro: 9–14, 15 **Ch 1:** 28–37, T29, 38, 48–49, 53 **Ch 2:** 66–73, T66, 74, 89 **Ch 3:** 104–109, 110, 125, T125 **Ch 4:** 138–145, 146, 165 **Ch 5:** 178–183, 184, 195–197, 198–202, 205, T205 **Ch 6:** 218–231, 232, 237–239, 249 **Ch 7:** 263–271, 272, 282, 283, 293 **Ch 8:** 306–314, 316–318, 337 **Ch 9:** T350–T351 **Ch 12:** 435 **Ch 13:** 465 **Ch 14:** 489 **Ch 15:** 509 **Ch 16:** 545 **Ch 17:** 571 **Ch 18:** 611 **Ch 19:** 635 **Ch 20:** 665 **Ch 21:** 691 **Ch 22:** 721 **Ch 23:** 737 **Ch 24:** 755 **Ch 25:** 777 **Ch 26:** 806 **QRH:** 939–952

(B) write in a voice and style appropriate to audience and purpose;

Intro: 10, 15 **Ch 1:** 29–30, 38, 48–49 **Ch 2:** 67–68, 74, T75 **Ch 3:** 105–106, T106, 110 **Ch 4:** 139–140, 165 **Ch 5:** 179, T182, 184, T186, 196–197, 202 **Ch 6:** 220–221, T220, 232, 237–239, 249 **Ch 7:** 264–266, T265, 272, 282, 283, 293 **Ch 8:** 307–309, 316–318, 337 **Ch 12:** 435 **Ch 13:** 465 **Ch 14:** 489 **Ch 16:** 545 **Ch 22:** 721 **Ch 23:** 737 **Ch 25:** 777 **Ch 26:** 806 **QRH:** 939–952

(C) organize ideas in writing to ensure coherence, logical progression, and support for ideas.

Intro: 10–11 **Ch 1:** 30–37, T36, 38 **Ch 2:** 70–73, T72, 74, T74 **Ch 3:** 106–109, 110 **Ch 4:** 141–145, 146 **Ch 5:** 181–183, T183, 184 **Ch 6:** 230–231, 232, 239 **Ch 7:** 271, T271, 272, T276, 283 **Ch 8:** 309–314, 316–318 **Ch 11:** 370–401 **Ch 15:** 509 **QRH:** 940–946

 Additional instruction, practice, and reinforcement for TEKS 10.1 can be found in the following ancillaries:

- Communications
- Preparation for TAAS
- TAAS Tool Kit
- Preparing for English II End-of-Course Examination
- Sentences, Paragraphs, and Compositions
- Grammar, Usage, and Mechanics
- HRW Internet Site

T = Teacher's Edition Page Number
Ch = Chapter
Intro = Introduction
QRH = Quick Reference Handbook

10.2 Writing/Writing Processes. The student uses recursive writing processes when appropriate. The student is expected to:

(A) use prewriting strategies to generate ideas, develop voice, and plan;

Intro: 10, 15 **Ch 1:** 28–29, T29, T30, T32, 31–34, T35, T36, T48 **Ch 2:** 66–67, T66, T69, 74, 89, T89 **Ch 3:** 104–105, T104, T107, T109, 110, 125, T125 **Ch 4:** 126–127, 138–139, T138, T139, T157 **Ch 5:** 178–179, T180, 184, T184, 196, T196 **Ch 6:** 218–220, T218, T219, T221, T227, T229, T231, T233, 249 **Ch 7:** 263–264, T263, T264, 282, 283 **Ch 8:** 306–307, T306, T307, T312, T316, T319, T329, T330, T332, T334 **Ch 11:** 376–378 **Ch 12:** 435 **Ch 13:** 465 **Ch 14:** 489 **Ch 15:** 509 **Ch 16:** 545 **Ch 17:** 571 **Ch 18:** 611 **Ch 19:** 635 **Ch 20:** 665 **Ch 21:** 691 **Ch 22:** 721 **Ch 23:** 737 **Ch 24:** 755 **Ch 25:** 777 **QRH:** 915, 952–957

(B) develop drafts both alone and collaboratively by organizing and reorganizing content and by refining style to suit occasion, audience, and purpose;

Intro: T10, 11, 15 **Ch 1:** T31, T33, T34, T36, 38, 42–43, T42, T43, T44, 48–49 **Ch 2:** T70, 72–73, 74, T74, 78–80, T78, T79, 82–83 **Ch 3:** 106, T106, T109, 110, T110, 114–115 **Ch 4:** T142, 143, 146, 150–153, T157, T165 **Ch 5:** T180, T181, T182, T183, 184, 188–191, T194, T205 **Ch 6:** T221, T229, 230, 232, T238, 239, 240–243, T242, T247, 249, T249 **Ch 7:** T264, T265, T267, T271, 272, 276–278, T277 **Ch 8:** T307, T311, T312, 316–318, T317, 321–323 **Ch 9:** T349, T350–T351 **Ch 10:** T358 **Ch 11:** T376, T379, T384, T391 **Ch 12:** 435 **Ch 25:** 777

(C) proofread writing for appropriateness of organization, content, style, and conventions;

Intro: 12–13 **Ch 1:** 42–44, T42, 46–47, T47, 48–49 **Ch 2:** T62, 78–81, T78, T79, 82–83 **Ch 3:** 114–117 **Ch 4:** 150–153, T151, 155, T155 **Ch 5:** 188–191, 197 **Ch 6:** 240–243, 244–245, **Ch 7:** 276–278, T276 **Ch 8:** 321–323, T323 **Ch 9:** 343 **Ch 10:** T368 **Ch 12:** 435 **Ch 13:** 465 **Ch 15:** 509 **Ch 20:** 665 **Ch 21:** 691 **Ch 22:** 721 **Ch 23:** 737 **Ch 24:** 755 **Ch 26:** 806 **QRH:** 957–958

(D) refine selected pieces frequently to publish for general and specific audiences;

Intro: 13 **Ch 1:** 46–47 **Ch 2:** 82–83 **Ch 3:** 118–119 **Ch 4:** 155–156 **Ch 5:** 193–194, T194, 197, 202, T205 **Ch 6:** 244–245 **Ch 7:** 280–281, T281 **Ch 8:** T321, 325–326 **Ch 9:** T350–T351 **Ch 14:** 489 **Ch 18:** 611 **Ch 21:** 691

(E) use technology for aspects of creating, revising, editing, and publishing texts.

Intro: 10–11 **Ch 1:** 34, T40, 45, T48, 53, T53 **Ch 2:** T68, T81, 83 **Ch 3:** 115, 117 **Ch 4:** T150, 153–154, T154, T159 **Ch 5:** T166, T183, 191, 202, T202 **Ch 6:** 219, 222–225, T225, T241, 243, T247, 249, T249 **Ch 7:** T266, 279, T283 **Ch 8:** 312, T312, T313, T318, 324, T329, T333 **Ch 9:** T344 **Ch 11:** 383 **Ch 13:** 465 **Ch 14:** 489 **Ch 16:** 545 **Ch 18:** 611 **Ch 19:** 635 **Ch 20:** 665 **Ch 22:** 721 **Ch 23:** T732, 737 **Ch 24:** 755 **Ch 25:** 777 **Ch 26:** 806 **QRH:** 849–855, 947

Additional instruction, practice, and reinforcement for TEKS 10.2 can be found in the following ancillaries:

- Communications
- Preparation for TAAS
- TAAS Tool Kit
- Preparing for English II End-of-Course Examination
- Sentences, Paragraphs and Compositions
- Grammar, Usage, and Mechanics
- Writer's Workshop 2 CD-ROM
- Language Workshop CD-ROM
- HRW Internet Site

10.3 Writing/Grammar/Usage/Conventions/Spelling. The student relies increasingly on the conventions and mechanics of written English, including the rules of usage and grammar, to write clearly and effectively. The student is expected to:

(A) produce legible work that shows accurate spelling and correct use of the conventions of punctuation and capitalization such as italics and ellipses;

Intro: 12–13, T13 Ch 1: T32, 46–47 Ch 2: 82 Ch 3: 118 Ch 4: 155 Ch 5: 193 Ch 6: T238, T242, 244 Ch 7: 280, T283 Ch 8: 325 Ch 9: 340–351, T348–T349 Ch 10: 352–369 Ch 12: 435 Ch 13: T459 Ch 14: 489 Ch 15: T494, 509 Ch 17: T561, T562 Ch 18: T578 Ch 19: T630 Ch 20: 665 Ch 21: 666–690, T668, T672, T674, T678, T683, T686, T687, 691 Ch 22: 692–720, T694, T695, T696, T701, T703, T704, T706, T708, T714, T716, T717, 721 Ch 23: 722–734, T724, T726, T727, T728, T730, T731, 737 Ch 24: 738–754, T740, T741, T742, T743, T746, T747, T751, 755 Ch 25: 756–776, T760, T761, T762, T763, T764, T765, T767, T768, T769, T770, T771, T772, T773, 777 Ch 26: 778–805, T779, T780, T782, T787, T792, T793, T794, T795, T796, T800, T802, 806 Ch 27: 810–843 QRH: 849, 960, 964–966, 967–968, 970–973, 975–976, 980–981

(B) demonstrate control over grammatical elements such as subject-verb agreement, pronoun-antecedent agreement, verb forms, and parallelism;

Intro: 12–13 Ch 1: 46–47 Ch 2: T78, 82 Ch 3: 118 Ch 4: 155 Ch 5: 192, 193 Ch 6: 244 Ch 7: 278, 280 Ch 8: 325 Ch 9: 340–351, T343 Ch 10: 352–369, T355, T359 Ch 11: T392–T393 Ch 12: 404–434, T405, T406, T409, T412, T413, T420, T424, T426, T427, T428, T431 Ch 13: 436–464, T438, T439, T440, T450, T451, T452, T453, T454, T458, T461 Ch 14: T468, T470, T473, T476 Ch 15: 490–508, T492, T493, T494, T496, T497, T499, T500, T501, T502, T505 Ch 16: 510–544, T511, T513, T514, T518, T523, T525, T533, T534, T536, T537, 545 Ch 17: 546–570, T550, T552, T554, T557, T558, T559, T560, T562, T565, T567, 571 Ch 18: 572–610, T575, T576, T586, T603, T605, 611 Ch 19: 612–634, T617, T619, T628, T630, 635 Ch 20: 636–664, T639, T642, T648, T649, T652, T653, 665 Ch 21: 691 Ch 22: T701, T706, T717, T718 Ch 23: T725 Ch 24: T746 Ch 27: 810–831, T814, T817, T821, T839 QRH: 960–985

(C) compose increasingly more involved sentences that contain gerunds, participles, and infinitives in their various functions;

Ch 1: 44 Ch 3: 116, T116, T117, 118 Ch 5: 189–190 Ch 9: 342–344 Ch 10: 355, 356, T365, 366–367, T366 Ch 12: T418 Ch 14: 472–483, T473, T475, T477, T480, T481, T483, T484, T486, 489 Ch 18: 572–581, T576, T577, T578, T580, T582, T583, T584, T587, T588, T589, T591, T592, T595, T597, T602 Ch 19: T615 Ch 22: 721 Ch 27: T819 QRH: 973, 978

(D) produce error-free writing in the final draft.

Intro: 13 Ch 1: 46–47 Ch 2: 83 Ch 3: 118 Ch 4: 155 Ch 5: 193 Ch 6: 244 Ch 7: 280 Ch 8: T323, 325, T326 Ch 9: 340–351 Ch 10: 352–369 Ch 12: 404–434 Ch 13: 436–464, 465 Ch 14: 466–488, 489 Ch 15: 490–508, 509 Ch 16: 510–544, 545 Ch 17: 546–570, 571 Ch 18: 572–610, T602, 611 Ch 19: 612–634, 635 Ch 20: 636–664, 665 Ch 21: 666–690, 691 Ch 22: 692–720, T716 Ch 23: 722–734, 737 Ch 24: 738–754, 755 Ch 25: 756–776, 777 Ch 26: 778–805, 806 QRH: 849, 939–952, 960–985

Additional instruction, practice, and reinforcement for TEKS 10.3 can be found in the following ancillaries:

- Grammar, Usage, and Mechanics
- Combining Sentences
- Preparation for TAAS
- TAAS Tool Kit
- Preparing for English II End-of-Course Examination
- Daily Language Activity Transparencies
- Language Workshop CD-ROM

Required Language and Composition TEKS

10.4 Writing/Inquiry/Research. The student uses writing as a tool for learning. The student is expected to:

(A) use writing to formulate questions, refine topics, and clarify ideas;

Ch 1: T17, T18, T24, T48 **Ch 2:** T56, T58 **Ch 3:** T92, T104, T117, 125 **Ch 4:** T139, T143, T150, T158, T165 **Ch 5:** T170, T179, T193, T200 **Ch 6:** 221–222, 249 **Ch 8:** T306, T316, T329 **Ch 9:** T348 **Ch 11:** T401

(B) use writing to discover, organize, and support what is known and what needs to be learned about a topic;

Ch 2: T56, T62, 89 **Ch 3:** T104, T109, 125 **Ch 4:** 138–145, T145, 165 **Ch 5:** 205 **Ch 6:** 218–231, T228, 249 **Ch 7:** 263–271, 293 **Ch 8:** 306–314, T307 **Ch 11:** T398–T399, T401 **QRH:** 914, 950–951, 959

(C) compile information from primary and secondary sources in systematic ways using available technology;

Intro: 10–11, 15 **Ch 2:** T67, 69–70, T78 **Ch 3:** 109, T109, T125 **Ch 4:** 140–141, T141, 158, T165 **Ch 5:** T182 **Ch 6:** 208, 214–215, 219–220, 222–229, T222, T224, T225, T240, T249 **Ch 7:** 266–270 **Ch 8:** 300, T300, 333

(D) represent information in a variety of ways such as graphics, conceptual maps, and learning logs;

Ch 1: T30, 33, T36 **Ch 2:** T65, 69–70, T72, T85, T88, 89, T89 **Ch 3:** T98, T109, T112, 117, 125 **Ch 4:** T126, 127, T137, T145, T157 **Ch 5:** T166, T180, 205, T205 **Ch 6:** 206–207, T219, T223, T227, 230–231, T231, T238, 246 **Ch 7:** 271, T273, 279 **Ch 8:** T295, 312–314, 316–318, T323, 324, 327–328, T330, T334 **Ch 11:** T389 **Ch 21:** 691 **QRH:** 855–860, 948–949

(E) use writing as a study tool to clarify and remember information;

Ch 1: T24, T43, T47, T51 **Ch 2:** T83 **Ch 3:** T119 **Ch 4:** T135, T156, T161, T164 **Ch 5:** T177, T189, T194, T202, T204 **Ch 6:** T223, T232, T237, T238, T245, T247, T249 **Ch 7:** T281 **Ch 8:** T303, T319, T329, T336 **Ch 11:** T387

(F) compile written ideas and representations into reports, summaries, or other formats and draw conclusions;

Intro: 15 **Ch 2:** 85, 89 **Ch 3:** 125 **Ch 4:** T165 **Ch 5:** T194, T200 **Ch 6:** 218–231, T228, 232, 239, 249 **Ch 8:** 327–328, 337 **QRH:** 914

(G) analyze strategies that writers in different fields use to compose.

Ch 1: T39 **Ch 4:** T149 **Ch 5:** 205, T205 **Ch 6:** T233, T234, T239, T246, T249 **Ch 7:** T253, T259, T273, 293 **Ch 8:** T297, T320, T327, 337, T337 **Ch 9:** T345 **Ch 10:** T368 **Ch 11:** T377, T394, T396, T397

Additional instruction, practice, and reinforcement for TEKS 10.4 can be found in the following ancillaries:

- Communications
- Designing Your Writing
- Preparation for TAAS
- TAAS Tool Kit
- Writer's Workshop 2 CD-ROM

10.5 Writing/Evaluation. The student evaluates his/her own writing and the writings of others. The student is expected to:

(A) evaluate writing for both mechanics and content;

Intro: 12–13, T12 Ch 1: T42, 43–44, T43, 46–47 Ch 2: T70, T79, T80, T81 Ch 3: 114–117, 118 Ch 4: 150–153, T153, 155 Ch 5: T181, T182, 188–191, T188, 193, T196 Ch 6: T237, 240–243, 244, T245 Ch 7: T275, 276–278, T277, 280 Ch 8: T303, T312, 321–323, 325, T326 Ch 9: T350–T351 Ch 10: T358 Ch 13: T438 Ch 16: T538 Ch 17: 571 Ch 18: T603 Ch 21: 691 Ch 22: T717 Ch 25: T772 Ch 26: T800

(B) respond productively to peer review of his/her own work.

Intro: 12, T12 Ch 1: 33, 42–43, T42, T43, 47 Ch 2: T70, T73, 78–79, T79 Ch 3: 114–115, T115 Ch 4: 150–153, T153 Ch 5: T181, T182, 188–189, T188, T189 Ch 6: T215, 240–242, T240 Ch 7: 276–277, T277 Ch 8: 321–322, 322–323 Ch 13: 465 Ch 16: T513, 545 Ch 17: T567, 571 Ch 20: 665 Ch 26: 806

Additional instruction, practice, and reinforcement for TEKS 10.5 can be found in the following ancillaries:

- Grammar, Usage, and Mechanics
- Communications
- Preparation for TAAS
- TAAS Tool Kit
- Preparing for English II End-of-Course Examination
- Language Workshop CD-ROM

10.14 Listening/Speaking/Critical Listening. The student listens attentively for a variety of purposes. The student is expected to:

(A) focus attention, interpret, respond, and evaluate speaker's message;

Ch 1: T31, T33, T49, T53 Ch 2: T84 Ch 3: 120–121 Ch 4: 161 Ch 7: 291–292 Ch 10: T363 QRH: 906

(B) engage in critical, empathic, appreciative, and reflective listening.

Ch 1: T31, T49 Ch 2: T84 Ch 3: T120 Ch 4: T161, 165 Ch 7: 291–292 Ch 9: T349 Ch 10: T363 QRH: 907–910

Additional instruction, practice, and reinforcement for TEKS 10.14 can be found in the following ancillaries:

- Media Literacy and Communication Skills
- Assessment Alternatives

10.15 Listening/Speaking/Evaluation. The student listens to analyze, appreciate, and evaluate oral performances and presentations. The student is expected to:

(A) listen and respond appropriately to presentations and performances of peers or published works such as original essays or narratives, interpretations of poetry, and individual or group performances of scripts;

Ch 1: T31, T49 **Ch 4:** T141 **Ch 5:** T198, T199, 204, 205 **Ch 7:** 290–291, T293 **Ch 9:** T357 **QRH:** 907

(B) identify and analyze the effect of artistic elements within literary texts such as character development, rhyme, imagery, and language;

Ch 1: 37, 49 **Ch 5:** 168, 173–175, 180, 195, T196, 204, 205 **Ch 7:** 293 **Ch 10:** T358 **QRH:** 907

(C) evaluate informative and persuasive presentations of peers, public figures, and media presentations;

Ch 3: 120–121 **Ch 4:** T152, T160, 161 **Ch 5:** 185, T198, T199 **Ch 7:** 291–292, T291 **Ch 8:** 315, 327–328 **QRH:** T907, 908, 932–935

(D) evaluate artistic performances of peers, public presenters, and media presentations;

Ch 1: T49 **Ch 5:** T198, T199, T201, 204, T204 **Ch 7:** T292 **Ch 8:** 327–328 **QRH:** 907

(E) use feedback to evaluate his/her own effectiveness and set goals for future presentations.

Ch 1: T49 **Ch 3:** 120–121 **Ch 4:** 160, T161 **Ch 5:** 204 **Ch 7:** 289, T289, T290 **Ch 8:** 336 **QRH:** 934

Additional instruction, practice, and reinforcement for TEKS 10.15 can be found in the following ancillaries:

- Media Literacy and Communication Skills
- Assessment Alternatives

10.16 Listening/Speaking/Purposes. The student speaks clearly and effectively for a variety of purposes and audiences. The student is expected to:

(A) use the conventions of oral language effectively;

Ch 1: 53 **Ch 3:** 120–121, 125 **Ch 4:** T141, 158–161, 165 **Ch 5:** T199, 203–204, T205 **Ch 6:** 248, 249 **Ch 7:** 288–291, 293 **Ch 8:** 337 **Ch 12:** 435 **QRH:** 896–905

(B) use informal, standard, and technical language effectively to meet the needs of purpose, audience, occasion, and task;

Ch 1: 53 **Ch 2:** 54–55 **Ch 3:** 90–91, 120–121, 124 **Ch 4:** 126–127, T141, 157, 159, T159, 165 **Ch 5:** 166–167, T205 **Ch 6:** 206–207, 248, 249 **Ch 7:** 250–251, 288, T289, 293 **Ch 8:** 294–295, 337 **QRH:** 864–865, 896–905

(C) prepare, organize, and present a variety of informative and persuasive messages effectively with an emphasis on persuasion;

Ch 1: 53 **Ch 2:** T73, 89 **Ch 3:** 125 **Ch 4:** 158–161, T159, 165 **Ch 5:** T191, T199 **Ch 6:** 249 **Ch 7:** 288–292, T289, T292, T293 **Ch 8:** 337 **QRH:** 897–903

(D) use effective verbal and nonverbal strategies in presenting oral messages;

Ch 2: 89 **Ch 4:** T141, 159, T159, 160 **Ch 5:** T190, 203–204, T204, 205 **Ch 6:** 249 **Ch 7:** 289–291, T289, 293 **QRH:** T897, 900

10.16 **(E)** ask clear questions for a variety of purposes and respond appropriately to the questions of others;
Ch 1: T31, T33 **Ch 3:** 120–121, 124 **Ch 4:** T132, T141, T159, 160–161, 165, T165 **Ch 5:** T199, 203 **Ch 8:** 337 **QRH:** 902–903

(F) make relevant contributions in conversations and discussions.
Ch 1: T16, T17, T18, T21, T22, T28, T33, T42, T43, T46, T53 **Ch 2:** 54–55, T56, T67, T73 **Ch 3:** 90–91, T92–T93, T94–T95, T118, 120–121, T120, T122 **Ch 4:** 126–127, T127, T128, T132, T133, T141, T143, T146, T155, T158, T160, T162, T164 **Ch 5:** 166–167, T167, T178, T180, T182, T183, T184, T188, T193, T198, T200 **Ch 6:** 206–207 **Ch 7:** 250–251 **Ch 8:** 294–295 **QRH:** 901–902, 904–905

Additional instruction, practice, and reinforcement for TEKS 10.16 can be found in the following ancillaries:

- Media Literacy and Communication Skills
- Assessment Alternatives

10.17 Listening/Speaking/Presentations. The student prepares and presents informative and persuasive messages. The student is expected to:

(A) present and advance a clear thesis and logical points, claims, or arguments to support messages;
Intro: 15 **Ch 1:** 53 **Ch 2:** T73, 89 **Ch 3:** 125 **Ch 4:** 158, 165 **Ch 5:** T199 **Ch 6:** 249 **Ch 7:** 288–289, T289, T293 **Ch 8:** 337 **QRH:** 897–903

(B) choose valid proofs from reliable sources to support claims;
Ch 2: 89 **Ch 3:** 125 **Ch 4:** 165 **Ch 5:** T199 **Ch 6:** 249 **Ch 7:** 289, T289, T293 **Ch 8:** 337 **QRH:** T897

(C) use appropriate appeals to support claims and arguments;
Ch 2: 89 **Ch 3:** 125 **Ch 4:** 158–161, 165 **Ch 6:** 249 **Ch 7:** 289, T289, 298 **QRH:** 896–897, T897

(D) use language and rhetorical strategies skillfully in informative and persuasive messages;
Intro: 15 **Ch 1:** 53 **Ch 2:** T73, 89 **Ch 3:** 125 **Ch 4:** T159, 165 **Ch 5:** T191 **Ch 6:** 249 **Ch 7:** 288–290, T289, T291, T293 **Ch 8:** 337 **QRH:** 897–903

(E) use effective nonverbal strategies such as pitch and tone of voice, posture, and eye contact;
Ch 2: 89 **Ch 3:** 125 **Ch 4:** 159, T159, 160, 165 **Ch 5:** 203–204, T204, 205 **Ch 6:** 249 **Ch 7:** 289–291, T289, T293 **Ch 8:** 337 **QRH:** T897, 900

(F) make informed, accurate, truthful, and ethical presentations.
Intro: 15 **Ch 2:** 89 **Ch 3:** 125 **Ch 4:** 158–161, 165 **Ch 6:** 249 **Ch 7:** 289, T293 **Ch 8:** 337 **QRH:** 896–903, T897

Additional instruction, practice, and reinforcement for TEKS 10.17 can be found in the following ancillaries:

- Media Literacy and Communication Skills
- Assessment Alternatives

10.19 Viewing/Representing/Interpretation. The student understands and interprets visual representations. The student is expected to:

(A) describe how meanings are communicated through elements of design such as shape, line, color, and texture;
   Intro: T2   **Ch 1:** T16   **Ch 2:** T54, T86   **Ch 3:** T90   **Ch 4:** T126, 153–154   **Ch 5:** T166   **Ch 6:** T206, T213   **Ch 7:** T250, 284–287, 293   **Ch 8:** T294, 296–300, T301, 303, T332, T337   **QRH:** 936

(B) analyze relationships, ideas, and cultures as represented in various media;
   Ch 2: 84–85   **Ch 3:** 122–124, T122, T123   **Ch 5:** 200   **Ch 7:** 284–287   **QRH:** 928–938

(C) distinguish the purposes of various media forms such as informative texts, entertaining texts, and advertisements.
   Ch 2: 84–85, T84   **Ch 7:** T250, 284–287, 293   **Ch 8:** T295, 296–300, 303, 327–328, 329–336, 337   **QRH:** 928–938

Additional instruction, practice, and reinforcement for TEKS 10.19 can be found in the following ancillaries:
- Media Literacy and Communication Skills
- Designing Your Writing
- HRW Internet Site

10.20 Viewing/Representing/Analysis. The student analyzes and critiques the significance of visual representations. The student is expected to:

(A) investigate the source of a media presentation or production such as who made it and why it was made;
   Ch 2: 84–85, 86–88   **Ch 3:** 122–124   **Ch 4:** 162–164   **Ch 6:** 247–248   **Ch 7:** 284–287   **QRH:** 932–935, 936–938

(B) deconstruct media to get the main idea of the message's content;
   Ch 1: T51   **Ch 2:** T68, 84–85, T84, 86–88, T87   **Ch 3:** 122–124, 125   **Ch 4:** 162–164   **Ch 5:** 198–202   **Ch 6:** 246, 247–248   **Ch 7:** T250, 284–287, T285   **Ch 8:** T301, 327–328, T327   **QRH:** 928–931, 932–935, 936–938

(C) evaluate and critique the persuasive techniques of media messages such as glittering generalities, logical fallacies, and symbols;
   Ch 2: 87–88, T87   **Ch 3:** 122–124   **Ch 4:** 163–164   **Ch 7:** 284–287   **Ch 8:** 296–300, T300, T301, 303, T315, 327–328, 337

(D) recognize how visual and sound techniques or design convey messages in media such as special effects, editing, camera angles, reaction shots, sequencing, and music;
   Ch 1: 50–52   **Ch 2:** 85, T86, 87–88, T87   **Ch 4:** 163   **Ch 5:** 200–203, T200, T201   **Ch 8:** 327–328, T327, 331–333, T331   **QRH:** 928–931, 932–935, 936–938

(E) recognize genres such as nightly news, newsmagazines, and documentaries and identify the unique properties of each;
   Ch 2: 84–85   **Ch 3:** 125   **Ch 4:** 162–164   **Ch 6:** 246   **Ch 7:** 284–287   **QRH:** 928–932, 934

10.20 (F) compare, contrast, and critique various media coverage of the same event such as in newspapers, television, and on the Internet.

Ch 2: 84–85, 86–88, 89   **Ch 3:** T125   **Ch 8:** T301, 337   **QRH:** 928–935

Additional instruction, practice, and reinforcement for TEKS 10.20 can be found in the following ancillaries:

- Media Literacy and Communication Skills
- Designing Your Writing
- HRW Internet Site

10.21 Viewing/Representing/Production. The student produces visual representations that communicate with others. The student is expected to:

(A) examine the effect of media on constructing his/her own perception of reality;

Ch 3: 122–124, T123   **Ch 7:** 284–287   **Ch 8:** 329–336   **QRH:** 933

(B) use a variety of forms and technologies such as videos, photographs, and web pages to communicate specific messages;

Ch 1: 45, 50–52, 53, T53   **Ch 3:** 125   **Ch 4:** 160, 165   **Ch 5:** 205   **Ch 7:** T285, 293   **Ch 8:** T308, T311, 312–314, 329–336, T329, T333, 337   **Ch 10:** T363   **Ch 24:** 755

(C) use a range of techniques to plan and create a media text and reflect critically on the work produced;

Ch 1: 50–52, T51, 53   **Ch 5:** T200   **Ch 7:** T285, 293   **Ch 8:** T308, T311, 312–314, T313, T314, 316–318, 329–336, T335, T336

(D) create media products to include a five- to six-minute documentary, a print ad, an editorial, a flier, a movie critique, or an illustrated children's book to engage specific audiences;

Ch 1: 50–52, 53   **Ch 3:** 125   **Ch 5:** 198–202, 205, T205   **Ch 7:** T285, 293   **Ch 8:** 306–314, T308, 315, 316–318, 319–320, 321–324, 329–336, T329, T335, 337, T337   **Ch 20:** 665

(E) create, present, test, and revise a project and analyze a response using data-gathering techniques such as questionnaires, group discussions, and feedback forms.

Ch 1: 50–52   **Ch 4:** 160–161, T160   **Ch 8:** T313, 329–336

Additional instruction, practice, and reinforcement for TEKS 10.21 can be found in the following ancillaries:

- Media Literacy and Communication Skills
- Designing Your Writing
- HRW Internet Site

Additional TEKS

This section of the Alignment covers those TEKS not required by the Texas Proclamation for language and composition textbooks.

10.6 Reading/Word Identification/Vocabulary Development. The student acquires an extensive vocabulary through reading and systematic word study. The student is expected to:

(A) expand vocabulary through wide reading, listening, and discussing;
Ch 1: T37   **Ch 3:** T110

(B) rely on context to determine meanings of words and phrases such as figurative language, idioms, multiple meaning words, and technical vocabulary;
Ch 1: 26   **Ch 2:** 64, T64   **Ch 3:** T110   **Ch 4:** 136   **Ch 6:** 216, 217   **Ch 8:** 304   **QRH:** 887, 921–922

(C) apply meanings of prefixes, roots, and suffixes in order to comprehend;
Ch 3: 102   **Ch 5:** 176   **Ch 26:** 781, 782   **QRH:** 887–888, 891–895, 979–980, 984

(D) research word origins as an aid to understanding meanings, derivations, and spellings as well as influences on the English language;
Ch 5: 176   **Ch 21:** T670   **Ch 24:** T741   **Ch 26:** T789   **QRH:** 847, 861–863, 890

(E) use reference material such as glossary, dictionary, thesaurus, and available technology to determine precise meanings and usage;
Ch 1: 26, T31   **Ch 2:** T64   **Ch 3:** 102   **Ch 6:** 216, T216   **Ch 7:** 261   **Ch 13:** T442   **Ch 16:** T520
Ch 17: T561   **Ch 18:** T577   **Ch 20:** 638, T638, T640, T641, T645, T652   **Ch 22:** T713   **QRH:** 846–848

(F) discriminate between connotative and denotative meanings and interpret the connotative power of words;
Ch 7: 259, 261, 269, T289   **QRH:** 888

(G) read and understand analogies.
Ch 2: T61   **Ch 7:** 285, 287   **Ch 10:** T363   **QRH:** 888, 918–920

Additional instruction, practice, and reinforcement for TEKS 10.6 can be found in the following ancillaries:

- Communications
- Vocabulary Workshop and Tests
- Alternative Readings
- Grammar, Usage, and Mechanics
- Preparing for English II End-of-Course Examination

T = Teacher's Edition Page Number   Intro = Introduction
Ch = Chapter   QRH = Quick Reference Handbook

10.7 Reading/Comprehension. The student comprehends selections using a variety of strategies. The student is expected to:

(A) establish a purpose for reading such as to discover, interpret, and enjoy;
Intro: 4–6, T5, 15 **Ch 2:** 56, T56 **Ch 3:** 96 **Ch 4:** 128, T129, T132 **Ch 5:** T167, 168 **Ch 6:** 208 **Ch 7:** 251 **Ch 8:** 296, T316 **QRH:** 883

(B) draw upon his/her own background to provide connection to texts;
Intro: 4–6, T8 **Ch 1:** 18–23, T18, T20, T21, 27, T28 **Ch 3:** T92–T93, T123 **Ch 4:** 128–134, T128 **Ch 5:** T167–T168, 168–173, T168–T169, T198 **Ch 6:** T207, T208, T218, T219, T229, T240, T248 **Ch 8:** T299 **QRH:** 877

(C) monitor his/her own reading strategies and make modifications when understanding breaks down such as by rereading, using resources, and questioning;
Intro: 5, 7, 15 **Ch 2:** T58–T59 **Ch 4:** T131, 137 **Ch 5:** T170, 177 **Ch 6:** 208–215, T210, 217 **Ch 7:** 262 **Ch 8:** T296–T297, 305

(D) construct images such as graphic organizers based on text descriptions and text structures;
Intro: T6, 8 **Ch 2:** T62, 63, T63, 89 **Ch 3:** T100, 101 **Ch 4:** T131, 135, 157 **Ch 5:** 205 **Ch 7:** 260 **QRH:** 878–881, 912

(E) analyze text structures such as compare and contrast, cause and effect, and chronological ordering for how they influence understanding;
Ch 1: 35–36 **Ch 2:** 56–62, T63 **Ch 3:** 92–101, T99, 109, T112, T123, T125 **Ch 4:** T129–T130, 137 **Ch 6:** T230 **QRH:** 876–877, 885–886

(F) produce summaries of texts by identifying main ideas and their supporting details;
Intro: 6–7 **Ch 1:** 22, T24 **Ch 2:** 56–59, 62–63, T62, 65, T84 **Ch 4:** 165 **Ch 5:** 177 **Ch 6:** 208–214 **Ch 11:** 371 **QRH:** 881, 884–885

(G) draw inferences such as conclusions, generalizations, and predictions and support them with text evidence and experience;
Intro: 4–8, 15 **Ch 1:** 18–23, T22, T24, 27 **Ch 2:** T56, 71, T84 **Ch 3:** 92–97, T94–T95, 103 **Ch 4:** 128–134, T129–T130, T131 **Ch 5:** 168–173 **Ch 8:** T296–T297 **Ch 11:** 396 **QRH:** 877–878, 881

(H) use study strategies such as skimming and scanning, note taking, outlining, and using study-guide questions to better understand texts;
Intro: 5–7, T6, 15 **Ch 1:** 27 **Ch 2:** T56, T58–T59, T62, T63 **Ch 3:** 103 **Ch 4:** 128–135, T129–T130 **Ch 5:** T170 **Ch 6:** T213, 231, T239 **Ch 7:** 252–260 **QRH:** 884, 909, 911–927, 950

(I) read silently with comprehension for a sustained period of time.
Intro: 4–8 **Ch 1:** T17, 19–20 **Ch 2:** T55, 57–59 **Ch 3:** T91, 93–94 **Ch 4:** T127, 129–131 **Ch 5:** T167, 169–171 **Ch 6:** T208, 209–212 **Ch 7:** T251, 253–254 **Ch 8:** T295

Additional instruction, practice, and reinforcement for TEKS 10.7 can be found in the following ancillaries:

- Alternative Readings
- Preparation for TAAS
- TAAS Tool Kit
- Preparing for English II End-of-Course Examination
- Communications

10.8 **Reading/Variety of Texts.** The student reads extensively and intensively for different purposes in varied sources, including world literature. The student is expected to:

(A) read to be entertained, to appreciate a writer's craft, to be informed, to take action, and to discover models to use in his/her own writing;

Intro: 4–8, 15 **Ch 1:** 16–17, 19–20, T24, T29, T37, T39, 53 **Ch 2:** 57–59, 75–77 **Ch 3:** 93–94, 110–113, T111 **Ch 4:** 129–131, T129–T130, T140, 147–149, T147, T149 **Ch 5:** 169–171, 178–183, T183, 185–187, T185, T196, 205 **Ch 6:** 209–212, T209, T217, T221, T224, T228, T230, 233–236, T233, T234, T239, T246, 249 **Ch 7:** 253–254, T259, 273–275 **Ch 8:** 297–299, T300, T305, T311, T315, 316–320, T316, 337 **Ch 10:** T368

(B) read in such varied sources as diaries, journals, textbooks, maps, newspapers, letters, speeches, memoranda, electronic texts, and other media;

Intro: 15 **Ch 1:** 16–17, T17, T24, 53 **Ch 2:** T55, T68, 71 **Ch 3:** T91 **Ch 4:** T127, T133 **Ch 5:** T167, 205 **Ch 6:** T208, T217, T221, T224, T228, T230, T233, T234, T239, T242, T246, T248 **Ch 7:** T251, T259 **Ch 8:** T295, 297–299, T297, T315, T316 **Ch 9:** T345 **Ch 10:** T358, T363 **QRH:** 866–875

(C) read world literature, including classic and contemporary works;

Ch 1: T17, 19–20 **Ch 2:** T55 **Ch 3:** T91 **Ch 4:** T127, 157 **Ch 5:** T167, 178–183 **Ch 6:** T208 **Ch 7:** T251 **Ch 8:** T295

Additional instruction, practice, and reinforcement for TEKS 10.8 can be found in the following ancillaries:

- Alternative Readings
- Communications
- HRW Internet Site

10.9 **Reading/Culture.** The student reads widely, including world literature, to increase knowledge of his/her own culture, the culture of others, and the common elements across cultures. The student is expected to:

(A) recognize distinctive and shared characteristics of cultures through reading;

Ch 1: T17, T21, T24 **Ch 2:** T55, 57–59 **Ch 3:** T91 **Ch 4:** T127 **Ch 5:** T167 **Ch 6:** T208 **Ch 7:** T251 **Ch 8:** T295

(B) compare text events with his/her own and other readers' experiences.

Ch 1: T20, T21, T24 **Ch 3:** T123, T125 **Ch 6:** T217 **Ch 7:** T254 **Ch 8:** T301, T319

Additional instruction, practice, and reinforcement for TEKS 10.9 can be found in the following ancillaries:

- Alternative Readings
- Communications
- HRW Internet Site
- Preparing for English II End-of-Course Examination

10.10 Reading/Literary Response. The student expresses and supports responses to various types of texts. The student is expected to:

(A) respond to informational and aesthetic elements in texts such as discussions, journals, oral interpretations, and enactments;

Ch 1: 16–17, 53 **Ch 2:** 61, 62, 63, 89 **Ch 3:** 103, 125 **Ch 4:** 134, 135, 157, 165 **Ch 5:** 166–167 **Ch 6:** 214 **Ch 7:** 270 **Ch 8:** 302, 303

(B) use elements of text to defend his/her own responses and interpretations;

Ch 1: 16–17, 19–20, 21, T24, 53 **Ch 2:** 57–59, 60, 89 **Ch 3:** 93–94, 95, 125 **Ch 4:** 129–131, 132, 157 **Ch 5:** 169–171, 172, 183, 184, 192 **Ch 6:** 209–212, 213 **Ch 7:** 253–254, 255 **Ch 8:** 298–299, 300 **Ch 10:** T363

Additional instruction, practice, and reinforcement for TEKS 10.10 can be found in the following ancillaries:

- Alternative Readings
- Communications
- Preparation for TAAS
- TAAS Tool Kit
- Preparing for English II End-of-Course Examination
- Media Literacy and Communication Skills
- HRW Internet Site

10.11 Reading/Literary Concepts. The student analyzes literary elements for their contributions to meaning in literary texts. The student is expected to:

(A) compare and contrast varying aspects of texts such as themes, conflicts, and allusions;

Ch 2: 61, 89 **Ch 3:** 125 **Ch 4:** 157 **Ch 5:** T167–T168, T168–T169, 173–175, 180–183, 196, 198–199, 203

(B) analyze the relevance of setting and time frame to text's meaning;

Ch 5: 173–175, 180–183, 196, 198–199, 203

(C) describe and analyze the development of plot and identify conflicts and how they are addressed and resolved;

Ch 3: 125 **Ch 4:** 157 **Ch 5:** 173–175, 180–183, 196, 198–199, 203

(D) analyze the melodies of literary language, including its use of evocative words and rhythms;

Ch 1: 48–49 **Ch 10:** T358, T363

(E) connect literature to historical contexts, current events, and his/her own experiences;

Ch 1: T20, T21 **Ch 3:** T100 **Ch 4:** T132 **Ch 7:** T254 **Ch 8:** T300

10.11 (F) understand literary forms and terms such as author, drama, biography, autobiography, myth, tall tale, dialogue, tragedy and comedy, structure in poetry, epic, ballad, protagonist, antagonist, paradox, analogy, dialect, and comic relief as appropriate to the selections being read.

Ch 1: 18–25, 48–49   **Ch 3:** 125   **Ch 4:** 157, 165   **Ch 5:** 173–175, 177, 180–183, 195–197, 198–199, 204, 205   **Ch 7:** 293

Additional instruction, practice, and reinforcement for TEKS 10.11 can be found in the following ancillaries:

- Alternative Readings
- Communications
- Preparation for TAAS
- TAAS Tool Kit
- Preparing for English II End-of-Course Examination

10.12 Reading/Analysis/Evaluation. The student reads critically to evaluate texts and the authority of sources. The student is expected to:

(A) analyze the characteristics of clearly written texts, including the patterns of organization, syntax, and word choice;

Intro: 6–8   **Ch 1:** 24–25   **Ch 2:** T75, T76   **Ch 3:** 92–94, 97–101, T106, T111   **Ch 4:** 128–131, 134–135   **Ch 5:** 173–175, T174, 180–183, T183, 184, T185   **Ch 6:** 214, T242   **Ch 7:** 252–257, T259, 262, T273   **Ch 8:** 296–302, 305, 315   **Ch 9:** T345   **Ch 10:** T357, T363

(B) evaluate the credibility of information sources, including how the writer's motivation may affect that credibility;

Intro: 8   **Ch 2:** T68   **Ch 4:** 132–133, T140, T142, T143   **Ch 6:** 213, 226, T248   **Ch 8:** 297–299

(C) recognize logical, deceptive, and/or faulty modes of persuasion in texts.

Ch 4: T133   **Ch 7:** 252–254, 257–260, T259, T273   **Ch 8:** 296–302, 305, 315   **QRH:** 882

Additional instruction, practice, and reinforcement for TEKS 10.12 can be found in the following ancillaries:

- Alternative Readings
- Communications
- Preparation for TAAS
- TAAS Tool Kit

10.13 Reading/Inquiry/Research. The student reads in order to research self-selected and assigned topics. The student is expected to:

(A) generate relevant, interesting, and researchable questions;

Ch 4: T132   **Ch 6:** 221–222, 249   **Ch 7:** 293   **Ch 8:** 337

(B) locate appropriate print and non-print information using text and technical resources, including databases and the Internet;

Intro: 15   **Ch 2:** 68–70, T68, T88, T89   **Ch 3:** T100, 109   **Ch 4:** T132, T143   **Ch 5:** 203   **Ch 6:** 222–225, 249   **Ch 7:** 268, 293   **Ch 8:** 311, 329–330, T333   **Ch 19:** 635   **Ch 21:** 691   **QRH:** 866–875

10.13 (C) use text organizers such as overviews, headings, and graphic features to locate and categorize information;
Ch 2: T56 **Ch 4:** 132 **QRH:** 912

(D) produce reports and research projects in varying forms for audiences;
Ch 4: T132 **Ch 6:** 218–245, 249 **Ch 7:** 293 **Ch 8:** 329–336, 337, T337

(E) draw conclusions from information gathered.
Ch 3: T105 **Ch 6:** 232, 249 **Ch 7:** T259, 284–287, 293 **Ch 11:** 393–396

Additional instruction, practice, and reinforcement for TEKS 10.13 can be found in the following ancillaries:

- Alternative Readings
- Communications
- Preparation for TAAS
- TAAS Tool Kit
- Designing Your Writing
- HRW Internet Site

10.18 Listening/Speaking/Literary Interpretations. The student prepares, organizes, plans, and presents literary interpretations. The student is expected to:

(A) make valid interpretations of a variety of literary texts;
Intro: 15 **Ch 4:** 157 **Ch 5:** 203–204 **QRH:** 905

(B) justify the choice of verbal and nonverbal performance techniques by referring to the analysis and interpretations of the text;
Ch 5: 204 **QRH:** 905

(C) present interpretations by telling stories, performing original works, and interpreting poems and stories for a variety of audiences.
Intro: 15 **Ch 1:** T29 **Ch 2:** 89 **Ch 5:** 203–204, 205 **QRH:** 905, 907, T907

Additional instruction, practice, and reinforcement for TEKS 10.18 can be found in the following ancillaries:

- Media Literacy and Communication Skills
- Assessment Alternatives

Alignment with the Exit Level TAAS Objectives
Based on the 1999–2000 TEA Update

The Texas Education Agency has aligned the Exit Level TAAS with targets that include some of the TEKS from grades 8, 9, and 10. The sections that are underlined are not tested in that objective but are tested in another objective. The sections that are bracketed and italicized are not tested on TAAS. The TEKS numbering is as follows:

The number to the left of the decimal is the grade level **(10)**. **10.1** The number to the right of the decimal is the TEKS number **(1)**.

TAAS Writing Objectives

▶ **Exit Level TAAS Writing Objective 1: The student will respond appropriately in a written composition to the purpose/audience specified in a given topic.**

10.1   Writing/Purposes. The student writes in a variety of forms, including business, personal, literary, and persuasive texts, for various audiences and purposes. The student is expected to:

(A) write in a variety of forms with an emphasis on persuasive forms, such as logical argument and expression of opinion, [*personal forms, such as response to literature, reflective essay, and autobiographical narrative, and literary forms, such as poems, plays, and stories*]

Intro: 9–14, 15   **Ch 1:** 28–37, T29, 38, 48–49, 53   **Ch 2:** 66–73, T66, 74, 89   **Ch 3:** 104–109, 110, 125, T125   **Ch 4:** 138–145, 146, 165   **Ch 5:** 178–183, 184, 195–197, 198–202, 205, T205   **Ch 6:** 218–231, 232, 237–239, 249   **Ch 7:** 263–271, 272, 282, 283, 293   **Ch 8:** 306–314, 316–318, 337   **Ch 9:** T350–T351   **Ch 12:** 435   **Ch 13:** 465   **Ch 14:** 489   **Ch 15:** 509   **Ch 16:** 545   **Ch 17:** 571   **Ch 18:** 611   **Ch 19:** 635   **Ch 20:** 665   **Ch 21:** 691   **Ch 22:** 721   **Ch 23:** 737   **Ch 24:** 755   **Ch 25:** 777   **Ch 26:** 806   **QRH:** 939–952

(B) write in a voice and style appropriate to audience and purpose

Intro: 10, 15   **Ch 1:** 29–30, 38, 48–49   **Ch 2:** 67–68, 74, T75   **Ch 3:** 105–106, T106, 110   **Ch 4:** 139–140, 165   **Ch 5:** 179, T182, 184, T186, 196–197, 202   **Ch 6:** 220–221, T220, 232, 237–239, 249   **Ch 7:** 264–266, T265, 272, 282, 283, 293   **Ch 8:** 307–309, 316–318, 337   **Ch 12:** 435   **Ch 13:** 465   **Ch 14:** 489   **Ch 16:** 545   **Ch 22:** 721   **Ch 23:** 737   **Ch 25:** 777   **Ch 26:** 806   **QRH:** 939–952

9.2   Writing/Writing Processes. The student uses recursive writing processes when appropriate. The student is expected to:

(B) develop drafts [*both*] alone [*and collaboratively*] by organizing and reorganizing content and by refining style to suit occasion, audience, and purpose

Intro: T10, 11, 15   **Ch 1:** T31, T33, T34, T36, 38, 42–43, T42, T43, T44, 48–49   **Ch 2:** T70, 72–73, 74, T74, 78–80, T78, T79, 82–83   **Ch 3:** 106, T106, T109, 110, T110, 114–115   **Ch 4:** T142, 143, 146, 150–153, T157, T165   **Ch 5:** T180, T181, T182, T183, 184, 188–191, T194, T205   **Ch 6:** T221, T229, 230, 232, T238, 239, 240–243, T242, T247, 249, T249   **Ch 7:** T264, T265, T267, T271, 272, 276–278, T277   **Ch 8:** T307, T311, T312, 316–318, T317, 321–323   **Ch 9:** T349, T350–T351   **Ch 10:** T358   **Ch 11:** T376, T379, T384, T391   **Ch 12:** 435   **Ch 25:** 777

▶ **Exit Level TAAS Writing Objective 2: The student will organize ideas in a written composition on a given topic.**

9.1 **Writing/Purposes.** The student writes in a variety of forms, including business, personal, literary, and persuasive texts, for various audiences and purposes. The student is expected to:

(C) organize ideas in writing to ensure coherence, logical progression, and support for ideas

Intro: 10–11 **Ch 1:** 30–37, T36, 38 **Ch 2:** 70–73, T72, 74, T74 **Ch 3:** 106–109, 110 **Ch 4:** 141–145, 146 **Ch 5:** 181–183, T183, 184 **Ch 6:** 230–231, 232, 239 **Ch 7:** 271, T271, 272, T276, 283 **Ch 8:** 309–314, 316–318 **Ch 11:** 370–401 **Ch 15:** 509 **QRH:** 940–946

9.2 **Writing/Writing Processes.** The student uses recursive writing processes when appropriate. The student is expected to:

(B) develop drafts [*both*] alone [*and collaboratively*] by organizing and reorganizing content <u>and by refining style to suit occasion, audience, and purpose</u>

Intro: T10, 11, 15 **Ch 1:** T31, T33, T34, T36, 38, 42–43, T42, T43, T44, 48–49 **Ch 2:** T70, 72–73, 74, T74, 78–80, T78, T79, 82–83 **Ch 3:** 106, T106, T109, 110, T110, 114–115 **Ch 4:** T142, 143, 146, 150–153, T157, T165 **Ch 5:** T180, T181, T182, T183, 184, 188–191, T194, T205 **Ch 6:** T221, T229, 230, 232, T238, 239, 240–243, T242, T247, 249, T249 **Ch 7:** T264, T265, T267, T271, 272, 276–278, T277 **Ch 8:** T307, T311, T312, T317, 316–318, 321–323 **Ch 9:** T349, T350–T351 **Ch 10:** T358 **Ch 11:** T376, T379, T384, T391 **Ch 12:** 435 **Ch 25:** 777

▶ **Exit Level TAAS Writing Objective 3: The student will demonstrate control of the English language in a written composition on a given topic.**

9.2 **Writing/Writing Processes.** The student uses recursive writing processes when appropriate. The student is expected to:

(C) proofread writing for appropriateness of [*organization, content, style, and*] conventions

Intro: 12–13 **Ch 1:** 42–44, T42, 46–47, T47, 48–49 **Ch 2:** T62, 78–81, T78, T79, 82–83 **Ch 3:** 114–117 **Ch 4:** 150–153, T151, 155, T155 **Ch 5:** 188–191, 197 **Ch 6:** 240–243, 244–245 **Ch 7:** 276–278, T276 **Ch 8:** 321–323, T323 **Ch 9:** 343 **Ch 10:** T368 **Ch 12:** 435 **Ch 13:** 465 **Ch 15:** 509 **Ch 20:** 665 **Ch 21:** 691 **Ch 22:** 721 **Ch 23:** 737 **Ch 24:** 755 **Ch 26:** 806 **QRH:** 957–958

9.3 **Writing/Grammar/Usage/Conventions/Spelling.** The student relies increasingly on the conventions and mechanics of written English, including the rules of usage and grammar, to write clearly and effectively. The student is expected to:

(A) produce legible work that shows accurate spelling and correct use of the conventions of punctuation and capitalization [*such as italics and ellipses*]

Intro: 12–13, T13 **Ch 1:** T32, 46–47 **Ch 2:** 82 **Ch 3:** 118 **Ch 4:** 155 **Ch 5:** 193 **Ch 6:** T238, T242, 244 **Ch 7:** 280, T283 **Ch 8:** 325 **Ch 9:** 340–351, T348–T349 **Ch 10:** 352–369 **Ch 12:** 435 **Ch 13:** T459 **Ch 14:** 489 **Ch 15:** T494, 509 **Ch 17:** T561, T562 **Ch 18:** T578 **Ch 19:** T630 **Ch 20:** 665 **Ch 21:** 666–690, T668, T672, T674, T678, T683, T686, T687, 691 **Ch 22:** 692–720, T694, T695, T696, T701, T703, T704, T706, T708, T714, T716, T717, 721 **Ch 23:** 722–734, T724, T726, T727, T728, T730, T731, 737 **Ch 24:** 738–754, T740, T741, T742, T743, T746, T747, T751, 755 **Ch 25:** 756–776, T760, T761, T762, T763, T764, T765, T767, T768, T769, T770, T771, T772, T773, 777 **Ch 26:** 778–805, T779, T780, T782, T787, T792, T793, T794, T795, T796, T800, T802, 806 **Ch 27:** 810–843 **QRH:** 849, 960, 964–966, 967–968, 970–973, 975–976, 980–981

9.3 **(B)** demonstrate control over grammatical elements, such as subject-verb agreement, pronoun-antecedent agreement, verb forms, and parallelism

Intro: 12–13 **Ch 1:** 46–47 **Ch 2:** T78, 82 **Ch 3:** 118 **Ch 4:** 155 **Ch 5:** 192, 193 **Ch 6:** 244 **Ch 7:** 278, 280 **Ch 8:** 325 **Ch 9:** 340–351, T343 **Ch 10:** 352–369, T355, T359 **Ch 11:** T392–T393 **Ch 12:** 404–434, T405, T406, T409, T412, T413, T420, T424, T426, T427, T428, T431 **Ch 13:** 436–464, T438, T439, T440, T450, T451, T452, T453, T454, T458, T461 **Ch 14:** T468, T470, T473, T476 **Ch 15:** 490–508, T492, T493, T494, T496, T497, T499, T500, T501, T502, T505 **Ch 16:** 510–544, T511, T513, T514, T518, T523, T525, T533, T534, T536, T537, 545 **Ch 17:** 546–570, T550, T552, T554, T557, T558, T559, T560, T562, T565, T567, 571 **Ch 18:** 572–610, T575, T576, T586, T603, T605, 611 **Ch 19:** 612–634, T617, T619, T628, T630, 635 **Ch 20:** 636–664, T639, T642, T648, T649, T652, T653, 665 **Ch 21:** 691 **Ch 22:** T701, T706, T717, T718 **Ch 23:** T725 **Ch 24:** T746 **Ch 27:** 810–831, T814, T817, T821, T839 **QRH:** 960–985

(C) compose increasingly more involved sentences that contain gerunds, participles, and infinitives in their various functions

Ch 1: 44 **Ch 3:** 116, T116, T117, 118 **Ch 5:** 189–190 **Ch 9:** 342–344 **Ch 10:** 355, 356, T365, 366–367, T366 **Ch 12:** T418 **Ch 14:** 472–483, T473, T475, T477, T480, T481, T483, T484, T486, 489 **Ch 18:** 572–581, T576, T577, T578, T580, T582, T583, T584, T587, T588, T589, T591, T592, T595, T597, T602 **Ch 19:** T615 **Ch 22:** 721 **Ch 27:** T819 **QRH:** 973, 978

▶ **Exit Level TAAS Writing Objective 4: The student will generate a written composition that develops/supports/elaborates the central idea stated in a given topic.**

9.1 **Writing/Purposes.** The student writes in a variety of forms, including business, personal, literary, and persuasive texts, for various audiences and purposes. The student is expected to:

(C) organize ideas in writing to ensure coherence, logical progression, and support for ideas

Intro: 10–11 **Ch 1:** 30–37, T36, 38 **Ch 2:** 70–73, T72, 74, T74 **Ch 3:** 106–109, 110 **Ch 4:** 141–145, 146 **Ch 5:** 181–183, T183, 184 **Ch 6:** 230–231, 232, 239 **Ch 7:** 271, T271, 272, T276, 283 **Ch 8:** 309–314, 316–318 **Ch 11:** 370–401 **Ch 15:** 509 **QRH:** 940–946

9.4 **Writing/Inquiry/Research.** The student uses writing as a tool for learning. The student is expected to:

(A) use writing to [*formulate questions, refine topics, and*] clarify ideas

Ch 1: T17, T18, T24, T48 **Ch 2:** T56, T58 **Ch 3:** T92, T104, T117, 125 **Ch 4:** T139, T143, T150, T158, T165 **Ch 5:** T170, T179, T193, T200 **Ch 6:** 221–222, 249 **Ch 8:** T306, T316, T329 **Ch 9:** T348 **Ch 11:** T401

(B) use writing to [*discover, organize, and*] support what is known [*and what needs to be learned*] about a topic

Ch 2: T56, T62, 89 **Ch 3:** T104, T109, 125 **Ch 4:** 138–145, T145, 165 **Ch 5:** 205 **Ch 6:** 218–231, T228, 249 **Ch 7:** 263–271, 293 **Ch 8:** 306–314, T307 **Ch 11:** T398–T399, T401 **QRH:** 914, 950–951, 959

▶ **Exit Level TAAS Writing Objective 5: The student will recognize appropriate sentence construction within the context of a written passage.**

8.17 **Writing/Grammar/Usage.** The student applies standard grammar and usage to communicate clearly and effectively in writing. The student is expected to:

(A) write in complete sentences, varying the types, such as compound and complex sentences, and use appropriately punctuated independent and dependent clauses
Ch 5: 189–190 **Ch 9:** 340–351 **Ch 10:** 358, 359–360, 366–367 **Ch 13:** 448, 451, 456 **Ch 15:** 490–503, 504–505 **Ch 17:** 558–559 **Ch 22:** 701, 703 **Ch 23:** 724–726

(B) use conjunctions to connect ideas meaningfully
Ch 9: 348 **Ch 10:** 357–368 **Ch 12:** 428–429 **Ch 15:** 492, 498–499

8.18 **Writing/Processes.** The student selects and uses writing processes for self-initiated and assigned writing. The student is expected to:

(C) revise [*selected drafts*] by [*adding, elaborating,*] deleting, combining, and rearranging text
Ch 1: 42–45 **Ch 2:** 78–81 **Ch 3:** 114–117 **Ch 4:** 150–151 **Ch 5:** 188–192 **Ch 6:** 240–243 **Ch 7:** 276–279 **Ch 8:** 321–324

9.3 **Writing/Grammar/Usage/Conventions/Spelling.** The student relies increasingly on the conventions and mechanics of written English, including the rules of usage and grammar, to write clearly and effectively. The student is expected to:

(C) compose increasingly more involved sentences that contain gerunds, participles, and infinitives in their various functions
Ch 1: 44 **Ch 3:** 116, T116, T117, 118 **Ch 5:** 189–190 **Ch 9:** 342–344 **Ch 10:** 355, 356, T365, 366–367, T366 **Ch 12:** T418 **Ch 14:** 472–483, T473, T475, T477, T480, T481, T483, T484, T486, 489 **Ch 18:** 572–581, T576, T577, T578, T580, T582, T583, T584, T587, T588, T589, T591, T592, T595, T597, T602 **Ch 19:** T615 **Ch 22:** 721 **Ch 27:** T819 **QRH:** 973, 978

▶ **Exit Level TAAS Writing Objective 6: The student will recognize appropriate English usage within the context of a written passage.**

9.3 **Writing/Grammar/Usage/Conventions/Spelling.** The student relies increasingly on the conventions and mechanics of written English, including the rules of usage and grammar, to write clearly and effectively. The student is expected to:

(B) demonstrate control over grammatical elements, such as subject-verb agreement, pronoun-antecedent agreement, verb forms, and parallelism
Intro: 12–13 **Ch 1:** 46–47 **Ch 2:** T78, 82 **Ch 3:** 118 **Ch 4:** 155 **Ch 5:** 192, 193 **Ch 6:** 244 **Ch 7:** 278, 280 **Ch 8:** 325 **Ch 9:** 340–351, T343 **Ch 10:** 352–369, T355, T359 **Ch 11:** T392–T393 **Ch 12:** 404–434, T405, T406, T409, T412, T413, T420, T424, T426, T427, T428, T431 **Ch 13:** 436–464, T438, T439, T440, T450, T451, T452, T453, T454, T458, T461 **Ch 14:** T468, T470, T473, T476 **Ch 15:** 490–508, T492, T493, T494, T496, T497, T499, T500, T501, T502, T505 **Ch 16:** 510–544, T511, T513, T514, T518, T523, T525, T533, T534, T536, T537, 545 **Ch 17:** 546–570, T550, T552, T554, T557, T558, T559, T560, T562, T565, T567, 571 **Ch 18:** 572–610, T575, T576, T586, T603, T605, 611 **Ch 19:** 612–634, T617, T619, T628, T630, 635 **Ch 20:** 636–664, T639, T642, T648, T649, T652, T653, 665 **Ch 21:** 691 **Ch 22:** T701, T706, T717, T718 **Ch 23:** T725 **Ch 24:** T746 **Ch 27:** 810–831, T814, T817, T821, T839 **QRH:** 960–985

▶ **Exit Level TAAS Writing Objective 7: The student will proofread for spelling, capitalization, and punctuation errors within the context of a written passage.**

9.2 **Writing/Writing Processes.** The student uses recursive writing processes when appropriate. The student is expected to:

(C) proofread writing for appropriateness of [*organization, content, style, and*] conventions

Intro: 12–13 **Ch 1:** 42–44, T42, 46–47, T47, 48–49 **Ch 2:** T62, 78–81, T78, T79, 82–83
Ch 3: 114–117 **Ch 4:** 150–153, T151, 155, T155 **Ch 5:** 188–191, 197 **Ch 6:** 240–243, 244–245
Ch 7: 276–278, T276 **Ch 8:** 321–323, T323 **Ch 9:** 343 **Ch 10:** T368 **Ch 12:** 435 **Ch 13:** 465
Ch 15: 509 **Ch 20:** 665 **Ch 21:** 691 **Ch 22:** 721 **Ch 23:** 737 **Ch 24:** 755 **Ch 26:** 806
QRH: 957–958

9.3 **Writing/Grammar/Usage/Conventions/Spelling.** The student relies increasingly on the conventions and mechanics of written English, including the rules of usage and grammar, to write clearly and effectively. The student is expected to:

(A) produce <u>legible work that shows</u> accurate spelling and correct use of the conventions of punctuation and capitalization [*such as italics and ellipses*]

Intro: 12–13, T13 **Ch 1:** T32, 46–47 **Ch 2:** 82 **Ch 3:** 118 **Ch 4:** 155 **Ch 5:** 193 **Ch 6:** T238, T242, 244
Ch 7: 280, T283 **Ch 8:** 325 **Ch 9:** 340–351, T348–T349 **Ch 10:** 352–369 **Ch 12:** 435 **Ch 13:** T459
Ch 14: 489 **Ch 15:** T494, 509 **Ch 17:** T561, T562 **Ch 18:** T578 **Ch 19:** T630 **Ch 20:** 665
Ch 21: 666–690, T668, T672, T674, T678, T683, T686, T687, 691 **Ch 22:** 692–720, T694, T695, T696, T701, T703, T704, T706, T708, T714, T716, T717, 721 **Ch 23:** 722–734, T724, T726, T727, T728, T730, T731, 737
Ch 24: 738–754, T740, T741, T742, T743, T746, T747, T751, 755 **Ch 25:** 756–776, T760, T761, T762, T763, T764, T765, T767, T768, T769, T770, T771, T772, T773, 777 **Ch 26:** 778–805, T779, T780, T782, T787, T792, T793, T794, T795, T796, T800, T802, 806 **Ch 27:** 810–843 **QRH:** 849, 960, 964–966, 967–968, 970–973, 975–976, 980–981

9.5 **Writing/Evaluation.** The student evaluates his/her own writing and the writings of others. The student is expected to:

(A) evaluate writing for [*both*] mechanics [*and content*]

Intro: 12–13, T12 **Ch 1:** T42, 43–44, T43, 46–47 **Ch 2:** T70, T79, T80, T81 **Ch 3:** 114–117, 118
Ch 4: 150–153, T153, 155 **Ch 5:** T181, T182, 188–191, T188, 193, T196 **Ch 6:** T237, 240–243, 244, T245
Ch 7: T275, 276–278, T277, 280 **Ch 8:** T303, T312, 321–323, 325, T326 **Ch 9:** T350–T351 **Ch 10:** T358
Ch 13: T438 **Ch 16:** T538 **Ch 17:** 571 **Ch 18:** T603 **Ch 21:** 691 **Ch 22:** T717 **Ch 25:** T772
Ch 26: T800

Additional instruction, practice, and reinforcement for the Exit Level TAAS Writing Objectives can be found in the following ancillaries:

- Communications
- Preparation for TAAS
- TAAS Tool Kit
- Preparing for English II End-of-Course Examination
- Sentences, Paragraphs, and Compositions
- Combining Sentences
- Daily Language Activity Transparencies
- Language Workshop CD-ROM
- Writer's Workshop 2 CD-ROM
- HRW Internet Site
- Grammar, Usage, and Mechanics

TAAS Reading Objectives

▶ **Exit Level TAAS Reading Objective 1: The student will determine the meaning of words in a variety of written texts.**

10.6 **Reading/Word Identification/Vocabulary Development.** The student acquires an extensive vocabulary through reading and systematic word study. The student is expected to:

(B) rely on context to determine meanings of words and phrases, such as figurative language, [idioms,] multiple-meaning words, and technical vocabulary

Ch 1: 26 **Ch 2:** 64, T64 **Ch 3:** T110 **Ch 4:** 136 **Ch 6:** 216, 217 **Ch 8:** 304 **QRH:** 887, 921–922

(C) apply meanings of prefixes, roots, and suffixes in order to comprehend

Ch 3: 102 **Ch 5:** 176 **Ch 26:** 781, 782 **QRH:** 887–888, 891–895, 979–980, 984

▶ **Exit Level TAAS Reading Objective 2: The student will identify supporting ideas in a variety of written texts.**

10.7 **Reading/Comprehension.** The student comprehends selections using a variety of strategies. The student is expected to:

(E) analyze text structures, such as compare and contrast, cause and effect, and chronological ordering, for how they influence understanding

Ch 1: 35–36 **Ch 2:** 56–62, T63 **Ch 3:** 92–101, T99, 109, T112, T123, T125 **Ch 4:** T129–T130, 137 **Ch 6:** T230 **QRH:** 876–877, 885–886

9.7 (F) identify main ideas and their supporting details

Intro: 6–7 **Ch 1:** 22, T24 **Ch 2:** 56–59, 62–63, T62, 65, T84 **Ch 4:** 165 **Ch 5:** 177 **Ch 6:** 208–214 **Ch 11:** 371 **QRH:** 881, 884–885

8.13 **Reading/Inquiry/Research.** The student inquires and conducts research using a variety of sources. The student is expected to:

(D) interpret and use graphic sources of information, such as maps, graphs, time lines, or tables, to address research questions

Ch 2: T56 **Ch 4:** 132 **QRH:** 912

▶ **Exit Level TAAS Reading Objective 3: The student will summarize a variety of written texts.**

9.7 **Reading/Comprehension.** The student comprehends selections using a variety of strategies. The student is expected to:

(F) identify main ideas and their supporting details

Intro: 6–7 **Ch 1:** 22, T24 **Ch 2:** 56–59, 62–63, T62, 65, T84 **Ch 4:** 165 **Ch 5:** 177 **Ch 6:** 208–214 **Ch 11:** 371 **QRH:** 881, 884–885

(G) summarize texts

Intro: 6–7 **Ch 1:** 22, T24 **Ch 2:** 56–59, 62–63, T62, 65, T84 **Ch 4:** 165 **Ch 5:** 177 **Ch 6:** 208–214 **Ch 11:** 371 **QRH:** 881, 884–885

TAAS Reading Objectives

9.11 Reading/Literary Concepts. The student analyzes literary elements for their contributions to meaning in literary texts. The student is expected to:

(A) recognize the theme (general observation about life or human nature) within a text

Ch 2: 61, 89   **Ch 3:** 125   **Ch 4:** 157   **Ch 5:** T167–T168, T168–T169, 173–175, 180–183, 196, 198–199, 203

▶ **Exit Level TAAS Reading Objective 4: The student will perceive relationships and recognize outcomes in a variety of written texts.**

10.7 Reading/Comprehension. The student comprehends selections using a variety of strategies. The student is expected to:

(E) analyze text structures, such as compare and contrast, cause and effect, <u>and chronological ordering,</u> for how they influence understanding

Ch 1: 35–36   **Ch 2:** 56–62, T63   **Ch 3:** 92–101, T99, 109, T112, T123, T125   **Ch 4:** T129–T130, 137   **Ch 6:** T230   **QRH:** 876–877, 885–886

(G) draw inferences, such as <u>conclusions, generalizations, and</u> predictions, and support them with text evidence and experience

Intro: 4–8, 15   **Ch 1:** 18–23, T22, T24, 27   **Ch 2:** T56, 71, T84   **Ch 3:** 92–97, T94–T95, 103   **Ch 4:** 128–134, T129–T130, T131   **Ch 5:** 168–173   **Ch 8:** T296–T297   **Ch 11:** 396   **QRH:** 877–878, 881

8.11 Reading/Literary Response. The student expresses and supports responses to various types of texts. The student is expected to:

(D) connect, compare, and contrast ideas, themes, and issues across texts

Intro: 5, 6, 15   **Ch 1:** 17, T17, T53   **Ch 2:** 55, T55, 56, 62–63, 66–77, 86–88, 89, T89   **Ch 3:** T91, 92, 97–101, 104–113   **Ch 4:** T127   **Ch 5:** 178–187, T188, T191, T194, 195–197   **Ch 6:** T208, 218–236, T221   **Ch 8:** T295, T301

▶ **Exit Level TAAS Reading Objective 5: The student will analyze information in a variety of written texts in order to make inferences and generalizations.**

10.7 Reading/Comprehension. The student comprehends selections using a variety of strategies. The student is expected to:

(G) draw inferences, such as conclusions, generalizations, <u>and predictions,</u> and support them with text evidence and experience

Intro: 4–8, 15   **Ch 1:** 18–23, T22, T24, 27   **Ch 2:** T56, 71, T84   **Ch 3:** 92–97, T94–T95, 103   **Ch 4:** 128–134, T129–T130, T131   **Ch 5:** 168–173   **Ch 8:** T296–T297   **Ch 11:** 396   **QRH:** 877–878, 881

10.11 Reading/Literary Concepts. The student analyzes literary elements for their contributions to meaning in literary texts. The student is expected to:

- **(B)** analyze the relevance of setting and time frame to text's meaning
  Ch 5: 173–175, 180–183, 196, 198–199, 203

- **(C)** describe and analyze the development of plot and identify conflicts and how they are addressed and resolved
  Ch 3: 125 **Ch 4:** 157 **Ch 5:** 173–175, 180–183, 196, 198–199, 203

9.11 (C) analyze characters [*and identify time and point of view*]
  Ch 3: 125 **Ch 5:** 173–175, T174, 180–181, 195, 197, 199, T199

8.12 Reading/Text Structures/Literary Concepts. The student analyzes the characteristics of various types of texts (genres). The student is expected to:

- **(K)** recognize how [*style, tone, and*] mood contribute to the effect of the text
  Ch 1: 30, 43–45, T43 **Ch 2:** 68, 79–81 **Ch 3:** 106, 115–117 **Ch 4:** 139, 151–154 **Ch 5:** 179, 189–193, 203 **Ch 6:** 221, 242–243 **Ch 7:** 266, 277–279 **Ch 8:** 308–309, 322–324

8.13 Reading/Inquiry/Research. The student inquires and conducts research using a variety of sources. The student is expected to:

- **(D)** interpret <u>and use</u> graphic sources of information, such as maps, graphs, timelines, or tables, to address research questions
  Ch 2: T56 **Ch 4:** 132 **QRH:** 912

- **(G)** draw conclusions from information gathered from multiple sources
  Ch 3: T105 **Ch 6:** 232, 249 **Ch 7:** T259, 284–287, 293 **Ch 11:** 393–396

▶ **Exit Level TAAS Reading Objective 6: The student will recognize points of view, propaganda, and/or statements of fact and opinion in a variety of written texts.**

9.12 Reading/Analysis/Evaluation. The student reads critically to evaluate texts. The student is expected to:

- **(D)** analyze texts, such as editorials, documentaries, and advertisements, for bias and use of common persuasive techniques
  Intro: 8 **Ch 2:** T68 **Ch 4:** 132–133, T133, T140, T142, T143 **Ch 6:** 213, 226, T248 **Ch 7:** 252–254, 257–260, T259, T273 **Ch 8:** 297–299, 305, 315 **QRH:** 882

8.10 Reading/Comprehension. The student comprehends selections using a variety of strategies. The student is expected to:

- **(J)** distinguish fact and opinion in various texts
  Ch 6: 228 **Ch 7:** 252, 255–257, 258, 262 **QRH:** 877

8.12 Reading/Text Structures/Literary Concepts. The student analyzes the characteristics of various types of texts (genres). The student is expected to:

(A) identify the purposes of different types of texts, such as to inform, influence, express, or entertain
  Intro: 10 **Ch 1:** 29 **Ch 2:** 67–68 **Ch 3:** 105 **Ch 4:** 127, 139 **Ch 5:** 167, 179 **Ch 6:** 207, 220 **Ch 7:** 251–252, 264 **Ch 8:** 295, 307 **QRH:** 876, 935

(H) describe how the author's perspective or point of view affects the text
  Ch 2: 87–88 **Ch 5:** 174, 180, 196, 198, 203 **QRH:** 876

Additional instruction, practice, and reinforcement for Exit Level TAAS Reading Objectives can be found in the following ancillaries:

- Preparation for TAAS
- TAAS Tool Kit
- Preparing for English II End-of-Course Examination
- Communications
- Vocabulary Workshop and Tests
- Alternative Readings
- Grammar, Usage, and Mechanics

Alignment with
English II End-of-Course Test Objectives
Based on the 1999–2000 TEA Update

The Texas Education Agency has aligned the English II End-of-Course Objectives with targets that include some of the TEKS from the tenth grade. The sections that are underlined are not tested in that objective but are tested in another objective. The sections that are bracketed and italicized are not tested on TAAS. The TEKS numbering is as follows:

The number to the left of the decimal is the grade level **(10)**.   **10.7**   The number to the right of the decimal is the TEKS number **(7)**.

Domain: Reading

▶ **English II End-of-Course Objective 1: The student will demonstrate a basic understanding of culturally diverse written texts.**

10.7 Reading/Comprehension. The student comprehends selections using a variety of strategies. The student is expected to:

(F) produce summaries of texts by identifying main ideas and their supporting details
   Intro: 6–7 **Ch 1:** 22, T24 **Ch 2:** 56–59, 62–63, T62, 65, T84 **Ch 4:** 165 **Ch 5:** 177 **Ch 6:** 208–214 **Ch 11:** 371 **QRH:** 881, 884–885

▶ **English II End-of-Course Objective 2: The student will demonstrate an understanding of the effects of literary elements and techniques in culturally diverse written texts.**

10.6 Reading/Word Identification/Vocabulary Development. The student acquires an extensive vocabulary through reading and systematic word study. The student is expected to:

(F) discriminate between connotative and denotative meanings and interpret the connotative power of words
   Ch 7: 259, 261, 269, T289 **QRH:** 888

10.9 Reading/Culture. The student reads widely, including world literature, to increase knowledge of his/her own culture, the culture of others, and the common elements across cultures. The student is expected to:

(B) compare text events with his/her own [*and other readers*'] experiences
   Ch 1: T20, T21, T24 **Ch 3:** T123, T125 **Ch 6:** T217 **Ch 7:** T254 **Ch 8:** T301, T319

10.10 Reading/Literary Response. The student expresses and supports responses to various types of texts.. The student is expected to:

(B) use elements of text to defend his/her own responses and interpretations
   Ch 1: 16–17, 19–20, 21, T24, 53 **Ch 2:** 57–59, 60, 89 **Ch 3:** 93–94, 95, 125 **Ch 4:** 129–131, 132, 157
   Ch 5: 169–171, 172, 183, 184, 192 **Ch 6:** 209–212, 213 **Ch 7:** 253–254, 255 **Ch 8:** 298–299, 300
   Ch 10: T363

10.11 Reading/Literary Concepts. The student analyzes literary elements for their contributions to meaning in literary texts. The student is expected to:

(A) compare and contrast varying aspects of texts, such as themes, conflicts, and allusions
   Ch 2: 61, 89 **Ch 3:** 125 **Ch 4:** 157 **Ch 5:** T167–T168, T168–T169, 173–175, 180–183, 196, 198–199, 203

10.11 (B) analyze relevance of setting and time frame to text's meaning
Ch 5: 173–175, 180–183, 196, 198–199, 203

(C) describe and analyze the development of plot and identify conflicts and how they are addressed and resolved
Ch 3: 125 **Ch 4:** 157 **Ch 5:** 173–175, 180–183, 196, 198–199, 203

(D) analyze the melodies of literary language, including its use of evocative words and rhythms
Ch 1: 48–49 **Ch 10:** T358, T363

▶ **English II End-of-Course Objective 3: The student will demonstrate the ability to analyze and critically evaluate culturally diverse written texts.**

10.6 Reading/Word Identification/Vocabulary Development. The student acquires an extensive vocabulary through reading and systematic word study. The student is expected to:

(F) discriminate between connotative and denotative meanings and interpret the connotative power of words
Ch 7: 259, 261, 269, T289 **QRH:** 888

10.7 Reading/Comprehension. The student comprehends selections using a variety of strategies. The student is expected to:

(G) draw inferences such as conclusions, generalizations, and predictions and support them with text evidence and experience
Intro: 4–8, 15 **Ch 1:** 18–23, T22, T24, 27 **Ch 2:** T56, 71, T84 **Ch 3:** 92–97, T94–T95, 103
Ch 4: 128–134, T129–T130, T131 **Ch 5:** 168–173 **Ch 8:** T296–T297 **Ch 11:** 396 **QRH:** 877–878, 881

10.9 Reading/Culture. The student reads widely, including world literature, to increase knowledge of his/her own culture, the culture of others, and the common elements across cultures. The student is expected to:

(B) compare text events with his/her own [*and other readers'*] experiences
Ch 1: T20, T21, T24 **Ch 3:** T123, T125 **Ch 6:** T217 **Ch 7:** T254 **Ch 8:** T301, T319

10.10 Reading/Literary Response. The student expresses and supports responses to various types of texts. The student is expected to:

(B) use elements of text to defend his/her own responses and interpretations
Ch 1: 16–17, 19–20, 21, T24, 53 **Ch 2:** 57–59, 60, 89 **Ch 3:** 93–94, 95, 125 **Ch 4:** 129–131, 132, 157
Ch 5: 169–171, 172, 183, 184, 192 **Ch 6:** 209–212, 213 **Ch 7:** 253–254, 255 **Ch 8:** 298–299, 300
Ch 10: T363

10.12 Reading/Analysis/Evaluation. The student reads critically to evaluate texts and the authority of sources. The student is expected to:

(A) analyze the characteristics of clearly written texts, including the patterns of organization, syntax, and word choice
Ch 2: 61, 89 **Ch 3:** 125 **Ch 4:** 157 **Ch 5:** T167–T168, T168–T169, 173–175, 180–183, 196, 198–199, 203

Domain: Writing

▶ **English II End-of-Course Objective 4: The student will, within a given context, produce an effective composition for a specific purpose.**

10.1 Writing/Purposes. The student writes in a variety of forms, including business, personal, literary, and persuasive texts, for various audiences and purposes. The student is expected to:

(A) write in a variety of forms with an emphasis on [*persuasive forms, such as logical argument and expression of opinion,*] personal forms, such as response to literature, reflective essay, [*and autobiographical narrative, and literary forms, such as poems, plays, and stories*]

Intro: 9–14, 15 **Ch 1:** 28–37, T29, 38, 48–49, 53 **Ch 2:** 66–73, T66, 74, 89 **Ch 3:** 104–109, 110, 125, T125 **Ch 4:** 138–145, 146, 165 **Ch 5:** 178–183, 184, 195–197, 198–202, 205, T205 **Ch 6:** 218–231, 232, 237–239, 249 **Ch 7:** 263–271, 272, 282, 283, 293 **Ch 8:** 306–314, 316–318, 337 **Ch 9:** T350–T351 **Ch 12:** 435 **Ch 13:** 465 **Ch 14:** 489 **Ch 15:** 509 **Ch 16:** 545 **Ch 17:** 571 **Ch 18:** 611 **Ch 19:** 635 **Ch 20:** 665 **Ch 21:** 691 **Ch 22:** 721 **Ch 23:** 737 **Ch 24:** 755 **Ch 25:** 777 **Ch 26:** 806 **QRH:** 939–952

(B) write in a voice and a style appropriate to audience and purpose

Intro: 10, 15 **Ch 1:** 29–30, 38, 48–49 **Ch 2:** 67–68, 74, T75 **Ch 3:** 105–106, T106, 110 **Ch 4:** 139–140, 165 **Ch 5:** 179, T182, 184, T186, 196–197, 202 **Ch 6:** 220–221, T220, 232, 237–239, 249 **Ch 7:** 264–266, T265, 272, 282, 283, 293 **Ch 8:** 307–309, 316 318, 337 **Ch 12:** 435 **Ch 13:** 465 **Ch 14:** 489 **Ch 16:** 545 **Ch 22:** 721 **Ch 23:** 737 **Ch 25:** 777 **Ch 26:** 806 **QRH:** 939–952

(C) organize ideas in writing to ensure coherence, logical progression, and support for ideas

Intro: 10–11 **Ch 1:** 30–37, T36, 38 **Ch 2:** 70–73, T72, 74, T74 **Ch 3:** 106–109, 110 **Ch 4:** 141–145, 146 **Ch 5:** 181–183, T183, 184 **Ch 6:** 230–231, 232, 239 **Ch 7:** 271, T271, 272, T276, 283 **Ch 8:** 309–314, 316–318 **Ch 11:** 370–401 **Ch 15:** 509 **QRH:** 940–946

10.2 Writing/Writing Processes. The student uses recursive writing processes when appropriate. The student is expected to:

(B) develop drafts [*both*] alone [*and collaboratively*] by organizing and reorganizing content and by refining style to suit occasion, audience, and purpose

Intro: T10, 11, 15 **Ch 1:** T31, T33, T34, T36, 38, 42–43, T42, T43, T44, 48–49 **Ch 2:** T70, 72–73, 74, T74, 78–80, T78, T79, 82–83 **Ch 3:** 106, T106, T109, 110, T110, 114-115 **Ch 4:** T142, 143, 146, 150-153, T157, T165 **Ch 5:** T180, T181, T182, T183, 184, 188–191, T194, T205 **Ch 6:** T221, T229, 230, 232, T238, 239, 240-243, T242, T247, 249, T249 **Ch 7:** T264, T265, T267, T271, 272, 276–278, T277 **Ch 8:** T307, T311, T312, 316-318, T317, 321-323 **Ch 9:** T349, T350-T351 **Ch 10:** T358 **Ch 11:** T376, T379, T384, T391 **Ch 12:** 435 **Ch 25:** 777

10.5 Writing/Evaluation. The student evaluates his/her own writing and the writings of others. The student is expected to:

(A) evaluate writing for <u>both mechanics and</u> content

Intro: 12–13, T12 **Ch 1:** T42, 43–44, T43, 46–47 **Ch 2:** T70, T79, T80, T81 **Ch 3:** 114–117, 118 **Ch 4:** 150–153, T153, 155 **Ch 5:** T181, T182, 188–191, T188, 193, T196 **Ch 6:** T237, 240–243, 244, T245 **Ch 7:** T275, 276–278, T277, 280 **Ch 8:** T303, T312, 321–323, 325, T326 **Ch 9:** T350–T351 **Ch 10:** T358 **Ch 13:** T438 **Ch 16:** T538 **Ch 17:** 571 **Ch 18:** T603 **Ch 21:** 691 **Ch 22:** T717 **Ch 25:** T772 **Ch 26:** T800

▶ **English II End-of-Course Objective 5:** The student will produce a piece of writing that demonstrates a command of the conventions of spelling, capitalization, punctuation, grammar, usage, and sentence structure.

10.2 **Writing/Writing Processes.** The student uses recursive writing processes when appropriate. The student is expected to:

(C) proofread writing for appropriateness of <u>organization, content, style, and</u> conventions

Intro: 12–13 **Ch 1:** 42–44, T42, 46–47, T47, 48–49 **Ch 2:** T62, 78–81, T78, T79, 82–83
Ch 3: 114–117 **Ch 4:** 150–153, T151, 155, T155 **Ch 5:** 188–191, 197 **Ch 6:** 240–243, 244–245,
Ch 7: 276–278, T276 **Ch 8:** 321–323, T323 **Ch 9:** 343 **Ch 10:** T368 **Ch 12:** 435
Ch 13: 465 **Ch 15:** 509 **Ch 20:** 665 **Ch 21:** 691 **Ch 22:** 721 **Ch 23:** 737 **Ch 24:** 755
Ch 26: 806 **QRH:** 957–958

10.3 **Writing/Grammar/Usage/Conventions/Spelling.** The student relies increasingly on the conventions and mechanics of written English, including the rules of usage and grammar, to write clearly and effectively. The student is expected to:

(A) produce legible work that shows accurate spelling and correct use of the conventions of punctuation and capitalization [*such as italics and ellipses*]

Intro: 12–13, T13 **Ch 1:** T32, 46–47 **Ch 2:** 82 **Ch 3:** 118 **Ch 4:** 155 **Ch 5:** 193 **Ch 6:** T238,
T242, 244 **Ch 7:** 280, T283 **Ch 8:** 325 **Ch 9:** 340–351, T348–T349 **Ch 10:** 352–369 **Ch 12:** 435
Ch 13: T459 **Ch 14:** 489 **Ch 15:** T494, 509 **Ch 17:** T561, T562 **Ch 18:** T578 **Ch 19:** T630
Ch 20: 665 **Ch 21:** 666–690, T668, T672, T674, T678, T683, T686, T687, 691 **Ch 22:** 692–720, T694,
T695, T696, T701, T703, T704, T706, T708, T714, T716, T717, 721 **Ch 23:** 722–734, T724, T726,
T727, T728, T730, T731, 737 **Ch 24:** 738–754, T740, T741, T742, T743, T746, T747, T751, 755
Ch 25: 756–776, T760, T761, T762, T763, T764, T765, T767, T768, T769, T770, T771, T772, T773,
777 **Ch 26:** 778–805, T779, T780, T782, T787, T792, T793, T794, T795, T796, T800, T802, 806
Ch 27: 810–843 **QRH:** 849, 960, 964–966, 967–968, 970–973, 975–976, 980–981

(B) demonstrate control over grammatical elements, such as subject-verb agreement, pronoun-antecedent agreement, verb forms, and parallelism

Intro: 12–13 **Ch 1:** 46–47 **Ch 2:** T78, 82 **Ch 3:** 118 **Ch 4:** 155 **Ch 5:** 192, 193 **Ch 6:** 244
Ch 7: 278, 280 **Ch 8:** 325 **Ch 9:** 340–351, T343 **Ch 10:** 352–369, T355, T359 **Ch 11:** T392–T393
Ch 12: 404–434, T405, T406, T409, T412, T413, T420, T424, T426, T427, T428, T431 **Ch 13:** 436–464,
T438, T439, T440, T450, T451, T452, T453, T454, T458, T461 **Ch 14:** T468, T470, T473, T476
Ch 15: 490–508, T492, T493, T494, T496, T497, T499, T500, T501, T502, T505 **Ch 16:** 510–544, T511,
T513, T514, T518, T523, T525, T533, T534, T536, T537, 545 **Ch 17:** 546–570, T550, T552, T554, T557,
T558, T559, T560, T562, T565, T567, 571 **Ch 18:** 572–610, T575, T576, T586, T603, T605, 611
Ch 19: 612–634, T617, T619, T628, T630, 635 **Ch 20:** 636–664, T639, T642, T648, T649, T652, T653,
665 **Ch 21:** 691 **Ch 22:** T701, T706, T717, T718 **Ch 23:** T725 **Ch 24:** T746 **Ch 27:** 810–831,
T814, T817, T821, T839 **QRH:** 960–985

(C) compose increasingly more involved sentences that contain gerunds, participles, and infinitives in their various functions

Ch 1: 44 **Ch 3:** 116, T116, T117, 118 **Ch 5:** 189–190 **Ch 9:** 342–344 **Ch 10:** 355, 356, T365,
366–367, T366 **Ch 12:** T418 **Ch 14:** 472–483, T473, T475, T477, T480, T481, T483, T484, T486, 489
Ch 18: 572–581, T576, T577, T578, T580, T582, T583, T584, T587, T588, T589, T591, T592, T595,
T597, T602 **Ch 19:** T615 **Ch 22:** 721 **Ch 27:** T819 **QRH:** 973, 978

10.5 Writing/Evaluation. The student evaluates his/her own writing and the writings of others. The student is expected to:

(A) evaluate writing for both mechanics and content

Intro: 12–13, T12 **Ch 1:** T42, 43–44, T43, 46–47 **Ch 2:** T70, T79, T80, T81 **Ch 3:** 114–117, 118 **Ch 4:** 150–153, T153, 155 **Ch 5:** T181, T182, 188–191, T188, 193, T196 **Ch 6:** T237, 240–243, 244, T245 **Ch 7:** T275, 276–278, T277, 280 **Ch 8:** T303, T312, 321–323, 325, T326 **Ch 9:** T350–T351 **Ch 10:** T358 **Ch 13:** T438 **Ch 16:** T538 **Ch 17:** 571 **Ch 18:** T603 **Ch 21:** 691 **Ch 22:** T717 **Ch 25:** T772 **Ch 26:** T800

▶ **English II End-of-Course Objective 6: The student will demonstrate the ability to revise and proofread to improve the clarity and effectiveness of a piece of writing.**

10.2 Writing/Writing Processes. The student uses recursive writing processes when appropriate. The student is expected to:

(C) proofread writing for appropriateness of organization, content, style, and conventions

Intro: 12–13 **Ch 1:** 42–44, T42, 46–47, T47, 48–49 **Ch 2:** T62, 78–81, T78, T79, 82–83 **Ch 3:** 114–117 **Ch 4:** 150–153, T151, 155, T155 **Ch 5:** 188–191, 197 **Ch 6:** 240–243, 244–245 **Ch 7:** 276–278, T276 **Ch 8:** 321–323, T323 **Ch 9:** 343 **Ch 10:** T368 **Ch 12:** 435 **Ch 13:** 465 **Ch 15:** 509 **Ch 20:** 665 **Ch 21:** 691 **Ch 22:** 721 **Ch 23:** 737 **Ch 24:** 755 **Ch 26:** 806 **QRH:** 957–958

10.3 Writing/Grammar/Usage/Conventions/Spelling. The student relies increasingly on the conventions and mechanics of written English, including the rules of usage and grammar, to write clearly and effectively. The student is expected to:

(A) produce legible work that shows accurate spelling and correct use of the conventions of punctuation and capitalization [*such as italics and ellipses*]

Intro: 12–13, T13 **Ch 1:** T32, 46–47 **Ch 2:** 82 **Ch 3:** 118 **Ch 4:** 155 **Ch 5:** 193 **Ch 6:** T238, T242, 244 **Ch 7:** 280, T283 **Ch 8:** 325 **Ch 9:** 340–351, T348–T349 **Ch 10:** 352–369 **Ch 12:** 435 **Ch 13:** T459 **Ch 14:** 489 **Ch 15:** T494, 509 **Ch 17:** T561, T562 **Ch 18:** T578 **Ch 19:** T630 **Ch 20:** 665 **Ch 21:** 666–690, T668, T672, T674, T678, T683, T686, T687, 691 **Ch 22:** 692–720, T694, T695, T696, T701, T703, T704, T706, T708, T714, T716, T717, 721 **Ch 23:** 722–734, T724, T726, T727, T728, T730, T731, 737 **Ch 24:** 738–754, T740, T741, T742, T743, T746, T747, T751, 755 **Ch 25:** 756–776, T760, T761, T762, T763, T764, T765, T767, T768, T769, T770, T771, T772, T773, 777 **Ch 26:** 778–805, T779, T780, T782, T787, T792, T793, T794, T795, T796, T800, T802, 806 **Ch 27:** 810–843 **QRH:** 849, 960, 964–966, 967–968, 970–973, 975–976, 980–981

(B) demonstrate control over grammatical elements, such as subject-verb agreement, pronoun-antecedent agreement, verb forms, and parallelism

Intro: 12–13 **Ch 1:** 46–47 **Ch 2:** T78, 82 **Ch 3:** 118 **Ch 4:** 155 **Ch 5:** 192, 193 **Ch 6:** 244 **Ch 7:** 278, 280 **Ch 8:** 325 **Ch 9:** 340–351, T343 **Ch 10:** 352–369, T355, T359 **Ch 11:** T392–T393 **Ch 12:** 404–434, T405, T406, T409, T412, T413, T420, T424, T426, T427, T428, T431 **Ch 13:** 436–464, T438, T439, T440, T450, T451, T452, T453, T454, T458, T461 **Ch 14:** T468, T470, T473, T476 **Ch 15:** 490–508, T492, T493, T494, T496, T497, T499, T500, T501, T502, T505 **Ch 16:** 510–544, T511, T513, T514, T518, T523, T525, T533, T534, T536, T537, 545 **Ch 17:** 546–570, T550, T552, T554, T557, T558, T559, T560, T562, T565, T567, 571 **Ch 18:** 572–610, T575, T576, T586, T603, T605, 611 **Ch 19:** 612–634, T617, T619, T628, T630, 635 **Ch 20:** 636–664, T639, T642, T648, T649, T652, T653, 665 **Ch 21:** 691 **Ch 22:** T701, T706, T717, T718 **Ch 23:** T725 **Ch 24:** T746 **Ch 27:** 810–831, T814, T817, T821, T839 **QRH:** 960–985

10.3 **(C)** compose increasingly more involved sentences that contain gerunds, participles, and infinitives in their various functions

Ch 1: 44 **Ch 3:** 116, T116, T117, 118 **Ch 5:** 189–190 **Ch 9:** 342–344 **Ch 10:** 355, 356, T365, 366–367, T366 **Ch 12:** T418 **Ch 14:** 472–483, T473, T475, T477, T480, T481, T483, T484, T486, 489 **Ch 18:** 572–581, T576, T577, T578, T580, T582, T583, T584, T587, T588, T589, T591, T592, T595, T597, T602 **Ch 19:** T615 **Ch 22:** 721 **Ch 27:** T819 **QRH:** 973, 978

(D) produce error-free writing in the final draft

Intro: 13 **Ch 1:** 46–47 **Ch 2:** 83 **Ch 3:** 118 **Ch 4:** 155 **Ch 5:** 193 **Ch 6:** 244 **Ch 7:** 280 **Ch 8:** T323, 325, T326 **Ch 9:** 340–351 **Ch 10:** 352–369 **Ch 12:** 404–434 **Ch 13:** 436–464, 465 **Ch 14:** 466–488, 489 **Ch 15:** 490–508, 509 **Ch 16:** 510–544, 545 **Ch 17:** 546–570, 571 **Ch 18:** 572–610, T602, 611 **Ch 19:** 612–634, 635 **Ch 20:** 636–664, 665 **Ch 21:** 666–690, 691 **Ch 22:** 692–720, T716 **Ch 23:** 722–734, 737 **Ch 24:** 738–754, 755 **Ch 25:** 756–776, 777 **Ch 26:** 778–805, 806 **QRH:** 849, 939–952, 960–985

10.5 **Writing/Evaluation.** The student evaluates his/her own writing and the writings of others. The student is expected to:

(A) evaluate writing for both mechanics and content

Intro: 12–13, T12 **Ch 1:** T42, 43–44, T43, 46–47 **Ch 2:** T70, T79, T80, T81 **Ch 3:** 114–117, 118 **Ch 4:** 150–153, T153, 155 **Ch 5:** T181, T182, 188–191, T188, 193, T196 **Ch 6:** T237, 240–243, 244, T245 **Ch 7:** T275, 276–278, T277, 280 **Ch 8:** T303, T312, 321–323, 325, T326 **Ch 9:** T350–T351 **Ch 10:** T358 **Ch 13:** T438 **Ch 16:** T538 **Ch 17:** 571 **Ch 18:** T603 **Ch 21:** 691 **Ch 22:** T717 **Ch 25:** T772 **Ch 26:** T800

Additional instruction, practice, and reinforcement for English II End-of-Course Objectives can be found in the following ancillaries:

- Preparing for English II End-of-Course Examination
- Alternative Readings
- Communications
- Preparation for TAAS
- TAAS Tool Kit
- Grammar, Usage, and Mechanics
- Combining Sentences
- Daily Language Activity Transparencies
- Language Workshop CD-ROM

Elements of Language

Fourth Course
Annotated Teacher's Edition

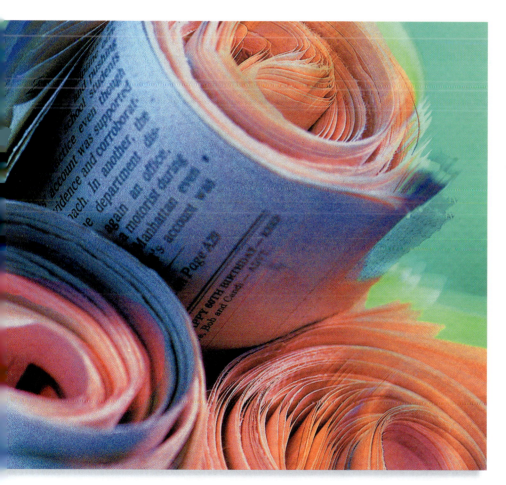

Lee Odell

Richard Vacca

Renée Hobbs

Grammar, Usage, and Mechanics
Instructional Framework by

John E. Warriner

HOLT, RINEHART AND WINSTON

A Harcourt Classroom Education Company

Austin • New York • Orlando • Atlanta • San Francisco • Boston • Dallas • Toronto • London

STAFF CREDITS

EDITORIAL

Director
Mescal Evler

Manager of Editorial Operations
Bill Wahlgren

Executive Editor
Kristine E. Marshall

Project Editors
Marcia L. Kelley
Suzanne Thompson

Annotated Teacher's Edition Editors
Eileen Joyce
Susan Lynch

Writing and Editing
Roger Boylan, David Bradford, Susan Britt, Karen Kolar, Barbara Knaggs, David Knaggs, Kevin Lemoine, Chi Nguyen, Kathryn Rogers, Jennifer Schwan, Mary Shaw

Copyediting
Michael Neibergall, *Copyediting Manager;* Mary Malone, *Senior Copyeditor;* Joel Bourgeois, Gabrielle Field, Suzi A. Hunn, Jane Kominek, Millicent Ondras, Theresa Reding, Désirée Reid, Kathleen Scheiner, Sarah Searcy, *Copyeditors*

Project Administration
Marie Price, *Managing Editor;* Lori De La Garza, *Editorial Operations Coordinator;* Tracy DeMont, Heather Cheyne, Mark Holland, Marcus Johnson, Jill O'Neal, Joyce Rector, Janet Riley, Kelly Tankersley, *Project Administration;* Gail Coupland, Elizabeth Dickson, Ruth Hooker, Margaret Sanchez, *Word Processing*

Editorial Permissions
Janet Harrington

ART, DESIGN AND PHOTO

Book Design
Senior Design Director
Diane Motz

Teresa Carrera-Paprota, *Designer*
Tim Hovde, *Design Associate*

Cover Design
Joe Melomo, *Design Director*

Graphic Services
Kristen Darby, *Manager*

PRODUCTION
Beth Prevelige, *Prepress Manager*
Simira Davis, *Supervisor*
Joan Lindsay, *Production Coordinator*

MANUFACTURING
Belinda Lopez, *Senior Production Coordinator*
Ben Saffer, *Production Assistant*

Copyright © 2001 by Holt, Rinehart and Winston

All rights reserved. No part of this publication may be reproduced or transmitted in any form or by any means, electronic or mechanical, including photocopy, recording, or any information storage and retrieval system, without permission in writing from the publisher.

Requests for permission to make copies of any part of the work should be mailed to the following address: Permissions Department, Holt, Rinehart and Winston, 1120 South Capital of Texas Highway, Austin, Texas 78746-6487.

Acknowledgments and other credits appear on pages 1032–1033 and 1034–1035, which are extensions of the copyright page.

Printed in the United States of America
ISBN 0-03-054798-9
1 2 3 4   048   03 02 01 00

PROGRAM AUTHORS

LEE ODELL helped establish the pedagogical framework for the composition strand of *Elements of Language*. In addition, he guided the development of the scope and sequence and the pedagogical design of the Writing Workshops. Dr. Odell is Professor of Composition Theory and Research and, since 1996, Director of the Writing Program at Rensselaer Polytechnic Institute. He began his career teaching English in middle and high schools. More recently he has worked with teachers in grades K–12 to establish a program that involves students from all disciplines in writing across the curriculum and for communities outside their classrooms. Dr. Odell's most recent book (with Charles R. Cooper) is *Evaluating Writing: The Role of Teacher's Knowledge about Text, Learning, and Culture* (1999). He is Past Chair of the Conference on College Composition and Communication and of NCTE's Assembly for Research.

RENÉE HOBBS helped develop the theoretical framework for the viewing and representing strand of *Elements of Language*. She guided the development of the scope and sequence; served as the authority on terminology, definitions, and pedagogy; and directed the planning for the video series. Dr. Hobbs is Associate Professor of Communication at Babson College in Wellesley, Massachusetts, and Director of the Media Literacy Project. Active in the field of media education, Dr. Hobbs has served as Director of the Institute on Media Education, Harvard Graduate School of Education; Director of The "Know TV" Project, Discovery Networks and Time Warner Cable; and Board Member, The New York Times Newspaper in Education Program. She works actively in staff development in school districts nationwide. Dr. Hobbs has contributed articles and chapters on media, technology, and education to many publications.

RICHARD VACCA helped establish the conceptual basis for the reading strand of *Elements of Language*. In addition, he guided the development of the pedagogical design and the scope and sequence of skills in the Reading Workshops. Dr. Vacca is Professor of Education at Kent State University. He recently completed a term as the forty-second President of the International Reading Association. Originally a middle school and high school teacher, Dr. Vacca served as the project director of the Cleveland Writing Project for several years. He is the co-author of *Content Area Reading; Reading and Learning to Read;* and articles and chapters related to adolescents' literacy development. In 1989, Dr. Vacca received the College Reading Association's A.B. Herr Award for Outstanding Contributions to Reading Education. Currently, he is co-chair of the IRA's Commission on Adolescent Literacy.

JOHN E. WARRINER was a high school English teacher when he developed the original organizational structure for his classic *English Grammar and Composition* series. The approach pioneered by Mr. Warriner was distinctive, and the editorial staff of Holt Rinehart, and Winston have worked diligently to retain the unique qualities of his pedagogy. For the same reason, HRW continues to credit Mr. Warriner as an author of *Elements of Language* in recognition of his groundbreaking work. John Warriner also co-authored the *English Workshop* series and was editor of *Short Stories: Characters in Conflict.* Throughout his long career, however, teaching remained Mr. Warriner's major interest, and he taught for thirty-two years in junior and senior high schools and in college.

PROGRAM CONSULTANTS

The program consultants reviewed instructional materials to ensure consistency with current research, classroom appropriateness, and alignment with curriculum guidelines.

Ann Bagley
Senior Administrator for Secondary English
Wake County Public Schools
Raleigh, North Carolina

Vicki R. Brown
Professor of Education, Grambling State University
Principal, Grambling Middle School
Grambling, Louisiana

Beth Johnson
Supervisor of Language Arts
Polk District Schools
Bartow, Florida

Kathleen Jongsma
Associate Professor, Department of Education Chair
Texas Lutheran University
Seguin, Texas

Lois King
Dallas Public Schools
Dallas, Texas

Bruce A. Marshall
Secondary Reading/Dyslexia Teacher
Cypress Falls High School
Houston, Texas

Baird Neville
Principal/Teacher
Communications Arts High School
San Antonio, Texas

Kaye Price-Hawkins
Language Arts Consultant
Abilene, Texas

Olga Samaniego
English Department Chair
Burges High School
El Paso, Texas

CRITICAL REVIEWERS

The critical reviewers read and evaluated pre-publication materials for this book.

Pupil's Edition

Geralann Barnes
Ozen High School
Beaumont, Texas

Elizabeth M. Colleran
Washington High School
Sioux Falls, South Dakota

Andrea Denton
Central Cabarrus High School
Concord, North Carolina

Leann Dixon
Hamilton Southeastern High School
Hamilton, Indiana

Kay Hannum
Hobbs High School
Hobbs, New Mexico

Carolyn E. Harris
Leesville Road High School
Raleigh, North Carolina

Patricia Hayes
West Brook High School
Beaumont, Texas

Margaret R. Karl
Florin High School
Elk Grove Unified, California

Jacquelyn Moore
Laguna Creek High School
Sacramento, California

Conni Shelnut
Lakeland Senior High School
Lakeland, Florida

Michelle Smith
Colleyville Heritage High School
Colleyville, Texas

Peggy A. Stover
Independence High School
San Jose, California

Pat Sturm
Weatherford High School
Weatherford, Oklahoma

Beverly A. Wixon
Kathleen High School
Lakeland, Florida

Debbie Zupancic
Dripping Springs High School
Dripping Springs, Texas

Annotated Teacher's Edition

Rebecca Danello
Curriculum Coordinator
Stafford County School District
Stafford, Virginia

Pat Sturm
Weatherford High School
Weatherford, Oklahoma

Char-Lene Wilkins
Morenci High School
Morenci, Michigan

Martha Woolery
Hickory High School
Chesapeake, Virginia

TEACHER/STUDENT CONTRIBUTORS

The following teachers and students worked with HRW's editorial staff to provide models of student writing for the book.

Teachers

Carolyn E. Harris
Leesville Road High School
Raleigh, North Carolina

Janet Meeks
Fairmont Junior High School
Boise, Idaho

Baird Neville
Communication Arts High School
San Antonio, Texas

Peggy A. Stover
Independence High School
San Jose, California

Students

Katie Baker
Holmes High School
Covington, Kentucky

Adam Caputo
Leesville Road High School
Raleigh, North Carolina

Yen Co
Independence High School
San Jose, California

Tabitha Henry
Weston High School
Cazenovia, Wisconsin

Gwen Miller
Fairmont Junior High School
Boise, Idaho

Jason Potterf
Communication Arts High School
San Antonio, Texas

Jeremy Schmidt
University High, University of Chicago
   Lab Schools
Chicago, Illinois

David Thompson
McNeil High School
Round Rock, Texas

FIELD TEST PARTICIPANTS

The following teachers participated in the pre-publication field test or review of prototype materials for the *Elements of Language* series.

Nadene Adams
Robert Gray Middle School
Portland, Oregon

Carol Alves
Apopka High School
Apopka, Florida

Susan Atkinson
O. P. Norman Junior High School
Kaufman, Texas

Sheryl L. Babione
Fremont Ross High School
Fremont, Ohio

Jane Baker
Elkins High School
Missouri City, Texas

Martha Barnard
Scarborough High School
Houston, Texas

Jennifer S. Barr
James Bowie High School
Austin, Texas

Leslie Benefield
Reed Middle School
Duncanville, Texas

Gina Birdsall
Irving High School
Irving, Texas

Sara J. Brennan
Murchison Middle School
Austin, Texas

Janelle Brinck
Leander Middle School
Leander, Texas

Geraldine K. Brooks
William B. Travis High School
Austin, Texas

Peter J. Caron
Cumberland Middle School
Cumberland, Rhode Island

Patty Cave
O. P. Norman Junior High School
Kaufman, Texas

Mary Cathyrne Coe
Pocatello High School
Pocatello, Idaho

Geri-Lee DeGennaro
Tarpon Springs High School
Tarpon Springs, Florida

Karen Dendy
Stephen F. Austin Middle School
Irving, Texas

Dianne Franz
Tarpon Springs Middle School
Tarpon Springs, Florida

Continued on page T6

FIELD TEST PARTICIPANTS *Continued*

Doris Frazier
East Millbrook Magnet Middle School
Raleigh, North Carolina

Shayne G. Goodrum
C. E. Jordan High School
Durham, North Carolina

Bonnie L. Hall
St. Ann School
Lansing, Illinois

Doris Ann Hall
Forest Meadow Junior High School
Dallas, Texas

James M. Harris
Mayfield High School
Mayfield Village, Ohio

Lynne Hoover
Fremont Ross High School
Fremont, Ohio

Patricia A. Humphreys
James Bowie High School
Austin, Texas

Jennifer L. Jones
Oliver Wendell Holmes Middle School
Dallas, Texas

Kathryn R. Jones
Murchison Middle School
Austin, Texas

Bonnie Just
Narbonne High School
Harbor City, California

Vincent Kimball
Lake Clifton/Eastern High School #40
Baltimore, Maryland

Nancy C. Long
MacArthur High School
Houston, Texas

Carol M. Mackey
Ft. Lauderdale Christian School
Ft. Lauderdale, Florida

Jan Jennings McCown
Johnston High School
Austin, Texas

Alice Kelly McCurdy
Rusk Middle School
Dallas, Texas

Elizabeth Morris
Northshore High School
Slidell, Louisiana

Victoria Reis
Western High School
Ft. Lauderdale, Florida

Dean Richardson
MacArthur High School
Houston, Texas

Susan M. Rogers
Freedom High School
Morganton, North Carolina

Sammy Rusk
North Mesquite High School
Mesquite, Texas

Carole B. San Miguel
James Bowie High School
Austin, Texas

Jane Saunders
William B. Travis High School
Austin, Texas

Gina Sawyer
Reed Middle School
Duncanville, Texas

Laura R. Schauermann
MacArthur High School
Houston, Texas

Stephen Shearer
MacArthur High School
Houston, Texas

Elizabeth Curry Smith
Tarpon Springs High School
Tarpon Springs, Florida

Jeannette M. Spain
Stephen F. Austin High School
Sugar Land, Texas

Carrie Speer
Northshore High School
Slidell, Louisiana

Trina Steffes
MacArthur High School
Houston, Texas

Andrea G. Freirich Stewart
Freedom High School
Morganton, North Carolina

Diana O. Torres
Johnston High School
Austin, Texas

Janice Voorhees
Whitesboro High School
Marcy, New York

Ann E. Walsh
Bedichek Middle School
Austin, Texas

Mary Jane Warden
Onahan School
Chicago, Illinois

Beth Westbrook
Covington Middle School
Austin, Texas

Char-Lene Reinhart Wilkins
Morenci High School
Morenci, Michigan

CONTENTS IN BRIEF

PART 1

Communications

Introduction: Thinking About Reading and Writing 2

1. Narration/Description: Reflecting on Experiences 16
2. Exposition: Exploring Comparisons and Contrasts 54
3. Exposition: Examining Causes and Effects 90
4. Exposition: Analyzing Problems 126
5. Exposition: Analyzing a Short Story 166
6. Exposition: Sharing Research Results 206
7. Persuasion: Persuading Others 250
8. Persuasion: Using Persuasion in Advertising 294

PART 2

Sentences and Paragraphs

9. Writing Complete Sentences 340
10. Writing Effective Sentences 352
11. Understanding Paragraphs and Compositions 370

PART 3

Grammar, Usage, and Mechanics

Grammar
12. Parts of Speech Overview 404
13. The Parts of a Sentence 436
14. The Phrase 466
15. The Clause 490

Usage
16. Agreement 510
17. Using Pronouns Correctly 546
18. Using Verbs Correctly 572
19. Using Modifiers Correctly 612
20. A Glossary of Usage 636

Mechanics
21. Capitalization 666
22. Punctuation: End Marks and Commas 692
23. Punctuation: Semicolons and Colons 722
24. Punctuation: Italics, Quotation Marks, and Ellipsis Points 738
25. Punctuation: Apostrophes, Hyphens, Dashes, Parentheses, Brackets 756
26. Spelling 778
27. Correcting Common Errors 810

PART 4

Quick Reference Handbook

- The Dictionary 846
- Document Design 849
- The History of English 861
- The Library/Media Center 866
- Reading and Vocabulary 876
- Speaking and Listening 896
- Studying and Test Taking 911
- Viewing and Representing 928
- Writing 939
- Grammar at a Glance 960

CONTENTS

Features T30
Communication Assignments T32
Overview of the Program T34
To Our Students T51

PART 1 — INTRODUCTION

Communications 1

Thinking About Reading and Writing 3
Reading as a Process 4
   Prereading 5
   While Reading 6
      Model Paragraph: from *Young Men and Fire*, Norman Maclean ... 7
   After Reading 8
Writing as a Process 9
   Prewriting 10
   Writing 11
   Revising 12
   Publishing 13
The Reading-Writing Connection 14

CHOICES: *Writing, Collaborative Reading, Careers, Literature* ... 15

CHAPTER 1 — Narration/Description

Reflecting on Experiences 16

Chapter Planning Guide T15A
Chapter Overview T15C
Preview 17
READING WORKSHOP: *Reading a Personal Reflection* ... 18
  Preparing to Read 18
     READING SKILL ▸ MAKING INFERENCES
     READING FOCUS ▸ NARRATIVE AND DESCRIPTIVE DETAILS
  Reading Selection: from *An American Childhood*, Annie Dillard ... 19
  Vocabulary Mini-Lesson: *Using Multiple-Meaning Words* ... 26
  Test-Taking Mini-Lesson: *Answering Inference Questions*
    on Reading Tests 27

WRITING WORKSHOP: *Writing a Personal Reflection* ... 28
  Prewriting 28
  Writing Mini-Lesson: *Using Figurative Language*
  Writing 38
  Framework for a Personal Reflection
  A Writer's Model: "Kicking Shyness" 39
  A Student's Model: "My Last Goodbye," Tabitha Henry ... 41

Revising 42
First Reading: *Content and Organization*
Second Reading: *Style*
   Focus on Sentences: *Combining Sentences to Add Sentence Variety*

Publishing 46
Proofreading: Grammar Link—*Subject-Verb Agreement*
Connections to Literature: *Writing a Free-Verse Poem*
   "Lost," Carl Sandburg 48

FOCUS ON VIEWING AND REPRESENTING
Making a Video Reflection 50

CHOICES: *Crossing the Curriculum: Social Studies, Literature, Careers, Viewing and Representing* 53

Exploring Comparisons and Contrasts 54

CHAPTER 2 — Exposition

Chapter Planning Guide T53A
Chapter Overview T53C

Preview 55

READING WORKSHOP: *Reading a Comparison-Contrast Article* 56
Preparing to Read 56
   READING SKILL ▶ IDENTIFYING MAIN IDEA AND SUPPORTING DETAILS
   READING FOCUS ▶ COMPARISON-CONTRAST STRUCTURE
Reading Selection: "Two Peoples Divided by Common Road Signs,"
   Norman Berdichevsky from *Contemporary Review* 57
Vocabulary Mini-Lesson: *Comparison-Contrast Context Clues* 64
Test-Taking Mini-Lesson: *Main Idea* 65

WRITING WORKSHOP: *Writing a Comparison-Contrast Essay* 66
Prewriting 66
Critical Thinking Mini-Lesson: *Synthesizing Information to Form a Thesis*

Writing 74
Framework for a Comparison-Contrast Essay
A Writer's Model: "Movie? Video? What Is the Difference?" 75
A Student's Model: "Higher than Society," Adam Caputo 77

Revising 78
First Reading: *Content and Organization*
Second Reading: *Style*
   Focus on Word Choice: *Avoiding Worn-out Adverbs*

Publishing 82
Proofreading: Grammar Link—*Using Comparative and Superlative Forms*
Connections to Life: *Distinguishing the Purposes of Media Forms* ... 84

FOCUS ON VIEWING AND REPRESENTING
Comparing and Contrasting Media Coverage 86

CHOICES: *Careers, Literature, Speaking and Listening,
Crossing the Curriculum: Science* 89

CHAPTER 3

Exposition

Examining Causes and Effects 90

Chapter Planning Guide T89A
Chapter Overview T89C

Preview 91

READING WORKSHOP: *Reading a Cause-and-Effect Article* 92
  Preparing to Read 92
    READING SKILL ▶ INFERRING CAUSES AND EFFECTS
    READING FOCUS ▶ CAUSE-AND-EFFECT STRUCTURE
  Reading Selection: "Yellowstone Makes a Triumphant Return Ten Years
    After Fires," Bruce Babbitt from the *Austin American-Statesman* 93
  Vocabulary Mini-Lesson: *Suffixes* 102
  Test-Taking Mini-Lesson: *Inferring Causes and Effects* 103

WRITING WORKSHOP: *Writing a Cause-and-Effect Explanation* 104
  Prewriting 104
    Critical Thinking Mini-Lesson: *Oversimplification and
      False Cause and Effect*

  Writing 110
  Framework for a Cause-and-Effect Essay
    A Writer's Model: "School Daze" 111
    A Student's Model: "TV Baby Sitters: Help or Hindrance?" Gwen Miller 113

  Revising 114
  First Reading: *Content and Organization*
  Second Reading: *Style*
    Focus on Sentences: *Using Infinitives and Infinitive Phrases as Openers*

  Publishing 118
  Proofreading: Grammar Link—*Dangling Modifiers*
  Connections to Life: *Participating in Group Discussions* 120

FOCUS ON VIEWING AND REPRESENTING
Analyzing the Effects of TV 122

CHOICES: *Careers, Viewing and Representing, Crossing the
Curriculum: Arts and Science; Literature* 125

CHAPTER 4

Exposition

Analyzing Problems 126

Chapter Planning Guide T125A
Chapter Overview T125C

Preview 127

READING WORKSHOP: *Reading a Problem-Analysis Article* 128
  Preparing to Read 128
     READING SKILL ▶ MAKING GENERALIZATIONS
     READING FOCUS ▶ PROBLEM-SOLUTION STRUCTURE
  Reading Selection: "Danger Beneath the Dash," Steven Levingston
    from *Reader's Digest* 129
  Vocabulary Mini-Lesson: *Context Clues: Definitions and Restatements* 136
  Test-Taking Mini-Lesson: *Answering Logic Questions* 137

WRITING WORKSHOP: *Writing a Problem-Analysis Essay* 138
  Prewriting 138
  Critical Thinking Mini-Lesson: *Coordinating and Subordinating Ideas*

  Writing 146
  Framework for a Problem-Analysis Essay
  A Writer's Model: "Licensed—but Safe?" 147
  A Student's Model: "Athletes Trying to Be Too Perfect,"
    David Thompson 149

  Revising 150
  First Reading: *Content and Organization*
  Second Reading: *Style*
    Focus on Word Choice: *Eliminating "Word Wasters"*

  Publishing 155
  Proofreading: Grammar Link—*Sentence Fragments*
  Connections to Literature: *Analyzing the Problems*
    of a Literary Character 157

FOCUS ON SPEAKING AND LISTENING
  Giving an Informative Speech 158

FOCUS ON VIEWING AND REPRESENTING
  Recognizing News Genres 162

CHOICES: *Careers, Crossing the Curriculum: Literature,
  Speaking and Listening, Media and Technology* 165

CHAPTER 5

Exposition

Analyzing a Short Story 166

Chapter Planning Guide T165A
Chapter Overview T165C

Preview 167

READING WORKSHOP: *Reading a Literary Analysis* 168
  Preparing to Read 168
    READING SKILL ▸ DRAWING CONCLUSIONS
    READING FOCUS ▸ LITERARY ELEMENTS
  Reading Selection: from "An Introduction to Charles Dickens's
    A Christmas Carol," John Irving from *You've Got to Read
    This: Contemporary American Writers Introduce Stories that
    Held Them in Awe* 169
  Vocabulary Mini-Lesson: *Using Roots* 176
  Test-Taking Mini-Lesson: *Literary Elements* 177

WRITING WORKSHOP: *Writing a Literary Analysis* 178
  Prewriting 178
  Writing 184
  Framework for a Literary Analysis
  A Writer's Model: "Characterization in 'A Man Called Horse'" ... 185
  A Student's Model: "Number One," Jeremy Schmidt 187
  Revising 188
  First Reading: *Content and Organization*
  Second Reading: *Style*
    Focus on Sentences: : *Using Complex Sentences*
  Writing Mini-Lesson: *Weaving Quotations into Your Essay*
  Publishing 193
  Proofreading: Grammar Link—*Using Quotation Marks in a Literary
    Analysis*
  Connections to Literature: *Writing a Short Story* 195

FOCUS ON VIEWING AND REPRESENTING
  Critiquing a Film 198

FOCUS ON SPEAKING AND LISTENING
  Presenting an Oral Interpretation 203

CHOICES: *Careers, Speaking and Listening, Media and Technology,
  Viewing and Representing* 205

CHAPTER 6

Exposition

Sharing Research Results 206

Chapter Planning Guide T205A
Chapter Overview T205C

Preview 207

READING WORKSHOP: *Reading a Research Article* 208
  Preparing to Read 208
    READING SKILL ▶ PARAPHRASING
    READING FOCUS ▶ PRIMARY AND SECONDARY SOURCES
  Reading Selection: "The Art of Money," David Standish
    from *Smithsonian* 209
  Vocabulary Mini-Lesson: *Specialized and Technical Terms* 216
  Test-Taking Mini-Lesson: *Using Context to Understand Specialized or
    Technical Terms* 217

WRITING WORKSHOP: *Writing a Research Paper* 218
  Prewriting 218
  Critical Thinking Mini-Lesson: *Evaluating Sources*

  Writing 232
  Framework for a Research Paper
  A Writer's Model: "The Rise of Radio" 233
  A Student's Model: "An Indecisive Conclusion," Yen Co 236

  Revising 240
  First Reading: *Content and Organization*
  Second Reading: *Style*
    Focus on Sentences: *Varying Sentence Length*

  Publishing 244
  Proofreading: Grammar Link—*Correcting Misplaced Modifiers*
  Connections to Life: *Research in the Media* 246

FOCUS ON VIEWING AND REPRESENTING
  Evaluating Web Sites 247

CHOICES: *Careers, Literature, Crossing the Curriculum: the Arts,
  Media and Technology* 249

CHAPTER 7

Persuasion

Persuading Others 250

Chapter Planning Guide T249A
Chapter Overview T249C

Preview 251

READING WORKSHOP: *Reading a Persuasive Newspaper Article* 252
    Preparing to Read 252
        READING SKILL ▸ DISTINGUISHING FACTS FROM OPINIONS
        READING FOCUS ▸ ELEMENTS OF PERSUASION
    Reading Selection: "Force-Fed Television," Adam Hochschild
      from *We the Media* 253
    Vocabulary Mini-Lesson: *Understanding Connotations and Denotations* 261
    Test-Taking Mini-Lesson: *Fact-and-Opinion Questions* 262

WRITING WORKSHOP: *Writing a Persuasive Essay* 263
    Prewriting 263
    Critical Thinking Mini-Lesson: *Evaluating Your Reasoning*

    Writing 272
    Framework for a Persuasive Essay
    A Writer's Model: "Do Something Good for the Earth" 273
    A Student's Model: "Uniforms Reduce Problems," Katie Baker 275

    Revising 276
    First Reading: *Content and Organization*
    Second Reading: *Style*
        Focus on Sentences: *Active and Passive Voice*

    Publishing 280
    Proofreading: *Grammar Link—Double Negatives*
    Test-Taking Mini-Lesson: *Analyzing a Writing Prompt*
    Connections to Life: *Writing Letters of Application* 283

FOCUS ON VIEWING AND REPRESENTING
    Analyzing Editorial Cartoons 284

FOCUS ON SPEAKING AND LISTENING
    Giving a Persuasive Speech 288

CHOICES: *Careers, Literature, Media and Technology, Crossing the
    Curriculum: Journalism and Art* 293

Using Persuasion in Advertising 294

CHAPTER 8

Persuasion

Chapter Planning Guide T293A
Chapter Overview T293C

Preview 295

READING WORKSHOP: *Reading a Persuasive Brochure* 296
  Preparing to Read 296
    READING SKILL ▶ IDENTIFYING PERSUASIVE TECHNIQUES
    READING FOCUS ▶ ANALYZING PERSUASIVE VISUAL ELEMENTS
  Reading Selection: "Adopt-A-Bison," The Nature Conservancy 297
  Vocabulary Mini-Lesson: *Synonym and Antonym Context Clues* 304
  Test-Taking Mini-Lesson: *Persuasive Devices* 305

WRITING WORKSHOP: *Creating a Persuasive Brochure* 306
  Prewriting 306
  Critical Thinking Mini-Lesson: *Evaluating Reasoning in Advertising*

  Writing 316
  Framework for a Persuasive Brochure
  A Writer's Model: "Tech Teens" 316
  A Student's Model: "Gourmet School Lunch," Jason Potterf 319

  Revising 321
  First Reading: *Content and Organization*
  Second Reading: *Style*
    Focus on Word Choice: *Eliminating Clichés*

  Publishing 325
  Proofreading: Grammar Link—*Consistent Verb Tenses*
  Connections to Life: *Analyzing Persuasion in the Media* 327

FOCUS ON VIEWING AND REPRESENTING
  Creating a Documentary on Print Advertising 329

CHOICES: *Careers, Literature, Crossing the Curriculum: History, Media and Technology* 337

PART 2 **Sentences and Paragraphs** 338

CHAPTER 9

Writing Complete Sentences 340

SENTENCE FRAGMENTS 340
    Phrase Fragments 342
        Verbal Phrases   342
        Appositive Phrases   343
        Prepositional Phrases   343
    Subordinate Clause Fragments 344

RUN-ON SENTENCES 347
    Revising Run-on Sentences 348

REVIEW A: Correcting Fragments and Run-on Sentences 350

REVIEW B: Revising Fragments and Run-on Sentences 351

CHAPTER 10

Writing Effective Sentences 352

COMBINING SENTENCES 352
    Inserting Words 353
    Inserting Phrases 355
        Prepositional Phrases   355
        Participial Phrases   355
        Appositive Phrases   355
    Using Compound Subjects and Verbs 357
    Creating a Compound Sentence 358
    Creating a Complex Sentence 359
        Adjective Clauses   359
        Adverb Clauses   359
        Noun Clauses   360

REVIEW A: Revising Sentences by Combining 361

REVIEW B: Revising a Paragraph by Combining Sentences 362

IMPROVING SENTENCE STYLE 362
    Using Parallel Structure 362
    Revising Stringy Sentences 363

Revising Wordy Sentences 365
Varying Sentence Beginnings 366
Varying Sentence Structure 368

REVIEW C: Writing a Paragraph Using a Variety of Sentence Structures 369

Understanding Paragraphs and Compositions 370

CHAPTER 11

HOW PARAGRAPHS AND COMPOSITIONS FIT TOGETHER 370

THE PARTS OF A BODY PARAGRAPH 370
Putting the Parts Together 372

QUALITIES OF PARAGRAPHS 374
Unity 374
Coherence 374
Elaboration 376
Looking at the Qualities of Paragraphs 378

REVIEW A: Analyzing Paragraphs 381

PARAGRAPHS WITHIN COMPOSITIONS 382

WHAT MAKES A COMPOSITION? 382

THE INTRODUCTION 382
Catching the Reader's Interest 383
Techniques for Writing Introductions 383
Setting the Tone 385
The Thesis Statement 386
The Structure of Introductions 388

THE BODY 391
Unity 391
Coherence 391
   Direct References   391
   Transitional Expressions   392
Elaboration 392

THE CONCLUSION 393

USING A BASIC FRAMEWORK 397

A WRITER'S MODEL 398

REVIEW B: Writing an Informative Composition 400

Contents **T17**

Teaching Strands T401A

PART 3 Grammar, Usage, and Mechanics 402

Parts of Speech Overview
Identification and Function 404

CHAPTER 12

DIAGNOSTIC PREVIEW: Determining the Parts of Speech of Words 404

NOUNS 405
   Common Nouns and Proper Nouns 406
   Compound Nouns 406
   Concrete Nouns and Abstract Nouns 407
   Collective Nouns 407

PRONOUNS 408
   Personal Pronouns 409
   Reflexive and Intensive Pronouns 409
   Demonstrative Pronouns 410
   Interrogative Pronouns 410
   Relative Pronouns 410
   Indefinite Pronouns 411

ADJECTIVES 412
   Articles 412
   Pronoun or Adjective? 414
   Noun or Adjective? 415

VERBS 417
   Main Verbs and Helping Verbs 417
   Action Verbs and Linking Verbs 418
   Transitive Verbs and Intransitive Verbs 421

ADVERBS 422
   Adverbs Modifying Verbs 422
   Adverbs Modifying Adjectives 423
   Adverbs Modifying Other Adverbs 424
   Noun or Adverb? 424

PREPOSITIONS 426
   Preposition or Adverb? 427

CONJUNCTIONS 428
   Coordinating Conjunctions 428
   Correlative Conjunctions 428

INTERJECTIONS 429

DETERMINING PARTS OF SPEECH 430

CHAPTER REVIEW 433
    A. Identifying the Parts of Speech in Sentences
    B. Identifying the Parts of Speech in a Paragraph
    C. Identifying Pronouns in Sentences
    D. Identifying Words as Nouns, Pronouns, or Adjectives
    E. Classifying Nouns

    Writing Application: *Using Adjectives in a Poem* 435

The Parts of a Sentence
Subjects, Predicates, Complements 436

CHAPTER 13

DIAGNOSTIC PREVIEW 436
    A. Identifying Subjects, Verbs, and Complements
    B. Classifying Sentences According to Purpose

WHAT IS A SENTENCE? 437

SUBJECTS AND PREDICATES 439
    The Subject 440
    The Predicate 441
    Finding the Subject 442
    Sentences Beginning with *There* or *Here* 446
    Sentences Asking Questions 446
    The Understood Subject 447
    Compound Subjects and Compound Verbs 447

COMPLEMENTS 450
    The Subject Complement 453
    The Object of a Verb 455

CLASSIFYING SENTENCES BY PURPOSE 459

CHAPTER REVIEW 463
    A. Identifying Subjects, Verbs, and Complements
    B. Identifying Subjects and Predicates
    C. Completing Sentences by Supplying Subjects and Verbs
    D. Identifying Predicate Nominatives and Predicate Adjectives
    E. Classifying Sentences as Declarative, Interrogative, Imperative, or Exclamatory

    Writing Application: *Using Varied Sentences in a Letter* 465

Contents **T19**

CHAPTER 14

The Phrase
Prepositional, Verbal, and Appositive Phrases **466**

DIAGNOSTIC PREVIEW: Identifying Prepositional, Verbal, and
Appositive Phrases 466

WHAT IS A PHRASE? 467

PREPOSITIONAL PHRASES 467
 Adjective Phrases 468
 Adverb Phrases 469

VERBALS AND VERBAL PHRASES 472
 The Participle 472
 The Participial Phrase 473
 The Gerund 476
 The Gerund Phrase 478
 The Infinitive 479
 The Infinitive Phrase 480

APPOSITIVES AND APPOSITIVE PHRASES 483

CHAPTER REVIEW 487
 A. Sentences with Prepositional Phrases
 B. Identifying Participles and Participial Phrases
 C. Identifying Phrases in Sentences
 D. Identifying Phrases in a Paragraph
 Writing Application: *Using Phrases in a Newspaper Article* 489

CHAPTER 15

The Clause
Independent Clauses and Subordinate Clauses **490**

DIAGNOSTIC PREVIEW 490
 A. Identifying and Classifying Clauses
 B. Classifying Sentences According to Structure

WHAT IS A CLAUSE? 492

INDEPENDENT CLAUSES 492

SUBORDINATE CLAUSES 493
 Complements and Modifiers in Subordinate Clauses 494

USES OF SUBORDINATE CLAUSES 495
    The Adjective Clause 495
    Relative Pronouns 496

THE ADVERB CLAUSE 498
    Subordinating Conjunctions 498

THE NOUN CLAUSE 501

SENTENCES CLASSIFIED ACCORDING TO STRUCTURE 504

CHAPTER REVIEW 507
    A. Identifying and Classifying Clauses
    B. Identifying and Classifying Subordinate Clauses
    C. Classifying Sentences According to Structure
    Writing Application: *Writing a Paragraph* 509

CHAPTER 16

Agreement
Subject and Verb, Pronoun and Antecedent 510

DIAGNOSTIC PREVIEW 510
    A. Identifying Subject-Verb Agreement and
       Pronoun-Antecedent Agreement
    B. Identifying Subject-Verb Agreement and
       Pronoun-Antecedent Agreement

AGREEMENT OF SUBJECT AND VERB 512
    Indefinite Pronouns 516
    Compound Subjects 520
    Special Problems in Subject-Verb Agreement 522

AGREEMENT OF PRONOUN AND ANTECEDENT 532
    Indefinite Pronouns 533
    Compound Antecedents 535
    Special Problems in Pronoun-Antecedent Agreement 536

CHAPTER REVIEW 543
    A. Identifying Subject-Verb and Pronoun-Antecedent Agreement
    B. Choosing Pronouns That Agree with Their Antecedents
    C. Identifying Subject-Verb Agreement and
       Pronoun-Antecedent Agreement
    Writing Application: *Using Agreement in a Letter* 545

Using Pronouns Correctly
Nominative, Objective, and Possessive Case; Clear Reference **546**

CHAPTER 17

DIAGNOSTIC PREVIEW 546
    A. Proofreading Sentences for Correct Pronoun Forms
    B. Proofreading Sentences for Correct Forms and Uses

CASE FORMS OF PERSONAL PRONOUNS 547
    The Nominative Case 549
    The Objective Case 553
    The Possessive Case 556

SPECIAL PROBLEMS IN PRONOUN USAGE 558
    The Relative Pronouns *Who* and *Whom* 558
    Appositives 561
    Reflexive and Intensive Pronouns 564
    Pronouns in Incomplete Constructions 565

CLEAR PRONOUN REFERENCE 566

CHAPTER REVIEW 569
    A. Using Pronouns Correctly in Sentences
    B. Selecting Pronouns to Complete Sentences Correctly
    C. Proofreading Sentences for Correct Pronoun Usage

    Writing Application: *Using Pronouns Correctly in a Letter* 571

Using Verbs Correctly
Principal Parts, Tense, Voice, Mood **572**

CHAPTER 18

DIAGNOSTIC PREVIEW 572
    A. Writing the Past and Past Participle Forms of Irregular Verbs
    B. Revising Sentences to Correct Problems in Verb Tense and Voice
    C. Determining Correct Uses of *Lie* and *Lay, Sit* and *Set,* and *Rise* and *Raise*

THE PRINCIPAL PARTS OF VERBS 574
    Regular Verbs 575
    Irregular Verbs 576

SIX TROUBLESOME VERBS 582
    Lie and *Lay* 582

Sit and *Set* 585
Rise and *Raise* 588

TENSE 590
  Verb Conjugation 590
  The Uses of the Tenses 594
  Consistency of Tense 597

MODALS 599

ACTIVE VOICE AND PASSIVE VOICE 601
  Using the Passive Voice 604

MOOD 606

CHAPTER REVIEW 608
  A. Writing the Past or Past Participle Form of Verbs
  B. Revising Verb Tense or Voice
  C. Determining Correct Use of *Lie* and *Lay*, *Sit* and *Set*, and *Rise* and *Raise* in Sentences
  D. Using the Different Tenses of Verbs
  E. Choosing the Correct Forms of Verbs

  Writing Application: *Using Verb Tense in an Essay* 611

Using Modifiers Correctly
CHAPTER 19
Forms, Comparison, and Placement 612

DIAGNOSTIC PREVIEW 612
  A. Revising Sentences to Correct Errors in the Use and Placement of Modifiers
  B. Revising a Paragraph to Correct Errors in the Use and Placement of Modifiers

WHAT IS A MODIFIER? 614
  One-Word Modifiers 614
  Phrases Used as Modifiers 616
  Clauses Used as Modifiers 617

EIGHT TROUBLESOME MODIFIERS 617
  Bad and *Badly* 617
  Good and *Well* 617
  Slow and *Slowly* 618
  Real and *Really* 618

COMPARISON OF MODIFIERS 620
    Regular Comparison 621
    Irregular Comparison 622
    Use of Comparative and Superlative Forms 623

DANGLING MODIFIERS 626

MISPLACED MODIFIERS 627
    Misplaced One-Word Modifiers 627
    Misplaced Phrase Modifiers 628
    Misplaced Clause Modifiers 630

CHAPTER REVIEW 633
    A. Correcting Errors in the Use of the Comparative and Superlative forms
    B. Revising Sentences by Correcting Dangling and Misplaced Modifiers
    C. Revising Sentences by Correcting Unclear Comparisons and Incorrect, Misplaced, and Dangling Modifiers
    Writing Application: *Using Comparison in a Consumer Guide* 635

A Glossary of Usage
Common Usage Problems 636

CHAPTER 20

DIAGNOSTIC PREVIEW 636
    A. Revising Errors in Usage
    B. Proofreading Paragraphs to Correct Usage Errors

ABOUT THE GLOSSARY 638

THE DOUBLE NEGATIVE 656

NONSEXIST LANGUAGE 659

CHAPTER REVIEW 661
    A. Revising Expressions by Correcting Errors in Usage
    B. Proofreading a Paragraph to Correct Usage Errors
    C. Identifying Standard Usage
    Writing Application: *Creating a Flier* 665

CHAPTER 21

Capitalization
Standard Uses of Capitalization 666

DIAGNOSTIC PREVIEW 666
  A. Capitalizing Sentences Correctly
  B. Capitalizing a Paragraph Correctly

USING CAPITAL LETTERS CORRECTLY 668
  Abbreviations 686

CHAPTER REVIEW 689
  A. Using Capitalization Correctly
  B. Capitalizing Words in a Paragraph Correctly
  C. Using Capitalization Correctly
  D. Correcting Sentences by Capitalizing Words

Writing Application: *Writing a Guidebook* 691

CHAPTER 22

Punctuation
End Marks and Commas 692

DIAGNOSTIC PREVIEW 692
  A. Correcting Sentences by Adding Periods, Question Marks, Exclamation Points, and Commas
  B. Correcting Paragraphs by Adding Periods, Question Marks, Exclamation Points, and Commas

END MARKS 694
  Abbreviations 696

COMMAS 700
  Items in a Series 700
  Independent Clauses 703
  Nonessential Clauses and Phrases 704
  Introductory Elements 707
  Interrupters 711
  Conventional Uses of Commas 714
  Unnecessary Commas 716

CHAPTER REVIEW 719
  A. Using End Marks
  B. Correcting Sentences by Adding Punctuation
  C. Correcting Paragraphs by Adding Punctuation

Writing Application: *Using Commas in Instructions* 721

CHAPTER 23

Punctuation
Semicolons and Colons 722

DIAGNOSTIC PREVIEW: Correcting Sentences by Adding Semicolons
and Colons 722

SEMICOLONS 724

COLONS 729

CHAPTER REVIEW 733
    A. Correcting Sentences by Using Semicolons and Colons
    B. Correcting Sentences by Adding Colons
    C. Correcting Sentences by Adding Semicolons and Colons

Writing Application: *Punctuating a Business Letter* 737

CHAPTER 24

Punctuation
Italics, Quotation Marks, and Ellipsis Points 738

DIAGNOSTIC PREVIEW: Correcting Sentences by Adding Italics
(Underlining), Quotation Marks, and Ellipsis Points 738

ITALICS 739

QUOTATION MARKS 743

ELLIPSIS POINTS 750

CHAPTER REVIEW 753
    A. Correcting Sentences by Adding Italics (Underlining)
       and Quotation Marks
    B. Correcting Sentences by Adding Italics (Underlining)
    C. Using Ellipsis Points Correctly

Writing Application: *Writing an Interior Dialogue* 755

Punctuation
Apostrophes, Hyphens, Dashes, Parentheses, Brackets 756

CHAPTER 25

DIAGNOSTIC PREVIEW 756
    A. Correcting Sentences by Using Apostrophes and Hyphens
    B. Correcting Sentences by Using Dashes, Parentheses, and Brackets

APOSTROPHES 758
    Possessive Case 758
    Contractions 763
    Plurals 766

HYPHENS 767
    Word Division 767
    Compound Words 768

DASHES 770

PARENTHESES 770

BRACKETS 772

CHAPTER REVIEW 775
    A. Using Apostrophes and Hyphens Correctly
    B. Using Dashes, Brackets, and Parentheses Correctly
    C. Writing the Possessive Forms of Nouns
    D. Proofreading a Paragraph for Errors in Punctuation
    Writing Application: *Punctuating a Poem* 777

Spelling
Improving Your Spelling 778

CHAPTER 26

DIAGNOSTIC PREVIEW: Correcting Misspelled and Misused Words
    and Numerals 778

GOOD SPELLING HABITS 779

SPELLING RULES 780
    ie and *ei* 780
    –*cede*, –*ceed*, and –*sede* 780
    Adding Prefixes 781

Contents **T27**

Adding Suffixes	782
Forming Plurals of Nouns	787
Writing Numbers	791

WORDS OFTEN CONFUSED 793

CHAPTER REVIEW 803
    A. Proofreading Sentences to Correct Spelling Errors
    B. Proofreading a Paragraph to Correct Spelling Errors
    C. Distinguishing Between Words Often Confused
    Writing Application: *Using Correct Spelling in an Application Letter* 805

SPELLING WORD LIST 807

CHAPTER 27

Correcting Common Errors
Key Language Skills Review 810

GRAMMAR AND USAGE 811
    Grammar and Usage Test: Section 1 827
    Grammar and Usage Test: Section 2 830

MECHANICS 832
    Mechanics Test: Section 1 840
    Mechanics Test: Section 2 842

PART 4 — Quick Reference Handbook 844

THE DICTIONARY 846
Information About Words 846

DOCUMENT DESIGN 849
Manuscript Style 849
Desktop Publishing 849
Graphics 855

THE HISTORY OF ENGLISH: ORIGINS AND USES 861
The History of English 861
Varieties of American English 864

THE LIBRARY/MEDIA CENTER 866
Using Print and Electronic Sources 866

READING AND VOCABULARY 876
Reading 876
Vocabulary 887

SPEAKING AND LISTENING 896
Speaking 896
Listening 906

STUDYING AND TEST TAKING 911
Study Skills and Strategies 911
Test-Taking Skills and Strategies 915

VIEWING AND REPRESENTING 928
Media Terms 928

WRITING 939
Skills, Structures, and Techniques 939

GRAMMAR AT A GLANCE 960

Diagramming Appendix 986
Index 1000
Acknowledgments 1032
Photography and Illustration Credits 1034

Features

Reading Skills and Focuses
Making Inferences... 21
Narrative and Descriptive Details 24
Main Idea and Supporting Details............................. 60
Comparison-Contrast Structure 62
Inferring Causes and Effects.................................. 95
Cause-and-Effect Structure 97
Making Generalizations 132
Problem-Solution Structure................................... 134
Drawing Conclusions 172
Literary Elements 173
Paraphrasing 213
Primary and Secondary Sources 214
Distinguishing Facts from Opinions........................... 255
Elements of Persuasion.. 257
Identifying Persuasive Techniques............................ 300
Analyzing Persuasive Visual Elements........................ 303

Vocabulary Mini-Lessons
Using Multiple-Meaning Words 26
Comparison-Contrast Context Clues 64
Suffixes.. 102
Context Clues: Definitions and Restatements 136
Using Roots 176
Specialized and Technical Terms 216
Understanding Connotations and Denotations................ 261
Using Context Clues—Synonyms and Antonyms 304

Reading Test Taking Mini-Lessons
Answering Inference Questions on Reading Tests 27
Main Idea 65
Inferring Causes and Effects.................................. 103
Answering Logic Questions 137
Literary Elements 177
Using Context to Understand Specialized or Technical Terms . 217
Fact-and-Opinion Questions................................... 262
Questions About Recognizing Persuasive Devices 305

Critical Thinking/Writing Mini-Lessons
Using Figurative Language.................................... 37
Synthesizing Information to Form a Thesis 71
Oversimplification and False Cause and Effect 108
Coordinating and Subordinating Ideas........................ 144
Weaving Quotations into Your Essay......................... 192
Evaluating Sources 226
Evaluating Your Reasoning.................................... 270
Evaluating Reasoning in Advertising......................... 315

Focus On Sentences/Word Choice
Combining Sentences to Add Sentence Variety 44
Avoiding Worn-out Adverbs 80

Using Infinitives and Infinitive Phrases as Openers............ 116
Eliminating "Word Wasters"............ 152
Using Complex Sentences............ 190
Varying Sentence Length............ 242
Active and Passive Voice............ 278
Eliminating Clichés............ 323

Grammar Links
Subject-Verb Agreement............ 46
Comparative and Superlative Forms............ 82
Dangling Modifiers............ 118
Sentence Fragments............ 155
Using Quotation Marks in a Literary Analysis............ 193
Correcting Misplaced Modifiers............ 244
Double Negatives............ 280
Consistent Verb Tenses............ 325

Writing Test Taking Mini-Lessons
Analyzing Literary Elements............ 177
Analyzing a Writing Prompt............ 282

Connections to Literature/Life
Writing a Free-Verse Poem............ 48
Distinguishing the Purposes of Media Forms............ 84
Participating in Group Discussions............ 120
Analyzing the Problems of a Literary Character............ 157
Writing a Short Story............ 195
Examining Research in the Media............ 246
Writing Letters of Application............ 283
Analyzing Persuasion in the Media............ 327

Designing Your Writing
Designing Your Web Page............ 45
Using Subheads............ 81
Using Flowcharts and Diagrams............ 117
Using Color............ 153
Formatting Your Essay............ 191
Using Site maps............ 243
Using Visuals to Support Position............ 279
Using Typefaces............ 324

Viewing and Representing/Speaking and Listening
Making a Video Reflection............ 50
Comparing and Contrasting Media Coverage............ 86
Analyzing the Effects of TV............ 122
Giving an Informative Speech............ 158
Recognizing New Genres............ 162
Critiquing a Film............ 198
Presenting an Oral Interpretation............ 203
Evaluating Web Sites............ 247
Analyzing Editorial Cartoons............ 284
Giving a Persuasive Speech............ 288
Creating a Documentary on Print Advertising............ 329

Major Communication Assignments

	Introductory Course	First Course	Second Course
Narration/ Description	• Writing About a Life Experience • Writing a Narrative Poem • Telling a Story • Writing a Descriptive Paragraph • Writing a Short Story	• Writing an Eyewitness Account • Writing a Descriptive Essay • Writing a Descriptive Poem • Writing a Short Story • Writing a Personal Narrative	• Writing a Personal Narrative • Writing a Descriptive Essay • Telling a True Story • Writing a Humorous "How-to" Poem
Exposition	• Writing a Newspaper Article • Writing a Newspaper's Advice Column • Producing a Newspaper • Producing TV News • Writing a "How-to" Paper • Writing a Comparison-Contrast Essay • Comparing Documentaries • Writing a Book Review • Writing About a Poem • Writing a Research Report • Giving a Research Presentation	• Writing Instructions • Giving Directions • Writing an Advantages/ Disadvantages Essay • Comparing Informative TV or Video Presentations • Making a Documentary Video • Creating Book Jacket Copy • Analyzing a Poem • Analyzing and Designing Book Covers • Writing an Information Report • Giving an Informative Speech	• Writing a Process Explanation • Writing a Cause-and-Effect Essay • Writing a Book Review • Creating a Slide Show Comparing a Book and Its Movie • Writing a Response to a Poem • Holding a Panel Discussion • Writing a Research Report • Giving an Informative Speech Using a Web Site as a Visual • Designing a Web Site
Persuasion	• Writing a Persuasive Letter • Writing an Advertisement	• Writing a Persuasive Essay • Creating a Print Advertisement • Creating Your Own Commercial	• Writing a Persuasive Essay • Writing a Short Story That Persuades • Giving a Persuasive Speech • Creating a Brochure
Research Skills	• Writing a Research Report • Giving a Research Presentation	• Writing a Research Report • Giving an Informative Speech	• Writing a Research Report • Giving an Informative Speech Using a Web Site as a Visual • Designing a Web Site
Creative Writing, Speaking, and Representing	• Writing a Narrative Poem • Telling a Story • Writing a Short Story	• Writing Haiku • Writing a Short Story • Performing a Dramatic Reading	• Writing a Humorous "How-to" Poem • Producing a Scene from a Book • Writing a Fable

Third Course	Fourth Course	Fifth Course	Sixth Course
• Writing a Description of a Place • Taking Field Notes • Creating a Video Postcard • Writing a Personal Narrative • Writing a Short Story • Presenting Oral Narratives	• Writing a Personal Reflection • Writing a Free-Verse Poem • Making a Video Reflection • Writing a Short Story • Presenting an Oral Interpretation	• Writing an Autobiographical Narrative • Writing a Narrative for an Application • Creating an Oral History • Writing a Poem that Defines • Writing a Dramatic Scene • Writing a Short Story • Adapting a Scene from a Novel for Film	• Writing a Reflective Essay • Writing a College Application • Creating an Oral History • Creating an Audiovisual Self-Reflection • Writing a Short Story • Planning a Trailer • Writing a Ballad • Writing a Dramatic Scene
• Writing a Comparison-Contrast Essay • Comparing and Contrasting Media Coverage • Writing a Cause-and-Effect Explanation • Writing a Literary Cause-and-Effect Essay • Presenting an Informative Speech • Writing an Analysis of a Poem • Presenting a Poetry Reading • Writing an I-Search Paper • Making a Video Documentary • Analyzing Network News	• Writing a Comparison/Contrast Essay • Distinguishing the Purposes of Media Forms • Comparing and Contrasting Media Coverage • Writing a Cause-and-Effect Explanation • Participating in Group Discussions • Writing a Problem-Analysis Essay • Giving an Informative Speech • Writing a Literary Analysis • Critiquing a Film • Writing a Research Paper	• Writing an Extended Definition • Comparing and Contrasting Media Coverage • Writing a Progress Report • Writing a Memo • Writing and Delivering an Informative Speech • Writing a Problem-Solution Essay • Writing a Literary Analysis of a Novel • Writing a Historical Research Paper • Exploring Uses of History in Fiction • Creating a Video Documentary	• Writing a Comparison-Contrast Essay • Comparing and Contrasting TV Entertainment Genres • Conducting Interviews • Writing a Causal Analysis • Creating an Informative Speech • Writing a Literary Analysis of a Drama • Writing a Literary Research Paper • Researching a Film • Creating an Investigative Documentary • Examining Characterization in TV Sitcoms • Analyzing TV News • Investigating Problem-Solution in Literature
• Writing a Persuasive Paper • Making a Persuasive Speech • Writing a Critical Review • Critiquing Persuasion in the Media	• Writing a Position Paper • Writing a Letter of Application • Giving a Persuasive Speech • Creating a Brochure • Creating a Documentary on Print Advertising	• Writing an Editorial • Writing a Sales Letter • Writing and Delivering a Persuasive Speech • Creating a Political Campaign • Writing a Book Review • Preparing and Delivering an Oral Critique • Writing an Ad Evaluation • Creating an Ad Campaign	• Writing a Persuasive Essay • Creating a Parody • Analyzing Media Persuasion • Making a Persuasive Speech • Reviewing a Documentary • Writing a Proposal • Conducting a Panel Discussion • Evaluating a Film Version of a Drama
• Writing an I-Search Paper • Researching for Fiction Writing • Making a Video Documentary	• Writing a Research Paper • Evaluating Web Sites • Analyzing Research in the Media	• Writing a Historical Research Paper • Exploring Uses of History in Fiction • Evaluating Web Sites	• Writing a Literary Research Paper • Researching a Film • Creating an Investigative Documentary
• Creating a Video Postcard • Writing a Short Story • Writing a Poem • Presenting a Poetry Reading	• Writing a Free-Verse Poem • Writing a Short Story • Presenting an Oral Interpretation • Making a Video Reflection	• Writing a Dramatic Scene • Writing a Poem that Defines • Writing a Short Story • Adapting a Scene for Film • Preparing and Presenting an Oral Interpretation	• Writing a Short Story • Writing a Ballad • Writing a Dramatic Scene • Creating a Dramatic Reading • Creating a Parody

Elements of Language

Designed for the Information Age

While reading and writing have been traditional topics of instruction for centuries, *what* and *how* students read and write have changed dramatically. Personal computers have become a staple in most homes and classrooms, and the variety of communications coming through television, radio, movies, and the Internet demands that students process information in a number of ways. That's why Holt, Rinehart and Winston has created *Elements of Language.*

Elements of Language is a comprehensive language arts program designed for the Information Age. Through its exciting visual design and use of real-world examples, *Elements of Language* helps students understand that—as global communications guru Marshall McLuhan said—"the medium is the message," whether that medium is a book, a television show, an advertisement, or a Web site.

Structured for Teacher Flexibility

Elements of Language is comprehensive in scope yet structured in a way that gives you the ability to pick and choose the instruction most appropriate for each class. Each book is divided into four main parts—the first three parts developing instructional topics in depth and the fourth part providing a comprehensive reference tool.

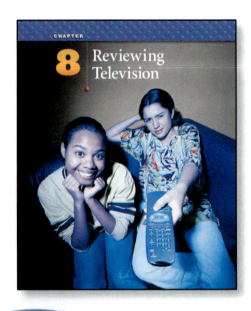

Part 1
Communications

Part 1: Communications is dedicated to an intensive study of a variety of literacies—reading, writing, speaking, listening, viewing, and representing—with an emphasis on writing. Each chapter uses nonfiction texts and real-world documents to explore different modes of communication, such as reviewing a television program, evaluating print ads, or writing a persuasive editorial.

Sentences and Paragraphs

Part 2: Sentences and Paragraphs gives students focused instruction in how to revise and improve their sentences through techniques such as combining sentences and varying sentence lengths. After mastering the skills of structuring sentences, students then learn the basics of good paragraphs, including how to achieve unity and coherence and how to use effective transitions between paragraphs in a longer piece of writing.

Grammar, Usage, and Mechanics

Part 3: Grammar, Usage, and Mechanics is organized in the classic and effective Warriner's format—rule, followed by example, followed by exercise. Part 3 also contains spelling instruction with spelling rules and an extensive list of words that are often confused.

Part 4

Quick Reference Handbook

Part 4: Quick Reference Handbook gives students an efficient way to access information to help them write, do research, hone speaking and listening skills, learn strategies for studying and taking tests, and develop visual literacy. The Handbook also includes "Grammar at a Glance," a concise overview and reference tool.

Part 1 Communications

The Reading Workshop

Taking Reading to the Next Level

All readers, even the best, sometimes struggle. **Part 1: Communications** offers strategies and skills developed by the experts to help you address the specific reading needs of your students.

Real-World Focus

Each Communications chapter opens with a **Reading Workshop** that focuses on a reading skill students need to become effective communicators. Each Reading Workshop features nonfiction texts drawn from real-world sources, such as magazines, newspapers, brochures, or Web sites, to model for students the different ways ideas are communicated through writing.

Reading Skills for Life

The **Reading Workshops** teach students strategies for reading and for understanding different kinds of texts.

READING SKILL

Each **Reading Workshop** targets one essential reading skill, demonstrating the strategies active readers use to maximize comprehension.

READING FOCUS

Each **Reading Workshop** focuses on a unique element characteristic of the informational or persuasive text students are studying.

Expert Advice

Dr. Richard Vacca, past president of the International Reading Association and author of *Reading in the Content Areas*, established the conceptual basis for the reading strand in *Elements of Language*. He was pivotal in shaping both the instructional design and the content of the program, and his classroom experience informs the program's practical, real-world strategies for improving communication.

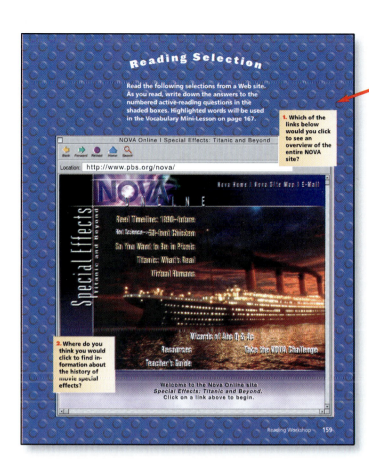

Active-Reading Questions model the thinking and questioning students need to acquire strong reading skills.

Mini-Lessons demonstrate strategies for acquiring an extensive vocabulary and scoring well on standardized tests.

Thinking It Through walks students through the steps needed to analyze a task and identify the critical path to success.

Expert Advice

Judith L. Irvin helped establish the conceptual basis for the middle school reading strand of *Elements of Language*. Dr. Irvin teaches courses in curriculum, middle school education, and educational leadership at Florida State University. She is also chair of the Research Committee of the National Middle School Association and was the editor of *Research in Middle Level Education* for six years.

T37

Part 1 Communications
The Writing Workshop

Writing by Design

A blank page can be one of the most terrifying things any writer faces. *Elements of Language* recognizes that fear, and through its **Writing Workshops** guides students step by step through the writing process with focused exercises for prewriting, writing, revising, and publishing.

Reading/Writing Connection

The *Pupil's Edition* provides clear connections between reading and writing, easing the transition from reading "writing" to writing "reading." In the Reading Workshop at the start of each chapter, students learn how to read a real-world text and identify the techniques authors use. This instruction prepares students to write a similar piece in the Writing Workshop.

Visual Delivery of Instruction

The step-by-step nature of the instruction is enhanced by its visual presentation. Throughout the Workshop, abundant, colorful graphics convey information and key concepts. A writer's model and a student model—both clearly structured and labeled—provide strong instructional cues for putting pen to paper or fingers to keyboard.

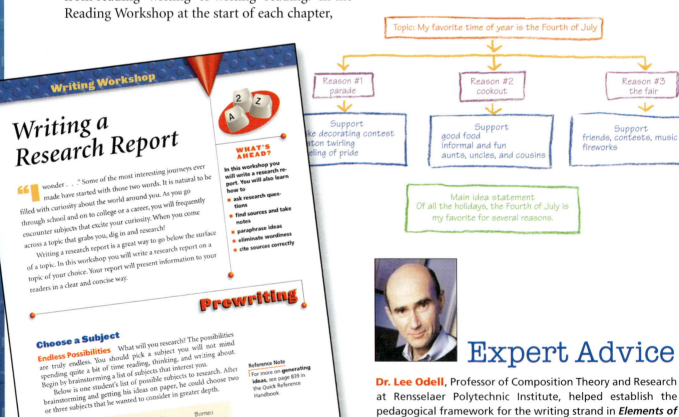

Expert Advice

Dr. Lee Odell, Professor of Composition Theory and Research at Rensselaer Polytechnic Institute, helped establish the pedagogical framework for the writing strand in *Elements of Language*. Coeditor of the recently published *Evaluating Writing: The Role of Teachers' Knowledge About Text, Learning, and Culture* (1999), Dr. Odell guided the development of both the scope and sequence and the instructional design of the Writing Workshops.

Mini-Lessons provide instruction for critical-thinking and writing skills.

A Writer's Model provides sample papers that model the assignment and that demonstrate how to use the Framework as a guide.

The **Framework** breaks down the parts of a written product, showing students exactly how to structure their papers.

Revision Charts identify evaluation questions, tips for revising, and appropriate techniques for revising.

Features for Developing Style

WORD CHOICE or SENTENCES

Additional instruction and practice help students refine one aspect of their writing style, such as revising wordy sentences or eliminating clichés.

Grammar Link

Instruction and practice show students how to identify and correct common grammatical problems.

Designing Your Writing

This feature teaches students about the visual aspects of writing, helping them choose the most effective design and layout and select the best graphics to convey their message.

T39

Part 1 Communications

Focus on
▶ Speaking and Listening
▶ Viewing and Representing

Media Literacy and Oral Communication

Today's teenagers are often delighted by the variety and frequency of media. Stimulated from all directions by a multitude of messages, from magazine and television advertising to billboards, movies, and the Internet, students must learn how to understand the power of these messages, how to evaluate them, and how to produce their own messages in a variety of formats. Teaching students to view the media with an analytical eye is a serious responsibility. Students must also learn to receive and interpret verbal messages, and to organize ideas and communicate them orally. *Elements of Language* is here to help.

At the end of each Communications chapter, one or more extensive lessons highlight speaking and listening or viewing and representing skills, offering meaningful instruction on ways students can learn to take advantage of the power of the media.

Focus on Viewing and Representing helps students become savvy, critical viewers and creative, responsible media communicators.

Focus on Speaking and Listening encourages students to improve the ways in which they receive and convey oral communications.

T40

Expert Advice

Renée Hobbs, one of the nation's leading authorities on media education, guided the development of the Viewing and Representing lessons in *Elements of Language*. As the director of the Media Literacy Project at Clark University in Worcester, Massachusetts, Dr. Hobbs works with school districts to develop programs that build the media literacy of students across the nation.

Your Turn puts students' new knowledge to work in real-world situations with hands-on activities.

Features That Connect to Literature and Life

Connections to Life/Connections to Literature features connect chapter concepts to the students' own lives, to the literature they may be reading, and to the communities in which they live.

Foundations for Writing

Part 2: Sentences and Paragraphs

In **Part 2: Sentences and Paragraphs,** *Elements of Language* focuses on the nuts-and-bolts knowledge students need to become successful writers.

The *Pupil's Edition* presents easy-to-follow instruction on writing complete and effective sentences; combining sentences; and correcting common errors such as fragments, wordiness, and lack of parallel structure.

Students also learn to develop strong paragraphs, focusing on unity and coherence. In grades 10, 11, and 12, students focus on composition structure.

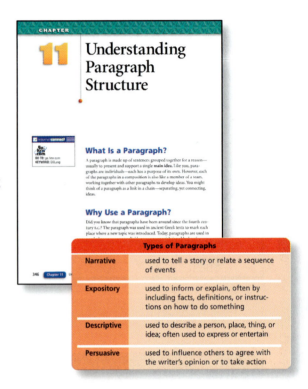

Part 3: Grammar, Usage, and Mechanics

A confident control of grammar, usage, and mechanics helps to ensure clear and effective communication. In **Part 3: Grammar, Usage, and Mechanics,** *Elements of Language* delivers a comprehensive language skills curriculum that's accessible and effective. Diagnostic Previews give opportunities for diagnosing students' strengths and weaknesses. Reviews A and B provide cumulative assessment, and Chapter Reviews offer additional exercises for ongoing assessments.

Time-Tested Model

Part 3 of *Elements of Language* is based on John Warriner's logical model of instruction—teach students the rule, show examples of the rule in action, and provide immediate practice to reinforce the skill or concept. This time-honored approach has been the authoritative standard for teaching grammar, usage, and mechanics skills for over fifty years.

Common Conjunctive Adverbs		
also	incidentally	next
anyway	indeed	nonetheless
besides	instead	otherwise
consequently	likewise	still
finally	meanwhile	then
furthermore	moreover	therefore
however	nevertheless	thus

Common Transitional Expressions		
after all	even so	in fact
as a result	for example	in other words
at any rate	for instance	on the contrary
by the way	in addition	on the other hand

Warriner's Model for Instruction

"Practice makes perfect," and a multitude of exercises, both written and oral, offer students ample opportunities to practice each rule and learn one concept at a time.

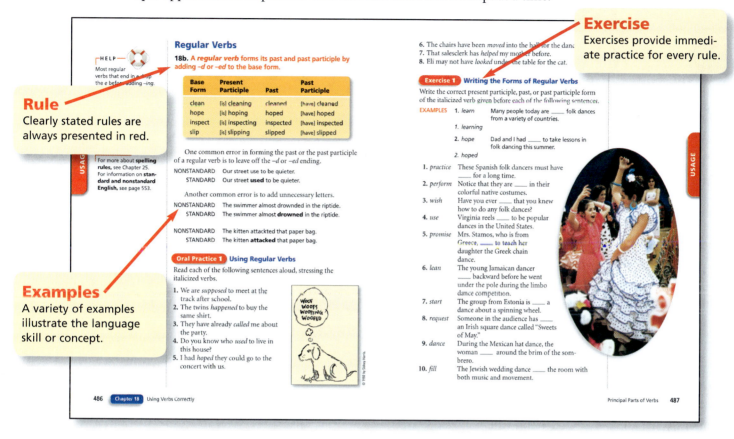

Grammar Expert

John E. Warriner, English teacher for thirty years in junior and senior high schools and college, developed the original organizational structure that serves as the basis for the Grammar, Usage, and Mechanics instruction in *Elements of Language*. His well-known and respected pedagogical concept, a clearly stated rule followed by examples and then immediate practice, continues to stand as the ideal model for authoritative grammar, usage, and mechanics instruction.

 # Quick Reference Handbook

Designed to give students quick and convenient access to key communication concepts, this handbook covers the following topics:

- ▶ The Dictionary
- ▶ Document Design
- ▶ The History of English: Origins and Uses
- ▶ The Library/Media Center
- ▶ Reading and Vocabulary
- ▶ Speaking and Listening
- ▶ Studying and Test Taking
- ▶ Viewing and Representing
- ▶ Writing
- ▶ Grammar at a Glance

Resources to Enrich the Learning Process

Support for Communications Chapters

The wide array of print, visual, and technological resources included with *Elements of Language* gives you the visual and academic support needed to make learning come alive for students.

The **Communications** booklet provides support and practice for the Reading and Writing Workshops with graphic organizers, teaching transparencies, and student worksheets. It includes

- writing prompts
- journal warm-ups
- revising charts
- proofreading practice
- fine art transparencies
- guidelines for peer evaluation and self-evaluation
- additional practice

Designing Your Writing transparencies and worksheets model effective techniques for presenting writing. They teach and demonstrate how the choice of formatting, graphics, and other design elements can affect the intended message.

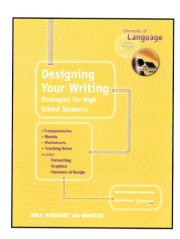

Media Literacy and Communications Skills provides chapter-by-chapter support for speaking, listening, viewing, and representing skills. The package includes videocassettes, *A How-to Handbook,* a set of *Support and Practice* transparencies and worksheets, and a *Teacher's Guide* that pulls these materials together. For more information, see Technology Resources on page T48.

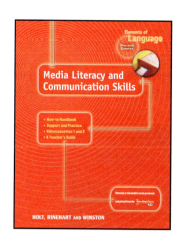

Alternative Readings booklet benefits struggling readers by offering an easier MiniRead, including active-reading questions, for each Reading Workshop. Additional reading strategy options target struggling readers and provide tools they can apply to a range of texts.

Language Skills

Elements of Language is a comprehensive program of language skills instruction that gives students a solid foundation for effective communication.

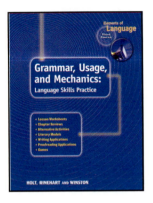

Grammar, Usage, and Mechanics: Language Skills Practice provides additional practice for all grammar, usage, and mechanics rules in Part 3 of the *Pupil's Edition*. Based on Warriner's rule-example-exercise model, this invaluable workbook features exercises, proofreading applications, writing applications, and literary-model activities.

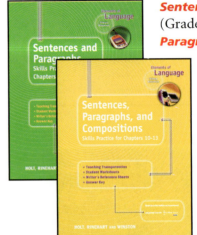

Sentences and Paragraphs (Grades 6–9) and ***Sentences, Paragraphs, and Compositions*** (Grades 10–12) provide up to two pages of additional practice for every exercise in Part 2 of the *Pupil's Edition*.

Spelling Lessons and Activities (Grades 6–8) focuses on both sound patterns and word analysis strategies. Analysis and additional practice are included for each word list.

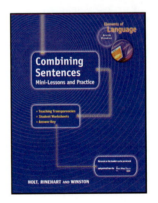

Combining Sentences provides instruction, models, and practice in sentence-combining strategies. This instruction addresses all the basic techniques, such as inserting prepositional or appositive phrases and using compound subjects and verbs.

Daily Language Activity Transparencies binder includes

- test-taking practice in analogies, sentence completion, and reading comprehension
- proofreading practice in grammar, usage, and mechanics
- sentence combining
- vocabulary building and word games

Additional Resource

Vocabulary Workshop helps students build their vocabularies and simultaneously prepare for standardized tests. Concepts and skills include analogies, context clues, prefixes, suffixes, roots, synonyms, antonyms, and etymologies.

Vocabulary Workshop Tests assess knowledge of the words and concepts taught in the *Vocabulary Workshop* and provide practice in standardized test formats.

Planning and Assessment

Elements of Language provides several options for planning and assessment, giving you more flexibility for today's diverse classroom.

One-Stop Planner CD-ROM with Test Generator for Macintosh® and Windows®

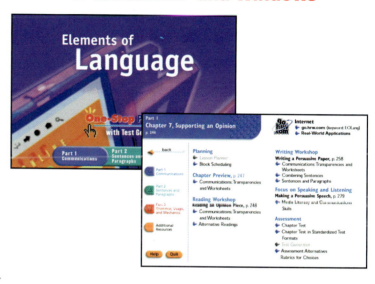

Planning and managing lessons has never been easier than with the *One-Stop Planner CD-ROM*. This convenient, all-in-one, planning software program includes all the teaching resources for *Elements of Language*, plus valuable planning and assessment tools. The *One-Stop Planner* provides

- editable lesson plans
- previews of teaching resources
- an easy-to-use test generator

To preview a video segment or transparency, or to print out tests and worksheets for your students, simply select and click.

The **Lesson Planner, Including Strategies for English-Language Learners** focuses on both classroom time and the independent working time needed for the reading, writing, speaking, listening, viewing, and representing lessons in the *Pupil's Edition*.

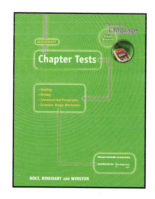

Chapter Tests provides short-answer questions in traditional formats for each chapter in the *Pupil's Edition*. The tests include assessment for the Reading and Writing Workshops in Part 1; for the sentences, paragraphs, and compositions instruction in Part 2; and for the grammar, usage, and mechanics skills in Part 3.

Assessment Alternatives includes inventory and evaluation forms for both teachers and students in writing, reading, listening, speaking, viewing, representing, working in groups, and working on projects. Scoring models demonstrate the use of both holistic and analytic rubrics and scales for assessment.

Chapter Tests in Standardized Test Formats offers an additional test for each chapter in the *Pupil's Edition*. Using a range of formats from the most commonly used standardized assessments, these tests include all of the content listed under **Chapter Tests**.

Technology
The Key to Learning in the Information Age

The wide range of dynamic and interactive resources available with *Elements of Language* gives students the opportunity to learn and retain more.

Media Literacy and Communication Skills

Designed to support the speaking, listening, viewing, and representing lessons in *Elements of Language*, this package contains the following materials:

Videocassettes provide video segments that show students and professionals giving speeches and making documentaries; the segments model camera angles and visual effects; and they demonstrate strategies for media analysis.

A How-to Handbook guides students step-by-step through speaking, listening, and media-based activities. The *Handbook* includes sample storyboards, an analysis of camera angles, tips on identifying persuasion in the media, and much more. A glossary of media terms is also included.

Support and Practice contains viewing guides, planning checklists, and transparencies to support each speaking, listening, viewing, and representing lesson in the *Pupil's Edition*. It also includes a summary of each video segment.

A Teacher's Guide includes options for teaching the oral-visual literacy lessons, including ideas for using the video segments and for guiding students through the projects suggested in the *Pupil's Edition*.

Internet references throughout the *Pupil's Edition* direct students to a new Web site for users of *Elements of Language*. This site links students to activities and projects for each Communications chapter and allows them to put their reading, writing, speaking, and listening skills into action in real-world situations.

When students see the **go.hrw.com** logo and a keyword in the textbook, they can go to the **go.hrw.com** site, enter the keyword, and link instantly to well-researched resources.

The *Elements of Language* Web site gives students a context and clear purpose for visiting Web sites. Carefully checked for instructional validity and appropriateness, **go.hrw.com** helps students make the most of the time they spend searching for information on the Internet.

Language Workshop Interactive Multimedia CD-ROM Software

This award-winning CD-ROM gives your students a complete course of study in grammar, usage, and mechanics.

Each *Language Workshop CD-ROM* includes

- grammar, usage, and mechanics rules in both English and Spanish
- interactive multimedia exercises
- tests and exercises scored by computer
- gradebook updated automatically
- online Diagnostic Pretest that evaluates a student's skill level and recommends a course of study

Writer's Workshop Interactive Multimedia CD-ROM Software

This award-winning interactive CD-ROM program guides students through the eight most common writing assignments, such as writing a personal narrative, preparing an informative report, or composing a persuasive essay.

Features include

- step-by-step guidance through the writing process, from prewriting to publishing
- thesaurus, dictionary, and spell-checker
- bibliography maker for MLA or APA style

All CD-ROMs are available for both Macintosh® and Windows®.

MODELS

READING SELECTIONS

- Bruce Babbitt, **"Yellowstone Makes a Triumphant Return Ten Years After Fires,"** from *Austin American-Stateman*
- Norman Berdichevsky, **"Two Peoples Divided by Common Road Signs,"** from *Contemporary Review*
- Annie Dillard, *An American Childhood*
- Adam Hochschild, **"Force-Fed Television,"** from *We the Media*
- John Irving, **"An Introduction to Charles Dickens's *A Christmas Carol,*"** from *You've Got to Read This*
- Steven Levingston, **"Danger Beneath the Dash,"** from *Reader's Digest*
- Norman Maclean, *Young Men and Fire*
- The Nature Conservancy, **"Adopt-A-Bison"**
- David Standish, **"The Art of Money,"** from *Smithsonian*

WRITING MODELS

- Robert D. Ballard, *Exploring the Titanic*
- Stephen Crane, **"The Bride Comes to Yellow Sky"**
- Ian Darragh, **"Prince Edward Island: A World Apart No More,"** *National Geographic*
- John L. Eliot, **"Snake Venom Strikes at Heart Attacks,"** *National Geographic*
- William Fleming, *Arts and Ideas*
- Wendy M. Grossman, **"Access Denied,"** *Scientific American*
- Kim Hubbard, **"Review of *The Eat a Bug Cookbook*,"** *Discover*
- John Elkington, Julia Hailes, Douglas Hill, and Joel Makower, *Going Green*
- Nicholas L. Johnson, **"Monitoring and Controlling Debris in Space,"** *Scientific American*
- Michael E. Long, **"The Vanishing Prairie Dog,"** *National Geographic*
- Steve Nadis, **"Bug Zappers Miss Their Mark,"** *Omni* magazine Web site
- Carl Sandburg, **"Lost"**
- Paul Theroux, *Riding the Iron Rooster*
- Mark Wheeler, **"Science Friction,"** *Discover*
- Harold M. Williams, **"Don't Ignore the Arts,"** *USA Today*
- Ethel Yari, **"Teenage Lincoln Sculptor,"** *American History*

STUDENT MODELS

- Katie Baker, **"Uniforms Reduce Problems"**
- Adam Caputo, **"Higher than Society"**
- Yen Co, **"An Indecisive Conclusion"**
- Tabitha Henry, **"My Last Goodbye"**
- Gwen Miller, **"TV Baby Sitters: Help or Hindrance?"**
- Jason Potterf, **"Gourmet School Lunch"**
- Jeremy Schmidt, **"Number One"**
- David Thompson, **"Athletes Trying to Be Too Perfect"**

TO OUR STUDENTS

Think about it: On any given day, you probably watch TV, skim the newspaper, listen to the radio, surf the Internet, glance at billboards, read magazines, listen to CDs, and watch videotapes. Each day you probably also talk to friends, write papers in school, send e-mails, make lists, and talk on the phone. The world of language around you is expanding rapidly. To keep up, you need to become a skilled language user. *Elements of Language* can be an important resource by helping you use language more effectively as you communicate in the twenty-first century.

Elements of Language is divided into four major parts:

PART 1 Communications shows you how to develop the skills you use to **receive** communications through **reading, listening,** and **viewing** and to **send** communications through **writing, speaking,** and **representing.**

PART 2 Sentences and Paragraphs shows you how to develop interesting, clear **sentences** and **paragraphs**—the forms you need to know to write and speak effectively.

PART 3 Grammar, Usage, and Mechanics provides instruction and practice with the basic **building blocks of language**—words, phrases, and clauses—the rules you need to know to convey meaning clearly.

PART 4 Quick Reference Handbook is a one-stop **reference guide** to a variety of skills and concepts. From **Document Design** to **Grammar at a Glance,** it contains the information you need in a concise, easily accessible form.

Think of *Elements of Language* as your personal resource for information on communication.

As you use this resource, remember that everything is here for a reason. For example, **boldface** type and color draw your attention to an important word or idea; **charts** present information so you can read and understand it easily; and **headings** and **subheadings** show the organization of ideas.

PART 1 chapters include

- **Reading Workshop** that shows you how to develop and improve your reading skills to understand a published selection (usually nonfiction)

- **Writing Workshop** that shows you how to use the writing process to develop and refine a piece of your own writing

- **Focus on Speaking and Listening** or **Focus on Viewing and Representing** that helps you master either the skills of speaking and listening or of viewing and representing

You will also encounter the following features in PART 1.

- **Mini-Lessons**—vocabulary and test-taking strategies, as well as writing or critical thinking skills

- **A Writer's Model**—a model of how you might organize and write your own paper

- **A Student's Model**—a paper written by a real student

- **Content and Organization Guidelines for Peer and Self-Evaluation** and **Style Guidelines**—questions, tips, and techniques to help you evaluate and revise *what* you say as well as *how* you say it

- **Designing Your Writing**—pointers on how to present ideas and information visually so your readers can grasp them more easily

- **Connections to Literature** and **Connections to Life**—communication activities related to literature or to the world at large

To Our Students

Here are some of the features you will come across in PART 2 and PART 3.

- **Rules**—the grammar, usage, and mechanics concepts in each Part 3 chapter, numbered in each chapter
- **Exercises**—practice for skills and concepts
- **Tabs**—colored corners on the Part 3 pages that show rule numbers
- **Tips & Tricks**—easy-to-use hints, from locating sentence fragments to choosing the correct pronoun
- **Style Tips**—information about formal and informal uses of English
- **Help**—pointers and hints to help you understand concepts and complete exercises
- **Computer Tips**—hints for using a computer to help you write better
- **Writing Applications**—activities that link grammar, usage, and mechanics skills and concepts with writing activities

Elements of Language on the Internet

Put the communication strategies in *Elements of Language* to work by logging on to the Internet. At the *Elements of Language* Internet site, you can dissect the prose of professional writers, crack the codes of the advertising industry, and find out how your communication skills can help you in the real world. Then, if you want to give your own work a home in cyberspace, you can submit it for publication in one of our online galleries. As you move through *Elements of Language,* you will find the best online resources at **go.hrw.com.**

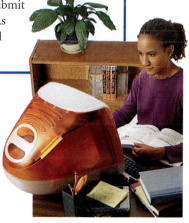

Where would you be without language? Let this book be your guide to developing your skill as an effective and critical language user—a communicator—in the twenty-first century.

The Authors and Editors

PART 1
Communications

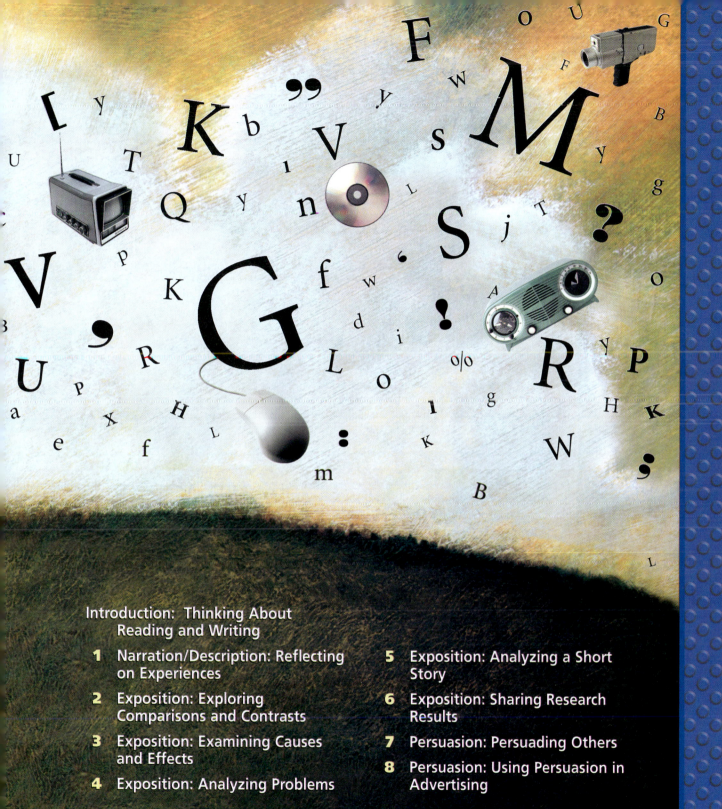

Introduction: Thinking About Reading and Writing

1. Narration/Description: Reflecting on Experiences
2. Exposition: Exploring Comparisons and Contrasts
3. Exposition: Examining Causes and Effects
4. Exposition: Analyzing Problems
5. Exposition: Analyzing a Short Story
6. Exposition: Sharing Research Results
7. Persuasion: Persuading Others
8. Persuasion: Using Persuasion in Advertising

Introduction

INTRODUCTION

PREVIEWING THE CHAPTER

- Successful readers and writers use processes and understand the relationships between reading and writing. In this chapter, students will learn about the stages of the reading and writing processes and the interconnections between the two. You may want to use this chapter to introduce the first reading and writing workshops, or you may choose to return to this chapter as necessary throughout the year.

VIEWING THE ILLUSTRATION (19A)

- As students look at the computer-generated illustration of two cars, discuss its colors, lines, and shapes. Explain that the illustration is abstract and that simple shapes and lines and bright colors suggest a scene of two cars at a city stoplight. Point out how rectangles suggest windowed buildings and a traffic light, and circles suggest lights. Ask students what eye-catching techniques appear in the illustration. [Students may mention the bright colors and the bright, "spray-painted" lines, which highlight or outline the shapes of the car, lights, and traffic.]

- Point out to students that messages, such as the ones on the license plates of the two cars, appear in many other places besides books, newspapers, and magazines. You might discuss with students other sources of messages. [Examples include television, billboards, brochures, bumper stickers, and street signs.]

CHAPTER RESOURCES

Planning
- *Lesson Planner,* Introductory Ch.
- *One-Stop Planner* CD-ROM

Practice
- *Communications,* TPs. 1–9, WS. pp. 1–5

Reinforcement
- *Daily Language Activity Transparencies*

Evaluation and Assessment
- *Assessment Package*
  —*Assessment Alternatives,* Introductory Ch.

Thinking About Reading and Writing

Think of all the different kinds of texts you might read or write in a given day: stories, notes, essays, advertisements, letters, song lyrics, poems, e-mail, and more. Not all of them are easy to read and write. See if the following situations are familiar to you.

- A book in your hand, you suddenly realize that you have read the same sentences several times, yet the words on the page have conveyed absolutely no meaning to you. What can you do to refocus your mind?
- You sit in front of a computer screen that contains a single sentence you have written. You cannot seem to write anything else. Is there anything that can help you get the words flowing again?

Practice the Process

Both reading and writing are *processes* with logical steps and strategies. Following the reading and writing processes will prepare you to tackle any reading or writing task that comes your way. In the following pages, you will become better acquainted with the strategies and skills you can use

- **before** you start reading or writing
- **while** you are reading or **while** you are putting your ideas on paper
- **after** you have read or **after** you have written down your ideas

YOUR TURN 1 — Thinking About Reading and Writing

With a partner, select and read a brief magazine article. Then, complete the following activities together.

- Think about your reading process. How did you choose an article? What steps did you take to understand the article? What thoughts did you have after reading it? Brainstorm and write down your ideas.
- Now, use your own experience as a writer to think about the writing process. What steps do you think the magazine article's writer took? What did he or she do before writing? while writing? after writing?

YOUR TURN 1

Check that each pair of students has created two lists of at least six or seven steps involved in reading and writing. Discuss with students their lists, and emphasize the steps they have listed in common. You may want to write these common elements on the chalkboard so that students can compare their ideas with the strategies listed on the following pages of the textbook.

Reading as a Process

WHAT'S AHEAD?

In this section, you will learn what effective readers do
- before reading
- while reading
- after reading

Imagine that you are browsing through a guide to national parks. As you glance at words and photographs, your mind ricochets from impression to impression. Then a heading, "The Petrified Forest," catches your attention. Your focus narrows, and you note details like *fossilized leaves* and *petrified logs*. What is happening as you read?

Think of reading as a dialogue between the writer and the reader of a text. Writers use words (and sometimes images) to communicate information to readers. In turn, readers use thinking strategies *before, while,* and *after* reading to understand and respond to the writer's messages.

What You Do During the Reading Process	
Before you read: Prereading	• Identify your **purpose** for reading. • **Preview** the text, and make **predictions** about what it contains. • Think about your **prior knowledge**—what you already know about the topic. • Develop your **interest** in the text you will be reading. • **Focus** your mind on what you are about to read.
While you read: Reading	• Identify **main ideas** and **details**, and look for **organizational patterns**. • Confirm or revise your **predictions** about the text. • Based on your purpose for reading, the difficulty of the text, and your prior knowledge of the subject, adjust your **reading rate** as needed to understand the text better. • Make **connections** between your prior knowledge of the topic and what you are reading. • Use **"fix-it" strategies** when you do not understand what you are reading. • Ask yourself **questions** about the text. • Determine the **writer's intent** by reading between the lines to understand what the writer does not actually say.
After you read: Exploring and Extending Your Reading	• Determine whether or not you have accomplished your **purpose** for reading. • Confirm your **understanding** of the text. • Draw **conclusions** and make **generalizations** based on the text. • **Evaluate** the text for accuracy, bias (author's point of view), and overall quality. • **Extend your thinking** by using the ideas you encountered while reading.

Prereading

Getting Ready

Much as athletes loosen their leg muscles before running, good readers stretch their *reading* muscles before charging into a text. Using the prereading strategies below will make you a sharper, deeper reader.

- **Identify your purpose.** Before you begin to read a text, ask yourself why you are reading it. Determining your purpose for reading will help you select a reading style and decide what to focus on as you read. For instance, when your purpose for reading is to acquire information, you will read slowly and deliberately as you look for key information and related details. However, when your purpose for reading is entertainment you might read more quickly, skimming over less important details to get to the next exciting part in the story.

- **Preview the text.** Identify major headings and subheadings to learn about the text's structure. Find out how illustrations and other graphic elements relate to the topic, and take note of any boldface or italicized terms. By skimming introductions and one or two random paragraphs, you can get a pretty accurate sense of a writer's subject matter and style. These first impressions help you focus your expectations for the text.

- **Make predictions.** Based on your preview, predict what you will find when you read the text. What important ideas do you think will be discussed? What overall message might the writer express? Making educated guesses about these matters—and then adjusting these guesses as you read—will keep you involved with the reading material.

- **Think about your prior knowledge.** What do you already know about the topic of the text from your own observations, experiences, or previous reading? Making connections to this prior knowledge will help you process and understand new information in the text.

- **Develop your interest.** From time to time you will be asked to read texts that at first glance you may not find very appealing. Try to overcome your hesitation by developing some curiosity about the subject. Think about the discoveries you might make as you read. Ask yourself why the text is so significant that people are encouraging you to read it.

- **Focus your mind on what you are about to read.** Find a comfortable place to read, and try to eliminate outside distractions, such as people talking or sound from the television.

TIP With practice, these prereading strategies will become second nature to you. Applying them every time you encounter a new text will help you become a more effective reader.

TEACHING TIP

Getting Ready
Point out to students that they will often be asked on standardized tests to read passages and to answer questions based on their reading. One way to set a purpose in such a situation is to read ahead to the questions they will need to answer. Students can rephrase the question as an answer statement with a blank. For example, they can rewrite the question *What does the author state is the leading cause of air pollution?* as *The author states that the leading cause of air pollution is ____.* Then students can read the test passage to find the answer that best fits the blank.

Reading, pp. 4–8
Alignments
TEKS 7A, 7B, 7C, 7D, 7F, 7G, 7H, 7I, 8A, 12A, 12B
TAAS R2, R3, R4, R5
English II End-of-Course 1, 3
Texas Resources
- *Lesson Planner,* Introductory Ch.
- *One-Stop Planner CD-ROM*
- *TAAS Tool Kit*
- *Preparation for TAAS*

Meeting INDIVIDUAL NEEDS

MODALITY
Visual Learners. One way students can make sense of what they read is by arranging the information they find into graphic organizers such as outlines or diagrams. Encourage students to keep paper and pen or pencil handy as they read. Depending on the material, students may also benefit from drawing maps or sketches to go along with their reading. After students have finished their reading, they can then review their organizers or drawings to check their accuracy.

TIP Reading is a **recursive process**—that is, you can return to earlier steps when needed. For example, in addition to confirming or revising your predictions as you read, you may also make new predictions—a prereading task.

While Reading

Making Sense

No matter what type of text you are reading—a narrative of the doomed Donner party, a technical essay on the complex social behavior of ants, or a magazine article about soccer star Mia Hamm—your primary goal is to interpret the words before you. Use the following strategies to help you understand and interpret any writer's message.

- **Identify the main ideas and details.** Every paragraph has a main idea. In informative or persuasive writing, the main idea is usually stated directly by the writer; in narrative or descriptive writing, the main idea is often implied. In either case, the rest of each paragraph should contain details, examples, or explanations that support the main idea. Often you can grasp a text's overall main idea by combining the main ideas of the individual paragraphs.

- **Look for organizational patterns.** Identifying a text's organizational pattern is an important part of figuring out its main idea. For instance, recognizing that an essay is constructed in a comparison-contrast pattern should alert you to look for information about two different subjects. Other common patterns of organization are cause-effect, chronological order, problem-solution, order of importance, and logical order.

- **Confirm or revise your predictions.** As you read, you should keep in mind the predictions you made about the text. Confirm the ones that prove to be correct, and rethink the ones that are not correct. Then, continue making and revising predictions as you make sense of the text.

- **Adjust your reading rate.** You might be called on to read a text that is difficult or one that is on a subject about which you know little. Based on the purpose you have set for reading, the difficulty of the text, and your knowledge of the subject, adjust how quickly or slowly you are reading.

- **Make connections.** Connect what you read in the text to your own prior knowledge and experience. Ask yourself if the text supports, contradicts, or adds to what you already know about its subject. Most new knowledge will have some sort of connection to what you already know. You just need to discover the link.

- **Use fix-it strategies.** If you are having trouble understanding the text, read difficult passages aloud, brainstorm the meanings of unfamiliar words, put difficult sentences in your own words, or use graphic organizers.

- **Ask yourself questions.** Treating reading like a dialogue helps your mind stay active and alert as you read. Ask questions, offer comments, and note details that confuse or intrigue you. In the margin below, you can see one reader's dialogue with the writer of a text about Smokejumpers—an elite crew of airborne firefighters employed by the United States Forest Service.
- **Determine the writer's intent.** Dig deep to interpret the writer's message. Ask yourself "What larger meaning is the writer expressing?" By making inferences and drawing conclusions, you get below the surface to comprehend a writer's intended meanings.

The chief danger from a ground fire is that it will become a "crown fire," that is, get into the branches or "crowns" of trees especially where the trees are close together and the branches interlace. So a crew has to be careful that a ground fire doesn't burn into a jack-pine thicket where the branches are close to the ground and can be set afire by low flames. But there is still a very different way for an ordinary-looking fire to explode. A fire doesn't always need flames to advance. A fire may seem under control, burning harmlessly under tall trees with branches too high to be touched by ground flames, but the fire is burning with such intensity that most of the oxygen has been burned out of the air near it, which is heated above the point of ignition. If the wind suddenly changes and fresh air is blown in loaded with oxygen, then the three elements necessary for a fire are suddenly present in the lower branches—flammable material, temperature above the point of ignition, and oxygen. An old-timer knows that, when a ground fire explodes into a crown fire with nothing he can see to cause it, he has not witnessed spontaneous combustion but the outer appearance of the invisible pressure of a "fire triangle" suddenly in proper proportions for an explosion. — Norman Maclean, *Young Men and Fire*	This sounds like a main idea. The writer is distinguishing the chief danger. This detail supports the main idea. I wonder where "jack-pine thickets" grow. Here's another detail —another way that a crown fire can get started. The writer has organized this information by explaining causes and effects. I wonder if these "three elements necessary for a fire" will be mentioned again—they're so basic to the writer's topic. Does "fire triangle" refer back to the "three elements"?

MULTIPLE INTELLIGENCES
Intrapersonal Intelligence. Encourage students to extend their reading by first focusing on how the reading has affected them personally. Students can ask themselves the following questions: *How has the reading changed my opinion or knowledge of the subject? How has it affected me emotionally? How does it relate to the world in which I live?* Students can then think of other ways that literature has affected them or think of ways to share the effects with others.

After Reading

Exploring and Extending

The reading process does not end at the last word of a text. Responding to the ideas you have just encountered will help you connect with the text. Use these postreading strategies to explore and extend your reading.

- **Determine whether you have accomplished your purpose.** Think back to your reasons for reading the text. Did you reach your goals?
- **Confirm your understanding.** Has the text stimulated any striking images, memories, or ideas? Has it raised any questions? Share your reactions with other readers; trading ideas may change or deepen your own understanding of the text. You can also create a graphic organizer such as a Venn diagram or a cluster.
- **Draw conclusions.** Combine the information in the text with your own knowledge and experience to draw conclusions about the writer's underlying messages or ideas.
- **Make generalizations.** Combine specific details or examples from the text with your own experience to make generalizations—broad statements that apply to the world around you.
- **Evaluate the text.** Step back, and evaluate the text with a critical eye. How well or poorly has the writer achieved his or her purpose? Is the work accurate, interesting, free of bias, intelligent, original, satisfying? Do you agree with the writer's message? Why or why not?
- **Extend.** Use the ideas you encountered while reading in one or more of the following ways.
    1. **Think up spinoff projects.** Make some creative response to the text. You might write a letter, a journal entry, or a poem; or you could create a painting, poster, or performance that connects to the text.
    2. **Continue reading.** Broaden your understanding by reading further in another text on a related topic or in another work by the same author.
    3. **Relate the text to the world.** Sometimes things you read help you solve problems, address issues, or enrich your own life. Plan and carry out a family or community project using ideas from your reading.

Reading and writing are flip sides of a single coin. Readers and writers must work together to communicate. In the following pages you will take a closer look at the writing process.

Writing as a Process

There are almost as many ways to write as there are kinds of texts. Some writers cannot produce a word unless they are poised behind a desk, while others prefer to write sitting outdoors or in noisy restaurants. Some writers create an entire work before going back to read what they have written, while others may rewrite a single paragraph a dozen times before moving on. While individual writers' techniques may vary, successful writers do have one thing in common: the writing process.

The writing process is made up of four stages, and each stage involves certain activities. The chart below summarizes what happens during each stage of the writing process.

WHAT'S AHEAD?

In this section, you will learn what effective writers do as they

- prewrite
- write
- revise
- publish

What You Do During the Writing Process	
Prewriting	• Choose your **topic**. • Identify your **purpose and audience**, and **select a writing form** appropriate to that purpose and audience. • Generate **ideas** and gather **information** about the topic. • Begin to **organize** the information. • Decide the **main point** you want to express.
Writing a Draft	• Grab your readers' attention in the **introduction**. • Provide **background information**. • State your **main points**, your **support**, and your **elaboration** of them. • Follow a **plan** of organization. • Wrap up with a **conclusion**.
Revising	• **Evaluate** your draft. • **Revise** the draft to improve its **content**, **organization**, and **style**.
Publishing	• **Proofread**, or edit, your final draft. • **Publish**, or share your finished writing with readers. • **Reflect** on your writing experience.

TIP The writing process is **recursive**, meaning that writers go back and forth between the stages as necessary. For example, as you revise an essay you may realize that one paragraph contains no details to support your main idea. You can go back and add more information to the paragraph.

Meeting INDIVIDUAL NEEDS

ADVANCED LEARNERS
Have students read the **What You Do During the Writing Process** chart on their own. Then, initiate a class discussion of the similarities between the reading process and the writing process. What are some steps in each process that seem to go well together? Why do students think the two processes are so similar? You may want to remind students that reading and writing are both forms of dialogue.

Writing, pp. 9–14
Alignments
TEKS 1A, 1B, 1C, 2A, 2B, 2C, 2D, 2E, 3A, 3B, 3D, 4C, 5A
TAAS W1, W2, W3, W4, W6, W7
English II End-of-Course 4, 5, 6

Texas Resources
- *Lesson Planner*, Introductory Ch.
- *One-Stop Planner* CD-ROM
- *TAAS Tool Kit*
- *Preparation for TAAS*

Meeting INDIVIDUAL NEEDS

MODALITY

Kinesthetic Learners. Encourage students to act out possible topics when they are getting ready to write. If students are writing about a process or event, they can mime the process or event and use the performance to remember steps in the process and to remember sensory details about the event. If a student has chosen a topic that is not easy to act out, he or she can meet with a partner to engage in a dramatic dialogue on the topic. Students can then use their performed dialogues to help them construct their written ones.

Cooperative Learning

Collaborative Groups. Explain to students that writing usually is a solitary task, but that working collaboratively to develop drafts is also a valuable experience. Collaborative planning and writing—such as organizing and reorganizing content and refining style to suit particular occasions, audiences, and purposes—will prepare students for similar real-world tasks.

Prewriting

Getting Ready

Just as musicians warm up before a concert, writers warm up in the *prewriting* stage. Prewriting prepares you to be informed, organized, and focused when you begin to write your first draft. Here are the steps you should follow during the prewriting stage.

TIP Do some preliminary research on your proposed topic to make sure sufficient resources are available.

- **Choose your topic.** Since you will spend a lot of time examining and writing about your topic, it pays to choose this topic carefully. Brainstorm, use trigger words, draw a cluster diagram, or use another strategy to generate topic ideas. Select a topic that genuinely interests and inspires you. Then, make sure the topic is appropriate for the writing task at hand. A topic that is too narrow may leave you without enough to say, and one that is too broad may overwhelm you.

- **Identify your purpose and audience, and select a writing form.** Focus your thoughts, and establish a direction for your writing by thinking carefully about why you are writing and who will read your work. Then, select the form for your writing that will most effectively achieve that purpose with the audience you have identified.

- **Generate ideas and gather information about the topic.** Zealously gather information from an array of sources. You need not limit yourself to using books or magazine and newspaper articles; you can often collect other valuable material from documentary videos, the Internet, or from interviews with professionals, other adults, family members, and peers. Take notes whenever you find anything that looks useful.

- **Begin to organize the information.** Depending on your topic, purpose, and form, arrange your information according to comparisons and contrasts, causes and effects, chronological order, order of importance, or some other appropriate plan of organization. In keeping your audience in mind, ask yourself, "What will my readers need to know first, next, and so on?" Consider constructing a map, an outline, or another type of visual organizer to order your ideas.

- **Decide the main point you want to express.** Before you begin drafting, you must figure out what overall point you wish to make. Then, for nonfiction, create a single sentence that contains this main point—your thesis statement. In writing fiction, you often do not state this main idea (the theme) directly. You only hint at it. Remember to stay flexible, though. You may change the focus of your composition.

Reference Note
For more on **outlining**, see page 950.

10 Introduction

Making A Start

One of the reasons that prewriting works so well is that it helps you begin to write gradually: You jot down words, phrases, and a sentence here or there as you get your thoughts together. Of course, writing a first draft involves writing for an audience other than yourself. Just remember that a first draft is never perfect; it is your initial attempt to present your ideas. Here are some of the things you need to do as you write your first draft.

- **Grab your readers' attention in the introduction.** Draw your readers in with a fascinating or unusual fact, a puzzling question, a tantalizing description, or even a brief anecdote that relates to your topic. The sooner—and deeper—you hook your readers' interest, the better the chances that they will read on and pay attention to everything you have to say.

- **Provide background information.** Give your readers whatever background information they will need to put your ideas and information in context. For instance, it might be necessary to define a few technical terms or to provide a historical overview of your subject.

- **State and support your main points, and elaborate on them.** Readers should not have to guess what you are saying about your topic. State the main idea of each paragraph clearly and concisely in a topic sentence, and then elaborate on the idea in the paragraph's remaining sentences. Elaboration adds texture to your writing by providing explanations, examples, illustrations, facts, and other kinds of details. For instance, rather than simply writing "Crash diets do more harm than good" and moving on, give statistics, scientific facts, or other evidence to prove your statement to readers who might be skeptical.

- **Follow a plan of organization.** Complete the organizational plan you began in the prewriting stage and, once you have committed to an organizational plan, adhere to it as you write your draft. Your paragraphs should be ordered in the way that most effectively supports your thesis statement and keeps your audience's attention.

- **Wrap up with a conclusion.** Since readers wish to come away from a text feeling that they have learned or experienced something significant, conclude by giving a distinct sense of your overall message. If necessary, make connections between key ideas again. Restate (not repeat) your thesis in some fresh way, and try to provide an image, question, or opinion that makes a vivid final impression.

TIP A fiction writer uses literary elements such as setting and plot, and details such as description and dialogue, to present his or her main idea, known as the **theme.**

Meeting INDIVIDUAL NEEDS

MULTIPLE INTELLIGENCES
Spatial Intelligence. When students begin writing their papers, encourage them to use the metaphor of building a lookout tower. The paper, like the tower, should have a broad and solid foundation, be constructed with adequate support, and offer a point of view that one could not have normally. Before writing, students might want to take a minute to visualize such a building and to think of the ways their papers offer a foundation, support, and a unique view on a topic.

Revising

Going Back Over Your Draft

Some of your most important work as a writer comes after you have written your draft. Drafts are often rough and incomplete. Examine your writing carefully and improve it so that your message is clear and memorable. Following these steps will help you make your draft as good as it can be.

- **Evaluate your draft.** Assess the effectiveness of your first draft by identifying its strengths and weaknesses. Reread your work at least three times, focusing first on **content**, then on **organization**, and finally on **style**. If possible, have a peer read your draft to offer feedback.

- **Revise the draft to improve its content and organization.** After evaluating your writing's strengths and weaknesses, correct any problems. You may want to ask a classmate to offer suggestions for changes. Use these five fix-it strategies to improve content and organization.

  1. **Add.** Give life to your writing by adding sensory details, interesting facts, examples, and illustrations. Clarify relationships among your ideas by adding connecting words and phrases such as *moreover, as a result, however, furthermore, also, yet, for example,* and *therefore.*

  2. **Delete.** Be ruthless about eliminating repetition and wordiness in your sentences. Omit any words, phrases, or sentences that do not contribute to the main idea of a given paragraph.

  3. **Replace.** Replace clichés and vague verbs and nouns with fresher, more precise language. A dictionary and a thesaurus are invaluable tools to help you do this type of revising.

  4. **Rearrange.** The sentences in each paragraph should flow logically and clearly from one to another. If any idea seems out of place, move it to a more appropriate paragraph.

  5. **Elaborate.** To support each of your main ideas adequately, you may need to elaborate with additional details, facts, examples, illustrations, sensory images, quotations, or anecdotes.

- **Revise the draft to improve its style.** Revise for style by considering some of the following strategies.

  1. **Eliminate** slang, clichés, and worn-out verbs.
  2. **Avoid** using the passive voice.
  3. **Vary** sentence length and sentence beginnings.
  4. **Combine** sentences to add variety or complexity.

TIP One of the best ways to get an accurate picture of your draft's strengths and weaknesses is to let it sit for a day before reading. This rest period will allow you to evaluate your work with a more objective eye.

TEACHING TIP 5B

Going Back Over Your Draft
Explain to students that in the publishing industry, writing is often a collaborative effort. For example, one story in a magazine might by reviewed by several editors or copyeditors, who make suggestions to improve the content, organization, and style of the writing. Similarly, students can improve their writing by incorporating feedback from peer reviewers. Tell students that accepting suggestions and corrections graciously is an important way to grow as a writer. Allow students the opportunity to practice giving and receiving constructive criticism by having them write a brief description of their dream house. Students can meet in small groups to review members' results and help one another evaluate, revise, and edit their writing.

Publishing

Going Public

You have created a piece of writing that no one has ever written (or read) before. Now you need to complete the last stage of the writing process to create a finished work to share with an audience.

- **Proofread, or edit, your final draft.** Re-read your final version to catch and correct each error. Proofreading is exacting work; use every available bit of mental focus as you read and re-read your draft. Proofread your draft three times—the second time aloud. Use a dictionary to double-check spellings of which you are unsure; use the Grammar, Usage, and Mechanics section of this book (page 402) to make sure your final draft follows the **conventions of written language.**

Here is a chart of proofreading guidelines you can use to identify and correct errors in your final draft. Use the proofreading symbols in the Writing section of the Quick Reference Handbook to indicate any changes you will need to make.

Guidelines for Proofreading

1. Is every sentence complete, not a fragment or run-on? (See pages 340 and 347.)
2. Are punctuation marks—such as end marks, commas, semicolons, colons, dashes, and quotation marks—used correctly? (See pages 692, 722, 738, and 756.)
3. Are the first words of sentences, proper nouns, and proper adjectives capitalized? (See page 668.)
4. Does every verb agree in number with its subject? (See page 512.)
5. Are verb forms and tenses used correctly? (See page 590.)
6. Are subject and object forms of personal pronouns used correctly? (See pages 549 and 553.)
7. Does every pronoun agree with its antecedent in number and in gender? Are pronoun references clear? (See pages 532 and 566.)
8. Are frequently confused words (such as *fewer* and *less*, *affect* and *effect*) used correctly? (See page 793.)
9. Are all words spelled correctly? Are the plural forms of words correct? (See pages 779 and 787.)
10. Is the paper neat and in correct form? (See page 849.)

TEACHING TIP 3A

Going Public
Remind students that producing legible work in their final product is an important strategy to follow because error-free essays make favorable impressions upon readers. Suggest that using accurate spelling and the correct conventions of capitalization, punctuation, and other mechanics of written English will show their careful attention to all phases of the writing process.

> **TIP** Publishing is a vital part of the writing process. Sharing what you have written with an audience gives you a clearer view of your current work and influences the shape of your next work.

- **Publish, or share, your finished writing with readers.** Writing is first and foremost a method of communication: Without readers, your work cannot fulfill its purpose. Publish what you have written in an appropriate place to reach your intended audience. Possibilities include school newspapers, magazines, or literary journals; brochures; speech contests; bulletin boards; library displays; and Web sites.

- **Reflect on your writing experience.** Each time you write—especially when you take the writing process seriously—you learn something more about yourself as a writer. Take time now to consider what this most recent experience was like for you. When did you struggle or stall? At what points did you shine? Were certain aspects of the writing process especially challenging for you? Why? How might you approach the writing process differently next time? If you decide to put this piece in your writing **portfolio** (a collection that reflects your writing skills and interests), think about why you chose to include it.

In this chapter, you have examined the reading and writing processes. You have probably already noticed that they are really just different sides of the same process—the process of written communication. The chart below compares the reading and writing processes step by step.

The Reading-Writing Connection

	Reading Process	Writing Process
Before	- Determine your purpose for reading. - Think about what you already know about the topic. - Preview the text to make predictions about what the text will include.	- Identify your purpose for writing and your intended audience. - Draw upon what you already know about the topic. Conduct research to find out more. - Plan what the text will include. Make notes or an outline to organize your information.
During	- Try to understand the writer's main idea(s). - Look for the writer's support for his or her main idea(s). - Notice how the writer has organized the text.	- Express your main idea(s) clearly. - Support your main idea(s) with specific details, facts, examples, or anecdotes. - Organize your writing so that readers can easily follow your ideas. Follow your prewriting notes or outline.
After	- Evaluate the text to decide how accurate it is and its overall quality. - Relate what you have read to the world around you and to your own experiences. - Reflect on what you have read.	- Evaluate and revise the text to improve its content, organization, and style. Decide how to use peer editors' comments. - Relate your writing to the world around you by publishing it. - Reflect on what you have written.

Choices

Choose one of the following activities to complete.

▶ **WRITING**

1. A New View Write a short **essay** in which you describe your writing process by comparing it to something else. Start by completing the sentence "My writing process is like _____." For example, you might write "My writing process is like building a house." Then, explain and elaborate on your comparison. Be prepared to share your essay with your class.

▶ **COLLABORATIVE READING**

2. Double the Process With a partner, choose a short nonfiction text to read aloud together. After figuring out your purpose for reading the text, talk through each step of the reading process. Take turns making predictions and connections, reading the text itself, asking questions, drawing conclusions, making evaluations, and reflecting on your shared reading experience. Expect both similarities and differences in the ways you and your partner interact with the text. Present an **oral report** to your class about what you and your partner discovered. If some of your partner's reading strategies seem effective, consider adopting them.

▶ **CAREERS**

3. Reading and Writing on the Job With a group of peers, brainstorm a list of occupations that involve reading and writing in some way. Be sure to include a variety of fields, such as nursing and police work. From this list, select an occupation that interests you, and do research (in print sources, through interviews, and on the Internet) on the job's various characteristics, features, and tasks. Then, collaborate with your group members to create a **flier** in which you explain how skillful reading and writing contributes to an individual's success in this career.

▶ **LITERATURE**

4. Approaching Different Texts Read four to five short passages from a variety of different sources—a newspaper, a short story, an article from a general-interest magazine, a play, an article from a technical journal, an instruction manual, a narrative poem, and so on. Then, analyze how your use of the reading process varied with the type of material you read. Jot down **notes**, and share your impressions with peers in a small group.

PORTFOLIO

Choices 15

Choices
Alignments
Choice 1   TEKS 1A, 1B; TAAS W1
Choice 2   TEKS 7A, 7C, 7G, 7H, 8A, 8B;
           TAAS R3, R4, R5
Choice 3   TEKS 2A, 2B, 4C, 4F, 13B;
           TAAS W1, W2
Choice 4   TEKS 7C, 7H, 8A, 8B

CHAPTER 1

Reflecting on Experiences

Use this guide to create an instructional plan that suits the individual needs of your students. Assignments marked by an asterisk (*) may be completed out of class. Times given for pacing lessons are estimated. See pp. 16–17 for chapter-wide resources. Resources listed in this guide are point-of-use resources only.

Curriculum Connections

Connections to Literature pp. 48–49
- Writing a Free-Verse Poem

Choices p. 53
- Crossing The Curriculum: Social Studies
- Literature
- Viewing and Representing

internet connect
GO TO: go.hrw.com
KEYWORD: EOLang 10–1

All resources for this chapter are available for preview on the *One-Stop Planner CD-ROM with Test Generator*. All worksheets and tests may be printed from the CD-ROM.

Texas Resources For a complete listing of all resources prepared for Texas teachers and students, please see the blue box at the beginning of each chapter.

	Chapter Opener pp. 16–17	**Reading Workshop: Reading a Personal Reflection** pp. 18–27
DEVELOPMENTAL PROGRAM	⏱ **30 minutes** • Personal Reflection p. 17 • Your Turn 1 in groups p. 17	⏱ **90 minutes** • Preparing to Read p. 18 • Reading Selection pp. 19–20 • First Thoughts on Your Reading 1–2 in groups p. 21 • Making Inferences pp. 21–23 • Your Turn 2 p. 23 • Narrative and Descriptive Details pp. 24–25 • Your Turn 3 p. 25 • Test Taking Mini-Lesson p. 27
CORE PROGRAM	⏱ **20 minutes** • Personal Reflection p. 17 • Your Turn 1 p. 17	⏱ **100 minutes** • Preparing to Read p. 18 • Reading Selection pp. 19–20 • First Thoughts on Your Reading 1–3 p. 21 • Making Inferences pp. 21–23 • Your Turn 2 p. 23 • Narrative and Descriptive Details pp. 24–25 • Your Turn 3 p. 25 • Vocabulary Mini-Lesson p. 26 • Test Taking Mini-Lesson p. 27
ADVANCED PROGRAM	⏱ **10 minutes** • Personal Reflection p. 17 • Your Turn 1 p. 17	⏱ **70 minutes** • Preparing to Read p. 18 • Reading Selection pp. 19–20 • First Thoughts on Your Reading 3 p. 21 • Making Inferences pp. 21–23 • Your Turn 2 p. 23 • Narrative and Descriptive Details pp. 24–25 • Your Turn 3 p. 25 • Vocabulary Mini-Lesson p. 26
RESOURCES – PRINT	• *Communications*, TP. 10, WS. p. 6	• *Alternative Readings*, Ch. 1 • *Communications*, TPs. 11, 12, WS. pp. 7–14
RESOURCES – MEDIA	• *One-Stop Planner* CD-ROM	• *One-Stop Planner* CD-ROM

TP.=Transparency   WS.=Worksheet

Writing Workshop: Writing a Personal Reflection *pp. 28–49*	**Focus on Viewing and Representing: Making a Video Reflection** *pp. 50–52*
🕐 **180 minutes** • Choosing an Experience *pp. 28–29* • Consider Purpose, Audience, Tone, and Voice *pp. 29–30* • Gathering Details *pp. 30–32* • Putting It All Together *pp. 33–34* • Reflect on the Meaning of Your Experience *pp. 34–35* • Organize Details and Your Turn 4 *p. 36* • Writing Mini-Lesson *p. 37* • Framework and Your Turn 5* *p. 38* • Writer's Model and Student's Model *pp. 39–41* • Evaluate and Revise and Your Turn 6* *pp. 42–43* • Focus on Sentences; Your Turn 7 in groups *pp. 44–45* • Proofread, Publish, and Reflect *pp. 46–47* • Grammar Link *p. 46* • Your Turn 8 *p. 47*	🕐 **30 minutes** • Putting Words into Motion *pp. 50–52* • Your Turn 10* *p. 52*
🕐 **170 minutes** • Choosing an Experience *pp. 28–29* • Consider Purpose, Audience, Tone, and Voice *pp. 29–30* • Gathering Details *pp. 30–32* • Putting It All Together *pp. 33–34* • Reflect on the Meaning of Your Experience *pp. 34–35* • Organize Details and Your Turn 4 *p. 36* • Writing Mini-Lesson *p. 37* • Framework and Your Turn 5* *p. 38* • Writer's Model and Student's Model *pp. 39–41* • Evaluate and Revise and Your Turn 6* *pp. 42–43* • Focus on Sentences and Your Turn 7 *pp. 44–45* • Proofread, Publish, and Reflect *pp. 46–47* • Grammar Link *p. 46* • Your Turn 8 *p. 47* • Connections to Literature and Your Turn 9* *pp. 48–49*	🕐 **20 minutes** • Putting Words into Motion *pp. 50–52* • Your Turn 10* *p. 52*
🕐 **120 minutes** • Choosing an Experience *pp. 28–29* • Consider Purpose, Audience, Tone, and Voice *pp. 29–30* • Gathering Details *pp. 30–32* • Reflect on the Meaning of Your Experience *pp. 34–35* • Organize Details and Your Turn 4 *p. 36* • Framework and Your Turn 5* *p. 38* • Writer's Model and Student's Model *pp. 39–41* • Evaluate and Revise and Your Turn 6* *pp. 42–43* • Proofread, Publish, and Reflect *pp. 46–47* • Your Turn 8 *p. 47* • Connections to Literature and Your Turn 9* *pp. 48–49*	🕐 **10 minutes** • Putting Words into Motion *pp. 50–52* • Your Turn 10* *p. 52*

• *Communications,* TPs. 13–16, WS. pp. 15–23
• *Designing Your Writing*
	• *Media Literacy and Communication Skills Kit*
	  —*Support and Practice,* Ch. 1
	  —*A How-to Handbook*
	  —*A Teacher's Guide,* Ch. 1

• *One-Stop Planner CD-ROM*	• *Media Literacy and Communication Skills Kit* —Videocassette 1, Segment A • *One-Stop Planner CD-ROM*

CHAPTER PLANNING GUIDE

CHAPTER 1: Reflecting on Experiences

CHAPTER OBJECTIVES
- To read a personal reflection
- To write a personal reflection
- To create a video reflection

Chapter Overview

Personal reflection helps students get to know themselves. By remembering defining moments and reflecting on them, students identify experiences that have shaped their lives. In this chapter, students learn to examine their lives by reading about others' experiences, by writing about important experiences of their own, and by making visual presentations of personal experiences. In the Reading Workshop, students read a passage from the autobiography of a Pulitzer Prize–winning writer that describes a defining moment in the author's life and how it affected her. In the Writing Workshop, students follow the steps in the writing process to plan, write, and publish their own personal narratives. The Focus on Viewing and Representing tells students how to create a video reflection on a topic of personal significance. While the sections of the chapter can be taught independently, as a unit they offer a broad view of personal reflection and introduce students to the various media for such self-expression.

Why Reflect on Experiences?

Reflection on experiences is a means of personal growth, of increasing one's understanding of the world and one's place within it. Personal reflection allows students to recall and analyze significant events in their lives. The personal reflections of others teach students new ways of examining their own lives. Through their reflections and through reflection on the lives of others, students learn how experiences help shape their personalities.

Teaching the Chapter

Option 1: Begin with Literature

If you prefer to begin with literature, you could study the use of personal experience in short stories, poetry, or drama before introducing this chapter. Whatever genre or genres you choose, focus on the events that form the narrative. How do they shape people's lives? What effect do they have on people's perceptions of themselves and others? Follow up by having students read the selection in this chapter (pp. 19–20), and discuss how personal experiences are reported in memoirs or autobiographical narratives. After students have read some personal reflections, they will be ready to write personal narratives of their own.

Option 2: Begin with Nonfiction and Writing

Use this chapter to introduce and develop the concept of personal reflection. Begin with the excerpt from Annie Dillard's autobiography, *An American Childhood*, in the Reading Workshop, encouraging students to be on the lookout for narrative and descriptive details and to make inferences based on the text and on their own knowledge and experience. Then have students follow the steps outlined in the Writing Workshop to compose their personal narratives. Writing a personal reflection will prepare students to recognize and interpret personal reflection when they return to literature. See also **Connections to Literature** on pp. 48–49.

Making Connections

■ To the Literature Curriculum

Literature often contains personal reflections of characters. Characters examining their lives can be found, for example, in "George Gray" by Edgar Lee Masters and "Hair" by Malcolm X with Alex Haley. In these stories, students are presented with George Gray reflecting on his life and Malcolm X beginning to find his identity.

Lesson Idea: Personal Reflection in "George Gray" by Edgar Lee Masters

1. Have students read "George Gray" by Edgar Lee Masters and outline the things George Gray avoided.

2. Ask students what contradictions Gray sees in his own life and at what point he sees them. What details does he share?

3. Ask students how Gray finally makes his personal discovery, and discuss what advice he wishes he had followed. Then ask what advice he would give others. How does he share this?

4. Next, introduce students to the selection from Annie Dillard's *An American Childhood* in the Reading Workshop (pp. 19–20). Make students aware that, like "George Gray," this passage from Dillard's autobiography is a personal reflection. The instruction on personal reflection (p. 17) focuses on narrative and descriptive details, which will help prepare students to write their own personal reflections.

■ To Careers

Reflecting on experiences is beneficial in the world of work as in other areas of life. Invite several people of different occupations to talk to your class about how personal reflection helps them in the workplace. In advance of the visit, ask students to prepare questions such as the following: Did personal reflection lead to or affect your choice of a job or career? How? How does personal reflection help you do your job? How does it affect your cooperation or interaction with others? The visitors' responses will teach students that reflecting on experiences plays an important role in people's jobs and careers.

■ To the Community

Have students interview an older relative, a neighbor, or a person they admire about a defining moment in the interviewee's life. Students should prepare questions that not only aim at a general outline of the experience, but also gather details about it. Students may share their findings with the class in oral reports. You may want to obtain permission from parents or guardians before students begin work on this assignment, and notify the interviewees that students will be reporting their findings to the class.

■ To the Art Curriculum

Explain to students that art, as well as writing, is a medium for self-reflection. Have students work individually or in small groups to create an artistic representation of a defining moment in their lives or in their school experience. Students' artwork need not be realistic; students may use symbols, shapes, and colors to create a drawing, painting, collage, or sculpture that represents the moment and expresses their thoughts and emotions about it. When students have completed their artistic representations, invite them to present their work to the rest of the class.

CHAPTER 1

Reflecting on Experiences

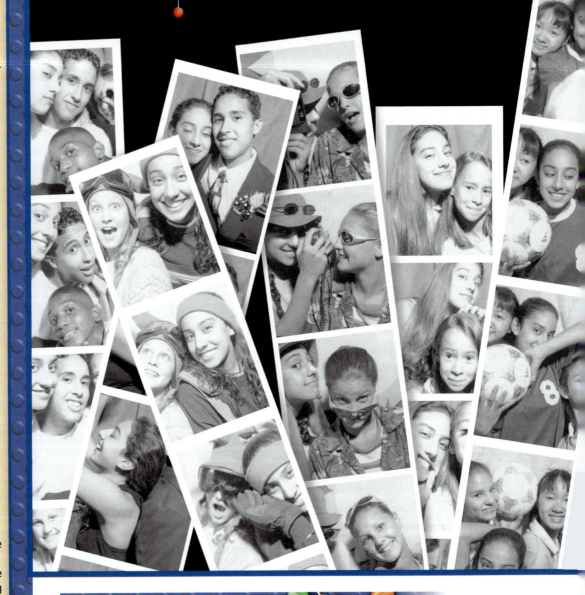

PREVIEWING THE CHAPTER

- The three workshops in this chapter focus on personal reflection. Although each of the workshops can be taught alone, the three workshops complement each other when taught together. The reading selection introduces students to elements of personal reflection and approaches to its interpretation, preparing students to write their own personal essays. Students' essays can then be used as the basis for a video reflection. To integrate this chapter with grammar, usage, and mechanics chapters, see pp. T401A–T401B.

INTRODUCING THE CHAPTER

- To introduce the chapter, use the Journal Warm-up, Transparency 10, in *Communications*.

VIEWING THE ILLUSTRATION (19A)

- The illustration is of six series of photos taken quickly by an automated camera in a small booth. One person appears in every photo, and this girl has selected these photos of herself and her friends to remember and share with others. Ask students how the photos reflect who the girl is and the experiences she has. Make the point that the process of choosing photos to share and that of choosing experiences to write about and share are very similar.

CHAPTER RESOURCES

Planning
- *Lesson Planner*, Ch. 1
- Block Scheduling, p. T15A (this book)
- One-Stop Planner CD-ROM

Practice
- *Communications*, Ch. 1

- Media Literacy and Communication Skills
- Writer's Workshop 2 CD-ROM

Extension
- Designing Your Writing

PREVIEW

Reading Workshop

Reading a Personal Reflection
PAGE 18

Writing Workshop

Writing a Personal Reflection
PAGE 28

Focus on Viewing and Representing

Making a Video Reflection
PAGE 50

Personal Reflection

- Driving down the street, you hear a song on the radio that makes you think of a summer weekend you spent at the beach.
- Your older sister goes off to college. As you sit in her room, looking at her things, you remember when you both were much younger.
- At a family reunion, a cousin says to you, "Boy, you sure have changed!" The remark makes you ask yourself, "How have I changed?"

When you can take advantage of opportunities like these to examine events in your life that have shaped your unique personality, you are making a **personal reflection**. Personal reflection helps you know yourself better by making you think about who you are and how you got to be the way you are. Many people write down their personal reflections as autobiographical narratives, memoirs, journal entries, or diary entries. When you read personal reflections like these, you not only get to know the thoughts, feelings, and experiences of other people, but you also learn new ways of reexamining your life through the examples set by others.

GO TO: go.hrw.com
KEYWORD: EOLang 10-1

YOUR TURN 1 — Thinking About Personal Reflection

Working with a partner, look through magazines, newspapers, or Web pages for two examples of personal reflections. Write down what you liked about the reflections and what they told you about the author. Be prepared to share your findings with your classmates.

Motivate

To stimulate thought about personal reflection, explain that students have been learning from stories of others' experiences from an early age. Prompt students to identify people who have shared personal experiences with them. Then, ask students to freewrite for ten minutes about that experience. What did it teach them about the person? about themselves? about life?

ELEMENTS OF Literature

Personal Reflection in Literature. In *Elements of Literature,* Fourth Course, see "Daddy Doll Under the Bed," by Erma Bombeck, p. 679, and "The Magic Happened," by John Steinbeck, p. 954, for examples of personal reflection.

YOUR TURN 1

Make sure each student in the pair comments in writing on both examples.

Chapter Opener, pp. 16–17
Alignments
TEKS 8A, 8B, 10A, 10B

Texas Resources
- *Lesson Planner,* Ch. 1
- *TAAS Tool Kit*
- *Preparation for TAAS*
- *Preparing for English II End-of-Course Examination*
- *One-Stop Planner CD-ROM*

Reinforcement
- *Communications,* Ch. 1
- *Alternative Readings,* Ch. 1
- *Daily Language Activity Transparencies*
- *Vocabulary Workshop* and *Tests*

Evaluation and Assessment
- *Test Generator* (One-Stop Planner CD-ROM)

- *Assessment Package*
  —*Chapter Tests,* Ch. 1
  —*Chapter Tests in Standardized Test Formats,* Ch. 1
  —*Assessment Alternatives,* Ch. 1

Internet
- go.hrw.com (keyword: EOLang 10–1)

Reading Workshop

OBJECTIVES

- To read a personal reflection in preparation for writing one
- To make inferences
- To analyze narrative and descriptive details
- To determine the meaning of multiple-meaning words in context

TEACHING TIP

Preparing to Read
The material on p. 18 introduces concepts that will be treated in greater detail on pp. 21–25. Narrative and descriptive details and making inferences are the basis of instruction in the Reading Workshop. Students have the opportunity to make inferences and analyze narrative and descriptive details in the reading selection, an excerpt from *An American Childhood* by Annie Dillard.

Quotation for the Day

"So when I was a little boy, I loved listening to my old people. The other little guys would go out and play around together, but I would go sit with the old people and listen to them."

(Wallace H. Black Elk, 1921– , Lakota shaman)

Have students focus on their earliest memories of their "old people." Ask them to write a paragraph or two about their memories, and allow volunteers to share with the class.

RESOURCES

Reading Workshop
Reinforcement
- *Alternative Readings*, Ch. 1

Reading Workshop

Reading a Personal Reflection

WHAT'S AHEAD?
In this section, you will read a personal reflection and learn how to
- make inferences
- analyze narrative and descriptive details

Have you ever had an experience that you thought was unimportant at the time, but that you later realized actually shaped your life? In the selection from *An American Childhood* that begins on the next page, Annie Dillard reflects on such a life-changing experience. As you read the selection, you may think of experiences or emotions you have had that are similar to the ones Dillard describes.

Sometimes the **significance**, or importance, of an experience is not immediately obvious. At other times, a small, insignificant experience can begin a series of events that cause major, life-altering changes.

Preparing to Read

READING SKILL

Making Inferences An **inference** is an educated guess you make based on the facts presented to you and on your personal knowledge and experience. For example, as you enter a freeway ramp, you find that traffic is backed up. Since it is too early for rush hour, you infer that there must be an accident or perhaps road repairs up ahead. Inferences are also important to understanding what you read. When you read, you make inferences by taking the details that writers give and connecting them to your own knowledge and experience. A good narrative unfolds with your active participation as a reader, uncovering details and making personal connections. As you read the following passage from *An American Childhood*, see if you can recognize places where the writer expects you to connect the details she has provided with your own knowledge and experience.

READING FOCUS

Narrative and Descriptive Details Writers of narratives mainly use two types of details to help the reader share their experiences. **Narrative details** specifically relate actions and events, while **descriptive details** describe important people, places, and objects. Be on the lookout for the details the writer has included in the following personal reflection.

18   Chapter 1   Narration/Description: Reflecting on Experiences

---

READING PROCESS

PREREADING
Activate Prior Knowledge. Help students connect the incident the author describes with their own experiences. Ask students if they have ever captured a caterpillar that spun a cocoon or if they have ever seen a moth or butterfly emerge from a cocoon or chrysalis. Encourage students to share with the class childhood experiences with moths or butterflies. You may wish to show a brief video about the stages in the metamorphosis of moths and butterflies.

Reading Selection

As a student, Pulitzer Prize–winning writer Annie Dillard encountered a moth that changed her life. In this passage from her autobiography, *An American Childhood*, she examines that encounter and its significance. As you read, write down your answers to the numbered active-reading questions.

from An American Childhood

BY ANNIE DILLARD

Everywhere, things snagged me. The visible world turned me curious to books; the books propelled me reeling back to the world.

At school I saw a searing sight. It turned me to books; it turned me to jelly; it turned me much later, I suppose, into an early version of a runaway, a scapegrace.[1] It was only a freshly hatched Polyphemus moth crippled because its mason jar[2] was too small.

The mason jar sat on the teacher's desk; the big moth emerged inside it. The moth had clawed a hole in its hot cocoon and crawled out, as if agonizingly, over the course of an hour, one leg at a time; we children watched around the desk, transfixed. After it emerged, the wet, mashed thing turned around walking on the green jar's bottom, then painstakingly climbed the twig with which the jar was furnished.

There, at the twig's top, the moth shook its sodden clumps of wings. When it spread those wings—those beautiful wings—blood would fill their veins, and the birth fluids on the wings' frail

1. How old do you think the writer was when this event occurred? What makes you think so?

2. What details about the Polyphemus moth's appearance does the writer include?

---

1. **scapegrace:** a graceless, unprincipled person.
2. **mason jar:** a jar with a wide mouth and screw-on lid.

Active-Reading Questions

The active-reading questions direct students to make inferences and to think about the use of detail in the Reading Selection. Students' answers will help you measure their ability to make inferences based on information in the text and assess their understanding of the use of detail in a personal narrative.

ANSWERS

1. She was probably of elementary-school age. The moth is in a jar on the teacher's desk, and the students stand around the teacher's desk for an hour, watching the moth emerge.

2. wings: "sodden clumps," "frail sheets," "wide," "hardened while they were still crumpled"; body: "big," "gold furred," "almost as big as a mouse"

The author writes that if the moth had not been in the jar, blood would have filled the veins of its wings; the fluids on the wings would have hardened to make the wings "tough as sails," and the moth's "brown, yellow, pink, and blue wings would have extended six inches from tip to tip." The moth "would have been as big as a wren."

Reading Workshop, pp. 18–25

Alignments
TEKS 7B, 7G, 8A, 11F, 12A
TAAS R4, R5
English II End-of-Course 3

Texas Resources
- *Lesson Planner*, Ch. 1
- *TAAS Tool Kit*
- *Preparation for TAAS*
- *Preparing for English II End-of-Course Examination*
- *One-Stop Planner CD-ROM*

sheets would harden to make them tough as sails. But the moth could not spread its wide wings at all; the jar was too small. The wings could not fill, so they hardened while they were still crumpled from the cocoon. A smaller moth could have spread its wings to their utmost in that mason jar, but the Polyphemus moth was big. Its gold furred body was almost as big as a mouse. Its brown, yellow, pink, and blue wings would have extended six inches from tip to tip, if there had been no mason jar. It would have been big as a wren.

The teacher let the deformed creature go. We all left the classroom and paraded outside behind the teacher with pomp and circumstance. She bounced the moth from its jar and set it on the school's asphalt driveway. The moth set out walking. It could only heave the golden wrinkly clumps where its wings should have been; it could only crawl down the school driveway on its six frail legs. The moth crawled down the driveway toward the rest of Shadyside,[3] an area of fine houses, expensive apartments, and fashionable shops. It crawled down the driveway because its shriveled wings were glued shut. It crawled down the driveway toward Shadyside, one of the several sections of town where people like me were expected to settle after college, renting an apartment until they married one of the boys and bought a house. I watched it go.

I knew that this particular moth, the big walking moth, could not travel more than a few more yards before a bird or a cat began to eat it, or a car ran over it. Nevertheless, it was crawling with what seemed wonderful vigor, as if, I thought at the time, it was still excited from being born. I watched it go till the bell rang and I had to go in. I have told this story before, and may yet tell it again, to lay the moth's ghost, for I still see it crawl down the broad black driveway, and I still see its golden wing clumps heave.

> **3.** What does this paragraph seem to reveal about the writer's attitude toward Shadyside?

> **4.** Do you think the writer is correct about what will happen to the moth? What makes you think this?

---

3. **Shadyside:** The neighborhood in east Pittsburgh, Pennsylvania, where Dillard was raised.

Active-Reading Questions
ANSWERS continued

3. She seems to be comparing the community to the mason jar in which the moth was trapped. In Shadyside, young people (like herself at the time) are cramped and unable to "spread their wings."

4. Yes; the moth cannot fly away because its wings are deformed.

READING PROCESS

READING (7B)
Make Personal Connections. Students will better understand the selection and derive more meaning from it if they are able to relate the incident and the author's reaction to it to an experience of their own. Invite students to explore in their journals situations in their lives when they recognized circumstances that prevented them from realizing their potential. What happened? What challenges remain for students to overcome in order to "spread their wings and fly"?

First Thoughts on Your Reading
Work with a partner to answer the following questions about *An American Childhood*. Put your answers on your own paper.

1. In the second paragraph, Dillard tells the reader that the moth's jar is too small—even though she goes on to make that point later. Why? What purpose is served by saying this early in the narrative?
2. List five words or phrases in the passage that describe the moth. Based on the words or phrases, how do you think the writer wants you to feel about this moth?
3. How does the writer feel about this experience? How do you know? In which two paragraphs does she provide the most details about how the experience affected her?

Making Inferences

Playing Detective To spur your interest, writers often give clues about what they want you, as the reader, to understand. As a reader, you must play the part of a detective, piecing together the clues and relating them to your own experiences. When you carry out this process, you are **making inferences**—educated guesses based on information in the text and on your own knowledge and experience. Inference can be used to

- **draw conclusions:** to make judgments that are *specific to the text* that you are reading

  Example:
  A writer describes her experience viewing Halley's comet from the hood of her car. You conclude that this reflection must have taken place in 1986—the only time Halley's comet has passed the earth since automobiles were invented.

- **make generalizations:** to make judgments that *apply to the world in general* and not just the text you are reading

  Example:
  After reading that the dahlia got its name from an eighteenth-century botanist named Anders Dahl, the magnolia was named for Pierre Magnol, a French botanist, and the zinnia's name came from J. G. Zinn, a German botanist, you could make the generalization that flowers often get their names from scientists who work with the plants.

READING SKILL

TIP Good writers will sometimes **create suspense** by leading readers to make invalid inferences. They do this by withholding details, providing misleading information, or going against the expectations readers have developed from past knowledge and experience.

First Thoughts on Your Reading
ANSWERS
Possible answers are suggested below.

1. The brief detail about the mason jar in the second paragraph helps explain why Dillard calls the moth in the jar "a searing sight," and motivates the reader to keep reading to find out more.
2. "crippled"; "crawled out, as if agonizingly"; "mashed thing"; "painstakingly climbed"; "shook its sodden clumps of wings." Dillard wants the reader to feel sorry, sad, and sympathetic.
3. She has been disturbed by it; it has haunted her for a long time. She describes it as "searing" and sees the moth as a ghost; she says she has told the story before and thinks she will tell it again. The second and the last paragraphs provide these details.

Cooperative Learning
Discussing the Effects of Culture. Remind students that their cultural experiences during childhood might differ from the one Annie Dillard describes. Divide the class into small groups, and ask them to take notes on their discussions. Ask students to explain how culture affects personal responses, first by defining the culture within the text, then by relating their personal knowledge to the text, and finally by describing their culture as well as the cultures represented by other group members. (These discussion topics may also be used to evaluate a visual text, such as the video reflection suggested on p. 50.)

**MULTIPLE INTELLIGENCES
Intrapersonal/Interpersonal Intelligences.** Students may benefit from investigating the different ways they have made inferences in previous readings. Have students re-read a work that related to their own experiences. What inferences did they make, and how? Students can meet in small groups to discuss their pieces, findings, and thought processes.

- **make predictions:** to foretell events

   Example:
   When a multiplex theater opens in the narrator's town, you predict that the single-screen theater her parents own will have trouble competing.

- **determine causes or effects:** to figure out the probable effect or the probable cause when only a cause or effect is stated

   Example:
   A writer tells about losing his dog and about his resulting sadness. He describes coming home to an open fence gate. You determine that someone might have left the gate open, and the dog ran out.

- **determine main idea:** to understand the unstated focus or key idea in a piece of writing

   Example:
   A passage of a memoir written by a World War I veteran describes a fear-filled night in the trenches during the battle of the Somme. The narrator later wins a Congressional Medal of Honor. You determine that the main idea of the passage was that even heroes feel fear when faced with great challenges.

Although inference serves a variety of purposes, in every case the process of making inferences can be illustrated by the following equation.

$$\boxed{\text{details from the reading}} + \boxed{\text{personal knowledge and experience}} = \boxed{\text{inference}}$$

One difficulty with making inferences, however, is that your knowledge and experience may sometimes fail to match a writer's expectations. When there are cultural or educational differences between a writer and his or her readers, some readers are likely to have problems making inferences—whether they are reading Shakespeare or *The New York Times.* For example, a politician's memoir might describe her New York City childhood as "growing up in the shadow of Lady Liberty." The writer expects her readers to make the inference that "Lady Liberty" is the Statue of Liberty, a symbol of political freedom and democracy, and that living near the statue influenced her political dreams. A reader unfamiliar with the term "Lady Liberty" or the symbolism of the monument might not be able to make the inference that the writer intended.

THINKING IT THROUGH Making Inferences

Watch how the three-step process of making an inference shown in the following Thinking It Through can be used to draw a reasonable conclusion from the following passage. These same steps can be applied to all types of inferences.

> When I returned home hours late, the only light that greeted me was the flickering television. The only sounds I heard were the TV's babble and my father's snores coming from his favorite chair.

▶ **STEP 1 Identify the details the writer has given.**

The narrator came home late. The TV is still on. No lights are on. The narrator's father is asleep in the chair.

▶ **STEP 2 Relate the details to your knowledge and experience.**

Normally people do not sleep in chairs with the TV on, except when exceptionally tired—maybe from staying up too late. My dad tends to fall asleep in front of the TV when he has stayed up too late. My dad sometimes waits up for me when I have been out too late.

▶ **STEP 3 Decide what you think the writer has left out and what you are being asked to infer.**

Based on the passage and my knowledge and experience, I conclude that the father may have fallen asleep while waiting for the narrator to return home.

YOUR TURN 2 Making Inferences

Using the Thinking It Through steps above, explain what conclusions you can infer about Annie Dillard's attitude toward the moth in the selection from *An American Childhood* on page 19. Pay close attention to the following key words.

- *would, would have, could have,* and *could not* in paragraph four
- *bounced, could, crawled, shriveled,* and *glued* in paragraph five

Write your answer on your own paper.

YOUR TURN 2
ANSWER

The mason jar prevented the moth from becoming all that it should have, yet there was vigor and beauty in its efforts to spread its wings. The author both pities the creature's condition and admires its determination and spirit.

RESOURCES

Your Turn 2

Practice
- *Communications,* WS. p. 7

Reinforcement
- *Communications,* TP. 11, WS. p. 8

Critical Thinking

Synthesis. To check students' understanding of narrative and descriptive details, have students write six to eight interview questions they can ask Annie Dillard about her experience with the Polyphemus moth. Then, have students answer the questions from Dillard's point of view. Students should base their questions and Dillard's hypothetical responses on details in the selection as well as inferences drawn from their reading. Students may present their interviews in oral or written form.

TIP Some details can be from more than one category. For example, the sentence "The lightning flashed around us like spears" tells what happened and to whom (both narrative details) and also illustrates what the lightning looked like (sensory detail) by using the simile *like spears* (figurative detail).

READING FOCUS

Narrative and Descriptive Details

The Spice of Life Do you have a favorite food? If you had to eat that favorite food every day for the next two weeks, do you think you would still like it as much? No matter how good that food is, you would probably be ready for a little variety. As a reader, you probably have a similar desire for variety in what you read. For example, when you read a narrative, you probably want to see a variety of **narrative** and **descriptive details.**

Narrative details are the elements that provide a basic framework for specifying the **people, things, places,** and **events** of a narrative. They give an account of not only the **actions** but also the **thoughts and feelings** of those people involved, and often include **dialogue**—the exact words of the speakers. Narrative details answer the questions *Who? What? When?* and *Where?* The narrative details in *An American Childhood* include the school (place), the teacher and students (people), the deformed moth (thing), and Dillard's sympathetic reaction to the moth's plight (feelings).

Added to the simple framework of narrative details are **descriptive details,** which elaborate on or "flesh out" the framework. Just as a leafless tree in the winter is still a tree, a narrative without descriptive details is still a narrative—though very stark and bare. Three key kinds of descriptive details help a narrative come alive for the reader: **sensory details, factual details,** and **figurative details.**

- **Sensory details** appeal to the five senses: sight, hearing, taste, touch, and smell. These details bring you into the narrative through elements you recognize from your own experiences. They answer the questions *How does it look? How does it sound? How does it taste? How does it feel?* and *How does it smell?*

  Example:
  Its *brown, yellow, pink, and blue wings* would have extended six inches from tip to tip, if there had been no mason jar. [Details of *sight* are provided.]

- **Factual details** give the straightforward, objective aspects of the events, people, places, and objects in the narrative. They often involve names, dates, and numbers.

  Example:
  It was only a freshly hatched *Polyphemus* moth crippled because its *mason* jar was too small. [*Polyphemus* and *mason* tell us what kind of moth and what kind of jar are being discussed.]

- **Figurative details** use figures of speech to compare things in imaginative ways that prompt readers to look at the things differently. The three

---

READING PROCESS

EXTENDING
Read Other Works. Have students read the excerpt "Typhoid Fever" from *Angela's Ashes* by Frank McCourt. Ask students what inferences they can make about the author from his experience. Then, discuss how details reveal the author's thoughts and feelings and help readers understand his experience more fully.

kinds of figurative details used most often are **simile**, **metaphor**, and **personification**. The following chart provides information that will help you recognize these details as you read.

Figure of Speech	How to Recognize	Example
Simile	uses the word *like* or *as* to compare two things	Maxwell's heart leapt **like a frightened cat** at the unexpected barks of the dog behind the fence. Explanation: The leaping feeling of his heart is compared to the leaping reaction of a frightened cat.
Metaphor	says that one thing *is* another thing; compares two things without using *like* or *as*	Mishka's **words were the shining ribbon on the wonderful gift** my day had been. Explanation: The girl's words enrich a wonderful day (which is compared to a gift).
Personification	gives animals or objects human characteristics	The **Colosseum proudly says,** "I was born of the Roman Empire; while I stand, the Romans shall not be forgotten." Explanation: An unliving thing cannot show pride or speak, but the writer imaginatively describes what the Colosseum would feel and say if it were alive.

YOUR TURN 3 — Identifying Narrative and Descriptive Details

For each sentence below, identify the italicized word or phrase as either a narrative detail or a descriptive detail.

- Label the narrative details as people, things, places, events, actions, or thoughts and feelings.
- Label the descriptive details as sensory, factual, or figurative.

Write your answers on your own paper.

1. ". . . the birth fluids on the wings' frail sheets would harden to make them *tough as sails*."
2. "A *smaller* moth could have spread its wings to their utmost in that mason jar. . . ."
3. "Nevertheless, it was crawling with what seemed wonderful vigor, as if, I thought at the time, *it was still excited from being born*."
4. "It *crawled down the driveway*. . . ."
5. "After it emerged, the *wet, mashed* thing turned around walking on the *green* jar's bottom. . . ."

Wrap It Up

Metacognition. Ask students to reflect on their own reading processes. Give students five minutes to write a brief answer to the following question.

1. What is your reaction to Dillard's story about the moth? What about the writing makes you feel that way?

Then, ask students the following question.

2. What is the equation for making an inference while reading? [details from the reading + personal knowledge and experience = inference]

YOUR TURN 3

ANSWERS

1. descriptive-figurative
2. descriptive-factual or sensory
3. narrative-thoughts and feelings
4. narrative-actions
5. descriptive-sensory; descriptive-sensory

RESOURCES

Your Turn 3

Practice
- *Communications,* WS. p. 9

Reinforcement
- *Communications,* TP. 12, WS. p. 10

TEACHING TIP

Using Multiple-Meaning Words
Point out that Dillard uses a multiple-meaning word when she writes, "We all left the classroom and paraded outside . . . with pomp and *circumstance*." *Circumstance* has several meanings, including "an influencing factor," "existing conditions," and "showy ceremony." If students know different meanings of a multiple-meaning word and the sentence or passage has helpful context clues, they can figure out the intended meaning. In the example, the context clue *paraded* indicates that *circumstance* means "showy ceremony."

MINI-LESSON VOCABULARY

Using Multiple-Meaning Words

ANSWERS
Possible responses are given below.

1. drop or decline in vigor or strength
2. with a central unit of a mother, a father, and a child or children
3. to put up with; endure
4. to abstain from food
5. a political party's formal declaration of principles

Taking a Second Look
Using Multiple-Meaning Words.
Have students rewrite the practice sentences or add other sentences so that the meanings for the italicized words can be inferred through context clues. Students can refer to a chart of context clues on p. 887 in the Quick Reference Handbook.

MINI-LESSON VOCABULARY

Using Multiple-Meaning Words

When you read the selection from *An American Childhood*, you encountered several multiple-meaning words. **Multiple-meaning words** are words that have more than one meaning and (sometimes) different pronunciations. **Homographs** are multiple-meaning words that have different origins.

To determine the intended meaning of multiple-meaning words in sentences, follow the steps in Thinking It Through below.

THINKING IT THROUGH — Understanding Multiple-Meaning Words

Take a look at the example sentence below and the steps following it.

Zane drank the orange juice with *relish*.

1. **Eliminate known meanings that will not work.** For example, if you think of *relish* as meaning only "chopped pickles," then either Zane has really odd tastes or you need to consider another meaning for the word.

2. **Use a dictionary to check the other meanings of the word.** Read the entire entry for that word. Most dictionaries define **homographs** in separate entries. Check to see if there is a second or even third entry that might match the intended meaning of the word.

   relish (rel´ish) *n.* [[ME *reles* < OFr *relais*, something remaining < *relaisser*: see RELEASE]] **1** distinctive or characteristic flavor [a *relish* of garlic in the stew] **2** a trace or touch (*of* some quality); hint or suggestion [a *relish* of malice in his action] **3** an appetizing flavor; pleasing taste **4** *a)* pleasure; enjoyment; zest [to listen with *relish*] *b)* liking or craving [showing little *relish* for the task] **5** anything that gives pleasure, zest, or enjoyment; attractive quality **6** any of a variety of foods, as pickles, olives, piccalilli, raw vegetables, etc., served with a meal to add flavor or as an appetizer —*vt.* **1** [Now Rare] to give flavor **2** to enjoy; like —*vi.* **1** to taste or have the flavor (*of* something) **2** to have a pleasing taste

3. **Determine which meaning fits best within the context of the sentence.** For the sentence about Zane's drinking juice, meaning number 4 of *relish* works best. The main idea is that Zane drank the juice with *pleasure* or *enjoyment*.

PRACTICE

Use the steps above to determine the meanings of the italicized words in the following sentences. Write on your own paper.

1. After six perfect innings, the pitcher felt his energy *flag*.
2. Many people look back to the 1950s and wonder whatever happened to the "perfect" *nuclear* family.
3. The senator said he would *brook* no opposition to his proposed amendment.
4. Many religions specify holidays as a time to *fast*.
5. There was great debate before the group could decide on a *platform*.

RESOURCES

Vocabulary
Practice
- *Communications*, WS. p. 11

Test Taking
Practice
- *Communications*, WS. pp. 12–14

Answering Inference Questions on Reading Tests

Reading tests often include questions that check your ability to make inferences from a reading passage. Here are a typical reading passage and inference test question.

> As a child, I watched my father grow old before his time. His hair grayed, and his skin grew rough and wrinkled. His walk slowed and became more purposeful with each passing day. Although I never saw him leave, each day I watched him return from the fields with the setting sun making him a scarecrow in silhouette. His eyes reflected only the flicker of our farmhouse candlelight, but little light of their own. The father I had known before the hard times seemed to be drying up like the dusty fields he worked.

Which of the following statements about the narrator's father can you infer from the passage?

A. He is confused about his family's future.
B. He lost his job because of the economy.
C. He is a farmer whose hard work has affected him physically and emotionally.
D. He feels sorry for his child and wants to make things better for his family.

THINKING IT THROUGH — Answering Inference Questions

Use the following steps to answer inference test questions like the one above.

1. **Skim the passage once for a general understanding; then, re-read it carefully.** Keep in mind that most of these questions are designed to measure your reading comprehension, not your reading speed.

2. **Locate key words and phrases in the answer choices that match similar words and phrases in the reading passage.** You may be able to eliminate some answers right away. Choices **A** and **D** discuss the father's feelings with *confused* and *feels sorry*. The reading passage does not say how the father feels. Choice **B** mentions *lost his job* and *the economy*, words that are not used in the reading passage. Choice **C** uses the words *farmer* and *hard work* along with the phrase *affected him physically*. The reading passage does evoke images of a farm with the words *fields*, *farmhouse*, and *scarecrow*. The father also has undergone physical changes, as evidenced by the descriptions of his hair, skin, and walk. Choice **C** seems the most likely answer.

3. **Confirm your answer by considering your prior knowledge about the subject of the passage.** The image of dusty fields might remind you of pictures of farms in the Dust Bowl you may have seen when studying the Great Depression in history class. This knowledge, combined with the details from the passage, makes the inference in answer **C** a safe (and correct) choice.

Reading Workshop 27

Looking Ahead to Writing

Students will write their personal reflections in this chapter's Writing Workshop (pp. 28–49). As they write and revise their personal narratives, students will recognize the importance of narrative and descriptive detail in reaching and connecting with their audience. Have students refer to the Reading Selection on pp. 19–20 and to the discussion of narrative and descriptive details on pp. 24–25 as they work on their essays.

Vocabulary
Alignments
TEKS 6B, 6E
TAAS R1

Test Taking
Alignments
TEKS 7B, 7G, 7H
TAAS R4, R5

Reading Workshop 27

Writing Workshop

OBJECTIVES

- To write a personal reflection
- To gather and organize details
- To reflect on the meaning of an experience
- To use figurative language
- To combine sentences to add sentence variety
- To check subject-verb agreement

Quotation for the Day

"I remember the green coat that I wore in fifth and sixth grades when you either danced like a champ or pressed yourself against a greasy wall, bitter as a penny toward the happy couples."

(Gary Soto, 1952– , Mexican American poet, from "The Jacket")

Ask students if they have any memories of clothing that call up particular experiences. Have them brainstorm lists of memorable clothing and any incidents associated with the clothing. Have students keep their lists as a source for possible ideas for an essay.

Writing Workshop

Writing a Personal Reflection

WHAT'S AHEAD?

In this workshop, you will write a personal reflection. You will also learn how to

- gather and organize details
- reflect on the meaning of an experience
- use figurative language
- combine sentences to add sentence variety
- check subject-verb agreement

Imagine that you receive an application to a college you really want to attend. One section asks you to write a thousand-word essay about a life experience that has prompted you to study a particular subject. What will you write? How will you write it?

This kind of essay calls for writing a **personal reflection**—an autobiographical narrative reflecting on an experience in your life that has helped make you the person you are today. People write personal reflections to share their experiences and life lessons with others. Some writers are famous people, telling the stories of their private lives. Other writers are simply ordinary people with extraordinary tales to tell. Still others have ordinary tales to tell but an extraordinary ability to tell them. In this Writing Workshop, you will learn how to choose an important experience you have had and to write a personal reflection describing that experience in an interesting way.

Prewriting

Choosing an Experience

Who Are You? To find an experience to use as the topic for a personal or autobiographical narrative, you should begin by exploring the experiences in your life that have made you who you are. You can think of the important experiences that have changed your life as **defining moments** because they have helped define your character. Follow the suggestions below to start thinking of experiences to write about in your personal reflection.

- **Look through old photo albums, diaries, and scrapbooks.** Take a few hours to look through them and stir up old memories. Write down notes about experiences they make you remember.

28 Chapter 1 Narration/Description: Reflecting on Experiences

- **List your hobbies**—the things you like to do. Then, think about the experiences in your life that got you interested in these hobbies. What about those experiences made them meaningful to you?
- **Interview a parent, teacher, or friend** to see whether these people remember any experiences that they think were important in your life. You might also ask what they find interesting about you. Then, you can think about any experiences in your life that may have helped to make you interesting.
- **Carry a notebook** with you for a day or two. When you find yourself thinking of interesting experiences from your past, you will have a handy place to write them down.

When choosing an experience in your life to write about, there are three things you should keep in mind.

- **The experience should be one important to you.** If it is not very significant to you, you will have a hard time interesting your reader.
- **The experience should stand out clearly in your memory.** Make sure you can remember the major details of the experience—they will form the core of your personal reflection.
- **The experience should not be too personal or too private to share.** Others will be reading your narrative. Make sure your topic is one you are willing to share with them.

After you have brainstormed a list of possible experiences, choose three or four that are of special interest to you. Show the list to your friends, parents, or teachers and get their opinions on which one would be the most interesting for them to read. Once you have chosen one of the experiences from your list, you are ready to begin.

TIP Do not reject an experience as a topic just because you do not immediately remember every single detail about it. Often, details from your memory will surface over time as you continue to think about past experiences.

Considering Purpose, Audience, Tone, and Voice

The Big Picture To write an interesting personal reflection, you must have a clear idea of your **purpose, audience, tone,** and **voice.** These will be the main forces that influence the choices you make while planning, writing, and revising your work.

Purpose The main **purpose** of a personal reflection is to express yourself. You examine an experience in your life and explore your thoughts and feelings about it. Unlike a diary or a journal entry, this is writing in which your purpose is also to write something that you can share with others. You must not only reach into yourself but also try to reach *out* to others.

ADVANCED LEARNERS
Suggest an alternative assignment in which students write a folk tale or fable about a personal experience. Students should determine the characteristics of such writings by analyzing a familiar folk tale or fable. They may then use the folk tale or fable as a model when they begin writing. Students who choose such an option can still work with the concepts and techniques presented in this chapter. Students may share their works by orally presenting the folk tales or fables to an audience of peers, faculty, or family.

Prewriting, pp. 28–37
Alignments
TEKS 1A, 1B, 1C, 2A
TAAS W1, W2, W4
English II End-of-Course 4

Texas Resources
- *Lesson Planner,* Ch. 1
- *TAAS Tool Kit*
- *Preparation for TAAS*
- *Preparing for English II End-of-Course Examination*
- *One-Stop Planner CD-ROM*

Meeting INDIVIDUAL NEEDS

MODALITY

Visual Learners. Suggest that students draw maps of the settings of their personal narratives. By visualizing and mentally walking through the rooms in the house, the areas of the yard, their neighborhood, or whatever the setting might be, students can generate more details for their essays. Students might note details directly on their maps or jot them down on a separate sheet of paper.

Audience It is especially important to have a specific **audience** in mind as you compose your personal reflection. That means you need to choose an appropriate audience *before* you begin writing. For example, if you are writing about an experience that involves a relative of yours, that relative might be an appropriate audience for your personal reflection. However, if you are writing an autobiographical narrative to send in with a college application, the choice is clear: Your audience is any college admissions counselor who might read the narrative. Before you begin writing, try listing everything you know about the audience for whom you plan to write. Here are some questions to help you form a clear mental image of your audience and what they will want to see in your personal reflection.

- Who might benefit from reading my personal reflection?
- What kind of things will this audience be expecting to read?
- How are my audience's experiences similar to mine? How are they different?
- Which people and places will be familiar to my audience? Which will I need to explain better?
- Will they understand or disapprove if I use informal language?

Tone **Tone** is the feeling or attitude you, the writer, convey about your topic. In a personal reflection, how you *feel* about the experience should come through clearly. For example, if the experience was funny, you should choose words and examples that are light and amusing—ones that give your narrative a humorous tone. Because personal expression is informal, you will also use first-person pronouns: *I, me, our,* and *we.*

Voice Isn't it great that your friends recognize your voice when you telephone them? **Voice** in writing is the unique sound and rhythm of a writer's language. By letting your own voice show through in your writing, you make the reader know that there is a real person behind the words on the page. Trying to adopt the voice of someone else (for example, by using overblown, pretentious language) often is a mistake because it will make your writing sound insincere.

Gathering Details

Putting the Pieces Together Gathering details is like sorting pieces of a complicated jigsaw puzzle. You reach into a box that holds hundreds of brightly colored parts of a picture. Your task is to turn the pieces over and see which ones fit into the section of the picture you are working on—with that picture in mind at all times as you work. Similarly, you should keep in mind the "big picture" for your personal reflection while you work on connecting all of its particular details.

Events After you have selected your topic, brainstorm a list of events central to the telling of the narrative—events that you need to relate so readers will understand and share the experience with you. Include **narrative details,** which tell about specific actions and events. List the events **chronologically,** in the order that they happened. One writer created the list of events below when she began gathering details for her personal reflection.

> **Events List**
> - I watched others practicing tae kwon do and imagined that I could do it, too.
> - I met an instructor who taught me techniques.
> - I practiced hard.
> - I entered a competition.
> - My mom and dad saw me compete for the very first time.

TIP Sometimes meeting with a small group of your peers to discuss the events you are focusing on helps you remember details better. If you use this strategy, be sure to employ effective **listening strategies.**
- Ask clear questions.
- Respond appropriately to others' questions.
- Be an empathic listener by responding to feelings, not just to facts.

People and Places Next, make a list of people and places you will need to include in your narrative. Who, besides yourself, played a part in your experience? Where did the experience take place? Use **descriptive details** to paint a clear image of the experience. What did the people look like? What did they say? What did the place look like? What did you hear there? Notice that most of these questions deal with your senses. When you describe details of sight, hearing, smell, touch, and taste, you use **sensory details,** which many of your readers will be able to identify. Other descriptive details include **figurative language** (such as **similes** and **metaphors**) and **factual details.** Below is an example of a list that includes a mix of details.

> **People and Places List**
> - **Me**—shy, not very confident, age 13, physically unimpressive
> - **People in the class**—graceful, like swaying trees
> - **Gwen**—college student, strong and swift, friendly smile
> - **Derek and Tamara**—brother (17) and sister (15), older, popular, smart
> - **Mom and Dad**—protective, amazed at what I did, proud
> - **YMCA**—pool, activity rooms, picnic place—really hot
> - **Practice room**—both youths and adults, white uniforms, noisy

Cooperative Learning
Storytelling Details. Students might benefit from telling their stories to one or more classmates who could write down the key details of the oral narratives. These details can then be given back to the speaker for use in his or her writing. Students can help the storyteller by asking questions that provide details for the writer to use. If possible, have each student serve as both a storyteller and a listener within a small group.

Meeting INDIVIDUAL NEEDS

ENGLISH-LANGUAGE LEARNERS
General Strategies. Some students settle for general adjectives to describe people and places, such as *tall, happy, big,* and *nice.* As a remedy, have students work with a partner, using a thesaurus to find synonyms, such as *lanky, elated, immense,* and *delightful.*

TEACHING TIP

Thoughts and Feelings
If students' experiences include other people, encourage them to imagine or ask what others might have been thinking or feeling at the time. Taking this angle may give the writer more insight into his or her experience and produce a more accurate picture of others involved.

Dialogue
As you introduce dialogue as a kind of detail, review with students how to punctuate dialogue by using the following guidelines and examples:

- Use quotation marks at the beginning and end of a direct quotation. ["I believe the test is on Friday."]

- Use a comma, question mark, or an exclamation point to set off a quotation from the rest of the sentence. ["We are going to the movies on Saturday," said Dawn. "May I join you?" Holly asked.]

- Place question marks and exclamation points that belong to a quotation inside quotation marks. [My little sister shrieked, "This is absolutely the best gift!"]

Thoughts and Feelings To make your reflection truly personal, you should let your reader know what you were thinking and how you felt during the experience. At times, this will appeal to similar thoughts and feelings your reader has had in other situations. At other times it will give readers an insight into thoughts and feelings with which they may not be familiar. Use actions, appearance, and dialogue to show externally what is going on with you internally. For example, to show that she was terrified of sparring, a writer might say that her knees were "like mashed potatoes." Here are some thoughts and feelings one writer wrote down while preparing a personal reflection.

Thoughts and Feelings List

- Envy—imagined being graceful, perfect techniques; afraid to join the group
- Surprise and fear—knees shaking, needed a compliment
- Accomplishment—Mom and Dad proud; photo in the newspaper; a good match

Reference Note
For more on **interviewing**, see page 910 in the Quick Reference Handbook.

TIP Interviewing other people who were involved in the experience will refresh your memory about details of the experience and give you different perspectives from which to view the experience.

KEY CONCEPT

Dialogue The final kind of detail is dialogue—another narrative detail. Because you are telling a story, you should use dialogue to add variety and to make the people in your narrative more real to your readers. Try to remember who said what, and use their own words. Keep in mind that **dialogue should fit the speaker and can be informal** (for example, it can include slang and sentence fragments). Here are a couple of pieces of dialogue one writer recorded.

DIALOGUE LIST

What happened?	What did they say?
Gwen was encouraging.	"Why don't you come help me practice? I could teach you some other techniques."
Friends teased me.	"Here comes Jackie Chan!"

Putting It All Together

Collect all your details and gather them in a chart like the one below.

Who or What	Details
Events	
I watched others practicing tae kwon do and imagined that I could do it, too.	Others practicing kicks, blocks, and stances
	I just watch, practice at home where no one can laugh at me
I met an instructor who taught me techniques.	Gwen offers to help; pretends that I am helping her
	I am scared; do it anyway because she is so friendly
I practiced hard.	Tough exercise; lots of sore muscles
	Eventually earn some belts
I entered a competition.	Confident; ready to show the world that I am good enough
My mom and dad saw me compete for the very first time.	They hear my name on loudspeaker
	See me in the ring
People	
Me	Shy, not very confident, age 13, physically unimpressive
People in the class	Graceful, like swaying trees
Gwen	College student, strong and swift, friendly smile
Derek and Tamara	Brother (17) and sister (15), older, popular, smart
Mom and Dad	Protective, amazed, proud
Places	
YMCA	Pool, activity rooms, picnic place—really hot
Practice room	Both youths and adults, white uniforms, noisy

(continued)

Cooperative Learning 16E, 16F

Detail Charts. Have students work in small groups to prepare their detail charts. Working with others on the details for their narratives may provide students with questions and feedback for their charts.

Before students get into groups to prepare their charts, give the class a short lesson on listening and speaking skills. Tell students that as speakers in group discussions or conversations, they have responsibilities for successfully communicating ideas. Tell students that effective speakers and listeners show the following behaviors.

Speakers
- make useful suggestions and relevant contributions by staying on the topic
- respond respectfully and appropriately to others and give attention to what has been said
- ask questions to clarify and expand on each other's ideas

Listeners
- focus on the speaker's message by being prepared to listen and by being attentive
- interpret the speaker's message by developing vocabulary and using their knowledge of language, such as clue words that signal the organization of the speaker's ideas
- monitor that they understand the speaker's message by asking relevant questions and by predicting what the speaker will say next
- formulate and provide effective verbal and nonverbal feedback, such as asking questions, making eye contact, smiling, etc.

(continued)

Thoughts and Feelings	
Envy	Imagined being graceful, perfect techniques
	Afraid to join the group
Surprise and fear	Knees shaking, needed a compliment
Accomplishment	Mom and Dad proud; photo in the newspaper—a good match
Dialogue	
Gwen was encouraging.	"Why don't you come help me practice? I could teach you some other techniques."
Friends teased me.	"Here comes Jackie Chan!"

COMPUTER TIP

Try dimming your screen while you are brainstorming a list of details at a computer. Because you will not see any typing mistakes you make, you will be able to focus more on the details themselves rather than on your typing ability.

KEY CONCEPT

List as many details as you can remember. When you write your personal reflection, you will not necessarily use all of the details that you put in this chart, and you can always add other details as you write. Remember, the goal of collecting details is not to make your notes perfectly grammatical or flawlessly neat—it is to write your ideas down as they come to you. However, make sure they are clear enough so that you will understand the notes when you come back to them.

Reflect on the Meaning of Your Experience

That Was Then, This Is Now A personal reflection about an experience should convey the significance of the experience. **Your readers should clearly see a difference between the way you were before the experience and what you became after it.** Your narrative will not be a personal reflection if it does not include actual **reflections**—your thoughts and feelings—about the significance of the experience you describe.

Give background information early in your personal reflection. Readers will not be able to recognize the change in you if they do not know what you were like before the experience. Unlike thesis statements in many essays, your thesis statement, which directly states the significance of your experience, does not appear in your narrative's introduction. Instead, you only hint at the meaning of your experience through the details of your background information. For example, if your introduction says, "When I was fourteen, I never really cared about sea life. Until then, I had never

Meeting INDIVIDUAL NEEDS

MULTIPLE INTELLIGENCES
Bodily-Kinesthetic Intelligence. Some students may benefit from exploring the meaning of an experience through acting or drawing. Students might visualize and quickly sketch how they felt and what they thought at the time of the experience. Then they can sketch their feelings and thoughts about it now. If students wish to act out a scene, have them prepare dialogue and meet with partners. Students can take turns acting out each other's scenes. Have students refer to their sketches and scenes as they explain the meaning of the experience.

seen a humpback whale," readers should sense that your reflection will be about how seeing a humpback whale changed your views on sea life. Save the direct statement of the significance of your experience for the conclusion of your narrative—after your readers have had a chance to share in your experience and possibly determine for themselves how it changed your life.

THINKING IT THROUGH

Interpreting Meaning

Use the following Thinking It Through steps to reflect on the meaning of your experience. One writer's responses are shown as an example.

▶ **STEP 1** Ask yourself if you were somehow different at the end of the experience. If so, what were you like at the beginning? How exactly did you change?

In the beginning I was shy and not very confident. I didn't ever really do my own thing. By learning tae kwon do, I think I became more confident.

▶ **STEP 2** Ask yourself whether you learned something new about yourself. What was it?

I never realized how much I was comparing myself to my brother and sister—like I was living in their shadows. I think I even unconsciously thought my parents didn't think I was anything special because I didn't have the achievements Derek and Tamara had.

▶ **STEP 3** Ask yourself if you learned something new about other people, human nature, or life in general. What was it?

I learned that my parents were proud of me no matter what. I was the one who needed to accomplish something on my own to feel like a real person.

▶ **STEP 4** Write one or two sentences about the meaning of the experience. These will become the focus of your essay. You can use a simple sentence structure like one of these to get started:

- At first, I _____ , but afterward I _____ .
- I realized that _____ .

At first, I was shy and lacked confidence, but afterward I was more self-assured. I realized that I had felt myself to be only a shadow of my older brother and sister, but now I had an accomplishment of my own to prove I was my own person.

TEACHING TIP

Interpreting Meaning
As students reflect on the meaning of an experience, they may discover that it had a negative impact on their lives. Students can still use the steps in the Thinking It Through on this page. However, you may want to provide students with the following examples that account for these kinds of experiences.

- At first, I _____, but afterward I _____. [At first, I was excited about moving to a new town, but afterward I was disappointed because it was hard to make friends.]
- I realized that _____. [I realized that my parents' divorce was final, and we would never be a family again.]

Remind students that they should only express thoughts they feel comfortable sharing with you and their classmates.

Meeting INDIVIDUAL NEEDS

INCLUSION
Students who have a difficult time organizing their details may work with a classmate, volunteer, or teacher. As the student dictates thoughts, his or her partner records them on index cards. This process could take the form of an interview, with the interviewer giving prompts such as *How did you feel?* and *What happened next?* Afterward, the cards can be sorted and sequenced for transfer to a draft.

To check that students have completed all the prewriting steps, have them organize their events, details, and thesis statements in charts. Also, remind students that gathering details is an ongoing process. To relate an experience and its meaning effectively, they may need to add additional details as they work on their drafts.

Reference Note
For more on **chronological order,** see page 375.

Organizing Your Details

Following the Leader   After listing the details of your experience, you need to put them in an order that will make the most sense to your readers. Commonly, **chronological order**—which shows the order in which the events occur over time—is the easiest for readers to follow. Another effective way of organizing a narrative is through the use of a **flashback.** In a flashback, the narrative starts in the middle or end, then "flashes back" to the beginning to relate the events leading up to that point. You should choose the order that best presents your personal reflection. The writer of the tae kwon do lesson ended up with the following arrangement.

> **Ordered Events List**
> 1. Watched others practicing tae kwon do
> 2. Imagined I could do it
> 3. Met Gwen
> 4. Learned some techniques from Gwen
> 5. Joined the class
> 6. Practiced hard
> 7. Entered a competition; had a great match
> 8. Picture in the paper

TIP   When you write your personal reflection, you need to give your readers time signals to show the order of events. You can signal the passage of time with **transitional expressions.** These expressions include words such as *next, then, eventually, soon, until, the next day,* and so on. Readers rely on these clue words to be able to follow a narrative.

YOUR TURN 4   Planning Your Personal Reflection

Review this list of prewriting steps to ensure that you have everything ready to begin writing your personal reflection. You should

- choose an experience that was a defining moment in your life and that your audience will find interesting
- gather details that will make your reflection vivid and engaging
- reflect on the meaning of the experience
- organize the events in the experience so that it will make sense

---

36   Chapter 1   Narration/Description: Reflecting on Experiences

RESOURCES

Your Turn 4
Practice
- *Communications,* WS. p. 15

Writing
Practice
- *Communications,* WS. p. 16

MINI-LESSON WRITING

Using Figurative Language

One important way of grabbing your readers' attention and creating interest in your personal reflection is to use **figurative language**—imaginative comparisons of something unfamiliar with something familiar. Using figurative language helps the reader to experience your events with you. These descriptions form memorable images that are clearer and more concrete.

Below are definitions and examples of three of the most common forms of figurative language.

If you do use figures of speech, you should be careful to avoid figures of speech that are **clichés**—tired and overused phrases. Clichés include similes such as "fog as thick as pea soup," metaphors such as "raining cats and dogs," and personification such as "raging blizzard" or "Old Man Winter." Clichés do not challenge readers to think of things in a new way and thus are not as fresh as figurative language should be.

A *simile* compares two things using *like* or *as*.	The smile spread across her face like autumn leaves across a crystal pond.
A *metaphor* says one thing *is* something else.	The smile was a lighthouse beacon illuminating the room.
Personification gives human characteristics to nonhuman things.	The smile knew it would make me look foolish, but it sprang forth regardless.

PRACTICE

Using the following chart, create five figures of speech by comparing one word in column A with one word in column B.

Then, use each new figure of speech in a sentence. Use each of the three different figures of speech at least once. Put your answers on your own paper.

Example:
child, stamp

The frightened child clung to his mother like a stamp to an envelope.

Column A	Column B
fog	sand
puppy	stamp
sailboat	leaf
bicycle	ball
child	tablecloth
canyon	river
music	book
pencil	paint

Writing Workshop 37

TEACHING TIP

Using Figurative Language
To help students understand how common figurative language is, have the class identify examples of figurative language used in advertising to compare a product to something desirable.

MINI-LESSON WRITING

Using Figurative Language

ANSWERS

Sample answers appear below. NOTE: Students can choose a word from one column when writing an example of personification.

1. fog, tablecloth

The fog was a heavy, gray tablecloth covering the town. (metaphor)

2. canyon, book

The canyon was like a geology book, revealing the composition of the earth. (simile)

3. puppy, ball

The puppy bounced around the room like a rubber ball. (simile)

4. music, river

The music was a river of joy flowing through the open door. (metaphor)

5. bicycle, leaf

The leaves covering the road quieted the singing bicycle. (personification)

Writing Workshop 37

Quotation for the Day

"Good writing is not the perfectly tailored garment of a Personage, perfectly pressed since he last wore it; it is the rumpled suit of a living person, still relaxing from the strain of his labors, its pockets stuffed with trash and with things worth getting at."

(Martin Joos, 1907–1979, American philologist)

Even though the first draft of a writing assignment needs a structure, students should know that it cannot be ready to publish at this stage. Discuss the importance of details as related to this quotation. Compare the "trash" with generalizations that clutter writing and the "things worth getting at" with the details that bring writing to life.

YOUR TURN 5

Check to see that students are following the framework. If students are having a difficult time, refer them to the margin notes next to **A Writer's Model** on pp. 39–40.

Timesaver

To quickly assess that students' drafts follow the framework, ask students to use two different colored pens, one for writing and one to label the introduction, the body, the conclusion, and one or two examples of transitional words, narrative details, and descriptive details.

Writing

Personal Reflection

Framework

Introduction
- Start with an interesting opener.
- Provide background information.
- Hint at the meaning of the experience.

Body
- Relate the events.
- Include details about people, places, thoughts, and feelings.

Conclusion
- Reflect on what the experience means to you.

Directions and Explanations

Capture Your Reader's Interest Include an interesting thought or image to grab your audience's attention.

Provide a Glimpse of You Before the Experience Give enough background information to provide an impression of what you were like prior to the experience.

No Mixed Signals Give your readers a clue about why this experience was important.

Watch the Clock Structure your essay so that your readers can follow it easily. Use **transitional words** or phrases to signal chronological order. If you feel adventurous, provide flashbacks.

Solid as a Rock Provide a solid basis of **narrative details** to help your readers see what happened. Write about people and places, but also describe thoughts and emotions.

A Large Palette and Beautiful Canvas Use **descriptive details** to paint vivid images. Provide a variety of **sensory details**. Where appropriate, include **figurative language** to show things from a new perspective.

Drive It Home Let your readers know how you feel now. Use this portion of your narrative to reflect on how this experience changed you.

YOUR TURN 5 Writing a First Draft

Using the above guidelines, write the first draft of your personal reflection on an experience. For an example of an essay that follows the same guidelines, see the Writer's Model on the next page.

38   **Chapter 1**   Narration/Description: Reflecting on Experiences

RESOURCES

Writing
Writing Prompts
- *Communications*, TP. 13, WS. p. 17

Your Turn 5
Practice
- *Communications*, TP. 14, WS. p. 18

A Writer's Model

The following short essay, which is a final draft, closely follows the framework on the previous page.

Kicking Shyness

My whole way of looking at the world began to change around the time I turned thirteen. That May, my parents began taking the family to a local YMCA. We could swim, play softball, and visit with other families. Without admitting it to myself, I always seemed to live in the shadows of my older brother and sister. However, beginning with those hot summer days at the center, I started to lose track of what my brother and sister did—because for the first time in my life I was too busy doing my own thing.

After about a month, I found a tae kwan do class and was mesmerized as I watched men and women, boys and girls practice moves and spar with each other. The room was filled with swishing white uniforms and the roar of *ki-hop* yells. I imagined I was one of these people, timing my strokes perfectly, blocking so gracefully, sneaking in the winning point. In reality I spent weeks blending into the wall farthest from the others, shadowboxing at home behind locked doors, too afraid to join the others.

Then, after weeks of my watching, one day it happened. The *sabom-nim* (instructor), a college student named Gwen who moved as if gravity did not apply to her, called to me just as I was just about to sneak out the door. "Hey, wallflower! Why don't you come help me practice some of my blocks?" she asked. I told her that I was not part of the class, but she insisted. "I promise I'll only block your moves. No countermoves until you're ready—and I can teach you some other techniques, too." If Gwen had not been so friendly, I might have tried to escape. Instead, I found myself on the mats, outfitted in all the protective gear. My knees were like mashed potatoes, my heartbeat thundering in my head. There was no place to go but forward—head tucked safely behind my pads so that I could barely see. After a few minutes, though, I started to relax and enjoy myself. "See?" Gwen said afterward. "Once you've loosened up, you're a natural." That was the

(continued)

INTRODUCTION
Interesting opening

Background information

Hint at meaning

BODY
Event 1
Sensory details

Thoughts

Narrative detail

Event 2

Dialogue

Sensory detail
Figurative details

Actions show thoughts/feelings

Connecting Reading and Writing

As students begin to write their first drafts, they may find it helpful to model their essays on **"Kicking Shyness."** Write the essay's framework on the chalkboard, and point out that such a framework allows students to add as many events and details as are necessary to narrate their experiences.

INTRODUCTION
- Interesting opening
- Background info
- Hint at meaning

Event 1
- Sensory details
- Thoughts
- Narrative detail

Event 2
- Dialogue
- Sensory detail
- Figurative details
- Actions → thoughts/feelings

Event 3
- Narrative detail
- Figurative detail
- Dialogue
- Narrative detail

Event 4
- Narrative detail
- Feelings
- Narrative detail
- Thoughts/feelings

— BODY

CONCLUSION
- Thoughts/feelings
- Significance of experience

Writing, pp. 38–41
Alignments
TEKS 1A, 1B, 1C, 2B, 8A
TAAS W1, W2, W4
English II End-of-Course 4

Writing Workshop

> **TECHNOLOGY TIP**
>
> Suggest that students use computer graphics software to create pictures or use word-processing software to create line drawings, such as maps or diagrams, to accompany their writing. Students may want to paste in clip art to add interest to their word processor documents, or they may use a CD-ROM drive and software to download photographic images to include in their essays.

(continued)

Event 3
Narrative detail

Figurative detail
Dialogue

Narrative detail

Event 4

Narrative detail

Feelings

Narrative detail

Thoughts/feelings

CONCLUSION
Thoughts/feelings
Significance of experience

right thing to say, then, because I needed praise.

That night, I convinced my parents to let me enroll in the class. I memorized all the moves: *ahre maggi* (down block), *guligi cha-gi* (hook kick), *poom sogi* (tiger stance), and so on. Believe me, this "natural" never worked so hard in her life. There is no doubt about it—tae kwon do is a tough, aerobic workout. Sometimes my muscles felt like limp noodles by the end of the day. My friends thought I was crazy. "Here comes Jackie Chan!" they would tease. Eventually, though, I was not just graceful but good enough to earn a yellow, then orange, and eventually a green belt.

My mother still likes to tell the next part of this story. The following March, I had invited her, Dad, and my brother and sister to the center one Saturday for the spring tournaments— not telling them that I was competing. While they were looking for me on the bench, they were surprised to hear my name blared over a loudspeaker. However, their shock was not over. Finally they noticed their younger daughter, poised confidently in the ring, waiting to spar in her first competition match. What a match it was! I didn't win, but I did get my picture in the newspaper (a close-up of my determined face) and had the reward of my parents' amazed and proud faces.

Looking back, I realize now that my parents did not need proof to think I was worth something—*I* did. I needed an accomplishment all my own, and tae kwon do was it. I learned confidence and greater respect for myself, not from winning, but from trying. From then on, I felt like a real person, not just a shadow.

A Student's Model

In the following reflection, Tabitha Henry of Weston High School in Cazenovia, Wisconsin, describes a personal experience that is familiar to many of us. Notice how she begins with background information that hints at what is to come.

My Last Goodbye

My life was perfect when I was twelve years old. I had a family, including my sister, Chrissy, and a little brother, Patrick, whom I loved greatly. Spring was coming, and I was excited about another summer with Grandma. She and I did a lot of things together. We used to talk to each other, go shopping, tell each other our secrets, and garden together. She was retiring this year, so that meant more time with her.

Then, on April 11, 1994, at 10:00 P.M., we were all going to bed when the phone rang. My mom answered; my uncle was calling to say that Grandpa had just taken Grandma to the hospital. . . .

My life fell apart that night. The next morning I was told that Grandma had had a heart attack and that she was gone. My heart stopped at that moment. I tried to be strong, but even my father cried. I just kept asking myself, "Why her?" I was so mad that I had not even gotten to say goodbye. I still thought that I could keep my feelings hidden until someone said of me, "This is the one that will miss her the most." I couldn't control my feelings anymore. I burst into tears. It finally hit me: She was gone forever. All I had left were memories in the garden—the hours we spent planting flowers and taking care of them. Although my aunt and I later tried to work the garden, it just was never the same.

I believe that my grandma is a star watching over me, just like she would be if she were still here. No one could ever fill that part of my heart that died with her. Still, my grandma would have wanted me to be strong and happy like her, even though there are good times and bad. My family and friends love me for who I am and support me for what I do, as I know my grandma would, too.

INTRODUCTION

Background information

Hint at what is to come

BODY

Event 1
Narrative detail

Event 2
Narrative detail

Dialogue

Thoughts/feelings
Figurative detail

CONCLUSION

Figurative detail

Significance of experience

Quotation for the Day

"The joy of life is variety."

(Samuel Johnson, 1709–1784, English lexicographer, critic, and writer)

Lead students in a discussion of the parts of their narratives that could be varied, such as vocabulary, sentence type, and sentence length.

TEACHING TIP

▶ **Elaboration**

Remind students that when they elaborate, they need to add information, not just words. One way to do that in a personal reflection is to build on or flesh out existing details. Urge students to include fine detail in their writing by asking questions. How did the cat flex her paws? What did the clouds look like? Were the ants headed in random directions or were they moving in a straight line? Fine detail in description makes writing vivid and memorable.

Cooperative Learning

Feedback on First Drafts. Have students form random groups of four and read their first drafts aloud to each other. Writers may ask for specific feedback from their peers, such as what part they liked best and why. Writers can also ask their peers to retell what happened to help develop clarity and vivid detail.

Revising

Evaluate and Revise Your Draft

Taking a Second Look Your task as a writer does not end with writing your first draft. You also need to evaluate and revise what you have written. You should work collaboratively with a peer to re-read each other's writing at least twice—first to focus on possible revisions of content and organization, and second to focus on style.

▶ **First Reading: Content and Organization** By yourself or with a peer, use the following guidelines to evaluate and revise your personal reflection.

Personal Reflection: Content and Organization
Guidelines for Peer and Self-Evaluation

Evaluation Questions	Tips	Revision Techniques
❶ Will the introduction grab the reader's attention? Does it provide background information and hint at the meaning of the experience?	**Circle** the sentences in the introduction that capture the reader's attention or provide background. **Bracket** the sentence or sentences that hint at the meaning of the experience. If there are no circles or brackets, revise.	**Replace** the opening sentences with one or two sentences that will grab the reader's attention. **Add** background or a hint of the meaning of the experience.
❷ Does the narrative include details that make the events, people, and places memorable?	**Underline** each sentence that begins a description of a separate event. **Double underline** each phrase or sentence that provides memorable details about each event. If there are no double underlines, revise.	**Add** memorable details or **elaborate** on existing details.
❸ Can the reader find descriptions of the writer's thoughts and feelings?	**Mark with a star** any sentences that describe thoughts and feelings. If you do not see any, revise.	**Add** or elaborate on details about your thoughts and feelings and those of other people in the narrative.
❹ Are the events of the narrative easy to follow? Are any events unnecessary to the experience?	**Number** the events in the narrative, looking for gaps. Put an *X* next to any event that does not seem to fit into the narrative.	**Reorder** the events in a way that will be clearer for the reader. **Cut** any events marked with an X.
❺ Does the conclusion state the significance or meaning of the experience?	**Highlight** any sentences that state why the experience was important to the writer. If there are none, revise.	**Add** one or two sentences to the conclusion that clearly state the significance or meaning of the experience.

42   Chapter 1   Narration/Description: Reflecting on Experiences

RESOURCES

Revising

Practice
- *Communications,* TPs. 15, 16, WS. pp. 19, 20, 21

Extension
- *Designing Your Writing*

ONE WRITER'S REVISIONS Here is how one writer used the content and organization chart to revise a section of the essay "Kicking Shyness," on page 39. After examining the changes, answer the questions following the paragraph.

> My knees were ~~shaking and my heart was pounding~~ *like mashed potatoes, my heartbeat thundering in my head.* There was no place to go but forward—head tucked safely behind my pads so that I could barely see. *After a few minutes, though,* I started to relax and enjoy myself.

replace

add

Analyzing the Revision Process
1. What do the changes in the first sentence add to the narrative?
2. Why did the writer insert *After a few minutes, though?*

YOUR TURN 6 Focusing on Content and Organization
Evaluate and revise the content and organization of your personal reflection using the guidelines on the previous page.

PEER REVIEW
Ask a classmate to read your paper and to answer the following questions:
1. Did the narrative keep your interest? Why or why not?
2. What else would you like to know about the writer's experience?

Second Reading: Style
During your second reading, you should focus on style. One stylistic change that will keep your readers interested in your narrative is to vary your sentence length. Uninterrupted stretches of long or short sentences make writing either drag on too long or sound choppy. **Sentence combining** is a way to improve sentence variety. You can use the style guidelines below to find and fix sentence monotony in your personal reflection.

Style Guidelines

Evaluation Question	Tip	Revision Technique
Is there a series of sentences that are the same length?	**Put a jagged line** beneath sentences of five to seven words. If you find more than two short sentences in a row, revise.	**Combine** sentences using participial phrases to add variety to sentence length.

Analyzing the Revision Process
ANSWERS
Possible answers follow.
1. The changes add figurative details that are memorable.
2. The phrase signals the passage of time and helps clarify the order of events.

YOUR TURN 6
Students should follow the tips in the chart for evaluating their essays and then use at least one of the revision techniques suggested.

Cooperative Learning
Mood. Have students work with a partner to discuss the mood, or predominant feeling, expressed in each other's personal reflection. Students may be able to suggest ways to improve each other's drafts so that readers may more easily re-create the mood felt by the author during his or her reminiscence.

Revising, pp. 42–45
Alignments
TEKS 2B, 2C, 2E, 3C, 5A, 5B
TAAS W1, W2, W3, W4, W5, W7
English II End-of-Course 4, 5, 6

Cooperative Learning 2B
Writing to Suit Occasion. Have students work in groups of three to revise a finished piece of writing to suit a different occasion. Students may choose a piece of writing from textbooks, newspapers, portfolios, or journals. Each student can take a role of focusing on how the style, the content, and the organization may change. For example, a personal reflection essay rewritten as a journal entry would be less formal; the content may not include figurative language or dialogue; and the organization would be less structured. Together, students should revise the piece to reflect the new occasion they list at the top of their papers.

Analyzing the Revision Process
ANSWERS
1. The paragraph flows more smoothly with one sentence instead of four.
2. No; the sentence is longer, but it is clear. The participial phrases modify the subject and are brief.

Focus on Sentences

Reference Note
For more on **participial phrases,** see page 473.

Combining Sentences to Add Sentence Variety

You can add variety to sentences by reducing some sentences to **participial phrases** and then inserting them into other sentences. A participial phrase consists of a **participle,** a verb form (usually ending in –*ing* or –*ed*) that can be used as an adjective, and any complements or modifiers the participle may have. Short sentences with words that are repeated from the previous sentence are often the best to combine. In each of the following sentences, the participial phrase is underlined, the participle is in boldface, and the noun or pronoun it modifies is underlined twice.

<u>**Running** through the trees,</u> <u><u>I</u></u> sped toward the camp.

My <u><u>brother,</u></u> <u>**rested** from an afternoon nap,</u> waited for me there.

> **ONE WRITER'S REVISIONS** The example below shows how the writer of the personal narrative on page 39 used the style guidelines to combine short sentences into a single sentence.
>
> **BEFORE REVISION**
>
> four sentences of similar length in a row
>
> I imagined I was one of these people. I timed my strokes perfectly. I was blocking so gracefully. I snuck in the winning point.
>
> **AFTER REVISION**
>
> three sentences reduced to participial phrases (in blue)
>
> I imagined I was one of these people, timing my strokes perfectly, blocking so gracefully, sneaking in the winning point.

Analyzing the Revision Process

1. How does reducing three sentences to participial phrases help the flow of the paragraph?
2. Do you think the sentence after the revision is too long or complicated? Why or why not?

RESOURCES

Focus on Sentences
Practice
- *Communications,* WS. p. 22

YOUR TURN 7 — Focusing on Style

Use the style guidelines on page 43 to revise any sentences in your essay that can be combined by using participial phrases. Remember to use sentences of *varying* length throughout your narrative—you do not need to eliminate *all* of your short sentences.

Designing Your Writing

Designing Your Web Page Uploading your personal reflection to the World Wide Web is a great way to reach an audience beyond your classroom and to incorporate visual elements into your narrative. However, creating an effective Web page takes more than just scanning or typing in your essay. Below are a few tips for designing your personal reflection Web page. Even if you do not have the technology to make a Web page, knowing about these basic design concerns will help you understand the choices Web designers make when creating the pages you see on the World Wide Web.

- **Limit the number of graphics you use.** Too many graphics make pages seem "busy" and cause them to take longer to download.

- **Keep your line lengths under two thirds of the page width.** Solid text across a screen can be difficult to read and hard on the eyes.

- **Try looking at your Web page on different computers,** especially ones with smaller screens, to see if all of your words fit on the page. Scrolling may be required if text runs off the right or bottom edge of the screen. Your readers will accept scrolling down the page only if the information in the top portion captures their interest.

- **Use strong visual contrasts.** Pages filled with solid blocks of text appear as a dull mass of words, as shown on the left below.

Dull, no visual focus

Strong visual contrasts

Quotation for the Day

"Watch your use of the word *because*. You don't have to link sentences up and make reasons for them. The juxtaposition speaks for itself. It is a matter of grammar. Don't get bogged down in the need to explain."

(Natalie Goldberg, American writer, poet, and teacher)

Use the quotation as a springboard to discuss the benefits of grammar. Obvious connections in students' writing may not intrigue readers, whereas grammatical choices that lead readers to make inferences will engage the readers.

Grammar Link
Subject-Verb Agreement
ANSWERS
1. I; runs
2. C
3. I; interests
4. C
5. C

Publishing

Proofread Your Essay

Putting on the Polish Have you ever read a piece of writing and found a typographical error or noticed that a word was omitted? When you run across errors of this kind, you become distracted—your attention focuses on the errors instead of the meaning of the writing. To avoid distracting your reader, work collaboratively to put the final polish on your writing by proofreading for errors. In your personal reflection, be especially careful to catch subject-verb agreement errors. Poor subject-verb agreement can leave a reader confused about the experience you are sharing.

Reference Note
For more on **subject-verb agreement with intervening phrases**, see page 513.

Grammar Link

Subject-Verb Agreement

Many sentences contain **intervening phrases,** phrases that separate a sentence's subject and verb. If a phrase comes between the subject and verb of a sentence, be sure that the verb agrees with the true subject and not with any nouns or pronouns within the phrase. A singular subject should have a singular verb, and a plural subject should have a plural verb.

Example:
Today my **brother,** together with his prize-winning dogs, **appears** in a special-interest story on the local news.

[The phrase *together with his prize-winning dogs* is an intervening phrase between the subject *brother* and the verb *appears.* The subject *brother* is singular, so the verb *appears* must be singular.]

Example:
The dogs with the black ears are sisters.

[The phrase *with the black ears* is an intervening phrase between the subject *dogs* and the verb *are.* The subject *dogs* is plural, so the verb *are* must be plural.]

PRACTICE

Identify the subject of each of the following sentences. Then, determine whether the verb (in italics) agrees in number with the subject. On your own paper, write *I* and the correct verb if the verb is incorrect. Write *C* if the verb is correct.

1. My mother, along with Mrs. Shapiro and Mr. Talbot, *run* a health fair at school every year.
2. The movies at the theater *were* all new that weekend.
3. Ms. Wyatt's class on movie icons *interest* many students.
4. The old mall, which was the first in town, *has* a renovated food court.
5. My grandfather on my mother's side of the family *tells* wonderful stories about his childhood in Mexico.

46 Chapter 1 Narration/Description: Reflecting on Experiences

RESOURCES

Grammar Link
Practice
- *Communications,* WS. p. 23

46 Narration/Description: Reflecting on Experiences

Publish Your Essay

Making the World a Little Smaller By sharing your personal reflection with others, you can connect your experiences with those of your readers. Here are some suggested ways to have others read and respond to your narrative:

- If your reflection is about a time spent in a special place, such as a national park, check to see if that place has a Web site that welcomes visitor feedback. If so, submit your essay for posting.
- Ask your teacher to arrange a "cultural exchange" of personal reflections with a class in another part of the country or world. You can see the ways in which you are all similar or different.
- Put old photos of the experience in your reflection together with your personal reflection to create a family memento.
- Many magazines publish personal reflections that are entertaining or that will provide readers with examples of positive growth experiences. Ask your teacher or parents to help you submit your reflection to a topic-appropriate magazine.

Reflect on Your Essay

Looking Back, Looking Forward Answering the following questions will help you think about what you have learned while writing your reflection and what you might do differently the next time you write one. If you include this essay in your portfolio, make sure to attach these responses to it.

- Which prewriting step did you find most difficult? Do you think it will be easier for you the next time you write a narrative? Why or why not?
- While writing your reflection, what new insights did you have into the experience you chose as a topic?

PORTFOLIO

YOUR TURN 8 Proofreading, Publishing, and Reflecting

Before you share your personal reflection with an audience, be sure to
- correct any spelling, punctuation, or grammatical errors
- find ways to follow through on any publishing ideas you have
- answer the reflection questions above

TEACHING TIP

Publish Your Essay
Before publishing their personal narratives, students should invent interesting titles. The title, like the essay's introduction, should grab readers' attention.

Wrap It Up

Metacognition. Ask each student to reflect on his or her writing process through a brief written response to the following question.

1. How can writing about yourself help you become a more effective writer?

Then, ask students the following questions.

2. What do details in a personal reflection describe? [events, people, places, thoughts, emotions, and dialogue]

3. What are two ways of organizing a personal narrative? [chronological order, flashback]

YOUR TURN 8

You may wish to have students proofread each other's papers. As students answer the reflection questions, ask them to think about which elements of personal narrative might be useful in other kinds of essays.

Publishing, pp. 46–47
Alignments
TEKS 2C, 2D, 3A, 3B, 3D, 5A
TAAS W3, W6, W7
English II End-of-Course 5, 6

TEACHING TIP

Writing a Free-Verse Poem
If students have difficulty writing poems, suggest that each student first write a brief descriptive paragraph on his or her topic. Then tell students to eliminate anything that does not contribute to the images they wish to create. Next, have students work with line breaks and add additional sensory details, figurative language, and sound elements as needed to shape their poems.

TECHNOLOGY TIP

To aid composition, students might write their free-verse poems using a word-processing program. Students can then revise using the cut, copy, and paste options. Encourage students to use the save as function to make copies of their original files when they do revisions so that they can return to the original wording if they find it more effective than the revisions.

Connections to Literature

Writing a Free-Verse Poem

Sometimes thoughts and feelings drawn to the surface when you reflect on an experience are more interesting to explore through verse rather than through prose.

One kind of poetry that is well suited to writing about feelings and images is **free verse**. Free-verse poems usually do not follow a regular pattern of rhythm or rhyme. Instead, words and lines are arranged according to natural speech patterns. In other words, line length is determined by natural **"breath rhythm"**—the line breaks coincide with natural pauses for breathing.

Learn from an Example The following free-verse poem describes a lonely harbor scene. Notice that the final word in each line is important to the meaning of the poem.

Lost
by Carl Sandburg

last word emphasized	Desolate and lone All night long on the lake
personification	Where fog trails and mist creeps,
imagery (sound)	The whistle of a boat Calls and cries unendingly,
	Like some lost child In tears and trouble
personification	Hunting the harbor's breast And the harbor's eyes.

Choosing a Topic You can write a free-verse poem on almost any topic. Here are some example topics that might work well:

- an item, activity, or person from your personal reflection
- a plant or animal that has interesting similarities to human beings
- sights, sounds, or smells that remind you of a friend or relative

Basic Elements Remember that free verse does not have a set rhythm or rhyme scheme. However, form is determined by the content of the poem.

- **Words that need special emphasis should be placed at the beginning or the ends of lines.** Key words should be placed on a line by themselves. Look at the last word on each line of "Lost."

- **A stream of words related in meaning should flow together in one line.** For example, "Where fog trails and mist creeps" is a description of the lake.

- **Line length is controlled to create a visual arrangement.** For example, the short lines of "Lost" might visually emphasize the loneliness of the scene, or the variation of line length could suggest waves.

Of course, free-verse poems should also contain some of the numbered items in the chart at the top of the next page.

48   Chapter 1   Narration/Description: Reflecting on Experiences

1. **sensory details** of sight, hearing, touch, taste, and smell to create vivid images

2. **figurative language,** like the following examples, to give readers new perspectives on familiar things
   - **simile:** a comparison of two basically unalike things, using the words *like* or *as*
     Like some lost child
   - **metaphor:** a direct comparison of two things without using the words *like* or *as;* says that something *is* something else
     The moonlight rays are the eyelashes of night
   - **personification:** giving human characteristics to nonhuman things
     (T)he harbor's eyes

   (For more on **figurative language,** see page 37.)

3. **sound elements** to help create mood and evoke images; these include
   - **assonance:** the repetition of vowel sounds in words or syllables
     Like some lost child
   - **alliteration:** the repetition of the same consonant sound in words or syllables
     All night long on the lake

TIP When you revise your poem, read it aloud. Do the words and line breaks follow your natural speech patterns? If not, make some adjustments.

YOUR TURN 9 Writing a Free-Verse Poem

Choose a topic that interests you, and write your own free-verse poem about it. Pay attention to line breaks and word choice. Try to include sensory details and figurative language to make your poem more vivid and memorable.

YOUR TURN 9

Have student partners read their poems aloud to each other and suggest line breaks and other improvements. Remind students to title their poems.

A sample poem follows.

Change in Seasons

Piled up by the chill breezes
That swept away summer,
Dry leaves huddle everywhere
As dove-gray clouds
Wait on the horizon
To blanket the earth
In glistening white.

Connections to Literature, pp. 48–49
Alignments
TEKS 1A, 1B, 11D, 11F
TAAS W1
English II End-of-Course 4

Focus on Viewing and Representing

OBJECTIVES
- To plan a visual presentation
- To create a storyboard
- To tape a video reflection

Quotation for the Day

"Revision means learning through the acknowledgment of limitation and failure. Creation in its largest sense, then, must be thought of as a process of creation, destruction, and re-creation."

(Robert Pack, 1929– , American poet and literary critic)

Write the quotation on the chalkboard or on an overhead transparency. Help students draw parallels between revision in writing and film editing. Point out that scenes in films are often reshot, cut, and edited in various ways before the film is considered finished.

TEACHING TIP

Every Picture Tells a Story
Remind students that when they sketch storyboards, they do not need to worry about artistic accuracy. Simple stick figures can show the basics of what they want in their shots.

Focus on Viewing and Representing

WHAT'S AHEAD?

In this section you will
- plan a visual presentation
- create a storyboard
- tape a video reflection

Making a Video Reflection

Just as you may sometimes prefer verse as a way of expressing yourself, you may at other times choose to express yourself using images—photographs, film, or video. One good way to develop your skills as a visual storyteller is to create a **video reflection**—a short series of videotaped scenes that visually tell a narrative. You can use the experience from your personal reflection essay as the basis for a video reflection, or you can base it on some other personal experience.

Putting Words into Motion

Planning a Visual Presentation If you have ever seen the film version of a book you have read, you know that filmmakers must choose which events, characters, dialogue, and scenes to include and which ones to omit. You, too, will have to decide what can go into your video reflection and what you must leave out. Use the steps below to plan.

- Break the narrative into a list of essential events.
- Determine the number of shots needed to illustrate each event.
- Decide how each shot will look. A close-up shot of someone's face? A long shot of the setting?
- Create a storyboard. (See the detailed instructions below.)

Every Picture Tells a Story A vital part of creating a film or video is **storyboarding**—the process of sketching out scenes before filming or taping. A storyboard is a series of sketches that chronologically depicts important narrative events. These sketches will become separate "shots" in the finished film or video. A completed storyboard looks very much like the pages of a comic book, with dialogue and descriptions written below or beside the illustrations.

Here are some terms for describing transitions from shot to shot.

RESOURCES

Focus on Viewing and Representing Practice
- *Media Literacy and Communication Skills*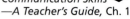
  —*Support and Practice,* Ch. 1
  —*A How-to Handbook*

Teaching Notes
- *Media Literacy and Communication Skills* —*A Teacher's Guide,* Ch. 1

- **Cut**—instantaneous change from one scene to another
- **Dissolve**—scene slowly disappears as the next slowly appears
- **Fade-in**—scene begins as black, and then slowly appears
- **Fade-out**—scene slowly disappears to a black screen
- **Wipe**—scene slowly replaces the previous scene, usually through use of a line moving across the screen

An Example Storyboard The following is a portion of the storyboard for a video presentation of the Writer's Model on page 39. Notice that the marginal notes give information that cannot be portrayed only with images. However, all of the information involves actions that will take place either on-screen or with camera and audio effects.

1 fade-in: long shot. Girl in foreground; tae kwon do class in background, moving in unison sounds: "ki-hop" yells, swishing of movements

2 close-up from front girl's face; she looks longingly at the class; after a moment, closes eyes sounds: same as last fade-out

3 fade-in, effects indicate a daydream; girl, confident, wearing headgear, eyes straight ahead takes three deep breaths sound: breathing

4 still daydream girl spars effortlessly with opponent sound: swish of movement fade-out

5 fade-in, daydream effect gone sound: same as scene 1 girl looks down, sighs fade-out

Critical Thinking

Evaluation. Show students part of a film that could be characterized as a personal reflection. Then have students evaluate the film as a visual presentation in a class discussion that focuses on questions such as these: Were the person's experiences clearly presented? How well did the film move from shot to shot? What techniques were used to make transitions? How effective were the sound and lighting? What techniques used in the film would you like to try in your own video reflection? Why?

Focus on Viewing and Representing, pp. 50–52
Alignments
TEKS 20D, 21B, 21C, 21D

TEACHING TIP

Basic Video Techniques
Backlighting—an effect created when the light behind a subject is brighter than the light in front—is one effect that can be used indoors or outdoors. Students may wish to use this technique as a special effect if they want their subjects to appear in silhouette. In most cases, however, the lighting source should be kept behind the camera so that the subject is well lit.

Camera movement can be used as a video technique. For instance, a student recording a marathon experience may want to tape while running to illustrate the action. However, caution students to use this technique sparingly, as too much movement can annoy and distract viewers.

Wrap It Up

Metacognition. Have students use the following questions to reflect on their experiences.

1. Which kind of personal reflection— essay, poem, or video—do you think best suits your topic? Why?

Then, ask students to answer the following question.

2. What are the four steps in planning a visual presentation? [Create a list of essential events, determine the number of shots needed, decide how each shot will look, and create a storyboard.]

YOUR TURN 10

Have students form small groups to critique each other's storyboards before filming. If you plan to show students' video reflections in class, you may wish to preview the videos first.

Roll the Tape If you do not have the editing technology available to professionals, you will instead need to use **in-camera editing**—taping your reflection in exactly the same sequence you planned in your storyboard.

Make sure that all people involved in your production are familiar with the storyboard and their parts in the video reflection. Rehearse the sequence of actions and any dialogue several times in the days before you begin taping. Still, if mistakes happen, relax. If you are using in-camera editing, view each scene as soon as you finish taping it. You can always rewind the video and tape over a weak scene. If you have editing equipment, you can tape the scene several times and insert the best version into the final tape.

Basic Video Techniques Here are a few tips to remember when preparing your video reflection.

- **Give your reflection sound.** Dialogue and background sound effects help you relate thoughts, feelings, and elements that you cannot portray visually. Consider using a **voice-over,** offscreen narration to describe on-screen events or the thoughts of the narrator in a first-person reflection. Voice-overs can be directly input to the video as you tape using a microphone, or added later with editing equipment.

  Keep in mind that unwanted noise may intrude on your audio. To avoid these distractions, add voice-over narration in a quiet room after the video has been shot. You add voice-overs by either using video editing equipment or simply taping the narration on an audiocassette to accompany your video. Just be careful to ensure that your audio and video stay in sync.

- **Make lighting work for—not against—you.** Taping in natural sunlight works best for most home video recorders—but do not be afraid to test your camera's indoor capabilities.

- **Use a tripod, or set your camera on a stable surface when taping.** No matter how steady you think your hand is, it will invariably move as you tape. Even the slightest movement can make the final videotape seem unsteady and sloppy.

YOUR TURN 10 Creating a Video Reflection

Create a storyboard for a five- to seven-minute video reflection (you may want to use a portion of the personal reflection you wrote in the Writing Workshop). Then, videotape your reflection using your storyboard as a guide. If you do not have access to a video camera, you may be able to present the narrative through a series of still photographs or drawings.

RESOURCES

Your Turn 10
Practice and Reinforcement

- *Media Literary and Communication Skills*
  —*Support and Practice,* Ch. 1, transparencies and worksheets
  —Videocassette 1, Segment A

CHAPTER 1 Choices

Choose one of the following activities to complete.

▶ CROSSING THE CURRICULUM: SOCIAL STUDIES

1. Snatched from the Headlines Choose a current event featured in a newspaper, magazine, TV, or Internet news source. Consider local, state, or national government decisions that have had a direct effect on you or your family. Produce a two-minute **audio commentary** on that news item, explaining how the event influenced you.

▶ LITERATURE

2. Join the Book Club Choose a book that has had special meaning to you, and submit a one-hundred-word **online review** to a book club or to a bookstore's customer comments section. Reading this book may have been a defining moment in your life, making you the person that you are today. Think of characters that you respect and have tried to emulate or ones that you despise and have tried hard not to be like. Consider books that have inspired you to reach for certain goals: playing a guitar, flying an airplane, or becoming a veterinarian. Include passages from the book as details to show your reader why it was so important.

▶ CAREERS

3. You're Hired! Often, when interviewing, potential employers will ask you to tell about a time when you failed. Their interest is not in seeing what you did wrong, but rather how you handled it. Prepare a **two-minute oral response** to an interviewer's question about your failure and your reaction. Your response should show that you have used the failure as a chance for personal reflection to help you learn from your mistakes.

▶ VIEWING AND REPRESENTING

4. The Land That Time Forgot Imagine that one million years from now, archaeologists will unearth your house. Create **a message** for these archaeologists. Keep in mind that they will probably not understand our language, so you will have to communicate to them through **illustrations** only. Your pictures should show who you were, how you lived, and what was important to you.

PORTFOLIO

▶ CROSSING THE CURRICULUM: SOCIAL STUDIES

You may wish to play an audio commentary for students before they execute their own. Tell students to summarize the decision briefly before explaining its influence on them.

▶ LITERATURE

Remind students to use a variety of details to explain the importance of the books. Interested students might work with the school or local librarian and a teacher with advanced computer skills to create a database of book recommendations for young people. Use students' reviews to launch the database.

▶ CAREERS

To help students get started, brainstorm with the class a list of common failures, such as not making a team, forgetting to do something, or not acting responsibly. When students have composed their oral responses, pair them with classmates and have the members of each pair take turns being interviewer and interviewee. Students can refer to the Speaking and Listening section of the Quick Reference Handbook on pp. 896–910 for help.

▶ VIEWING AND REPRESENTING

Have students work in small groups to devise a message and execute it in pictures. Then, have groups decipher each other's messages.

Choices   53

RESOURCES

Reflecting on Experiences

Assessment
- *Assessment Package*
  —*Chapter Tests,* Ch. 1
  —*Chapter Tests in Standardized Test Formats,* Ch. 1
  —*Assessment Alternatives,* Ch. 1
- *Test Generator* (One-Stop Planner CD-ROM)

Choices

Rubrics
- *Assessment Package*
  —*Assessment Alternatives,* Ch. 1

Choices
Alignments
Choice 1   TEKS 8B, 16A, 16B, 16C
Choice 2   TEKS 1A, 2E, 8A, 10A, 10B; TAAS W1
Choice 3   TEKS 16A, 16B, 16C
Choice 4   TEKS 21B, 21C, 21D

Choices   53

CHAPTER 2

Exploring Comparisons and Contrasts

Use this guide to create an instructional plan that suits the individual needs of your students. Assignments marked by an asterisk (*) may be completed out of class. Times given for pacing lessons are estimated. See pp. 54–55 for chapter-wide resources. Resources listed in this guide are point-of-use resources only.

Curriculum Connections

Choices p. 89
- Literature
- Speaking and Listening
- Crossing the Curriculum: Science

GO TO: go.hrw.com
KEYWORD: EOLang 10-2

All resources for this chapter are available for preview on the *One-Stop Planner CD-ROM with Test Generator*. All worksheets and tests may be printed from the CD-ROM.

Texas Resources For a complete listing of all resources prepared for Texas teachers and students, please see the blue box at the beginning of each chapter.

CHAPTER PLANNING GUIDE

	Chapter Opener pp. 54–55	**Reading Workshop: Reading a Comparison-Contrast Article** pp. 56–65
DEVELOPMENTAL PROGRAM	⏱ **30 minutes** • Similarities and Differences p. 55 • Your Turn 1 in groups p. 55	⏱ **100 minutes** • Preparing to Read p. 56 • Reading Selection pp. 57–59 • First Thoughts on Your Reading 1–2 p. 60 • Main Idea and Supporting Details pp. 60–62 • Your Turn 2 p. 62 • Comparison-Contrast Structure pp. 62–63 • Your Turn 3 p. 63 • Test Taking Mini-Lesson p. 65
CORE PROGRAM	⏱ **20 minutes** • Similarities and Differences p. 55 • Your Turn 1 p. 55	⏱ **90 minutes** • Preparing to Read p. 56 • Reading Selection pp. 57–59 • First Thoughts on Your Reading 1–3 p. 60 • Main Idea and Supporting Details pp. 60–62 • Your Turn 2 p. 62 • Comparison-Contrast Structure pp. 62–63 • Your Turn 3 p. 63 • Vocabulary Mini-Lesson p. 64 • Test Taking Mini-Lesson p. 65
ADVANCED PROGRAM	⏱ **10 minutes** • Similarities and Differences p. 55 • Your Turn 1 p. 55	⏱ **70 minutes** • Preparing to Read p. 56 • Reading Selection pp. 57–59 • First Thoughts on Your Reading 3 p. 60 • Main Idea and Supporting Details pp. 60–62 • Your Turn 2 p. 62 • Comparison-Contrast Structure pp. 62–63 • Your Turn 3 p. 63 • Vocabulary Mini-Lesson p. 64
RESOURCES — PRINT	• *Communications*, TP. 17, WS. p. 24	• *Alternative Readings*, Ch. 2 • *Communications*, TPs. 18, 19, WS. pp. 25–32
RESOURCES — MEDIA	• *One-Stop Planner CD-ROM*	• *One-Stop Planner CD-ROM*

TP.=Transparency   WS.=Worksheet

Writing Workshop: Writing a Comparison-Contrast Essay pp. 66–85	**Focus on Viewing and Representing: Comparing and Contrasting Media Coverage** pp. 86–88
180 minutes • Choose Two Subjects *pp. 66–67* • Consider Purpose, Audience, and Tone *pp. 67–68* • Gather Information and Determine Features *pp. 68–70* • Write a Thesis Statement *p. 70* • Arrange Your Supporting Details *pp. 72–73* • Your Turn 4 *p. 73* • Framework and Your Turn 5* *p. 74* • Writer's Model and Student's Model *pp. 75–77* • Evaluate and Revise and Your Turn 6* *pp. 78–80* • Focus on Word Choice and Your Turn 7 *pp. 80–81* • Proofread, Publish, and Reflect *pp. 82–83* • Grammar Link and Your Turn 8 *pp. 82–83*	**30 minutes** • Looking at the News *pp. 86–88* • Your Turn 10* *p. 88*
150 minutes • Choose Two Subjects *pp. 66–67* • Consider Purpose, Audience, and Tone *pp. 67–68* • Gather Information and Determine Features *pp. 68–70* • Write a Thesis Statement *p. 70* • Critical Thinking Mini-Lesson *p. 71* • Arrange Your Supporting Details *pp. 72–73* • Your Turn 4 *p. 73* • Framework and Your Turn 5* *p. 74* • Writer's Model and Student's Model *pp. 75–77* • Evaluate and Revise and Your Turn 6* *pp. 78–80* • Focus on Word Choice and Your Turn 7 *pp. 80–81* • Proofread, Publish, and Reflect *pp. 82–83* • Grammar Link and Your Turn 8 *pp. 82–83* • Connections to Life and Your Turn 9* *pp. 84–85*	**20 minutes** • Looking at the News *pp. 86–88* • Your Turn 10* *p. 88*
120 minutes • Choose Two Subjects *pp. 66–67* • Consider Purpose, Audience, and Tone *pp. 67–68* • Gather Information and Determine Features *pp. 68–70* • Write a Thesis Statement *p. 70* • Critical Thinking Mini-Lesson *p. 71* • Your Turn 4 *p. 73* • Framework and Your Turn 5* *p. 74* • Writer's Model and Student's Model *pp. 75–77* • Evaluate and Revise and Your Turn 6* *pp. 78–80* • Proofread, Publish, and Reflect *pp. 82–83* • Your Turn 8 *p. 83* • Connections to Life and Your Turn 9* *pp. 84–85*	**10 minutes** • Looking at the News *pp. 86–88* • Your Turn 10* *p. 88*
• *Communications*, TPs. 20–23, WS. pp. 33–41 • *Designing Your Writing*	• *Media Literacy and Communication Skills Kit* —*Support and Practice*, Ch. 2 —*A How-to Handbook* —*A Teacher's Guide*, Ch. 2
• *One-Stop Planner CD-ROM*	• *Media Literacy and Communication Skills Kit* —Videocassette 1, Segment B • *One-Stop Planner CD-ROM*

CHAPTER 2
Exploring Comparisons and Contrasts

CHAPTER OBJECTIVES

- To read a comparison-contrast article and analyze its structure
- To write a comparison-contrast essay
- To compare and contrast media coverage of events

Chapter Overview

Comparing and contrasting is an effective method of evaluating things or ideas. This chapter explains and demonstrates comparison-contrast techniques and invites students to identify and practice these techniques in reading, writing, and viewing. The Reading Workshop introduces students to the concepts of main idea and supporting details and outlines comparison-contrast structure through a comparison-contrast article. In the Writing Workshop, students have the opportunity to explore these concepts and methods further as they follow the steps in the writing process to compose their own comparison-contrast essays. The third section, Focus on Viewing and Representing, teaches students how to analyze news stories and compare and contrast media coverage of events. You may choose to teach just one or two of the workshops. When all sections are taught together, however, they provide a broader view of comparison and contrast, helping students understand and implement their use in different contexts.

Why Study Comparing and Contrasting?

Recognizing comparison-contrast structures in reading and viewing and applying these structures in writing will help students in many areas of their lives. Students face many choices now and in the future, and comparison-contrast skills will enable them to make wise decisions. Students will discover that thorough and thoughtful evaluation of options, in which significant features are identified, researched, and analyzed, helps making decisions in their personal, civic, and professional lives easier.

Teaching the Chapter

Option 1: Begin with Literature

If you prefer to make literature your starting point, you could introduce this chapter after comparing and contrasting two pieces of literature or after examining the use of comparison and contrast in literature to establish setting, portray characters, or evoke theme. Then, you could assign the magazine article in this chapter to show students how comparison and contrast techniques work in nonfiction. Once students understand how comparison and contrast are used in fiction and nonfiction, they will be ready to write their own comparison-contrast essays.

Option 2: Begin with Nonfiction and Writing

Use this chapter to teach students about comparison-contrast structure as well as the uses of comparing and contrasting. After you introduce the Reading Workshop, have students plan and write comparison-contrast essays of their own in the Writing Workshop (pp. 66–85). When students return to literature, they should have a firm grounding in the general writing framework of main idea and supporting details and a clear understanding of comparison-contrast organization. This understanding will help them to recognize and write about comparisons and contrasts in literature as well as to compare literary pieces.

Making Connections

■ To the Literature Curriculum

Comparison is a common technique in literature and in writing about literature. William Shakespeare's sonnet "Shall I Compare Thee to a Summer's Day" compares a woman to a summer's day. "Moons," by John Haines, and "The Moon Was but a Chin of Gold," by Emily Dickinson, both compare the moon to familiar objects. In literature, comparing and contrasting often helps the reader understand the writer's vision.

Lesson Idea: Comparison and Contrast in "Shall I Compare Thee to a Summer's Day" by William Shakespeare

1. Have students list the qualities of a summer's day that Shakespeare believes are not fine enough to represent the woman in the poem.
2. Ask students why Shakespeare chooses to compare the woman to a summer's day when summer does not adequately represent her.
3. From the comparison, have students infer the qualities that Shakespeare admires in the woman. Discuss what these implied rather than stated qualities reveal about the woman.
4. After students have discussed the comparisons in the sonnet, introduce the article "Two Peoples Divided by Common Road Signs" (pp. 57–59). Explain that this article is also structured around similarities and differences. Then, use the material about main idea and supporting details on pp. 60–62 and comparison-contrast structure on pp. 62–63 to help students to organize information about two subjects in a comparison-contrast essay.

■ To Careers

To help students understand the use of comparison and contrast in the world of work, explain that one way companies evaluate their products is to compare them to the competition. A competitive analysis describes common characteristics and important differences between similar products. It may include ideas for product improvement.

Have students work in pairs to write a competitive analysis of two products. Show students examples of product comparisons in consumer magazines. Then, have students brainstorm products to compare. Students may gather information about the products by comparison shopping, reading advertisements, talking to people who use or are familiar with the products, and doing research in consumer periodicals. Students will need to analyze the data they collect, draw conclusions, and write an analysis of their findings. Instruct students to review the material on pp. 72–73 on organizing and presenting data. Students' analyses should include a thesis statement, a presentation of their points of comparison, and a logical conclusion.

■ To the Community

To enhance understanding of the magazine article in the Reading Workshop, you may wish to invite someone from the community who is familiar with the British road system to speak to your class. Ask the speaker to explain how the British system differs from the American system and to describe problems he or she may have experienced driving on American roads. You may wish to provide the speaker with a copy of the article in advance of the visit so that he or she may elaborate on significant differences mentioned in the article, such as *roundabouts*.

■ To the Social Studies Curriculum

Have students work in small groups to research criteria American voters use to choose between candidates in an election. Students should identify criteria such as political affiliation, political or other experience, stand on major issues, appearance, ethnicity, gender, and socioeconomic status. Ask each group to present their findings to the class. Then, have students compare and contrast the groups' findings in a class discussion.

CHAPTER 2

PREVIEWING THE CHAPTER

- The three workshops in this chapter explore comparing and contrasting. Although each workshop can be taught separately, teaching the three as a unit provides students with a thorough understanding of the uses of comparison and contrast. Reading a comparison-contrast article prepares students to write effective comparison-contrast essays of their own. Students will then compare and contrast media coverage of events. To integrate this chapter with grammar, usage, and mechanics chapters, see pp. T401A–T401B.

INTRODUCING THE CHAPTER

- To introduce the chapter, use the Journal Warm-up, Transparency 17, in *Communications*.

VIEWING THE PHOTOGRAPH (19A)

- William Wegman's photograph *Tame Animals* shows two dogs in similar poses. Ask students to compare and contrast the dogs in the photograph. [Comparison: dogs with similar expressions and poses, both on pedestals. Contrast: dogs of different breeds, shape, fur color, eye color, ears, and pedestals. One has a collar.] Discuss with students how the background color contributes to the contrast in the photograph. [The dog on the right and its pedestal seem to be absorbed by the gold background, which makes the dog on the left stand out.]

CHAPTER 2

Exploring Comparisons and Contrasts

CHAPTER RESOURCES

Planning
- *Lesson Planner*, Ch. 2
- *Block Scheduling*, p. T53A (this book)
- *One-Stop Planner CD-ROM*

Practice
- *Communications*, Ch. 2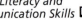

- *Media Literacy and Communication Skills*

Extension
- *Designing Your Writing*

Reinforcement
- *Communications*, Ch. 2

PREVIEW

Reading Workshop
Reading a Comparison-Contrast Article
PAGE 56

Writing Workshop
Writing a Comparison-Contrast Essay
PAGE 66

Focus on Viewing and Representing
Comparing and Contrasting Media Coverage
PAGE 86

Similarities and Differences

- Two creeks run through your community. You discover that one is polluted, while the other is clean. What differences in the environments that surround the creeks make one polluted and one not?
- You meet a new friend who shares your interest in snowboarding, and you swap stories. What similar snowboarding experiences have you had?

In these situations, you **compare** and **contrast** things or ideas to get more information or to explain something to someone. When you compare two things, you look at their similarities. For instance, as you compare your snowboarding experiences with those of a friend, you may find out about similar experiences you have had. When you contrast two things, you look at their differences. As you contrast the environment around a clean creek with that around a polluted creek, you may discover differences in the two environments that explain why one is polluted and the other is not.

internet connect

GO TO: go.hrw.com
KEYWORD: EOLang 10-2

YOUR TURN 1 — Comparing and Contrasting

How important is comparison and contrast in the real world? Consider the times when you have had to evaluate two things based on their similarities or differences. For instance, think about when you made decisions or judgments about two hobbies, experiences, products, or TV shows. Work with a partner to create a list of these instances, and be ready to share your list with the class.

- *Alternative Readings*, Ch. 2
- *Daily Language Activity Transparencies*
- *Vocabulary Workshop* and *Tests*

Evaluation and Assessment
- *Test Generator* (One-Stop Planner CD-ROM)

- *Assessment Package*
  —*Chapter Tests*, Ch. 2
  —*Chapter Tests in Standardized Test Formats*, Ch. 2
  —*Assessment Alternatives*, Ch. 2

Internet
- go.hrw.com (keyword: EOLang 10-2)

Reading Workshop

OBJECTIVES

- To read a comparison-contrast magazine article in preparation for writing a comparison-contrast essay
- To identify main idea and supporting details
- To analyze comparison-contrast structure
- To use comparison-contrast context clues to determine word meanings

Quotation for the Day

"So before writing, learn to think."

(Nicolas Boileau-Despréaux, 1636–1711, French critic and poet)

Ask students to list five films or TV shows they have enjoyed watching. Then, in random groups of four, have students look for similarities and differences among the films or shows. To encourage students to think about comparing and contrasting, ask each group to write a brief statement about how the quotation relates to learning.

TEACHING TIP

Preparing to Read
Preparing to Read on this page introduces the concepts of main idea and supporting details as well as comparison-contrast structure. These concepts form the instructional focus of the Reading Workshop and are treated more fully on pp. 60–63. They are also illustrated in the Reading Selection, **"Two Peoples Divided by Common Road Signs."**

Reading Workshop

Reading a Comparison-Contrast Article

WHAT'S AHEAD?

In this section, you will read a magazine article and learn how to

- identify the main idea and supporting details
- analyze comparison-contrast structure

Imagine hopping in a car and heading out to school on the wrong side of the road. How long would it be before you created a traffic jam, or worse? When Americans drive on British roads or when British people drive on American roads, they have to switch sides of the road and obey different driving rules. The article on the next page, "Two Peoples Divided by Common Road Signs," compares and contrasts American and British road systems and the frustration they bring to tourists.

Preparing to Read

READING SKILL

Main Idea and Supporting Details To understand an article or other type of writing, you must first figure out its **main idea**—the message, opinion, or insight on which the writing is focused. Once you determine the main idea, you can look for **supporting details,** the information that develops and explains the main idea.

READING FOCUS

Comparison-Contrast Structure Writers usually organize their discussion of comparison and contrast in one of two ways: the **block method** or the **point-by-point method.** Writers use the block method when they want to discuss all of the points about each subject separately. They use the point-by-point method to deal with both subjects at the same time, making a point about one subject, then following it with a comparable point about the other.

As you read "Two Peoples Divided by Common Road Signs," look for clues that will help you determine how the writer, Norman Berdichevsky, organized his discussion.

PREREADING 7G, 7H
Make Predictions. As a preview of the selection, invite students to read the selection's title and the headnote that precedes it. Also direct students to scan the subheads and active-reading questions. Then, have students write brief paragraphs predicting the content of the article, based on their preview. Explain that making predictions sparks interest and provides a purpose for reading. Students should save their paragraphs to check their predictions.

Reading Selection

In the following satirical article, the writer makes frequent use of exaggeration and humor to point out some confusing differences between British and American (U.S.) road systems. As you read, write down answers to the active-reading questions.

from Contemporary Review

TWO PEOPLES DIVIDED BY COMMON ROAD SIGNS

By Norman Berdichevsky

As an American in Britain, it is my firm belief that the confusion stemming from the two different road systems and their portrayal on maps is the single most irritating factor causing frustration, anger and a shrug of the shoulders accompanied by mutterings of . . . those crazy Brits (Americans)."

1. According to the writer, what causes anger and frustration among Americans driving in Britain and British tourists driving in America?

Squares versus Circles

It is not, as many might believe, the Left v. Right hand side of the road conundrum which is the source of the most awful aggravation, and cursing (swearing), but rather the totally opposing circulatory systems. Americans are "squares"—a condition which stems from the geometric lay-out based on the cardinal directions of the compass and lines of latitude and longitude on which North America was shaped (French Canada, Louisiana and the Spanish-Mexican land grant systems being the exceptions). The American systems of grids and rectangles stand in sharp contrast to the devious British who move in gyratory arcs, curves and circles frequently interrupted by dead ends leading nowhere. Put in simpler terms, this simply means that almost anywhere in North America, a motorist can, even without a map, make three consecutive right (or even left) turns and come back to where he started. In Britain, there is practically no chance of returning to one's starting point.

Roundabouts versus Grids

During many years of driving in the United States, I have encountered one roundabout (it was in Cape Cod, Massachusetts, and stands out in my

2. What aspects of driving in Britain and in America does this paragraph contrast?

Reading Workshop 57

Active-Reading Questions

The purpose of the active-reading questions is to help students look closely at the structure and content of the article, focusing on the main idea and supporting details as well as on how the essay is subdivided.

ANSWERS

1. the confusion stemming from the two different road systems and their portrayal on maps

2. circulatory systems (Americans use grids and rectangles, while the British use arcs, curves, and circles.)

Reading Workshop, pp. 56–63

Alignments
TEKS 7D, 7E, 7F, 8A, 9A
TAAS R2, R3, R4

Texas Resources
- *Lesson Planner,* Ch. 2
- *TAAS Tool Kit*
- *Preparation for TAAS*
- *Preparing for English II End-of-Course Examination*
- *One-Stop Planner CD-ROM*

Reading Workshop
Reinforcement
■ *Alternative Readings,* Ch. 2

Reading Workshop 57

Active-Reading Questions
ANSWERS continued

3. a circle with four spin-offs or straight roads coming off it

4. Road names often change along commercial stretches, and odd and even numbers are not always on opposite sides of the street or in close numerical order.

5. that they are posted for both major thoroughfares and minor abutting streets and that they are not shared or repeated in the same area

---

memory as a freak occurrence). Along a stretch of a few miles of road in the UK [United Kingdom], I have often encountered a dozen or more roundabouts. This means that the chances of taking a wrong road in the UK as compared to the US are on the order of 12:1 (i.e., an American intersection of two roads meeting at right angles compared to a half a dozen roundabouts each of which contain four spin-offs). In America, [it would be difficult] to make an unwanted U-turn and go back on the same road but in the opposite direction, whereas this has frequently happened to me in the UK after driving round a roundabout and exiting by the same road I entered it (in spite of a Ph.D. in geography).

Traveling within a city also presents a nightmare of what Americans consider gross violations of the most elementary "rules of thumb" for finding an address. The American grid systems with few exceptions apply in cities everywhere and not just Manhattan so that a newcomer can easily orient himself in terms of numbered streets and lettered avenues. Washington D.C. is an "exotic" variation on this theme due to its diagonally trending avenues and pentagonal street pattern rather than the standard square. In Britain however, roads have names which often change along commercial stretches (frequently called "Parades") and then return to their original name. This often results in Americans being convinced that they have already made a wrong turn somewhere along the line. Odd and even numbers which are always on the opposite sides of the street and close in numerical order in the US may be neither in British cities.

Street Names
Road signs with street names are often absent from major thoroughfares in British cities although every minor abutting street is prominently named. To add to the confusion, it is common practice for many streets to bear the same patronymic but be distinguished by a confusion of appendages, i.e. Wallace Road, Wallace Street, Wallace Avenue, Wallace Crescent, Wallace Close, Wallace Parade, Wallace Gardens, etc. Even more absurd is the existence of a dozen or more streets in the same city with exactly the same name! The most recent edition of the famous London *A to Z* (pronounced A to Zed) Street Atlas contains sixteen Essex Roads, thirteen Durham Roads, etc. in widely different parts of the city. One of the most helpful items for an American motorist to obtain is a map of London's postal zones (not obtainable in Post Offices). These practices have convinced me and other Americans that the British must have devised all this to intentionally thwart a German invasion

3. A roundabout is compared with an intersection of two roads. What is a roundabout?

4. What facts does the writer provide to show that British street addresses break American "rules of thumb"?

5. What does the writer imply about American road names?

58   Chapter 2   **Exposition:** Exploring Comparisons and Contrasts

---

READING PROCESS

READING (7C, 7H)
Ask Questions. Suggest that, in addition to answering the active-reading questions, students formulate questions of their own as they read to increase their understanding of the selection. Copy the following chart on the chalkboard to explain the four types of questions students can ask about a reading selection. Then, have students write four questions about the selection, one for each of the four types of questions. Use students' questions to prompt class discussion.

58   Exposition: Exploring Comparisons and Contrasts

in 1940 and then forgot to restore helpful information.

Compass Points versus "Clockwise"
As far back as the novels of Sir Arthur Conan Doyle, an American character, the Mormon refugee in *A Study in Scarlet*, comments on his work in London as a cab driver (a horse-drawn cab that is): "The hardest job was to learn my way about, for I reckon that of all the mazes that ever were contrived, this city [London] is the most confusing." Nothing offends the American sensibility as much as coming to a divided highway without being clearly informed far in advance which lane turns East or West, North or South. Instead, the signs tell you the destinations of the next major towns—often three, four, or more bunched together on the sign. This creates problems of visibility and recognition as well as taxing one's memory even after a careful pre-journey perusal of the map. This is especially so in unfamiliar territory. On quite a few occasions, I found that the drivers or pedestrians I asked for help were really not speaking the same language as me because they spoke only of the "clockwise" and "anti-clockwise" (counter clockwise) flows of traffic rather than the points of the compass.

Many times I have approached a huge sign informing me of the approaching highway with its boldly emblazoned number but without having a clue as to how I should proceed to get to the same numbered highway leading in the opposite direction. In the United States, not a few drivers make good use of a compass mounted on the dashboard but I have yet to observe one anywhere inside an automobile in Britain.

"Get Out of the Way!" versus "Please Go First!"
Then there is the strange British preference to do major road works during rush hour traffic rather than on week-ends and late at night and the many urban roads too narrow for two cars to pass each other at the same time. Someone has to give way. Here too, there is room for maximum confusion for an American recently arrived in the UK. Courteous British drivers will flash their headlights which in the US would signify "Get out of the way. I have the right of way and even if I don't, I'm coming through now!" In Britain, this sign actually means the opposite—"Please go first!"

Although Britain is now the only European nation which drives on the left hand side of the road (Sweden went over to the right more than a decade ago), in most other respects, European and British driving habits, rules, and regulations coincide. If an American-British reunion were ever attempted, it would immediately founder on the absolute incompatibility of the square grid *v.* the roundabout. It's no wonder that at the Battle of Yorktown which ended the American Revolution in 1783, the British military band at the surrender ceremony played "The World Turned Upside Down."

6. What do the subheads tell you about the organization of this article?

Active-Reading Questions
ANSWERS continued

6. The subheads show that the essay is organized by the point-by-point method.

Types of Questions	
Right There	The answer is stated in one place in the text.
Think and Search	The answer is in the text, but to find it, you have to put together different pieces of information from different places in the text.
Author and You	The answer is not in the text; to figure it out, you use both what you already know and what the author tells you.
On My Own	The answer is not in the text; to respond, you draw on your own knowledge and experience.

Reading Workshop 59

First Thoughts on Your Reading

ANSWERS

Possible answers follow.

1. that some British roads often lead to nowhere and the road system does not allow one to return to one's starting point easily
2. British road layouts, by contrast, follow arcs, curves, and circles.
3. that Americans do not do road repairs during busiest times; students may disagree, pointing out that road repairs are frequently done on highways during peak driving hours

---

First Thoughts on Your Reading

The following questions will help you analyze and understand "Two Peoples Divided by Common Road Signs." Write your answers on your own paper.

1. Look back at the second paragraph of this article. What does the writer think is the real cause of aggravation among Americans driving in Britain?
2. The writer says Americans are "squares" when it comes to road layouts. How do British road layouts contrast with those in America?
3. In the eighth paragraph, the writer claims that the British frequently do road repairs during the busiest times for traffic. What do you think this implies about Americans? Do you agree or disagree?

READING SKILL

Main Idea and Supporting Details

What's the Point? When you read an article or essay, you want to make sure you get the point. Being able to identify the main idea of an article ensures that you get the point the writer is trying to make. The **main idea** of an article, also called the **thesis,** is the idea on which the entire piece is focused. In an article that is several paragraphs long, the main idea or thesis is sometimes sketched out in one or two sentences, often near the beginning of the piece. These one or two sentences, known as the **thesis statement,** declare the topic of the entire piece and the main idea about it. Some pieces of writing, however, lack a thesis statement and instead have an **implied main idea.** When this is the case, the reader must determine the main idea by examining and combining the details found in each paragraph.

TIP An implied main idea is often found in narrative and descriptive writing.

Each paragraph in the piece focuses on a specific point, its own **paragraph main idea,** that helps complete the picture outlined by the thesis. The paragraph main idea often appears in a topic sentence, and **supporting details** make up the rest of each paragraph. Sensory details, facts or statistics, examples, or anecdotes are all details that can support the main idea of a paragraph.

The diagram on the next page shows how the thesis, the main idea of each paragraph, and the supporting details all relate to each other in a piece of writing.

Main Idea and Supporting Details

```
                    main idea of article (thesis)
            ↙                    ↓                    ↘
   paragraph main idea   paragraph main idea   paragraph main idea
      ↙        ↘          ↙         ↘          ↙          ↘
 supporting  supporting  supporting  supporting  supporting  supporting
  details     details     details     details     details     details
```

TIP Many essays and articles you read deal with only one subject. Comparison-contrast articles, however, always deal with at least two subjects. In professional writing, if one of the subjects is unfamiliar and the other is more familiar, a writer might **imply** details about the familiar subject because the writer assumes the reader already knows those details. For example, in a comparison of the two sports baseball and cricket, a writer might give all the details about cricket bats without fully describing the more familiar baseball bats.

THINKING IT THROUGH

Identifying Main Idea and Supporting Details

You can use the following process to identify the main idea and supporting details of a reading selection. The examples below are based on an article titled "British English vs. U.S. English."

▶ **STEP 1** Read the piece and identify the subjects. Pay special attention to the title and to repeated words and phrases. Think about what the writer is addressing. Based on the title, it would be reasonable to guess that Britain and the U.S. are probably the two subjects.

▶ **STEP 2** Look for a clearly stated thesis. A thesis statement often appears in the introduction or in the conclusion of a piece. A piece of this kind might contain a thesis statement like this one: Although U.S. citizens and the British both speak English, there are differences in the ways they communicate.

▶ **STEP 3** If the writer does not include a thesis statement, re-read each paragraph of the selection. As you finish each paragraph, write a

---

Critical Thinking

Synthesis. An analogy is another type of comparison in which the relationship between two objects or ideas is compared. Writers commonly use analogies to simplify complex relationships, such as "the scattering of billiard balls on a pool table is a good picture of what happens to atomic particles during nuclear fission."

Ask students to write their own analogies to show comparisons between relationships. Some possible examples are life and a Ferris wheel, the writing process and building a house, and a football game plan and playing chess.

Timesaver

Have students work in pairs on **Your Turn 2** and organize their answers as a diagram like the one on the preceding page. Their arrangement of answers in diagram form will allow you to check their work quickly for missing elements. Students can mark their implied ideas with asterisks.

YOUR TURN 2

ANSWERS
Here are possible answers.

Main idea: The differences between the American and British road systems are confusing and irritating.

Supporting details:

1. The American system uses grids and rectangles; the British system follows curves and circles.
2. The British have roundabouts with spin-offs; American roads meet at right angles.
3. Street names change along commercial stretches in Britain, and odd and even numbers may be on the same side.
4. In Britain, street names are absent from major thoroughfares, and many roads have the same name.
5. Traffic flow is clockwise or counterclockwise in Britain rather than by compass points, as in the United States.
6. The British do road work during rush hour instead of at night.
7. Many urban roads in Britain are too narrow for cars.

The author implies that the opposite is true in the United States for supporting details 3, 4, 6, and 7.

---

sentence that expresses the main idea of the paragraph. Main idea of paragraph 1: Some words are spelled differently in Britain than they are in the U.S. Main idea of paragraph 2: Different words are used to name the same things. Main idea of paragraph 3: Some words sound different.

▶ **STEP 4** **Look for details that support the main idea of each paragraph.** In paragraph 1, the writer might support the main idea with details about the spellings of specific words: U.S. citizens write *gray, labor,* and *license,* while the British write *grey, labour,* and *licence.*

▶ **STEP 5** **After looking at each paragraph, write a statement that combines the main ideas of *all* the paragraphs.** This means you will have to *infer* the main idea of the whole piece—that is, you will determine the main idea based on the information in the individual paragraphs. In this case, you would end up with a statement that looks very much like the thesis statement in step 2.

YOUR TURN 2 — Identifying Main Idea and Supporting Details

Use the Thinking It Through steps above to identify the overall main idea (or thesis) and the supporting details of "Two Peoples Divided by Common Road Signs." As you re-read the article, watch for implied details about American roads.

READING FOCUS

Comparison-Contrast Structure

Recognize How It's Organized When you read a comparison-contrast essay, you can expect to find details about the two subjects organized with either the **block method** or the **point-by-point method**.

Writers use the block method to separate all of the points about one subject from all of the points about the other subject. This type of organization is called the block method because it presents all of the information about the first subject in a block of paragraphs and then presents all of the information about the second subject in a block of paragraphs.

Writers use the point-by-point method to group each point about the first subject with its corresponding point about the second subject. A point about the first subject is made in one or more sentences and then that point is followed by the corresponding point about the second subject. The writer will continue pairing up each subject until all of the points have been made.

READING PROCESS

EXTENDING
Apply What You Read. To check understanding of the concept of a main idea, have each student select an appropriate essay he or she has written and create a subhead for each paragraph or section. Emphasize that the subheads should reflect the main ideas of the paragraph or section. Then, challenge students to come up with a better way of arranging and expressing support for their essays' main ideas, based on what they have just learned in reading the article.

The following diagram illustrates the difference between the two methods.

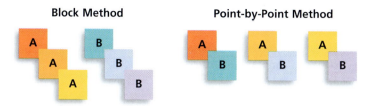

Block Method   Point-by-Point Method

The following graphic organizers compare cricket with baseball. Look at the differences in how the two subjects are presented using the block method and the point-by-point method.

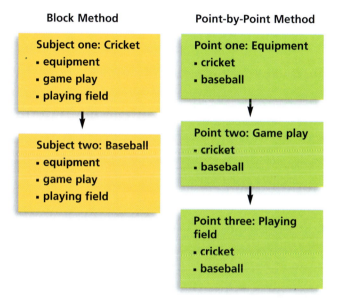

YOUR TURN 3 — Analyzing Comparison-Contrast Structure

Analyze the structure of "Two Peoples Divided by Common Road Signs." First, decide which organizational method the writer uses; then, create a graphic organizer to list the differences between British and American road systems. Remember that details about American road systems may be implied because the writer assumes you are already familiar with them.

Connecting Reading and Writing

With students' help, create a graphic organizer that applies the block method to the Reading Selection. Would the selection have been easier to follow if the writer had used this method? Point out that more involved concepts are easier for readers to understand when presented point by point.

Wrap It Up

Metacognition. Ask students to reflect on their reading processes by writing a brief response to the following questions:

1. What methods do you find most useful for identifying main idea and supporting details? Why?

Then, have students answer the following question:

2. What are the two comparison-contrast structures? [block method and point-by-point method]

YOUR TURN 3

The author uses the point-by-point method. Students' graphic organizers should be modeled after the point-by-point diagram on this page, with the British road system as the first subject and the American system as the second, and with a box for each detail listed for **Your Turn 2**; both stated and implied details should be included.

RESOURCES

Your Turn 2
Practice
- *Communications*, WS. p. 25

Reinforcement
- *Communications*, TP. 18, WS. p. 26

Your Turn 3
Practice
- *Communications*, WS. p. 27

Reinforcement
- *Communications*, TP. 19, WS. p. 28

MINI-LESSON VOCABULARY

Comparison-Contrast Context Clues

When you encounter an unfamiliar word in a comparison-contrast piece, consider its **context,** or surrounding words. Look for nearby **comparison-contrast clue words** that signal a comparison (such as *like, similar, also,* and *as*) or a contrast (*however, but, contrast,* and *conversely*).

In a comparison, an unfamiliar word might have a meaning similar to a familiar word or phrase in the sentence.

British *car parks* are **like** U.S. parking lots. (*Like* signals a comparison between *car parks* and *parking lots.* A car park is probably the same as a parking lot.)

In a contrast, an unfamiliar word might have a meaning dissimilar to a familiar word.

The *lift* is faster, **but** I usually take the stairs. (*But* signals contrast between *lift* and *stairs.* A lift is probably the same as an elevator.)

THINKING IT THROUGH Using Comparison-Contrast Context Clues

Look at the steps to determine the meaning of the italicized word below.

> When the orangutans are free to move around, they are filled with energy. When confined in their cages, however, they are overcome with *torpor*.

1. **Look for comparison-contrast clue words.** The word however signals a contrast.
2. **Look for a word or phrase that might have the same (for comparison) or the opposite (for contrast) meaning as the unfamiliar word.** The word energy is probably an opposite of the word torpor.
3. **Use the comparison or contrast to help you determine the unfamiliar word's meaning.** If energy is contrasted with torpor, then torpor probably means "a lack of energy" or "dullness."

PRACTICE

Use the steps above to find the meanings of the italicized words in the following sentences. Write your answers on your own paper.

1. Driving on the left side of the road is a *conundrum* for Americans. Roundabouts also are a point of confusion.
2. British and European drivers seem to get along; however, a union of British and American drivers would certainly *founder*.
3. American and British drivers may agree about gasoline prices, but the conflicting road systems are a large source of *discord*.
4. British streets may share a name but have a different *appendage*, like "street" or "road." U.S. streets have similar extensions.

MINI-LESSON VOCABULARY

Comparison-Contrast Context Clues

ANSWERS
Possible answers are given.

1. point of confusion
2. fail
3. disagreement
4. extension

Taking a Second Look

Comparison-Contrast Context Clues. Instead of using context clues, have students consult a dictionary to find definitions for the italicized words and to choose the most appropriate definition for each word. To evaluate their strategies, students may then compare the dictionary definitions with the meanings they have derived from context clues.

Sample dictionary definitions are provided.

1. problem with no satisfactory solution
2. collapse or break down; fail
3. lack of agreement among persons, groups, or things
4. something attached as a supplement; attachment

RESOURCES

Vocabulary
Practice
- *Communications,* WS. p. 29

Test Taking
Practice
- *Communications,* WS. pp. 30–32

Exposition: Exploring Comparisons and Contrasts

Main Idea

Many reading tests feature questions that require you to identify the main idea of a reading passage. Below are a reading passage and a typical comprehension question that you might find on a reading test.

> Many people think that bacteria and viruses are the same thing. After all, both are extremely small. They both can cause infectious diseases and are scientifically classified as microbes. However, even though they may seem similar, bacteria and viruses are very different.
>
> Bacteria can live independently of host organisms and can reproduce without any outside aid. In fact, they can live in soil and thrive without any direct contact with other organisms.
>
> Viruses, on the other hand, are completely inert or dormant outside of a host organism. Viruses can reproduce only by using the machinery of a host cell's nucleus; they must hijack the cells of host organisms to make copies of themselves.

1. Which of the following best states the main idea of the third paragraph?
   A. Bacteria can reproduce on their own.
   B. Viruses and bacteria are almost the same.
   C. Viruses are dependent on a host organism.
   D. Viruses use cell machinery to reproduce.

THINKING IT THROUGH — Answering Questions About Main Idea

The following steps will help you identify the main idea on reading tests.

▶ **STEP 1 Read through the entire paragraph or passage.** Many tests include answer choices meant to catch those who only skim through a passage. Choice **A** is true, but it is stated in the second paragraph, not the third.

▶ **STEP 2 Look for a directly stated main idea—a sentence that all the other sentences support.** This is often the first sentence of a paragraph or passage. Choice **D** appears in the third paragraph, but it only supports the sentence that comes before it. Choice **C** is a restatement of the paragraph's main idea; the remaining paragraph sentences provide details that support that idea.

▶ **STEP 3 If the passage includes no directly stated main idea, try summarizing the paragraph or passage in your own words.** Read each sentence in the paragraph or passage, and try to come up with a summary that states the main idea that unites them. Then, look for an answer choice that matches this inferred main idea. The passage makes the point that bacteria and viruses are different. Choice **B** states the opposite. The correct answer has to be Choice **C**.

Looking Ahead to Writing

Students will write their own comparison-contrast essays in the Writing Workshop (pp. 66–85). Encourage students to refer to the graphic organizers on p. 61 (Main Idea and Supporting Details) and p. 63 (Block Method and Point-by-Point Method) as they plan their essays and organize their ideas.

Vocabulary Alignments
TEKS 6B
TAAS R1

Test Taking Alignments
TEKS 7F
TAAS R3

Writing Workshop

OBJECTIVES

- To write an essay comparing and contrasting two subjects
- To determine relevant features
- To form a thesis
- To use either the block method or the point-by-point method
- To use comparative and superlative forms
- To avoid worn-out adverbs

Quotation for the Day

"He who does not expect a million readers should not write a line."

(J. W. Goethe, 1749–1832, German poet, dramatist, and thinker)

Write the quotation on the chalkboard or on an overhead transparency, and ask students to freewrite about the importance of audience when choosing a subject for a paper. Challenge students to imagine a large audience for what they have to say on some possible subjects.

TEACHING TIP

Choose Two Subjects
Ask students what the term *comparison shopping* suggests or means to them. Explain that smart shoppers get the best value for their money by comparing the quality and price of similar products. Invite students to describe in one or two short paragraphs situations in which they have done comparison shopping. Students might have compared and contrasted different brands of jeans, sneakers, or CD players, for example. Students may draw on their shopping experiences for essay subjects.

Writing Workshop

WHAT'S AHEAD?

In this workshop, you will write an essay comparing and contrasting two subjects. You will also learn how to

- determine relevant features
- form a thesis
- use the block method or the point-by-point method
- use comparative and superlative forms
- avoid worn-out adverbs

Writing a Comparison-Contrast Essay

Picture this situation: You have just moved to a new neighborhood and attended your first day at a new school. Your best friend at your old school is dying to know what your new school is like. Is your new science teacher as spirited as your last one? Are your classes still on block schedule? Are the graduation requirements similar? Does the new school offer the same extracurricular activities, or are there different ones? In an e-mail to your friend, you describe the similarities and differences between your new school and your old one. That is, you **compare and contrast** the two schools to help your friend more easily understand your ideas.

Comparing and contrasting are two natural ways you seek to understand the world around you. This understanding can help you to make informed decisions and sound judgments. In this Writing Workshop, you will have a chance to plan, organize, and write a comparison-contrast essay about two subjects that you choose on your own.

Prewriting

Choose Two Subjects

Pick and Choose When you write a comparison-contrast essay, you focus on the similarities or the differences (or both) of two subjects in order to understand them better. To get started, you first must decide which two subjects you will compare and contrast.

- If you have ever wondered how two things are different or similar, you could compare and contrast them to find out. For example, you might wonder how the trumpet and the trombone are alike and different.

Chapter 2 Exposition: Exploring Comparisons and Contrasts

- Think about any time you have to make a choice between two things. If your family is thinking about buying a computer or a car, for instance, but can't decide between two models, you could compare and contrast the models to help make the choice clearer.
- Think about your hobbies and interests. If you are a fan of the *Star Wars* movies, you might compare and contrast the latest movie in the series with an earlier one. Similarly, if you are a sports enthusiast who likes both snowskiing and waterskiing, you might compare and contrast the two sports.

As you think of possible subjects, ask yourself the following questions to determine whether the subjects can be developed well in a comparison-contrast essay.

- **Do the subjects have something in common?** The subjects must have at least one basic similarity. For instance, you could compare watching movies on videotape to watching movies in theaters because both are ways to view a common form of entertainment—movies.
- **Do the subjects have significant differences?** The subjects you choose must be different enough to be interesting. For example, the differences in the cost, the convenience, and the experience of watching videos at home and seeing movies in theaters are significant enough to make for an interesting essay.

Remember to choose subjects that can be easily compared in a short essay. Comparing all forms of live entertainment with all forms of pre-recorded entertainment, for instance, would be too much to accomplish. However, comparing home video viewing with watching movies in theaters is manageable. After you have found two subjects that you think will work, jot them down in a notebook or journal.

TIP The word *compare* is sometimes used to mean "look at both similarities and differences, not just similarities." If a teacher asks you to compare two subjects, check to see if you should look for differences as well as similarities.

Consider Purpose, Audience, and Tone

Thinking of the Why, the Who, and the How You will communicate more clearly with your audience if you are sure of why you are writing—that is, if you have your **purpose** clearly in mind. The main purpose of this comparison-contrast piece is to inform your readers about your subjects. To begin, you must first determine which aspects of your subjects you want to discuss: their similarities, their differences, or both. To do this, think about the focus of your paper.

- If your purpose were to show your readers how softball and baseball are alike, you would write an essay about their **similarities**.

TIP Comparison-contrast structure is often used only to present information about two subjects. However, it can be used for persuasive purposes—to convince you that one subject is better, or worse, than the other.

Writing Workshop 67

TECHNOLOGY TIP

If students choose to compare two brands of the same item, suggest that they visit the Web sites of the companies that produce the items to learn what each company lists as its product's strengths. Remind students that they must evaluate the truth of these claims before they include them in their papers, and emphasize that company Web sites should be only one of several sources students consult for information. *You need to be aware that Internet resources are sometimes public forums, and their content can be unpredictable.*

- If your purpose were to inform your readers about the differences between owning a cat and owning a dog, you would write an essay about **differences.**
- If your purpose were to explain to your readers how the Sahara and the Mojave deserts have both similar and different characteristics, you would write an essay about **both similarities and differences.**

In order for your writing to be as informative as it can be, you should carefully consider who your intended **audience** is—who your readers are. You must also consider what those readers already know about your subject so you can define terms and provide necessary background information. For example, suppose that you were planning to write an essay contrasting owning a cat and owning a dog. If you were writing for an audience of cat owners, you would include more details about owning a dog. Your readers would already be familiar with cat ownership—you would not have to include as many details about it.

To help you decide what kinds of information you should include for your readers, ask yourself the following questions.

- What do your readers already know about your two subjects?
- Is one subject more familiar to them than the other?
- What facts and information will your readers want to know about the two subjects?

Finally, you should decide on the **tone** of your writing, or how you will present your message. Tone is like the personality of your writing. Whether you are serious, funny, casual, or formal, your tone is created by the details, words, rhythms, and sounds of language that you choose. Writers of informative pieces, such as comparison-contrast essays, usually use a clear, authoritative tone because they want to sound knowledgeable about their subjects. You might decide, however, that a humorous tone is more fitting for your essay. For example, humor might be appropriate in an essay comparing and contrasting a satirical novel with its movie version. The tone you use depends on the purpose of your writing, on your intended audience, and on the subjects you are comparing and contrasting.

Gather Information and Determine Relevant Features

Get the Facts In order to discuss your two subjects seriously, you must gather information about them. Information you will want to gather includes definitions, facts, statistics, and descriptions of the distinct characteristics of each subject. Some of this information may come from your own knowledge or experience, but most often you will need to research information, even if only to support the claims you make based on what you know.

Where you get the information for your essay will depend on your two subjects. You might go to a library for books or articles written about the subjects. You might search the Internet for information as well, or interview people who are experts on the subjects. Once you have gathered the information that you will include in your comparison-contrast essay, you will begin to identify your two subjects' *relevant features*. **Relevant features are the important characteristics of your two subjects; they provide the main points for supporting your thesis.** These features are called *relevant* because they are important, or significant, to the understanding of the two subjects.

▶ KEY CONCEPT

The relevant features you choose depend on your audience. If you are writing for the general public, you might contrast features of general interest. On the other hand, if your intended audience consists of experts or enthusiasts on your subjects, you might choose specific relevant features that would interest them more.

THINKING IT THROUGH

Discovering Relevant Features

Take the following steps to determine possible relevant features for your subjects. The chart that follows the steps shows how a student determined relevant features for an essay contrasting watching movies in the theater with watching videos at home.

▶ **STEP 1 Freewrite a list of the details of the two subjects you have chosen.** Try to list as many as possible. Note that a detail of one subject may trigger a corresponding detail of the other subject.

▶ **STEP 2 Label the items in your list.** For instance, if you have a detail that relates to a subject's cost, then label it "cost." Labeling the details you have discovered will help you organize and compare your details later. You can always go back and relabel an item if necessary.

▶ **STEP 3 Create a two-column chart like the one on the following page. Within each column, group all details with the same label, or details that seem to belong together. Cross out any details that do not have a corresponding detail in the other column.** The group labels, shown on the chart in boldface type, are the relevant features. The details are the specifics the essay will address.

Meeting INDIVIDUAL NEEDS

MODALITIES

Visual Learners. Have students create a Venn diagram as they brainstorm or identify similarities and differences between their subjects.

Kinesthetic Learners. Encourage students to choose subjects involving an activity that can be replicated or mimed while writing. For example, a student comparing and contrasting how to throw a curveball and how to throw a fastball can mimic throwing a baseball while freewriting for relevant features. A student comparing and contrasting ballet and jazz dancing can perform different steps to jog his or her memory; a student writing on different architectural styles can take notes while on a walking tour of a historic neighborhood, and so on.

Timesaver

Because the thesis statement determines the general content and direction of an essay, spending time now to help students formulate appropriate thesis statements will save time during the revision and assessment stages. Direct students to exchange thesis statements with a partner and check off each of the following essential elements in each other's statements: introduction of subjects, indication of relevant features, and a suggestion of the evaluative criteria.

TEACHING TIP

Write a Thesis Statement
Remind students that their thesis statements should be adjusted to reflect changes in focus, if the need arises during writing. A thesis statement with an emphasis on differences might be changed to a statement that emphasizes both similarities and differences. For example, "You will want to take into account differences in space, exercise, and food requirements when considering what size dog to get" might become "Although you will certainly take into account differences in space, exercise, and food requirements when deciding what size dog to get, common characteristics such as companionship and affection will also play a part in your decision."

RELEVANT FEATURES	
Movies in theaters	Videotapes at home
Comfort • seating may be limited • people may block your view of the screen	**Comfort** • can sit where you want • usually no one will block your view
Cost • expensive tickets • snacks very expensive	**Cost** • rental price a few dollars • can eat whatever is in the house
Control • cannot rewind bits you miss • going to the restroom or snack bar, you miss out on the movie • chatty patrons are annoying	**Control** • can rewind, pause, and so on • easy to take restroom breaks and snack runs to the refrigerator • can talk during the movie or stop movie to chat
Movie quality • big screen; sharp sound	**Movie quality** • smaller screen size; poorer sound

From the chart you can see that the relevant features of the two subjects are comfort, cost, control, and movie quality.

TIP When writing your essay, you may have to adjust your thesis a little to represent your essay's final focus better and to capture your readers' interest.

Write a Thesis Statement

State Your Case You must state a thesis, or main idea, in the introduction of your comparison-contrast essay to let your readers know what to expect as they read. Your thesis statement should identify the subjects of your essay and alert your readers to the approach you will use—whether you will discuss mostly similarities, mostly differences, or both similarities and differences. For an example, look at the following thesis statement.

> When deciding between watching a video at home or watching a movie in a theater, most people base their choices on differences in comfort, cost, control and quality.

MINI-LESSON: CRITICAL THINKING

Synthesizing Information to Form a Thesis

Synthesizing information is a critical thinking skill that involves putting together parts into a unified whole. For example, you are synthesizing information when you draw conclusions about the similarities and differences between two subjects you have chosen as the subjects of a comparison-contrast essay. The conclusion you reach is your thesis.

THINKING IT THROUGH: Synthesizing Information

Use the following steps to synthesize information and create a thesis statement about the subjects of your essay. The responses are based on the subjects baseball and cricket.

▶ **STEP 1** List the relevant features of each subject. For example, the relevant features for baseball and cricket are: equipment, game play, and playing field.

▶ **STEP 2** List details for each relevant feature. Then, determine which details are similarities and which are differences between the two subjects. Game play is different for baseball and cricket, in that there are more innings played in baseball, but a baseball game is shorter. The playing field in baseball has four bases that make up a diamond-shaped running path, while the field in cricket is called the pitch and has two wickets that stand at each end. Lastly, only the wicketkeepers use gloves in cricket, and a cricket bat is flat-edged.

▶ **STEP 3** Write a sentence that states whether there are more similarities, more differences, or a balance of both, for your subjects. When it comes to the equipment, the playing field, and actual game play, there is little that would make someone confuse cricket with baseball.

PRACTICE

For each pair of subjects, use the steps above to synthesize information and create a thesis statement for a comparison-contrast essay.

1. News in newspapers; news on TV
2. Shopping in a mall; shopping online
3. Driving to school or work; taking the bus
4. Live music; recorded music (CDs, cassettes)
5. Video games; board games

MINI-LESSON: CRITICAL THINKING

Synthesizing Information to Form a Thesis

ANSWERS
Here are sample thesis statements.

1. Although both newspapers and TV report the same events, the two media differ in methods and depth of reporting.

2. Differences in convenience, cost of transportation or equipment, selection of goods, and the overall shopping experience separate shopping in a mall and online shopping.

3. Before choosing whether to drive or to take the bus to work or school, you may want to consider the differences in expense, time involved, and accommodation of special needs.

4. Although both live and recorded music are entertaining, significant differences exist between the two with regard to cost, accessibility, and the experience itself.

5. Price, portability, player interaction, and skills used are the main differences between video games and board games, both of which are favorite leisure-time activities.

RESOURCES

Critical Thinking
Practice
- *Communications*, WS. p. 33

Critical Thinking
Alignments
TEKS 7G, 8B
TAAS R5
English II End-of-Course 3

TEACHING TIP

Arrange Your Supporting Details
Remind students that when they use the point-by-point method, the order in which they discuss the features in the body of their papers should follow the order in which the features are listed in the thesis statement. For example, if the thesis statement is "Michelangelo and Leonardo da Vinci share many similarities in their achievements, innovations, and major works," the three body paragraphs will be about achievements, innovations, and major works, in that order.

MODALITY
Visual Learners. Make copies of a blank chart such as the organizational diagram on p. 63 with columns labeled *Block Method* and *Point-by-Point Method*. Students can use the chart to manipulate their information to see which method is the better format for their essays.

KEY CONCEPT

TIP When you are organizing your ideas, you may come up with new ones. If so, include them where they seem to fit naturally.

Arrange Your Supporting Details

Get It Together! To support the main idea expressed in your thesis statement, **you can arrange the information you have gathered in one of two ways: the block method or the point-by-point method.**

Use the **block method** when you want to discuss all of the points about each subject separately. The block method presents all of the information about the first subject in a block of one or more paragraphs and then presents all of the information about the second subject in a block of paragraphs. Consider this method if you plan on discussing only a few features. The following diagram shows how the relevant features and supporting details on page 70 could be arranged according to the block method.

ORGANIZATION DIAGRAM

Block Method

Subject 1: Viewing videos at home
Feature 1: Comfort—choice of seating; no one blocks your view
Feature 2: Cost—a few dollars for tape rental; low-cost snacks
Feature 3: Control—can pause and rewind
Feature 4: Quality—smaller screen size; poorer sound

Subject 2: Seeing a movie in a theater
Feature 1: Comfort—seating may be limited, people may block view
Feature 2: Cost—several dollars admission per person; high prices for snacks
Feature 3: Control—no control of viewing (pause, stop, rewind)
Feature 4: Quality—big screen and sharp sound

Use the **point-by-point method** to deal with both subjects at the same time. With this method, you make a point about one subject and then follow it with a corresponding point about the second subject. Then, you continue pairing up each subject until all of the points have been made. This method is extremely helpful when comparing or contrasting subjects that are very similar or very different, because it is easier to see the similarities and differences when the points about each subject are discussed together. The diagram on the next page shows an example of the point-by-point method of organization.

Chapter 2   Exposition: Exploring Comparisons and Contrasts

ORGANIZATION DIAGRAM
Point-by-Point Method

Feature 1: Comfort
Subject 1: Video—choice of seating; no one blocks your view
Subject 2: Theater—seating may be limited; people may block view

Feature 2: Cost
Subject 1: Video—a few dollars for tape rental; low-cost snacks
Subject 2: Theater—several dollars admission per person; high prices for snacks

Feature 3: Control
Subject 1: Video—can pause and rewind
Subject 2: Theater—no control of viewing (pause, stop, rewind)

Feature 4: Quality
Subject 1: Video—smaller screen size; poorer sound
Subject 2: Theater—big screen and sharp sound

TIP In an essay that explores differences, you might begin with the one or two similarities the subjects have in common and then explore their differences. In the same way, you might explore similarities by beginning with the one or two differences between the subjects and then devoting most of your paper to exploring similarities.

YOUR TURN 4 — Planning Your Comparison-Contrast Essay

Review the prewriting steps on the previous pages to be sure you have everything in place to plan your comparison-contrast essay.

- Choose two subjects that have enough differences or similarities to provide sufficient material for a comparison-contrast essay.
- Think about your purpose, your audience, and the tone of your essay.
- Gather information in order to discover the relevant features of your two subjects.
- Write a thesis statement that clearly identifies your two subjects and indicates the approach you plan to use.
- Arrange your information using either the block method or the point-by-point method.

Cooperative Learning

Panel Discussion. Ask students to form groups of two panels of two students each to practice determining and organizing relevant features. One panel will tell about a sport or type of music, and another will tell about a sport or type of music to which the first will be compared. Possible pairs for comparison include football and soccer or hip-hop music and rock music. Be sure that the pairs of students work together to determine relevant features for comparison. Their presentations should maintain an informative dialogue, rather than become an argument about which is best. The panels might use the point-by-point method, with one side and then the other citing a parallel fact, or they might use the block method, with one side listing its facts first, followed by the other side. Have the panels present their discussions to the class.

YOUR TURN 4

Students may run into obstacles as they plan their comparison-contrast essays. Organize students in random groups of three to discuss problems they have encountered and to brainstorm solutions. If the group cannot offer a solution to a particular problem, open the discussion to the entire class for additional ideas.

Then, have students use **Your Turn 4** as a checklist before beginning to write. Students who have not completed one or more steps should review the relevant pages in the Prewriting section of the Writing Workshop.

RESOURCES

Your Turn 4
Practice
- *Communications*, WS. p. 34

Quotation for the Day

"How many good books suffer neglect through the inefficiency of their beginnings!"

(Edgar Allan Poe, 1809–1849, American story writer and poet)

Use the quotation to emphasize the importance of creating interesting introductory paragraphs. Ask students to think about times when they have made judgments about people or places based on first impressions. Explain that readers also make judgments based on first impressions, so good writers try to make an impression with their introductions that will pique their readers' interest.

TEACHING TIP

Writing a First Draft
If students are having difficulty getting started, suggest that they begin with the thesis statement and then organize and write the body of their essays, writing paragraphs to discuss the points they have identified. Once the thesis statement and body are drafted, show students how transitional phrases, an introduction, and a conclusion can be added to complete their essays.

YOUR TURN 5

Suggest that in their first drafts students label the introduction, body, and conclusion and their parts, as is done in **A Writer's Model** on p. 75. This will help students see what elements, if any, still need to be supplied.

Writing

Comparison-Contrast Essay

Framework	Directions and Explanations
Introduction ■ Open with an attention getter. ■ Give background information. ■ Include a thesis statement.	**Get Their Attention** Make your readers eager to see what you have to say by starting with a "hook"—a high-interest opener that pulls readers into your essay. **Give Some Background** If one or both of your subjects are unfamiliar to your readers, provide background information to help them understand the subjects. **Declare Your Thesis** Include a clear thesis statement that identifies your subjects and indicates whether you will compare them, contrast them, or both.
Body ■ Organize your information into multiple paragraphs using either the block method or the point-by-point method.	**Inform Your Readers** Present the information that supports your thesis, using either the block or point-by-point method. Use transitional words and phrases to connect and clarify ideas. Words and phrases like *also, similarly, both,* and *just as* signal a comparison. *By contrast, however, unlike,* and *on the other hand* signal a contrast.
Conclusion ■ Connect your points back to your thesis. ■ Leave your readers with something to remember.	**Stress the Point** Be sure your readers understand your main idea: Remind them how the points you have made in your body paragraphs support your thesis. **Wrap It Up** Finish with an engaging fact or insight to leave your readers thinking about the points you have made about your subjects.

YOUR TURN 5 Writing a First Draft

Using the framework and the directions and explanations above as a guide, write the first draft of your comparison-contrast essay.

74   Chapter 2   Exposition: Exploring Comparisons and Contrasts

---

RESOURCES

Writing
Writing Prompts
■ *Communications,* TP. 20, WS. p. 35

Your Turn 5
Practice
■ *Communications,* TP. 21, WS. p. 36

Exposition: Exploring Comparisons and Contrasts

A Writer's Model

The following essay, which is a final draft, closely follows the framework on the previous page, using the point-by-point method to contrast watching movies in a theater with watching videos at home.

Movie? Video? What Is the Difference?

You and a couple of friends are trying to decide what to do on a Friday night. One friend asks, "Want to go to the movies?" The other chimes in with, "A movie? No way! How about a video?" As they argue back and forth you may be tempted to say, "Movie, video—who cares? What difference is there anyway?" When you stop to think about it, though, you will realize that there are very real differences in comfort, cost, control, and quality between watching movies and watching videos.

Comfort is one way that watching a video at home and watching a movie in a local theater differ. At home, you can stretch out on the sofa, curl up in a recliner, or even sprawl out on the floor as you watch. Also, when you enjoy a video at home, you can relax and talk with your friends. In a theater, you are confined to one seat—often behind someone who is so tall that you cannot see. If you happen to whisper a comment to a friend, you are likely to get a glare or a disgusted "Sh!" from someone else in the audience.

Another obvious difference between the two ways of watching a film relates to cost. You can rent a video to play at home for just a few dollars—no matter how many people watch it. Furthermore, you can buy inexpensive grocery-store snacks to enjoy with the video. Admission for a movie in a theater, on the other hand, can cost twice as much as a video rental—and that is the price for just one person. If the high prices for popcorn, drinks, and other snacks are added, the cost can really mount up.

An additional point to consider is control. Thanks to the VCR's versatility, viewers can stop a video if they need to leave the room, and then hit PLAY when they return—and not miss a single line of dialogue. If your attention is lagging or you are just too tired to finish a video, you can stop the tape and finish watching it the next day. At a theater, if a person

(continued)

INTRODUCTION
Attention getter

Thesis statement
(focus on differences)

BODY
Relevant feature 1:
Comfort

Videos

Theater

Relevant feature 2:
Cost

Videos

Theater

Relevant feature 3:
Control

Videos

Theater

Connecting Reading and Writing

As students examine **A Writer's Model**, point out that the audience (young moviegoers) influences word choice in the essay (use of *you*, for example) and the overall tone of the piece, which is informal. Have students compare the essay in **A Writer's Model** with the comparison-contrast article in the Reading Workshop (pp. 57–59). Students should note that the latter's audience is adult travelers, and that its tone is somewhat formal but spiced with humor. Remind students to identify their audience and the tone or voice they will adopt before beginning to write.

Writing, pp. 74–77
Alignments
TEKS 1A, 1B, 1C, 2A, 2B, 8A
TAAS W1, W2, W4
English II End-of-Course 4

Critical Thinking

Analysis. Discuss the transitions used at the beginnings and ends of the paragraphs in the essays in this chapter to help students understand how transitions tie the comparison-contrast subjects together. Here are some questions students can ask to focus their analyses:

1. How does the author make transitions between ideas?
2. What ideas, words, or phrases does the author repeat to connect paragraphs?
3. Does the author refer to the thesis statement? Where? Why?

(continued)

tries heading out to the concession stand for another bag of popcorn, he or she will be sure to miss the most dramatic part of the movie—with no way to rewind it and see what was missed. Since you have to pay the full admission price every time you see a movie at a theater, you will probably choose to sit through the entire movie in spite of lagging attention or tiredness.

Relevant feature 4: Quality

Videos

Theater

When just the differences in comfort, cost, and control are considered, watching videos at home seems like the clear choice. So what, if anything, is better about watching a movie in a theater? That question can be answered in a single word: *quality*. A movie seen on a TV screen does not compare to the rich color and clarity of a movie seen on a big screen in a theater. Some may argue that home theater quality is getting better with large digital televisions, surround sound, and digital sound and video technology. Still, theater technology keeps improving on already excellent sound and projection quality, promising to continue surpassing home theater systems. For some people, the difference in quality far outweighs any other considerations.

CONCLUSION: Connection of support to thesis

When you think about comfort, cost, control, and quality, it is easy to see how friends could disagree about whether watching a movie at home or in a theater is better. Maybe one is not better than the other. Clearly, they both have their advantages. It is true—videos are cheaper and controllable, but would you want to see the latest action-packed movie on a TV set or on the big screen?

Exposition: Exploring Comparisons and Contrasts

A Student's Model

In the following excerpt, Adam Caputo of Leesville High School in Raleigh, North Carolina, examines similarities and differences between characters in two of literature's most famous works.

Higher than Society

A massive gap of more than two millennia separates Creon of Sophocles' Antigone (442 B.C.) and Torvald Helmer of Henrik Ibsen's A Doll's House (A.D. 1879). Nevertheless, these characters share common hardship and suffering as they confront the omnipresent conflict between higher laws and the laws of society. **[Thesis statement]**

Both Creon and Torvald stubbornly view the human-created laws of society as the supreme law—superior to the higher laws of morality, conscience, and respect of the divine. Torvald displays this by forcing his wife Nora to be subordinate to him. He establishes his superiority by naming Nora with such words as little, squirrel, and foolish. These derogatory comments illustrate that Torvald feels he is superior to Nora, and that women should be subservient to their husbands—a common idea at the time. By controlling Nora like a child, Torvald follows society's law that women are inferior to men while breaking the higher law of equality for all. Similarly, King Creon supports his society's law when he punishes his niece Antigone. When Creon puts in place a law that anyone who buries Antigone's dead brother Polyneices (a traitor) would be stoned to death, Antigone, respecting the higher law of respect for the dead, defies Creon's edict. To establish that his law is supreme, Creon punishes Antigone with death. Through their actions, Creon and Torvald show parallel traits of stubbornness and disrespect for higher causes by overruling laws that are the keystones of life. These personality traits lead them further into conflict between higher laws and the laws of society. **[Relevant feature 1]**

Eventually, Torvald and Creon face peak moments of conflict between higher laws and the law of society. . . . **[Relevant feature 2]**

Quotation for the Day

"Boredom, after all, is a form of criticism."

(William Phillips, 1907– , American writer and editor)

As students begin evaluating and revising their first drafts, share the quotation with the class. Encourage students to revise parts of their essays that might bore or confuse readers. One way to do this is to make sure that they as the writers of the pieces are engaged by and enthusiastic about their subjects.

Meeting INDIVIDUAL NEEDS

ENGLISH-LANGUAGE LEARNERS
General Strategies. Many English-language learners will benefit from individual attention at the revision stage. If feasible, meet with students privately and have them read their essays aloud. Immediate feedback will build confidence and will give students the necessary information to make effective revisions. Besides making suggestions about content and organization, point out specific areas of grammar, vocabulary, and syntax that students should focus on as they revise their work.

TEACHING TIP

▶ **Elaboration**
Suggest that students use quotations from authorities on their subjects to develop or support a point. An authority may be an expert in the field or a friend, family member, or teacher with special knowledge or experience. Explain that quotations often provoke thought and keep readers interested.

Revising

Evaluate and Revise Your Draft

Check It Out Look at your draft to see which parts are working well and which parts you might change to make your writing even better. Read your entire essay at least twice. First, focus on content and organization; then, evaluate and revise sentence style.

▶ **First Reading: Content and Organization** Use the chart below to evaluate and revise your essay. Answer the questions in the left-hand column; then, use the tips to find possible places for revision. Finally, use the techniques in the right-hand column to guide you in revising your work.

Comparison-Contrast Essay: Content and Organization Guidelines for Peer and Self-Evaluation

Evaluation Questions	Tips	Revision Techniques
❶ Does the introduction grab your attention?	**Underline** the parts of the introduction designed to get readers interested. If you find none, revise.	**Add to** the introduction by including an interesting scenario, fact, or question about your subjects.
❷ Does the thesis statement clearly identify the subjects and the main idea of the essay?	**Circle** the subjects being discussed. **Highlight** the thesis statement. If the subjects and main idea are not clearly stated, revise.	**Add** a thesis that identifies the two subjects being discussed and tells whether the essay focuses on similarities, differences, or both.
❸ Does the essay fully develop relevant features of both subjects, and are there transitional words and phrases between the features?	**Put an A** next to points about the first subject. **Put a B** next to points about the second subject. If similar points are not made about both subjects, or if points are not clearly connected, revise.	**Add** points about one subject that correspond to those made about the other subject. **Elaborate** on points about a subject. **Add** transitional words or phrases between ideas.
❹ Is the body organized by the block method or by the point-by-point method?	**Look at each A and B you marked.** All the As should be in one part and all the Bs in another (block); or, each A should be followed by a B (point-by-point). If the organization does not follow either of these patterns, revise.	**Reorder** the ideas into either a block or point-by-point pattern.
❺ Is the conclusion effective?	**Double underline** the parts of the conclusion that restate or support the thesis. If you underline nothing, revise.	**Add** a restatement of your thesis, and **add** a statement that summarizes the information in your essay.

78   Chapter 2   **Exposition:** Exploring Comparisons and Contrasts

RESOURCES

Revising
Practice
- *Communications,* TPs. 22, 23, WS. pp. 37, 38, 39

Extension
- *Designing Your Writing*

ONE WRITER'S REVISIONS The example below shows how one writer used the content and organization guidelines to revise part of the comparison-contrast essay on page 75. Look at the revisions carefully, and answer the questions that follow.

> ~~An~~ *Another* obvious difference between the two ways of watching a film relates to cost. You can rent a video to play at home for just a few dollars—no matter how many people watch it. *Furthermore,* Admission for a movie in a theater, on the other hand, can cost twice as much as a video rental—and that is the price for just one person. If the high prices for popcorn, drinks, and other snacks are added, the cost can really mount up. ~~You can buy inexpensive grocery-store snacks to enjoy with the video.~~

replace

add

reorder

Analyzing the Revision Process

1. How did changing the first word of this paragraph more effectively connect the paragraph to the one before it?
2. How did reordering the sentences enhance the writer's presentation of ideas?

YOUR TURN 6 Focusing on Content and Organization

Use the guidelines on the previous page and the sample revisions above to revise the content and organization of your essay.

▶ **Second Reading: Style** Now that you have revised your essay for content and organization, read it a second time and examine your sentence style. Look carefully at the adverbs you have used. Adverbs are an easy way to add emphasis to your points about similarities and differences—so easy, in fact, that many adverbs tend to be overused and worn out. Use the style guidelines on the next page to help you eliminate overused adverbs. If you need more help, see the Focus on Word Choice on page 80.

PEER REVIEW

Ask someone in your class to read your essay and respond to the following questions:

1. How did the essay's organization make it easy (or difficult) to follow the writer's points?
2. Did you want more information about one of the subjects? If so, what did you want to know?

Cooperative Learning

Evaluation Techniques. Assign students to groups of four, and have each group member take on a different evaluation task. One student could evaluate the effectiveness of the opening sentences written by the individual members. Another could evaluate support for each thesis statement. A third student could evaluate transitions, and the fourth could evaluate concluding paragraphs. Students should use their peers' feedback to revise their papers.

Analyzing the Revision Process
ANSWERS

1. Changing the first word of the paragraph shows that there is a series of obvious differences and that this is the next point in the series.

2. When all of the information about the cost of watching a movie at home is in one place, the discussion is less confusing. The paragraph is organized more logically and reads more smoothly.

YOUR TURN 6

Along with his or her essay, each student should submit a list of responses to the evaluation questions included in the chart as well as a brief description of any action taken. Students may do the same for the **Peer Review** questions on this page.

Revising, pp. 78–81
Alignments
TEKS 2B, 2C, 5B
TAAS W1, W2, W3, W7
English II End-of-Course 4, 5, 6

Style Guidelines

Evaluation Question	Tip	Revision Technique
▶ Are worn-out adverbs used in the essay?	▶ **Highlight** worn-out adverbs, such as *very, really, awfully, rather, extremely,* and *somewhat*.	▶ **Replace** the overused adverbs with more precise words, or **delete** the adverbs.

Focus on Word Choice

COMPUTER TIP

Do not use the grammar checker in your word-processing program as a substitute for stylistic editing. Grammar checkers can be helpful, but they cannot recognize many common style problems.

Avoiding Worn-out Adverbs

When you are drafting a comparison-contrast essay, it is natural to use adverbs because you are explaining the degree to which two subjects are alike or different. However, worn-out adverbs like *very, really,* and *somewhat* are imprecise. Eliminate imprecise adverbs by replacing them, and often the words they modify, with more precise words. For example, a more precise word for *very large* is *enormous*. Other times, the worn-out adverb is completely unnecessary in the sentence, in which case you can just delete it. In the phrase *extremely enormous,* for example, *extremely* is unnecessary because *enormous* itself is an extreme word.

ONE WRITER'S REVISIONS Here is how the writer of the essay on page 75 used the guidelines above to eliminate overused adverbs.

BEFORE REVISION

Overused adverbs are highlighted.

In a theater, you are confined to one seat— **very** often behind someone who is so **extremely** tall that you cannot see. If you happen to whisper a comment to a friend, you are **really** likely to get an **awfully** dirty look or a disgusted "Sh!" from someone else in the audience.

AFTER REVISION

delete
delete
delete, replace

In a theater, you are confined to one seat—often behind someone who is so tall that you cannot see. If you happen to whisper a comment to a friend, you are likely to get a glare or a disgusted "Sh!" from someone else in the audience.

TEACHING TIP

Avoiding Worn-out Adverbs
Remind students that worn-out adverbs may also be replaced by more precise verbs. The example "who is so extremely tall that you cannot see" could also be revised to read "who towers above the seat, blocking your view."

RESOURCES

Focus on Word Choice
Practice
- *Communications,* WS. p. 40

Analyzing the Revision Process

1. Why did the writer delete the words "very" and "extremely"?
2. How does replacing "awfully dirty look" with "glare" improve the paragraph?
3. How is "likely" better than "really likely"?

 Focusing on Style

Use the style guidelines on the previous page to eliminate or replace overused adverbs in your essay. Use the sample revisions as a model.

Designing Your Writing

Subheads Long essays that are not broken up into clearly labeled sections can sometimes be overwhelming for readers. Writers often make such essays more readable by introducing **subheads** into them. Subheads are words or short phrases that identify the topics of sections of a paper. They stand alone on the line above the section they identify.

Subheads benefit both the reader and the writer. Readers can focus better on a single paragraph or group of paragraphs, and they can easily move to the parts of the essay that they want to read. For the writer, subheads provide a succinct transition from one section to the next.

You might find it useful to add subheads to your comparison-contrast essay. If you use them, they should be flush with the left margin. For a point-by-point organization, you could label each paragraph with a subhead that names the main point you will discuss in that paragraph. With the block method, you could still use subheads, but you might use fewer—one for each subject. Here is how the writer of the Writer's Model might have used a subhead to identify the topic of a paragraph.

Cost

Another obvious difference between the two ways of watching a film relates to cost. You can rent a video to play at home for just a few dollars—no matter how many people watch it. Furthermore, you can buy inexpensive grocery-store snacks to enjoy with the video.

Analyzing the Revision Process
ANSWERS
Here are some possible answers.

1. Both of these adverbs are overused and do not add meaning to the sentence.
2. The description is more precise when "awfully dirty look" is replaced by "glare."
3. It is more concise, because "really" does not add anything to the meaning of "likely."

Before assigning **Your Turn 7,** have students brainstorm a list of overused adverbs so that they have a more specific idea of which adverbs in their essays might need to be eliminated or replaced.

After students have completed **Your Turn 7,** have them exchange papers. A partner may be better able to spot overused adverbs. Have students submit "Before" and "After" versions of their essays.

TECHNOLOGY TIP

Even if your school computers are not arranged in a network, students can evaluate and revise each other's essays by using highlighting techniques and typing comments next to the highlighted text. Students can save their work on disks, and other students can work with the disks.

Point out to students that they can use the find function of most word-processing programs to locate key words in their papers. Locating key words will help students to revise the organization of their points of comparison and to eliminate repetition.

Quotation for the Day

"Sloppily prepared pieces, peppered with mechanical glitches that could easily have been caught and corrected by the writer, are rarely going to sell—and the few that do are bound to be heavily edited."

(David Petersen, 1946– , American author and editor)

Copy the quotation on the chalkboard or on an overhead transparency, and ask students to comment on what the author means by "sloppily prepared" and "mechanical glitches." Discuss why writing that has good content but displays poor spelling and grammar as well as typographical errors is not likely to be accepted without heavy revision.

Grammar Link

Using Comparative and Superlative Forms

ANSWERS

1. C
2. Of the two movies, this one is clearly the better.
3. Books are better than movies because they make you imagine.
4. C
5. Playing computer games for hours is worse than watching television all evening.

Publishing, pp. 82–83
Alignments
TEKS 2C, 2D, 2E, 3A, 3B, 3D
TAAS W3, W6, W7
English II End-of-Course 5, 6

Publishing

Proofread Your Essay

Reference Note
For more information and practice on **comparative and superlative forms,** see page 623.

Double-Check Yourself   Be sure your essay is free of grammar, spelling, and punctuation errors. Check for proper use of comparative and superlative forms of modifiers (adjectives and adverbs) because they are frequently used in comparison-contrast writing.

Grammar Link

Using Comparative and Superlative Forms

When you compare or contrast two subjects, you will often rely on **adjectives and adverbs** to make comparisons. These modifiers change form to show different degrees of comparison: **positive, comparative,** and **superlative.**

- Most one-syllable modifiers form the comparative degree by adding *–er* and the superlative degree by adding *–est.*

  big   bigger   biggest

- The same is true for most two-syllable modifiers, but they may also form the comparative degree by using *more* and the superlative degree by using *most.*

  quickly   more quickly   most quickly

- Modifiers that have three or more syllables always use *more* and *most.*

  dramatic   more dramatic   most dramatic

- The comparative and superlative forms of some modifiers are irregular.

  good   better   best

  Use the **comparative degree** when comparing *two* items; use the **superlative degree** when comparing *more than two* items.

| Comparative | Ala likes biology better than chemistry. |
| Superlative | Of all her classes, she likes math best. |

Avoid double comparisons. A **double comparison** is one that uses both *–er* and *more* (or *less*) or *–est* and *most* (or *least*).

| Incorrect | more louder, least brightest |
| Correct | louder, least bright |

PRACTICE

Read each sentence below. Correct any incorrect modifiers. If the sentence is correct, write **C.** Write your answers on your own paper.

1. Juan thinks that writing with a computer is easier than writing with pencil and paper.
2. Of the two movies, this one is clearly the best.
3. Books are more better than movies because they make you imagine.
4. Newspapers give more in-depth information than television news shows.
5. Playing computer games for hours is badder than watching television all evening.

82   Chapter 2   Exposition: Exploring Comparisons and Contrasts

RESOURCES

Grammar Link
Practice
- *Communications,* WS. p. 41

Publish Your Essay

Tell the World Here is a list of ideas for publishing your comparison-contrast essay.

- If your essay is about two subjects that are appropriate for a particular section of your school newspaper (sports, entertainment, and so on), try to get your paper published in the newspaper.
- If your essay is about two subjects that might interest other students (two movies or two CDs, for instance), post your paper where everyone in the class can read it. You might also make copies of your paper to pass out to class members.
- If you can find a Web site that deals with one or both of the subjects of your essay—and that publishes outside material—submit your essay to the site for publication.

TIP Remember to create a title for your essay. The title should give your readers a clue to your thesis. If you need help thinking of a title, look for the most memorable phrase in your essay.

PORTFOLIO

Reflect on Your Essay

Looking Back Think about and jot down answers to the following questions. Your answers will increase your awareness of what you have learned in this workshop.

- How easy or hard was it to identify the relevant features that supported your thesis? What might you try next time to refine your process?
- What new things did you learn about the subjects you compared or contrasted?
- What do you think is the most important revision you made to your writing? Why?

If you put your essay in your portfolio, be sure to include your responses to the above questions.

YOUR TURN 8 — Proofreading, Publishing, and Reflecting

Review each of the sections on this page and on the previous page. Before you hand in your comparison-contrast essay, be sure you have

- proofread your writing carefully
- considered how to publish your work
- answered the reflecting questions above

Connections to Life

Distinguishing the Purposes of Media Forms

Media Purposes Every day, you are surrounded by messages from various **media forms,** such as radio, television, newspapers, magazines, compact discs, and the Internet. Just as you have a purpose when you write, each media message you see or hear is created by someone with a purpose in mind. Using comparison and contrast techniques can help you analyze those messages and understand the purposes behind them as an important part of being an informed, active media consumer.

Media Genres In order to analyze media purposes, you must understand media *genres.* **Genres** are categories into which media products can be classified. For example, genres of television shows include news broadcasts, game shows, soap operas, and talk shows. Each genre generally has one primary purpose that it has been created to fulfill. The following chart describes four common purposes of media messages and gives examples of some media genres that fulfill these purposes.

MEDIA PURPOSES		
Purpose	**Explanation**	**Genres**
to inform	These messages primarily provide information.	• TV and radio news programs • news articles in newspapers • educational Web sites • magazine articles
to entertain	These messages use drama, comedy, or other means to engage an audience.	• movies • TV dramas and sitcoms (situation comedies) • comic books • novels
to advertise	These messages attempt to persuade an audience to buy something or take some sort of action.	• TV and radio commercials • banner advertisements on Web pages • billboards • movie previews
to teach	These messages show an audience how to do something, or they explain concepts or subjects of study.	• "how-to" TV shows and videos, such as those that teach how to cook or repair a car • textbooks educational journals, magazines, and newspapers

Mixed Purposes Although we usually associate a media genre with one **primary purpose**, most genres also have at least one **secondary purpose**. For example, a TV commercial's primary purpose may be to advertise a product, but it may also try to entertain in order to keep the viewer's interest. A "how-to" video might teach how to repair a car's brakes and also give information on different kinds of brakes and how they work.

Sometimes it is hard to determine the primary purpose of a media genre because it may have a disguised purpose. Consider, for instance, the **infomercial.** Infomercials are advertisements (commercials) disguised as informational programs. Although they do always give a great deal of information about the product they advertise, infomercials are created with a single goal: to sell a product.

Another media genre with mixed or disguised purposes is the **infotainment program.** These programs can be highly informative and highly entertaining at the same time. An example of an infotainment program is a children's TV show that teaches science in a way that is entertaining and appealing to children.

A third media genre, the **docudrama,** presents factual or historical information in a dramatic format. The reenacted life story of a famous person, for instance, would be classified as a docudrama. Like the children's science show, docudramas are meant to be both informative and entertaining.

It's That Important The fact that most media genres have mixed purposes can make identifying a particular message's purpose difficult. However, identifying media purposes is a vital part of analyzing media. Knowing why a message was created helps you understand a message's intended effect on you, and it will allow you to evaluate whether the message accomplishes its purpose. In addition, a knowledge of mixed purposes can help you create your own highly effective media messages.

YOUR TURN 9 — Distinguishing Media Purposes

Select three different types of media messages. For example, you might choose a billboard, a radio talk show, and an Internet Web site. For each message, identify the media form used to deliver the message, the message's genre, and the purposes you believe the message is meant to fulfill. To identify purposes, ask yourself

- what the message's creators hope to gain
- what action the creators want you to take
- why the creators chose this media form for their message

From those purposes, identify the message's primary purpose and one or more secondary purposes. Be prepared to discuss your findings with the rest of your class and to explain your conclusions.

TEACHING TIP
Distinguishing Media Purposes

Students who do not have access to TV programming or the Internet may work with print media such as newspapers and magazines. You may want to provide printed materials in the classroom for students to use, or tape TV or radio programming for students to study at school.

YOUR TURN 9

Have students use a chart such as this to organize their findings. Using a chart will help students complete each part of the activity and will make it easier for you to check each of the steps.

Media Message	Media Form	Genre	Purpose
1.			
2.			
3.			

Focus on Viewing and Representing

OBJECTIVES

- To compare and contrast media messages
- To analyze how news stories are put together
- To compare and contrast different media coverage of the same event

Quotation for the Day

"... [T]he medium is the message."
(Herbert Marshall McLuhan, 1911–1980, Canadian philosopher and media expert)

Discuss with students the connection between the method of delivery and the content of some media messages with which students are familiar. Does the medium affect the message? How? One way to answer the question is to imagine the message in another medium. Remind students of the various types of media, including TV, radio, newspapers, magazines, and Internet sources.

Focus on Viewing and Representing

WHAT'S AHEAD?

In this section, you will compare and contrast media messages. You will also learn to

- analyze how news stories are put together
- compare and contrast different media coverage of the same event

Comparing and Contrasting Media Coverage

Ask two friends to tell you what happened in geometry class when you were absent, and chances are you will hear two different **accounts,** or retellings, of what happened. "We talked about how to calculate the area of a circle and then reviewed yesterday's homework," one friend tells you. "First, Ms. Garcia passed back yesterday's homework for a class review," another says. Although your friends start with the same basic facts, they construct different accounts by focusing on different details. The truth is people rarely retell events in exactly the same way.

Looking at the News

How They Put It Together   Just as people rarely retell events in the same way, media sources often give differing accounts of a news event. This is because all news stories—on TV, on the radio, in magazines, in newspapers, and on the Internet—are *constructions* of events. Just as your friends decide which details to include when they retell a story, news writers and editors make **editorial decisions** about how news stories are put together. It is important to be aware of these editorial decisions because, whether intentional or not, the news you see, read, or hear may present only one side of the story and may carry personal or political bias.

Perception or Reality?   The editorial decisions writers and editors make shape your view of events. Compare your reactions to the following headlines describing the same event:

Files Missing from Government Office
FBI Officials Say Top-Secret Files Lost

86   Chapter 2   Exposition: Exploring Comparisons and Contrasts

---

RESOURCES

Focus on Viewing and Representing Practice

- *Media Literacy and Communication Skills*
  —*Support and Practice,* Ch. 2
  —*A How-to Handbook*

Teaching Notes

- *Media Literacy and Communication Skills*
  —*A Teacher's Guide,* Ch. 2

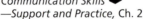

Did you react more strongly to one of the headlines? Did the headlines cause you to picture the same event differently? The second headline was probably more attention getting. It mentions the FBI, an important government agency, and labels the missing files as "top secret." The first headline is less specific and, therefore, less interesting.

By comparing how different media sources present the same story, you can see the types of editorial decisions media professionals make to affect your perception of events. Two aspects of news stories that vary depending on editorial decisions are **attention getters**—how words, images, and sounds are arranged to get attention—and **point of view**—the writer's angle, or viewpoint, on the subject. When you view or read a news story, be aware of how the writers or producers handle both aspects.

Attention Getters Media sources compete for your attention. To get you to pay more attention to *its own* media messages, each media source uses its own unique blend of three common **attention-getting techniques:**

- **Controversy**—focusing on an issue that stirs opposing views in readers or viewers. (For example, a source might use a quotation or a sound bite from someone blaming damages on some person or group.)
- **Suspense**—designing the narrative to create curiosity in viewers or readers about the outcome of an event. (For example, a news article or TV news report might begin with, "Yesterday this family had a home. Today, they're living with nearby relatives.")
- **Juxtaposition**—placing opposing images or words near each other to create tension. (For example, a media source might show "before" and "after" photos or video of a town devastated by a tornado.)

Media professionals make key editorial decisions about how to arrange words, sounds, and images for the greatest impact. Depending on the form of the message, news stories usually include one or more of the following **attention-getting elements** to draw you in. These elements are easily recognized if you are looking out for them.

- **Headlines** are brief summaries printed in larger type at the top of a newspaper, magazine, or Internet news article. Some TV news programs begin with summary descriptions of the top stories.
- **Startling images** include shocking photographs (newspapers, magazines, or Internet) or video images (television or Internet) of an event.
- **Teasers** are promotional messages for news stories that will appear in an upcoming broadcast, often including startling images (see above) and brief, often alarming, statements designed to entice you into watching an

> **TIP** Keep in mind these other aspects of news stories also determined by editorial decisions:
> - **Complexity**—the level of detail given about the subject, including background information and details from multiple sources
> - **Sequence of information**—the order in which the story is presented
> - **Emotional impact**—the story's appeal to its audience's feelings rather than reason

TEACHING TIP

Attention Getters
Share extreme examples of attention-getting elements with students, such as headlines in tabloid newspapers or magazines or startling images or teasers in advertisements or commercials. Have students compare these elements with the information actually provided. Point out that media forms may distort the facts to grab readers', listeners', or viewers' attention.

Meeting INDIVIDUAL NEEDS

MULTIPLE INTELLIGENCES
Linguistic Intelligence. Point out to students that the difference between a mundane headline and an attention getter is often like the difference between a passive verb and an active verb. When looking for attention-getting headlines, students should look for verbs performing a vivid action.

Focus on Viewing and Representing, pp. 86–88
Alignments
TEKS 20A, 20B, 20C, 20D, 20F

TECHNOLOGY TIP

Students may wish to search online editions of newspapers and magazines for articles to evaluate. Make sure that students access a complete article and not simply a synopsis. *You need to be aware that Internet resources are sometimes public forums, and their content can be unpredictable.*

YOUR TURN 10

Have students work in pairs or small groups and share their findings with the rest of the class in an oral presentation or as a poster or chart. Students can use a chart to help display their findings.

Medium	Attention-Getting Technique	Point of View	Evaluation

Wrap It Up

Metacognition. Have each student reflect on and respond to the following questions:

1. How has what you have learned in this section of the chapter affected the way you evaluate news items? Why?

Then, have students answer the following questions:

2. What are three common attention-getting techniques? [controversy, suspense, juxtaposition] What are three attention-getting elements found in news stories? [headlines, startling images, teasers]

3. What is *point of view* in a news story? [the angle a news report takes on the reported event]

---

upcoming news broadcast. Newspapers, magazines, and Internet news sites occasionally include teasers about articles in future editions.

Point of View: Not Just the Facts Most of us assume that news stories are objective accounts that contain only the facts about an event. Honest media professionals try to avoid distorting the facts with personal interpretations and subjective statements. However, they must also make choices about what angle—or **point of view**—to use in a news story. By identifying the point of view that a news report is taking, you can keep your mind open to, and possibly search for, alternative points of view. When you examine more than one point of view, you are better able to make your own informed decisions about the news being presented. To explore a media source's point of view, answer the following questions about a news story.

- **What terms are used to describe the main subject? Are these terms positive or negative?** For example, a politician might be described in one article as a rabble-rouser but as a statesman in another article.

- **How is the main subject shown in visual images?** Is the photograph or video of the subject flattering, or is it unfavorable? How is the subject dressed? What is in the background? Is the lighting bright or dark?

- **What kind of sources are used in the story?** Does the story include statements only from people on one side of the issue?

YOUR TURN 10 Comparing and Contrasting Media Coverage of an Event

Find a news story that was covered in at least two different news media—newspapers, magazines, TV, or the Internet. Choose two of the news sources, and find examples of attention-getting techniques and elements in each one. Identify the point of view in each story. Then, compare and contrast each media source's coverage of the event by writing answers to the following questions. Be prepared to share your answers with the class.

- How did the attention-getting techniques in each story shape your impression of the event? How would your view of the event be different if your knowledge of it came from only one of these stories?

- Did the stories have similar points of view, or did they differ? Give evidence to support your answer.

- Do you think one media source did a better job of covering the event? Why do you think so?

Chapter 2   Exposition: Exploring Comparisons and Contrasts

RESOURCES

Your Turn 10

Practice and Reinforcement

- *Media Literary and Communication Skills*
  —*Support and Practice*, Ch. 2, transparencies and worksheets
  —Videocassette 1, Segment B

CHAPTER 2 Choices

Choose one of the following activities to complete.

▶ CAREERS

1. Chart Your Future Like most students your age, you are probably facing decisions about what you will do when you graduate from high school. Perhaps you are comparing schools to attend or jobs to pursue. To help you make your decisions, use what you know about comparison and contrast. Make a chart like the Relevant Features chart you created in the prewriting section of the Writing Workshop (page 70). In it, list all of the relevant features of the subjects (careers, for example, or different colleges) you are comparing. Then, write a **paragraph** that synthesizes the information in the chart.

▶ LITERATURE

2. Movie vs. Book Think of a movie you have seen that is based on a book. Select a scene from the movie, and read or re-read the corresponding portion of the book. Then, create a **chart** or other graphic that shows the similarities and differences between the movie version and the book. Post your chart or graphic in your classroom or somewhere else at your school.

▶ SPEAKING AND LISTENING

3. People Are Talking Imagine that you are a news reporter, perhaps for your school newspaper. Think of an event that happened in your community or school recently, making sure that it is an event you did not witness. Ask two friends separately to tell you their accounts of the event. With your friends' permission, create a two-column list to compare and contrast their accounts. Then, integrate your two friends' stories into your own retelling of the event. Make a **tape-recording** of your story.

▶ CROSSING THE CURRICULUM: SCIENCE

4. Concentrate on Comparisons Many chemical compounds that look similar are actually very different. For instance, it might be difficult to tell the difference between an unlabeled bottle of ammonia and an unlabeled bottle of water just by looking at them. Choose two chemical compounds that look very similar, and write a short **explanation** of how to tell them apart.

▶ CAREERS

Encourage students to gather information by consulting guidance counselors, individuals who have pursued the educational or career paths they are considering, or Internet college or career sites. *(You need to be aware that Internet resources are sometimes public forums, and their content can be unpredictable.)* Suggest that students focus on the three most important points of comparison in their paragraphs.

▶ LITERATURE

To get started, have the class brainstorm a list of movies based on books. Students who do not have easy access to movies on TV, on video, or in the theater might compare books with similar plots in the same genre or books by the same author and focus on aspects such as characterization and plot.

▶ SPEAKING AND LISTENING

You may wish to create guidelines regarding the kinds of events that can be covered, explaining that real journalists also have guidelines to follow. Guidelines that have students focus on newsworthy events will eliminate stories that focus on people or personalities. If you have students play their tapes in class, preview their content.

▶ CROSSING THE CURRICULUM: SCIENCE

Ask a science teacher to help students select similar compounds and identify their properties. Students should not handle or experiment with compounds without teacher supervision. Offer students the option of presenting their comparisons in the form of a poster.

RESOURCES

Exploring Comparisons and Contrasts Assessment
- *Assessment Package*
  —Chapter Tests, Ch. 2
  —Chapter Tests in Standardized Test Formats, Ch. 2
  —Assessment Alternatives, Ch. 2

- *Test Generator* (One-Stop Planner CD-ROM)

Choices Rubrics
- *Assessment Package*
  —Assessment Alternatives, Ch. 2

Choices Alignments
Choice 1   TEKS 4B, 4D, 4F; TAAS W4
Choice 2   TEKS 7D, 10B, 20F
Choice 3   TEKS 1A, 2A; TAAS W1
Choice 4   TEKS 1A, 2A; TAAS W1

CHAPTER 3

Examining Causes and Effects

Use this guide to create an instructional plan that suits the individual needs of your students. Assignments marked by an asterisk (*) may be completed out of class. Times given for pacing lessons are estimated. See pp. 90–91 for chapterwide resources. Resources listed in this guide are point-of-use resources only.

Curriculum Connections

Choices *p. 125*
- Viewing and Representing
- Crossing the Curriculum: Arts & Science
- Crossing the Curriculum: Literature

internet connect
GO TO: go.hrw.com
KEYWORD: EOLang 10-3

All resources for this chapter are available for preview on the *One-Stop Planner CD-ROM with Test Generator*. All worksheets and tests may be printed from the CD-ROM.

Texas Resources For a complete listing of all resources prepared for Texas teachers and students, please see the blue box at the beginning of each chapter.

T89A

		Chapter Opener pp. 90–91	Reading Workshop: Reading a Cause-and-Effect Article pp. 92–103
DEVELOPMENTAL PROGRAM		**30 minutes** • Cause and Effect *p. 91* • Your Turn 1 in groups *p. 91*	**100 minutes** • Preparing to Read *p. 92* • Reading Selection *pp. 93–94* • First Thoughts on Your Reading 1–2 in groups *p. 95* • Inferring Causes and Effects *pp. 95–96* • Your Turn 2 in groups *p. 97* • Cause-and-Effect Structure *pp. 97–100* • Your Turn 3 *p. 101* • Test Taking Mini-Lesson *p. 103*
CORE PROGRAM		**20 minutes** • Cause and Effect *p. 91* • Your Turn 1 *p. 91*	**90 minutes** • Preparing to Read *p. 92* • Reading Selection *pp. 93–94* • First Thoughts on Your Reading 1–3 *p. 95* • Inferring Causes and Effects *pp. 95–96* • Your Turn 2 *p. 97* • Cause-and-Effect Structure *pp. 97–100* • Your Turn 3 *p. 101* • Vocabulary Mini-Lesson *p. 102* • Test Taking Mini-Lesson *p. 103*
ADVANCED PROGRAM		**10 minutes** • Cause and Effect *p. 91* • Your Turn 1 *p. 91*	**70 minutes** • Preparing to Read *p. 92* • Reading Selection *pp. 93–94* • First Thoughts on Your Reading 3 *p. 95* • Inferring Causes and Effects *pp. 95–96* • Your Turn 2 *p. 97* • Cause-and-Effect Structure *pp. 97–100* • Your Turn 3 *p. 101* • Vocabulary Mini-Lesson *p. 102*
RESOURCES	**PRINT**	• *Communications,* TP. 24, WS. p. 42	• *Alternative Readings,* Ch. 3 • *Communications,* TPs. 25, 26, WS. pp. 43–50
	MEDIA	• *One-Stop Planner CD-ROM*	• *One-Stop Planner CD-ROM*

TP.=Transparency   WS.=Worksheet

Writing Workshop: Writing a Cause-and-Effect Explanation pp. 104–121	**Focus on Viewing and Representing: Analyzing the Effects of TV** pp. 122–124
⏱ **180 minutes** • Choose a Situation or Event pp. 104–105 • Narrow Your Topic p. 105 • Consider Purpose, Audience, and Tone pp. 105–106 • Write Your Thesis pp. 106–107 • Gather and Organize Support; Your Turn 4 p. 109 • Framework and Your Turn 5* p. 110 • Writer's Model and Student's Model pp. 111–113 • Evaluate and Revise and Your Turn 6* pp. 114–115 • Focus on Sentences and Your Turn 7 pp. 116–117 • Proofread, Publish, and Reflect pp. 118–119 • Grammar Link p. 118 • Your Turn 8 p. 119	⏱ **30 minutes** • Television and the Real World pp. 122–124 • Your Turn 10 p. 124
⏱ **160 minutes** • Choose a Situation or Event pp. 104–105 • Narrow Your Topic p. 105 • Consider Purpose, Audience, and Tone pp. 105–106 • Write Your Thesis pp. 106–107 • Critical Thinking Mini-Lesson p. 108 • Gather and Organize Support; Your Turn 4 p. 109 • Framework and Your Turn 5* p. 110 • Writer's Model and Student's Model pp. 111–113 • Evaluate and Revise and Your Turn 6* pp. 114–115 • Focus on Sentences and Your Turn 7 pp. 116–117 • Proofread, Publish, and Reflect pp. 118–119 • Grammar Link p. 118 • Your Turn 8 p. 119 • Connections to Life and Your Turn 9 pp. 120–121	⏱ **20 minutes** • Television and the Real World pp. 122–124 • Your Turn 10 p. 124
⏱ **120 minutes** • Choose a Situation or Event pp. 104–105 • Narrow Your Topic p. 105 • Consider Purpose, Audience, and Tone pp. 105–106 • Write Your Thesis pp. 106–107 • Critical Thinking Mini-Lesson p. 108 • Your Turn 4 p. 109 • Framework and Your Turn 5* p. 110 • Writer's Model and Student's Model pp. 111–113 • Your Turn 6* p. 115 • Focus on Sentences and Your Turn 7 pp. 116–117 • Proofread, Publish, and Reflect pp. 118–119 • Your Turn 8 p. 119 • Connections to Life and Your Turn 9 pp. 120–121	⏱ **20 minutes** • Television and the Real World pp. 122–124 • Your Turn 10 p. 124
• *Communications*, TPs. 27–30, WS. pp. 51–59 • *Designing Your Writing*	• *Media Literacy and Communication Skills Kit* —*Support and Practice*, Ch. 3 —*A How-to Handbook* —*A Teacher's Guide*, Ch. 3
• *One-Stop Planner CD-ROM*	• *Media Literacy and Communication Skills Kit* —Videocassette 1, Segment C • *One-Stop Planner CD-ROM*

CHAPTER 3
Examining Causes and Effects

CHAPTER OBJECTIVES

- To read a cause-and-effect article and examine its structure
- To write a cause-and-effect explanation
- To analyze how TV affects the way viewers see the world

Chapter Overview

Causes and effects are vital to most explanations of events. In this chapter, students will learn to recognize and use cause-and-effect patterns as readers, writers, and viewers. The Reading Workshop is structured around an article that demonstrates cause-and-effect patterns and requires students to infer causes and effects that are not directly stated. The Writing Workshop offers students an opportunity to write cause-and-effect explanations of their own, and the Focus on Viewing and Representing helps students understand how television affects their view of the world. Although each section of the chapter may be taught separately, students usually gain a more thorough understanding of cause and effect if the three sections are taught as a unit.

Why Study Cause and Effect?

Cause and effect is the basic structure of most actions and reactions in both the natural world and society. Studying cause and effect not only makes students more aware of relationships between events in their world but also teaches them that their actions and behaviors have consequences. An awareness of causes and effects and causal chains helps students identify connections between events and recognize linkages between themselves and others.

Teaching the Chapter

Option 1: Begin with Literature

If you prefer to examine cause and effect in literature first, you could introduce the chapter after studying cause-and-effect relationships in novels, dramas, epics, or short stories. In any of these genres, you might emphasize how characters affect each other, how events cause characters to change or behave in certain ways, or how characters affect the complications and outcome of the plot. After they look at cause-and-effect relationships in literature, have students read the article in the Reading Workshop and identify causes and effects and their uses in nonfiction. Examining cause-and-effect relationships in various genres will prepare students to write their own cause-and-effect explanations.

Option 2: Begin with Nonfiction and Writing

Use the material in this chapter to introduce cause-and-effect relationships to students. The cause-and-effect article and accompanying instruction in the Reading

Workshop (pp. 93–101) illustrate cause-and-effect structure and give students practice making inferences about causes and effects that may not be obvious. Students may apply these concepts and skills in the Writing Workshop (pp. 104–119) as they plan, write, revise, and publish their own cause-and-effect essays. With this foundation in recognizing and setting up cause-and-effect relationships in reading and writing nonfiction, students will be better able to identify such relationships in literature.

Making Connections

■ To the Literature Curriculum

Cause-and-effect relationships are a basic component of literature. Erma Bombeck's personal essay "Daddy Doll Under the Bed," Anna Akhmatova's poem "I am not one of those who left the land," and William Shakespeare's play *The Tragedy of Julius Caesar* show the effects of a father's death, the causes of an exile's suffering, and the motives and results of two rivals' actions. Causes and effects shape conflicts and resolutions as well as events in stories.

Lesson Idea: Cause and Effect in *The Tragedy of Julius Caesar* by William Shakespeare

1. In a class discussion, brainstorm a list of motives or reasons (causes) Brutus and Cassius had for killing Caesar. Make a separate list for each character and label the motives as noble or selfish.

2. The actions of Brutus and Cassius affected not only the society in which they lived, but also the two characters themselves. Help students identify the effects for each character.

3. Prompt students to discuss each character's motives and the effects of their actions, identifying similarities and differences between them. Then, discuss Brutus's choice of actions and how he might have tried more wisely to protect Rome from Caesar. Finally, consider how good motives coupled with unwise actions can lead to negative effects.

4. After discussion, direct students' attention to the article on pp. 93–94. Point out that the article, like Shakespeare's play, illustrates unexpected effects from a particular cause. Use the instruction on cause-and-effect organizational patterns and on inferring causes and effects to ready students to write their own cause-and-effect essays.

■ To Careers

This chapter is designed to complement your literature book by relating cause and effect to students' experiences both in school and out of school. Invite a small business owner or human resources manager from a local company to talk to your class about qualities, behaviors, and actions that lead to promotions and raises or loss of a job. Tell students to take notes during the talk to develop a list of reasons people are promoted, given a raise, or lose their jobs. Following the visit, have students work in small groups to create a poster-size diagram that shows the cause-and-effect relationship between workplace habits and behaviors and promotions and raises or loss of employment.

■ To the Community

The article in the Reading Workshop may provide students with a new perspective on forest fires. To help students see a relationship between what they are learning and their world, encourage interested students to investigate local policies regarding wildfire management or controlled burning. Then, discuss the causes and effects of the policies. Compare the effects of such policies with the effects of wildfires like those in Yellowstone. Is controlled burning a good idea? Why or why not?

■ To the Social Studies Curriculum

Students are often called on to identify and analyze cause and effect in their study of history. Take time in class to hold a workshop on how to implement a cause-and-effect chart. Have students draw a line down the center of one page to create two columns with the following headings: *What happened? (Cause)* and *What was the result? (Effect)*. Then, ask students to work in pairs to review a history text and enter three incidents from the text in the chart. Also, suggest that students keep a reader's journal in which they can note their speculations about causes and effects as they read their history texts. Remind students that one cause may have more than one effect or that more than one cause may have the same effect.

T89D

CHAPTER 3

Examining Causes and Effects

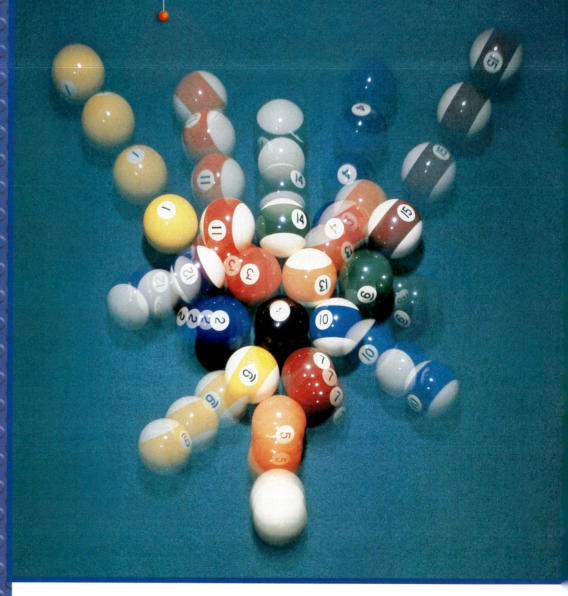

PREVIEWING THE CHAPTER

- The three workshops in this chapter examine causes and effects. The workshops may be taught separately, but taught together they provide a complete view of cause-and-effect relationships. After reading a cause-and-effect article, students follow the steps in the writing process to compose their own cause-and-effect essays. Reading and writing about causes and effects prepares students to analyze the effects of TV through a comparison of TV representations and real life. To integrate this chapter with grammar, usage, and mechanics chapters, see pp. T401A–T401B.

INTRODUCING THE CHAPTER

- To introduce the chapter, use the Journal Warm-up, Transparency 24, in *Communications*.

VIEWING THE PHOTOGRAPH (19A)

- The stroboscopic photograph shows the effect of a white cue ball striking a group of billiard balls. A stroboscope is a device that flashes light at the rate of 100 flashes per second. The frequency of the flashes allows the eye (or camera) to see minute changes in an object's movement. Point out how the photo reveals causes and effects. [The photo shows the cause of the movement, the white cue ball striking the group of balls; and the effect, the movement of the billiard balls outward after the cue ball strikes the group.]

CHAPTER RESOURCES

Planning
- *Lesson Planner*, Ch. 3
- Block Scheduling, p. T89A (this book)
- One-Stop Planner CD-ROM

Practice
- *Communications*, Ch. 3
- *Media Literacy and Communication Skills*

- *Writer's Workshop 2 CD-ROM*

Extension
- *Designing Your Writing*

Reinforcement
- *Communications*, Ch. 3
- *Alternative Readings*, Ch. 3

PREVIEW

Reading Workshop

Reading a Cause-and-Effect Article
PAGE 92

Writing Workshop

Writing a Cause-and-Effect Explanation
PAGE 104

Focus on Viewing and Representing

Analyzing the Effects of TV
PAGE 122

Curiosity is a basic human characteristic. From the time you began to talk, "Why?" was probably one of your favorite questions: "Why does it get dark?" or "Why do I have blue eyes while my friend has brown eyes?" As you grew older you probably began to ask "What-if" questions. For example, you might have wondered "What if I become a lawyer?" "What if I take Spanish class instead of French?" or "What if my parents really *are* space aliens?"

When you began to ask yourself these questions, you started to develop the skill of examining **cause-and-effect relationships**—a process also known as **causal analysis**. Curiosity about causes and effects accounts for much of the human knowledge in the world. People have searched for the causes of diseases, tidal currents, blue skies, and rainbows. People have also wondered about the effects of sailing west to India, earthquakes, and pet ownership.

internet connect
GO TO: go.hrw.com
KEYWORD: EOLang 10-3

YOUR TURN 1 — Considering Causes and Effects

To gain a better understanding of the importance of causes and effects in the world around you, write down at least five inventions that are part of the world in which you live. With a classmate, make a list of the possible **causes** that drove each inventor to come up with the idea for each invention. Think about how the world has changed because of these inventions. Then, write down a few of the positive and a few of the negative **effects** of these inventions.

Motivate

Point out to students that they have been dealing with causes and effects since they first started exploring the world as small children. Many behaviors and activities they engage in they do to have a desired effect. They brush their teeth to avoid cavities. They play a sport to have fun and exercise. Have students list behaviors from childhood and the present, the reasons (causes) for them, and their desired and actual effects.

Cause and Effect in Literature.
In *Elements of Literature*, Fourth Course, examples of characters who deal with causes and effects are in Sophocles' *Antigone*, pp. 691–737 and in *I Never Sang for My Father* by Robert Anderson, pp. 636–675.

YOUR TURN 1

If students have difficulty identifying inventions, tell them to make a list of everyday items that make our lives easier. To help students generate a list of causes and effects, ask them to imagine what life was like before the items were available and how life changed afterward.

Preview   91

- Daily Language Activity Transparencies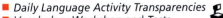
- Vocabulary Workshop and Tests

Evaluation and Assessment
- Assessment Package
  —*Chapter Tests*, Ch. 3
  —*Chapter Tests in Standardized Test Formats*, Ch. 3
  —*Assessment Alternatives*, Ch. 3

- Test Generator
  (One-Stop Planner CD-ROM)

Internet
- go.hrw.com
  (keyword: EOLang 10-3)

Chapter Opener, pp. 90–91
Alignments
TEKS 16B, 16F

Texas Resources
- *Lesson Planner*, Ch. 3
- *TAAS Tool Kit*
- *Preparation for TAAS*
- *Preparing for English II End-of-Course Examination*
- *One-Stop Planner CD-ROM*

Preview   **91**

Reading Workshop

OBJECTIVES

- To read a cause-and-effect article in preparation for writing a cause-and-effect explanation
- To infer causes and effects
- To analyze cause-and-effect patterns
- To use suffixes to identify the meanings of unfamiliar words

Quotation for the Day

"Shallow men believe in luck. . . . Strong men believe in cause and effect."

(Ralph Waldo Emerson, 1803–1882, American poet, essayist, and philosopher)

Write the quotation on the chalkboard or on an overhead transparency, and ask students to freewrite for five minutes about what the quotation means to them. Then invite students to share their interpretations of Emerson's observation.

TEACHING TIP

Preparing to Read
The brief section preceding the Reading Selection describes methods and structures that will be treated at greater length on pp. 95–100. Inferring causes and effects and cause-and-effect structures form the instructional basis of the Reading Workshop. The reading selection **"Yellowstone Makes a Triumphant Return Ten Years After Fires"** illustrates cause-and-effect patterns and requires students to practice inferring cause-and-effect relationships.

RESOURCES

Reading Workshop Reinforcement
- *Alternative Readings,* Ch. 3

Reading Workshop

Reading a Cause-and-Effect Article

WHAT'S AHEAD?

In this section, you will read a newspaper article and learn how to
- infer causes and effects
- analyze cause-and-effect patterns

"Fire! Fire!" someone yells. What do you do? You move fast because you know that fires can be dangerous and destructive. In newspapers and on television, you have seen dramatic images of raging fires destroying buildings or forests. Keep in mind, however, that although news stories typically focus on the negative effects of fire, fires can also have positive effects. The article on the next page, "Yellowstone Makes a Triumphant Return Ten Years After Fires," describes the positive effects that the massive forest fires of 1988 had on Yellowstone National Park.

Preparing to Read

READING SKILL

Inferring Causes and Effects Often when you read, you recognize a cause-and-effect relationship because the writer directly states that relationship. At other times, the relationships are less obvious, and you have to make an **inference**—an educated guess based on your own knowledge and experience—about the causes or the effects. The article on the next page deals with several cause-and-effect relationships. The writer directly states some; others are not as obvious.

READING FOCUS

Cause-and-Effect Structure Writers organize their explanations of cause-and-effect relationships by focusing on **causes,** on **effects,** or on **causal chains.** (Causal chains begin with the first cause and follow with a series of intermediate actions or events to the final effect.) For example, an essay focusing on causes identifies and explains several causes of one effect. An essay focusing on effects identifies and explains several effects resulting from one cause. An essay focusing on a causal chain identifies and explains multiple causes and effects. As you read the following article, see if you can tell whether the author focuses on causes, on effects, or on a causal chain.

Chapter 3   **Exposition:** Examining Causes and Effects

READING PROCESS

PREREADING (7B)
Activate Prior Knowledge. Before assigning the Reading Selection, ask students to respond to the following questions in the context of a class discussion.
1. What causes forest fires?
2. How do fires affect wildlife and the environment in general?

Reading Selection

The following article from the *Austin American-Statesman* describes the effects that the immense forest fires of 1988 had on the wild lands of Yellowstone National Park. As you read, jot down answers to the numbered active-reading questions.

Yellowstone Makes a Triumphant Return Ten Years After Fires

BY BRUCE BABBITT

What a difference a decade makes. Ten years ago this month, Yellowstone National Park was a sea of flames. Some of the largest wildfires in U.S. history swept restlessly across the park's magnificent terrain, incinerating forests, threatening historic buildings. The news media and politicians fanned the flames even higher. Yellowstone, they said, was devastated.

Night after night, horrific images of ash and flame flashed across America's TV screens. One evening, after showing an enormous expanse of blackened forest, network news anchor Tom Brokaw solemnly concluded: "This is what's left of Yellowstone tonight."

But guess what? Fire didn't destroy Yellowstone. Ten years later, we realize fire had the opposite effect. Fire rejuvenated Yellowstone. Elk and other wildlife are healthy. Tourism is thriving. Biodiversity is booming. New forests are rising from the ashes of old ones. The recovery is so dramatic it deserves a closer look.

First, a bit of background: The 1988 fires were gigantic. They swept over roughly 793,000 of Yellowstone's 2.2 million acres—one third of the park. Some were lightning-caused; others were of human origin. The $120 million firefighting effort amassed against them has been called the largest in U.S. history. The heroic work saved many key structures. But in the wild lands, it made almost no difference. What put Yellowstone's fires out was not retardant-dropping planes or armies of firefighters on the ground. It was a quarter inch of autumn rain.

In July and August, as fires raged across the park, business owners fumed. Our future is ruined, they said. Tourism is dead. But today, tourism is very much alive. Yellowstone has set numerous visitation records since 1988. Fire has not repelled tourists; it has attracted them—just as it attracts many species of wildlife. Ten years later, the number one question asked of Yellowstone naturalists remains "What are the effects of the fires?"

The answer is simple: The fires were therapeutic. Since 1988, some seventy scientific research projects have looked

1. As the fires raged, what long-term consequences did people expect?

2. What caused the fires?

Connecting Reading and Writing

Have students note that Babbitt's article opens with the expected effects of the Yellowstone fires and then goes on to show how this perception of forest fires is not always correct. Discuss with students how a similar opening that debunks a popular perception could be effective in their own writing.

Active-Reading Questions
ANSWERS continued

3. The fires "planted" a new forest of lodgepole pines.

4. Controlled fires may be a way of protecting wildlife communities and making forests healthier.

5. grizzly bears, three-toed woodpeckers, mountain bluebirds, tree swallows, and other birds and mammals that nest in cavities

---

at various aspects of the Yellowstone fires. Not one has concluded the fires were harmful. That sounds too good to be true. But it is. The science is there to prove it.

Come to Yellowstone this summer and see for yourself. Pull off the road near Ice Lake, east of the Norris Geyser Basin. Here the fire burned especially savagely. Hundreds of thousands, perhaps millions, of mature lodgepole pine trees were destroyed. But today, the forest floor is a sea of green—knee-high lodgepoles planted, literally, by the fires of 1988.

Yellowstone's lodgepole forest is a place of mystery. In order to live, it must first die. It must burn. The fire that swept through here worked an ancient magic: It scorched lodgepole cones, melted their sticky resin, and freed the seeds locked inside. Within minutes, a new forest was planted.

By suppressing wildfire, as Smokey Bear has taught us to do, we interrupt nature's cycles. We rob our western forests of something they need desperately. We steal their season of rebirth. Without fire, pine forests grow senile, prone to disease, and unnaturally thick. There are lessons in these lodgepoles. Too much protection is no virtue. We can harm what we try to save. I'm not suggesting that we worship fire—that we let it run wild outside of natural parks and wilderness areas. But we can respect its wisdom. We can treat it, when possible, as an ally, not an enemy, and use it more frequently under controlled conditions to protect communities and make forests healthier.

Look closely around Ice Lake and you will almost surely see something else: wildlife. Bison, elk, mule deer, white-tailed deer, bighorn sheep, and mountain goats have all prospered since 1988. Just as fire rejuvenated lodgepoles, so, too, did it revitalize plants that grazing animals eat. Walt Disney got it wrong: Bambi and his forest friends have nothing to fear—and much to gain—from fire.

If you're lucky, you may also see Yellowstone's king of beasts: the grizzly bear. To a grizzly, wildfire is a meal ticket. Fires kill trees, which fall to the ground and fill up with insects: grizzly sushi. Others enjoy the feast, too. Before 1988, three-toed woodpeckers were almost nonexistent in Yellowstone. After 1988, one ornithologist spotted thirty in one day. But dead lodgepoles are more than lunch counters; they are housing opportunities, home sites for mountain bluebirds, tree swallows, and other "cavity-nesting" birds and mammals.

Ten years ago, the news media said fire "blackened" Yellowstone. Today, we know the reverse is true. Fire has painted the park brighter, added color and texture to its ecosystem, and increased the diversity and abundance of its species. As Yellowstone scientist John Varley put it recently, "The biodiversity story over the past ten years has been fascinating. Biodiversity has gone through a revolution at Yellowstone."

3. What is one effect of the Yellowstone fires?

4. What conclusion does the writer draw about forest fires?

5. What animals benefit from fallen trees?

READING PROCESS

READING
Make Predictions. Making predictions as they read will help students see how the author of the article develops the story of the causes and effects of the Yellowstone fires. Direct students to pause after reading every two or three paragraphs to write a quick prediction of how the article will end. When students have finished reading, ask them to share their series of predictions.

First Thoughts on Your Reading

Work with a partner to answer the following questions about "Yellowstone Makes a Triumphant Return." Jot down your answers on a sheet of paper.

1. The first two paragraphs of the article describe the fire and devastation of 1988. What reaction do you think the writer is trying to provoke in his readers?
2. Who do you think was the original intended audience for this article? Was it the general public? park service workers? Yellowstone business owners? What makes you think your choice is right?
3. What effect do you think the lessons taught by the 1988 Yellowstone fires will have on future conservation efforts?

Inferring Causes and Effects

Making a Connection When you read that one action or event is the result of another action or event, you are reading about a cause-and-effect relationship. A **cause** makes something happen; an **effect** is what happens as a result of that cause. The link between cause and effect can sometimes be very obvious; at other times you may be required to make an educated guess about the connection.

When writers want to make cause-and-effect relationships very obvious for the reader, they do so with clue words that signal the cause-and-effect relationship. The Yellowstone article, for example, notes that some of the fires were "lightning-*caused*." The relationship between lightning and the fires is very clearly signaled by the word *caused*. A few more words and phrases that can signal cause-and-effect relationships are

accordingly	because	effect	in order that	since
affect	cause	for	reason	therefore
as a result	consequently	if . . . then	results in	why

At times a writer only hints at a cause-and-effect relationship. In such cases, you will have to combine details in the text with your own knowledge and experience to make an educated guess about a cause-and-effect relationship. When you make an educated guess about probable causes or probable effects, you are **inferring** the presence of a cause-and-effect relationship that the writer has **implied**. For example, in "Yellowstone Makes a

READING SKILL

TIP Be careful. Sometimes clue words and phrases have uses unrelated to cause-and-effect relationships, as in the sentences, "His **cause** is just" or "She has not visited **since** she was a baby."

First Thoughts on Your Reading
ANSWERS
Possible answers are suggested below.

1. shock, concern, hopelessness

2. The general public; the author invites readers to visit the park and refers to wildlife and other sights tourists might see there. In addition, the author seems to be trying to explain the effects of the fires in terms the average person would understand, and the tone of the article is lighter than it might be if it were intended for park service workers or business owners.

3. Conservation efforts in the future may include the tolerance of fire to encourage new growth and healthy conditions in forests.

Discuss how students' predictions change as the emphasis of the article shifts and supporting details are added. Point out as well that the author guides the reader from the established belief that forest fires are devastating to the understanding that fires can renew forests.

Triumphant Return Ten Years After Fires," the writer states that though some fires were caused by lightning, "others were of human origin." The writer assumes that you are familiar enough with forest fires to infer what the "human" causes might have been: campers leaving a campfire unattended or out of control, or children playing with matches, for example.

THINKING IT THROUGH: Inferring Causes and Effects

You can use the following steps to infer, or make an educated guess, about implied cause-and-effect relationships. The process is modeled for you using a sentence from the article about the Yellowstone fires.

Example:
"Without fire, pine forests grow senile, prone to disease, and unnaturally thick."

▶ **STEP 1** Ask yourself, "What happens in the passage?" (What is the effect?) Forests become physically deteriorated, likely to contract diseases, and denser than they would naturally.

▶ **STEP 2** Ask, "Why does it happen?" (What is the cause?) The lack of fire.

▶ **STEP 3** Rewrite the passage using an explicit cause-and-effect signal word like *cause, effect,* or *because.* Notice that the *cause* is lack of fire; the *effect* is that the pine forests grow senile, prone to disease, and unnaturally thick. I can infer that the lack of fires causes pine forests to grow senile, prone to disease, and unnaturally thick.

You can also discover cause-and-effect relationships by paying careful attention to the verbs the writer uses. Certain verbs are **causative verbs**—verbs that express cause-and-effect relationships. For example, here is a sentence from the Yellowstone article: *Fire rejuvenated Yellowstone.* In this sentence, *rejuvenated* is a causative verb meaning "to make seem new or fresh again." The cause-and-effect relationship is built into the verb *rejuvenated.* Fire is the cause; making Yellowstone seem new or fresh again is the effect of fire. If you are unsure whether a verb is a causative verb, look it up in a dictionary to see whether the verb describes an effect one thing has on another. Here are some other common causative verbs:

contract	destroy	expand	make
create	dissolve	inflate	produce
darken	energize	lighten	sharpen

Chapter 3 Exposition: Examining Causes and Effects

YOUR TURN 2 — Identifying Implied Causes and Effects

Using the steps in Thinking It Through, identify the cause-and-effect relationships in the following passages from the reading selection. It may not be necessary to go through every step for every passage.

1. But today, the forest floor is a sea of green—knee-high lodgepoles planted, literally, by the fires of 1988.
2. What put Yellowstone's fires out was not retardant-dropping planes or armies of firefighters on the ground. It was a quarter inch of autumn rain.
3. Fire has not repelled tourists; it has attracted them—just as it attracts many species of wildlife.
4. Before 1988, three-toed woodpeckers were almost nonexistent in Yellowstone. After 1988, one ornithologist spotted thirty in one day.
5. Just as fire rejuvenated lodgepoles, so, too, did it revitalize plants that grazing animals eat.

Cause-and-Effect Structure

I'm Beginning to Sense a Pattern . . .

Newton's third law of motion says that for every action there is an equal and opposite reaction. The "butterfly" effect, an example of the chaos theory of physics, states that the movement of a butterfly wing somewhere in China can cause a chain reaction of events that affects the weather in California weeks later. With all the actions and "equal and opposite" reactions going on in the world, how can anyone keep up with them? How can you, as a reader, make sense of it all?

Here is one way: try to determine the writer's **organizational pattern.** For causal analysis, writers generally start with one of three patterns:

- patterns that emphasize causes
- patterns that emphasize effects
- patterns that trace a causal chain

From these simple organizational patterns, writers often develop more complex patterns to describe more complex cause-and-effect relationships. These **composite patterns** show a mixture of two or more of the simple patterns. By identifying the organizational pattern a writer uses, you will be better able to understand and follow the cause-and-effect relationships the writer explains.

Meeting INDIVIDUAL NEEDS

MODALITY
Kinesthetic Learners. Encourage students to move around the room to look for or act out simple processes that involve cause and effect. For example, students can trace the steps in the causal chain set off by flipping the classroom light switch, or enact the effects that might follow from teaching a friend how to kick a soccer ball. Then students can organize the steps of the processes they investigate in graphics such as the diagrams given on these two pages.

> **TIP** Sometimes a writer discusses **underlying causes** in an analysis. For example, an obvious cause of a car wreck might be an equipment malfunction, while the underlying cause might be neglected maintenance.

▶ **Pattern 1: Focus on Causes** Some pieces of writing focus on explaining what has caused a certain event to happen. Writers usually begin these pieces by presenting a clearly observed effect; then, they proceed to analyze the causes that have led to the effect. Sometimes these causes are obvious and easily explained. At other times, a writer will present only *possible* causes, because no one is certain of the exact reasons for the effect.

If a piece you are reading focuses on causes, you are likely to find an effect presented in the introductory paragraph as part of the thesis statement. Then, the body paragraphs will explain the causes of the effect.

The following diagram illustrates an example of a "focus on causes" organizational pattern. One cause, drought conditions, is inferred.

▶ **Pattern 2: Focus on Effects** Sometimes a writer describes a cause and analyzes its effects. If the writer is discussing a recent situation, with effects not yet observed, the writer may speculate about *possible* effects.

In a piece that focuses on effects, you will likely find the cause presented as part of the thesis statement. The effects that result from the cause will be the topics of the piece's body paragraphs. Much of the Yellowstone article's focus was on the effects of the fire. The following illustration shows the pattern in which some of the effects are presented in the article.

It is important for you as a reader to pay close attention to whether the writer of an article has pointed out both long-term and short-term causes and effects. **Short-term effects** are usually the most immediately identifiable, but **long-term effects** are often the most important. For example, as the article on the Yellowstone fires points out, most people recognized only the short-term destruction caused by the fires. Some saw a once beautiful Yellowstone National Park devastated by fire. Others saw an end to businesses that thrived on tourism. However, the long-term *positive* effects of rejuvenation turned out to be more important (and more surprising), although several years passed before they became obvious. The diagram below illustrates both the long- and short-term effects.

▶ **Pattern 3: Causal Chain** A causal chain is like a row of toppling dominoes—one event causing another, repeated until a final effect is reached. The event that begins a causal chain—known as the **initial cause**—is followed by an effect that becomes the cause of another effect. This process is repeated until the **final effect**—the effect that ends the chain—is reached. Each **intermediate** (in-between) **cause** or **effect** is like a link in a chain. Though one link may not be as important or as strong as the other links, they are all necessary to the chain. If just one of these intermediate causes were absent, the final effect would not be reached.

Typically, you will find an initial cause stated in the thesis of an article. Within the body of the article, you will then read explanations of each link in the chain of events through the final effect. In the Yellowstone article, you probably noticed that the writer discussed a few causal chains. This diagram shows part of a causal chain from that article.

Reading Workshop   99

Meeting INDIVIDUAL NEEDS

MULTIPLE INTELLIGENCES
Musical Intelligence. To check comprehension of cause-and-effect patterns, organize students in four groups, one for each cause-and-effect pattern. Ask each group to create a rap, song, or chant that explains its assigned pattern and then illustrates it with causes and effects from the article about the Yellowstone fires. Students should refer to the text and diagrams on pp. 97–100 as they compose their raps, songs, or chants. Allow time for each group to perform its rap, song, or chant and teach it to the rest of the class.

Pattern 4: The Composite Pattern When you read a causal analysis, you may not always find a single organizational pattern that covers all the information given. A situation or process may be too complicated to be effectively described using a simple pattern. The following diagram illustrates a composite cause-and-effect pattern that explains the relationship between causes and effects in a volcanic eruption.

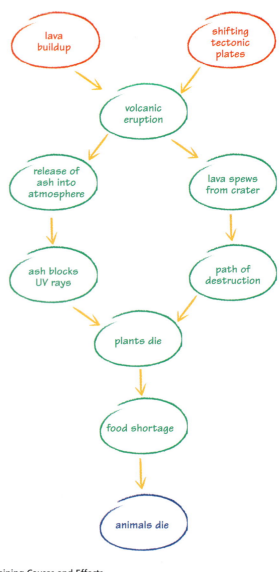

Your Turn 3 — Analyzing Cause-and-Effect Structure

To analyze the complex cause-and-effect relationships in "Yellowstone Makes a Triumphant Return," redraw and fill in the causal-chain diagram below. Draw a red circle around the initial cause, green circles around the intermediate causes, and a blue circle around the final effect. Identify at least one long-term and one short-term effect.

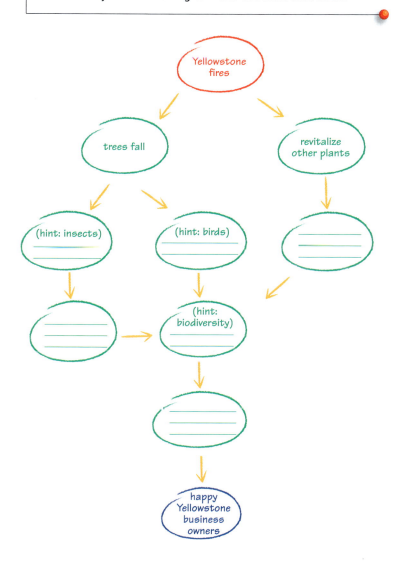

Your Turn 3

ANSWERS
A completed diagram might look like this:

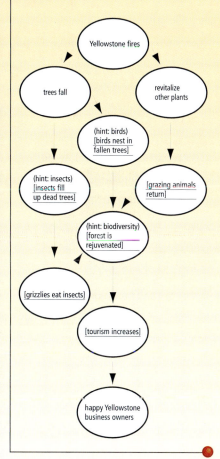

Wrap It Up

Metacognition. Ask students to reflect on their reading processes. Give students five minutes to answer this question:

> What text clues helped you infer the cause-and-effect relationships in the article?

RESOURCES

Your Turn 3

Practice
- *Communications*, WS. p. 45

Reinforcement
- *Communications*, TP. 26, WS. p. 46

MINI-LESSON VOCABULARY

Suffixes

ANSWERS
Sample responses follow.

1. *horri–fic; specific;* when you are specific about something, you are exact about it, and based on the meaning of the suffix *–fic,* being *specific* means "making exact"; then *horrific* must mean "making or causing horror"

2. *revital–ize; emphasize;* when you emphasize something, you show that it is important, and based on the meaning of the suffix *–ize, emphasize* means "make or cause to be important"; then *revitalize* must mean "make or cause to be alive again"

3. *rejuven–ate; abbreviate;* when you abbreviate something, you make it shorter, and based on the suffix *–ate, abbreviate* means "cause to be short"; then *rejuvenate* must mean "cause to be young again"

4. *terri–fic; pacific; pacific* describes something that evokes calm or peace, and based on the suffix *–fic, pacific* means "causing peace"; then *terrific* means "causing terror" or maybe "causing excitement"

5. *black–en; soften;* when you soften something, you make it soft, and based on the meaning of the suffix *–en, soften* would mean "cause to be soft"; then *blacken* must mean "cause to be black"

MINI-LESSON VOCABULARY

Suffixes

When you read complicated cause-and-effect explanations like Bruce Babbitt's article on the Yellowstone fires of 1988, you might run into some unfamiliar words. One way to prepare yourself to identify the meanings of unfamiliar words is to learn some basic suffixes. A **suffix,** a word part of one or more syllables, is added to the end of a word to alter its meaning or to change its part of speech. The suffixes in the chart at right often act as indicators of changes, causes, or effects.

Suffix	Meaning	Example
–ate	become, cause	activate
–ation	the result of ____ing	summation
–en	cause to be, become	cheapen
–fic	making, causing	horrific
–ic	caused by	acidic; choleric
–ize	make, cause to be	terrorize

THINKING IT THROUGH Using Suffixes

Use these steps to figure out the meanings of many words with suffixes.

▶ **STEP 1 Write the word down, but put a long dash between the root and the suffix.** Suppose you needed to figure out the meaning of the word *compilation.* compil—ation

▶ **STEP 2 Write down a known word that has the same suffix.** relaxation

▶ **STEP 3 Write down everything you know about the known word and about the suffix.** Relaxation means taking a break, or relaxing. Based on the meaning of the suffix *–ation,* it means "the result of relaxing."

▶ **STEP 4 Now, use what you know to make an inference—an educated guess—about the definition of the unfamiliar word.** If relaxation is the result of relaxing, then compilation must be the result of compiling. For example, when a music group puts out a compilation disc, it must be the result of compiling, or gathering together, all their best songs.

Be careful, though; many suffixes have multiple meanings. For example, *–ic* can also mean "like," as in the word *angelic.*

PRACTICE

Using the steps in Thinking It Through, above, write definitions for the words at right. Then, look up the words in a dictionary to check the accuracy of your definitions.

1. horrific
2. revitalize
3. rejuvenate
4. terrific
5. blacken

Chapter 3 Exposition: Examining Causes and Effects

RESOURCES

Vocabulary
Practice
■ *Communications,* WS. p. 47

Test Taking
Practice
■ *Communications,* WS. pp. 48–50

Exposition: Examining Causes and Effects

MINI-LESSON: TEST TAKING

Inferring Causes and Effects

Reading tests often measure your ability to infer, or make an educated guess about, causes or effects not directly stated in a reading passage. Because inference reading passages will not include clue words or phrases such as *because* or *as a result*, you must figure out the cause-and-effect relationship within them yourself.

Here is a typical reading passage and test question:

> Damage by pollution to ecosystems can be slow but sure. Acid rain, for instance, changes the quality of the water in ponds and streams. When frogs and toads lay eggs in acidic water, fewer of their offspring reach maturity. When there are fewer frogs and toads, the insect population explodes. The insects, in turn, feed on plants and crops, which may prompt farmers and gardeners to use more pesticides. These pesticides can eventually get washed by rain into waterways, where they might create further problems.

1. From this paragraph, what can you infer about the effects of frogs and toads on their ecosystems?

   A. American factories are the largest cause of acid rain.

   B. Frogs and toads help to keep insect populations down.

   C. Fish, which eat tadpoles, suffer when frog and toad populations decline.

   D. Frogs and toads eat plants and crops.

THINKING IT THROUGH: Inferring Causes and Effects

Use the following steps to answer cause-and-effect inference test questions like the sample question above.

▶ **STEP 1 Skim the passage once for a general understanding; then re-read it carefully.** Keep in mind that most of these questions are designed to measure your reading comprehension, not your reading speed.

▶ **STEP 2 Locate key words and phrases in the sample answers that match similar words and phrases in the reading passage.** Answers **A** and **C** share few key words with the reading passage. The reading passage does not mention *factories* or *fish*. Answers **B** and **D** contain key words which are in the reading passage.

▶ **STEP 3 Apply your knowledge to the remaining answers.** The passage states that *insects* (not frogs and toads) eat plants and crops, so **D** is wrong. Your knowledge that frogs and toads eat large numbers of insects confirms that **B** is correct.

Looking Ahead to Writing

In the Writing Workshop, students will need to choose a pattern for organizing their own cause-and-effect explanations. Have students review the four patterns described and diagrammed on pp. 97–100 as they plan their papers.

Vocabulary
Alignments
TEKS 6C, 6E
TAAS R1

Test Taking
Alignments
TEKS 7G, 7H
TAAS R4, R5

Reading Workshop 103

Writing Workshop

OBJECTIVES

- To write a cause-and-effect essay
- To narrow a topic effectively
- To write a thesis statement
- To recognize oversimplification and false cause and effect
- To use verbals to vary sentence beginnings
- To correct dangling modifiers

Quotation for the Day

"As I see it, writing is applied psychology because it is the art of creating desired effects. It follows from this that our chief need is to know *what* effects are desirable and *how* to create them."

(John R. Trimble, 1940– , American educator and writer)

Ask students to freewrite about the quotation. Encourage them to discuss the effects they will want to cause in their readers with their writing.

Critical Thinking

Evaluation. Help students evaluate topics for possible use in exploring cause-and-effect relationships. Ask students to name situations or events—international, national, or local—that are of interest to them. List their ideas on the chalkboard and have students ask "Why did the event happen?" or "What is the result?" with respect to each situation or event they named. Point out that if it is possible to ask one or both of these questions, they can explain the situation or event in terms of causes, effects, or both.

Writing Workshop

WHAT'S AHEAD?

In this workshop, you will write a cause-and-effect essay. You will also learn to

- narrow your topic effectively
- write a thesis statement
- recognize oversimplification and false cause and effect
- use verbals to vary sentence beginnings
- correct dangling modifiers

Writing a Cause-and-Effect Explanation

Imagine that you and your friends are on the way to play basketball at a local park when you see a bulldozer tearing up the court. You have been playing there for years, and now, without any notice, it is being destroyed. You decide to send letters to the newspaper and the city council to express your concern. However, before you put pen to paper, you will want to consider two questions: *What caused this event to happen?* and *What will the effects of this event be?*

These are typical questions to ask yourself when you are preparing a **cause-and-effect explanation,** or a **causal analysis,** such as the one you will write in this Writing Workshop. By following the steps in this workshop, you will learn how to examine both the causes and effects of an event or situation and how to create an effective, well-supported essay on any cause-and-effect topic that you choose.

Prewriting

Choose a Situation or Event

Pulling Order from Chaos The world around you is an immensely complex cause-and-effect system—an almost infinite number of actions and reactions are constantly taking place. With so many cause-and-effect topics to choose from, focusing in on one good topic for a cause-and-effect essay can be difficult. Here are a few good ways to narrow the list.

- **Create an If-Then Log.** Look at the world around you and jot down if-then situations or events. Ask yourself, "**If** (a certain event or situation) occurred, **then** what effects would it cause?" Some areas where you might search for events and situations are local and professional sports,

104   Chapter 3   **Exposition:** Examining Causes and Effects

grades, and driving. For example, **if** your school's star quarterback were injured, **then** what effect would it have on the rest of the team?

- **Investigate news sources,** including radio and TV programs or newspaper and magazine articles. Look for thought-provoking stories about important political events or recent scientific discoveries. Ask yourself "Why did that happen?" or "What will happen because of this?"

- **Write about what you know.** Use your personal experiences or collaborate with other writers and use their experiences as a source of cause-and-effect topics. For example, you may know firsthand the causes of soil erosion or the effects of exercise on appetite.

Make a list of promising topics. Then, review the list and choose the one topic you find most interesting.

Narrow Your Topic

Sharpen the Focus Once you have found an interesting topic, you must decide whether it is too general or too specific to cover in the amount of space you have for your essay. For example, if you chose to write on the effects of the invention of the personal computer, you could easily have a book-length project on your hands—a short paper would not do justice to the topic. However, if you narrowed the topic to the effects that the personal computer has had on writing school essays, you might be able to cover the subject adequately.

In a short paper, plan to discuss only the most important or most immediate causes or effects associated with your topic. Trying to cover too many causes or effects or trying to discuss a chain of causes and events with too many links would be overwhelming for you and your readers.

> **TIP** Cause-and-effect may also be used as an **elaboration technique in a persuasive essay.** For example, if you were writing to persuade the school board to devote more of their budget to school music programs, you might stress the positive effects of music education.

Consider Purpose, Audience, and Tone

Who Wants to Know? The main **purpose** of your essay is to explain clearly a causal relationship to your **audience,** or readers. You will be giving your readers information that you think will be useful or interesting to them. Knowing your audience can help you decide what information to include in your essay. If your readers are already familiar with your cause-and-effect topic, how will you maintain their interest? Do you have new information that they do not know? If your readers are unfamiliar with your topic, how much background detail will you need to give them so that your explanation makes sense? Will you need to explain technical

Meeting INDIVIDUAL NEEDS

MODALITY

Auditory Learners. Hearing their drafts read aloud by another person will help students evaluate the tone and voice of their writing. Throughout the writing process, you may want to pair students so that they can read aloud each other's writing.

TEACHING TIP

Write Your Thesis
Remind students that the focus of their causal analysis (causes, effects, or both causes and effects) will determine their main idea, or thesis. Provide examples of thesis statements with the three different focuses:

Causes: There are three basic reasons most teenagers feel the need to buy a car.

Effects: While buying a car seems like a liberation, it may bring consequences that are not so pleasant.

Causes and Effects: Many teenagers have good reasons for buying a car, but some effects of purchasing a car may be negative.

---

terms? Often it is best to think of a broad audience composed of some readers who are familiar with your topic and some readers who are unfamiliar with it. Provide enough background information for readers to understand your topic, but not so much that you will bore readers who are already familiar with it.

Knowing your audience will also help you determine what tone you should use in your writing. **Tone** is the reflection of your attitude toward your subject and your audience. Your tone can be happy, angry, serious, lighthearted, disgusted, or any other feeling. **You express tone in writing through your style—your choice of words, details, and sentence structure.** You might be tempted to write your causal analysis in a serious, conservative tone—but you do not have to. You should adjust your tone to your subject and your audience. For example, if you are writing a humorous essay for your class or a club to which you belong, your tone can be informal and breezy. If you are writing to the school board requesting that new courses be added to the curriculum, your tone should be formal and respectful.

A word closely associated with tone is **voice**. Your speaking voice is recognizable to people who know you; similarly, your writing **style** should reflect your uniqueness. Even though a causal analysis may be on a serious topic, this does not mean that your language has to be stuffy and overly formal. You are much more likely to impress people by sounding natural than you are by using unnecessarily big words or complex sentence structures. Still, you should avoid being too informal or colloquial—don't use slang or other words that might put off your audience.

> KEY CONCEPT

Write Your Thesis

Focus the Vision A **thesis statement** is a precise statement of the main idea of your essay as a whole. Creating a thesis statement is like focusing a camera lens to get the clearest possible view of a photographic subject. **To write a thesis statement for a causal analysis, take all of your thoughts and ideas about your topic and focus them into one clear main idea**—stating whether you are focusing on causes, on effects, on causes and effects, or on a chain of causes and effects. Remember that your thesis statement can change. You might discover a better approach to your topic as you develop your paper. Refining your thesis is part of the writing process. Begin by using the following Thinking It Through steps to determine the focus of your essay.

> KEY CONCEPT

THINKING IT THROUGH: Focusing on Causes or Effects

Use the following steps to form a thesis statement for your essay. Model student responses are based on an essay written about the causes and effects of falling asleep in class.

▶ **STEP 1** Write your topic on a piece of paper. Fold the paper in half lengthwise. On one half of the paper, write the question *Why did (or does) it happen?*, and then, under the question, list the probable cause or causes associated with your topic.

▶ **STEP 2** On the other half of the paper, write the question *What are the results?* Then, list all the effects associated with your topic.

TOPIC: FALLING ASLEEP IN CLASS

Why does it happen? (causes)	What are the results? (effects)
after-school jobs	disrupts class
extracurricular activities	miss important class information
physical problems	detention
lack of sleep	embarrassing
	grounded by parents

▶ **STEP 3** Compare the number of items on each side of the page. Did you end up listing more causes or more effects? Which seem more significant—the causes you listed, or the effects—or do they seem equally significant? Based on your responses, decide whether to write about causes, effects, or both. *There are nearly the same number of significant causes and effects. My essay will focus on both.*

▶ **STEP 4** Write a thesis statement that clearly indicates the approach you will take in your essay: a cause-centered approach, an effects-centered approach, or an approach that involves discussing both causes and effects. A thesis can be written as a formula:

   thesis = topic + your focus on causes, effects, or both

Example:

topic   *causes*
Teenagers fall asleep in class for many reasons, and as a

   effects
consequence, suffer many negative results.

Cooperative Learning

Thesis Statements. You may want to give students practice developing thesis statements for different focuses of a subject. Divide the class into groups of three. One member of the group will focus on causes, another on effects, and the third on causes and effects. Give each group a subject, and instruct each member to write a thesis statement on his or her assigned focus. You may want to give each group more than one subject and switch the members' focus assignments. The groups should present their thesis statements to the whole class for discussion and evaluation. Ask students to comment on difficulties they experienced in writing thesis statements to reflect a particular focus.

MINI-LESSON: CRITICAL THINKING

Oversimplification and False Cause and Effect

ANSWERS

1. false cause-and-effect statement
2. oversimplification
3. valid cause-and-effect statement
4. oversimplification
5. oversimplification
6. false cause-and-effect statement
7. valid cause-and-effect statement
8. valid cause-and-effect statement
9. false cause-and-effect statement
10. oversimplification

Taking a Second Look

Oversimplification and False Cause and Effect. For each of the invalid statements, have students create a question that reveals the fallacy in the statement.

1. Does the parrot squawk only then?
2. Are there other reasons for sleeplessness?
4. Does practice alone guarantee you a position on a pro team?
5. Did the Revolution have only one cause?
6. What else contributes to good health?
9. What is the scientific explanation for rain?
10. Are there other causes of hearing loss?

MINI-LESSON: CRITICAL THINKING

Oversimplification and False Cause and Effect

You must think critically about causal relationships—how causes and effects are connected. For example, in looking at a friend's wilted houseplant you might assume that the owner had neglected the plant. However, a critical investigation might reveal that the owner in fact overwatered the plant in an effort to take care of it. By making a thorough investigation of causes and effects, you can avoid two common fallacies, or errors in thinking, in cause-and-effect explanations: **oversimplifying** and **false cause and effect**.

- **Oversimplifying:** Most events have more than one cause. When you identify a single major cause but ignore all other causes, you are oversimplifying. Clues to oversimplification are words such as *only, never,* and *always* or phrases such as *the cause is* or *the effect is*. To remedy many oversimplification problems, you can limit, or qualify, your cause-and-effect statement with such phrases as *an important factor, the three major effects,* or *one of the main reasons.*

    Oversimplification: Human overpopulation is responsible for the decline in the African cheetah population.

    Revised: Human overpopulation is *one of many contributing factors* in the decline in the African cheetah population.

- **False Cause and Effect:** This error in thinking is made when you incorrectly assume that just because one event follows another in time, the first event caused the second.

    False Cause and Effect: Every time I attend a school soccer game, the team wins. The team must win because I am there.

    Revised: Although I'd like to think that I cause our school soccer team to win whenever I attend a game, *there are other causes for* the wins.

PRACTICE

Identify each of the following statements as an oversimplification, a false cause-and-effect statement, or a valid cause-and-effect statement. Be prepared to explain your answers.

1. Our parrot squawks whenever my sister's boyfriend comes in the room. It must not like him.
2. Stress causes sleeplessness.
3. Many people with perfect eyesight begin to experience some vision problems as they age.
4. Practicing a sport every day will guarantee you a position on a pro team.
5. Taxation without representation was the cause of the American Revolution.
6. An apple a day keeps the doctor away.
7. Freezing rain caused the cancellation of the football game.
8. Carolyn's improved energy probably comes from her new habits: regular exercise and proper eating.
9. If I forget my umbrella today, it will rain.
10. Hearing loss is caused by listening to too much loud music.

RESOURCES

Critical Thinking
Practice
- *Communications,* WS. p. 51

Your Turn 4
Practice
- *Communications,* WS. p. 52

Gather and Organize Support

Find and Assemble Your Essentials To make your essay convincing, you will need to include details that support your points. These supporting details come from **facts, statistics, real-life examples,** and **expert opinions.** Where do you find this support?

- To locate facts and statistics, look at **reference materials** such as encyclopedias, newspapers, magazines, and Web pages and newsgroups.
- Some details may even come from **personal experiences** or the experiences of those you know. Depending on your topic, you might also interview friends, neighbors, or relatives for real-life examples.
- **Interviewing people who are knowledgeable about your topic** is often very helpful. Appropriate people to interview for expert opinions may include professors, government officials, or law officers.

A Balancing Act A well-supported cause-and-effect essay relies on a variety of supporting details. How well you organize these supporting details determines the effectiveness of your explanation. Well-balanced and well-organized support presented in a coherent, **logical progression** makes your essay easier to write and easier for your audience to read.

Your causal analysis may involve a clear causal chain—beginning with the first cause and following a series of intermediate actions or events to the final effect. For explanations of causal chains, you should consider arranging your information in **chronological order,** beginning your explanation with the initial cause and working through subsequent events to end your explanation with the final effect. If your focus is primarily on causes or on effects rather than on a causal chain, consider arranging your information in **order of importance**—moving from the least important to the most important factor, or vice versa.

TIP Reverse chronological order starts with an effect or series of effects and then traces them back to the original cause.

YOUR TURN 4 Preparing to Write

Review each of these prewriting steps before you begin your essay.
- Choose a cause-and-effect situation to write about and narrow it down to a manageable topic.
- Remember your purpose for writing this essay. Keep your audience in mind and write with an appropriate voice and tone.
- Write a clear thesis statement.
- Gather and organize your supporting evidence.

TECHNOLOGY TIP

Suggest that students use e-mail to interview friends and relatives. Students may also use e-mail to contact and interview experts on a topic, such as professors and government officials. *You need to be aware that Internet resources are sometimes public forums, and their content can be unpredictable.*

Meeting INDIVIDUAL NEEDS

LEARNERS HAVING DIFFICULTY
To help students remember to provide supporting details for the causes and/or effects in their essays, have them write each cause and/or effect on a separate index card. As students gather information, they may write supporting details on the appropriate cards. When students are ready to organize their essays, they can lay the index cards out on their desks and rearrange them until they find the most effective order.

YOUR TURN 4

Ask each student to list the topic of his or her essay; its purpose, audience, and tone; and the thesis statement, supporting details, and chosen order for arranging information. This allows both you and the students to see whether students are ready to begin writing.

Quotation for the Day

"An idle reason lessens the weight of the good ones you gave before."

(Jonathan Swift, 1667–1745, English satirist)

Use this quotation to emphasize the importance of citing valid reasons as supporting details. As students write their first drafts, they should be reminded that each cause or effect needs supporting reasons or evidence to prove its accuracy.

Meeting INDIVIDUAL NEEDS

ENGLISH-LANGUAGE LEARNERS
General Strategies. Some students may need help with the idiomatic language and technical terms used to describe the content of a cause-and-effect essay. The idioms *listen up, back story,* and *hook* may not be immediately comprehensible to some students. You may also need to elaborate on technical terms such as *causal chain, thesis statement,* and *chronological order.* Ask students to define the terms in their own words; then elicit specific examples of each.

YOUR TURN 5

Students may find it easier to draft the body of their essays first, describing causes and effects and providing details, and then to go back to check whether there is sufficient support for their theses. If not, students should revise their theses or find additional supporting evidence before drafting their introduction and conclusion.

Cause-and-Effect Essay

Framework	Directions and Explanations

Introduction
- Get your readers interested.
- Provide background information.
- Include a clear thesis.

Listen Up Like the opening scene of a movie, your introduction should hook your audience and make them want to see what comes next. Surprise your readers: Make a bold statement. Present an interesting statistic, fact, or example. Surprise them with what they don't know.

The Back Story Give information to set the stage for your cause-and-effect explanations. Show your readers why your explanation is important and worth reading.

Announce the Main Event Clarify your purpose for your readers by providing them with a well-focused thesis statement at the end of your introduction.

Body
- Present the causes and/or effects of your topic in a clear sequence.
- Support the causes and/or effects with adequate detail.

Telling the Tale If your essay involves an analysis of a **causal chain,** consider using **chronological order.** Otherwise, use **order of importance.** Whatever order you choose, be sure there is a logical progression of ideas. Make sure that you back up each of your cause-and-effect statements with supporting details such as statistics, facts, examples, and expert opinions.

Conclusion
- Remind your readers of your thesis and bring your essay to a close.

The Curtain Call Summarize your essay's main points completely but concisely. Consider ending with a question, prediction, or thought-provoking statement.

 Writing a First Draft

Write the first draft of your cause-and-effect essay, using the framework above and the Writer's Model on the next page as guides.

110 Chapter 3 Exposition: Examining Causes and Effects

RESOURCES

Writing
Writing Prompts
- *Communications,* TP. 27, WS. p. 53

Your Turn 5
Practice
- *Communications,* TP. 28, WS. p. 54

A Writer's Model

The following short essay, which is a final draft, closely follows the framework on the previous page. As you read the essay, notice how the highlighted words—cause-effect clue words—help communicate the writer's explanation of the causes and effects of sleeping in class.

School Daze

In the middle of presenting a lesson to the class, your teacher unexpectedly stops speaking. Everyone in the class becomes expectantly silent—nothing is heard except a faint sound from somewhere in the back of the room, a noise that sounds like . . . snoring? Suddenly, with a loud *thwack!*, your teacher claps a book shut, and the snoring culprit is jarred from his sleep, lifting his head from his desk with a startled, bleary-eyed look on his face. Read old comic strips or watch really old TV shows, and you will see a similar scene. There is a history of schooltime dozing. You would think times have changed. Unfortunately, though, falling asleep in class is actually an all-too-common occurrence among today's active teenagers—one which has both complex causes and serious consequences.

Why do students sometimes fall asleep in class? An obvious reason is lack of sleep. However, there are also causes for getting too little sleep. Homework is a daily occurrence for most students, one that can take three to four hours per night. A teenager who wants to be able to participate in any activity besides homework must frequently stay up late in order to fit everything in. Club activities, sports, computer-game playing, and TV viewing, for example, all contribute to teens having less time for both homework and sleep. Sometimes teens lack sleep because of after-school jobs that are taken on to earn extra money for college, family expenses, or simply for clothes and recreation. For students with jobs, losing sleep is often preferable to quitting their job or even cutting back on their hours.

Physical problems are another factor that can cause students to fall asleep in class. For example, insomnia—the inability to sleep—may keep a student up at night, causing exhaustion during class hours. Insomnia, which may be triggered by stress and

(continued)

INTRODUCTION
Interesting opener

Background information

Thesis

BODY
Cause 1
Support for cause 1
Facts

Cause 2
Support for cause 2

Connecting Reading and Writing

Because students often find writing an introduction challenging, ask them to examine the opening paragraph of **"School Daze"** closely. Point out the three elements of an introduction (hook, background information, thesis) in the model. Focus on the vivid vignette that opens the essay and discuss why, considering the audience, it is particularly effective. Then, have students identify the three elements of an introduction in the cause-and-effect article on pp. 93–94. What makes the introduction to that essay effective?

Writing, pp. 110–113
Alignments
TEKS 1A, 1B, 1C, 2A, 2B, 8A
TAAS W1, W2, W4
English II End-of-Course 4

Meeting INDIVIDUAL NEEDS

STUDENTS WITH SPECIAL NEEDS
Create a chart on which students can outline the framework of the cause-and-effect explanation in the **A Writer's Model**. On the lines provided for the introduction, students can copy the interesting opener, background information, and thesis statement from the model. For the body, have them write the causes and effects and supporting details. For the conclusion, they can copy the restatement of the thesis and prediction.

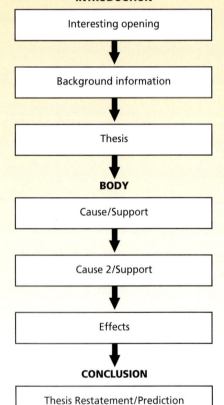

(continued)

anxiety, is a serious problem that may **require** medical attention. Medical evidence also supports the idea that each person has an internal clock that helps to **determine** his or her individual sleep pattern. Unfortunately, these internal clocks are not always synchronized with school class schedules.

Effects

The **effects** of falling asleep in class can be quite serious. First of all, sleeping in class is not a good way to endear yourself to teachers, who are not likely to tolerate it for very long. (It is extremely embarrassing to awaken from a blissful nap to find your teacher standing next to your desk, glowering at you.) In addition, napping students run the risk of becoming the target of jokes and disparaging comments—not to mention the occasional paper wad—leveled by classmates. However, the most detrimental **effect** of sleeping in class is missing out on important instruction and suffering the **consequences**. In the long run, chronic sleepers may end up serving a great deal of detention time and, in serious cases, failing classes. These students might also wind up being grounded by their parents for long periods of time.

Causal chain: fall asleep in class→miss instruction→fail classes→get grounded

CONCLUSION Restatement of thesis

Prediction

To stay more alert in class, teens should think about these **effects** and do something to deal with the **causes**. Since teens are probably not going to address the problem, falling asleep in class will probably remain an all-too-common occurrence. It will likely continue until more teens find a way to balance their personal and social lives with school and work, while still finding enough time for those precious *z*'s.

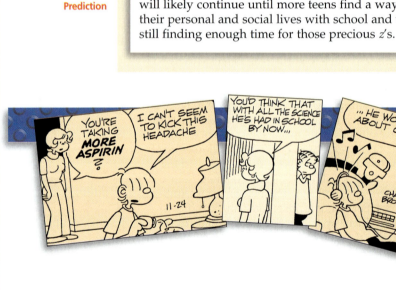

Chapter 3 Exposition: Examining Causes and Effects

A Student's Model

The following excerpt from a cause-and-effect essay is by student writer Gwen Miller of Fairmont Junior High School in Boise, Idaho. Her parenthetical citations refer to the sources she used as support for her essay.

TV Baby Sitters: Help or Hindrance?

The TV blaring disrupts the peace of the apartment complex. A child's eyes are glued to the character dancing on the screen. He has been sitting there for hours. The child's father sits exhausted, not sure what to do when the children's shows are replaced with the evening news. His built-in baby sitter is about to quit its job, so he makes the decision to buy a video machine. However, is feeding his child a diet of nothing but TV really good for his child? Along with the many reasons parents leave their children to be baby-sat by the TV, there are also many negative effects of this electronic caregiver.

TV is the only way many parents know to keep their children entertained. They are not aware of the many dangerous sides of television. For example, according to the Center for Media Education, children who watch an abundance of TV have a greater chance of obesity and increased alcohol and drug use (Jones 22). The Center also states that the American Medical Association, the American Psychological Association, and others believe that viewing TV violence can have lifelong harmful effects on children's health (Jones 33). A 1999 policy statement from the American Academy of Pediatrics suggests parents avoid all television for children under two. The statement says, "While certain television programs may be promoted to this age group, research on early brain development shows that babies and toddlers have a critical need for direct interactions with parents and other significant caregivers for healthy brain growth and the development of appropriate social, emotional, and cognitive skills" (26). Instead of turning on the TV for entertainment, parents can do other fun activities with their children. . . .

INTRODUCTION
Interesting opening

Hypothetical scenario to set the stage

Thesis statement

BODY
Major support for thesis statement

Expert testimony as support

More expert testimony as support

Alternatives to negative effects

Quotation for the Day

"You write the first draft really to see how it's going to come out."

(James Michener, 1907–1997, American novelist and Pulitzer Prize winner)

Share the quotation with students, pointing out the importance of evaluating how the first draft "came out" and then revising it as needed. Emphasize that a draft is very rarely a finished product; it is much more often a kind of rough drawing that hints at the finished picture.

TEACHING TIP

▶ **Elaboration**

As students consider which parts of their essays need elaboration, remind them that less obvious causes and effects may need more supporting information (facts, statistics, examples, expert opinions) than causes and effects that are more evident.

Revising

Evaluate and Revise Your Draft

Take Two There are two key areas to consider when you set out to evaluate and revise your paper: the first is content and organization; the second is style. Work collaboratively with a peer to review your essay once, using the content and organization guidelines on this page, and then review it a second time, using the style guidelines on page 115.

▶ **First Reading: Content and Organization** What have you done especially well in your draft? Where might you make improvements? Use the following chart to find out. Ask yourself the questions in the left-hand column of the chart. The tips in the middle column will help you answer the questions. If you identify a problem in your paper, use the revision technique suggested in the right-hand column to fix it.

Cause-and-Effect Essay: Content and Organization Guidelines for Peer and Self-Evaluation

Evaluation Questions	Tips	Revision Techniques
❶ Will the introductory paragraph make a reader want to keep reading?	▶ **Highlight** attention-getting phrases or sentences. If there are none, revise.	▶ **Add** an anecdote, fact, question, or example that will get readers interested in your topic.
❷ Does the introduction contain a clear thesis statement?	▶ **Underline** the cause-and-effect thesis statement. If there is not one, or if it is not very clear, revise.	▶ **Add** a sentence that clearly states the essay's main idea and focus.
❸ Are the cause-and-effect statements adequately developed?	▶ **Draw arrows** between each cause or effect and the sentences used as support for each one. If there are not at least two arrows pointing to sentences supporting each cause and effect, revise.	▶ **Elaborate** on cause-and-effect statements by supporting them with facts, statistics, examples, and expert opinions.
❹ Does the paper present information in an organized format?	▶ **Number** the causes and effects in your paper. If the numbers do not seem to reflect an ordering strategy such as order of importance or chronological order, revise.	▶ **Rearrange** your causes and effects. Consider using order of importance or chronological order.
❺ Does the essay have a reasonable and logical conclusion?	▶ **Double underline** the sentence in the conclusion that restates the thesis of your essay. If you cannot find one, revise.	▶ **Add** a sentence that restates the focus of your essay.

114 Chapter 3 Exposition: Examining Causes and Effects

RESOURCES

Revising

Practice

- *Communications,*
  TPs. 29, 30, WS. pp. 55, 56, 57

Extension

- *Designing Your Writing*

ONE WRITER'S REVISIONS Here is how one writer used the content and organization guidelines to revise some sentences from the cause-and-effect essay on page 111. Study the revisions and answer the questions that follow.

> In the long run, chronic sleepers ~~might~~ **These students/also** wind up being grounded by their parents for long periods of time, ~~and these students~~ may ~~also~~ end up serving a great deal of detention time **and, in serious cases, failing classes**.
>
> reorder
>
> elaborate

Analyzing the Revision Process

1. Why did the writer add "failing classes" to her list of effects?
2. Why did the writer switch the order of effects? In your opinion, is this order better? Why or why not?

YOUR TURN 6 Focusing on Content and Organization

Revise your essay using the content and organization guidelines on page 114. Use the example revisions shown above as a model.

▶ **Second Reading: Style** In your first reading, you focused on content and organization. In the second reading, you will look at how you *express* your ideas—your style. Unless you revise for style, you may develop habits that make your writing monotonous. For example, when writing your causal analysis, you might start many of your sentences with "The cause is . . ." or "The effect is . . ." To avoid such repetitive sentence structure, you might try to vary some of your sentence beginnings by using **infinitives** and **infinitive phrases.**

Style Guidelines

Evaluation Question	Tip	Revision Technique
Do many of the sentences begin the same way? Are some structures overused?	▶ Put parentheses around the first six words of each sentence. Revise half of the sentences that have both a subject and a verb in the first six words.	▶ Reword sentences to begin with infinitives or infinitive phrases.

PEER REVIEW

Ask a classmate to read your essay and to answer the following questions:
1. Does the thesis statement prepare you for the rest of the paper?
2. What is the most significant cause or effect in the paper? Why do you think so?

COMPUTER TIP

Most word-processing programs have an Undo command. The Undo command lets you revert to material that you prefer to your revision.

Writing Workshop **115**

Analyzing the Revision Process
ANSWERS
Possible answers follow:

1. because failing classes is the most serious effect, and it strengthens the writer's thesis
2. The author switched the order to begin with the more serious effects. The new order is better because it emphasizes the more serious effects.

Encourage student writers who have a good grasp of the revision process to help students who need guidance in revising their first drafts. Have students include copies of both their rough and revised drafts so you can quickly check the completed revisions.

Revising, pp. 114–117
Alignments
TEKS 2B, 2C, 2E, 4D, 5A, 5B
TAAS W1, W2, W3, W7
English II End-of-Course 4, 5, 6

Writing Workshop **115**

Cooperative Learning

Infinitives and Infinitive Phrases. Have students form small groups, and provide students with newspapers, magazines, and books from which each group can find a cause-and-effect explanation. Ask each student in the group to choose a sentence in the group's explanation and to revise the sentence by including infinitives or infinitive phrases that help clarify *why* the described action is performed. Post both the original and revised versions of groups' explanations for the class to compare.

Focus on Sentences

Reference Note

For more information and practice on **infinitives** and **infinitive phrases**, see page 479.

Using Infinitives and Infinitive Phrases as Openers

Good writers, like good chefs, know that making their work appealing requires excellent presentation. One way to clarify *why* an action is performed is to use an infinitive or infinitive phrase. To vary sentence beginnings, use an infinitive or infinitive phrase as the opener of the sentence. Look at the following examples.

He had the car's engine checked **to ensure a safe trip**. [*To ensure a safe trip* is the infinitive phrase that tells *why*.]

To ensure a safe trip, he had the car's engine checked. [The infinitive phrase opens the sentence, but still tells *why*.]

ONE WRITER'S REVISIONS Here is how the writer of the model cause-and-effect essay on page 111 used the guidelines on page 115 to revise some sentence beginnings.

BEFORE REVISION

(Teens should think about these effects) and do something to deal with the causes to stay more alert in class. (Since teens are probably not going) to address the problem, falling asleep in class will probably remain an all-too-common occurrence. (It will likely continue until more) teens find a way to balance their personal and social lives . . .

The subject and the verb appear within the first six words of these sentences.

reword

AFTER REVISION

To stay more alert in class, teens should think about these effects and do something to deal with the causes. Since teens are probably not going to address the problem, falling asleep in class will probably remain an all-too-common occurrence. It will likely continue until more teens find a way to balance their personal and social lives . . .

Chapter 3 Exposition: Examining Causes and Effects

RESOURCES

Focus on Sentences

Practice

- *Communications*, WS. p. 58

Focus on Sentences
Alignments
TEKS 2C, 3C
TAAS W3, W5
English II End-of-Course 5, 6

Exposition: Examining Causes and Effects

Analyzing the Revision Process

1. Why did the writer move the infinitive phrase to the beginning of the first sentence? Does it change the sentence's meaning?
2. Why did the writer not revise the final sentence?

 Focusing on Style

Revise your essay using the style guidelines on page 115. Use the example revision shown on page 116 as a model.

Designing Your Writing

Flowcharts and Diagrams Two types of visuals commonly used in causal analysis are *flowcharts* and *diagrams*. A **flowchart** illustrates a series of causes-and-effects using geometric shapes (such as squares, circles, and triangles) connected by lines or arrows to indicate movement in a cause and effect chain. **Diagrams** use illustrations also with lines or arrows to indicate the relationship between causes and effects.

Whether you create graphics on a computer or draw them by hand, the following tips will help you make your graphics effective illustrations of your cause-and-effect essay.

- Include only graphics that are explained or reinforced by information in your text. Graphics never *replace* information from your text.
- Your graphics should read left to right, top to bottom. The initial cause should be on the far left and the end result to the farthest right.
- When you illustrate a causal chain, clearly indicate the starting or initial cause in the chain and the ending effect in the chain.
- Use dark, thick arrows to ensure that the connections between causes and effects are easy to see.
- Briefly and clearly state only essential details. Do not try to fit all the details from your essay into your graphic. Instead, use only the important details that will help your reader understand the information in your essay.
- Use consistent sizes and shapes for similar types of information.

Reference Note
For more on **flowcharts** and **diagrams,** see pages 857 and 858 of the Quick Reference Handbook.

Analyzing the Revision Process
ANSWERS
Possible answers include the following:

1. The change emphasizes *why* teens should consider the effects and deal with the causes of the behavior, and it varies sentence beginnings; the change does not change the meaning of the sentence, but it makes the sentence more interesting for readers.

2. In the final sentence, the infinitive phrase "to balance their personal and social lives with school and work" follows the word "way" and cannot stand on its own at the beginning of the sentence without changing the sentence's meaning.

YOUR TURN 7

Have students label and provide reasons for the infinitives and infinitive phrases they introduce into their drafts.

Timesaver

Have students jot down questions they have about revising their essays. Discuss each student's questions anonymously with the class. Answering questions now will help students identify and correct specific problems in their essays and will save time later when you assess their work.

Quotation for the Day

"In a very real sense, the writer writes in order to teach himself, to understand himself, to satisfy himself; the publishing of his ideas, though it brings gratifications, is a curious anticlimax."

(Alfred Kazin, 1915–1998, American literary critic)

Write the quotation on the chalkboard or on an overhead transparency, and discuss the kinds of rewards the writing process offers a writer. Ask students whether they would find publishing their own writing anticlimactic. Students should explain their responses.

Grammar Link
Dangling Modifiers

ANSWERS
Sample answers are given.

1. While driving to school, I saw flashing lights in the road.
2. Running to catch the bus, Kara tripped on her shoestrings.
3. Having selected a college, she planned a trip to the campus.
4. To be a good ballplayer, you must practice daily.
5. When hosting a dinner party, provide a variety of food.

Publishing

Proofread Your Essay

Getting it Right Before you prepare a final copy of your essay, work collaboratively with a peer to make sure that the essay is free of errors in grammar, spelling, and punctuation. As you proofread, check your essay for **dangling modifiers**—modifying words, phrases, or clauses that do not clearly and sensibly modify a word or a group of words in a sentence. Dangling modifiers confuse your reader and muddle your explanation.

Grammar Link
Dangling Modifiers

In a causal analysis, the relationships between causes and effects must be clear. This connection can be confusing if your reader cannot understand to which word each modifier refers.

When you use **verbal phrases**, be careful to avoid **creating dangling modifiers**. Be sure that the noun immediately after the verbal phrase is the one the phrase modifies. You may correct a dangling modifier by adding a word or words that the dangling phrase can sensibly modify or by adding a word or words to the dangling phrase.

Dangling	**To earn extra spending money,** Sachi's **summer** was spent working for her father. [Did the summer earn money?]
Correct	**To earn extra spending money,** Sachi spent her summer working for her father. [adds a word *(Sachi)* that the dangling phrase can sensibly modify]
Dangling	**While reaching into my pocket for change,** my **car** rolled into the tollbooth. [Was the car reaching?]
Correct	**While I was reaching into my pocket for change,** my car rolled into the tollbooth. [adds words *(I was)* to the dangling phrase]

Reference Note
For more information and practice on **dangling modifiers,** see page 626. For more information on **verbal phrases,** see page 472.

PRACTICE

Revise the following sentences to correct their dangling modifiers. Write your answers on your own paper.

1. While driving to school, flashing lights appeared in the road.
2. Running to catch the bus, Kara's shoestrings tripped her up.
3. Having selected a college, a trip to the campus was planned.
4. To be a good ballplayer, daily practice is extremely important.
5. When hosting a dinner party, a variety of food should be provided.

Chapter 3 Exposition: Examining Causes and Effects

RESOURCES
Grammar Link
Practice
- *Communications,* WS. p. 59

Exposition: Examining Causes and Effects

Publish Your Essay

Your Name in Lights Try reaching an audience for your cause-and-effect essay through one of these publishing ideas.

- **Submit your local sports-related or school-related essay to your school's newspaper and to club or sports newsletters.** For example, fellow students might want to read an essay discussing how recent school board decisions will affect their daily lives.

- **If your topic relates to a historical event, try submitting your essay to a historical society newsletter.** For example, an essay on the impact of the railroad on your town's development might interest members of a local historical society.

- **Showcase your illustrated science-related cause-and-effect essay by participating in a science fair.** For example, you might explain the causes and effects of damage to the earth's ozone layer.

Reflect on Your Essay

A Job Well-Done To think about the writing skills you gained while working on your essay and the decisions you made along the way, write responses to these questions.

- Did you have trouble finding enough causes or effects to discuss, or were there too many? Could you have broadened or narrowed your topic? Explain your answer.
- How did you choose whether to focus on causes, on effects, on both causes and effects, or on a causal chain?
- Did you find any dangling modifiers in your essay? How will you remember to check for dangling modifiers in future essays?

If this essay will be part of a writing portfolio, be sure to include your answers to these questions along with your essay.

YOUR TURN 8 — Proofreading, Publishing, and Reflecting

Before you turn in your essay, make sure to
- proofread it carefully
- consider how you might publish it
- reflect on your essay by considering the writing process you went through to create it

---

Metacognition. Ask each student to write a brief response to the following question:

1. What was the most important cause-and-effect relationship in your essay? How did you structure your essay to show its importance?

Then, have students answer the following questions:

2. What is the formula for a thesis in a cause-and-effect explanation? [thesis = topic + your focus on causes, effects, or both]

3. What are two common fallacies in cause-and-effect explanations? Explain each. [oversimplifying (identifying a single major cause for an event and ignoring all other causes); false cause and effect (incorrectly assuming that just because one event follows another in time, the first event caused the second)]

YOUR TURN 8

Students may find it easier to spot errors if they exchange papers with a partner and proofread each other's essays. Collect copies of students' published essays in a binder so that students can review and compare their work.

Publishing, pp. 118–119
Alignments
TEKS 2D, 3A, 3B, 3C, 3D, 5A
TAAS W3, W5, W6, W7
English II End-of-Course 5, 6

TEACHING TIP

Participating in Group Discussions
To encourage participation by everyone in the group, suggest that the leader call on each member of the group to respond to the topic under discussion. Remind students that people in discussion groups may have different points of view or unique points to make and that both respect for others' opinions and patience are essential qualities for participation in group discussions.

Playing a Part
A tape recorder is a useful tool for the recorder or secretary in a group. The recorder may take notes as the discussion is being taped and then use the tape later to confirm and flesh out the notes. He or she may also tape the discussion without taking notes and then transcribe significant portions of the tape, pausing to rewind and replay as necessary to reconstruct the discussion.

Connections to Life

Participating in Group Discussions

One good way to share your causal analysis with an audience is through a group discussion. A **group discussion** involves face-to-face communication among a small number of people who meet **for a specific purpose, such as to brainstorm ideas, share information, solve a problem, or arrive at a decision.** By taking part in a group discussion, you can receive feedback on your ideas—and learn about other people's ideas at the same time.

Playing a Part Effective group discussions require that each participant have a role: either leader, recorder, or participant. Each role is defined by its key responsibilities, summarized in the following chart.

Leader	<ul><li>announces the discussion topic</li><li>keeps the discussion moving and on the topic</li><li>encourages each member to participate</li><li>manages group interaction</li></ul>
Recorder (secretary)	<ul><li>records significant information, such as all major points of agreement and disagreement, and any decisions made</li><li>prepares a final report</li></ul>
Participant	<ul><li>contributes to the discussion</li><li>cooperates, asks clear questions, and shares information</li><li>listens carefully to others</li><li>responds appropriately</li></ul>

Be aware that you may be called upon to play any of these roles in a discussion. Also, make sure that each role and its responsibilities are clear to every group member before the discussion begins.

Being Prepared All members of a group discussion should be well prepared. If there is an outline, or **agenda,** that the discussion will follow, you should look it over and be ready to ask questions or provide information on each item listed. Being prepared may involve doing some research if you do not know much about a particular item on the agenda. Allow yourself ample time to research topics before the discussion takes place.

Listening During a discussion, concentrate on what other participants are saying, instead of on what you want to say next. Make sure you **ask questions to clarify** anything that you do not understand. Take notes on what other participants have to say, and keep the following questions and ideas in mind while others are speaking.

- **What is the source of the speaker's information?** Is the source reliable? Focus your attention on the speaker's message.

- **Do the speaker's details support his or her message?** Are any facts or ideas contradictory? Interpret what the speaker is saying.

- **Does the speaker's conclusion follow logically from the details presented?** Does the speaker avoid logical errors, such as over-simplification and false cause and effect? Evaluate how well the speaker has presented the message.

Speaking Speak loudly enough to be heard and clearly enough to be understood. Be sure that your **tone of voice** is appropriate for your **audience** and the topic being discussed. For group discussions among your peers, a relaxed "be yourself" tone is usually fine. However, even in informal situations you should follow these guidelines:

- Be considerate of other participants.
- Let others finish talking before you comment on their ideas.
- Ask appropriate questions.
- If you want to disagree with the ideas of a participant, do so with courtesy and tact.
- Focus your own comments on the facts and issues of the discussion.
- Respect others' opinions.

Feedback A final factor in developing group discussion skills is **feedback**—offering others an evaluation of the strengths and weaknesses of their discussion points and accepting their evaluation of yours. You can ask the following questions after a group discussion to evaluate the success of the discussion and the participants' discussion skills. Be sure to consider the individual participants (including yourself) and the group as a whole.

- Was the group goal clearly stated at the beginning of the discussion?
- Did the group have a discussion agenda or outline? If so, was it followed?
- Was everyone prepared?
- Did each participant perform the key responsibilities of his or her role as leader, recorder, or participant?
- Did all group members participate?
- Were all participants listening actively and speaking clearly?
- Was there any conflict? Was it resolved respectfully?

YOUR TURN 9   Participating in Group Discussions

- Form a small group of five to six students to discuss the topic of one or more of the causal analysis essays you and your classmates wrote for the Writing Workshop (or another topic, if your teacher prefers).
- Before beginning the discussion, be sure to determine who will be the leader, who will be the recorder, and who will be participants.
- Decide among yourselves whether or not you will have an agenda to follow for your discussion. If you decide to have an agenda, follow it.
- Be prepared to take notes during your discussion and to write evaluations of yourself and your peers to hand in to your teacher.

YOUR TURN 9

You may wish to assign students to groups, balancing more forceful and more reserved personalities. Include points in your rubric for participation of all members of the group. This will encourage group members to allow others to be heard.

Connections to Life, pp. 120–121
Alignments
TEKS 14A, 15C, 15E, 16A, 16B, 16E, 16F

Focus on Viewing and Representing

OBJECTIVES

- To analyze how television depicts a real-life career
- To recognize how TV both mirrors and molds people's view of the world
- To compare TV representations with real life

Quotation for the Day

"... [T]elevision reporting allows no opportunity for revisiting and rethinking the text. It's easy to 'suspend belief' and become passive receptors of whatever sounds, messages, and dramatic stories the producers choose to convey. The result is we become less critical and evaluative in our thinking."

(Regie Routman, American educator)

Use the quotation as a springboard to discussion of TV viewing. Ask students: *Does TV viewing involve less critical thinking than reading a book or newspaper?*

TEACHING TIP

Television and the Real World
Point out to students that as TV affects one's view of the world, it also affects one's view of other people. How accurate are these depictions? Have students analyze a TV show for its view of a particular culture—for example, Mexican, Canadian, or African American culture. Challenge students to compare TV's depiction to what they know from their own experience. Students should note instances in which they think the representation rings true and when it seems false. Ask volunteers to share their ideas and discuss with the class the limitations that might make it difficult for TV to portray such a real-life diversity of cultures.

Focus on Viewing and Representing

Analyzing the Effects of TV

WHAT'S AHEAD?

In this section, you will analyze how television depicts a real-life career. You will also learn how to

- recognize how TV both mirrors and molds your view of the world
- compare TV representations with real life

No one would deny that television is a powerful medium. Indeed, since the 1950s, television has been recognized as a very influential form of mass media. Television has had an impact on the educational, political, and economic systems of countries around the world. Television has also reshaped the patterns of family life. Some critics believe that television has weakened personal and community relationships by isolating people in their living rooms. Others believe there is a definite cause-and-effect relationship between television and practically every malady of modern society.

Television and the Real World

Mold or Mirror? From one point of view, the reason television is such a powerful medium is that television programs are reflections of the world. According to this point of view, the psychiatrist in a sitcom and the detective in a police drama **represent,** or portray, real-life people going about the business of real life. Television, then, is seen as a mirror that reflects a true image of life in our society.

Another point of view is that television molds—at least partially—the way that people see the world around them. Many media critics argue that television shapes people's values and attitudes, especially those of children. For example, some believe that a child who regularly watches a television program in which violence is the ultimate solution to problems will accept, perhaps even use, violence as a solution to his or her own problems.

The truth is that both points of view—television as mirror and television as mold—are partially true. To some degree, **television reflects the real world,** and, to some degree, **television molds people's views of the real world.** The important question for you to ask yourself is "To what extent does television influence *my* view of the world?" To answer this question, you must become a critical viewer—an analyzer of television.

122 | Chapter 3 | Exposition: Examining Causes and Effects

RESOURCES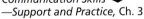

Focus on Viewing and Representing
Practice
- *Media Literacy and Communication Skills*
  —*Support and Practice,* Ch. 3
  —*A How-to Handbook*

Teaching Notes
- *Media Literacy and Communication Skills*
  —*A Teacher's Guide,* Ch. 3

True Lies? One way television mirrors the real world is in the number of careers and walks of life that are depicted in entertainment programming. On any given night of television programming, you might see

- a doctor performing an emergency operation
- a lawyer defending a murder suspect
- a sportscaster preparing for a broadcast
- a parent giving advice to a teenager

People of these types exist in the real world, of course—and all of the scenarios occur in the real world. The question is "How realistic and accurate are television's **representations,** or depictions, of these people and scenarios?" To find out, you must do a **comparative analysis.** For example, you might first analyze, or **deconstruct,** programs that show a particular career as it is represented on television. Then, you could find out how realistic that representation is by talking to people who actually work in that field.

Through Rose-Colored Glasses Imagine that your favorite television series is about a nurse in a big-city hospital. You watch the hour-long series every week. In fact, you like the main character, Lucinda, so much that you watch re-runs, refuse to answer the phone during the broadcast, and dream of a career as a nurse. How would you answer someone who asked you why being a nurse is so appealing to you? The chart below lists some reasons and examples you might provide to answer such a question.

Reasons that a career as a nurse appeals to me	Examples from the TV program
Nurses are highly-trained, well-paid professionals.	In one episode, Lucinda saved a patient's life because she recognized unusual symptoms in the patient. She refused to give the patient medicine that would have proved fatal. She has a fabulous apartment in the city, so she must make a lot of money.
Nurses are compassionate people who care about all of their patients and their co-workers, too.	In last week's episode, Lucinda took great care of one really rude patient. She also covered a mistake that another nurse had made.
Nurses lead very exciting, full lives.	In every episode, Lucinda has to deal with emergencies that are a matter of life and death. She has a glamorous life outside of work, too.
Nurses are respected by the people they work with and the patients they serve.	The medical staff and the patients look up to Lucinda. They all think she is great.

Critical Thinking

Analysis. Point out to students that TV also presents many short, fast-paced, attention-grabbing cause-and-effect situations to viewers in commercials. A commercial for a laundry detergent, for example, might show dirty clothes (effect) unaffected by an inferior detergent brand (cause), and then the commercial might state that Brand X (cause) will produce cleaner clothes (effect).

Students may want to work together to videotape some commercials that present cause-and-effect situations. Then, they could show the tapes to the class. They can identify the causes and effects and explain the reasons for their own reactions to the ads.

Cooperative Learning

TV's Portrayal of People of Various Cultures. Put students in groups of three to four and have them discuss how television portrays career opportunities for people of various cultural groups. Here are some questions students can use to guide their discussions: Are people of one cultural group always portrayed in similar careers? Are certain positions shown as being filled predominately by people of one group? How do these depictions compare to your own experience? How does your own cultural background affect how you think about television and about the relationship between people's careers and their cultures? Tell students to be prepared to share and support their responses.

Focus on Viewing
and Representing,
pp. 122–124
Alignments
TEKS 16B, 16E, 19B, 20B

Wrap It Up

Metacognition. Use the following question to prompt students to reflect on their viewing:

1. Were you surprised to learn that TV can shape people's view of the real world? Explain.

Then, have students answer the following question:

2. How can you find out how realistic a TV representation is? [by doing a comparative analysis of the TV representation and the real thing]

YOUR TURN 10

If students are contacting people in the community who practice certain careers, you may want to obtain permission slips from parents or guardians and from the people students will contact before sending students into the community. After students share their findings, follow up with a general discussion of the accuracy of TV representations of the real world.

TEACHING TIP

Checking TV Representations of Reality
Some students may not have access to television at home. Have these students use literature as a source for depictions of careers for **Your Turn 10**.

Reality Check Now, suppose that you talk about your dream of a career in nursing to your best friend. Your friend responds with surprising news: Her uncle is a veteran nurse at Megalopolis Memorial Hospital. With your friend's help, you call her uncle to find out what being a nurse is *really* like.

Reasons that a career as a nurse appeals to me	What a real nurse told me
Nurses are highly trained, well-paid professionals.	Lou said that while it is true that nurses are highly trained, the pay is not as good as it should be. Nurses often have to "struggle to make ends meet, like everybody else."
Nurses are compassionate people who care about all of their patients and co-workers.	Lou said that as a rule nurses are compassionate people who want their patients to get better, but that patients and co-workers are not always easy to like.
Nurses lead very exciting, full lives.	Lou said that this is so true that he "stays at the point of exhaustion all the time." He also said that the pressures on a nurse make for a lot of "wear and tear on the nerves."
Nurses are respected by the people they work with and the patients they serve.	Lou said that most health care professionals treat nurses with respect, although some don't. Patients, he said, often are more demanding than respectful, though the appreciative patients more than make up for the unappreciative ones.

As the example shows, the difference between "TV life" and real life can be great. Therefore, a critical viewer of television should never lose sight of the fact that what he or she sees on television is a just a *representation* of something that exists in real life, and that some TV *representations* of the real world are not very accurate or realistic at all.

YOUR TURN 10 Checking TV Representations of Reality

Working in groups of three or four, brainstorm a list of three prominent careers that are commonly depicted on prime-time television. Then, brainstorm a list of characteristics of each career as television represents it. Finally, contact people who actually practice each career and ask them to comment on your list of career characteristics. Finally, create a third list of the information often omitted from TV representations of these careers. Share your group's results with the rest of the class.

124   Chapter 3   Exposition: Examining Causes and Effects

RESOURCES

Your Turn 10
Practice and Reinforcement
- *Media Literacy and Communication Skills*
  —*Support and Practice*, Ch. 3, transparencies and worksheets
  —Videocassette 1, Segment C

CHAPTER 3 Choices

Choose one of the following activities to complete.

▶ CAREERS
1. To Be or Not to Be Choose a career that interests you. List three positive and three negative effects this career choice might have on your life. For example, if you decided to become a doctor, you might list "opportunity to help people" as a positive effect. Under negative effects you might list "possibly being on call at all hours." Create a **poster** for your classmates highlighting the pros and cons of this career choice.

▶ VIEWING AND REPRESENTING
2. A Double Take Videotape a nightly news report. As you review it, take notes on news stories that involve cause and effect. For example, you might see a news report on the effects of new medical research, or the causes of reading problems among high school students. Look carefully for examples of oversimplification or false cause-and-effect. Use your notes to prepare a short **oral presentation** for your class about the news story.

▶ CROSSING THE CURRICULUM: ARTS & SCIENCE
3. Make It Work! Rube Goldberg (1883–1970) was a cartoonist famous for dreaming up complex cause-and-effect inventions to accomplish simple tasks. With a small group of peers, draw your own **Rube Goldberg machine** to perform a simple task such as turning on a radio, feeding a pet, or emptying the garbage. Include at least five steps between start and finish. Be prepared to explain your causal chain to your classmates.

▶ CROSSING THE CURRICULUM: LITERATURE
4. Motivations and Consequences Writers of fiction often shape their characters and plots around cause-and-effect. Choose a character from a work of fiction and write a **short analysis** of the causes, or motives, of the character's behavior. What effects do his or her actions have on fellow characters or the plot? For example, in Shakespeare's *Julius Caesar*, what are the *causes* and *effects* of Brutus's betrayal of Caesar?

PORTFOLIO

▶ CAREERS
Students might need to research some of the positives and negatives of their career choices to create valid lists. They may also wish to use information gathered in **Your Turn 10** if relevant. Hold an informal career fair in your classroom at which students can share their posters with both their classmates and other students.

▶ VIEWING AND REPRESENTING
You may wish to encourage students to watch or read other versions of the event to gain a more balanced perspective on the event and to recognize oversimplification or false cause and effect more easily. Pair students who do not have access to TV or a VCR with those who do, and have them complete the assignment together.

▶ CROSSING THE CURRICULUM: ARTS & SCIENCE
To help students get started, have small groups brainstorm a number of simple, repetitive tasks that they do every day. Before actually designing their machines, students should list the steps involved in doing the task. Then they can begin to sketch their machines.

▶ CROSSING THE CURRICULUM: LITERATURE
Instruct students to focus on just a few causes and effects of the character's behavior. Remind students that limiting their focus will force them to evaluate more critically the causes and effects they choose to discuss. Suggest that students present their analyses in the form of a book review that others in the class may read.

RESOURCES
Examining Causes and Effects
Assessment
- Assessment Package
  —Chapter Tests, Ch. 3
  —Chapter Tests in Standardized Test Formats, Ch. 3
  —Assessment Alternatives, Ch. 3
- Test Generator (One-Stop Planner CD-ROM)

Choices
Rubrics
- Assessment Package
  —Assessment Alternatives, Ch. 3

Choices Alignments
Choice 1   TEKS 2A, 21B, 21D
Choice 2   TEKS 1A, 10B, 11F
Choice 3   TEKS 21B, 21D
Choice 4   TEKS 16A, 16C, 20B, 20E

CHAPTER 4

Analyzing Problems

Use this guide to create an instructional plan that suits the individual needs of your students. Assignments marked by an asterisk (*) may be completed out of class. Times given for pacing lessons are estimated. See pp. 126–127 for chapter-wide resources. Resources listed in this guide are point-of-use resources only.

Curriculum Connections

Connections to Literature *p. 157*
- Analyzing the Problems of a Literary Character

Choices *p. 165*
- Crossing the Curriculum: Literature
- Speaking and Listening
- Media and Technology

internet connect
GO TO: go.hrw.com
KEYWORD: EOLang 10-4

 All resources for this chapter are available for preview on the *One-Stop Planner CD-ROM with Test Generator*. All worksheets and tests may be printed from the CD-ROM.

Texas Resources For a complete listing of all resources prepared for Texas teachers and students, please see the blue box at the beginning of each chapter.

T125A

		Chapter Opener *pp. 126–127*	**Reading Workshop: Reading a Problem-Analysis Article** *pp. 128–137*
DEVELOPMENTAL PROGRAM		⏲ **30 minutes** • Analyzing Problems *p. 127* • Your Turn 1 *p. 127*	⏲ **100 minutes** • Preparing to Read *p. 128* • Reading Selection *pp. 129–131* • First Thoughts on Your Reading 1–2 in groups *p. 132* • Making Generalizations *pp. 132–134* • Your Turn 2 *p. 134* • Problem-Solution Structure *pp. 134–135* • Your Turn 3 *p. 135* • Test Taking Mini-Lesson *p. 137*
CORE PROGRAM		⏲ **20 minutes** • Analyzing Problems *p. 127* • Your Turn 1 *p. 127*	⏲ **90 minutes** • Preparing to Read *p. 128* • Reading Selection *pp. 129–131* • First Thoughts on Your Reading 1–4 *p. 132* • Making Generalizations *pp. 132–134* • Your Turn 2 *p. 134* • Problem-Solution Structure *pp. 134–135* • Your Turn 3 *p. 135* • Vocabulary Mini-Lesson *p. 136* • Test Taking Mini-Lesson *p. 137*
ADVANCED PROGRAM		⏲ **15 minutes** • Analyzing Problems *p. 127* • Your Turn 1 *p. 127*	⏲ **70 minutes** • Preparing to Read *p. 128* • Reading Selection *pp. 129–131* • First Thoughts on Your Reading 3–4 *p. 132* • Making Generalizations *pp. 132–134* • Your Turn 2 *p. 134* • Problem-Solution Structure *pp. 134–135* • Your Turn 3 *p. 135* • Vocabulary Mini-Lesson *p. 136*
RESOURCES	**PRINT**	• *Communications*, TP. 31, WS. p. 60	• *Alternative Readings*, Ch. 4 • *Communications*, TPs. 32, 33, WS. pp. 61–68
	MEDIA	• *One-Stop Planner CD-ROM*	• *One-Stop Planner CD-ROM*

TP.=Transparency   WS.=Worksheet

Writing Workshop: Writing a Problem-Analysis Essay *pp. 138–157*	**Giving an Informative Speech** *pp. 158–161*, **Recognizing News Genres** *pp. 162–164*
⏱ **200 minutes** • Find a Problem to Analyze *pp. 138–139* • Consider Purp., Occasion, Aud., Tone *pp. 139–140* • Investigate Your Problem *pp. 140–141* • Analyze Your Problem and Your Turn 4 *pp. 141–142* • Provide Support *pp. 142–143* • Write Your Thesis Statement *p. 143* • Organize Your Essay and Your Turn 5 *p. 145* • Framework and Your Turn 6* *p. 146* • Writer's Model and Student's Model *pp. 147–149* • Evaluate and Revise and Your Turn 7 *pp. 150–151* • Focus on Word Choice and Your Turn 8 *pp. 152–153* • Proofread, Publish, and Reflect *pp. 155–156* • Grammar Link and Your Turn 9 *pp. 155–156*	⏱ **120 minutes** • Prepare a Memorable Speech *pp. 158–159* • Deliver Your Speech *p. 160* • Conduct a Question-and-Answer Session *pp. 160–161* • Listen Actively to a Speech *p. 161* • Your Turn 11 *p. 161* ⏱ **40 minutes** • What Are News Genres? *pp. 162–163* • Knowing What You Are Getting *pp. 163–164* • Your Turn 12* *p. 164*
⏱ **190 minutes** • Find a Problem to Analyze *pp. 138–139* • Consider Purp., Occasion, Aud., Tone *pp. 139–140* • Investigate Your Problem *pp. 140–141* • Analyze Your Problem and Your Turn 4 *pp. 141–142* • Provide Support *pp. 142–143* • Write Your Thesis Statement *p. 143* • Critical Thinking Mini-Lesson *p. 144* • Organize Your Essay and Your Turn 5 *p. 145* • Framework and Your Turn 6* *p. 146* • Writer's Model and Student's Model *pp. 147–149* • Evaluate and Revise and Your Turn 7* *pp. 150–151* • Focus on Word Choice and Your Turn 8 *pp. 152–153* • Proofread, Publish, and Reflect *pp. 155–156* • Grammar Link and Your Turn 9 *pp. 155–156* • Connections to Literature and Your Turn 10 *p. 157*	⏱ **100 minutes** • Prepare a Memorable Speech *pp. 158–159* • Deliver Your Speech *p. 160* • Conduct a Question-and-Answer Session *pp. 160–161* • Listen Actively to a Speech *p. 161* • Your Turn 11 *p. 161* ⏱ **30 minutes** • What Are News Genres? *pp. 162–163* • Knowing What You Are Getting *pp. 163–164* • Your Turn 12* *p. 164*
⏱ **120 minutes** • Find a Problem to Analyze *pp. 138–139* • Consider Purp., Occasion, Aud., Tone *pp. 139–140* • Investigate Your Problem *pp. 140–141* • Analyze Your Problem and Your Turn 4 *pp. 141–142* • Provide Support and Write Thesis Statement *pp. 142–143* • Critical Thinking Mini-Lesson *p. 144* • Your Turn 5, Framework, and Your Turn 6* *pp. 145–146* • Writer's Model and Student's Model *pp. 147–149* • Evaluate and Revise and Your Turn 7* *pp. 150–151* • Focus on Word Choice and Your Turn 8 *pp. 152–153* • Proofread, Publish, Reflect and Your Turn 9 *pp. 155–156* • Connections to Literature and Your Turn 10* *p. 157*	⏱ **90 minutes** • Prepare a Memorable Speech *pp. 158–159* • Deliver Your Speech *p. 160* • Conduct a Question-and-Answer Session *pp. 160–161* • Listen Actively to a Speech *p. 161* • Your Turn 11 *p. 161* ⏱ **20 minutes** • What Are News Genres? *pp. 162–163* • Knowing What You Are Getting *pp. 163–164* • Your Turn 12* *p. 164*
• Communications, TPs. 34–37, WS. pp. 69–78 • *Designing Your Writing*	• *Media Literacy and Communication Skills Kit* —Support and Practice, Ch. 4 —A How-to Handbook —A Teacher's Guide, Ch. 4
• *One-Stop Planner CD-ROM*	• *Media Literacy and Communication Skills Kit* —Videocassette 1, Segment D • *One-Stop Planner CD-ROM*

CHAPTER 4
Analyzing Problems

CHAPTER OBJECTIVES

- To read a problem-analysis article in preparation for writing a problem-analysis essay
- To write an analysis of a problem
- To prepare and deliver an informative speech
- To recognize news genres and analyze news coverage

Chapter Overview

Knowing how to analyze problems is a necessary skill for students if they are to understand and improve their surroundings. This chapter is designed to help students analyze problems when they read, write, speak, and listen. Students will read a magazine article in the Reading Workshop and will analyze problem-analysis structure. Students will write their own problem-analysis essays in the Writing Workshop.

Focus on Speaking and Listening gives students the opportunity to present an informative speech, and Focus on Viewing and Representing will assist students in analyzing the coverage of news programs. Although each section can be taught independently, the sections taught together provide a comprehensive interpretation of problem-analysis structure.

Why Study Analyzing Problems?

Because people must solve problems every day, analyzing problems is important both in and out of the classroom. In the language arts classroom, analyzing problems helps students use reading strategies, understand content, and communicate possible solutions to the problems in a text. Outside the classroom, analyzing problems helps students look for true sources of problems and for effective solutions. Because problems are often more complex than they appear, the "obvious" solution may not solve the problem at all. Analyzing problems is essential to reach effective solutions.

Teaching the Chapter

Option 1: Begin with Literature

If you choose to focus first on literature, introduce this chapter before or after studying the way characters analyze and resolve problems in short stories, novels, epics, and dramas. The instructional emphasis is on analyzing characters' problems, examining how the author solves problems within the story, or deciding how the problems and solutions affect the outcome of the piece. When students have completed the literature segment, they can read "Danger Beneath the Dash" to see how nonfiction writers develop problem-analysis articles. When students understand how the problem-analysis process works, they will be ready to write their own problem-analysis essays.

Option 2: Begin with Nonfiction and Writing

Beginning with the material in this chapter, make students aware of problem analysis and its structure. The article "Danger Beneath the Dash" and the Reading Workshop instruction provide a framework for students' understanding of generalization and problem-solution structure. Students will then select and analyze a problem, finding support for their ideas and writing a problem-analysis essay in the Writing Workshop. With this framework for understanding problem analysis, students will be prepared to examine and write about problem-solution structure when they encounter it in literature.

Making Connections

■ To the Literature Curriculum

Conflict, or a series of problems which the characters analyze and solve, provides the foundation for most literature. The narrator in "By the Waters of Babylon," by Stephen Vincent Benét, must decide whether to make his journey despite his father's warning not to go east. Problem analysis provides the basis for stories, which in turn give strategies for overcoming real-life problems.

Lesson Idea: Problem Analysis in "By the Waters of Babylon" by Stephen Vincent Benét.

1. With students, make a chart like the one below, showing the problems the narrator faces, his analysis of the problems, and the action resulting from that analysis.

Problem	Analysis	Action Taken

2. Have students work in groups to determine what has prepared the narrator for his journey and for solving his problems. Then, ask students to discuss in their groups whether, when they tried something new, they ever experienced feelings similar to the narrator's on the raft, however well prepared they thought they were.

3. Invite students to debate whether the narrator chose the best solutions for his problems and to state the reasons for their opinions.

4. Introduce students to the magazine article on pp. 129–131. Explain that the author has analyzed a problem and proposed a solution based on the information he has gathered. Use the instruction on problem-solution structure and making generalizations to help students write their problem-analysis essays.

■ To Careers

To demonstrate to students that problem analysis is a necessary strategy in life, suggest that students interview a parent, guardian, or other adult, asking what types of problems they must solve in the workplace. Because many people do not see problem solving as a separate part of their jobs, you may wish to have students brainstorm types of common work-related problems before the interviews. After the interviews are complete, have students create a chart or poster of various careers and the problems workers must solve. Before you send students into the community, you may wish to alert parents or guardians about the activity.

■ To the Community

The Reading Selection for this chapter discusses a serious problem of concern to all drivers. To increase local awareness among students, invite a police officer to your classroom to discuss the effect of distractive devices on local motorists, particularly teenagers, and any local regulations related to the problem. This activity may help students understand their responsibilities as drivers and avoid potential problems.

■ To the Health Curriculum

Have interested students work in small groups to research how health investigators find the sources of tainted food or a serious epidemic and decide what action to take. Each group member should contact a different agency, such as the local health department, the state health department, the Centers for Disease Control, and any other agencies which might become involved in a serious health crisis. The agencies' Web sites may also offer excellent information. When students have completed their research, invite them to report their findings to the class.

CHAPTER 4

Analyzing Problems

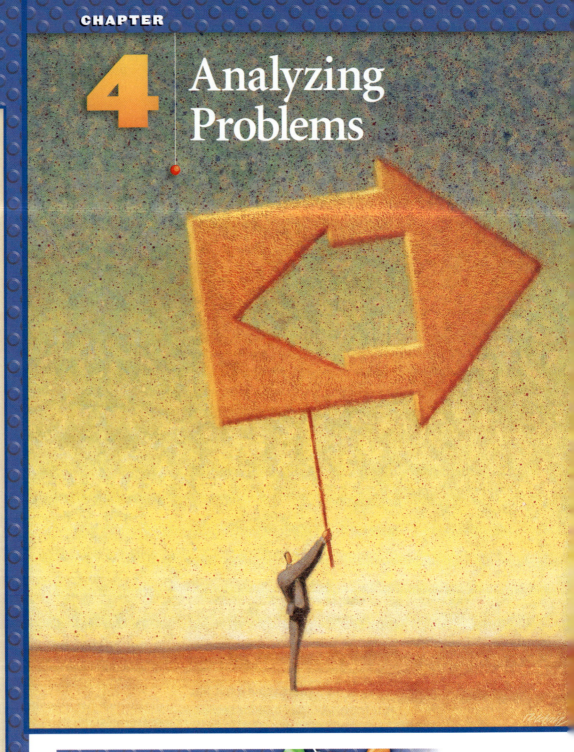

PREVIEWING THE CHAPTER

■ Taught separately or taught together, each workshop demonstrates how problem solving applies to reading, writing, speaking, and viewing. Reading a problem-analysis article prepares students to write their own problem-analysis essays. When students understand the problem-solution structure, they will be able to apply it to giving a speech and recognizing news genres. For help in integrating this chapter with grammar, usage, and mechanics chapters, see the chart on pp. T401A–T401B.

INTRODUCING THE CHAPTER

■ To introduce the chapter, use the Journal Warm-up, Transparency 31, in *Communications*.

VIEWING THE ILLUSTRATION (19A)

■ The illustration shows a man holding an arrow-shaped sign. Point out that the arrows in the illustration create confusion for the viewer. Direct students to analyze the illustration for clues that might help them understand the sign. [The larger arrow and the man's body point to the right. The other arrow is smaller, so it seems less important. The sign suggests going or looking to the right.]

Representing. Invite students to create illustrations of problems and solutions. Display the illustrations for students to analyze.

CHAPTER RESOURCES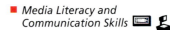

Planning
- Lesson Planner, Ch. 4
- Block Scheduling, p. T125A (this book)
- One-Stop Planner CD-ROM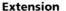

Practice
- *Communications*, Ch. 4

- Media Literacy and Communication Skills

Extension
- Designing Your Writing

Reinforcement
- *Communications*, Ch. 4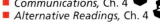
- Alternative Readings, Ch. 4

PREVIEW

Reading Workshop
Reading a Problem-Analysis Article
PAGE 128

Writing Workshop
Writing a Problem-Analysis Essay
PAGE 138

Focus on Speaking and Listening
Giving an Informative Speech
PAGE 158

Focus on Viewing and Representing
Recognizing News Genres
PAGE 162

Analyzing Problems

- There are traffic jams every afternoon at a traffic light near your school.
- Your dog keeps discovering new ways to get out of the yard, costing you time and aggravation in trying to find him.
- Your grades are falling. Between your part-time job and extracurricular activities, you have less and less time for homework.

A good way to deal with problems like these is to analyze the **factors** (conditions or situations) that help cause them. By **analyzing** (looking at all the parts that contribute to the whole) you can better understand what causes a problem and maybe how to solve it. Problem analysis helps to create an awareness of problems and, through awareness, to motivate others to find solutions. News media, community meetings, and governmental assemblies are only a few of the many public forums where people exchange ideas and seek ways to make the world a better place.

GO TO: go.hrw.com
KEYWORD: EOLang 10-4

YOUR TURN 1 — Analyzing Problems

With a partner, brainstorm a list of problems that affect not just you personally, but others as well. Make a two-column chart. In the first column, list three or four problems, and in the second column, list some of the factors that you think cause or contribute to each problem. Next, discuss the problems with your partner. Be prepared to share your chart and discussion notes with your class.

Motivate

Have students form small groups to analyze the problem of a hypothetical student's transportation. Tell the class that the student must arrive at school early and leave late, and that he or she cannot take the school bus. Groups should analyze possible solutions, such as taking public transportation, carpooling, or purchasing a used car. Then, have a member of each group discuss its main points with the class. Remind students that brainstorming possible solutions in groups of people is often an effective way to solve problems.

ELEMENTS OF Literature

Problem Analysis in Literature. In *Elements of Literature,* Fourth Course, see "The Sword in the Stone," by Sir Thomas Malory, pp. 951–953, and *The Tragedy of Julius Caesar,* by William Shakespeare, pp. 775–877, for examples of characters who analyze problems.

YOUR TURN 1

Remind students to look beneath the surface for problem factors. For example, if a roof collapses after a heavy snowfall, people might blame the snow instead of the weak roof.

Chapter Opener, pp. 126–127
Alignments
TEKS 2A, 16B, 16F

Texas Resources
- *Lesson Planner,* Ch. 4
- *TAAS Tool Kit*
- *Preparation for TAAS*
- *Preparing for English II End-of-Course Examination*
- *One-Stop Planner CD-ROM*

- *Daily Language Activity Transparencies*
- *Vocabulary Workshop* and *Tests*

Evaluation and Assessment
- *Test Generator* (*One-Stop Planner CD-ROM*)

- *Assessment Package*
  —*Chapter Tests,* Ch. 4
  —*Chapter Tests in Standardized Test Formats,* Ch. 4
  —*Assessment Alternatives,* Ch. 4

Internet
- go.hrw.com (keyword: EOLang 10–4)

Reading Workshop

OBJECTIVES

- To read a problem-analysis article in preparation for writing a problem-analysis essay
- To make and evaluate generalizations
- To analyze problem-solution structure
- To learn how to use definition and restatement context clues
- To answer logic questions

Quotation for the Day

"I think you should learn, of course, and some days you must learn a great deal. But you should also have days when you allow what is already in you to swell up inside of you until it touches everything."

(*From the Mixed-up Files of Mrs. Basil E. Frankweiler,* E. L. Konigsburg, 1930– , American writer)

Write the quotation on the chalkboard or on an overhead transparency. Lead students in a discussion of what they already know about solving problems. Encourage them to draw on their own experiences to help them understand the problem-analysis article.

TEACHING TIP

Preparing to Read
The concepts of making generalizations and understanding problem-solution structures are introduced at right and will be covered in detail on pp. 132–135. Understanding problem-solution structure and making generalizations are the focus of instruction for the Reading Workshop, and the Reading Selection **"Danger Beneath the Dash"** illustrates both concepts.

Reading Workshop

Reading a Problem-Analysis Article

WHAT'S AHEAD?

In this section, you will read a problem-analysis article and learn how to

- make and evaluate generalizations
- analyze problem-solution structure

Have you ever been told, "Be careful what you wish for. You just might get it"? Often, when people make wishes, they fail to anticipate the consequences that their wishes might have. For example, we wish for technological advances to make our lives easier, but we fail to foresee some of the problems these advances can cause. The following article, "Danger Beneath the Dash," examines an unintended problem created by cellular phone use and discusses some of the factors that contribute to the problem.

Preparing to Read

READING SKILL

Making Generalizations   You make a **generalization** whenever you combine information in a text with what you already know to make a statement or judgment that applies to the world in general. For example, if you read an article stating that late out-of-town games leave your school's volleyball team ill-prepared for the next school day, you might make the generalization that athletes in other sports may be similarly affected. From the specific case of the volleyball team, you generalize about *all* school athletes.

READING FOCUS

Problem-Solution Structure   When you read about problems, pay special attention to the way the writer has organized the information. You will find that although the following elements are present, writers arrange them in different ways.

- a clear statement of the problem
- evidence (facts, statistics, and anecdotes) of the problem
- discussion of contributing factors—situations that help cause the problem
- suggested ways to solve the problem

Exposition: Analyzing Problems

RESOURCES

Reading Workshop
Reinforcement
- *Alternative Readings,* Ch. 4

Reading Selection

As you read the following article, notice how the writer raises your awareness of a problem and the factors that contribute to it. Jot down answers to the numbered active-reading questions as you read.

from Reader's Digest

Danger Beneath the Dash

BY STEVEN LEVINGSTON

Sharon Fultz, 38, had her mind on the future as she drove her car south on Morgan Ross Road in Morgan Township, Ohio. It was July 1, 1997, and she was chatting on her hand-held phone with her fiancée, Christopher Congdon, about their wedding plans. Apparently engrossed in her conversation, she sailed through a stop sign. Congdon heard his fiancée cry out . . . as a truck broad-sided her car at about 50 miles an hour.

The car's fuel tank ruptured, and flames engulfed the car and the truck's front end. The truck driver, who couldn't avoid the collision, escaped and tried to rescue Fultz, but the flames pushed him back. Sharon Fultz, who was to be married later in the month, died at the scene.

This tragic accident is a searing reminder of a growing danger: distracting electronic gadgetry in our cars. It's no surprise that we love cellular phones, which now are used by more than 62 million Americans. We're a society on the run, and to save time, we conduct business, chat with friends, make our arrangements—all from the car.

Experts warn, however, that cell phones and other devices in a car can drive us straight to disaster if we're not careful. In a study published in 1997, University of Toronto researchers Donald Redelmeier and Robert Tibshirani analyzed data from Toronto drivers with cell phones who were involved in crashes. Their shocking conclusion: Drivers talking on a cell phone were *four* times as likely to have an accident as those not on the phone. That's similar to the risk of driving with a blood-alcohol level at the legal limit.

"Nothing's quite as wonderful as

1. Why do you think the article begins with a real-life example instead of first stating the problem?

2. Why do so many people use cell phones?

3. What specific details raise your awareness of the dangers of cell phone use?

Reading Workshop 129

Active-Reading Questions

The purpose of the active-reading questions is to encourage students to think about the structure and support necessary for a problem-analysis essay and to think of how readers draw generalizations from the material. Students' answers will provide an informal evaluation of their understanding of problem-solution structure.

ANSWERS
Possible answers are given below.

1. The real-life example catches the reader's interest and emphasizes the deadly consequences of the problem.

2. Because people are busy, they use cell phones to save time.

3. Drivers using cell phones are four times more likely to have an accident as those not on the phone and are as dangerous as drivers whose blood-alcohol levels are at the legal limit.

Reading Workshop, pp. 128–135
Alignments
TEKS 7B, 7D, 7G, 7H, 8A, 12A, 12B
TAAS R5
English II End-of-Course 3

Texas Resources
- *Lesson Planner,* Ch. 4
- *TAAS Tool Kit*
- *Preparation for TAAS*
- *Preparing for English II End-of-Course Examination*
- *One-Stop Planner CD-ROM*

READING PROCESS

Continued on p. 130

PREREADING
Set a Purpose for Reading the Selection.
The purpose set for students in this chapter is to analyze problem-solution structure.

Before students begin to read, have them look at the **Active-Reading Questions** and the **First Thoughts on Your Reading.** Point out to students that the questions focus

Reading Workshop 129

Active-Reading Questions
ANSWERS continued

4. not dialing and driving simultaneously

5. thinking about conversation instead of driving, cell phone conversation requires more concentration than conversing with a passenger, objects in peripheral vision tend to be suppressed

---

a cell phone if you have a traffic problem," says Stephanie Faul, communications director for the AAA Foundation for Traffic Safety. "But there's no question they contribute to crashes."

To remain safe, experts suggest applying these new rules of the road:

Don't dial and drive

Just the mechanics of dialing or answering the phone can prove dangerous. A twenty-six-year-old tow-truck driver was heading to work in his truck on a Sunday morning in June 1997, according to police. After he entered Cedar Lake, Indiana, he drove along U.S. 41 toward 133rd Avenue. Realizing he was late, he picked up his cell phone and looked down to punch in his work number, police said.

In front of him, Richard and Barbara Francis were heading to church when the light turned red at 133rd Avenue. Richard glanced in his rearview mirror and spotted the truck bearing down on him.

"Barb, we're going to get hit," he yelled after realizing he couldn't get out of the way. The truck plowed into the car's rear, devouring the entire back end, according to police. Barbara, cut and bruised, had to be extricated from the wreck. (Charges of speeding against the driver were later dismissed.)

> **4.** What possible solution does the subhead above suggest?

The Insurance Institute for Highway Safety says the safest way to make calls from your car is just before or after your trip. Others suggest using your cell phone while stopped at a traffic light, or asking a passenger to field the call.

Some experts say that cautiously pulling over to the side of the road and finding a place to park before making a call is a safe way to use your cell phone. This may seem inconvenient, but "when your conversation is over," says James Solomon of the National Safety Council, "you can focus on driving again."

Don't think dialing is the only problem

Initially experts believed that the problems with car phones lay mostly with its mechanical use—dialing, holding the phone, putting it back— and that hands-free speakerphones might offer an advantage. But a bigger problem is the mental distraction caused by talking on the phone.

"I've been run off the road by people on a car phone," says Alvin Yamaguchi, a motorcycle officer with the California Highway Patrol. "When you're on the phone, you're thinking about your conversation—not about the road."

Talking on a car phone is often more distracting than listening to the

> **5.** What evidence of mental distractions is given in the next three paragraphs?

130 Chapter 4 **Exposition:** Analyzing Problems

READING PROCESS

primarily on making generalizations and on understanding the structure of the problem-analysis article. Students' reading should concentrate on these two concepts.

Students' personal purposes for reading will differ and must be explored. One purpose might be seeking knowledge of problem-solution structure to prepare for writing. Ask students how their purposes might differ if they were reading the article for a driver's education class.

A sign in Brooklyn, Ohio, where it is a misdemeanor to use a cell phone while driving unless both hands are on the steering wheel

radio or the tape deck. Moreover, it's a greater drain on our mental faculties than chatting with a passenger, experts say. A voice on a cell phone is usually not as distinct and requires more concentration to comprehend. What's more, a passenger can alert you to road dangers. The person in the car with you is aware of traffic, whereas the person not in the car isn't," says Roger Koppa of the Texas Transportation Institute.

Walter Wierville, a fellow at Virginia Tech's Center for Transportation Research, says that a driver may be looking at the road while talking on the phone, but still miss important cues. "In particular, objects in your peripheral vision often tend to be suppressed," he says.

Beware of more high-tech distractions

Sophisticated communication and navigation devices are now showing up in rental cars and in high-end luxury models. They help us pinpoint our location, browse the Internet, check e-mail, receive and send faxes by voice command all while seated behind the wheel.

In 1997, one automaker demonstrated a prototype car with Internet access, complete with a computer screen in the center of the dashboard. "Companies are creating these devices because people want them," says Julie Rochman of the Insurance Institute for Highway Safety. "We know that more and more will be coming on the market, and they can be very distracting. These items can be beneficial in reporting impaired drivers to law enforcement, calling for help, keeping you from getting lost. But these new technologies have to be used responsibly."

"Driving is a full-time job," concludes National Safety Council's James Solomon. "You should not be doing anything else behind the wheel."

6. Does Dr. Rochman see similarities between cell phones and other electronic gadgets? Why do you think so?

Active-Reading Questions
ANSWERS continued

6. She sees similarities between cell phones and cars with computers. She believes they both can interfere with driving safely, but both can also be helpful to drivers.

Reading Workshop 131

READING PROCESS

READING
Self-Check. Students should work through the **Active-Reading Questions** while they read the article and then move on to the **First Thoughts on Your Reading.** As students are reading the selection, have them create charts listing evidence and logical generalizations that the evidence supports. This will help them remain focused on the article, maintaining attention and comprehension levels. Students should list at least three generalizations.

Reading Workshop 131

First Thoughts on Your Reading

ANSWERS
Possible responses are given below.

1. A driver using a cell phone is apt to concentrate more on the conversation than on the road. In addition, the conversation partner, unlike the passenger in a car, is unaware of traffic conditions.

2. The author uses subheads to highlight cautions for cell phone use.

3. The cellular phone information shows the dangers of distracting the driver; other electronic devices are likely to do the same.

4. The writer focuses more on solutions—probably because the problem is familiar and his purpose is to suggest safety steps.

First Thoughts on Your Reading
Working with a partner, write the answers to the following questions on your own paper.

1. Explain in your own words why talking on a cell phone is more distracting than talking with a passenger.
2. Why do you think the writer uses subheads in the article?
3. How does the evidence of the cellular phone problem support the point that other high-tech devices will also create problems?
4. Does the writer focus more on the problem or its solution? Why do you think this is the case?

READING SKILL

Making Generalizations

Beyond Specifics   A **generalization** goes way beyond a specific case to make a general statement about a whole group of cases. You make generalizations all the time—combining your **prior knowledge** (what you already know) with details from your reading, observations, and experiences to make a statement that applies to an entire classification of things or people. For instance, what statement could you make about the following sentences that would apply to all of them?

> One auto company decided to name its new pickup truck the Mountain Lion. Their new four-door sedan is called the Stallion. Another company named its new sports utility vehicle the Grizzly and its new sports car the Cheetah.

If you said, "It seems that automobile companies are basing the names of their new vehicles on animals," then you would be making a generalization. You have created a general statement based on the key words and the pattern in the passage's details—animals' names and new automobiles. As a reader, you use generalizations in two ways.

- **You identify writers' generalizations.** In "Danger Beneath the Dash," for instance, the writer provides real-world examples, facts, statistics, and quotes from experts. From all this specific information, the writer makes generalizations about *all* drivers who talk on cell phones. Determining what generalizations a writer makes helps you evaluate the accuracy of his or her writing. If a writer bases generalizations on insufficient evidence or faulty logic, then you should be skeptical about what the writer presents. When you read a problem analysis, consider also

---

132   Chapter 4   **Exposition:** Analyzing Problems

READING PROCESS

EXTENDING
Connect to the World. Review with students the purposes they set for themselves in reading the article. Ask them to evaluate whether they achieved their goals, and then assign students to small groups. Each group should contact a driver education instructor. Have students investigate the matter of cell phone use. What instruction is given about using electronic devices while driving? Then, have students report their findings to the class.

whether the writer's own opinions (bias) about the problem affect the generalizations he or she makes.

- **You make your own generalizations** based on information in your reading to help you discover the essential meaning of a passage.

True or Not? Just because a statement sounds like a generalization doesn't make it valid, or true. "All pigs have wings" and "Every sun has nine planets" are invalid, or unsound, generalizations. To evaluate a writer's generalization and your own, use these questions:

- **Is the generalization based on sufficient information?** Generalizations require support—a great many facts, statistics, and real-life experiences. A generalization based on only one example or a single experience is a **fallacy** (error in thinking) known as a **hasty generalization.** Beware of making your own hasty generalizations and watch out for writers who fail to support their generalizations with sufficient information.

- **Is the generalization relevant?** Stick to the point. For instance, a generalization about the cost of cell phone service would not be relevant to the problem discussed in "Danger Beneath the Dash."

- **Does the generalization contain qualifying words?** Words like *many, most, usually,* and *often* limit the claim a generalization makes. Since most generalizations do not apply to every single situation, these qualifying words often signal a valid generalization. Be suspicious of too-broad statements that contain words like *every, all, always,* and *never;* most generalizations have exceptions.

TIP When you are asked to make a generalization about a reading passage on a test, base your generalization *only* on the information given in the passage.

Critical Thinking

Analysis. Place students in small groups, and provide each group with samples of advertisements for cell phones. Ask students to look for the generalizations the ads make and the persuasive appeals, especially any appeals that suggest a problem-solution relationship. Then, discuss whether the generalizations are relevant and have sufficient support and whether they contain qualifying words. Ask students to note what the advertisement does not say and to consider whether the arguments are valid.

THINKING IT THROUGH — Making Valid Generalizations

Use the following steps to make valid generalizations based on a reading passage. The example responses are based on another article about safe cellular phone use.

▶ **STEP 1 List key details (facts, statistics, and other evidence) from the reading passage.** Each day, fifty thousand highway and neighborhood emergencies are reported with cellular phones. Dialing 911 on a cellular phone is a free call with most service providers. The use of cellular phones can reduce emergency response times in many situations.

▶ **STEP 2 Consider your own knowledge or experience that relates to what you have read.** I once had a flat tire and had to walk two miles to find a phone. A cellular phone would have been helpful then. Imagine my trouble if I had been in a serious accident. My parents once used their cellular phone to report a reckless driver to the police.

▶ **STEP 3 Combine your prior knowledge with the text information to make a generalization.** In many situations, cellular phones are helpful, possibly even life saving.

▶ **STEP 4 Evaluate your generalization. Is it valid? Is it based on sufficient information? Is it relevant?** There are two facts, a statistic, and two examples from my own life. The generalization is related to the data and observations about cell phone use. <u>Many</u> and <u>possibly</u> are words that qualify, or limit, the statement. This is a <u>valid</u> generalization.

YOUR TURN 2 — Making Generalizations

Use the Thinking It Through steps above and information from "Danger Beneath the Dash" to evaluate the three generalizations below. Is each generalization valid, relevant, and based on sufficient evidence? Be prepared to discuss each generalization with the class.

1. Traffic safety professionals are very concerned about improper cell phone use.
2. People should never use a car phone while driving.
3. It can be dangerous for people to read a map while driving.

YOUR TURN 2 ANSWERS

1. The generalization is valid, relevant, and based on sufficient evidence.
2. The word *never* makes it invalid.
3. This statement is irrelevant.

| READING FOCUS

Problem-Solution Structure

One Step at a Time One good way to work through an analysis of a problem is to examine how the writer organizes his or her explanation. When you look closely at the organizational structure, you may discover that it follows one of the patterns common to problem-analysis articles. Once you recognize a pattern, then you can map the organizational structure, either in writing or in your head. Knowing the pattern is like having a map of the text that helps you see and understand the writer's main points and important supporting details.

There are several ways writers organize an analysis of a problem. The focus may be either on the problem or on its possible solutions—or sometimes both. "Danger Beneath the Dash" focuses more on evidence and contributing factors and less on solutions because the solution to the problem is obvious: Don't talk on the phone while you are driving.

The chart on the next page shows the organization of "Danger Beneath the Dash." Notice how many sections of the essay focus on the problem.

RESOURCES

Your Turn 2
Practice
- *Communications*, WS. p. 61

Reinforcement
- *Communications*, TP. 32, WS. p. 62

Your Turn 3
Practice
- *Communications*, WS. p. 63

Reinforcement
- *Communications*, TP. 33, WS. p. 64

Focus on the Problem	
1. State the problem.	The increasing use of cellular phones while driving is a growing problem.
2. Give evidence.	The article provides many different warnings and statistics from experts.
3. Examine contributing factors.	Drivers look away from the road to dial or pick up the phone.
4. Propose a solution.	Don't talk on a cell phone while driving.

Imagine an article that, unlike "Danger Beneath the Dash," is about a problem with a less-obvious solution: hunger in developing countries. Few people would argue that hunger in developing countries is not a problem; therefore, the article would focus more on the solution and less on the problem. By focusing on solutions, a writer draws your attention to thinking about what is most important—finding answers.

Focus on the Solution	
1. State the problem.	While industrialized countries have plenty of food, many people in developing countries do not have enough.
2. Give evidence.	Statistics show the prevalence of starvation and malnutrition in developing countries.
3. Propose and examine solutions.	Governments and charities could direct aid in the form of food supplies.
	Governments and charities could create programs to develop business and industry.
	Governments could institute reforms to eliminate blocks to distribution of food.

TIP Although problem-analysis articles primarily explain a problem, they can also have a secondary persuasive purpose. For example, "Danger Beneath the Dash" is trying to persuade drivers to stay off the phone while they are driving.

YOUR TURN 3 — Analyzing Problem-Solution Structure

The chart at the top of the page does not list all the ideas and information in the "Danger Beneath the Dash" article. Copy the chart onto your own paper and fill it in with more evidence, contributing factors, and proposed solutions discussed in the article.

Timesaver

Divide the class into small groups to work on **Your Turn 3** together. Each group should take only one of the different tasks: evidence, contributing factors, or proposed solutions. Have each group report orally to the class.

YOUR TURN 3

ANSWERS
Possible answers are shown.

Evidence includes statistics from University of Toronto researchers, the tow-truck driver's accident, the motorcycle officer's being run off the road, and quotations from various experts.

Contributing factors include mental distraction and suppressed peripheral vision.

Solutions include using cell phones only when pulled over or when stopped at a traffic light, and using technologies responsibly.

Wrap It Up

Metacognition. Have students respond to the following question:

1. How did the **Active-Reading Questions** help you understand problem-solution structure?

Then, have students respond to the following question:

2. List three ways to evaluate a generalization. [Look for sufficient evidence, decide whether it is relevant, and determine whether it is valid or contains qualifying words.]

MINI-LESSON VOCABULARY

Context Clues: Definitions and Restatements

ANSWERS

1. The restating word is *absurd*. *Absurd* does fit in. The meaning of *ludicrous* must be similar to *absurd*—"ridiculous."

2. The definition is *totally absorbed*. *Totally absorbed* does fit. The meaning of *engrossed* must be similar to *totally absorbed*—"concentrating completely."

3. The restating phrase is *tried unsuccessfully*, which does fit. The meaning of *futile* must be similar to *tried unsuccessfully*—"useless."

4. The restating word is *swallowed*, and it fits. The meaning of *engulfed* must be similar to *swallowed*—"to take in or absorb completely."

5. The definition is *freed*, and it fits. *Extricated* must be similar to *freed*—"taken out."

MINI-LESSON VOCABULARY

Context Clues: Definitions and Restatements

When you read problem-analysis articles, you may encounter unfamiliar words—technical terms, for example. A good way to find the meanings of these terms is to look for **definition and restatement context clues.** These are words or phrases defining an unfamiliar term or restating it. Commas or dashes that set off a definition or restatement from the rest of the sentence can signal these context clues. Words or phrases like *are, is, or, that is, also known as, which is to say, sometimes called,* and *meaning* can also signal a definition or restatement:

Airtime, actual time spent talking on a cell phone, often determines the billing rate for cellular phone users. [The definition is underlined; the commas provide a context clue.]

You will often find that both clue words and punctuation signals appear together in a sentence.

THINKING IT THROUGH — Using Context Clues

Use the steps below to apply definition and restatement context clues. The sample responses are based on the following sentence.

Cell phone use while driving is an *impediment,* or obstacle, to safe driving.

1. **Find a word or phrase that restates the unfamiliar word.** Check for signal words or for commas or dashes that set off the definition or restatement from the unfamiliar word. The word obstacle is set off from the rest of the sentence with commas; the clue word or also signals a restatement.

2. **Try replacing the unfamiliar word with the definition or restatement to see if the sentence still makes sense.** Cell phone use while driving is an obstacle to safe driving.

3. **Write your best guess about the meaning of the unfamiliar word.** The meaning of impediment must be similar to obstacle—a hindrance or obstruction.

PRACTICE

Use the steps above to find the meanings of the italicized words in the following sentences. Write answers on your own paper.

1. The very thought of surfing the Internet while driving seems *ludicrous*—that is, absurd—to some people.

2. Sharon Fultz was *engrossed*—totally absorbed in a conversation.

3. The truck driver made *futile* attempts to avoid the collision, which is to say he tried unsuccessfully to miss her car.

4. Her car was completely *engulfed* in flames. Fire quickly swallowed the entire car.

5. Barbara was carefully *extricated* from the wreck, meaning that she was freed by rescue workers using special equipment.

RESOURCES

Vocabulary
Practice
■ *Communications,* WS. p. 65

Test Taking
Practice
■ *Communications,* WS. pp. 66–68

MINI-LESSON TEST TAKING

Answering Logic Questions

Reading tests often test your ability to see how the relationship of two or more details in a passage fit logically into an overall pattern. These patterns include comparisons, contrasts, and chronologies (time orders). Below are clue words and phrases that signal each of these patterns.

- comparison—*equally, like,* and *similar*
- contrast—*but, however,* and *nonetheless*
- chronological—*after, before, later,* and *next*

Matching the same clue words in the passage with those in an answer choice indicates the best answer. Here is a typical reading passage and a logic question.

In the past few years, approximately thirty-five out of every 100,000 sixteen-year-old drivers have died. Some states are tackling this problem head-on by adopting graduated licensing programs for new teen drivers. Most plans begin with an ordinary learner's permit and then progress to daytime-only driver's licenses before granting unrestricted licenses. By adopting a similar graduated licensing program, the country of New Zealand reduced teen driving deaths nearly 13 percent.

1. The writer provides information about New Zealand in order to
   A. contrast driving in New Zealand with driving in the U.S.
   B. show that New Zealand had graduated licensing programs before the U.S.
   C. point out that teen driving is a problem
   D. show that graduated licensing programs like those in New Zealand can effectively reduce teen driving deaths

THINKING IT THROUGH Answering Logical Questions

Keep the following steps in mind as you answer a logic question.

1. **Read the question carefully, and then locate specific details in the passage.** Information about New Zealand is in the last sentence of the paragraph.

2. **Look for clue words that signal what kind of relationship the details have with the rest of the passage. Then, look for clue words that show the same relationship.** The sentence about New Zealand uses the clue word *similar*, which indicates that this detail is making a comparison. Only answer D uses a clue word that indicates a comparison—*like*.

3. **Eliminate answers that show inaccurate relationships.** Remember, even though the statement made in a possible answer may be true, it may not show the same relationship indicated in the passage. Answer A uses the word *contrast*, which is a contrast clue, making it an incorrect choice. B uses the chronology clue word *before*, making it incorrect. C doesn't have any clue word and is clearly wrong. Only D has a comparison clue word, so D is the correct answer.

Looking Ahead to Writing

Writing a problem-analysis essay will be the focus of the Writing Workshop in this chapter. As each student researches a topic, he or she will decide whether to focus on the problems or the solutions for the paper's structure. Remind students that the organizational charts on p. 135 can help them structure either type of essay.

**Vocabulary
Alignments**
TEKS 6B
TAAS R1

**Test Taking
Alignments**
TEKS 7C, 7E
TAAS R4

Writing Workshop

OBJECTIVES

- To write an analysis of a problem
- To investigate the factors that contribute to a problem
- To gather and organize support for an analysis of a problem
- To coordinate and subordinate ideas
- To eliminate "word wasters"
- To recognize and correct sentence fragments

Quotation for the Day

"Natural curiosity is the fuel of all powerful writing and is also the best tool for discovering what's important and what wants to be written about."

(Barry Lane, 1955– , American educator and writer)

After you read the quotation to the class, have students brainstorm a list of problems or issues about which they are curious. Remind students that subjects they find interesting or are curious about make the best writing topics.

TEACHING TIP

Find a Problem to Analyze

You might suggest that students avoid controversial problems about which they have strong feelings. Strong opinions may blind them to some of the important causes of the problem and may affect their objectivity.

Writing Workshop

WHAT'S AHEAD?

In this workshop, you will write an analysis of a problem. You will also learn how to

- investigate the factors that contribute to a problem
- gather and organize support for an analysis of a problem
- coordinate and subordinate ideas
- eliminate "word wasters"
- recognize and correct sentence fragments

Writing a Problem-Analysis Essay

What makes some problems so difficult to solve? Often it is their complexity. Complex problems are usually made up of several different parts. When you **analyze** a problem, you break it into its parts in order to understand it better. For example, imagine that your school has recently adopted the baboon as its mascot. You know this adoption is a problem, but in order to understand this problem fully and explain it to others, you will need to analyze it. What factors make this situation—having the baboon as the school mascot—problematic? An analysis of the problem might reveal that

- a majority of students are unhappy with the choice
- it makes the school vulnerable to ridicule
- it is unlikely that a baboon suit can be found or that anyone would be willing to wear it if it were

In this Writing Workshop, you will learn how to analyze a problem by identifying and discussing the parts that make up the problem.

Prewriting

Find a Problem to Analyze

The Needs of the Many Everyone has problems, but not every problem will interest a general audience of readers. You need to choose a problem that will. For example, you would probably not want to write a detailed analysis of your Aunt Bertha's battle with the tomato worms that have invaded her garden. "Who cares?" your readers would say. Instead, choose a problem that matters both to you and to your readers.

For instance, one writer, whose essay you will read later in this chapter, chose to write about the high rate of traffic accidents involving teenage drivers—a problem that will certainly interest many readers. To begin looking for an interesting problem to analyze and discuss in your essay, try the following suggestions.

- **Read a weekly newsmagazine or watch the national and local news on TV each evening for a week.** Keep on the lookout for stories about ongoing problems that will interest you and your readers.
- **Browse the Web.** Find information about government and community groups devoted to raising awareness of specific problems.
- **Check your local and school newspapers.** Look at the editorials and letters to the editor. Check items about school board and city council meetings to identify problems your community is currently facing.

After using one or more of these suggestions, list two or three problems that you think might be good topics for an analysis. Share your list of problems with your classmates. Then, choose one problem that you would like to analyze.

TIP You might want to work collaboratively on this problem–solution essay. If so, work with your teacher so that you and your fellow students are sure of your individual responsibilities.

Consider Purpose, Occasion, Audience, and Tone

The Right Style How can you show readers that the problem you are writing about is significant and that your analysis of it is sensible? Start by considering your **purpose** (goal for writing), **occasion** (opportunity for writing), **audience** (readers), and **tone** (your feelings toward the problem).

Purpose and Occasion Generally, **the purpose for writing an analysis of a problem is to raise readers' awareness of the problem and to explain the problem so that readers have a better understanding of it.** In addition, you may have **occasion**, or a real-life reason, to write about the particular problem you chose. For instance, if you are about to get your driver's license, you might have occasion to analyze the high rate of accidents among teenage drivers. ◀ **KEY CONCEPT**

Audience and Tone You need to tailor your writing to your particular audience—that includes both what you say to them and how you say it. To help you tune in to your audience's needs, ask yourself the questions in the following Thinking It Through.

Meeting INDIVIDUAL NEEDS

LEARNERS HAVING DIFFICULTY
Provide a quick outline, such as the following, for all students to fill in with information on their prospective topics.

Topic: _____

Purpose: _____

Occasion: _____

Audience: _____

Tone: _____

Students' responses will indicate whether they understand these terms. As you walk around to check work, you can offer immediate, specific feedback. If time permits, work individually with students having difficulty.

MULTIPLE INTELLIGENCES
Interpersonal Intelligence. To help students anticipate the needs of their audience, encourage them to role-play with partners. First, have them role-play explaining to their friends why they did not get their homework done, and then have them role-play explaining the same situation to a teacher. Tell students to note that different information is stressed or minimized in each account, depending on the audience. They will need to be just as aware of their audience when writing.

Prewriting, pp. 138–145
Alignments
TEKS 1A, 1B, 1C, 2A, 4B, 4C
TAAS W1, W2, W4
English II End-of-Course 4

Texas Resources
- *Lesson Planner*, Ch. 4
- *TAAS Tool Kit*
- *Preparation for TAAS*
- *Preparing for English II End-of-Course Examination*
- *One-Stop Planner CD-ROM*

THINKING IT THROUGH

Analyzing Audience

▶ **Who is my audience?** Figure out who might be interested in learning about the problem you have chosen. What do you know about the concerns and interests of those readers? Which aspects of the problem will interest them most?

▶ **What do my readers already know about this problem?** Some readers will need background information; others may want to know more about certain aspects of the problem. For example, if you are writing about the high rate of auto accidents involving teenagers (the problem) and parents are your audience, you might assume that they are painfully aware of the high cost of insuring teenage drivers.

▶ **What tone is appropriate for addressing my audience?** Remember, your **tone** reveals your attitude toward your topic and your readers. You achieve a particular tone through word choice and sentence style. For your analysis of a problem, use a tone formal enough so that you will be taken seriously, but informal enough to avoid seeming stuffy and dry. If you were writing to your state representatives, for example, your tone would be more formal than if you were writing for your classmates.

TIP A word closely related to tone is voice. **Voice** is the identifiable characteristics of your writing that make it sound like you. What voice will you want to show through your writing? Do not write long, complicated sentences or use certain words just because you think they sound important or intelligent. The best words to use are the ones you are most comfortable using—words that sound like you, not like someone else. Be careful, however, to maintain a voice that is appropriate to your audience. In classroom writing, you should avoid slang and other overly informal language.

Investigate Your Problem

First Things First Before you can explain your problem to an audience, you need to get a better understanding of it yourself. Do some initial research or investigation into the problem, keeping these two goals in mind:

- getting a better understanding of the problem you have chosen
- gathering specific facts, quotations, and examples you can include in your essay to support your ideas

---

TEACHING TIP

Investigate Your Problem
As students visit the library, remind them to use only unbiased and serious sources. Tell students to avoid tabloids, materials published by special interest groups, and magazines that cover only the surface of issues. You may wish to provide guidelines for what you will or will not accept as source material. Also, remind students that they must ask permission before taping interviews, including telephone interviews.

To find sources, look at the suggestions below. Use at least two types of sources to obtain information.

- **Visit a library.** Check current magazines, journals, newspapers, or books to get up-to-date information on your problem.
- **Conduct interviews.** If you know or can find someone who is knowledgeable about your problem, make an appointment with him or her for an interview. Be sure to prepare a list of questions ahead of time and to take detailed notes during the interview. You might also want to tape-record the interview.
- **Search the Internet.** You can find ongoing—even *endless*—discussions of specific problems posted on Internet newsgroups and on mailing lists. Remember, though, that anyone can post a comment on the Internet. Make sure you use information only from reputable individuals or organizations—information that can be verified in other sources.
- **Observe directly.** If your problem is local, go out and do some direct observations to gather information. For example, if you are writing about stray dogs and cats, visit a local animal shelter or an organization that helps stray pets. Take notes on where and when stray animals gather and who is feeding them.

Reference Note
For more on **interviewing,** see page 902 in the Quick Reference Handbook.

TIP As you do your research, keep track of your sources of information; you may need to cite them in your essay. For information on **citing sources,** see page 237.

Analyze Your Problem

Questions and Answers After gathering information, you can begin to analyze the problem. One of the best ways to begin analyzing a problem is to ask yourself the *5W-How?* questions (*Who, What, When, Why, Where,* and *How?*). The chart below shows how one writer used the *5W-How?* questions to analyze the problem of teenage auto accidents.

Problem: The high rate of traffic accidents involving teenage drivers	
Who is affected by the problem?	Parents, teenagers, police, insurance companies, doctors, and the general public
Why are they concerned?	Everybody wants to save lives and money, but teenage drivers want to retain their freedom.
When did this problem become evident?	The problem has probably been around as long as teenagers have been driving. Maybe it seems worse now because more teens are driving.

(continued)

TEACHING TIP

- **Conduct Interviews**
Before students contact people to interview them for information, give the class a mini-lesson on interviewing. Remind students that in interviews they will play two roles, one as speaker and one as listener. As speakers, students should ask clear questions, respond appropriately to any questions the interview subject has, and ask follow-up questions if they do not understand an answer. As listeners, students need to focus their attention, respect the interview subject's opinions, monitor their nonverbal communications (facial expressions and gestures), and evaluate what the interview subject says. For more information on interviewing, see p. 902 in the **Quick Reference Handbook.**

STUDENTS WITH SPECIAL NEEDS
Students with special needs may find videos and television newsmagazines particularly helpful as sources. You may wish to check with colleagues in audiovisuals to begin building a library of suitable clips. Using a short video clip, demonstrate how to take notes and record the appropriate bibliographic information.

(continued)

Where is this a problem—locally, statewide, nationally, or globally?	It is a national problem—maybe even a worldwide problem. I have heard that some other countries have much better teenage-driver safety records than the United States does.
What are the causes of the problem?	Inexperienced drivers, peer pressure to take risks while driving, the perception that accidents only happen to other people
How does this problem affect me and my audience?	Bad driving puts everyone at risk, and makes adults view teenagers as irresponsible. Teenagers and their parents pay high insurance rates.

Choose Key Points Look through your notes and your answers to the *5W-How?* questions and select three to five key points to cover in your essay. These should be the ideas that you think are the most important for your readers to know. The writer who created the chart above chose these three key points (the answers to the *How?* question).

TIP When drafting your essay you will most likely revise these key points for content and style and then use them as topic sentences for your body paragraphs.

Key Points:
Bad driving puts everyone at risk
Unsafe driving makes adults view teens as irresponsible.
Teenagers and their parents pay high insurance rates.

YOUR TURN 4 Choosing and Analyzing a Problem

Use the guidelines above to choose, investigate, and analyze a problem for a problem-analysis essay.

Provide Support

Legs to Stand On You pick up your newspaper one morning and find the following headline on the front page: "Local Penguins Attack Again." Unless you live in Antarctica or in the far reaches of the Southern Hemisphere, you are going to have a hard time believing that headline. You read on. Aha! The news story explains that your local zoo had five penguin handlers roughed up by the little tuxedo-wearing birds in the last three weeks. Now you understand that there really is a local penguin problem.

What changed your mind was that the news story provided **supporting details** for the headline. You, too, will need to provide a variety of supporting details for your key points in order to explain your problem to readers. Here are four types of support you can use.

- **Facts** (objective statements that can be checked) and **statistics** (number facts) give strong support. The student writing about teenage auto accidents found that in the United States more than six thousand teenagers die in auto accidents every year. Be sure that your facts are accurate and up-to-date. Record the original sources of your facts since most teachers will require you to cite them.

- **Expert testimony** (quotations and comments) carries weight because it comes from someone who has already studied or experienced the problem. For example, if you were writing about fire safety problems, you might quote a representative of your local fire department. Whenever you use quotations, make sure they are accurate—a person's exact words.

- **Examples** (specific cases that illustrate a point) can come from your personal knowledge or from research. The student writing about teenage auto accidents found examples of ways that teenagers can lower their car insurance rates.

- **Anecdotes** (brief stories about a real person or event) provide a human element and add interest to your essay. An anecdote about a student from your high school who crashed her car makes the topic of teenage auto accidents more personal and compelling.

To find facts, expert testimony, examples, and anecdotes that support your key points, look carefully at the information you gathered during your initial research. If these sources do not provide enough supporting details, do more research—and keep looking until you find what you need.

Write Your Thesis Statement

Make a Statement After gathering support for your key points, your next step is to generate a preliminary **thesis statement**—a sentence stating your topic plus your controlling (main) idea about the topic. Your thesis statement should state your problem and alert your readers to its seriousness, and it should relate directly to the key points you have chosen as your focus. Here is one writer's preliminary thesis statement.

> The distressing safety record of teenage drivers is still a real problem in the United States today.

TIP If you find as you write that you need to change or add to your key points, you can go back and revise your thesis statement to reflect the changes or additions you make.

Critical Thinking

Synthesis. Because students come in contact with many first-person accounts, ranging from tabloid articles to Web sites, they must be able to evaluate which sources are valid. Have students form small groups to create guidelines for "expert testimony" and the reliability of sources. When the groups have finished, have them share their lists and create class guidelines for research.

TEACHING TIP

Write Your Thesis Statement
Remind students that including the key points of their essays can be particularly helpful in focusing their thesis statements. For example, the thesis statement at left could read: "The distressing safety record of teenage drivers is still a real problem in the United States today, resulting in negative images of teens, high insurance rates, and the loss of many teens' lives."

MINI-LESSON: CRITICAL THINKING

Coordinating and Subordinating Ideas

ANSWERS

1. A. S
   B. C
   C. S
   D. S

2. A. S
   B. S
   C. C
   D. S

3. A. C
   B. S
   C. S
   D. S

Taking a Second Look

Have students look at each item in each set and determine what types of sources they might use to support each point. Possible answers follow.

1. A. interviews, direct observation
   B. library, interviews, Internet
   C. interviews, direct observation
   D. interviews

2. A. interviews, direct observation
   B. interviews, direct observation
   C. interviews, direct observation
   D. interviews, direct observation

3. A. library, Internet, direct observation
   B. interviews, library, Internet
   C. interviews, library
   D. interviews, library, Internet

MINI-LESSON: CRITICAL THINKING

Coordinating and Subordinating Ideas

As you look through your notes you may ask yourself, "How can I distinguish the problem from its contributing factors?" or "Which of these ideas should I choose to include in my essay?" One way to begin making sense of your ideas is to group related ideas and then classify them as either *coordinate* or *subordinate*.

Coordinate ideas are equal in importance to one another. These are often your key points that become the main ideas of your body paragraphs. These ideas, for example, are coordinates: *Kerry plays the guitar. Marcus creates computer games. Ann is a talented dancer.*

Subordinate ideas are less important ideas. They are supporting details that elaborate on broader or more important points. With the preceding statements about Kerry, Marcus, and Ann, the following would be a subordinate point: *Ann specializes in bolero and flamenco styles.*

Your first step in organizing your ideas should be to try to find the relationship between them. That is, you need to look at each idea and ask, "Is this idea equal in importance to other ideas on the list, or is it a less important point that supports another idea?"

PRACTICE

For each item, write S (for *subordinate*) for every statement that is subordinate to the boldface statement. Write C (for *coordinate*) for every statement that is coordinate to the boldface statement.

Write your answers on your own paper.

1. **Crowded classrooms are a major problem.**
   A. There are as many as forty students in some classrooms.
   B. New legislation may alleviate most of the class-size problems through increased state funding of teacher certification programs.
   C. Some classrooms present a fire hazard because of overcrowding.
   D. One in five teachers says she feels overwhelmed by the number of students in each class.

2. **Construction of the new elementary school has fallen behind schedule.**
   A. Severe weather conditions have caused many delays.
   B. The school board had trouble choosing a final design.
   C. The old building was poorly designed.
   D. Obtaining permits took longer than originally estimated.

3. **The price of movie tickets keeps increasing.**
   A. Video rental prices also are rising.
   B. Theaters must continually pay to upgrade their sound systems.
   C. Theater owners' taxes increase yearly.
   D. Distributors charge theater owners more money to rent films.

RESOURCES

Critical Thinking
Practice
- *Communications,* WS. p. 70

Your Turn 5
Practice
- *Communications,* WS. p. 71

Organize Your Essay

Put Things in Order In your essay, **your key points and supporting details should follow a logical progression so that your readers can easily comprehend your explanation.** To make sure that your essay follows a logical progression, use one of these three organizational patterns:

- **Order of importance** Begin with the least important point and build up to the most important one, or the reverse.
- **Chronological order** Present your problem as it has developed over time.
- **Cause-and-effect order** Choose this order to show what caused your problem or to indicate what the effects of the problem are.

For her essay on the high rate of auto accidents among teenage drivers, this writer arranged her key points by order of importance, from least to most important. She created the following chart to reflect that plan.

Initial thesis	The distressing safety record of teenage drivers is still a real problem in the United States today.
Key point 1 (least important)	Unsafe driving makes adults view teens as irresponsible.
Key point 2 (next important)	Teenagers and their parents pay high insurance rates.
Key point 3 (most important)	Bad driving puts everyone at risk.

KEY CONCEPT

TIP You may use more than one order in your essay, but choose one as the dominant, overall pattern. If a detail does not fit the pattern, ask yourself whether it is worth keeping. If your answer is yes, find a place to fit it in.

YOUR TURN 5 Getting Ready to Write

Make sure that you have completed each of the following prewriting steps before drafting your essay.

- Provide facts, quotations, and examples to support your key points.
- Write a thesis statement that states your problem and alerts readers to its seriousness.
- Organize your essay by order of importance, chronological order, or cause-and-effect order.

Quotation for the Day

"Write to discover what you have to say. You do not have to know what you want to say to be able to say it. Just the opposite. You have to write to find out what you have to say."

(Donald M. Murray, 1924– , American writer and educator)

Write the quotation on the chalkboard or on an overhead transparency. Have students freewrite in response to the quotation, drawing on their own experiences if possible. Invite volunteers to share their responses with the class.

YOUR TURN 6

As students begin writing, remind them to provide sufficient support for each key point. While less obvious points will require the most convincing and detailed support, strong points also need valid support.

Writing

Problem-Analysis Essay

Framework

Introduction
- Catch your audience's attention.
- State the problem in your thesis.

Body
- State the key points in your analysis of the problem.
- Provide support for your key points.
- Organize ideas in a way that makes sense.

Conclusion
- Restate your thesis.
- Emphasize the seriousness of the problem and its importance to your audience.

Directions and Explanations

Start with Something Interesting A good way to get an audience's attention is to start with an intriguing question or with an anecdote to which an audience can relate on a personal level.

Make Yourself Clear The key to your entire essay is your thesis statement. It should clearly and concisely outline the problem you discuss in the essay.

Close to Home One way to help your readers recognize the seriousness of your problem is to help them realize how the problem affects them. If you can show that the problem has an impact on your readers' lives, they are more likely to be interested in what you are saying.

Do Not Confuse the Issue Focus on only one key point in each body paragraph of your essay. Provide enough supporting details—facts, statistics, quotations, examples, and anecdotes—to create a well-developed paragraph. Use transitions to help coherence.

Repeat Yourself Do not simply copy the thesis sentence from your introduction and insert it in your conclusion. Restate the thesis in terms that will remind your audience how the problem should matter to them.

 Writing a First Draft

Using the framework above, write a first draft of your own problem analysis. Before you begin, read the Writer's Model that follows.

146 Chapter 4 Exposition: Analyzing Problems

Writing
Writing Prompts
- *Communications,* TP. 34, WS. p. 72

Your Turn 6
Practice
- *Communications,* TP. 35, WS. p. 73

A Writer's Model

This first draft of an essay closely follows the framework on the previous page.

Licensed—but Safe?

How safe on the road are today's teenage drivers? Few people will deny that the safety features built into today's cars are more advanced than ever. Driver's education students today graduate with a greater awareness of road dangers thanks to the efforts of their teachers, to public service announcements in the media, and to student groups such as Students Against Drunk Driving (SADD) and Youth Against Road Rage (YARR). Some states have even enacted graduated licensing programs that ease teenagers into driving privileges and responsibilities. Therefore, teenage drivers today *should* be safer on the road than they have ever been, right? Well, it may be too early for congratulations. To tell the truth, the distressing safety record of teenage drivers is still a real problem in the United States today.

Part of the problem is that teenagers' bad driving record creates a negative image of teens. How often are words like *irresponsible* and *reckless* used to describe teenagers? Comments like the following, from a recent poll taken at the East Towne Mall, are common from adults. "What do you expect when you give a kid the keys? Trouble, that's what." "It's not a matter of if a sixteen-year-old will have an accident; it's a question of when." Never mind that many teenagers drive perfectly well—some adults still expect the worst.

Insurance companies know that teenage drivers are a greater risk, so they charge them higher premiums. Parents who add a teenager to their policy may find that their insurance premiums double, because insurance companies know that half of all teenage drivers have an accident within a year of getting a license. Not all teenagers have a bad record, but teenagers are the group with the highest accident rate among American drivers. Taking driver's education, having good grades and a good driving record, and driving a less-expensive car bring down the premiums a little, but the high rates still make things tough for whoever makes the payments.

(continued)

INTRODUCTION

Facts

Thought-provoking question

Thesis

BODY
Point 1

Quotations

Point 2

Statistic

Fact

Fact

Connecting Reading and Writing

Have students re-read the opening paragraph of **A Writer's Model,** noting the way the author changes direction at the end of the first paragraph by moving the reader from complacency to the realization that a problem remains. Remind students that *this* is an effective way to stimulate an audience and move them to consider possible solutions.

Writing, pp. 146–149
Alignments
TEKS 1A, 1C, 2B, 8A
TAAS W1, W2, W4
English II End-of-Course 4

(continued)

Point 3

Statistics

Fact

Anecdote

However, the greatest cost associated with poor teenage driving is not monetary—it is the cost in human lives. Car crashes are a leading killer of American teenagers—more than six thousand teenagers die in auto accidents every year. That is like having everyone in three high school homerooms die every week. Although teenagers make up only 7 percent of the American driving population, they are involved in an astonishing 14 percent of all fatal auto accidents. Even crashes that do not kill can cause long-term problems for both drivers and victims. For example, when she was sixteen, Tara Davis (not her real name) crashed her mother's car head-on into a pickup truck, seriously injuring two people. Though she was not injured physically, the accident devastated Tara emotionally. In fact, she was unable to move on with her life and her plans for her future until she asked for and received forgiveness from the people she injured. "I've never tried to forget what I caused to happen," she says, "because I don't want to cause something like that again."

CONCLUSION

Restatement of thesis

Every teenager looks forward to a driver's license and the freedom associated with driving. Even so, teenagers need to realize that along with that freedom come responsibilities and some significant risks. Those risks will be reduced only when teenagers realize that the high rate of accidents among teenage drivers is a serious but preventable problem.

A Student's Model

The following passage from a problem-solution analysis was written by David Thompson, a student from McNeil High School in Austin, Texas. It focuses on a problem he is concerned about—eating disorders in athletes his own age.

Athletes Trying to Be Too Perfect

The gymnast's vault scores a 9.5! She is a successful athlete, so obviously she is in great physical condition, the picture of health, right? Incredibly, this gymnast is extremely unhealthy and, in fact, is at high risk for cardiac arrest. She is secretly fighting bulimia, an eating disorder that is characterized by a cycle of binge eating followed by purging to try ridding the body of calories. This girl is not alone, either; eating disorders are on the rise for both male and female athletes.

Two of the most prevalent eating disorders affecting athletes are anorexia nervosa and bulimia nervosa. People with anorexia lose enormous amounts of weight from excessive dieting. These people usually do not know or admit they have a problem, and they consider themselves fat no matter what their real weight is. Anorexics will often do anything not to eat, and even when they weigh as little as eighty pounds will continue to say they are fat. Medical complications from anorexia include hair loss, irregular heartbeats, constipation, loss of bone mass, kidney and liver damage, and finally cardiac arrest and death. According to the Harvard Eating Disorder Center, "a young woman with anorexia is twelve times more likely to die than other women her age without anorexia." (www.hedc.com) Victims with bulimia nervosa indulge in a cycle of binge eating and then purging to get rid of unwanted calories. Bingeing, though, does not have to mean eating thousands of calories. To many bulimics, eating just one cookie could be considered bingeing. Purging is accomplished in several ways, including self-induced vomiting, excessive exercise, fasting, diuretics, and diet pills. Unlike anorexia, bulimics usually realize they have a health problem. . . .

INTRODUCTION
Attention-getting opening

Thesis

BODY
Point 1

Facts

Statistic

Facts

Connecting Reading and Writing

Before beginning their essays, students may wish to re-read the opening of **"Danger Beneath the Dash"** on p. 129 to see how the writer captures the reader's attention. Students should notice that showing an actual example of the problem is more effective than proposing a hypothetical situation.

Quotation for the Day

"After a lifetime of writing I still revise every sentence many times and still worry that I haven't caught every ambiguity; I don't want anyone to have to read a sentence of mine twice to find out what it means."

(William Zinsser, 1922–   , American teacher and author)

Ask students to recall reading a piece of writing that was unclear, and discuss reasons why the author may have failed to revise. Ask how they felt about the writing and why clarity was important to them. Point out that their papers also need careful revision so that readers can understand the message.

TEACHING TIP

▶ **Elaboration**

As students locate additional support for their key points, encourage them to use the keyword function on computerized searches, whether in an online library catalog, an online reference source, or a Web site. You need to be aware that Internet resources are sometimes public forums, and their content can be unpredictable.

Meeting INDIVIDUAL NEEDS

ENGLISH-LANGUAGE LEARNERS
General Strategies. Ask English-language learners to answer the evaluation questions in the "Problem Analysis" chart on this page. Then, during individual conferences, discuss the guidelines. Clarify any points that students do not understand, explain what they need to revise, and brainstorm possible revisions with them.

Revising

Evaluate and Revise Your Draft

Take a Second Look   Before you share your problem-analysis essay with readers, read through it at least twice: One reading should focus on your content (have you clearly and thoroughly discussed the problem?) and organization (does your analysis follow a logical progression?). The second reading should focus on your style, or how you express your ideas. Then, revise your essay to make it the best it can be.

▶ **First Reading: Content and Organization**   By yourself or with a partner, use the chart below to evaluate the content and organization of your essay.

Problem Analysis: Content and Organization Guidelines for Peer and Self-Evaluation

▶ Evaluation Questions	▶ Tips	▶ Revision Techniques
❶ Does the introduction get readers interested in the problem discussed in the essay?	▶ **Circle** any sentence in the introduction that grabs a reader's attention. If you do not find one, revise.	▶ **Add** an attention-getting opener; **cut** any material that does not build up to the thesis of the essay.
❷ Does the thesis state the problem clearly?	▶ **Double underline** the thesis statement. If it does not clearly state the problem, revise.	▶ **Add** a thesis statement that presents the problem clearly.
❸ Does the writer present a reasoned analysis of the problem that includes at least three key points?	▶ **Bracket** the sections in each body paragraph that introduce a key point. If you do not see at least three sets of brackets or if each bracketed section does not focus on one aspect of the problem, revise.	▶ **Add** key points so that at least three points discuss each different part of the problem.
❹ Does each body paragraph include support for the key point?	▶ **Put a star** beside each fact, statistic, example, and so forth that supports a key point. If there are not at least two stars for each key point, revise.	▶ **Elaborate** by supplying facts, statistics, expert testimony, examples, and anecdotes to support each key point.
❺ Does the conclusion restate the thesis of the essay?	▶ **Highlight** any sentence in the conclusion that restates the thesis. If you do not find one, revise.	▶ **Add** a sentence that clearly restates—but does not repeat word-for-word—the thesis.

RESOURCES

Revising
Practice
■ *Communications*, TPs. 36, 37, WS. pp. 74, 75, 76

Extension
■ *Designing Your Writing*

ONE WRITER'S REVISIONS Below is a passage from an early draft of the essay on page 147. The handwritten revisions show how the writer revised the passage based on the guidelines from the previous page.

> Parents who add a teenager to their policy may find that their insurance premiums ~~rise~~ *double*, because insurance companies know that ~~many~~ *half of all* teenage drivers have *an* accident*s within a year of getting a license.*

replace

elaborate

Analyzing the Revision Process
1. What key point does the writer seem to be making in this passage?
2. How do the revisions strengthen this point?

YOUR TURN 7 Focusing on Content and Organization

Evaluate and revise your problem-analysis essay using the content and organization guidelines on the previous page.

▶ **Second Reading: Style** An analysis of a complex problem can be hard for readers to follow—even without unnecessary words and phrases such as "at the present period of time" and "in my opinion I think." In fact, faced with these "word wasters," some readers may decide it is just not worth the time and trouble needed to read your analysis. Hold your readers' attention by eliminating unnecessary repetition and padding. Say what you mean clearly and directly. Use the following guidelines to eliminate "word wasters" from your writing.

PEER REVIEW

Have a classmate read your essay and answer the questions below.
1. For what audience was this essay intended?
2. Are there any aspects of the problem that have not been considered?

COMPUTER TIP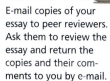

E-mail copies of your essay to peer reviewers. Ask them to review the essay and return the copies and their comments to you by e-mail.

Style Guidelines

Evaluation Question	▶ Tip	▶ Revision Technique
Do sentences contain redundant phrases or flabby phrases and clauses?	▶ **Underline** words or phrases that add length but not meaning. **Circle** the words *which* and *that,* and check to see if the clauses they introduce can be revised.	▶ **Cut** or **replace** any underlined words or phrases that dilute the meaning of a sentence. **Replace** unnecessary clauses and phrases.

Writing Workshop **151**

Meeting INDIVIDUAL NEEDS

MODALITY

Auditory Learners. Have students listen to radio and television advertisements or a political speech. Ask students to jot down five "word wasters" they hear. Then, have students work in pairs to revise them. Alert students to listen for more subtle examples of "word wasters," such as *lead pencil* or *smile on her face*.

Focus on Word Choice

Eliminating "Word Wasters"

Do you want to know a great way to frustrate your readers? Load your essay with unnecessary phrases and clauses. On the other hand, if you want your readers to understand your ideas, try this instead: Make every word in the essay count. Take a look at the examples of "word wasters" below—phrases or clauses that add length to sentences but no substance. All these "word wasters" can be reduced so that a reader does not have to wade through extra words to get to the message.

Redundant Phrases: *in the morning about nine o'clock A.M., repeat again, but nevertheless, because of the fact that, and moreover, surrounding circumstances, few in number* [The underlined words can be omitted without changing the meaning of the phrase.]

Flabby Phrases: *at the present time (now), for the reason that (because), with regard to (about), with the result that (so that)* [The words or phrases within parentheses can replace the flabby phrase.]

Flabby Which and That Clauses: *problems which are frequent (frequent problems), solutions which require creative thinking (solutions requiring creative thinking), examples that were worthwhile (worthwhile examples)* [The phrase in parentheses can replace the *which* or *that* clause.]

ONE WRITER'S REVISIONS Below is a sentence from an early draft of the problem-analysis essay on page 147, along with a revised version of the same sentence. Study the sentences, and then answer the questions that follow them.

BEFORE REVISION

How safe on the road are today's teenage drivers? Few people will deny that the safety features (that) people build into the present cars of today are more advanced than ever.

flabby *that* clause

redundant phrase

Chapter 4 Exposition: Analyzing Problems

RESOURCES

Focus on Word Choice
Practice
■ *Communications*, WS. p. 77

Exposition: Analyzing Problems

AFTER REVISION

How safe on the road are today's teenage drivers? Few people will deny that the safety features built into today's cars are more advanced than ever.

"Word wasters" have been cut or replaced.

Analyzing the Revision Process

1. Why do you think the writer replaced the phrase "the present cars of today"?
2. How did reducing the *that* clause to a phrase help the sentence?

YOUR TURN 8 Focusing on Style

Using what you have learned about "word wasters," search your essay for phrases or clauses that dilute your writing. Cut "word wasters" to create a more effective essay.

Designing Your Writing

Using Color Now that color printers and color copiers are widely available, color can be used to clarify messages and to speed up readers' comprehension—both things that are especially important in an essay that analyzes a complex, potentially confusing problem. You can use color to

- highlight a point
- tell the reader where to look first
- group related items

Should you make your essay a rainbow of color? You shouldn't if you want your audience to be able to read it. Here are some guidelines for using color.

- **Use color for clarity and emphasis, not decoration.** Color attracts the eye—you want readers to be drawn to your content, not to the decoration.
- **Remember that bright colors attract the eye more strongly than dull colors.**

Writing Workshop 153

TECHNOLOGY TIP

If equipment with color monitors is available, have students look at a Web site that uses different colors within the text. Have students discuss why they think the color is important on the screen and how it helps the reader. Be aware that Web sites are sometimes public forums, and their content can be unpredictable.

- **Use colors that strongly contrast with the background.** Contrast is the reason black letters on white are the easiest to read. Yellow on white is nearly impossible to read. On the other hand, yellow is effective against a dark background—for example, in a magazine print advertisement or on a Web page.
- **Stick to a few colors.** Using too many colors can confuse readers—the last thing you want to do.
- **Use color to unify your essay.** If you begin highlighting your subheads in green, do not switch to blue later in the essay.

Here is how one writer used color to emphasize an attention-getting sentence.

> **No more helium-filled balloons!** Environmentalists and animal rights groups are boycotting balloons because they are concerned about wild animals that die from eating such balloons.

Another student writer used color to differentiate heads from subheads in this way:

> **Crowded Classrooms**
> **Not Enough Teachers** One major factor in the problem of overcrowded classrooms is that there are not enough teachers to go around. The ratio of students to teachers worsens with the start of each new school year. . . .

Here is how one writer used color to liven up a chart and to make the lines clearly distinguishable.

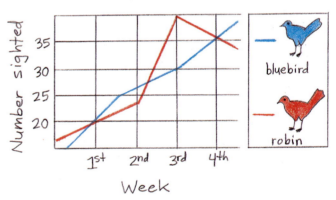

154 Chapter 4 **Exposition:** Analyzing Problems

Publishing

Proofread Your Essay

A Real Fixer Upper Who will enjoy reading your essay if it is full of errors? You want your audience to focus on what you say—not on spelling and grammar errors. Work with a peer to proofread your essay carefully to eliminate errors. Use the guidelines in the following Grammar Link to deal with one all-too-common error: sentence fragments.

Reference Note
For more on **sentence fragments**, see page 340.

Grammar Link

Sentence Fragments

A group of words may begin with a capital letter and end with a period, but that is no guarantee that it forms a sentence. **Sentence fragments** are groups of words that look like sentences but are not. To decide whether a particular group of words is a sentence or a fragment, use these tests:

1. Does the group of words have a subject?
2. Does it have a verb?
3. Does it express a complete thought?

If the group of words fails to meet even one of the tests, it is not a complete sentence.

Most fragments occur in writing when an explanation, example, or some other addition is added to the main statement. Many fragments can be corrected just by joining them to a sentence. If not, you may have to add words to make a complete sentence.

Here are examples of two types of fragments.

Prepositional Phrase Fragment	In the other room. Ray yawned.
Sentence	In the other room, Ray yawned. [The fragment is joined to the sentence.]
Verbal Phrase Fragment	Using creative thinking.
Sentence	Burke's greatest skill is using creative thinking. [A subject and a verb are added.]

PRACTICE

Correct any sentence fragments in each of the following items. If an item does not contain a fragment, write *C* for *correct*. Write your answers on your own paper.

1. Having more accidents. Teenagers must pay more for insurance.
2. Police enforcing the speed limit.
3. It was especially difficult for me. Learning to drive can be difficult.
4. Before having a flat tire myself. I didn't realize how important it was to carry a spare.
5. Studying more. I made better grades.

Quotation for the Day

"The writer of any work, and particularly any nonfiction work, must decide two crucial points: what to put in and what to leave out."

(Annie Dillard, 1945– , American author)

Write the quotation on the chalkboard or on an overhead transparency. Then, guide students through a discussion of criteria for deciding what needs to be eliminated and what needs to be kept in their problem-analysis essays.

TEACHING TIP

Proofread Your Essay
Suggest that students proofread their essays, beginning at the end and reading backward one sentence at a time. Because this method separates the reader from the flow of the content, spotting errors is often much easier.

Grammar Link
Sentence Fragments

ANSWERS
Possible answers follow.

1. Having more accidents, teenagers must pay more for insurance.
2. Police started enforcing the speed limit.
3. C
4. Before having a flat tire myself, I didn't realize how important it was to carry a spare.
5. Studying more, I made better grades.

RESOURCES

Grammar Link
Practice
- *Communications*, WS. p. 78

Publishing, pp. 155–156
Alignments
TEKS 2C, 2D, 3A, 3B, 3D, 5A
TAAS W3, W6, W7
English II End-of-Course 4, 5, 6

Wrap It Up

Metacognition. Ask students to reflect on their writing processes. Allow students five minutes to answer the following question:

1. Look back at the order of the main points of your essay. Explain why you placed them in that order and why that order is most effective.

Then, ask students to respond to the following questions:

2. List four types of support for key points. [facts, expert testimony, examples, and anecdotes]

3. List four types of research sources. [library materials, interviews, the Internet, direct observation]

YOUR TURN 9

Ask students to submit their reflections with their final copy. As you evaluate their essays, you may wish to use each student's reflections to help you provide detailed feedback on his or her strengths and make specific, practical suggestions for improvement.

TIP If you handwrite your analysis, make sure your writing is **legible**—clear, clean, and easy to read.

PORTFOLIO

Publish Your Essay

Put the Gears in Motion You want others to recognize the seriousness of the problem you have analyzed and to begin working toward solutions. Try one or more of the ideas listed below to share your essay with an appropriate audience.

- **Create a problem bank.** Gather copies of your class's problem-analysis essays, put them into a binder, and ask your school librarian to place the binder in the library for use as a "problem bank." Other students at your school who are interested in problem solving and problem analysis may use the problem bank as a resource.

- **Schedule a debate.** If your school has a debate team, share your essay with the debate coach and ask him or her to consider using your problem as the topic for a schoolwide debate.

- **Form a task force if your problem is school related.** Does your problem directly affect students at your school? Is it something your school, as a community, may be able to solve? If so, submit your problem-analysis essay to your school newspaper and invite students, teachers, and parents to form a task force to discuss possible solutions to the problem.

Reflect on Your Essay

Look Back After you have completed your essay, take a moment to answer the following questions and find out what you have learned from this experience.

- What new ideas or information did you discover about your problem?
- What was the most helpful skill you learned from writing an analysis of a problem?
- What, if anything, do you think you will do differently when you next write a problem analysis?

YOUR TURN 9 Proofreading, Publishing, and Reflecting

Why write an essay if no one is going to read it? Proofread your essay carefully, and then share it with an audience. Finally, use the questions above to reflect on what you learned.

156 Chapter 4 Exposition: Analyzing Problems

Connections to Literature

Analyzing the Problems of a Literary Character

Daily life seems to be full of problems. You read about them in the newspaper, hear about them on the radio, and watch them on the television. Like real life, literary works also present readers and audiences with a variety of problems that characters must confront and resolve by the end of the story. These problems are called **conflicts**. When you analyze a problem in literature, you are examining the story's **plot** elements.

The following chart analyzes the problems of the title character in the play *Antigone* by Sophocles. The plot elements are listed in the left column, with key terms shown in boldface, and examples provided from the play are given in the right column.

The **basic situation** (the major characters and the circumstances in which they find themselves)	A man named Polyneices is killed while leading an attack on the city of Thebes (from which he has been exiled). Creon, the city's king, decrees that anyone who attempts to bury Polyneices will be punished with execution.
The **conflict** (the major problem between opposing forces, characters, or emotions)	The conflict in Antigone is between the law of conscience and the law of the land. Antigone (Polyneices' sister) faces a difficult choice: leave her brother's body unburied (a terrible sacrilege in ancient Greek religion) or defy Creon's decree and risk execution.
Complications (developments that take place because of the existing conflict, or any elements that intensify the conflict)	Antigone's personality complicates the problem. She makes her choices because she is a brash, outspoken person who will follow her beliefs—no matter the consequences.
The **climax** (the moment of greatest suspense or tension)	Creon sentences Antigone to death for sprinkling earth over her brother's body. She tragically chooses to take her own life.
The **resolution** (the final solution to the problem or conflict)	Creon's son (who loves Antigone) kills himself in grief, an act that causes Creon to realize that he was wrong.

YOUR TURN 10 — Analyzing the Problems of a Literary Character

Analyze the problems of a main character in one of your favorite literary works. Make a chart like the one above for your character; then, present your findings to your classmates in a brief oral presentation.

Focus on Speaking and Listening

OBJECTIVES

- To prepare a memorable speech
- To deliver a speech in an interesting way
- To conduct a question-and-answer session
- To listen actively to a speech

Quotation for the Day

❝When you speak and write, there is no law that says you have to use big words. Short words are as good as long ones, and short, old words—like *sun* and *grass* and *home*—are best of all.❞

(Richard Lederer, 1938–   , American teacher and linguist)

After reading the quotation aloud, have students write journal entries about why short words may be especially appropriate for a speech. Ask student volunteers to share their responses.

Focus on Speaking and Listening

WHAT'S AHEAD?

In this section, you will learn how to

- prepare a memorable speech
- deliver your speech in an interesting way
- conduct a question-and-answer session
- listen actively to a speech

Giving an Informative Speech

Suppose that you have analyzed the problem of pollution in a neighborhood creek, and you want to alert local businesspeople, homeowners, and elected officials to the problem. One way you can share your information is to write an informative speech and deliver it during a community meeting.

In this section, you will learn how to create and deliver an informative speech. Creating a speech is in many ways like writing an essay. You choose a subject, determine your audience, and then gather and organize your information in an interesting and logical way. Informative speeches and informative essays share these characteristics:

- a clearly defined purpose
- language appropriate for the audience
- an engaging introduction
- a well-supported thesis statement
- a logical progression of ideas
- a conclusion that summarizes the main points

Prepare a Memorable Speech

Zoom In   The topic for your speech should interest you and be something you already know about. However, it must have a narrow focus so that you can cover it adequately in a limited amount of time. For example, "pollution" is much too broad a topic for a speech, but "pollution in Brushy Creek" is manageable. Gather information you may need from interviews, surveys, books, reference works, periodicals, or Web sites. Once you have chosen a topic and researched it (if needed), write a **thesis statement** that expresses your most important idea about your

158   Chapter 4   Exposition: Analyzing Problems

RESOURCES

Focus on Speaking and Listening
Practice

- Media Literacy and Communication Skills
  —Support and Practice, Ch. 4
  —A How-to Handbook

Teaching Notes

- Media Literacy and Communication Skills
  —A Teacher's Guide, Ch. 4

Exposition: Analyzing Problems

topic. Think also about **occasion,** the setting for your speech and what motivated you to give it. Will it be a city council chamber, where strict, formal procedures must be followed or will it be an informal classroom setting? Are you giving the speech because you are passionate about the topic and wish to share this interest with others? Consider the **task** you are trying to accomplish with your speech. If your speech is on a problem you have researched, your task is to help your audience become aware of the problem and understand the seriousness of the problem.

Who's Out There? Consider your **audience**—the people who will be listening to your speech. If you are lucky, they are ready and willing to learn something new. Sometimes, though, they are a captive audience, present only because they are required to be there. Part of your goal is to make sure that audience members go away from your speech feeling that they have learned something interesting and important.

> **TIP** To maintain your audience's attention, adapt your speech to suit their interests and knowledge. If your audience is your classmates, you might consider polling them to find out what they already know about your topic.

Good Form! The structure of your speech is very similar to the three-part structure of an essay. Use the following framework as a guide.

Introduction	• Get your audience's attention. Begin with a startling statement, an interesting story, or a thought-provoking question. • Gain your audience's goodwill. If your audience likes or respects you, they will be more likely to listen to and think about what you say.
Body	• Give supporting information for your main points. • Organize the main points of your speech in one of the following ways: **Chronological Order**—Arrange events and details as they developed over time. **Order of Importance**—Arrange information from least important to most important. **Cause-and-Effect Order**—Arrange information to show causes and effects (results of those causes). **Comparison-and-Contrast Order**—Arrange details to show similarities or differences.
Conclusion	• Summarize and emphasize the main points of your speech. • Leave your audience with a greater interest in your topic.

Watch Your Language Make sure that what you say is immediately understandable. Because this is a formal speech, be sure to choose **standard language,** that is, standard English, to communicate your ideas. Standard language is the kind of English people are expected to use in school and business situations.

> **TIP** When you speak to an audience that is familiar with your subject, you can use **technical language** your audience will recognize. On the other hand, define any technical terms when an audience is unfamiliar with your subject.

Focus on Speaking and Listening   **159**

TEACHING TIP

Deliver Your Speech in an Interesting Way

Ask students to listen to a speech given on television or by someone in the community. You may wish to bring in a videotape of a speech for students who do not have access to television. Give students the following rubric to evaluate the quality of the speech, using four as a high rating and one as a low rating. Discuss with students the ratings they gave the speech.

Characteristic	Rating
clearly defined purpose	1 2 3 4
language appropriate for audience	1 2 3 4
engaging introduction	1 2 3 4
well-supported thesis	1 2 3 4
logical progression of ideas	1 2 3 4
conclusion summarizing main points	1 2 3 4

Timesaver

To evaluate students' informative speeches more efficiently, design a chart. You may wish to use the bulleted list on this page or the steps listed in **Your Turn 11**.

Deliver Your Speech in an Interesting Way

Here are some tips that will help you make the presentation of your speech more interesting.

- **Be enthusiastic.** If you show genuine interest in your topic, it will be easier for you to get your audience interested in it.
- **Know your speech well.** Before you deliver your speech, practice it several times. Be sure of the pronunciation of key terms, and note places where you might add verbal emphasis.
- **Speak from notes.** Once you know your speech well, write notes to use as you speak. Don't try to memorize your speech (you may get stuck) or read it word for word. Know your general points and details, and glance at your note cards whenever you need reminding.
- **Maintain eye contact.** Do not keep your head down and your eyes locked on your notes. Look out at your audience and use eye contact to keep your listeners involved in your speech.
- **Say it with feeling.** Speak loudly enough so everyone can hear you, and vary your **rate of speaking, volume,** and **pitch.**

Think Visual Readers can read and re-read a written paper as many times as they want until they feel they understand it. However, listeners must actively listen and try to understand and remember your speech the first time through, because they cannot ask you to give it a second time. You can help your listeners remember your speech by making use of **visuals**—materials that an audience can see, such as charts, graphs, slides, transparencies, and films. If you use visuals with your speech,

- clearly explain the content of the visual to your audience and connect the visuals to your speech
- don't overdo—use only as many visuals as you need to illustrate or emphasize the most important points of your speech
- test audio or video equipment before your speech to be sure it is working properly

Conduct a Question-and-Answer Session

If possible, end your speech with a question-and-answer period. Listeners will have a chance to become more actively involved, and you will have a chance to clear up any misunderstandings. The **feedback** you get from your audience can help you to **set goals** for improving future speeches or other presentations. Use the following suggestions to make your question-and-answer period more productive.

TIP **Feedback** from your audience, such as smiles, nods of agreement, fidgeting, or confused looks, can help you know how to adjust your presentation. If your audience seems confused, slow your pace or repeat key ideas. If they seem bored, try varying your rate of speaking, volume, and pitch.

Feedback also helps you to evaluate your effectiveness and to set goals for future presentations.

- **Call on people from all over the audience.** Try to involve everyone—including those at the back and on the sides of the audience.
- **Respond to questions clearly and succinctly.** Instead of responding with words repeated directly from your speech, give short, clear responses that build on points you have already made.
- **Don't worry if you can't answer every question.** Rather than try to bluff your way through an answer, tell your audience that you will try to locate the information and forward it later to anyone who is interested.

Listen Actively to a Speech

When it is your turn to be a listener, pay careful attention to what the speaker is saying. Even if you are already a good listener, these tips will help improve your critical-listening skills.

- **Take notes.** As the speaker talks, jot down notes about each key point.
- **Think ahead.** To stay actively involved, you should try to anticipate the points the speaker might make next and then confirm and adjust your predictions as you listen. Jot down questions you want to ask the speaker later.
- **Relate what the speaker is saying to your own life.** For example, if the speaker is talking about the importance of wearing bicycle helmets, you might briefly recall a bicycle accident you had as a child and relate what the speaker is saying to that experience.
- **Participate in the question-and-answer period.** Ask the speaker to clarify anything you found confusing. You can also use the time to give the speaker positive comments, telling him or her about specific parts of the speech that you found particularly informative.

TIP Part of your task as a listener is to analyze, evaluate, and appreciate the presentation. As you actively listen to a speech, you may want to use what you have learned about purpose, audience, tone, and delivery to create your own criteria (standards of judgement) to analyze, evaluate, and appreciate.

YOUR TURN 11 — Creating and Delivering an Informative Speech

Follow the guidelines in the previous section to create and deliver an informative speech. Make sure to follow each of these steps:
- Deliver your speech in an interesting way, using eye contact and variations in your rate of speech, volume, and pitch.
- Plan appropriate visuals and demonstrations that will make your speech memorable.
- Conduct a question-and-answer session after your speech, if possible.

RESOURCES

Your Turn 11

Practice and Reinforcement

- *Media Literacy and Communication Skills—Support and Practice,* Ch. 4, transparencies and worksheets

Focus on Viewing and Representing

OBJECTIVES

- To recognize three common news genres
- To analyze the coverage of individual news programs

Quotation for the Day

"Television is not merely one of a number of important influences upon today's child. Through the changes it has made in family life, television emerges as *the* important influence in children's lives today."

(Marie Winn, 1937– , Czech-born American writer)

Read the quotation aloud to students, and discuss the impact of television news in their lives. Then, discuss whether they agree or disagree with the quotation. Students should give reasons for their opinions.

Focus on Viewing and Representing

WHAT'S AHEAD?

In this section, you will learn how to

- recognize three common news genres
- analyze the coverage of individual news programs

Recognizing News Genres

What kind of news would there be if the world had no problems? Consider how much of the news you receive is about local, national, and global problems. One of the main ways this "problem news" and other kinds of news reaches you is through television news programs, many of which fit into the three genres described below.

What Are News Genres?

National nightly news broadcasts mostly present breaking news stories about events that have happened since the previous evening. Within a half-hour broadcast (including commercials), each news item may receive less than a minute of airtime, so the depth of coverage is limited.

Newsmagazines are often broadcast once a week (sometimes more). They provide more detailed coverage of topics, not just breaking news. A weekly newsmagazine will generally present only a handful of stories—four or five at the most—in the space of an hour, so the depth of coverage is greater than that on the nightly news. Many of the stories presented on weekly newsmagazines are **human-interest** stories, stories that are designed to evoke emotional responses, such as joy, compassion, outrage, and sympathy. Human-interest stories may or may not actually provide much factual information about a topic.

Documentaries are creatively constructed *interpretations* of actual events, people, or groups. They are often broadcast as "specials"—not according to a daily or weekly schedule. Like newsmagazines, documentaries usually do not deal with breaking news. Instead, a one-hour (sometimes less) news-related documentary generally deals with a single topic, and therefore treats that topic in much greater depth than either a nightly news broadcast or a multiple-story newsmagazine can. Keep in mind that documentaries often reflect the filmmaker's bias or point of view. Documentaries have been made on such varied topics as the music of India, the Battle of Gettysburg, the rain forests of Peru, presidential campaigns, Michael Jordon, Michelangelo, and the *Titanic*. Most

162   Chapter 4   **Exposition:** Analyzing Problems

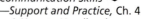

RESOURCES

Focus on Viewing and Representing
Practice

- Media Literacy and Communication Skills
  —Support and Practice, Ch. 4
  —A How-to Handbook

Teaching Notes

- Media Literacy and Communication Skills
  —A Teacher's Guide, Ch. 4

news-related documentaries are about historical events or people or are about news items that are still developing or that show possible long-lasting consequences.

Why Do They Do It?   Sometimes it is easy to forget that a news program does anything more than inform, but nonfiction TV can serve one or more of a **variety of purposes**: to inform, to educate, to entertain, to persuade, for self-expression, and for profit. For example, a newsmagazine program about the latest record-breaking multiple birth can inform you by showing you the problems parents go through when an event like this happens. The program can also entertain you by showing cute videotape of the adorable babies, and it may additionally attempt to persuade you by interviewing doctors about the risks associated with fertility drugs.

Also, when watching news programs, consider who the **target audience**—the people to whom the programs are designed to appeal—might be. To remain on the air, any television program must attract enough viewers to encourage advertisers to sponsor the show. To attract viewers, producers must shape the content of their programs to suit the interests and desires of their target audience. Oftentimes, the commercials that are shown during the program will give you some clue about who the producer expects will be watching.

When you watch nightly news programs, newsmagazines, and documentaries, you may begin to notice that each can have purposes and target audiences that are very specific to its genre.

Knowing What You Are Getting

To help you analyze the news genres that you see on television, use the following questions whenever you conduct a focused news-viewing session. Not all questions will be relevant to each news genre, since, for example, documentaries focus specifically on one news item instead of on several. Remember, too, to record pertinent information, such as the program's name, the topics it covers, its length, and the number of news items it includes.

> **TIP**   To spot stories designed to manipulate your feelings, be on the lookout for emotional background music, an overdose of stirring images, and a narrow focus on individual people and their problems. Stories with these characteristics often fail to provide enough facts or statistics to give a big-picture view of the problem and the number of people it affects.

- How much of the program is devoted to breaking news? What other kinds of stories are presented?
- What aspects of the topic (or topics) were *not* covered at all?
- Does the program provide factual information, or does it just leave you with an emotional reaction? Explain your answers.
- Which purpose or purposes do you think the news stories serve? Explain your response.

Focus on Viewing and Representing   **163**

Focus on Viewing and Representing, pp. 162–164
Alignments
TEKS 20A, 20B, 20C, 20E

YOUR TURN 12

If you do not show videos of the three types of news programs in the classroom, you may need to create an alternative assignment for those students who lack access to television, such as listening to the radio, or reading newspapers and magazines. Class discussion based on answers to the questions could help students look more critically at television news programs.

Wrap It Up

Metacognition. Ask students to reflect on the following questions. Allow five minutes for a written response.

1. Which type of news program did you find most enjoyable? How did the producer make that show attractive to you, and how did that affect the factual content?

Then, have students answer the following questions:

2. List three genres of news programs. [national nightly news broadcasts, newsmagazines, and documentaries]

3. List four possible purposes for nonfiction television. [Possible answers include to inform, to educate, to entertain, to persuade, for self-expression, for profit.]

- What advertisements aired during the broadcast? What target audience is reflected in the commercials? Why?
- What unanswered questions do you have after watching the program?

The following is an example portion of an analysis one student made using the questions that begin on page 163 as a guide.

National Nightly News	Does the program provide factual information, or does it just leave you with a feeling? Explain.
Name: Nightly World News **Topic(s):** forest fire, Senate budget deadlock, former baseball commissioner passed away, floods in Asia, latest election campaign news **Length:** 21 minutes **Number of news items:** 18	Most of the program seemed factual. The political coverage seemed fair—neither side was being blamed in the budget negotiations. However, there were some upsetting images of the results of a forest fire and of the Asian floods. I am not sure how the producers could really present information on these two topics without some sort of emotional impact.
Newsmagazine **Name:** In Focus	

YOUR TURN 12 — Analyzing the Content and Depth of Coverage in News Programs

Watch three types of news programs: a national nightly news broadcast, a newsmagazine, and a news-related documentary. Using the questions on page 163 and above, analyze the program. Then, use your notes to answer the following questions. Explain all your answers.

- Which type of news program leaves you with the most factual information? The most emotional reactions?
- Which type of news program shows the least bias?
- Does each genre have the same purposes? The same target audience?
- In your judgment, does each of these programs provide more than enough, enough, or not enough coverage for each news item?

164 Chapter 4 Exposition: Analyzing Problems

RESOURCES

Your Turn 12

Practice and Reinforcement

- *Media Literacy and Communication Skills*
  —*Support and Practice*, Ch. 4, transparencies and worksheets
  —Videocassette 1, Segment D

CHAPTER

 4 Choices

Choose one of the following activities to complete.

▶ CAREERS

1. Give a Checkup Conduct an interview with a health professional (a nurse, doctor, or dentist, for example). Ask about the health problems he or she treats: What kinds of problems are typical, how are they treated, and what research needs to be done to treat them? After completing the interview, present a brief **oral report**—a short profile of the health professional and of the methods he or she uses to research and treat problems.

▶ CROSSING THE CURRICULUM: LITERATURE

2. Hatch a Plot Make some trouble for a fictional character. Think of a problem that interests you, and write a **summary** of a short-story plot based on the problem. Remember that the main character's responses to the problem should create a conflict to be resolved in the story.

▶ SPEAKING AND LISTENING

3. Join the Debate Go to your school's drama or debate coach and ask to sit in on a debate class or competition. Take notes on how the debaters discuss the problems they have researched. What rules do they follow? How do they argue a point without erupting in anger? If debaters present a solution to the problem, how do they convince you that their solution is a good one? Create a **"how-to" booklet** about debate that you can share with others.

▶ MEDIA AND TECHNOLOGY

4. Tune It In Some TV and radio stations show the government in action with live or taped broadcasts of trials, hearings, city council meetings, school board meetings, and so on. Watch or listen to one of these broadcasts and make notes on

- problems discussed
- people discussing the problems
- any solutions discussed

Use your findings to write a **profile** of how governmental officials try to solve problems. Consider including this profile in your portfolio.

 PORTFOLIO

▶ CAREERS 2B
Remind students to develop their questions before scheduling interviews. Students can work in groups to create possible interview questions and advance information about the assignment for interviewees. Students can work together to develop outlines for these materials and then divide the tasks equally among themselves. The same system can be used to work collaboratively to write the report and give the presentation. Discuss with students other strategies for working collaboratively. You should obtain permission from parents or guardians and inform the interviewees of the project before sending students into the community.

▶ CROSSING THE CURRICULUM: LITERATURE
Challenge students to create a problem that is not simplistic. They should be sure that solutions are consistent with how the character would respond.

▶ SPEAKING AND LISTENING
If your school has no debate class or team, help interested students find a debate program at a neighboring high school or college. Students may wish to attend and report on a debate or to videotape a debate for class viewing.

▶ MEDIA AND TECHNOLOGY
If this type of broadcast is unavailable in your area, you might, with permission, videotape a school board or local government meeting to show during class. If viewing occurs outside of class, be sure to provide an alternative assignment for students lacking access to television.

Choices   **165**

 RESOURCES

Analyzing Problems
Assessment
- Assessment Package
  —Chapter Tests, Ch. 4
  —Chapter Tests in Standardized Test Formats, Ch. 4
  —Assessment Alternatives, Ch. 4
- Test Generator (One-Stop Planner CD-ROM)

Choices
Rubrics
- Assessment Package
  —Assessment Alternatives, Ch. 4

Choices
Alignments
Choice 1   TEKS 16A, 16B
Choice 2   TEKS 1A, 1B, 11F; TAAS W1
Choice 3   TEKS 1A, 1B, 14B; TAAS W1
Choice 4   TEKS 1A, 1B, 14B; TAAS W1

Choices   **165**

CHAPTER 5

Analyzing a Short Story

Use this guide to create an instructional plan that suits the individual needs of your students. Assignments marked by an asterisk (*) may be completed out of class. Times given for pacing lessons are estimated. See pp. 166–167 for chapterwide resources. Resources listed in this guide are point-of-use resources only.

Curriculum Connections

Connections to Literature *pp. 195–197*
- Writing a Short Story

Choices *p. 205*
- Speaking and Listening
- Media and Technology
- Viewing and Representing

internet connect

 GO TO: go.hrw.com
KEYWORD: EOLang 10-5

 All resources for this chapter are available for preview on the *One-Stop Planner CD-ROM with Test Generator*. All worksheets and tests may be printed from the CD-ROM.

Texas Resources For a complete listing of all resources prepared for Texas teachers and students, please see the blue box at the beginning of each chapter.

		Chapter Opener *pp. 166–167*	**Reading Workshop: Reading a Literary Analysis** *pp. 168–177*
DEVELOPMENTAL PROGRAM		**30 minutes** • Analysis *p. 167* • Your Turn 1 in groups *p. 167*	**100 minutes** • Preparing to Read *p. 168* • Reading Selection *pp. 169–171* • First Thoughts on Your Reading 1–2 *p. 172* • Drawing Conclusions *pp. 172–173* • Your Turn 2 *p. 173* • Literary Elements *pp. 173–175* • Your Turn 3 in groups *p. 175* • Test Taking Mini-Lesson *p. 177*
CORE PROGRAM		**20 minutes** • Analysis *p. 167* • Your Turn 1 *p. 167*	**90 minutes** • Preparing to Read *p. 168* • Reading Selection *pp. 169–171* • First Thoughts on Your Reading 1–3 *p. 172* • Drawing Conclusions *pp. 172–173* • Your Turn 2 *p. 173* • Literary Elements *pp. 173–175* • Your Turn 3 *p. 175* • Vocabulary Mini-Lesson *p. 176* • Test Taking Mini-Lesson *p. 177*
ADVANCED PROGRAM		**10 minutes** • Analysis *p. 167* • Your Turn 1 *p. 167*	**70 minutes** • Preparing to Read *p. 168* • Reading Selection *pp. 169–171* • First Thoughts on Your Reading 3 *p. 172* • Drawing Conclusions *pp. 172–173* • Your Turn 2 *p. 173* • Literary Elements *pp. 173–175* • Your Turn 3 *p. 175* • Vocabulary Mini-Lesson *p. 176*
RESOURCES	**PRINT**	• *Communications,* TP. 38, WS. p. 79	• *Alternative Readings,* Ch. 5 • *Communications,* TPs. 39, 40, WS. pp. 80–87
	MEDIA	• *One-Stop Planner CD-ROM*	• *One-Stop Planner CD-ROM*

TP.=Transparency   WS.=Worksheet

Writing Workshop: Writing a Literary Analysis *pp. 178–197*	**Critiquing a Film, Presenting an Oral Interpretation** *pp. 198–204*
🕐 **220 minutes** • Choose a Story *p. 178* • Read and Respond and Your Turn 4 *pp. 178–179* • Consider Purpose; Analyze Your Story *pp. 179–180* • Develop a Thesis and Your Turn 5 *pp. 181–182* • Gather Support *pp. 182–183* • Organize Your Analysis and Your Turn 6 *p. 183* • Framework and Your Turn 7* *p. 184* • Writer's Model and Student's Model *pp. 185–187* • Evaluate and Revise and Your Turn 8* *pp. 188–189* • Focus on Sentences and Your Turn 9 *pp. 190–191* • Writing Mini-Lesson *p. 192* • Proofread, Publish, and Reflect *pp. 193–194* • Grammar Link and Your Turn 10 *pp. 193–194*	🕐 **10 minutes** • Watching and Forming an Opinion *pp. 198–200* • Identifying and Critiquing Technical Elements *pp. 200–201* • A Model Critique *pp. 201–202* • Your Turn 12* *p. 202* • Select and Analyze a Short Story *p. 203* • Create and Practice Your Interpretation* *p. 204* • Evaluate an Oral Interpretation *p. 204* • Your Turn 13* *p. 204*
🕐 **200 minutes** • Choose a Story *p. 178* • Read and Respond and Your Turn 4 *pp. 178–179* • Consider Purpose; Analyze Your Story *pp. 179–180* • Develop a Thesis and Your Turn 5 *pp. 181–182* • Gather Support *pp. 182–183* • Organize Your Analysis and Your Turn 6 *p. 183* • Framework and Your Turn 7* *p. 184* • Writer's Model and Student's Model *pp. 185–187* • Evaluate and Revise and Your Turn 8* *pp. 188–189* • Focus on Sentences and Your Turn 9 *pp. 190–191* • Writing Mini-Lesson *p. 192* • Proofread, Publish, and Reflect *pp. 193–194* • Grammar Link and Your Turn 10 *pp. 193–194* • Connections to Literature and Your Turn 11* *pp. 195–197*	🕐 **90 minutes** • Watching and Forming an Opinion *pp. 198–200* • Identifying and Critiquing Technical Elements *pp. 200–201* • A Model Critique *pp. 201–202* • Your Turn 12* *p. 202* • Select and Analyze a Short Story *pp. 203–204* • Create and Practice Your Interpretation* *p. 204* • Evaluate an Oral Interpretation *p. 204* • Your Turn 13* *p. 204*
🕐 **160 minutes** • Choose a Story *p. 178* • Read and Respond and Your Turn 4 *pp. 178–179* • Consider Purpose; Analyze Your Story *pp. 179–180* • Develop a Thesis and Your Turn 5 *pp. 181–182* • Gather Support *pp. 182–183* • Organize Your Analysis and Your Turn 6 *p. 183* • Framework and Your Turn 7* *p. 184* • Writer's Model and Student's Model *pp. 185–187* • Evaluate and Revise and Your Turn 8* *pp. 188–189* • Proofread, Publish, and Reflect; Your Turn 10 *pp. 193–194* • Connections to Literature and Your Turn 11* *pp. 195–197*	🕐 **80 minutes** • Watching and Forming an Opinion *pp. 198–200* • Identifying and Critiquing Technical Elements *pp. 200–201* • A Model Critique *pp. 201–202* • Your Turn 12* *p. 202* • Select and Analyze a Short Story *pp. 203–204* • Create and Practice Your Interpretation* *p. 204* • Evaluate an Oral Interpretation *p. 204* • Your Turn 13* *p. 204*
• *Communications,* TPs. 41–44, WS. pp. 88–98 • *Designing Your Writing*	• *Media Literacy and Communication Skills Kit* —*Support and Practice,* Ch. 5 —*A How-to Handbook* —*A Teacher's Guide,* Ch. 5
• *One-Stop Planner CD-ROM*	• *Media Literacy and Communication Skills Kit* —Videocassette 2, Segment E • *One-Stop Planner CD-ROM*

CHAPTER 5
Analyzing a Short Story

CHAPTER OBJECTIVES
- To read and analyze a literary analysis
- To write a literary analysis
- To view and critique a film

Chapter Overview

People use analytical skills in many areas of their personal and professional lives. This chapter is designed to teach students how to approach and critique works of literature. The Reading Workshop presents a literary analysis from which students can draw conclusions and learn how literary elements function in a story. The Writing Workshop guides students in writing their own literary analyses, and the Focus on Viewing and Representing has students use a similar process to critique a film. Each section can be taught independently, but taught together they provide students with a more thorough understanding of literary analysis.

Why Study Literary Analysis?

The study and analysis of literary elements (plot, setting, character, point of view, theme, and language) enriches students' experience of literature. Students will learn how these basic elements of literature interact to illustrate the theme or message an author wishes to convey. Learning how to analyze a short story will help students to evaluate the analyses of others and will both deepen their understanding of various literary works and increase their appreciation of the writer's craft.

Teaching the Chapter

Option 1: Begin with Literature

If you choose to introduce literary analysis through literature, you might focus on literary elements in novels, short stories, drama, or epics, showing students how these elements function in such works. Then, have students examine John Irving's analysis of Charles Dickens's *A Christmas Carol* (pp. 169–171) to learn more about literary elements and their functions. This introduction will help prepare students to write their literary analyses.

Option 2: Begin with Nonfiction and Writing

You may choose to begin teaching literary analysis with the material in this chapter. Using the selection in the Reading Workshop (pp. 169–171) as an example of a literary analysis, identify and explain the literary elements critiqued by Irving and help students draw conclusions about Dickens's work from Irving's discussion. Then, walk students through the steps in the writing process to compose their own literary analyses of a short story in the Writing Workshop (pp. 178–197). When students return to literature, they will have the skills needed to explore and write about the techniques authors use to compose engaging plots, create memorable characters, or express meaningful themes. See also **Connections to Literature** on pp. 195–197, where interested students may compose short stories using what they have learned about literary elements and their interplay.

T165C

Making Connections

▪ To the Literature Curriculum

Literary analysis is fundamental to understanding literature. It enables the reader to identify literary elements in a story and explore how the elements work together to support a theme or message. By analyzing characters in "The Bet" by Anton Chekhov or the expectations of the characters in "A Very Old Man with Enormous Wings" by Gabriel García Márquez, for example, students can discover the story's meaning.

Lesson Idea: Literary Analysis of "A Very Old Man with Enormous Wings" by Gabriel García Márquez

1. Review the concept of satire with the class.
2. Have students select details from the story that show the author's use of satire when describing the townspeople. Then, prompt students to identify other satirical aspects of the story.
3. Ask students to develop a statement of the author's view of humanity based on his use of satire. Then, discuss how the author shows the people's willingness to accept only what fits their stereotypes. What conclusions can be drawn about the meaning of the story?
4. After this discussion, introduce students to the Reading Selection (pp. 169–171) and point out that to develop his literary analysis, John Irving focuses on the same literary elements and uses the same kinds of details from *A Christmas Carol* as are found in Márquez's story. The instruction on basic elements of literature, key points, and supporting details (pp. 173–175) will help students compose their analyses of a short story in the Writing Workshop (pp. 178–197).

▪ To Careers

Advertising analysts look critically at how advertising affects readers and viewers. Help students develop similarly critical stances toward advertising by having them apply the critical reading and viewing strategies they have learned in this chapter to an advertisement and then write critical analyses. You may want to provide an advertisement or allow small groups of students to select their own. Advertisements can be in print or video format.

Remind students that advertisements usually contain elements similar to those in a short story; they may have a specific setting, characters who reveal themselves through actions or words, a plot, and a distinct point of view. Students' critical analyses should focus on identifying the message of the advertisement and should include a thesis statement, a description of the ad, supporting evidence, and a conclusion. Publish students' analyses by displaying them with copies of the ads. If the ads are on video, have students show the videos and then read aloud their analyses.

▪ To the Community

Help students use what they have learned about literary analysis to practice being critical listeners. Ask students to attend a community event that features a speaker. Students should make a critical analysis of the speech, noting key points and supporting evidence. Each student might share his or her analysis of the speech in an article about the event for the school or local newspaper. Following the activity, discuss the importance of critical listening as a citizenship skill. Good citizens stay informed and base their actions and votes on a critical analysis of information.

▪ To the Science Curriculum

Have students investigate how scientists use analysis to assess the quality of their water supply, to determine the amount of air pollution in the area, or to pinpoint the extent of seasonal airborne allergens. Students can contact or interview meteorologists from local TV stations or government officials. Students may work in small groups or individually. Ask them to share their findings with the class.

CHAPTER 5

PREVIEWING THE CHAPTER

- Literary analysis is the focus of the three workshops in this chapter. Each workshop can be taught on its own, but as a group the three provide a more complete understanding of the composition and applications of a critical analysis. Reading and analyzing a literary analysis helps prepare students to write their own analyses. Students can then apply their analytical skills to critiquing a film. For help in integrating this chapter with grammar, usage, and mechanics chapters, see the interleaf chart on pp. T401A–T401B.

INTRODUCING THE CHAPTER

- To introduce the chapter, use the Journal Warm-up, Transparency 38, in *Communications*.

VIEWING THE ILLUSTRATION (19A)

- This illustration shows a mechanical drawing of a machine. The background color and lines suggest the texture of parchment. Perspective is achieved by the angled lines of the base and by the white and shadow on the curve of the spout. Have students identify the machine's purpose. [To identify a story's key elements.]

Representing. Ask students to design a machine that writes stories. Students may draw by hand or use a computer graphics program.

CHAPTER 5 | Analyzing a Short Story

character
PLOT
setting
theme STYLE

CHAPTER RESOURCES

Planning
- *Lesson Planner*, Ch. 5
- Block Scheduling, p. T165A (this book)
- One-Stop Planner CD-ROM

Practice
- *Communications*, Ch. 5

- Media Literacy and Communication Skills

Extension
- Designing Your Writing

Reinforcement
- *Communications*, Ch. 5

PREVIEW

Reading Workshop

Reading a Literary Analysis
PAGE 168

Writing Workshop

Writing a Literary Analysis
PAGE 178

Focus on Viewing and Representing

Critiquing a Film
PAGE 198

Focus on Speaking and Listening

Presenting an Oral Interpretation
PAGE 203

Analysis

- An automobile mechanic working on a car uses the process of elimination to confirm her initial diagnosis of an engine malfunction.
- A book reviewer closely examines a new thriller to determine how its author builds suspense.

What do these scenarios have in common? Both involve **analysis:** the process of breaking something into parts and then examining the parts to discover how they work together. For example, during the telecast of a diving competition, commentators might play back each dive in slow motion, discussing every twist and turn. Their analysis would help viewers understand what made each dive successful or unsuccessful.

A writer of a **literary analysis** uses a similar process to explore the techniques an author uses to create memorable characters or to convey meaningful themes throughout a work. That is, the writer might focus on certain *literary elements* to better understand the work as a whole. In turn, readers use literary analyses to increase their understanding of a work and to form opinions about it.

GO TO: go.hrw.com
KEYWORD: EOLang 10-5

YOUR TURN 1 — Analyzing Literature

Think about one of your favorite novels as a whole. Then, jot down notes about the characters, scenes, and other parts of the novel that you enjoyed most. Finally, discuss your notes with a small group.

- *Alternative Readings,* Ch. 5
- *Daily Language Activity Transparencies*
- *Vocabulary Workshop* and *Tests*

Evaluation and Assessment

- *Test Generator* (One-Stop Planner CD-ROM)

- *Assessment Package*
  —*Chapter Tests,* Ch. 5
  —*Chapter Tests in Standardized Test Formats,* Ch. 5
  —*Assessment Alternatives,* Ch. 5

Internet

- go.hrw.com (keyword: EOLang 10–5)

Reading Workshop

OBJECTIVES

- To read a literary analysis in preparation for writing a literary analysis
- To draw conclusions
- To identify literary elements
- To use word roots to build vocabulary

Quotation for the Day

"The critic's job is to *explain and evaluate*—that is, to bring his reader to a *better* understanding of his subject."

(John R. Trimble, 1940– , American professor of English)

Read the quotation to students and ask them what *they* expect from book and movie reviews. Do they read a critical review to get a better understanding of a work, or do they also have other purposes?

TEACHING TIP

Preparing to Read
The concepts introduced in **Preparing to Read** will be developed further on pp. 172–175 of the Reading Workshop. The purpose of the Reading Workshop is to teach students how to draw conclusions and to identify and analyze literary elements as they read. The Reading Selection, which excerpts John Irving's **"An Introduction to Charles Dickens's *A Christmas Carol,"** includes a discussion of the work's key literary elements and requires students to draw conclusions.

RESOURCES

Reading Workshop Reinforcement
- *Alternative Readings,* Ch. 5

Reading Workshop

Reading a Literary Analysis

WHAT'S AHEAD?

In this section, you will read a literary analysis and learn how to
- draw conclusions
- identify literary elements

Consider this scene: A dark room in an old house whose sole human occupant hears the sound of clanking chains as someone—or something—climbs the stairs. Could this ominous scene appear in some Christmas story? Indeed it does, and the story has become a classic: *A Christmas Carol,* by Charles Dickens. In the essay you will read next, the contemporary American novelist John Irving analyzes how Dickens crafted this haunting holiday tale.

Preparing to Read

READING SKILL

Drawing Conclusions When you read a literary analysis, you are presented with a wealth of information about a work. To understand this information, you must **draw conclusions** as you read. A conclusion is a type of **inference,** an educated guess that you make by combining details from the text with your own knowledge and experience.

You draw conclusions all the time. For example, when you try to find an address in an unfamiliar city, you take in details from a map and from street signs. You combine these details with what you already know about street-numbering systems. From all of this, you can decide if you are on the right track. As you read Irving's analysis, begin to draw some conclusions about his overall opinion of *A Christmas Carol.*

READING FOCUS

Literary Elements Many things can be broken into parts. For example, the elements of the game of tennis include a court, two players, and rackets. Likewise, stories all have certain basic elements:

| plot | character | theme |
| setting | point of view | language |

As you read John Irving's introduction to *A Christmas Carol,* see if you notice which of these elements he focuses on in his analysis.

READING PROCESS

PREREADING
Activate Prior Knowledge. Before students read Irving's analysis of *A Christmas Carol,* write *Scrooge* on the chalkboard and ask students what the name calls to mind. Organize their ideas in a concept map. Then explain, if necessary, that Scrooge is the main character in Charles Dickens's story

Reading Selection

A Christmas Carol is a novella, a fictional work longer than a short story but shorter than a novel. In this excerpt from Irving's introduction he analyzes how Dickens uses some key literary elements. As you read the excerpt, write down answers to the numbered active-reading questions.

from an Introduction to Charles Dickens's

A Christmas Carol

by John Irving

A Christmas Carol was originally subtitled "Ghost Story of Christmas"; the accent on the ghostly (*not* the Christmas-y) elements of the tale was further emphasized in Dickens's Preface to the 1843 edition. "I have endeavoured in this Ghostly little book, to raise the Ghost of an Idea, which shall not put my readers out of humour with themselves, with each other, with the season, or with me."

If that doesn't alert his readers sufficiently, Dickens titles the first stave[1] of his carol "Marley's Ghost," *and* the author states no less than four times in the first four paragraphs that Marley is dead. "Marley was dead: to begin with"—the first sentence of the first paragraph. "Old Marley was as dead as a door-nail"—the last sentence of the first paragraph. "You will therefore permit me to repeat, emphatically, that Marley was as dead as a door-nail"—the last sentence of the second paragraph. And, finally: "There is no doubt that Marley was dead. This must be distinctly understood, or nothing wonderful can come of the story I am going to relate"—the second and third sentences of the fourth paragraph. I think we get the idea. An editor of today's less-is-more school of fiction would doubtless have found this repetitious, but Dickens never suffered a minimalist's[2] sensibilities; in Dickens's prose, the refrain is as common as the semicolon.

From the beginning, Scrooge's cantankerous character is unsparing with his cynicism; his miserliness—more so, his utter shunning of humanity—

> **1. What point about Dickens's writing style do you think Irving is trying to make in this paragraph?**

---

1. Dickens divided *A Christmas Carol* into five sections called staves.
2. A minimalist uses simple structures and forms, often repetitiously.

Active-Reading Questions

The purpose of the active-reading questions is to familiarize students with the structure and focus of a literary analysis and to prompt them to draw conclusions as they read. Students' answers will provide an informal measure of their ability to draw conclusions from text materials.

ANSWERS
Possible answers follow.

1. Dickens is not afraid to repeat an idea to make sure the reader understands.

A Christmas Carol. Ask how many students have read *A Christmas Carol* or seen a movie or cartoon adaptation of it. Tell students to pay particular attention as they read the selection to Irving's comments about Scrooge and to other elements of the story. Students should compare and contrast what Irving says with their own ideas and images of the character and story.

Reading Workshop, pp. 168–175
Alignments
TEKS 7B, 7G, 8A, 11A, 11B, 11C, 11F, 12A
TAAS R3, R5
English II End-of-Course 2, 3

Texas Resources
- *Lesson Planner,* Ch. 5
- *TAAS Tool Kit*
- *Preparation for TAAS*
- *Preparing for English II End-of-Course Examination*
- *One-Stop Planner CD-ROM*

Active-Reading Questions
ANSWERS continued

2. Scrooge is cold, miserly, cynical, and isolated, and he likes being that way.

3. People can change dramatically.

4. his imaginative, childlike point of view

---

makes him seem a fair match for any ghost. "The cold within him froze his old features," as Dickens describes him. "He carried his own low temperature always about with him; he iced his office in the dog-days; and didn't thaw it one degree at Christmas." Beggars don't dare to approach him. "Even the blindmen's dogs" give Scrooge a wide berth. "It was the very thing he liked. To edge his way along the crowded paths of life, warning all human sympathy to keep its distance"—Ebenezer Scrooge is the original Bah-Humbug man. "If I could work my will," Scrooge declares, "every idiot who goes about with 'Merry Christmas,' on his lips, should be boiled with his own pudding, and buried with a stake of holly through his heart."

> **2.** After reading this paragraph, what can you quickly determine about Ebenezer Scrooge?

Scrooge is such a pillar of skepticism, he at first resists believing in Marley's Ghost. "You may be an undigested bit of beef, a blot of mustard, a crumb of cheese, a fragment of an underdone potato. There's more of gravy than of grave about you, whatever you are!" Yet Scrooge is converted; beyond the seasonal lessons of Christian charity, *A Christmas Carol* teaches us that a man—even a man as hard as Ebenezer Scrooge—can change. What is heartening about the change in Scrooge is that he learns to love his fellowman; in the politically correct language of our insipid times, Scrooge learns to be *more caring*. But, typical of Dickens, Scrooge has undergone a deeper transformation; that he is persuaded to believe in ghosts, for example, means that Scrooge has been miraculously returned to his childhood—and to a child's powers of imagination and make-believe.

> **3.** What theme, or underlying message, from *A Christmas Carol* does Irving seem to be discussing in this paragraph?

Dickens's celebration of ghosts, and of Christmas, is but a small part of the author's abiding faith in the innocence and magic of children; Dickens believed that his own imagination—in fact, his overall well-being—depended on the contact he kept with his childhood. Furthermore, his popularity with his fellow Victorians, which is reflected by the ongoing interest of young readers today, is rooted in Dickens's remarkable ability for rendering *realistically* what many adults condescendingly call "fantasy." . . .

> **4.** What aspect of Dickens's writing does Irving discuss in this paragraph?

This is a Christmas story, yes; as such, it has a happy ending. But, as Marley's Ghost tells Scrooge, the tale is truly a warning. We had best improve our capacity for human sympathy—or else! We must love one another or die unloved.

READING PROCESS

READING (7C, 7H)
Ask Questions. Suggest that as students read, they outline Irving's analysis of *A Christmas Carol*, making each main idea in his discussion a main heading in their outlines with supporting details as subheads. When students have completed their outlines, have them recast the main headings as questions similar to the active-reading questions. Students may use the questions either to review the main points in Irving's analysis or to test a partner's comprehension of the analysis.

Most of us have seen so many renditions of *A Christmas Carol* that we imagine we know the story, but how long has it been since we've actually *read* it? Each Christmas, we are assaulted with a new carol; indeed, we're fortunate if all we see is the delightful Alastair Sim.[3] One year, we suffer through some treacle[4] in a western setting; Scrooge is a grizzled cattle baron, tediously unkind to his cows. Another year, poor Tiny Tim hobbles about in the Bronx or in Brooklyn; old Ebenezer is an unrepentant slum landlord. In a few years, I'll be old enough to play the role of Scrooge in one of those countless amateur theatrical events which commemorate (and ruin) *A Christmas Carol* every season. We should spare ourselves these sentimentalized enactments and reread the original—or read it for the first time, as the case may be.

It may surprise us to learn that there is not one scene of Scrooge interacting with Tiny Tim, although that is a cherished moment in many made-for-television versions; it is also surprising that, in the epilogue, Dickens anticipates his own detractors. Of Scrooge, the author writes, "Some people laughed to see the alteration in him, but he let them laugh, and little heeded them; for he was wise enough to know that nothing ever happened on this globe, for good, at which some people did not have their fill of laughter in the outset; and knowing that such as these would be blind anyway, he thought it quite as well that they should wrinkle up their eyes in grins, as have the malady in less attractive forms. His own heart laughed: and that was quite enough for him." . . .

5. By making this statement, what objections about the character of Scrooge do you think Dickens may have been anticipating?

To his readers, Charles Dickens called himself "Their faithful Friend and Servant." In his Preface to the 1843 edition of *A Christmas Carol*, Dickens bestowed a generous benediction; he confessed his hopes for his "Ghostly little book" *and* for his readers—"May it haunt their houses pleasantly." In truth, . . . 150 years after the carol was written—Dickens's "Ghost Story of Christmas" continues to haunt us pleasantly. "And so, as Tiny Tim observed, God bless Us, Every One!"

---

3. An actor who played Scrooge in a 1972 film version of *A Christmas Carol*.
4. treacle: anything excessively sweet.

Active-Reading Questions
ANSWERS continued

5. that the change in his character was superficial, had some ulterior motive, or would not last

First Thoughts on Your Reading

ANSWERS

Sample responses are provided.

1. It is a wonderful story with an enduring message: It is never too late to begin caring about others, and that innocence and imagination help us to be reborn.

2. Students may choose among various details mentioned by Irving. As Irving especially seems to enjoy Dickens's characterization of Scrooge, students may cite a detail and example sentence from the third paragraph of Irving's analysis.

3. character; because the change in Scrooge is the focus of the story and illustrates its theme

---

First Thoughts on Your Reading

Answer the following questions about John Irving's introduction to *A Christmas Carol*. Write your answers on your own paper.

1. What is Irving's overall opinion of *A Christmas Carol*?
2. Describe a specific detail from *A Christmas Carol* that Irving seems especially to enjoy. Give an example sentence from the essay to support your answer.
3. Which literary element (plot, setting, character, point of view, theme, or language) does Irving seem to discuss most fully? Why do you think he focuses on that element?

READING SKILL

Drawing Conclusions

Put Two and Two Together As you read John Irving's essay, you probably drew some conclusions about the story and about Irving's view of it. To draw those conclusions, you had to "put two and two together"—to combine what you read with what you already know. When you draw a conclusion from your own reading, you use information from the text along with your prior knowledge to make a judgment about the text.

When you read fiction or nonfiction, drawing conclusions helps you more fully understand the author's meaning. Often, especially in fiction, authors "show" rather than "tell." For example, a writer might describe a single tear coming from a character's eye instead of directly stating, "He suddenly felt sad." In his essay, Irving says of Scrooge that "Beggars don't dare to approach him." From that detail, he expects you to understand—to draw the conclusion—that Scrooge is stingy.

The following Thinking It Through provides a general set of steps that you can use to draw conclusions as you read.

THINKING IT THROUGH **Drawing Conclusions**

Read through the passage below, and then use the steps on the following page to draw some conclusions about it.

> Dickens's *A Christmas Carol* was a great success with the readers of his day, and it remains a very popular story even now. The idea of a ghost story in which a seemingly unredeemable man is transformed for the better will continue to intrigue readers around the world for many years to come.

▶ **STEP 1 Identify the topic of the passage.** The phrases <u>remains very popular</u> and <u>will continue to intrigue readers</u> suggest that the topic may be the lasting popularity of A Christmas Carol.

▶ **STEP 2 Relate the topic and contents of the passage to your own knowledge and experiences.** I know that A Christmas Carol is a ghost story and that it is performed every year at my school. I also know that several movie versions are shown each year. I have no doubts that it is still very popular.

▶ **STEP 3 Use your knowledge and experiences to draw a conclusion about the topic of the passage.** The writer never directly states, "The lasting popularity of A Christmas Carol is due to the idea behind it: a ghost story about a bad man who becomes good." However, based on my knowledge and experiences, I think that is the conclusion the writer wants readers to make.

YOUR TURN 2 — Drawing Conclusions

Use the steps above to answer each of the following questions about John Irving's essay. Write your answers on your own paper.

1. Based on the last sentence of the fifth paragraph, what conclusions can you draw about Irving's opinion of "fantasy" and about the differences in the attitudes of adults and young readers toward it? Support your answer with quotations from this reading.

2. Based on Irving's statements in the seventh paragraph, what conclusion can you draw about his attitude toward recent versions of A Christmas Carol? Support your answer with quotations from this reading.

Literary Elements

Building Blocks   Plot, setting, character, point of view, theme, and language are the most important elements an author uses to create the overall effect of a story. As a reader of a literary analysis, you must be familiar with these elements so that you can decide whether you agree with the writer's analysis of them. The chart on the following page explains the most important of these elements and provides important questions to ask about each.

YOUR TURN 2

ANSWERS
Here are possible answers.

1. Irving believes that "fantasy" is an important part of being alive, unlike most adults, who think that fantasy is childish and that it no longer has a place in their lives. Irving clearly believes that fantasy enriches one's experiences as an adult.

2. He believes that recent versions distort and wreck the story; he thinks people should read the original. The descriptive words Irving uses to characterize recent versions show his displeasure with them.

RESOURCES

Your Turn 2
Practice
■ *Communications,* WS. p. 80
Reinforcement
■ *Communications,* TP. 39, WS. p. 81

TEACHING TIP

Literary Elements
To help students begin to think like literary critics, have them select and re-read a familiar short story and respond to the literary elements in the story in a chart such as the following.

Literary Elements	Comments
Plot	
Setting	
Characters	
Point of View	
Theme	
Language	

Students should briefly describe each element and then write comments on each element in the right-hand column. Then, have each student share his or her reaction to the story with a small group of classmates by writing and then reading aloud a brief paragraph titled "What I Liked or Didn't Like in [title of story] and Why."

Literary Elements	Questions
Plot is the term used to describe the actions and events in a story. Key terms related to plot include **conflict**—the problems a character faces in a story, and **climax**—the high point of a plot, the scene that settles the story's main conflict and determines how the story turns out.	Does the analysis contain a detailed discussion of the sequence of events in the story, or of the problems or difficulties the main character faces?
Setting is the time and place in which a story takes place. It may provide background for understanding characters and events in the story or for creating a particular mood or atmosphere.	Is there much discussion of the time or place in which the story happens?
Characters are the individuals in a story. **Characterization** is the way that an author reveals the qualities and traits of these individuals—either directly through description, thoughts, or feelings or indirectly through dialogue.	Is much of the analysis devoted to discussing the traits or qualities of the main character, or of another character in the story?
Point of view is the vantage point or "angle" from which a story is told. In **first-person point of view** the narrator is a character in the story and speaks using the pronoun *I*. A first-person narrator can tell only what he or she sees, hears, is told, or believes—but not what any other character sees, hears, is told, or believes. In **third-person point of view**, the narrator speaks from outside the story—not as a character—and uses third-person pronouns such as *he, she,* and *them*. A **third-person omniscient** narrator can reveal the thoughts of all characters or describe any event. A **limited third-person** narrator reveals the thoughts of just one character; that is, the story's events are filtered through the mind of that one person.	Does the writer of the analysis seem to spend much time discussing the "angle" or vantage point from which the story is told?
Theme is an important idea about life or human nature revealed in a story. It is not just a subject, like "war," but an insight, such as "war wounds are not only physical." (Authors usually don't state their themes directly, so readers have to draw their own conclusions about theme by analyzing the characters, events, setting, and dialogue the author uses.)	Is much of the analysis given over to discussing the story's message—an important idea about life or about people that the story reveals?
Authors of fiction, just like poets, use **language** to achieve certain effects. For example, an author may use *alliteration* (repeated consonant sounds) or *assonance* (repeated vowel sounds) to create a particular mood in a story. Another author may use a *refrain* (a repeated word or phrase) to try to drive home an important point.	Does the writer of the analysis seem especially interested in the writing style (word choices, figurative language, and so on) used by the author of the story?

Elements at Work A literary analysis can enhance even the most critical reader's appreciation of a story by explaining how a writer uses various elements to create certain effects. Just as a tennis commentator might discuss a player's agility, endurance, and great backhand return, a literary analysis can explain each story element's

■ **function** (how the element works in the story; what its purpose is)

174   Chapter 5   Exposition: Analyzing a Short Story

READING PROCESS

EXPLORING
Analyze Literary Elements. Have students read *A Christmas Carol* or view a true-to-the-text video of Dickens's story. Then, lead a discussion in which students analyze the story's literary elements and evaluate Irving's analysis.

- **effect** (what the reader feels or understands because of the presence of the element)
- **development** (how the writer creates or builds on the element—to set a mood or emphasize a theme, for instance)

For example, Irving begins with Dickens's use of language—specifically, Dickens's use of repetition—as the following quotation shows.

> ". . . Dickens titles the first stave of his carol 'Marley's Ghost,' *and* the author states no less than four times in the first four paragraphs that Marley is dead."

Irving then supports this statement by quoting four passages from the story that repeat the same idea: Marley is dead. However, he does not just *identify* the repetition—he actually begins by explaining its function: to emphasize that Marley is a ghost, and that the story is therefore a ghost story, something a reader might otherwise not have noticed right away.

YOUR TURN 3 — Analyzing Literary Elements

Read each of the following passages from the reading selection. Think about the specific literary element Irving discusses in each passage. Then, for each passage, write an answer to the following questions.

- Which literary element does Irving focus on in this passage?
- Does he discuss the element's function, effect, or development? Why?

Compare your responses with those of two or three other students. Keep in mind that you may not come to exactly the same conclusions because readers respond to texts differently.

1. "But, typical of Dickens, Scrooge has undergone a deeper transformation; that he is persuaded to believe in ghosts, for example, means that Scrooge has been miraculously returned to his childhood—and to a child's powers of imagination and make-believe."
2. "This is a Christmas story, yes, as such, it has a happy ending. But, as Marley's Ghost tells Scrooge, the tale is truly a warning. We had best improve our capacity for human sympathy—or else!"
3. "From the beginning, Scrooge's cantankerous character is unsparing with his cynicism; his miserliness—more so, his utter shunning of humanity—makes him seem a fair match for any ghost."

YOUR TURN 3 — ANSWERS

1. character; development; to point out that Scrooge's transformation illustrates the theme of the story
2. theme; effect; to explain what the reader should understand as the meaning of the story
3. character; function; to highlight Scrooge's qualities and compare them with those of the ghosts in the story

RESOURCES

Your Turn 3

Practice
- *Communications,* WS. p. 82

Reinforcement
- *Communications,* TP. 40, WS. p. 83

VOCABULARY

Using Roots

ANSWERS

1. b
2. d
3. a
4. d

Taking a Second Look
Demonstrating Understanding of New Vocabulary. Call on students to use the words *dictatorial, pensive, subvert,* and *diction* in additional sentences that illustrate their meanings.

MINI-LESSON VOCABULARY

Using Roots

One way to deal with unfamiliar words is to study **word roots**, the basic blocks of meaning on which words are built. For example, knowing that the root *–ject* means "to cast or throw" will help you to understand words such as *dejected*, which means "cast down; discouraged." In this word, the root *–ject–* is combined with the prefix *de–* (meaning "down") to create the word's meaning. Here are three common roots and their definitions:

1. *–dict–, –dictat–* to say, command, or speak
2. *–vert–, –verse–, –verg–* to turn
3. *–pend–, –pens–* to hang or weigh

THINKING IT THROUGH — Using Word Roots

Use these steps to strengthen your vocabulary using root words.

1. **Remember the root meaning by associating it with a word you already know.** To remember *–dict–*, meaning "to say, command, talk, or speak," you might associate it with *contradict*, which means "to speak against."

2. **Keep in mind that some roots have alternative spellings.** For example, *–dict–* can also appear as *–dictat–*, as in the word *dictate*, meaning "to speak or read for a person to transcribe."

3. **When you recognize the root in a word you do not know, see if you can figure out its meaning.** If the word can be divided into roots and prefixes and suffixes, you will have to put the meanings of parts together. For example, the word *edict* is made up of the prefix *e–*, meaning "out," and the root *–dict–*. You can conclude that the word means "a speech or command given out."

4. **Test your meaning to see if it fits the context of the sentence.** For example, in the sentence *The officer's edict was obeyed by all,* you could say that "a speech or command given out" fits well with something that is obeyed.

PRACTICE

Using the steps above, choose the correct meanings of the boldface words. Put your answers on your own paper.

1. They resented his **dictatorial** methods. **(a)** very childish **(b)** controlling **(c)** extremely difficult **(d)** obviously untrustworthy

2. The last day of summer camp caused my sister's **pensive** mood. **(a)** joyous **(b)** indifferent **(c)** excited **(d)** sad

3. The rebels tried to **subvert** the movement toward peace. **(a)** overturn **(b)** instigate **(c)** support **(d)** create

4. They discussed the novelist's **diction**, **(a)** use of character **(b)** thematic ideas **(c)** plot complication **(d)** word choice

176 Chapter 5 Exposition: Analyzing a Short Story

RESOURCES

Vocabulary
Practice
- *Communications,* WS. p. 84

Test Taking
Practice
- *Communications,* WS. pp. 85–87

MINI-LESSON: TEST TAKING

Literary Elements

Reading tests often include questions that ask you to describe certain literary elements in reading passages of literary selections. Below is a sample reading passage and a multiple-choice question about it that might appear on a test. Following the question is a set of steps you can use to find the correct answer.

> To Dr. Kresta's query about how they were doing, Mr. Barrow replied, "So far, so good, as long as the weather holds."
>
> Suddenly, unpredictable gusts of wind threatened to rip apart the hot-air balloon they had been riding in as they tried to complete their around-the-world flight. High-altitude temperatures froze the controls, increasing the chance for a potentially fatal crash landing. Below the balloonists, vast stretches of sparsely populated terrain—deserts and mountains—offered scant hope for rescue should they be forced to land.

1. Based on the passage above, the setting could be described as
   A. a mountain range
   B. thousands of feet in the air
   C. the desert
   D. a cold rain forest

THINKING IT THROUGH — Describing Literary Elements

The following steps will help you answer test questions about literary elements.

▶ **STEP 1** Read the question and choices *before* you read the passage so you know exactly what to look for in the passage. *The question clearly asks about the setting of the passage. I know I must look for details of setting.*

▶ **STEP 2** Be sure you understand the literary element you are asked to find. *Setting involves when and where the story takes place.*

▶ **STEP 3** Look for information in the passage that relates to the literary element you are asked to find. *I see from the passage that the two people are in a "hot-air balloon" at a "high altitude." The passage says nothing about when the story takes place.*

▶ **STEP 4** Choose the answer that most correctly relates to the details in the passage. *Choice A is incorrect; mountains are mentioned, but the balloon is high above them. Choice B could be correct; hot-air balloons are usually found high in the air. Choice C is incorrect; the desert is mentioned but lies far below the balloon. Choice D is incorrect because a rain forest is not even mentioned in the passage. The answer must be B.*

Reading Workshop 177

Wrap It Up

Metacognition. Ask students to reflect on their reading processes in a written answer to the following question:

1. How did reading Irving's analysis change your preconceptions about *A Christmas Carol*?

Then, have students answer the following questions:

2. What is the method of drawing conclusions about a literary passage? [identify the topic of the passage; relate the passage's topic and contents to your own knowledge and experiences; use your knowledge and experiences to draw a conclusion about the topic]

3. What are the building blocks of a story? [plot, setting, characters, point of view, theme, and language]

Looking Ahead to Writing

Students will compose their own literary analyses in the Writing Workshop for this chapter (pp. 178–197). In their papers, students will focus on literary elements of a story and how the author uses them to create the story. As they consider the suitability of stories for analysis and plan their papers, students may wish to review the chart of literary elements on p. 174.

Vocabulary
Alignments
TEKS 6C
TAAS R1

Test Taking
Alignments
TEKS 7C, 7H, 11F

Writing Workshop

OBJECTIVES

- To write a literary analysis
- To focus the analysis and develop a thesis
- To collect, elaborate on, and organize supporting details
- To express ideas in complex sentences
- To use quotation marks

Quotation for the Day

"The good critic is one who tells of his mind's adventures among masterpieces."

(Anatole France, 1844–1924, French novelist and Nobel Prize winner)

Read the quotation to the class. What books or stories would students call masterpieces? Ask each student to name a favorite story and tell why he or she considered reading it an "adventure."

TEACHING TIP

Read and Respond Personally to Your Story
If lack of library resources is a problem, or if students simply do not know where to begin, suggest that they look for an appropriate short story in their literature book. If available, literature books from previous years are a useful source of stories. Try to match students having difficulty responding to a story with stories that revolve around their interests or situation (science, sports, rural or urban environment, and so on). If students can choose their stories fairly quickly, they will have more time to analyze and write.

WHAT'S AHEAD?

In this workshop, you will write a literary analysis. You will also learn how to

- focus your analysis and develop a thesis
- collect, elaborate on, and organize details
- use complex sentences
- use quotation marks

Writing a Literary Analysis

You have just read the last page of a book that you really enjoyed. In fact, several days later you are still thinking about it. You begin to wonder where you can read a discussion about the workings of the story or about the author. One place is in an **analysis**—a literary analysis.

A **literary analysis** is an in-depth look at a work of literature. In this Writing Workshop you will plan, organize, and write a literary analysis of a short story of your choice. Your goal as you write should be to create something that you would be proud to share.

Prewriting

Choose a Story

The Choice Is Yours   What kinds of stories do you like to read? Your personal taste in reading is a good place to start when choosing a story to analyze. You might also think about authors whose stories you have enjoyed. The chances are that other stories by the same authors will interest you.

Read and Respond Personally to Your Story

Dig In   As you read, it is a good idea to respond personally to what you are reading. When you involve yourself in what you read, you become an active reader. An active reader of a story

- **forms opinions** by asking, "How do I feel about the story?"
- **judges or measures** the characters and plot by asking, "How do I feel about the characters, events, and situations in the story?"
- **questions things** by asking, "What about the story is confusing?"
- **predicts** by asking, "What will happen next?"

TIP   Remember that personal responses to stories are neither right nor wrong. Two people can read the same story and come away with completely different views of it. Your response is unique to you.

Choosing and Responding to a Story

Review the two prewriting steps on the previous page. Then, choose a short story and read it through, noting your responses to the story as you read.

Consider Purpose, Audience, and Tone

Get Things Straight When you write an analysis of a short story, your **purpose** is to provide a clear and detailed explanation of how the author uses literary elements to shape the entire piece. Because you can assume that your **audience** has already read your story, you do not need to retell the plot.

You should maintain a formal tone in your literary analysis. **Tone** is your attitude toward your subject; it is conveyed through your use of language. Writing in the third person (using the pronouns *he, she,* and *they*) and avoiding the contractions and colloquialisms of conversational expressions will help you achieve a formal tone.

TIP A literary analysis, like many other forms of nonfiction, is meant to be somewhat persuasive. To some degree, writers of literary analyses want their readers to agree with their opinions of the story and of the story's author.

Analyze Your Story

Take a Closer Look Authors manipulate literary elements—the components of stories—to achieve different effects. You analyze a short story to discover the important elements in a story and how the author uses them. Analyze the elements in a story by answering the questions below.

Literary Element	Analysis Questions
Plot—the action or series of events in a story. **Conflicts** are the problems the characters face. These conflicts can be internal or external. The **climax** is the point in the story at which the main conflict is resolved.	• What important problems or difficulties do the characters face? • How are the characters' problems resolved? • Do the events happen logically?
Setting—the time and place in which the story occurs. The setting provides important background for understanding people and events in the story.	• Where and when does the story take place? • Do the time and place affect characters and events, cause a conflict, or set a mood?
Characters—the individuals in a short story. *Characterization* is how the characters' qualities are revealed: *directly* through description, thoughts, or feelings, or *indirectly* through dialogue.	• What is the main character like? • How are the characters' qualities revealed? • What motivates the character? • Does the main character change? If so, how and why?

(continued)

Discuss the active-reading questions in **Read and Respond Personally to Your Story** to be sure students understand them. Emphasize that the questions address literary elements and represent useful strategies for approaching any reading selection. Suggest that each student copy the questions on a sheet of paper and write responses while reading the short story he or she has chosen.

Prewriting, pp. 178–183
Alignments
TEKS 1A, 1B, 1C, 2A, 8A, 8C, 10B, 11A, 11B, 11C, 11F, 12A
TAAS R3, R5, W1, W2, W4
English II End-of-Course 2, 3, 4

Texas Resources
• *Lesson Planner,* Ch. 5
• *TAAS Tool Kit*
• *Preparation for TAAS*
• *Preparing for English II End-of-Course Examination*
• *One-Stop Planner CD-ROM*

Your Turn 4
Practice
■ *Communications,* WS. p. 88

Meeting INDIVIDUAL NEEDS

STUDENTS WITH SPECIAL NEEDS
To provide motivation for writing, have students view a videotaped version of a piece of literature and allow them to write about aspects of the videotaped version. Have students use a viewing guide similar to the analysis log at right that lists the literary elements and includes a short definition of each. Students may make notes in the Responses column of the guide as they view the videotape. Afterward, place students in small discussion groups to help inspire them and to help them develop ideas before writing comments on the literary piece.

(continued)

Point of view—the angle from which the story is told. The angle can be from a character in the story (signaled by first-person pronouns such as *I*) or from an outside person (signaled by third-person pronouns such as *he* or *she*). In some short stories the point of view shifts.	• How does point of view affect your response? • Does the narrator speak with the pronoun *I*? (This point of view is called **first person**.) • Can the narrator reveal the thoughts of any character? (This point of view is called **third-person omniscient**.) • Does the narrator relate events from the view of just one character? (This point of view is called **third-person limited**.)
Foreshadowing—a hint or suggestion of coming events.	• Does the author hint at events that might take place later? If so, where and how?
Irony—a surprising contrast between appearance or expectation and reality. Irony can be humorous or bitter, but it always makes us think.	• Do the author or characters ever say one thing, but mean something different? (This contrast is **verbal irony**.) • Do characters face situations surprisingly unlike their expectations? (This contrast is called **situational irony**.) • At any point, do you know more than the characters do? (This contrast is called **dramatic irony**.)
Theme—an important idea about life or human nature. Rather than stating a theme directly, writers often expect readers to figure out the theme.	• What important idea about life or human nature does the story reveal? • How is this theme developed?

Here is part of an analysis log one writer created to record information about literary elements in a story titled "A Man Called Horse."

Analysis Log: "A Man Called Horse"

Literary Element	Responses
Plot	Main character has problems with his feelings of self-worth. These problems are resolved when he moves to the West and is captured by Crow Indians—with whom he "earns" his future.
Setting	The story takes place on the northern plains of the American frontier near the middle of the nineteenth century. The location gives the story a feeling of danger and adventure.
Characters	The main character is a New England man who eventually calls himself Horse. His traits are revealed by direct and indirect characterization. He is motivated by a need for a sense of self-worth.
Theme	The theme of this story is that a person has to earn a sense of self-worth. The author develops this theme by describing the events Horse goes through to gain self-worth.

Find a Focus and Develop a Thesis

Pick Your Target Once you have analyzed how literary elements are used in your story, you can decide which elements will serve as the focus of your analysis. You can zero in on a single element, or you can discuss how two elements work together. For example, the student writing about "A Man Called Horse" might choose to discuss the way the author shows how the man's character changes through events in the story.

Next, draft a preliminary **thesis statement**. Your thesis statement is important because it identifies the element or elements on which you will focus, *and* it states your main idea about those elements.

KEY CONCEPT

THINKING IT THROUGH

Finding a Focus and Developing a Thesis

Use the following steps to find a focus and construct a thesis statement for your analysis. The example responses are based on "A Man Called Horse."

▸ **STEP 1 Recall what went through your mind after you first read the story.** Your initial reaction to the story is often a clue to insights you might want to share with your readers. *The main character changed a lot from the beginning to the end of the story.*

▸ **STEP 2 Review your answers to the analysis questions about story elements on pages 179 and 180.** Think about the literary element for which you seem to have the most interesting information. *The most interesting information in my answers concerns the story's main character.*

▸ **STEP 3 Compare your response in step 1 to your response in step 2.** It is likely that your most interesting answers to the analysis questions will support your overall reaction to the story. *Since my first reaction was to the main character and I have a lot of notes about the main character, I'll focus on characterization.*

▸ **STEP 4 Decide what you want to say about the element or elements you find most important.** Your thoughts about these elements will be your **main idea**, or **thesis**. *The author's use of characterization shows how the main character changes through the story.*

▸ **STEP 5 Form your thesis statement by joining the literary element(s) with your main idea about them.** Write a sentence that includes the story's title, the author, the literary element(s) on which you will focus, and your main idea. *In the short story "A Man Called Horse," Dorothy M. Johnson traces the changes that one nineteenth-century young man undergoes in his search for self-worth.*

TEACHING TIP

Find a Focus and Develop a Thesis
Have students work in small groups as peer reviewers to focus on avoiding the problems of thesis statements that are too broad or too vague. Instruct students to check one another's work for a single literary element as the focus of their analysis. Students should also be sure they are working with a manageable topic—the plot of a short story, for example, rather than of a novel.

YOUR TURN 5

Students should make certain that each aspect of their analyses (purpose, audience, tone, focus, and thesis) is compatible with the others. Point out to students that their choice of audience will have a major influence on what they say in their analyses and how they say it. In the same way, the tone of their writing will determine to a great extent who will be interested in reading the piece.

Timesaver

Before students begin their rough drafts, have them present to a small group the evidence from their stories that supports their thesis statements. The group should judge whether the evidence is sufficient and specific enough to prove each thesis. Students can also suggest ways for the presenters to strengthen their theses. This type of peer critique at the prewriting stage will save you conferencing time now and at later stages in the writing process.

TEACHING TIP

Supporting Details
Tell students that when they select a direct quotation from a story for use in their analyses, they should write it down on a note card with the page number and paragraph or line number of the quotation. When they begin to write, students can relocate the quotation easily in the text to check its accuracy and appropriateness.

YOUR TURN 5 Laying the Groundwork for Your Analysis

Delve into your short story by using the preceding steps. Remember to consider your purpose, audience, and tone, analyze your story, and find a focus and develop your thesis.

Gather Support

Focusing In Your readers are not likely to accept your ideas if you do not support them. In a literary analysis, support consists of **key points** to support your thesis, **details** from the story to support key points, and **elaboration** that explains the details and ties them to the key points.

Key Points The key points you make should relate directly to your thesis. There are several techniques you can use to determine your key points.

- **Try asking questions about the thesis.** Consider the example thesis about "A Man Called Horse" in the Thinking It Through on page 181. A student writer could ask, "What has to be in this essay to reflect Horse's change? What does Horse say or do that shows the change?"

- **Set up contrasts and freewrite about them.** Seeing contrasts often helps you discover ideas. At the beginning of the story Horse is discontented and longing. At the end of the story, Horse is content, proud, and confident.

- **Create a map showing how the main idea develops through the story.** This technique works well when writing about characterization.

KEY CONCEPT

TIP When discussing events from a story, always use the **literary present tense.** That is, always refer to the events in the story as if they were happening in the present—not in the past.

Supporting Details Supporting details are the evidence you include to support your key points. When you establish the points you want to make about a story, you will discover supporting details in the text. You can include supporting details by using three methods:

182 Chapter 5 Exposition: Analyzing a Short Story

RESOURCES

Your Turn 5
Practice
- *Communications,* WS. p. 89

Your Turn 6
Practice
- *Communications,* WS. p. 90

- **paraphrasing,** or restating a passage in your own words
- **summarizing** the main points of a passage in a condensed form
- **direct quotations,** or using the exact words from a story

TIP Use strong, active verbs in your literary analysis. Replace words such as *show* and *use* with more descriptive ones such as *mirror* and *trace*. Make passive sentences active whenever possible.

Elaboration Supporting a key point with a detail from the story is not enough. You must elaborate on details to explain *how* they support your key points. The following portion of a chart shows the three key points that a writer makes to support a thesis statement about "A Man Called Horse."

Thesis: In the short story "A Man Called Horse," Dorothy M. Johnson traces the changes that one nineteenth-century young man undergoes in his search for self-worth.

Key Point	Story Detail	Elaboration
Johnson first characterizes her main character as a person discontented with a life others might envy.	**Quotation:** . . . the man has "every comfort and privilege his father's wealth could provide."	This description mirrors his casual acceptance of a privileged life.
Later on, when this man is captured by Indians, Johnson uses the man's thoughts and feelings to show his personal growth.	**Summary:** After months of hearing an unfamiliar language, one day he is surprised to discover that he understands a phrase he overhears.	This boost to his spirits is shown by his decision to try to marry into the family he serves.
As Horse takes his final steps from alienation to self-worth, Johnson shifts her focus to Horse's outer life.	**Paraphrase:** Unexpectedly, Horse decides to stay and care for his destitute mother-in-law.	His unselfish decision to stay and care for her shows just how much he has changed.

Organize Your Analysis

Get It in Order Often, your topic and your ideas will suggest a natural way to arrange your points and supporting details. For example, to address how an author uses plot to build suspense, you might discuss the events in **chronological order.** You can also order information by **order of importance.**

 Collecting and Organizing Your Ideas

Use the preceding steps to collect and organize details. Remember to collect details (quotations, paraphrases, or summaries) that support your key points and elaborate on each detail you provide.

Connecting Reading and Writing

To make students aware of how direct quotations can enhance a literary analysis, refer students to the Reading Selection (pp. 169–171). Have students identify direct quotations in Irving's analysis. Then, discuss how the author uses them to develop his thesis.

TECHNOLOGY

Students may find it useful to save a set of notes or an outline along with their developing draft and to use the multiple-window feature of their word-processing program to view their prewriting notes and their plan or outline at the same time.

YOUR TURN 6

Tell students that if they have too many supporting details, they can be selective, using only those that best support their key points. If students have too few details, however, they will need to gather more evidence. Emphasize that students should decide how they will order their key points and supporting details before beginning their rough drafts. They can always change the order if, once they start writing, they find that their original arrangements do not help advance their theses.

Writing Workshop 183

Quotation for the Day

"Nothing is ended with honour which does not conclude better than it began."

(Samuel Johnson, 1709–1784, English lexicographer, essayist, and poet)

Use the quotation to initiate a discussion of the framework for writing a literary analysis: introduction, body, and conclusion. Brainstorm with students ways in which a writer can conclude an essay with a flourish.

YOUR TURN 7

Allot a half hour or more of class time for students to begin their rough drafts. Use this time to help students avoid frustration by dealing with questions and difficulties immediately. You may also wish to schedule at least one more day in class for writing, based on student progress and their questions and problems with the assignment.

Writing

Literary Analysis

Framework

Introduction
- Open with an interesting comment on the story.
- Include a thesis statement.

Body
- State first key point with support and elaboration.
- State second key point with support and so on.

Conclusion
- Restate your thesis.
- Summarize your key points.

Directions and Explanations

A Good Start Use an observation, a question, or a quotation related to your thesis to describe a connection you made to the story.

Set Your Focus Your thesis statement should include the title and author of the story, the literary element or elements on which you will focus, and your main idea about the element or elements.

Make Your Point Develop a paragraph for each of your other key points. Arrange them in a logical order.

Back It Up Support each point by quoting, paraphrasing, or summarizing details from the story. Elaborate by explaining how the details connect to each point.

Finish with a Flourish Leave your readers with something to consider. One good way to close your essay is with a general comment about the story that relates to your thesis.

YOUR TURN 7 Writing a First Draft

Using the framework and the directions and explanations above as a guide, write a first draft of your literary analysis. Read the Writer's Model on the next page to see how one writer developed a thesis.

RESOURCES

Writing
Writing Prompts
- *Communications,* TP. 41, WS. p. 91

Your Turn 7
Practice
- *Communications,* TP. 42, WS. p. 92

184 Exposition: Analyzing a Short Story

A Writer's Model

The following literary analysis closely follows the framework on the previous page.

"A Man Called Horse"

"Who am I?" and "Where do I belong?" are questions people have always asked themselves as they approach adulthood. In the short story "A Man Called Horse," Dorothy M. Johnson traces the changes that one nineteenth-century young man undergoes as he finds answers to those questions in his search for self-worth.

Johnson first characterizes her main character, an unnamed young man, as a person discontented with a life others might envy. The author tells readers that living in a "gracious old Boston home," the man has "every comfort and privilege his father's wealth could provide." This description mirrors his casual acceptance of a privileged life. The author goes on to explain that the man knows himself so little that he does not even know why he is unhappy. Vaguely sensing that he does not belong and hoping to find his "equals," he moves to the West, where he believes "all white men" are "kings." His money allows him to surround himself with men he respects, but who show no interest in being his friends.

Later on, when this man is taken captive by a band of Crow Indians, Johnson uses the man's thoughts and feelings to show his first steps toward personal growth. She first displays the character's humiliation by describing how he is tethered and forced into servitude: "They took him along in a matter-of-fact way, as they took the captured horses." The man knows he is being treated as a nonperson, but he is too afraid for his life to fight against his captors. Johnson reveals the man's growing ingenuity when she describes how he pretends to be a horse, a meek "bearer of burdens." The man knows that it is shrewd to do so, because it helps him fare much better. Then, Johnson shows a spark of happiness in him: After months of being ordered around in an unfamiliar language, one day he is surprised to discover that he understands a phrase he overhears. This boost to his spirits is shown by his decision to try to marry into the family he serves. He reasons

(continued)

INTRODUCTION

Thesis

BODY
First key point

Support and elaboration

Second key point

Support and elaboration

Connecting Reading and Writing

Have students re-read the introductory paragraphs of both the Reading Selection (pp. 169–171) and the analysis titled **"Characterization in 'A Man Called Horse,'"** before they draft their own introductions. Point out that Irving begins with historical information about the work and a quotation from Dickens to make the point that *A Christmas Carol* is a ghost story. The author of the analysis featured in **A Writer's Model** uses generic questions about identity to lead into the thesis that **"A Man Called Horse"** is about a young man's search for a sense of self-worth. Encourage students to create similarly engaging openings for their own analyses.

Writing, pp. 184–187
Alignments
TEKS 1A, 1B, 1C, 2A, 2B, 8A, 10B, 12A
TAAS W1, W2, W4
English II End-of-Course 3, 4

Meeting INDIVIDUAL NEEDS

ENGLISH-LANGUAGE LEARNERS
General Strategies. Remind English-language learners that they should avoid the words *I*, *me*, *my*, and *mine* when writing a literary analysis. They can avoid these terms by rewording statements or by using the pronoun *one*. Provide students with models like these:

1. I didn't understand the motives of Dr. Frankenstein. [Dr. Frankenstein's motives were unclear.]

2. I expected the ending to be happier. [One might have expected the ending to be happier.]

(continued)

that doing so will help him to escape. Thus, Horse, as he now calls himself, sets out to win the Crows' respect.

Third key point

As Horse takes his final steps away from alienation toward self-worth, Johnson shifts her focus to Horse's outer life. He kills a member of an enemy tribe and steals two horses—actions the Crows view as brave. Then, by gaining a wife and wealth, he wins the respect he sought from the Crows and the sense of worth he sought for himself. His hard-won self-respect is tested, however, when he loses all his possessions, the entire camp moves away, and his wife dies in childbirth. Unexpectedly, Horse decides to stay and care for his destitute mother-in-law. His unselfish decision to stay and care for her shows just how much he has changed: "He could afford to be magnanimous, for he knew he was a man."

Support and elaboration

CONCLUSION
Summary of key points

Johnson's characterization of Horse parallels his personal growth. By describing his life in Boston, she underscores his sense of alienation, even though he has all the material things he could want. She then shifts to reveal the thoughts and feelings behind his actions as he takes the initiative to secure a future as a more giving, noble man. Perhaps her story suggests that for many people, the path to self-worth ultimately lies in taking action to achieve it.

General comment related to the thesis

Crow Warriors

A Student's Model

The following is an excerpt from a literary analysis written by Jeremy Schmidt, a student from University High, University of Chicago Lab Schools in Chicago, Illinois.

Number One

Everybody strives to be recognized as an individual, but this is often a difficult task. This idea is illustrated in Kurt Vonnegut's short story, "The Lie." At the beginning of the story, Sylvia thinks of her son Eli only as one of many Remenzels; by the end, she begins to think of him as an individual. The change that occurs in Eli's mother has an important effect on their relationship and on Eli himself.

Throughout the early part of the story Sylvia Remenzel thinks of her son as the next Remenzel to attend Whitehill, not as a distinct individual. While they are driving to school Sylvia says to Eli, "If I were you, I'd be so excited I could hardly stand it." She is pressuring Eli to feel "excited" or happy about his entrance into high school. She then tells him that his four years at the Whitehill school will be the "best" years of his life. Rather than inquiring about his feelings, she is telling him how to feel. Sylvia assumes that since all the Remenzel men have attended, been successful at, and enjoyed Whitehill, Eli will also. She fails to even consider the possibility that Eli is not "excited" about going to Whitehill or that this school is not right for Eli because of his individual character. . . .

Sylvia eventually recognizes her own misconception of her son. During the Remenzels' talk with the headmaster of Whitehill, he explains that Eli was not accepted to the school due to his previous grades and his poor score on the entrance exam. He tells them that "to expect him to do Whitehill work would be both unrealistic and cruel." Sylvia's mind momentarily goes "blank." This suggests that Sylvia has been shocked into completely reassessing her son's life and needs.

INTRODUCTION

Thesis

BODY: First key point

Support and elaboration

Second key point
Support and elaboration

Quotation for the Day

"True ease in writing comes from art, not chance, / As those move easiest who have learn'd to dance."

(Alexander Pope, 1688–1744, English poet)

Write the quotation on the chalkboard or on an overhead transparency. Then, ask students to share their own experiences of when and why writing was easy or difficult. Point out that, as with any learned skill, the more writing students do, the easier it will become.

TEACHING TIP

▶ **Elaboration**

Tell students that allusion is an effective method of elaborating. Students might refer to another piece of literature, a historical event, or some aspect of mythology to help the reader understand a detail from the story. To explain the faithfulness of a female character in a story, for instance, a writer might make an allusion to the circumstances or behavior in *The Odyssey*, of Odysseus's wife, Penelope, who never gave up hope that her husband would return home eventually.

Cooperative Learning 5B

Peer Review. Point out to students that peer review is a powerful tool to help a writer communicate ideas to an audience. Peer review should always be constructive. Likewise, the writer should always respond productively, considering seriously each suggestion the reviewer makes. Arrange students in small groups to review one another's drafts. Emphasize to students that they should work together as a team to make each draft the best it can be.

Revising

Evaluate and Revise Your Draft

Check It Twice   Carefully read your whole paper at least twice. First, examine content and organization using the guidelines below. Then, use the guidelines on the next page to help you focus on sentence style.

▶ **First Reading: Content and Organization**   The following chart will help you evaluate and revise the content and organization of your analysis. First, answer the questions in the left-hand column. If you need help, use the tips in the middle column. Then, use the revision techniques in the right-hand column to make any needed changes.

Literary Analysis: Content and Organization Guidelines for Peer and Self-Evaluation

▶ Evaluation Questions	▶ Tips	▶ Revision Techniques
❶ Does the opening capture the reader's attention?	**Underline** the sentences that hook the reader. If no sentences are underlined, revise.	**Add** a quotation, a question, or a personal connection you made to the story.
❷ Does the thesis statement provide the title of the story, the author, the literary element(s) discussed, and the main idea about the element(s)?	**Put a 1** over the title, a **2** over the author, a **3** over key words that signal the literary element(s) discussed, and a **4** over the main idea. If any number is missing, revise.	**Add** any missing parts to the thesis statement.
❸ Do details from the story support each key point? Is sufficient elaboration provided for each story detail?	**Put an A** next to the sentence that states the key point in each body paragraph. **Put a B** next to details that support the key points. **Put a C** next to any sentence that explains how a detail connects to the key point. If an **A, B,** or **C** is missing from a body paragraph, revise.	**Add** one or more sentences that quote, summarize, or paraphrase story details to support your key points. **Elaborate** by explaining how the details connect to the paragraph's key point. **Cut** any sentences that are not connected to the key point of a paragraph.
❹ Is the language in the analysis appropriate for the intended audience, purpose, and tone?	**Draw a box** around any contractions, colloquial expressions, or other informal language. Revise the boxed parts.	**Replace** informal expressions with words that set a more formal tone. For sentences not in the third person, **rewrite** them from the third-person point of view.
❺ Does the conclusion restate the thesis and summarize the key points? Does it leave readers with something to **consider**?	**Highlight** the restatement of the thesis and **circle** the summary of the key points. If any of these parts is missing, revise.	**Add** a restatement of the thesis and a summary of the key points. **Add** a thought that applies the thesis to a more general world.

188   Chapter 5   Exposition: Analyzing a Short Story

RESOURCES

Revising

Practice
- *Communications,* TPs. 43, 44, WS. pp. 93, 94, 95

Extension
- *Designing Your Writing*

Exposition: Analyzing a Short Story

ONE WRITER'S REVISIONS Here is how one writer used the content and organization guidelines to revise part of the literary analysis on page 185. Study the revisions carefully, and then answer the questions that follow.

> Johnson first characterizes her main character, an unnamed young man, as a person discontented with a life others might envy. The author tells readers that living in a ~~ritzy house~~ "gracious old Boston home," the man has "every comfort and privilege his father's wealth could provide." This description mirrors his casual acceptance of a privileged life.

replace

elaborate

Analyzing the Revision Process
1. Why did the writer revise her description of the house?
2. Why did the writer add a sentence after the quoted material?

YOUR TURN 8 — Focusing on Content and Organization
Using the guidelines on page 188, revise the content and organization of your literary analysis. Use the example revisions above as a model.

PEER REVIEW
Ask a classmate to read your analysis and answer these questions.
1. Which quotations, summaries, or paraphrases from the story most effectively support the writer's key points? Why?
2. What is the writer's thesis? Does the writer close with a final thought about this thesis? What is that thought?

▶ **Second Reading: Style** An engaging literary analysis should not use too many short, choppy sentences. Instead, combine such sentences into **complex sentences** by using **adjective clauses**—subordinate clauses introduced by **relative pronouns** (such as *who, whom, which,* and *that*) that modify a noun or pronoun. Use the following guidelines to incorporate more of these kinds of complex sentences into your paper.

Style Guidelines

Evaluation Question	Tip	Revision Technique
Does the paper include too many short, choppy sentences?	**Underline** repeated nouns in back-to-back sentences. Consider revising these sentences.	**Eliminate** choppy sentences by using adjective clauses to combine sentences. **Replace** a repeated noun with the relative pronoun of the adjective clause.

Writing Workshop **189**

Analyzing the Revision Process
ANSWERS
Possible answers follow.
1. The phrase "ritzy house" is too slangy. "Gracious old Boston home" is both more formal and more specific.
2. to elaborate on the key point of the paragraph

YOUR TURN 8
In addition to using the guidelines on p. 188 to evaluate and revise their analyses, students should evaluate and implement the feedback they received from the peer review. One way to check students' revisions is to have each student write a brief paragraph explaining how the changes he or she made improved the overall quality of the paper.

Critical Thinking
Synthesis. Revision may seem complicated to students. Emphasize that revising consists of just four techniques: replacing, cutting, adding, and reordering. These techniques can be used for evaluating and revising almost anything. To demonstrate, ask students to think of ways to redesign their school using the four revision techniques. [They might replace buildings, cut unused lockers, add parking space or a place for students to gather, and rearrange classrooms.]

Revising, pp. 188–191
Alignments
TEKS 2B, 2C, 2E, 5A, 5B
TAAS W1, W2, W3, W7
English II End-of-Course 4, 5, 6

Meeting INDIVIDUAL NEEDS

ENGLISH-LANGUAGE LEARNERS
General Strategies. Exchanging papers for peer evaluation can help students understand the value of constructive criticism. Because some students may feel uncomfortable giving criticism, they may need help phrasing valuable constructive criticism. You may want to model the following examples for students to use when making suggestions to classmates:

1. I wonder if there is a better way to say this.
2. You might want to . . .
3. How about changing this to . . . ?

Focus on Sentences

Using Complex Sentences

When you are writing about specific key ideas from a short story, you will sometimes write short sentences whose ideas are so closely related that you use some of the same words in each sentence. Because these short sentences are logically connected, you can combine them by using adjective clauses. The examples below show how two sentences containing a repeated noun can be combined into a single complex sentence by using an adjective clause. In combining sentences this way, you embed one sentence inside the other by replacing the repeated noun with a relative pronoun.

> **Sentences containing a repeated noun (*Poe*):** Edgar Allan **Poe** was a writer. **Poe** was born in Boston.
>
> **Sentences combined using an adjective clause that is introduced with a relative pronoun (*who*):** Edgar Allan Poe, **who** was born in Boston, was a writer.

ONE WRITER'S REVISIONS Here is how the writer of the model literary analysis on page 185 used a relative pronoun to combine two simple sentences into a complex sentence.

BEFORE REVISION

In the short story "A Man Called Horse," one nineteenth-century young man undergoes <u>changes</u>. He experiences <u>changes</u> as he finds answers to those questions in his search for self-worth. Dorothy M. Johnson traces those changes.

The word changes *is repeated unnecessarily.*

AFTER REVISION

In the short story "A Man Called Horse," Dorothy M. Johnson traces the changes **that** one nineteenth-century young man undergoes as he finds answers to those questions in his search for self-worth.

Sentences are combined using a relative pronoun.

190 Chapter 5 Exposition: Analyzing a Short Story

RESOURCES

Focus on Sentences
Practice
- *Communications*, WS. p. 96

Analyzing the Revision Process
1. What did the writer accomplish by combining the sentences?
2. Is there any advantage of not combining the sentences? If so, what is it?

 Focusing on Style

Use the style guidelines on page 189 to locate repetition in your paper and to eliminate it by creating complex sentences.

Designing Your Writing

Formatting Your Essay Your teacher will probably give you specific directions about formatting your literary analysis. If not, you can use the following MLA guidelines.

- **Use one-inch margins** all around so that your pages are easy to read.
- **Double-space** lines of text, and **indent the first line of paragraphs** five spaces. **Align text** on the left, but **leave the right margins ragged.**
- **Center the title** of your essay at the top of the first page. In the upper left-hand corner, **include your name, the course name, your teacher's name,** and **the date. Number the pages** (except the first page) in the top right-hand corner.
- If your teacher requires a title page, **center the title, your name, the course name, the teacher's name,** and **the date** on a separate page.

TIP These guidelines specifically address essays written with word-processing software, but several apply also to handwritten essays.

Essay Without Title Page

Name   1
Course
Teacher
Date
              Title
_____
_____
_____
_____.

Title Page

Title
Name

Course
Teacher
Date

Analyzing the Revision Process
ANSWERS
Possible answers follow.

1. The writer avoided repeating the noun *changes* and expressed the idea more concisely.

2. yes; to emphasize that Dorothy M. Johnson is the one who traces the changes described; (Note: The purpose of this question is to show students that there are appropriate times *not* to combine sentences.)

YOUR TURN 9

Refer students to p. 359 for further discussion of complex sentences and additional practice combining sentences.

Meeting INDIVIDUAL NEEDS

ADVANCED LEARNERS
When they have finished their short story analyses, students might enjoy the challenge of selecting a novel and a film based on it and analyzing how accurately the film represents the novel. When students have finished, have them share their analyses with the class.

Cooperative Learning

Incorporation of Quotations. You might have students work in pairs to complete the practice items. Ask student pairs to combine each quotation and sentence in two different ways. This will discourage students from using the same pattern for each quotation and sentence.

MINI-LESSON: WRITING

Weaving Quotations into Your Essay

ANSWERS

Sample responses are provided.

1. Poe uses sensory details such as "his room was black as pitch with the thick darkness" to create a feeling of terror.

2. Edgar Allan Poe uses comparison for description, likening the beating of an "old man's heart" to the sound "a watch makes when enveloped in cotton."

3. "Nervous—very, very dreadfully nervous" are the words Poe uses to establish the narrator of "The Tell-Tale Heart" as troubled.

4. Poe's poetic language, especially his use of personification in phrases such as "when all the world slept," reinforces the atmosphere of terror.

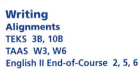

Writing Alignments
TEKS 3B, 10B
TAAS W3, W6
English II End-of-Course 2, 5, 6

MINI-LESSON: WRITING

Weaving Quotations into Your Essay

You know one way to support a key idea in your analysis is to include supporting quotations from the story. However, if you fail to integrate these quotations skillfully, you will affect the communication of your ideas. An effective way to use short quotations is to weave them into your sentences, at the beginning, middle, or end. Look at the following examples:

Beginning: "He was envious still, even among the horses," which are capable of fending for themselves.

Middle: Because he amused the Crows "like a strange pet," they gave him food in the winter.

End: Forced into servitude, he is filled with rage, "although anger was an emotion he knew he could not afford."

When you integrate a quotation into a sentence, be sure that the quoted material fits grammatically into the sentence. For example, be sure that what you end up with is a complete sentence and not a sentence fragment.

Sentence Fragment	"A future," he realizes, "something to be earned." [lacks a verb]
Complete Sentence	"A future," he realizes, is "something to be earned."

You can also use a short phrase to introduce a quotation into a sentence, as in the following example:

According to Johnson, "One of the customs of courtship involved sending a gift of horses to a girl's older brother and bestowing much buffalo meat upon her mother."

TIP When the material you quote takes up more than four lines in your analysis, create a **block quotation.** In MLA style, block quotations begin on a new line; each line of the quotation is indented one inch (about ten spaces). When you set off a quotation this way, do not enclose it in quotation marks.

PRACTICE

For each practice item below, weave the quotation into the sentence. You do not have to use all the words in a quotation, and you may add or revise words in the sentence.

1. **Sentence** Poe uses sensory details to create a feeling of terror.
   Quotation "His room was as black as pitch with the thick darkness. . . ."

2. **Sentence** Edgar Allan Poe uses comparisons for description.
   Quotation "old man's heart" and "sound, such as a watch makes when enveloped in cotton"

3. **Sentence** In "The Tell-Tale Heart," Poe immediately establishes the narrator as troubled.
   Quotation "nervous—very, very dreadfully nervous"

4. **Sentence** Poe's use of personification, reinforces the atmosphere of terror.
   Quotation "when all the world slept"

RESOURCES

Writing

Practice

- *Communications*, WS. p. 97

Publishing

Proofread Your Analysis

A Last Look Before publishing your analysis, work collaboratively to proofread it at least twice for errors in grammar, spelling, and punctuation. In a literary analysis, it is important to pay particular attention to your punctuation of the title of the story and of direct quotations.

Reference Note
For more information on **quotation marks**, see page 743.

Grammar Link

Using Quotation Marks in a Literary Analysis

In a literary analysis it is particularly important that quotation marks be used correctly.

- **Enclose titles of short stories in quotation marks.**

  I read the story "The Cold Equations."

- **Use quotation marks at the beginning and the end of material quoted directly from a story.** Place commas and periods inside closing quotation marks; place semicolons and colons outside closing quotation marks. Exclamation points and question marks are placed inside the closing quotation marks only when they are part of the quoted material.

  Godwin reinforces the stowaway's innocence by saying she "belonged in that world of soft winds and a warm sun, music, and moonlight."

  At one point in the story, Barton says, "You're afraid, but you're not a coward"; this statement reflects Barton's admiration of his stowaway.

  Marilyn says, "I've caused everyone I love to be hurt, haven't I?"

- **Use single quotation marks to enclose a quotation within a quotation.**

  To reinforce the idea that technology is frightening and cold, Godwin includes Marilyn's comments on the spaceship, "'Isn't it—' She stopped, and he looked at her questioningly. 'Isn't it cold in here?'"

PRACTICE

On your own paper, correct errors in the punctuation of story titles and quotations in the following sentences.

1. In Leslie Marmon Silko's The Man to Send Rain Clouds," imagery reinforces the story's conflict: The wind pulled at the priest's brown Franciscan robe and swirled away the cornmeal and pollen".

2. Louise wants to be sure that Teofilo 'won't be thirsty.'

3. The priest asks, What brings you here?

4. Leon "took a piece of string out of his pocket and tied a small gray feather in the old man's long white hair;' here he observes tradition.

5. Why does Leon say "now the old man could send big thunder-clouds for sure?"

Writing Workshop **193**

Quotation for the Day

"Patience is not only a virtue, but it pays."

(B. C. Forbes, 1880–1954, American businessperson and editor of *Forbes Magazine* from 1917 to 1954)

Share the quotation with students, and have them freewrite about a time in their own experience when patience paid off in writing, or when impatience had a price. Encourage students to share their experiences. Then, discuss how patience might pay off when proofreading or publishing.

Grammar Link

Using Quotation Marks in a Literary Analysis

ANSWERS
Possible responses are given.

1. In Leslie Marmon Silko's "The Man to Send Rain Clouds," imagery reinforces the story's conflict: "The wind pulled at the priest's brown Franciscan robe and swirled away the cornmeal and pollen."

2. Louise wants to be sure that Teofilo "won't be thirsty."

3. The priest asks, "What brings you here?"

4. Leon "took a piece of string out of his pocket and tied a small gray feather in the old man's white hair"; here he observes tradition.

5. Why does Leon say, "Now the old man could send big thunderclouds for sure"?

RESOURCES

Grammar Link
Practice
- *Communications,* WS. p. 98

Publishing, pp. 193–194
Alignments
TEKS 2D, 3A, 3B, 3D, 5A
TAAS W3, W6, W7
English II End-of-Course 5, 6

Cooperative Learning

Publishing. Some students might combine their literary analyses and create casebooks with artfully designed construction-paper or cardboard covers. These might be kept on file as examples for future students.

Casebooks might focus on a particular story or on a literary element such as plot or theme. Students might collaborate on a brief introduction to the story or literary element that provides a short synopsis of each analysis in the collection. The jobs of making copies of the analyses, assembling the pieces, adding an introduction or table of contents, and providing art for the cover can be divided equally among each group's members.

Encourage students not to neglect these steps in the writing process, particularly the last step. You might model possible answers to the reflective questions to help students understand how to use the questions as a self-check.

Wrap It Up

Metacognition. Ask students to respond to the following question.

1. What was the most difficult part of writing your literary analysis? Why? How did you overcome this difficulty?

Then, have students answer the following question:

2. What are three methods for including supporting details in a literary analysis? [paraphrasing, summarizing, quoting directly from the story]

TIP If you write your analysis by hand, make sure it is **legible**—that is, clear and easy to read.

PORTFOLIO

Publish Your Analysis

Share Your Work Here are a few ways you might share your literary analysis with an audience.

- Try to publish your analysis on a Web site that accepts reviews or analyses from the public.
- Submit your analysis to the school newspaper or to a literary magazine that accepts student writing.
- Tape-record a reading of your analysis, and start an audio library of analyses with other students.
- Contact a local book club, and ask to read your analysis at a meeting.

Reflect on Your Analysis

Looking Back To help you think about what you have learned from this workshop, answer the following questions about your literary analysis.

- What process did you use to choose the story you read for your analysis? Would you use this process with other stories?
- How did your understanding of the story change after writing your analysis? Does this new understanding increase your enjoyment of the story? Will the deeper understanding gained through analysis change how you approach other stories? Explain.
- What was the most important revision you made to your first draft? How did this change mprove the presentation of your analysis?

If you put your essay in your portfolio, be sure to include your responses to these questions.

YOUR TURN 10 — Proofreading, Publishing, and Reflecting on Your Analysis

Review each of the steps discussed in this section. Before you turn in your literary analysis, be sure to

- proofread it carefully, looking especially for errors in the use of quotation marks
- consider ways to publish your essay
- reflect on your writing process by answering the reflective questions above

Connections to Literature

Writing a Short Story

Up to this point you have learned to analyze how authors put stories together. Now you can create a story of your own, using what you have learned.

Imagine That Creating a short story often means focusing on a single fictional character. That character can be almost anyone. A brief experience in the character's life—a musician's best performance, a pilot's first solo flight, a student's field trip—is described.

Where to Start Short-story writers concentrate on four basic literary elements: plot, character, point of view, and setting. As you know from your analysis, a writer can emphasize certain elements more than others. When you write a short story, it is up to you to decide which elements are most important.

Plot Plot is what happens in a story—the actions and events. In most stories, the plot opens with some sort of **conflict,** or problem. An **external conflict** is a problem a character faces with another character or group or with nature. An **internal conflict** is a problem a character faces with himself or herself.

The plot of your story should unfold through the events you describe. After an initial conflict occurs, smaller complications build suspense that leads to the story's climax. The **climax** is the high point of a story—the moment of tension. Each event in the plot should build on the previous event until the conflict is resolved or a goal is attained at the end of the story. Answer the following questions to help you plot your story.

- What conflict will your character face when your story begins?
- What events will lead to a resolution of the conflict?
- What will be the climax of the story?
- What loose ends will you have to tie up?
- How will you end the story?

Character Since the main character is very important to the short story, you have to consider what he or she thinks and feels and how he or she would react in a situation or speak to another character. To get a good picture of your main character, freewrite about

- the physical appearance and actions of the character
- the thoughts and feelings of the character
- the kinds of things the character might say
- the changes the character might undergo
- the thoughts of others about the character

Character development means showing what the character learns or how the character changes as a result of the events in the story.

TIP Pay special attention to your use of dialogue. **Dialogue** should be realistic, and develop the plot.

TEACHING TIP

Writing a Short Story
Explain that authors sometimes use their own experiences as a basis for their short stories. Students may choose to write short stories that reflect personal experience, but remind them that short stories are a form of fiction: they may reflect, but should not exactly represent a real person, event, or setting. If students choose to base their stories on actual events, suggest that they change some elements to serve their individual writing purposes. Students who base a character on a real person, for example, might depict the person not as he or she was, but in a way that reflects the theme of the story.

Connections to Literature, pp. 195–197
Alignments
TEKS 1A, 1B, 2C, 2D, 11A, 11B, 11C, 11F
TAAS R5, W1, W3, W7
English II End-of-Course 2, 4, 5, 6

TEACHING TIP

Point of View
Students who write a story using a first-person or third-person omniscient narrator may choose to include interior monologue to reveal the characters' feelings and thoughts. For an example of this technique, you may wish to examine with students Amy Tan's story "Two Kinds."

Meeting INDIVIDUAL NEEDS

LEARNERS HAVING DIFFICULTY
Students who have never attempted fiction writing may be wary of this assignment. Their anticipation of problems may be their biggest obstacle to getting started. Remind students that writing problems frequently resolve themselves during the writing process. Once they have identified the basic elements of their stories and how they might develop them, students should begin writing. Tell students not to be too critical of their work until they finish their first drafts. Then they can cut, add, and replace, building on and developing interesting aspects of the various story elements. Students may find that once they start writing, their stories take a different direction from the original plan.

Point of View Stories are told from somebody's perspective. The literary term for this is **point of view**—who is telling the story. You have several points of view to pick from for your story, and each has its advantages. After deciding which one is right for your story, be sure that you use it consistently; carelessly shifting points of view can confuse readers. Here are three basic points of view:

- **First-person point of view:** One of the characters tells the story (using the first-person pronoun *I*). This character can reveal only his or her own thoughts and feelings.

- **Third-person omniscient (all-knowing) point of view:** The narrator, who is not a character, can tell what all characters are thinking and feeling and what is happening in other places in the story.

- **Third-person limited point of view:** The narrator, who is not a character, tells the story through the mind of one character.

Setting Once you have determined plot and point of view, you can consider the **setting**: the time, place, and **mood** (the atmosphere or feeling a story conveys). The more detailed your descriptions of setting are, the more interesting the setting will be to readers.

What's the Big Idea? Many stories are built around a **theme**—a meaning an author tries to convey about life or human nature. You can convey a theme in your story by hinting at it in the story's title or through dialogue spoken by characters.

Learn by Example Read the following excerpts from "The Bride Comes to Yellow Sky" by Stephen Crane. Note that some of the excerpts illustrate more than one literary element. The annotations explain how the literary elements function in the excerpt.

Setting—Crane includes specific descriptions of the setting—the plains of Texas.

> The great Pullman was whirling onward with such dignity of motion that a glance from the window seemed simply to prove that the plains of Texas were pouring eastward. Vast flats of green grass, dull-hued spaces of mesquite and cactus, little groups of frame houses, woods of light and tender trees, all were sweeping into the east, sweeping over the horizon, a precipice.

Plot (conflict), Point of view—Internal conflict begins with the town marshal returning with his new bride to Yellow Sky, afraid of how the people will react. The story is told from the third-person omniscient point of view.

> He, the town marshal of Yellow Sky, a man known, liked, and feared in his corner, a prominent person, had gone to San Antonio to meet a girl he believed he loved, and there, after the usual prayers, had actually induced her to marry him, without consulting Yellow Sky for any part of the transaction. He was now bringing his bride before an innocent and unsuspecting community.

The California Express on the Southern Railway was due at Yellow Sky in twenty-one minutes. There were six men at the . . . "Weary Gentleman." . . . A young man . . . suddenly appeared in the open door. He cried: "Scratchy Wilson's . . . turned loose with both hands."

"Don't know whether there'll be a fight or not," answered one man grimly. "But there'll be some shootin'— some good shootin'."

Presently they heard from a distance the sound of a shot, followed by three wild yowls. It instantly removed a bond from the men in the darkened saloon. There was a shuffling of feet. They looked at each other. "Here he comes," they said.

Potter and his bride walked sheepishly and with speed. . . . As they circled the corner, they came face to face with a man in a maroon-colored shirt who was feverishly pushing cartridges into a large revolver. Upon the instant the man dropped his revolver to the ground, and, like lightning, whipped another from its holster.

"Married!" said Scratchy, not at all comprehending. . . . "Well," said Wilson at last, slowly, "I s'pose it's all off now." . . . He was not a student of chivalry; it was merely that in the presence of this foreign condition he was a simple child of the earlier plains. He picked up his starboard revolver, and placing both weapons in their holsters, he went away.

Plot (complication), Character— The plot becomes more complicated when Scratchy Wilson, the town troublemaker, starts a fight. The one man who handles him is the marshal. Scratchy is characterized as a troublemaker who often goes wild and looks for a gunfight with Marshal Potter. This is the story's external conflict.

Plot (suspense)— Crane builds suspense by describing how the men in the saloon wait for Scratchy to come.

Plot (climax)— The climax of the story comes when Jack Potter and his new wife are making their way to Potter's house and bump into Scratchy Wilson as he is loading his gun.

Character (development), Plot (resolution)— Upon noticing the marshal's new wife, Scratchy Wilson no longer wants to fight him. Crane reveals another side of this villain—his simplicity. This scene is also the plot's resolution. Potter's new status as a married man ends Wilson's torment of the town.

YOUR TURN 11 Writing Your Short Story

Using the guidelines above, write the story you would like to tell. Once you have finished your first draft, give your story a title. Then, revise, proofread, and publish the story.

Cooperative Learning

Peer Review. When students have completed rough drafts of their short stories, divide the class into small groups for peer review. Have each student read his or her story to the group. Members of the group should share what they like best about the story, what they want to know more about, and what parts need clarification. Many times a peer group can help a writer identify what a story is really about if he or she has been merely touching on a theme.

YOUR TURN 11

You may want to specify a particular length for students' stories, such as 1,500 to 2,000 words. Students need to recognize that developing a short story will take some space. Students will also need time to develop their stories, so be sure to allow adequate time for them to plan, draft, and revise their stories.

Focus on Viewing and Representing

OBJECTIVES
- To identify and critique literary elements in a film
- To identify and critique technical elements in a film

Quotation for the Day
"It is in the hard, hard rock-pile labor of seeking to win, hold, or deserve a reader's interest that the pleasant agony of writing again comes in."

(John Mason Brown, 1900–1969, American drama critic, essayist, and lecturer)

Lead students in a discussion of the oxymoron "pleasant agony." You might ask them to cite examples from their own lives of learning a new skill or of drafting a particular piece of writing.

TEACHING TIP

Critiquing a Film
Provide an alternative assignment for students who are not able to view a video or go to a theater to see a film. Students might critique a speech, a school play or musical, a sports event, or some other public performance in their community.

WHAT'S AHEAD?
In this section you will learn to
- identify and critique literary elements in a film
- identify and critique technical elements in a film

Critiquing a Film

Critiquing a film is much like analyzing a story. In both cases, you evaluate how the creator conveys thoughts, ideas, images, and events. The writer of a story has only one way to do this: words. A filmmaker uses many elements to tell a story—dialog, action, visual images, music, and other elements. These elements must combine seamlessly to contribute to the overall effect. This seamlessness makes a good movie difficult to analyze. It is hard to pay attention to the separate elements when you are holding your breath to see if the heroine escapes!

Watching and Forming an Opinion

Presenting the Elements   Stories you see on the big screen contain the same elements as stories you read—point of view, setting, character, plot, theme, and so on. Although many movies are based on stories previously published in books or magazines, filmmakers must handle these literary elements differently because film itself is different. Aside from presenting literary elements through spoken dialogue and occasional narration, a filmmaker must *show* the literary elements of a story.

Point of View   One key difference between stories in books and stories on film is that most films lack a narrator. That is, in most films, the camera becomes the narrator, the point of view from which the story is told. The filmmaker uses the camera to show the audience what he or she wants them to see. Of course, there are exceptions. Some movies have a narrator that tells part of the film's story in a **voice-over**—that is, the narrator is heard but not seen.

Setting   You can identify a film's setting by watching, listening, and noting details, such as clothing styles. For instance, if a film opens with a character wearing clothes that were in style twenty years ago, you quickly get an idea of the time in which the story occurs. One way that place is often conveyed is through the depiction of landmarks, such as the New York City skyline.

RESOURCES

Focus on Viewing and Representing
Practice
- Media Literacy and Communication Skills
  —Support and Practice, Ch. 5
  —A How-to Handbook

Teaching Notes
- Media Literacy and Communication Skills
  —A Teacher's Guide, Ch. 5

A filmmaker can also convey a setting directly by superimposing a temporary title on the screen at a film's beginning or at scene changes. For example, a film or a scene in a film might open with the words *London, 1602* temporarily shown at the bottom of the screen.

Character Characters in a film are not usually described through **direct characterization** (descriptions provided by a narrator). Instead, their appearance and actions are depicted by actors for viewers to see with their own eyes. Sometimes a character's thoughts will be heard in a voice-over so the audience can get a more direct understanding of the character.

Plot Plot development in a film works very much as it does in stories in books. There is a conflict with complications that build to a climax. Of course, as a film viewer, you actually see events and characters' actions instead of reading descriptions of them.

Theme A theme of a film is also similar to a theme of a story in a book. However, instead of inferring a story's theme from written words, a viewer must determine a movie's theme based on what is seen and heard.

Evaluating the Elements To critique a film well, you must work from a set of **evaluation criteria:** standards for judging the effectiveness of individual elements of the film. Just as you have to meet standards to get an A in a course or to qualify for one of your school's teams, a film should measure up to certain standards to be judged a good film. The following chart lists some basic criteria you can use to evaluate the use of literary elements in film.

Element	Criteria
Point of View	• The film presents the story from a point of view that helps the characters seem real.
Setting	• The filmmaker creates a setting that is realistic, believable, and consistent.
Characters and Actors	• The characters seem like real people. • The characters/actors interact well with each other.
Plot	• The story holds a viewer's interest. • The story presents believable problems or conflicts for characters to resolve.

**MULTIPLE INTELLIGENCES
Interpersonal Intelligence.**
You might want students to cooperate for paired film critiques. Assign one student the main critique of the film, which he or she will give first. The other student should develop ideas to present in his or her own critique, but also must be ready to respond spontaneously to the other student's main critique. Both students should deliver their critiques orally with the help of notes.

If possible, have each pair of students create a videotape of their critique and then exchange their tape with another pair for evaluation and feedback. The pair of students can use the feedback to revise their videotape before final presentations. If students critique current movies or recent additions to video rental stores, they might submit a written version of their paired critiques to the school newspaper.

TEACHING TIP

Evaluating the Elements
Point out to students that the criteria presented in the chart on this page and in the chart on p. 200 can also be used to evaluate artistic performances such as plays, dramatic readings, and TV shows. Have students attend an artistic performance or watch one on TV and evaluate the performance by using the criteria. Students' evaluations should be one to two pages long. Students can share their evaluations by presenting them to the class.

Focus on Viewing and Representing, pp. 198–202
Alignments
TEKS 1A, 1B, 2E, 11A, 11B, 11C, 11F, 19B, 20D
TAAS R5, W1
English II End-of-Course 2, 4

TEACHING TIP

Identifying and Critiquing Technical Elements

Because technical aspects of films may be new to students, you may wish to walk them through a critique of these elements. Before viewing a short film on videotape, suggest that each student make a chart of the technical elements used in film.

Technical Elements	Notes
Lighting	
Sound	
Camera Techniques	

Have students make notes on their charts when you pause the video to point out technical elements. When students have finished watching the video, help them formulate critical observations about the technical elements of the film that you identified during the viewing.

Critical Thinking

Metacognition. Ask students what they have learned in this chapter, besides how to critique literature and films. Point out that most people do not read literature or see films to marvel at the writer's craft or to analyze elements. They simply hope the story will engage them and give them some insight into their own lives. Lead students to observe that what they have learned in this chapter will let them respond more personally, critically, and insightfully to literature or film.

Of course, this list of criteria is just a starting point. When you critique a film, you will also have to consider your specific personal preferences about what makes a movie good or bad and use those preferences as additional criteria.

Identifying and Critiquing Technical Elements

When reading a story in a book, you must picture the setting, characters, and events in your mind. However, in a film, all story elements are displayed, portrayed, and acted for you under the direction of a filmmaker.

To present these story elements in a movie, a filmmaker must manage many **technical elements** (lighting, sound, and camera techniques) specific to movies. Therefore, in addition to identifying and critiquing the literary elements in a film, you should identify and critique how effectively a filmmaker deals with some common technical elements. The following chart

Element	Criteria
Lighting—the way in which each scene is lit (bright or dark or soft or harsh, for example)	• Lighting should help the filmmaker create a mood, tone, or atmosphere. • It may enhance the aesthetic (artistic) experience of watching the film; some scenes may take on the qualities of fine paintings.
Sound—the sound effects, music, and dialogue that accompany the images in the film	• Sound should be appropriate to each scene; for example, lighthearted music and comical sound effects should not accompany a solemn scene (unless the filmmaker intends to create a contrast to achieve a certain effect).
Camera Techniques—the techniques used by the filmmaker to alter the audience's view of the characters and scenes. These include adjustments in camera angles and movement, zooms, and close-ups.	• Camera techniques should help to keep viewers involved and interested in the characters and scenes. • They should not distract from the story the filmmaker is telling. • They may be used for a variety of effects: to depict visual confusion, for example, or to help create a humorous mood.

The chart above presents just some of the basics. There are many more specific technical elements that you can evaluate in a film. However, for a film critique intended for a general audience (not for filmmakers or film students), the elements and criteria above are a good starting point.

TIP To achieve a booklike narration, a film director may include the voice of a **narrator**. The narrator can be presented in third person or in first person, as in Arthur Penn's film *Little Big Man*.

A Model Critique

Below is a model critique built from the lists of criteria on pages 199 and 200. The writer begins with a one-sentence description of the film, then comments on the filmmaker's use of literary and technical elements, and closes with a one-sentence summary of his overall opinion of the movie. (The film the writer discusses is an imaginary one, not a real movie.)

Young Guinevere

As you might guess from the title, *Young Guinevere* tells the story of the young woman who became queen to the legendary King Arthur. However, this Arthurian story is told in a unique way—not from the vantage point of Arthur or his knights, but from that of the woman who eventually stood with Arthur at the center of the legends. This point of view adds a new dimension to the tales, making the characters seem more genuine and lively than they have in any other film version of the story. The plot the characters find themselves in (a retelling of Guinevere's young life up to and including her courting by Arthur) drifts into silliness at times but never leaves viewers bored. The principal actors the film brings together always keep things interesting, playing off each other for both comic and tragic effects. The one exception is Jenny Osgood, who plays a wildly over-the-top older sister to the title character. However, Allison Harvey's brilliant performance as a smart, self-confident, completely charming Guinevere more than makes up for any shortcomings in the rest of the cast. With some minor lapses, the film's director and crew also make the setting come alive; the costumes, sets, and other details all help to create a world that is at the same time both fantastic and believable.

(continued)

- One-sentence description
- Point of view
- Characters
- Plot
- Actors

TEACHING TIP

A Model Critique
Challenge students to reconstruct the plot of *Young Guinevere* from the critique of the film. When students have difficulty doing so, point out that a good critique does not include a plot summary. When students write their own critiques, remind them that they are only to evaluate the plot as in the sample, not retell it.

MULTIPLE INTELLIGENCES
Musical Intelligence. Encourage students to evaluate the film's soundtrack in their critiques. Students might comment on the nature and quality of the music and how it interacts with and supports other elements of the film.

	(continued)
Lighting	The director handles the film's technical elements nicely. In the festive scenes, the lighting often brings out the brilliant colors of the period costumes. In the grittier scenes (such as the battle scenes) the director makes appropriate use of darkness to remind viewers of the misery and terror that lurked in the shadows of the legends. A great deal of thought also went into the film's soundtrack; the music heard in many scenes fits the world of the film perfectly. However, the film has one flaw that is hard to ignore: the director sometimes slips into using "stylish" camera techniques that have no real purpose and only serve to distract viewers from the characters and the story.
Sound	
Camera techniques	
Summary of overall opinion	Overall, though, *Young Guinevere* is a fascinating visit to Guinevere's world and its people, skillfully crafted by a director who shows a great love for the subject.

YOUR TURN 12

You may wish to provide guidelines for the kinds of films that are acceptable for this assignment. Students might post their critiques on the school Web site or on a bulletin board at school.

Wrap It Up

Metacognition. Ask students to respond to the following question in a brief paragraph:

1. How did your viewing of a film change when you were critiquing it rather than watching it for entertainment? Give examples.

Then, have students answer this question:

2. What technical elements do filmmakers use to present the story elements of a film? [lighting, sound, and camera techniques]

YOUR TURN 12 Critiquing a Film

Choose a film to critique, and watch it (either on video or at a theater). Make sure the film is one you would be comfortable discussing aloud with your teacher and classmates at school.

When watching the film, take notes about the filmmaker's use of literary and technical elements. Be sure to

- indicate how the film's setting is conveyed
- write down character names and descriptions
- note any special uses of camera techniques, lighting, or sound

After you have watched the film, use the lists of criteria on pages 199 and 200 to evaluate it. You may need to watch the film a second time to focus on how the story is told. Then, using the model on page 201 as a guide, write your critique. Make sure to share it with classmates or others who have seen the same film, and discuss similarities and differences in your opinions of the film. Try to publish your review on a class Web page or school Web site, or add your review to a class book of movie reviews.

RESOURCES

Your Turn 12

Practice and Reinforcement

- *Media Literacy and Communication Skills*
  —*Support and Practice,* Ch. 5, transparencies and worksheets
  —Videocassette 2, Segment E

Focus on Speaking and Listening

Presenting an Oral Interpretation

An **oral interpretation** of a short story is a dramatic reading that communicates the story's meaning and artistry to a group of listeners. In this workshop you will sharpen your analytic and acting skills by crafting and performing an oral interpretation of a short story.

WHAT'S AHEAD?

In this section you will learn to
- select and analyze a short story for oral interpretation
- present and evaluate an oral interpretation

Select and Analyze a Short Story

You Choose   Select a short story that you like. The more a story interests you, the better able you will be to communicate its meaning and **mood**, or atmosphere, to others. Consider these factors in choosing a selection.

- The story should have **technical quality**—it should be well written.
- Stories that deal with **universal themes** appeal to a wide range of listeners.
- The **length** of the short story is important. If you do not have time to read the entire story, you might use an excerpt or choose a shorter work.

Pick It Apart   To present the **meaning,** or message, of a short story to others, you must first understand it yourself. To discover the story's meaning, analyze its literary elements, such as plot, characters, and theme.

Point of view   In adapting a short story for an oral interpretation, the **point of view**—the vantage point from which a writer tells a story—will determine what reading voice you use.

- In stories told from the **first-person point of view,** an "I" tells the story. Tell first-person stories as though you were the main character.
- Many stories are told from the **omniscient,** or "all-knowing," **point of view.** The omniscient narrator can reveal the thoughts and feelings of all the characters. Use your own voice to present a story told from the omniscient point of view.

Mood   Writers create **mood,** or atmosphere, through descriptive details and evocative language. Adapt your tone of voice to the story's mood.

TIP   Even if you present an excerpt of a short story, you should shorten the story by cutting **dialogue tags,** such as "Jose stated." You can also eliminate references to characters or events that are not part of the passage you are reading.

Focus on Speaking and Listening   203

RESOURCES

Focus on Speaking and Listening
Practice
- Media Literacy and Communication Skills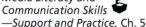
  —Support and Practice, Ch. 5
  —A How-to Handbook

Teaching Notes
- Media Literacy and Communication Skills
  —A Teacher's Guide, Ch. 5

TEACHING TIP 15D

Presenting and Evaluating an Oral Interpretation

You may want to provide students with the option of listening to a performance by someone in the community or on TV. Students can use the following rubric in their evaluations.

Criteria	Yes	No
The introduction prepares the listener for the performance.		
The performer speaks clearly and smoothly.		
The performer varies volume, pitch, and rate of speech to convey meaning and mood.		
The performer uses gestures and facial expressions to convey meaning and mood.		

YOUR TURN 13

You might suggest to students that they use the evaluation questions in the chart at right as a checklist as they prepare their presentations. To save time, you might have students count off from 1 to 4. Have the "1's" evaluate the "3's," the "2's" evaluate the "4's," and so on. Students should turn in their evaluations following the class discussion.

Wrap It Up

Metacognition. Ask students to respond to the following question:

1. Why did you select the short story you chose for an oral interpretation?

Then, ask students to answer the following question:

2. What are the steps for putting an oral interpretation together? [know your text, use your voice to convey meaning, use gestures and facial expressions to aid communication]

TIP To mark your manuscript
- Use commas, semicolons, periods, and dashes for pauses.
- Use underlining for louder volume.
- Use question marks for rising inflection.

For more on oral interpretation, see page 905 in the Quick Reference Handbook.

Create, Practice, and Evaluate

Begin with an Introduction In your introduction, name the author and the title of the piece you will present. If you are presenting an excerpt, describe the characters and the action preceding the passage.

Put It All Together After you have analyzed your selection, marked the manuscript, and planned an introduction, use the following tips to craft and practice your performance.

- **Know your text well.** Read your story aloud several times so that you are very familiar with it. Find out how to pronounce difficult words.
- **Use your voice to convey meaning.** Portray different characters by changing the pitch of your voice, and vary your rate of speech to indicate changes in the story's action.
- **Use gestures and facial expression to aid communication.** Use your body, hands, and facial expressions to convey meaning and mood.

Be an Appreciative Listener These questions are for evaluating your own and your peers' oral interpretations. Use your peers' feedback to set goals for future presentations.

Evaluation Questions	Yes	No
1. Does the reader's introduction prepare the listener for the story?		
2. Does the reader speak clearly and smoothly and change his or her voice as necessary to portray the story's narrator and characters?		
3. Does the reader vary his or her volume, pitch, and rate of speech to help convey the story's meaning and mood?		
4. Does the reader use gestures and facial expressions to help convey the story's meaning and mood?		
5. Does the reader make frequent eye contact with the audience?		

YOUR TURN 13 Presenting and Evaluating an Oral Interpretation

Choose a short story, and analyze it carefully. Create and practice an oral interpretation of the story, and then present it to the class. Evaluate your peers' performances, and be prepared to share your evaluations with your classmates.

204 Chapter 5 Exposition: Analyzing a Short Story

RESOURCES

Your Turn 13
Practice and Reinforcement
- *Media Literacy and Communication Skills* *—Support and Practice,* Ch. 5, transparencies and worksheets

204 Exposition: Analyzing a Short Story

CHAPTER 5 Choices

Choose one of the following activities to complete.

▶ CAREERS

1. Analysis at Work Besides movie and book reviewers, many other professionals use the techniques of analysis in their work. They closely examine parts of something to see how the parts work together. Write a **paragraph** about how you might use analysis skills in a career you are considering.

▶ SPEAKING AND LISTENING

2. Discover Writing Strategies Writers often give readings of their works at bookstores. Attend one of these readings, and ask the writer some specific questions about the writing strategies he or she uses. Write down the writer's responses. After the reading, take the strategies you think would be helpful to you and combine them with your own writing strategies to form a **writing checklist**. Make copies of the checklist and distribute them to your classmates. If you cannot attend a reading, try mailing your questions to the writer in care of his or her publisher.

▶ MEDIA AND TECHNOLOGY

3. Analyze an Analysis Find a review to analyze. You might choose a movie review or a magazine article reviewing a new software program. Then, create a **graphic organizer** by dividing a piece of paper into three columns, and labeling them "Strengths," "Weaknesses," and "Other." As you read the review, jot down strengths and weaknesses in the appropriate columns. If any of your responses do not fit either of these categories, write them in the third column. Finally, discuss your organizer with other students.

▶ VIEWING AND REPRESENTING

4. Illustrate a Children's Book Create an **illustrated children's book**. Focus on these four literary elements: plot, character, setting, and point of view. Once you have written the story, draw or paint illustrations of the more interesting characters and events in the plot. Be sure your story is appropriate for children. When finished, share your story with students in a local elementary school.

▶ CAREERS
Students might gather information about analysis skills needed in various careers by interviewing people in those careers. (You may want to obtain permission slips for the interviews from parents or guardians and from the people students will be contacting.) Suggest that students present their findings in the form of classified ads for jobs in the careers they have identified.

▶ SPEAKING AND LISTENING
Discuss with students the need for writers to use strategies to help them compose. Point out that just as writers will have different strengths and weaknesses, they will also have differing strategies. As strategies will differ depending on the purpose of a piece of writing, students will need to analyze possible strategies before writing to make sure they will work for them. Students can ask themselves, *What is the purpose of what I am writing? How does this purpose relate to my strengths and weaknesses as a writer? Which strategies will work best?*

▶ VIEWING AND REPRESENTING
Tell students to think of a simple theme or lesson for their stories, such as "Look before you leap." Then, have students follow these steps:

1. Consider your audience.
2. Decide on your plot, characters, setting, and point of view.
3. Write your story.
4. Storyboard the plot and illustrations.
5. Draw the pictures and copy the story on the illustrated pages.
6. Read your book to your audience.

RESOURCES

Analyzing a Short Story
Assessment
- Assessment Package
  —Chapter Tests, Ch. 5
  —Chapter Tests in Standardized Test Formats, Ch. 5
  —Assessment Alternatives, Ch. 5

- Test Generator
  (One-Stop Planner CD-ROM)

Choices
Rubrics
- Assessment Package
  —Assessment Alternatives, Ch. 5

Choices Alignments
Choice 1   TEKS 1A, 4B; TAAS W1, W4
Choice 2   TEKS 4B, 4D, 4G; TAAS W4
Choice 3   TEKS 7D, 8A, 8B, 12A
Choice 4   TEKS 1A, 11F, 21B; TAAS W1

CHAPTER 6

Sharing Research Results

Use this guide to create an instructional plan that suits the individual needs of your students. Assignments marked by an asterisk (*) may be completed out of class. Times given for pacing lessons are estimated. See pp. 206–207 for chapter-wide resources. Resources listed in this guide are point-of-use resources only.

Curriculum Connections

Choices *p. 249*
- Literature
- Crossing the Curriculum: The Arts
- Media and Technology

internet connect

GO TO: go.hrw.com
KEYWORD: EOLang 10-6

 All resources for this chapter are available for preview on the *One-Stop Planner CD-ROM with Test Generator*. All worksheets and tests may be printed from the CD-ROM.

Texas Resources For a complete listing of all resources prepared for Texas teachers and students, please see the blue box at the beginning of each chapter.

CHAPTER PLANNING GUIDE

T205A

		Chapter Opener pp. 206–207	Reading Workshop: Reading a Research Article pp. 208–217
DEVELOPMENTAL PROGRAM		🕒 **25 minutes** • Investigation *p. 207* • Your Turn 1 in groups *p. 207*	🕒 **100 minutes** • Preparing to Read *p. 208* • Reading Selection *pp. 209–212* • First Thoughts on Your Reading 1–2 *p. 213* • Paraphrasing *pp. 213–214* • Your Turn 2 *p. 214* • Primary and Secondary Sources *pp. 214–215* • Your Turn 3 *p. 215* • Test Taking Mini-Lesson *p. 217*
CORE PROGRAM		🕒 **20 minutes** • Investigation *p. 207* • Your Turn 1 in groups *p. 207*	🕒 **90 minutes** • Preparing to Read *p. 208* • Reading Selection *pp. 209–212* • First Thoughts on Your Reading 1–3 *p. 213* • Paraphrasing *pp. 213–214* • Your Turn 2 *p. 214* • Primary and Secondary Sources *pp. 214–215* • Your Turn 3 *p. 215* • Vocabulary Mini-Lesson *p. 216* • Test Taking Mini-Lesson *p. 217*
ADVANCED PROGRAM		🕒 **15 minutes** • Investigation *p. 207* • Your Turn 1 *p. 207*	🕒 **60 minutes** • Preparing to Read *p. 208* • Reading Selection *pp. 209–212* • First Thoughts on Your Reading 3 *p. 213* • Paraphrasing *pp. 213–214* • Primary and Secondary Sources *pp. 214–215* • Your Turn 3 *p. 215* • Vocabulary Mini-Lesson *p. 216*
RESOURCES	**PRINT**	• *Communications,* TP. 45, WS. p. 99	• *Alternative Readings,* Ch. 6 • *Communications,* TPs. 46, 47, WS. pp. 100–107
	MEDIA	• *One-Stop Planner CD-ROM*	• *One-Stop Planner CD-ROM*

TP.=Transparency   WS.=Worksheet

Writing Workshop: Writing a Research Paper *pp. 218–246*	**Focus on Viewing and Representing: Evaluating Web Sites** *pp. 247–248*
⏱ **300 minutes** • Choose a Subject; Narrow Your Subject *pp. 218–220* • Think About Purpose, Audience, and Tone *pp. 220–221* • Develop Research Questions and Your Turn 4 *pp. 221–222* • Find Sources; Create Source Cards; Your Turn 5 *pp. 222–225* • Prepare to Take Notes; Take Notes *pp. 227–229* • Write a Thesis Statement; Organized Ideas *pp. 229–230* • Create a Formal Outline and Your Turn 6 *pp. 230–231* • Framework and Your Turn 7* *p. 232* • Models; Credit Sources; Integrate Quotations *pp. 233–239* • Evaluate and Revise and Your Turn 8 *pp. 240–242* • Focus on Sentences and Your Turn 9 *pp. 242–243* • Proofread, Publish, and Reflect *pp. 244–245* • Grammar Link and Your Turn 10 *pp. 244–245*	⏱ **30 minutes** • The World Wide Web *pp. 247–248* • Your Turn 12 in groups *p. 248*
⏱ **260 minutes** • Choose a Subject; Narrow Your Subject *pp. 218–220* • Think About Purpose, Audience, and Tone *pp. 220–221* • Develop Research Questions and Your Turn 4 *pp. 221–222* • Find Sources; Create Source Cards; Your Turn 5 *pp. 222–225* • Critical Thinking Mini-Lesson *p. 226* • Prepare to Take Notes; Take Notes *pp. 227–229* • Write a Thesis Statement; Organized Ideas *pp. 229–230* • Create a Formal Outline and Your Turn 6 *pp. 230–231* • Framework and Your Turn 7* *p. 232* • Models; Credit Sources; Integrate Quotations *pp. 233–239* • Evaluate and Revise and Your Turn 8 *pp. 240–242* • Focus on Sentences and Your Turn 9 *pp. 242–243* • Proofread; Grammar Link; Your Turn 10 *pp. 244–245* • Connections to Life and Your Turn 11 in groups *p. 246*	⏱ **20 minutes** • The World Wide Web *pp. 247–248* • Your Turn 12 in groups *p. 248*
⏱ **210 minutes** • Choose a Subject; Narrow Your Subject *pp. 218–220* • Think About Purpose, Audience, and Tone *pp. 220–221* • Develop Research Questions and Your Turn 4 *pp. 221–222* • Find Sources and Your Turn 5 *pp. 222–225* • Critical Thinking Mini-Lesson *p. 226* • Take Notes; Write a Thesis *pp. 228–230* • Create a Formal Outline and Your Turn 6 *pp. 230–231* • Framework and Your Turn 7* *p. 232* • Models; Credit Sources; Integrate Quotations *pp. 233–239* • Evaluate and Revise and Your Turn 8* *pp. 240–242* • Proofread; Your Turn 10* *pp. 244–245* • Connections to Life and Your Turn 11 *p. 246*	⏱ **15 minutes** • The World Wide Web *pp. 247–248* • Your Turn 12 *p. 248*

• *Communications*, TPs. 48–51, WS. pp. 108–118
• *Designing Your Writing*
	• *Media Literacy and Communication Skills Kit*
	  —*Support and Practice*, Ch. 6
	  —*A How-to Handbook*
	  —*A Teacher's Guide*, Ch. 6

• *One-Stop Planner CD-ROM*	• *Media Literacy and Communication Skills Kit* —Videocassette 2, Segment F • *One-Stop Planner CD-ROM*

CHAPTER 6
Sharing Research Results

CHAPTER OBJECTIVES
- To read a research article and determine primary and secondary sources
- To write a research paper
- To evaluate a Web site

Chapter Overview

Research is frequently required in many areas of life, from personal to professional. Accurately sharing the results of this research is often a necessary step. This chapter is designed to help students not only conduct research but also share that research in a format that readers and viewers understand. The Reading Workshop provides a magazine article that will help students identify both primary and secondary sources. The Writing Workshop leads students through researching and writing their own research papers, and the Focus on Viewing and Representing will help students evaluate Web sites. While each section may be taught independently, taught together they provide students with a comprehensive background in the research process and the structure of a research paper.

Why Study Sharing Research Results?

Understanding how to research a topic and how to present that research to an audience will help students find answers to their questions and present their ideas effectively. Students need to know not only how to search for resources but also how to evaluate the validity of those resources. Students must also learn to combine information into a well-constructed presentation that others can understand. To help them understand their world, students need to know how to find and share information at school, on the job, and in their personal and civic lives.

Teaching the Chapter

Option 1: Begin with Literature

If you choose to begin your study of research with literature, you could introduce the chapter after studying how authors of plays, short stories, and poetry often do research to provide credibility to their writing. The emphasis in literature would be on the research required to write the piece and why it is important. Then, have students read the article in this chapter (pp. 209–212), and show students the importance of research in nonfiction. Once students understand the value of research and how writers use it, they will be ready to write essays based on their research.

T205C

Option 2: Begin with Nonfiction and Writing

The article in the Reading Workshop and its accompanying instruction provide basic groundwork for students' understanding of using research in nonfiction writing. The skills of paraphrasing and correctly citing primary and secondary sources are highlighted. Next, students will apply their knowledge of research as they write essays in the Writing Workshop (pp. 218–246). When students return to literature, they will have a better understanding of how writers use research and will be better able to examine and write about the way research is incorporated into literature.

Making Connections

■ To the Literature Curriculum

By reading "R.M.S. Titanic" by Hanson W. Baldwin, students can learn many facts about the *Titanic* and see how the author incorporated these facts into his report. This article not only tells the reader what happened aboard the sinking ship, but also follows up with information about the investigations of the sinking.

Lesson Idea: Sharing research results in "R.M.S. Titanic" by Hanson W. Baldwin

1. Have students list examples of different types of information provided in the article.
2. Ask students to identify the types of sources the author could have used to gather the information.
3. This account is considered an excellent example of reporting. Have students discuss why such an account is important after this type of disaster. Then, ask students to identify details that would be relevant in fiction and nonfiction accounts of the tragedy.
4. Next, introduce students to the article **"The Art of Money"** found on pp. 209–212 of this chapter. Point out that this author had to research his facts just as the author of "R.M.S. Titanic" did. Use the instruction on primary and secondary sources and paraphrasing (pp. 213–215) to help prepare students for including researched facts in their essays.

■ To Careers

Asking students to think about how research is used in different careers helps them see how their ability to conduct research can be used outside of school. Have each student select three careers and explore at least one example of what research each career might require. For example, a person who works in marketing might gather facts on consumer spending trends and analyze them. Remind students that research on the job can include anything from searching for the best mixture of lawn seed to seeking a cure for a deadly disease.

■ To the Community

The Reading Selection will acquaint students with currency from foreign countries. Invite someone from a local bank to discuss exchange rates between countries and what determines the rates. You may wish to have students research other countries' currency and exchange rates and find pictures of the currency to share with the class.

■ To the Social Studies Curriculum

Ask interested students to use the research skills taught in this chapter to investigate a historical event to find out how it affected their communities. Rather than presenting a traditional research paper, have students create a videotape to present their research. To prepare students for making a video, show them segments of Ken Burns's documentaries on baseball, women's suffrage, or the American West.

CHAPTER

6

PREVIEWING THE CHAPTER

- This chapter contains three workshops that focus on sharing research results. Although each workshop may be taught independently, taught together they reinforce the concepts, helping students understand how to present research. Reading a research article and writing research essays will help students understand the components of research and prepare them to evaluate Web sites as research sources. To integrate this chapter with grammar, usage, and mechanics chapters, see pp. T401A–T401B.

INTRODUCING THE CHAPTER

- To introduce the chapter, use the Journal Warm-up, Transparency 45, in *Communications*.

VIEWING THE ILLUSTRATION

- Ask students to identify the objects and symbols in the computer-generated collage. [arrow, globe, gears, letters, computer keys, money, mathematical symbols and figures] Point out shapes that are circular, square, rectangular, and triangular, and explain how shading makes some shapes look three-dimensional. Ask students for their reactions to the artists' mixture of concrete and abstract images. [Students may feel challenged to discover the connections between objects.] Invite students to explain how the illustration represents this chapter on sharing research results.

CHAPTER

6 Sharing Research Results

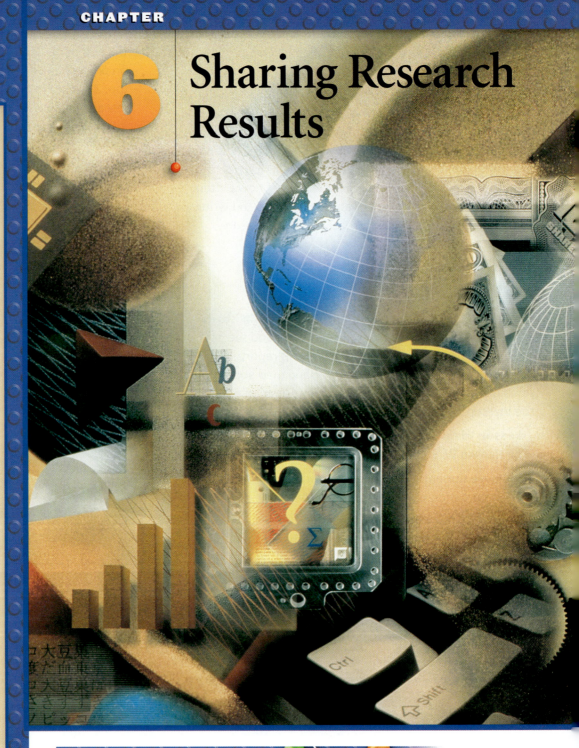

CHAPTER RESOURCES

Planning
- *Lesson Planner,* Ch. 6
- Block Scheduling, p. T205A (this book)
- *One-Stop Planner* CD-ROM

Practice
- *Communications,* Ch. 6

- *Media Literacy and Communication Skills*

Extension
- *Designing Your Writing*

Reinforcement
- *Communications,* Ch. 6

PREVIEW

Reading Workshop

Reading a Research Article
PAGE 208

Writing Workshop

Writing a Research Paper
PAGE 218

Focus on Viewing and Representing

Evaluating Web Sites
PAGE 247

Investigation

- A screenwriter is writing a screenplay for a movie about Michelangelo. In order for the movie to be historically accurate, she must gather information for the story's events, setting, costumes, and so on.

- On a family vacation, you read a roadside historical marker. You discover you are at the site of a famous battle in which one of the participants has the same last name as you. You become curious about whether you may be related.

- One day during lunch, you stop and think about the name of your school. Until now, you have never wondered why your school is named for a person or even who the person was. You decide to find out.

Research is used all around you. People research when they want to explore, discover, or learn about something or when they just want to satisfy their curiosity. People do research to learn about another culture or time period and to understand the world we live in.

internet connect
GO TO: go.hrw.com
KEYWORD: EOLang 10-6

YOUR TURN 1 — Brainstorming About Research and Investigation

With two or three classmates, make a two-column chart. In the first column, list people or professionals whom you think would use research in their lives or in their work. In the second column, provide reasons you think they would use research. Share your results with your class.

Motivate

Have students brainstorm lists of questions they researched during the past week. These could include the location of a business, how much a grocery item costs, and so forth. Have students explain how they found the answers to their questions.

YOUR TURN 1 (16E, 16F)

Before students get into groups, explain that effective speakers and listeners show these behaviors:

Speakers
- make relevant contributions by staying on topic
- respond respectfully and appropriately to others and give attention to what has been said
- ask questions to clarify and expand on each other's ideas

Listeners
- are attentive and prepared to listen
- interpret the speaker's message by developing vocabulary and using their knowledge of language, such as clue words that signal the organization of the speaker's ideas
- monitor their understanding of the speaker's message by asking relevant questions and by predicting what the speaker will say next
- formulate and provide effective verbal and nonverbal feedback, such as asking questions, making eye contact, and smiling

Chapter Opener, pp. 206–207
Alignments
TEKS 4D, 16B, 16F

Texas Resources
- *Lesson Planner,* Ch. 6
- *TAAS Tool Kit*
- *Preparation for TAAS*
- *Preparing for English II End-of-Course Examination*
- *One-Stop Planner CD-ROM*

- *Alternative Readings,* Ch. 6
- *Daily Language Activity Transparencies*
- *Vocabulary Workshop* and *Tests*

Evaluation and Assessment
- *Test Generator* (One-Stop Planner CD-ROM)

- *Assessment Package*
  —*Chapter Tests,* Ch. 6
  —*Chapter Tests in Standardized Test Formats,* Ch. 6
  —*Assessment Alternatives,* Ch. 6

Internet
- go.hrw.com (keyword: EOLang 10–6)

Reading Workshop

OBJECTIVES

- To read a research article in preparation for writing a research paper
- To paraphrase material
- To identify primary and secondary sources
- To understand the meanings of specialized and technical terms

Quotation for the Day

"We shall not cease from exploration and the end of all our exploring will be to arrive where we started and know the place for the first time."

(T. S. Eliot, 1888–1965, American-born English poet and dramatist)

Lead students to understand that just as travelers explore new lands or astronauts explore space, researchers explore information.

TEACHING TIP

Preparing to Read
The **Preparing to Read** section on this page introduces two concepts, paraphrasing and primary and secondary sources in research. These concepts will be taught in depth on pp. 213–215. The Reading Selection, **"The Art of Money,"** illustrates both of these concepts.

Research in Literature. In *Elements of Literature,* Fourth Course, see "Trap of Gold" by Louis L'Amour, pp. 249–256, or "The Pit and the Pendulum" by Edgar Allan Poe, pp. 289–305. These short stories reflect the authors' research into historical settings.

Reading Workshop

Reading a Research Article

WHAT'S AHEAD?

In this section, you will read a research article and learn how to

- paraphrase what you have read
- identify primary and secondary sources

Suppose you are preparing for an around-the-world trip, but you know nothing about the countries to which you are traveling. Your only clues are the spending money you obtained ahead of time. When you look at this money, you notice that each country has its own uniquely designed currency. What can you learn about each country by looking at the artwork on the currency? Who are the people on the bills? The research article on the following pages, "The Art of Money," can help you answer these questions.

Preparing to Read

READING SKILL

Paraphrasing   A **paraphrase** is a restatement of someone's ideas or words in your own words. Paraphrasing is a valuable tool when you read. You can paraphrase to check your comprehension of the main ideas and details of a piece. A paraphrase can also help you explain ideas expressed in complicated or unusual terms, as in a poem or in a symbolic piece of writing such as a myth or fable. After you have read "The Art of Money" and answered some questions about it, you will have a chance to go back and paraphrase parts of it in order to check your understanding of the piece.

READING FOCUS

Primary and Secondary Sources   A researcher may include both primary and secondary sources in a report. A **primary source** is firsthand, original information. For example, the letters John Adams wrote to his wife during the drafting of the Declaration of Independence are a primary source of information about that time period. A **secondary source** is information derived from or about a primary source. Books (such as history books) written by authors who read and interpreted Adams's letters are secondary sources. Both types of sources can be valuable when doing research. As you read "The Art of Money," see if you can determine which sources the writer mentions are primary and which are secondary.

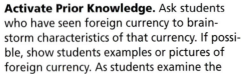

PREREADING 7B
Activate Prior Knowledge. Ask students who have seen foreign currency to brainstorm characteristics of that currency. If possible, show students examples or pictures of foreign currency. As students examine the currency, list on the chalkboard the information that can be deduced about the issuing country. Then, tell students that this article discusses what a country's currency reveals about its culture.

Reading Selection

The writer of the following article researched the images found on paper money from around the world. As you read the article, jot down answers to the numbered active-reading questions.

from Smithsonian

The Art of Money

BY DAVID STANDISH

Across the globe, the images on a country's currency offer a window on its culture

1. Based on the title and subtitle, what do you think the article will be about?

When I'm traveling outside the country, I generally think about the local currency only in terms of how many—or how few—pounds, francs, kroner, yen, or pesos constitute one U.S. dollar. Even with a calculator, I'm usually too confused or flustered to pay much attention to what the money looks like. Compared with our own currency, most foreign notes seem too colorful and too cute, anyway. Haven't we all referred to exotic dough as "play money" at least once? Since you know you'll be coming back to good old greenbacks, foreign money is hard to take seriously—beyond figuring out the exchange rate, that is. But the images and designs on paper money say a lot about the country that issues it.

Money and National Self-Image

Through their money, countries project their self-image—to themselves and to foreigners—and reveal what's important to them, and how they want to be seen by the rest of the world. I first began noticing this on a trip to China some years ago. This wasn't too long after Richard Nixon's presidential visit [1972], and the Chinese had come up with two separate currencies, one for regular folks and one for the new influx of tourists. The tourist yuan bills were new and crisp and looked like cigarette coupons from the '50s. Engraved on the front were tranquil bucolic scenes, while on the back were instructions in English on the currency's proper use. The other notes were worn, dingy, somewhat smaller than the tourist yuan, and emblazoned with images not of the Chinese landscape but of socialism and industrialization on the march: happy workers bearing hoes, a mighty freighter steaming along. China was supposed to evoke images of waterfalls for us, but happy, communal socialist work for the Chinese people.

The dual Chinese currencies reminded me of the vast difference between most Caribbean island currencies and

2. What is the author's source for the information in this paragraph?

Active-Reading Questions
ANSWERS continued

3. He has visited Jamaica and has read Jamaican history.

4. Jamaica's currency shows two leaders of resistance against Britain and a sketch demonstrating the unity of peoples. Other Caribbean islands display nature images and portraits of Queen Elizabeth on their currency.

5. The section may talk about different designs and forms of money.

6. It seems slippery and untrustworthy. It also seems too busy and has lots of color and designs.

TEACHING TIP
Active-Reading Question 6
To help students understand the writer's tone toward and feelings about Australian money, you might want to further explain the allusion to Athena. Tell students that the goddess Athena supposedly sprang fully-formed out of Zeus's forehead, just as the horses on Australian bills seem to be leaping out of Banjo's neck and shoulder. Explain further that the allusion to Athena is meant to be comic.

Jamaican money. The face of the Cayman Islands' dollar bill, for instance, bears a portrait of Queen Elizabeth II. To her left, there's an open undersea pirate treasure chest filled with gold coins (which could be taken as a subliminal advertisement for Cayman banking practices, I guess), while the back depicts a coral reef scene of serene tropical fish.

Bermuda's turquoise two-dollar bill bears a familial resemblance, too: Queen Elizabeth on the front, flanked by a sea horse and an anemone. And most of the Netherlands Antilles' bills feature adorable engravings of birds, the only exceptions being the nostalgic port view on the one-gulden note, and an airliner in flight (presumably whisking in tourists) on the 2½-gulden note. But Jamaican money offers nowhere near as much soothing escapism.

One of the appealing things about Jamaica is that it's a country, not just a beach; you can see this on the money. I happen to love the place, and have read Jamaican history, so I know about the guys on the two-dollar bill and the ten—Paul Bogle and George William Gordon, respectively. Both were leaders of the failed Morant Bay Rebellion of 1865—a movement to give greater rights to newly freed slaves—and both were executed for their trouble. True, the two-dollar bill (no longer printed but still legal tender) does have a lovely emerald streamertail hummingbird (also called the "doctor bird") hovering next to Bogle. But on the back is a happy, racially mixed group of kids, a shining sun, and the words "Out of Many, One People." . . .

Plastic and Op Art

A new wrinkle in money—or maybe the absence thereof—is plastic. Australia no longer prints its notes on paper. They're now made of a polymer that looks and feels fairly paperish, but has a certain slipperiness to it that seems somehow untrustworthy. The notes also have a clever new anticounterfeiting device: little see-through cellophane-like windows with hologram designs embedded in them. The overall look of the bills is eye-catchingly busy. On the front of the ten, for instance, is emblazoned the central head shot of A. B. "Banjo" Paterson (the poet who wrote the lyrics to "Waltzing Matilda") wearing an understated Western hat. To Paterson's left, a cowboy gallops on horseback, flicking a whip at a group of wild horses that seem to be racing out of Banjo's right neck and shoulder like spooked equine[1] Athenas.[2] These images are superimposed on a profusion[3] of op-art circles and curves, in a smear of colors including blue, yellow, green, and violet, plus the see-through window with a windmill in it. Little danger of nodding off while handling Australian money.

> **3.** How does the author know so much about Jamaica?
>
> **4.** In your own words, explain the differences between the currencies of Jamaica and of the Caribbean islands.
>
> **5.** Based on this subhead, what do you think this section will be about?
>
> **6.** How does the author feel about the new Australian money?

1. **equine:** of, like, or characteristic of a horse.
2. **Athena:** the Greek goddess of wisdom, skills, and warfare.
3. **profusion:** an abundance.

READING PROCESS

READING
Self-Check. As students read the selection, remind them that successful readers monitor their comprehension as they read. If students realize they are off track, they should slow their reading rate or stop and re-read. Encourage them to place sticky notes next to any passages they found particularly difficult. After students finish reading the selection, have them work with others to figure out the meaning of their marked passages.

National Heroes

Something else that's interesting about various currencies is that the national heroes depicted on the bills generally don't mean anything two doors away. Banjo Paterson, for instance, was certainly somebody I'd never heard of before I began looking into this. Also J. Abelardo Quiñones. As someone who takes a certain pride in blabbing out quiz show answers in front of my kids, to prove I'm not as completely dumb as they think I am, encountering these famous unknowns was a seriously humbling experience.

I figured the people pictured on the most common bills would generally be those best known or most important to a particular country. (I based this assumption on our choice of George Washington for the one-dollar bill.)

Given the standard cultural bias in what has passed for my education, I didn't feel too bad about not knowing who D. Sukhbaatar was on the Mongolian fifty-tugrik note, say, or Alhaji Sir Abubakar Tafawa Balewa (who gets the prize for the longest name I encountered) on Nigeria's five-naira bill. I was relieved to find that my *Encyclopaedia Britannica* knew them both. Sukhbaatar was a revolutionary leader in the Mongolian war of independence from China after World War I, and Balewa was Nigeria's first federal prime minister, killed in an army coup in 1966.

But I felt I ought to know who the distinguished gent in the stiff white collar on Canada's five-dollar bill is. Sir W. Laurier? I didn't have a clue. But then I didn't know who J. A. Macdonald on the ten-dollar bill was either. You probably do. Laurier was prime minister between 1896 and 1911, and Macdonald was Canada's first prime minister, serving two terms between 1867 and 1891. "Though accused of devious and unscrupulous methods," the *Britannica* says, "he is remembered for his achievements." Not by me, until now. I'm proof of why our neighbors to the north think we're arrogant and ignorant when it comes to them. . . .

Favorite and Not-So-Favorite Bills

I am not alone in liking [my favorite bill] best. Several people I talked to at an international travel agency, who spend their working lives shuffling 164 various currencies, agreed. It's the face of the Netherlands' fifty-gulden note, to me the prettiest of them all. The image is a close-up of a bee on a single sunflower, colored a cheery yellow with some orange and green, and detailed with quintessential Northern Renaissance precision. It is money fit for framing.

Which is something that can't be said for our own money, which gets my vote as the world's most boring. I think it is the only national currency that's based on a dreary green color. If that isn't emblematic[4] of our puritan past, in which money

---

4. **emblematic:** symbolic.

was viewed as a necessary evil instead of something that should be colorful and beautiful, I don't know what is. Our money is also fairly weird. I mean, what must people of other countries think when they see that enigmatic, glowing eye, balanced on a pyramid on the back of the one-dollar bill? That the United States traces its origins back to visitors from outer space who purportedly founded Egypt?

And what sort of country would put Salmon P. Chase on what was its largest circulating bill—now outmoded but still legal tender—the ten thousand dollar note? Civil War buffs will recall that Chase was Secretary of the Treasury under Lincoln, but really, wouldn't W C. Fields or Marilyn Monroe or William Faulkner or Mickey Mouse have been better?

The new fifties and hundreds aren't much of an improvement. They have buildings on the back—the Capitol and Independence Hall, respectively—and the portraits on the front are still U. S. Grant and Ben Franklin, but the heads, well, they're too big. And with the new, bigger print to go with them, as a friend of mine noted, they seem to have been designed by aging baby boomers for aging baby boomers—all of us who can no longer read without our glasses. MONEY: THE LARGE-PRINT EDITION.

Actually, the weirdest picture is on the back of the ten-dollar bill. Stare at it for a while sometime. In the first place, it's an etching of the U.S. Treasury Building, which is an institutional narcissism[5] that a number of other currencies also indulge in. (It would be more forgivable if the backs of most of our U.S. bills didn't also feature representations of buildings. More of our uptightness about money, if you ask me.)

10. What does the author think about the United States' money?

The ten-dollar bill is also one of our few notes with ordinary citizens on it. I count seven tiny figures standing in front of the imposing neoclassical[6] Treasury Building, which is the star of the etching. Except for a single 1920s-vintage vehicle, the street in the foreground is empty.

11. How does the author know about the figures on the United States' ten-dollar bill?

I look at this and wonder: What does this say about America? For one thing, in this driving-besotted[7] land, it's disturbingly appropriate that we felt compelled to depict an automobile. There's an everyday bleakness to the scene, which might have been painted by Edward Hopper[8] or photographed by Walker Evans.[9] There's a lonely, nondemocratic feeling to it that I'm sure no one ever intended—but it's there.

But unlike the Netherlands' lovely fifty-gulden note, at least this bleak scene will pay our bills.

---

5. **narcissism:** self-love; excessive interest in one's own importance.
6. **neoclassical:** of a revival of classic style and form in art, literature, and so on.
7. **besotted:** silly.
8. **Edward Hopper** (1882–1967): an American realist painter known for his bleak depictions of everyday American big-city life.
9. **Walker Evans** (1903–1975): an American photographer best known for his photographs of poverty in the rural South during the Great Depression.

Active-Reading Questions
ANSWERS continued

10. He feels that it is the world's most boring and weird.

11. The author knows about the figures from his personal experience as a U.S. citizen and by studying the bill.

First Thoughts on Your Reading

Work with a partner to answer the following questions about "The Art of Money." Put your answers on your own paper.

1. How does the writer's use of mostly primary sources add to your interest in the article? Would it have been as interesting if the writer had used mostly secondary sources? Why or why not?
2. Why do you think the writer wrote this article?
3. If the author could redesign U.S. currency, what changes do you think he would probably make?

Paraphrasing

Telling It Your Way "The Art of Money" is an informational article describing the images on paper money from many countries. If you wanted to explain the article to a friend, one way would be to *paraphrase* the writer's words. When you **paraphrase,** you retell information in your own words, making sure to keep the meaning of the original text. Thus, paraphrasing is a good way to check your understanding of what you are reading. If you can retell someone's words or ideas in your own words, you have a good understanding of what you have read.

Keep in mind that a paraphrase is somewhat different from a *summary*. In a **summary,** you retell only the most important information or details of a text, a fact that makes a summary almost always shorter than the original text. On the other hand, a paraphrase is more detailed, often includes your interpretation, and is usually as long as the original piece. The chart below shows how one student paraphrased a sentence from "The Art of Money." Notice that the paraphrase is about as long as the original; the ideas are just expressed in simpler terms.

READING SKILL

 TIP Whether you use a paraphrase or a summary, you can include a direct quotation. Just make sure to set it off with quotation marks and to give credit to the original source.

Original	Paraphrase
Through their money, countries project their self-image—to themselves and to foreigners—and reveal what's important to them, and how they want to be seen by the rest of the world.	The money that different countries use reveals three things about them: their identities, their values and their philosophies.

First Thoughts on Your Reading
ANSWERS
Possible answers follow.

1. The use of primary sources allows the writer to be present as a storyteller who interjects personal opinion in the article. It would probably have been less interesting with only secondary sources because the personal element would have been missing.
2. The writer wrote this article to inform and to entertain with his reflections on foreign and American currency.
3. He would add color and eliminate the portraits and the buildings, including the pyramid, on bills. He would replace these with pictures more representative of the people and the land.

TEACHING TIP

Paraphrasing
Suggest that when students paraphrase material, they read a sentence and then cover the original sentence with a sheet of paper while paraphrasing. Often, students find it easier to be original if they work from memory rather than looking at the actual material.

READING PROCESS

EXTENDING
Apply What You Read. Have students form groups of four. Assign each group a denomination of U.S. currency. Have the groups brainstorm images representative of American culture. Then, ask them to use these images to design a new bill, either hand-drawn or computer-generated. Have them present and explain their new designs to the class.

YOUR TURN 2

ANSWER
A possible answer follows.

   The use of two different currencies in China brings to mind that Jamaican currency is very different from that of the majority of Caribbean currencies. Queen Elizabeth's portrait is on the front of the Cayman Island's dollar bill. She shares the space with a pirate's chest full of gold coins (representing Cayman banking practices, perhaps) while the back of the bill shows calm tropical fish and a coral reef.
   Queen Elizabeth also appears on Bermuda's two-dollar bill, along with an anemone and a sea horse. Drawings of birds, a harbor scene, and an airplane probably bringing in visitors appear on the Netherlands Antilles' bills. However, Jamaican currency does not offer such lovely scenes.
   One of the inviting things about Jamaica is that it is a nation, not just a tropical paradise; anyone can see this by looking at the money. The men on their two- and ten-dollar bills are Paul Bogle and George William Gordon. Having led the failed Morant Bay Rebellion of 1865, both were executed for their attempts to obtain more freedom for recently freed slaves. Although a beautiful green streamertail hummingbird (known also as the "doctor bird") is next to Bogle on the two-dollar bill (no longer being made, but still in use legally), the picture on the back of the bill is a group of racially mixed, joyful children; a glowing sun; and the motto "Out of Many, One People."

THINKING IT THROUGH
Paraphrasing a Passage

Use the following steps to paraphrase a reading passage.

▶ **STEP 1 Re-read the passage to make sure you get the overall meaning.** You might have to look up unfamiliar words to understand the entire passage.

▶ **STEP 2 Identify the main ideas of the passage.** Look for topic sentences and thesis statements. Make sure the ideas in your paraphrase are the same as those in the original passage.

▶ **STEP 3 Restate the ideas in your own words.** You can use synonyms in place of key words from the passage. Stick closely to the original, using your own sentence structure to follow the passage point by point.

▶ **STEP 4 Compare the original passage with your paraphrase to make sure you have kept the original ideas but explained them in your words.** Your restatement should be about the same length as the original passage but phrased in your own words.

YOUR TURN 2 Paraphrasing

Using the steps above, paraphrase paragraphs three ("The dual Chinese currencies . . .") through five ("One of the appealing things . . .") of "The Art of Money."

READING FOCUS

Primary and Secondary Sources

First- or Secondhand News? It is important for readers to recognize the sources a writer uses in a research paper or article; when you know the sources of information, you can judge whether the information is reliable and accurate. You can also judge whether a source is current or outdated. For example, a 1980 edition of an encyclopedia would not be a current source for an article about today's space exploration. Sources of information in research articles are divided into two types: *primary sources* and *secondary sources*.

   A **primary source** is the first recording of the information. Primary sources include historical documents, letters, transcripts or tapes of interviews or speeches, lab reports, eyewitness accounts, and statistical surveys. If you were reading an article about the Declaration of Independence, and the writer cited a passage from Thomas Jefferson's own journal, then the passage would be a primary source. Primary sources usually carry more weight since they come directly from an authority. Just remember that a primary source could be mistaken or could show bias.

On the other hand, if the writer cited an article about Jefferson written by someone else, the article would be a **secondary source.** Secondary sources include encyclopedias, documentaries, biographies, and history books. You will use secondary sources on virtually any research project.

It is easier to identify sources in **formal research** articles than in **informal research** articles. In a formal research article, the writer includes clear documentation of where he or she obtained the information in the article. This documentation usually appears as footnotes or as a list of works cited in the piece. (A **list of works cited** includes print and nonprint sources, unlike a bibliography, which lists only print sources.) The sources may also be cited in parentheses immediately after the information in the article.

An informal research article, on the other hand, contains no footnotes or detailed list of the works cited. Instead, a sentence might begin with a short introductory phrase such as "According to the president of the company."

If a research article includes a list of works cited, use the information there to determine which sources are primary and which are secondary.

YOUR TURN 3 — Identifying Primary and Secondary Sources

The following sentences from "The Art of Money" contain references to primary and secondary sources. Identify the type of source cited in each sentence, and write a short explanation of why the source is primary or secondary.

1. I first began noticing this on a trip to China some years ago. (page 209, paragraph 2)
2. I happen to love the place, and have read Jamaican history, so I know about the guys on the two-dollar bill and the ten—Paul Bogle and George William Gordon, respectively. (page 210, paragraph 2)
3. I was relieved to find that my *Encyclopaedia Britannica* knew them both. (page 211, paragraph 3)
4. Several people I talked to at an international travel agency, who spend their working lives shuffling 164 various currencies, agreed. (page 211, paragraph 5)
5. I count seven tiny figures standing in front of the imposing neoclassical Treasury Building. . . . (page 212, paragraph 4)

Reading Workshop   215

Timesaver

Students working in random groups of three can check one another's paraphrasing. Have students compare each other's paraphrases with the original, making certain that the passages have been properly rephrased to avoid plagiarism. After this peer evaluation, paraphrases should be more easily and quickly graded.

YOUR TURN 3

ANSWERS

1. primary—based on personal experience
2. secondary—He read history books based on other sources.
3. secondary—Encyclopedias are based on other sources.
4. primary—These people have worked directly with the currency and have firsthand experience.
5. primary—He is looking directly at the bill as he describes it.

RESOURCES

Your Turn 2

Practice
- *Communications,* WS. p. 100

Reinforcement
- *Communications,* TP. 46, WS. p. 101

Your Turn 3

Practice
- *Communications,* WS. p. 102

Reinforcement
- *Communications,* TP. 47, WS. p. 103

Reading Workshop   215

VOCABULARY

Specialized and Technical Terms

ANSWERS

Possible answers include the following.

1. Context clues indicate that *numismatics* means "the study of coins."

2. Because the sentence says they are over something and can be seen, *superimposed* must mean "put over."

3. The context indicates that *etching* means "a design," and the dictionary states that it is "a drawing or design printed on metal or glass."

4. The context indicates that a *greenback* was issued by the U.S. government, and the dictionary says it is "any U.S. paper money printed with green ink on the back."

5. The context indicates that *gulden* comes from the Netherlands, and the dictionary indicates that it is "short for golden florin, a coin."

TECHNOLOGY TIP

If online dictionaries are available, have students use them to complete the **Vocabulary Mini-Lesson** on this page. *You need to be aware that Internet resources are sometimes public forums, and their content can be unpredictable.*

Specialized and Technical Terms

Knowing the meanings of the specialized and technical terms related to the topic of a research paper will increase your understanding of the piece. For instance, in "The Art of Money," the writer uses the word *note* to mean "a piece of paper money or a bill." This use of *note* is called jargon. **Jargon** refers to language that has a special meaning for a particular group of people. People working in money-related fields refer to paper money as *notes*. To a musician, however, the word *note* would more commonly mean "a tone with a certain pitch."

THINKING IT THROUGH

Understanding the Meanings of Specialized and Technical Terms

Use the guidelines below to determine the meanings of jargon.

1. **Use context clues.** Examine the context— the way the term is used in a sentence. Good writers will usually give readers a short explanation of technical terms within a sentence or paragraph.

2. **Look for the terms in reference books.** Dictionaries, encyclopedias, or other reference books provide information on particular subjects. Pay special attention to technical terms that have other meanings in popular use.

3. **Ask someone who is familiar with the subject.** A club or professional organization might be another good source of information.

4. **Use online sources.** You could use a search engine on the Internet to find sites where the specialized terms might be used, discussed, or defined.

PRACTICE

Using the methods described above, determine the meanings of the italicized words in each of the following sentences. Put your answers on your own paper.

1. The museum had over 400,000 coins in its *numismatics* exhibition.

2. On the front of the Australian ten, the images of Banjo Paterson and the group of wild horses are *superimposed* over the op-art circles and curves.

3. The back of the American ten-dollar bill contains an *etching* of the U.S. Treasury Building.

4. The *greenback* was issued in the U.S. during the Civil War.

5. The Netherlands' fifty-*gulden* note features a bee on a sunflower.

216   Chapter 6   Exposition: Sharing Research Results

RESOURCES

Vocabulary

Practice

- *Communications,* WS. p. 104

Test Taking

Practice

- *Communications,* WS. pp. 105–107

MINI-LESSON: TEST TAKING

Using Context to Understand Specialized or Technical Terms

On many reading tests, you may be asked to find the meaning of a specialized or technical term in a reading passage in order to test your vocabulary and ability to reason. If you do not already have the word in your vocabulary, consider its **context**—that is, look at how the word is used in the sentence in order to figure out the meaning.

Read the following passage, and use the Thinking It Through steps below to figure out the answer to the reading question.

The Bureau of Engraving and Printing, an agency of the U.S. Treasury Department, issues all of the paper money for the United States. The money is printed by pressing paper between felt pads and metal plates that have been cut, or engraved, with special designs and brushed with ink. Money printed with this *intaglio* process is the most difficult to counterfeit.

1. In the passage, *intaglio* is another name for
   A. an agency of the U.S. Treasury Department
   B. a printing technique
   C. paper money
   D. a method of counterfeiting

THINKING IT THROUGH

Using Context to Understand Specialized or Technical Terms

Use the following steps to find the meanings of specialized terms.

1. **Read the question and the answer choices, and then read the passage again.** Re-reading the passage with the question and answer choices in mind might help you find the writer's explanation of the specialized or technical term.

2. **Look at the word's context for clues to the word's meaning.** In the last sentence of the passage above, *intaglio* refers to a kind of process for making money. Much of the passage describes how the money is made.

3. **Cross out the answers that do not seem correct.** You could eliminate choice **A** and choice **C** because neither an agency nor paper money are processes.

4. **Review the context of the specialized or technical term again, and make an educated guess at the word's meaning.** Choices **B** and **D** are both possibilities. However, the passage says the intaglio process is the most difficult to counterfeit. Choice **B** must be the correct answer.

Looking Ahead to Writing

Students will be asked to write research papers in the Writing Workshop that follows. As they research their papers, students will use primary and secondary sources and may wish to review the definitions and examples on pp. 214–215 when judging the reliability of their material.

Metacognition. Ask students to reflect on their reading processes. Give students ten minutes to jot down answers to the following questions:

1. What information about using sources was most helpful to you? Why?

Then, have students answer the following questions:

2. What is the difference between primary and secondary sources? [Primary sources are firsthand, original information, while secondary sources are compiled from primary sources.]

3. What is paraphrasing? [restating someone's ideas in your own words while keeping the same meaning as the text]

Vocabulary
Alignments
TEKS 6B, 6E
TAAS R1

Test Taking
Alignments
TEKS 6B, 7C
TAAS R1

Reading Workshop

Writing Workshop

OBJECTIVES

- To write a research paper
- To gather and document sources on a topic
- To create a thesis and an outline
- To evaluate sources
- To revise for variety in sentence length
- To correct misplaced modifiers

Quotation for the Day

"Who can confidently say what ignites a certain combination of words, causing them to explode in the mind?"

(E(lywn) B(rooks) White, 1899–1985, American essayist)

Ask students to recall passages of writing that have been particularly meaningful to them, or provide examples from your own reading. Remind students that elements like fresh imagery or clear, precise language create powerful writing.

TEACHING TIP

Choose a Subject
If students are having difficulty selecting a subject, suggest that they discuss ideas with a partner. Partners can take turns brainstorming for subjects that interest them and asking each other questions about a favorite subject area or an area about which their partners want to learn more. Possible subject areas include school subjects, sports, community issues, events, works of art, and technology.

Writing a Research Paper

WHAT'S AHEAD?

In this workshop, you will write a research paper and you will

- gather and document sources on a topic
- create a thesis and an outline
- evaluate sources
- revise for variety in sentence length
- correct misplaced modifiers

Does a person's handwriting really reflect his or her personality? What food sources will eventually be grown on the bottom of the ocean? Will computers someday have artificial intelligence? What kind of breakthroughs have been found to halt the aging process?

To find the answers to these questions you would probably have to research—or, as some people put it, explore. In fact, research is a way of exploring your world, of learning what information is out there waiting to be discovered. Like explorers, researchers delight in digging up and sharing their finds. That is exactly what you will be doing in this workshop—exploring to discover information and sharing it with others in a research paper.

Prewriting

Choose a Subject

The Right Foot You have probably heard the expression "starting off on the right foot." In writing a research paper, the "right foot" is an interesting subject that you can develop into a suitable topic. Start with your interests. Below are some places for finding possible subjects to research.

- **Hit the books.** Browse through your textbooks, as well as the nonfiction section of your school's library or media center, a bookstore, or a video store. What subjects intrigue you more than others?
- **Skim the media.** Skim current newspapers and magazines, and watch news programs and public television shows. What issues or subjects catch and hold your attention?

- **Surf the Web.** Pick a search engine and search a subject or term related to one of your interests. Which results of the search would you be interested in pursuing further?
- **Talk to the experts.** Talk to your neighbors and relatives about their jobs and hobbies. What are your questions, and what are their answers? Which answers inspire more questions?
- **Pound the pavement.** Observe your surroundings, noting the sights and sounds (for example, the old radio collecting dust in your basement) that might be interesting subjects to research.

Before moving on, use one or more of the ideas above to list at least three possible research subjects.

Narrow Your Subject to Refine Your Topic

Approach and Landing In orbit, space shuttle astronauts gain a truly global view of the planet. However, as the shuttle descends toward Earth, they begin to see the planet in increasingly greater detail.

Similarly, as you begin a research paper, you first identify a subject and gain an overview of it. Then, you make your "approach," examining the subject in greater detail until you "land" on a suitable topic. Here are some ways you can move from an overview of your subject to a more specific, manageable research subject.

- **Read two or three general articles about your subject in reference books such as encyclopedias.** Notice headings and subheadings in the articles, and consider using one as the topic of your paper.
- **Search the World Wide Web** for pages or sites containing key words related to your subject.
- **Look up your subject in the** *Readers' Guide to Periodical Literature* or in your library's card catalog or online catalog. Note the topics listed under the subject headings.
- **Discuss your subject with someone** (a teacher, neighbor, parent, or friend, for example) who has expert knowledge about it. Ask for help with narrowing your subject down to a workable topic.

Once you have arrived at a suitable topic, jot down a short description of it. For example, a writer who began with radio as a subject might decide to narrow his topic to "the effects of early radio on life in the United States."

The questions in the Thinking It Through on the next page will help you evaluate whether topics you are considering are suitable for a research paper. The student responses show how the same writer used the questions to evaluate his topic.

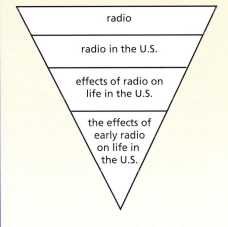

Meeting INDIVIDUAL NEEDS

ENGLISH-LANGUAGE LEARNERS
General Strategies. You may want to encourage English-language learners who were born outside the United States to research current events in their native countries. This strategy reinforces the links between students and their native cultures and offers them topics that may be of personal interest.

MODALITY
Visual Learners. Suggest that students create idea pyramids, using the structure to move from a few general words to several specific words on the subject. An example follows.

Prewriting, pp. 218–231
Alignments
TEKS 1A, 1B, 1C, 2A, 2E, 4A, 4C, 4D, 4F, 12B
TAAS W1, W2, W4
English II End-of-Course 4

Texas Resources
- *Lesson Planner,* Ch. 6
- *TAAS Tool Kit*
- *Preparation for TAAS*
- *Preparing for English II End-of-Course Examination*
- *One-Stop Planner CD-ROM*

THINKING IT THROUGH: Selecting and Evaluating a Topic

▶ **Does this topic interest you enough that you will be able to interest others in it?** The more a topic interests you, the more likely you will be able to bring it to life for your readers. Most people take the radio for granted, but I can't imagine life without it. Readers would probably be surprised to learn how much early radio changed people's lives.

▶ **Is the topic objective rather than subjective?** Your experiences and opinions are not suitable for a research paper because they are personal, subjective topics. For example, "my trip to Mexico" would not be a good choice, because *you* would be the only source of information. Your topic should be one you can research in information sources. "The effects of early radio on life in the United States" is an objective topic, one that I can research in print and nonprint sources.

▶ **Are enough different sources of information on the topic readily accessible?** What kinds of books, articles, and nonprint sources might have information on your topic? You may have trouble gathering enough information on your topic if it is too recent or too technical or if the source material is not available locally. Encyclopedias and books about radio history would probably have information on the development of radio, and business and entertainment magazines of the early radio days likely covered it, too. The Internet might also be a good source for material on how radio changed people's lives.

Think About Purpose, Audience, and Tone

KEY CONCEPT

Your Mission Is . . . The basic **purpose** of a research paper is to inform. As you research your topic, you will **uncover information and develop your own ideas about the topic.** When you write your paper, you will inform your readers about what you have learned.

Think, too, about the needs and interests of your potential **audience**—your readers. Readers expect to come away from a research paper with a better understanding of the topic or a new way of looking at it. The following questions will help you consider your readers' needs and interests.

- **What aspects of the topic might interest my readers?** How does the topic relate to their lives?
- **What do my readers probably already know about the topic?** What background information might they need?
- **How might I increase my readers' understanding of the topic** or give them a new way to think about it? What would they like to learn?

TEACHING TIP

Think About Purpose, Audience, and Tone
Professional writers sometimes choose a less formal tone or colloquial language for effect. Remind students that a more formal tone is more appropriate for them, particularly if their writing will have an adult audience.

Think about your **tone**—your attitude toward your topic and readers. The typical academic research paper, like the one you will write for this chapter, and the typical professional research report, like the ones you may do for your job someday, are *formal* in tone. A formal tone usually has the following characteristics of style.

- **Third-person point of view.** Use third-person pronouns, such as *he, she,* and *they,* to reflect your objective stance. First-person pronouns, such as *I* and *we,* reflect a subjective stance. Your purpose in a research paper is to convey information, not a personal opinion.
- **Relatively formal language.** Avoid casual and informal language, such as slang, colloquial expressions, and contractions.

Your **voice**—the unique sound and rhythm of a writer's language—can still sound natural although you are writing in a serious, formal tone. Through your choice of words, sentence structure, and punctuation, you can strike a balance by sounding authoritative and informed without being dry and boring.

Develop Research Questions

What Was the Question? Remember that a research paper should ask and answer good questions. Before you consult sources on your topic, jot down some specific questions to explore. Your natural curiosity will suggest some questions, and the ones in the following chart will help you round out your investigation. Working with a list of research questions will make it easier for you to sort through the information you find.

General Questions	Specific Questions on Your Topic
What is the topic, and how can you define it?	What was life in the United States like when radio was introduced?
What are the topic's parts, and how do they work together?	How did early radio affect entertainment, information delivery, and the economy?
How has the topic changed over time?	How has the impact of radio changed over time?
How is the topic similar to or different from related topics?	How do the effects of early radio compare to the effects of other, more recent technological innovations?
What are the topic's advantages or disadvantages?	What advantages did early radio have over existing media?

Critical Thinking

Analysis. Provide articles from both magazines designed primarily to entertain and magazines written primarily to inform. Have students skim the articles, looking for clues that illustrate the purpose, audience, and tone of each article.

Cooperative Learning

Generating Questions. Ask students working in small groups to answer the questions in the chart individually. When each person has done so, students can pass the papers around the group for further questions, comments, potential problems, or possible sources. Each student should initial his or her suggestions on the sheet.

YOUR TURN 4

Have students write their refined topics, their audience and tone, and their list of research questions on a piece of paper to turn in. This way you can check that students have chosen a suitable topic and considered their audience before they begin the research process.

TEACHING TIP

Find Sources
You might want to work with the school librarian or media specialist to design a library assignment. Your goal in doing so is to refamiliarize students with library resources and how to locate them.

YOUR TURN 4 Preparing for Research

Before you proceed with your research, make sure to
- choose a general subject and gain an overview of it
- narrow the subject to a suitable, refined topic
- consider your purpose, audience, tone, and voice
- compile a list of research questions

Find Sources

Inquiring Minds The first step in finding information on your topic is knowing where to look. The following chart lists some library and community resources you can use for your research. **Remember that some sources are primary (firsthand information, such as a copy of a historical document) and others are secondary (information derived from or about a primary source, such as an encyclopedia article about a historical document).**

KEY CONCEPT

Reference Note
For more information on **using the library**, including online catalogs, online databases, and the Internet, see page 866 of the Quick Reference Handbook.

Library and Community Resources	
Resource	**Source or Information**
Card catalog or online catalog	Books listed by title, author, and subject (most libraries also list audiovisual materials)
Readers' Guide to Periodical Literature or *National Newspaper Index*	Subject and author index to magazine and journal articles, index to major newspapers
Microfilm or microfiche	Indexes to major newspapers such as *The New York Times* and *The Washington Post*, back issues of newspapers and magazines
General reference books or CD-ROMs	Encyclopedias, encyclopedia yearbooks, dictionaries
Specialized reference books or CD-ROMs	Biographical reference sources, encyclopedias of special subjects (sports, arts, and so on), atlases, almanacs
Videotapes and audiotapes	Movies, documentaries, filmstrips, audiotapes of books
The librarian	Help in finding and using sources
World Wide Web and online services	Articles, interviews, bibliographies, pictures, videos, sound recordings

222   Chapter 6   Exposition: Sharing Research Results

RESOURCES

Your Turn 4
Practice
- *Communications,* WS. p. 108

---

222   Exposition: Sharing Research Results

Local government offices	Facts and statistics, information on local government policies, experts on government
Local offices of state and federal officials	Voting records of government officials, recent or pending legislation, experts on state and federal government
Museums and historical societies	Special exhibits, libraries and bookstores, experts on various subjects
Schools and colleges	Libraries, experts on various subjects
Local newspaper offices	Clippings, files on local events and history

Create Source Cards

Keeping Track   Before you take notes *from* a source, record information *about* the source. That way, you will not find yourself with a great quotation you really want to use but have no idea where you found it. Keeping track of your sources is essential for giving credit within your paper as well as for preparing the Works Cited list that accompanies your final version.

For each of your sources, record the author, title, and publication information on an index card or sheet of paper or in a computer file. Then, assign each source a number. (Source cards are sometimes called *bibliography cards*.)

Here is an example of a source card for a book with a single author. Notice that along with the source information, the card includes a **source number,** the **location** where the source was found, and the book's **call number.**

```
                                           3
Henderson, Amy. On the Air: Pioneers of American
     Broadcasting. Washington, D.C.:
     Smithsonian Institution Press, 1998.


                    Public Library
                       384.54H
```

TEACHING TIP

Create Source Cards
You may want to model the process of creating a source card for students. Select a book or magazine article and show students where to find the author's name, the title, and the publication information. Then, using the chart on pp. 224–225, show students how to record the source information accurately. Remind students to refer to this chart as they fill out their source cards.

Meeting INDIVIDUAL NEEDS

LEARNERS HAVING DIFFICULTY
It may help students to see how the information they are recording will be used later in their essays. Point out that the citations in the body of **A Writer's Model** on pp. 233–235 include information from their source cards. Then, show students the list of Works Cited at the end of the model. Point out that the sources in the list will be the sources they record on their cards and will appear in the same format. Remind students that because the information they write down on their source cards will be used later, it is important that it be recorded accurately and that it follow the punctuation set forth in the chart on pp. 224–225.

The following guidelines tell you how to record the necessary information for different types of sources. As you fill out your source cards, refer to these guidelines and note the special uses of punctuation.

Reference Note
For more on **capitalizing and punctuating titles,** see page 682.

Guidelines for Recording Source Information

1. **Book with One Author.** Write the author's or editor's name, last name first (follow the names of editors with a comma and the abbreviation *ed.*); the title of the book; the place of publication; the publishing company's name; and the year of publication. (To make it easier to locate a book later, put its call number in the lower right-hand part of the index card, paper, or computer file.)

    Collins, Philip. Radios: The Golden Age. San Francisco: Chronicle Books, 1987.

2. **Source with More Than One Author.** For the first listed author, write the last name first. For all other authors, write the first name first. Then, follow the format for books with one author to complete the record.

    Buxton, Frank, and Bill Owen. Radio's Golden Age: The Programs and Personalities. New York: Easton Valley Press, 1966.

3. **Magazine or Newspaper Article.** Write the author's name (if given), last name first; the title of the article; the name of the magazine or newspaper; the day (if given), month, and year of publication; and page numbers on which the article begins and ends. For an article in a newspaper that has different editions or multiple sections, specify the editions (use *ed.*) and/or sections before the page number.

    Stark, Phyllis. "On the Air." Billboard 1 Nov. 1994: 120–124.

4. **Encyclopedia Article.** Write the author's name (if given), last name first; the title of the article; the name of the encyclopedia; the edition (if given); and the year of publication. (Use the abbreviation *ed.* for *edition*.)

    "Radio as a Medium of Communication." The Encyclopedia Americana. 1998 International ed.

5. **Radio or TV Program.** Write the program title; the name of the network; the call letters and city of the local station (if any); and the broadcast date.

    NBC Nightly News. NBC. WNBC, New York. 13 Feb. 2000.

6. **Movie or Video Recording.** Write the title of the work and the director or producer's name (use *Dir.* for *Director* and *Prod.* for *Producer;*) for movies, write the original distributor's name (for movies not available on video) and the year of release; for video recordings, write the word *Videocassette* or *Videodisc,* the distributor's name, and the year the video recording was released.

    A Brief History of Time. Dir. Errol Morris. Videocassette. Paramount Studios, 1992.

7. **Interview.** Write the interviewee's name, last name first; the type of interview (personal or telephone); and the day, month, and year of the interview.

    Strohmer, Joseph. Telephone interview. 12 Dec. 2000.

8. **CD-ROM.** Write the author's name (if given), last name first; title (include print publisher, date, and page numbers if material was first in a print source); type of CD-ROM or database; the word *CD-ROM;* city (if given); distributor; date of publication.

   Foote-Greenwell, Victoria. "The Life and Resurrection of Alexandre Dumas." Smithsonian July 1996: 110+. Middle Search. CD-ROM. EBSCO Publishing. Nov. 1996.

9. **Online Source.** Write the author's name (if given), last name first; title of the work; title of the site; volume number, issue number, or other identifying number; posting date; name of any institution or organization associated with the site; date of access; and internet address.

   Baker, Robert T. "100 Years of Radio." CyberProfile Journal. 16 Mar. 1997. RTB Web Design. 30 Nov. 1998. <http://rtb.home.texas.net/history.htm>.

TECHNOLOGY TIP

Students using CD-ROM or online sources should record the source on the copy of the article immediately after printing the article. Finding the source material later may be difficult without this information. *You need to be aware that Internet resources are public forums, and their content may be unpredictable.*

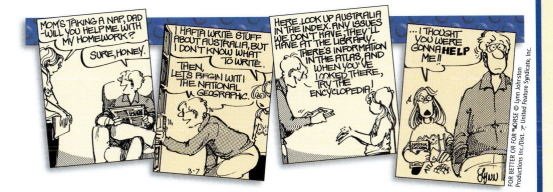

TIP The format for recording source information shown on these pages is the one recommended by the **Modern Language Association of America (MLA).** Your teacher may ask you to use a different format, such as that of the **American Psychological Association (APA).** Be sure you know which format your teacher requires.

YOUR TURN 5 — Gathering Sources

Review the prewriting steps related to finding sources and creating source cards. Find at least five possible sources for your topic and create a source card for each.

YOUR TURN 5

Have students test each of their sources with the 4R test described on p. 226. Each source should be relevant, reliable, recent, and representative. If the sources do not pass the test, have students continue to search for sources.

RESOURCES

Your Turn 5
Practice
- *Communications,* WS. p. 109

MINI-LESSON: CRITICAL THINKING

Evaluating Sources

GIGO—garbage in, garbage out—is as true for a research paper as it is for the output from a computer. The quality of your research paper will be only as good as the sources you use. Before you decide whether to use a particular source, evaluate it carefully. Putting your sources to the **4R** test will help you judge whether a source is worth using.

- **Relevant** Does the source have information that directly relates to your research questions? For a print source, check the table of contents and the index. For a nonprint source, read a review or a summary. For example, the table of contents entry "The Rise of Broadcast Journalism" indicates that the book *On the Air* contains information about radio news shows.

- **Reliable** Can you trust the source to be accurate and objective? Well-respected magazines and newspapers, such as *Smithsonian* and *National Geographic,* have earned the trust of their readers.

- **Recent** Is the copyright date of the source recent? Even for a history topic, you should have some up-to-date sources that present modern perspectives.

- **Representative** If your topic is controversial, you need to find sources that address more than one side of the issue so that you can take an objective, balanced approach. For example, if some scientists say that exercise lengthens life span and others say that it does not, report both theories.

PRACTICE

Use the 4R test to evaluate the items listed below. They are potential sources for the topic: "the effects of early radio on life in the United States." Compare and discuss your results with those of three or four classmates.

1. A book titled *History of Radio to 1926,* published by the American Historical Society in 1938
2. A Web page titled "Stories from Early Radio," first published on the Internet in 1998
3. A magazine article titled "The latest fashions in designer radio equipment," published in 1999
4. A book titled *Radio: The Only Useful Mass Medium,* published in 1985
5. A book titled *Demographic Vistas: Television in American Culture,* published in 1984
6. A play script titled *The Fall of the City: A Verse Play for Radio,* published in 1937
7. An article titled "Radio as a Medium of Communication," published in *Encyclopedia Americana* in 1994
8. A Web page titled "My Favorite Radio Programs," first published on the Internet in 2000
9. A book titled *Growing Up with the Radio: A Journey Through the Tunes of the 1960s,* published in 1998
10. A novel titled *Radio Life,* published in 1962

MINI-LESSON: CRITICAL THINKING

Evaluating Sources

ANSWERS

1. This meets three of the four. It is not recent, but the topic is historical.
2. Because this is a Web page with no given source or ability to be evaluated, it may not be reliable; based on the title, it is unlikely to be relevant, depending on the actual content.
3. This is not relevant to the topic.
4. The book may or may not be relevant, but the copyright is dated.
5. This book does not fit the topic.
6. This is not relevant other than to see what was written for radio broadcast, and it may not fit into the *early* criteria.
7. The reliability and date are fine, although the information seems too broad.
8. This does not appear to be a reliable source.
9. The book covers a later period than does the paper being planned.
10. The book is not a reliable source since it is not factual.

RESOURCES

Critical Thinking
Practice
- *Communications,* WS. p. 110

Prepare to Take Notes

Plan Your Route   Before you begin taking notes, take some time to create an **early plan**, which might take the form of a **list** or a **conceptual map**, to guide the rest of your research. This plan is tentative and will probably change as you read and learn more. Your early plan should include

- your refined topic
- headings that are suggested by your reading
- subdivisions that you think you might pursue

Refer to your early plan as you take notes, using its headings to decide what information to record. Remember, though, that you are free to add, delete, or rearrange parts of your early plan at any time. As you create your plan, be sure to consider the **relative value** of significant facts. Here is the early plan the writer made for the research paper on the effects of radio.

> Early Plan
> The Effects of Radio on Life in the United States
>   Background
>   Effects on entertainment
>   Original types of programs
>   Later types of programs
>   News events
>   Politics
>   Effects on information delivery
>   Effects on the economy
>   Manufacturers of sets
>   Other segments of the economy

TIP   To help you revise your plan, keep these points in mind.
- If you have too little information about a major heading, delete that heading and substitute another heading for which you have more information.
- If you have too much information about a major topic, subdivide that topic into two.
- If you have new information, alter or replace a major heading to include the new information.

Meeting INDIVIDUAL NEEDS

MULTIPLE INTELLIGENCES
Spatial Intelligence. Some students may benefit from other methods of organizing material. For example, students could use flowcharts to plan their papers and then organize their note cards based on the flowcharts.

> **TEACHING TIP**
>
> **Take Notes**
> You may want to give students practice using the three note-taking techniques before they begin researching on their own. Give students copies of a page from their history textbook, and have them take notes from the source by quoting, paraphrasing, and summarizing. Students can refer to the chart on this page and the instruction on paraphrasing on pp. 213–214. Have volunteers share some of their sample notes with the class, and discuss as a class any difficulties students had.

Take Notes

Bookmarks and Key Words Begin gathering information by skimming a source. Use self-sticking notes or slips of paper to mark pages with information on your topic. (Bookmark Web sites that look promising.) After deciding what information you want to use from the source, think about how that information fits into your early plan. Then, take notes from the source by **quoting, paraphrasing,** or **summarizing** it. The chart below shows how one writer used the three techniques to take notes from Neil Weiner's "Early Internet Business—Stories from Early Radio."

Technique	Example
Quote only when the author's exact words, as well as the ideas, are important. Copy the material word for word, and put quotation marks around it.	"The big taboo, the unthinkable moral violation in this new, pure instrument of democracy, was blatant paid advertising."
Paraphrase when you need to explain an idea in detail. A **paraphrase** is a restatement in your own words—your own sentence structure and vocabulary—that allows for more detail.	Because radio was seen as a tool of democracy, paid advertising was considered improper.
Summarize when you have to remember only the main idea. Read or listen to the passage, and then write a summary in your own words. Remember that a **summary** is a highly condensed version—one-fourth to one-third the length of the original.	Paid advertising was considered distasteful.

> **TIP** When taking notes, be sure that you distinguish information that is **fact** from information that is **opinion** by using phrases such as "Mr. Honeyton says" or "according to Mr. Honeyton."

> **TIP** Try color-coding your note cards. For example, you could put all the sources of information for one book on blue cards and all the citations for another book on yellow cards.

Follow these steps to ensure that your notes are clear and easy to use.

- **Use a separate 4" × 6" note card, sheet of paper, or computer file for each item of information.**
- **In the upper left corner, write a key word or key phrase** (perhaps a heading from your early plan) so that you can tell at a glance what the note is about.
- **In the upper right corner, write the source card number** (see page 223).
- **Write the text of the note** (a quotation, a summary, or a paraphrase).
- **Write the page number** on which you found the information.

After you have completed a note card, double-check to make sure that you have recorded quotations exactly and that you have correctly interpreted the information. Below is an example of a properly formatted note card.

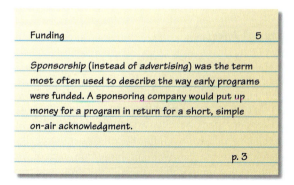

TIP Unless you quote a source directly, always take notes in your own words. Change the sentence structure, too. When you use someone else's words or ideas without giving proper credit, you commit *plagiarism*, a serious academic offense. Avoid plagiarism by always crediting your sources—even when restating the author's ideas.

Write a Thesis Statement

The Driving Force The thesis statement for a research paper states your main idea about your topic, and it lets your readers know what you plan to cover. Drafting a preliminary thesis statement will help you identify which aspects of the topic you want to emphasize. It will also help you organize the information you have collected. These three steps will help you draft your thesis statement:

- **Review the information you have gathered,** especially the main ideas you put on each note card.
- **Think about what possible approaches your notes suggest.** Will your paper explore new information? examine how the topic has changed over time? demonstrate a cause-and-effect relationship? demonstrate a comparison-contrast relationship?
- **Draw conclusions by writing a sentence that concisely illustrates the approach supported by the information in your notes.** The writer who chose "the effects of early radio" for a topic drafted this preliminary thesis statement: *Early radio dramatically affected American entertainment, information delivery, and business.*

Reference Note
For more on **writing thesis statements,** see page 386.

TEACHING TIP

Organized Ideas
Direct students to identify the order of ideas in the Reading Selection on pp. 209–212 and **A Writer's Model** on pp. 233–235. [The Reading Selection uses logical order; A Writer's Model uses a combination of chronological and logical order.] Students can use these essays as models as they organize their papers.

Remember that your preliminary thesis statement will serve as a *working* main idea. Think of it as a guidepost, not as a predetermined road. You may decide to revise it, perhaps more than once, as you continue shaping your paper.

Organized Ideas

Put Your Ducks in a Row Once you have written your thesis statement, you can review the information you have gathered and begin to develop an **organizational plan**—a preliminary outline for your paper. It is important for you to **organize your paper so that your ideas flow in a logical progression and there is adequate support for each idea.**

> KEY CONCEPT

You may be wondering how you will create order out of all the sources you collected. First, use the key word or phrase from each of your notes to group all notes with similar information. These groups may suggest the main sections or ideas of your paper. Then, you can decide how best to order the ideas within each group of cards and which supporting details to use. Although you may be able to order your information exclusively in one of the following ways, you will probably find a combination of the orders necessary.

- **Chronological order** gives events in the order they happen.
- **Logical order** groups related ideas together.
- **Order of importance** begins with the most important detail and moves to the least important (or the reverse).

Reference Note
For more on **orders of organization,** see page 374.

Create a Formal Outline

Where's the Map? If you were planning to visit a number of sites in each of several different states, a map would help you plan your trip. You might change your itinerary along the way, but at least you would have a clear idea about where you planned to go.

An **outline** is like the plan for such a trip. Once you have chosen an order for your information, you can begin creating your *working outline*. A **working outline** is a plan that allows you to arrange details in groups without using numbers or letters. To do this, you first must group the notes you have made under the major headings in your early plan. Then, subdivide the notes under each heading into smaller sets and give each set a subheading.

230   Chapter 6   **Exposition:** Sharing Research Results

You may be asked to create a formal outline for your research paper. Here is the beginning of the outline one writer prepared after researching early radio. (A complete outline would contain more specific details under each capital letter.) A *formal* outline like this, with Roman numerals and capital letters, can also be made after a report is written to serve as a table of contents for the research paper.

Reference Note
For more on **creating outlines,** see page 950 in the Quick Reference Handbook.

Thesis: Early radio dramatically affected American entertainment, information delivery, and business.

I. The invention of radio
   A. Earlier developments
      1. Discovery of radio waves
      2. Wireless transmission of Morse code signals
      3. Wireless transmission of sounds
   B. Early equipment
II. Effects on entertainment
   A. Duplication of existing forms
   B. Creation of new forms
III. Effects on information delivery

TIP In organizing your ideas, it may help to work collaboratively with another student. Discuss which order you each think will be most effective for your paper and why. Listening to others' ideas can help to clarify your own ideas.

TIP Outline entries may be words, word phrases, or complete sentences. Another way to determine the organization of your research paper is to **map your ideas.** For more on **mapping,** see page 948 of the Quick Reference Handbook.

 Preparing to Write

Before you begin to draft your research paper, make sure to
- create an early plan
- take notes from the sources you have identified
- review the information you find
- write a thesis statement that expresses your main idea and suggests your approach
- organize your notes and prepare an outline

RESOURCES

Your Turn 6
Practice
- *Communications,* WS. p. 111

Quotation for the Day

"The only sure weapon against bad ideas is better ideas."

(Whitney Griswold, 1909–1963, American educator)

Have students freewrite about a time when they replaced a bad idea in writing with a better idea. Discuss what was involved in replacing the bad idea. Remind students that while good ideas may require more thought and more research, better writing is the reward.

Before students begin their drafts, you may wish to review parenthetical documentation. If students cite sources as they draft, they are less likely to confuse sources or to forget to cite the material.

Writing

Research Paper

Framework	Directions and Explanations
Introduction ■ Arouse interest with an attention-getter. ■ Include your thesis statement. ■ Suggest which aspects of the topic your paper covers.	**Make a Good First Impression** Begin with an informative title that gives a clue to the controlling idea of your thesis statement. Then, get your readers' attention right away, perhaps by using an interesting detail you found in your research. **Create a Thesis to Remember** Your thesis sentence may open your paper, or it may work well as the last sentence of your introductory paragraph. **Guide Your Readers** Prepare readers by indicating in the thesis the main points of the paper.
Body ■ Develop your first main point with related supporting details. ■ Develop each of your additional main points with related supporting details.	**Develop Your Information** Create one or more paragraphs for each of the main points in your outline. Each paragraph should include a topic sentence and supporting details such as summaries, paraphrases, or quotations. Don't forget to show how your research information connects to your topic sentences.
Conclusion ■ Restate your thesis. ■ Leave readers with an insight.	**Final Impression** To close your paper, remind your readers of your thesis. Also, leave your readers with an insight or a question or thought to ponder.

 Writing a First Draft

Using the framework, write the first draft of your research paper. Also, look at the Writer's Model on the next page.

232 Chapter 6 Exposition: Sharing Research Results

RESOURCES

Writing
Writing Prompts
■ *Communications,* TP. 48, WS. p. 112

Your Turn 7
Practice
■ *Communications,* TP. 49, WS. p. 113

A Writer's Model

The following final draft of a research paper closely follows the framework on the preceding page. Note the use of parentheses to show sources of information. These parenthetical citations are explained on page 237.

The Rise of Radio

It nestles on your night stand, occupies a prominent place in your entertainment center, and rules the road from the dashboard of your car: the radio. This simple appliance is so common that most people take it for granted, yet radio is a relatively new invention. In fact, the first commercial radio station, KDKA in Pittsburgh, did not go on the air until 1920 (Stark 120). Before long, however, the new medium dramatically affected the nation's entertainment, information delivery, and economy.

The invention of radio was made possible by a number of earlier developments. German physicist Heinrich Hertz, drawing on established mathematical principles, discovered the existence of radio waves in 1887. Eight years later, in Italy, Guglielmo Marconi successfully completed the first wireless transmission of Morse code signals. An American invention helped move radio closer to reality: Lee De Forest's 1907 Audion, which made it possible to transmit sounds, not just signals. A full decade before KDKA debuted, De Forest broadcast a live performance by famed Italian tenor Enrico Caruso from New York City's Metropolitan Opera House (Yenne 77).

Few people were equipped to hear that landmark broadcast, however, because radio was still very much a do-it-yourself project; most people built their own receivers. In 1921, one such "tinkerer," twenty-eight-year-old Franklin Malcolm Doolittle of New Haven, Connecticut, even used his homemade transmitter to broadcast the Yale-Princeton football game from his home (Gelman 80). The first commercially produced receivers became available in 1920, when a Pittsburgh department store began offering sets for ten dollars. The response was so enthusiastic that Westinghouse began mass producing the appliances (Baker).

When radio found its way into the majority of American

(continued)

INTRODUCTION
Attention getter

Source with one author

Thesis

Background information

Paraphrase

Background information

Paraphrase

Summary
Online Source

BODY: First main point

Connecting Reading and Writing

Before students begin their papers, have them re-read **A Writer's Model**, paying particular attention to the writer's method of citing sources. Compare and contrast this practice with the firsthand experiences of the writer of the Reading Workshop article.

Writing, pp. 232–239
Alignments
TEKS 1A, 1B, 1C, 2B, 4F, 8A
TAAS W1, W2, W4
English II End-of-Course 4

Critical Thinking

Synthesis. This model illustrates the use of synthesis in crafting a research paper. Work with students to point out the ways the writer blended personal thoughts with a variety of factual sources. Ask students to locate a place in their drafts where they can weave personal experience and documented sources.

(continued)

households, it brought the nation together in an unprecedented way. Radio reached into "once dreary homes, reducing the isolation of the hinterlands and leveling class distinctions" (Henderson 44). At first radio programming simply duplicated existing forms of entertainment: singers, musicians, comedians, lecturers. Coping with technical difficulties left little time for creating new types of shows. Later, as the technical problems were resolved, programmers began adapting existing formats and experimenting with new types of shows, including variety shows, serials, game shows, and amateur hours ("Radio as a Medium of Communication"). As programming expanded, radio truly became, in researcher Amy Henderson's words, "a theater of the mind" (144).

    The introduction of radio also radically altered the way people learned about events in the outside world. For the first time in history, everyone could receive the same information simultaneously. As sociologists Robert and Helen Lynd, writing in the 1920s, noted, "With but little equipment one can call the life of the rest of the world from the air . . ." (qtd. in Monk 173). Live coverage gave news events an immediacy far greater than newspapers or newsreels could provide. In fact, most people first learned of such historic events as the 1941 Japanese attack on Pearl Harbor from the radio (Stark 120).

    Equally important was radio's impact on the economy. The first, and most noticeable, effect was to add a new consumer product to people's wish lists. Most early sets were strictly functional—"a box, some wire, and headphones" (Baker). Once the initial demand was satisfied, however, manufacturers began stimulating repeat sales by offering new models each year, with the goal of placing a "radio in every room" (Collins 10).

    The demand for sets was a boon to manufacturers, but it struck fear into some other segments of the economy. Newspapers worried that radio would drive them out of business (Henderson 90). Similarly, members of the traditional entertainment industry feared that the new technology would cut into the sales of tickets and recordings (Stark 120).

    Surprisingly, advertisers were slow to realize the opportunities radio offered. At first, most business people assumed that profits would come solely from the sale of sets and

Annotations (margin labels):
- Phrase/clause quotation
- Supporting details
- Source with no author given
- Author's name in text
- Second main point
- Indirect source
- Summary
- Third main point
- Supporting details
- Short quotation
- Additional supporting details
- Additional supporting details

replacement parts. In addition, paid advertising was considered improper for what was initially viewed as a "new, pure instrument of democracy" (Weiner). Instead, early programs were underwritten by "sponsors," with companies receiving only a brief, discreet acknowledgment in return for their support (Weiner). Eventually, however, this approach gave way to the direct advertising that is familiar today.

Reviewing the rise of radio makes clear how instrumental the medium was in shaping the nation's entertainment, information delivery, and economy. Today, with the advent of television and the Internet, radio is no longer the primary source of news and entertainment for most people, nor is its impact on the economy as far-reaching. Still, each day millions of listeners wake, work, and play to the rhythms of radio, and many would be lost without it. The radio may have been muted, but it has not been unplugged.

Summary

CONCLUSION
Restatement of thesis

Concluding thought

Works Cited

Baker, Robert T. "100 Years of Radio." CyberProfile Journal. 16 Mar. 1997. RTB Web Design. 30 Nov. 1998. <http://rtb.home.texas.net/history.htm>.

Collins, Philip. Radios: The Golden Age. San Francisco: Chronicle Books, 1987.

Gelman, Morrie. "75 Years of Pioneers." Broadcasting and Cable. 6 Nov. 1995: 80–92.

Henderson, Amy. On the Air. Washington, DC: Smithsonian Institution Press, 1988.

Monk, Linda R., ed. Ordinary Americans. Alexandria, VA: Close Up, 1994.

"Radio as a Medium of Communication." The Encyclopedia Americana. 1998 International ed.

Stark, Phyllis. "On the Air." Billboard 1 Nov. 1994: 120–124.

Weiner, Neil. "Stories from Early Radio." Background Briefing. 14 April 1996. 28 Mar. 1999. <http://www.backgroundbriefing.com/radio.html>.

Yenne, Bill. 100 Events That Shaped World History. San Francisco: Bluewood, 1993.

TIP Generally, the Works Cited list of a research report begins on a separate page from the report itself. In all other respects, however, the Works Cited list for this Writer's Model can be used as a model for the form of your Works Cited list.

A Student's Model

The following passages are excerpted from a research paper written by Yen Co of Independence High School in San Jose, California, about her state's Teenage Driving Act.

An Indecisive Conclusion

Background — ... The Teenage Driving Act regulates the actions of teenagers by limiting the allowable number of passengers, the hours during which a teenager can drive, and the driving experience needed before the issuance of a license. **Thesis statement** — Although the new Teenage Driving Act contributes to road safety and saves the state money, its efficiency is questionable.

Main point — ... Statistics show that motor collisions are the leading cause of death among teenagers, responsible for nearly one-third of teenage deaths **(Source with one author)** (Smith). **Supporting statistics** — Teenagers account for 17 percent of the driving population, but are involved in 14 percent of all fatal traffic accidents and nearly 20 percent of total crashes. More than 6,300 drivers and passengers aged fifteen to twenty died in traffic crashes in 1996—an average of more than seventeen deaths each day ("Seeking to Reduce"). **Summary** — Since most accidents involving teenagers happen between the hours of 9 P.M. and 6 A.M. (Willis), the new regulations aim to decrease accidents in this range of time by requiring first-year drivers to be accompanied by a parent, guardian, or licensed driver over the age of twenty-five when driving between midnight and 5 A.M. ...

Works Cited

"Seeking to Reduce Teen Driver Deaths." *USA Today*. Dec. 1997. Apr. 1999. <http://www.elibrary.com/s/edumark>.

Smith, Donna. "Graduated Licensing." Parents Against Speeding Teens. Aug. 1996. Apr. 1999. <http://www.pastnh.org/grad.htm>.

Credit Your Sources

Credit Where Credit Is Due You need to give credit to any writer from whose work you have gathered specific information. The challenge is in deciding *when* and *how* to do this.

- **When?** Give credit for specific data (facts, statistics, numbers, dates, and so on), original ideas, opinions, insights, or any other information that you found in the work of another writer.

    The only instances when you do not need to give credit are **common knowledge,** information the average person should know (such as "Television is a more recent invention than radio"); **familiar proverbs** ("A fool and his money are soon parted"); and **well-known quotations** ("Ask not what your country can do for you . . .").

- **How?** Give credit within the body of your paper using MLA-style parenthetical citations, unless your teacher gives you other directions. **Parenthetical citations** are simply credits given within parentheses immediately following borrowed information. You need to give only enough information in the parenthetical citation to aid the reader in finding the full citation on the Work Cited page and to show exactly where in that source you found the information. Be sure you include a Works Cited list at the end listing all of the works you have cited. (See the example on page 235.)

    This sentence from the Writer's Model on page 233 includes a parenthetical citation: "The first radio station, KDKA in Pittsburgh, did not go on the air until 1920 (Stark 120)." A reader then could consult the Works Cited list to learn that the information was taken from an article written by Phyllis Stark in the November 1, 1994, issue of *Billboard* magazine.

    The following chart provides specific guidelines for citing sources within your report, using MLA-style parenthetical citations.

Guidelines for Giving Credit Within a Paper

Place the information in parentheses at the end of the sentence in which you used someone else's words or ideas. Examples taken from the research paper on page 233 are indicated with an asterisk (*).

1. **Source with one author.** Author's last name followed by page number(s). (Stark 120)*

2. **Sources by authors with the same last name.** First and last names of each author followed by the page number(s). (Jackson Smith 38), (Leslie Smith 78)

3. **Source with more than one author.** All authors' last names followed by page number(s). (Burton and Owen 3)

(continued)

Meeting INDIVIDUAL NEEDS

LEARNERS HAVING DIFFICULTY Determining when to give credit to a source may be difficult for some students. To help them distinguish between common knowledge and material that should be credited, give them the following examples, and ask students to determine whether the material should be credited.

1. George Washington was the first president of the United States. [common knowledge]

2. Cancer is the second leading cause of death in children under fourteen years of age. [material that should be credited]

3. There is enough concrete in Hoover Dam to pave a standard highway, 16 feet wide, from San Francisco to New York City. [material that should be credited]

4. The United States has a representative form of government. [common knowledge]

Meeting INDIVIDUAL NEEDS

ENGLISH-LANGUAGE LEARNERS
General Strategies. Before preparing their Works Cited pages, students might need help assimilating the information about bibliographic form. Pair English-language learners with English-proficient speakers, and give the pairs source information for several works. Then, have the pairs organize the material properly, comparing the information to the sample list of Works Cited in **A Writer's Model** (pp. 233–235).

Timesaver

Before students turn in their papers, arrange the class in small groups. Have group members check each other's citations and Works Cited pages for proper punctuation and format.

(continued)

4. **Source with no author given.** Title or a shortened form of it and the page number(s). ("Radio Daze" 152)

5. **One-page source, unpaginated source, CD-ROM or online source, or article from an encyclopedia or other work arranged alphabetically.** Author's name only. If no author's name is given, title only. (Weiner)*

6. **More than one source by the same author.** Author's last name and the title or a shortened form of it followed by the page number(s). (Allen, "Only Yesterday" 7), (Allen, "Since Yesterday" 19)

7. **Author's name given in paragraph.** Page number only. (144)

8. **Indirect source.** *Qtd. in* ("quoted in") before the source and a page number. (qtd. in Monk 173)*

The next chart provides specific guidelines on how to correctly cite sources in a Works Cired list at **the end of your report.** Readers can turn to this list when they want complete publication information about the sources you have cited in your report.

Guidelines for Preparing the List of Works Cited

1. On a separate sheet of paper, center the words *Works Cited* (or *Bibliography* if all of your sources are print sources) one inch from the top.

2. For each entry on the list, follow the format you used for your source cards (page 223).

3. Organize your list using the following conventions.
   - List your sources in alphabetical order by the authors' last names.
   - If no author is given, alphabetize by the first important word in the title.
   - If you use two or more sources by the same author, write the author's name in the first entry only. For all other entries, use three hyphens where the author's name would be, followed by a period. Then, give the title, publication information, and page number(s). Arrange multiple entries alphabetically by the first important word in the title.

   Example:

   Allen, Frederick Lewis. <u>Since Yesterday: The 1930's in America</u>. New York: Harper, 1939.

   ---. <u>Only Yesterday: An Informal History of the 1920's</u>. New York: Harper, 1951.

4. Begin each listing at the left margin. If a listing is longer than one line, indent all the following lines five spaces.

   Example:

   Henderson, Amy. <u>On the Air</u>. Washington, DC: Smithsonian Institution Press, 1988.

Chapter 6   Exposition: Sharing Research Results

Integrate Direct Quotations into Your Paper

And I Quote . . . Using direct quotations in your research paper adds credibility to your writing. Just be sure to avoid using too many long quotations, and vary the pattern of your sentences to make your writing read smoothly. Also, make sure you do not use quotations just to fill out your paper. If you overuse quotations, your paper will look like a cut-and-paste version of other authors' works. The chart below shows some examples of ways to weave quotations from the book *On the Air* by Amy Henderson (Smithsonian Institution Press, 1988) into a paper.

Type of Quotation	Directions	Example
phrase or clause	Place the quotation within your own sentence and enclose it in quotation marks.	Researcher Amy Henderson states that radio became "a theater of the mind" as people experimented with imaginative new formats (144).
short quotation (four lines or less)	Introduce the quotation in your own words and enclose it in quotation marks.	According to Henderson, "The dramatic works of Norman Corwin, Orson Welles, and Archibald MacLeish showcased radio as a theater of the mind, with an imaginative scope beyond that of any other arena" (144).
long quotation (more than four lines)	Set off the quotation by indenting each line ten spaces from the left margin. Introduce it in your own words, followed by a colon. Do not use quotation marks.	Once the technical challenges involved with radio broadcasting were under control, new forms could be explored: The dramatic works of Norman Corwin, Orson Welles, and Archibald MacLeish showcased radio as a theater of the mind, with an imaginative scope beyond that of any other arena. Made possible by network willingness to experiment with creative programming on a sustained (that is, unsponsored) basis, these dramas proved that radio—though a mass commercial enterprise—was capable of producing eloquence. (Henderson 144)

Cooperative Learning

Group Analysis. Have students, working in groups of four or five, analyze **A Writer's Model** on pp. 233–235 for its use of direct quotations. Students should note the different ways the writer weaves quotations into the essay. Ask groups to share some of the examples they find with the class. Remind students to look back at these examples as they integrate direct quotations into their own papers.

Quotation for the Day

"Writing that is read is built from revealing details that are specific, insightful, and interesting."
(Donald Murray, 1924– , American writer and teacher)

Write the quotation on the chalkboard or on an overhead transparency. Ask students to recall particularly interesting articles they have read and to think about why the articles were interesting. Focus on the way details can make a paper interesting, and stress that students may need to add more details to their writing.

TEACHING TIP

Evaluate and Revise Your Draft
Inform students that often peer revision can generate a good title. Peer readers may spot a phrase or idea that seems to represent the entire paper. Remind students that while a title is not a label, it should provide the reader with a sense of what the paper includes.

▶ **Elaboration**
Suggest that students needing to gather more information from sources make an appointment with the school librarian or media specialist. This person has been trained to assist in research needs and can help students locate information, particularly more obscure facts.

Revising

Evaluate and Revise Your Draft

Read and Read Again Read your draft at least twice. The first time, focus on content and organization. The second time, concentrate on style.

▶ **First Reading: Content and Organization** The content and organization guidelines below will help you examine your paper and consider possible changes. First, answer the questions on the left. Next, use the tips in the middle to mark changes. Finally, use the suggestions in the column on the right to make revisions to your writing.

TIP You may also want to ask a classmate to use the chart below to review your essay and give you feedback.

Research Paper: Content and Organization Guidelines for Peer and Self-Evaluation

Evaluation Questions	Tips	Revision Techniques
❶ Does the opening grab the reader's attention?	**Put brackets** around the sentence(s) intended to hook the reader's interest. If no sentences are bracketed, revise.	**Add** an interesting fact, question, or observation.
❷ Does the thesis statement appear early in paper? Does it identify the topic and main idea and suggest which aspects of the topic are covered?	**Underline** the thesis statement. **Double underline** the words that suggest which aspects of the topic the paper covers. If any part is missing, revise.	**Add** a sentence identifying your topic and main idea. **Elaborate** by mentioning the aspects of the topic covered in your paper.
❸ Is each main point supported with relevant information—summaries, paraphrases, or quotations?	**Put a capital A** by the first main point. **Put a lowercase a** at the beginning of each sentence that supports that point. Continue this pattern with each point. If any capital letters are not followed by lowercase ones, revise.	**Elaborate** by adding your own ideas or information and summaries, paraphrases, or quotations. **Rearrange** information so that it clearly supports the appropriate main point.
❹ Is proper credit given for each source of information?	**Put a number** at the end of each sentence that uses information from an outside source. **Put the same number** over the corresponding citation. If any numbered sentence has no citation, revise.	**Add** citations for any information (other than common knowledge) summarized, paraphrased, or quoted from an outside source. **Delete** citations for any information that is common knowledge.
❺ Does the conclusion restate the paper's thesis?	**Put a wavy line** under the restatement of the thesis. If no sentence has a wavy line, revise.	**Add** a paraphrase of the thesis.

240 Chapter 6 **Exposition:** Sharing Research Results

RESOURCES

Revising
Practice
- *Communications,* TPs. 50, 51, WS. pp. 114, 115, 116

Extension
- *Designing Your Writing*

ONE WRITER'S REVISIONS The following example shows how one writer used the content and organization guidelines to revise a part of the research report on page 233. Examine the revisions carefully, and then answer the questions that follow.

> The invention of radio was made possible by a number of *, drawing on established mathematical principles,* earlier developments. German physicist Heinrich Hertz discovered the existence of radio waves in 1887. Eight years later, in Italy, Guglielmo Marconi successfully completed the first wireless transmission of Morse code signals. An American invention helped move radio closer to reality: Lee De Forest's 1907 Audion*, which made it possible to transmit sounds, not just signals.* A full decade before KDKA debuted, De Forest broadcast a live performance by famed Italian tenor Enrico Caruso from New York City's Metropolitan Opera House (Yenne 77).

add

elaborate

Analyzing the Revision Process

Use the following questions to help you consider the reasons for the author's revisions.
1. Why did the writer add the phrase to the second sentence?
2. How does the elaboration in the fourth sentence help the reader understand the paragraph's main points?

YOUR TURN 8 Focusing on Content and Organization

Use the guidelines on page 240 and the model furnished by One Writer's Revisions above to revise the content and organization of your research paper.

▶ **Second Reading: Style** Research reports are packed with information, much of it new to the audience. To make your report as "reader friendly" as possible, you need to make sure the information is presented in a manner that will retain your reader's interest. One way to accomplish this goal is to vary the length of your sentences.

PEER REVIEW

Ask a classmate to read your research paper and to answer the following questions:
1. After reading the introduction, were you clear about the paper's topic and approach? Why or why not?
2. Which main point was developed most completely? Why do you think so?
3. What new information did you learn by reading this paper?

Writing Workshop 241

TECHNOLOGY TIP

Remind students to print a copy of each draft of their essays in case of computer crashes or failures. Computer failure should not be an excuse for a late paper.

Analyzing the Revision Process
ANSWERS
1. The writer added the phrase to provide an example of earlier developments leading to the invention.
2. The elaboration helps explain how radio moved from signals to sound.

YOUR TURN 8

To make revising easier for students, you may suggest that they create checklists of revisions they need to make, based on the **Content and Organization Guidelines** and peer review.

Revising, pp. 240–243
Alignments
TEKS 2B, 2C, 2E, 5A, 5B
TAAS W1, W2, W3, W7
English II End-of-Course 4, 5, 6

Writing Workshop 241

Style Guidelines

Evaluation Question	▶ Tip	▶ Revision Technique
Are too many sentences in the research paper long and complicated?	**Underline** every other sentence with a colored marker. Use a different colored marker to underline the remaining sentences. If there are several long sentences in succession (longer than twenty to twenty-five words), revise.	**Rearrange** overly long sentences to create two or more shorter sentences.

Focus on Sentences

Varying Sentence Length

When you include quotations and paraphrases in your first draft, you may find yourself using too many long sentences. Long sentences can be a good way to emphasize a point by building up to it, as a sort of climax. However, using *only* long sentences can make your writing monotonous for readers. Long sentences also demand closer attention on the part of the reader and can produce confusion.

Reference Note
For more on **varying sentence length,** see page 352.

ONE WRITER'S REVISIONS Here is how the writer of the model research paper on page 233 used the Style Guidelines to vary sentence length.

BEFORE REVISION

one 35-word sentence

When radio found its way into the majority of American households, it brought the nation together in an unprecedented way, reaching into "once dreary homes, reducing the isolation of the hinterlands and leveling class distinctions" (Henderson 44).

AFTER REVISION

two sentences created from one

When radio found its way into the majority of American households, it brought the nation together in an unprecedented **way. Radio reached** into "once dreary homes, reducing the isolation of the hinterlands and leveling class distinctions" (Henderson 44).

Analyzing the Revision Process

1. How did the writer divide one sentence into two?
2. How did breaking the long sentence into two shorter sentences improve the paragraph?

YOUR TURN 9 Varying Sentence Length

Use the style guidelines on page 242 to evaluate the length of sentences in your research paper and to divide sentences if necessary.

Designing Your Writing

Site Maps Another way to share your research is to transform the information into a Web site. The **home page,** the first page of information in your Web document, should introduce your research topic. If you decide to publish your research this way, remember that a well-constructed Web site often starts with a *site map* to help site visitors understand what information is included. A **site map** is a visual depiction of the general structure and organization of a Web site. A site map usually lists every page on the site that includes a *hyperlink* to the home page. (A **hyperlink** is an image or highlighted section of text that takes you to another Web page when you click on it.) Site maps can be simple listings or more complicated image maps. To create your site map, list your ideas and organize them into four or five main sections; you can use the major points in the outline for your research paper. These points then become the main pages of your site. Organize your specific or detailed information under these pages. Here is an example of how to set up a site map with just the home page and main pages.

COMPUTER TIP
You can use a word-processing program's save-as command to save alternate versions of your paper while experimenting with changes. That way, you will always have a copy of the original in case you want to revert to it.

Analyzing the Revision Process
ANSWERS

1. The revision shows that the writer repeated the subject *radio* and changed the participle to a verb.
2. Making two sentences helped the pace of the writing, slowing it so the reader could more easily comprehend the ideas in the paragraph.

YOUR TURN 9

Have students mark their revisions in a different color of pen or marker so that you can easily make sure they have followed the guidelines.

Quotation for the Day

"Good swimmers are oftenest drowned."

(Thomas Fuller, M.D., 1654–1734, English physician, writer, and compiler)

Discuss with students examples of confidence leading to tragedy, such as an overconfident driver losing control of a vehicle. Suggest to students that the same principle holds true in proofreading. Those who are confident of their spelling and usage abilities still need to check their work carefully.

Grammar Link

Correcting Misplaced Modifiers

ANSWERS

1. Television, which was a novelty when it first came out, is common today.
2. At first it was thought that television would be too expensive for most people.
3. Television was demonstrated for the first time to many people attending a World's Fair.
4. When television came along, many people thought that it would do away with radio.
5. Showcasing their talents on television, entertainers found new audiences.

Publishing

Proofread Your Essay

Reference Note

For more information and practice on avoiding **misplaced modifers,** see page 627.

Perfect It So that your work looks polished and credible, work collaboratively with a peer to read your paper at least twice more, checking for grammar, spelling, and punctuation errors. Be sure to notice, for instance, whether you have misplaced any modifiers. Remember that modifying words, phrases, and clauses should be placed as close as possible to the words they modify.

Grammar Link

Correcting Misplaced Modifiers

When you are informing your readers about the results of your research, a **misplaced modifier** can muddle your meaning. This mistake also might be taken as carelessness and undermine your credibility. **A modifier (a word, phrase, or clause that makes the meaning of another word or word group more specific) should be placed as near as possible to the word or group of words it modifies.** Otherwise, you may confuse or mislead a reader. To understand how to correct misplaced modifiers, review these examples.

Misplaced Word	Most families almost listened to the radio daily. [The adverb *almost* seems to modify *listened*.]
Clear	Most families listened to the radio almost daily.
Misplaced Phrase	Some people had problems with reception living in remote areas. [The participial phrase *living in remote areas* seems to modify *reception*.]
Clear	Some people living in remote areas had problems with reception.
Misplaced Clause	Entire families that dominated the living room would gather around the device. [The adjective clause *that dominated the living room* seems to modify *families*.]
Clear	Entire families would gather around the device that dominated the living room.

PRACTICE

Revise each of the following sentences by correcting the misplaced modifier. You may need to add words and punctuation to make the meaning of a sentence clear.

1. Television is common today, which was a novelty when it first came out.
2. At first it was thought that television for most people would be too expensive.
3. Television was demonstrated to many people attending a World's Fair for the first time.
4. Many people thought that television would do away with radio when it came along.
5. Entertainers found new audiences showcasing their talents on television.

Chapter 6 Exposition: Sharing Research Results

RESOURCES

Grammar Link

Practice

- *Communications,* WS. p. 118

Publish Your Essay

Spread the Word   Here are some ways to share the results of your research with an audience.

- Show your paper to content-area teachers who are knowledgeable about your topic. They may have some helpful comments or suggestions about your research.
- Ask a media specialist in your school if you can set up a display of research reports written by your peers and yourself. Other students will be able to use the display as sources of ideas for research subjects.
- Record a reading of your report and offer the audiotape to your school's media specialist. He or she might be able to play it for other students.
- Publish your paper on the Web so that others interested in the topic can use it as a resource.

Reflect on Your Essay

Learning from Experience   You are nearing the end of a complex project requiring persistence and skill. Take a moment to reflect on your experience with the research paper by answering the following questions in writing.

- How did researching and writing about your topic (as opposed to other ways of learning about it, such as hearing a lecture) affect what and how much you learned?
- The next time you research and write about a topic, which parts of the process will you definitely use? What will you do differently?

If you add your report to your portfolio or learning log, date your responses to these questions and include them in your portfolio or learning log as well.

YOUR TURN 10 Proofreading, Publishing, and Reflecting

Review each of the steps explained in this section. Before you turn in your research paper, be sure to
- proofread it carefully
- consider publishing options
- record reflections on your writing experience

TIP   If you have written your essay for a general audience and now wish to publish it for a more specific audience—local experts on the topic, for example—you may need to refine your essay a bit. Always keep in mind what your audience already knows about the topic and how you might further inform them.

PORTFOLIO

TEACHING TIP

Research in the Media
Before assigning this exercise, you may wish to model the assignment with a videotape of a news broadcast or a copy of a newsmagazine article. Show students various sites where the credits or sources may be found, and brainstorm other locations of sources and their reliability.

Meeting INDIVIDUAL NEEDS

ADVANCED LEARNERS
Consider contacting your local television station to request a speaker for the class. Ask the person to focus on how he or she has researched various news stories or to discuss the research resources available to television reporters.

Check that students have listed at least three pieces of researched information for each media message. Then, check that the source for the information seems logical. You might want to discuss some of students' findings with the class.

Connections to Life

Research in the Media

Research skills come in handy for more than just writing research papers. People who create various kinds of media messages must do research. Here are just two examples of the ways research is used in the media.

- A television news reporter must research the background of an investigative story.
- A Web site designer must research information on her topic to create accurate hyperlinks for sites.

Often, many pieces of factual information—information that can be proven or verified—in a media message have been researched by someone.

Stay for the Credits Not only must creators of many media messages do research, but they must also, just like you, give credit to their sources. Often, sources are acknowledged during the credits at the end of a film or television show. Sometimes, however, credit is given in a way that is a little harder to spot. For instance, a reporter might say, "According to meteorologist Joe Whitey, this was the first tornado ever to hit New Hampshire." Who is the source of the information about tornadoes? Joe Whitey, the meteorologist, is.

Seeing Is Believing? You've probably heard the expression "Don't believe everything you read." Well, don't believe everything you see, either. To be a critical media viewer, try to identify the source of any information given. Always consider the reliability of the information, whether or not a source is given.

YOUR TURN 11 — Identifying Research in Media Messages

With one or two classmates, consider two different kinds of media messages. For example, you might consider a nightly news report and a Web site, or a newsmagazine and a documentary film. As you view or read each media message, try to identify at least three pieces of researched information. Then, see if you can identify the sources used. Make a chart like the one below to organize your findings.

Medium	Fact	Source
Newspaper article	Sixty percent of Americans agree with the recent Supreme Court decision.	The Gallup Poll

246 Chapter 6 Exposition: Sharing Research Results

Connections to Life
Alignments
TEKS 4D, 20B, 20E

Exposition: Sharing Research Results

Focus on Viewing and Representing

Evaluating Web Sites

Searching on the World Wide Web is like opening a floodgate: Waves of information come surging into your computer. Sometimes the amount of information can be overwhelming. How can you navigate the hundreds of Web pages on your topic without an online librarian to help you? Once you find a site that seems helpful, how can you determine whether the site gives reliable, accurate, and up-to-date information? By using the techniques described in this section, you can ride these waves of information without going under.

The World Wide Web

Getting What You Want When you type keywords about a research topic into a search engine, you often get results that seem overwhelming. Many times the search engine will produce hundreds or thousands of matches or near matches to a search. Where do you begin? Instead of visiting the sites one at a time, there are a couple of simple ways to determine whether a site will be useful to you.

Check the Meter Many search engines will tell you how useful a Web site will be by placing a number or other indicator alongside the site's address. This number signifies the percentage of the Web site that matches your research topic. If you were researching the history of animation, for instance, and you found a site devoted entirely to the history of animation, the number alongside the address might be *98*. On the other hand, if you found a site that is devoted to animation in the last decade, the number might be somewhat smaller. To save time and to keep your research on track, choose only the sites with the highest percentages. All search engines will list the highest percentages (the closest matches) first.

Be Specific Whittle your search down by being as specific as possible. If you were searching for the history of a certain cartoon character, the keyword *animation* might be too broad and would produce results related to *all* animation. Searching for the character's name, however, probably would produce the best results.

WHAT'S AHEAD?

In this section, you will learn to
- find Web sites related to a topic
- evaluate Web sites for reliability and validity

Focus on Viewing and Representing

OBJECTIVES

- To find Web sites related to a topic
- To evaluate Web sites for reliability and validity

Quotation for the Day

"Penetrating so many secrets, we cease to believe in the unknowable. But there it sits nevertheless, calmly licking its chops."

(H. L. Mencken, 1880–1956, American journalist, editor, and critic)

Remind students that new information is uncovered daily. If their topics are current, their information must also be current, and reliable Web sites are the most current sources of information. Learning how to evaluate Web sites is key to good research.

Cooperative Learning

Search Engines. Pair each student who is less proficient with using the Internet with one who is knowledgeable. As the more proficient student demonstrates how to use search engines, the less proficient student should write down the steps for accessing information. He or she can create a set of directions for using search engines in the future.

RESOURCES

Focus on Viewing and Representing
Practice
- Media Literacy and Communication Skills
  —Support and Practice, Ch. 6
  —A How-to Handbook

Teaching Notes
- Media Literacy and Communication Skills
  —A Teacher's Guide, Ch. 6

Focus on Viewing and Representing, pp. 247–248
Alignments
TEKS 16A, 16B, 20A, 20B

TECHNOLOGY TIP

If the equipment is available, you may wish to connect a computer to an overhead projector and demonstrate how to use a search engine and how to evaluate a sample Web site. *You need to be aware that Internet resources are sometimes public forums, and their content can be unpredictable.*

Wrap It Up

Metacognition. Have students reflect on their thinking processes by answering the following questions:

1. What was the most important evaluation tool you learned to apply to Web sites? Why?

Then, have students answer the following question:

2. Which Web sites are most likely to be reliable and how can you tell what they are? [sources that include *edu* or *org* in their URLs]

YOUR TURN 12

When students share their findings with the class, check that they have applied the guidelines on this page and that they have stated specific reasons for their choices.

What Can You Depend On? There are a couple of ways to make sure that a Web site is a reliable source of information. You can choose a site from a university (indicated by the abbreviation *edu* in the Web address, which is also called the URL, or uniform resource locator) or a library. These sites usually are more reliable than others. The suffix *org* in the URL also indicates a more reliable source. Many national magazines and newspapers will reference these sites. You can also visit individual home pages (those that are personal and not affiliated with any organization), but always double-check them against at least one other source since the individual may not be an expert or part of a respected and trusted organization.

A Whale of a Resource Ultimately, it will be up to you to determine whether a site is valid. A site is valid to your research if the site is relevant, meaningful, and appropriate to the topic. To check the validity of a Web site, remember the acronym ORCCCA:

> **O**bjective: Make sure the site is objective and not overly biased toward one side of an issue. If a site is sponsored by a single corporation, for instance, determine whether personal interests influence the information.
>
> **R**eliable: Verify that the site is produced by a reliable source—an expert in the field, a respected organization, or a trusted publication.
>
> **C**omplete: Make sure that the information is detailed and complete. Points should be supported with sufficient evidence, such as examples. All points of view (all views on the topic) should be presented.
>
> **C**lear: Consider whether the information is readable, easy to navigate, and well organized. Remember, though, that clarity usually is a matter of opinion.
>
> **C**urrent: Confirm that the information is up-to-date. Check for dates when the information was updated, added, or otherwise modified.
>
> **A**ccurate: Determine whether the information is correct. Names and dates should be included for all sources cited. If no citations are provided, confirm the information with another source.

YOUR TURN 12 Evaluating Web Sites

Working with a partner, think of a name, word, or phrase related to each of your research topics and type it into a search engine. Once the search engine produces a list of sites, select three or four of them by applying the guidelines above. Determine which site is the most reliable and valid, and provide your reasons. Share your results, explaining how you applied the guidelines, with the rest of the class.

248   Chapter 6   **Exposition:** Sharing Research Results

RESOURCES

Your Turn 12

Practice and Reinforcement

- *Media Literacy and Communication Skills*
  —*Support and Practice,* Ch. 6, transparencies and worksheets
  —Videocassette 2, Segment F

CHAPTER

 # Choices

Choose one of the following activities to complete.

▶ CAREERS
1. Research Your Future Pick a career, or field, you think might match your interests and talents, and brainstorm some questions about it. In a media center or bookstore, find some resources that contain information about research strategies used in that field. Skim the materials, and **take notes** about the answers you find. Present your findings in an **oral or video presentation**.

▶ LITERATURE
2. Your Very Own Book Club Select an author whose work you admire. Then, research the author's life to discover how it might have influenced his or her writing. Are there any events, themes, or character types that are present in both? Why might this be true? Share your discoveries in a **letter** to a friend or classmate who also enjoys the author's work.

▶ CROSSING THE CURRICULUM: THE ARTS
3. Your Art Form Think of an art form—modern dance, sculpture, hip-hop—that appeals to you, and write a sentence explaining how you feel about the art form and why. For example, "The blues cheer me up, because I let go of sad feelings when I listen to them." Then, use keywords to locate Web sites related to your topic, and search for other people's views on it. Using your original statement (or a revised version of it) as the topic sentence, write a **paragraph** about your art form, incorporating some of the views you found on the Internet.

▶ MEDIA AND TECHNOLOGY
4. One Research Report Leads to Another A research paper can serve as a source of inspiration. After reading your classmates' research reports, you may have questions that could be clarified by further research. Work collaboratively in small groups to compile a set of research questions suggested by each group member's report. Then, choose one topic, conduct an online search, and create an **early plan** for a possible group research report.

▶ CAREERS
Discuss with students the need for writers to use research strategies to help them compose. Point out that just as writers will have different strengths and weaknesses, they will also have differing strategies. Strategies will also differ depending on the purpose of a piece of writing. Have students answer the questions *What strategies would a writer use in the field I chose? How would I adapt these strategies to my own strengths and weaknesses as a writer?*

▶ LITERATURE
Remind students that reference tools in the library contain considerable author information. The school librarian or media specialist can point out specific works, such as biographical dictionaries, that would make this assignment simpler.

▶ CROSSING THE CURRICULUM: THE ARTS
Remind students that their sentences need to be specific or they may have problems finding related sites. Also, remind them to acknowledge the sources of the views found on the Internet. *You need to be aware that Internet resources are sometimes public forums, and their content can be unpredictable.*

▶ MEDIA AND TECHNOLOGY
Encourage students to use their individual strengths in working together on the early plan. Some students will naturally develop questions, organize material, conduct online searching, and so on. Students may wish to "think aloud" while one student records and then edits the ideas into written form.

RESOURCES
Sharing Research Results

Assessment
- *Assessment Package*
  —Chapter Tests, Ch. 6
  —Chapter Tests in Standardized Test Formats, Ch. 6
  —Assessment Alternatives, Ch. 6
- Test Generator
  (One-Stop Planner CD-ROM)

Choices Rubrics
- *Assessment Package*
  —Assessment Alternatives, Ch. 6

Choices Alignments
Choice 1 TEKS 13B, 13D, 16A, 16B
Choice 2 TEKS 1A, 1B, 8A, 13D; TAAS W1
Choice 3 TEKS 1A, 2A, 2E; TAAS W1
Choice 4 TEKS 2A, 2B, 2E, 4A; TAAS W1, W2, W4

CHAPTER PLANNING GUIDE

CHAPTER 7

Persuading Others

Use this guide to create an instructional plan that suits the individual needs of your students. Assignments marked by an asterisk (*) may be completed out of class. Times given for pacing lessons are estimated. See pp. 250–251 for chapter-wide resources. Resources listed in this guide are point-of-use resources only.

Curriculum Connections

Choices *p. 293*
- Literature
- Media and Technology
- Crossing the Curriculum: Journalism
- Art

---

internet connect

GO TO: go.hrw.com
KEYWORD: EOLang 10-7

 All resources for this chapter are available for preview on the *One-Stop Planner CD-ROM with Test Generator*. All worksheets and tests may be printed from the CD-ROM.

Texas Resources For a complete listing of all resources prepared for Texas teachers and students, please see the blue box at the beginning of each chapter.

	Chapter Opener *pp. 250–251*	**Reading Workshop: Reading a Persuasive Newspaper Article** *pp. 252–262*
DEVELOPMENTAL PROGRAM	⏱ **20 minutes** • Choosing Sides *p. 251* • Your Turn 1 in groups *p. 251*	⏱ **90 minutes** • Preparing to Read *p. 252* • Reading Selection *pp. 253–254* • First Thoughts 1–2 in groups *p. 255* • Distinguishing Facts from Opinions *pp. 255–257* • Your Turn 2 *p. 257* • Elements of Persuasion *pp. 257–260* • Your Turn 3 *p. 260* • Test Taking Mini-Lesson *p. 262*
CORE PROGRAM	⏱ **15 minutes** • Choosing Sides *p. 251* • Your Turn 1 *p. 251*	⏱ **80 minutes** • Preparing to Read *p. 252* • Reading Selection *pp. 253–254* • First Thoughts 1–3 *p. 255* • Distinguishing Facts from Opinions *pp. 255–257* • Your Turn 2 *p. 257* • Elements of Persuasion *pp. 257–260* • Your Turn 3 *p. 260* • Vocabulary Mini-Lesson *p. 261* • Test Taking Mini-Lesson *p. 262*
ADVANCED PROGRAM	⏱ **15 minutes** • Choosing Sides *p. 251* • Your Turn 1 *p. 251*	⏱ **60 minutes** • Preparing to Read *p. 252* • Reading Selection *pp. 253–254* • First Thoughts 3 *p. 255* • Your Turn 2 *p. 257* • Elements of Persuasion *pp. 257–260* • Your Turn 3 *p. 260* • Vocabulary Mini-Lesson *p. 261*
RESOURCES — PRINT	• *Communications,* TP. 52, WS. p. 119	• *Alternative Readings,* Ch. 7 • *Communications,* TPs. 53, 54, WS. pp. 120–127
RESOURCES — MEDIA	• One-Stop Planner CD-ROM	• One-Stop Planner CD-ROM

TP.=Transparency   WS.=Worksheet

Writing Workshop: Writing a Persuasive Essay pp. 263–283	**Analyzing Editorial Cartoons** pp. 284–287, **Giving a Persuasive Speech** pp. 288–292
⏰ **160 minutes** • Choose an Issue *pp. 263–264* • Write an Opinion Statement *p. 264* • Consider Your Purpose, Audience, and Tone *pp. 264–266* • Gather Support for Your Opinion *pp. 266–269* • Organize Support and Your Turn 4 *p. 271* • Framework and Your Turn 5* *p. 272* • Writer's Model and Student's Model *pp. 273–275* • Evaluate and Revise and Your Turn 6* *pp. 276–277* • Focus on Sentences and Your Turn 7 *pp. 278–279* • Proofread, Publish, and Reflect *pp. 280–281* • Grammar Link and Your Turn 8 *pp. 280–281* • Test Taking Mini-Lesson *p. 282*	⏰ **30 minutes** • What is an Editorial Cartoon? *pp. 284–287* • Your Turn 10 *p. 287* ⏰ **120 minutes** • Persuasive Speech *pp. 288–291* • Becoming the Listener *pp. 291–292* • Your Turn 11 *p. 292*
⏰ **150 minutes** • Choose an Issue *pp. 263–264* • Write an Opinion Statement *p. 264* • Consider Your Purpose, Audience, and Tone *pp. 264–266* • Gather Support for Your Opinion *pp. 266–269* • Critical Thinking Mini-Lesson *p. 270* • Organize Support and Your Turn 4 *p. 271* • Framework and Your Turn 5* *p. 272* • Writer's Model and Student's Model *pp. 273–275* • Evaluate and Revise and Your Turn 6* *pp. 276–277* • Focus on Sentences and Your Turn 7 *pp. 278–279* • Proofread, Publish, and Reflect *pp. 280–281* • Grammar Link and Your Turn 8 *pp. 280–281* • Test Taking Mini-Lesson *p. 282* • Connections to Life and Your Turn 9* *p. 283*	⏰ **20 minutes** • What is an Editorial Cartoon? *pp. 284–287* • Your Turn 10 *p. 287* ⏰ **100 minutes** • Persuasive Speech *pp. 288–291* • Becoming the Listener *pp. 291–292* • Your Turn 11 *p. 292*
⏰ **100 minutes** • Choose an Issue *pp. 263–264* • Write an Opinion Statement *p. 264* • Consider Your Purpose, Audience, and Tone *pp. 264–266* • Gather Support for Your Opinion *pp. 266–269* • Framework and Your Turn 4 and 5* *pp. 271–272* • Writer's Model and Student's Model *pp. 273–275* • Evaluate and Revise and Your Turn 6* *pp. 276–277* • Proofread, Publish, and Reflect *pp. 280–281* • Your Turn 8 *p. 281* • Connections to Life and Your Turn 9* *p. 283*	⏰ **10 minutes** • What is an Editorial Cartoon? *pp. 284–287* • Your Turn 10 *p. 287* ⏰ **80 minutes** • Persuasive Speech *pp. 288–291* • Becoming the Listener *pp. 291–292* • Your Turn 11 *p. 292*
• *Communications,* TPs. 55–58, WS. pp. 128–137 • *Designing Your Writing*	• *Media Literacy and Communication Skills Kit* —*Support and Practice,* Ch. 7 —*A How-to Handbook* —*A Teacher's Guide,* Ch. 7
• *One-Stop Planner CD-ROM*	• *Media Literacy and Communication Skills Kit* —*Videocassette 2, Segment G* • *One-Stop Planner CD-ROM*

CHAPTER 7
Persuading Others

CHAPTER OBJECTIVES

- To read a persuasive newspaper article and analyze its structure
- To write a persuasive essay
- To understand and analyze persuasive elements in editorial cartoons
- To prepare and evaluate a persuasive speech

Chapter Overview

From peer pressure to media messages, students are surrounded by persuasion. This chapter is designed to help students use and recognize persuasive techniques in reading, writing, viewing and representing, and speaking and listening. The Reading Workshop provides students with a newspaper article in which they will distinguish fact from opinion and identify elements of persuasion. The Writing Workshop focuses on the steps students need to follow to write a persuasive essay. The Focus on Viewing and Representing offers instruction in interpreting editorial cartoons. The Focus on Speaking and Listening provides criteria for preparing and evaluating a persuasive speech. The four sections of the chapter may be taught independently; when taught together, however, they give students more thorough practice with persuasive techniques.

Why Study Persuasion?

Every day students encounter people and media attempting to sway their views. At the same time, students frequently need to take stands on issues that are important to them. Distinguishing between facts and opinions and understanding the elements of persuasion allow students to analyze others' persuasive communications intelligently and to construct logical and convincing persuasive arguments of their own.

Teaching the Chapter

Option 1: Begin with Literature

If you begin the study of persuasion using literature, introduce this chapter after examining the use of persuasion in drama, novels, short stories, or poetry. Students will analyze the persuasive techniques within the chosen genre, whether used by the author to sway readers to relate to a view of life or agree with a point of view, or by characters trying to persuade other characters to share their beliefs or join them in taking a particular course of action. Following the literature study, have students read the newspaper article in the Reading Workshop (pp. 253–254). Discuss how persuasive techniques are used in nonfiction to influence readers. With a broad reading knowledge of persuasive techniques that encompasses both fiction and nonfiction, students will be well prepared to write their own persuasive essays.

Option 2: Begin with Nonfiction and Writing

The material in this chapter will make students aware of the pervasive use of persuasion in nonfiction. The persuasive newspaper article in the Reading Workshop and its accompanying instruction (pp. 252–262) provide students with a basic understanding of the elements of persuasion and the difference between facts and opinions. Next, students gain firsthand experience of persuasive techniques as they learn how to research and build an argument and write their own persuasive essays in the Writing Workshop. The understanding they have gained through the study of persuasive techniques in nonfiction and through writing persuasive essays will help students recognize, analyze, and write about persuasion in literature.

Making Connections

■ To the Literature Curriculum

Literature often is persuasive. Both Mark Twain's "The Lowest Animal" and Alice Walker's "Everyday Use" attempt to convince the reader to accept a particular point of view. Students need to be aware that literature has long been used to persuade readers to correct societal ills and to change people's behavior.

Lesson Idea: Persuasion in "Everyday Use" by Alice Walker

1. Work with students to determine the opinion Alice Walker is presenting. Help students formulate a statement that summarizes Walker's point of view.

2. Have students list characteristics of Dee and Maggie and examine how these characteristics support Walker's opinion.

3. Prompt students to consider the setting of the story and discuss how the author uses it to help the reader see her point of view.

4. After students have finished discussing "Everyday Use," direct their attention to the newspaper article on pp. 253–254. Explain that the article is a more obvious example of persuasion than Walker's fictional work, as it includes a clear opinion statement and directly supports it with reasons and evidence. To acquaint students with the elements of persuasion and prepare them to write persuasive pieces of their own, guide them through the text on pp. 257–260.

■ To Careers

Persuasion is used for many purposes in the workplace. As students learn in this chapter, a letter of application for employment is one form of persuasive writing in the workplace. This activity will make students aware of other times and places in the workplace in which persuasive techniques are useful. Invite someone from the human resources department of a company, a local business owner, or a successful businessperson to speak to the class. The speaker might discuss the use of persuasive techniques in the following situations: job interview, request for a promotion or raise, and complaints about working conditions. Allow time for students to ask the speaker questions. Have students role-play various workplace situations in which they might use persuasive techniques.

■ To the Community

Community issues inspire position papers of various kinds. Public advertising is common in many communities. Before students read the article **"Force-Fed Television,"** identify and discuss forms of public advertising in students' own community. Do students find these forms of advertising intrusive? Why or why not? Ask students to write brief paragraphs describing their feelings about public advertising. After students have read the persuasive newspaper article, ask them what kind of information they would need to write persuasive essays on public advertising and where they would get the information.

■ To the Journalism Curriculum

Have students work as a group to write a persuasive letter to the editor of the local newspaper. Students should research both sides of the issue before forming an opinion. Once students have written an opinion statement and gathered support for it, suggest that they read some published letters to the editor to get some idea of their length and style. Students should ask a teacher to read and evaluate their letter. When they have carefully proofread their letter, encourage students to send it to the local newspaper. Students should explain why they think the letter will persuade readers.

CHAPTER

PREVIEWING THE CHAPTER

- Persuasion is the subject of the four sections in this chapter. Although you may wish to teach the sections separately, taught together they complement and reinforce each other. Reading a persuasive newspaper article introduces students to the elements of persuasive writing, preparing them to write their own persuasive essays. Students can identify persuasive techniques used in writing and illustrating in the third section as they consider the impact of editorial cartoons. Then, students can practice giving and evaluating a persuasive speech. To integrate this chapter with grammar, usage, and mechanics chapters, see pp. T401A–T401B.

INTRODUCING THE CHAPTER

- To introduce the chapter, use the Journal Warm-up, Transparency 52, in *Communications*.

VIEWING THE PHOTOGRAPH

- The advertisement features baseball star Cal Ripken, Jr., with a milk mustache. Explain that Ripken holds the record in his sport for number of consecutive games played. Point out that the text in the corner of the ad refers to this record. Then, ask why Ripken's photograph is effective in this ad. [Since Ripken is associated with consistency, readers of the ad might be persuaded to drink milk every day.]

CHAPTER 7 Persuading Others

CHAPTER RESOURCES

Planning
- *Lesson Planner*, Ch. 7
- Block Scheduling, p. T249A (this book)
- One-Stop Planner CD-ROM

Practice
- *Communications*, Ch. 7

- Media Literacy and Communication Skills

Extension
- *Designing Your Writing*

Reinforcement
- *Communications*, Ch. 7

PREVIEW

Reading Workshop

Reading a Persuasive Newspaper Article
PAGE 252

Writing Workshop

Writing a Persuasive Essay
PAGE 263

Focus on Viewing and Representing

Analyzing Editorial Cartoons
PAGE 284

Focus on Speaking and Listening

Giving a Persuasive Speech
PAGE 288

Choosing Sides

- The high school four miles up the road is the same size as yours but has four times as many computers. Is that fair?
- Advertisers spend about $700 million annually on TV ads aimed at young people. Do you think that is right?
- The state legislature is proposing to raise the legal driving age in your state. Do you think it would be a good idea?

Like many students, you probably have opinions on these and other issues concerning the world, the nation, your community, and your personal life. Maybe you have read articles or heard speeches in which writers or speakers voiced opinions on issues ranging from world peace to whether there is enough parking space for students at your school.

When people try to convince you to agree with their opinions, they are trying to **persuade** you. Advertisers, politicians, teachers, parents, and friends all use persuasion. You also persuade others when you take a stand on something important to you.

GO TO: go.hrw.com
KEYWORD: EOLang 10-7

YOUR TURN 1 — Talking About Persuasion

In a small group of classmates, share recent experiences in which you have tried to persuade someone to do or believe something. Note whether the attempts at persuasion were successful. Keep a list of everyone's contributions. Be ready to share your list with the class.

- **Alternative Readings**, Ch. 7
- **Daily Language Activity Transparencies**
- **Vocabulary Workshop** and *Tests*

Evaluation and Assessment

- *Test Generator* (One-Stop Planner CD-ROM)

- **Assessment Package**
  —*Chapter Tests*, Ch. 7
  —*Chapter Tests in Standardized Test Formats*, Ch. 7
  —*Assessment Alternatives*, Ch. 7

Internet
- go.hrw.com (keyword: EOLang 10–7)

Motivate

To emphasize the role of persuasion in everyday life, have pairs of students role-play common situations in which they might persuade someone to agree with them. Possible scenarios include convincing a parent or guardian to allow them to stay out late for a special event or talking a friend into joining a club. After each brief skit, discuss with students the techniques and arguments they used.

ELEMENTS OF Literature

Taking a Stand in Literature. In *Elements of Literature*, Fourth Course, see "The Man in the Water," by Roger Rosenblatt, pp. 471–475, and "The Unknown Rebel," by Pico Iyer, pp. 489–490, for examples of two real people who took a position in life-threatening situations.

YOUR TURN 1

Possible examples include experiences sharing views on school policies, social issues, political topics, entertainment news, and environmental issues. Ask a group member to share one experience with the class.

Chapter Opener, pp. 250–251
Alignments
TEKS 16B, 16F

Texas Resources
- *Lesson Planner*, Ch. 7
- *TAAS Tool Kit*
- *Preparation for TAAS*
- *Preparing for English II End-of-Course Examination*
- *One-Stop Planner CD-ROM*

Reading Workshop

OBJECTIVES

- To read a persuasive newspaper article in preparation for writing a persuasive essay
- To distinguish facts from opinions
- To identify elements of persuasion
- To understand connotations and denotations of words
- To answer fact-and-opinion questions

TEACHING TIP

Preparing to Read
The material on this page introduces concepts that form the instructional basis of the Reading Workshop—distinguishing facts from opinions and identifying elements of persuasion. For an in-depth discussion of both concepts, see pp. 255–260. The Reading Selection offers students practice in distinguishing facts from opinions and helps them recognize techniques writers often use to persuade others to agree with their position.

Quotation for the Day

"The best cause requires a good pleader."

(Dutch proverb)

Write the quotation on the chalkboard or on an overhead transparency and have students list in their writing journals some causes for which they would be willing to take a stand. Students may wish to refer to their lists later when they are deciding on topics for position papers.

RESOURCES

Reading Workshop
Reinforcement
- *Alternative Readings,* Ch. 7

Reading Workshop

Reading a Persuasive Newspaper Article

You probably read newspaper articles and magazine articles that are informative, entertaining, or both. Some articles, however, serve another purpose—persuasion. The writer of a persuasive article is trying to convince you to agree with his or her position on some issue. For instance, maybe you have noticed that television sets seem to be everywhere, in places where you never expected to see them—in a grocery store, for example. The author of the following article, "Force-Fed Television," expresses a very definite opinion on this abundance of television sets. As you read the article, think about what the author's position is and whether you agree with it.

WHAT'S AHEAD?

In this section you will read a persuasive newspaper article and learn how to
- distinguish facts from opinions
- identify the elements of persuasion

Preparing to Read

READING SKILL

Distinguishing Facts from Opinions When deciding whether you agree with a writer's position, you must consider the facts he or she provides. Since persuasive writing includes both *facts* and *opinions*, it is important to distinguish between the two. A **fact** is information that can be proven true; an **opinion** is a judgment or belief that cannot be proven true. As you read the article on the next page, look for points that are facts and for statements that are opinions.

READING FOCUS

Elements of Persuasion Persuasive pieces always contain certain techniques that are intended to persuade you to agree with a position and, sometimes, to take action for or against something. Persuasive techniques include **opinion statements** that directly state or imply a position, **reasons** and **evidence** that support a position, and **emotional appeals** that engage your feelings. As you read "Force-Fed Television," see if you can spot any of these persuasive techniques.

252   Chapter 7   Persuasion: Persuading Others

READING PROCESS

PREREADING
Make Predictions. After students have read **Preparing to Read,** direct their attention to the title of the Reading Selection. As a preview of the selection, ask the following questions:
- When or how have you heard the term "force-fed" used?

Reading Selection

See if you can determine the writer's position in the following article. As you read, write down answers to the numbered active-reading questions.

from We The Media

FORCE-FED TELEVISION

by Adam Hochschild

Some friends from Moscow once introduced me to a lovely Russian custom. Before embarking on a trip, you "sit for the journey." Sitting quietly for a few minutes, you guarantee yourself a safe return by getting into the right, meditative frame of mind as you begin a major voyage.

Anyone looking for a few quiet moments in the place where most Americans begin longer voyages these days—an airport departure gate—is in for big trouble. Besides all the other distractions, there's often a new one: a flickering TV set. I first began encountering these TVs some months ago, and did some research to find out how widespread they are. It turns out that TVs are now installed at more than a thousand gates in more than twenty-five major American airports. The number is growing rapidly.

These TVs usually hang from the ceiling, exasperatingly out of reach of an angry foot or a hand trying to turn the sound off. Woe to the traveler who has an extra hour or two and hopes to read a book. You can't escape. And surely many people want to. At gates cursed with these TVs, most passengers are trying to talk, work, or read. But with little luck, for that penetrating TV sound relentlessly needles its way into a conversation or onto the page.

Nobody can claim that this is a service that travelers have asked for. They haven't. The TVs are there because there's big money to be made from them. Last year, Nielsen Media Research reported that 8.4 million people a month saw airport TV ads. Many millions in advertising dollars get divided between three parties to a deal: the airport, the airline whose gate it is, and the CNN Airport Network, which provides the programming. CNN employs retired baseball home run king Hank Aaron to sign up new airlines and airports.

1. What does the author do in this paragraph to capture your interest?

2. What information does the author provide to convince you that there is a problem with television in public places?

Reading Workshop 253

A TV set in a public place is different from one in your home. You can't turn it off. This force-fed TV is proliferating in part precisely because advertisers know that air travelers are likely to be working-age professionals—who usually watch less TV than children, housewives, retired people, and the poor. Furthermore, at home, everybody is more likely to turn off the sound during commercials. But airport TV is zap proof.

Not only in airports is television busy finding captive audiences, a phenomenon known in the advertising business as "place-based media." Despite strenuous opposition from parent and teacher groups, Channel One carries its commercials into thousands of school classrooms. Café USA is a TV network aimed at shopping-mall food courts. The Commuter Channel's silent screens hang above many cities' subway platforms. Happily, a recent Turner empire attempt aimed at supermarket shoppers, the Checkout Channel, failed. (NBC has been test-marketing the idea, however. "Our mission is to sell eyeballs to advertisers," the executive running the program has said.) Specially tailored TV programming is already creeping into doctors' waiting rooms. What sort of captive audience will they find next? Watch out for the Traffic Jam & Toll Plaza Network.

What is to be done the next time you fly? It won't work to courteously ask airport ticket agents to turn the TV off. They can't. Inadvisable for different reasons is using a sledgehammer or wire cutters to do the job yourself: This could land you in a place where you'd *really* be a captive audience, with nothing to do except watch TV all day long.

But there are other things you can do. You can support one of the organizations working to reduce the noxious effects of TV on American life, like UNPLUG or TV-Free America. And you can complain to the public authority that runs your local airport. What is a public place if not a spot where you can carry on an uninterrupted conversation?

In public places, TV is a form of pollution, like cigarette smoke. Smoke can at least be partly sucked away by a good ventilation system. The noise of an unwanted TV can't be. Regulation of unwanted noise is nothing new: many communities place restrictions on jet skis, leaf blowers, and snowmobiles. Thirty years ago people would have laughed at the idea of limiting smoking in public, but today, in the airport in my home city of San Francisco and in many others, smokers have to go to a special room. Why not a room for TV watchers?

3. How does the author try to stir your emotions in this paragraph?

4. What does the author want his readers to do?

5. What sentence in this paragraph seems to sum up the author's opinion, or point of view?

Active-Reading Questions
ANSWERS continued

3. He uses the word "captive" to describe the TV audiences, pointing out that people are powerless to turn the TVs off. He also uses strong words such as "strenuous" and "creeping" to portray advertisers' attempts as sneaky, damaging, and unwanted.

4. The author wants readers to support one of the organizations working to reduce the harmful effects of TV on American life and complain to the public authority that runs the airport.

5. "In public places, TV is a form of pollution, like cigarette smoke."

READING PROCESS

READING 7B

Make Personal Connections. The Reading Selection may make more sense to students if it is related to their lives. After they have read the selection, ask students if they have ever tried to read, study, or have a conversation with the TV or radio on or with some other distracting noise in the background. How did it affect their concentration? Have students write briefly about such a situation. Ask a few students to share their ideas to eliminate such distractions.

> **First Thoughts on Your Reading**
>
> Get together with a partner or small group to answer the following questions about "Force-Fed Television." Write your answers on your own paper.
>
> 1. Why do you think the author decided to put his opinion statement in the final paragraph instead of in the introduction?
> 2. What words and images did the author use to appeal to some of your emotions?
> 3. Did the author convince you to agree with his position? Why or why not?

Distinguishing Facts from Opinions

The Facts About Facts and Opinions "Force-Fed Television" includes some of the author's **opinions** on the problem of television in public places. Opinions cannot be proven true because they are simply judgments, beliefs, or interpretations based on emotions or speculations. The following statement is an example of an opinion in the article:

> In public places, TV is a form of pollution, like cigarette smoke.

There is no way to prove this statement right or wrong; it is just the author's opinion.

> **TIP** Keep in mind that writers sometimes disguise opinions by stating them with authority as if they were facts.
>
> **Example:**
> It is a well-known fact that all students' test scores will rise when students spend less time watching television.
>
> Putting the phrase "It is a well-known fact" in a sentence does not make the content of the sentence factual. Obviously, there is no way to prove that *every* student's scores will rise. Therefore, this statement is not a fact; it is an opinion.

If the author of the article had stated his opinion that TVs in public places are a form of pollution and had stopped there, the article would not be very convincing. However, good authors realize that in order to convince you, they have to back up their opinions with relevant **facts.** For

READING SKILL

First Thoughts on Your Reading
ANSWERS

1. By putting his opinion statement in the final paragraph, the author leads readers to agree with it as a logical conclusion following the supporting information provided throughout the article. In the last paragraph, the opinion statement also is effective as a final emotional appeal.

2. Words: "big trouble," "exasperatingly," "escape," "cursed," "penetrating," "relentlessly," "needles," "force-fed," "proliferating," "zap proof," "captive audiences," "aimed," "empire," "creeping," "noxious." Images: angry, exasperated travelers; travelers, children, shoppers, and patients as victims of TV networks; TV networks and others making millions of dollars from TV advertising; use of sledgehammer or wire cutters to turn off TV; TV as pollutant.

3. Answers may vary based on the students' enjoyment of television; students should, however, pick up the ideas that airport TV is intrusive, prevents a choice of activities, and is highly profitable for some at the expense of others' wishes or needs.

example, the author of "Force-Fed Television" includes the following fact about TVs in airports:

> It turns out that TVs are now installed at more than a thousand gates in more than twenty-five major American airports.

What makes this statement a fact? It is a fact because it can be proven true. Some facts, as in the example above, are **statistics,** which are simply facts based on numbers. Your job as a reader of a persuasive piece of writing is to determine which statements are opinions and which are facts. Making this distinction will help you to understand the writer's motivation and to evaluate how credible, or believable, the writer is. If you are not sure whether a particular statement is an opinion or a fact, you can use the following Thinking It Through steps to find out.

THINKING IT THROUGH: Distinguishing Facts from Opinions

Use the following steps to determine whether this statement from "Force-Fed Television" is a fact or an opinion.

> CNN employs retired baseball home run king Hank Aaron to sign up new airlines and airports.

▶ **STEP 1** Read the statement carefully.

▶ **STEP 2** Use the following checklist to make an initial decision about whether the statement is a fact or an opinion.

Fact	Opinion
_X_ Gives information such as statistics or specific examples that can be proven true	___ Gives information that cannot be proven true
_X_ Cannot be argued	___ Can be argued
___ May tell source of information	___ May include indefinite terms, such as *lots* or *many*
	___ May include generalization clue words, such as *all, every, always,* or *never*
	___ May include opinion clue words, such as *should* or *must*
	___ May include "value" clue words, such as *good, bad, worst,* or *best*

The information about Hank Aaron can be proven true: He works for CNN; he hit a record 755 home runs; and he is signing up new airlines and airports for the CNN Airport Network. The statement is a fact.

256 Chapter 7 **Persuasion:** Persuading Others

▶ **STEP 3** To confirm that a statement is a fact, double-check by asking yourself, "How and where could I find proof for this statement?"

A source at CNN could probably confirm the statement about Hank Aaron, or you might find the information in a news article.

YOUR TURN 2 Identifying Facts and Opinions

Use the steps in Thinking It Through to decide which of the following sentences from "Force-Fed Television" are opinions and which are facts. Write **O** for opinion and **F** for fact. Put your answers on your own paper, and be prepared to explain your answers.

1. Anyone looking for a few quiet moments in . . . an airport departure gate—is in for big trouble.
2. Café USA is a TV network aimed at shopping-mall food courts.
3. Last year, Nielsen Media Research reported that 8.4 million people a month saw airport TV ads.
4. Furthermore, at home, everybody is more likely to turn off the sound during commercials.
5. Regulation of unwanted noise is nothing new; many communities place restrictions on jet skis, leaf blowers, and snowmobiles.

Elements of Persuasion

The Main Ingredients "Force-Fed Television" contains many elements that clearly identify it as a persuasive piece of writing. Many readers of persuasive writing do not notice these separate elements. On your first reading, you will probably be aware only of your immediate response to the piece—agreement or disagreement. Critical readers go further by asking themselves why they responded as they did. They know that what they are really responding to are the three key elements of persuasive writing:

- **a strong opinion (or main idea)**—a directly stated or implied opinion about an issue on which people might disagree
- **logical appeals**—convincing reasons and evidence that support the writer's opinion
- **emotional appeals**—anecdotes and words with strong connotations that are intended to stir feelings in a reader

◀ READING FOCUS

YOUR TURN 2
ANSWERS

1. O; can be argued, includes "value" phrase: *big trouble*
2. F; gives information that can be proven true, cannot be argued
3. F; gives statistic, tells source of information
4. O; generalization, signaled by terms *everybody* and *more likely*
5. F; provides specific examples that can be proven true

RESOURCES

Your Turn 2

Practice
- *Communications,* WS. p. 120

Reinforcement
- *Communications,* TP. 53, WS. p. 121

TEACHING TIP

Opinion
Point out that good writers rarely use *I believe* or *I think* when stating an opinion. Such phrases personalize and often weaken an argument. When opinions are stated directly, without a personal reference, they sound more authoritative.

TIP Writers do not always directly state their opinions; instead, they **imply**, or suggest, them. In these cases, readers must analyze the text and **infer**, or figure out, the writers' opinions.

Opinion An opinion is the main idea of a persuasive piece of writing. It can be stated directly in a single sentence, or it can be implied throughout the piece or even by the title. An opinion also can be the topic sentence of an individual paragraph within a longer piece. When you are trying to recognize opinion statements, it might help to know that they can be worded in several ways, as shown in the following chart:

Judgment Opinion	Teenagers can improve their lives by watching less television.
"Why" Opinion	The concert tour failed because of a lack of advertising funds.
Prediction Opinion	TV advertisements soon will be seen in every building in America.
"Should" Opinion	City governments should restrict the number of TV sets in airports.

Logical appeals Writers must also provide support for an opinion in order for it to be considered seriously. The main way that writers of persuasive pieces support their opinions is through **logical appeals**. Logical appeals are the convincing **reasons** (common-sense statements that appeal to a reader's sense of logic) and the **evidence** (facts, statistics, expert opinions, examples, and anecdotes) that supports those reasons. The evidence an author provides can make or break a persuasive piece of writing. Without evidence, a writer's opinion would not be considered seriously.

The following chart contains a reason that might be used to support the opinion statement, "Teenagers can improve their lives by watching less television," and five forms of evidence that might be used to support the reason.

Reason: Even though most teenagers think they need television in their lives, they really do not.	
Fact	TV is by far the favored medium for advertising to children.
Statistic	In a study by CNN, 28 percent of teens reported that they could manage without a television.
Expert Opinion	Dr. Victor Strasburger, Director of Adolescent Medicine and Professor of Pediatrics at the University of New Mexico School of Medicine, says that American children and adolescents spend more time watching TV than in any other activity except sleeping.

258 Chapter 7 **Persuasion:** Persuading Others

READING PROCESS

EXTENDING
Connect to the World. After they complete the Reading Selection, encourage students to look for persuasive writing in other contexts. For example, have students describe commercials or advertisements they like. Prompt students to explain what makes the commercials and ads convincing or appealing. How do the

Example	Instead of watching TV, teenagers could read more books.
Anecdote	Some parents on my street have completely removed television sets from their homes.

Emotional appeals Emotional appeals stir feelings like happiness, sadness, or anger in a reader. You might say that they are techniques that writers use to "tug at your heartstrings."

One of the ways writers appeal to readers' emotions is to include words with strong **connotative meanings**—sometimes referred to as **loaded language.** These words have undertones that link attitudes or feelings with the words and, in this way, heighten the seriousness of the issue for readers. As a reader, be aware, though, of too much loaded language in persuasive writing. Overuse of loaded language might also signal a lack of solid logical appeals in support of the opinion statement. Another technique writers of persuasion often use is to include an **anecdote,** or brief story, in which they describe experiences or events that appeal to a reader's emotions.

Unlike opinion statements and logical appeals, which are essential to almost any piece of persuasive writing, emotional appeals are not used by every writer of persuasive pieces. However, they do appear very often. Look at the following examples of emotional appeals.

Emotional Appeals		
Type	Examples	Explanation
Loaded Language (Connotative Words)	Will you be an *unsuspecting victim* of this electronic mall the next time you are unlucky enough to *stumble,* however briefly, on a shopping channel while channel-surfing?	*Unsuspecting victim* has strong connotations of mistreatment or suffering. *Stumble* suggests an accidental event.
Anecdote	Last year, a man reportedly spent his entire savings on items he purchased from a shopping channel.	This anecdote might make you feel sorry for the man.

It is important for you to recognize emotional appeals when you read. While they are a valid tool for persuading readers, you must be sure to form your response to a writer's opinion based on the logic of his or her reasons and evidence, not just on emotions. Sometimes, though, you will find that a writer has used evidence that appeals to *both* logic and emotions, as in the example on the next page.

Critical Thinking
Analysis. To increase their awareness of the elements of persuasive writing, have students read a newspaper editorial. Students should identify the key elements of persuasion in the editorial, noting the writer's opinion and listing both the logical appeals (reasons and evidence) and the emotional appeals (loaded language and anecdotes) used to support it. Then, ask students to share their responses to the editorial. Are the persuasive techniques effective? Do students agree with the writer's position?

commercials and ads appeal to the audience's logical side? to their emotions? Discuss the content of the commercials and ads.

Then, have each student select a commercial or ad that makes a strong logical and/or emotional appeal. Students can make a chart that identifies the opinion (main idea) and details the specific examples that support the opinion.

ANSWERS
A sample chart is shown below.

OPINION: TV is forced on people in public places.

REASON: You can't turn off TVs in public places.
SUPPORT:
- **Fact:** These TVs usually hang from the ceiling, out of reach. *L*
- **Statistic:** TVs are now installed at more than 1,000 gates in more than 25 major American airports. *L*
- **Expert Opinion:** Last year, Nielsen Media Research reported that 8.4 million people a month saw airport TV ads. *L*
- **Example:** Channel One, Café USA, Commuter Channel. *L*
- **Anecdote:** opening paragraph, *E*
- **Connotative Words:** "force-fed," "big trouble," "you can't escape," "cursed," "penetrating," "relentlessly," "needles," "zap proof," "captive," "creeping," "noxious," "pollution;" *E*

Wrap It Up

Metacognition. Use the following questions to encourage students to reflect on their own reading processes. Give students five minutes to answer the following questions.

1. What evidence presented by the author of **"Force-Fed Television"** did you find most convincing? Why?

Then, ask students the question below.

2. What is the difference between a fact and an opinion? [A fact is information that can be proven true; an opinion is a belief or judgment that cannot be proven true.]

260 Persuasion: Persuading Others

Example:
American young people waste 15,000 hours watching television by the time they graduate from high school.

In the example above, the details about how much time children spend watching television is factual but also might touch people's feelings about the future of today's youth. This kind of evidence packs a double persuasive punch. It convinces readers that the writer's opinion is valid, and at the same time it involves readers' emotions. As a reader, it is important to note both the logical and emotional appeal of such statements.

YOUR TURN 3 Identifying Elements of Persuasion

Copy the chart below on your own paper. Then, get together with two or three of your classmates to complete the chart. First, write down the opinion expressed in "Force-Fed Television" on page 253. Remember that a writer's opinion, or main idea, can be implied by the title of a piece of writing. Then, examine the essay for an example of one reason and of each type of support listed in the chart. Put an *E* beside each emotional appeal; put an *L* beside each logical appeal. If the support is both, put both letters. Be aware that you might not find every kind of support listed in the chart. For effective persuasion, writers must include logical appeals, but they need not include all types.

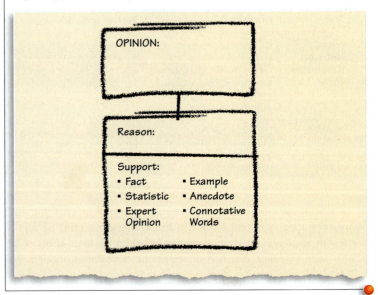

260 Chapter 7 Persuasion: Persuading Others

RESOURCES

Your Turn 3
Practice
- Communications, WS. p. 122

Reinforcement
- Communications, TP. 54, WS. p. 123

Vocabulary
Practice
- Communications, WS. p. 124

MINI-LESSON VOCABULARY

Understanding Connotations and Denotations

An effective persuasive writer chooses words not only for their **denotations** (meanings found in the dictionary) but also for their **connotations** (the feelings and emotions associated with words). In the following examples, note how the second sentence reads quite differently from the first when the italicized words are replaced with more neutral words.

1. The *penetrating* sound from the TV *needled* its way into the room.
2. The *noticeable* sound from the TV *made* its way into the room.

THINKING IT THROUGH — Understanding Connotations and Denotations

Use the following steps to understand the connotations of *creeping* in this sentence from "Force-Fed Television."

> Specially tailored TV programming is already *creeping* into doctors' waiting rooms.

1. Be sure you understand the denotation of the word by checking its definition in a dictionary. Creeping means "to advance gradually."

2. Using a dictionary or thesaurus, if needed, brainstorm words or phrases that could replace the word. entering, sneaking, slinking.

3. Categorize the replacement words as negative, positive, or neutral by determining if they have any associations or feelings for you. Neutral: entering. Negative: sneaking, slinking. Both negative words seem threatening, like snakes and bugs moving.

4. Decide if the original word is more like the neutral, the negative, or the positive synonyms. Creeping seems more like the negative words. It has a threatening feeling (connotation).

PRACTICE

Use the steps above to identify the connotations of each italicized word.

1. Woe to the traveler who has an extra hour or two and hopes to read a book. You can't *escape*.
2. This force-fed TV is *proliferating* in part precisely because advertisers know that air travelers are likely to be working-age professionals . . .
3. Not only in airports is television busy finding *captive* audiences . . .
4. Happily, a recent Turner *empire* attempt aimed at supermarket shoppers, the Checkout Channel, failed.
5. You can support one of the organizations working to reduce the *noxious* effects of TV on American life . . .

MINI-LESSON VOCABULARY

Understanding Connotations and Denotations

ANSWERS
Possible answers follow.

1. negative; get away from something bad, dangerous, or annoying
2. negative; growing uncontrollably
3. negative; trapped, powerless
4. negative; a huge and extreme power
5. negative; poisonous

Vocabulary
Alignments
TEKS 6E, 6F
English II End-of-Course 3

Looking Ahead to Writing

Students will be asked to write persuasive essays in the Writing Workshop for this chapter (pp. 263–283). As they plan, write, and revise their papers, students may find it helpful to refer to the examples of the key elements of persuasive writing discussed on pp. 257–260 of the Reading Workshop.

MINI-LESSON TEST TAKING

Fact-and-Opinion Questions

Standardized tests often include questions designed to check your ability to distinguish between facts and opinions. Here is a typical reading passage and multiple-choice question.

People with children should keep the family's television sets under lock and key. The concern over children and television comes from the constant bombardment of violent behavior on TV.

A recent study showed that 44 percent of network television and 85 percent of premium cable programming contains violence. The amount of violence on TV continues to grow each year. Over three years, the number of prime time shows depicting violence rose from just over a half to well over two thirds.

Parental monitoring of what children and teens view is not the complete answer. Only 38 percent of parents say they watch television with their children on a fairly regular basis. The best way to avoid the damaging effects of TV violence is to remove televisions from the reach of vulnerable children and young adults.

Which statement from the selection is an opinion?

A. The amount of violence on TV continues to grow each year.

B. Only 38 percent of parents say they watch television with their children on a fairly regular basis.

C. Violence on TV is always damaging to children and teens.

D. People with children should keep the family's TV sets under lock and key.

THINKING IT THROUGH Answering Fact-and-Opinion Questions

Use the following steps to answer fact-and-opinion questions.

▶ **STEP 1** Read each statement carefully.

▶ **STEP 2** Ask yourself, "Can the statement be proved true?" Cross out the statements that can be proven true. **A** is a fact that is clearly proven in the selection. **B** is a statistical fact signaled by the use of the word *percent*.

▶ **STEP 3** Look for clue words that signal an opinion. Words such as *should, must, always,* and *never* signal an opinion. **C** makes a judgment that violence on TV is *always* damaging. **D** states something the author thinks *should* be done.

▶ **STEP 4** Continue through all the answer choices. When you think you have found the correct answer, check to see that the fact or opinion is actually stated in the passage. Do not settle on the first fact or opinion you find. In this case **C** is an opinion; however, it does not appear in the passage. Therefore, **D** is the correct answer.

262 Chapter 7 Persuasion: Persuading Others

RESOURCES

Test Taking

Practice

- *Communications,* WS. pp. 125–127

Test Taking
Alignments
TEKS 7C, 12A
English II End-of-Course 3

Writing Workshop

Writing a Persuasive Essay

Imagine this situation: City officials plan to decrease traffic on the street in front of your high school by making the street one-way. This means that you and many of your friends would have to drive several blocks out of your way before turning around toward home. You believe that the city should find another way to decrease traffic on the street, but how can you share your views? One way is to express and support them in a persuasive essay.

In this Writing Workshop, you will learn how to do just that—create a persuasive essay on a topic about which you have a strong opinion. Your goal in the essay will be to state your opinion clearly and to support it with reasons and evidence.

WHAT'S AHEAD?

In this workshop, you will write a persuasive essay and learn how to

- form an opinion statement
- gather support for your opinion
- evaluate your reasoning
- avoid overusing the passive voice
- find and correct double negatives

Choose an Issue

A Powerful Issue A good topic for a persuasive essay is an issue that brings up strong feelings in you and in others. Be on the lookout for these issues in your everyday life. Consider what sets off your "unfairness meter." Think about situations or events that make you feel angry, sad, or enthusiastic, for example. Once you have come up with a few possible issues for your persuasive essay, ask yourself the following questions.

- **Is the issue important to me?** If the issue is one that matters deeply to you, it will be easier to persuade your readers to care about it.

Writing Workshop

OBJECTIVES

- To write a persuasive essay
- To form an opinion statement
- To gather support for an opinion
- To evaluate reasoning
- To avoid overusing the passive voice
- To find and correct double negatives

Quotation for the Day

"All men have a reason, but not all men can give a reason."

(John Henry Cardinal Newman, 1801–1890, English theologian and writer)

Use the quotation to discuss using reasons to support an opinion. Ask students to brainstorm situations in which a person might have trouble giving reasons for an opinion.

TEACHING TIP

Choose an Issue

Warn students not to choose an issue that is so emotional that they are not able to acknowledge opposing arguments. Students must be objective enough to see some validity in other viewpoints and to weigh the support for opposing views realistically.

Prewriting, pp. 263–271
Alignments
TEKS 1A, 1B, 1C, 2A, 4C, 4D
TAAS W1, W2, W4
English II End-of-Course 4

Texas Resources
- *Lesson Planner,* Ch. 7
- *TAAS Tool Kit*
- *Preparation for TAAS*
- *Preparing for English II End-of-Course Examination*
- *One-Stop Planner CD-ROM*

Meeting INDIVIDUAL NEEDS

LEARNERS HAVING DIFFICULTY
Have the class brainstorm five or six possible topics and form groups of five based on students' common interests. Have each group choose one of the topics, develop a thesis, and then brainstorm possible reasons and support for it. Students should take notes of their group's ideas. Students may wish to use the ideas generated in their group as a basis for their individual papers.

TEACHING TIP

Write an Opinion Statement
To help students evaluate their opinion statements or theses, have them create antitheses—thesis statements for the opposing point of view. If they cannot come up with an antithesis, their issues probably lack two sides and are not suitable for persuasive essays. Provide students with the following example.

Opinion Statement: Students should be required to complete thirty hours of community service before they graduate.

Antithesis: Students should do community service only when it is their own choice.

- **Do I have an opinion on the issue?** Just being able to say you do or do not like a situation is not enough. You have to describe in detail how things would be different or better if you had the power to do something about the issue.
- **Do people have different opinions on the issue?** If everyone agrees with your views on the issue, there is no one to persuade. Remember the saying "There are two sides to every story," and pick an issue about which people disagree.
- **Is my opinion supportable?** Will you be able to gather enough facts and examples to make a case that your audience will consider seriously? Will you be able to respond effectively to any **opposing arguments** (objections to your opinion)?

After you have chosen and considered a few possible issues, write down the one that you think you can deal with best in a persuasive essay.

Write an Opinion Statement

Get on Your Soapbox When you write a persuasive essay, your first job is to create a preliminary opinion statement (sometimes called a thesis). You can always revise your opinion statement later. This statement should clearly state your issue and your opinion on it. The following chart shows that good opinion statements contain both elements.

Issue	Opinion
The proposed one-way street	would cause problems for many students.
Recycling	is something good that people can do for the earth.
The preservation of natural resources	is a very important benefit of recycling.

TIP Avoid using words such as *all, every, never, worst,* or *best* in opinion statements. Statements that include these words are often **broad generalizations**, as opposed to **valid opinions** that can be supported with facts.

Consider Your Purpose, Audience, and Tone

Your Readers Await You As the writer of a persuasive essay, your **purpose** is to persuade your readers. More specifically, you want to convince them to think differently about an issue or to follow the course of action you suggest. To persuade your readers effectively, you must understand them well. To get a better understanding of your audience, ask yourself the following questions.

- **What will my readers already know about the issue?** Consider how much background information you will have to provide in order for your readers to understand your position on the issue.
- **What will make my readers care about this issue?** Think about how the topic affects the lives of your readers.
- **What objections might my readers raise to my opinion?** Anticipate opposing arguments so you can respond to readers' concerns and persuade them to see things your way.
- **What will they want to know more about?** Consider aspects of the issue about which readers might want more information.

The writer who created the Writer's Model that begins on page 273 used the following chart to organize his responses to the preceding questions. After you have identified the audience for your persuasive essay, create a chart like this one and fill it out.

TIP Before you start to analyze your audience, you have to know who the members of that audience will be. To identify your audience, ask yourself, "Who is affected by this issue?" and "Who has power to take action on this issue?"

ISSUE: RECYCLING

Audience	Responses to Questions
Readers of my local newspaper	**What they know:** They probably know about the need to recycle—about the amount of garbage that we all produce. **What will make them care:** Help them recognize just how serious the garbage problem is and how recycling can help. **What objections they might raise:** They might think that recycling costs too much—but I could counter with details about how it saves money in the long run. **What they will want to know more about:** They will probably expect specific facts and statistics about how much garbage we produce and the problems it creates.

Meeting INDIVIDUAL NEEDS

MODALITY

Visual Learners. Students may use the following strategy to get to know their audience. Have students mentally picture individual members of their audience. Then, have students imagine how the audience members might respond to their opinions. Encourage students to develop support for their theses based on their visualization of their audience's reactions.

TECHNOLOGY TIP

If possible, have students e-mail local experts, appropriate departments at colleges and universities, and organizations for information to support their positions. E-mail addresses can be found in newspapers, magazines, ads, and university catalogues. Students may ask specific questions or request facts or statistics supporting their reasons. Make sure students keep their requests polite and to the point. *Remind students that their letters will not be confidential because of the nature of the Internet.*

TIP Your writing **voice** (the unique style with which you express your ideas) should further the goal of the essay: to present your opinion and to support it with convincing reasons and evidence.

KEY CONCEPT

Your choice and arrangement of words determines your tone—your attitude and feelings about your issue. Choose your words to suit your audience and your purpose for writing (in this case, persuasion). If your readers are put off by your tone, they may not take your opinion seriously. In a persuasive essay, your tone should be as serious and as carefully considered as your opinion.

Gather Support for Your Opinion

Getting Your Facts Together You must support your opinion in a persuasive essay, or you won't convince readers. To be convincing, you must use **logical appeals**, which include **reasons** and **evidence**. As the diagram below shows, reasons support your opinion, and evidence supports your reasons.

Reasons These are logical statements that answer the question *Why?*

Opinion	People should recycle.
Reasons that answer the question *Why?*	1. Recycling reduces the mountains of garbage we produce. 2. Recycling saves water and energy. 3. Much of the garbage we throw away could be recycled with very little effort.

THINKING IT THROUGH

Finding Your Reasons

Use the following strategies to help you think of supporting reasons for your opinion.

▶ **STEP 1** Ask yourself, "What are the advantages of agreeing with my opinion?" Think of ways that agreeing with your opinion will **help** the people in your audience—for example, by making them healthier or happier. *Advantage of recycling: It helps to make people healthier by reducing the waste that ends up in ground water.*

▶ **STEP 2** Ask yourself, "What are the disadvantages of agreeing with my opinion?" Think of ways that agreeing with your opinion might **make things more difficult** for the people in your audience—for example, by requiring them to sacrifice time or money. *Disadvantage of recycling: It takes too much time for people to separate recyclable materials from the rest of the garbage they throw out.*

▶ **STEP 3** Turn your responses about advantages and disadvantages into reasons that support your opinion. An advantage becomes a reason when you simply state the advantage. A disadvantage becomes a reason when you refute (prove wrong through argument) the disadvantage as you would an opposing argument. *Advantage as a reason: Recycling helps to make people healthier by reducing the waste that ends up in ground water. Disadvantage as a reason: The small amount of personal time each of us takes to recycle can save all of us time by reducing the amount of garbage that we, as a society, must take time to process.*

TIP A persuasive essay differs from a **formal logical argument**—a line of reasoning that attempts to explain or to prove by logic. Formal logical arguments include research reports, business proposals, and some school essays.

Evidence Evidence includes the facts, statistics, expert opinions, anecdotes, and examples that support your reasons.

Types of Evidence	Examples
Facts statements that can be checked by testing, observation, or research	In older landfills, toxins leached into the soil and eventually into the ground water.
Statistics facts that are numerical and are tabulated to present information about a subject	People in the United States throw away 40 percent of all the garbage in the world.

(continued)

TIP You might have to do some research in order to gather support for your opinion. Besides traditional sources, you could contact local resources, such as a recycling center. You could find expert opinions in news articles. You could search on Web sites.

(continued)

Expert Opinions statements made by a recognized authority on the subject	The Environmental Protection Agency estimates that in the next decade 10 percent of our cities will run out of landfill space.
Anecdotes extended examples, or stories, used to support a main idea	While driving to a relative's house yesterday, I noticed that mountaintops once covered by beautiful pine trees were now completely bare.
Examples specific instances, or illustrations, of a general idea	Recycling paper instead of making paper from trees reduces water use and energy use.

Use a chart like the one below to collect support for your opinion. In the left column, the student listed reasons. In the right-hand column, the student showed specific evidence to support each reason.

OPINION: People really need to throw away less by recycling more.

Reasons (Why?)	Supporting facts, statistics, expert opinions, anecdotes, and examples
Much of the garbage that is now tossed out could be recycled.	• Statistic: Government officials estimate that 60 percent of all this trash could be recycled. • Statistic: Environmentalists suggest a much higher figure—as much as 70 to 90 percent.
Recycling more of our garbage can also save precious resources.	• Example: Every week, for example, 50,000 trees are sacrificed to produce Sunday newspapers in the United States. • Fact: By recycling newspapers we can rescue trees from destruction.
Recycling more can reduce the mountains of garbage produced—and reduce the costs associated with all the landfills where the garbage is dumped.	• Fact: Garbage, unfortunately, does not just disappear like magic after it is hauled away. • Fact: Garbage usually goes into landfills—many of which have created toxic pollution problems and monumental cleanup costs. • Expert Opinion: The Environmental Protection Agency estimates that in the next decade 10 percent of our cities will run out of landfill space.

Emotional Impact An **emotional appeal** is support that targets readers' feelings and emotions. Persuasive writers appeal to their readers' feelings and emotions by using **examples, anecdotes,** and, most commonly, **words with strong connotations.**

Examples pack emotional power because they show the impact of your issue on a specific place, situation, or person. Look at the general statement and the specific example below.

General Statement	Runoff from landfills pollutes creeks.
Specific Example	Dog Run Creek, once a favorite community swimming and fishing spot, is now a lifeless, weed-choked gully marked with large signs warning the unwary not to swim in or eat fish from the cloudy water.

The specific example might have a strong impact on a reader who calls to mind his or her own favorite creek and who might, therefore, be alarmed at the idea of landfill runoff polluting this creek.

Anecdotes are brief stories that illustrate a point. They can affect readers' emotions by showing how your issue affects people like them. Look at the following anecdote about the use of trees for paper products.

Anecdote	Ed Chafee recently visited his old hometown. He looked forward to seeing some familiar faces, but most of all he wanted once again to wander through the forests he had loved as a boy. When he got there, the forests were gone, replaced by evenly spaced saplings. The entire forest had been turned into paper towels.

Words with strong connotations (loaded language) can also affect readers' emotions. Words such as *grimy, rotten, fresh,* and *clear* can make your reader feel disgusted by or attracted to what you are describing. In the chart below, notice how the italicized words in the right-hand column add emotional impact to the original sentences in the left-hand column.

Original Sentences	Revised Sentences with Connotative Words Added
People can help save a forest.	People can help *rescue priceless* forests *from destruction.*
People can help just by recycling newspapers.	People can *have a far-reaching impact* just by recycling newspapers.

TIP Use connotative words carefully. If you use too many of them, you risk overstating the importance of your issue so much that your readers might not take it, or you, seriously.

Meeting INDIVIDUAL NEEDS

STUDENTS WITH SPECIAL NEEDS
To help students understand the difference between emotional and logical appeals, have them role-play a conversation between a student and a teacher about why the student deserves a higher grade than the one given for an assignment. Before the role-play, help students by brainstorming with the class reasons a student might give for deserving a better grade. Categorize the reasons as logical or emotional. Then, have pairs of students role-play as follows. First, have the "teacher" probe for facts while the "student" responds with primarily emotional appeals. Then, have the two students play the same roles, this time with the "student" responding with logical reasons and evidence. The role-play should demonstrate to students that emotional appeals are not as effective when used alone.

MINI-LESSON: CRITICAL THINKING

Evaluating Your Reasoning

ANSWERS
1. E
2. H
3. E
4. H
5. H

Taking a Second Look
Evaluating Your Reasoning.
Emphasize logical reasoning rather than faulty reasoning in this exercise. Have students rewrite each practice item as a logical statement. Possible answers follow.

1. Recycling paper is one way of saving forests.
2. Glass recycling would be more effective if contamination by unrecyclable glass could be controlled.
3. Recycling helps control pollution.
4. Because recycling newspapers saves trees, newspaper subscribers should be urged to recycle.
5. Although recycled newspapers save more landfill space than other recycled materials, all kinds of recycling help save the environment.

MINI-LESSON: CRITICAL THINKING

Evaluating Your Reasoning

As you gather the reasons and evidence that support your opinion, it is important to find and correct statements that contain faulty reasoning—statements that sound like logical reasons but really are not. If readers detect faulty reasoning in your essay, they might decide that your support is not valid or that you are trying to fool them. Consider the two following common errors in reasoning—errors you could make if you are not careful. Both of these errors result from oversimplifying a complicated situation, that is, from failing to take all the facts and alternatives into account.

Hasty Generalizations Don't fall into the trap of basing conclusions on inadequate evidence. Make sure that you consider all the facts before you generalize. Also, keep in mind that there may be exceptions to your generalization; therefore, you should use qualifying words such as *many, most, generally,* and *some* where needed to turn a hasty generalization into a valid one.

> **Inadequate Evidence:** The first time I played baseball, I hit a home run.
>
> **Hasty Generalization:** Baseball is an easy game that I can play well without having to practice.

The fact that someone hits a home run once does not mean he or she can play baseball well without practicing.

Either-Or Reasoning This error involves describing a situation in terms of two extreme alternatives and suggesting that there is only one correct choice. Usually there are several choices between the two extremes.

> **Either-Or Reasoning:** If you do not call me every night, you do not love me.

Obviously, there can be several reasons why someone does not call every night.

PRACTICE

Identify the type of faulty reasoning used in each of the numbered items below. On your own paper, write **H** if the item is a hasty generalization. Write **E** if it uses either-or reasoning.

1. People cannot save forests if people do not recycle paper.
2. Loads of glass for recycling are often contaminated by unrecyclable glass. Therefore, it is not worthwhile to recycle glass.
3. If people do not recycle, the earth will become completely polluted.
4. Recycling a stack of newspaper piled one meter high saves a ten-meter-tall evergreen tree. People should not be allowed to subscribe to daily newspapers.
5. More landfill space is saved by recycling paper than by recycling any other material. Recycling materials other than paper does not accomplish anything.

RESOURCES

Critical Thinking
Practice
- *Communications,* WS. p. 128

Your Turn 4
Practice
- *Communications,* WS. p. 129

Organize Your Support

Get Your Information in Order Before writing, you should decide how to order the reasons for your opinion logically. Keep in mind that the parts of your essay that readers will remember the most—the high-profile parts—are at the end of the essay and at the beginning. Therefore, one way to show a **logical progression** of your reasons is to put your strongest reason last, where it is most likely to be remembered by your readers, and your second strongest reason first—in the beginning of the essay. Place remaining reasons in the middle of the essay.

To determine the strength of your reasons, think about the impact each will have on your readers. The strongest reason will have the most impact. Use a chart like the one below to organize your reasons. As you add to your chart, add numbers to show the strength for each reason. Use the number *1* to show the strongest, the number *2* for the next strongest, and so on.

KEY CONCEPT

OPINION: People really need to throw away less by recycling more.

Reasons:

2   Much of the garbage that is now tossed out could be recycled.
3   Recycling more of our garbage can save precious resources.
1   Recycling more can reduce the mountains of garbage produced—and reduce the costs associated with all the landfills where the garbage is dumped.

YOUR TURN 4 Planning Your Persuasive Essay

Review each of the prewriting steps; before you start writing your persuasive essay, remember to

- choose an issue that stirs strong feelings in you and that is likely to capture the interest of your readers
- create a clear opinion statement (thesis)
- consider your audience, purpose, and tone
- determine the reasons for your opinion, anticipate opposing arguments, and gather support for each reason.
- organize reasons and evidence for your opinion

TEACHING TIP

Organize Your Support
To help students organize their support, have them write each reason and its evidence on individual note cards or on half-sheets of paper. Students can rearrange their reasons until they have placed the reason with the most impact last. Suggest that students insert transitions between their reasons so the ideas will flow smoothly when they write their first drafts. Refer students to p. 959 for a list of transitions.

YOUR TURN 4

Review the prewriting steps with each student to see that each one has been completed and that students have sufficient evidence to support their opinions. If not, be sure that the students complete the steps before beginning to write.

Quotation for the Day

"The human brain is the laziest apparatus in the world. If you start to revise before you've reached the end you're likely to begin dawdling with the revisions, and putting off the difficult task of writing."

(Pearl Buck, 1892–1973, American novelist)

Ask students to share ways they become sidetracked when they are writing. Discuss ways students can refocus on their drafts. Make sure that students understand the importance of writing their ideas first and working on revisions later.

TEACHING TIP

Your Opinion (Re)Statement Suggest that when students revisit their opinion statements, they attempt to use synonyms for the terms they presented at the beginning of the paper. This will prevent boring the reader through rote repetition.

YOUR TURN 5

See that students are following the framework on this page. Also, refer students to the notes in the margin of **A Writer's Model** on pp. 273–274. If students are having trouble getting started, suggest that they begin their writing with their opinion statements and wait until after they have completed the rest of their papers to compose attention-getter openings.

Writing

Persuasive Essay

Framework

Introduction
- Open with an attention-getter.
- Give background information.
- Present your opinion statement.

Body
- Provide reasons and support.
- Refute opposing arguments.

Conclusion
- Restate your opinion.
- Include a call to action.

Directions and Explanations

Interest Earning Start with a statement, statistic, story, or question that will draw your readers into the issue. The author of the Writer's Model on page 273 uses *Garbage!* to hook readers.

Looking Back Give your readers whatever background information you think they will need in order to understand the issue.

Your Two Cents Near the beginning of your paper, provide a clear, powerful opinion statement expressing your position.

Sound Reasoning, Good Support Focus each body paragraph on a different reason. Provide facts, statistics, expert opinions, anecdotes, or examples to support each reason. Strive for three reasons.

The Other Side Predict and respond to any opposing arguments your readers might have.

Emotions in Motion Use language that will inspire strong feelings in your readers, or provide an example or anecdote that will appeal to their emotions.

Your Opinion (Re)statement Restate what you are trying to convince your readers to think, believe, or do—or just summarize your reasons.

Get Busy! The conclusion of a persuasive essay often asks the audience to do something or suggests ways they can get involved. The author of the Writer's Model makes a call to action when he asks, "Do you care enough to do your part by recycling?"

YOUR TURN 5 Writing a First Draft

Follow the framework and the directions and explanations above as you write a first draft of your persuasive essay. Also, read through the Writer's Model on the next page.

272 Chapter 7 Persuasion: Persuading Others

RESOURCES

Writing
Writing Prompts
- *Communications*, TP. 55, WS. p. 130

Your Turn 5
Practice
- *Communications*, TP. 56, WS. p. 131

A Writer's Model

The following is a final draft of a persuasive essay that closely follows the framework on the previous page.

Do Something Good for the Earth

Garbage! It smells bad and looks disgusting. Most people prefer not to think about trash more than once a day, and that is only when they take it out. People in the United States should be thinking about garbage more, however, because they throw away 40 percent of all the garbage in the world. People really need to throw away less by recycling more.

Much of the garbage that is now tossed out could be recycled. Of the 200 million tons of garbage that U.S. citizens produce yearly, about 42 percent is paper (from trees), 8 percent is glass, 9 percent is metal (from ore, a natural resource), 7 percent is plastic (from petroleum, a natural resource), 8 percent is rubber (mostly from rain forests), 8 percent is food waste, and 18 percent is yard waste. Government officials estimate that 60 percent of all this trash could be recycled. Environmentalists suggest a much higher figure—as much as 70 to 90 percent.

Recycling more of our garbage can also save precious resources. Every week, for example, fifty thousand trees are sacrificed to produce Sunday newspapers in the United States. By recycling newspapers, we can rescue trees from destruction. We can also save water and energy by recycling. Recycling paper instead of making paper from trees reduces the amount of water used to make the paper by 60 percent and the amount of energy by 70 percent. Aluminum cans show the biggest savings from recycling. To produce a can from recycled aluminum takes 95 percent less energy than from ore.

Recycling more can reduce the mountains of garbage produced—and reduce the costs associated with all the landfills where the garbage is dumped. Garbage, unfortunately, does not just disappear like magic after it is hauled away. It usually goes into landfills—many of which have created toxic pollution problems and monumental cleanup costs. People often object to recycling by saying that it costs too much. What they need to understand is that recycling actually <u>saves</u> money by reducing waste and by eliminating the costs that go along

(continued)

Annotations:
- INTRODUCTION
- Attention grabber
- Background
- Opinion statement
- BODY: Reason 1
- Evidence—facts and statistics
- Reason 2
- Emotional appeal—connotative words
- Reason 3
- Evidence—facts
- Opposing argument
- Response to opposing argument

Connecting Reading and Writing

To help students strengthen the emotional impact of their writing, review pp. 259–260 in the Reading Workshop. Then, have students examine the author's use of emotional appeals with reasons and evidence in **A Writer's Model**. Note how the use of emotional appeal helps make the reader sympathetic to the writer's position.

Cooperative Learning

Analyze a Thesis. To help students understand the development of a thesis, have them analyze the Declaration of Independence, which is an example of a persuasive essay. Distribute copies of the document to random groups of four or five students. Using the framework outlined on p. 272, have students identify the different parts of a persuasive essay. Students may present their analysis as a graphic organizer similar to that on p. 266.

Writing, pp. 272–275
Alignments
TEKS 1A, 1B, 1C, 2B, 8A
TAAS W1, W2, W4
English II End-of-Course 4

(continued)

CONCLUSION
Restatement of opinion/summary of reasons

Emotional appeal

Call to action

with solid-waste disposal and landfill cleanup.

Much of what is thrown away now <u>can</u> be recycled—and recycling is the best way to preserve natural resources and to reduce the costs of processing all the garbage. Anyone who loves the earth can help make it a better place by recycling. Garbage makes our shared home, this planet, less livable for the people of today and for the children of tomorrow. People have caused this garbage crisis, and only people can solve it. Do you care enough to do your part by recycling?

A Student's Model

The following persuasive essay is by Katie Baker of Holmes High School in Covington, Kentucky. She begins the essay by stating her opinion and listing three reasons for it in the introduction. Notice how she then focuses each body paragraph on one of the reasons.

Uniforms Reduce Problems

Students enrolled in a public high school should be required to wear a school uniform. Many studies show that when school-uniform policies are put into place, there is an improvement in both attitude and schoolwork. Wearing uniforms would also reduce clothing costs and many problems related to competition in dress. *[Statement of opinion (thesis); Overview of 3 reasons]*

Mrs. Chung, a principal at a high school, conducted research on the results of wearing uniforms. She said, "In the past two or three years, several schools in the nation have begun to require a school uniform. All of these schools are reporting improved student grades and improved student behavior." *[Support for reason 1]*

Uniforms are also less expensive than regular clothing. An outfit for a student can easily cost sixty dollars. A uniform would cost fifty-four dollars or less and would save money. This would be especially helpful to families on a low budget. *[Support for reason 2]*

Last, uniforms would reduce the competition in dress among students. Students who do not have as much money as others would not have to be embarrassed about their parents' income. *[Support for reason 3]*

Uniforms would not cause a threat to a student's individual freedom because there are lots of other things that make you "you" besides clothing. *[Response to opposing arguments]* Wearing uniforms would reduce many problems and would improve grades and behavior. Therefore, students enrolled in public high school should be required to wear a school uniform. *[Restatement of opinion]*

Critical Thinking

Evaluation. Challenge students to use the framework from p. 272 to evaluate the model on this page. How well does the author meet the criteria given in the framework? What would students do differently, and why? Discuss with students their evaluations and suggest that they keep their insights in mind as they evaluate their own papers.

Quotation for the Day

❝What makes me happy is rewriting. In the first draft you get your ideas and your theme clear . . . But the next time through it's like cleaning house, getting rid of all the junk, getting things in the right order, tightening things up.❞

(Ellen Goodman, 1941– , American columnist)

Ask students to share their approaches to revising: what they eliminate, what they add, how they reorder their ideas, what they do to tighten their writing. Point out that the revision stage is a time to bring a topic into sharper focus and to eliminate anything that weakens the development of the position.

TEACHING TIP

▶ **Elaboration**
Remind students that elaboration helps readers make connections between opinions, reasons, and evidence, and takes ideas a step further by making them personal or more understandable.

Meeting INDIVIDUAL NEEDS

ENGLISH-LANGUAGE LEARNERS
General Strategies. When helping students with their first drafts, avoid correcting every grammatical error. Instead, pay strict attention to content and organization to help students focus on what they are saying. You might state the main idea of each paragraph to help each student notice how the essay as a whole is organized. Once the content and organization of their essays are clear, students can work on grammar.

Revising

Evaluate and Revise Your Draft

Perfecting Your Persuasive Essay Read your whole essay carefully at least twice. During the first reading, use the guidelines below to evaluate and revise **content** and **organization**. When you read the second time, use the guidelines on page 277 to evaluate and revise for **style**.

▶ **First Reading: Content and Organization** The chart below will help you evaluate and revise your writing. First, work collaboratively to answer the questions in the left-hand column. If you need help in answering, refer to the tips in the middle column. Then, make the changes suggested in the right-hand column.

Persuasive Essay: Content and Organization Guidelines for Peer and Self-Evaluation

Evaluation Questions	Tips	Revision Techniques
❶ Does the beginning grab the reader's attention, include necessary background information, and provide a clear opinion statement?	▶ **Put brackets** around any sentence that is intended to get the reader interested. **Put a check mark** by any background information. **Circle** the writer's opinion. If any of these parts is missing, revise.	▶ **Add** an interesting statement, question, or anecdote. **Add** background facts the reader would need to understand the issue. **Elaborate** on background. **Add** an opinion statement.
❷ Are there adequate reasons and sufficient evidence to support the opinion statement?	▶ **Underline** each reason. **Number** the sentences that provide evidence for each reason. If underlining or numbers are missing, revise.	▶ **Add** reasons or **elaborate** on existing reasons. **Add** evidence (facts, statistics, expert opinions, anecdotes, and examples) that supports them. **Cut** any unnecessary sentences.
❸ Are opposing arguments addressed?	▶ **Put a plus sign** by any sentence that anticipates and responds to an opposing argument. If a plus sign is missing, revise.	▶ **Add** sentences that identify and convincingly respond to opposing arguments. **Elaborate** on existing responses.
❹ If appropriate, does the paper contain any emotional appeals?	▶ **Put the letter E** by emotional appeals. If you have none, revise—only if appropriate.	▶ **Add** connotative words and examples that will appeal to the reader's emotions.
❺ Is the writer's opinion restated in an effective conclusion? If appropriate, does the conclusion include a call to action?	▶ **Put a box** around the sentence that restates the writer's opinion. **Highlight** any call to action. If either part is missing, revise.	▶ **Add** a sentence that restates your position. **Rewrite** your conclusion to make it effective. **Add** a call to action (if appropriate).

276 Chapter 7 Persuasion: Persuading Others

RESOURCES

Revising
Practice
■ *Communications,*
TPs. 57, 58, WS. pp. 132, 133, 134

Extension
■ *Designing Your Writing*

ONE WRITER'S REVISIONS Here is how one writer used the guidelines to revise part of the persuasive essay on page 273. Look over the revisions and answer the questions that follow.

> Recycling more of our garbage can also save precious resources. Every week, for example, ^fifty thousand^ trees are ~~used~~ ^sacrificed^ to produce Sunday newspapers in the United States. By recycling newspapers, we can ~~make a difference~~ ^rescue trees from destruction^.

add, replace

replace

Analyzing the Revision Process

1. Why did the writer add information to the second sentence?
2. Why do you think the writer replaced the word *used* and the phrase *make a difference*?

 Focusing on Content and Organization

Revise your persuasive essay using the content and organization guidelines on the previous page. Use the revisions above as a model.

PEER REVIEW

Work collaboratively to peer edit. Ask a classmate to read your persuasive essay and to answer the following questions:

1. What was convincing about the way the writer supported his or her opinion?
2. How did the writer appeal to your emotions?

▶ **Second Reading: Style**   Your first reading focused on your content and organization. Your second reading will focus on style. One common stylistic error that writers often make is overuse of **passive-voice verbs**. The way to correct this error is to replace passive-voice verbs with their **active-voice** counterparts (verbs expressing action done by the subject). Using the active voice in a persuasive essay makes your writing direct, forceful, and authoritative—in short, more persuasive. Use the following style guidelines to replace passive-voice verbs in your writing.

Style Guidelines

Evaluation Question	▶ Tip	▶ Revision Technique
Does the essay contain too many passive-voice verbs?	**Underline** each *be* verb (*am, is, are, was, were, be, being, been*) in the essay. Do not underline *be* verbs used to express a state of being. Do not underline *be* verbs in quotations.	**Reword** two thirds of your passive-voice verbs so that the subject of the sentence performs the verb.

Writing Workshop

Analyzing the Revision Process

ANSWERS
Possible answers follow.

1. The writer added information to provide concrete supporting evidence.
2. The writer replaced the words to make an emotional appeal with words that have strong connotations.

Check to see whether students have marked their essays according to the tips in the **Content and Organization Guidelines** chart on p. 276. To make sure that students do not simply recopy the draft as a final copy, ask that they submit lists of their revisions with their essays.

Cooperative Learning (5B)

Peer Review. Point out to students that peer review is a powerful tool to help a writer communicate ideas to an audience. Peer review should always be constructive—that is, intended to help the writer improve the work. Likewise, the writer should always respond productively, thanking the reviewer for his or her help and considering seriously each suggestion the reviewer makes. Allow students to practice these skills by pairing students together to review one another's drafts. Tell students to make at least one suggestion the writers can use to improve their papers.

Revising, pp. 276–279
Alignments
TEKS 2B, 2C, 2E, 3B, 4D, 5A, 5B
TAAS W1, W2, W3, W6, W7
English II End-of-Course 4, 5, 6

Focus on Sentences

Active and Passive Voice

A verb in the **active voice** expresses an action performed *by* the subject of the sentence. A verb in the **passive voice** expresses an action done *to* the subject of the sentence. In the passive voice, the verb always contains a form of *be* (such as *am, is, are, was,* or *were*) and a past participle form of the main verb (such as *flooded* or *estimated*). As the examples below show, the active voice is generally more compelling, while the passive voice often seems weak.

Passive Voice   The earth **is polluted** by people.
[This sentence seems weak because it fails to emphasize who does the polluting.]

Active Voice   People **pollute** the earth.
[This sentence is more compelling because it clearly emphasizes who pollutes—people.]

TIP You do not have to use the active voice all of the time. You might use the passive voice when
- you do not know who performed the action
- you do not want to reveal the performer
- you want to emphasize the receiver of the action

ONE WRITER'S REVISIONS Here is how the writer of the model persuasive essay on page 273 revised a part of his draft.

BEFORE REVISION
Our shared home, this planet, <u>is</u> made less livable for people and for the children of tomorrow by garbage. This garbage crisis <u>was</u> caused by people, and it can only <u>be</u> solved by people.

The underlined be *verbs could signal the use of passive voice.*

AFTER REVISION
Garbage makes our shared home less livable for the people of today and for the children of tomorrow. People caused this garbage crisis, and only people can solve it.

Both sentences now are in the active voice.

Reference Note
For more on **active voice,** see page 601.

Analyzing the Revision Process
1. Why are the sentences with active-voice verbs more effective?
2. Why might these revisions be especially important in the conclusion of a persuasive essay?

278   Chapter 7   Persuasion: Persuading Others

Analyzing the Revision Process
ANSWERS
Possible answers follow.

1. The sentences are more effective because garbage and people, the focus of the paper, are prominently featured as the subjects of the sentences.

2. The revisions are important because the sentences now emphasize that people can take action on the problem the author is describing.

RESOURCES
Focus on Sentences
Practice
- *Communications,* WS. p. 135

TIP Use a word-processing program's *Find* command to look for *be* verbs (*am, is, are, was, were,* etc.). When you find one, check to see if it is part of a passive-voice construction that you might want to make active.

YOUR TURN 7 — Focusing on Style

Revise the style of your essay. Use the guidelines on page 277 to eliminate any overuse of passive-voice verbs.

Designing Your Writing

Using Visuals You know that support is essential to any persuasive essay: Readers will more likely agree with a writer's position if opinions are supported by plenty of relevant reasons and evidence. To make your support more appealing and clearer to readers, you could present this information in visuals such as graphs, charts, tables, or pictures. These tools might make it easier for readers to grasp statistics and other factual information. Here are some suggestions to make your support stand out:

- **Put statistical information in a chart or table.** Sometimes numbers and other statistical information are easier to read and to compare when presented in a chart or table.

- **Use pie charts and bar graphs to illustrate compared amounts, times, or dates.** You could clearly illustrate, for instance, the proportions of waste products produced by Americans every year. Most word-processing programs include a tool for creating graphs.

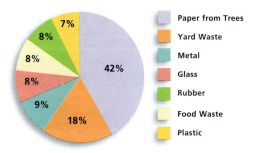

- **If appropriate, include photographs or drawings to support an opinion and possibly to appeal to readers' emotions.** For instance, a picture of mountains of garbage would be appropriate to illustrate the results of not recycling.

Quotation for the Day

"Words are but the signs of ideas."

(Samuel Johnson, 1709–1784, English writer, lexicographer, and essayist)

Write the quotation on the chalkboard and discuss how words communicate ideas. Suggest to students that errors in grammar, spelling, punctuation, capitalization, and usage make it difficult to understand words and the ideas they convey.

Grammar Link
Double Negatives

ANSWERS
Possible answers follow.

1. The school library does not have any computers for student use.
2. The football team was so muddy that you could not see any of the numbers on their uniforms.
3. The bus had a flat tire, and the driver could not do anything about it.
4. When school is out for the summer, there is scarcely anyone on the campus.
5. Most high school seniors can hardly wait for college.

Publishing

Proofread Your Persuasive Essay

Reference Note
For more on finding and correcting **double negatives**, see page 656.

Last Look Now that you have polished the content, organization, and style of your essay, proofread it to be sure it conforms to the **conventions of written language**—in other words, that it is free of grammar, spelling, and punctuation errors. Take special note of whether you have included any double negatives.

Grammar Link

Double Negatives

A **double negative** is the use of two negative words in one sentence when one will do. If you use double negatives, you end up delivering a message that is the opposite of what you intend—which could be disastrous in persuasive writing. Here are two simple rules that will help you find and correct double negatives.

1. **Do not use *no*, *none*, *nothing*, *not*, or *–n't* with another negative word.**

Nonstandard	There is not no reason to close the beach. (If there is not *no* reason, then there must be *some* reason.)
Standard	There is no reason to close the beach.
Standard	There is not any reason to close the beach.

2. **Do not use the words *hardly* or *scarcely* with another negative word.**

Nonstandard	The swimmer could not hardly finish the race.
Standard	The swimmer could hardly finish the race.
Nonstandard	There is not scarcely enough in this glass to cover the bottom.
Standard	There is scarcely enough in this glass to cover the bottom.

PRACTICE

Each of the following sentences contains a double negative. Rewrite each sentence to correct the double negative, being careful not to change the intended meaning. Write your answers on your own paper.

1. The school library does not have no computers for student use.
2. The football team was so muddy that you could not see none of the numbers on their uniforms.
3. The bus had a flat tire, and the driver could not do nothing about it.
4. When school is out for the summer, there is not scarcely anyone on the campus.
5. Most high school seniors cannot hardly wait for college.

RESOURCES

Grammar Link
Practice
- *Communications*, WS. p. 136

Publish Your Persuasive Essay

Have Your Say Persuasive writing is meant to be shared. Here are some ways you might share your persuasive essay with an audience.

- Send your persuasive essay to an organization interested in your issue or empowered to make the changes called for in your essay.
- Submit your persuasive essay to your school newspaper or to a newspaper or magazine that publishes articles on issues like yours.
- If possible, try to get your essay published on a Web page.

TIP If you wish to publish your essay for a more specific audience (a local organization, for example) than you originally intended, you may need to refine your essay a bit. Keep in mind what your audience knows and how they might be convinced.

PORTFOLIO

Reflect on Your Persuasive Essay

Taking a Deeper Look Every time you write and reflect on your writing, you can learn something new. To reflect on what you have learned in this workshop, provide short responses to these questions.

- What difficulties did you have finding reasons to support your opinion, or evidence to support your reasons? How did you solve these problems?
- What revisions do you think strengthened your essay the most? Why?

Use your responses to these questions to help you **evaluate your writing** and **set future goals as a writer**.

YOUR TURN 8 Proofreading, Publishing, and Reflecting

Review each of the steps discussed in this section. Before you turn in your persuasive essay, remember to

- proofread it carefully, looking for double negatives
- consider publishing options
- reflect on the skills you used to create your persuasive essay

BORN LOSER reprinted by permission of Newspaper Enterprise Association, Inc.

Writing Workshop **281**

MINI-LESSON: TEST TAKING

Analyzing a Writing Prompt

Many writing tests begin with a set of directions, called a **prompt,** for which you are asked to write a response. A prompt usually specifies the topic and form you should use, along with the audience and purpose for which you should write.

In order to be successful on a writing test, you must analyze the prompt to understand *exactly* what you are being asked to write. If you misread or misunderstand a prompt, your score will not be as high as it could be—no matter how well written your response is. Looking for key words or phrases in the prompt—such as *write* or *explain*—will help you be successful. Also, be aware that words and phrases such as *think about* and *include* are actually clues to the required information. Here is an example of a typical writing prompt.

> You have a new principal in your school. She has asked for input about changes to make the school better. Think about the change you want to suggest, and write a letter to persuade your principal to make the change at your school. Remember to include the reasons for the change and the supporting evidence for your reasons.

THINKING IT THROUGH: Analyzing a Prompt

The following steps will help you analyze writing prompts.

1. **Read through the entire prompt.** Start by getting a general idea of what is being asked of you.

2. **Re-read the prompt, noticing key words and phrases that signal four specific requirements for your writing:**
   - the *topic:* the specific subject you are asked to address
   - the *form:* the shape and structure of the writing—for example, a letter or an essay
   - the *purpose:* the reason for writing—for example, to inform or to persuade
   - the *audience:* the intended reader of your writing—for example, another student, a reader of a local newspaper, or a teacher

   Example:
   Then, write a letter [**form**] to persuade [**purpose**] your principal [**audience**] to make the change at your school [**topic**].

3. **Jot down, underline, or highlight the required elements signaled by the key words or phrases you discovered.**

   Topic: the change that I think should be made at the school
   Form: a letter
   Purpose: to persuade
   Audience: the school principal

Test Taking
Alignments
TEKS 1A, 1B, 2A
TAAS W1
English II End-of-Course 4

RESOURCES
Test Taking
Practice
- *Communications,* WS. p. 137

Connections to Life

Writing Letters of Application

One practical form of persuasive writing is a letter of application. Here are some guidelines for effective letters of application.

Opinion   State why you think you are the best person to choose.

Reasons   Provide reasons why you believe you are the right person.

Evidence   Back up your reasons with details about your education and experience. You might also include a professional recommendation.

The model letter below is in response to a classified job ad in a city newspaper.

6523 Farley Road
Duluth, MN 55807
January 23, 2001

Michael Chumchal
Michael's Photography
1371 Gault Street
Duluth, MN 55805

Dear Mr. Chumchal:

    I believe that I am an ideal candidate for the job of photographer's assistant you recently advertised in *The City Gazette*.
    I have academic qualifications. I take photography classes at Jackson High School, and I am president of the school photography club.
    I completed a work/study program last semester with Superior Photography and am a photographer for the school newspaper.
    Please let me know if you need more information.

Sincerely yours,

Isabel Tovar
Isabel Tovar

— **Opinion Statement**

— **Reason and evidence**

— **Reason and evidence**

YOUR TURN 9 — Writing a Letter of Application

Choose a classified job ad from a local newspaper. Then, use the information at the top of the page to write a letter of application for the job.

TECHNOLOGY TIP

Have students use a computer to compose and print their letters. Remind students that accuracy and neatness are important to employers. Using a word-processing program will allow students to check and correct spelling and will produce professional-looking documents. Students may also wish to save the letters on disk for future use.

YOUR TURN 9

Have students meet with partners to evaluate each other's letters. Students should check for an opinion statement, reasons, evidence, and correct letter form in their classmates' letters. Ask them also to respond to the following questions: Would this letter persuade you to hire the applicant? Why or why not?

Connections to Life
Alignments
TEKS   1A, 1B, 1C, 2A
TAAS   W1, W2, W4
English II End-of-Course   4

Writing Workshop

Focus on Viewing and Representing

OBJECTIVES

- To analyze an editorial cartoon
- To identify symbolism
- To understand exaggeration and caricature
- To find and interpret analogies
- To recognize irony

TEACHING TIP

What Is an Editorial Cartoon?
Ask the school librarian for help in creating a file of editorial cartoons of interest to students. Students may refer to the file for additional examples of editorial cartoons. Students who do not have access to a newspaper may use cartoons from the file to complete **Your Turn 10**.

Quotation for the Day

" By persuading others, we convince ourselves. "

(Junius, pseudonym of the author of "The Letters of Junius," a series of letters printed in the London *Public Advertiser* during the years 1769–1771)

Discuss with students what this quotation means. Ask students to consider whether this would apply to someone designing an editorial cartoon. [Students may say that in order to draw such a cartoon, the artist would have to have a strong opinion about an issue already. Therefore, the artist would be convinced before trying to persuade others.]

Focus on Viewing and Representing

WHAT'S AHEAD?

In this section, you will analyze an editorial cartoon. You will also learn how to

- identify symbolism
- understand exaggeration and caricature
- find and interpret analogies
- recognize irony

Analyzing Editorial Cartoons

Here is a riddle for you: When are cartoons not funny? Answer: When they are editorial cartoons that you don't understand. On the comics page of your newspaper, the cartoons are meant only to entertain, and the humor is easy to recognize. However, editorial cartoons, sometimes called political cartoons, can be completely different.

What is an Editorial Cartoon?

Editorial cartoons are illustrations. Located in the editorial section, sometimes called the Op-Ed section, of newspapers, they are designed to make you think about current issues and to sway you toward the cartoonist's point of view. If you understand the techniques used to create them, you will have a better chance of getting the point and appreciating the humor. Here are some common elements of editorial cartoons:

- **Symbolism:** Using a picture to stand for a more abstract concept
- **Exaggeration/Caricature:** Overstating an aspect of a problem or exaggerating a person's physical features
- **Analogy:** Comparing two things; for instance, directly or indirectly comparing a situation or event with a historical or fictional event
- **Irony:** Contrasting (often humorously) between appearance or expectation and reality

Symbolism Instead of using several words or sentences to convey an idea, editorial cartoonists often use symbolism. They use pictures as symbols for larger ideas, people, organizations, and so on.

Exaggeration/Caricature Exaggeration and caricature are tools that editorial cartoonists use to make their opinions clear. Without exaggeration and caricature, the cartoonist's opinion might not be clear enough, or the problem might not be obvious. In the example that appears

284   Chapter 7   **Persuasion:** Persuading Others

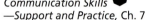

RESOURCES

Focus on Viewing and Representing
Practice

- *Media Literacy and Communication Skills*
  —*Support and Practice*, Ch. 7
  —*A How-to Handbook*

Teaching Notes

- *Media Literacy and Communication Skills*
  —*A Teacher's Guide*, Ch. 7

to the right, Mr. Spock from the *Star Trek* series is made to have ears that extend above his head. The cartoonist does this to exaggerate the fact that Mr. Spock has large ears.

Analogy Like symbolism, an analogy can often express an idea that might otherwise take many words to describe or explain. It is sometimes easier to describe a situation or event by comparing it to a historical or fictional situation or event.

Irony Cartoonists often use irony to emphasize a point because it suggests the absurdity of a problem.

Other Elements Editorial cartoons may include **dialogue bubbles** (bubbles in which the characters' speech appears), **captions,** and **labels** to make clear to the reader what people and objects are being represented. For instance, the camera-toting monkeys in the cartoon on page 287 would look confusing if the evil castle were not labeled "Tabloids."

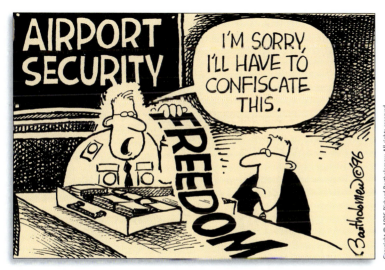

Personal freedom and civil rights are two of the concepts often treated in editorial cartoons. In the cartoon above, the cartoonist **exaggerates** the security worker's job by having him confiscate the man's freedom. Here, the word *freedom* **symbolizes** the idea of personal freedom. The cartoonist is suggesting that airport security measures have gone too far and that travelers' personal freedoms are being taken away.

The man in the cartoon above is seeking clean air in a world filled with smog. It is **ironic** that the only source for this clean air is at a gas station that fuels the cars that cause the pollution in the first place. It is also **ironic** that the air is intended to fill the tires of cars and not the lungs of people. The cartoonist **exaggerates** the problem of air pollution by filling the frame with smog and by suggesting that the man's only source for clean air is from a gas station air machine.

This cartoon on academics and sports recruiting also uses **exaggeration** to illustrate its point that colleges recruiting athletes do not care enough about the education an athlete receives. Notice that the cartoonist uses a **label** on the recruiter's briefcase to tell readers who is being represented in the cartoon.

The cartoon above **exaggerates** the problem of privacy-invading photographers sent out by tabloid newspapers (the kind you find at supermarket checkouts) by making an **analogy** between them and the flying monkeys from the movie *The Wizard of Oz*. In the movie, the monkeys are portrayed as evil and menacing, which is how many people view tabloid photographers.

YOUR TURN 10 Analyzing an Editorial Cartoon

Find an example of an editorial cartoon in a newspaper, and briefly analyze it by answering the following questions on your own paper. Then, share and discuss your cartoon and analysis with a group of two or three classmates.

- What is the issue addressed in the cartoon? What do you think is the cartoonist's opinion about the issue?
- Which techniques (symbolism, exaggeration/caricature, analogy, or irony) are used in the cartoon?
- Is the cartoon humorous? What makes it humorous?
- What is another opinion a person could have about the issue treated in the cartoon? How could the cartoon be revised to communicate that opinion?

Timesaver

Keep a file of editorial cartoons from both newspapers and magazines. Using preselected cartoons will save you time grading students' analyses, since you will already understand the cartoon's issue and techniques.

YOUR TURN 10

You may wish to collect and review students' responses to the questions. Each group might revise one cartoon to represent another opinion and then share both cartoons on an overhead transparency.

Wrap It Up

Metacognition. Have students reflect on what is involved in analyzing editorial cartoons. Then, ask them to respond to the following questions.

1. What problems did you encounter in understanding editorial cartoons?
2. How might you overcome these problems?

Finally, ask students to answer the question below.

3. What are four common elements of editorial cartoons? [symbolism, exaggeration/caricature, analogy, irony]

RESOURCES

Your Turn 10

Practice and Reinforcement

- *Media Literacy and Communication Skills —Support and Practice,* Ch. 7, transparencies and worksheets

Focus on Speaking and Listening

Giving a Persuasive Speech

OBJECTIVES
- To give a persuasive speech
- To use logical and emotional appeals
- To improve speaking style
- To evaluate a persuasive speech

Quotation for the Day

"It takes two to speak the truth—one to speak, and another to hear."

(Henry David Thoreau, 1817–1862, American writer and naturalist)

Read the quotation aloud to the class and discuss the importance of an audience to a speaker. Ask students to relate their experiences as part of an audience at a public speech. What made the speech memorable? Did the speaker convince them to think in a certain way or do something?

TEACHING TIP

A Recipe for Success   17A, 17B, 17C

Explain to students that giving a persuasive speech has the same goal as writing a persuasive essay—to present an opinion and provide evidence to support that opinion. Review the relationship between the terms used in the Writing Workshop and the terms mentioned in this section by using the following chart.

Writing Workshop	Focus on Speaking and Listening
opinion statement	thesis
reasons	claims, arguments
logical appeals	logical appeals
facts, statistics, expert opinions	proofs
emotional appeals	emotional appeals

WHAT'S AHEAD?

In this section, you will give a persuasive speech. You will also learn how to
- use logical and emotional appeals
- improve your speaking style
- evaluate a persuasive speech

Cellular phones, e-mail, satellite dishes; no matter how many advancements are made in communications technology, the spoken word remains the most powerful persuasive force of all. Whether they come from a politician making a campaign speech at your local community center or from a news anchor hosting a televised round-table debate on a hot issue, spoken words have enormous impact. Although making a speech can be scary, it does not have to be. Giving a speech is a way to make your words come alive and give color and depth to an issue.

Persuasive Speech

Match Topic to Task   When you are faced with giving a persuasive speech, your first consideration must be your **task**. Your task might be to give a speech assigned by your teacher or to speak as a candidate for student council. You need to know the exact requirements of the task set forth by your teacher or required by the **occasion** of your speech. Occasion refers not only to such physical considerations as time, location, availability of audiovisuals, and time limits, but also to real-life events that might prompt your speech, such as a serious accident prompting you to speak on the need for a new traffic light. Once you have considered task and occasion you can select a topic to match, preferably one about which you have definite opinions. You might wish to adapt material from the persuasive essay you wrote in the Writer's Workshop for your persuasive speech.

A Recipe for Success   Because the purpose of your speech is to convince the members of your audience to think or do something, it is important that you tailor your speech to them. You need to decide upon your **thesis, support,** and **tone** with them in mind.

Thesis   The **thesis** of your speech states your position on the issue. How you state this position depends on your audience. For instance, here are

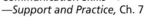

288   Chapter 7   Persuasion: Persuading Others

RESOURCES

Focus on Speaking and Listening
Practice
- *Media Literacy and Communication Skills*
  —*Support and Practice,* Ch. 7
  —*A How-to Handbook*

Teaching Notes
- *Media Literacy and Communication Skills*
  —*A Teacher's Guide,* Ch. 7

two thesis statements for a speech adapted to two different audiences.

Bikers: Motorcycle helmets save your lives and should be required by law.

Lawmakers: You are helping to make streets safer by passing a law to require bikers to wear motorcycle helmets.

Support No one is going to be convinced if you don't back up your thesis with convincing claims or arguments. You can use two persuasive techniques to support your thesis:

- **Logical appeals.** Even a skeptical audience will be convinced when you support your thesis with solid reasons and support those reasons with **valid proofs** from **reliable sources**.
- **Emotional appeals.** To affect the audience's feelings so that they will agree with you, use statements that arouse strong feelings—pleasure, anger, joy, sadness, and so forth.

No matter how you choose to support your thesis, your presentation should demonstrate that you are informed and concerned. Your purpose is to persuade, but your obligation is to be accurate, truthful, and ethical.

Tone The tone of your speech reflects your attitude toward your topic and your audience. You indicate tone in speech not only by your choice of words, but by facial expressions, physical gestures, and your **tone of voice**. Depending upon your audience and your topic, your tone might be dignified, respectful, ironic, or a combination of these and more. For example, if you are trying to persuade your city council of the need for a recreation center for teenagers, you would probably want to use objective, mature language and a dignified, sincere, and respectful tone of voice.

Once you decide upon your thesis, support, and tone, you must organize your speech. Persuasive speeches are usually organized according to one of two approaches. With the **deductive** approach, you state your thesis first, then deliver your reasons and support. With the **inductive** approach, you present reasons and support first, building to a thesis statement.

Practice Makes Perfect To ensure that your speech runs smoothly and to avoid embarrassment, you will need to be well rehearsed. If you are prepared, you will be less likely to be unnerved. In addition, thorough rehearsal will help you to develop the best nonverbal behavior and vocal skills for your particular speech and audience. Just be sure to practice in front of an audience so that you can get used to speaking in front of a group and to use your visuals as you practice delivering your speech. If you will use them during your speech, practice using your note cards. Also, experiment with a timer or watch as you practice to ensure that you stay within a certain time limit.

> **TIP** To make your speech as persuasive as possible, you should use **effective language**, language that is appropriate for your topic and your audience. To emphasize particular points, you can use **rhetorical strategies** such as **repetition** (saying exact words more than once), **restatement** (using different words to repeat an idea or point), **parallelism** (rhythmically repeating words, phrases, clauses, or sentences to emphasize a point), and **announcement** or **sign-posting** (emphasizing a point by announcing its importance).

Critical Thinking

Analysis. Ask student pairs to analyze the rhetorical strategies used in live or recorded professional speeches. You might suggest Dr. Martin Luther King, Jr.'s "I Have a Dream" speech or one of Franklin Delano Roosevelt's or Winston Churchill's World War II speeches. After students present their analyses to the class, they should then incorporate these language and rhetorical strategies in their speeches.

TEACHING TIP

Tone

Students may have the greatest difficulty in adapting their tone to their audience. Tell students that a speech's tone comes from the speaker's verbal and nonverbal behavior, elements of which are given in the charts on p. 290. Another part of the tone lies in the structure of the speech's sentences, which should probably be shorter, more direct, and more full of examples, images, and connotative language than the sentences of a written paper. To help students gauge the connotations of words, encourage them to use a graphic such as the one below to determine the best word from a spectrum of possibilities.

Negative	Neutral	Positive
criminal	unlawful	rule-bending

Focus on Speaking and Listening, pp. 288–292
Alignments
TEKS 14A, 14B, 15C, 16A, 16B, 16C, 16D, 17A, 17B, 17C, 17D, 17E, 17F

Cooperative Learning

Improving Delivery. Some students may write good speeches but have trouble with delivery. Pair these students with students who have strong speaking skills. Have the partners deliver the speeches to their writers. This approach will help writers see the power of their ideas and possibly ways to improve delivery.

Critical Thinking

Metacognition. If equipment is available, videotape each speaker and put the tapes on reserve in the school library or media center for viewing. Have students evaluate their own speeches according to the criteria in the charts on this page, listing and explaining the three strongest features of their presentation. Then, have students list three areas that could be improved and describe how they would work on them. If time allows, you might want students to retape their speeches and compare the two presentations.

TIP Avoid making unjust attacks or exaggerations about the opposing side, as the audience will rapidly lose faith in your ethics, or moral standards.

Seeing and Hearing Nonverbal behavior can affect the impact you have on your audience as much as your words can. **Nonverbal behavior** includes eye contact, facial expressions, gestures, and posture. The chart below shows the important points to keep in mind for nonverbal behavior.

Appearance	Good appearance, in both your clothing and your grooming, is not going to guarantee a good speech, but poor appearance can lessen your chances of achieving your goal.
Eye Contact	Eye contact means direct visual contact with the eyes of the people in your audience. The key is to look at someone or some group at all times—for instance, for a few seconds talk to people on the left side of the front row; then talk to people at the right rear, and so on.
Facial Expressions	Concentrate on what you are saying, not on the fact that you are giving a speech. Avoid the deadpan expression—an expressionless facial appearance, and avoid a conflicting expression—a facial expression that does not match your words or actual feelings.
Effective Gestures	Use the same natural gestures that you use in ordinary conversation.
Good Posture	Stand up straight with both feet firmly on the ground. Good posture creates an impression of confidence and authority.

Verbal behavior, or your speaking skill, is another factor that can determine how persuasive you are. The way you use your voice plays a major role in your success as a speaker. The chart below shows important elements of good verbal behavior.

Enthusiasm	You should show **enthusiasm**—a strong positive feeling for your topic—through your voice. Listeners who believe that a speaker is enthusiastic will become enthusiastic themselves.
Vocalized Pauses	**Vocalized pauses**—the meaningless sounds speakers use to fill time—weaken your effectiveness. Some common pauses are *uh, well uh, um,* and *you know*.
Enunciation	**Enunciation** refers to the distinctness of the sounds you make. Be sure your enunciation is clear and precise. Sloppy enunciation, such as saying *gunna* for *going to,* causes problems for the audience.
Vocalization	Speak at the **pitch** (highness or lowness of sound) at which you feel the least strain and have the best resonance. Practice controlling your speaking **volume**, the loudness or intensity of speech. Don't speak too softly or too loudly. Practice speaking at a steady **rate**, neither too quickly nor too slowly. Your audience should not have to struggle to keep up with you; neither should they seem to be impatient for you to speed up.

Becoming the Listener

Evaluating Time   To evaluate the effectiveness of an essay, you have to consider only the words on the page. However, evaluating a speech is a little more complicated. After all, a speech involves not only words but also a speaker. To decide if a classmate's persuasive speech (or your own) is effective, you must consider the **message** and **delivery**.

Get the Goods   In order to evaluate a speech's **content**, you must become a **critical listener**. It is easy to focus on a speaker's voice or mannerisms and miss what the person actually says. It is also important to remember that a polished delivery does not guarantee good content, and a poor delivery can mask valid thoughts and ideas. The ability to distinguish between content and delivery is an important life skill. As you focus your attention to listen, use the following questions to analyze the speech.

- What is the speaker's message—his or her opinion? Was it stated clearly?
- Does the speaker adequately support this opinion or claim?
- Does the speaker use valid logical appeals?
- Does the speaker use emotional appeals appropriately?
- Does the speaker use the **conventions of oral language** effectively?

Special Delivery   Is a clearly stated, well supported opinion all it takes to convince you? Probably not. A speech must also be delivered well to be effective. Your reaction to a speaker's **delivery** is probably immediate and instinctive. You stifle a yawn, make a mental list of things to do when you get home, or sit up and take notice. Many elements of delivery combine to have this effect. To evaluate a speaker's delivery, ask yourself the following questions as you listen.

- Does the speaker make eye contact with the audience and use natural facial expressions?
- Does the speaker show enthusiasm?
- Does the speaker avoid vocalized pauses and enunciate words distinctly?
- Are the pitch and volume of the speech appropriate?
- Does the speaker have a good pace?

Is critical listening just a classroom skill? Of course not. In addition to evaluating your classmates' speeches, you can also use the preceding questions about content and delivery to evaluate media presentations and live speeches by public figures.

Cooperative Learning

Evaluating Others. Show students a tape of a persuasive speech by someone in their community or some other public figure. Ask students to meet in small groups to evaluate the speech using the same questions they asked when evaluating their peers and themselves. If the speaker uses visuals, students may ask additional questions such as these: Are the visuals clear and easy to see? How do the visuals support the speaker's position? Groups may share their critique with the class, replaying the tape as necessary to point out the parts of the speech that support their evaluation.

YOUR TURN 11

Before delivering their speeches to the class, students should rehearse, applying the feedback they received from the small group of their classmates. Use the criteria in the charts on p. 290 to evaluate students' speeches, alerting students in advance of additional criteria you might use to grade their speeches.

Wrap It Up

Metacognition. Ask students to reflect on what they have learned by giving and evaluating a persuasive speech. Prompt students with the questions below.

1. What did you like most about giving a speech? least?
2. What did you learn about persuasive speaking from others' speeches?

Then, ask students the following questions.

3. What are some examples of nonverbal behavior? verbal behavior? [nonverbal: appearance, eye contact, facial expressions, gestures, posture; verbal: enthusiasm, vocalized pauses, enunciation, pitch, volume, rate]

Fair Play A special problem in evaluating a persuasive speech is judging the speech based on the opinion it expresses. Imagine that you are an active member of a community group that promotes the spaying and neutering of pets. One of your classmates gives a persuasive speech titled "Neuter or Spay—It's the Only Way." You obviously agree with the speech before the speaker has even opened her mouth. You might also be tempted to say that she gave a good speech because you agree with it. Try to put aside your opinion and focus on the speech itself to make a fair evaluation.

Support Your Local Speaker When you evaluate a speech, put yourself in the speaker's shoes. Be aware that the speaker and audience are constantly sending one another signals. Do you think that a speaker can give exactly the same speech to a polite, interested audience and a rude, bored audience? Chances are that the better audience will hear the better speech. Here are some things you can do to give speakers a better chance of success.

- Welcome each speaker with enthusiasm.
- Focus your attention to look at the speaker and be willing to make eye contact.
- Let your natural reactions to the speech show on your face and in your body language. If you look puzzled, then the speaker will have a chance to clarify the point.
- Note any questions that occur to you, and save them for the question and answer period.

Feedback Loop Use feedback from your classmates to evaluate the effectiveness of your speech. What parts of your speech worked well? What needed improvement? Then set goals for the content and delivery of your next speech.

YOUR TURN 11 — Practicing, Delivering, and Evaluating a Persuasive Speech

Create and deliver a persuasive speech. Practice your speech in front of a few classmates before presenting it to your entire class. When it's time to deliver the speeches, use the preceding questions to help you evaluate your own and others' speech presentations.

RESOURCES

Your Turn 11

Practice and Reinforcement

- *Media Literacy and Communication Skills*
  —*Support and Practice,* Ch. 7, transparencies and worksheets
  —Videocassette 2, Segment G

CHAPTER 7 Choices

Choose one of the following activities to complete.

▶ CAREERS
1. Persuasion That Pays
Interview a professional whose career involves persuasive writing, such as a salesperson, fund-raiser, or speech writer. Then, write a **paragraph** about the specific writing strategies and persuasive skills that are involved in his or her daily work.

▶ LITERATURE
2. Poetically Persuasive
Not all persuasive pieces have to take the form of a formal persuasive essay or letter. Some forms of persuasion can be very creative. Using the opinion from the persuasive essay you wrote, draft a **poem** or **song lyric** that expresses your position and the reasons for it.

▶ MEDIA AND TECHNOLOGY
3. Web of Persuasion Using the opinion from the persuasive essay you wrote, create a **Web page** that might convince others to take a stand on the issue. Think about what would make the Web page persuasive. Should your page have a persuasive title? persuasive pictures? In deciding how to approach this task, you may want to visit some existing persuasive Web pages to see what kind of elements they use.

▶ CROSSING THE CURRICULUM: JOURNALISM
4. Editorially Yours Write an **editorial** that expresses your views on an issue. You may choose an entirely different issue from the subject of your essay. For instance, there may be a social, technological, or environmental situation that stirs a strong reaction in you. If you need to, do research on the issue to form a stronger opinion about it. Look at editorials in your local newspaper and notice their content and tone.

▶ ART
5. In Your Opinion Convert your persuasive essay into an **editorial cartoon.** Keep the basic elements of editorial cartoons in mind: symbolism, exaggeration/caricature, analogy, and irony. (For more on **editorial cartoons,** see page 284.)

 PORTFOLIO

▶ CAREERS (4G)
To identify and analyze strategies people in different career fields use to write persuasively, direct students to include these questions in their interview: Who is your audience? What issues concern them? Are they generally well-informed or do they need to be educated about issues? What tone do you use to address them? What special strategies do you use to persuade your audience? Collect students' paragraphs in a binder so that students can compare and contrast their findings.

▶ MEDIA AND TECHNOLOGY
Students may work in pairs or groups to create a Web page. You may also choose to set some guidelines or to remind students of school guidelines regarding appropriate content on school computers.

▶ CROSSING THE CURRICULUM: JOURNALISM (21D)
Tell students that their editorials should state a clear opinion early, use logical reasons and evidence, and include a call to action, if appropriate. Remind students of the **Thinking It Through** steps on p. 267 if they have trouble generating reasons to support their opinions. Have students deliver their editorials orally, as is done on radio and television.

Choices **293**

RESOURCES
Persuading Others
Assessment
- *Assessment Package*
  —*Chapter Tests,* Ch. 7
  —*Chapter Tests in Standardized Test Formats,* Ch. 7
  —*Assessment Alternatives,* Ch. 7
- *Test Generator* (One-Stop Planner CD-ROM)

Choices
Rubrics
- *Assessment Package*
  —*Assessment Alternatives,* Ch. 7

Choices
Alignments
Choice 1 TEKS 1A, 4G, 16A, 16B; TAAS W1
Choice 2 TEKS 1A, 1B, 11F; TAAS W1
Choice 3 TEKS 21B, 21C
Choice 4 TEKS 1A, 1B, 4G; TAAS W1
Choice 5 TEKS 19A, 19C, 21B, 21C

Choices **293**

CHAPTER 8

Using Persuasion in Advertising

Use this guide to create an instructional plan that suits the individual needs of your students. Assignments marked by an asterisk (*) may be completed out of class. Times given for pacing lessons are estimated. See pp. 294–295 for chapter-wide resources. Resources in this guide are point-of-use resources only.

Curriculum Connections

Choices *p. 337*
- Literature
- Crossing the Curriculum: History
- Media and Technology

internet connect
GO TO: go.hrw.com
KEYWORD: EOLang 10–8

All resources for this chapter are available for preview on the *One-Stop Planner CD-ROM with Test Generator*. All worksheets and tests may be printed from the CD-ROM.

Texas Resources For a complete listing of all resources prepared for Texas teachers and students, please see the blue box at the beginning of each chapter.

	Chapter Opener pp. 294–295	**Reading Workshop: Reading a Persuasive Brochure** pp. 296–305
DEVELOPMENTAL PROGRAM	⏱ **25 minutes** • Persuading Others *p. 295* • Your Turn 1 in groups *p. 295*	⏱ **100 minutes** • Preparing to Read *p. 296* • Reading Selection *pp. 297–299* • First Thoughts on Your Reading 1 *p. 300* • Identifying Persuasive Techniques *pp. 300–302* • Your Turn 2 *p. 302* • Analyzing Persuasive Visual Elements *p. 303* • Your Turn 3 *p. 303* • Test Taking Mini-Lesson *p. 305*
CORE PROGRAM	⏱ **20 minutes** • Persuading Others *p. 295* • Your Turn 1 in groups *p. 295*	⏱ **90 minutes** • Preparing to Read *p. 296* • Reading Selection *pp. 297–299* • First Thoughts on Your Reading 1–2 *p. 300* • Identifying Persuasive Techniques *pp. 300–302* • Your Turn 2 *p. 302* • Analyzing Persuasive Visual Elements *p. 303* • Your Turn 3 *p. 303* • Vocabulary Mini-Lesson *p. 304* • Test Taking Mini-Lesson *p. 305*
ADVANCED PROGRAM	⏱ **15 minutes** • Persuading Others *p. 295* • Your Turn 1 *p. 295*	⏱ **60 minutes** • Preparing to Read *p. 296* • Reading Selection *pp. 297–299* • First Thoughts on Your Reading 2 *p. 300* • Identifying Persuasive Techniques *pp. 300–302* • Analyzing Persuasive Visual Elements *p. 303* • Your Turn 3 *p. 303* • Vocabulary Mini-Lesson *p. 304*
RESOURCES – PRINT	• *Communications,* TP. 59, WS. p. 138	• *Alternative Readings,* Ch. 8 • *Communications,* TPs. 60, 61, WS. pp. 139–146
RESOURCES – MEDIA	• *One-Stop Planner CD-ROM* 💿	• *One-Stop Planner CD-ROM* 💿

TP.=Transparency   WS.=Worksheet

Writing Workshop: Creating a Persuasive Brochure *pp. 306–328*	**Focus on Viewing and Representing: Creating a Documentary on Print Advertising** *pp. 329–336*
⏱ **260 minutes** • Choose a Product, Service, or Cause *pp. 306–307* • Consider Purp., Aud., Tone and Your Turn 4 *pp. 307–309* • Consider Your Style *pp. 309–310* • Determine the Primary Idea *pp. 310–311* • Provide Support; Know Your Format *pp. 311–313* • Plan Your Visual Elements and Your Turn 5 *pp. 313–314* • Framework and Your Turn 6 *pp. 316–320* • Writer's Model and Student's Model *pp. 316–320* • Evaluate and Revise; Your Turn 7 *pp. 321–322* • Focus on Word Choice and Your Turn 8 *p. 323* • Proofread, Publish, and Reflect *pp. 325–326* • Grammar Link and Your Turn 9 *pp. 325–326*	⏱ **140 minutes** • Preproduction *pp. 329–335* • Production* *p. 335* • Postproduction *p. 336* • Your Turn 11* *p. 336*
⏱ **180 minutes** • Choose a Product, Service, or Cause *pp. 306–307* • Consider Purp., Aud., Tone and Your Turn 4 *pp. 307–309* • Consider Your Style *pp. 309–310* • Determine the Primary Idea *pp. 310–311* • Provide Support; Know Your Format *pp. 311–313* • Plan Your Visual Elements and Your Turn 5 *pp. 313–314* • Critical Thinking Mini-Lesson *p. 315* • Framework and Your Turn 6* *pp. 316–320* • Writer's Model and Student's Model *pp. 316–320* • Evaluate and Revise; Your Turn 7 *pp. 321–322* • Focus on Word Choice and Your Turn 8* *p. 323* • Proofread, Publish, and Reflect *pp. 325–326* • Grammar Link and Your Turn 9 *pp. 325–326* • Connections to Life and Your Turn 10* *pp. 327–328*	⏱ **120 minutes** • Preproduction *pp. 329–335* • Production* *p. 335* • Postproduction *p. 336* • Your Turn 11* *p. 336*
⏱ **150 minutes** • Choose a Product, Service, or Cause *pp. 306–307* • Consider Purp., Aud., Tone and Your Turn 4 *pp. 307–309* • Determine the Primary Idea *pp. 310–311* • Provide Support; Know Your Format *pp. 311–313* • Plan Your Visual Elements and Your Turn 5 *pp. 313–314* • Critical Thinking Mini-Lesson *p. 315* • Framework and Your Turn 6* *pp. 316–320* • Writer's Model and Student's Model *pp. 316–320* • Evaluate and Revise; Your Turn 7 *pp. 321–322* • Proofread, Publish, Reflect; Your Turn 9 *pp. 325–326* • Connections to Life and Your Turn 10* *pp. 327–328*	⏱ **100 minutes** • Preproduction *pp. 329–335* • Production* *p. 335* • Postproduction *p. 336* • Your Turn 11* *p. 336*
• *Communications*, TPs. 62–65, WS. pp. 147–156 • *Designing Your Writing*	• *Media Literacy and Communication Skills Kit* —*Support and Practice*, Ch. 8 —*A How-to Handbook* —*A Teacher's Guide*, Ch. 8
• *One-Stop Planner CD-ROM* 💿	• *Media Literacy and Communication Skills Kit* —Videocassette 2, Segment H • *One-Stop Planner CD-ROM*

CHAPTER 8
Using Persuasion in Advertising

CHAPTER OBJECTIVES
- To read a persuasive brochure
- To create a persuasive brochure
- To create a documentary on print advertising

Chapter Overview

Persuasion is a common element in advertising, politics, and literature. This chapter is designed to help students identify and use persuasive techniques and visual elements in their reading and writing, and will also help them create a documentary which analyzes advertising. Students will read a persuasive brochure in the Reading Workshop, then identify persuasive techniques and analyze illustrations. In the Writing Workshop, students will create advertising brochures. Students will analyze the use of persuasion in advertising through creating a documentary video in the Focus on Viewing and Representing. While the sections of the chapter can be taught separately, taught together they provide your students with an overview of the use of persuasion in advertising.

Why Study Persuasion in Advertising?

Students are surrounded by persuasive media messages advertising many products, services, and causes. Understanding persuasion in advertising helps students not only to understand persuasive elements but also to become more educated consumers. Students need to understand how advertising appeals to their emotions and how to evaluate persuasive materials logically. They also need to understand the use of persuasive techniques to market their own products and services. Students will also be able to use the knowledge gained from this chapter to evaluate other persuasive messages in their worlds.

Teaching the Chapter

Option 1: Begin with Literature

To use literature as the point of departure for studying persuasion, introduce this chapter after studying the use of persuasion in drama, poetry, or fiction. The emphasis in any genre would be persuasion: how characters try to influence each other or how the writer attempts to influence the reader toward a particular viewpoint. Have students read the persuasive brochure in this chapter (pp. 297–299) to illustrate the use of persuasion in advertising as well as in literature. With a reading knowledge of persuasive techniques, students will be prepared to write advertising brochures.

Option 2: Begin with Nonfiction and Writing

Familiarize students with persuasive techniques, starting with the material in this chapter. The Reading Selection and the accompanying instruction (pp. 297–303) provide a basis for student understanding of persuasive techniques. Then, guide students in creating a persuasive brochure in the Writing Workshop (pp. 306–328). When students return to literature, they will have a more complete understanding of persuasive techniques and will be better prepared both to understand persuasion in other genres and to write persuasively about literature.

Making Connections

■ To the Literature Curriculum

In *The Tragedy of Julius Caesar*, Brutus and Mark Antony use persuasion to move the crowd after Caesar's assassination and to affect the political outcome in Rome. Mark Twain in "The Lowest Animal" tries to persuade readers that humans are incurably foolish. In literature as in life, persuasion shapes a viewpoint or moves people to action.

Lesson Idea: Persuasion in *The Tragedy of Julius Caesar* by William Shakespeare

1. Have students read and outline Brutus's and Mark Antony's funeral speeches in Act 3, Scene 2.

2. Have students label the persuasive techniques each character uses, as well as other persuasive devices (timing, tears, and so forth).

3. Ask students what Brutus might have done to make the crowd accept his position.

4. Introduce students to the brochure on pp. 297–299. Point out that the brochure uses persuasive techniques just as Antony and Brutus do. Then, use the instructional material on persuasive techniques to help prepare students to write their own persuasive brochures.

■ To Careers

Gather sample brochures or advertisements from local politicians, business leaders, media representatives, or small business owners. Have students working in groups evaluate the persuasive techniques used in each ad or brochure, looking at both the visual and written elements.

■ To the Community

Check with the public relations departments of local nonprofit organizations in your community, such as hospitals and animal shelters. Invite a speaker to the classroom to explain the special advertising challenges in the not-for-profit segment. Ask the speaker to bring brochures, posters, or overhead transparencies to illustrate his or her points. Students should prepare questions about advertising or community outreach for discussion after the presentation.

■ To the Social Studies Curriculum

Work with the social studies teacher to have groups of students create persuasive brochures supporting or attacking a political issue from history. Challenge students to re-create the writing and visuals that might have been used during the historical period. This activity will help students understand how persuasion can be used to support political positions as well as to sell services and products.

CHAPTER 8

Using Persuasion in Advertising

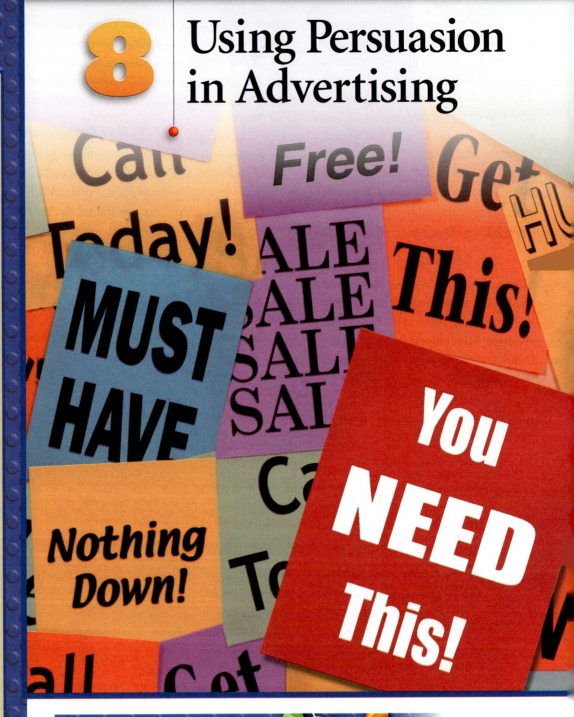

PREVIEWING THE CHAPTER

- The three workshops in this chapter explore persuasion. Each can be taught independently, but taught together they reinforce one another to give students a full understanding of persuasive techniques. Reading a persuasive brochure prepares students to write and design their own brochures. After reading and writing about persuasion in advertising, students will be better prepared to analyze print advertising in a documentary format. To integrate this chapter with grammar, usage, and mechanics chapters, see pp. T401A–T401B.

INTRODUCING THE CHAPTER

- To introduce the chapter, use the Journal Warm-up, Transparency 59, in *Communications*.

VIEWING THE ILLUSTRATION (19A)

- As students look at the illustration, they should notice how the use of vivid colors and bold typefaces grab the viewer's attention and how this bold style supports persuasive statements. Ask them which message stands out the most and why. [Students will probably say the red poster in the lower right corner because of the bright background color, contrasting typeface color, and overlapping placement on the page.] Remind students that it is a combination of elements—color, typeface, and wording—that makes advertisements persuasive.

CHAPTER RESOURCES

Planning
- *Lesson Planner*, Ch. 8
- Block Scheduling, p. T293A (this book)
- One-Stop Planner CD-ROM

Practice
- *Communications*, Ch. 8

- Media Literacy and Communication Skills

Extension
- Designing Your Writing

Reinforcement
- *Communications*, Ch. 8

PREVIEW

Reading Workshop

Reading a Persuasive Brochure
PAGE 296

Writing Workshop

Creating a Persuasive Brochure
PAGE 306

Focus on Viewing and Representing

Creating a Documentary on Print Advertising
PAGE 329

Persuading Others

- Island Mini-Cars puts your life into the fast lane!
- Aggressor Athletics gear is for you. Take your game to the next level.
- Give a gift from the heart: Donate to your local blood bank today.

It is easy to find enticements like these printed on brightly colored brochures in the lobbies of hotels and restaurants, in airport kiosks, in racks at the travel agency, or on bulletin boards around your community. **Brochures**—print advertisements that fold to create several pages—use both words and images to persuade you to buy a product or a service or to support an organization or a cause. Most brochures catch your eye with exciting images, then draw you into in-depth information. Brochures have one great advantage over other forms of advertising: their portable size makes them easy for their maker to distribute and for an audience to read at its convenience.

GO TO: go.hrw.com
KEYWORD: EOLang 10-8

YOUR TURN 1 — Brainstorming About Brochures

With a few of your classmates, discuss any brochures you have seen. List the products, services, or causes advertised, along with the places you found the brochures. What do you remember most about them? What types of goods or services do you think are most commonly advertised through brochures? Take notes on your discussion and be prepared to discuss your findings with your class.

Motivate

Divide the class into small groups. Ask each group to select a well-known product they use and to brainstorm ways the product is advertised. Groups should discuss the image they feel advertisers are trying to create and the techniques used to create that image.

Persuasion in Literature. In *Elements of Literature,* Fourth Course, have students study "The Man in the Water," by Roger Rosenblatt, pp. 471–475, and an excerpt from *Letter from Birmingham Jail* by Dr. Martin Luther King, Jr., pp. 744–748, for examples of persuasive writing.

YOUR TURN 1

You may wish to collect brochures from travel agencies, mailings, or store displays for students to peruse as they complete the assignment. Students can list their answers in a chart such as the following one.

Brochure	Memorable Qualities

Chapter Opener, pp. 294–295
Alignments
TEKS 16B, 16F

Texas Resources
- Lesson Planner, Ch. 8
- TAAS Tool Kit
- Preparation for TAAS
- Preparing for English II End-of-Course Examination
- One-Stop Planner CD-ROM

- Alternative Readings, Ch. 8
- Daily Language Activity Transparencies
- Vocabulary Workshop and Tests

Evaluation and Assessment

- Test Generator (One-Stop Planner CD-ROM)
- Assessment Package
  —Chapter Tests, Ch. 8
  —Chapter Tests in Standardized Test Formats, Ch. 8
  —Assessment Alternatives, Ch. 8

Internet
- go.hrw.com (keyword: EOLang 10-8)

Reading Workshop

OBJECTIVES

- To read a persuasive brochure in preparation for writing a brochure
- To identify persuasive techniques
- To analyze persuasive visual elements
- To use synonym or antonym context clues to define words

Quotation for the Day

"We read a written text *and hear the writer.*

And in that hearing we make the decision to stop or read on, to distrust or believe the writer, to reject or accept the writer's view of the world."

(Donald Murray, 1924– , American teacher and writer)

Read the quotation to the class. Have students discuss how the quotation might apply to persuasion: How does persuasion promote a particular "view of the world"?

TEACHING TIP

Preparing to Read
The material on p. 296 introduces the skills that will be taught in more depth on pp. 300–303. Identifying persuasive techniques and analyzing persuasive visual elements will be the focus of the Reading Workshop. The brochure **"Adopt-A-Bison"** provides opportunities to practice both skills.

RESOURCES

Reading Workshop
Reinforcement
- *Alternative Readings,* Ch. 8

Reading Workshop

Reading a Persuasive Brochure

WHAT'S AHEAD?

In this section you will read a persuasive brochure and learn how to

- identify persuasive techniques
- analyze persuasive visual elements

Fun parks, athletic wear, and blood banks are just some of the many products, services, and organizations that are advertised in brochures. Since brochures can present much information in a small space, they are used to advertise a wide variety of interesting and surprising things. For example, the brochure on the following page, "Adopt-A-Bison," will try to gain your support for a program that is rebuilding bison herds in the prairies of Oklahoma.

Preparing to Read

READING SKILL

Identifying Persuasive Techniques Advertising works to persuade you to buy products and services or to support causes. How do advertisements like brochures convince you to take action? They use **persuasive techniques,** including logical and emotional appeals. Some advertisements, however, rely very heavily on emotion and not as much on logic and evidence. If you are not aware of the emotional appeals used to get your attention—and your money—you might be misled into paying for or supporting something without really knowing why. As you read the following brochure, think about the techniques it uses to accomplish its purpose—to convince you to adopt a bison.

READING FOCUS

Analyzing Persuasive Visual Elements Unlike persuasive articles, brochures use **persuasive visual elements**—columns, graphics, headings, and colors—to convince readers. Besides being tools for persuasion, these elements attract readers' attention, help make reading easier, and emphasize the points that their creators believe deserve special attention. As you read the brochure that begins on the next page, notice which items first catch your attention. These items probably highlight key ideas that the writer wants you to remember.

296 Chapter 8 Persuasion: Using Persuasion in Advertising

READING PROCESS

PREREADING
Make Predictions. Have students preview the reading selection and make predictions based on the following questions. Sample answers are provided.

1. Based on the headline and pictures on the opening pages, what do you think the brochure is about? [The brochure is about a campaign to save the bison.]

Reading Selection

In the following persuasive brochure, The Nature Conservancy tries to convince you to protect America's native bison. As you read, answer the numbered active-reading questions on your own paper.

ADOPT-A-BISON

And help The Nature Conservancy save part of America's vanishing heritage!

The Nature Conservancy

Here's how to adopt a bison and what you get when you do:

By adopting a bison, you're playing a vital role in restoring and preserving one of the last great expanses of tallgrass prairie. It's easy and inexpensive to do.

Simply choose the animal you prefer. Then, mail your contribution of $25 or more. Or call 1-800-555-BISON toll-free.

You will receive a handsome adoption certificate, suitable for framing, complete with your name along with the name and photo of your bison. We'll keep you updated on The Nature Conservancy's Tallgrass Prairie Preserve throughout the year with our lively quarterly newsletter, *Prairie Thunder*.

Connecting Reading and Writing

Students may be able to read and understand brochure format more easily if they consider differences in style when writing brochures and writing essays. For example, brochures tend to have simpler, shorter sentences and paragraphs, and they use lively action verbs. Brochures also rely on design elements such as graphics and illustrations. Direct students to the instruction on style on pp. 309–310.

2. Based on the headlines and pictures, what does the rest of the brochure encourage readers to do? [The brochure encourages people to adopt a bison.]

Discuss responses before students read the Reading Selection. Encourage students to make additional predictions that they can check as they read.

Reading Workshop, pp. 296–303
Alignments
TEKS 8A, 12A, 12C, 19A, 19C, 20C
TAAS R6
English II End-of-Course 3

Texas Resources
- *Lesson Planner*, Ch. 8
- *TAAS Tool Kit*
- *Preparation for TAAS*
- *Preparing for English II End-of-Course Examination*
- *One-Stop Planner CD-ROM*

"Oh give me a home..."

1. Why do you think the writer chose this headline?

The Tallgrass Prairie Preserve: Restoring a Lost Ecosystem.
As settlers turned the prairie into the nation's breadbasket, an entire ecosystem that supported hundreds of plants and animals disappeared.

It could have been gone forever, if it weren't for The Nature Conservancy and its 37,000-acre Tallgrass Prairie Preserve in Osage County, Oklahoma. Here you can journey back in time and experience the prairie as our ancestors did with 8-foot-tall grasses, breathtaking wildflower displays, and roaming bison.

Why the bison must graze for the prairie to bloom.
The prairie depends on climate, fire, and bison to survive.

The fire—which The Nature Conservancy manages through controlled burns—prevents trees and brush from overwhelming the prairie and removes dead vegetation, allowing new plants to sprout.

The bison, attracted by this new growth, graze it and then move on, giving the land time to recover. They also wallow in the grasses and rub against the trees and boulders. This in turn affects the growth of plants and the patterns of fires.

But while nature will take care of the 30 to 50 pounds of forage a bison consumes each day, there are many other expenses the Conservancy must cover to ensure that the tallgrass prairie is not just a legend, but a reality.

Adopt a bison—and help keep the legend alive.
Your tax-deductible gift of $25 will give you a personal stake in the future of the tallgrass prairie:

- It will help us track the herd and research its role in sustaining the prairie.
- It will let us re-create the "wide open spaces" of yesteryear and secure the perimeter with fencing that can stand up to a one-ton charge.
- It will help make sure the herd remains disease-free.

2. How do the brochure's photographs help you understand its message?

Act today—make a lasting mark on tomorrow!
You're the key to our success at the Tallgrass Prairie Preserve. Because the prairie depends on the bison. The bison depend on us. And we depend on *you*.

So please act now. Adopt a bison, and help us to restore this precious legacy, so that it will be here for our children . . . and their children . . . and their great-great-grandchildren.

3. Why do you think the brochure includes this section?

Which bison will be your bison?

4. Why did the writer give contributors a choice of bison to support?

Prairie Chief. Weighing close to a ton and boasting a massive mane, this mature bull likes to spend most of his time alone, wallowing in the prairie dust or shining up his horns by rubbing them on trees. In July and August, however, he can be found fighting with the other bulls as they compete for females in their annual courtship ritual called rutting.

Wildfire. A young bull just hitting his prime. He enjoys hanging out with his pals, and it's always a contest to prove who's the strongest and toughest. He's also proving to be quite a flirt with the heifers.

Buster. He's just cutting his horns and going through that awkward adolescent stage. Poor Buster is easily recognizable by his "spotted" face, dark legs, and fur now the dark brown of an adult. Sometimes it's tough growing up— even for a bison!

Sweet Pea. This two-year-old pregnant female is about to become a first-time mother. After a 9 1/2-month gestation period, she will give birth to a 50-pound baby. During her pregnancy, you will find her spending most of her time with her own mother and the other mature females. And of course, she's also busy "eating for two."

Penny. She is a lovable little newborn who spends most of her day at Mom's side. Her cute voice is a squeaky grunt, and she'll remain the coppery red color of a penny until she's three months old.

Pick your favorite, and mail your gift. Or call toll-free: 1-800-555-BISON.

ADOPT-A-BISON

5. What impression of Penny do words such as *luvable*, *cute*, and *squeaky* give you?

Active-Reading Questions
ANSWERS continued

4. Choosing a category of bison makes the adoption seem more personal.

5. The words make her seem almost like a pet.

READING PROCESS

READING 7B
Personal Connections. Relating brochure content to something familiar makes the reading more meaningful and will help students' comprehension. Have students brainstorm about other endangered species and natural resources, or other similar causes, that are important to them. How would they persuade others to support their cause?

First Thoughts on Your Reading

ANSWERS
Possible answers follow.

1. Students may comment on the headlines, illustrations, or colors of the brochure.
2. Students may mention feeling protective of the bison. The language also promotes feelings of connection and empathy.

TEACHING TIP

Identifying Persuasive Techniques
Have students bring in examples of advertisements that display techniques listed and label the techniques. So that students can see common uses of these persuasive techniques, post the examples in the classroom.

First Thoughts on Your Reading

With a partner or on your own, answer the following questions about "Adopt-A-Bison." Write your answers on your own paper.

1. What part of the brochure's design first attracted your attention? Why?
2. What feelings did the descriptions of different bison give you as you read the brochure?

READING SKILL

Identifying Persuasive Techniques

Act Now! All advertisements use **persuasive techniques**—methods used to convince you to purchase a product or service or to support a cause. Have you ever seen a commercial that made you feel that you could be more attractive by using a particular cologne, shampoo, or deodorant? If so, you have experienced persuasive techniques that play on your emotions or on your perceptions of the product to make the sale. These kinds of persuasive techniques are not all necessarily bad. However, some advertisements rely too much on emotional persuasive techniques to convince you and do not provide enough facts or evidence.

In order to make good choices about what you do with your money and time, you need to be able to distinguish between real evidence and persuasion aimed purely at your emotions. Look for the reasons and evidence, and make your decisions based on those elements. The persuasive techniques that follow are based solely on emotion.

TIP Persuasive writing used for purposes other than advertising should rely primarily on logical appeals (reasons and evidence) and less on emotional appeals.

- **The bandwagon technique attempts to persuade the reader to do something because everyone else is doing it.** The bandwagon technique invites readers to "join the crowd" or "join the winning side," and it reinforces people's natural desire to be accepted and admired. Its opposite is **plain folks,** which promotes a product or service because it is effective and sensible rather than popular—the sort of thing plain folks (regular people like you) use or buy.

    Bandwagon: Join the stampede to save the bison.
    Plain folks: Bison are down-to-earth, just like you.

- **Transfer** projects the positive or negative qualities of one person, entity, object, or value on to another. Transfer is used to make the second item in a comparison more acceptable or to discredit it. For example, a car ad may show a cheetah, trying to draw a connection between the car and the cheetah's grace and speed. A **testimonial** is one

---

READING PROCESS

EXTENDING
Connect to the World. Have students investigate an endangered animal or natural resource native to their area and list the arguments for preserving or not preserving the animal or resource. Make sure they include the sources for their information.

kind of transfer in which famous people endorse a product or cause. The positive qualities of the famous person are transferred to the product or cause they endorse.

> **Testimonial:** "Show your support for nature today by contributing to the Homes for Wildlife fund."—Koko Markelli, star of TV's *Mother Nature*.

- **Emotional words attempt to create a strong feeling in the reader.** Their connotations evoke either positive or negative emotions about someone or something. Value words, such as *love, happiness, security,* and *wisdom* call up positive emotions because of their association with the readers' beliefs.

> **Emotional words:** Cute, furry prairie dogs once frolicked on the open plains. Now, colonies of these playful animals are scarce.

- **Glittering generalities focus on highly valued concepts and beliefs such as patriotism, peace, freedom, glory, and honor.** The "glitter" and positive emotional appeal of these concepts sometimes cause readers to lower their guards and to accept information that is not adequately supported. **Name-calling** is the counterpoint to glittering generalities. This technique uses words with intense negative emotional appeal to make readers condemn a product or idea without examining the evidence.

> **Glittering generality:** The gray wolf is a hero of the American wilderness. It roams freely, evading the fenced-in areas provided for it by well-meaning supporters. Help the wolf stay free.
>
> **Name-calling:** The gray wolf is a sneak thief and scavenger that preys upon the helpless stock of hard-working families.

TIP Two or more persuasive techniques can be used at the same time. For example, *transfer* is used if an advertisement portrays Uncle Sam—the positive qualities of this fictional character would be transferred to a product, service, or cause. However, the advertisement would also be using *glittering generalities,* because Uncle Sam symbolizes the highly valued concepts of patriotism, freedom, and democracy.

THINKING IT THROUGH
Recognizing Emotional Persuasive Techniques

The steps on the next page will help you recognize emotional persuasive techniques in a brochure or in other advertisements. The sample responses are based on the following excerpt from "Adopt-A-Bison."

Critical Thinking

Analysis. Allow students to form small groups and select a controversial national issue or upcoming election that is the subject of media focus. Students should analyze three articles, speeches, editorials, letters to the editor, or cartoons on the topic to identify the persuasive techniques used. Then, have each group report their findings to the class.

Meeting INDIVIDUAL NEEDS

LEARNERS HAVING DIFFICULTY
Reproduce an advertisement on an overhead transparency. Use a guided exercise to show students that every element is designed to produce a specific, desired effect on the viewer.

Penny. She is a lovable little newborn who spends most of her day at Mom's side. Her cute voice is a squeaky grunt, and she'll remain the coppery red color of a penny until she's three months old.

▶ **STEP 1** Read the passage carefully.

▶ **STEP 2** To analyze the passage for emotional persuasive techniques, ask yourself the following questions:
- Does this passage make you think that everyone else is supporting the cause (bandwagon)? *No.*
- Does it project the qualities of one person, group, or object onto another (transfer)? *No.*
- Does it use emotional words to create a strong feeling in you? *Yes. The section uses words like "lovable little newborn," "cute," and "squeaky grunt."*
- Does it refer to highly valued, abstract ideas, such as freedom and democracy (glittering generalities)? *No.*

▶ **STEP 3** Decide which emotional persuasive techniques are being used and what reaction the passage is trying to evoke. *This passage uses emotional words that make me feel as if I should protect this "baby."*

YOUR TURN 2 — Identifying Persuasive Techniques

Using the steps in Thinking It Through above, identify the persuasive techniques used in the examples below. Write your answers on your own paper.

1. Adopt-A-Bison—And help The Nature Conservancy save part of America's vanishing heritage!
2. **Buster.** He's just cutting his horns and going through that awkward adolescent stage. Poor Buster is easily recognizable by his "spotted" face, dark legs, and fur now the dark brown of an adult. Sometimes it's tough growing up—even for a bison!
3. School classes, community organizations, and business associations from across the country: These are some of the people who have already adopted their own bison. Won't you and your organization be next?
4. Like another of America's symbols, the bald eagle, the bison rely on us to limit our encroachment into their environment.

YOUR TURN 2 ANSWERS

1. glittering generalities
2. emotional words
3. bandwagon
4. transfer

RESOURCES

Your Turn 2

Practice
- *Communications,* WS. p. 139

Reinforcement
- *Communications,* TP. 60, WS. p. 140

Your Turn 3

Practice
- *Communications,* WS. p. 141

Reinforcement
- *Communications,* TP. 61, WS. p. 142

Analyzing Persuasive Visual Elements

READING FOCUS

Designed to Grab You You may have had an experience like this one. You are on vacation with your family. While your parents are checking into your hotel, you spot a stand full of brochures. Maybe you can find an interesting museum or park to visit, or a fun shopping district. As you pause in front of the stand, there is much competition for your attention. **Visual elements** such as headlines, graphics, colors, and type style most likely will determine which brochure you choose to pick up and read. Once the brochure is in your hands, the same visual elements reinforce the brochure's message, making you more interested in buying the product, visiting the place, or joining the cause. The following chart lists some of these visual elements and their uses.

Persuasive Visual Elements	
Headings and subheadings	- divide up, or group, related information - contain key words that instantly identify each section - help readers predict what information is contained in the brochure and locate the information that interests them
Warm colors (reds, yellows, and oranges)	- give readers a sense of warmth and good feeling - work well for brochures that urge readers to get involved, take action, or make an impulsive decision
Cool colors (blues, purples, and greens)	- give readers a feeling of distance and professionalism - can help a brochure seem more factual and informative
Graphics	- emphasize major points - provide images of unfamiliar places, animals, objects, or people - combine with captions to reinforce text - draw readers to any text that wraps around the graphic
Type sizes and fonts	- can encourage the reader's eye to slow down when type is small—slow reading pace helps a reader absorb complex ideas or persuasive points - can catch the reader's attention with headings in large type

YOUR TURN 3 Analyzing Visual Elements

Working with a partner, find in the "Adopt-A-Bison" brochure on page 297 an example of each of the visual elements explained above. Then, explain how each of the examples you found makes the brochure more persuasive.

Wrap It Up

Metacognition. Ask students to reflect on their own reading processes, and give them five minutes to write a response to the following questions.

1. How did the visual elements affect your reaction to the text of the brochure? Why?

Then, have students answer the following items.

2. List four types of persuasive techniques. [bandwagon, glittering generalities, transfer, and emotional words]

3. List four types of visual persuasive techniques. [headings and subheadings, colors, graphics, type sizes and fonts]

YOUR TURN 3

As students share their responses with the class, discuss how changes in these elements of the brochure could produce different effects.

Reading Workshop

MINI-LESSON VOCABULARY

Synonym and Antonym Context Clues

ANSWERS
Possible answers follow.

1. The words *whose need for food* suggests *food* could be a synonym for *forage*. "The prairie provides plenty of *food* for the bison. . . ." Therefore, *forage* must mean *food*.

2. The word *but* is the clue word suggesting *boon* is an antonym for *curse*. "Fire is a *boon*. . . ." Therefore, if a *boon* is the opposite of a *curse*, *boon* must mean a *benefit*.

3. The word *unlike* indicates an antonym follows, and *boundless* could be the antonym. A *perimeter* is the opposite of *boundless*, so *perimeter* means *boundary*.

4. The word *though* indicates an antonym. *Future* might be the antonym for *heritage*. If *heritage* is the opposite of *future*, *heritage* must mean *our past*.

5. The word *was* indicates a synonym, and *large* could be the synonym for *vast*. Therefore, *vast* could mean *extremely large*.

Taking a Second Look
Using Synonyms and Antonyms.
Have students use the italicized words in original sentences of their own. Sample answers follow.

1. Deer must seek *forage* during the winter.

2. The invention of the electric light bulb has been a *boon* to humankind.

3. The *perimeter* of the triangle was outlined in red.

4. Our *heritage* includes defending democracy.

5. The *vast* ocean spread before the shipwrecked sailors.

MINI-LESSON VOCABULARY

Synonym and Antonym Context Clues

To make sure their messages come through clearly, ad writers often use **synonyms**—words with similar meanings to those of other words—and **antonyms**—words with opposite meanings to those of other words. Look for synonym or antonym context clues when you encounter unfamiliar words. Signals for synonym context clues are *be* verbs and words like *or* and *and*. Signals for antonym context clues are words such as *different, unlike, though, opposite, contrast,* or *but*.

Synonym Context Clue: The Citizens' Coalition **is** an alliance of neighborhood groups.

Antonym Context Clue: Our new dog is **not** *ornery*, **but** easygoing.

If no clues are given, sometimes common sense will lead you to a familiar word that is a synonym or antonym of the unfamiliar word.

THINKING IT THROUGH — Using Synonyms and Antonyms

Use the steps below to help you define unknown words using synonyms and antonyms. The sample responses are based on the following example sentence.

> . . . there are many other expenses the Conservancy must cover to ensure that the tallgrass prairie is not just a *legend*, but a reality.

1. **Find clue words that might signal a synonym or antonym.** The word *but* may indicate that an antonym follows.

2. **Find a word you think may be the synonym or antonym.** The word *reality* could be an antonym for *legend*.

3. **Replace the unfamiliar word with the familiar synonym or with a word or phrase that expresses the familiar word's opposite.** ". . . to ensure that the tallgrass prairie is not just the opposite of reality."

4. **Use the meaning of the synonym or antonym to come up with your own definition.** A *legend* is the opposite of reality—imaginary or a fantasy.

PRACTICE

Use the steps above to define the italicized words in the sentences below. Write your definitions on your own paper.

1. The prairie provides plenty of *forage* for the bison, whose need for food is provided for by grasses and other plants.

2. Fire is not a curse, but a *boon* to the prairie.

3. Unlike the boundless prairies of old, today's prairies have a *perimeter*.

4. Bison are part of America's *heritage*. With careful planning, though, they can be part of our future, too.

5. To the early settlers, the *vast* tallgrass prairie was as large as the sea.

RESOURCES

Vocabulary
Practice
- *Communications,* WS. p. 143

Test Taking
Practice
- *Communications,* WS. pp. 144–146

MINI-LESSON: TEST TAKING

Persuasive Devices

Because the ability to recognize persuasive devices is so important in making informed decisions, this ability is often tested on standardized reading tests. Read the passage and the question below, and then use the Thinking It Through steps to determine the correct answer.

The bison, or buffalo, which once provided food and clothing to many American Indians, should be the symbol of America. This animal, like the American spirit, reflects the strength to survive against enormous odds. Bison numbered nearly 50 million prior to European colonization; but hunters had almost wiped them out by the late 1800s—leaving only 835 alive in 1885. However, with the help of conservationists like zoologist William Temple Hornaday, this animal now numbers as many as 200,000. Thus, because it was nurtured and has survived in the freedom of our vast western plains, the untamable bison best embodies American perseverance.

1. The writer tries to convince the reader that the bison should be the American symbol by
   A. relating that bison provided food and clothing for American Indians
   B. explaining that even though hunters nearly wiped out the bison, it survived
   C. stating that William Temple Hornaday helped save the bison from extinction
   D. showing that the bison once numbered 50 million

THINKING IT THROUGH: Recognizing Persuasive Devices

1. **Rephrase the statement as a question to be answered with one of the possible choices.** Which choice supports the idea that the bison should be the American symbol?

2. **Read each answer choice to see if it supports the question.**
   - "A" says that American Indians relied on bison for food and clothing. This is true for some American Indians, but it does not support the idea that bison would make a good American symbol. "A" must be incorrect.
   - "B" states that bison are survivors. The passage says that the bison, "like the American spirit, reflects the strength to survive." "B" is probably correct.
   - "C" is a supporting fact about how the bison survived, but does not directly support the writer's idea. "C" is incorrect.
   - "D" shows that there were great numbers of bison once, but it is illogical to think that great numbers reflect the spirit of America. "D" must be incorrect.

3. **Decide which is the best answer.** Choice "B" is correct.

Looking Ahead to Writing

In the Writing Workshop for this chapter (pp. 306–328), students will be asked to create and design persuasive brochures. As they do so, students will recognize the importance of visual elements and their power to persuade the reader. Have them refer to the chart on p. 303 to review those elements.

Vocabulary
Alignments
TEKS 6B
TAAS R1

Test Taking
Alignments
TEKS 7C, 12A, 12C
TAAS R6
English II End-of-Course 3

Writing Workshop

OBJECTIVES

- To write a persuasive brochure
- To determine a primary idea
- To create an eye-catching design
- To evaluate reasoning in advertising
- To eliminate clichés
- To use consistent verb tenses

Quotation for the Day

"When you write to persuade, you're trying to influence what someone thinks, feels, or does. You're trying to affect the audience's behavior or attitudes, or both."

(Tom Sant, American consultant and writer)

Write the quotation on the board and have students freewrite on a topic or topics about which they have strong feelings. Urge students to keep this freewriting exercise as a possible starting point for their persuasive brochures.

TEACHING TIP

Choose a Product, Service, or Cause

You may wish to set guidelines regarding what products, causes, or services students may choose for their brochures. Remind students that brochures cannot promote illegal substances or actions and must be in good taste.

Writing Workshop

Creating a Persuasive Brochure

WHAT'S AHEAD?

In this workshop you will write a persuasive brochure and learn how to

- determine a primary idea
- create an eye-catching design
- evaluate reasoning in advertising
- eliminate clichés
- use consistent verb tenses

Imagine that you have been making a little extra money mowing lawns in your neighborhood. The school year is almost over, and you would love to make enough money to go on the class trip. Maybe you could create a brochure to get more customers.

Perhaps you and a friend volunteer at the local animal shelter. Every day, you see pets that need a loving home. Surely more people would adopt a lovable dog or cat if they knew how important and affordable adoption is. Maybe you could create a brochure to help your fuzzy friends.

These examples are only two of the many practical uses for a persuasive brochure that you could create. In this workshop, you will learn how to create a brochure that persuades readers to take action or change their ways of thinking.

Prewriting

Choose a Product, Service, or Cause

What's Your Angle? Considering all the products, services, or causes that you could advertise, how will you decide which one to choose? Try these tips to find a good topic for your brochure:

- **Think about your hobbies and interests.** Could any of them be the basis for your own part-time business? Lawn work, baby-sitting, painting, and car washing are all services that could earn you some extra entertainment (or college) money. Advertise your own service.

- **Consider your community's unique attractions.** Does your town boast an old frontier fort, a great boating lake, or the world's largest chicken statue? Persuade people to visit your local attractions.

- **Think about school festivals, celebrations, or events.** Check with your school office for upcoming events such as science fairs, dances, or special presentations. Spur your community's interest in these events.
- **Close your eyes and think of the perfect world.** What problems would you solve? Would litter disappear overnight? Maybe you could convince people to stop running yellow traffic lights. Convince readers of a problem and prompt them to help solve it.

Here is what one student wrote after considering her hobbies.

> My friends and I enjoy working on computers. Our computer club has talked about fund-raising through setting up and maintaining computers. I will create a brochure for our computer service.

Consider Your Purpose, Audience, and Tone

Give the People What They Want The **purpose** of your brochure is to persuade its readers that your product, service, or cause meets their needs or is something they want to support. To begin doing that, you must identify your audience. Your **audience** consists of the people whom you expect to read your brochure. To identify your audience, you must ask the following questions about your product, service, or cause: Who needs it? Who wants it? Who has the time and money for it?

Here is how the computer club student determined her audience.

> **Who needs our service?** anyone who has trouble understanding computers, software, the Internet
>
> **Who wants our service?** people who want to improve their computer skills—people who cannot get help through work or school. Adults who are not in college might find that help is hard to find.
>
> **Who has the time and money for our service?**
>
> **Time**—would be determined a lot by when we are available: nights and weekends. That is when most students and people with 9–5 jobs would more likely also have free time.
>
> **Money**—Since most people in school can get free assistance with computers, they might not pay for the service. Adults who are not in college should be able to pay for our help.
>
> **My audience:** adults who are not familiar with computers and do not have access to training at work or school

TIP The audience of an advertisement is often referred to as a **target market,** a name that makes sense if you think of the ad as "aimed" at a very specific group of people.

Cooperative Learning

Creating a Flier. Define a *flier* as a small circular or handbill prepared for extensive distribution. Then, have groups of students follow these steps.

1. Have each group select a topic.
2. Show groups some sample fliers, noting the type size, white space, and information included.
3. Have groups decide what information and appropriate visuals should be included in their fliers.
4. If equipment is available, have groups lay out their fliers on the computer, experimenting with type fonts and sizes as well as placement. Students can also lay out brochures by hand.
5. Have groups complete and proofread their fliers.
6. After you have approved the fliers, post them in the classroom.

You may want to allow students the option of using the same information they use for their brochures to create fliers. Remind them that since fliers are generally one page and more concise, they may have to eliminate details from their planned brochure copy.

Once you have determined your audience, or target market, then you must analyze what they want and need from your product, service, or cause, and how you can meet those wants and needs. The following Thinking It Through can help you analyze your audience.

THINKING IT THROUGH — Analyzing Audience

Use the following Thinking It Through steps to analyze your brochure's audience. The examples provided are responses one student had when making a brochure for a computer service.

▶ **STEP 1** Write a statement defining your audience. *My audience is adults who are not familiar with computers and do not have access to training at work or at school.*

▶ **STEP 2** List your audience's wants and needs.
  1. staying in touch with family and friends
  2. overcoming difficulty getting computers set up
  3. contacting people with similar interests
  4. staying current with technology for the workplace

▶ **STEP 3** Explain how your product, service, or cause can address each of your audience's wants or needs.
  1. staying in touch: teach the use of e-mail
  2. getting computers set up: help set up computer systems and software
  3. contacting people: teach about the Internet, chat rooms, and newsgroups
  4. staying current with technology for the workplace: help develop up-to-date computer skills

TIP Keep in mind that your audience's wants include emotional desires, such as the desire to feel intelligent, attractive, or compassionate.

TIP Sometimes you will find **contractions** and sentence fragments in advertisements. Some advertisers feel this informal style choice is very effective. However, remember that these grammatical choices are unacceptable in most business and academic writing.

The **tone** of your brochure (the attitude or feeling that you express about the subject and your readers) is very important in persuading your readers that your product, service, or cause is worthwhile. Choose words and phrases that have a positive tone to make your audience feel good about themselves and what you are promoting. Avoid negative words and phrases that might make your audience feel uncomfortable. For example, the student trying to raise money for her computer club wants to make sure her tone is proper for adults. She should choose her words to make her readers feel good about the service but not bad about their own lack of skills. She must also decide on a proper balance of formal and informal language—informal enough to make the readers feel relaxed and comfortable, but not so informal as to make them feel that she and her friends are

308 Chapter 8 Persuasion: Using Persuasion in Advertising unprofessional. Formal and informal language choices include those of vocabulary, pronunciation, spelling, and grammar.

TIP Always keep in mind your **occasion**—the motivating force behind your writing. Often there is more than one motivating factor. For example, the student from the computer club was motivated both by being given a classroom assignment *and* by her club's need to raise funds.

YOUR TURN 4 Designing Your Brochure

Choose a product, service, or cause that you would like to advertise or promote in a brochure. Answer the questions on page 307 to identify your audience. Then, follow the Thinking It Through steps to analyze your audience's wants and needs. Lastly, determine the tone you will use to persuade your audience.

Consider Your Style

Point Fingers The whole purpose of your brochure is to get your reader to act or think in a certain way. Your **style,** or word choice, has an effect on your reader. Use your text to address your audience directly. You are probably familiar with the classic Uncle Sam image shown in the margin. Notice how it directly addresses *you,* asking for *your* personal involvement. You, too, should use the personal pronouns *you* and *our* to establish a person-to-person connection with your readers. Here is an example of how one writer changed a sentence to be more inclusive of her audience and to establish a person-to-person connection.

Before: Whenever the customer needs help, the Tech Teens will be there.

After: Whenever you need us, the Tech Teens will be there.

TIP In most of your classroom writing, second-person pronouns are not appropriate. However, brochures present a unique exception to this rule.

Short and Sweet The message in your brochure should be concise and to the point. Your reader should be able to find and understand the important information about your product, service, or cause quickly. To avoid cramming too much information into your brochure, thereby making it difficult to read, consider the guidelines on the next page.

YOUR TURN 4

Be sure that each student has chosen a suitable product, service, or cause to promote. You may wish to provide students with graphic organizers on which to work through questions of audience and tone.

Audience	Tone
• defined	• word choice
• wants and needs	• formal/informal language
• how the product addresses those wants and needs	

RESOURCES
Your Turn 4
Practice
- *Communications,* WS. p. 147

- **Limit your sentences to fifteen words or fewer.** Short sentences help readers to read the information rapidly and to hold onto ideas more easily.
- **Write paragraphs of only two to four sentences.** Readers can then find the information they want more quickly.
- **Use strong, action-oriented verbs.** They encourage readers to take action.

Determine the Primary Idea

What's the Big Idea? Your brochure should have one main point, or **primary idea.** For example, the main point for a beach-vacation brochure is that the audience should go to the beach. A brochure for highway litter control focuses on the fact that drivers should not litter our roadways. **Think about the one primary idea, suggestion, or recommendation on which you want the readers of your brochure to act.** All of your writing should focus on that one main idea. For example, the primary idea for the computer club service was "We help customers solve their computer problems."

To express their primary idea, most brochures use a *slogan*, which is similar to the thesis statement of an essay. **Slogans** are short, catchy phrases that are designed to be remembered. Good slogans show the audience how the product or service can fulfill their wants and needs. For example, the slogan "Bananas equal energy" appeals to its audience's desire to be energized.

Teaser slogans grab an audience's attention and make the audience want to know more. The slogan "Share the power of reading with a friend" is intriguing because it makes readers wonder, "How can I share it?" Once curiosity is aroused, readers will probably want to read more of the brochure to find out how they can do their part.

Some slogans use **repeated words or phrases** to catch our attention, as in the slogan "Eat right. Eat rice." Other slogans include **rhymes,** such as "Great advice: Rice is nice!" Some writers use **alliteration,** the repetition of consonant sounds, to make their slogans memorable. For instance, the following slogan uses the sound of alliterative *t*'s to create a memorable slogan for a roller coaster: "The untamable tornado—Can you take it?"

To come up with a catchy slogan, consider your primary idea and then look at the most important parts of that idea—the key focus. For the computer service brochure, the student thought her key focus should be that she and her friends would *help* their customers and not just do things *for* them, and, of course, that their expertise is in computers. Once you have the key focus in mind, brainstorm some catchy words that relate to it. Combine these catchy words with strategies such as repeated words or phrases, rhyme, and alliteration to create a memorable slogan.

Here is how the student working on the computer service brochure came up with some slogan ideas.

> **Primary Idea:** We help customers solve their computer problems.
> **Audience's Most Important Desire or Need:** They want to use computers in work or hobbies but need help or guidance in setting up, operating, and maintaining computers.
> **Key Focus:** help and computers
> **Catchy Words:** guiding, leading, helping, technology, future, troubles
> **Possible Slogans:** "Tackling Technology Troubles," "Guiding You into the Future," "Leading You Toward Future Technology"

Provide Support for Your Primary Idea

Back It Up   Once you have a slogan, you need to consider what the rest of your brochure will say. One way to start is by reviewing the responses you made to the Thinking It Through on page 308. This information on how your product, service, or cause meets the wants and needs of your audience will provide the content of your brochure. Follow the guidelines below to elaborate on your ideas for this persuasive brochure.

- **Use one idea for one paragraph.** Focus on a single idea in each paragraph to help your readers focus on and understand your message. Use **subheadings**—section titles that state or hint at the main idea for each section.
- **Support your claims.** Just claiming that your product meets readers' needs is not persuasive. As in any persuasive writing, you need to support your claims and declarations with concrete examples or statistics. Brainstorm a list of examples that support your claims about your product. Use your local library or the Internet to research facts, statistics, and other information to support your claims.
- **Anticipate your audience's questions.** Good persuasive brochures should anticipate and answer questions that many readers will probably have. Try to put yourself in your audience's place to brainstorm a list of questions. Then, be sure to answer them in your brochure.
- **Include a call for action.** Once your readers are persuaded, they will be ready to take action. Include a section in your brochure that tells readers what specific actions they need to take to purchase the product or service or to get involved with the cause.

TEACHING TIP

Know Your Format
Remind students that although fancy fonts such as Old English are attractive, they are difficult to read. Since a main goal is a readable brochure, ornate fonts should generally be avoided.

If computers are not available, students can create their brochures using pens, pencils, crayons, and markers, as well as graphics cut from other sources.

Brochure Panels
Remind students that most readers look at an average brochure only for a few seconds. If a brochure does not catch the reader's interest quickly, it probably will be ignored. Have each student write one or two sentences explaining why their designs will capture an audience's immediate interest.

Meeting INDIVIDUAL NEEDS

MULTIPLE INTELLIGENCES
Spatial Learners. Encourage students to construct cardboard brochure "skeletons" on which they can paperclip different sheets of designs to see which configurations are most appealing.

Know Your Format

InFORMATion It should be obvious at first sight that brochures are different from essays. Brochures have an easily recognizable **format**, or physical design, created through the use of shapes, sizes, and folds. The most common brochures are tri-fold or quad-fold designs, in which a sheet of paper is folded into three or four parts. The brochure you create for this workshop will be a tri-fold design. Below is a diagram of how this design works.

> **TIP** When visualizing your final tri-fold brochure, remember that as you look at the inside spread, the middle panel will fold over from the back of the right side of the paper, and the front panel will fold in from the left.

COMPUTER TIP
If you are using a word-processing program, you can create a professional-looking brochure. First, change your page orientation from portrait (8.5 x 11 inches) to landscape (11 x 8.5 inches). Then, use the column-formatting features to create a tri-fold brochure.

Brochure Panels The front and back panels are very important for selling your product, service, or cause. The **front panel** is likely to be the first part of your brochure that your readers will see. Imagine a potential customer or supporter picking up your brochure. How will you capture that person's attention and draw him or her into reading further? Be sure to identify your intended audience and the product, service, or cause, so that your audience will keep reading for more information.

Commonly, after looking at the front panel, a reader will flip the brochure over and look at the **back panel**—where many *5W-How?* questions are answered: *How can I contact a representative for this cause? When is this business open? Where can I find this festival?*

The **middle panel** is often a transitional space between the alluring front panel and the *inside spread*, which provides the bulk of the information in the brochure. The middle panel can begin to provide more substantial information while continuing to provide a visually persuasive element to draw readers into the inside spread. The degree to which information and enticement are mixed depends on the writer.

The **inside spread** (made of three panels) is where you will provide the majority of information on your product, service, or cause. You will need to persuade through valid, logical arguments supported with facts and evidence. You will still want to use visuals, mainly as supports for the claims you make in persuading your audience. For example, the writer of the brochure promoting teen help for computer users thought this would be a good place for a chart showing the increase in the number of local homes with Internet access—something that would have been more difficult using only text. At the same time, she also thought a cartoon might add a lighthearted element to the inside spread of her brochure. She thought her audience would appreciate the blend of serious information and informality, rather than a straightforward, serious brochure.

Plan Your Visual Elements

Picture This Brochures combine visual and textual elements to make persuasive points and grab a reader's attention. As you create your brochure, think about how its *look* will achieve these goals. **Graphics such as graphs, charts, photos, and drawings emphasize the strong selling points of your product or service.** Each panel of your brochure should contain at least one graphic to keep it from becoming too **text-heavy**. You can find graphics in old magazines or books, on the Internet, or possibly in computer software you or your school own. You can also draw your own graphics or create them with a computer to jazz up your brochure or give it a personal touch. Remember, though, that all your graphics should be clearly connected to the text around them.

Graphics in persuasion can play different roles: They can capture attention and visually support ideas or descriptions in your text. Keep your audience and product, service, or cause in mind as you choose graphics. For some audiences and products, bold graphics work well; for others, more subdued, practical graphics are best. Good visual elements make readers think, feel, and wonder.

KEY CONCEPT

Reference Note
For more on **graphics and visual design,** see page 855 of the Quick Reference Handbook.

TIP Remember that you must get permission to reproduce any copyright materials (like most visuals from magazines and books).

Location, Location, Location **Page layout,** also called **visual** or **graphic design,** is how the elements of your brochure are arranged on the page. The positions of your visual and textual elements are nearly as important as their content. Too little or too much visual design can make your brochure either too dull or too busy, respectively. Here are some guidelines to help you make decisions about your page layout.

- **Identify the purpose of your brochure by placing your slogan on the front panel.** Write the slogan in a font sized eighteen points or larger. If you create your brochure by hand, letters should be 1/2 to 3/4 inches high.
- **Use a readable type size of ten or twelve points** in the brochure's body. Ten to twelve points for letters will be about 1/4 inch for handwritten text.
- **Insert headings that identify each major section of your brochure** to help your audience quickly find the information they want.
- **Use section headings, also known as subheadings,** above each section. These act as titles to the sections and state or hint at the main idea for each section. Section headings guide readers to the information that is most important to them. For example, the student creating the computer service brochure put section headings over each section that discusses an individual service. Readers, then, are able to quickly find and read about the services they desire and skip over the services they don't need.
- **Use single spacing between lines in your paragraphs and double-space between paragraphs to organize support for your primary idea and help readability.** You do not have to indent new paragraphs because you are using a block format.
- **Align your type only to the left-hand side of the page.** By leaving the right margin unjustified, or free from rigid alignment, you will reduce eyestrain for your reader.
- **Balance your text and visuals with white space (the unprinted portions of the page).** Brochures without white space look cluttered and are difficult to read.

YOUR TURN 5 Designing Your Brochure

Decide on one primary idea for your brochure and formulate a slogan before gathering support for your primary idea. Then, decide on the visual elements of your brochure, such as graphics and page layout. Create a **mock-up**, or rough sketch, of your brochure to help you make sure it will fold and look the way you want it to.

TEACHING TIP

Designing Your Brochure
Students may wish to use bulleted or numbered lists to emphasize important points.

YOUR TURN 5

Have students submit their primary ideas and slogans before beginning their mock-ups. Students creating their brochures on computer should first outline their work using a piece of folded paper to determine what should be placed on each panel.

RESOURCES

Your Turn 5
Practice
- *Communications,* WS. p. 148

Critical Thinking
Practice
- *Communications,* WS. p. 149

Evaluating Reasoning in Advertising

Persuasive advertising, like all persuasion, should include sound reasons and factual evidence. However, advertisers also use certain persuasive techniques to encourage target audiences to believe in something or to do something to benefit the advertiser, not necessarily the consumer. It is possible for an advertiser to go too far in trying to show a product, service, or cause in the best light and actually to deceive the public. However, informed, critical readers want to feel that advertisements appeal to their honest judgment and will resent any writing that merely manipulates them. If you use any of the following persuasive techniques in your brochure, keep in mind that if you do not also include sound reasons and factual evidence, you risk discrediting yourself and your product, service, or cause.

Technique	Example
Assertion is presenting statements as facts without any supporting evidence. True or not, assertions imply that what is stated needs no further proof.	It goes without saying: Baseball is the greatest American sport. So who would turn down a chance to bring a Class AA team to town?
Attacking the person is name-calling that criticizes the person who holds an opinion, rather than the opinion itself. It does not deal with the real issues.	No one as unpatriotic as Bob Jones deserves to be our congressman.
Card-stacking is providing only those facts that support your case, hoping that the audience will not notice the facts that have been left out.	The debate boils down to just one inescapable fact: The adoption of school uniforms would deny teens their personal freedom.
Circular reasoning is restating an opinion or conclusion in different words and trying to pass it off as a reason or supporting evidence.	Sheika is the best choice for class president because she would make the best leader.
Either-or reasoning is describing a situation as if there are only two choices.	If you really care, you should buy your sweetheart roses for Valentine's Day.

Identify each statement below as attacking the person, circular reasoning, either-or reasoning, card-stacking, or assertion.

1. Xlurp: For your thirst, it's either this or nothing at all.
2. Xlurp is the best thirst quencher because nothing else satisfies your thirst so well.
3. Victory sports drink is for people from Dullsville.
4. Xlurp puts you on top of your game. Period.
5. Comparing Xlurp to Victory, you'll find that Xlurp has the vitamin C, electrolytes, and carbohydrates your body needs.

Meeting INDIVIDUAL NEEDS

ADVANCED LEARNERS

Students who are successful in understanding the fallacies of logic presented in this lesson might want to research other fallacies, such as denying the antecedent, biased or insufficient statistics, or the genetic fallacy. After students have had time to get familiar with the vocabulary and reasoning used in logic syllogisms, have them present their fallacies to the class in a forum as Greek philosophers might have done. Pairs of students could present short discussions using fallacious thinking.

MINI-LESSON CRITICAL THINKING

Evaluating Reasoning in Advertising

ANSWERS

1. either-or reasoning
2. circular reasoning
3. attacking the person
4. assertion
5. card-stacking

Critical Thinking Alignments
TEKS 12A, 12C
TAAS R6
English II End-of-Course 3

Quotation for the Day

"Writing is communication, and unless you communicate with somebody, it's just busy work."

(Andre Norton, 1912– , American author)

Read the quotation aloud to the class. Then have students freewrite on what they hope to communicate through their brochures. Have volunteers share their entries with the class.

Timesaver

Before students begin their rough drafts, you may wish to have them list the information they will use for each item on each page of the framework. Then you can quickly check to see that students have each item ready to use before they start drafting.

Connecting Reading and Writing

It will help students in their own writing if they read **A Writer's Model** with an awareness of persuasive visual elements. Using a guided reading process may assist students who are having difficulties. Before students read **A Writer's Model,** refer them to p. 303. As they read the model, have them note the ways that the visual elements help persuade the reader.

Writing

Framework

Front Panel
- Open with a catchy slogan.
- Identify the product, service or cause and its intended audience.
- Use eye-catching visual elements.

Directions and Explanations

Send Up a Flare Catch your reader's attention by using a memorable slogan. Make your slogan 18-point type or larger.

Take Aim Your intended audience should know this brochure is aimed at them. Some brochures use illustrations or photos to identify the intended audience.

Bait Your Hook Use persuasive techniques to draw your readers into reading further.

A Writer's Model

Eye-catching visual

Guiding You into the Future — Slogan

Computers are not always user-friendly. When you need reliable help with your computer, call the Tech Teens.

555-TECH

How Can We

✓ **Internet and E-mail Tutoring**
Isn't it time to get connected? Discover what the World Wide Web has to offer you. Take the bold step toward utilizing connectivity to make your business hum—or just jot a note to a Navy buddy!

Visual element (chart)

✓ **Computer and Printer Maintenance**
Tech Teens can keep your computer system in top order. Call us if your system fails, and we will get things running again.

Whenever you need us, we will be there.

316 | Chapter 8 | **Persuasion:** Using Persuasion in Advertising

---

RESOURCES

Writing

Writing Prompts
- *Communications,* TP. 62, WS. p. 150

Inside Spread
- Include sections that sell the primary idea.
- Include section headings.
- Emphasize major points visually.

Directions and Explanations

One and Only Each paragraph or section should contain one idea that supports the primary idea expressed in your slogan.

Use Your Head(ings) Each section should have a heading that identifies it. Headings help readers predict the content of each section and locate the information they want.

A Solid Center Use facts, concrete examples, and statistics to support each point. Supporting evidence makes your brochure more persuasive.

Visualize It Use graphics to catch the reader's eye and to help explain your message.

Help You? — Heading

√ **Software Tutoring** — Subheading

Let Tech Teens help you learn that new software program in a few simple lessons. We can teach you in your home or office or in our classroom lab.

√ **Computer System Setups**

Don't waste your precious time with wires, cords, and packing bubbles—call the Tech Teens. We can set up a new system or add hardware such as printers and scanners to existing systems. Tech Teens can even install new software.

Visual element (illustration)

Hey, You're Just a Bunch of Kids!

Don't feel bad if that's the first thing that comes to your mind! We get that often! Sure, we don't have degrees, but together we do have experience.

Between us we have:
- 50 years of experience on computers
- Expertise in over 40 different programs
- 1000s of hours logged in online
- 75 operational Web pages on the Internet

Visual element (photo)

All proceeds from Tech Teens go to fund the Marshall High School Computer Club for further education and equipment.

(continued)

Meeting INDIVIDUAL NEEDS

STUDENTS WITH SPECIAL NEEDS

You may wish to hold individual conferences with students who are having difficulty organizing information. Folding a piece of blank paper and writing down the appropriate information on each panel may help students create a more organized brochure. If individual conferences are not possible, have students work in pairs as you walk around the room to help.

Writing, pp. 316–320
Alignments
TEKS 1A, 1B, 1C, 2B, 4D, 8A, 21C, 21D
TAAS W1, W2, W4
English II End-of-Course 4

TECHNOLOGY TIP

Remind students that many brochures now include Web page or e-mail addresses as well as standard addresses and phone numbers. If students wish to include Web addresses in their brochures, remind them not to reveal any personal contact information.

Middle Panel
- Continue drawing your readers' attention.
- Use additional eye-catching graphics.
- Begin providing information.

Reel Them In You have caught the attention of your reader; now, continue to draw them into your brochure by using persuasive graphics and text.

Back Panel
- Provide necessary contact information.
- Tell readers what actions to take.

Be a Spark The back of your brochure tells readers what action to take to acquire the product or service or to contribute to the cause.

Call, Write, or Visit Provide necessary contact information, such as addresses, telephone numbers, maps, or directions.

Translator, Please!

Learning to use computers can feel like a trip to another planet. Every day you hear a new phrase connected with computers or the Internet. We translate and bring you into the tech community faster than you can double-click!

Information on service

Call Us for Home/Office Consultation, or Visit Us at Marshall High

Tech Teens are the Marshall High School Computer Club. You can find us at Marshall High School, 1234 Thompson St., Smith, Idaho.

Call Tech Teens for
- Internet and E-mail Tutoring
- Software Tutoring
- Computer System Setup
- Computer and Printer Maintenance

Contact information

Tech Teens are available:
Monday–Friday, 3–7 P.M.
Saturday, 9 A.M.–2 P.M.

Call 555-TECH

318 Chapter 8 **Persuasion:** Using Persuasion in Advertising

A Student's Model

The following are the front and back panels, followed by the first two panels of the inside spread, of a brochure created by Jason Potterf, a student at Communications Arts High School in San Antonio, Texas. Notice how the front panel directly addresses his readers and tempts them with the image of delicious food. He uses rhyme to make his slogan catchy and memorable.

Visual element (eye-catching photo)

Turn Your Cafeteria into a **Slogan**

Gourmet Cafe

Tired of the same cafeteria food every day? Let **Direct address**

Gourmet School Lunch

deliver the best to your school. **Identifies audience**

Call Today!
1-555-GOURMET

Visual element (color)

How Can I Contact You?

Contact information

Write, call, or e-mail us at:

12345 W. Main

Anytown, USA 90210

1-555-GOURMET

info@scholasticgourmet.com

Connecting Reading and Writing

Explain that students have many different tasks to consider when they are prearranging a brochure, such as choosing interesting visuals, creating catchy slogans, and providing accurate information. Ask students to freewrite for a few minutes about which elements of a brochure are most important to them as the creators of a brochure. Then, ask students if they identified the same elements that are important to them as readers of a brochure.

Subheading

Hungry for a Change?

Visual element (photo)

Tired of the same choices every day in your school's cafeteria? We are the solution to your problem.

Gourmet School Lunch delivers delectable meals to local schools every day, bringing you the very best in midday cuisine.

We offer a broad selection of deli sandwiches for your dining pleasure. We also offer real Italian calzones and even pizza!

The best part of our service is the price. We offer superior food at affordable prices. This way you can eat like a king and not end up in the poorhouse.

Subheading

Delectable Midday Dining

Visual element (photo)

Order one of our many classic sandwiches, or create your own. We stock a wide variety of lunch meats, vegetables, and quality hand-baked bread to satisfy any sandwich craving.

YOUR TURN 6

If students have difficulty getting started, suggest they reexamine the sample brochures and the formats to see how other writers incorporated information into actual brochures. Students may also wish to draft their text first and decide how and where to add the visuals later.

YOUR TURN 6 — Writing a First Draft

Use the framework beginning on page 316 to help you write a first draft of your persuasive brochure. The Writer's Model that begins on the same page is an example of a brochure.

320   Chapter 8   Persuasion: Using Persuasion in Advertising

---

RESOURCES

Your Turn 6

Practice

- *Communications*, TP. 63, WS. p. 151

Revising

Evaluate and Revise Your Draft

Give It the Once-Over You would never participate in a sports tournament or give a musical performance without practicing, would you? Even the best performers practice constantly, working toward perfection. Writing a brochure is no different. Your first draft is not ready for an audience yet. You should read over your brochure at least twice before publishing it. In the first reading, use the guidelines below to evaluate content and organization. The second time through, use the guidelines on page 322 to revise for style.

▶ **First Reading: Content and Organization** The chart below will help you evaluate and revise your persuasive brochure. Answer the questions in the left-hand column. If you need help answering the questions, refer to the tips in the middle column. Finally, if you need to revise, use the techniques in the right-hand column.

Persuasive Brochure: Content and Organization Guidelines for Peer and Self-Evaluation

Evaluation Questions	Tips	Revision Techniques
❶ Does the front panel contain a catchy slogan?	**Put brackets** around the slogan. If there is no slogan, revise.	**Add** a slogan or **replace** ordinary words and phrases with catchier ones.
❷ Does the front panel identify the intended audience and product, service, or cause?	**Circle** the sentence, phrase, or graphic that identifies the audience. **Underline** the product, service, or cause. If you do not find both, revise.	**Add** sentences, phrases, or graphics that identify the audience and the product, service, or cause.
❸ Does each section include headings or subheadings?	**Put the letter H** by each heading or subheading. If a section does not have an H, revise.	**Add** a heading or subheading to any section that does not have one.
❹ Does each section contain concrete facts, examples, and statistics?	**Put a star** next to each fact, example, or statistic in each section. If there are no stars in a section, revise.	**Elaborate** by using facts, examples, or statistics to support claims made in sections with no stars.
❺ Does the brochure use graphics, such as illustrations and charts?	**Put a check mark** next to each graphic. If each panel does not have a graphic, revise.	**Replace** text-heavy sections with a balance of graphics and text.
❻ Does the back panel contain a call to action?	**Highlight** the specific actions that the reader is to take. If you do not find any, revise.	**Cut** any text that does not encourage action. **Add** specific actions for your reader to take.

Writing Workshop **321**

RESOURCES

Revising

Practice
- *Communications,* TPs. 64, 65, WS. pp. 152, 153, 154

Extension
- *Designing Your Writing*

Quotation for the Day

"I don't know of any writer of consequence or any writer at all, any writer who survived to be remembered, who was not sometimes part of a group—"

(John Ciardi, 1916–1986, American writer and translator)

Read the quotation to students and then discuss what they have gained and can gain from peer revision groups. Later, as students begin revising their papers, remind them of the benefits of feedback from others.

TEACHING TIP

Give It the Once-Over
Remind students that using statistics can strengthen persuasion. Students should credit the sources of statistics and of any charts they use.

▶ **Elaboration**
Remind students that including quotations from satisfied customers or supporters can strengthen their brochures. Students need to request permission to quote, and then quote the individual accurately.

Revising, pp. 321–324
Alignments
TEKS 2B, 2C, 2E, 4D, 5A, 5B
TAAS W1, W2, W3, W6, W7
English II End-of-Course 4, 5, 6

ONE WRITER'S REVISIONS Below are the revisions one writer made using the content and organization guidelines on page 321. Read the revisions and then answer the questions below.

> add
>
> elaborate
>
> ✔ **Computer System Setups**
> Don't waste your precious time with wires, cords, and packing bubbles—call the Tech Teens. We can set up a new system or add hardware ∧ to existing systems.
>   *such as printers and scanners*

Analyzing the Revision Process

1. What does adding a heading to the beginning of the section do for the reader?
2. How did adding the two examples improve the brochure?

 Focusing on Content and Organization

Revise your essay using the content and organization guidelines on page 321. Use the example revisions shown above as a model.

▶ **Second Reading: Style** The first time you read through your brochure, you focused on content and organization. Your second reading should focus on style. Style is an important part of persuasion because the words you use can get readers' attention, help them feel comfortable, and encourage them to trust you. Advertising writers sometimes use common phrases to make their writing more familiar or folksy. However, some of these phrases (called **clichés**) have been used so much that readers do not even notice them. Do not run the risk of boring and turning off your reader—avoid using clichés in your persuasive brochure.

Style Guidelines

Evaluation Question	▶ Tip	▶ Revision Technique
Does the brochure include clichés?	▶ **Double underline** any sayings you have heard often before. Revise any underlined phrases.	▶ **Replace** each cliché with a fresh, original saying.

PEER REVIEW
Revise collaboratively by asking a classmate to review your brochure and answer the following questions:
1. What element of the brochure first grabbed your attention?
2. Which support did you find most convincing? Which did you find least convincing? Why?

Analyzing the Revision Process
ANSWERS

1. It helps the reader locate the section, catches interest, and breaks up the text.
2. Examples make the service offered more concrete.

Students may wish to work in peer groups of four as they revise their papers. Peer reviewers should note any language or visuals that may not be effective with the intended audience and should note any unanswered questions about the product.

322 Chapter 8 Persuasion: Using Persuasion in Advertising

Eliminating Clichés

Word Choice

A **cliché** is a tired expression that once was fresh and original but over time has become stale through overuse. The first person to compare an upset stomach to a stomach "full of butterflies" had a fresh and original thought. By now, though, that phrase has been repeated so many times that it has become a cliché. Here are some clichés that seem to sneak into writing.

| believe it or not | the last straw | sink or swim |
| crying shame | let's face it | too good to pass up |

If an advertisement uses a cliché, its audience may think that the product or service is as stale and unimaginative as the cliché.

ONE WRITER'S REVISIONS The writer of the persuasive brochure on page 316 used the style guidelines on page 322 to eliminate clichés.

BEFORE REVISION

We translate and bring you into the tech community faster than the blink of an eye.   *cliché*

AFTER REVISION

We translate and bring you into the tech community faster than you can double-click!   *reword*

Analyzing the Revision Process

1. How does the revision change your image of the service?
2. What other original expressions can you think of to replace the cliché in the Before Revision example?

YOUR TURN 8 Focusing on Style

Revise your brochure to eliminate clichés using the style guidelines on page 322. Use the example revisions shown above as a model.

RESOURCES

Focus on Word Choice
Practice
- *Communications*, WS. p. 155

Designing Your Writing

Typefaces A professional-looking brochure effectively uses **typefaces,** sometimes referred to as **fonts.** If you have access to a computer and a word-processing or desktop publishing program, you can use different typefaces to create various effects. There are four common groups of typefaces: serif, sans-serif, script, and novelty. Here are descriptions and examples of the most common typefaces with some suggestions for their use:

a serif

serif

- A **serif** typeface has lines or curves (called serifs) at the ends of its letters. For some people, a serif typeface is easier to read because the serifs create a visual base line for reading, making them the best choice for body text. Common serif typefaces include Garamond, Palatino, and Times.

H

sans-serif

- **Sans-serif** typefaces do not have fine lines on the ends of each letter. This simplicity of style can make words seem bold and eye-catching, which is why they are often used in headings, slogans, and captions. Common sans-serif typefaces include Arial, Futura, and Helvetica.

script

- **Script** typefaces, which imitate cursive handwriting with the letters connected to each other, are more difficult to read. They are more suitable for items such as invitations or menus. Some common script typefaces are Brush, Chaucer, and Zapf Chancery.

H

novelty

- **Novelty,** or display, typefaces are very "showy" and expressive. They capture the reader's attention. However, they should not be used in body text since they are very difficult to read at length. Novelty typeface names often reflect the mood of the type; for example, Daisy, Neon, Salsa, and Stencil.

Notice that the Tech Teens brochure on page 316 effectively mixes both serif and sans-serif typefaces. A sans-serif typeface is used in the headings and subheadings, making them seem bolder, while a serif typeface is used in the body text to aid readability and text flow. The student model on page 319 makes good use of a script typeface on the front panel to draw an implied, natural connection between the brochure and a menu.

Remember these tips while you design your writing using typefaces:

- Too many typefaces will make your brochure look busy and disjointed. **Use only one or two in your finished product.**
- **Text set in all capital letters can slow down reading speed;** use all caps only in headings or subheadings.

Publishing

Proofread Your Brochure

The Final Run-Through   Once you have revised the content, organization, and style of your brochure, you still need to proofread it. Proofreading helps you make sure that your brochure is free from grammar, spelling, and punctuation errors. Readers tend to assume that an error-filled brochure advertises a low-quality product or service.

Reference Note
For more information and practice on **consistent verb tenses**, see page 597.

Grammar Link

Consistent Verb Tenses

An advertisement that catches your eye reads "Everything must go! Our district manager saw our prices and says they are too high—so he marked everything down 20%!" You might wonder "He *says* the prices are too high? Does that mean they are *still* too high?" Persuasive advertising must communicate clearly and make a good first impression. Grammatically incorrect or awkward writing can confuse the reader and spoil this impression. Make sure your writing is the best it can be by maintaining **consistent verb tenses**. Verb tense indicates the time of the action or state of being expressed in the verb.

Do not change from one verb tense to another unless you need to show a change in the time of the action or state of being you are describing.

Incorrect	The Lawn King **cut** my grass, **waters** my plants, and **took** care of all my lawn and garden maintenance. [Was the work done in the past or present?]
Correct	The Lawn King **cut** my grass, **watered** my plants, and **took** care of all my lawn and garden maintenance. [past tense]
Correct	The Lawn King **cuts** my grass, **waters** my plants, and **takes** care of all my lawn and garden maintenance. [present tense]

PRACTICE

Rewrite each of the following sentences to correct verb tense problems. Write your answers on your own paper.

1. Super Software organized your files and stores your documents.
2. Software Co. sells Super Software and offered all products through mail order.
3. Customers say Super Software makes computing fun. They also said it is the best software on the market.
4. Super Software was developed by the same people who brought you Simple Spreadsheets and who collaborate on the Winning Word-Processing Program.
5. If Super Software did not meet your standards, send it back for a full refund.

Writing Workshop **325**

Quotation for the Day

"I rewrite a lot, over and over again, so that it looks like I never did. I try to make it look like I never touched it, and that takes a lot of time and a lot of sweat."

(Toni Morrison, 1931– , American novelist and Nobel Prize winner for literature)

Write the quotation on the chalkboard and discuss with students the ways in which a writer can make sure his or her work is easy for a reader to follow and understand. Point out to students that, as with any sport or any other art, making something look easy takes a lot of hard work.

Grammar Link

Consistent Verb Tenses

ANSWERS
Possible answers follow.

1. Super Software organizes your files and stores your documents.
2. Software Co. sells Super Software and offers all products through mail order.
3. Customers say Super Software makes computing fun. They also say it is the best software on the market.
4. Super Software was developed by the same people who brought you Simple Spreadsheets and who collaborated on the Winning Word-Processing Program.
5. If Super Software does not meet your standards, send it back for a full refund.

RESOURCES

Grammar Link
Practice
- *Communications*, WS. p. 156

Publishing, pp. 325–326
Alignments
TEKS 2D, 3A, 3B, 3D, 5A
TAAS W3, W6, W7
English II End-of-Course 5, 6

Wrap It Up

Metacognition. Have students reflect on their writing. Allow them five minutes to write a response to the following questions.

1. What elements in your brochure most please you? Why?

Then, have students answer the following items.

2. List three elements needed on the front panel of a brochure. [a catchy slogan, identification of the product, service or cause, and eye-catching visuals]

3. Why should clichés be eliminated? [because they are overused expressions that make the writing less original]

YOUR TURN 9

Remind students that eliminating errors on the final copy is vital, since any material distributed to the public reflects the competence of the distributor. Students may wish to have several peers proofread their final copies, looking for written errors or any visual elements that detract from the brochure.

Publish Your Brochure

Show It Off If you have an actual product, service, or cause you are promoting, try one of these ideas to get your brochure into the hands of your intended audience:

- Hand out copies of your brochure around your neighborhood or at a local store.
- Display your brochure on public bulletin boards in your neighborhood.
- If your brochure is for a cause, send it to an organization involved with that cause. Perhaps they will use your brochure to help the cause.
- If your brochure is for a product or service that might interest your classmates, share your brochure with them. Be sure to get permission from school officials to do this.

PORTFOLIO

Reflect on Your Brochure

Looking Back Every chance to write is a chance to learn something you did not know before. To make the most of this opportunity, think about the process you went through to write your persuasive brochure. Then, write answers to the questions below on your own paper.

- Do the visual elements you chose make your brochure more persuasive? If so, how? If not, what other visual elements might you have chosen?
- Are you satisfied with the tone of your brochure? If so, why? If not, how might you have set a more engaging, persuasive tone?
- What did you like about writing a brochure as opposed to an essay? What did you find more difficult?

YOUR TURN 9 Proofreading, Publishing, and Reflecting

Use the information above to help you
- proofread your brochure, paying close attention to clichés
- eliminate unnecessary shifts in verb tense
- choose a way to publish your brochure
- reflect on the writing process used to create your brochure to help you become a more thoughtful writer

Connections to Life

Analyzing Persuasion in the Media

Thirty seconds or less—that is all it takes to sell a brand-new car, a cereal, or a video game. In spite of their time limits, television commercials are one of the most dominant forms of advertising used today. Unlike a brochure, which can be picked up and taken along by a reader, a commercial must get the message across to its audience in one minute or less. Good commercials have to be creative and attention-grabbing to get their messages across to viewers in this short time span.

Why? Why? Why? Every year, companies pay millions of dollars to have their products or services broadcast on local or national television. Why?

The main reason is that commercials are effective. They combine some of the best elements of all forms of advertising—the audio of a radio spot and the best visual elements from a print ad. The ability of the commercial to tell a story or to present intriguing scenarios has made it an art form. In short, commercials work at two levels: selling a product, service, or cause and enhancing the image of a product through creative storytelling.

Make It Quick In a commercial's short time, it first must get the viewer's attention. Some commercials rely on a story line or the familiar faces of actors, sports celebrities, or animated characters to hook viewers. Other commercials grab viewers by quickly cutting scenes into a montage of fast-paced video and music. You can even find commercials that rely on an "anti-" appeal. Instead of creating an attention-grabbing beginning, they rely on quiet music or even silence—hoping that the absence of sound will attract the viewer.

Once a commercial has a viewer's attention, it must convey information or create a feeling. Some commercials focus on presenting as much information as possible—leaving viewers with a thorough knowledge of what they are promoting. Other commercials convey only an emotional feeling that can override any logical consideration.

Who's the Target? Every ad has a **target audience** for whom the ad is especially created—the people who are most likely to purchase the product or service or to support the cause. Advertisers try to broadcast commercials when the target audience will be watching. For example, cars and trucks are usually advertised at different times than toys.

The target audience is also crucial in determining the content of the commercial. Products likely to be used or purchased by one age group, for example, may be advertised as part of an adventurous or glamorous lifestyle, while products that appeal to another age group may focus more on a prosperous, safe life. Note that the same kind of product can be advertised in two very different ways, depending on the target audience. For example, think of how differently an economy car is advertised compared to a luxury car.

Meeting INDIVIDUAL NEEDS

MULTIPLE INTELLIGENCES

Musical Intelligence. You may wish to tape several commercials from television or radio. Students can view or listen to the commercials and analyze the way music sets the mood or contributes to the image of the product.

Critical Thinking

Analysis. Ask students to recall advertising slogans or jingles. Write students' examples on the chalkboard. Then, have students analyze why advertisers use slogans or jingles and how they increase product recognition.

Connections to Life,
pp. 327–328
Alignments
TEKS 4D, 4F, 19C, 20B, 20C, 20D

To determine the target audience for a commercial, pay attention to these elements:

- **the age and gender of the actors**—a commercial showing only 40-year-old men is probably targeted at 40-year-old men
- **the music played either in the background or foreground**—music from the 1960s or 1970s appeals to people who grew up during those decades
- **the cost of the product or service being advertised**—the more expensive the item, the more likely the commercial will target an audience of above-average income
- **slogans or catch phrases that may identify the target audience**—a commercial that states "your children are your number one concern" is obviously targeting parents

Also, consider who wants or needs the product being advertised. For example, an advertisement for diapers would be targeted at parents with young children.

Logging On Here is part of a chart one student made to log his observations on television commercials.

Commercial	Time of Broadcast	Target Audience	How the Advertisement Appeals to the Target Audience
1. Toughie Toy Trucks	9 A.M. Saturday	young children	The trucks are driving around without any help. My brother has one of these trucks, and they do not operate that way. They look more fun in the commercial, even to someone older like me.
2. Smile Juice	3 P.M. Tuesday (videotaped)	parents—The mother in the ad addresses the viewer as if he or she is a peer.	There are four happy preschool-aged children playing while the mother makes them juice. Most of the message is about thevitamins and how healthy the juice is for "growing children."

YOUR TURN 10 — Analyzing Persuasion in the Media

Over the period of a week, make a log of the television commercials you see. Pay attention to differences in kinds of commercials that appear at different times of the day and on different days of the week.

Then, draw conclusions about the effect a target audience has on an advertisement's content. What was used in the commercials to address the target audience? Why were the commercials broadcast at this specific time? Share your findings with your classmates.

YOUR TURN 10

You may wish to determine a minimum number of entries in the logs students will keep. Allow students without access to television to analyze radio commercials.

Focus on Viewing and Representing

Creating a Documentary on Print Advertising

With thirty-one million teens in the United States spending about $140 billion annually, there is no question that teenagers are an appealing target for advertisers. Money is not the only thing such a large group has to offer. Advertisers also target teens to support causes, follow certain career paths, and adopt certain lifestyles. As a member of this **target audience**—people for whom certain ads are especially created—you should use your knowledge of persuasive techniques to spend your money wisely, to support worthy causes, and to make informed decisions. In this workshop you and a group of classmates will use the information you have gained in this chapter to create your own **documentary**—an informative nonfiction film or video that explores and analyzes the real world. Your documentary's topic will be the persuasive methods used in a print advertisement targeted specifically at teenagers.

WHAT'S AHEAD?

In this section you will make a documentary that analyzes and evaluates persuasive techniques in advertising. You will also learn how to

- set limits on time and topic for a video production
- plan text, visuals, and music
- get feedback on your documentary

Preproduction

In Search of . . . The first steps in creating your video are similar to the steps of prewriting an essay. You need to determine an approach to covering your topic. Beginning your research could be as simple as sitting down and flipping through some magazines or newspapers to look for advertisements you feel are specifically aimed at you and your peers. Another approach is to look at what brand names are popular around your school or neighborhood; then, you can investigate what role advertising has had in the choices you and your peers have made. Look not only in magazines and newspapers that are popular with your friends, but also in magazines read by your parents, teachers, or other adult friends and

Reference Note

For more on **persuasive techniques,** see page 300.

relatives. Looking at advertisements aimed at another target audience gives you a comparative basis for seeing how you and your peers are targeted.

Know Your Limits It is tempting to try to do too much when you make your first documentary. Although you may have movie-length dreams, your first documentary should have a more limited scope. By limiting the time and narrowing your topic, you can make your focus more in-depth.

Limit Your Time Focus your documentary so that it takes *five to seven minutes*. Do not, however, overpack those few minutes with too much information. You want to create memorable impressions of a select few main points rather than overload your audience.

Narrow Your Topic Narrow your topic so that you can cover it in a short time period. One way to do this is to find one specific print advertisement and look at the many persuasive techniques that ad uses. Another approach is to choose a persuasive technique and show many ads that illustrate that technique. Here is how one student narrowed his topic:

> As I looked through several magazines and newspapers, one advertisement really grabbed my attention because of how different it was from the others. Instead of bright colors or images of people having fun, it was toned down and had a serious-looking guy up front. It was an advertisement for the Navy. My documentary will examine how different persuasive techniques are used in this one ad.

The Audience Is Listening Before you proceed, ask yourself questions about your **audience.** Who would best benefit from seeing your video? How will you make your information appealing to them? Your program content will also vary depending on the **gender, economic status, education,** and **age** of the members of your intended audience. Keep the following guidelines in mind—they apply to all audiences.

- **Engage your audience's emotions.** Logical evaluations can often grow from initial emotional reactions. Consider how you want your audience to feel after viewing your documentary.

- **Make your audience care about the subject.** Your documentary should relate to the lives of the audience, or else why would they care? Allow your audience to share in your experience as you search for answers to questions. People enjoy learning about new and interesting things.

Here is what the student who found the Navy advertisement wrote down about his audience.

> The audience for my documentary will most likely be my classmates and teacher; but if I like the final product, I might show it to my other friends and family—a pretty diverse group.

Talk the Talk As with any special area of knowledge, video making and filmmaking have a vocabulary all their own. **Technical language,** or **jargon,** can be useful when you are writing or speaking to a group of peers who share the same profession, field of study, or hobby. When properly used, technical language compresses complex information into a precise word or two. Learn and use the following terms when writing or speaking with your peers as you make your documentary.

Term	Definition
Close-up	a camera shot (see below) in which the camera is perceived to be very close to the subject
Cover shot	a long camera shot that establishes the setting of the scene
Fade-in	a technique for beginning a scene in which the scene begins as black, then slowly appears
Fade-out	a technique for ending a scene in which the scene slowly disappears to a black screen
Full shot	a camera shot that shows a person from head to toe
Shot	the frame of a video; a shot can be wide (far away from the subject), medium (closer to the subject), or close-up
Sound effects	a sound added to a video to enhance actions in the video
Stills	photographs used in a video
Voice-over	narration that is dubbed over live action or stills
Zoom	a movement toward or away from the subject, usually through use of a zoom lens

A Show-and-Tell Agenda Before you begin taping your documentary, plan exactly what you want to show and tell your audience. The more planning you do before taping, the better your final project will come out. Begin by writing a scene-by-scene outline of your documentary that lists the main points you want to present and the order in which you will present them. On the next page is the script outline for the documentary on the Navy ad.

Reference Note
For more on **outlining,** see page 230.

Meeting INDIVIDUAL NEEDS

LEARNERS HAVING DIFFICULTY
Make a videotape or use clips from commercial videos to show examples of each of the techniques listed in the chart on this page. Students who have seen the techniques demonstrated are more likely to incorporate those techniques in their own work.

Meeting INDIVIDUAL NEEDS

MODALITY

Visual Learners. Encourage students to draw rough sketches of the possible scenes and visual elements they plan to incorporate in their videos.

TIP Planning is especially important if you do not have film-editing equipment and must tape your documentary in the sequence in which it will be shown. This technique is known as **in-camera editing.**

Scene 1: Introduction: hook. Student in class reading magazine, sees the advertisement, and then has a daydream about it.

Scene 2: The daydream: student dressed as sailor, saluting.

Scene 3: Focus in on brochure. Voice-over explains how persuasive advertising can be and explains some common persuasive techniques.

Scene 4: Voice-over explains that one target audience for this advertisement is young adults. "Person-on-the-Street" interviews: We ask students passing by what they think of the advertisement. See how many of the persuasive techniques catch their attention. Prompt them to give initial reactions first, and then to look more closely at the techniques. (For example, "What do you think of the slogan 'Navy. Let the journey begin'?" or "What impression does the image make on you?")

Scene 5: Voice-over explains that we will talk in depth with an advertising professional about persuasive techniques.

Scene 6: Final commentary on the research done. Has the research shown that the persuasive techniques used in this ad are effective for the target audience?

TIP As you plan your documentary production, take a few minutes to examine how media affects your own and others' perceptions of reality. Specifically, think about how viewing your documentary will affect audience's perception of reality and how creating your documentary will affect your own views.

Sound and Vision Next, add details to your **script** outline to describe exactly how and where **words, visual elements,** and **music** will be included in the documentary. Keep in mind that you want to give your scenes variety. Who is going to want to watch a video screen showing a magazine or newspaper ad for five minutes? Use the chart below to incorporate effectively words, visual elements, and music into your documentary.

Words	<ul><li>Use a conversational style with short, concise sentences.</li><li>Identify the subject for the audience: for example, the advertisement you are analyzing, the product or service advertised, or the people you interview.</li><li>Explain on-screen action that is not readily obvious to the viewer.</li><li>Use words to ease transitions between scenes.</li><li>Provide background information that can't be shown on-screen.</li></ul>
Visual elements	<ul><li>Show any speakers to establish identification.</li><li>Combine wide shots of whole scenes with close-ups.</li><li>Signal scene transitions through use of zoom or fade features.</li></ul>

| Music | • Signal scene transitions.
• Add moods to scenes. |

Keep the following facts in mind as you create your script.

- Normally, scenes are about five to ten seconds long.
- The two most important segments of your documentary are the beginning, which captures your audience's attention, and the ending, which should leave a positive impression.

People Power A golden rule of documentary writing is that you *must* use people to convey ideas to the audience. A great documentary about Mount Everest chronicles *people* climbing Mount Everest. Great documentaries about war have focused on tales of *human* suffering or triumph. Your documentary should also have a human face to it. Instead of saying that ads for Brand-X athletic shoes have strong emotional appeal, show how emotionally attached teens who wear Brand-X are to their shoes.

Face to Face Another way to put human faces behind your facts is to interview your peers, your parents, or experts in your community. See what opinions or special knowledge they have that might prove useful. For example, an advertising expert could help you analyze your advertisement. Consider the following questions when selecting people to interview.

- **Is the person knowledgeable about the topic of your documentary?** You might consider people who are associated with the product, service, or cause advertised. You could interview people who have used the product or service, or who have supported the cause advertised.
- **Does the person have primary or secondary knowledge of your topic?** That is, will the person give you information from personal experience or information gained through study?
- **Is the person a reliable source?** What sort of qualifications does this person have—years of experience or a degree, perhaps? Keep in mind that although experience often comes with age, some younger people may have more up-to-date information. Also, consider that your source may have a biased point of view on your topic, that is, a partiality for or against the product, service, or cause in your documentary.

TIP Firsthand knowledge often adds to an interviewee's credibility; however, in some cases, people with secondary knowledge may be more objective.

Make an appointment by phone or mail with your interviewee. Keep your appointment and be sure to call in advance if you need to reschedule. If it is not practical for you to arrange an in-person interview (for example, if the person lives too far away), try conducting your interview over the phone.

TECHNOLOGY TIP

Students who cannot interview either personally or by phone may wish to interview using e-mail. When e-mailing their questions, students need to include a return due date so the information will arrive in time to be included.

TEACHING TIP

Face to Face
If students plan to tape their interviews, remind them that it is a federal offense to tape a phone conversation without the other party's consent.

Students who have access to film-editing tools can enliven interviews by showing background footage of people, events, or objects being spoken of in the interview and by dividing the interview into five- to ten-second segments.

Here are some tips for conducting interviews.

- **Prepare a list of questions ahead of time for the interview.** Include a variety of **open questions,** which encourage the interviewee to talk at length, and **closed questions,** which can be answered with "yes" or "no."
- **Ask only one question at a time and allow the interviewee time to answer without interruption.**
- **Listen carefully and paraphrase (state in your own words) any answers you find to be unclear.** This will give the interviewee a chance to clear up any confusion.

Avoid having one person talking on-screen any longer than is necessary to establish who is speaking. Instead, show what the person is discussing—for example, the product or service—and use the speaker's comments as narration.

Putting It All Together   Here is the script of the first two scenes of the documentary on the Navy advertisement. Directions for the scene are in italic print, and narration and dialogue are in regular print. Technical terms are in italic bold. If you handwrite your script, substitute underlining for italic print, and use all capital letters for italic bold print.

> **Scene 2:** *Tape-recorded music ("Navy Hymn") provides transition from Scene 1 to Scene 2. Scene will begin out of focus (to show daydream), then come into focus. The scene shows the student, dressed in sailor uniform, saluting. To the right and behind student, slide photos of sailors working with technology will be shown on the wall. Voice-over reads the slogan from the ad.*
>
> *Voice-over:* Navy. Let the journey begin.
>
> *Fade-out.*
>
> **Scene 3:** *Fade-in. Close-up of advertisement. Tape-recorded, light, instrumental music (to add an upbeat feel to the scene) plays for background to voice-over.*
>
> *Voice-over:* Advertising can be very persuasive. What you have just seen is a typical reaction to good advertising. Notice how the words in this advertisement work with the visual elements to effectively create a strong emotional appeal.
>
> *Zoom in on time line at top of ad.*
>
> *Voice-over:* The time line begins when the young man enters the Navy, and it includes technological training and travel to

---

TEACHING TIP

Putting It All Together
Students may want to use different-colored markers for the directions, narration, dialogue, and technical terms. Have students prepare a color-coding system and use it consistently.

exotic places. It concludes with the young man leaving the Navy for a high-tech career in the civilian world—continuing his journey.

Zoom out to focus on the young man and satellite dishes.

Voice-over: The words and image combine to appeal to some teenagers' desire to work in a cutting-edge, high-tech career. Also, the serious-looking young man would appeal to teenagers who have a sense of personal maturity.

Now Boarding . . . After writing a script, create a **storyboard**—a series of sketches of key scenes with notes on visuals, narration, dialogue, and music. Your storyboard will show the progression of your documentary from the first scene to the final closing credits. Each segment of the storyboard should have a picture to represent the visuals, as well as annotations to the side that indicate key dialogue, narration, or music. Do not worry if you are not a great artist—storyboards are meant to be rough sketches. Like all forms of writing, your storyboard probably will not be perfect on your first try.

Reference Note
For more on **storyboarding,** see page 50.

Production

Get Your Gear To film your documentary, you will need equipment, such as a handheld video camera, videotapes, and microphones. Make sure every member of your group knows how to use the equipment. You may want to have one member of your group take care of all of the equipment and make sure it is in working order.

TIP If one member of your group is especially proficient with the camera, you may want him or her to tape the entire documentary.

Talking Pictures Once you have finalized your script and gathered your equipment, it is time to film. Take advantage of areas around your school or neighborhood. Vary your shots to include live action and still, close-up, medium, and wide shots. Your visuals should be easy to see, to identify, and to understand. This may mean you will need to add voice-overs to explain. For example, you may need to point out where a specific persuasive technique appears in an ad. At other times, you should let your visuals speak for themselves. Whenever possible, use a tripod to ensure that your camera is steady during filming.

Make sure your documentary includes credits. Your credits should show the names of each member of your group and how each contributed to the documentary (for example, narrator, cameraperson, set designer).

Focus on Viewing and Representing **335**

TEACHING TIP

Now Boarding
Remind students that the storyboard is also a good place to put estimates of how much time each scene should take, so that the completed video remains within a five- to seven-minute time frame.

Talking Pictures
Suggest that students may want to videotape credits written on a chalkboard or sheets of paper.

Wrap It Up

Metacognition. Ask students to reflect on the production of their documentaries. Allow them five minutes to freewrite on the following question.

1. What was the most difficult aspect of making your documentary? Explain why it was difficult.

Then, have students answer the following question.

2. What three qualities should you consider when determining the reliability of an interviewee? [Is this person knowledgeable about the topic? Is the person a reliable source? Does the person have primary or secondary knowledge?]

YOUR TURN 11

You may wish to view the documentaries before students show them to the class. In evaluating the videos, place emphasis on students' analysis of persuasive techniques within the documentary.

Postproduction

High Polish, or Diamond in the Rough? Even after you have shot your documentary, you still may be able to make changes if your school or your community has film-editing facilities. Preview your finished documentary, and use the questions below to help you revise and edit.

- What is the main point of your documentary? Does every scene relate to that main point?
- Does any of the narration seem too obvious? Is there too much narration or too little?
- Are all of the shots clear and easy to follow? Are any jerky or out of focus?

Once you have reviewed your video with the questions above in mind, redo any of the scenes that are unclear or confusing.

Opening Night Once your documentary is finished, you will want to show it off. Consider arranging a showing for your class or invite the whole school to a screening before or after school. Finally, you may want to consider asking classmates to join with you in hosting a film festival at your school.

The Reviews Are In After your documentary has debuted, get feedback from your audience. Ask viewers to answer a few questions to determine how clearly you communicated your information. You might give out a questionnaire or ask a few audience members to stay behind for brief interviews. Ask your viewers questions such as the ones below.

- What is the strongest point of the video?
- What is the weakest point of the video?
- What is the overall quality of the filming?
- Are any sections of the narration unclear?
- In one sentence or phrase, what is the main point of the video?

Use the answers to these questions to evaluate your effectiveness, revise your documentary, and to set goals for your next documentary project.

YOUR TURN 11 Creating Your Documentary

Using the above instruction, create a documentary on persuasive techniques in print advertising. Pay as careful attention to the prefilming and postfilming process as you do to the actual filming.

RESOURCES

Your Turn 11

Practice and Reinforcement

- *Media Literacy and Communication Skills*
  —*Support and Practice,* Ch. 8, transparencies and worksheets
  —Videocassette 2, Segment H

CHAPTER 8 Choices

Choose one of the following activities to complete.

▶ CAREERS

1. In the Ad Game Contact a local advertising firm to learn about strategies people in advertising careers use to compose their writing. To analyze these strategies, ask an interviewee how he or she approaches the three stages of the writing process: prewriting, writing, and revision. Also ask about the special challenges and rewards of this kind of writing career and what a typical day is like. Share your findings with your classmates in an **oral presentation,** or invite the interviewee to come speak to your class.

▶ LITERATURE

2. Come to Sunny Mars Think of your favorite book's setting—possibly another planet, an imaginary world, a desert island, or a real place. Create a **print advertisement** for that place, convincing vacationers that this is the ideal place to visit. Use compelling visual elements such as graphics and color to catch your reader's attention. Then, continue the appeal with tempting descriptions of your place. Share your advertisement with other fans of the book or people you think might be interested in reading the book.

▶ CROSSING THE CURRICULUM: HISTORY

3. Rabble-Rousing Many of the great movements in world history occurred because a person with an idea persuaded more people, who persuaded even more, and so on. Pick a major event or movement in history, such as the Boston Tea Party or the women's movement. Then, write a **brochure** persuading your audience to join in your movement.

▶ MEDIA AND TECHNOLOGY

4. Apples vs. Oranges Pick a product that is widely advertised. Then, find a print advertisement, television commercial, radio spot, and brochure for that product. You might even check to see if there is a Web site for the product. Finally, create a chart in which you compare and contrast the persuasive elements of the advertisements. Which form of advertisement do you think is the most effective? Why? Share your findings in a **group discussion** or in an **multimedia presentation.**

 PORTFOLIO

Choices   **337**

▶ CAREERS

Discuss with students the need for people in advertising careers to use strategies to help them compose advertisements. Point out that just as writers will have different strengths and weaknesses, they will also have differing strategies. Strategies will also differ depending on the purpose of a piece of writing. Students can answer the questions *What strategies would be useful in writing advertisements? How could I adapt these strategies to my own strengths and weaknesses as a writer?*

▶ LITERATURE

Have available examples of print ads from magazines and newspapers for students to use as models. Point out that while print ads may include the same type of information as brochures, ads are compressed into a page or less. Review with students the use of graphic design elements such as illustrations and font choice.

▶ CROSSING THE CURRICULUM: HISTORY

Remind students to research the historical event before beginning their brochures. You may wish to work with the history teacher on this assignment. Display completed brochures in the classroom.

▶ MEDIA AND TECHNOLOGY

Remind students who are having difficulty choosing a product that tourist locations are also options for the assignment.

RESOURCES

Using Persuasion in Advertising

Assessment
- *Assessment Package*
  —*Chapter Tests,* Ch. 8
  —*Chapter Tests in Standardized Test Formats,* Ch. 8
  —*Assessment Alternatives,* Ch. 8
- *Test Generator* (One-Stop Planner CD-ROM)

Choices

Rubrics
- *Assessment Package*
  —*Assessment Alternatives,* Ch. 8

Choices Alignments
Choice 1   TEKS 4G, 16A, 16B
Choice 2   TEKS 8A, 21B, 21D
Choice 3   TEKS 1A, 1B; TAAS W1
Choice 4   TEKS 19C, 20C, 20F

Choices   **337**

PART 2 Sentences and Paragraphs

- **9** Writing Complete Sentences
- **10** Writing Effective Sentences
- **11** Understanding Paragraphs and Compositions

CHAPTER 9

PREVIEWING THE CHAPTER

- Complete sentences are the building blocks of good compositions. In this chapter, students will learn to revise sentence fragments and run-on sentences to create complete sentences. This chapter is a useful review for evaluating sentences for completeness, and may be used throughout the year as a writing resource.

INTRODUCING THE CHAPTER

- To introduce the chapter, use Transparency 1 in *Sentences, Paragraphs, and Compositions.*

CHAPTER 9

Writing Complete Sentences

internet connect

GO TO: go.hrw.com
KEYWORD: EOLang

Sentence Fragments

A *sentence fragment* is a group of words that is only a part of a sentence. Since a fragment of something is not the whole thing, it will not be as useful to you as it could be. Just as a fragment of a bowl cannot hold much food, a fragment of a sentence may not communicate what you want to say. To communicate clearly, whether at school or in the workplace, you must write complete sentences.

To be complete, a sentence must (1) have a subject, (2) have a verb, and (3) express a complete thought. If any of these requirements is not met, the group of words is a fragment rather than a complete sentence.

FRAGMENT	Is a large, hairy spider. [The subject is missing. *What* is a large, hairy spider?]
SENTENCE	The tarantula is a large, hairy spider.
FRAGMENT	Some tarantulas of South America to a body length of 3 1/2 inches. [The verb is missing. *What* do they do to a length of 3 1/2 inches?]
SENTENCE	Some tarantulas of South America can grow to a body length of 3 1/2 inches.
FRAGMENT	Although tarantulas of the United States are feared. [The word group has a subject and a verb, but it does not express a complete thought.]
SENTENCE	Although tarantulas of the United States are feared, their bite is only as dangerous as a bee sting.

340   Chapter 9   Writing Complete Sentences

CHAPTER RESOURCES

Planning
- *Lesson Planner,* Ch. 9
- *One-Stop Planner CD-ROM*

Practice and Extension
- *Sentences, Paragraphs, and Compositions,* for Ch. 9

Evaluation and Assessment
- *Assessment Package*
  —*Chapter Tests,* Ch. 9
  —*Chapter Tests in Standardized Test Formats,* Ch. 9
- *Test Generator (One-Stop Planner CD-ROM)*

Fragments usually occur when you are writing in a hurry or when you are a little careless. For example, you might create a fragment by leaving out an important word or two. Also, you might chop off part of a sentence by putting in a period too soon.

To find out if what you have written is a fragment, you can use the following simple three-part test:

1. Does the group of words have a subject?
2. Does it have a verb?
3. Does it express a complete thought?

If even one of your answers is no, then you have a fragment.

NOTE By itself, a sentence fragment does not express a complete thought. However, a fragment can be used for effect in writing if it is clearly related to a sentence that comes before or after it. Read the following groups of words:

        The stark mountains. The lush valley.
    The quiet lake.

By themselves, these fragments do not make sense because we do not know to what they relate. Now, read them along with a sentence placed before them:

    When he reached the peak, the hiker
    stopped to take in the beauty. The stark
    mountains. The lush valley. The quiet lake.

As you can see, the sentence gives the fragments meaning. It fills in the missing parts.

Experienced writers sometimes use sentence fragments for effect. In most of your formal writing, however, you should avoid using fragments. As you gain more experience as a writer, you may feel comfortable enough to experiment in your informal writing. Still, it is important to master the basics first.

Exercise 1 Identifying Sentence Fragments

Try the three-part test on each group of words on the next page. In each case, identify what, if anything, is missing. If the group of words is missing a subject, write *S*. If it is missing a verb, write *V*. If the group of words has both a subject and a verb but does not express a complete thought, write *I* for incomplete. Write *C* if the words form a complete sentence.

COMPUTER TIP

You or your school may have word-processing programs that have tools to check grammatical construction. These tools can find sentence fragments and run-on sentences for you to revise. However, these tools are not foolproof, so you should always proofread your own work carefully.

Sentence Fragments

OBJECTIVES

- To identify sentence fragments
- To create complete sentences from phrase fragments
- To identify and correct subordinate clause fragments in a paragraph
- To use subordinate clauses in sentences
- To identify and correct fragments in a paragraph

Quotation for the Day

"Whate'er is well conceived is clearly said, and the words to say it flow with ease."

(Nicolas Boileau-Despréaux, 1636–1711, French poet and literary critic)

Discuss with students the difficulty that might arise in writing when the writer has not fully thought through what he or she wants to say. Discuss how unclear thinking might affect the clarity of a person's writing. Point out that while a first draft might contain errors, every sentence in a revised draft should express a clear and complete thought.

Writing Complete Sentences, pp. 340–351

Alignments
TEKS 3A, 3B, 3D
TAAS W3, W6, W7
English II End-of-Course 5, 6

Texas Resources
- *Lesson Planner*, Ch. 9
- *TAAS Tool Kit*
- *Preparation for TAAS*
- *Preparing for English II End-of-Course Examination*
- *One-Stop Planner CD-ROM*

Internet
- go.hrw.com (keyword: EOLang)

RESOURCES

Sentence Fragments Practice
- *Sentences, Paragraphs, and Compositions*, TPs. 2, WS. pp. 1, 2, 3, 4, 5, 6, 7, 8, 9, 10

Exercise 1

ALTERNATIVE LESSON
After students have identified the sentence fragments in **Exercise 1**, ask them to revise the fragments to make them complete sentences. You may wish to have students underline added words. Possible answers are shown below.

1. Vampire bats <u>live</u> only in the tropics of Central and South America.
2. no change
3. Vampire bats <u>are</u> very small mammals.
4. Although they do bite other animals, <u>they infrequently attack humans</u>.
5. <u>Some people do not realize</u> that they do not drain their victims of blood.
6. no change
7. While animals are sleeping, <u>the bats are out on their nocturnal flights</u>.
8. <u>They are often harmless</u> but can be dangerous.
9. Some vampire bats <u>can be</u> carriers of rabies.
10. no change

LEARNERS HAVING DIFFICULTY
For **Exercise 1,** have students prepare a note card with the following questions to ask themselves after reading each sentence. *Who or what did something? What did the subject do? What happened during the main action?*

If students cannot answer one of these questions, they will know that the sentence is a fragment and is lacking, respectively, a subject, a verb, or a main independent clause. Students can use their cards until they feel comfortable identifying fragments without them.

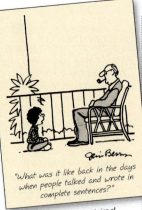

"What was it like back in the days when people talked and wrote in complete sentences?"

BERRY'S WORLD reprinted by permission of Newspaper Enterprise Association, Inc.

Reference Note
For more on **verbal phrases,** such as **participial phrases, gerund phrases** and **infinitive phrases,** see page 472.

1. Vampire bats only in the tropics of Central and South America.   **1. V**
2. Most horror tales about vampire bats are not true.   **2. C**
3. Vampire bats very small mammals.   **3. V**
4. Although they do bite other animals.   **4. I**
5. That they do not drain their victims of blood.   **5. I**
6. Their small teeth are as sharp as needles.   **6. C**
7. While animals are sleeping.   **7. I**
8. But can be dangerous.   **8. S**
9. Some vampire bats carriers of rabies.   **9. V**
10. The greatest danger to victims is infection.   **10. C**

Phrase Fragments

A *phrase* is a group of words that does not contain a subject and a verb. Because it does not have all the basic parts of a sentence, a phrase by itself is a fragment. Three kinds of phrases are often mistaken for sentences: *verbal phrases, appositive phrases,* and *prepositional phrases.*

Verbal Phrases

A *verbal* is a word that is formed from a verb but is used as another part of speech. Because verbs and verbals are look-alikes, it is sometimes hard to tell the difference between them. That is why **verbal phrases** (phrases that contain verbals) are easily mistaken for sentences—they can appear to have verbs in them when they really don't.

Watch for verbals in phrases. Some verbals have endings such as *–ing, –d,* or *–ed.* Another kind of verbal often has the word *to* in front of it (*to run, to look*). A verbal phrase alone does not express a complete thought.

FRAGMENT	Our class interested in deserts.
SENTENCE	Our class was interested in deserts.
FRAGMENT	Found in hot and cold climates.
SENTENCE	Found in hot and cold climates, deserts are created when the earth's surface receives little or no rain.
FRAGMENT	Learning about the Gobi Desert.
SENTENCE	Learning about the Gobi Desert made me interested in studying deserts.
FRAGMENT	To find information about deserts.
SENTENCE	We went to the library to find information about deserts.

NOTE When a verbal phrase modifies, or describes, another word in a sentence, it is usually best to place the phrase as close as possible to the word it modifies. However, some verbal phrases make sense either at the beginning or at the end of the sentence.

Appositive Phrases

An *appositive* is a noun or pronoun that identifies or describes a nearby word in the sentence. An *appositive phrase* consists of an appositive and its modifiers. Because an appositive phrase does not express a complete thought, it cannot stand alone as a complete sentence.

| FRAGMENT | A strange rock formation. |
| SENTENCE | Devils Tower, a strange rock formation, has sage moss and grass on its flat top. |

Prepositional Phrases

A *prepositional phrase* is a group of words that contains a preposition, a noun or pronoun called the object of the preposition, and any modifiers of the object.

| FRAGMENT | Of volcanic rock. |
| SENTENCE | Devils Tower is an 865-foot-tall tower of volcanic rock. |

Exercise 2 Revising Phrase Fragments

Using the photograph on the next page to help spark your imagination, create a sentence from each of the following phrase fragments. You may (1) add the fragment to a complete sentence or (2) develop the fragment into a complete sentence by adding a subject, a verb, or both.

TIPS & TRICKS

You can correct one kind of verbal phrase fragment—a participial phrase fragment—by adding a helping verb to the participle. This action transforms the participle into a predicate verb. Some of the more common helping verbs are *is, was, do, can, will, had, may,* and *would.*

Relating to Usage

Remind students that in an imperative sentence the subject "you" is understood. Therefore, although no subject is directly given in a sentence such as *Please pass the salt,* the sentence is complete.

Critical Thinking

Synthesis. As students study this chapter, have them keep a log of ways to revise and avoid creating sentence fragments and run-ons. At the end of the chapter, have students work in small groups to create handbooks for avoiding fragments and run-ons. Ask students to define and explain in their own words the different types of fragments and run-ons and then to create examples and explain how to revise them. Encourage students to include tips to help avoid such errors.

Sentence Fragments **343**

Exercise 2 Revising Phrase Fragments

ANSWERS
Sample revisions are shown below.

1. Curious about what might be in outer space, NASA scientists launch space exploration equipment such as *Mars Pathfinder.*
2. Space vehicles travel through asteroid fields on the way to distant planets.
3. The desire to discover the unknown has led scientists to send space vehicles to other planets.
4. Sampling rocks and soil, *Sojourner* crossed the Martian landscape.
5. Excited and surprised, scientists studied the reports on the samples *Sojourner* examined.
6. *Sojourner,* a remote-controlled vehicle, was designed as a part of the *Mars Pathfinder* mission.
7. Fueled by scientists' imaginations, the *Pathfinder* mission provided us with information about Mars.
8. On the planet's horizon was the setting sun.
9. Vehicles traveling in outer space must have protective shields so that they will not be shattered by asteroids.
10. One of *Sojourner's* missions was to probe the surface of Mars.

TECHNOLOGY TIP

Have each student type five fragments and five complete sentences on the computer. Then, have students exchange computer files with partners and ask the partners to identify the fragments. When students finish, have them use the grammar-checking feature to check their answers. Remind students to proofread their own work to check for sentence fragments rather than rely on grammar-checking software.

EXAMPLE
1. moving slowly and deliberately on the surface of Mars
1. *Moving slowly and deliberately on the surface of Mars,* the space vehicle Sojourner *looked like a large bug.*

or

The space vehicle Sojourner *was moving slowly and deliberately on the surface of Mars.*

1. in outer space
2. through asteroid fields
3. to discover the unknown
4. sampling rocks and soil
5. excited and surprised
6. a remote-controlled vehicle
7. fueled by scientists' imaginations
8. on the planet's horizon
9. shattered by asteroids
10. to probe the surface of Mars

Reference Note
For more on **independent and subordinate clauses,** see pages 492 and 493.

Subordinate Clause Fragments

A *clause* is a group of words that has a subject and a verb. One kind of clause, an **independent clause,** expresses a complete thought and can stand alone as a sentence. For example, the independent clause *I missed the bus* is a complete sentence. However, another kind of clause, the **subordinate clause,** does not express a complete thought and cannot stand alone as a sentence. A subordinate clause fragment is easy to identify because it suggests a question that it does not answer.

FRAGMENT When flocks of scarlet ibises come to roost in the mangrove trees of the Caroni Swamp. [*What* happens when the ibises roost in the mangrove trees?]

SENTENCE When flocks of scarlet ibises come to roost in the mangrove trees of the Caroni Swamp, the trees seem to blossom in bright red.

FRAGMENT Which is the national bird of Trinidad. [Note that this group of words would be a complete sentence if it ended with a question mark. However, as a statement, it does not express a complete thought. It does not tell *which* is the national bird of Trinidad.]

SENTENCE The scarlet ibis, which is the national bird of Trinidad, begins its flight at sunset.

FRAGMENT That was established by the government. [*What* was established by the government?]

SENTENCE Part of the Caroni Swamp is a bird sanctuary that was established by the government.

NOTE A subordinate clause telling *why, where, when,* or *how* (an adverb clause) generally may be placed before or after the independent clause. When you combine sentences by inserting an adverb clause, try the clause in both positions to see which reads better to you.

EXAMPLES **Because it wanted to protect the beautiful bird,** the government of Trinidad established the Caroni Bird Sanctuary.

or

The government of Trinidad established the Caroni Bird Sanctuary **because it wanted to protect the beautiful bird.**

When the adverb clause comes first, remember to separate it from the independent clause with a comma.

Exercise 3 Revising Subordinate Clause Fragments

Use what you have learned about subordinate clause fragments to correct the following paragraph. First, find the clause fragments. Then, revise the paragraph by combining the subordinate clauses with independent clauses. (There may be more than one way to combine them.) Change the punctuation and capitalization as necessary.

```
    Before and during the Civil War, the
Underground Railroad helped hundreds of
slaves to escape to the North. The Under-
ground Railroad was a system of travel. That
moved the slaves from one house to another.
Until they reached the North and freedom.
"Conductors" on the Underground Railroad
would plan the slaves' journey to the next
"station." One conductor on the Underground
Railroad was Harriet Tubman. Who was born a
slave in 1821. After she escaped from the
South in 1849. She dedicated herself to
helping other slaves escape. Because Harriet
Tubman was brave. More than three hundred
people were able to reach freedom.
```

Exercise 4 Using Subordinate Clauses in Sentences

ANSWERS

Possible answers appear below.

1. When I watch films, I often see an actor who inspires me.
2. When I rented the movie, I found that Rita Moreno was one of the main actors.
3. I especially appreciated the movie because I enjoy her acting.
4. If the performance is good, I enjoy watching any actor.
5. Acting, dancing, and singing must work together in a musical that wins the award.
6. Rita Moreno is an actor whose singing is wonderful.
7. Once I controlled my excitement, I sat down to watch the movie.
8. Ms. Moreno looked as if she were dancing on air.
9. Although I never saw her in person, I felt that I knew her by the end of the movie.
10. Ms. Moreno's role, which she portrayed with great skill, required showing a number of complex emotions.

Exercise 4 Using Subordinate Clauses in Sentences

Use your skills and your imagination to make a complete sentence from each of the following subordinate clauses. To make a complete sentence, add an independent clause at the beginning or end of the subordinate clause. Add capitalization and punctuation wherever necessary.

EXAMPLE
1. because she is a versatile performer
1. Because she is a versatile performer, the actor Rita Moreno has had a long, successful career on stage, in films, and on television.

1. who inspires me
2. when I rented the movie
3. because I enjoy her acting
4. if the performance is good
5. that wins the award
6. whose singing is wonderful
7. once I controlled my excitement
8. as if she were dancing on air
9. although I never saw her in person
10. which she portrayed with great skill

NOTE You have seen that it is easy to mistake phrases and subordinate clauses for complete sentences. It is also easy to mistake a series of items for a complete sentence. In the following example, the series of items in boldface type is a fragment. It may make sense along with the sentence that comes before it, but it cannot stand on its own because it does not express a complete thought.

FRAGMENT   My brother enjoys different types of science. **Biology, chemistry, and astronomy.**

To correct the series fragment, you can

- **make it into a complete sentence**
- **link it to the previous sentence with a colon**

Corrections appear in boldface type.

SENTENCE   My brother enjoys different types of science. **He enjoys** biology, chemistry, and astronomy.

or

My brother enjoys different types of science**:** biology, chemistry, and astronomy.

Exercise 5 Identifying and Revising Fragments

The writer of the following paragraph is explaining why she wants to be an oceanographer. However, the sentence fragments in the paragraph make the meaning unclear. Help make the paragraph clearer by finding and revising the fragments. To correct each fragment, you can (1) link it to an independent clause or (2) develop it into a complete sentence.

```
    Whenever I am at the beach. I think
about the vast world that exists beneath
the ocean's surface.  Though the marine
life is interesting. The ocean floor is what
really interests me. The deepest known spot
in the Pacific Ocean is the Marianas Trench.
Which is the deepest known spot in any
ocean. It lies 36,198 feet below sea level.
In 1960, the bathyscaph Trieste dove to a
record depth in the trench. Plunging 35,810
feet. The Atlantic Ocean is the shallowest
ocean. With an average depth of 11,700
feet. The deepest known spot in the
Atlantic Ocean is the Milwaukee Depth. It
lies 27,493 feet below the surface. In the
Puerto Rico Trench. These trenches exceed
the average depth of the ocean floor.
Reaching deep into the earth's surface.
```

Run-on Sentences

A *run-on sentence* is two or more complete sentences that are written as one sentence. Because run-on sentences do not show where one idea ends and another begins, they can confuse readers. There are two kinds of run-on sentences: the *fused sentence* and the *comma splice*.

In a *fused sentence*, the writer has joined two or more sentences with no punctuation between them.

RUN-ON	Measurements originally were related to the sizes of people's hands, arms, and feet an inch was once defined as the width of a thumb.
CORRECT	Measurements originally were related to the sizes of people's hands, arms, and feet. **A**n inch was once defined as the width of a thumb.

TIPS & TRICKS

To identify run-on sentences, try reading your writing aloud. A natural, distinct pause in your voice usually means that you have come to the end of a thought. If your voice pauses, but your sentence keeps going, you may have a run-on.

Another way to spot run-ons is to look for subjects and verbs. This strategy will help you see where one complete thought ends and another one begins.

RESOURCES

Run-on Sentences
Practice
- *Sentences, Paragraphs, and Compositions,* TP. 3, WS. pp. 11, 12, 13, 14, 15, 16

Quotation for the Day

"Talking and eloquence are not the same: to speak, and to speak well, are two things. A fool may talk, but a wise man speaks."

(Ben Jonson, 1572–1637, English dramatist and poet)

Have students look up the definition of eloquence and discuss why they would want their writing to be considered eloquent. Discuss how complete sentences, free from errors, contribute to eloquence.

TEACHING TIP

Revising Run-on Sentences
Remind students that changing a run-on sentence into a complete sentence is not always the best revision. A string of independent clauses joined by a series of coordinating conjunctions is usually a poor sentence. This type of sentence needs to be divided, unless there is a good stylistic reason for using such sentences (to indicate excitement, for example).

Crossing the Curriculum

Foreign Language/History. The early Greek language had no system of punctuation between sentences, and most early Latin books used no punctuation. Ask students to write briefly about what might happen if English followed this same practice today. Then, ask why students think punctuation developed in languages, over time.

In a *comma splice,* the writer has joined two or more sentences with only a comma to separate them.

RUN-ON   A foot was the length of a person's foot, a yard was the distance from a person's nose to the end of his thumb when his arm was outstretched.

CORRECT A foot was the length of a person's foot**.** **A** yard was the distance from a person's nose to the end of his thumb when his arm was outstretched.

Revising Run-on Sentences

There are several ways to revise a run-on sentence. As shown in the previous examples, you can always make two separate sentences. However, you can also make a compound sentence if the independent clauses in the run-on are closely related.

Reference Note
For more on **forming compound sentences,** see page 358.

1. You can make a compound sentence by adding a comma and a coordinating conjunction (*and, but, for, nor, or, so,* or *yet*).

   RUN-ON   In photography, an aperture controls the amount of light exposing the film a shutter controls how long the film is exposed to the light.

   REVISED In photography, an aperture controls the amount of light exposing the film**, and** a shutter controls how long the film is exposed to the light.

2. You can make a compound sentence by adding a semicolon.

   RUN-ON   A slower shutter speed allows more light to expose the film a faster shutter speed allows less light to expose the film.

   REVISED A slower shutter speed allows more light to expose the film**;** a faster shutter speed allows less light to expose the film.

348   Chapter 9   Writing Complete Sentences

Punctuating Sentences. Offer these reminders to help students decide whether to use a colon or a semicolon when punctuating sentences.

- Colons emphasize the information that follows the colon.

- Semicolons join related independent clauses that are not joined by a comma and coordinating conjunction.

Have students practice using colons and semicolons by correctly inserting them in the following sentences.

3. You can make a compound sentence by adding a semicolon and a *conjunctive adverb*—a word such as *therefore, instead, meanwhile, still, also, nevertheless,* or *however.* A conjunctive adverb should be followed by a comma.

Reference Note
For a list of **conjunctive adverbs,** see page 724.

RUN-ON   Cameras have been greatly improved over time, controlling exposure with the aperture and shutter has remained the same.
REVISED   Cameras have been greatly improved over time**; nevertheless,** controlling exposure with the aperture and shutter has remained the same.

Exercise 6 Revising by Correcting Run-ons

The following items are confusing because they are run-on sentences. Using the method of revision indicated in parentheses, correct each run-on sentence.

1. Cambodia is a Southeast Asian country it is bordered by Thailand, Laos, and Vietnam. (Make into two sentences.)
2. Most of the people living in Cambodia belong to the Khmer ethnic group, people belonging to other ethnic groups also live there. (Use a semicolon and a conjunctive adverb.)   2. ; however,
3. Cambodia has a famous river called the Mekong it also has a large lake called Tonle Sap. (Use a comma and a coordinating conjunction.)   3. , and   4. ; therefore,
4. Like many other Asian countries, Cambodia has a climate that is good for growing rice, no one should be surprised to find out that rice is the country's principal crop. (Use a semicolon and a conjunctive adverb.)
5. More than 200,000 people from other countries visit Cambodia each year most of them are tourists. (Make into two sentences.)
6. In the northwestern part of Cambodia, there is an area known as Angkor it is now a popular site for visitors to the country. (Use a semicolon.)

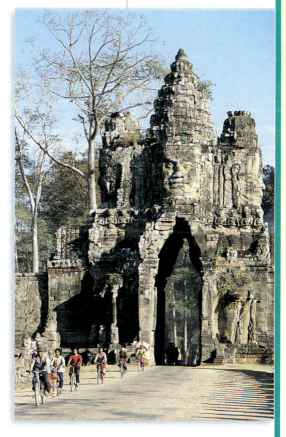

Meeting INDIVIDUAL NEEDS

ENGLISH-LANGUAGE LEARNERS
General Strategies. Reading aloud the run-on sentences in **Exercise 6** may help students understand the problems with run-ons. Have pairs of students take turns reading the sentences. Tell students to exaggerate the confusing effect of run-ons by reading them faster than normal. Then, have students re-read the sentences aloud after proper punctuation has been inserted. Again, have students exaggerate the pauses a little to hear how punctuation works as an organizer to make sentences clear and understandable.

Critical Thinking

Evaluation. Have students write for five to seven minutes on topics of their choice. Encourage students to write as much information as they can on their topics. Then, have students exchange papers to evaluate each other's writing for run-ons and fragments. Students should use their evaluations to check for clarity and organization.

---

1. The soccer team played games in four cities[:] Memphis, Atlanta, Charleston, and Mobile.
2. Our team won three of the four games[;] injuries to our goalie in the fourth game contributed to our loss.
3. When the team arrived home, a band greeted the bus[;] however, a traffic jam prevented the crowd of fans from reaching the victory parade.

Review A — Correcting Fragments and Run-on Sentences

ANSWERS
Possible answers are shown below.

1. Explorers have found many kinds of forests in the world, including tropical rain forests, temperate forests, and evergreen forests.

2. In rain forests, trees form a dense canopy, which shuts out much of the sunlight.

3. C

4. In order to live, animals need forests, which provide places to live and sources of nourishment.

5. The carefully balanced food chain in forests is nourishing all forest creatures.

6. Although some countries that cut down rain forests institute programs to help maintain the forest as a resource, rare species of life may still face extinction as their habitats are destroyed.

7. C

8. Forests perform several vital functions for other living things; among them are cleaning carbon dioxide from the air and preventing soil erosion.

9. People have been clearing forests for thousands of years, but deforestation has increased as the earth's population has increased.

10. C

RESOURCES

Writing Complete Sentences
Assessment
- Assessment Package
  —Chapter Tests, Ch. 9
  —Chapter Tests in Standardized Test Formats, Ch. 9
- Test Generator (One-Stop Planner CD-ROM)

---

7. Some of the structures in Angkor are more than eight hundred years old; they are world renowned for their beautifully carved details. (Make into two sentences.)

8. Angkor, an area in the northwestern part of the country, is the most popular tourist destination in Cambodia; many people visit the country just to see it. (Use a semicolon.)

9. Angkor Wat, the most famous monument at Angkor, was originally built as a temple it also served as an astronomical observatory. (Use a comma and a coordinating conjunction.) **9. , but**

10. Another monument, called Angkor Thom, features a structure called the Bayon; two hundred stone faces decorate its surface. (Use a semicolon.)

Review A — Correcting Fragments and Run-on Sentences

Most of the items below contain fragments or run-on sentences. Correct the fragments and run-on sentences in any of the ways you have learned. If an item is correct, write C. Change the punctuation and capitalization wherever necessary.

1. Many kinds of forests in the world, including tropical rain forests, temperate forests, and evergreen forests.

2. In rain forests, trees form a dense canopy. Which shuts out much of the sunlight.

3. After falling to the warm, damp forest floor, plants decay and release nutrients.

4. Animals need forests in order to live forests provide places to live and sources of nourishment.

5. The carefully balanced food chain in forests nourishing all forest creatures.

6. Although some countries that cut down rain forests institute programs to help maintain the forest as a resource.

7. Some forests have been damaged by acid rain, a product of air pollution mixing with rain to develop sulfuric acid.

8. Forests perform several vital functions for other living things, among them are cleaning carbon dioxide from the air and preventing soil erosion.

9. People clearing forests for thousands of years but increased deforestation as the earth's population has increased.

10. In order to help save our forests, people have set aside national parks and have replaced felled trees with new ones.

Learning for Life

Effective Communication. Knowing how to write complete sentences will help students in settings other than school. Many jobs require the writing of reports, for example, that describe a product or event clearly and concisely. The accuracy of such communication is often of vital importance to a business. Have students practice their reporting skills by writing brief reports on an event of their choice—a game, a school council

Review B **Revising Fragments and Run-on Sentences**

When you read the following paragraphs, you will notice several sentence fragments and run-on sentences. First, identify each fragment and run-on. Then, rewrite the passage correctly. Change the punctuation and capitalization wherever necessary.

```
    Heroes come in all shapes and sizes.
Women and men, adults and children. However,
one hero looked quite different from what
you might imagine. Living in Czechoslovakia
after World War II and named Antis. This
hero was a German shepherd dog.
    Shortly before World War II, Antis was
adopted by a man named Jan Bozdech. Bozdech
served in the British Air Force during the
war, afterwards, he returned to his home-
land, Czechoslovakia. Because the Soviet
Union controlled his country. Bozdech even-
tually decided to escape to Austria with his
dog. During the journey, Antis alerted his
master to the presence of police and border
patrols, when Bozdech almost drowned trying
to cross a fast-flowing river in the dark,
Antis grabbed his master's jacket and pulled
him to safety.
    Near the end of their journey to freedom.
A border guard began to walk toward Bozdech.
Who was sleeping. Antis diverted the guard's
attention by leaping around and distracting
him. The guard did not find Bozdech, he and
his faithful dog made it to safety.
```

CHAPTER 10

PREVIEWING THE CHAPTER

- Effective sentences are vital in writing clear, smooth, and interesting paragraphs. In this chapter, students will learn to combine sentences and improve sentence style to make effective sentences. You may choose to use this chapter to focus on effective sentences directly. You may also find it valuable as a review and a reference when teaching composition.

INTRODUCING THE CHAPTER

- To introduce the chapter, use Transparency 4 in *Sentences, Paragraphs, and Compositions*.

CHAPTER 10 Writing Effective Sentences

GO TO: go.hrw.com
KEYWORD: EOLang

Combining Sentences

Whether you are writing a school or workplace assignment or a personal letter, your goal is to communicate your ideas. Therefore, you want your writing to be clear, effective, and interesting. Short sentences can be effective, but too many of them make writing sound choppy. For example, notice how the many short sentences in the following paragraph make it boring to read.

```
A geyser is a spring. A geyser shoots
hot water into the air with great force.
Some geysers erupt continually. Some gey-
sers remain inactive for long periods.
The water seeps into the earth's surface
through cracks. The water expands into
steam when it reaches extremely hot rocks.
```

Sentence combining is a way to improve choppy writing. Below and on the next page, you can see how the paragraph about geysers can be improved by combining the short sentences into longer, smoother sentences.

Notice that even though the sentences are longer, the revised paragraph is shorter and more precise. That is because sentence combining has helped to eliminate repeated words and ideas.

```
A geyser is a spring that shoots hot
water into the air with great force. Some
geysers erupt continually, while some remain
```

352 Chapter 10 Writing Effective Sentences

CHAPTER RESOURCES

Planning
- *Lesson Planner,* Ch. 10
- One-Stop Planner CD-ROM

Practice and Extension
- *Sentences, Paragraphs, and Compositions,* for Ch. 10

- *Combining Sentences,* Teaching Notes

Evaluation and Assessment
- Assessment Package
  —Chapter Tests, Ch. 10
  —Chapter Tests in Standardized Test Formats, Ch. 10

inactive for long periods. The water seeps into the earth's surface through cracks and expands into steam when it reaches extremely hot rocks.

Inserting Words

You can combine short sentences by taking a key word from one sentence and inserting it into another sentence. When you do this, you may have to delete one or more words. You may also have to change the form of the word you insert.

Using the Same Form	
ORIGINAL	Andrew Lloyd Webber composed the music for several Broadway musicals. The musicals were popular.
COMBINED	Andrew Lloyd Webber composed the music for several **popular** Broadway musicals.
Changing the Form	
ORIGINAL	Webber is best known for his melodic scores. The scores flow.
COMBINED	Webber is best known for his **flowing** melodic scores.

NOTE When you change the form of a word before inserting it into a sentence, you often add an ending that makes the word an adjective or an adverb. The endings you will use most frequently are –*ed*, –*ful*, –*ing*, and –*ly*.

Exercise 1 Combining Sentences by Inserting Words

On the next page are ten sets of sentences about the many uses of common plants. Combine each set into one sentence by inserting the italicized word(s) from the second sentence into the first sentence. The directions in parentheses will tell you how to change the form of a word if it is necessary to do so. Possible combinations follow.

EXAMPLE 1. You can find books that describe the uses of herbs. These books describe the *many* uses that herbs have.
1. You can find books that describe the many uses of herbs.

Combining Sentences 353

Combining Sentences

OBJECTIVES

- To combine sentences by inserting words and phrases
- To combine sentences by using compound subjects and verbs
- To combine sentences into compound and complex sentences

Quotation for the Day

"You never want to bore your readers. It's the biggest sin, next to misleading them and lying. One way to stay interesting is to change the length of your sentences, so that the rhythm is interesting."
(Ethel Grodzins Romm, 1925– , American writer)

Ask students to brainstorm problems that make writing boring. Then, point out to students that this chapter may help them address some of these problems in their own writing.

RESOURCES

Combining Sentences
Practice
- *Sentences, Paragraphs, and Compositions,* TP. 5, WS. pp. 17–32
Extension
- *Combining Sentences,* TPs. 1–7, WS. pp. 1–20

- Test Generator (One-Stop Planner CD-ROM)
Internet
- go.hrw.com (keyword: EOLang)

Writing Effective Sentences, pp. 352–369
Alignments
TEKS 3A, 3B, 3D
TAAS W3, W6, W7
English II End-of-Course 5, 6

Texas Resources
- Lesson Planner, Ch. 10
- TAAS Tool Kit
- Preparation for TAAS
- Preparing for English II End-of-Course Examination
- One-Stop Planner CD-ROM

Combining Sentences 353

Meeting INDIVIDUAL NEEDS

MODALITY

Kinesthetic Learners. As students complete **Exercise 1**, they may benefit from writing the sentences on index cards and writing the words to be inserted on self-stick notes. Then, students can move the word from place to place on the index card until they find an acceptable placement.

Timesaver

You may wish to have students underline the inserted words in **Exercises 1** and **2** to make the inserted words easier to identify.

Exercise 1

ALTERNATIVE LESSON

Have students look at their revised sentences for **Exercise 1** and label each inserted word's function in the sentence. After students have labeled each inserted word as an adjective or an adverb, discuss with them any changes they made to the original form of the word to insert it into the sentence.

TIPS & TRICKS

One effective way to vary sentences is to insert an adverb ending in –ly at the beginning of a sentence.

EXAMPLE
Slowly the noise filled the room.

---

1. Plants have always been valued for their properties. ~~These properties are~~ *medicinal*.   **1.** medicinal
2. Digitalis, a medicine for heart failure, is extracted from the foxglove plant. ~~Digitalis is an~~ *effective* ~~medicine~~.   **2.** an effective
3. The recipes for many old-fashioned herbal remedies have been lost. ~~The loss of these recipes is~~ *unfortunate*. (Add –ly.)   **3.** Unfortunately,
4. Some herbal remedies have been passed down through many generations of families. ~~The families~~ *trust* ~~these remedies~~. (Add –ed.)
5. Plants are still used to make products such as shampoos and hair dyes. ~~These products are~~ *beauty* ~~products~~.   **4.** trusted   **5.** beauty
6. The ancient Egyptians used dill in healing. ~~This healing was~~ *herbal*.
7. Research shows that dill helps relax the muscles of the digestive tract. ~~These muscles are the~~ *smooth* ~~muscles~~.   **6.** herbal   **7.** smooth
8. Another herb, echinacea, was adopted by plains settlers as a remedy for stings and snakebites. ~~This was a~~ *folk* ~~remedy~~.   **8.** folk
9. Many recent European studies show that echinacea has remarkable properties. ~~These properties can~~ *heal*. (Add –ing.)   **9.** healing
10. Did you know that cinnamon was used by the Ancient Chinese as a treatment for digestive problems? ~~The cinnamon was a~~ *powder*. (Add –ed.)   **10.** powdered

Exercise 2 Combining Sentences by Inserting Words

In Exercise 1, the key words were italicized for you. Now it is up to you to decide which words to insert. There may be more than one way to combine each set of sentences; choose the combination you think is best. Change the forms of words wherever necessary.

Here are possible combinations.

1. The Statue of Liberty, a copper sculpture on Liberty Island, towers over a bay. ~~The bay is Upper New York Bay~~.   **1.** Upper New York Bay
2. In 1884, France gave the statue to the United States as a gift of friendship. ~~The statue is massive~~.   **2.** massive
3. The people of France donated the money to construct the statue. ~~Their donation was generous~~.   **3.** generously
4. French sculptor Frederic Auguste Bartholdi tried to complete the statue in time for the centennial celebration of the Declaration of Independence. ~~He was not successful~~.   **4.** unsuccessfully
5. In 1986, a restoration of the Statue of Liberty was completed. ~~The restoration was extensive~~.   **5.** an extensive

Inserting Phrases

You can also combine closely related sentences by reducing one sentence to a phrase and inserting it into the other sentence. When it is inserted, the phrase gives additional information about an idea expressed in the sentence.

Prepositional Phrases

A *prepositional phrase* contains a preposition, its object, and any modifiers of the object. Usually, you can move a prepositional phrase from one sentence into another without changing the phrase in any way.

ORIGINAL   Great Salt Lake is an inland body of saltwater. The lake is in northwestern Utah.

REVISED   Great Salt Lake is an inland body of saltwater **in northwestern Utah.**

Participial Phrases

A *participle* is a word that is formed from a verb and that can be used as an adjective. A participle usually ends in *–ing* or *–ed*. A *participial phrase* contains a participle and any modifiers or complements the participle has. The whole participial phrase acts as an adjective in a sentence.

Sometimes you can combine sentences by reducing one sentence to a participial phrase. When you insert the participial phrase into the other sentence, place it close to the noun or pronoun it modifies. Otherwise, you may confuse your reader.

ORIGINAL   Juanita Platero describes the conflict between old and new ideas. She does this as she writes about Navajo culture.

REVISED   **Writing about Navajo culture,** Juanita Platero describes the conflict between old and new ideas.

Appositive Phrases

An *appositive phrase* is made up of an appositive and its modifiers. It identifies or describes a noun or pronoun in a sentence. Sometimes you can change one sentence into an appositive phrase and insert it into another sentence. Like a participial phrase, an appositive phrase should be placed directly before or after the noun or pronoun it modifies. The phrase should be separated from the rest of the sentence by a comma (or two commas if you place the phrase in the middle of the sentence).

Reference Note
For more on **the different kinds of phrases,** see page 467.

Relating to Usage

Remind students that modifying phrases should be placed as closely as possible to the words they modify. To give students practice placing modifying phrases correctly, write the following sentences on an overhead transparency or on the chalkboard and have students revise them to eliminate misplaced modifiers.

1. Growing in my garden, she loved the snapdragons. [*She loved the snapdragons growing in my garden.*]

2. He read about her scientific achievements in the journal. [*In the journal, he read about her scientific achievements.*]

3. Ignacio found his sister's doll mowing the lawn. [*Mowing the lawn, Ignacio found his sister's doll.*]

4. Leaping gracefully, we watched the dancers. [*We watched the dancers leaping gracefully.*]

5. Isabelle described hang gliding in class. [*In class, Isabelle described hang gliding.*]

Combining Sentences

Exercise 3 — Combining Sentences by Inserting Phrases

ANSWERS
Here are possible answers.

1. Searching for work, migrant laborers move constantly.
2. Many live in extreme poverty, without adequate food, shelter, and medical care.
3. Lacking education, many migrant laborers are unable to find other kinds of work.
4. Cesar Chavez, a labor union organizer, championed the rights of migrant farmworkers.
5. Chavez was born on a farm in Arizona.
6. His family became migrant workers after losing their farm.
7. Organizing grape pickers in the 1960s, Chavez helped make the voices of farmworkers heard.
8. He established a union, the National Farm Workers Association.
9. Committed to nonviolent protest, Chavez organized strikes and boycotts.
10. Through his organizing efforts, he helped to improve working conditions for migrant laborers.

ORIGINAL Neil Armstrong is best known for his historic first steps on the moon. Neil Armstrong is a former U.S. astronaut.

REVISED Neil Armstrong**, a former U.S. astronaut,** is best known for his historic first steps on the moon.

Exercise 3 Combining Sentences by Inserting Phrases

Insert phrases to combine each of the following pairs of sentences into one sentence. (There may be more than one way to combine each pair.) For each sentence pair, the hints in parentheses will tell you when to change the forms of words and when to add commas. To help you get started, the words you need to insert are italicized in the first five sentence pairs.

EXAMPLE
1. Migrant farmworkers move from region to region. They *follow the seasonal crop harvests.* (Change *follow* to *following*, and add a comma.)

1. Following the seasonal crop harvests, migrant farmworkers move from region to region.

1. Migrant laborers move constantly. They *search for work.* (Change *search* to *searching*, and add a comma.)
2. Many live in extreme poverty. They live *without adequate food, shelter, and medical care.*
3. Many migrant laborers are unable to find other kinds of work. They *lack education.* (Change *lack* to *lacking*, and add a comma.)
4. Cesar Chavez championed the rights of migrant farmworkers. He was *a labor union organizer.* (Add two commas.)
5. Chavez was born in Arizona. He was born *on a farm.*
6. His family became migrant workers. They became migrant workers after losing their farm.
7. Chavez helped make the voices of farmworkers heard. He organized grape pickers in the 1960s. (Change *organized* to *organizing*, and add a comma.)
8. He established a union. It was called the National Farm Workers Association.
9. Chavez organized strikes and boycotts. He was committed to nonviolent protest. (Add a comma.)
10. He helped to improve working conditions for migrant laborers. He did this through his organizing efforts.

Using Compound Subjects and Verbs

You can also combine sentences by using compound subjects and verbs. Just look for sentences that have the same subject or the same verb. Then, use coordinating conjunctions (such as *and, but, for, nor, or, so,* and *yet*) to make a compound subject, a compound verb, or both.

ORIGINAL Jaguars are large, spotted cats. Leopards are large, spotted cats.
REVISED **Jaguars and leopards** are large, spotted cats. [compound subject with the same verb]

ORIGINAL Jaguars live in the Americas. Jaguars hunt in the Americas.
REVISED Jaguars **live and hunt** in the Americas. [compound verb with the same subject]

ORIGINAL Jaguars hunt and attack other animals. Leopards hunt and attack other animals. These cats rarely attack humans.
REVISED **Jaguars and leopards hunt and attack** other animals **but** rarely **attack** humans. [compound subject and compound verb]

NOTE When you combine sentences by using compound subjects and compound verbs, make sure your subjects and verbs agree in number.

ORIGINAL Asia is home to the leopard. Africa is home to the leopard.
REVISED Asia and Africa **are** home to the leopard.

Exercise 4 Combining Sentences by Using Compound Subjects and Verbs

Here are five pairs of short, choppy sentences. Combine each pair into one sentence by using a compound subject, a compound verb, or both.
Possible combinations appear below.
1. Glaciers shape landforms over time. ~~Volcanoes also shape landforms over time~~. **1. and volcanoes**
2. Antarctica is mostly covered by glaciers. ~~Greenland is mostly covered by glaciers~~. **2. and Greenland are**
3. ~~Glaciers move slowly~~. Glaciers shape the land as they flow across it.
4. A volcano begins as molten rock beneath the earth's surface. ~~It~~ gradually rises upward. **3. move slowly and   4. and**
5. Volcanoes can create land area. ~~Glaciers can also create land area. They both can destroy land area~~. **4. and glaciers/and destroy**

STYLE TIP

So is often overworked in writing. Think twice before using it.

Reference Note

For more on **subject-verb agreement,** see page 512.

TEACHING TIP

Using Compound Subjects and Verbs
Point out to students that when a compound subject is joined by *or* or *nor,* the verb should agree in number with the part of the subject that is closest to the verb. For example, in the sentence "Neither the casserole nor the corn muffins are done," the verb (*are*) agrees with the closest half of the compound subject (*muffins*).

Critical Thinking

Analysis. Provide students with a well-written paragraph that includes several compound subjects and verbs. Have students analyze how the writer uses compound subjects and verbs to convey information more effectively.

Relating to Literature

James Weldon Johnson's poem "The Creation" includes many compound sentences joined by *and*. Have students read the poem, if available, and ask them what effect the large number of compound sentences has on the poem. [*Students might say that the repetition of the compound sentence structure creates intensity and gives the poem a regular rhythm.*] Tell students that a regular rhythm is one of the characteristics of the oral storytelling tradition because it helps the storyteller remember the story and because it holds the listener's attention.

Crossing the Curriculum

Science. Have students look at the directions for an experiment in their science books. Working in groups of four, students should combine these directions into longer sentences. Then, each group can exchange papers with another group and compare the new directions with the original ones. [*The new directions should be more difficult to follow.*] Discuss with students why, in some writing, using many short sentences may be necessary. [*to provide directions that might otherwise be confusing*]

Creating a Compound Sentence

If the thoughts in two sentences are related to one another and are equal in importance, you can combine the sentences to form a *compound sentence.* A compound sentence is two or more independent clauses joined by

- a comma and a coordinating conjunction

  or

- a semicolon

  or

- a semicolon and a conjunctive adverb

Reference Note
For a list of **common conjunctive adverbs,** see page 724.

ORIGINAL   Veins carry blood to the heart. Arteries carry blood away from the heart.

REVISED   Veins carry blood to the heart**,** **but** arteries carry blood away from the heart. [comma and coordinating conjunction]

or

Veins carry blood to the heart**;** arteries carry blood away from the heart. [semicolon]

or

Veins carry blood to the heart**;** **however,** arteries carry blood away from the heart. [semicolon and conjunctive adverb]

Exercise 5 Combining Sentences into Compound Sentences

The following sentences are fine by themselves, but together they would make a choppy paragraph. Using the above methods, combine each pair of sentences into a compound sentence. Try to use each method at least once. Be sure to use the correct punctuation.

Possible combinations follow.

1. In 1881, a French company began building a canal through the Isthmus of Panama. The United States took over construction of the canal in 1903. **1. , but**
2. Workers labored for ten years to complete the canal. One of the toughest obstacles was disease. **2. , and**
3. The Panama Canal is a valuable engineering achievement. Ships using the canal can shorten their journeys by thousands of miles.
4. The canal is about 50 miles long. Because of its winding course, ships come out only 27 miles east or west of their entrance point.
5. The United States controlled the Panama Canal Zone after 1914. On January 1, 2000, the Republic of Panama assumed complete control of the canal. **4. , but**   **5. ; however,**

Creating a Complex Sentence

If two sentences are unequal in importance, you can combine them into a *complex sentence.* Just turn the less important idea into a subordinate clause, and attach it to the other sentence (the independent clause).

Adjective Clauses

You can make a sentence into an adjective clause by replacing its subject with *who, whom, whose, which,* or *that.* Then you can use the adjective clause to give information about a noun or pronoun in another clause.

ORIGINAL   Christopher Columbus noted the unusual quantity of floating seaweed. He crossed the Sargasso Sea.

REVISED   Christopher Columbus, **who crossed the Sargasso Sea,** noted the unusual quantity of floating seaweed.

ORIGINAL   The Sargasso Sea is a strange, still area. It is part of the Atlantic Ocean.

REVISED   The Sargasso Sea is a strange, still area **that is part of the Atlantic Ocean.**

NOTE If an adjective clause is not essential to the meaning of the sentence, set it off with commas. If it is essential to the meaning, no commas are necessary.

NONESSENTIAL   This fireplace, **which my brother built,** is a replica of one in Williamsburg, Virginia.

ESSENTIAL   The fireplace **that my brother built** is a replica of one in Williamsburg, Virginia.

Adverb Clauses

You can also combine sentences by turning one sentence into an adverb clause. The adverb clause modifies a verb, an adjective, or another adverb in another clause.

To make a sentence into an adverb clause, add a subordinating conjunction (*although, after, because, if, when, while*) at the beginning. The conjunction shows the relationship between the ideas in the adverb clause and the ideas in the independent clause. If the adverb clause comes first, set it off from the independent clause with a comma.

Reference Note
For more on **independent** and **subordinate clauses,** see pages 492 and 493.

Reference Note
For a list of **common subordinating conjunctions,** see page 498.

ORIGINAL	Sailing ships were sometimes trapped in the Sargasso Sea. There wasn't enough wind to sail.
REVISED	Sailing ships were sometimes trapped in the Sargasso Sea **when there wasn't enough wind to sail.**
ORIGINAL	Sailors used to fear the Sargasso Sea. They heard strange tales about it.
REVISED	**Because they heard strange tales about it,** sailors used to fear the Sargasso Sea.

Noun Clauses

You can make a sentence into a noun clause by adding a word like *that*, *how*, *what*, *whatever*, *who*, or *whoever*. Then you can insert the clause into another clause. When you combine the sentences, you may need to change or delete some words.

ORIGINAL	Someone will arrive first. That person will get the best seat.
REVISED	**Whoever arrives first** will get the best seat.
ORIGINAL	The players were informed. The game had been forfeited.
REVISED	The players were informed **that the game had been forfeited.**

Exercise 6 Combining Sentences into a Complex Sentence

Here are ten pairs of sentences about Napoleon I. Combine each pair by turning the second sentence into a subordinate clause and inserting it into the first sentence. For the first six pairs, you are given hints about how to create the subordinate clauses. For the last four, you will have to use your own judgment. You may have to add or delete some words in the sentences. Add commas where necessary.

1. Napoleon I conquered much of Europe. He crowned himself emperor of France in 1804. (Use *who*.)
2. In 1769, Napoleon was born on the French island of Corsica. The island had been purchased from Italy the year before. (Use *which*.)
3. Napoleon gained control of the French government in 1799. The French people had lost faith in the five-member Directory. (Use *because*.)
4. Napoleon married Marie Louise, daughter of the emperor of Austria, in 1810. France's principal enemy by 1796 was Austria. (Use *although*.)
5. After Paris was captured in 1814, Napoleon was exiled to the small island of Elba. Napoleon gave up the throne. (Use *who*.)

Exercise 6 Combining Sentences into a Complex Sentence

ANSWERS
Possible answers appear below.

1. Napoleon I, who crowned himself emperor of France in 1804, conquered much of Europe.
2. In 1769, Napoleon was born on the French island of Corsica, which had been purchased from Italy the year before.
3. Napoleon gained control of the French government in 1799 because the French people had lost faith in the five-member Directory.
4. Although France's principal enemy by 1796 was Austria, Napoleon married Marie Louise, daughter of the emperor of Austria, in 1810.
5. After Paris was captured in 1814, Napoleon, who gave up the throne, was exiled to the small island of Elba.
6. Troops that had been sent to arrest Napoleon praised him as their emperor on his march back to Paris.
7. French troops and combined forces from several countries soon clashed in Belgium, although Napoleon had assured his enemies that he would not make war.
8. Napoleon, who had won many military battles, was defeated on June 18, 1815, at the Battle of Waterloo.
9. While Napoleon was trying to escape to the United States, he was captured by a British battleship.
10. Napoleon was exiled to the British island of St. Helena in the Atlantic Ocean because he was considered a threat to peace.

HELP
Before you begin Exercise 6, review the words that can be used to introduce subordinate clauses. These words are included in the explanations on pages 359 and 360.

6. Troops praised Napoleon as their emperor on his march back to Paris. The troops had been sent to arrest Napoleon. (Use *that*.)
7. French troops and combined forces from several countries soon clashed in Belgium, although Napoleon had assured his enemies of something. He would not make war.
8. Napoleon was defeated on June 18, 1815, at the Battle of Waterloo. He had won many military battles.
9. Napoleon was captured by a British battleship. At the time, Napoleon was trying to escape to the United States.
10. Napoleon was exiled to the British island of St. Helena in the Atlantic Ocean. Napoleon was considered a threat to peace.

Review A Revising Sentences by Combining

Using all the sentence-combining skills you have learned, revise and rewrite each of the following sets of sentences into one sentence. You may combine by inserting words or phrases, by creating compounds, or by creating complex sentences. You may have to add or delete some words. Add punctuation where necessary.

1. Espionage is the secret collection of intelligence information. The history of espionage goes back over two thousand years.
2. Around 500 B.C., Sun Tzu wrote a book giving instructions on organizing an espionage system. Sun Tzu was a Chinese military theorist.
3. In the nineteenth century, Joseph Fouché, duc d'Otrante, worked to create a network of police agents and spies. Fouché was the French minister of police.
4. In World War I, one of the most famous German spies was Mata Hari. She posed as an Indian dancer in Paris.
5. World War II saw an enormous growth in worldwide espionage. Countries needed quick, accurate information about their enemies.
6. One of the most remarkable intelligence operations in World War II was Operation Double Cross. In Operation Double Cross, almost all the German spies in Great Britain were captured. These German spies were turned into double agents.
7. Japan's most successful espionage led to the attack on the U.S. naval base at Pearl Harbor. This attack was a surprise, and it happened in World War II.
8. Today in the United States, the Central Intelligence Agency gathers secret information. This information is about national security. The Central Intelligence Agency is also called the CIA.

Review A Revising Sentences by Combining

ANSWERS

Sample answers appear below.

1. The history of espionage, the secret collection of intelligence information, goes back over two thousand years.
2. Around 500 B.C., Sun Tzu, a Chinese military theorist, wrote a book giving instructions on organizing an espionage system.
3. In the nineteenth century, Joseph Fouché, duc d'Otrante, who was the French minister of police, worked to create a network of police agents and spies.
4. In World War I, one of the most famous German spies was Mata Hari, who posed as an Indian dancer in Paris.
5. World War II saw an enormous growth in worldwide espionage because countries needed quick, accurate information about their enemies.
6. One of the most remarkable intelligence operations in World War II was Operation Double Cross; almost all of the German spies in Great Britain were captured and turned into double agents.
7. Japan's most successful espionage during World War II led to the surprise attack on the U.S. naval base at Pearl Harbor.
8. Today in the United States, the Central Intelligence Agency, also called the CIA, gathers secret information about national security.

> **Review A** Revising Sentences by Combining
>
> **ANSWERS continued**
>
> 9. The Federal Bureau of Investigation, which was formed in 1908, is responsible for counterespionage within the United States.
> 10. It is difficult to know the exact number of espionage agents in the world today, since they work to keep information about themselves hidden.

Improving Sentence Style

OBJECTIVES

- To revise sentences to create parallel structure
- To revise stringy and wordy sentences
- To revise sentences to vary sentence beginnings

---

9. The Federal Bureau of Investigation is responsible for counterespionage within the United States. The FBI was formed in 1908.
10. It is difficult to know the exact number of espionage agents in the world today. Espionage agents work to keep information about themselves hidden.

> **Review B** Revising a Paragraph by Combining Sentences

Using all the sentence-combining skills you have learned, revise and rewrite the following paragraph. Use your judgment about which sentences to combine and how to combine them. Try for smooth, varied sentences that are easy to understand, but do not change the original meaning of the paragraph.

Here are possible combinations.

Prairie dogs are very sociable. ~~They~~ live in communities called towns. The towns can be large. ~~The towns~~ consist of numerous burrows. The word *dog* is part of this animal's name. ~~The~~ prairie dog is actually a rodent. It gets its name from the sound it makes. ~~The sound~~ is similar to a dog's bark. ~~L~~ivestock might step into the burrows that prairie dogs make. (Some ranchers fear) ~~this~~. However, horses usually do not step into prairie dog burrows. ~~Cows do not usually step into prairie dog burrows~~.

Edits in margin: , which / and / , but / , which / that / and cows

> **TIPS & TRICKS**
>
> Begin to look for parallel structure in sentences when you combine words, phrases, and clauses by using the coordinating conjunction *and*.

Improving Sentence Style

In the first part of this chapter, you learned how to reduce choppiness in your writing by combining sentences. Now you will learn more ways to polish your sentence style and make your writing more effective.

Using Parallel Structure

When you join several equal or related ideas in a sentence, it is important that you express these ideas in a similar way. You can do this by balancing the structure of your sentence parts. For example, you should balance an adjective with an adjective, a phrase with a phrase, and a clause with a clause. This kind of balance in writing is called *parallel structure.*

> **RESOURCES**
>
> **Improving Sentence Style Practice**
>
> - *Sentences, Paragraphs, and Compositions,* TP. 6, WS. pp. 33–44

NOT PARALLEL	He learned three things: shooting, passing, and how to dribble. [two gerunds and a phrase]
PARALLEL	He learned three things: **shooting, passing,** and **dribbling.** [three gerunds]
NOT PARALLEL	A good coach must learn to communicate with players, to organize a schedule, and adversity. [two phrases and a noun]
PARALLEL	A good coach must learn **to communicate with players, to organize a schedule,** and **to handle adversity.** [three phrases]
NOT PARALLEL	My sister decided that she would study coaching techniques and to work with the youth basketball league. [a clause and a phrase]
PARALLEL	My sister decided **that she would study coaching techniques** and **that she would work with the youth basketball league.** [two clauses]

Exercise 7 Revising Sentences to Create Parallelism

Some of the following sentences are out of balance. Bring balance to them by using parallel structure. You may have to delete or add some words. If a sentence is already correct, write C.

Possible revisions appear below.

1. Athens, the capital of Greece, is known for its ancient ruins, busy lifestyle, and ~~enjoying~~ fine Greek food.
2. Because it is nearly three thousand years old and its rich history, Athens attracts many visitors. 2. has a
3. Athens attracts artists, and historians, and ~~is attractive to~~ tourists.
4. People often drive very fast in Athens and scare the pedestrians. 4. C
5. I like seeing the sights in Athens ~~to learn~~ about its history.
   5. and learning

Revising Stringy Sentences

What is a *stringy sentence*? Read this one:

```
I was going on a fishing trip with my
uncle, and I knew I would need a lot of
luck, and I always fish in the same spot that
my uncle does, but he always catches more
than I do, but this time I brought all of my
fishing lures so that I would be prepared.
```

Quotation for the Day

"A sentence should read as if its author, had he held a plow instead of a pen, could have drawn a furrow deep and straight to the end."

(Henry David Thoreau, 1817–1862, American philosopher and writer)

With this analogy, Thoreau seems to be saying that a good sentence gets straight to the point. Ask students to formulate their own analogies that describe effective sentences. Have them write their analogies on poster board and then display them around the room.

Meeting INDIVIDUAL NEEDS

ADVANCED LEARNERS

You may wish to have students choose examples of well-written sentences from their favorite literary selections. Students can then write their own sentences that imitate the structural elements used in those model sentences. Have students analyze and evaluate the structures they emulate.

Relating to Speaking and Listening

A good example of parallel sentence structure can be provided by Dr. Martin Luther King, Jr.'s speech "I Have a Dream." Ask a student volunteer to read aloud all or part of this speech. Afterward, discuss with students where Dr. King uses parallel structure and how it contributes to the power of his speech.

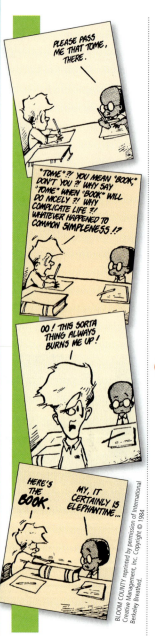

The *stringy sentence* on the previous page has too many independent clauses strung together with coordinating conjunctions like *and* or *but*. Because the ideas are all treated equally, it is difficult to see how they are related to one another. To fix a stringy sentence, you can

- **break the sentence into two or more shorter sentences**
- **turn some of the independent clauses into subordinate clauses or phrases**

Now read the following sentences aloud and hear the difference. Notice how the writer has broken up the stringy sentence into three shorter sentences and turned an independent clause into a subordinate clause.

```
I was going on a fishing trip with my
uncle, and I knew I would need a lot of
luck. Although I always fish in the same spot
that my uncle does, he always catches more
than I do. This time I brought all of my
fishing lures so that I would be prepared.
```

There are usually several ways to revise a stringy sentence. The most important thing is to make the meaning clear for your reader.

Exercise 8 Revising Stringy Sentences

Revise each of the following stringy sentences. For some items, you can just break the stringy sentence into two or more shorter sentences. For others, you will have to turn an independent clause into a subordinate clause or a phrase to show the relationship between the ideas. Change the punctuation wherever necessary.

1. Music is used for entertainment, relaxation, and self-expression, and it is used in every culture, and it is a very important part of our lives.
2. Music is an ancient art, and people learned to make flutes around 10,000 B.C., and they began to write music around 2500 B.C.
3. Today, much popular music is electronically produced, and many musicians play electric guitars and synthesizers, and some even play electric violins.
4. Different countries have different kinds of music, but some kinds of music are internationally popular, and those kinds include rock music and rap music.
5. Rock music first became popular in the 1950s, and it was inspired by blues and jazz music, but its sound was different from anything people had heard.

Exercise 8 Revising Stringy Sentences

ANSWERS

Possible revisions are listed below.

1. In every culture, people use music for entertainment, relaxation, and self-expression. It is a very important part of our lives.
2. Music is an ancient art. People learned to make flutes around 10,000 B.C. and began to write music around 2500 B.C.
3. Today, much popular music is electronically produced. Many musicians play electric guitars and synthesizers, and some even play electric violins.
4. Different countries have different kinds of music, but some kinds of music, such as rock and rap, are internationally popular.
5. Rock music first became popular in the 1950s. Although it was inspired by blues and jazz music, its sound was different from anything people had heard.

Revising Wordy Sentences

Read the following sentence.

```
Anticipating that tomorrow's forthcoming
examination may be perplexing, I have made
the astute conclusion that we should dili-
gently scrutinize our scholarly tomes at
the decline of day.
```

When you read sentences like this, you probably wonder what language the writer is using. How much easier and clearer it is to say "The test tomorrow may be hard, so let's study tonight." Here are three tips for creating sentences that are not too wordy:

- **Do not use more words than you need.**
- **Do not use fancy, difficult words where plain, simple ones will do.**
- **Do not repeat words or ideas unless it is absolutely necessary.**

WORDY	Our sofa has a lot of weight to it.
IMPROVED	Our sofa is heavy.
WORDY	The reason I am undertaking the task of photographing the exteriors of these abandoned buildings is that I have an interest in architecture.
IMPROVED	I am taking pictures of these abandoned buildings because I am interested in architecture.
WORDY	Greg speaks Spanish well, and his Spanish is clear and fluent.
IMPROVED	Greg speaks clear, fluent Spanish.

Exercise 9 Revising Wordy Sentences

Some of the following sentences are wordy. For each sentence, ask the following questions: Does it have unnecessary words? Does it have fancy words that can be replaced with simple ones? Does it repeat ideas? If you answer yes to any question, revise the sentence to reduce the wordiness. If a sentence doesn't need improvement, write *C*.

Possible revisions follow.

1. Caves are dark, damp areas ~~that don't have any light~~.
2. Many caves have beautiful, icicle-like mineral formations called speleothems.   **2. C**
3. Luray Caverns, ~~which is~~ a cave system ~~that is situated~~ in the area of northern Virginia, is famous for its colorful speleothems.   **3. in**

Relating to Usage

You may want to introduce students to two kinds of phrases that can be used to combine sentences or to reduce wordiness. Explain to students that a gerund phrase includes a verb form ending in *–ing* that is used as a noun. An infinitive phrase usually begins with *to*, contains a verb form, and is used as a noun, an adjective, or an adverb. Write the following sentences on the chalkboard, and work with students to reduce and/or combine sentences by using gerund and infinitive phrases.

1. That she finished her book was important. [*Finishing her book was important.*—gerund phrase]
2. Yosef gave a birthday party. He wanted to surprise his brother. [*To surprise his brother, Yosef threw a birthday party.*—infinitive phrase]

Then, have students working in groups compose three or four sentences of their own that contain gerund and infinitive phrases. Groups can share their sentences with the class.

TECHNOLOGY TIP

If students in your class have access to computers and e-mail software, pair them with e-mail partners in another class and have them discuss by e-mail possible revisions to the sentences in **Exercise 9**. This activity will require students to use writing to explain how and why they made their revisions.

Cooperative Learning

Practice with Sentence Beginnings. Have students work in pairs to write sentences that begin with each of the following grammatical forms:

1. adverb clause [*When Sam arrived at the park, he was ready to play.*]
2. noun clause [*How he could catch the big fish puzzled Sean.*]
3. participial phrase [*Pleased by the present, the child grinned broadly.*]
4. prepositional phrase [*In the morning we will start our journey.*]
5. single-word modifier [*First, we must read the instructions.*]

---

4. Lascaux Cave, a famous cave in southwestern France, has many ~~ancient,~~ prehistoric wall paintings.
5. Cavefish are small, cave-dwelling fish that ~~are not equipped with optical organs~~. 5. do not have eyes.

Varying Sentence Beginnings

You would probably get bored if you ate the same food at every meal. Variety is as important in your writing as it is in your diet. The basic subject-verb sentence pattern is fine sometimes, but if it is all you ever use, your writing will be monotonous.

Read the following paragraph. Notice that while the paragraph is correct, it is boring because every sentence follows the same subject-verb pattern.

```
The pool was nearly empty on an early
weekend morning. Dedicated swimmers swam
multiple laps. A few sunbathers and parents
with small children sat on the grass at the
edge of the pool and watched. The day grew
hotter, and the sun rose higher. The pool
became more crowded. The pool was soon
filled with young people. They laughed as
they played games and splashed each other.
```

Now read a revised version of the paragraph. Notice how the varied sentence beginnings break the monotony of the subject-verb pattern.

```
On an early weekend morning, the pool
was nearly empty. Dedicated swimmers swam
multiple laps. A few sunbathers and parents
with small children sat on the grass at the
edge of the pool and watched. As the day
grew hotter and the sun rose higher, the
pool became more crowded. Soon the pool was
filled with young people. Laughing, they
played games and splashed each other.
```

Instead of starting all your sentences with subjects, try opening sentences in a variety of ways. Begin with single-word modifiers, with phrases, and with subordinate clauses. Remember to add commas as necessary after introductory words, phrases, or clauses.

Commas with Introductory Elements. Some students may need additional practice to punctuate introductory elements correctly. Remind students to use a comma after introductory words such as *well, no,* or *yes,* after an introductory participial phrase, after two or more introductory prepositional phrases, and after an introductory adverb clause.

Write the following sentences on the board and have students insert commas where needed.

Varying Sentence Beginnings

Single-Word Modifiers	**Grotesquely,** Dr. Frankenstein's monster began to rise from the table. [adverb]
	Frightened, Dr. Frankenstein jumped back. [participle]
	Cackling, Igor ran from the room. [participle]
Phrases	**With little hope,** Sam entered the writing contest. [prepositional phrase]
	Excited that he had won, Sam accepted the award. [participial phrase]
Subordinate Clauses	**Because Manuel was tall,** people expected him to play basketball.
	Although Manuel wasn't interested in playing basketball, he always went to the games.

Exercise 10 Varying Sentence Beginnings

Using what you have learned about varying sentence beginnings, revise each of the following sentences. The hint in parentheses will tell you whether to begin with a phrase, a clause, or a single-word modifier.

EXAMPLE 1. Astronomy is one of the oldest of the sciences, and it still intrigues scientists today. (phrase)

1. *Still intriguing scientists today, astronomy is one of the oldest of the sciences.*

1. Maps of the heavens were first drawn on stone parchment, and they were created by the ancient Chinese. (phrase)
2. Early humans started watching the sun, moon, and stars when they learned that understanding the heavens could help their harvests. (subordinate clause)
3. Astronomers work with large radio and optical telescopes and space probes today. (single-word modifier)
4. The moon lacks wind, atmosphere, and weather and would be an ideal location for an observatory. (phrase)
5. The early Egyptians planned their festivals and events by studying the heavens, but the ancient Greeks were the first to study the sky scientifically. (subordinate clause)
6. Galileo supported Ptolemy's idea that the sun was the center of the universe and was threatened with punishment. (phrase)

Improving Sentence Style 367

---

1. In the middle of the night [,] they began their ascent of the summit.
2. Grabbing a towel and the sunscreen [,] Sam headed out to the pool.
3. No [,] I am not going to the play.
4. When she answered the door [,] she was surprised to see him.
5. Up the stairs to the left [,] there is a storage closet.

Exercise 10 Varying Sentence Beginnings

ANSWERS continued

7. Using a homemade telescope, William Herschel discovered the planet Uranus.
8. Because Newton proved that gravity rules the universe, astronomers have been able to predict the paths of planets.
9. In 1990, the Hubble Space Telescope was placed in orbit.
10. Initially, the Hubble Space Telescope's vision was blurry, but it was repaired in 1993 by astronauts.

TEACHING TIP

Varying Sentence Structure
Point out to students that writers sometimes use a series of short sentences for a specific purpose. For example, if a writer wants to create a sense of urgency, he or she may use several short, simple sentences to quicken the pace of a longer piece of writing.

Critical Thinking

Metacognition. Have each student re-read a paper he or she has written. Students can then write a brief evaluation of their sentences. Have students suggest revisions that would make their papers more interesting and clearer, and then have students describe how the strategies they have learned have affected the way they write and revise.

---

7. William Herschel discovered the planet Uranus by using a homemade telescope. (phrase)
8. Astronomers have been able to predict the paths of planets because Newton proved that gravity rules the universe. (subordinate clause)
9. The Hubble Space Telescope was placed in orbit in 1990. (phrase)
10. The Hubble Space Telescope's vision was initially blurry, but it was repaired in 1993 by astronauts. (single-word modifier)

Varying Sentence Structure

You have learned to create different kinds of sentences by combining sentences and varying sentence beginnings. Now you can use this skill to create a better writing style. For varied, interesting paragraphs, it sometimes is not enough just to create sentences of different lengths. You also need to use a variety of sentence structures. That means using a mix of simple, compound, and complex (and sometimes even compound-complex) sentences in your writing.

Read the following short paragraph, which is made up of only simple sentences.

```
My sister went to college. She was nervous at first. She was determined to be a success. She worked hard every day. She graduated at the top of her class. I was proud of her. We celebrated after the ceremonies. We ate a big meal. My mother took pictures of the whole family.
```

Now read the revised version of the paragraph. The writer has included a variety of sentence structures to break the monotony of the first version.

```
Although she was nervous at first, my sister went to college. Because she was determined to be a success and because she worked hard, she graduated at the top of her class. I was proud of her. We celebrated after the ceremonies as we ate a big meal, and my mother took pictures of the whole family.
```

Notice how the use of subordinate clauses improved some sentences and made the paragraph clearer. Besides adding variety, subordinate clauses help show how the ideas in a sentence are related.

Reference Note
For more on **types of sentence structures,** see page 504.

Effective Professional Writing. To show students how sentence style in news writing differs from sentence style for academic writing, have them evaluate copies of news stories you provide them. Ask them to examine the first few paragraphs of the article and evaluate why the sentences are effective. Students should be able to refer to specific strategies the writers used.

You might also ask a journalism teacher to present a lesson on the criteria for effective news writing.

NOTE Be sure you understand the type of relationship each subordinating conjunction expresses.

CONTRAST *although, even though, though,* and *while*

REASON *as, because, considering that, if, since,* and *so that*

TIME *after, as, as long as, as soon as, before, when,* and *while*

Exercise 11 Revising a Paragraph to Create a Variety of Sentence Structures

Using what you have learned about combining sentences and varying structure, revise the following paragraph to make it smoother and more varied. A combination of different kinds of sentences will make the paragraph much more fun to read.

```
    My friends and I had lunch. We ate at a
food court on the second floor of a mall.
The food court has food from different
countries. About twenty restaurants are
there. Lin had soup and salad. I had a bur-
rito. It was delicious. Joe and Debbie
split a pizza. Then we walked around and
looked at the people. We all imagined what
they were thinking. There was a fashion
show on the main floor. Debbie and I admired
the clothes. Lin and Joe liked estimating
the costs of the outfits. We looked at a
display of new cars. We talked about the
kinds of cars we would like to have.
```

Review C Writing a Paragraph Using a Variety of Sentence Structures

You are the director of a music video for a new song called "The Edge of Dreams." Write a paragraph explaining which singers, dancers, and musicians you will cast in your video. Their names may be real or fictional. If you want your reader to understand and be interested in your casting choices, you will need to make your paragraph lively and clear. Capture your reader's attention by using a variety of interesting sentence structures. Avoid wordy and stringy sentences, and be sure to check for parallel structure as you revise.

COMPUTER TIP

You can use a word-processing program's cut and paste functions to move subordinate clauses within a document. If you change your mind, you can always move the text again.

TIPS & TRICKS

Use the strategies you have learned in this chapter to revise your own writing. Look for opportunities to better your work by combining sentences and improving sentence style.

CHAPTER 11

Understanding Paragraphs and Compositions

PREVIEWING THE CHAPTER

- Paragraphs are the building blocks of a composition—each paragraph expresses a main idea of its own and all the paragraphs work together to develop and support the thesis, or controlling idea, of the composition as a whole. This chapter explains the parts of both a paragraph (topic sentence, supporting sentences, and clincher sentence) and a composition (introduction, body, and conclusion). The chapter also describes and models three important qualities of well-written paragraphs and compositions: unity, coherence, and elaboration. You may wish to use this chapter as a review before beginning the composition chapters or as a reference throughout the year.

INTRODUCING THE CHAPTER

- To introduce the chapter, use Transparency 7 in *Sentences, Paragraphs, and Compositions*.

internet connect
GO TO: go.hrw.com
KEYWORD: EOLang

How Paragraphs and Compositions Fit Together

A paragraph is made up of sentences grouped together for a reason—usually to present and support a single **main idea.** In the same way, a composition is made up of a group of paragraphs. The paragraphs in a composition are a bit like the players on a football team. Each player on a football team is assigned a position, and each has an individual contribution to make. However, it is teamwork—the players working together—that usually wins the game. Similarly, each paragraph in a composition expresses a main idea of its own, but the paragraphs also work together to develop and support a **thesis,** or controlling idea, that makes the composition work as a whole.

The Parts of a Body Paragraph

While paragraphs in narrative writing do not always have a central focus, paragraphs in most other types of compositions do usually emphasize a main idea. These paragraphs, often called **body paragraphs,** usually have three major parts: a *topic sentence, supporting sentences,* and (sometimes, but not always) a *clincher sentence.* The table that follows provides more details about each of these parts.

370 | Chapter 11 Understanding Paragraphs and Compositions

CHAPTER RESOURCES

Planning
- *Lesson Planner,* Ch. 11
- One-Stop Planner CD-ROM

Practice and Extension
- *Sentences, Paragraphs, and Compositions,* for Ch. 11

Internet
- go.hrw.com (keyword: EOLang)

Evaluation and Assessment
- Assessment Package
  —Chapter Tests, Ch. 11
  —Chapter Tests in Standardized Test Formats, Ch. 11

Parts of Paragraphs	
Main Idea	• provides the central focus of the paragraph
Topic Sentence	• directly states the paragraph's main idea • often is the first sentence in the paragraph • may be found at the end of the paragraph, for emphasis or variety

Supporting Sentences	• support the main idea of the paragraph
	• use the following kinds of details:
	  sensory details: information collected using the five senses (sight, hearing, smell, touch, and taste)
	  facts: information that can be proven
	  statistics: facts based on numbers
	  examples: specific instances or illustrations of a general idea
	  anecdotes: an extended example or brief story, often entertaining or amusing

Clincher Sentence	• sometimes (but not always) is found at the end of longer paragraphs • emphasizes or summarizes the main idea of a paragraph • adds zing to a paragraph • often includes a transitional phrase • most often is used with longer, complicated paragraphs to reinforce the main idea.

STYLE TIP

Clincher sentences should not be overused. Weak clinchers like "Those are the reasons I dislike snow" make your writing dull. They lack the punch that effective clinchers have.

Keep in mind that paragraphs may be developed by using either one kind of supporting detail or by combining several kinds together. For example, if you were writing an autobiographical narrative, you might use a combination of sensory details, anecdotes, and examples.

NOTE Some paragraphs lack topic sentences. Instead of being directly stated, the main idea of these paragraphs is said to be *implied,* or unstated. For example, paragraphs in fiction rarely contain topic sentences. However, in your school essays, using topic sentences helps you focus on your topic and helps your readers easily identify and understand your main ideas.

■ Test Generator (One-Stop Planner CD-ROM)

 RESOURCES

The Parts of a Body Paragraph
Practice
■ *Sentences, Paragraphs, and Compositions,* TP. 8, WS. p. 45

Meeting INDIVIDUAL NEEDS

LEARNERS HAVING DIFFICULTY
To help students understand the typical structure of a paragraph, show them a visual representation of the relationship between the topic sentence, supporting sentences, and the clincher sentence. Point out that the arrows show that each part of a paragraph should directly or indirectly support the topic sentence.

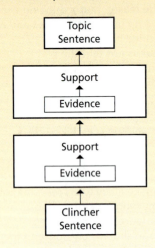

Cooperative Learning

Parts of Paragraphs. Have students work in groups of three to complete **Exercise 1**. One student can identify the topic sentences, one the supporting sentences, and one the clincher sentences. Students can rotate roles for each paragraph. Group members can then discuss each sentence's function in the paragraph and the way all three types of sentences work together in each of the paragraphs. Call on three groups of students to share their conclusions about the three paragraphs with the class. If students disagree on the function of any sentence, have them share their views until they come to a consensus.

TIPS & TRICKS
Often a paragraph that describes a sequence of events or actions has no topic sentence. To identify the main idea and create a topic sentence for such a paragraph, think of a one-sentence summary of what happens in the paragraph.

Putting the Parts Together

The following passage shows how the parts of a paragraph work together to support a main idea.

Topic Sentence
Supporting Sentences
(Facts and Statistics)
Clincher Sentence

> Electric insect traps, or "bug zappers," are effective killing machines, but they kill the wrong kind of insects, claims University of Delaware entomologist Doug Tallamy. Over the course of a summer, Tallamy and a high school student, Tim Frick, analyzed the victims of the electric traps installed in six yards in Newark, Delaware. Of the 13,789 insects killed, just 31—less than one-quarter of one percent—were biting insects. Tallamy and Frick estimate that the millions of traps employed in the U.S. needlessly kill 71 billion to 350 billion "nontarget insects" each year, causing untold damage to ecosystems. Bug zappers, they conclude, are "worthless" as well as "counterproductive."
>
> Steve Nadis, "Bug Zappers Miss Their Mark," *Omni* magazine Web site

Notice that the topic sentence immediately calls the reader's attention to the paragraph's main idea: These traps kill the wrong insects. Each supporting sentence contains information that supports this main idea, with the writer using facts and statistics to provide more detailed support. The final sentence, a clincher sentence, emphasizes the main idea by presenting a judgment based on the facts and statistics in the supporting sentences.

Exercise 1 Identifying Parts of Paragraphs

See if you can identify the parts of paragraphs in the three paragraphs that begin on the following page. First, locate the topic sentence in each paragraph. Then, identify each supporting sentence as either a sensory detail, a fact, a statistic, an example, or an anecdote. Finally, determine whether any of the paragraphs have a clincher sentence.

1. Animals bitten by some snakes bleed internally, because the venom contains an anticoagulant. For the past decade researchers have studied snake venom in search of a drug that would prevent blood clots that can trigger heart attacks. Robert Gould of Merck Research Laboratories thinks his company has found one: "We tested eleven kinds of vipers and found proteins in their venom that keep human blood platelets from sticking together." Merck synthesized one of the proteins of the saw-scaled viper's venom and used the knowledge gained to design a drug called Aggrastat. It may save thousands of lives a year.

   John L. Eliot, "Snake Venom Strikes at Heart Attacks," *National Geographic*

2. On Prince Edward Island [Canada] change has often come slowly. Some parts of the island got paved roads and "the lights," as electricity was called, only in the early sixties. The 1970s finally saw the demise of the one-room schoolhouse, and even more recently small family farms have given way to agribusinesses—operations of up to 3,000 acres that grow potatoes to feed the North American appetite for french fries. How islanders come to accept this newest—and potentially most far-reaching—form of change remains to be seen.

   Ian Darragh, "Prince Edward Island: A World Apart No More," *National Geographic*

3. Prairie dogs are talented linguists. "They possess the most sophisticated natural animal language so far decoded," says Con Slobodchikoff of Northern Arizona University. Researching alarm calls of Gunnison's [a species of prairie dog], he found that they discriminated among predators—humans, hawks, coyotes, and dogs. Moreover, the prairie dogs

   (continued)

Exercise 1 Identifying Parts of Paragraphs

ANSWERS

1. A. fact
   B. topic sentence
   C. fact (or statistic)
   D. fact
   E. clincher
2. A. topic sentence
   B. example
   C. example
   D. clincher
3. A. topic sentence
   B. fact
   C. fact
   D. clincher

(continued)
distinguished between people of different sizes, and when they gave the same call for a man—wearing the same clothes—after not seeing him for two months, "that blew me away," says Slobodchikoff.

Michael E. Long, "The Vanishing Prairie Dog," *National Geographic*

Qualities of Paragraphs

Having the parts of a paragraph in place is just the beginning of developing a good paragraph. The next step is to consider the three qualities of any well-written paragraph: *unity, coherence,* and *elaboration.* You can think of these qualities as the strong glue that holds the parts of a paragraph together.

Unity

Unity is the quality achieved when all of the sentences in a paragraph work together as a unit to express or support one main idea. Unrelated ideas spoil unity and distract the reader. Unity is present in a paragraph when at least one of the following is true:

- **All sentences in a paragraph relate to the main idea stated in the topic sentence.**
- **All sentences in a paragraph relate to an implied main idea.** When there is no stated topic sentence, all the sentences support the paragraph's unstated main idea, or **implied main idea**.
- **All sentences in a paragraph relate to a sequence of events.** In a narrative paragraph, unity is achieved when all the sentences work together to narrate the event.

Coherence

Along with unity, good paragraphs have *coherence.* Coherence is achieved when all of the details and ideas in a paragraph are logically arranged and clearly connected. To ensure that the ideas in a paragraph are arranged in a way that makes sense, pay attention to the **logical**

To identify an implied main idea of a paragraph, determine the topic of the first sentence, and then refine and adjust this idea as you continue reading the supporting sentences of the paragraph.

progression or **organizational pattern,** of the ideas. Use one of the orders described in the chart below.

Building Coherence: Types of Order		
Order	When To Use	How It Works
Chronological	• to tell a story • to explain a process	• presents actions and events according to the order in which they occur
Spatial	• to describe a place or object	• arranges details or ideas according to their location in space
Logical	• to explain or classify (by defining, dividing a subject into parts, or comparing and contrasting)	• groups related details or ideas together to show their relationship
Order of Importance	• to inform or to persuade	• arranges details or ideas from most important to least important, or vice versa

At times, multiple orders may be used to add variety to writing. For example, within a narration (which typically follows chronological order) a description of a scene or place may follow a spatial order.

In addition to presenting details in an order that makes sense, a paragraph that has coherence should also show *how* these details are connected. You can show connections by using **direct references** or **transitional expressions.**

Building Coherence: Connecting Ideas	
Connecting Strategy	How It Works
Direct References	• use a noun or pronoun that refers to a noun or pronoun used earlier • repeat a word used earlier • use a word or phrase that means the same thing as one used earlier

(continued)

Meeting INDIVIDUAL NEEDS

MULTIPLE INTELLIGENCES
Interpersonal Intelligence. Have pairs of students practice elaborating with sensory details by playing a quick game. One person in each pair thinks of a location or event and gives his or her partner one vivid detail for each of the senses. The other student should try to guess the location or event. Point out to students that when elaborating with sensory details, they should try to choose details that are vivid and evocative.

TEACHING TIP

Elaboration
Have students suggest several topics to write on the chalkboard, and ask students to suggest ways in which the topics could be developed using one of the four elaboration strategies presented in the chart. Students with similar interests might work collaboratively to complete this activity on a topic of their choice.

(continued)

Building Coherence: Connecting Ideas	
Transitional Expressions (including prepositions that show chronological or spatial order and conjunctions)	• compare ideas (*also, and, besides, in addition, similarly, too*) • contrast ideas (*although, but, however, instead, nevertheless, otherwise, yet*) • show cause and effect (*as a result, because, consequently, so, therefore, thus*) • show time (*after, before, eventually, finally, first, meanwhile, then, when*) • show place (*above, across, around, beyond, from, here, in, on, over, there, to, under*) • shows importance (*first, last, mainly, then, to begin with*)

STYLE TIP
There are many types of information you can provide as elaboration: examples, descriptions, expert opinions, reasons, evidence, personal experience, statistics. You should use a combination of these to give your writing variety.

Elaboration

Along with unity and coherence, a good paragraph should have *elaboration*. A paragraph has elaboration when it contains supporting sentences (supporting details) that thoroughly develop its main idea. A paragraph lacks elaboration when it does not contain enough supporting sentences, or when its supporting sentences do not sufficiently develop a paragraph's main idea. A lack of elaboration can confuse readers and cause them to doubt whether the writer understands what he or she is trying to say.

To help you think of ideas to use for elaboration, try one of the following strategies. For the examples provided, the writer's topic was the clean-up of a neighborhood vacant lot.

Purpose: Description
Strategy: Freewrite a list of details based on the five senses

Smell: garbage
rotting fruit

Sight: rusty old cans
broken glass
old shoes

Taste: smelled so bad I thought I could taste the trash

Touch: cold to start, warm sun came out eventually

Hearing: chatter about what we would do with area once cleaned up

---

376 Chapter 11 Understanding Paragraphs and Compositions

Purpose: Exposition
Strategy: Use *5W-How?* questions

Who was involved?
   neighborhood association
   Councilmember White
   my family

What was changed?
   neighborhood lot was cleaned up

When was it changed?
   last October

Where did it happen?
   corner lot on Fifth and Willow streets

Why did it happen?
   citizens were concerned

How did it happen?
   neighborhood association arranged clean-up day
   city provided dumpsters, gloves

The *5W-How?* questions are especially useful for generating ideas to answer questions on an essay test. Just use the topic of the question as the basics for each of the six questions.

Purpose: Persuasion
Strategy: Cluster

(continued)

Meeting INDIVIDUAL NEEDS

MODALITY

Visual Learners. Have students take a few minutes to evaluate the graphic organizers given in the chart for persuasion and narration. Do they find these graphics helpful, or are there other methods students find more useful for organizing ideas? Tell students that graphic organizers are particularly useful in organizing one's ideas for a composition. Students should experiment with using different graphics until each finds a method that works well for him or her.

Critical Thinking

Evaluation. Tell students that writers of newspaper articles make sure their reports answer as many of the *5W-How?* questions as possible in the first few paragraphs. Have small groups of students each select a newspaper article and evaluate how quickly and efficiently the reporter answers the *5W-How?* questions. Does the reporter sacrifice any necessary details in trying to answer these questions quickly? Have spokespersons from the groups share their groups' findings with the class.

(continued)

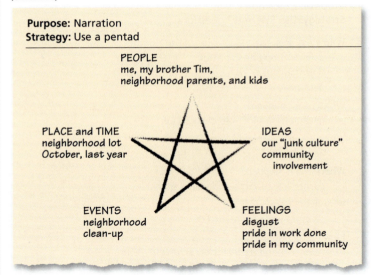

Purpose: Narration
Strategy: Use a pentad

PEOPLE
me, my brother Tim,
neighborhood parents, and kids

PLACE and TIME
neighborhood lot
October, last year

IDEAS
our "junk culture"
community
involvement

EVENTS
neighborhood
clean-up

FEELINGS
disgust
pride in work done
pride in my community

NOTE When you speak with someone face-to-face, you are able to respond directly to questions from that person. When you write, you cannot actually speak to your readers. However, you can try to anticipate, or guess, the questions they might ask, and then answer these questions using elaboration.

Looking at the Qualities of Paragraphs

The following paragraph describes Picasso's *Guernica* (1937), a mural painted after a German air raid on the Spanish town of Guernica. The paragraph is unified because all of its sentences support and elaborate on the main idea of the composition—the allegorical nature of *Guernica*. First, the writer presents his topic sentence, then gives supporting examples from the painting. To give the paragraph coherence, the writer arranges his points **logically** (moving from images of dark to light) and **spatially** (giving directional clues to the elements of the painting being discussed). Notice how he uses **transitional devices** (shown in boldface) to shift the reader's attention from one part of the painting to another. Coherence is also given to the paragraph through **direct references** (shown with asterisks). Finally, notice how the final sentence follows the cue of the painting by providing the contrast of the flower of hope to the darkness of the other images of the paragraph.

Critical Thinking

Synthesis. Have students use the paragraph on Picasso's *Guernica* as a model for writing their own descriptions of a work of art. Tell students that the main idea of their paragraphs should be the meaning or overall effect of the artwork. They should elaborate on their main ideas in a coherent fashion by arranging their points logically and spatially. Students can present their descriptions and the artworks to the class.

According to Picasso, *Guernica* is allegorical.* He* explained some of the symbolism.* The horse with the spear in its back, the inevitable victim* of bullfights, signifies* victimized* humanity overwhelmed by brute* force. The motif of the shrieking mouth is repeated in that of the screaming woman with her dead child **at the left**, the face of the soldier **below**, and the victim* of the flames **at the right**. The bull, standing* for brutality,* is the only triumphant figure in this symbolic* struggle between the forces of darkness and those of light, between barbarism and civilization. **Above**, an arm reaches forward to hold the lamp of truth over the whole gruesome scene. **Amid** the general havoc and gloom the artist sounds one soft note* of optimism. **Above** the victim's* severed arm and broken sword **in the bottom center** is a tiny plant in bloom to signify* the force of renewal.

William Fleming, *Arts and Ideas*

Topic Sentence

Example 1

Example 2

Example 3

Example 4

Example 5

Example 6

TIPS & TRICKS

Notice the direct references indicated with asterisks. For example, *He*, in the second sentence, refers back to *Picasso*, in the first sentence. *Allegorical*, in the first sentence, is repeatedly referred to by similar-meaning words and phrases such as *symbolism, standing for, symbolic,* and *signify*. Variations of *victim* and *brutality* are also repeated throughout the paragraph.

Pablo Picasso. *Guernica*, 1937, oil on canvas, 11' 5½" x 25' 5¾". Museo del Prado, Madrid.

NOTE To check your own writing for elaboration, coherence, and unity, ask whether your writing is "on **TOP**":

- **T = Topic** Are all points and sentences about the topic? This ensures **elaboration**.
- **O = Order** Is there a logical/clear order of ideas? This ensures **coherence**.
- **P = Points of development** Is there sufficient development of ideas? This ensures **unity**.

TECHNOLOGY TIP

If computer equipment is available, students may prefer working on **Exercise 2** (pp. 380–381) on a computer and using the copy, cut, and paste functions to organize the sentences into effective paragraphs.

Meeting INDIVIDUAL NEEDS

MULTIPLE INTELLIGENCES
Spatial Intelligence. Have students write the sentences from the paragraphs in **Exercise 2** (pp. 380–381) on strips of paper. Then, have students determine which type of order would work best for each paragraph, and arrange the strips in that order. Students can then work to revise the sentences and eliminate sentence strips that are unnecessary.

Relating to Literature

Refer students to the Dr. Martin Luther King, Jr., speech "I Have a Dream." Ask students to work in small groups to analyze the speech to understand its elaboration, coherence, and unity using the "TOP" criteria on p. 379.

Exercise 2 — Improving the Qualities of Paragraphs

ANSWERS
Possible answers are shown below.

1. To tie-dye fabric, select 100% cotton fabric and pretreat it in a solution of soda ash and water. Then, twist your fabric in spirals or fold it into interesting patterns, and tie it using either rubber bands or string. Mix the dyes in glass jars; then place them in squirt bottles. Squirt dyes on tied materials, being careful to protect your eyes, skin, clothes, and work area from spills. Allow the dye to react with the fabric by placing the items in a plastic bag for twenty-four hours. Then, rinse the fabric first in cool, then in warmer water until the water runs clear. [*This paragraph needs a chronological sequence because it is explaining a process.*]

2. Politics and entertainment seem strangely intertwined. Early in life, Ronald Reagan appeared in a total of fifty-two feature movies. Later in his life, his political career went from Republican governor of California (1967–75) to fortieth president of the United States (1981–89). Sonny Bono was half of the Sonny and Cher variety team before entering politics. Starting as mayor of Palm Springs, California, in 1988, Bono eventually became the U.S. Representative from California's 44th District in 1994. Minnesota even elected a former professional wrestler and actor, Jesse "The Body" Ventura, to the office of governor in 1998. [*This paragraph should be organized so that each entertainment personality who was elected to office is covered in full before moving on to the next.*]

Exercise 2 — Improving the Qualities of Paragraphs

In the following three paragraphs, the ideas are poorly arranged, making it difficult to make sense of what the writers are saying. Also, some of the information in each paragraph may detract from that paragraph's unity. After you determine which type of order would make sense for each paragraph, revise each paragraph by rearranging sentences into that order. Eliminate any sentences that are unrelated to the main idea and incorporate direct references and transitions. Finally, decide whether there is sufficient elaboration to support the main idea. Be prepared to explain your revisions.

1. Pre-treat all fabric by soaking it in a solution of soda ash and water. Allow the dye to react with the fabric by placing the items in a plastic bag for twenty-four hours. Squirt dyes on tied material. Use only 100% cotton material. Protect your eyes, skin, clothes, and work area from spills. Twist your fabric in spirals or fold it into interesting patterns. Mix dyes in glass jars, then place in squirt bottles. Tie, using either rubber bands or string. Rinse first in cool, then warmer water until the water runs clear.

2. Politics and entertainment seem strangely intertwined. Early in life, Ronald Reagan appeared in a total of fifty-two feature movies. Minnesota even elected a former professional wrestler and actor, Jesse "The Body" Ventura, to the office of governor in 1998. Singer/actor Sonny Bono was half of the Sonny and Cher variety team before entering into politics. Cher continued in music and film, even earning an Academy Award. Starting as mayor of Palm Springs, California in 1988, Bono eventually became the U.S. Representative from California's 44th District in 1994. Ronald Reagan's political career went from Republican governor of California (1967–75) to fortieth president of the United States (1981–89). Australian

Peter Garrett, lead singer of Midnight Oil, is active in his country's politics. Whether in politics or entertainment, some people seem destined for the spotlight.

3. Only ten percent of visitors to the Grand Canyon actually hike into the canyon. The first sight of the Grand Canyon is enough to make your heart leap into your mouth. A trip to the Grand Canyon is not the same without a hike down into the canyon itself. Gift shops, food concessions, and a hotel all have been run by the famous Fred Harvey Company since 1876. Do not even try to hike down to the river and back in one day. Tours into the canyon on the backs of mules are conducted daily. The Grand Canyon is approximately one mile deep, 277 miles long, and up to eighteen miles across. The Colorado River snakes across the bottom of the canyon. Reservations are always recommended. Las Vegas is in nearby Nevada. The mules are sure-footed and they provide an excellent photo opportunity for the brave adventurer.

Review A — Analyzing Paragraphs

With two or three classmates, look through a variety of sources to find four different kinds of paragraphs—one that explains, one that describes, one that persuades, and one that narrates. You might look in magazine and newspaper articles and advertisements, instruction manuals, and reviews of movies, CDs, or books. After you have found the paragraphs, identify their **parts** (topic, support, and clincher sentences) and **qualities** (coherence, unity, and elaboration). Then, identify which paragraphs are particularly weak or strong. If you decide that a paragraph is weak, explain why. For example, write "fails to provide support" or "lacks unity."

Exercise 2 — Improving the Qualities of Paragraphs

ANSWERS continued

3. The first sight of the Grand Canyon is enough to make your heart leap into your mouth. It is approximately one mile deep, 277 miles long, and up to eighteen miles across; the Colorado River snakes across the canyon floor. Although they find the canyon breathtaking, only ten percent of visitors actually hike into the canyon, but every day sure-footed mules take riders into the canyon on tours for the brave adventurer. [*This paragraph has far too many ideas and not enough development of any of them. The author needs to stick to one main idea.*]

Review A — Analyzing Paragraphs

Make certain that students have examples of each type of paragraph and that they correctly identify parts and qualities of the paragraphs. Also, be sure that students can explain why a paragraph is weak

What Makes a Composition?

OBJECTIVES

- To analyze thesis statements
- To analyze introductions on the basis of technique, tone, and structure
- To analyze body paragraphs on unity, coherence, and elaboration
- To improve a poorly written conclusion

Quotation for the Day

"People ought to be reading all the time when they're writing, or while they're learning to write, because they are going to learn a lot of what they write from other writers."

(Wallace Stegner, 1909–1993, American writer)

Have each student bring to class a reading selection written by a favorite author. Have students explain what captures their attention and why the selections are favorites. Encourage students to note techniques the writer has used that make the reading more interesting. How does the writer set the tone in the introduction? How has the topic been developed? What is compelling or satisfying about the conclusion?

STYLE TIP

Introductions can vary in length from one short sentence to several paragraphs. Length is determined by the scope of the thesis.

Paragraphs Within Compositions

Just as individual sentences function as parts of a paragraph, paragraphs function as parts of longer pieces of writing called *compositions*. Within a composition, paragraphs are used for a variety of reasons:

- to explain another step in a process or another part of a subject
- to introduce another kind of support for an opinion
- to show movement in time or place
- to indicate a change in speaker in dialogue
- to break up unusually long sections of text

What Makes a Composition?

In much the same way that paragraphs are built from different types of sentences, compositions are built from different types of paragraphs. Some complex main ideas require more detailed elaboration than one paragraph can supply. **Compositions** consist of paragraphs that individually elaborate on specific points of a complex main idea, which is the main focus of the composition. You will remember that a paragraph has three parts: a topic sentence, supporting sentences, and (sometimes) a clincher sentence. Compositions may also have three parts: an *introduction*, a *body*, and a *conclusion*. Paragraphs and compositions are also similar in that they both require unity, coherence, and elaboration to support their main ideas.

The Introduction

Because the **introduction** is the first thing your readers see, you will want to be sure it creates a good impression. This means that the time you take in writing an introduction is well spent. After all, if an introduction is not well written, your reader might not bother reading the rest of your composition. You will write good introductions if you keep in mind that an introduction should do these three things:

- catch the *reader's interest*
- set the *tone of the composition*
- present the *thesis statement*

382   Chapter 11   Understanding Paragraphs and Compositions

RESOURCES

What Makes a Composition?
Practice
- *Sentences, Paragraphs, and Compositions*, TPs. 11, 12, 13, WS. pp. 47, 48, 49, 50

Catching the Reader's Interest

To understand the importance of good introductory sentences, think about TV commercials. The first few seconds of a good commercial will quickly grab your attention and make you want to watch the rest. Similarly, the first few sentences of a good introduction will immediately attract your readers and give them a reason for reading more.

Techniques for Writing Introductions

If you have trouble beginning a composition, try using one of the following six techniques. Each is illustrated by a sample introduction about roadside attractions throughout the United States. You can also try combining techniques for variety.

1. **Begin with a question.** Some introductions begin with a question that contradicts the thesis. Others use a rhetorical question—one with no answer expected. Any question that applies to the reader can be intriguing, as in this introduction:

   > What would possess a man to dig giant holes in the ground, and then plunge ten vintage Cadillacs nose-first into the holes, burying them with just the back ends sticking out? Would you believe it was done for "artistic" purposes? Stanley Marsh III claims that is why he created his "Cadillac Ranch" in 1973 just west of Amarillo, Texas, on Interstate 40. His creation has led many people to question: *Is* it art?

> **COMPUTER TIP**
>
> Experiment with different types of introductions for the same composition. Type several different introductions in a separate file, then cut-and-paste your best one into your first draft. Be sure to save the others in case you change your mind or think of ways to improve one to make it fit better.

Meeting INDIVIDUAL NEEDS

ADVANCED LEARNERS
Challenge students to find examples of each introduction technique in their own reading. Students can meet to gather and compare their examples of each type and then discuss the strengths and weaknesses of each. Students can put their examples, along with their brief notes of evaluation, in a folder to be used as a resource by the entire class.

Cooperative Learning

Writing Introductions. Arrange students in groups of six. Have each group choose a well-known topic and have each group member take one of the types of introductions. Students can compose brief introductions, using their assigned types, on their group's topic. Then, group members can meet to share their introductions and their ideas about each introduction type. Are the types of introductions suited to certain tones? Are some more efficient or more interesting than the others? Have group spokespersons share their groups' insights with the class.

2. **Begin with an anecdote or example.** An *anecdote* is a little story, or real-life incident, that may be humorous or just intriguing. An *example* is a specific instance or illustration of a general idea. Going to a concert is an example of a good time you might have with a group of your friends. An introduction to a composition on tornadoes could begin with an example describing a place where a tornado has struck. The following introduction begins with an anecdote.

> I remember when I was in kindergarten and my parents bought me my first yo-yo. To me, it was like magic the way my father, sister, mother—nearly everyone but me—could make it bob down, and then shoot right back up where it started. If you could do tricks with it, then you were definitely some sort of genius. After I had gained a modest amount of skill with the yo-yo, I grew bored with it. Now, though, after visiting the National Yo-Yo Museum in Chico, California, and seeing the world's largest yo-yo (256 pounds!), a little bit of that magic has come back.

3. **State a startling fact or an unusual opinion.** This method will grab your readers' attention: They will want to see how you will support your main idea or defend your opinion.

> It is not the Statue of Liberty, the Liberty Bell, or even Mount Rushmore that best exemplifies the true spirit of America. Instead, it is the monument to the boll weevil in Enterprise, Alabama. Built in 1919, this monument is dedicated to the swarm of insects that destroyed this cotton town's main crop. It symbolizes the town's turning its attention to other crops that eventually brought prosperity. This is an example of the true spirit of America—facing adversity and triumphing while maintaining a sense of humor.

4. **Begin with background information.** Facts and other specific details not only help your reader understand your main idea but also may create interest in your topic.

384   Chapter 11   Understanding Paragraphs and Compositions

> For years Kissimmee, Florida, could boast having the world's largest alligator. Standing adjacent to the Gator Motel, this roadside attraction was a full 126 feet long. However, the reptile had to give up its title in 1992, when 200 foot long (and one inch thick) "Swampy" appeared in Christmas, Florida. Of course, these are not real alligators—just human-made tributes to the creatures that are a part of so many Floridians' lives.

5. **Set the scene.** Just as a short story may begin with a description of the setting (when and where the events take place), you might describe the setting of your topic.

> Driving across a seemingly endless North Dakota highway, with fields of rye blowing in the wind, weary travelers may not quite believe their eyes. Off in the horizon, starting as barely a speck, comes in to view what appears to be a cow—a very BIG cow. Travelers are drawn to her like a magnet. She is known as "Salem Sue." Standing thirty-eight feet tall, she is the proud symbol of the small dairy town of New Salem.

6. **Begin with a simple statement of your thesis.** You do not always have to be clever. You can be direct and get right to your main idea.

> Roadside attractions are a time-honored tradition of American culture, reflecting our big attitudes and sense of humor.

Setting the Tone

As you introduce the topic of your composition, the words you choose, the details you include, and the rhythm of your sentences all set the composition's *tone*—your attitude toward your audience and topic. The tone of a composition may be serious, humorous, formal, informal, critical—even outraged. For example, the author of the paragraph about the painting *Guernica* (page 379) discusses a serious subject, and his tone remains formal.

> **TEACHING TIP**
>
> **The Thesis Statement**
> Remind students that their thesis statements may change as they develop their compositions. The thesis is like a map that shows where a composition is headed. If, as students explore the ideas of their compositions, they decide that their maps no longer accurately describe their compositions, the thesis statements can be revised.
>
> **Meeting INDIVIDUAL NEEDS**
>
> **MULTIPLE INTELLIGENCES**
> **Interpersonal Intelligence.** Have students work in pairs to write three thesis statements. Students should include a topic and main idea in each, with one student providing the topic and the other student the main idea. Review students' work to evaluate their understanding of the concept of a thesis statement.

The Thesis Statement

The *thesis statement* is a sentence or two in the introduction that announces your topic and what you want to say about it. Your entire composition will support the ideas presented in this statement.

Some thesis statements simply state the topic, for example: *Vinnie Ream was commissioned by Congress in 1866 to sculpt a memorial statue of Abraham Lincoln.* This introduces the topic of the sculptor commissioned to do the Lincoln sculpture, which stands in the rotunda of the U.S. Capitol in Washington, D.C.

Other thesis statements, including the ones you are often asked to write, do more. They also identify a main idea the writer is trying to prove in the composition. Here is one example of this kind of thesis statement:

Vinnie Ream

> Congress's 1866 decision to award a $10,000 commission to 18-year-old Vinnie Ream for a marble statue memorializing the nation's recently assassinated president, Abraham Lincoln, vaulted the young sculptor into the center of a storm of controversy.
>
> Ethel Yari, "Teenage Lincoln Sculptor,"
> *American History*

In this thesis sentence we are introduced to the topic *and* the main idea of the composition, which is about the controversy that Ream's commission caused.

Hints for Writing and Using a Thesis Statement

1. **Develop your thesis statement from information you have gathered.** Review your prewriting material—the many facts and details you have gathered. Ask yourself: *What main idea do the facts and details suggest?*

2. **Include both a topic and your main idea about it.** Most thesis statements answer these two questions: *What is my topic? What am I saying about my topic?* To make sure you have included both parts, underline the topic and circle the main idea.

   For example, read this thesis statement: *"If you take sensible precautions with clothing, equipment, and safety, you can enjoy bicycling all year long."* It is clear that this writer is going to discuss year-round bicycling (topic) and specific precautions you need to make with clothing, equipment, and safety (main idea).

386 Chapter 11 Understanding Paragraphs and Compositions

MINI-LESSON

Limiting a Topic. To create a thesis statement, each student must first choose a topic and then develop a main idea about it. When a topic is too broad, it is difficult to develop a main idea. Have students narrow each of the following topics to a more specific topic that lends itself to the development of a main idea that could be presented in a thesis statement. Possible answers are given in brackets.

1. women's basketball [*televising women's games during prime time*]

Hints for Writing and Using a Thesis Statement
3. **Be clear and specific.** Keep your language and ideas sharp and definite. Compare this vague thesis statement with the actual one you have just read: "If you want to continue bicycling, you need to take care of a lot of things."
4. **Keep your thesis statement in front of you as you plan and write.** It will help keep you on track. Every idea and detail should directly support your thesis statement, so be focused and get rid of any that do not.

NOTE Your *preliminary thesis statement*, the first one you develop before you actually write your composition, is probably direct and straightforward. You may even think it is a little dull. Later on, you can revise it to give it more zing, as professional writers do. Here is an example of how one writer revised a thesis statement.

PRELIMINARY Although rain seldom comes to the Sonoran Desert, when it does, flash flooding often accompanies it, creating major changes in the lives of animals, plants, and landscape of the region.

REVISED "Flash flood!" That wall of water racing down the dry creek bed is the first rain to come to the Sonoran Desert in months—and whether beast, plant, or the very landscape itself, life is about to change in an instant.

Exercise 3 Analyzing Thesis Statements

On your own paper, identify the specific topic and the main idea of each of the following thesis statements.

EXAMPLE
1. The habitat of the Cuban bee hummingbird—the world's smallest bird—must maintain its perfect balance to support such a fragile creature.
   1. Topic: Cuban bee hummingbird habitat
      Main idea: The bird's habitat must be maintained.

1. Professional sports lost three greats to retirement in 1999: basketballs's Michael Jordan, hockey's Wayne Gretzky, and football's John Elway.
2. Pet owners seem to come in two antagonistic species: cat people and dog people; but, members of both sides should recognize that the two species of pet actually do share many characteristics.

STYLE TIP

Sometimes in longer papers, of five hundred or more words, it is a good idea to use a **multipoint thesis,** in which you list the main point of each body paragraph. Here is a multipoint thesis with the three points underlined:

The introduction of printing <u>encouraged writing,</u> <u>furthered literacy,</u> and <u>expanded the flow of information.</u>

Generally, a multipoint thesis promotes good organization and coherence, because it gives the framework for the body of your composition.

Critical Thinking

Metacognition. Have students re-read compositions they wrote earlier in the year. Ask each student to write his or her thesis statement on a separate sheet of paper. (It may be implied or directly stated.) Then, have students write brief evaluations of how well the compositions support the theses. What have they learned about composition since they wrote those papers? What would they do differently, and why?

Exercise 3 Analyzing Thesis Statements

ANSWERS

1. Topic: retired professional athletes
   Main idea: Three professional star athletes retired in 1999.

2. Topic: cat and dog owners
   Main idea: Cat and dog owners may seem to be different types of people, but their pets share some characteristics.

---

2. ecology [*preservation of the Kirtland warbler*]
3. war [*the treatment of prisoners of war under the terms of the Geneva Convention*]
4. national parks [*high levels of tourism in Yosemite National Park*]
5. careers [*training programs for arborists*]

> **Exercise 3** Analyzing Thesis Statements
>
> **ANSWERS continued**
>
> 3. Topic: car depreciation
>   Main idea: Know the causes of car depreciation before buying a car.
> 4. Topic: the printing press
>   Main idea: The printing press changed the English language.
> 5. Topic: LP turntables
>   Main idea: Outdated LP turntables may have value.
> 6. Topic: rhythm
>   Main idea: Many living things use rhythmic movement.
> 7. Topic: Dingo Fence
>   Main idea: The Dingo Fence has had a greater ecological impact than originally imagined.
> 8. Topic: language formulas
>   Main idea: The formulas for greeting and leave-taking are odd.
> 9. Topic: history of food and dining words
>   Main idea: The history of food and dining words reveals exploration during the Renaissance.
> 10. Topic: wildlife conservation
>   Main idea: It is necessary to understand the relationship between an animal and its habitat.
>
> ### TEACHING TIP
>
> **The Structure of Introductions**
> Show students that the funnel-like structure of the beginning of a composition allows a writer to warm up to a topic slowly. As a result, the first paragraph of a rough draft may be too general. Students may often find that their second paragraphs make better introductions because they have had time to strengthen their focus, and their first paragraphs can be discarded.

3. When you consider buying your first car, keep in mind the factors that can cause it to depreciate, or lose value, over just the first year.
4. With the advent of the printing press, cheap books became readily available in England and the English language was forever changed.
5. While CDs have virtually replaced LPs, think twice before you chuck that turntable into the trash.
6. Although humans may believe that they are the only ones on the planet who have rhythm, many living things use some form of rhythmic movement in their everyday patterns.
7. Designed to protect sheep from a highly destructive predator, the 1553-mile long Dingo Fence of Australia has had a greater ecological impact than originally imagined.
8. The formulas that languages use to create their words for greeting and leave-taking are odd.
9. Exploring the history of many words for food and dining reveals the story of exploration during the Renaissance.
10. In order to understand wildlife conservation, people must first understand the relationship between an animal and its habitat.

The Structure of Introductions

To shape introductions in both formal and informal writing, writers often follow a common format: They move from general information to a more specific statement—often a thesis statement. Think of a funnel. The wide opening at the top of the funnel is like the general opening of an introduction. The slender end of the funnel is like the precise thesis to which the introduction narrows.

Reference Note
For more on **writing introductions,** see page 943 in the Quick Reference Handbook.

In the following example introduction, notice how the sentences grow increasingly more specific, with the last statement serving as a thesis.

> Human civilizations are always questioning and changing the requirements they have for the people who lead and represent them. William Shakespeare, the great Elizabethan dramatist, recognized this tendency in himself and in his audience and explored the nature of leadership in a great majority of his plays. The characters he portrays as leaders or aspiring leaders often are models for the strengths and weaknesses of particular leadership types. In *Julius Caesar,* he focuses his attention upon three types of revolutionary leaders represented by the idealistic Brutus, the self-serving Cassius, and the popular Antony.

Another type of introduction is one that you might think of as a "twist." It begins by stating commonly accepted knowledge, but adds a twist that calls this knowledge into question. This kind of introduction is known as a **"But" introduction,** because the thesis begins with a word or phrase indicating an opposite, such as *but, however,* or *on the other hand.* "But" introductions can be very effective in capturing a reader's attention. For example, in the following paragraph, the thesis twist begins with "But no."

> With all the advances toward equality for women, you've got to assume there are lots of women programmers, right? After all, it's not as though computer science is a discipline that requires more brawn than brains. But no: According to statistics compiled by Tracy K. Camp, then an assistant professor of computer science at the University of Alabama, the number of undergraduate degrees in computer science that is awarded to women has been shrinking steadily, both in real numbers and as a percentage of degrees awarded.
>
> Wendy M. Grossman, "Access Denied,"
> *Scientific American*

TIPS & TRICKS

In formal writing, you should avoid beginning a sentence with a conjunction such as *but.* Instead, choose one of the synonym forms *however* or *on the other hand* to begin a "But" introduction.

Critical Thinking

Analysis. Have each student use a funnel-shaped graphic organizer to show exactly how each of the example introductions proceeds from the general to the specific. Students should break the paragraphs into parts and write the parts on their organizers. They should find that even the "But" introduction goes from general to the specific, as is shown below:

- general: advances toward equality for women
  - does this apply to programmers?
  - one would expect it to, but . . .
  - specific: the number of undergraduate degrees in computer science awarded to women is shrinking, both in real numbers and in percentage of degrees awarded.

Exercise 4 Analyzing Introductions

ANSWERS
Possible answers are shown below.

1. • The writer uses a startling opinion to begin.
   • The shocking opening works well to keep me reading and wanting to know more.
   • The tone is humorous and practical, stating that bugs are more efficient to raise and that we could cut down on pesticide use by eating bugs.
   • The introduction follows the funnel structure, moving from general to specific.

2. • The writer begins with background information on the topic.
   • The technique works well because it leads to the problem of untracked scraps in space, which is an interesting and surprising problem.
   • The tone is serious; the writer uses facts to emphasize the danger for spacecraft operators.
   • Yes, the introduction follows the funnel pattern.

Exercise 4 Analyzing Introductions

For each of the two published introductions below, answer the following questions.

- What technique does the writer use in the beginning of the introduction? (Look back over the techniques on pages 383–385.)
- How well do you think the technique works? Would you continue reading the article?
- How would you describe the tone—the writer's attitude toward the topic? What words and details in the introduction reveal the tone?
- Does the introduction follow the structure you learned about on page 388? If not, how does it differ?

1. Entomophagy, or bug eating, writes David George Gordon in *The Eat a Bug Cookbook*, is good for the planet. It takes only a quarter as much feed to raise a pound of roach meat as it does to raise a pound of beef. "And consider this: Many of our common garden pests are edible. If everyone served rapacious critters such as vine weevils and tomato hornworms at the dinner table, we'd have little need for most over-the-counter pesticide[s]."

    Kim Hubbard, Review of *The Eat a Bug Cookbook, Discover*

2. Since the space age began four decades ago, rockets have lifted more than 20,000 metric tons of material into orbit. Today 4,500 tons remain in the form of nearly 10,000 "resident space objects," only five percent of which are functioning spacecraft. These objects are just the large ones that military radars and telescopes can track. Of increasing interest to spacecraft operators are the millions of smaller, untrackable scraps scattered into orbits throughout near-Earth space, from only a few hundred kilometers to more than 40,000 kilometers (25,000 miles) above the surface of the planet.

    Nicholas L. Johnson, "Monitoring and Controlling Debris in Space," *Scientific American*

The Body

Your composition would read like a telegram if you simply stated your main ideas without supporting them. To have an effective composition you need to include a *body* of supporting paragraphs. These paragraphs, which are the core of your composition, support, or prove, the thesis or main idea by developing it with supporting details. All body paragraphs should relate directly to the thesis statement and should connect smoothly with one another. In other words, the body of a composition should have the qualities of unity, coherence and elaboration.

Unity

It is a strain to try to listen to someone whose thoughts leap illogically from one idea to another. A composition has *unity* when instead of leaping between ideas, its paragraphs work smoothly together to support a single main idea—your thesis. Unity is lost when any detail or statement detracts from the sense of "oneness" in the composition.

Coherence

Coherence means that ideas within the composition are strongly connected. In a coherent composition, the ideas are easy to follow from paragraph to paragraph and the writing seems to flow smoothly from beginning to end. The reader does not have to agonize over what something means; nothing sounds awkward or disjointed. You can make your composition coherent by arranging ideas sensibly and by using *direct references* and *transitional expressions* to show how ideas are connected.

Direct References
One way to connect ideas from paragraph to paragraph is to make *direct references* to something you have already mentioned. Here are three ways to use direct references.

1. Use pronouns to refer to nouns or ideas in previous paragraphs. For example, by using the pronouns *she*, *they*, or *this*, you can avoid awkwardly repeating nouns.
2. Repeat key words or phrases. Tie paragraphs together by reminding the reader of what is important.
3. Use synonyms or slight rewordings of ideas and key words introduced in previous paragraphs. Too much repetition sounds awkward.

Reference Note
When you write the body of a composition, it is often helpful to draft a plan, whether an **early plan** (sometimes called a **rough outline**), or a **formal outline**. For more information about early plans and formal outlines, see pages 950 and 951 of the Quick Reference Handbook.

Reference Note
For more on **direct references** and **transitional words and phrases**, see pages 375 and 376.

Timesaver

Assign students to groups of three to answer the questions in **Exercise 5.** One student will record the answers for the group and submit the answers with all group members' names. This approach will cut grading time and provide another opportunity for students to discuss the elements of body paragraphs.

Exercise 5   Analyzing Body Paragraphs

ANSWERS
Possible answers are shown below.

1. why people visit the Science Center

2. There are several reasons for the popularity of the Los Angeles Science Center.

3. *First off:* transitional expression

   Most important: transitional expression

   museum: direct reference

   science: direct reference

4. All three sentences elaborate on the main idea, explaining why the Science Center is a popular place to visit.

TIPS & TRICKS

To check that the details you select for elaboration fit your purpose, audience, and topic, you can use the following questions.
- Did I include details that helped me achieve my purpose?
- What details will make my main ideas stronger?
- Do these details answer the questions my audience might have about my topic?

Transitional Expressions   You can also use *transitional expressions*—words and phrases like *for example, therefore, of course,* or *on the other hand*—to connect ideas and make relationships clear.

Elaboration

Elaboration, the third element of good compositions, is the technique of supporting and explaining the thesis of a composition completely. This is achieved by including details, reasons, and evidence. Without proper elaboration, readers will be left confused or unconvinced. In some cases, such as in scientific reports, several paragraphs of elaboration may be needed to explain a certain point completely. In other cases, just a few paragraphs of elaboration may be sufficient. The amount of elaboration that you need depends on what you are trying to show. However, you should always strive to develop your thesis thoroughly and convincingly.

Exercise 5   Analyzing Body Paragraphs

Analyze the following pair of body paragraphs by answering these questions. Be prepared to explain your answers.

1. Identify the main idea that creates unity between the paragraphs.
2. Write a thesis statement that summarizes the main idea.
3. Identify examples of direct references and transitional expressions that the writer uses to show coherence between the two paragraphs.
4. Identify sentences in the second paragraph that elaborate on the main idea.

> I had come to the Science Center because I'd heard of its booming popularity and wondered what it was doing right. L.A. is, after all, a place of many diversions. It's got amusement parks galore, it's got beaches, it's got mountains, it's got celebrities out and about, along with year-round SPF-15 sun. In addition, there is the dismal 1996 report from the National Science Foundation, which states that "only 49 percent of Americans know that the Earth revolves around the sun once each year."
>
> *(continued)*

392   Chapter 11   Understanding Paragraphs and Compositions

MINI-LESSON

Clarifying Pronoun References. Some students may need additional practice with using pronouns correctly when making direct references to build coherence in a paragraph. Remind students that ambiguous references occur when pronouns do not have clear antecedents. Have students correct the following sentences to eliminate ambiguous pronoun references. Possible answers appear in brackets.

1. When Elisha visited Sue in Washington, D.C., they met her aunt. [*When Elisha*

(continued)

So I wondered just what it takes these days to propel people . . . to visit, of all things, a science museum.

First off is free admission, although you do have to pony up five dollars for parking. There's the appeal of a big, airy, and all-around impressive brand-new building. Most important, presumably, are all the interactive exhibits that the museum hopes will generate some wonder about science in all these potential [National Science Foundation] grant applicants.

Mark Wheeler, "Science Friction," *Discover*

The Conclusion

The third element of compositions, the **conclusion,** is just as important as the introduction. Take advantage of the fact that the conclusion is the last thing your reader will see in your composition, and write a solid conclusion that completes the work of your introduction and body paragraphs. A strong conclusion should give the reader a sense that all of your ideas have been properly tied together and explained thoroughly. A composition that lacks a strong conclusion can leave the reader feeling puzzled. The following are some techniques that you can use to create effective conclusions.

1. **Restate the main idea.** Say it again, but use different words. This is probably the easiest kind of conclusion to write. When you use this technique, it works well to put the reworded version of your thesis statement at the beginning of the last paragraph. The following conclusion restates the thesis illustrated in the first model introduction on page 383.

> Is the Cadillac Ranch art? That is not for any one person to decide yes or no. However, if you are ever passing through Amarillo, Texas, why not make a stop at this roadside attraction and let your own eyes, mind, and heart continue the debate for yourself? Just watch your step for cacti and rattlers.

STYLE   TIP

Oftentimes, descriptive and narrative compositions do not need distinctive conclusions separate from and following the body paragraphs. The description or experience is self-contained and does not require further elaboration or summarization.

Exercise 5

ALTERNATIVE LESSON
Have students rewrite the paragraphs in **Exercise 5** using a more formal tone. A sample revision follows.

The Los Angeles Science Center is well known and heavily visited in spite of the city's many other attractions, including amusement parks, beaches, sun, and celebrities. The fact that a 1996 National Science Foundation report stated that "only 49 percent of Americans know that the Earth revolves around the sun once each year" makes the attendance even more surprising. Clearly, the Science Center is very resourceful when it comes to attracting visitors.

One of the center's major draws is free admission (although parking fees are five dollars). Also, the impressive new building is large and airy, and most importantly, the interactive exhibits create wonder about science among young visitors who may someday become scientists themselves.

T E A C H I N G   TIP

The Conclusion
Point out to students that a conclusion that includes "In this essay I told you . . ." or a similar statement is weak and unengaging. To be effective, a conclusion should strengthen the main idea of the essay in a concise, creative fashion.

---

visited Sue in Washington, D.C., they met Sue's aunt.]
2. Jim and Maria met Raoul and Sara as they were leaving the art museum. [*As Jim and Maria were leaving the art museum, they met Raoul and Sara.*]
3. The differences in the team members became apparent as the judges marked each of their scorecards. [*The differences in team members became apparent as the judges marked each player's scorecard.*]

Cooperative Learning

Writing Conclusions. Arrange students in groups of six. Each group member should choose a different conclusion type and find one to three examples of his or her type in textbooks, newspapers, or magazines. Students should share their examples with their groups and give their opinions as to the strengths and weaknesses of the conclusion type.

Crossing the Curriculum

Science and History. Have students analyze two or more scientific or historical articles from textbooks, specialized magazines, or newspapers. Arrange students in small groups and have them share their findings. Is a certain type of introduction, conclusion, and tone used in the articles—or does it depend on the audience for whom the article is written? Discuss with students as a class how scholarly articles in certain subject areas may differ in tone and style from informative or entertaining articles in the same areas. Point out, however, that unity and coherence are important no matter the audience or subject area.

2. **Refer to the introduction.** Bring the reader back full circle by referring to something in your introduction other than just the thesis.

> Returning home from my trip to the National Yo-Yo Museum, I searched in the attic, under the bed, and at the back of the closet, but found no yo-yos. Like fairies in Peter Pan, maybe yo-yos disappear when we stop believing in them. A 256-pound yo-yo demands attention and belief. Thanks to the people in Chico, California, though, this American treasure will continue to spark magic in all those who see it.

3. **End with a thoughtful comment, a personal reaction, or a look to the future.** Think of this kind of conclusion as a way to "extend" your thesis.

> Like Swampy the Gator in Christmas, Florida, or Salem Sue the cow in New Salem, North Dakota, roadside attractions are more than just humorous attempts at being "the biggest and the best." They are icons of pride in community. While they may not have the longevity of the pyramids or Stonehenge, they should stand as reminders to future generations of who we were and what we considered important.

4. **Use a quotation.** A quotation that is startling or moving works well to end a composition. Be sure to show how the quotation is relevant to your composition.

> Romain Gary wrote in *Promise at Dawn* "humor is an affirmation of dignity, a declaration of man's superiority to all that befalls him." The dignity of Enterprise, Alabama, is evident in the Boll Weevil Monument, which remains the centerpiece of the downtown district. Through humor, the people of Enterprise have shown their superiority to the 1915 agricultural disaster that befell them.

5. **End with a call to action.** Persuasive essays often end by asking the reader to take a specific action. This method can make an effective ending for other kinds of compositions, too.

> Do not let America's proud tradition of roadside attractions fade into the past like its drive-in movie theaters and Burma Shave signs. Do your part to maintain any giant fiberglass animals or balls of twine in your town. Support retailers with colossal Muffler Men and anyone with the audacity to place giant pink inflatable gorillas in bikinis anywhere on their establishment. If your community does not have a "world's largest," don't you think perhaps it is time it did?

6. **Summarize the main points developed in the body.** Rephrase the topic sentences of each of your body paragraphs.

> Roadside attractions serve a purpose in asking the motorist speeding by at seventy-plus mph to slow down, stop by, and take a moment to see that our communities are more than just highway markers, gas stations, and blurs on the periphery. Giant yo-yos invite you to learn the history of this popular toy. Salem Sue and Swampy the Gator tell of the local economy or wildlife. Boll Weevil monuments tell the tale of perseverance in the face of adversity. However, behind it all are the people of America you might not ordinarily meet. As you stop and share a laugh with a fellow traveler or listen to a local tell his or her story, you are enriched in ways you never could have been if that roadside attraction had not prompted you to stop.

Meeting INDIVIDUAL NEEDS

LEARNERS HAVING DIFFICULTY
Some students may not grasp the differences among techniques 1, 2, and 6. Explain the difference between a restatement and a summary, and compare a few examples of each. Tell students that referring to the introduction doesn't mean restating or summarizing the composition's main idea. It means mentioning something specific that was stated in the introduction.

Relating to Literature
Have students read "No News from Auschwitz" by A. M. Rosenthal, if it is contained in their literature textbook. Ask students which of the six techniques for writing conclusions Rosenthal uses. [*He refers to the introduction.*] Then have each student use one of the other techniques to write a different conclusion for the essay. Ask for volunteers to read aloud their new conclusions.

Exercise 6 Improving a Conclusion

ANSWER
A possible answer is shown below. Suggestions for improvement:

The author tells what he has told the reader, introduces a new topic, and ends with a weak statement. It could be improved with more development.

  Because people with disabilities should have access to public facilities, ramps must be made part of the design of any new construction and older facilities must be remodeled for easier access. A sense of justice should make us support public access for all people, not just those who can climb stairs.

In formal compositions, writers often conclude with a restatement of the thesis followed by summaries of their main points. The structure for a formal conclusion is similar to reversing the "funnel" approach you learned for introductions (see page 388). In these conclusions, writers move from the specifics of their composition into a general final statement.

STYLE TIP
Although conclusions can vary in length, the typical conclusion to an in-school essay will have 3–4 sentences. Longer conclusions may indicate that material was not adequately covered within the body paragraphs or that too lengthy a restatement of the points presented is being given.

Exercise 6 Improving a Conclusion

Here are the first drafts of conclusions for two compositions. With a partner, decide what is wrong with each conclusion. How can they be improved? Then, write better conclusions. You will need to infer the main idea of the compositions from the details in the paragraphs. You can change the paragraphs any way you like, make up details, or even start over completely.

1. That is why I think there should be ramps for people in wheelchairs and some sort of help for people with other disabilities. That does not even mention the problems they have getting decent jobs. I hope you will agree.

2. In conclusion, it is obvious that scuba diving is a hobby that people of all ages can enjoy. As I said in my introduction, "Scuba diving is a relaxing and unusual pastime that parents and children can share." Plus, scuba diving can be less expensive if you buy used equipment.

Using a Basic Framework

The following framework shows in a general way how an introduction, body, and conclusion come together to form a complete composition. Each of the Writing Workshops in this book has a more specific framework that provides guidelines for a particular type of writing.

Framework for Composition	
Introduction	• catches the reader's interest • sets the tone for the composition • presents the thesis statement
Body	• states the main points • provides support for the main points
Conclusion	• reinforces the main idea stated in the thesis statement • ties together the main points of the body • leaves the reader with a sense that the composition has been "wrapped up"

Crossing the Curriculum

Journalism. Have students read newspaper and magazine articles and then meet in small groups to discuss the framework the articles seem to follow. How is it different from or similar to the framework given on this page? Then, ask students to write their own very brief informative articles, following the framework they have uncovered in their reading. Students can rely on newspaper and magazine reports for information, but each article should exhibit the student's perspective on the event. Have students share their articles with the class and discuss their methods and framework.

Relating to Reading

Knowledge of the basic structure of good writing is helpful when taking notes on reading. Ask students how knowledge of topic sentences, thesis statements, and supporting details could help them in their note-taking. Point out to students that recognizing a thesis statement and analyzing the support given in the body of the piece of writing will help them to remember the main points of a piece and to evaluate its argument.

Have students each read a newspaper editorial article, using their identification of the thesis, support, and conclusion to evaluate the argument. Discuss with students how their familiarity with the parts of a composition makes them more careful, objective readers.

A Writer's Model

The following is the final draft of a composition on bicycle touring. You might want to use this composition as a model for a composition of your own.

Two-Wheel Holidays

INTRODUCTION

Automobiles speed along highways at sixty-five miles an hour or more. Bullet trains rocket down their tracks at nearly two hundred miles an hour. If that is not fast enough for you, the Concorde jet carries passengers faster than the speed of sound! However, despite faster means of transportation, more and more people are choosing to take day trips, overnights, or extended tours the slow way—by bicycle. If you are interested in bicycle touring, you will need to make some specific preparations involving your bike, yourself, your clothing, and your route.

Thesis statement

BODY
Major point: Your bike

The first thing to consider is your bicycle. With so many types to choose from (road bikes, off-road bikes, mountain bikes, and all-terrain bikes) you can pick one that is appropriate for the kind of terrain on which you will be traveling. Whichever bike you choose, it should be in excellent condition. Equip the bike with a map, a light, a bicycle-repair kit, a first-aid kit, saddlebags for food and clothing, and a water carrier.

Major point: Your physical condition

Your bike may be in good shape, but what about you? Whether your trip is a few miles to the next town or across country, you need to get yourself in good physical condition. Start an exercise program and build up your muscles and endurance gradually. You should be able to cycle ten to fifteen miles a day easily.

Major point: Your clothing

Now think about clothing. What you pack will depend on the season, but always prepare for possible bad weather. Pack rain gear and clothing that allows freedom of movement as it protects you from strong winds, wet, and cold. In general, avoid clothing that might interfere with your mobility or comfort, and be sure to wear a helmet. Head injuries are a cyclist's biggest worry.

Major point: Safety

Bicycle safety does not end when you put on your helmet. Helmets provide some protection in case of an accident, but

398   Chapter 11   Understanding Paragraphs and Compositions

Learning for Life

Writing a Personal Statement. As students begin to think about looking for employment or applying to colleges and universities, remind them that many applications will ask students to write personal statements revealing their past experience and plans for the future. Ask students to practice writing such statements by describing experiences they have had that will prepare them to achieve future goals. Tell students that their statements should clearly explain how the experience and their current efforts you are still better off avoiding accidents altogether—especially when you are sharing the road with motorists. Remember to ride to the right, on the shoulder or far in the right lane. Avoid busy roads if at all possible. Use lights, reflectors, and bright or light-colored clothing to make yourself visible to motorists. Finally, remember, always use hand signals to indicate turns or lane changes, just as you would use turn signals when driving a car.

Finally, talk to experienced cyclists and read books and magazines to plan your route. You may want to join the American Youth Hostels (AYH), which offers its members inexpensive lodging and group rides. Bicycling magazines appear each month with information and special features about bicycle touring. An organization called the Adventure Cycling Association publishes guidebooks, maps of the U.S. National Bicycle Trails Network, and a list of bicycle tour operators.

Major point: Planning your route

If you plan your trip well, you will discover that bicycle touring—alone or with a group—is more fun than faster ways of travel. Before you go, give yourself time to get your bike, your body, your clothing, and your route in top condition. Careful advance planning practically guarantees a safe trip.

CONCLUSION

Restatement of thesis

Cooperative Learning

Analyzing a Model. Arrange students in groups of six. Each group member should analyze a different part of the Writer's Model: the introduction, the four body paragraphs, and the conclusion. Each student should be able to report to the group on the unity, coherence, and elaboration in his or her assigned paragraph, as well as the tone of the paragraph and the use of any attention-getting or clincher techniques. Students reporting on the introduction or conclusion should name the type used. Group members should then come to a consensus about the tone and method of organization of the model as a whole. Discuss groups' findings as a class.

contribute to achieving a goal. Point out to students that their statements could be organized as follows:
- Introduction
- Past experience
- Present efforts
- Future plans
- Conclusion

Suggest that students keep their statements in their portfolios for future reference. Remind students not to share information that would be considered too personal.

> **Review B** Writing an Informative Composition
>
> **ANSWER**
> A possible composition follows.
>
> Little did Sioux Chief Henry Standing Bear know, when he wrote to Korczak Ziolkowski in 1939, that his dream of a monument to Chief Crazy Horse was about to take form. That summer Korczak was assisting in the carving of Mount Rushmore, and Chief Standing Bear commented, "My fellow chiefs and I would like the white man to know the red man has great heroes, too." His words began the process of creating the mountain monument, an effort that has lasted decades and produced impressive results.
>
> When the U.S. government failed to comply with the Treaty of 1868, Chief Crazy Horse of the Lakota (Sioux) people began an armed uprising. When asked, "Where are your lands now?" Chief Crazy Horse responded, "My lands are where my dead lie buried." In 1877, Chief Crazy Horse, only thirty-four years old, died.
>
> A fitting memorial to the great chief, the completed monument will stand 563 feet high and 641 feet long. The arm will be nearly the length of a football field, the head as large as the four Mount Rushmore heads combined, the face will be nine stories tall, and the horse's nostrils will be large enough to hold a five-room house. To carve the monument, Korczak had to climb up and down a 741-step staircase to deal with his gas-fueled compressor as many as nine times a day.
>
> Korczak died in 1982 and his family continues to carry on his vision. In 1998, on the fiftieth anniversary of the memorial, the face was unveiled and dedicated. Thanks to the words of Chief Henry Standing Bear, and the tireless efforts of Korczak Ziolkowski and his family, the memory of the great hero Crazy Horse is in no danger of dying out.

> **COMPUTER TIP**
> While composing on the computer, remember to save your work every ten to fifteen minutes as you write, and keep backup copies of all your work.

NOTE First person (I) and second person (you) points-of-view are typically used only in informal writing. Formal writing requires a sense of objectivity toward the topic and distance from the reader. For this type of writing, the third person (he, she, it, they) is the most acceptable. Consider your audience when deciding the level of formality you will be required to achieve.

Review B Writing an Informative Composition

You have learned that a composition has three parts:

introduction + body + conclusion = composition

You can use this structure for many **writing purposes**—to inform, to persuade, to describe, and to narrate. Use the facts below and on the following page to write a short informative composition about the Crazy Horse Memorial in South Dakota. You do not have to use all the information provided, but use as much as you need to make a complete composition. You may also add any information you can find through research or your own knowledge. Begin by developing a thesis statement. Then, create a good introduction and conclusion for the main points and elaboration in the body. Review the framework on page 397 to see how the parts should come together. Finally, evaluate and revise your composition to make sure that it demonstrates unity, coherence, and elaboration.

The Warrior, the Sculptor, and
the Crazy Horse Memorial

1. Crazy Horse signed no treaties and refused to move to a reservation.
2. Crazy Horse began an armed uprising when the U.S. government did not comply with the Treaty of 1868.
3. Crazy Horse, of the Lakota (Sioux) people, died in 1877 at age thirty-four.
4. When asked "Where are your lands now," Chief Crazy Horse responded "My lands are where my dead lie buried."
5. Korczak Ziolkowski assisted Gutzon Borglum in the carving of Mount Rushmore in the summer of 1939.
6. Interestingly, Mr. Ziolkowski is often referrred to simply as Korczak.
7. In 1939, Sioux Chief Henry Standing Bear wrote to Korczak asking him to sculpt a mountain memorial: "My fellow chiefs and I would like the white man to know the red man has great heroes, too." This

was in reference to Mount Rushmore, on which work continued until 1941.

8. During early work on the memorial, Korczak had to climb up and down a 741-step staircase to deal with his gas-fueled compressor as many as nine times a day.
9. Korczak died in 1982, and his family continues working on the memorial to carry on his vision.
10. The fiftieth anniversary of the Crazy Horse Memorial was celebrated in 1998 with the unveiling and dedication of the completed face.
11. The completed memorial will be 563 feet tall and 641 feet long.
    - The arm will be nearly the length of a football field.
    - The head will be as big as all the Mount Rushmore heads combined.
    - The completed head will be nearly seven stories tall.
    - The horse's nostril will be large enough to hold a five-room house.

Teaching Strands

This teaching-strand chart shows you some connections between grammar instruction and the writing assignments in Part 1 of this textbook.

The *Elements of Language* grammar handbook is designed to be a flexible teaching tool that accommodates many teaching philosophies and styles. For example, some teachers will prefer to use the handbook as a reference source, having students refer to it only as the need for explicit grammar instruction arises. Others will use the handbook as a teaching text, having their classes work through the instruction, examples, and exercises in a more methodical fashion. Your personal teaching style and the needs of your students will determine the best way for you to teach this material.

GO TO: go.hrw.com
KEYWORD: EOLang

 All resources for this chapter are available for preview on the *One-Stop Planner CD-ROM with Test Generator*. All worksheets and tests may be printed from the CD-ROM.

Texas Resources For a complete listing of all resources prepared for Texas teachers and students, please see the blue box at the beginning of each chapter.

Writing Assignments	Rationale
PERSONAL REFLECTION (Chapter 1)	Writing a personal reflection requires describing past actions clearly and sequentially through verb tenses. Pronouns in correct cases, precise, well-placed adjectives and adverbs, and accurately punctuated and capitalized dialogue help to convey the writer's story. Fragments may appear in dialogue.
COMPARISON-CONTRAST ESSAY (Chapter 2)	One key to writing a successful comparison-contrast essay is the use of fresh adjectives and adverbs accurately compared and spelled. Clear connections made with subordinating conjunctions and relative pronouns guide the reader.
CAUSE-EFFECT ESSAY (Chapter 3)	A successful cause-effect essay relies on strong verbs, often clarified by prepositional phrases, and clear connections signaled by conjunctions that indicate intent. Varied sentence structures, correctly punctuated, can stress links between reasons and actions.
PROBLEM ANALYSIS (INFORMATIVE) (Chapter 4)	Problem-analysis essays ask and answer questions such as *who* and *what* through clear nouns and pronouns; *when, where,* and *how* through adverbs or adverb phrases and clauses; and *why* with subordinate clauses. Quoted support must be correctly punctuated.
LITERARY ANALYSIS OF A SHORT STORY (Chapter 5)	Literary analysis may hinge on understanding point of view, which requires correct pronoun case and person. Story events may be related in the literary present tense. Titles and supporting quotations need correct capitalization and punctuation.
RESEARCH PAPER (Chapter 6)	Research reports require formal language, detailed support, and third-person point of view, as well as correctly cited and punctuated quotations and credits. Because incorporating this information may lead to many complicated sentence structures, sentence variety and clarity are critical.
PERSUASIVE ESSAY (Chapter 7)	Using active-voice verbs intensifies the force of supporting opinions in persuasive essays, while avoiding double negatives helps keep support clear. Careful word selection helps avoid loaded and often confused words. Questions and exclamations can add emotional punch.
PERSUASIVE BROCHURE (Chapter 8)	Persuasive writing mixes logical and emotional appeals using correctly punctuated short sentences, strong verbs, fresh vocabulary, clear information, and sound reasoning.

Links to Grammar	Links to Usage	Links to Mechanics
▶ verbs (Ch. 12)	▶ verb tense, sequence (Ch. 18)	
▶ pronouns, adjectives, adverbs (Ch. 12)	▶ pronoun case (Ch. 17); placement of adverbs (Ch. 19)	
▶ fragments, sentences (Ch. 13)		▶ punctuation and capitalization of quotations (Ch. 22)
▶ adjectives, adverbs (Ch. 12)	▶ comparison of modifiers (Ch. 19)	▶ spelling words with suffixes (Ch. 26)
▶ conjunctions, relative pronouns (Ch. 12)	▶ pronoun reference and case (Ch. 17)	▶ punctuating compound and complex sentences (Ch. 22 & Ch. 23)
▶ verbs (Ch. 12)	▶ active, passive voice (Ch. 18)	
▶ phrases (Ch. 14); clauses (Ch. 15)	▶ placement of phrase and clause modifiers (Ch. 19)	▶ commas with phrases and subordinate clauses (Ch. 22)
▶ subjects, predicates, sentences (Ch. 13)	▶ agreement of subject and verb with compound subjects or intervening phrases (Ch. 16)	▶ semicolons (Ch. 23)
▶ nouns, pronouns (Ch. 12)	▶ *who* and *whom* (Ch. 17)	
▶ adverbs, phrases, clauses (Ch. 12, Ch. 14, & Ch. 15)	▶ comparing and placing modifiers (Ch. 19)	▶ commas with clauses (Ch. 22)
▶ fragments, sentences (Ch. 13)		▶ using quotations (Ch. 24)
▶ pronouns (Ch. 12)	▶ pronoun case, person (Ch. 17)	▶ capitalization of *I* (Ch. 21)
▶ verbs (Ch. 12)	▶ literary present tense (Ch. 18); subject-verb agreement when using literary titles (Ch. 16)	▶ capitalization of titles (Ch. 21); punctuation of quotations and titles (Ch. 24)
▶ parts of speech (Ch. 12)	▶ formal English (Ch. 20)	
▶ pronouns (Ch. 12)	▶ pronoun case, person (Ch. 17)	▶ words often confused (Ch. 26)
▶ sentences classified by structure (Ch. 15)		▶ punctuating sentences (Ch. 22 & Ch. 23)
▶ linking, action verbs (Ch. 12)	▶ active, passive voice (Ch. 18)	▶ syllable division (Ch. 26)
▶ parts of speech (Ch. 12)	▶ double negatives, formal English (Ch. 20)	▶ words often confused (Ch. 26)
▶ sentences classified by purpose (Ch. 13)		▶ end marks (Ch. 22)
▶ sentences classified by purpose, fragments (Ch. 13)	▶ subject-verb agreement (Ch. 16)	▶ end marks (Ch. 22)
▶ linking, action verbs (Ch. 12)	▶ consistency of tense (Ch. 18)	▶ changing word forms (Ch. 26)

PART 3
Grammar, Usage, and Mechanics

Grammar
- **12** Parts of Speech Overview
- **13** The Parts of a Sentence
- **14** The Phrase
- **15** The Clause

Usage
- **16** Agreement
- **17** Using Pronouns Correctly
- **18** Using Verbs Correctly
- **19** Using Modifiers Correctly
- **20** A Glossary of Usage

Mechanics
- **21** Capitalization
- **22** Punctuation: End Marks and Commas
- **23** Punctuation: Semicolons and Colons
- **24** Punctuation: Italics, Quotation Marks, and Ellipsis Points
- **25** Punctuation: Apostrophes, Hyphens, Dashes, Parentheses, Brackets
- **26** Spelling
- **27** Correcting Common Errors

CHAPTER 12

Parts of Speech Overview
Identification and Function

PREVIEWING THE CHAPTER

- This chapter discusses the eight parts of speech and their grammatical functions.

- The chapter closes with a **Chapter Review**, which includes a **Writing Application** feature that asks students to write a poem describing themselves as an animal or an object, using at least ten vivid adjectives.

- For help in integrating this chapter with writing chapters, use the **Teaching Strands** chart on pp. T401A–T401B.

USING THE DIAGNOSTIC PREVIEW

- The **Diagnostic Preview** asks students to identify the parts of speech of italicized words in sentences. You could use the **Diagnostic Preview** to assess students' understanding of the parts of speech and to determine how much instruction is needed.

  If only a few students are unable to demonstrate mastery, you might have them work cooperatively to review definitions and complete exercises. You may want to assess student progress periodically.

Diagnostic Preview

Determining the Parts of Speech of Words

Identify the part of speech of each italicized word or word group in the following paragraphs.

EXAMPLES What were the [1] *most* common forms of transportation [2] *between* [3] *colonial* times and the twentieth [4] *century*?
1. adverb
2. preposition
3. adjective
4. noun

n. = noun   adv. = adverb
adj. = adjective   conj. = conjunction
prep. = preposition   v. = verb
pro. = pronoun

1. n.   2. adj.
3. n.   4. adv.
5. pro. 6. pro.
7. adj.
8. conj.
9. n.
10. prep.

Since the [1] *condition* of the roads prevented [2] *extensive* use of wheeled vehicles, the most reliable means of transportation in colonial times was the [3] *saddle horse*. Some [4] *exceptionally* wealthy people kept carriages, but [5] *these* were usually heavy vehicles [6] *that* were pulled by two or more horses. Such carriages were [7] *satisfactory* for short trips, [8] *but* they were not practical for long journeys.

Stagecoaches were introduced in [9] *America* in about 1750. [10] *By* this time roads ran between such major cities as New York and

404   Chapter 12   Parts of Speech Overview

CHAPTER RESOURCES

Planning
- One-Stop Planner CD-ROM

Practice and Extension
- Grammar, Usage, and Mechanics, p. 1
- Language Workshop CD-ROM

Internet
- go.hrw.com (keyword: EOLang)

Evaluation and Assessment
- Assessment Package
  —Chapter Tests, Ch. 12
  —Chapter Tests in Standardized Test Formats, Ch. 12
- Test Generator (One-Stop Planner CD-ROM)

Boston. Although these roads [11] *were* little more than muddy tracks, [12] *most* were wide enough for a four-wheeled coach. [13] *Three* or four pairs of horses [14] *were harnessed* to a coach. Generally, however, the vehicles were so heavy that [15] *coach* horses tired [16] *quite* [17] *rapidly* [18] *and* had to be either rested frequently [19] *or* changed at post houses along the route. The design of horse-drawn vehicles soon improved, and until the early years of the twentieth century, buggies and wagons remained a common [20] *form* of transportation.

11. v.
12. pro.　13. adj.
14. v.
15. adj.　16. adv.
17. adv.　18. conj.
19. conj.
20. n.

Nouns

12a. A *noun* names a person, a place, a thing, or an idea.

Persons	hero	teachers	audience	Mai Ling
Places	museum	countries	rain forest	San Diego
Things	stereo	songs	fences	Pacific Ocean
Ideas	sympathy	fairness	generosity	Impressionism

Exercise 1 Identifying Nouns in Sentences

Identify the nouns in the following sentences. Treat as single nouns all capitalized names containing more than one word.

HELP——
You do not need to include years, such as *1815*, in your answers for Exercise 1.

EXAMPLE 1. Elizabeth Cady Stanton was born in the state of New York in 1815.

　　1. Elizabeth Cady Stanton, state, New York

1. As a young woman, Elizabeth Cady Stanton studied mathematics and the classics both at home and at Troy Female Seminary, from which she graduated in 1832.
2. Beginning at an early age, she recognized the injustices suffered by women, especially in education and politics.
3. In 1840, she married Henry Stanton, a prominent abolitionist.
4. At an antislavery convention in London, England, Mrs. Stanton was outraged at the treatment of the female delegates.
5. She later helped to organize the first meeting to address the rights of women.
6. At that convention, she read her "Declaration of Sentiments," outlining the inferior status of women and calling for reforms.

Nouns　**405**

RESOURCES

Nouns
Practice
- *Grammar, Usage, and Mechanics,* pp. 2, 3
- *Language Workshop CD-ROM,* Lesson 1

Nouns
Rule 12a *(pp. 405–408)*

OBJECTIVES
- To identify nouns in sentences
- To replace common nouns with proper nouns

Meeting INDIVIDUAL NEEDS

ENGLISH-LANGUAGE LEARNERS
General Strategies. To illustrate the concept of nouns, have students develop charts similar to the one on this page in which they name persons, places, things, and ideas that are familiar to them. Then, have students classify the names in their charts as common or proper nouns.

Parts of Speech Overview, pp. 404–434
Alignments
TEKS 3B, 3D
TAAS W3, W6
English II End-of-Course 5, 6

Texas Resources
- *TAAS Tool Kit*
- *Preparation for TAAS*
- *One-Stop Planner CD-ROM*

Nouns　**405**

> **TEACHING TIP**
>
> **Activity.** To give the class practice in identifying the different types of nouns, provide students with magazines and newspapers. Have each student find and identify at least one example of each kind of noun: common, proper, compound, concrete, abstract, and collective. Then, have students work in groups of three to check one another's work.
>
> **Meeting INDIVIDUAL NEEDS**
>
> **ENGLISH-LANGUAGE LEARNERS**
> **Spanish.** The names of the months of the year, days of the week, languages, nationalities, and the first-person singular pronoun *yo* (I) are among the words not capitalized in Spanish. Emphasize to Spanish-speaking students that in English, these words generally are capitalized.

7. Among these reforms, the most controversial one was giving women the right to vote.
8. In 1850, Stanton began working with Susan B. Anthony.
9. These two women did much work for the suffrage movement.
10. Stanton remained adamant about effecting change for the remainder of her life.

Reference Note
For more on **capitalizing proper nouns,** see page 669.

Common Nouns and Proper Nouns

A *common noun* names any one of a group of persons, places, things, or ideas. A *proper noun* names a particular person, place, thing, or idea. Generally, common nouns are not capitalized; proper nouns are.

Common Nouns	Proper Nouns
mountain	Mount McKinley
novelist	Louisa May Alcott
museum	Museum of Fine Arts
ship	Queen Elizabeth 2
movie	Casablanca

Reference Note
For information about **capitalizing the parts of a compound noun,** see page 669.

Compound Nouns

A *compound noun* consists of two or more words that together name a person, a place, a thing, or an idea. The parts of a compound noun may be written as one word, as separate words, or as a hyphenated word.

One Word	Separate Words	Hyphenated Word
basketball	civil rights	no-hitter
newspaper	Arts and Crafts Club	sister-in-law

NOTE If you are not sure how to write a compound noun, look it up in an up-to-date dictionary. Some dictionaries may give two correct forms for a word. For example, you may find the word *vice-president* written both with and without the hyphen. Generally, use the form the dictionary lists first.

Exercise 2 **Replacing Common Nouns with Proper Nouns and Identifying Compound Nouns**

For each of the following common nouns, give a proper noun. Then, write *compound* next to each compound noun that you write.

EXAMPLE
1. river
1. *Mississippi River—compound*

1. play
2. state
3. street
4. song
5. president
6. newspaper
7. ocean
8. writer
9. poem
10. car
11. planet
12. poet
13. country
14. friend
15. continent
16. actor
17. explorer
18. scientist
19. religion
20. document

Concrete Nouns and Abstract Nouns

A *concrete noun* names a person, a place, or a thing that can be perceived by one or more of the senses (sight, hearing, taste, touch, and smell). An *abstract noun* names an idea, a feeling, a quality, or a characteristic.

Concrete Nouns	Abstract Nouns
dog	liberty
sunset	beauty
thunder	kindness
silk	success
Nile River	Buddhism

Collective Nouns

A *collective noun* names a group of people, animals, or things.

Collective Nouns		
audience	crowd	orchestra
batch	flock	pride
bouquet	gaggle	set
bunch	jury	staff
cluster	litter	swarm

Reference Note
For information on **using verbs with collective nouns,** see page 522.

HELP
The singular form of a collective noun names a group. Other kinds of nouns must be made plural to name a group.

Exercise 2 **Replacing Common Nouns with Proper Nouns and Identifying Compound Nouns**

POSSIBLE ANSWERS

1. *A Raisin in the Sun*—compound noun
2. North Dakota—compound noun
3. Rodeo Drive—compound noun
4. "Home on the Range"—compound noun
5. Thomas Jefferson—compound noun
6. *USA Today*—compound noun
7. Indian Ocean—compound noun
8. S.E. Hinton—compound noun
9. "Sea Fever"—compound noun
10. Toyota Celica—compound noun
11. Jupiter
12. Robert Frost—compound noun
13. France
14. Kay Meier—compound noun
15. South America—compound noun
16. Jim Carrey—compound noun
17. Admiral Byrd—compound noun
18. Jonas Salk—compound noun
19. Buddhism
20. Mayflower Compact—compound noun

Review A — Classifying Nouns

ANSWERS

1. common, concrete, collective
2. proper, concrete, compound
3. common, concrete
4. common, abstract
5. common, concrete
6. common, concrete
7. common, concrete
8. common, concrete
9. common, abstract
10. proper, concrete, compound

Pronouns
Rule 12b (pp. 408–412)

OBJECTIVE

- To identify pronouns in sentences

Reference Note

For information about **choosing pronouns that agree with their antecedents,** see page 532.

Review A — Classifying Nouns

Identify each of the italicized nouns in the following paragraph as *proper* or *common* and as *concrete* or *abstract*. Also, identify each *compound noun* and each *collective noun*.

EXAMPLE   [1] Doesn't the Cajun *dish* in the picture look delicious?
   1. common, concrete

Cajuns are descended from a [1] *group* of French settlers who were expelled from Acadia by the British in 1755. When some of these displaced people settled in the [2] *Atchafalaya Basin* in southeastern Louisiana, they had to invent [3] *ways* to use local foods in their traditional French recipes. If you've never tried Cajun food, the crawfish in this picture may be unfamiliar to you. In [4] *addition* to the plentiful crawfish, shrimp, oysters, and other seafood, freshwater fish, alligator meat, [5] *rice,* and many [6] *spices* find their way into Cajun cooking. Gumbos are soups flavored with [7] *filé,* which is powdered sassafras leaves. [8] *Gumbos* often contain okra and sausage, chicken, or seafood. The [9] *popularity* of these and other Cajun dishes has spread throughout the [10] *United States* in recent years.

Pronouns

12b. A *pronoun* takes the place of one or more nouns or pronouns.

EXAMPLES   Susan watched the monkey make faces at her little brother and sister. **She** laughed at **it** more than **they** did. [*She* is used in place of *Susan, it* in place of *monkey,* and *they* in place of *brother* and *sister.*]

When others saw the monkey, **they** began laughing, too. [*They* takes the place of the pronoun *others.*]

The word or word group that a pronoun stands for is called the **antecedent** of the pronoun. In the first example above, *Susan* is the antecedent of *she, monkey* is the antecedent of *it,* and *brother* and *sister* are the antecedents of *they.* In the second example, *others* is the antecedent of *they.*

408 Chapter 12 Parts of Speech Overview

RESOURCES

Pronouns

Practice

- *Grammar, Usage, and Mechanics,* pp. 4, 5, 6, 7, 8
- *Language Workshop CD-ROM,* Lesson 1

Personal Pronouns

A *personal pronoun* refers to the one(s) speaking (*first person*), the one(s) spoken to (*second person*), or the one(s) spoken about (*third person*).

	Singular	Plural
First Person	I, me, my, mine	we, us, our, ours
Second Person	you, your, yours	you, your, yours
Third Person	he, him, his, she, her, hers, it, its	they, them, their, theirs

EXAMPLES **I** hope that **you** can help **me** with **my** homework.

He said that **they** would meet **us** outside the theater.

NOTE This textbook refers to the words *my, your, his, her, its, our,* and *their* as possessive pronouns. However, because these words can come before nouns and tell *which one* or *whose,* some authorities prefer to call them adjectives. Follow your teacher's instructions regarding these possessive forms.

Reflexive and Intensive Pronouns

First Person	myself, ourselves
Second Person	yourself, yourselves
Third Person	himself, herself, itself, themselves

A *reflexive pronoun* refers to the subject of a sentence and functions as a complement or as an object of a preposition.

EXAMPLES I'm not quite **myself** today. [*Myself* is a predicate nominative identifying *I*.]

Cecilia let **herself** in through a trapdoor. [*Herself* is the direct object of *let*.]

They chose costumes for **themselves**. [*Themselves* is the object of the preposition *for*.]

Reference Note

For more information about **complements**, see page 450. For more about **objects of prepositions**, see page 426.

Meeting INDIVIDUAL NEEDS

ENGLISH-LANGUAGE LEARNERS
Spanish. Spanish does not have a neuter personal pronoun like *it* that can be used as a subject. Moreover, Spanish speakers seldom use a pronoun in sentences that in English require the impersonal or neuter subject pronoun (for example, "It is raining" = "Está lloviendo").

Spanish speakers use a pronoun that is of the same gender as the antecedent, which could lead to English translations such as "I do not have my pencil; *he* is in my locker." Point out that except for humans and for animals of known gender, almost everything else (including abstractions such as the weather) is considered neuter in English and requires the pronoun *it*.

General Strategies. Some students may have difficulty knowing when to use possessive pronouns in English. For example, because the Spanish language does not regard a body part as something to be possessed, Spanish speakers may say, "I have broken *the* arm." Explain that possessive pronouns are necessary in such expressions in English.

Meeting INDIVIDUAL NEEDS

ENGLISH-LANGUAGE LEARNERS

Spanish. The English possessive pronouns *your, his, her, its,* and *their* can all be translated in Spanish as *su* (or *sus* if more than one thing is possessed). *Yourself, himself, herself, itself,* and *themselves* can all be translated as *se*. Watch for any difficulties that students may have in distinguishing among pronouns, and offer them the opportunity to decide which pronouns they should have used in place of any incorrect ones. Provide quick feedback on the students' revisions of their work.

Spanish. In Spanish, the interrogative pronouns include a written accent (*qué = what; quién = who[m]; cuál = which, what*); the relative pronouns do not (*que = who[m], which, that; quien = who[m], that; cuyo = whose*). Reminding Spanish-speaking students of this distinction may help them distinguish between interrogative and relative pronouns in English.

TIPS & TRICKS

To tell whether a pronoun is reflexive or intensive, use this simple test: Read the sentence aloud, and omit the pronoun. If the meaning of the sentence stays the same, the pronoun is most likely intensive. If not, the pronoun is probably reflexive.

EXAMPLE
She changed the tire herself. [*She changed the tire* makes sense. The pronoun *herself* is intensive.]

Reference Note

For more about **demonstrative adjectives,** see page 414.

Reference Note

For more about **relative pronouns** and **subordinate clauses,** see page 496.

An *intensive pronoun* emphasizes its antecedent and has no grammatical function in the sentence.

EXAMPLES   Ray painted the mural **himself.**

The children dyed the eggs **themselves.**

Demonstrative Pronouns

A *demonstrative pronoun* points out a person, a place, a thing, or an idea.

| this | that | these | those |

EXAMPLES   **This** is our favorite campsite.

The tomatoes we grew in the garden taste better than **these.**

NOTE   The words that can be used as demonstrative pronouns can also be used as adjectives.

PRONOUN   **This** tastes good.
ADJECTIVE   **This** hummus tastes good.

Interrogative Pronouns

An *interrogative pronoun* introduces a question.

| who | whom | which | what | whose |

EXAMPLES   **What** is the address of this house?

Whose is the red truck parked outside?

Relative Pronouns

A *relative pronoun* introduces a subordinate clause.

| that | which | who | whom | whose |

EXAMPLES   The dog **that** you trained is very well behaved.

She is the candidate **who** promises to listen to the people.

Indefinite Pronouns

An *indefinite pronoun* refers to a person, place, idea, or thing that may or may not be specifically named.

all	each other	most	one another
another	either	much	other
any	everybody	neither	several
anybody	everyone	nobody	some
anyone	everything	none	somebody
anything	few	no one	someone
both	many	nothing	something
each	more	one	such

EXAMPLES **Everything** we will need is packed in the trunk.

Has **anyone** called for Mr. Reynolds?

NOTE Many of the pronouns you have studied so far may also be used as adjectives.

EXAMPLES **that** oyster   **whose** pearl   **some** shells

Exercise 3 Identifying Pronouns in Sentences

Identify the pronouns in each of the following sentences.

EXAMPLE   1. Let me tell you about one of the camping trips that I took last summer.

1. me, you, one, that, I

1. All of the other members of my family like to go camping, but few of them enjoy the outdoors more than I do.
2. Last summer several of my cousins and I stayed at a rustic camp in the Rocky Mountains, which are not far from our hometown.
3. At camp we learned how to build a campfire and how to keep it going ourselves.
4. A group of us even went beyond that—we learned to cook meals over the open fire.
5. One of our counselors showed those who were interested how to cook themselves simple meals.
6. Each of his recipes was delicious and easy to follow, and everyone ate everything in sight.
7. All of us enjoy anything cooked over an open fire.

Reference Note
For information about **distinguishing between pronouns and adjectives,** see page 414.

HELP
In Exercise 3, if a pronoun is used more than once, note it each time it appears.

Exercise 3

ALTERNATIVE LESSON
Have students review types of nouns by identifying the following items in the specified sentences.

1. compound common noun [*outdoors*]
2. compound proper noun [*Rocky Mountains*]
4. collective noun [*group*]

Adjectives

Rule 12c (pp. 412–416)

OBJECTIVES

- To identify adjectives and the words they modify
- To identify words as adjectives or pronouns

Relating to Literature

If the Elizabeth Bishop poem "The Fish" is in your literature textbook, have different students read parts of the poem aloud. Then, ask the class to identify the adjectives that help to convey the personality of the fish. [*The adjectives* grunting, battered, venerable, *and* homely, *combined with other descriptive language such as* frightening gills, fresh and crisp with blood, *suggest that the fish is a noble warrior that deserves to live.*]

ENGLISH-LANGUAGE LEARNERS
General Strategies. In some languages, nouns are never used without articles. Therefore, some students may have difficulty learning when to use articles correctly in English. If possible, pair such students with proficient English-speakers, and have the pairs write simple sentences with articles.

COMPUTER TIP

Using a computer software program's thesaurus can help you choose appropriate adjectives. To make sure that an adjective has exactly the connotation you intend, look up the word in a dictionary.

Reference Note
For more information on **predicate adjectives,** see page 454.

---

8. We also enjoy telling stories while sitting beside the fire.
9. Sometimes everybody tells ghost stories.
10. Who wants to go to sleep afterward?

Adjectives

12c. An *adjective* modifies a noun or a pronoun.

To modify means "to describe" or "to make the meaning of a word more specific." An adjective is a modifier that tells *what kind, which one, how many,* or *how much.*

What Kind?	Which One?	How Many?	How Much?
spilled ink	**this** park	**twenty** miles	**no** salt
English tea	**these** papers	**two** men	**enough** water
howling winds	**that** house	**several** apples	**some** food

An adjective may be separated from the word it modifies.

EXAMPLES   She is **clever.**

The sky had become **cloudy** suddenly.

NOTE An adjective that is in the predicate and that modifies the subject of a clause or sentence is called a **predicate adjective.**

Articles

The most frequently used adjectives are *a, an,* and *the.* These words are usually called **articles.**

A and *an* are called **indefinite articles** because they refer to any member of a general group. *A* is used before a word beginning with a consonant sound; *an* is used before a word beginning with a vowel sound.

EXAMPLES   **A** park ranger helped us.

Shady Lane is **a** one-way street. [*One-way* begins with a consonant sound.]

They planted **an** acre with corn.

We kept watch for **an** hour. [*Hour* begins with a vowel sound.]

RESOURCES

Adjectives

Practice
- *Grammar, Usage, and Mechanics,* pp. 9, 10, 11
- *Language Workshop CD-ROM,* Lesson 1

The is called the **definite article** because it refers to someone or something in particular.

EXAMPLES **The** park ranger helped us.

They planted **the** acre with corn.

The hour dragged by.

Exercise 4 Identifying Adjectives and the Words They Modify

For the following sentences, identify each adjective and the word it modifies. (Do not include the articles *a*, *an*, and *the*.)

EXAMPLE 1. In the latter part of the nineteenth century, bicycling became a popular sport in the United States.

1. *latter—part; nineteenth—century; popular—sport*

1. By the 1890s, an extraordinary craze for bicycling had swept the nation.
2. Though bicycles had been available for years, the early versions made for an awkward ride.
3. Ungainly cycles like the one in the picture had a very large wheel in the front and a small wheel in the back.
4. In 1885, however, a more sensible model was introduced, one that resembled the modern cycle.
5. Energetic people everywhere took to this kind of bicycle.
6. Bicycling soon became a national sport.
7. Cyclists joined special clubs that took vigorous tours through the countryside.
8. A typical ride might cover twenty miles, with a welcome stop along the way for refreshments.
9. Races were also popular with enthusiastic spectators, who often outnumbered those at ballgames.
10. The fans enjoyed watching these tests of endurance, which sometimes lasted six days.

Relating to Writing

Point out to students that using precise, descriptive adjectives will clarify the images they want to convey in their writing.

Write the following short paragraph on the chalkboard or on a transparency, and ask students to rewrite it, adding descriptive adjectives. Encourage students to consult thesauruses and dictionaries to find precise adjectives.

> The snow fell on me as I trudged up the hill toward my house. I was cold and tired, and I could hardly wait to change my clothes and lie down in my bed.

Meeting INDIVIDUAL NEEDS

ENGLISH-LANGUAGE LEARNERS
Spanish. Spanish demonstrative adjectives and demonstrative pronouns are identical, except that demonstrative pronouns have a written accent. If your students have learned this accentuation rule, reminding them of it may help them distinguish between these two parts of speech. (The Spanish demonstrative pronouns that have demonstrative adjective equivalents are *éste, éstos, ésta, éstas, ése, ésos, ésa, ésas, aquél, aquéllos, aquélla,* and *aquéllas.*)

TEACHING TIP

Exercise 5 You may want to use the first ten items in the exercise as guided practice. Then, have students complete the exercise as independent practice.

Pronoun or Adjective?

Some words may be used either as adjectives or as pronouns. In this book, demonstrative, interrogative, and indefinite terms are called pronouns when they stand for other nouns or pronouns. They are called adjectives when they modify nouns or pronouns.

PRONOUN	**Which** did you choose, Roberto?
ADJECTIVE	**Which** book did you choose to read, Alex?
PRONOUN	**Those** are excited fans.
ADJECTIVE	**Those** fans are excited.

NOTE The words *this, that, these,* and *those* are called **demonstrative adjectives** when they modify nouns or pronouns and are called **demonstrative pronouns** when they take the place of nouns or other pronouns.

In this book, the words *my, your, his, her, its, our,* and *their* are considered possessive pronouns. However, some authorities consider them to be adjectives. Follow your teacher's instructions on labeling these words.

Exercise 5 Identifying Words as Adjectives or Pronouns

Tell whether each italicized word in the following paragraph is used as a *pronoun* or an *adjective*. For each adjective, give the word it modifies.

EXAMPLES Of ants and wasps, [1] *which* do you think are considered [2] *antisocial*?

1. pronoun
2. adjective—which

Although ants are related to wasps, there are [1] *many* differences between [2] *these* two kinds of insects. [3] *All* ants are social insects. They live together in colonies, [4] *each* made up of three castes: a queen, males, and workers. Unlike ants, [5] *most* wasps are solitary insects. [6] *Most* of the 20,000 known species of wasps are solitary. Of [7] *these,* [8] *many* are hunting wasps [9] *that* make individual nests. [10] *These* wasps usually build their nests in the ground. [11] *Some* nest in wood or mud. However, not all wasps are antisocial; [12] *some* behave more like their cousins the ants. [13] *These* wasps live in permanent colonies of adults and young. While [14] *most* wasps are solitary, there are about 1,000 species of social wasps. Among the best-known social wasps are [15] *those* within a group that, like ants, has a caste system in [16] *its* societies. The queen builds a small nest consisting of a [17] *few* cells, and then she lays eggs. [18] *These* hatch into workers. The workers enlarge the nest, [19] *which* is made of material that has been chewed, regurgitated, and mixed with saliva. [20] *Some* of the best-known social wasps are yellow jackets and hornets.

Noun or Adjective?

When a word that can be used as a noun modifies a noun or pronoun, it is called an adjective.

EXAMPLES **salad** bowl   **chicken** dinner

New England states   **gold** medal

NOTE Notice in the preceding examples that the proper noun *New England* remains capitalized when it is used as an adjective. An adjective that is formed from a proper noun is called a ***proper adjective.***

Reference Note
For more information about capitalizing **proper adjectives,** see page 669. For more about **compound nouns,** see page 406.

Some word groups are considered compound nouns.

EXAMPLES salad dressing   chicken hawk   New England clam chowder

By checking an up-to-date dictionary, you can avoid mistaking a word that is part of a compound noun for a word that is considered a separate adjective.

Review B Identifying Nouns, Pronouns, and Adjectives

Identify the nouns, pronouns, and adjectives in the following sentences. For each adjective, give the word it modifies. (Do not include the articles *a*, *an*, and *the*.)

EXAMPLE 1. Several different kinds of butterflies flew around us.

1. nouns—kinds; butterflies

    pronoun—us

    adjectives—several (kinds); different (kinds)

1. Our teacher, Mr. López, identified the various trees along the nature trail.
2. Many people are working to clean up polluted rivers and streams to make them livable environments for wildlife again.

1. trees/trail

2. people/rivers; streams/environments

3. sight/travelers
4. doll/hat/suit
5. cake/table
6. leaves/splashes
7. bowl
8. girl/tenets/tenets/people
9. feeder/tree
10. anthology/anthology/days

3. The flag over the hotel was a (welcome) sight to the (two) travelers.
4. The (antique) doll was dressed in a (sailor) hat and a (blue) suit.
5. A (large) cake sat in the center of the (kitchen) table.
6. Along the Hudson River, (autumn) leaves colored the highway with (bright) splashes of orange and red.
7. Someone has filled the (fruit) bowl with dates and walnuts.
8. As a (young) girl, Susan B. Anthony was taught (Quaker) (religious) tenets, which include the belief in the equality of (all) people.
9. The (bird) feeder in the (elm) tree in my yard attracts cardinals, robins, and chickadees.
10. The dust jacket of (that) (literature) anthology has certainly seen (better) days.

Review C — Identifying Nouns, Pronouns, and Adjectives

Identify each numbered, underlined word in the following paragraph as a *noun*, a *pronoun*, or an (adjective).

EXAMPLE The Spanish built the first *ranchos,* or ranches, that were in the [1] United States.
1. noun

Californians Catching Wild Horses with Riata by Hugo Wilhelm Arthur Nahl (1833–1889), Oil on canvas mounted on masonite 19 5/8 x 23 3/4. Collection of the Oakland Museum, Kahn Collection.

The [1] man in this picture is a *vaquero,* but you can call [2] him a cowboy. *Vaqueros* got their name from the [3] Spanish word *vaca,* which means "cow." In fact, cowboys were at [4] home on the range in Mexico long before they gained [5] legendary status in the United States. Notice that this *vaquero* wears [6] leather chaps (*chaparejos*) to protect his legs and uses a [7] lariat (*la reata*) to rope the steer. [8] Many other words that we associate with cowboys came into the English language from [9] Spanish. [10] These include *rodeo, stampede,* and *bronco.*

Verbs

12d. A *verb* expresses action or a state of being.

In this textbook, verbs are classified in three ways: (1) as main or helping verbs, (2) as action or linking verbs, and (3) as transitive or intransitive verbs.

Main Verbs and Helping Verbs

A *verb phrase* consists of one *main verb* and one or more *helping verbs* (also called *auxiliary verbs*).

EXAMPLES   I **am reading** Thomas Hardy's novel *Under the Greenwood Tree*. [*Am* is a helping verb. *Reading* is the main verb.]

We **should have been listening** instead of talking. [*Should, have,* and *been* are helping verbs. *Listening* is the main verb.]

Commonly Used Helping Verbs				
Forms of *Be*	am	be	being	was
	are	been	is	were
Forms of *Have*	had	has	have	having
Forms of *Do*	did	do	does	
Modals	can	might	shall	would
	could	must	should	
	may	ought	will	

NOTE A *modal* is an auxiliary verb that is used to express an attitude toward the action or state of being of the main verb.

EXAMPLE   I **may** go to the concert after all. [The modal *may* expresses an attitude of possibility in relation to the main verb *go*.]

Helping verbs may be separated from the main verb.

EXAMPLE   **Did** she **paint** the house?

NOTE The word *not* and its contraction, *n't*, are never part of a verb phrase. Instead, they are adverbs telling *to what extent*.

Reference Note
For more about **modals**, see page 599.

Reference Note
For more about **adverbs**, see page 422.

Verbs

Rule 12d (pp. 417–422)

OBJECTIVES

- To identify verbs and verb phrases
- To identify action verbs and linking verbs
- To write sentences using verbs as both linking and action verbs
- To identify verbs as transitive or intransitive

RESOURCES

Verbs
Practice
- *Grammar, Usage, and Mechanics,* pp. 12, 13, 14, 15, 16
- *Language Workshop CD-ROM,* Lesson 2

Relating to Literature

You might want to have students read and discuss the Emily Dickinson poem "I Like to See It Lap the Miles." Have them list the verbs that describe the train's actions. [*lap, lick, stop, step, peer, pare, crawl, complaining, chase,* and *neigh*] What kind of verbs are these? [*They are action verbs.*] Is there anything unusual about this verb usage? [*With the exception of* stop, *the verbs are not typically used to describe the actions of a train.*] How does the verb usage affect the meaning of the poem? [*The verbs give life to an inanimate object by describing its actions as though it were a living animal.*]

HELP

Some sentences in Exercise 6 have more than one verb or verb phrase.

Exercise 6 Identifying Verbs and Verb Phrases

Identify the verbs and verb phrases in the following sentences. Be sure to include all helping verbs.

EXAMPLE
1. The marching band would be performing during half time.

   1. would be performing

1. Because of the cold weather, the members of the band worried about their half-time performance.
2. Marcia and the other saxophone players were clapping their hands vigorously so that their fingers wouldn't become even more numb in the raw, icy air.
3. They imagined what would happen if their fingers froze to the keys of their instruments.
4. Instead of music, harsh noise would blare out and probably startle the spectators.
5. The other band members would likely skip a beat, and chaos would soon spread across the field.
6. Out of step, the flute players might well stumble into the clarinet players, collide with the trombone players, or even trip over the drummers.
7. When half time was called, Marcia and her friends rolled their eyes and laughed about the dreadful scene they had just pictured.
8. Such a disaster couldn't possibly happen, could it?
9. As the band marched onto the field, large, white snowflakes swirled in the air and settled on the brand-new uniforms and shiny instruments.
10. Some people were leaving the stands when the principal announced over the loudspeaker: "Ladies and gentlemen, the band will now play 'Jingle Bells.'"

Action Verbs and Linking Verbs

An *action verb* expresses either physical or mental activity.

| PHYSICAL | bring | say | shout | jump | breathe |
| MENTAL | ponder | trust | review | evaluate | guess |

EXAMPLES   Please **return** this book. [*Return* expresses physical action.]

Do you **know** Han? [*Do know* expresses mental action.]

A *linking verb* connects the subject to a word or word group that identifies or describes the subject. Such a word or word group is called a *subject complement*.

EXAMPLES   Kelp **is** the scientific name for seaweed. [The subject complement *name* identifies the subject *Kelp*.]

Kelp **has been** a good source of iodine. [The subject complement *source* identifies the subject *Kelp*.]

Kelp **tastes** good in salads. [The subject complement *good* describes the subject *Kelp*.]

As it ages, kelp **becomes** brown. [The subject complement *brown* describes the subject *kelp*.]

Reference Note
For more information about **subject complements,** see page 453.

Commonly Used Linking Verbs

Forms of *Be*

be	were	shall have been	should be
being	shall be	will have been	would be
am	will be	can be	could be
is	has been	may be	should have been
are	have been	might be	would have been
was	had been	must be	could have been

Others

appear	feel	look	seem	sound	taste
become	grow	remain	smell	stay	turn

Some of the verbs listed as *Others* in the previous chart can be used as action verbs as well as linking verbs.

LINKING   Emilia **felt** calm at the seashore.
ACTION   Emilia **felt** the waving strands of kelp.

The forms of *be* are not always used as linking verbs. That is, they do not always link a subject to a subject complement. Instead of a subject complement, an adverb that tells *where* or *when* may follow the form of *be*. In such cases, the verb *be* is called a *state-of-being verb*.

EXAMPLE   My friends and I **were** there yesterday. [The verb *were* is followed not by a subject complement but by *there,* which tells *where,* and by *yesterday,* which tells *when.*]

TIPS & TRICKS

To determine whether a verb in a sentence is a linking verb, substitute a form of the verb *be*. If the sentence makes sense, the verb is most likely a linking verb.

LINKING
Emilia **felt** calm at the seashore. [The verb *was* can sensibly replace *felt: Emilia was calm at the seashore.*]

ACTION
Emilia **felt** the waving strands of kelp. [The verb *was* cannot sensibly replace *felt.*]

TEACHING TIP

Exercise 8 Encourage students to use the test from **Tips & Tricks** on p. 419 to check their sentences for correct verb usage.

Exercise 8 Writing Sentences Using Verbs as Both Linking and Action Verbs

ANSWERS

Responses will vary. Examples of sentences with linking (L) and action (A) verbs are provided.

1. (L) The sea gulls appear calm.
   (A) The sea gulls appear every morning.
2. (L) The guards sound excited.
   (A) The guards sounded the alarm.
3. (L) The rooms smelled musty.
   (A) The girls smelled smoke.
4. (L) The baby grew sleepy.
   (A) Mr. Reyes grows figs.
5. (L) Trudy looks lovely today.
   (A) Trudy looks both ways before crossing the street.
6. (L) The shirt felt soft.
   (A) Jorge felt the sand between his toes.
7. (L) I remain convinced.
   (A) Nothing remained of the village.
8. (L) They stayed calm.
   (A) The governor stayed at my house.
9. (L) The milk tasted sour.
   (A) She tasted the soup.
10. (L) The sky turned gray.
    (A) I turned the doorknob.

Exercise 7 Identifying Verbs as Action Verbs or Linking Verbs

Identify each italicized verb in the following sentences as an *action verb* or a *linking verb*.

EXAMPLE 1. The ancient Egyptians *built* a grand temple for Amon-Re, their chief deity.

1. action verb

1. Situated on the banks of the Nile River in Egypt, these ruins at Karnak *are* some of the most impressive sights in the world.
2. The largest structure there *is* the Great Temple of Amon-Re.
3. As you can see, its immense size *dwarfs* people.
4. The 42-meter-high gateway *amazes* visitors who follow the avenue of sphinxes that leads to the entrance.
5. The ceiling of the temple *rests* more than 23 meters above the floor.
6. Of course, the central columns that support the stone roof *look* enormous.
7. Carvings *decorate* the surfaces of these huge columns.
8. Even an amateur engineer *can appreciate* the tremendous efforts that must have gone into the completion of this temple.
9. We now *know* that inclined planes, combined with levers and blocking, enabled the ancient Egyptians to raise the large stones.
10. A remarkable technical achievement, the Great Temple of Amon-Re today *remains* a monument to the ancient builders' skills.

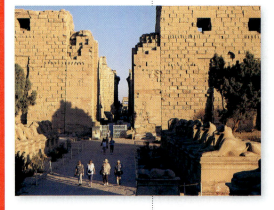

Exercise 8 Writing Sentences Using Verbs as Both Linking and Action Verbs

For each of the following verbs, write two sentences. In the first sentence, use the verb as a linking verb; in the second sentence, use it as an action verb.

EXAMPLE 1. become

1. We become older by the day.
   That hat becomes her.

| 1. appear | 3. smell | 5. look | 7. remain | 9. taste |
| 2. sound | 4. grow | 6. feel | 8. stay | 10. turn |

MINI-LESSON

Subject Complements. Explain to students that a subject complement is a noun, a pronoun, or an adjective that completes the meaning of a linking verb by identifying or describing the subject of the verb. If the complement is a noun or pronoun, it is called a predicate nominative; if it is an adjective, it is called a predicate adjective.

Write the following sentences on the chalkboard or on a transparency. Ask students to identify each subject complement as a predicate nominative or a predicate adjective.

Transitive Verbs and Intransitive Verbs

A *transitive verb* has an *object*—a word that tells who or what receives the action of the verb.

EXAMPLES   She **trusts** her friend. [The object *friend* receives the action of the verb *trusts*.]

Zora Neale Hurston **wrote** novels. [The object *novels* receives the action of the verb *wrote*.]

An *intransitive verb* does not have an object.

EXAMPLES   The audience **applauded.**

The train **stops** here.

The same verb may be transitive in one sentence and intransitive in another.

TRANSITIVE   Elsa **swam** the channel. [The object *channel* receives the action of the verb *swam*.]

INTRANSITIVE   Elsa **swam** for many hours. [no object]

TRANSITIVE   Miss Castillo **weeds** the garden every day. [The object *garden* receives the action of the verb *weeds*.]

INTRANSITIVE   Miss Castillo **weeds** every day. [no object]

Reference Note
For more about **objects of verbs,** see page 455.

"I MISS THE GOOD OLD DAYS WHEN ALL WE HAD TO WORRY ABOUT WAS NOUNS AND VERBS."

NOTE Action verbs can be transitive or intransitive. All linking verbs are intransitive.

ACTION   I **studied** my geometry notes for an hour. [transitive]

Luis also **studied** for an hour. [intransitive]

LINKING   We **are** ready for the quiz. [intransitive]

Like a one-word verb, a verb phrase may be classified as *transitive* or *intransitive* and as *action* or *linking*.

EXAMPLES   We **are planting** some cactus dahlias. [transitive action]

They **should bloom** in about six weeks. [intransitive action]

The flowers **will be** deep red. [intransitive linking]

HELP—
If you are not sure whether a verb is transitive or intransitive, look in a dictionary. Most dictionaries group the definitions of verbs according to whether the verbs are used transitively (*v.t.*) or intransitively (*v.i.*).

---

1. Mario is a good soccer <u>player</u>. [*pred. nom.*]
2. The hyacinths along the path smelled <u>sweet</u>. [*pred. adj.*]
3. The woman who called was <u>she</u>. [*pred. nom.*]
4. Were you <u>late</u> for class? [*pred. adj.*]
5. Ming sounded <u>happy</u>. [*pred. adj.*]

For more about subject complements, see **Chapter 13: The Parts of a Sentence.**

Adverbs

Rule 12e (pp. 422–426)

OBJECTIVES

- To identify adverbs and the words they modify in sentences
- To use words as adverbs and as adjectives in sentences

Meeting INDIVIDUAL NEEDS

ENGLISH-LANGUAGE LEARNERS
Spanish. Point out to Spanish-speaking students that the English suffix –ly is equivalent to the Spanish suffix –mente. Both suffixes can be used to convert many adjectives to adverbs.

French and Portuguese. The English suffix –ly is equivalent to the French suffix –ment and the Portuguese suffix –mente.

---

12 e

TIPS & TRICKS

Many adverbs end in –ly. However, not all words ending in –ly are adverbs. For instance, the following words are adjectives: *homely, kindly, lovely,* and *deadly.* To tell whether a word is an adverb, ask yourself these questions:

- Does the word modify a verb, an adjective, or an adverb?
- Does the word tell *when, where, how,* or *to what extent*?

Exercise 9 Identifying Verbs as Transitive or Intransitive

Identify the verb in each of the following sentences, and tell whether it is *transitive* or *intransitive.*

EXAMPLE 1. We eagerly anticipated our trip to the seashore.
         1. anticipated—transitive

1. The strong winds died down.
2. We quickly packed a lunch for our trip to the seashore.
3. The whitecaps on the ocean disappeared.
4. The sunlight sparkled on the splashing surf.
5. At low tide, Rosita suddenly spotted a starfish.
6. She noticed its five purplish arms.
7. She touched a soft, brown sponge floating nearby.
8. Three shore crabs swam in the tidal pool.
9. The beach was alive with interesting creatures.
10. Have you seen the ocean?

Adverbs

12e. An **adverb** modifies a verb, an adjective, or another adverb.

An adverb tells *how, when, where,* or *to what extent* (*how much, how long,* or *how often*).

Adverbs Modifying Verbs

EXAMPLES The bird was chirping **outside.** [where]
          The bird chirped **today.** [when]
          The bird chirped **loudly.** [how]
          The bird **never** chirped. [to what extent]

Exercise 10 Identifying Adverbs and the Verbs They Modify

Identify the adverbs in the following sentences. For each adverb, give the verb that it modifies.

EXAMPLE 1. The Montgolfier brothers worked steadily and earnestly to build the first hot-air balloon.
         1. steadily—worked, earnestly—worked

RESOURCES

Adverbs
Practice
- *Grammar, Usage, and Mechanics,* pp. 17, 18
- *Language Workshop CD-ROM,* Lesson 2

1. Birds, bats, and bugs fly effortlessly.
2. During the eighteenth century, a few creatures involuntarily entered the skies.
3. In 1783, an unpiloted balloon was tested, and a hot-air balloon carrying a sheep, rooster, and duck was launched later in the year.
4. Humans successfully flew for the first time in November of 1783.
5. The first balloonists floated gently above Paris in a hot-air balloon that had been cleverly designed by the Montgolfier brothers.
6. Although their earlier attempts had failed, the Montgolfiers kept trying and finally settled on a balloon made of paper and linen.
7. Early balloons differed significantly from modern balloons like those pictured, which are sturdily constructed of coated nylon.
8. Despite their ingenuity, the Montgolfiers originally thought that smoke, rather than hot air, would effectively push their balloon skyward.
9. In their experiments, they initially produced hot smoke by burning straw and wool.
10. Balloonists greatly appreciated the discovery that dense smoke was not a requirement for flight.

Adverbs Modifying Adjectives

EXAMPLES It was a **fiercely** competitive game. [The adverb *fiercely* modifies the adjective *competitive*.]

The **exceptionally** brave police officer was given an award. [The adverb *exceptionally* modifies the adjective *brave*.]

Exercise 11 Identifying Adverbs and the Adjectives They Modify

In each of the following sentences, an adverb modifies an adjective. Identify the adverb and the adjective it modifies.

EXAMPLE 1. A wagon train traveling to northern California carried a considerably large number of pioneers.

1. adverb—*considerably*; adjective—*large*

1. The immensely long wagon train started out from Denver, Colorado.
2. Both oxen and mules were used to pull unusually large wagons.
3. Even in good weather, the long trail through the mountains was fairly hazardous.
4. A moderately hard rain could turn the trail into a swamp.
5. When the trail was too muddy, the heavier wagons became mired.

STYLE TIP

Some of the most frequently used adverbs are *too, so, really,* and *very.* In your writing, try to avoid these overused words. Some adverbs that are less common are given below:
completely
dangerously
definitely
dreadfully
entirely
especially
generally
particularly
rather
surprisingly
unusually

Crossing the Curriculum
Music. You might point out to students that the system of musical notation is a code or shorthand method of giving musicians and singers adverbs that tell them how to play or sing a piece. For example, *piano* means to play or sing softly, and *pianissimo* means to play or sing extremely softly. If you have students who are familiar with musical notation, ask them to share musical terms with the rest of the class. If not, have students find some terms and their meanings in an encyclopedia or a music book. To extend the activity, you might ask students who play instruments or sing to demonstrate the use of terms to the rest of the class.

Meeting INDIVIDUAL NEEDS

MODALITIES
Visual Learners. To help visual learners better understand adverbs, have students work cooperatively to create drawings, cartoons, or collages to illustrate the following sentences:

1. In the footrace, Anita ran incredibly fast. [*The adverb* incredibly *modifies the adverb* fast, *telling* to what extent. *The adverb* fast *modifies the verb* ran, *telling* how.]

2. Anita triumphantly crossed the finish line first. [*The adverb* triumphantly *modifies the verb* crossed, *telling* how. *The adverb* first *modifies the verb* crossed, *telling* when.]

3. Anita was extremely happy, for she had finally broken the school record. [*The adverb* extremely *modifies the adjective* happy, *telling* to what extent. *The adverb* finally *modifes the verb* had broken, *telling* when.]

Reference Note
For information on adverbs used to join words or word groups, see **relative adverbs** on page 497, and **conjunctive adverbs** on pages 492.

---

6. Wagons that were extremely heavy had to be unloaded before they could be moved.
7. Stopping for the night along the trail was a consistently welcome experience.
8. It offered relief to thoroughly tired bones and muscles.
9. Nights in the mountains could be quite cold.
10. On terribly cold nights, the travelers would roll up in blankets and sleep near their campfires.

Adverbs Modifying Other Adverbs

EXAMPLES The guide spoke **extremely** slowly. [The adverb *extremely* modifies the adverb *slowly,* telling *to what extent* the guide spoke *slowly.*]

We will go to the mall **later** today. [The adverb *later* modifies the adverb *today,* telling *when* today.]

Noun or Adverb?

Some words may be used as either nouns or adverbs. When identifying parts of speech, classify words that are used to modify verbs, adjectives, and adverbs as adverbs.

NOUN	I was at **home.**
ADVERB	"Be **home** by nine o'clock," Dad said.
NOUN	**Tomorrow** is another day.
ADVERB	Do you want to go to the zoo **tomorrow**?

Exercise 12 Identifying Adverbs and the Words They Modify

Identify the adverb or adverbs in each of the following sentences. After each adverb, give the word it modifies and the part of speech of that word.

EXAMPLE 1. My sister Juana and I often had talked about getting a houseplant for our room.
1. often—had talked (verb)

1. verb — 1. A couple of months ago, Juana and I finally decided to buy a houseplant for the kitchen.
2. adjective — 2. The large ones we saw were too expensive for us.
3. verb — 3. Suddenly, Juana had a brainstorm.
4. verb — 4. "Let's buy some seeds and grow them indoors."

424 Chapter 12 Parts of Speech Overview

5. At the seed store, the owner, Mrs. Miller, greeted us cheerfully.
6. We explained that we wanted to grow a large plant but that our room never gets bright sunlight and that in the winter it can be especially chilly and dark.
7. "These are seeds of the bo tree, an unusually hardy member of the fig family native to India," said Mrs. Miller.
8. "There, this tree is sacred to Buddhists because it is said that the Buddha received enlightenment under a bo tree."
9. When we got back to our house, we planted the seeds.
10. In a short time, they sprouted, and we now have an unusual houseplant that is suited to our environment.

5. verb
6. verb/adjectives

7. adjective

8. verb

9. verb
10. verb

Exercise 13 Using Words as Adjectives and Adverbs

Write a pair of sentences for each word. In the first sentence, use the word as an adjective; in the second, use it as an adverb.

EXAMPLE
1. kindly
    1. She had a kindly manner.—adjective
       She spoke kindly.—adverb

1. daily
2. fast
3. late
4. more
5. far
6. early
7. further
8. hard
9. straight
10. right

Review D Identifying Parts of Speech

Identify the part of speech of each italicized word or word group in the following paragraphs. If the word is an adjective or an adverb, be prepared to tell what it modifies.

n. = noun   pro. = pronoun
v. = verb   adv. = adverb
adj. = adjective

EXAMPLES Without warning, the [1] *serenity* of the [2] *snow-covered* mountains is assaulted.
1. noun
2. adjective

With a [1] *thunderous* roar, a mighty avalanche [2] *crashes* [3] *headlong* down the mountainside. [4] *Some* of these slides travel at speeds of more than 200 miles an hour and pose a [5] *deadly* threat to skiers, mountain climbers, and the people [6] *who* live and work in the mountains.

One [7] *common* suggestion for surviving an avalanche is to make swimming motions to remain on top of the snow. However, people caught in avalanches [8] *rarely* can save [9] *themselves*. They are [10] *usually* immobilized, and the slide [11] *forces* snow into their nose and mouth.

HELP
In the example for Review D, the adjective *snow-covered* modifies the noun *mountains*.

1. adj.   2. v.
3. adv.   4. pro.
5. adj.
6. pro.

7. adj.

8. adv.   9. pro.
10. adv.   11. v.

Adverbs   425

GRAMMAR

Prepositions
Rule 12f *(pp. 426–427)*

OBJECTIVES
- To write sentences using words as prepositions and as adverbs

Relating to Listening
To show how the position of an adverb can affect the meaning of a sentence, read the following sentences aloud and have students discuss how the position of the adverb *just* affects the meaning of each sentence.

1. One student **just** solved the first riddle. [*modifies the verb* solved, *emphasizing that the student solved the riddle a very short time ago*]

2. One student solved **just** the first riddle. [*modifies the adjective* first, *emphasizing that the student solved only the first riddle*]

3. **Just** one student solved the first riddle. [*modifies the adjective* one, *emphasizing that only one student solved the first riddle*]

---

12. n.   13. adv.
14. adj. 15. n.
16. v.   17. adv.
18. n.   19. v.
20. n.   21. adj.
22. adj. 23. adv.
24. n.   25. adj.

STYLE TIP
In formal writing and speaking, you should avoid using a preposition at the end of a sentence when possible.

INFORMAL
Jaime asked me to name some people whom I look **up to.**

Sometimes rearranging such sentences results in an awkward or pretentious construction.

AWKWARD
Jaime asked me to name some people **up to whom** I look.

In formal situations, therefore, it is often best to reword sentences to avoid using such expressions.

FORMAL
Jaime asked me to name some people whom I **admire.**

Reference Note
For more about **prepositional phrases,** see page 467.

Avalanche workers in the [12] United States and abroad have [13] long realized the [14] potential [15] destructiveness of certain slide paths. The workers [16] have concluded that an avalanche can be [17] greatly reduced if [18] explosives [19] are used to trigger a [20] series of [21] smaller slides before [22] one large mass of snow can build up. [23] Today, the detonation of explosives has become a standard [24] practice for controlling avalanches in [25] this country.

Prepositions

12f. A *preposition* is a word that shows the relationship of a noun or a pronoun, called the *object of the preposition,* to another word.

Notice in the following examples how the prepositions show different relationships between the verb *rode* and *village,* the object of each preposition.

EXAMPLES
I rode **past** the village.	I rode **near** the village.
I rode **through** the village.	I rode **around** the village.
I rode **toward** the village.	I rode **beyond** the village.

NOTE A preposition, its object, and any modifiers of the object form a *prepositional phrase.*

Commonly Used Prepositions			
aboard	below	for	past
about	beneath	from	since
above	beside	in	through
across	besides	inside	to
after	between	into	toward
against	beyond	like	under
along	but (meaning except)	near	underneath
amid		of	until
among	by	off	up
around	concerning	on	upon
at	down	onto	with
before	during	outside	within
behind	except	over	without

426 Chapter 12 Parts of Speech Overview

RESOURCES
Prepositions
Practice
- *Grammar, Usage, and Mechanics,* pp. 19, 20
- *Language Workshop CD-ROM,* Lesson 3

A preposition that consists of two or more words is called a *compound preposition.*

EXAMPLES The soccer game was delayed **because of** rain.

Who is sitting **in front of** Arturo?

Commonly Used Compound Prepositions		
according to	in addition to	instead of
because of	in front of	on account of
by means of	in spite of	prior to

Preposition or Adverb?

Some words may be used as either prepositions or adverbs. Remember that an adverb is a modifier and does not have an object.

PREPOSITION Marge climbed **down** the ladder.
ADVERB Marge climbed **down** carefully.

PREPOSITION **Above** the dry riverbed, buzzards circled lazily.
ADVERB **Above,** buzzards circled lazily.

NOTE As a preposition, the word *to* precedes a noun or a pronoun to form a prepositional phrase. Do not confuse such a prepositional phrase with an *infinitive*—a verb form preceded by *to*.

PREPOSITIONAL PHRASES	to the library	to her	to Louisiana
INFINITIVES	to create	to play	to compare

Reference Note
For more information on **infinitives,** see page 479.

Exercise 14 Writing Sentences Using Words as Prepositions and as Adverbs

For each of the following words, write two sentences. In the first sentence, use the word as a preposition and underline the prepositional phrase. In the second sentence, use the word as an adverb. Be prepared to tell which word the adverb modifies.

EXAMPLE 1. in
1. We are going in the house now.
   We are going in now.

1. around   3. inside   5. up   7. outside   9. by
2. under   4. on   6. below 8. past   10. aboard

HELP
In the second example sentence for Exercise 14, the adverb *in* modifies the verb phrase *are going.*

Prepositions 427

Conjunctions

Rule 12g (pp. 428–429)

OBJECTIVE

- To identify coordinating conjunctions and correlative conjunctions in sentences

TEACHING TIP

Activity. Explain to students that conjunctions join related ideas and that the relationship between the ideas determines which conjunction is appropriate.

Write the following pairs of sentences on the chalkboard or on a transparency, and have students decide which conjunction or conjunctions should be used to combine each of the pairs.

1. Sako likes milk.
   Milk is good for her. [*and*]

2. Frank likes cats.
   Cats don't like Frank. [*but* or *yet*]

3. Maria will go with us to the movies.
   She will stay home and study. [*or* or *either . . . or*]

Reference Note

For a discussion of using **conjunctions in sentence combining,** see page 353. For the rules governing the use of **punctuation with conjunctions,** see pages 357, 703, and 724.

TIPS & TRICKS

You can remember the coordinating conjunctions as FANBOYS:
For
And
Nor
But
Or
Yet
So

Reference Note

Another kind of conjunction, the **subordinating conjunction,** is discussed with **subordinate clauses,** on page 498.

Conjunctions

12g. A *conjunction* joins words or word groups.

Coordinating Conjunctions

Coordinating conjunctions join words or word groups that are used in the same way.

Coordinating Conjunctions			
and	but	for	nor
or	so	yet	

EXAMPLES The orchestra played waltzes **and** polkas. [*And* joins two nouns.]

We can walk to the neighborhood pool **or** to the park. [*Or* joins two prepositional phrases.]

I looked for Hal, **but** he had already left. [*But* joins two clauses.]

Correlative Conjunctions

Correlative conjunctions are pairs of conjunctions that join words or word groups that are used in the same way.

Correlative Conjunctions	
both . . . and	not only . . . but also
either . . . or	whether . . . or
neither . . . nor	

EXAMPLES **Neither** the baseball team **nor** the soccer team has practice today.

Both the track team **and** the volleyball team enjoyed a winning season.

Their victories sparked the enthusiasm **not only** of students **but also** of teachers and townspeople.

Chapter 12 Parts of Speech Overview

RESOURCES

Conjunctions

Practice

- *Grammar, Usage, and Mechanics,* p. 21
- *Language Workshop CD-ROM,* Lesson 3

Exercise 15 **Identifying Coordinating and Correlative Conjunctions**

Identify the coordinating conjunctions and correlative conjunctions in the following sentences.

EXAMPLE 1. When did whaling and the whaling industry begin to decline?
1. and

1. Once, Nantucket and New Bedford, Massachusetts, were home ports of huge whaling fleets.
2. Whaling brought tremendous profits into these ports, but the golden days of whaling ended about the same time as the U.S. Civil War.
3. Even when it was successful, a whaling trip was no pleasure cruise for either the captain or the crew.
4. The living conditions were often quite dreadful, so maintaining order was no easy task on a long voyage.
5. Inevitably, the sailors had time on their hands, for they didn't encounter a whale every day.
6. To relieve the monotony and resulting boredom, the crews of whaling ships often would exchange visits.
7. Both the captains and their crew members looked forward to such visits.
8. The sailors enjoyed the opportunity not only to chat but also to exchange news.
9. The decline of whaling and of the whaling industry was signaled by the development of a new fuel.
10. By 1860, our country no longer needed large quantities of whale oil because kerosene, a cheaper and better fuel, had replaced it.

Interjections

12h. An *interjection* expresses emotion. An interjection has no grammatical relation to the rest of the sentence.

Interjections						
ah	ouch	ugh	wow	oops	hey	oh

STYLE TIP

Interjections are common in casual conversation. In writing, however, they are usually used only in informal notes and letters, in advertisements, and in dialogue.

Interjections
Rule 12h (pp. 429–430)

OBJECTIVE

- To complete sentences using interjections

RESOURCES

Interjections
Practice
- *Grammar, Usage, and Mechanics,* p. 22
- *Language Workshop CD-ROM,* Lesson 3

12 i

STYLE TIP

When you write an interjection, make sure the punctuation after it reflects the intensity of emotion you intend.

HELP

Check to see that you have punctuated your interjections with exclamation points or commas as needed and that you have capitalized the sentences correctly.

Answers will vary. Here are some possibilities.
1. Ouch,
2. Oops!
3. Whew,
4. Excellent!
5. Well,
6. Hey,
7. Wow!
8. Hey,
9. Wow!
10. Yow!

An interjection is generally set off from the rest of the sentence by an exclamation point or by a comma or commas. Exclamation points indicate strong emotion. Commas indicate mild emotion.

EXAMPLES **Whew!** What a day I've had!

Well, I'm just not sure.

There must be, **oh my,** a dozen snakes there.

Exercise 16 Using Interjections

Using the interjections from the list provided, complete the following sentences. Be sure to use the words as interjections and not as adjectives or adverbs.

EXAMPLE 1. _____ Wait for me!
1. Hey!

| excellent | well | whoa | ouch | wow |
| oops | whew | hey | cool | yow |

1. _____ that's hot!
2. _____ I forgot to do my homework.
3. _____ our teacher didn't collect the assignments today.
4. _____ tomorrow is a holiday!
5. _____ I can't decide; both puppies are adorable.
6. _____ he didn't know you were an athlete.
7. _____ she won the race!
8. _____ what time are you going home?
9. _____ my name was drawn in the raffle!
10. _____ our runner was passed inches away from the finish line!

Determining Parts of Speech

12i. The way a word is used in a sentence determines what part of speech the word is.

The same word may be used as different parts of speech. To figure out what part of speech the boldface word is in each of the sentences below, read the entire sentence. What you are doing is studying the **context**—the way the word is used in the sentence. From the context, you can identify the part of speech that *light* or *help* is in each of the following sentences.

Determining Parts of Speech

Rule 12i (pp. 430–432)

OBJECTIVES

- To identify parts of speech in sentences
- To use words as different parts of speech in sentences

RESOURCES

Determining Parts of Speech
Practice
- *Grammar, Usage, and Mechanics,* p. 23
- *Language Workshop CD-ROM,* Lesson 4

EXAMPLES
Rich heard the **light** patter of raindrops. [adjective]
The flash of **light** hurt her eyes. [noun]
Use care when you **light** the fire. [verb]
Please **help** your sister with her homework. [verb]
I will provide **help**, but I won't do your work for you. [noun]
If you can't find the answer in the instruction manual, you may have to call the **help** desk. [adjective]

Exercise 17 Determining the Parts of Speech of Words

Determine the part of speech of the italicized word in each of the following sentences. Be prepared to explain your answers.

EXAMPLES
1. Marisa holds the school *record* for the 100-meter dash.
1. noun
   n. = noun   v. = verb   adj. = adjective
   adv. = adverb   prep. = preposition
   conj. = conjunction
2. Marisa ran the race in *record* time.
2. adjective

1. They decided that the hedge needed a *trim*. **1.** n.
2. Their hedges always look *trim* and neat. **2.** adj.
3. We usually *trim* the tree with homemade ornaments. **3.** v.
4. Mom always *shears* a couple of inches off the top of the tree. **4.** v.
5. Later, she uses *shears* to cut straggling branches. **5.** n.
6. I wasn't thirsty, but I did *down* one glass of water before finishing my workout. **6.** v.
7. Dale ran *down* the stairs and hugged his sister. **7.** prep.
8. "If heights bother you, don't look *down*," the guide warned. **8.** adv.
9. I asked for Tuesday off, *but* my boss gave me Monday off instead. **9.** conj.
10. All *but* two of the students voted in the class elections. **10.** prep.

HELP
In the first example, *record* is a noun functioning as the direct object of the verb *holds*. In the second example, *record* functions as an adjective modifying *time*.

Review E Writing Sentences Using Words as Different Parts of Speech

Write two sentences for each of the following words, using the word as a different part of speech in each sentence. At the end of the sentence, write what part of speech the word is in that sentence.

EXAMPLE
1. hand
1. Jesse hurt his hand. (noun)
   Please hand me the biscuits. (verb)

| 1. long | 3. back | 5. iron | 7. tie | 9. outside |
| 2. cut | 4. fast | 6. some | 8. for | 10. empty |

Review E Writing Sentences Using Words as Different Parts of Speech

POSSIBLE ANSWERS

1. We all long for the lazy days of summer. (verb) We took the long way home. (adjective) We did not work long enough. (adverb)
2. Erris cut the cake into twenty-four neat pieces. (verb) The burglary suspect has a suspicious cut on his back. (noun) Nothing sparkles like cut glass. (adjective)
3. Please back the car into the garage carefully. (verb) She turned her back and walked away. (noun) The back door slammed. (adjective)
4. Some people fast to purify their minds and bodies. (verb) In ancient times, this was the main purpose of a fast. (noun) Now, some people who go without eating are usually looking for a fast way to lose weight. (adjective)
5. Will you iron my new shirt? (verb) She had to wait until the iron was hot. (noun) Her iron will and determination will see her through the audition. (adjective)
6. Have some cake. (adjective) Some of my friends don't want to go. (pronoun)
7. Tie your shoe. (verb) Your tie is hanging in the closet. (noun)
8. He is waiting for the bus. (preposition) The test was hard, for he didn't study. (conjunction)
9. Eagerly, the dog ran outside. (adverb) The team decided to seek outside help. (adjective) Outside the door, Stephen hesitated. (preposition)
10. Empty your glass into the sink. (verb) The empty theater seemed spooky. (adjective)

Learning for Life

Public Service Announcements. Point out to students that the parts of speech are basic building blocks of grammar and will be important to them in any speaking or writing situation in which formal, standard English is required.

Continued on p. 432

Ask each student to write a public service announcement (PSA) about a meeting of a neighborhood association. The announcement should tell the name of the organization; the date, time, and place of the meeting; two main topics to be discussed;

Review F — Determining Parts of Speech of Words

ANSWERS

1. adjective
2. noun
3. conjunction
4. adjective
5. pronoun
6. preposition
7. noun
8. preposition
9. pronoun
10. verb
11. adverb
12. preposition
13. conjunction
14. adjective
15. adverb
16. verb
17. adverb
18. conjunction
19. adverb
20. adjective

Review G — Writing Sentences with Words used as Different Parts of Speech

POSSIBLE ANSWERS

1. Maija had a novel idea. (adjective)
2. The movie was set on Park Avenue. (noun)
3. This week went fast! (adjective)
4. The children are laughing. (verb)
5. Yesterday I saw Donna. (adverb)
6. Tomorrow is Tuesday. (adverb)
7. Mariah or Sam may win the prize. (conjunction)
8. Speak quietly. (adverb)
9. Both the baby and the kitten are sweet. (conjunction)
10. Grandpa collects silver dollars. (adjective)
11. Jay hiked three miles. (verb)
12. Oh! Congratulations! (interjection)
13. The cereal tasted good. (verb)
14. Not Tom but I won. (conjunction)
15. We picnic there often. (adverb)
16. The boys are inside. (adverb)

Review F — Determining the Parts of Speech of Words

Identify the part of speech of each italicized word or word group in the following paragraph.

EXAMPLES The [1] *homes* of many [2] *of* the early farmers on the Great Plains [3] *were* [4] *quite* [5] *primitive*.

1. noun   3. verb   5. adjective
2. preposition   4. adverb

[1] *Early* farmers on the [2] *Great Plains* eked out a rough existence, [3] *for* there were few towns, stores, or other signs of civilization. [4] *Many* farm homes were constructed mostly of sod bricks, [5] *which* were cut [6] *out of* the prairie. Trees were in short supply on these windswept lands, but the resourceful settler might find a few [7] *cottonwoods* growing [8] *along* a creek or river. [9] *These* [10] *could be used* to build a frame for the roof, which was then covered [11] *lightly* with grassy earth. Grass, both [12] *on* the roof [13] *and* in the sod, helped to hold the house together. Some of [14] *these* rugged homes had a door made of timber, but [15] *quite* often a cowhide [16] *was draped* across the entrance. [17] *Inside* was a dirt floor covered with a bearskin [18] *or* a buffalo hide. As more settlers moved [19] *west*, bringing furnishings and [20] *building* materials, farmers eventually abandoned these first, primitive dwellings and built homes that were more conventional.

Review G — Writing Sentences with Words Used as Different Parts of Speech

Use each of the following words or groups of words in a sentence. Then, indicate what part of speech the word or word group is.

EXAMPLE 1. gold
1. Tamisha bought a gold bracelet. (adjective)

1. novel
2. Park Avenue
3. this
4. are laughing
5. yesterday
6. tomorrow
7. or
8. quietly
9. both . . . and
10. silver
11. hiked
12. oh
13. tasted
14. but
15. often
16. inside
17. underneath
18. appeared
19. whew
20. in

Learning for Life

and an appeal for people to come to the meeting. Ask students to use each of the parts of speech in their announcements. After students have finished writing their PSAs, they may want to read them aloud to the rest of the class or to record the PSAs and play the recordings for the class.

CHAPTER

Chapter Review

A. Identifying the Parts of Speech in Sentences

For each of the following sentences, identify the part of speech of each italicized word as a *noun*, an *adjective*, a *verb*, an *adverb*, a *pronoun*, a *conjunction*, or an *interjection*.

1. In the late nineteenth century, many men *worked* as cowboys on *cattle* drives. **1. v./adj.**
2. There *were few* comforts on the trail. **2. v./adj.**
3. Some *improvement* came after *Charles Goodnight* put together the first chuck wagon. **3. n./n.**
4. A hinged lid swung *down* from the wagon to reveal a simple *but* complete kitchen. **4. adv./conj.**
5. The *first* chuck wagons were pulled *by* oxen. **5. adj./prep.**
6. *These* were later replaced by mules *or* horses. **6. pro./conj.**
7. *Most* of the cowhands who took part in the historic cattle drives remain *nameless*. **7. pro./adj.**
8. Cowboys were *instrumental* in opening trails that were later used by the men and women who *settled* the frontier. **8. adj./v.**
9. *Railroads soon* began to crisscross the country; the cowboy was no longer needed to drive cattle. **9. n./adv.**
10. *Hey!* Did you know that ranchers still hire *cowboys* to brand and herd cattle, repair fences, and do many other jobs? **10. int./n.**

B. Identifying the Parts of Speech in a Paragraph

Identify the part of speech of the italicized word or words in each sentence in the following paragraph. For abbreviation keys, see Chapter Review A.

11. adj./prep.
12. n./v.
13. conj./v.
14. pro./adj.
15. n./adv.
16. int./v.

[11] In the *thirty* years following the Civil War, millions of longhorn cattle were driven *over* long trails from ranches in Texas to railroads in Kansas. [12] During this *period*, the cowboy *became* an American hero. [13] Novels *and* magazine articles *glorified* life on the range. [14] The men *who* rode this rugged land, however, had to endure *many* hardships. [15] Cowboys spent most of their *time* in the saddle, rounding up strays and moving the herd *along*. [16] Caring for sick animals, repairing fences, and, *well*, doing what had to be done *were* all part of a normal working day. [17] At the end of such a day, each cow-

---

Review G Writing Sentences with Words used as Different Parts of Speech

POSSIBLE ANSWERS continued

17. The puppy hid underneath the bed. (preposition)
18. The rain appeared unexpectedly. (verb)
19. Whew! It's over! (interjection)
20. When the rain began, we went in. (adverb)

Using the Chapter Review

To assess student progress, you may want to compare the types of items missed on the **Diagnostic Preview** to those missed on the **Chapter Review**. You may want to work on specific goals for mastering essential information with individual students who are still having difficulty.

Cooperative Learning

To give students a better understanding of the definitions of the parts of speech, have them study the etymologies of the names of the parts of speech. Divide the class into eight groups, if possible. Assign each group one part of speech to research. Have groups consult various works—such as a standard dictionary, an abridged dictionary, a specialized reference work on word origins (if available), and the *Oxford English Dictionary*—to obtain thorough information. Within a group, each student could be assigned a specific task, such as checking one of the sources, taking notes, and reporting back to the rest of the group. Ask the members of the group to work together to compile their findings and write down the information. Have each group select one member to report its findings to the class. You could compile the information and give the students copies to keep for reference.

17. conj./pro.
18. n./adj.

19. adv./adj.
20. prep./adv.

boy *not only* had to look after his horse *but also* had to cook dinner for *himself* and do a host of other chores. [18] The quiet *evenings* gave cowboys a chance to relax by telling stories and singing *campfire* songs. [19] Such details of trail life are *realistically* portrayed in the *popular* paintings of Charles M. Russell. [20] *Because of* these images and our need for a *truly* American hero, cowboys have become a colorful part of our history.

C. Identifying Pronouns in Sentences

Identify the pronouns in each sentence as *personal, reflexive, intensive, demonstrative, interrogative, relative* or *indefinite*.

21. pers./pers./ints.
22. ind./pers./refl.
23. pers./demo.

24. intr.
25. ind./rel.

21. They delivered their supplies themselves.
22. One of their colleagues spent all summer teaching himself French.
23. A few pooled their resources and decided to send these to Aunt Joan.
24. Who has been raking the leaves in the backyard?
25. Anybody who has done the homework could do this exercise.

D. Identifying Words as Nouns, Pronouns, or Adjectives

Tell whether each *italicized* word in the following paragraph is used as a *noun*, a *pronoun*, or an *adjective*. For each adjective, give the word it modifies. (Do not include the articles *a, an,* and *the*.)

26. pro./n.
27. adj./n./n./adj.
28. pro./n.
29. pro./n./adj.
30. adj.
31. pro./adj./pro.
32. n./adj./pro./pro./n.

33. n./adj./n.

34. adj.
35. adj./n.

[26] Nearly *everybody* has heard a Strauss *waltz*. [27] The waltz is a form of *ballroom* dance that originated in *Germany* and *Austria* in the *eighteenth* century. [28] Johann Strauss was the most famous and, *some* say, the best *composer* of waltzes. [29] *He* was born in *Vienna*, the *capital* city of Austria, in 1825. [30] Strauss came from a *well-established* family of musicians. [31] *His* father and brothers Eduard and Josef were *respected* composers and conductors in *their* own right. [32] Johann toured with an *orchestra* for many years, but in 1870, when his *first* wife said *she* would like *him* to write operettas, he turned his attentions to writing *music*. [33] His most famous compositions are Die Fledermaus (The Bat), an *operetta*, and "The Blue Danube" waltz, which later became *famous* as one of the *themes* of the 1968 movie 2001: A Space Odyssey. [34] Johann Strauss wrote more than *five hundred* orchestral compositions. [35] When he died in Vienna in 1899, his *worldwide* reputation as the "*Waltz King*" was assured.

RESOURCES

Parts of Speech Overview

Review
- *Grammar, Usage, and Mechanics,* pp. 24, 25, 26

Assessment
- *Assessment Package*
  —Chapter Tests, Ch. 12
  —Chapter Tests in Standardized Test Formats, Ch. 12
- *Test Generator (One–Stop Planner CD–ROM)*

E. Classifying Nouns

Identify each italicized noun in the following sentences as *proper* or *common* and *concrete* or *abstract*. Also, tell if a noun is *compound*.

36. On *Sunday*, the neighbor's *dog* barked all night.
37. To our *surprise*, the *zebras* cantered noisily across the path.
38. A painting by *Monet* that always gives me a feeling of *serenity* hangs in the *Metropolitan Museum of Art* in New York.
39. "As you know," said *Mr. Cima* proudly, "*knowledge* is *power*."
40. Seeking *solitude*, Kathryn hiked across the hills of *Connemara*.

36. prop.—con./ comm.—con.
37. comm.—abs./ comm.—con.
38. prop.—con./ comm.—abs./ prop.—con.—comp.
39. prop.—con.—comp./ comm.—abs./ comm.—abs.
40. comm.—abs./ prop.—con.

Writing Application
Using Adjectives in a Poem

Vivid Adjectives   The Czech author Franz Kafka wrote about a man who becomes an insect! Imagine that you are changed into an animal or an object. Using at least ten carefully chosen adjectives, write a poem describing yourself.

Prewriting   Select an object or an animal that you think you would like to be. Next, freewrite descriptive words about the object or animal. You may want to consult an article in an encyclopedia for additional details or pictures of your chosen topic.

Writing   As you write your first draft, concentrate on using the most vivid adjectives that you have listed.

Revising   Read through your first draft, and underline each adjective. For each one, ask yourself whether any other word more precisely describes the noun or pronoun. Be sure that you have used at least ten different adjectives.

Publishing   Check your poem to make sure that all words are spelled correctly, especially any adjectives that you do not use very often in writing. Proofread your poem for any errors in grammar, punctuation, and spelling. Your class may want to share your poems by reading them aloud or displaying them on a bulletin board.

Chapter Review   **435**

RESOURCES
Writing Application
Extension
- *Grammar, Usage, and Mechanics*, p. 29
- *Language Workshop CD-ROM*, Lessons 1–4

CHAPTER

13 The Parts of a Sentence
Subjects, Predicates, Complements

PREVIEWING THE CHAPTER

- This chapter shows the differences between word groups that are complete sentences and those that are sentence fragments. In addition, the chapter discusses complete and simple subjects and predicates, as well as subject complements and objects of verbs. The chapter also teaches students how to classify sentences as declarative, imperative, interrogative, or exclamatory.

- The chapter closes with a **Chapter Review** including a **Writing Application** feature that asks students to write a short letter using a variety of sentence structures.

- To integrate this chapter with the writing chapters, use the **Teaching T/Strands** chart on pp. T401A–T401B.

USING THE DIAGNOSTIC PREVIEW

- You may want to use the **Diagnostic Preview** along with an assessment of students' writing to evaluate their understanding of sentences.

- The **Diagnostic Preview** does not assess students' abilities to distinguish a sentence fragment from a sentence; therefore, you may want to use **Exercise 1** to assess students' understanding of that distinction.

Diagnostic Preview

A. Identifying Subjects, Verbs, and Complements

Identify each of the italicized words and word groups in the following sentences as a *subject*, a *verb*, a *predicate adjective*, a *predicate nominative*, a *direct object*, or an *indirect object*.

EXAMPLE   1. Robotics is the *science* or *technology* of robots.
            1. science—predicate nominative; technology— predicate nominative

1. s.   1. Have *you* ever met a robot?
2. d.o.   2. In the field of robotics, scientists have built vastly complex *robots*.
3. v.   3. Today, these machines *are put* to work in factories, laboratories, and outer space.
4. s.   4. How were these complex *machines* first used?
5. s.   5. There are a *number* of interesting early examples of robots at work.
6. p.n.   6. One of the first robots was a mechanical *figure* in a clock tower.
7. d.o.   7. It raised a hammer and struck a *bell* every hour.
8. p.n.   8. At the 1939 New York World's Fair, Elektro and Sparko were very popular *attractions*.
9. p.a.   9. Elektro was *tall*, more than seven feet high.
10. i.o.   10. Electric motors gave *Elektro* power for a variety of amazing tricks.

436   Chapter 13   The Parts of a Sentence

CHAPTER RESOURCES

Planning
- *One-Stop Planner CD-ROM*

Practice and Extension
- *Grammar, Usage, and Mechanics*, p. 30
- *Language Workshop CD-ROM*

Internet
- go.hrw.com (keyword: EOLang)

Evaluation and Assessment
- *Assessment Package*
  —*Chapter Tests*, Ch. 13
  —*Chapter Tests in Standardized Test Formats*, Ch. 13
- *Test Generator (One-Stop Planner CD-ROM)*

11. Sparko was Elektro's *dog*.   11. p.n.
12. Sparko *could bark* and even *wag* his tail.   12. v./v.
13. Today, *some* of the simplest robots are the drones in laboratories.   13. s.
14. Basically, drones are *extensions* of the human arm.   14. p.n.
15. They can be *useful* in many different ways.   15. p.a.

B. Classifying Sentences According to Purpose

Punctuate each of the following sentences with an appropriate end mark. Then, classify the sentence as *declarative*, *interrogative*, *imperative*, or *exclamatory*.

EXAMPLE   1. There's a twenty-five-foot robot named Beetle
          1. There's a twenty-five-foot robot named Beetle.—declarative

16. Can you picture a robot twenty-five feet tall **?**   16. int.
17. Step up and say hello to Beetle **.**   17. imp.
18. Perhaps you have heard of CAM, an even more advanced robot **.**   18. dec.
19. It can travel on long legs across rough terrain as rapidly as thirty-five miles per hour **.**   19. dec.
20. What an amazing creation it is **!**   20. exc.

What Is a Sentence?

In conversation, people can often leave out part of a sentence without confusing their listeners. In formal writing and speaking, though, it is usually better to use complete sentences. They help to make meaning clear to your audience.

13a. A *sentence* is a word group that contains a subject and a verb and that expresses a complete thought.

A *sentence fragment* is a word or word group that is capitalized and punctuated as a sentence but that does not contain both a subject and a verb or that does not express a complete thought.

SENTENCE FRAGMENT	The magazine's essay contest for tenth-grade American history students. [no verb]
SENTENCE	The magazine's essay contest for tenth-grade American history students ends Tuesday.

Reference Note

For information on how to correct **sentence fragments**, see page 340.

Cooperative Learning

Emphasize to students that using sentence fragments in most formal writing situations (for example, research papers, book reports, and business letters) is unacceptable. Point out, however, that in many informal writing situations, the use of sentence fragments is not only acceptable but also appropriate. For example, many songwriters often use sentence fragments to convey a mood or to create a desired rhythm or rhyme.

Organize the class into groups of three, and have each group choose a popular song with lyrics appropriate for the classroom. Ask each group to write down the lyrics of the song, to identify the sentences and the sentence fragments in the lyrics, and to present their findings orally to the rest of the class.

After the oral presentations, you may want to have the class suggest other writing situations in which the use of sentence fragments is appropriate (for example, ads, dialogues, poems).

TEACHING TIP

Exercise 1 You may want to use the first ten items in the exercise as guided practice. Then, have students complete the exercise as independent practice.

COMPUTER TIP

Many style-checking software programs can help you identify sentence fragments. If you have access to such a program, use it to help evaluate your writing.

Reference Note

For more about the **understood subject**, see page 447.

HELP

Example 1 of Exercise 1 contains a subject and verb and expresses a complete thought. Example 2 does not contain a subject and does not express a complete thought.

SENTENCE FRAGMENT	Was chosen as the best one from over two thousand entries. [no subject]
SENTENCE	Her essay was chosen as the best one from over two thousand entries.
SENTENCE FRAGMENT	When the judges announced the winner. [not a complete thought]
SENTENCE	When the judges announced the winner, everyone applauded.

NOTE Some sentences contain an understood subject (you).

EXAMPLES [You] Wait!
[You] Hold on to the reins.

Exercise 1 Identifying Sentences and Sentence Fragments

Identify each of the following word groups as a *sentence* or a *sentence fragment*. Be prepared to explain your answers.

EXAMPLES
1. Willa Cather wrote poetry, fiction, and nonfiction.
1. sentence
2. Grew up in the Midwest.
2. sentence fragment

1. Willa Cather was born in Back Creek Valley in northern Virginia. **1. sent.**
2. In 1883, when she was nine years old. **2. frag.**
3. Her family moved to the treeless prairie of Nebraska. **3. sent.**
4. She tracked buffalo and collected prairie flowers. **4. sent.**
5. Fascinated by the wild and rolling plains. **5. frag.**
6. Listening to the stories of neighboring settlers. **6. frag.**
7. They told memorable tales about the harsh struggles of the homesteaders. **7. sent.**
8. After she graduated from high school in the village of Red Cloud, Nebraska. **8. frag.**

438   Chapter 13   The Parts of a Sentence

Learning for Life

Writing a Personal Letter. Tell students that using some sentence fragments is common in informal personal letters. Organize students into pairs, and have each student write a one-page letter about a memorable experience. (Students should pick a subject that they are comfortable sharing with others.) Have students tally the sentences and sentence fragments in their completed letters, and then assess the effectiveness of using both complete and incomplete sentences in the letters.

9. The picture of Red Cloud on the previous page shows shops and people that would have been familiar to Willa Cather. **9. sent.**
10. And the Opera House at the end of the street where Cather and her classmates graduated in 1890. **10. frag.**
11. In college, Willa Cather discovered her talent for writing. **11. sent.**
12. Contributing stories and reviews to local newspapers. **12. frag.**
13. At first, her writing failed to reach a wide audience. **13. sent.**
14. She succeeded in establishing herself as a writer. **14. sent.**
15. After years earning a living as a schoolteacher and an editor in New York City. **15. frag.**
16. Although Cather enjoyed living in New York. **16. frag.**
17. She never lost touch with the sights and sounds of her childhood. **17. sent.**
18. She describes how farmers turned the open plains into orderly fields of wheat and corn. **18. sent.**
19. In *O Pioneers!*, her second novel. **19. frag.**
20. In a later novel, *My Ántonia*, the immigrant neighbors of her childhood play prominent roles. **20. sent.**

Subjects and Predicates

13b. Sentences consist of two basic parts: subjects and predicates.

The *subject* tells whom or what the sentence or clause is about, and the *predicate* tells something about the subject.

Notice in the following examples that the subject may come before or after the predicate or between parts of the predicate.

SUBJECT	PREDICATE
Some residents of the desert	can survive a long drought.

PREDICATE	SUBJECT
Particularly noteworthy is	the Australian frog.

PREDICATE	SUBJECT	PREDICATE
For up to three years	it	can live without rainfall.

PREDICATE	SUBJECT	PREDICATE
How can	an animal	survive that long?

In each example above, all the words labeled *subject* make up the **complete subject**; all the words labeled *predicate* make up the **complete predicate**.

Meeting INDIVIDUAL NEEDS

MODALITIES

Visual Learners. Everyday speech often contains sentence fragments. Ask students to create comic strips in which two characters speak in sentence fragments. Then, have students exchange comic strips and rewrite the dialogues by using complete sentences. Ask students which dialogue—the one written in sentence fragments or the one written in complete sentences—is more effective in their comic strips. Have students give reasons to support their opinions.

Subjects and Predicates

Rules 13b–g (pp. 439–450)

OBJECTIVES

- To identify complete subjects and complete predicates in sentences
- To identify verbs and verb phrases in sentences
- To identify subjects and verbs in sentences
- To complete sentences by supplying complete predicates
- To complete sentences by supplying subjects and verbs

RESOURCES

Subjects and Predicates

Practice
- *Grammar, Usage, and Mechanics,* pp. 32, 33, 34, 35, 36, 37, 38, 39, 40
- *Language Workshop CD-ROM,* Lesson 24

Meeting INDIVIDUAL NEEDS

MODALITIES

Visual Learners. Have students look in books and magazines to find pictures of people performing actions, such as a baseball player hitting a ball or an adult reading to a child. Ask students to describe the subject in each picture and to tell what the subject is doing. Write on the chalkboard a sentence based on each description, and ask students to identify the complete subject and the complete predicate in each sentence.

ENGLISH-LANGUAGE LEARNERS

Japanese and Korean. In Japanese, the subject is always followed by the functional word *wa* or *ga*. In Korean, the subject is always followed by *i* (ee) or *ga*. Speakers of these languages should consider which word(s) in English sentences would be followed by one of these functional words in each of their native languages.

HELP
In Excercise 2, the subject may appear anywhere in a sentence.

Exercise 2 — Identifying Subjects and Predicates

Identify the complete subject and the complete predicate in each of the following sentences.

EXAMPLE 1. When was the precious metal platinum discovered?
1. complete subject—the precious metal platinum
   complete predicate—When was discovered

1. People from a variety of countries have been credited with the discovery of platinum.
2. Spanish explorers in search of gold supposedly discovered this precious metal in the rivers of South America.
3. However, the explorers considered it a worthless, inferior form of silver.
4. Their name for platinum was *platina,* meaning "little silver."
5. Back into the river went the little balls of platinum!
6. The platinum might then become gold, according to one amazing theory.
7. Europeans later mixed platinum with gold.
8. This mixture encouraged the production of counterfeit gold bars and coins.
9. Platinum commands a high price today because of its resistance to corrosion.
10. Such diverse products as jet planes and jewelry include platinum in some form.

The Subject

13c. The main word or word group that tells whom or what the sentence is about is called the *simple subject*.

The *complete subject* consists of the simple subject and any words or word groups that modify the simple subject.

EXAMPLES A dog with this pedigree is usually nervous.
  Complete subject A dog with this pedigree
  Simple subject dog

  Both of these cockatiels are for sale.
  Complete subject Both of these cockatiels
  Simple subject Both

440   The Parts of a Sentence

MINI-LESSON — Continued on pp. 441–442

Spelling Compound Nouns. Direct students' attention to the **Reference Note** at the top of p. 441. Then, explain that some compound nouns are written as one word (*bedspread*), some as separate words (*bulletin board*), and others as hyphenated words (*cave-in*). Point out that because there are no rules governing the spellings of compound nouns, writers must consult a dictionary if they are in doubt about the

440 The Parts of a Sentence

The Taj Mahal in India is one of the most beautiful buildings in the world.

Complete subject   The Taj Mahal in India
Simple subject   Taj Mahal

NOTE In this book, the term *subject* usually refers to the simple subject unless otherwise indicated.

The Predicate

13d. The ***simple predicate,*** or ***verb,*** is the main word or word group that tells something about the subject.

The ***complete predicate*** consists of the verb and all the words that modify the verb and complete its meaning.

EXAMPLES   Spiders snare their prey in intricate webs.

Complete predicate   snare their prey in intricate webs
Simple predicate   snare

Rosa has been looking for you all morning.

Complete predicate   has been looking for you all morning
Simple predicate   has been looking

Have my keys been found?

Complete predicate   Have been found
Simple predicate   Have been found

Notice in the preceding examples that the simple predicate may be identical to the complete predicate. Also, the simple predicate may be a one-word verb or a ***verb phrase*** (a main verb and one or more helping verbs).

Commonly Used Helping Verbs

am	did	has	might	was
are	do	have	must	were
can	does	is	shall	will
could	had	may	should	would

NOTE In this book, the term *verb* usually refers to the simple predicate unless otherwise indicated.

Reference Note
A compound noun, such as *Taj Mahal,* functions as a single unit. For more about **compound nouns,** see page 406.

Reference Note
For more about **verbs** and **verb phrases,** see page 417.

TIPS & TRICKS

When you are identifying the simple predicate in a sentence, be sure to include all parts of a verb phrase.

EXAMPLE
Should Dad have painted the walls light gray? [The simple predicate is the verb phrase *Should have painted.*]

Subjects and Predicates   441

---

form of a compound noun. As you read the following words aloud, have students write the words. Then, have students consult a dictionary to check the spellings.

1. backyard
2. air conditioner
3. car pool
4. court-martial
5. doorknob

Exercise 3 Identifying Verbs and Verb Phrases in Sentences

Identify the verb in each of the following sentences. Be sure to include all parts of any verb phrases.

EXAMPLE 1. The giant panda of China is considered an endangered species.

1. *is considered*

1. Scientists throughout the world have expressed concern about the fate of the giant panda.
2. In recent years this animal's natural habitat has slowly become smaller.
3. Many forests of bamboo, the panda's favorite food, have died.
4. A panda like the one in the picture on this page may devour as much as forty pounds of bamboo daily.
5. However, each tender green shoot of bamboo contains only a very small amount of nutrients.
6. In addition, the large but sluggish panda is not known as a successful hunter.
7. In their concern for the panda's survival, scientists are now studying the habits of this animal.
8. A captured panda is held in a log trap for several hours.
9. During this time, scientists attach a radio to the panda's neck.
10. The radio sends the scientists valuable information about the animal's behavior in the wild.

Finding the Subject

To find the subject of a sentence, find the verb first. Then, ask "Who?" or "What?" before the verb.

EXAMPLES My cousin from Finland will arrive this afternoon. [The verb is *will arrive.* Who will arrive? *Cousin* will arrive. *Cousin* is the subject.]

On the other side of the brook stands a cabin. [The verb is *stands.* What stands? *Cabin* stands. *Cabin* is the subject.]

MINI-LESSON

To extend the lesson, you could have students look through a dictionary to find other examples of the three forms of compound nouns. For more information on compound nouns, refer students to **Chapter 12: Parts of Speech Overview** and **Chapter 26: Spelling.**

Exercise 4 Identifying Subjects and Verbs

Identify the subject and the verb in each of the following sentences. Be sure to include all parts of any verb phrases.

EXAMPLE   1. Our science class has been studying the migratory flights of different species of butterflies.
   1. subject—*class;* verb—*has been studying*

1. Despite their fragile appearance, butterflies have a great deal of stamina.
2. They often fly more than one thousand miles during migration.
3. The painted lady butterfly, for example, has been seen in the middle of the Atlantic Ocean.
4. In fact, this species was once spotted over the Arctic Circle.
5. During the spring, millions of these insects flutter across North America.
6. Huge flocks of colorful butterflies fly from their winter home in New Mexico to places as far north as Newfoundland, Canada.
7. The brilliant orange-and-black monarch butterfly flies south each September from Canada toward Florida, Texas, and California.
8. The migratory flight of the monarch may cover a distance of close to two thousand miles.
9. Every winter for the past several decades, monarchs have gathered in a small forest not far from San Francisco.
10. The thick clusters of their blazing orange wings make this forest very popular with tourists.

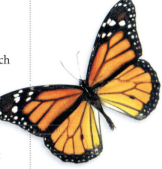

13e. The subject of a verb is never in a prepositional phrase.

A *prepositional phrase* consists of a preposition, the object of the preposition, and any modifiers of that object.

EXAMPLES   for the team   of mine   through the years
           on the top shelf at all times   along with my niece

Do not mistake a noun or pronoun in a prepositional phrase for the subject of a sentence.

EXAMPLES   One of my cousins has visited Ghana. [Who has visited? *One* has visited. *Of my cousins* is a prepositional phrase.]

           On top of the building is an up-to-date observatory. [What is? *Observatory* is. *On top* and *of the building* are prepositional phrases.]

Reference Note
For more information about **prepositional phrases,** see page 467.

Exercise 5

ALTERNATIVE LESSON

To reinforce what students have learned about complete subjects and complete predicates, have them point out each sentence in which the subject appears between parts of the predicate. Then, call on volunteers to read aloud the complete subject in each of these sentences. [4. *the earliest Chinese immigrants;* 5. *only men;* 6. *they;* 7. *the close-knit society of America's Chinatowns;* 8. *you;* 10. *Victor G. Nee and Brett de Bary Nee*]

HELP

Remember, the subject is never in a prepositional phrase.

Exercise 5 Identifying Subjects and Verbs

Identify the subject and the verb in each of the following sentences.

EXAMPLE
1. How much do you know about the Chinese experience in the United States?

1. subject—*you*
   verb—*do know*

1. The people in this picture are celebrating the arrival of the New Year in accordance with an ancient Chinese tradition.
2. These festivities, however, are occurring in the United States.
3. The Chinese New Year celebration, with its dragon parades and festive decorations, is a colorful addition to American culture.
4. In the 1850s the earliest Chinese immigrants came to the United States for jobs in the gold mines and on the railroads.
5. At first, only men could immigrate.
6. Not until much later could they send home to China for their wives and sweethearts.
7. As a result, not until the 1920s did the close-knit society of America's Chinatowns develop.
8. Have you read about the experience of Chinese immigrants in America?
9. I recommend the book *Longtime Californ': A Documentary Study of an American Chinatown.*
10. In this book, Victor G. Nee and Brett de Bary Nee trace the history of Chinese immigration to the United States and the development of the Chinese American community in San Francisco.

444   Chapter 13   The Parts of a Sentence

Exercise 6 — Completing Sentences by Supplying Complete Predicates

Finish each of the following sentences by adding a complete predicate. Then, underline the simple subject once and the verb twice.

Answers will vary.

EXAMPLE 1. One of the horses _____.
1. One of the horses has escaped from the corral.

1. Those lions _____. — 1. look fierce
2. A white fence _____. — 2. surrounded the yard
3. The surf _____. — 3. was pounding the shore
4. The road by my house _____. — 4. is bumpy
5. Students in our school _____. — 5. enjoy dancing
6. The school bus _____. — 6. is just turning the corner
7. The old, half-blind cat _____. — 7. still keeps me company
8. Sitting in innertubes, the tourists _____. — 8. floated down the river
9. The stone wall _____. — 9. needs repair
10. Last month _____. — 10. was warm

Review A — Identifying Complete Subjects, Complete Predicates, Simple Subjects, and Verbs

Identify the complete subject and the complete predicate in each sentence in the following paragraph. Then, underline the simple subject once and the verb twice.

EXAMPLE [1] For what is Benjamin Banneker best remembered?
1. complete subject—Benjamin Banneker
   complete predicate—For what is best remembered

[1] Benjamin Banneker (1731–1806) was born near Baltimore, Maryland, of a free mother and an enslaved father. [2] Considered free, Banneker could attend an integrated private school. [3] There he began his lifelong study of science and math. [4] Despite having only an eighth-grade education, this young man became a noteworthy astronomer and mathematician. [5] His astronomical research led to his acclaimed prediction of the solar eclipse of 1789. [6] A few years later, the first of his almanacs was published. [7] Banneker's almanacs contained tide tables and data on future eclipses. [8] Some bits of practical advice, as well as famous sayings, were also included. [9] These popular almanacs came out every year for more than a decade. [10] In addition to his scientific discoveries, Banneker is known for his work as a surveyor during the planning of Washington, D.C.

TIPS & TRICKS

In many sentences, you can find the subject and the verb more easily if you first cross out any prepositional phrases.

EXAMPLE
The team ~~with the best record~~ will play ~~in the state tournament~~.
Subject   team
Verb   will play

Review A — Identifying Complete Subjects, Complete Predicates, Simple Subjects, and Verbs

ANSWERS

1. CS: Benjamin Banneker (1731–1806); CP: was born near Baltimore, Maryland, of a free mother and an enslaved father
2. CS: Considered free, Banneker; CP: could attend an integrated private school
3. CS: he; CP: There began his lifelong study of science and math
4. CS: this young man; CP: Despite having only an eighth-grade education became a noteworthy astronomer and mathematician
5. CS: His astronomical research; CP: led to his acclaimed prediction of the solar eclipse of 1789
6. CS: the first of his almanacs; CP: A few years later was published
7. CS: Banneker's almanacs; CP: contained tide tables and data on future eclipses
8. CS: Some bits of practical advice, as well as famous sayings; CP: were also included
9. CS: These popular almanacs; CP: came out every year for more than a decade
10. CS: Banneker; CP: In addition to his scientific discoveries is known for his work as a surveyor during the planning of Washington, D.C.

Sentences Beginning with There or Here

The word *there* or *here* may begin a sentence, but it is almost never the subject. Often, *there* or *here* is used as an adverb telling *where*.

EXAMPLES   There are your **gloves**. [What are? *Gloves* are. *Gloves* is the subject. *There* tells where your gloves are.]

Here is my **nephew**. [Who is? *Nephew* is. *Nephew* is the subject. *Here* tells where my nephew is.]

NOTE   Sometimes, *there* begins a sentence but does not tell *where*. In this use, *there* is not an adverb but an **expletive**—a word that fills out the structure of a sentence but does not add to the meaning.

EXAMPLE   There is not much **time** left. [What is left? *Time* is left. *Time* is the subject. *There* does not add any meaning to the sentence, which may be rewritten without *there*: Not much time is left.]

Sentences Asking Questions

Questions usually begin with a verb, a helping verb, or a word such as *what, when, where, how,* or *why*. In most cases, the subject follows the verb or part of the verb phrase.

EXAMPLES   Where is your **parakeet**?

Did **you** make the team?

In a question that begins with a helping verb, such as the second example above, the subject generally comes between the helping verb and the main verb. To find the subject in any question, however, turn the question into a statement, find the verb, and then ask "Who?" or "What?" before the verb.

EXAMPLES   Were your friends early?
becomes
Your friends were early.
[Who were? *Friends* were.]

Where did the horses cross the river?
becomes
The horses did cross the river where.
[What did cross? *Horses* did.]

Exercise 7 **Identifying Subjects and Verbs**

Identify the subject and the verb in each of the following sentences.

EXAMPLE
1. There are several thousand asteroids in our solar system.

1. subject—*asteroids*
   verb—*are*

1. There were three questions on the final exam.
2. Here is my topic for the term paper.
3. What did you choose for a topic?
4. Will everyone be ready at eleven o'clock?
5. There will be a study-group meeting tomorrow.
6. When should we go to the library?
7. There were very few books on the subject.
8. Have you outlined the next chapter?
9. Where will our conference be held?
10. Are there many magazine articles about Nelson Mandela?

The Understood Subject

In a request or a command, the subject is usually not stated. In such sentences, *you* is the **understood subject**.

REQUEST   [**You**] Please rake the yard.
COMMAND   [**You**] Pick up the fallen branches.

When a request or command includes a name, the name is not the subject but a ***noun of direct address.*** *You* is still the understood subject.

EXAMPLE   Jason, [**you**] wash the dishes.

Reference Note

For information on using commas with **nouns of direct address,** see page 711.

Compound Subjects and Compound Verbs

13f. A *compound subject* consists of two or more subjects that are joined by a conjunction and that have the same verb.

The parts of a compound subject are generally joined by the coordinating conjunction *and* or *or*.

EXAMPLES   **Mr. Olivero** and his **daughter** planted the garden. [Who planted? *Mr. Olivero* and *daughter* planted.]

Either **Mr. Olivero** or his **daughter** planted the garden. [The two parts of the compound subject are *Mr. Olivero* and *daughter*.]

TEACHING TIP

Exercise 7 Reminding students that the subject of a verb never appears in a prepositional phrase may help them identify the subjects in **Exercise 7.** You may want students to find all of the prepositional phrases in each sentence before they attempt to identify the subject and verb in the sentence.

13g. A *compound verb* consists of two or more verbs that are joined by a conjunction and that have the same subject.

The parts of a compound verb are usually joined by the coordinating conjunction *and*, *but*, or *or*.

EXAMPLES   At the street festival, we **danced** the rumba and **sampled** the meat pies.

I **have written** the letter and **addressed** the envelope but **have** not **gone** to the post office yet.

Both the subject and the verb of a sentence may be compound.

EXAMPLE   Yesterday, **Jamal** and **I built** a box kite and **painted** it bright yellow and green.

NOTE   There are other cases in which a sentence may contain more than one subject and verb.

```
                              S                        V
COMPOUND     The unification of Italy in 1861 was a victory
SENTENCE     for Giuseppe Garibaldi,
                       S                    V
             and the event ended centuries of civil strife.

                        S         V                        S
COMPLEX      After the painter finished his self-portrait, he
SENTENCE      V        V
             went out and ate dinner.
```

Exercise 8   Identifying Subjects and Verbs

Identify the subject(s) and the verb(s) in each of the following sentences. If the subject is understood, write *(You)*.

EXAMPLE   1. Sarah, please return the overdue video and pay the late charges.

    1. subject—*(You)*
       verbs—*return, pay*

1. Jackets and ties are required in that restaurant.
2. Do any bears or wildcats live in these woods?
3. On our math test, Ann and Mark scored the highest.
4. Bring both a pencil and a pen to the history exam. **4.** *(You)*
5. Miguel neither sings nor plays an instrument.
6. Where do you and Liz buy CDs?

STYLE TIP

The helping verb may or may not be repeated if it is the same for all parts of the compound verb.

EXAMPLES
My aunt **will arrive** tomorrow and **will stay** with us for the holidays.
[The helping verb *will* is repeated.]

My aunt **will arrive** tomorrow and **stay** with us for the holidays.
[The helping verb *will* is not repeated.]

Reference Note

For more information on **compound sentences,** see page 504. For more information on **complex sentences,** see page 505.

7. The front and back tires are low and need air.
8. Play ball! **8. (You)**
9. Humor and wisdom are often used in folk sayings.
10. Either Bill or Jan may stay and help us.

Exercise 9 Completing Sentences by Supplying Subjects and Verbs

Complete each of the sentences below with an appropriate complete subject or complete predicate. Underline the subject of each sentence once, and underline the verb twice. **Answers will vary.**

EXAMPLE 1. Usually, the _____ leaves on time.
1. *Usually, the north-bound train leaves on time.*

1. _____ pull sleds through the snow. **1. Horses**
2. Houseplants _____ sunlight. **2. need**
3. Several of the football players _____ the sports drink. **3. tried**
4. After sunset, the neighbor's dog _____. **4. slept peacefully**
5. During daylight savings time, Don and Beth _____ their bikes after work. **5. rode**
6. _____ arrive every day. **6. Huge ships**
7. The _____ of Congress voted against the bill. **7. majority**
8. _____ enjoyed the beautiful day. **8. Everyone**
9. Unsure of the correct direction, he _____ at the map. **9. had stared**
10. _____ laughed. **10. Dorothy and Liam**

Review B Identifying Subjects and Verbs

Identify the subject(s) and the verb(s) in each of the following sentences. If the subject is understood, write *(You)*.

EXAMPLE 1. Most birds and many insects can fly.
1. *subjects—birds, insects*
   verb—can fly

1. How do birds fly?
2. Their wings lift and push them through the air.
3. Look carefully at an insect's wings. **3. (You)**
4. Most have two sets of wings.
5. The pair in front covers the pair in back.
6. Other animals can move through the air without flying.
7. The flying fish swims fast and leaps out of the water.
8. How does the flying squirrel glide from tree to tree?

Critical Thinking

Metacognition. After students have completed **Review B,** have them analyze the process they used to identify the subjects and verbs. Did they first find the verb and then ask "Who?" or "What?" before the verb to find the subject? Did they notice anything that the difficult sentences had in common? Did they refer to the instructional material in the textbook when they had trouble with a sentence? Did they use diagramming to help them find the subjects and verbs?

Complements

Rules 13h–k (pp. 450–459)

OBJECTIVES

- To write sentences with subjects, verbs, and complements
- To identify subjects, verbs, and complements in sentences
- To identify predicate nominatives and predicate adjectives in sentences
- To identify verbs and direct objects in sentences
- To identify direct objects and indirect objects in sentences

Meeting Individual Needs

ENGLISH-LANGUAGE LEARNERS

General Strategies. English commonly uses a subject-verb-complement (SVC) sentence structure. Some other languages use a subject-complement-verb or a verb-subject-complement structure. Consequently, some of your English-language learners may need extra practice in using the SVC structure. To help these students, you may want to write several subjects, verbs, and complements on separate strips of paper and to ask students to tape the strips together to form examples of the SVC sentence structure. After students have finished, encourage them to add words to the examples to form meaningful sentences.

---

9. There are flaps of skin between its legs.
10. Because of its webbed feet, the flying frog can make long, gliding leaps through the air.

Complements

13h. A *complement* is a word or word group that completes the meaning of a verb.

A group of words may have a subject and a verb and still not express a complete thought. Notice how the boldface complements complete the meanings of the verbs in the following examples.

EXAMPLES
    S V   C
That book is an **autobiography.**

  S   V   C
Bob felt **confident.**

   S   V   C
Joey hit a **home run.**

 V   S V C   C
Did you send **her** a birthday **card**?

 S V   C
This is **what I want.**

A complement may be compound.

EXAMPLES
         S   V   C   C
Sandra Cisneros writes **poetry** and **fiction.**

  V   S   V   C   C   C
Did you buy paper **plates, cups,** and **napkins**?

A complement may be a noun, a pronoun, or an adjective.

EXAMPLES
  S   V   C
Tino wants a new tennis **racket.** [noun]

      S   V   C
Aunt Sophie watched **us** fishing. [pronoun]

          S   V   C
The elephants in the safari park appear **happy.** [adjective]

RESOURCES

Complements

Practice

- *Grammar, Usage, and Mechanics,* pp. 41, 42, 43, 44, 45, 46, 47
- *Language Workshop CD-ROM,* Lesson 25

Do not mistake an adverb for a complement.

ADVERBS	At the next intersection, should we turn **right**? [*Right* tells *where* we should turn.]
	Lucy works **hard**. [*Hard* tells *how* Lucy works.]
COMPLEMENTS	You have the **right** to express your opinion. [*Right*, a noun, completes the meaning of the verb *have*.]
	These pears are **hard**. [*Hard*, an adjective, completes the meaning of the verb *are*.]

Complements are never in prepositional phrases.

EXAMPLES   Christopher quoted from the poem. [*Poem* is part of the prepositional phrase *from the poem*.]
Christopher quoted the **poem**. [*Poem* is the complement.]

NOTE Both independent and subordinate clauses contain subjects and verbs and may contain complements.

```
                S      V        C
EXAMPLES  Although he appeared sluggish at the start,

            S     V    C
          Ricardo won the race.

           S   V    C      S      V           C
          Josie is an engineer who designs computer hardware.
```

Reference Note
For more about **adverbs**, see page 614.

Reference Note
For more about **prepositional phrases**, see page 467.

Reference Note
For information about **independent** and **subordinate clauses**, see Chapter 15.

Exercise 10   Writing Sentences with Subjects, Verbs, and Complements

Construct ten sentences from the following groups of sentence parts. Add more than only a word or two to each group.

	SUBJECT	VERB	COMPLEMENT
EXAMPLES	1. pilot	flew	mission

1. *The pilot flew a dangerous mission over Germany.*

	2. baby	became	sleepy

2. *The baby became sleepy after her bath.*

Subject	Verb	Complement
1. cyclists	planned	trip
2. musicians	performed	duet

(continued)

Crossing the Curriculum

Geometry. You may want to point out to students that the term *complement* is used in geometry to denote a relationship between two angles. Explain to students that when the sum of the measures of two angles is 90 degrees, the angles are called *complementary angles*. For example, if the measure of one angle is 30 degrees, the measure of its *complement* is 60 degrees. You may want to demonstrate this concept by drawing and labeling a pair of complementary angles on the chalkboard, or you could encourage student participation by having a volunteer draw the angles.

Exercise 10   Writing Sentences with Subjects, Verbs, and Complements

ANSWERS

Sentences will vary. Here are some possibilities.

1. The cyclists carefully planned the twenty-mile trip.
2. Famous musicians from Africa performed the duet.

Exercise 10 Writing Sentences with Subjects, Verbs, and Complements

ANSWERS continued

3. The speaker looked enthusiastic when the crowd applauded.
4. The dancer tapped the complex rhythm of the song with her feet.
5. The novel is even more suspenseful than the movie.
6. Dennis became president of the Student Honor Society.
7. My brother's tambourine sounds very funny in small rooms.
8. Great Britain's prime minister gave her first speech to Parliament.
9. The foraging raccoon ate all of the banana peels we had put in the compost pile.
10. The shivering Girl Scout built a blazing fire in only ten minutes.

Relating to Literature

Poets sometimes invert the usual subject-verb-complement order to maintain the rhyme scheme of a poem or to emphasize a particular word by placing it at the end of a line. Have students read a poem that includes at least one such inversion. Possible poems include "I Wandered Lonely as a Cloud" by William Wordsworth and "Ozymandias" by Percy Bysshe Shelley.

Have students point out any inversions of the subject-verb-complement order and discuss as a class what effect the poet achieves by using the inversions.

Timesaver

Ask students to make a chart like the one in **Exercise 10**. Have students write the answers for **Exercise 11** under the appropriate headings.

(continued)

Subject	Verb	Complement
3. speaker	looked	enthusiastic
4. dancer	tapped	rhythm
5. novel	is	suspenseful
6. Dennis	became	president
7. tambourine	sounds	funny
8. prime minister	gave	speech
9. raccoon	ate	banana peels
10. Girl Scout	built	fire

Exercise 11 Identifying Subjects, Verbs, and Complements

Identify the subject(s) and the verb(s) in the following sentences. Then, identify any complement(s) the sentence contains.

EXAMPLE
1. Have you ever seen a storm surge during a hurricane?
   1. subject—you
      verb—Have seen
      complement—storm surge

1. A hurricane is a powerful storm, often measuring two or three hundred miles in diameter.
2. Such storms are notorious for their destructive power.
3. To be classified as a hurricane, a storm must have winds of at least seventy-four miles per hour.
4. These winds swirl around the *eye,* an area of calm in the center of the storm.
5. *Wall clouds* surround the eye of a hurricane.
6. Within these clouds the strongest winds and heaviest rain of the storm occur.
7. The winds and rain, along with the force of the sea, often produce enormous waves.
8. In a storm surge, tides rise well above normal.
9. Huge waves produce floods.
10. In fact, most hurricane-related deaths result from drowning in floods.

The Subject Complement

13i. A *subject complement* is a word or word group that completes the meaning of a linking verb and identifies or modifies the subject.

EXAMPLES   We may be the only **ones** here. [*Ones,* a pronoun, completes the meaning of the linking verb *may be* and identifies the subject *We.*]

Roscoe seems **worried**. [*Worried,* an adjective, completes the meaning of the linking verb *seems* and modifies the subject *Roscoe.*]

Did you know that Lani is a soccer **player**? [*Player,* a noun, completes the meaning of the linking verb *is* and identifies the subject *Lani.*]

A subject complement may consist of more than one word.

EXAMPLES   Michelangelo's full name was **Michelangelo di Lodovico Buonarroti Simoni.** [*Michelangelo di Lodovico Buonarroti Simoni,* a compound noun, completes the meaning of the linking verb *was* and identifies the subject *name.*]

A ring with her birthstone is **what she wants for her birthday.** [*What she wants for her birthday,* a noun clause, completes the meaning of the linking verb *is* and identifies the subject *ring.*]

NOTE Subject complements complete the meanings of linking verbs only. A word that completes the meaning of an action verb is generally a direct object or an indirect object.

There are two kinds of subject complements: the *predicate nominative* and the *predicate adjective.*

(1) A *predicate nominative* is a word or word group that is in the predicate and that identifies the subject or refers to it.

EXAMPLES   Some caterpillars become **butterflies.** [*Butterflies* identifies the subject *caterpillars.*]

The winners should have been **they.** [*They* refers to the subject *winners.*]

She is the next **speaker.** [*Speaker* refers to the subject *She.*]

Reference Note

For lists of commonly used **linking verbs**, see page 419. For more about **compound nouns**, see page 406. For a discussion of **noun clauses**, see Chapter 15.

Reference Note

For more about **direct objects** and **indirect objects**, see page 456.

STYLE TIP

The use of the nominative case pronoun, as in the sentence *The winners should have been they*, is uncommon in everyday speech. You will often hear such expressions as *That's him* and *It is her.* In formal English, however, you should use the nominative case pronoun in such expressions: *That's **he*** and *It is **she.***

Reference Note

For more about the **cases of pronouns**, see Chapter 17.

Complements   **453**

Meeting INDIVIDUAL NEEDS

LEARNERS HAVING DIFFICULTY

Rule 13i states that a subject complement completes the meaning of a linking verb. Some students, however, may have difficulty identifying linking verbs. To help these students, refer them to the list of commonly used linking verbs on p. 419 of Chapter 12: Parts of Speech Overview.

Relating to Writing

Ask each student to write a short poem (about ten lines) that uses an extended metaphor to compare a storm to something else. Tell students to begin their comparisons by writing a line that includes a form of the verb *be* and a predicate nominative. Examples are *A storm is a child* or *The storm was an angry god.* Encourage students to include vivid, expressive verbs, nouns, and adjectives to strengthen their comparisons.

Relating to Writing

Have each student write a personal letter describing himself or herself to a pen pal. When they have finished writing, have students find all the subject complements in their letters and label each complement as a predicate nominative or a predicate adjective.

TIPS & TRICKS

Do not assume that every adjective in the predicate is a predicate adjective. Remember that a predicate adjective modifies only the subject.

EXAMPLES
This antique clock is **valuable**. [The adjective *valuable* is a predicate adjective because it modifies the subject *clock*.]

This antique clock is a valuable timepiece. [The adjective *valuable* is not a predicate adjective. It modifies the predicate nominative *timepiece*, not the subject *clock*.]

HELP

Some sentences in Exercise 12 have more than one subject complement.

A predicate nominative may be compound.

EXAMPLE Our cats' names are **Wimpy** and **Henry**. [*Wimpy* and *Henry* identify the subject *names*.]

A predicate nominative may precede the subject and the verb.

EXAMPLE What a fine **speaker** you are! [*Speaker* identifies the subject *you*.]

(2) A **predicate adjective** is an adjective that is in the predicate and that modifies the subject of a sentence or a clause.

EXAMPLES You look **happy**. [*Happy* modifies the subject *You*.]

When she left, Norma appeared **calm**. [*Calm* modifies the subject *Norma*.]

A predicate adjective may be compound.

EXAMPLE He said that the yogurt tasted **sweet** and **creamy**. [*Sweet* and *creamy* modify the subject *yogurt*.]

A predicate adjective may precede the subject and the verb.

EXAMPLE How **silly** that commercial is! [*Silly* modifies the subject *commercial*.]

Exercise 12 Identifying Predicate Nominatives and Predicate Adjectives

Identify the subject complements in the following sentences. Then, tell whether each complement is a *predicate nominative* or a *predicate adjective*.

EXAMPLE 1. Kimchi is a spicy Korean dish of pickled cabbage and peppers.

1. dish—predicate nominative

1. The last scene of the play is very intense.
2. Those two small birds are finches.
3. The music sounded lively.
4. It is difficult to choose a winner when each contestant's costume looks so elegant.
5. My goldfish Alonzo grows larger every day.
6. Andrea's report on digital recording is a highly detailed and technical one.
7. When did Uncas become a chief of the Mohegans?
8. Your solution to this algebra problem is clever.

454   Chapter 13   The Parts of a Sentence

9. We felt full after we had eaten Thanksgiving dinner.
10. The setting of the story is a Spanish castle that looks old and deserted.

Review C Identifying Subjects, Verbs, and Subject Complements

Each of the following sentences contains at least one subject complement. Identify each subject, verb, and subject complement. Make a chart like the following one, and fill in the correct words.

EXAMPLE   1. Jazz was originally the music of African Americans.

	SUBJECT	VERB	SUBJECT COMPLEMENT
1.	Jazz	was	music

1. The style of 1920s musicians, such as Jelly Roll Morton, was smooth.
2. With the development of swing, the rhythm of jazz became more regular.
3. Practitioners of swing became known for their solo improvisation.
4. Billie Holiday was one of those practitioners.
5. She became the greatest singer in the history of jazz.
6. A typically American musical form, jazz was the sound of Louis Armstrong, "Count" Basie, Scott Joplin, and Ella Fitzgerald.
7. Created in the early twentieth century, jazz is a blend of elements from African and European music, but its irregular, or syncopated, rhythms are strictly African.
8. Early jazz was a combination of the cakewalk, a dance that was popular with many African Americans in the 1800s, and ragtime, which was mainly instrumental music.
9. After 1917, when jazz phonograph records became popular, the future of jazz appeared bright.
10. People remain fascinated by jazz, perhaps because it sounds new with each playing.

HELP
A sentence in Review C may have more than one subject, verb, and subject complement.

The Object of a Verb

An *object of a verb* is a complement that, unlike a subject complement, does not identify or modify the subject. An object of a verb is a noun, pronoun, or word group that completes the meaning of a *transitive verb*—a verb that expresses an action directed toward a person, a place, a thing, or an idea.

Reference Note
For more about **transitive verbs**, see pages 421.

Review C Identifying Subjects, Verbs, and Subject Complements

ANSWERS

SUBJECT	VERB	SUBJECT COMPLEMENT
1. style	was	smooth
2. rhythm	became	regular
3. Practitioners	became	known
4. Billie Holiday	was	one
5. She	became	singer
6. jazz	was	sound
7. jazz	is	blend
rhythms	are	African
8. jazz	was	combination
that	was	popular
which	was	music
9. records	became	popular
future	appeared	bright
10. People	remain	fascinated
it	sounds	new

Complements 455

EXAMPLES   The cat was chasing a **moth**. [*Moth* completes the meaning of the transitive verb *was chasing*.]

Jeff's mother gave **him** some **grapes**. [*Him* and *grapes* complete the meaning of the transitive verb *gave*.]

Kevin and I enjoy **playing** chess. [*Playing,* a gerund, completes the meaning of the transitive verb *enjoy*.]

An object of a verb may consist of more than one word.

EXAMPLES   The journalist interviewed the **Secretary of State**. [*Secretary of State,* a compound noun, completes the meaning of the transitive verb *interviewed*.]

Do you know **what this is**? [*What this is,* a noun clause, completes the meaning of the transitive verb *Do know*.]

Reference Note
For more about **compound nouns**, see page 406. For more about **noun clauses**, see Chapter 15.

> **NOTE** Objects of verbs, like other kinds of complements, can appear in subordinate clauses as well as independent clauses.
>
> EXAMPLE   After she had read **us** the **story,** the teacher gave **us** a **quiz** on it. [*Us* and *story* complete the meaning of *had read* in the subordinate clause. *Us* and *quiz* complete the meaning of *gave* in the independent clause.]

Two kinds of objects of verbs are *direct objects* and *indirect objects.*

13j. A ***direct object*** **is a noun, pronoun, or word group that tells *who* or *what* receives the action of a transitive verb or shows the result of the action.**

A direct object answers the question "Whom?" or "What?" after a transitive verb.

EXAMPLES   I took my little **sister** to the movie *Mulan.* [I took whom? *Sister.*]

She had already seen **it** four times. [She had seen what? *It.*]

A direct object may be compound.

EXAMPLE   The parrot said **"Good morning"** and **"Cat free to good home."** [The parrot said what? *"Good morning"* and *"Cat free to good home."*]

A direct object may precede the subject and verb.

EXAMPLE   What remarkable **tricks** the illusionist performed! [The illusionist performed what? *Tricks.*]

Direct objects are never found in prepositional phrases.

EXAMPLES Tom was driving in his car. [*Car* is part of the prepositional phrase *in his car*. The sentence has no direct object.]

Tom was driving his **car**. [*Car* is the direct object.]

Exercise 13 Identifying Verbs and Their Direct Objects

Identify the verbs and the direct objects in the following sentences.

EXAMPLE 1. My parents recently bought a 35-mm camera.
1. verb—*bought*; direct object—*camera*

1. I borrowed my parents' new camera.
2. First, I loaded the film into the camera.
3. Then, I set the shutter speed.
4. I focused the camera on a distant object.
5. I could read the shutter speed in the viewfinder.
6. A flashing red light signals an incorrect setting.
7. Slowly and carefully, I pressed the button.
8. I then advanced the film for the next shot.
9. By the end of the day, I had snapped thirty-six pictures.
10. Have you ever taken photographs?

13k. An *indirect object* is a noun, pronoun, or word group that often appears in sentences containing direct objects. An indirect object tells *to whom* or *to what* (or *for whom* or *for what*) the action of a transitive verb is done.

EXAMPLES Meli read **us** her report. [Meli read it to whom? *Us.*]

They fed the **horses** some oats. [They fed oats to what? *Horses.*]

Juan left **you** this message. [Juan left it for whom? *You.*]

Carly knitted her pet **dachshund** a blanket. [Carly knitted it for what? *Dachshund.*]

If the word *to* or *for* is used, the noun or pronoun following it is part of a prepositional phrase and cannot be an indirect object.

PREPOSITIONAL PHRASE Jeff wrote a note to me. [*Me* is part of the prepositional phrase *to me*.]

INDIRECT OBJECT Jeff wrote **me** a note. [*Me* is the indirect object.]

---HELP---
An indirect object generally comes between a verb and a direct object.

TIPS & TRICKS

When identifying complements, check first to see whether the verbs in the sentences are action or linking verbs. Remember that only action verbs may have direct objects and indirect objects and that only linking verbs may have predicate nominatives and predicate adjectives.

TEACHING TIP

Exercise 14 Before students begin the exercise, you may want to provide the following list of verbs and to point out that these verbs commonly take both direct and indirect objects.

ask   tell   sell   cost   pay
give teach lend   send   offer

Meeting INDIVIDUAL NEEDS

LEARNERS HAVING DIFFICULTY
Write the following incomplete sentences on the chalkboard, and have students fill in each blank (a possible answer appears in brackets).

1. During the baseball game only one player hit a _____. [home run]
2. My sister helped _____ with my homework. [me]
3. Mario gives his _____ gifts on their birthdays. [friends]
4. We bought our pet _____ a new bed. [terrier]

Point out to students that the words they supply will serve as objects of the verbs in the sentences. When students have filled in the blanks, have them identify each object as either direct [sentences 1 and 2] or indirect [sentences 3 and 4].

TEACHING TIP

Review D Before students begin the exercise, you may want to direct their attention to **Tips & Tricks** on p. 457. In addition, you may want to remind them that a list of linking verbs appears in **Chapter 12: Parts of Speech Overview**, p. 419.

An indirect object may be compound.

EXAMPLE The ski trip had given **Lucia** and **me** a wonderful vacation.
[The trip had given it to whom? *Lucia* and *me*.]

Exercise 14 Identifying Direct and Indirect Objects

Identify the direct objects and indirect objects in the following sentences. Not all sentences contain indirect objects.

EXAMPLE
1. His athleticism has earned Leroy many awards.
1. direct object—awards; indirect object—Leroy

1. Last summer, Leroy told us his plans for the future.
2. He wants a place on the U.S. swim team in the next Olympic games.
3. Of course, this goal demands hours of hard practice.
4. Every day, Leroy swims one hundred laps in the college pool and works out with weights for an hour.
5. Such intense training could cost him his social life.
6. With his rigorous schedule, Leroy doesn't have much time to spend with friends.
7. However, we all understand and give him much encouragement and support.
8. We can't teach him the fine points of competitive swimming.
9. His coach does that.
10. Maybe we'll see Leroy at the next Olympics!

Review D Identifying Sentences, Fragments, Subjects, Verbs, and Complements

Identify each of the following word groups as a *sentence* or a *sentence fragment*. If a word group is a sentence, identify its subject(s) and verb(s). If a sentence has a complement, label the complement as a *predicate adjective*, a *predicate nominative*, a *direct object*, or an *indirect object*.

EXAMPLE
1. Will you be attending the Cinco de Mayo celebration?
1. sentence; subject—you; verb—will be attending; direct object—celebration

1. Has the planning committee announced the date of the school carnival? 1. sent.—d.o.
2. Perhaps next week. 2. frag.
3. Linda gave us a summary of her science project.
4. It was long and interesting. 4. sent.—p.a./p.a.

458 Chapter 13 The Parts of a Sentence

5. Books and papers covered the desk and spilled onto the floor.   5. sent.—d.o.
6. Although it was well written. **6. frag.**
7. One of those dogs is not very obedient. **7. sent.—p.a.**
8. Ming Chin gave the children a handful of oatmeal cookies.   8. sent.—i.o./d.o.
9. Kim, Juan, and Tracey were winners at the track meet last Saturday.
10. How happy they were! **10. sent.—p.a.**   9. sent.—p.n.

Classifying Sentences by Purpose

13l. Depending on its purpose, a sentence may be classified as *declarative, imperative, interrogative,* or *exclamatory.*

(1) A *declarative sentence* makes a statement and ends with a period.

EXAMPLES Toni Morrison won the Nobel Prize for literature in 1993.

Although we were tired after working all day, we still wanted to go dancing.

(2) An *imperative sentence* gives a command or makes a request. Most imperative sentences end with a period. A strong command ends with an exclamation point.

EXAMPLES Be careful. [mild command]

Please open the window. [request]

Wait! [strong command]

Notice in the examples above that a command or a request has the understood subject *you.*

(3) An *interrogative sentence* asks a question and ends with a question mark.

EXAMPLES Can you speak Spanish?

Did you say that you were taking French?

(4) An *exclamatory sentence* shows excitement or expresses strong feeling and ends with an exclamation point.

EXAMPLES What a beautiful day this is!

How I enjoy autumn!

Reference Note
For a discussion of how **sentences** are **classified by structure,** see page 504. For more on **end marks,** see Chapter 22.

STYLE TIP

Sometimes a writer will use both a question mark and an exclamation point to express the combined emotions of disbelief and surprise.

EXAMPLE
"How could you have said that?!" she gasped.

You should limit the use of such combined punctuation to informal writing and dialogue.

RESOURCES

Classifying Sentences by Purpose
Practice
- *Grammar, Usage, and Mechanics,* pp. 48, 49
- *Language Workshop CD-ROM,* Lesson 26

Review E — Understanding the Parts of a Sentence

ANSWERS

Responses will vary. Each response should include a basic definition and an example.

1. A sentence is a word group that contains a subject and a verb and that expresses a complete thought.
2. A complete subject tells whom or what the sentence or clause is about and consists of the simple subject and words or word groups that modify the simple subject.
3. A verb is the main word or word group that tells something about the subject.
4. A verb phrase consists of a main verb and one or more helping verbs.
5. A complete predicate is the part of a sentence or clause that says something about the subject and consists of the verb and all the words that modify the verb and complete its meaning.
6. A simple subject is the main word or word group that tells whom or what the sentence or clause is about.
7. A subject complement is a word or word group that completes the meaning of a linking verb and identifies or modifies the subject.
8. A direct object is a noun, pronoun, or word group that tells who or what receives the action of a transitive verb or shows the result of the action.
9. An understood subject is the unstated subject, *you,* of a request or command.
10. An indirect object is a noun, pronoun, or word group that appears in some sentences containing direct objects and tells to whom or to what (or for whom or what) the action of a transitive verb is done.

NOTE Any sentence may be spoken so that it becomes exclamatory or interrogative. When writing dialogue, use an exclamation point or a question mark to show how you intend a sentence to be read.

EXAMPLES "It's snowing." [declarative]

"It's snowing!" [exclamatory]

"It's snowing?" [interrogative]

Exercise 15 Classifying Sentences According to Purpose

Punctuate each of the following sentences with an appropriate end mark. Then, classify the sentence as *declarative*, *imperative*, *interrogative*, or *exclamatory*.

EXAMPLE 1. What kinds of music do you like

1. What kinds of music do you like?—interrogative

1. The loudspeakers in our living room are small yet powerful. **1. dec.**
2. Turn down the sound. [*or* !] **2. imp.**
3. How loud that is! **3. exc.**
4. Listening to loud music can damage a person's hearing. **4. dec.**
5. How many watts does your amplifier produce? **5. int.**
6. Sound levels are measured in units called decibels. **6. dec.**
7. Do you know that an increase of ten decibels represents a doubling in the sound level? **7. int.**
8. Do not blast your sound system. [*or* !] **8. imp.**
9. Keep it quiet! **9. imp.**
10. Music played softly is relaxing. **10. dec.**

Review E Understanding the Parts of a Sentence

In your own words, define each of the following terms, and write a sentence in which the term is illustrated.

EXAMPLE 1. a transitive verb

1. A transitive verb is an action verb that takes an object. Babe Ruth played baseball.

1. a sentence
2. a complete subject
3. a verb (simple predicate)
4. a verb phrase
5. a complete predicate
6. a simple subject

7. a subject complement 9. an understood subject
8. a direct object 10. an indirect object

Review F Identifying Subjects, Verbs, and Complements

Identify each italicized word or word group in the following paragraphs as a *subject*, a *verb*, a *predicate nominative*, a *predicate adjective*, a *direct object*, or an *indirect object*.

EXAMPLE   The photograph below shows the [1] *Great Pyramid of Khufu.*
   1. direct object

The Great Pyramid of Khufu is [1] *one* of the wonders of the ancient world. [2] *It* was once encased with blocks of polished limestone. However, [3] *weather and thievery* [4] *have combined* to destroy the original structure. As you [5] *can see,* the pyramid [6] *looks* [7] *weather-beaten.* Still, it is an impressive [8] *sight.*

Hundreds of years ago, one invading Arab [9] *ruler* decided to rob the tomb of Khufu. With many workers at his disposal, he gave the [10] *men* his [11] *instructions.* The workers [12] *hacked* through the incredibly hard solid blocks of granite. Unexpectedly, [13] *they* broke into a tunnel. Imagine their [14] *excitement*! All too soon, however, they [15] *discovered* an enormous [16] *plug* of granite blocking their way. They cut around the plug and finally reached the inner [17] *chamber.*

Strangely enough, there was no [18] *gold.* No vast treasures [19] *sparkled* under the light of the torches. The tomb probably [20] *had been robbed* many centuries earlier by Egyptians familiar with its secret entrances.

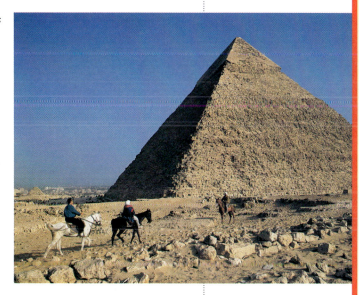

Classifying Sentences by Purpose   461

Review G Writing Sentences

Write sentences according to the following guidelines. Underline the subject once and the verb twice in each sentence. If the subject is understood, write *(You)*. Answers will vary.

EXAMPLES
1. Write a sentence containing a direct object.
1. *(You)* <u>Have</u> another glass of milk.

2. Write a sentence beginning with *Here*.
2. *Here <u>are</u> the missing puzzle <u>pieces</u>.*

1. Write a declarative sentence containing a verb phrase.
2. Write a sentence beginning with *There*.
3. Write an interrogative sentence.
4. Write an exclamatory sentence.
5. Write an imperative sentence.
6. Write a sentence containing a compound subject.
7. Write a sentence containing a predicate nominative.
8. Write a sentence containing a compound verb.
9. Write a sentence containing a predicate adjective.
10. Write a sentence containing an indirect object and a compound direct object.

Review G
Possible responses:
1. <u>I</u> <u>should have planted</u> more trees on Earth Day.
2. There <u>are</u> many <u>types</u> of plants.
3. <u>Have</u> <u>you</u> <u>studied</u> the plant life on our planet?
4. How interesting <u>plants</u> <u>are</u>!
5. (You) <u>Go</u> to the library and <u>read</u> about the types of plants in the world.
6. <u>Eucalyptuses</u> and <u>tree ferns</u> <u>can be found</u> in Australia's forests.
7. The <u>mula mula</u> <u>is</u> a plant.
8. The <u>vegetation</u> <u>grows</u> quickly and <u>forms</u> a series of distinct layers of trees of differing heights.
9. The forest <u>vegetation</u> <u>is</u> lush in tropical regions.
10. The <u>forest</u> <u>provides</u> scientists fascinating plants and ecosystems to study.

CHAPTER 13

Chapter Review

A. Identifying Subjects, Verbs, and Complements

Identify the italicized word or word group in each of the following sentences as a *subject*, a *verb*, a *predicate adjective*, a *predicate nominative*, a *direct object*, or an *indirect object*.

1. Native *cactuses* in the Southwest are in trouble. **1. s.**
2. Some species are already *vulnerable* to extinction. **2. p.a.**
3. Cactuses *are being threatened* by landscapers, tourists, and collectors. **3. v.**
4. Many people illegally harvest these wild *plants*. **4. d.o.**
5. There are many unique cactus *species* in Arizona. **5. s.**
6. Arizona is, therefore, an active *battlefield* in the war against the removal of these endangered species. **6. p.n.**
7. "Cactus cops" *patrol* the streets of Phoenix on the lookout for places with illegally acquired cactuses. **7. v.**
8. Authorized dealers must give *purchasers* permit tags as proof of legal sale. **8. i.o.**
9. First violations are *punishable* by a fine of five hundred dollars. **9. p.a.**
10. Illegally owned cactuses *may be confiscated* by the police. **10. v.**
11. What a thorny problem cactus *rustling* has become! **11. s.**
12. Why are illegal harvesters so *hard* to keep track of? **12. p.a.**
13. Many work at night and sometimes use permit *tags* over and over. **13. d.o.**
14. If you purchase a large cactus, always *examine* it for bruises. **14. v.**
15. A legally harvested cactus *should* not *show* any damage. **15. v.**

B. Identifying Subjects and Predicates

Identify the complete subjects and complete predicates in each of the following sentences.

16. The invention of motion pictures | is attributed to many people.
17. Chief among the inventors | are the French brothers Auguste and Louis Lumière.
18. A laboratory assistant of Thomas Edison named Dickson | had invented a type of simple "peep-hole" viewing device called the Kinetoscope.
19. The Edison-Dickson Kinetoscope | was displayed in Paris in 1894.

HELP
A sentence in Part B may contain more than one subject and predicate.

Using the Chapter Review

To assess student progress, you may want to compare the types of items missed on the **Diagnostic Preview** with those missed on the **Chapter Review.** You may want to work out specific goals with individual students who are still having difficulty mastering essential information.

20. Auguste and Louis were determined to improve upon it.
21. In 1895, their determination paid off, and the *cinématographe* was patented.
22. The *cinématographe* functioned as a camera and printer as well as a projector.
23. Everyday French life in the 1890s can be glimpsed in the Lumière brothers' first films.
24. Their 1895 film "Workers Leaving the Lumière Factory" is considered the first motion picture.
25. Ironically, *Lumière* means "light."

C. Completing Sentences by Supplying Subjects and Verbs

Complete each of the following sentences with an appropriate subject or verb. Identify your answer as a *subject* or a *verb*. Answers will vary.

26. run—verb
27. met—verb
28. Indians—sub.
29. cried—verb
30. returned—verb
31. Roofs—sub.
32. need—verb
33. howled—verb
34. Grandpa—sub.
35. draws—sub.

26. Greyhounds ____ races.
27. A few of the sophomores ____ after class.
28. Many ____ of the Great Plains were nomadic.
29. The audience ____ at the deathbed scene.
30. To get out of the maze, he ____ to where he had started.
31. ____ came tumbling down in the gale.
32. Dogs ____ to be walked regularly.
33. The wind ____ through the branches.
34. ____ smiled.
35. Every day after school, Maggie ____ pictures.

HELP—
A sentence in Part D may contain more than one subject complement.

D. Identifying Predicate Nominatives and Predicate Adjectives

Write each subject complement in the following sentences, and then identify it as a *predicate nominative* or a *predicate adjective*.

36. We felt exhausted after the marathon. **36. p.a.**
37. Sitting in the shade was pleasant when the sunlight was so intense. **37. p.a./p.a.**
38. Those dogs are Dalmatians. **38. p.n.**
39. Your explanation is very clear. **39. p.a.**
40. My colleague Eric grows calmer every day. **40. p.a.**
41. Abdullah II became king of Jordan in February, 1999. **41. p.n.**
42. Our neighbor Gary's new car is a very sleek and sporty model. **42. p.n.**

RESOURCES

The Parts of a Sentence

Review
- *Grammar, Usage, and Mechanics,* pp. 50, 51, 52, 53

Assessment
- *Assessment Package*
  —Chapter Tests, Ch. 13
  —Chapter Tests in Standardized Test Formats, Ch. 13
- *Test Generator (One-Stop Planner CD-ROM)*

43. The painting looked <u>somber</u>. **43.** p.a.
44. The first part of the movie is very <u>funny</u>. **44.** p.a.
45. Their apartment is in a building that looks <u>new</u> and <u>clean</u>. **45.** p.a./p.a.

E. Classifying Sentences as Declarative, Interrogative, Imperative, or Exclamatory

Classify each of the following sentences as *declarative*, *interrogative*, *imperative*, or *exclamatory*.

46. Read this article about imperiled cactuses. **46.** imp.
47. The author describes a trip into the desert with a legal hauler. **47.** dec.
48. Can you imagine a saguaro worth three hundred dollars? **48.** int.
49. A crested saguaro is even rarer and can sell for thousands of dollars. **49.** dec.
50. No wonder illegal harvesting is booming! **50.** exc.

Writing Application
Using Varied Sentences in a Letter

Sentence Variety Your neighborhood Residents' Council would like to sponsor a dance for the teenagers in your area. However, the council is not sure what kind of dance teens would like. You have decided to write a short letter to the council to give your opinion.

Prewriting Decide how you feel about this issue. Then, jot down a few notes about what kind of dance you would like to have. Next, write some different opening sentences. Choose the opener that you think will be the most interesting and effective.

Writing As you write your letter, refer often to your prewriting notes. Use a variety of sentence structures.

Revising Ask an adult you know to listen to your letter. Does he or she think your opening sentence is interesting? Does he or she find your letter persuasive? Revise any sections that are unclear or that lack sentence variety.

Publishing Proofread your letter for any errors in grammar, punctuation, and spelling. You and your classmates may want to post the letter on the class bulletin board or Web page.

Writing Application
(p. 465)

OBJECTIVE

- To write a short letter using a variety of sentence structures

Writing Application

Tip. Ask students to brainstorm possible opening sentences that will catch their readers' attention. Remind students that the flow of ideas is the most important element of brainstorming. Encourage students to generate as many ideas as possible and wait until later to evaluate them. For an example of persuasive writing, refer students to **A Student's Model** in **Chapter 7: Persuading Others,** p. 275.

Scoring Rubric. While you will want to pay particular attention to students' use of subjects, predicates, and complements, you will also want to evaluate overall writing performance. You may want to give a split score to indicate development and clarity of the composition as well as grammar skills.

RESOURCES
Writing Application
Extension
- *Grammar, Usage, and Mechanics,* p. 56
- *Language Workshop CD-ROM,* Lessons 24–26

**Writing Application
Alignments**
TEKS 1A, 1B, 2A, 2C, 2E, 3D
TAAS W1, W3, W7
English II End-of-Course 4, 5, 6

Texas Resources
- One-Stop Planner CD-ROM

CHAPTER

PREVIEWING THE CHAPTER

- This chapter focuses on defining and illustrating various kinds of phrases: prepositional, verbal, and appositive. In addition, the chapter provides students with opportunities to practice identifying and using each kind of phrase.

- The chapter closes with a **Chapter Review** including a **Writing Application** feature that asks students to write a short news article, using at least three verbal phrases and three appositive phrases.

- For help integrating the chapter with writing chapters, use the **Teaching Strands** chart on pp. T401A–T401B.

USING THE DIAGNOSTIC PREVIEW

- The **Diagnostic Preview** asks students to identify prepositional, participial, gerund, infinitive, and appositive phrases in paragraphs. You can use the results of the **Diagnostic Preview** to determine how you will organize your presentation of the material in **Chapter 14**.

CHAPTER 14

The Phrase
Prepositional, Verbal, and Appositive Phrases

Diagnostic Preview

Identifying Prepositional, Verbal, and Appositive Phrases

Identify each italicized phrase in the following paragraphs as a *prepositional* phrase, a *participial* phrase, a *gerund* phrase, an *infinitive* phrase, or an *appositive* phrase.

EXAMPLES An interesting profession [1] *to consider as a career* is [2] *practicing law.*

1. to consider as a career—infinitive phrase
2. practicing law—gerund phrase

HELP—
For items in the Diagnostic Preview, you do not need to identify separately a prepositional phrase that is part of another phrase.

1. app.   2. inf.
3. prep.
4. prep.
5. part.
6. ger.
7. app.
8. ger.
9. inf.   10. inf.
11. part.
12. part.   13. inf.
14. prep.

Susana, [1] *our next-door neighbor,* wanted [2] *to become an attorney.* After she earned a degree [3] *from a four-year college,* she took the Law School Admissions Test and was admitted [4] *to a prominent law school.* [5] *Having completed three full years of law school,* Susana was then awarded a J.D. degree. Before [6] *practicing law,* however, she took the state bar exam, [7] *a test required by the state board of bar examiners.* Only after [8] *passing this exam* had she completed the requirements [9] *to be admitted to the bar* and [10] *to practice law.*

[11] *Working as an attorney,* Susana provides service and advice [12] *relating to legal rights.* Even though she tries hard [13] *to keep cases out of court,* Susana enjoys the challenge [14] *of presenting cases*

466 Chapter 14 The Phrase

CHAPTER RESOURCES

Planning
- One-Stop Planner CD-ROM

Practice and Extension
- *Grammar, Usage, and Mechanics,* p. 57
- *Language Workshop CD-ROM*

Internet
- go.hrw.com (keyword: EOLang)

Evaluation and Assessment
- *Assessment Package*
  —*Chapter Tests,* Ch. 14
  —*Chapter Tests in Standardized Test Formats,* Ch. 14
- *Test Generator* (One-Stop Planner CD-ROM)

to a jury. **[15]** *Representing a client in court,* however, is only part **[16]** *of Susana's job.* She devotes hours to **[17]** *gathering enough evidence* **[18]** *to defend a client.* She also spends time **[19]** *on research* and is required **[20]** *to write numerous reports.*

15. ger.   16. prep.
17. ger.
18. inf.   19. prep.
20. inf.

What Is a Phrase?

14a. A *phrase* is a group of related words that is used as a single part of speech and that does not contain both a verb and its subject.

PREPOSITIONAL PHRASE   for you and her [no subject or verb]
INFINITIVE PHRASE   to be the best [no subject or verb]

NOTE A group of words that has both a subject and a verb is called a *clause.*

EXAMPLES   They will be here soon. [*They* is the subject of *will be.*]

after she leaves [*She* is the subject of *leaves.*]

Reference Note
For more about **clauses,** see Chapter 15.

Prepositional Phrases

14b. A *prepositional phrase* includes a preposition, the object of the preposition, and any modifiers of that object.

EXAMPLES   A koala is a marsupial, a mammal **with an external abdominal pouch.** [The noun *pouch* is the object of the preposition *with.*]

To me a koala looks **like a cuddly teddy bear.** [The pronoun *me* is the object of the preposition *To.* The compound noun *teddy bear* is the object of the preposition *like.*]

Koalas, **along with several other marsupials,** are native **to Australia.** [The noun *marsupials* is the object of the compound preposition *along with.* The noun *Australia* is the object of the preposition *to.*]

Reference Note
For lists of **commonly used prepositions,** see page 426.

NOTE Do not confuse a prepositional phrase beginning with *to*—as in *to me* or *to Australia*—with an infinitive, such as *to be* or *to learn.*

Reference Note
For more on **infinitives,** see page 479.

Prepositional Phrases   **467**

Prepositional Phrases
Rules 14b–d (pp. 467–471)

OBJECTIVES

- To identify adjective phrases and the words they modify in sentences
- To identify adverb phrases and the words they modify in sentences

RESOURCES

Prepositional Phrases
Practice
- *Grammar, Usage, and Mechanics,* pp. 58, 59, 60, 61, 62
- *Language Workshop CD-ROM,* Lesson 19

The Phrase, pp. 466–488
Alignments
TEKS 3C, 3D
TAAS W3, W5
English II End-of-Course 5, 6

Texas Resources
- *TAAS Tool Kit*
- *Preparation for TAAS*
- *One-Stop Planner CD-ROM*

Prepositional Phrases   **467**

Meeting INDIVIDUAL NEEDS

GRAMMAR

LEARNERS HAVING DIFFICULTY
To reinforce the correct use of prepositions, organize students into pairs and give each partner a similar set of pictures, such as those from a comic strip. (Each student's set should have one and only one picture that exactly matches one in his or her partner's set.) After instructing each student to look at only his or her own set of pictures, have partners ask questions about each other's pictures—for example, "Where are Snoopy and Charlie Brown?" Have partners respond by using sentences with prepositional phrases—for example, "Snoopy is lying *on his doghouse,* and Charlie Brown is standing *in front of the doghouse.*" Have students continue the activity until they have discovered which picture is the same in both sets. Point out to students that they were able to identify the cartoon they had in common by the use of prepositional phrases.

TIPS & TRICKS
Unlike single-word adjectives, adjective phrases almost always follow the noun or pronoun they modify.

HELP
Remember that adjective phrases modify only nouns or pronouns.

An object of a preposition may be compound.

EXAMPLE   Koalas feed **on only eucalyptus buds and leaves.** [The nouns *buds* and *leaves* are the compound object of the preposition *on.*]

Adjective Phrases

14c. A prepositional phrase that modifies a noun or a pronoun is called an **adjective phrase.**

An adjective phrase tells *what kind* or *which one.*

EXAMPLES   We ordered a dish **of salsa** and a basket **of tortilla chips.** [*Of salsa* modifies the noun *dish,* telling *what kind* of dish. *Of tortilla chips* modifies the noun *basket,* telling *what kind* of basket.]

No one **in the class** has seen the movie yet. [*In the class* modifies the pronoun *no one,* telling *which one.*]

Two or more adjective phrases may modify the same noun or pronoun.

EXAMPLE   The picture **of their candidate in today's newspaper** is not at all flattering. [Both *of their candidate* and *in today's newspaper* modify the noun *picture.*]

An adjective phrase may also modify the object of another prepositional phrase.

EXAMPLE   The coconut palms in the park **near the bay** were planted a long time ago. [*Near the bay* modifies *park,* the object of the preposition *in.*]

Exercise 1   Identifying Adjective Phrases

Identify the <u>adjective phrase</u>(s) in each of the following sentences. After each adjective phrase, give the <u>word it modifies</u>.

EXAMPLE   1. Julius Caesar was one of the most successful generals in ancient Rome.

1. *of the most successful generals*—*one*
   in ancient Rome—*generals*

1. Roman roads were one reason for Caesar's military successes.
2. The roads of ancient Rome linked the far corners of the empire.
3. Large blocks of hard stone provided a sound foundation for most major routes.
4. Caesar's interest in military roads showed his understanding of the vital importance of communication.
5. Close communication among the empire's provinces strengthened the power of the Roman rulers.
6. The need for roads was addressed in 312 B.C., when the 160-mile Via Appia was begun.
7. The curved surfaces of the road system facilitated drainage.
8. Heavy use of the highways lasted many centuries.
9. Some roads from the old empire still exist.
10. The Romans built nearly 50,000 miles of roads crossing Europe.

Adverb Phrases

14d. A prepositional phrase that modifies a verb, an adjective, or an adverb is called an *adverb phrase*.

EXAMPLES The mole burrowed **under the lawn.** [*Under the lawn* modifies the verb *burrowed.*]

Althea Gibson was graceful **on the tennis court.** [*On the tennis court* modifies the adjective *graceful.*]

The child speaks quite clearly **for a two-year-old.** [*For a two-year-old* modifies the adverb *clearly.*]

Adverb phrases tell *when, where, why, how,* or *to what extent* (*how much, how long,* or *how far*).

EXAMPLES **After the storm,** the town grew quiet. [*when*]

He glanced **out the window.** [*where*]

Most street musicians play **for tips.** [*why*]

This summer we're going **by car** to Kansas. [*how*]

She won the contest **by two points.** [*to what extent*]

STYLE TIP

Be sure to place prepositional phrases carefully so that they express the meaning you intend.

MISPLACED
In its nest at the top of the tree, we could see the great blue heron with binoculars. [The sentence suggests that we are in the heron's nest at the top of the tree and that the heron has binoculars.]

IMPROVED
With binoculars, we could see the great blue heron **in its nest at the top of the tree.**

Reference Note

For more about **misplaced modifiers,** see pages 627.

Adverb phrases may come before or after the words they modify, and more than one adverb phrase may modify the same word.

EXAMPLE **In the first inning** she pitched **with great control.** [*In the first inning* modifies the verb *pitched*, telling *when*; *with great control* modifies *pitched*, telling *how*.]

Exercise 2   Identifying Adverb Phrases

Identify the adverb phrases in the following sentences.

EXAMPLE 1. The plane taxied down the runway.
         1. down the runway

HELP—
Some sentences in Exercise 2 contain more than one adverb phrase.

1. The porters hiked toward the summit.
2. The chicken walked across the road.
3. During Ramadan, Muslims fast from sunrise to sunset.
4. Tamara and Dawn floated down the river on a raft.
5. We walked past many beautiful meadows and streams.
6. Beneath the waves, the ocean is calm.
7. We flew across the international date line.
8. After dinner, everyone slept.
9. Spinning out of control, we tumbled into the powdery snow and, laughing, brushed ourselves off.
10. The kayakers rested beside the river.

Exercise 3   Identifying Adverb Phrases

Identify the adverb phrase(s) in each of the following sentences. Then, give the word or word group the phrase modifies.

EXAMPLE 1. For several months no one has lived in the house next to ours.
         1. For several months—has lived
            in the house—has lived

HELP—
Remember that adverb phrases modify only verbs, adjectives, or adverbs. A prepositional phrase that modifies a noun or pronoun is an adjective phrase.

1. On Friday, Dad and I were alarmed by plaintive sounds that came from the abandoned house.
2. We searched inside the whole house, from the dusty attic to the cold, damp basement.
3. In the basement we found two stray kittens.
4. They were crying for food.

Meeting INDIVIDUAL NEEDS

LEARNERS HAVING DIFFICULTY
Ask students to find prepositional phrases in sources they enjoy reading. You may want to set a time limit or require them to find a specific number of phrases. Then, have students write each phrase and indicate whether it tells *which one, what kind, when, where,* or *to what extent.* Have students use the questions to help them classify the prepositional phrases as *adjective* or *adverb.*

5. The noises we'd heard had been made by them.
6. I found an empty box in the corner and gently placed both of the kittens in it.
7. They seemed happy with their temporary home.
8. Then, we took the kittens to our house.
9. We lined the box with some soft, old towels and set it in the warm kitchen.
10. Now the plaintive sounds come from our house at all hours of the night and day.

Review A — Sentences with Prepositional Phrases

Provide a prepositional phrase to complete each of the following sentences. After the sentence, identify the phrase as an *adjective phrase* or an *adverb phrase*. Answers will vary.

EXAMPLE   1. _____ Mrs. Bowen reads the newspaper.
1. In the evening Mrs. Bowen reads the newspaper.—adverb phrase

1. I watched a spider climb _____.   1. up the drainpipe—adv.
2. _____ the children played hopscotch.   2. In the park—adv.
3. We planned a drive _____.   3. to Grandmother's house—adj.
4. Her team played _____.   4. after ours—adv.
5. The sky divers jumped fearlessly _____.   5. from the plane—adv.
6. Hundreds _____ stared.   6. of people—adj.
7. _____ the cyclists unpacked their lunches.   7. At the rest area—adv.
8. There _____ winds a narrow road.   8. in the outback—adv.
9. This movie will be playing _____.   9. during the week—adv.
10. _____ the dancers swayed with the music.   10. Around the dance floor—adv.
11. Katherine always finishes her homework _____.   11. on time—adv.
12. _____, the children found some coins.   12. On the sidewalk—adv.
13. The beans _____ are very fresh.   13. in this bowl—adj.
14. Bao wrote a book _____.   14. about zebras—adj.
15. The group was silent _____.   15. for three minutes—adv.
16. Alice went _____.   16. through the looking glass—adv.
17. Everyone _____ was cheering.   17. in the stadium—adj.
18. We traveled _____ to the river.   18. on foot—adv.
19. The trees _____ are growing fast.   19. in their yard—adj.
20. The children _____ are being very cautious.   20. on that team—adj.

GRAMMAR

The Participle and the Participial Phrase

Rules 14e, f (pp. 472–476)

OBJECTIVES

- To revise sentences by adding participles
- To identify participial phrases and the words they modify in sentences

Meeting INDIVIDUAL NEEDS

ENGLISH-LANGUAGE LEARNERS

Spanish. The English present participle suffix *–ing* is equivalent to the Spanish *–ando* and *–iendo* (for example, *hablando,* "speaking," from *hablar,* "to speak," and *comiendo,* "eating," from *comer,* "to eat"). The English past participle suffix *–(e)d* is equivalent to the Spanish *–ado* and *–ido* (for example, *marcado,* "marked," and *adquirido,* "acquired"). In English and in Spanish, past participles can be used as adjectives.

Portuguese and French. The English *–ing* suffix corresponds to *–ando, –endo,* and *–indo* in Portuguese and *–ant* in French; the English *–(e)d* suffix corresponds to *–ado* and *–ido* in Portuguese and *–é(e)* in French.

Verbals and Verbal Phrases

Verbals are formed from verbs and are used as adjectives, nouns, or adverbs. The three kinds of verbals are the *participle,* the *gerund,* and the *infinitive.*

A **verbal phrase** consists of a verbal and its modifiers and complements. The three kinds of verbal phrases are the *participial phrase,* the *gerund phrase,* and the *infinitive phrase.*

The Participle

14e. A *participle* is a verb form that can be used as an adjective.

EXAMPLES   What is the temperature of the **boiling** water? [*Boiling,* formed from the verb *boil,* modifies the noun *water.*]

A **chipped** fingernail can be annoying. [*Chipped,* formed from the verb *chip,* modifies the noun *fingernail.*]

Your **chosen** topic is too broad, I think. [*Chosen,* formed from the verb *choose,* modifies the noun *topic.*]

Two kinds of participles are *present participles* and *past participles.*

(1) Present participles end in *–ing.*

EXAMPLES   The **smiling** graduates posed for the photographer. [*Smiling,* formed from the verb *smile,* modifies the noun *graduates.*]

For an hour we sat there **reminiscing.** [*Reminiscing,* formed from the verb *reminisce,* modifies the pronoun *we.*]

Standing and **applauding,** the audience cheered the cast of the musical *The Lion King.* [*Standing,* formed from the verb *stand,* and *applauding,* formed from the verb *applaud,* modify the noun *audience.*]

Reference Note

For lists of commonly used **irregular past participles,** see page 576.

(2) Most *past participles* end in *–d* or *–ed.* Some are formed irregularly.

EXAMPLES   For dinner we prepared **grilled** salmon, **baked** potatoes, and **tossed** salad. [*Grilled,* formed from the verb *grill,* modifies the noun *salmon; baked,* formed from the verb *bake,* modifies the noun *potatoes;* and *tossed,* formed from the verb *toss,* modifies the noun *salad.*]

RESOURCES

The Participle and the Participial Phrase
Practice
- *Grammar, Usage, and Mechanics,* pp. 63, 64, 65
- *Language Workshop CD-ROM,* Lesson 20

For years the treasure had remained **hidden** under tons of **fallen** rock. [*Hidden,* formed from the verb *hide,* modifies the noun *treasure; fallen,* formed from the verb *fall,* modifies the noun *rock.*]

> **NOTE** Do not confuse a participle used as an adjective with a participle used as part of a verb phrase.
>
> ADJECTIVE   The shrimp gumbo, **simmering** on the stove, smelled delicious.
> VERB PHRASE The shrimp gumbo **was simmering** on the stove.

Reference Note
For more about **verb phrases,** see pages 417 and 441.

Exercise 4 Revising Sentences by Adding Participles

After each of the following sentences is a participle in parentheses. Revise each sentence by inserting the participle next to the noun it modifies.

Answers may vary slightly.

EXAMPLE 1. We collected funds for the restoration of the building. (*damaged*)
         1. We collected funds for the restoration of the damaged building.

1. The space shuttle was greeted with loud cheers. (*returning*)
2. The parents named shows they found unacceptable. (*protesting*)
3. My sister did not hear the doorbell. (*ringing*)
4. The carpenter will show us how to fix this chair. (*broken*)
5. In 1949, Luis Muñoz Marín became Puerto Rico's first governor. (*elected*)
6. The stream crosses the farmer's land at three places. (*winding*)
7. We handed the envelope to the mail carrier. (*crumpled*)
8. This book includes many interesting facts about dinosaurs. (*illustrated*)
9. The Douglas fir behind our house has become a haven for several small creatures. (*fallen*)
10. The plane narrowly missed a radio antenna. (*circling*)

The Participial Phrase

14f. A *participial phrase* consists of a participle and any modifiers or complements the participle has. The entire phrase is used as an adjective.

Meeting INDIVIDUAL NEEDS

MODALITIES

Auditory Learners. To reinforce students' understanding of participles, write on separate strips of paper each of the following commands. Divide the class into groups of four students each. Then, make enough copies so that each group of four receives a full set.

1. Use the present participle of <u>win</u> as an adjective.
2. Use the present participle of <u>win</u> as part of a verb phrase.
3. Use the present participle of <u>dance</u> as an adjective.
4. Use the present participle of <u>dance</u> as part of a verb phrase.
5. Use the past participle of <u>pave</u> as an adjective.
6. Use the past participle of <u>pave</u> as part of a verb phrase.
7. Use the past participle of <u>toss</u> as an adjective.
8. Use the past participle of <u>toss</u> as part of a verb phrase.

Ask students to take turns drawing from the set and stating sentences using the verb forms as specified. Have group members who are listening to the sentence determine whether the verb form is used as an adjective or as part of a verb phrase.

Verbals and Verbal Phrases   473

MINI-LESSON   *Continued on p. 474*

Punctuating Participial Phrases. Explain to students that a participial phrase containing information that could be omitted without changing the meaning of the sentence is considered *nonessential* and is set off by commas. A participial phrase containing information that is needed to understand the main idea of the sentence is considered *essential* and is not set off by commas. An essential phrase could not be

| STYLE TIP |

When writing a sentence that contains a participial phrase, be sure to place the phrase as close as possible to the word or words it modifies.

MISPLACED The Scouts spotted the white-tailed deer and her twin fawns gathering wood for a campfire. [The sentence suggests that the deer and her two fawns are gathering wood.]

IMPROVED **Gathering wood for a campfire,** the Scouts spotted the white-tailed deer and her twin fawns.

Reference Note

For more information on the correct **placement of participial phrases,** see page 355. See page 711 for more on the **punctuation of participial phrases.**

Reference Note

For more information about **using commas with participial phrases,** see page 711.

In each of the following sentences, an arrow connects the participial phrase with the noun or pronoun the phrase modifies.

EXAMPLES **Climbing the tree,** the monkey disappeared into the branches. [The participial phrase modifies the noun *monkey*. The noun *tree* is the direct object of the present participle *Climbing*.]

I heard him **whispering to his friend.** [The participial phrase modifies the pronoun *him*. The adverb phrase *to his friend* modifies the present participle *whispering*.]

We watched the storm **blowing eastward.** [The participial phrase modifies the noun *storm*. The adverb *eastward* modifies the present participle *blowing*.]

Voted back into office, the mayor thanked her supporters. [The participial phrase modifies the noun *mayor*. The adverb *back* and the adverb phrase *into office* modify the past participle *Voted*.]

The concert **scheduled for tomorrow at the park** has been postponed until next week. [The participial phrase modifies the noun *concert*. The adverb phrases *for tomorrow* and *at the park* modify the past participle *scheduled*.]

NOTE When placed at the beginning of a sentence, a participial phrase is followed by a comma.

Exercise 5 Identifying Participial Phrases

Each of the following sentences contains at least one participial phrase. Identify each participial phrase and the word or words it modifies.

EXAMPLE 1. Robert Scott, commanding a British expedition to the South Pole, learned that another expedition was ahead of him.
 1. commanding a British expedition to the South Pole—Robert Scott

1. Hoping to be the first to reach the South Pole, Robert Scott (back row, center, in the photograph on the next page) took these four men with him on his final dash to the pole in November 1911.

474 Chapter 14 The Phrase

MINI-LESSON

omitted without changing the meaning of the sentence, for the phrase tells *which one(s) of two or more*. Finally, point out that an introductory participial phrase is always followed by a comma, whether the phrase is essential or nonessential.

If students need more information on punctuating participial phrases, refer them to **Chapter 22: Punctuation**.

2. Leading Scott, a British explorer, by sixty miles, a Norwegian expedition commanded by Roald Amundsen was moving swiftly, however.
3. Learning about Amundsen, Scott realized a race to the pole was on.
4. Plagued by bad weather and bad luck, Scott fell farther behind Amundsen.
5. Reaching the pole on January 17, the British found that the Norwegians had already been there.
6. Weakened by scurvy, frostbite, and exhaustion, the five explorers in the photograph set out on the eight-hundred-mile journey back to their base camp.
7. One member of the party, overcome by exhaustion and injuries, died before half the journey had been completed.
8. On March 15 another member, leaving the camp at night, crawled deliberately to his death in a violent blizzard.
9. Eight months later, a rescue mission, sent to find out what had happened, found the bodies of Scott and his companions.
10. Today, the ill-fated Scott expedition, acclaimed for its heroism, is more famous than the successful Amundsen expedition.

The Granger Collection, New York.

Review B Identifying Participles

Identify the participial phrases and the participles that are used as adjectives in the following sentences. Give the noun or pronoun each participle or participial phrase modifies.

HELP—
Sentences in Review B may contain more than one participle or participial phrase.

EXAMPLE   1. We have been studying one of the most feared animals in the sea—the killer whale.
   1. feared—animals

1. Killer whales, long known and feared as wolves of the sea, are not nearly as vicious as many people have thought.
2. Seeking to test the supposedly ferocious nature of the killer whale, scientists studied the whales' behavior.
3. After extensive study, scientists discovered that there is no proven case of an attack on a human by a killer whale.
4. In fact, scientists working with killer whales have confirmed that their charges are intelligent and can be quite gentle.
5. Most killer whales gathered in Johnstone Strait, which is a narrow channel between Vancouver Island and British Columbia in Canada, spend the summer and fall in large family groups.

Exercise 5

ALTERNATIVE LESSON
You may want to use **Exercise 5** to reinforce students' understanding of prepositional phrases. Have students point out the prepositional phrase that is part of the participial phrase in each of the following sentences from **Exercise 5**:

- sentence 4 [*by bad weather and bad luck*]
- sentence 5 [*on January 17*]
- sentence 8 [*at night*]
- sentence 10 [*for its heroism*]

Then, ask students to tell how each of the prepositional phrases is used. [*Each is used as an adverb modifying the participle in the participial phrase.*]

Meeting INDIVIDUAL NEEDS

LEARNERS HAVING DIFFICULTY
Identifying participial phrases may be difficult for some students. To give students extra practice in distinguishing participles used as adjectives from participles used as parts of verb phrases, hand out copies of a newspaper or magazine article and have students circle all the participles. Then, ask students to use the list of helping verbs on p. 417 to help them identify which of the participles they circled are used as adjectives and which are parts of verb phrases.

GRAMMAR

The Gerund and the Gerund Phrase
Rules 14g, h (pp. 476–479)

OBJECTIVES

- To identify gerunds and to tell how they are used in sentences
- To identify participles and the words they modify in sentences
- To complete sentences by adding gerunds or gerund phrases

TEACHING TIP

As you discuss with students the examples for **Rule 14g,** you may want to present the following ways for finding sentence parts:

1. Subject—Ask "What?" before the main verb.
2. Predicate Nominative—Ask "What?" after the main linking verb.
3. Direct Object—Ask "What?" after the main action verb.
4. Indirect Object—Ask "To or for whom or what?" after the main action verb.
5. Object of a Preposition—Ask "What?" after a preposition.

Reference Note

For more about **subjects,** see page 440. For more about **predicate nominatives,** see page 453. For more about **direct** and **indirect objects,** see page 456. For more about **objects of prepositions,** see page 467.

6. Choosing this spot to observe the mammals, researchers were able to identify more than one hundred whales.
7. The team of scientists, noting the unique shape of each whale's dorsal fin, named each whale in order to keep more accurate records.
8. Impressed by the long life span of killer whales, scientists have estimated that males may live fifty years and females may survive a century.
9. Cruising in groups called pods, most killer whales are highly social animals.
10. During the summer and fall in Johnstone Strait, many pods gather, splashing and playing in "superpods."

The Gerund

14g. A *gerund* is a verb form that ends in *–ing* and that is used as a noun.

A gerund can be used as a subject, a predicate nominative, a direct object, an indirect object, or an object of a preposition.

SUBJECT	**Reading** will improve your vocabulary. [*Reading,* formed from the verb *read,* is the subject of the verb *will improve.*]
PREDICATE NOMINATIVE	One popular summer sport is **swimming.** [*Swimming,* formed from the verb *swim,* is a predicate nominative identifying the subject *sport.*]
DIRECT OBJECT	Both Dad and Mom enjoy **cooking** together. [*Cooking,* formed from the verb *cook,* is the direct object of the verb *enjoy.*]
INDIRECT OBJECT	Before she decided to become a lawyer, she had given **teaching** thoughtful consideration. [*Teaching,* formed from the verb *teach,* is the indirect object of the verb *had given.*]
OBJECT OF A PREPOSITION	After **studying,** how do you relax? [*Studying,* formed from the verb *study,* is the object of the preposition *After.*]

476 Chapter 14 The Phrase

RESOURCES

The Gerund and the Gerund Phrase
Practice
- *Grammar, Usage, and Mechanics,* pp. 66, 67, 68, 69
- *Language Workshop CD-ROM,* Lesson 20

NOTE Gerunds, like present participles, end in *–ing*. Do not confuse a gerund, which is used as a noun, with a present participle, which may be used as an adjective or as part of a verb phrase.

GERUND I have enjoyed **reading** about the different species of dinosaurs. [*Reading* is used as the direct object of the verb *have enjoyed*.]

PRESENT PARTICIPLE I have spent several hours in the library, **reading** about different species of dinosaurs. [*Reading* is used as an adjective modifying the pronoun *I*.]

PRESENT PARTICIPLE I have been **reading** about the different species of dinosaurs. [*Reading* is used as part of the verb phrase *have been reading*.]

Exercise 6 Identifying Gerunds and Participles

Identify the verbal in each of the following sentences, and tell whether it is a *gerund* or a *participle*. If the verbal is a gerund, tell how it is used: as a *subject*, a *predicate nominative*, a *direct object*, an *indirect object*, or an *object of a preposition*. If the verbal is a participle, tell which word it modifies.

EXAMPLES
1. Sleeping on the job is foolish.
1. *Sleeping, gerund—subject*

2. Let sleeping dogs lie.
2. *sleeping, participle—dogs*

1. Their giggling annoyed the other viewers. **1.** s.
2. Virginia gave cycling a try. **2.** i.o.
3. Sneezing, the enemy scout revealed his location.
4. Fascinated, my sister asked to hear more about our wild plot.
5. Making friends in a new school can be difficult, but I am getting better at it. **5.** s.
6. The highlight of the season was watching our team win the regional tournament. **6.** p.n.
7. Spinning one full turn, the ballerina gracefully performed a pirouette.
8. During the summer, Carlota sometimes makes money by walking dogs for her neighbors. **8.** o.p.
9. My grandmother and I enjoy digging for clams. **9.** d.o.
10. Sensing the danger nearby, he shouted for help.

TEACHING TIP

Activity. Since both gerunds and present participles end with *–ing*, you may want to share with students the following tip for distinguishing between these kinds of verbals or between their phrases:

If a pronoun such as *it* or *that* can be substituted for the word or phrase in question, the word is a gerund or the phrase is a gerund phrase.

Write the following sentences on the chalkboard, and have students use the tip to classify the underlined words.

1. Studying often makes me hungry. [*gerund*]

2. Ana likes walking in the rain. [*gerund phrase*]

3. Howling loudly, the wind frightened us. [*participial phrase*]

Verbals and Verbal Phrases **477**

The Gerund Phrase

14h. A *gerund phrase* consists of a gerund and any modifiers or complements the gerund has. The entire phrase is used as a noun.

SUBJECT	**The sudden shattering of glass** broke the silence. [The gerund phrase is the subject of the verb *broke*. The article *The,* the adjective *sudden,* and the adjective phrase *of glass* modify the gerund *shattering*.]
PREDICATE NOMINATIVE	One of my chores in the summer is **mowing the lawn.** [The gerund phrase is a predicate nominative identifying the subject *One*. The noun *lawn* is the direct object of the gerund *mowing*.]
DIRECT OBJECT	She enjoys **hiking in the mountains occasionally.** [The gerund phrase is the direct object of the verb *enjoys*. The adverb phrase *in the mountains* and the adverb *occasionally* modify the gerund *hiking*.]
INDIRECT OBJECT	Ms. Yashima, a part-time reporter for the local newspaper, is giving **working full time** careful thought. [The gerund phrase is the indirect object of the verb *is giving*. The adverb *full time* modifies the gerund *working*.]
OBJECT OF THE PREPOSITION	By **reading the works of Pat Mora,** I have learned much about Mexican culture. [The gerund phrase is the object of the preposition *By*. The noun *works* is the direct object of the gerund *reading*. The adjective phrase *of Pat Mora* modifies *works*.]

Reference Note

For more about the **possessive forms of nouns and pronouns,** see page 758.

NOTE A noun or pronoun directly before a gerund should be in the possessive case.

EXAMPLES **Eli's** dancing won him first prize in the contest.
His dancing has greatly improved since last year.

Exercise 7 Using Gerunds and Gerund Phrases

Use gerunds or gerund phrases to fill in the blanks of the following sentences. *Answers will vary.*

EXAMPLE 1. The sign on the wall said "No ____."
1. The sign on the wall said "No Smoking."

1. Walking 1. ____ daily is a healthy hobby.

2. Fred Astaire was known for his ____.
3. ____ is advised for those who live in sensitive ecological zones.
4. After moving to England, Rick had to get used to many things, such as ____.
5. ____ is one of my claims to fame.
6. The ranger enjoys ____.
7. Most dentists recommend ____.
8. One way to increase your aerobic capacity is ____.
9. ____ helps me concentrate.
10. Give ____ your best effort.

The Infinitive

14i. An *infinitive* is a verb form that can be used as a noun, an adjective, or an adverb. Most infinitives begin with *to*.

Infinitives	
Used as	Examples
Nouns	**To err** is human. [*To err* is the subject of the verb *is*.] His dream is **to travel**. [*To travel* is a predicate nominative identifying the subject *dream*.] Betty wants **to act**. [*To act* is the direct object of the verb *wants*.]
Adjectives	The candidate **to believe** is Villegas. [*To believe* modifies the noun *candidate*.] She is the one **to ask**. [*To ask* modifies the pronoun *one*.]
Adverbs	Grandmother is coming **to visit**. [*To visit* modifies the verb *is coming*.] The favored team was slow **to score**. [*To score* modifies the adjective *slow*.]

NOTE The word *to* plus a noun or a pronoun (for example, *to Tokyo, to the movies, to her*) is a prepositional phrase, not an infinitive.

2. dancing
3. Recycling
4. drinking tea
5. Juggling
6. hiking through the woods
7. flossing daily
8. climbing stairs
9. Closing my eyes
10. skiing

Reference Note
For more about **prepositional phrases,** see page 467.

Verbals and Verbal Phrases **479**

---

14 i, j

GRAMMAR

Exercise 7

ALTERNATIVE LESSON
To extend **Exercise 7** have students identify how the gerunds or gerund phrases they have added in sentences 2, 3, 6, 8, 9, and 10 are used. The answers are as follows:

2. object of the preposition *for*
3. subject of *is advised*
6. direct object of *enjoys*
8. predicate nominative identifying *way*
9. subject of *helps*
10. indirect object of *give*

The Infinitive and the Infinitive Phrase

Rules 14i, j (pp. 479–483)

OBJECTIVES

■ To identify infinitives and to tell how they are used in sentences

■ To identify infinitive phrases and infinitive clauses and to tell how they are used in sentences

---

RESOURCES

The Infinitive and the Infinitive Phrase
Practice
■ *Grammar, Usage, and Mechanics,* pp. 70, 71, 72, 73–74
■ *Language Workshop CD-ROM,* Lesson 20

Verbals and Verbal Phrases **479**

Meeting INDIVIDUAL NEEDS

MULTIPLE INTELLIGENCES

Spatial Intelligence. Some students may find diagramming helpful in discerning the functions of infinitives. After they have studied the information on p. 479, you could lead students through diagramming the first sentence from **Exercise 8.**

Then, ask students to diagram two other sentences from **Exercise 8.** For more information on diagramming infinitives and infinitive phrases, refer students to the **Diagramming Appendix.**

ENGLISH-LANGUAGE LEARNERS

Spanish and Portuguese. Point out to students that the word *to* in English infinitives (*to speak, to sell, to part*) corresponds to the Spanish and Portuguese infinitive endings *–ar, –er,* and *–ir* (*hablar, vender,* and *partir* in Spanish; *falar, vender,* and *partir* in Portuguese).

French. In French, the infinitive ends in *–er, –ir, –oir,* or *–re* (for example, *aimer, finir, recevoir, rompre*).

HELP

Some sentences in Exercise 8 contain more than one infinitive.

STYLE TIP

Placing a word or word group between the sign of the infinitive, *to,* and the verb results in a **split infinitive.** Generally, you should avoid split infinitives in formal writing and speaking.

SPLIT
The director wants to, before rehearsal, speak with both the stage crew and the cast.

IMPROVED
The director wants **to speak** with both the stage crew and the cast before rehearsal.

Occasionally, however, you may need to use a split infinitive so that your meaning is clear.

UNCLEAR
He hoped to avoid carefully causing delays. [Does the adverb *carefully* modify the gerund *causing* or the infinitive *to avoid*?]

UNCLEAR
He hoped carefully to avoid causing delays. [Does the adverb *carefully* modify the verb *hoped* or the infinitive *to avoid*?]

CLEAR
He hoped **to carefully avoid** causing delays.

Exercise 8 **Identifying and Classifying Infinitives**

Identify the infinitives in the following sentences, and tell how each is used: as a *subject,* a *predicate nominative,* a *direct object,* an *adjective,* or an *adverb.*

EXAMPLE
1. What do you want to do after you graduate from high school?
1. to do—direct object

1. We are waiting to perform.   1. adv.
2. This summer she hopes to travel.   2. d.o.
3. I am ready to leave.   3. adv.
4. Do you want to drive?   4. d.o.
5. To forgive is sometimes difficult.   5. s.
6. To excel, one must practice.   6. adv.
7. We are eager to go.   7. adv.
8. A good way to learn is to live.   8. adj./p.n.
9. The soup is still too hot to eat.   9. adv.
10. I said to Jo, "One way to improve is to practice."   10. adj./p.n.

The Infinitive Phrase

14j. An *infinitive phrase* consists of an infinitive and any modifiers or complements the infinitive has. The entire phrase can be used as a noun, an adjective, or an adverb.

NOUN   **To hit a curveball solidly** is very difficult. [The infinitive phrase is the subject of the verb *is.* The noun *curveball* is the direct object of the infinitive *To hit,* and the adverb *solidly* modifies *To hit.*]

NOUN   She wants **to study marine biology.** [The infinitive phrase is the direct object of the verb *wants.* The noun *biology* is the direct object of the infinitive *to study,* and the adjective *marine* modifies *biology.*]

ADJECTIVE   His efforts **to trace his ancestry** led to greater appreciation of his heritage. [The infinitive phrase modifies the noun *efforts.* The noun *ancestry* is the direct object of the infinitive *to trace,* and the possessive pronoun *his* is used to modify *ancestry.*]

ADVERB   I found his explanation difficult **to accept.** [The infinitive phrase modifies the adjective *difficult.*]

480   Chapter 14   The Phrase

NOTE Unlike other verbals, an infinitive may have a subject. An *infinitive clause* consists of an infinitive with a subject and any modifiers or complements the infinitive has. The entire infinitive clause functions as a noun.

EXAMPLE I wanted **him to come to our powwow.** [*Him* is the subject of the infinitive *to come.* The entire infinitive clause is the direct object of the verb *wanted.*]

Sometimes *to*, the sign of the infinitive, is omitted.

EXAMPLES Did you watch her [to] **play** volleyball?

He will help us [to] **paddle** the canoe.

We don't dare [to] **go** outside during the storm.

Exercise 9 Identifying and Classifying Infinitive Phrases and Infinitive Clauses

Identify the infinitive phrases and infinitive clauses in the following sentences, and tell how each is used: as a *subject*, a *predicate nominative*, a *direct object*, an *adjective*, or an *adverb*.

EXAMPLE 1. Everyone in the class was eager to learn more about the life of Maya Angelou.

1. *to learn more about the life of Maya Angelou—adverb*

1. Our assignment was to read *I Know Why the Caged Bird Sings*. **1.** p.n.
2. I decided to write a report on Maya Angelou's descriptions of her childhood. **2.** d.o.
3. To grow up in Stamps, Arkansas, in the 1930s was to know great hardship. **3.** s./p.n.
4. Maya Angelou tried to show the everyday lives of African Americans during the Great Depression. **4.** d.o.
5. To accomplish this purpose meant including many descriptions; one such passage told about the process for curing pork sausage. **5.** s.
6. Angelou has an extraordinary ability to capture vivid details in her writing. **6.** adj.
7. She helps us see her grandmother's store through the eyes of a fascinated child. **7.** [to] d.o.
8. Angelou was eager to experience life beyond her hometown. **8.** adv.

COMPUTER TIP

Some style-checking software programs can identify and highlight split infinitives. Using such a program will help you eliminate unnecessary split infinitives from your writing.

HELP

Some sentences in Exercise 9 contain more than one infinitive phrase or infinitive clause. Remember that the sign of the infinitive, *to*, may be omitted.

Link to Literature

Cooperative Learning

To give students practice working with infinitives, divide the class into groups of four. Have one student in each group write an infinitive on a sheet of paper and then pass the paper to the right. Have the next student add words to the infinitive to create an infinitive phrase and also pass the paper to the right. Ask the next student to create a sentence using the infinitive phrase. Finally, have the last member of each group determine whether the infinitive phrase in the sentence is used as a noun, an adjective, or an adverb. If the infinitive phrase is a noun, have the group determine what its function is in the sentence (subject, predicate nominative, or direct object). If the infinitive phrase is an adverb or adjective, have the group identify the word or words the phrase modifies. Repeat the activity four times, with each member of the group performing each step once. Then, ask groups to exchange sentences and to check each other's work.

9. Her talents and ambition enabled her to achieve success as a writer, a dancer, and an actress. **9.** d.o.
10. To dramatize her African American heritage was a dream she realized by writing a television series. **10.** s.

HELP
Remember that *to*, the sign of the infinitive, may be omitted.

Review C — Identifying Types of Verbals and Verbal Phrases

Identify the verbal phrases in the following paragraph. Then, tell whether each verbal phrase is a *participial phrase*, a *gerund phrase*, or an *infinitive phrase*.

EXAMPLE [1] Looking at these control panels in the flight deck of a jumbo passenger jet, most of us feel completely lost.

1. Looking at these control panels in the flight deck of a jumbo passenger jet—participial phrase

[1] Intensive training is required for pilots. [2] Traveling the airways has become much easier because of modern technology. [3] Fortunately, in the flight deck sit people trained in the uses of these controls and instruments. [4] Sitting in front of identical control panels, both the captain and the first officer can fly the plane. [5] The captain, who uses the left-hand panel, operates a lever that controls the wing flaps and helps steer the plane. [6] Operating the brake panels is another one of the captain's jobs. [7] To the captain's right is the first officer, whose job is to help the captain. [8] The throttle, which governs the engines' ability to move the plane forward, is located between the captain and the first officer. [9] Some of the other instruments shown here are parts of the plane's navigation, autopilot, and communication systems. [10] At another station in the flight deck, the flight engineer monitors gauges and operates switches to control the plane's generators and the pressure and temperature in the cabin.

Review D — Identifying Verbal Phrases

Identify the verbal phrases in the following paragraph. Then, tell whether each verbal phrase is a *participial phrase*, a *gerund phrase*, or an *infinitive phrase*.

EXAMPLE [1] Would you like to have a summer job?
1. to have a summer job—infinitive phrase

[1] If you are not offered a job right away, remember that contacting a number of agencies and following up with phone calls and thank-you notes will increase your chances. [2] To persevere in the job hunt is very important. [3] Finding a summer job can be a difficult task. [4] The first step is to scan the classified ads listed in your local newspaper. [5] After discovering available opportunities, you can embark on the second step, which is matching your skills with the requirements of a specific job. [6] In most cases you can then contact a prospective employer by making a phone call or by writing a letter requesting an interview. [7] If you are asked to interview for a job, be sure to take care in preparing for the interview. [8] To make a good impression, be sure to arrive on time, to dress neatly, and to speak courteously. [9] Remember to avoid such nervous habits as constantly checking your watch or shuffling your feet. [10] By presenting yourself as calm, confident, and courteous, you may hear the magic words "We'd like you to work for us."

1. ger./ger.
2. inf.
3. ger.
4. inf./part.
5. ger./ger.
6. ger./ger./part.
7. inf./inf./ger.
8. inf./inf./inf./inf.
9. inf./ger./ger.
10. ger./inf.

Appositives and Appositive Phrases

14k. An *appositive* is a noun or pronoun placed beside another noun or pronoun to identify or describe it.

EXAMPLES My cousin **Bryan** is my best friend. [The appositive *Bryan* identifies the noun *cousin*.]

Our football team has won its first two games, **one** by three points and the **other** by six. [The appositives *one* and *other* identify the noun *games*.]

Soledad, a cautious **driver,** has never had an automobile accident. [The appositive *driver* describes the proper noun *Soledad*.]

14l. An *appositive phrase* consists of an appositive and any modifiers it has.

EXAMPLES The Vescuzos live on Milner Lane, **a wide street lined with beech trees.** [The appositive phrase identifies the noun *Milner Lane*. Note that the participial phrase *lined with beech trees* is part of the appositive phrase because the participial phrase, like the adjectives *a* and *wide*, modifies the appositive *street*.]

RESOURCES

Appositives and Appositive Phrases
Practice
- *Grammar, Usage, and Mechanics,* pp. 75, 76, 77
- *Language Workshop CD-ROM,* Lesson 21

Mount Kosciusko, **a part of the Australian Alps,** is the highest peak in Australia. [The appositive phrase describes the noun *Mount Kosciusko.* The prepositional phrase *of the Australian Alps* is an adjective phrase modifying the appositive *part.*]

An appositive phrase usually follows the noun or pronoun it identifies or describes. Sometimes, though, it precedes the noun or pronoun.

EXAMPLE **A diligent and quick-witted student,** Mark always gets good grades. [The appositive phrase identifies the noun *Mark.*]

Reference Note
For more information on **how to punctuate appositives and appositive phrases,** see page 711.

Appositives and appositive phrases that are not essential to the meaning of the sentence are set off by commas. However, an appositive that tells *which one of two or more* is essential to the meaning of the sentence and should not be set off by commas.

NONESSENTIAL Is Karen's sister, **Marcia,** also a sophomore? [The appositive *Marcia* is not essential because Karen has only one sister.]

ESSENTIAL Jorge's sister **Selena** is a sophomore. [The appositive *Selena* is essential because Jorge has more than one sister. Which one of the sisters is a sophomore? *Selena.*]

Exercise 10 Identifying Appositives and Appositive Phrases

Identify the appositive or appositive phrase in each of the following sentences, and give the word it identifies or describes.

EXAMPLE 1. Dr. Rosen, our family dentist, is a marathon runner.
1. our family dentist—Dr. Rosen

1. Soccer, my favorite sport, is very popular in South America and Europe.
2. The internationally famous soccer star Pelé is from Brazil.
3. Hausa, a Nigerian language, is widely used in western Africa.
4. Have you met my teacher Mr. Zolo?
5. Roseanne's youngest sister, Susan, speaks fluent Spanish.
6. Is your friend Greg getting married?
7. Cindy, a student at the community college, is studying computer-aided drafting.
8. The New York City Marathon, one of the largest spectator sports in the United States, is held each November.

484 Chapter 14 The Phrase

Learning for Life

Conversation. To show that the use of phrases, particularly verbal phrases, is not limited to formal writing, organize the class into groups of four or five and ask students to have a conversation. Encourage each group to try to choose a topic that interests all of its members. Ask the group to discuss the topic for five minutes and to tape-record the conversation. Then, have each group play back its conversation, stopping frequently so that they can note all the sentences containing verbal phrases (each

9. The Himalayas, the highest mountains on earth, are magnificent.
10. Always the one to object, Blair said, "Not on your life!"

Review E   Identifying Verbal and Appositive Phrases

The following paragraph contains ten verbal and appositive phrases. Identify each phrase as a *participial phrase*, a *gerund phrase*, an *infinitive phrase*, or an *appositive phrase*.

EXAMPLE   [1] Who was responsible for designing the Brooklyn Bridge?

   1. designing the Brooklyn Bridge—gerund phrase

[1] The Brooklyn Bridge, a remarkable feat of design, spans the East River in New York City. [2] Linking the boroughs of Brooklyn and Manhattan, it was once the longest suspension bridge in the world. [3] Most of the pedestrians who cross the bridge are impressed by the grandeur of its graceful cables, a majesty that the postcard below cannot fully evoke. [4] To support the twin towers on the bridge, the brilliant John A. Roebling, its engineer, designed airtight caissons filled with concrete. [5] Working underwater on the caissons was painstakingly slow and extremely dangerous. [6] The workers also faced great danger when they had to spin the cables from one side of the river to the other. [7] Because of these hazards, the bridge is remembered not only for being a masterpiece of engineering but also for having cost the lives of many of its builders.

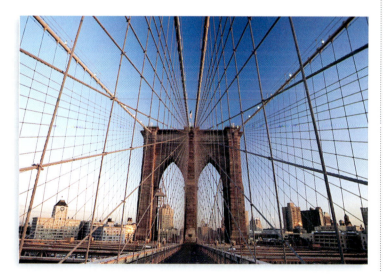

STYLE TIP

Using too many short sentences will make your writing choppy. By using prepositional, verbal, and appositive phrases, you can avoid the unnecessary repetition of words and can improve the flow of your ideas.

CHOPPY
The Appalachian National Scenic Trail is more than 2,000 miles long. The trail stretches from Mount Katahdin to Springer Mountain. Mount Katahdin is in Maine. Springer Mountain is in Georgia.

SMOOTH
Stretching from Mount Katahdin in Maine to Springer Mountain in Georgia, the Appalachian National Scenic Trail is more than 2,000 miles long.

GRAMMAR

Relating to Literature

To review with students the kinds of phrases discussed in this chapter, select a short story from the students' literature textbook. Create enough student groups so that each group has a different page to read. Then, have the members of each group work cooperatively to find all the phrases on the page and to classify each phrase as *prepositional, participial, gerund, infinitive,* or *appositive,* and ask students to explain the specific function of each phrase.

After students have completed their analyses, have each group share its findings with the rest of the class. You may want to conclude this activity by recording on the chalkboard the total number of each kind of phrase that appears in the story. This statistical summary of the author's use of phrases will reinforce students' understanding that good writing includes a variety of phrases.

Review F — Writing Sentences with Phrases

Write ten sentences, following the directions below for each sentence. Underline the given phrase in each sentence. **Answers will vary.**

EXAMPLE 1. Use *to get there from here* as an infinitive phrase acting as an adjective.
1. What is the fastest way <u>to get there from here</u>?

1. Use *in the garage* as an adjective phrase.
2. Use *for our English class* as an adverb phrase.
3. Use *from an encyclopedia* as an adjective phrase.
4. Use *by train* as an adverb phrase.
5. Use *walking by the lake* as a participial phrase.
6. Use *playing the piano* as a gerund phrase that is the subject of a verb.
7. Use *to hit a home run* as an infinitive phrase that is the direct object of a verb.
8. Use *to find the answer to that question* as an infinitive phrase acting as an adverb.
9. Use *the new student in our class* as an appositive phrase.
10. Use *my favorite writer* as an appositive phrase.

1. The toolbox <u>in the garage</u> should contain the screwdriver you need.
2. We will be presenting a scene from *Julius Caesar* <u>for our English class</u>.
3. Information <u>from an encyclopedia</u> is considered reliable.
4. The raw materials were shipped <u>by train</u>.
5. <u>Walking by the lake</u>, we could hear the loons calling.
6. <u>Playing the piano</u> is a skill that requires much practice.
7. Jesse hoped <u>to hit a home run</u>.
8. Shannon was finding it difficult <u>to find the answer to that question</u>.
9. Claudia, <u>the new student in our class</u>, is an exchange student from Argentina.
10. The teacher read aloud a short story by Mark Twain, <u>my favorite writer</u>.

Chapter 14 Review

A. Sentences with Prepositional Phrases

Provide a prepositional phrase for the blank in each of the following sentences. After writing the sentence, identify the phrase as an *adjective phrase* or an *adverb phrase*. Answers will vary.

1. The tall building ____ is the art museum.   **1. on your left—adj.**
2. *Brian's Song* is an inspiring story ____.   **2. about a football player—adj.**
3. The selection committee was impressed ____.   **3. by his achievements—adv.**
4. ____, we decided to spend the evening quietly at home.   **4. After a while—adv.**
5. I saw a raccoon ____.   **5. in a tree—adv.**
6. Early ____, my family holds a big reunion for all of our relatives.   **6. in the summer—adv.**
7. Last Christmas, Mother used a recipe similar to that ____.   **7. on the cooking show—adj.**
8. ____, my father fought as a soldier in the U.S. Army during the Persian Gulf Conflict.   **8. In 1991—adv.**
9. After protesting that he wanted to stay up late, my young brother finally went ____.   **9. to his room—adv.**
10. That rosebush ____ had seen better days.   **10. near the house—adj.**

B. Identifying Participles and Participial Phrases

HELP — Some sentences in Part B contain more than one participle or participial phrase.

Identify the participial phrases and participles that are used as adjectives in the following sentences. Give the noun or pronoun each participle or participial phrase modifies.

11. She heard <u>me</u> <u>sighing loudly</u>.
12. <u>Aided by good weather and clear skies</u>, the <u>sailors</u> sailed into port a day early.
13. <u>Searching through old clothes in a trunk</u>, <u>Ricardo</u> found a <u>map</u> <u>showing the location of a buried treasure</u>.
14. <u>Sparta</u> and <u>Athens</u>, <u>putting aside their own rivalry</u>, joined forces to fight the Persians.
15. I would love to see <u>it</u> <u>blooming</u>; it must be quite a sight!
16. The cat hissed at the <u>dog</u> <u>barking in the yard next door</u>.
17. <u>Waxing his car in the driveway</u>, <u>Joe</u> overheard a bit of song from an open window nearby.

Chapter Review 487

18. Known as Johnny Appleseed, John Chapman distributed apple seeds and saplings to families headed west.
19. Locked doors contradicted the "open" sign in the window.
20. Switching its tail, the leopard closed in on its prey.

C. Identifying Phrases in Sentences

Identify each italicized phrase in the following sentences as a *prepositional*, *participial*, *gerund*, *infinitive*, or *appositive phrase*.

21. The sundial was one of the first instruments used for *telling time*.
22. *Regarded chiefly as garden ornaments*, sundials are still used in some areas *to tell time*.
23. The shadow-casting object *on a sundial* is called a gnomon.
24. Forerunners of the sundial include poles or upright stones *used as gnomons by early humans*.
25. *To improve the accuracy of the sundial*, the gnomon was set directly parallel to the earth's axis, *the imaginary line running through the planet's poles*.
26. The development of trigonometry permitted more precise calculations *in the construction* of sundials.
27. For everyday use, *owning a watch* has obvious advantages over using a sundial.
28. *In the past*, sundials were used *to set and check the accuracy of watches*.
29. The heliochronometer, *a sundial of great precision*, was used until 1900 *to set the watches of French railway workers*.
30. The difference *between solar time and clock time* is correlated by the use of tables *showing daily variations in solar time*.

D. Identifying Phrases in a Paragraph

Identify each italicized phrase in the following paragraph as a *prepositional*, *participial*, *gerund*, *infinitive*, or *appositive phrase*.

[31] A sundial is not difficult *to make with simple materials*. [32] First find a stick *to use as a gnomon*. [33] At high noon, plant the stick *in the ground*, tilting it slightly northward. [34] *To mark the first hour*, place a pebble at the tip of the shadow *made by the stick*. [35] An hour later, put another pebble at the tip *of the shadow*. [36] Continue this process *throughout the afternoon*. [37] *Starting the*

next morning, repeat the hourly process. **[38]** Be sure *to place the last pebble at high noon*. **[39]** Observing the completed sundial, you will note that the hour markers, *the pebbles*, are not equidistant. **[40]** *Your spacing of the markers* has demonstrated that shadows move faster in the morning and the evening than during the middle of the day.

38. inf.
39. app.
40. ger.

Writing Application
Using Phrases in a Newspaper Article

Verbal and Appositive Phrases As a reporter for the local newspaper, you have just attended the final contest of your community's annual dog show. Now, you have to write a short news article on the show. Be sure you use at least three verbal phrases and three appositive phrases.

Prewriting First, make a list of the top dogs in the show. Give their names, their breeds, their owners, and their personalities. Interview the winner's owner for "the human perspective."

Writing Newspaper articles usually present the most important information first, so be sure to include the *who, what, when,* and *where* of the dog show in the beginning of the article. Describe how the winners were chosen, and explain why each winner was judged to be the best in its class. You may also want to describe other features of the show, such as the setting, the size and enthusiasm of the crowd, or the owners' preshow grooming of contestants.

Revising Read your first draft to a friend or family member, and ask for his or her reactions. Determine that you have given adequate information in as clear a manner as possible.

Publishing Check to make sure that you have used at least three verbal phrases and three appositive phrases. Also, check your spelling, especially of the names of dog breeds with which you may not be familiar. Proofread your article for any errors in grammar, usage, and mechanics. You and your classmates may wish to read your finished articles aloud. Post the article on a class bulletin board or Web page.

Chapter Review **489**

GRAMMAR

Writing Application
(p. 489)

OBJECTIVE
■ To write a short news article on the community's annual dog show, using at least three verbal phrases and three appositive phrases

Writing Application

Tip. To help students get started on their articles, you could have any dog owners in your class share information about dog breeds and, perhaps, about dog shows. Students could also find information in the library. Students will need to have general ideas about the kinds of events in a dog show and about the criteria used by the judges to rank the dogs.

Before students begin writing their articles, you may want to check their lists of top dogs and see if the students can describe or explain the dogs using appositive and verbal phrases.

Scoring Rubric. While you will want to pay particular attention to students' use of phrases, you will also want to evaluate overall writing performance. You may want to give a split score to indicate development and clarity of the composition as well as grammar skills.

RESOURCES
Writing Application
Extension
■ *Grammar, Usage, and Mechanics,* p. 83
■ *Language Workshop CD-ROM,* Lessons 19–21

Writing Application
Alignments
TEKS 1A, 1B, 2A, 3A, 3C, 3D
TAAS W1, W3, W5, W7
English II End-of-Course 4, 5, 6

Texas Resources
• One-Stop Planner CD-ROM

Chapter Review **489**

CHAPTER 15

PREVIEWING THE CHAPTER

- This chapter defines independent clauses and then goes on to discuss the three types of subordinate clauses—adjective, adverb, and noun. The last section discusses sentences classified according to structure—simple, compound, complex, and compound-complex.

- The chapter concludes with a **Chapter Review,** including a **Writing Application** feature that asks students to write paragraphs that each contain at least five subordinate clauses.

- For help in integrating the chapter with writing chapters, use the **Teaching Strands** chart on pp. T401A–T401B.

USING THE DIAGNOSTIC PREVIEW

- **Part A** of the **Diagnostic Preview** asks students to identify clauses as independent or subordinate and then to determine how subordinate clauses are used in sentences; **Part B** requires students to classify sentences according to structure. You may want to analyze the results of **Part A** of the **Diagnostic Preview** and to assign specific exercises for students who missed adjective clauses, items 1, 3, and 5; adverb clauses, items 6, 8, and 9; or noun clauses, items 4 and 7. After students have classified the sentences in **Part B,** help them to understand the importance of sentence variety by discussing whether the paragraph would have been as effective without a variety of sentence types.

CHAPTER 15 The Clause
Independent Clauses and Subordinate Clauses

Diagnostic Preview

A. Identifying and Classifying Clauses

Identify the italicized clause in each of the following sentences as an *independent clause* or a *subordinate clause*. Then, identify each of the subordinate clauses as an *adjective clause*, an *adverb clause*, or a *noun clause*.

EXAMPLES
1. The New York bridge *that most people recognize* is the Brooklyn Bridge.
1. subordinate clause—adjective clause
2. Known around the world, *the Brooklyn Bridge may be the most famous bridge in the United States.*
2. independent clause

1. The Brooklyn Bridge, *which spans the East River between Brooklyn and Manhattan in New York City*, is one of the engineering wonders of the world.   1. adj.
2. *The bridge was designed and built by John Roebling and Washington Roebling, a father-and-son engineering team* who were pioneers in the use of steel-wire cables.
3. The steel-wire cables give the bridge a graceful appearance *that resembles a spider's web.*   3. adj.
4. *What impresses many people* who see the bridge is the strength and beauty of its design.   4. n.
5. Massive granite towers *that are supported by concrete-filled shafts* are among its remarkable features.   5. adj.

490   Chapter 15   The Clause

CHAPTER RESOURCES

Planning
- *One-Stop Planner CD-ROM*

Practice and Extension
- *Grammar, Usage, and Mechanics,* p. 84
- *Language Workshop CD-ROM*

Internet
- go.hrw.com (keyword: EOLang)

Evaluation and Assessment
- *Assessment Package*
  —*Chapter Tests,* Ch. 15
  —*Chapter Tests in Standardized Test Formats,* Ch. 15
- *Test Generator (One-Stop Planner CD-ROM)*

6. *Although she was not an engineer,* Nora Roebling assisted in the efforts to complete the bridge.   6. adv.
7. The Roeblings discovered *that construction work could be both slow and dangerous.*   7. n.
8. *Because they were required at times to work underwater in airtight chambers called caissons,* many workers, including the designer Washington Roebling, suffered from caisson disease, or decompression sickness.   8. adv.
9. *Since they were used to working in ships' rigging at great heights,* sailors were hired to string the miles of cable.   9. adv.
10. *John Roebling injured his foot at the work site,* and as a result, he died of tetanus shortly after construction began.

B. Classifying Sentences According to Structure

Classify each of the sentences in the following paragraph as *simple*, *compound*, *complex*, or *compound-complex*.

EXAMPLE   [1] Washington and Nora Roebling worked together to complete the project.

   1. simple

[11] After succeeding his father on the project, Washington Roebling was stricken by caisson disease; therefore, he was confined to bed. [12] The Roeblings lived in a house that was near the construction site, and Washington supervised the work through a telescope. [13] He dictated instructions to Nora, and she relayed them to the work crew. [14] Whether the work on the bridge could have continued without her assistance is doubtful. [15] When the bridge was finally completed in 1883, President Chester A. Arthur attended the dedication ceremony. [16] Because of his illness, Washington Roebling was unable to attend the ceremonies. [17] Instead, the President visited Roebling's home to honor the man who had struggled so valiantly to complete the bridge. [18] The bridge took thirteen years to build. [19] At the time of its completion, it was the world's longest suspension bridge. [20] The bridge is now more than a century old, and it still stands as a monument to the artistry, sacrifice, and determination of all the people who planned and built it.

11. cd.
12. cd.-cx.
13. cd.
14. cx.
15. cx.
16. simp.
17. cx.
18. simp.
19. simp.
20. cd.-cx.

The Clause, pp. 490–509
Alignments
TEKS 3B, 3D
TAAS W3, W6
English II End-of-Course 5, 6

Texas Resources
• *TAAS Tool Kit*
• *Preparation for TAAS*
• *One-Stop Planner CD-ROM*

GRAMMAR

What Is a Clause?

Rules 15a–c *(pp. 492–495)*

OBJECTIVES

- To identify independent and subordinate clauses in sentences
- To identify subjects, verbs, and complements in subordinate clauses

TEACHING TIP

Activity. Have students use the comics section of a newspaper to practice identifying independent clauses. Give students pages of black-and-white comics from daily newspapers (a page of comics for each student), and ask them to highlight all the independent clauses they find. Students could pair up to check each other's identification of clauses.

HELP

A subordinate clause that is capitalized and punctuated as if it were a sentence is a *sentence fragment*.

Reference Note

For information about correcting **sentence fragments**, see page 340.

Reference Note

For more about **commas**, see page 700.

Reference Note

For more information on using **semicolons to join independent clauses**, see page 724.

What Is a Clause?

15a. A *clause* is a word group that contains a verb and its subject and that is used as a sentence or as part of a sentence.

Every clause has a subject and a verb, but not all clauses express complete thoughts. Those that do are called *independent clauses*. Those that do not are called *subordinate clauses*.

Independent Clauses

15b. An *independent* (or *main*) *clause* expresses a complete thought and can stand by itself as a sentence.

EXAMPLE   The **outfielders missed** easy fly balls.
                     S   V

Independent clauses that express related ideas can be joined together in a single sentence. Often, the clauses are linked by a comma and one of the coordinating conjunctions (*and, but, or, nor, for, so,* or *yet*).

EXAMPLE   The **outfielders missed** easy fly balls, and the **infielders**
                     S   V   S
          were throwing wildly.
                     V

Independent clauses can also be linked by a semicolon.

EXAMPLE   The **outfielders missed** easy fly balls; the **infielders**
                     S   V   S
          were throwing wildly.
                     V

A conjunctive adverb or a transitional expression can be used after the semicolon to express the relationship between the independent clauses.

EXAMPLES The **outfielders missed** easy fly balls; moreover, the
                     S   V
          infielders were throwing wildly.
                     S   V

          The **outfielders missed** easy fly balls; in addition, the
                     S   V
          infielders were throwing wildly.
                     S   V

---

492   Chapter 15   The Clause

RESOURCES

What Is a Clause?

Practice

- *Grammar, Usage, and Mechanics*, pp. 85, 86, 87, 88–89
- *Language Workshop CD-ROM*, Lesson 22

Common Conjunctive Adverbs		
also	however	nevertheless
anyway	instead	otherwise
besides	likewise	still
consequently	meanwhile	then
furthermore	moreover	therefore

Common Transitional Expressions		
as a result	for example	in other words
at any rate	in addition	on the contrary
by the way	in fact	on the other hand

Subordinate Clauses

15c. A *subordinate* (or *dependent*) *clause* does not express a complete thought and cannot stand alone as a sentence.

EXAMPLES   whom we spoke to yesterday

because no students have applied for them

The thought expressed by a subordinate clause becomes part of a complete thought when the clause is combined with an independent clause.

EXAMPLES   The woman **whom we spoke to yesterday** told us about sources of financial aid for college applicants.

Some scholarships are still available **because no students have applied for them.**

Exercise 1 Identifying Independent and Subordinate Clauses

For each of the following sentences, identify the italicized clause as *independent* or *subordinate*.

EXAMPLE   1. One of the guests *who spoke at the ceremony* was Barbara Jordan.
1. subordinate

1. *Whenever I think of Barbara Jordan*, I imagine her as she looks in a picture taken at my mother's college graduation in 1986.

Meeting INDIVIDUAL NEEDS

ENGLISH-LANGUAGE LEARNERS
General Strategies. Describing a subordinate clause by using expressions such as "does not express a complete thought" and "cannot stand alone" may not help your English-language learners. It may be helpful to describe this clause structurally as having a subject and a verb as well as a subordinating conjunction, relative pronoun, or relative adverb that links it to another clause.

MODALITIES
Auditory Learners. To help auditory learners understand how independent and subordinate clauses function in writing, read aloud the sentences from **Exercise 1**. As you read, emphasize each italicized clause. Then, ask students whether the clause could stand alone as a complete thought.

Continued on p. 494

Punctuating Compound Sentences.
Remind students that when independent clauses are joined together in a single sentence, the result is a compound sentence. Put the following reminders on the chalkboard:

1. Use a comma before a coordinating conjunction joining two independent clauses. If the independent clauses are very short and the sentence cannot be misunderstood, the comma may be left out.

Critical Thinking

Analysis. The sentences in Exercise 1 present facts about the life of Barbara Jordan. Ask students to find three facts used in the sentences. For example, the statement that the photograph was taken when Jordan delivered a commencement address in 1986 is a fact because it can be proved. When students complete their lists, have them compare and discuss their findings.

Looking at Language

Word Origins. Point out to students that the etymology of the word *subordinate* is derived from the Latin prefix *sub–,* which means "under," plus *ordinare,* which means "to order." Have students consult a dictionary to find the meaning of *subordinate* and the different parts of speech it can be. [*adjective, noun, verb*] Ask students to work in pairs to compose three sentences using *subordinate,* once as an adjective, once as a noun, and once as a verb. Then, have pairs of students read their sentences aloud to another pair. (Point out to students that *subordinate* has a different pronunciation as a verb than it does as an adjective or noun.)

Reference Note

For more about the different kinds of **complements,** see page 450. For more about **adjectives** and **adverbs,** see page 614. For more about **prepositional phrases,** see page 467.

2. According to my mother, *Jordan spoke eloquently about the importance of values in our society.*
3. *Of course, her choice of subject matter surprised no one* since Jordan had long been known as an important ethical force in American politics.
4. *When Jordan began her public service career in 1966,* she became the first African American woman to serve in the Texas legislature.
5. In 1972, she won a seat in the U.S. House of Representatives, *where only one other black woman—Shirley Chisholm—had ever been a member.*
6. However, Jordan was still not widely recognized *until she gave the keynote speech at the 1976 Democratic National Convention.*
7. Seen on television by millions of people, *Jordan immediately gained national attention.*
8. Two years after the speech, Jordan decided *that she would retire from national politics.*
9. After she returned to Texas in 1978, *Jordan taught at the University of Texas at Austin.*
10. From 1991 until her death in 1996, she served on various government committees and used *what she had learned in her many years of public service* to fight corruption in politics.

Complements and Modifiers in Subordinate Clauses

A subordinate clause may contain complements and modifiers.

EXAMPLES since she told **us the truth** [*Us* is the indirect object of the verb *told,* and *truth* is the direct object of *told. The* modifies *truth.*]

when I am **busy** [*Busy* is a predicate adjective modifying the subject *I.*]

after he had cooked **for us** [*For us* is a prepositional phrase modifying the verb *had cooked.*]

that he **recently** painted [*That* is the direct object of the verb *painted; recently* is an adverb modifying *painted.*]

who they were [*Who* is a predicate nominative identifying the subject *they.*]

MINI-LESSON

2. Use a semicolon between independent clauses if they are not joined by a coordinating conjunction.
3. Use a semicolon before and a comma after a conjunctive adverb or transitional expression that joins two independent clauses.
4. A semicolon may be needed to separate independent clauses joined by a coordinating conjunction if there are commas within the clauses.

Exercise 2 — Identifying Subjects, Verbs, and Complements in Subordinate Clauses

Identify the subject and the verb in the italicized subordinate clause in each of the following sentences. Then, identify each complement in the clause as a *predicate adjective*, *predicate nominative*, *direct object*, or *indirect object*.

EXAMPLE 1. *After he shows us his new boat,* we will go swimming.
1. he—subject; shows—verb; us—indirect object; boat—direct object

1. We couldn't see *who had won the race.* 1. d.o.
2. They couldn't tell *who the winner was.* 2. p.n.
3. She is the celebrity *whom we saw at the restaurant.* 3. d.o.
4. Kelly says *that her new house is beautiful.* 4. p.a.
5. The horse *that you rode yesterday* was skittish. 5. d.o.
6. *After we passed the test,* we celebrated. 6. d.o.
7. Do you know which *country she is touring?* 7. d.o.
8. *Because you had not given us the right address,* we missed the party. 8. i.o./d.o.
9. Look for the mouse *that you heard last night.* 9. d.o.
10. *Until Mike lent me this book,* I had never heard of the author Rudolfo A. Anaya. 10. i.o./d.o.

Uses of Subordinate Clauses

Subordinate clauses can be used as adjectives, adverbs, or nouns.

The Adjective Clause

15d. An ***adjective clause*** is a subordinate clause that modifies a noun or a pronoun.

An adjective clause tells *what kind* or *which one* and generally follows the word or words it modifies.

EXAMPLES I am now reading this book, **which is a historical novel about the Irish revolt of 1798.** [The adjective clause modifies the noun *book,* telling what kind of book.]

A photograph of those **who had participated in the school's Earth Day celebration** appeared on the front page of the local newspaper. [The adjective clause modifies the pronoun *those,* telling which ones.]

HELP

Before doing Exercise 2, you may want to review **complements** in Chapter 13.

STYLE TIP

Although a series of short, simple sentences can be effective, a variety of sentence structures is usually more effective. To make choppy sentences into smoother writing, combine shorter sentences by changing some into subordinate clauses. Also, avoid unnecessary repetition of subjects, verbs, and pronouns.

CHOPPY
  Ted runs every day. Ted is in training. He is training for a marathon.

SMOOTH
  Ted, who is in training for a marathon, runs every day.

In the example above, two of the short sentences are combined into a single subordinate clause.

Exercise 2
ALTERNATIVE LESSON
In sentence 3, have students identify the word group *at the restaurant.* [prepositional phrase] Remind students that the object of a preposition cannot be a direct or indirect object.

The Adjective Clause
Rule 15d (pp. 495–498)

OBJECTIVES

- To identify in sentences adjective clauses, the relative pronoun or relative adverb that introduces the clause, and the word or words to which the relative word relates

---

RESOURCES

The Adjective Clause
Practice
- *Grammar, Usage, and Mechanics,* pp. 90–91, 92
- *Language Workshop CD-ROM,* Lesson 23

Meeting INDIVIDUAL NEEDS

LEARNERS HAVING DIFFICULTY
If students need additional practice with adjective clauses, have them complete each of the following sentences by writing an adjective clause that begins with the word shown in parentheses. Answers will vary.

1. The swimmer (*who*) _____ won the race. [*who came from my high school*]
2. The dog (*that*) _____ woke up the neighborhood. [*that barked so loudly*]
3. The singer (*whose*) _____ sang at the concert. [*whose album was just released*]

Students might work together in pairs or in small groups and then share their sentences with the rest of the class.

TIPS & TRICKS

Generally, an adjective clause that modifies a proper noun, such as *Emil* in the second example, is nonessential and is therefore set off by commas.

Reference Note
See page 711 for more about **essential** and **nonessential clauses.**

NOTE Depending on how it is used, an adjective clause is either *essential* or *nonessential*. An **essential** (or **restrictive**) **clause** contains information necessary to the sentence's meaning. A **nonessential** (or **nonrestrictive**) **clause** contains information that can be omitted without affecting the sentence's basic meaning. An essential clause is not set off by commas; a nonessential clause is set off by commas.

ESSENTIAL The oboe is the only instrument **that I can play well.** [The adjective clause is essential because omitting it would change the basic meaning of the sentence.]

NONESSENTIAL Emil, **who can play many instruments,** taught me how to play the oboe. [The adjective clause is nonessential because omitting it would not affect the basic meaning of the sentence.]

Relative Pronouns

An adjective clause is usually introduced by a *relative pronoun*.

Common Relative Pronouns				
who	whom	whose	which	that

These pronouns are called **relative pronouns** because they are used to relate an adjective clause to the word or word group the clause modifies. That word or word group is called the **antecedent** of the relative pronoun. Each relative pronoun also serves a grammatical function within the adjective clause.

EXAMPLES Isabella Baumfree was an abolitionist **who is most often remembered as Sojourner Truth.** [*Who* relates the adjective clause to the noun *abolitionist*. *Who* also serves as the subject of the verb *is remembered* in the adjective clause.]

The topic **about which he is writing** is controversial. [*Which* relates the adjective clause to the noun *topic*. *Which* also serves as the object of the preposition *about* in the adjective clause.]

She is the person **whom I trust most.** [*Whom* relates the adjective clause to the noun *person*. *Whom* also serves as the direct object of the verb *trust* in the adjective clause.]

Do you know the name of the group **whose recording is number one on the charts**? [*Whose* relates the adjective clause to the noun *group*. *Whose* also serves as a possessive pronoun modifying *recording* in the adjective clause.]

Sometimes the relative pronoun is left out of a sentence. In such a sentence, the pronoun is understood and still serves a grammatical function within the adjective clause.

EXAMPLE   Ms. Chung is the legislator [**that** or **whom**] we met. [*That or whom* is understood. The understood relative pronoun relates the adjective clause to *legislator* and serves as the direct object of the verb *met* in the adjective clause.]

NOTE   *Who* and *whom* refer to persons only; *which* refers to things only; *that* refers to persons or things.

Occasionally, an adjective clause is introduced by the word *where* or *when*. When used in such a way, these words are called **relative adverbs**.

EXAMPLES   Here is the spot **where we will have lunch.** [*Where* relates the adjective clause to the noun *spot*.]

This is the season **when it rains almost every day.** [*When* relates the adjective clause to the noun *season*.]

Reference Note
For information on using **who** and **whom** correctly, see pages 558.

Exercise 3 Identifying Adjective Clauses

Identify the adjective clauses in the following sentences, and underline the relative pronoun or relative adverb in each clause. Then, give the word or words to which the relative pronoun or relative adverb relates. If a sentence contains an adjective clause from which the relative pronoun has been omitted, add the relative pronoun in parentheses and underline it.

EXAMPLES   1. The topic that Melissa chose for her essay was difficult.
   1. *that* Melissa chose for her essay—*topic*

   2. The other topics she had considered were just as difficult.
   2. *(that)* she had considered—*topics*

HELP
Some sentences in Exercise 3 contain more than one adjective clause.

1. A speech community is a group of people who speak the same language.
2. There are speech communities that contain millions of people and some that have only a few people.
3. The first language you learn is called your native language.   3. *(that)*
4. People who master a second language are bilingual.
5. Those who conduct business internationally often need to know more than one language.
6. English, French, and Spanish, which many diplomats can speak, are among the six official languages of the United Nations.

TEACHING TIP

Activity. Explain to students that an adjective, an adjective prepositional phrase, and an adjective clause all function exactly the same way in a sentence—that is, they modify a noun or pronoun. Write the following phrases on the chalkboard:

<u>strong</u> women
women <u>of strength</u>
women <u>who are strong</u>

Ask students to identify the underlined words. [adjective, adjective prepositional phrase, adjective clause]

Write the following word groups on the chalkboard. Have students identify the form of each word group, then convert each word group into the other two forms so that each is in the form of an adjective, an adjective prepositional phrase, and an adjective clause. (Students' answers will vary.)

1. Water with ice [*ice water, water that has ice in it*]
2. Dress of blue [*blue dress, dress that is blue*]
3. Students who show ability [*able students, students of ability*]
4. Quiet time [*time of quiet, time when there is quiet*]

GRAMMAR

The Adverb Clause

Rule 15e (pp. 498–501)

OBJECTIVES

- To identify adverb clauses and the subordinating conjunctions that introduce them
- To complete sentences by adding adverb clauses

Reference Note

Introductory adverb clauses are usually set off by **commas.** See page 707.

---

7. Russian, Chinese, and Arabic are the other three languages that are used officially at the UN.
8. People for whom language study is important include telephone operators, hotel managers, and police officers.
9. Tourists traveling to countries where they do not know the local languages can find themselves at a disadvantage.
10. French is a language that is widely understood in parts of Europe, Africa, Southeast Asia, and the Middle East.

The Adverb Clause

15e. An *adverb clause* is a subordinate clause that modifies a verb, an adjective, or an adverb.

An adverb clause tells *how, when, where, why, to what extent,* or *under what condition.*

EXAMPLES Donna sounds **as if she has caught a cold.** [The adverb clause modifies the verb *sounds,* telling how Donna sounds.]

Before we left, we lowered the blinds. [The adverb clause modifies the verb *lowered,* telling when we lowered the blinds.]

You will see our house **where the road turns right.** [The adverb clause modifies the verb *will see,* telling where you will see our house.]

Will you move **so that I can see**? [The adverb clause modifies the verb *will move,* telling why you will move.]

Your stereo is louder **than it should be.** [The adverb clause modifies the adjective *louder,* telling to what extent the stereo is louder.]

André can type faster **than anyone else in his computer class can.** [The adverb clause modifies the adverb *faster,* telling to what extent Andre can type faster.]

As long as he starts early, he will arrive on time. [The adverb clause modifies the verb *will arrive,* telling under what condition he will arrive on time.]

Subordinating Conjunctions

An adverb clause is introduced by a *subordinating conjunction*—a word that shows the relationship between the adverb clause and the

498   **Chapter 15**   The Clause

RESOURCES

The Adverb Clause

Practice

- *Grammar, Usage, and Mechanics,* pp. 93–94, 95, 96
- *Language Workshop CD-ROM,* Lesson 23

word or words that the clause modifies. Unlike a relative pronoun, which introduces an adjective clause, a subordinating conjunction does not serve a grammatical function in the clause it introduces.

Common Subordinating Conjunctions

after	before	unless
although	even though	until
as	if	when
as if	in order that	whenever
as long as	provided that	where
as soon as	since	wherever
as though	so that	whether
as well as	than	while
because	though	why

Reference Note
Some of the words in this chart can be used as **adverbs** (see page 422) or **prepositions** (see page 426).

Exercise 4   Identifying Adverb Clauses and Subordinating Conjunctions

Identify the adverb clause in each of the following sentences, and circle the subordinating conjunction.

EXAMPLE   1. While the others worked inside the house, Ruth, Lou, and I worked in the yard.
   1. (While) the others worked inside the house

1. (Because) the house had been vacant for so long, the lawn and gardens were overgrown.
2. The grass in the front looked (as if) it hadn't been cut in months.
3. Ruth began mowing the lawn (while) Lou and I weeded the flower beds.
4. We decided to borrow some tools (because) the weeds were extremely thick.
5. We were unable to cut through the heavy undergrowth (until) we started using a machete.
6. (Before) we pulled out the weeds, we couldn't even see the roses.
7. We piled the debris in a huge mound (so that) it could be hauled away later.
8. (After) Ruth had mowed the lawn, she was exhausted.
9. We all stretched out in the shade (when) we stopped for a rest.
10. Long hours in the sun had made us feel (as though) the day would never end.

COMPUTER TIP

Because an adverb clause usually does not have a fixed location in a sentence, the writer must choose where to put the clause. The best place for it is usually a matter of personal taste and style, but often the placement is determined by the context.

If you use a computer, you can easily experiment with the placement of adverb clauses in sentences. Print out different versions of the same sentence containing the adverb clause along with the sentences that immediately precede and follow it. Read each version aloud to see how the placement of the clause affects the flow, rhythm, and overall meaning of the passage.

Uses of Subordinate Clauses   **499**

Critical Thinking

Analysis. Students sometimes have trouble analyzing the relationships among ideas presented in written material. This difficulty is particularly apparent when student writers use inappropriate connecting words—*and* for *but* or *since* for *although,* for example. Provide practice in making correct word choices by asking students to insert appropriate subordinating conjunctions in the following sentences.

1. We will not pay the repair bill _____ the television is fixed. [*until, unless, before*]

2. _____ it rained, the baseball game was postponed. [*Because, Since*]

3. Mother served dinner early _____ we could get to the concert on time. [*so, so that*]

MINI-LESSON   Continued on p. 500

Nominative Case with *Than* and *As*.
Explain to students that in clauses using the subordinating conjunctions *than* and *as,* often the predicate of the clause is left out; for example, "He is taller than I (am tall)." Remind students that in standard usage, the pronoun subject of an incomplete construction must be in the nominative case. Ask students to choose the pronoun that conforms to standard usage in the follow-

Uses of Subordinate Clauses   **499**

Exercise 5 Using Adverb Clauses

POSSIBLE ANSWERS

1. Because of the sleet storm, the show was canceled.
2. After we finished eating, the telephone rang.
3. The child was scared when the lights failed.
4. Constance will work until the project is finished.
5. Wherever she goes, her dog goes with her.
6. Danny and Sandra plan to go biking as long as the weather is clear.
7. Let me know if your plans change.
8. Cindy is going to the bookstore unless the car fails to start.
9. I carry my passport although I have never been out of the country.
10. Even though he has studied music for only a short time, Hiroshi is an accomplished pianist.

Meeting INDIVIDUAL NEEDS

ENGLISH-LANGUAGE LEARNERS

General Strategies. Ask students to reserve pages in their notebooks for collecting sentences that contain subordinating conjunctions ending with the word *that: now that, in that, such that, provided that, so that,* and so forth. *That,* a word with a variety of functions in English, is often mistakenly omitted by students. Keeping a notebook of sentences to be reviewed periodically may help students master these connectors more easily.

Exercise 5 Using Adverb Clauses

Complete the following sentences by adding adverb clauses.

EXAMPLE 1. _____, I usually go straight home.
1. When I finish work, I usually go straight home.

1. _____, the show was canceled.
2. _____, the telephone rang.
3. The child was scared _____.
4. Constance will work _____.
5. _____, her dog goes with her.
6. Danny and Sandra plan to go biking _____.
7. Let me know _____.
8. Cindy is going to the bookstore _____.
9. I carry my passport _____.
10. _____, Hiroshi is an accomplished pianist.

Review A Identifying Adjective and Adverb Clauses

Identify the subordinate clauses in the following paragraph. Then, tell whether each is an *adjective clause* or an *adverb clause*.

EXAMPLE [1] Someone who pilots a balloon is an aeronaut.
1. who pilots a balloon—adjective clause

[1] In 1978, the aeronauts Ben Abruzzo, Max Anderson, and Larry Newman, whose home was Albuquerque, New Mexico, became the first people ever to pilot a balloon across the Atlantic Ocean. [2] Although Abruzzo and Anderson had been forced to land in the ocean in an

---

MINI-LESSON

ing sentences and to supply the missing words in the clause.

1. Melissa is as old as (him, he). [*is old*]
2. The Carsons have lived in this neighbor-

hood longer than (we, us). [*have lived*]

For more information on pronouns in incomplete construction, refer students to **Chapter 17: Using Pronouns Correctly.**

earlier attempt in *Double Eagle*, they had not given up. [3] Instead, they had acquired a new balloon, which they had named *Double Eagle II*. [4] Newman joined them because experience had shown the need for a third crew member. [5] On its journey from Maine to France, *Double Eagle II* was airborne for 137 hours, which is a little less than six days. [6] Although *Double Eagle II* relied on the wind's force, the balloon didn't just drift across the Atlantic; the aeronauts piloted it. [7] Abruzzo, Anderson, and Newman had to understand meteorology so that they could take advantage of favorable winds. [8] They also had to regulate their altitude constantly by adjusting their supply of helium and by losing ballast, as the balloonists shown on the previous page are doing. [9] When the balloon gained too much altitude, the crew lowered the aircraft by releasing some of the gas. [10] If the balloon lost altitude, the crew raised it by discarding ballast.

The Noun Clause

15f. A *noun clause* is a subordinate clause that is used as a noun.

A noun clause may be used as a subject, a predicate nominative, a direct object, an indirect object, or the object of a preposition.

SUBJECT	**What I need** is my own room.
PREDICATE NOMINATIVE	The happiest time in my life was **when we went to Costa Rica for the summer.**
DIRECT OBJECT	She believes **that lost time is never found again.**
INDIRECT OBJECT	We will give **whoever wins the contest** a prize.
OBJECT OF PREPOSITION	She has written an article about **how she was elected to the Senate.**

Common Introductory Words for Noun Clauses		
how	where	whoever
that	whether	whom
what	which	whomever
whatever	whichever	whose
when	who	why

Reference Note

For more about **subjects**, see page 439. For more about **predicate nominatives**, see page 453. For more about **direct** and **indirect objects**, see page 456. For more about **objects of prepositions**, see page 426.

Reference Note

Some of the words in this chart can be used to introduce **adjective clauses** (see page 495) and **adverb clauses** (see page 498).

RESOURCES

The Noun Clause

Practice

- *Grammar, Usage, and Mechanics*, pp. 97–98, 99–100
- *Language Workshop CD-ROM*, Lesson 23

Meeting INDIVIDUAL NEEDS

MULTIPLE INTELLIGENCES
Bodily-Kinesthetic Intelligence.
To provide practice in working with noun clauses, ask students to write the following word groups on separate strips of paper: *that the game was lost, whoever reaches the finish line first, what classes she wanted to take, the winner will be, the new student didn't know, became obvious in the third quarter.* Then, ask students to match the strips of paper to form three sentences. Finally, have students identify the functions of the noun clauses.

1. The winner will be *whoever reaches the finish line first.* [predicate nominative]
2. The new student didn't know *what classes she wanted to take.* [direct object]
3. *That the game was lost* became obvious in the third quarter. [subject]

Reference Note
For information about another kind of noun clause—**the infinitive clause**—see page 481.

HELP
Some sentences in Exercise 6 have more than one noun clause.

Sometimes the introductory word serves a grammatical function within the noun clause, and sometimes it does not.

EXAMPLES

                PN   S   V
Do you know **what the problem is**? [The introductory word *what* is a predicate nominative of the subject *problem—the problem is what*.]

          S   V
I know **that she is worried.** [The introductory word *that* has no grammatical function in the clause.]

In some sentences the word that introduces a noun clause can be omitted.

EXAMPLES He told us **[that] attendance is improving.** [The introductory word *that* is understood.]

The judge mentioned **[that] she was born in Guyana.** [The introductory word *that* is understood.]

Exercise 6 Identifying and Classifying Noun Clauses

Identify the noun clauses in the following sentences. Then, tell how each clause is used: as a *subject*, a *predicate nominative*, a *direct object*, an *indirect object*, or an *object of a preposition*.

EXAMPLE 1. Mr. Perkins, the band director, announced that we would play at half time this week.

1. *that we would play at half time this week*—direct object

1. Mr. Perkins did not tell us, however, what we would be playing during the half-time show.   1. d.o.
2. What we can never predict is whether he will choose a familiar march or a show tune.   2. s./p.n.
3. He always gives whoever is asked to play each selection a chance to express an opinion about it.   3. i.o.
4. He is genuinely interested in what we think of his sometimes unusual choices.   4. o.p.
5. A drummer once told Mr. Perkins she did not like most show tunes.   5. d.o.
6. How she could say that was a mystery to me.   6. s.
7. Mr. Perkins told us we would play a medley of marches.   7. d.o.
8. What everyone wanted to know immediately was who would play the solos.   8. s./p.n.
9. He understands why that was our first question.   9. d.o.
10. The crowd always applauds enthusiastically for whoever plays a solo.   10. o.p.

Review B   Identifying Adjective, Adverb, and Noun Clauses

Each sentence in the following paragraph contains at least one subordinate clause. Identify each subordinate clause, and tell whether it is an *adjective clause*, an *adverb clause*, or a *noun clause*.

EXAMPLE   [1] What's so special about the Blue Grotto, which the Italians call *Grotta Azzurra*?

1. which the Italians call *Grotta Azzurra*—adjective clause

[1] In the painting below, you can see that the color and the hidden location of the Blue Grotto have made it famous. [2] The grotto is a cavern that can be entered only from the sea. [3] Do you know where the Blue Grotto is located? [4] It is on the west side of the Italian island of Capri, which lies at the entrance to the Bay of Naples. [5] Since the only opening to the cavern is approximately three feet high, visitors must lie down in a rowboat to enter the grotto. [6] The sapphire blue of the water inside the spacious, oval cavern is created by light that is refracted through the deep pool. [7] Although the calm, blue water looks inviting, the grotto is no longer a swimming hole. [8] In the past, however, people who lived in the area greatly enjoyed swimming there. [9] Tour guides tell whoever goes there that centuries ago Tiberius, a Roman emperor, used the Blue Grotto as his private swimming pool. [10] Seeing it today, you would agree that it's a pool fit for an emperor.

1. n.
2. adj.
3. n.
4. adj.
5. adv.
6. adj.
7. adv.
8. adj.
9. n./n.
10. n.

Sandro Chia, *Grotto azzurra* (1980). Oil on canvas (147 cm x 208 cm). Courtesy Galerie Bruno Bischofberger, Zurich, Switzerland. © 1998 Sandro Chia/Licensed by VAGA, New York.

Viewing the Art

About the Artist. The Italian-born painter Sandro Chia is part of a group of artists known as postmodernists. In the 1980s, these artists rejected the modern pop style and pioneered a new aesthetic that ironically combines the traditional and the modern.

As illustrated in *Blue Grotto,* Chia's art often combines the abstract and the representational. Chia specializes in plump figures that look inflated or bloated—thus producing an ironic, barren sensuality.

Sentences Classified According to Structure

Rule 15g (pp. 504–506)

OBJECTIVE

- To classify sentences as simple, compound, complex, or compound-complex

Relating to Literature

James Weldon Johnson's poem "The Creation" includes a variety of sentence types. Have students read the poem carefully, and ask them how Johnson uses compound and complex sentences effectively. [*Johnson creates a powerful, rhythmic, melodic effect with the parallel structure of repeated independent clauses introduced by* And, *as in lines 10–12, and with the parallel structure of repeated adjective clauses introduced by* Who, *as in lines 81–83.*]

Reference Note
Sentences may also be **classified according to purpose.** See page 459.

Reference Note
See pages 703 and 724 for more information on **punctuating compound sentences.**

Sentences Classified According to Structure

The *structure* of a sentence is determined by the number and types of clauses it has.

15g. A sentence can be classified, depending on its structure, as *simple, compound, complex,* or *compound-complex*.

(1) A *simple sentence* contains one independent clause and no subordinate clauses.

A simple sentence may contain a compound subject, a compound verb, and any number of phrases.

EXAMPLES   **Cora** and **Kareem bought** party supplies at the mall. [compound subject]

Later, **they drove** to school and **decorated** the cafeteria for the Ecology Club's annual banquet. [compound verb]

(2) A *compound sentence* contains two or more independent clauses and no subordinate clauses.

A compound sentence is two or more independent clauses joined together by (1) a comma and a coordinating conjunction, (2) a semicolon, or (3) a semicolon and a conjunctive adverb such as *therefore, however,* or *consequently* followed by a comma.

EXAMPLES   **Cora hung** colorful streamers from the ceiling, and **Kareem set** party favors on the tables.

After an hour, **they took** a short break; then **they went** back to work.

They agreed not to take any more breaks; otherwise, **they would be** late getting home.

504   Chapter 15   The Clause

RESOURCES

Sentences Classified According to Structure Practice

- *Grammar, Usage, and Mechanics,* pp. 101–102
- *Language Workshop CD-ROM,* Lesson 26

NOTE Do not mistake a simple sentence with a compound subject or compound verb for a compound sentence.

	S V
SIMPLE SENTENCE	To pass the time, **they talked** about school and
	V
	told stories about their families. [compound verb]
	S V
COMPOUND SENTENCE	To pass the time, **they talked** about school, and
	S V
	they told stories about their families.

(3) A *complex sentence* contains one independent clause and at least one subordinate clause.

	S V S
EXAMPLES	When **they had finished** their work, **they**
	V
	complimented each other on the results.

(4) A *compound-complex* sentence contains two or more independent clauses and at least one subordinate clause.

	S V
EXAMPLE	**Cora waited** for just the right moment to ask
	S V
	Kareem to the banquet, and **he** promptly **accepted** her
	S V
	invitation, adding that **he had been planning** to ask her.

Exercise 7 — Classifying Sentences According to Structure

Classify each of the sentences in the following paragraph as *simple*, *compound*, *complex*, or *compound-complex*.

EXAMPLE 1. The Key Club decided to sponsor a rummage sale.
 1. simple

1. Organizing the rummage sale, the Key Club requested donations from everyone at school.   **1. simp.**
2. The club members accepted whatever was donated, but they welcomed housewares most.   **2. cd.-cx.**

STYLE TIP

Paragraphs in which all the sentences have the same structure can be monotonous to read. To keep your readers interested in your ideas, evaluate your writing to see whether you've used a variety of sentence structures. Then, use revising techniques—adding, cutting, replacing, and reordering—to enliven your writing by varying the structure of your sentences.

COMPUTER TIP

A word processor can help you check for varied sentence structure in your writing. Make a copy of your document. By inserting a return or a page break after every period, you can view the sentences in a vertical list and compare the structures of each sentence in a particular paragraph. Make any revisions on the properly formatted copy of your document.

Crossing the Curriculum

Math. Explain to students that using a variety of sentence structures makes writing more interesting. Tell students that they will use a technique from math, the bar graph, to analyze a piece of their writing. Ask them first to count the total number of sentences and then the number of each of the four types of sentences classified according to structure. Then, have them make bar graphs like the one shown below. The bar graph shown here is for an essay containing fifty sentences, of which twenty-five are simple, five are compound, ten are complex, and ten are compound-complex.

Discuss with students how this visual representation gives them a clear idea of how varied their sentence structures are. To extend the lesson, ask students to practice combining sentences in the pieces they have analyzed and then to make new bar graphs reflecting the changes. For more information on sentence combining, refer students to **Chapter 10: Writing Effective Sentences.**

Learning for Life

continued on p. 506

Storytelling. Tell students that storytelling is part of many jobs, such as camp counselor, disc jockey, or minister. Storytelling is also a part of conversation; students may not be aware that they already use a variety of sentence structures in daily conversations. Divide the class into groups of three or four students each. Ask one person in each group to volunteer to "tell a story," that is, to relate a brief incident, real or imaginary, to the rest of the group. (Three minutes should be sufficient.) Provide

3. The principal donated a vacuum cleaner; the soccer coach contributed a set of dishes; and several of the teachers provided towels and sheets. **3. cd.**
4. The club sold almost everything that had been donated, and the members celebrated their success with pitchers of lemonade. **4. cd.-cx.**
5. Afterward, they gave all the profits that they had made from the sale to the city's homeless shelter. **5. cx.**
6. The shelter's employees were very grateful for the donations. **6. simp.**
7. They offered the members of the Key Club the chance to tour the facility. **7. simp.**
8. John took photos, and I interviewed both staff members and clients of the shelter. **8. cd.**
9. After we had finished our article, we took it to the editor of the school newspaper. **9. cx.**
10. The story was published in the next issue, and we received many compliments even though we hadn't expected any praise. **10. cd.-cx.**

Review C Writing Sentences with Varied Structures

Write your own sentences according to the following guidelines.

EXAMPLE 1. Write a simple sentence containing a compound subject.
  1. *My aunt and uncle live nearby.*

1. Write a simple sentence containing a compound verb.
2. Write a compound sentence containing two independent clauses joined by a comma and the conjunction *but*.
3. Write a compound sentence containing two independent clauses joined by a semicolon, a conjunctive adverb, and a comma.
4. Write a complex sentence containing an adjective clause.
5. Write a complex sentence beginning with an adverb clause.
6. Write a complex sentence ending with an adverb clause.
7. Write a complex sentence containing a noun clause used as the direct object.
8. Write a complex sentence containing a noun clause used as the subject.
9. Write a complex sentence containing a noun clause used as the object of a preposition.
10. Write a compound-complex sentence.

Review C Writing Sentences with Varied Structures

POSSIBLE ANSWERS

1. After dinner, Peter washed and dried the dishes.
2. Ed tried to install the new windows himself, but the process was very difficult.
3. Trish Doyle is usually a very good student; however, her grades have gone down this year.
4. At Monday's concert, I got to hear the piece that I like.
5. After they had lunch, the Garcias went to the beach.
6. Tim and Shelley will meet us there if they have time.
7. We discussed how to persuade our neighbors to cut their grass.
8. Whether we should vote or not was the topic of debate.
9. She photocopied the instructions for whoever has to organize the fire drills.
10. Max thought that Kate was just kidding, but he had to make sure.

Learning for Life

groups with tape recorders so they can record the stories. Then, ask students to play back the taped stories, pausing at the end of each sentence to classify it according to structure. One person in the group should make a tally of the types of sentence structures. If there are fragments, ask students to convert them to complete sentences and then to classify them. Finally, ask groups to report their findings to the rest of the class.

Chapter Review

A. Identifying and Classifying Clauses

For each of the following sentences, identify the italicized clause as *independent* or *subordinate*. Tell whether each subordinate clause functions in the sentence as an *adjective clause*, an *adverb clause*, or a *noun clause*.

1. Scientists have recently discovered *that chameleons are not masters of disguise.* **1. n.**
2. *Their changes of color are not attempts at camouflage;* they are responses to changes in light and temperature.
3. Chameleons, *which dislike any contact*, will tolerate it for the purpose of breeding. **3. adj.**
4. *When two chameleons cross paths*, they do their best to frighten each other by hissing, snapping, and changing color. **4. adv.**
5. Some scientists think *that such encounters control the chameleons' changes in color.* **5. n.**
6. Males occasionally fight, but *most chameleons try to avoid physical confrontation.*
7. Almost all of the species *that make up the chameleon family* live in trees. **7. adj.**
8. *Because the chameleon moves slowly*, it would become an easy prey without its natural green and brown coloration. **8. adv.**
9. *The chameleon's tongue is sticky and has numerous folds and furrows* that are lined with hooklike cells.
10. The tongue is propelled by a set of muscles *that can extend it as far as one and one-half times the length of the chameleon's body.* **10. adj.**

B. Identifying and Classifying Subordinate Clauses

Identify each subordinate clause in the following sentences. Then, tell whether each subordinate clause is an *adjective clause*, an *adverb clause*, or a *noun clause*.

11. adv. 11. Before you buy the sweater, try it on.
12. adj. 12. Chang, whose mother is a dentist, just lost his retainer.

13. n.	13. Do you know who won the speech contest?
14. adj.	14. The dog that scattered our garbage has annoyed all of us.
15. adv.	15. Don't agree to do the project if you don't like to paint.
16. n.	16. Lisa said that she would provide food for the trip.
17. adv.	17. Until you pay back the money, I will charge you interest.
18. n.	18. Reynaldo was thrilled with what you gave him for his birthday.
19. adj.	19. We saw a movie that scared even the bravest of us.
20. adj.	20. The CD that you borrowed yesterday belongs to my brother.
21. adv.	21. After we have dinner, let's remember to call Grandpa.
22. n.	22. Do you know what the capital of Nigeria is?
23. adj.	23. Lilliput, which was invented by Jonathan Swift, is the land of tiny people in Swift's *Gulliver's Travels*.
24. n.	24. Ariana was a bit worried about what you said about her.
25. adj.	25. The boy who climbed the tree to save the parakeet has endeared himself to everybody.
26. adj.	26. Our parents heard a song that moved them deeply.
27. n.	27. Have you heard what happened at the intersection this morning?
28. adv.	28. If you don't like camping, don't go on the trip.
29. n.	29. Tom and Phyllis said they would pay our dog's boarding costs.
30. n.	30. We know exactly who is responsible, but we will point the finger at no one.

C. Classifying Sentences According to Structure

Classify each of the following sentences as *simple*, *compound*, *complex*, or *compound-complex*.

31. simp.	31. The Bugatti Motor Club hosted an exhibit of old motoring prints.
32. cd.-cx.	32. When our team finished the project, we all went out to lunch at the Mumbai Grill, and our friend Amrit met us there.
33. cx.	33. The hotel guests were surprised when the alarm went off.
34. cd.	34. Bill gave a speech, and I took notes.
35. cx.	35. Georges Bizet was the French composer who wrote "Carmen," which is definitely my favorite opera.
36. cd.	36. The store employees decorated the storefront, the manager put on his best suit, and the customers arrived promptly at eight.
37. simp.	37. We students were very proud of our prize-winning principal.

RESOURCES

The Clause
Review
- *Grammar, Usage, and Mechanics,* pp. 103, 104, 105, 106

Assessment
- *Assessment Package*
  —*Chapter Tests,* Ch. 15
  —*Chapter Tests in Standardized Test Formats,* Ch. 15
- *Test Generator (One-Stop Planner CD-ROM)*

38. The weather inland was unseasonably cold and frosty, but on the coast a mild wind was blowing from the south.
39. Our short film was shown in one of the theaters downtown; despite our dire predictions, it was fairly well received.
40. Under the foundations of many an old building in Rome, especially near the Forum and Colosseum, are even older foundations, some dating back to the late Empire.

38. cd.
39. cd.
40. simp.

Writing Application
Writing a Paragraph

Using Subordinate Clauses The student council has decided to decorate your school with posters of popular artworks. To decide on the posters, the council has asked for recommendations, along with brief descriptions, for artworks that students would like to see. Write two paragraphs about two works (one paragraph on each work) that you would like to recommend. Use specific details and include at least five subordinate clauses.

Prewriting Think of two paintings that you like, and find a picture of each one. If you do not know their titles, try looking in books or asking a librarian or art teacher. Think about why you particularly like these works, and jot down your reasons.

Writing As you write, you may think of additional details and reasons. If you do, pause for a moment and consider how they fit in with the rest of your notes. Add to your rough draft any new information that fits in smoothly.

Revising Read through your paragraphs to be sure they each have a topic sentence supported by your reasons for recommending each artwork. Check to see that you have used a total of at least five subordinate clauses in the two paragraphs. If you have not, try combining sentences by creating adjective, adverb, or noun clauses.

Publishing Proofread your paragraphs for any errors in grammar, punctuation, and spelling. You and your classmates may want to present two or three of the class's recommendations to the school board or parent-teacher organization.

Chapter Review **509**

Writing Application
(p. 509)

OBJECTIVE
- To recommend and describe works of art in paragraphs containing subordinate clauses

Writing Application

Tip. This assignment allows students to form opinions about visual art and to articulate those opinions in written paragraphs. The assignment further encourages students to develop maturity and variety in their writing by having each student include at least five subordinate clauses in the paragraphs.

Scoring Rubric. While you will want to pay particular attention to students' use of clauses, you will also want to evaluate overall writing performance. You may want to give a split score to indicate development and clarity of the composition as well as grammar skills.

GRAMMAR

RESOURCES
Writing Application
Practice
- *Grammar, Usage, and Mechanics*, p. 109
- *Language Workshop CD-ROM*, Lessons 22–23, 26

Writing Application
Alignments
TEKS 1C, 2A, 2C, 3A, 3D
TAAS W1, W2, W3, W4, W5, W7
English II End-of-Course 4, 5, 6

Texas Resources
- *One-Stop Planner CD-ROM*

Chapter Review **509**

CHAPTER 16

Agreement
Subject and Verb, Pronoun and Antecedent

PREVIEWING THE CHAPTER

- This chapter is divided into two main parts: **Agreement of Subject and Verb** and **Agreement of Pronoun and Antecedent**. Instead of presenting the rules and exercises in the order in which they appear in the chapter, you may want to design lesson plans by pairing similar rules, such as **Rules 16b** and **16q**, which both relate to the use of indefinite pronouns.

- The chapter concludes with a **Chapter Review**, which includes a **Writing Application** feature that asks students to write a personal letter using correct subject-verb and pronoun-antecedent agreement.

- For help in integrating the chapter with writing chapters, use the **Teaching Strands** chart on pp. T401A–T401B.

USING THE DIAGNOSTIC PREVIEW

- Both **Part A** and **Part B** of the **Diagnostic Preview** ask students to find and revise errors in subject-verb agreement and in pronoun-antecedent agreement. You may want to use the results of the preview to determine how much reteaching is necessary. For example, if the results show that only a few students have difficulty determining which verb forms to use with subjects that are indefinite pronouns, you may want to have proficient learners help you guide those few students through the discussion of **Rule 16b** and through the completion of **Exercises 4** and **5** and **Review B**.

Diagnostic Preview

A. Identifying Subject-Verb Agreement and Pronoun-Antecedent Agreement

In most of the following sentences, either a verb does not agree with its subject or a pronoun does not agree with its antecedent. For each incorrect verb or pronoun, write the correct form. If a sentence is already correct, write *C*.

EXAMPLES   1. Every leaf, flower, and seedpod were glimmering with frost.
1. *was*

2. Were any tickets left at the box office for me?
2. *C*

1. were
2. C
3. are
4. is

1. There was women, as well as men, who set out on the perilous journey into new territory.
2. The Morenos, I think, have the best chance of winning.
3. The store, the hotel, and the airport is all in a ten-mile radius of the beach.
4. *Bronzeville Boys and Girls* are a collection of poems by Gwendolyn Brooks.

510   Chapter 16   Agreement

CHAPTER RESOURCES

Planning
- One-Stop Planner CD-ROM

Practice and Extension
- *Grammar, Usage, and Mechanics,* p. 110
- Language Workshop CD-ROM

Internet
- go.hrw.com (keyword: EOLang)

Evaluation and Assessment
- Assessment Package
  —Chapter Tests, Ch. 16
  —Chapter Tests in Standardized Test Formats, Ch. 16
- Test Generator (One-Stop Planner CD-ROM)

5. Neither of the candidates has prepared ~~their~~ statement. — 5. his or her
6. Mr. Ortega, along with other members of his firm, ~~have~~ established a scholarship fund for art students. — 6. has
7. To apply for the scholarship, a student must submit at least four samples of ~~their~~ work. — 7. his or her
8. The test results showed that about 80 percent of the respondents ~~was~~ in the average group. — 8. were
9. A hostile crowd gathers outside the courtroom to show ~~their~~ disapproval of the verdict. — 9. its [or gather . . . their]
10. The committee ~~was~~ preparing their speeches for the meeting with the new governor. — 10. were

B. Identifying Subject-Verb Agreement and Pronoun-Antecedent Agreement

For each sentence in the following paragraph, write the correct form of each incorrect verb or pronoun. If a sentence is already correct, write C.

EXAMPLE [1] Aunt Bonnie, along with several other Peace Corps volunteers, are going to Kenya.

1. is going

[11] Neither my brothers nor my dad ~~were~~ surprised to hear that Aunt Bonnie is going to Kenya as a Peace Corps volunteer. [12] First, she and the other members of the Kenya group ~~gathers~~ in Philadelphia for a few days of orientation. [13] Their focus at this point ~~are~~ to meet one another and get acquainted. [14] Then the whole group travels together to Nairobi, Kenya, where everyone will have ~~their~~ last chance for months to enjoy hot running water! [15] After one night in Nairobi, half of them ~~leaves~~ for the town of Naivasha for eleven weeks of cultural sensitivity training. [16] Each of the volunteers ~~get~~ to live with a Kenyan family during this period of training. [17] The close daily contact will help them learn to converse in Swahili, one of the languages that is spoken in Kenya. [18] Bonnie ~~don't~~ know yet where exactly in Kenya she is going to be posted. [19] She, as well as the other members of her group, expects to be assigned to the area of greatest need. [20] No one in the group has been told ~~their~~ specific job assignment, but Bonnie says she will probably be helping Kenyans develop small businesses.

11. was
12. gather
13. is
14. his or her
15. leave
16. gets
17. are
18. doesn't
19. C
20. his or her

Agreement of Subject and Verb

Rules 16a–o *(pp. 512–532)*

OBJECTIVES

- To identify words as singular or plural
- To select verbs that agree in number with their subjects
- To read aloud correct sentences with indefinite pronouns as subjects
- To write sentences with verbs that agree with their subjects
- To correct errors in subject-verb agreement in sentences
- To read aloud sentences with compound subjects
- To select verbs that agree in number with their subjects
- To write sentences with singular and plural collective nouns
- To revise sentences so that the verbs agree with their subjects
- To proofread sentences for correct subject-verb agreement
- To use *don't* and *doesn't* correctly in sentences

Reference Note
For more about forming the **plurals of nouns**, see page 787.

HELP
Most of the time, nouns ending in *–s* are plural (*aunts, bushes, cities, tacos, friends*); verbs ending in *–s* are generally singular (*gives, takes, does, has, is*). Note, though, that verbs used with the pronouns *I* and *you* do not end in *s*.

Agreement of Subject and Verb

16a. A verb should agree in number with its subject.

A word that refers to one person, place, thing, or idea is *singular* in number. A word that refers to more than one is *plural* in number.

Singular	video	child	I	thief	herself
Plural	videos	children	we	thieves	themselves

Exercise 1 Identifying Words as Singular or Plural

Identify each of the following words as either *singular* or *plural*.

EXAMPLES
1. uncles
1. plural

2. leaf
2. singular

1. stories **1. p**   6. mouse **6. s**   11. he **11. s**   16. pods **16. p**
2. one **2. s**   7. genius **7. s**   12. has **12. s**   17. donates **17. s**
3. several **3. p**   8. teeth **8. p**   13. both **13. p**   18. donation **18. s**
4. applies **4. s**   9. ability **9. s**   14. toy **14. s**   19. key **19. s**
5. people **5. p**   10. says **10. s**   15. woman **15. s**   20. many **20. p**

(1) Singular subjects take singular verbs.

EXAMPLES **Earline attends** college. [The singular verb *attends* agrees with the singular subject *Earline*.]

That **boy delivers** newspapers. [The singular verb *delivers* agrees with the singular subject *boy*.]

(2) Plural subjects take plural verbs.

EXAMPLES **They attend** college. [The plural verb *attend* agrees with the plural subject *They*.]

Those **boys deliver** newspapers. [The plural verb *deliver* agrees with the plural subject *boys*.]

In a verb phrase, the first helping (auxiliary) verb agrees in number with the subject.

EXAMPLES **Earline is attending** college.
They are attending college.

Reference Note
For more about **helping verbs**, see page 417.

RESOURCES

Agreement of Subject and Verb
Practice
- *Grammar, Usage, and Mechanics,* pp. 111, 112–113, 114–115, 116–117, 118, 119, 120, 121, 122, 123
- *Language Workshop CD-ROM,* Lessons 5, 6, 7

A **boy** in my class **has been delivering** newspapers.
Two **boys** in my class **have been delivering** newspapers.

NOTE A gerund phrase or an infinitive phrase used as a complete subject takes a singular verb. Do not be misled by any particular noun or pronoun in the phrase. The gerund or infinitive serves as a singular simple subject.

EXAMPLES **Working with you and the others has been** a privilege.
[The singular verb *has been* is used because the gerund *Working*, not the pronoun *you* or *others*, is the subject of the verb.]

To finish our science projects is our immediate goal.
[The singular verb *is* is used because the infinitive *To finish*, not the noun *projects*, is the subject of the verb.]

Reference Note
For more about **gerund phrases** and **infinitive phrases**, see page 478 and page 480.

Exercise 2 Selecting Verbs That Agree with Their Subjects

Choose the verb in parentheses that agrees with each subject given.

EXAMPLE 1. bells (*is ringing, are ringing*)
         1. are ringing

1. people (*walks, walk*)
2. you (*is, are*)
3. house (*has stood, have stood*)
4. we (*talks, talk*)
5. Joan (*was, were*)
6. cattle (*is running, are running*)
7. result (*is, are*)
8. they (*believes, believe*)
9. crews (*sails, sail*)
10. women (*seems, seem*)
11. Lauren and Sierra (*laughs, laugh*)
12. everyone (*is, are*)
13. otters (*has swum, have swum*)
14. students (*graduates, graduate*)
15. boulder (*weighs, weigh*)
16. firefighting (*saves, save*)
17. Phoebe (*reads, read*)
18. jets (*flies, fly*)
19. children (*sings, sing*)
20. to whisper (*is, are*)

(3) The number of a subject usually is not determined by a word in a phrase or clause following the subject.

SINGULAR A **book** of poems **is** on the shelf. [The prepositional phrase *of poems* does not affect the number of the subject *book*.]

PLURAL The **dinosaurs** from the Jurassic Period **include** the Seismosaurus. [The prepositional phrase *from the Jurassic Period* does not affect the number of the subject *dinosaurs*.]

Reference Note
For more about **phrases**, see "Chapter 14: The Phrase." For more about **clauses**, see "Chapter 15: The Clause."

Agreement of Subject and Verb 513

Cooperative Learning

After students have completed **Exercise 1,** organize the class into four groups. Assign each group four of the nouns or pronouns from **Exercise 1,** and ask the group members to write a sentence using each word as the subject. Encourage students to refer to the examples at the bottom of p. 512 and at the top of p. 513 as models for their sentences. Have students underline each subject once and each verb twice. Next, have groups check each other's work for errors in subject-verb agreement.

Then, have groups revise the sentences they have assessed. Instruct group members to change each singular subject and verb to plural and each plural subject and verb to singular. Finally, have groups exchange papers again to check each other's revisions.

Meeting INDIVIDUAL NEEDS

LEARNERS HAVING DIFFICULTY
If students need extra practice with the examples for **Rule 16a (3)** and **16a (4),** choose from a newspaper or magazine a short article that you think students will find interesting. Rewrite the article, adding errors that pertain to each of the parts of **Rule 16a.**

Provide students with copies of the error-filled article, tell them the number of errors in it, and have them correct the errors. You may want to guide students through the article by asking them to strike through the modifying phrase or clause or the negative construction that comes between each subject and verb.

MINI-LESSON   Continued on pp. 514–515

Appositive Phrases. To extend the discussion about the kinds of phrases that may separate subjects from verbs (see **Alternative Lesson,** p. 514), point out to students that an appositive phrase identifying or explaining the subject may also appear between the subject and the verb. Explain to students that although the appositive phrase adds information about the subject, the phrase does not determine the number of the subject and verb.

Write the following sentences on the

Meeting INDIVIDUAL NEEDS

ENGLISH-LANGUAGE LEARNERS

Spanish. In Spanish, *la gente* (people) is a singular noun, so Spanish-speaking students might use sentences such as "The people is going to the game." You might want to provide extra practice in subject-verb agreement using *people* as the subject.

TEACHING TIP

Exercise 3 Remind students that the subject in a sentence answers the question *Who?* or *What?* before the verb and that the answer to the question does not appear in a modifying phrase or clause. You may want to suggest to students that before they choose the verb form for each sentence in **Exercise 3**, they omit any modifying phrase or clause that comes before the verb.

Exercise 3

ALTERNATIVE LESSON
To reinforce students' understanding of the different kinds of phrases, ask students to identify the kind of phrase that comes between the subject and the verb in each of the following sentences from **Exercise 3**:

sentence 1 [*prepositional phrase*]

sentence 3 [*prepositional phrase*]

sentence 8 [*participial phrase*]

Remind students that one kind of phrase may be part of another kind of phrase. Ask students to identify the object of the prepositional phrase in sentence 3 [*collecting (stamps)*]. Then, ask students to tell what kind of phrase *collecting stamps* is [*gerund phrase*].

Note: At this time, you may want to use the **Mini-Lesson,** pp. 513–515, since it discusses appositive phrases, which can also appear between subjects and verbs.

SINGULAR   The only **mammal** that has wings **is** the bat. [The subordinate clause *that has wings* does not affect the number of the subject *mammal*.]

PLURAL   **Frogs,** which live both on land and in water, **are** amphibians. [The subordinate clause *which live both on land and in water* does not affect the number of the subject *Frogs*.]

NOTE *Together with, in addition to, as well as,* and *along with* are compound prepositions. Words in phrases beginning with compound prepositions do not affect the number of the subject or verb.

EXAMPLES   His technical **skills,** together with his delightful sense of humor, **have enabled** Enrique to become a successful computer consultant.

His delightful **sense** of humor, together with his technical skills, **has enabled** Enrique to become a successful computer consultant.

(4) A negative construction following the subject does not change the number of the subject.

EXAMPLE   **Carl,** not Juan and I, **is doing** the artwork.

Exercise 3 Choosing Verbs That Agree with Their Subjects

Identify the subject in each of the following sentences. Then, choose the verb in parentheses that agrees in number with the subject.

EXAMPLE   1. The price of haircuts (*has, have*) gone up.
1. price—has

1. A heaping basket of turnip greens (*was, were*) sitting on the counter.
2. The cost of two new snow tires (*was, were*) more than I had expected.
3. The community college course on collecting stamps always (*attracts, attract*) many people.
4. The members of the Pak family (*meets, meet*) for a reunion every year.
5. The carpeting you saw in the upstairs and downstairs rooms (*is, are*) going to be replaced.
6. The turquoise stones in this Navajo ring certainly (*is, are*) pretty.
7. One friend of my brothers (*says, say*) that I look a little like Whitney Houston.
8. The package sent by my cousins (*was, were*) smashed in the mail.

MINI-LESSON

chalkboard. (Do not underline any words until students have given their responses.) For each sentence, ask students to identify the appositive phrase, choose the correct verb form in parentheses, and tell why the verb form is correct.

1. Kiole, one of the basketball team's best players, (*averages,* average) fifteen points per game. [*Averages* is correct because it agrees with the singular subject, *Kiole,* not with any word in the appositive phrase.]

9. Not all the singers who tried out for the school choir (*sings*, *sing*) equally well.
10. Burt, not Anne and Laura, (*has*, *have*) borrowed the bicycle pump.

Review A — Completing Sentences That Demonstrate Agreement

Anna Mary Robertson Moses (1860–1961), better known as "Grandma Moses," became famous for her paintings of rural America. Add words to the following word groups to complete ten sentences about this Grandma Moses painting, titled *The Barn Dance*. Make sure that all verbs agree with their subjects. Be prepared to identify the subject and verb in each sentence.

EXAMPLE   1. barn are
         1. *The doors of the barn are wide open.*

1. clouds look
2. musician is playing
3. horse is drinking
4. barn dance are enjoying
5. buildings in the distance is
6. green wagon are waving
7. along with laughter and conversation, fills
8. guests have noticed the cloudy
9. who are at this barn dance
10. horses pulls

HELP—
In the example sentence in Review A, *doors* is the subject, and *are* is the verb.

The Barn Dance by Grandma Moses, 1860–1961, Copyright 1989. Grandma Moses Properties Co., New York.

Agreement of Subject and Verb

2. Oranges, a delicious source of vitamin C, (*is*, *are*) part of my daily diet. [*Are* is correct because it agrees with the plural subject, *Oranges*, not with any word in the appositive phrase.]

For more information on appositive phrases, refer students to **Chapter 14: The Phrase**.

Review A — Completing Sentences That Demonstrate Agreement

POSSIBLE ANSWERS

1. The clouds look like fluffy elephants.
2. A musician is playing to warm up for the dance.
3. A horse is drinking from the trough.
4. All of the people at the barn dance are enjoying the music.
5. One of the buildings in the distance is my house.
6. The people on the green wagon are waving.
7. Fiddle music, along with laughter and conversation, fills the air as the band begins a new dance.
8. The guests have noticed the cloudy sky.
9. Many of the folks who are at this barn dance are making new friends.
10. A pair of horses pulls each of the wagons.

Relating to Writing

After the class has completed **Review A,** ask each student to write a brief story using the sentences he or she created for **Review A.** Encourage students to imagine they are part of the scene depicted in the painting by Grandma Moses. Explain that as they write, they may need to revise some of their sentences from **Review A** and add sentences in order to show a clear and meaningful relationship between ideas. Stress to students that when they proofread their stories, they should look particularly for errors in subject-verb agreement.

The words *one*, *thing*, and *body* are singular, and so are the indefinite pronouns that contain these words.

EXAMPLES
Was any**one** hurrying?

Every**body welcomes** the good weather.

No**thing has** been clarified.

Indefinite Pronouns

An *indefinite pronoun* refers to a person, a place, a thing, or an idea that may or may not be specifically named.

EXAMPLES Has **anyone** loaded the van?

Some of the campsites **are** vacant.

Please pack **everything** we will need for camping.

All of the space in the back seat **is** filled.

16b. Some indefinite pronouns are singular; others are plural. Certain indefinite pronouns may be either singular or plural, depending on how they are used.

(1) The following indefinite pronouns are singular: *anybody, anyone, anything, each, either, everybody, everyone, everything, neither, nobody, no one, nothing, one, somebody, someone,* **and** *something.*

EXAMPLES **Neither** of the animals in the pen **has been fed** this morning.

Somebody is bringing a CD player to the birthday party on Saturday.

Was everyone on the volleyball team on time for the class picture at noon?

One of the puppies **has chewed** a hole in your tennis shoe.

NOTE *Either* and *neither* can be used as adjectives and correlative conjunctions as well as indefinite pronouns. When either word is used as an adjective or a correlative conjunction, it cannot be the subject of a sentence. Carefully identify the subject when you are deciding what form of a verb to use.

ADJECTIVE **Neither** animal has been fed. [The verb agrees with the subject *animal. Neither* modifies *animal.*]

CORRELATIVE CONJUNCTION **Neither** the cows nor the pigs have been fed yet. [The verb agrees with the subject that is nearer to it—*pigs. Neither* is part of the correlative conjunction *Neither . . . nor.*]

INDEFINITE PRONOUN **Neither** of the animals **has been fed.** [The verb agrees with the subject *Neither.*]

(2) The following indefinite pronouns are plural: *both, few, many,* and *several.*

EXAMPLES
Have **both** of them **been** informed?

A **few** in the crowd **were** rowdy.

Many of the staff **write** and **edit** on word processors.

Several of the women **are** pilots.

(3) The following indefinite pronouns may be either singular or plural, depending on how they are used: *all, any, more, most, none,* and *some.*

These pronouns are singular when they refer to singular words and are plural when they refer to plural words.

SINGULAR **Most** of the job **was finished.** [*Most* refers to the singular noun *job*.]

PLURAL **Most** of the jobs **were finished.** [*Most* refers to the plural noun *jobs*.]

SINGULAR **Has any** of the shipment **arrived**? [*Any* refers to the singular noun *shipment*.]

PLURAL **Have any** of the shipments **arrived**? [*Any* refers to the plural noun *shipments*.]

SINGULAR **None** of the test **was** difficult. [*None* refers to the singular noun *test*.]

PLURAL **None** of the tests **were** difficult. [*None* refers to the plural noun *tests*.]

In each of the examples above, the object of the prepositional phrase following the indefinite pronoun provides a clue to the number of the pronoun.

> NOTE In a sentence that does not include a phrase after the subject, you must find the number of the noun to which the pronoun refers. Make sure the verb has the same number as the antecedent.
>
> EXAMPLES **Most was** interesting. [The pronoun *Most* may be referring to a portion of a book, of a movie, of a conversation, or some other thing.]
>
> **Most were** interesting. [The pronoun *Most* may be referring to a number of books, photographs, ideas, or other things.]

HELP
Many of the words listed in Rule 16b, (1)–(3), can be used either as pronouns or as adjectives.

ADJECTIVES
One child is there.
Many children have left.
Some children remain.

PRONOUNS
One is there.
Many have left.
Some remain.

TEACHING TIP

Mnemonic. To help students learn the indefinite pronouns that can be either singular or plural, you may want to share with them the following rhyme:

> It could be one
> Or more than one:
> All, any, more,
> Most, some, or none!

Agreement of Subject and Verb

TEACHING TIP

Oral Practice 1 You may want to extend **Oral Practice 1** to reinforce students' understanding that some indefinite pronouns may be singular or plural. Write on the chalkboard the following sentences:

1. <u>Some</u> of the cheese <u>was</u> eaten.
2. <u>Most</u> of the milk cartons <u>are</u> empty.
3. <u>None</u> of the fruit <u>is</u> ripe.

As soon as students have read aloud sentence 5, 6, or 8 from **Oral Practice 1**, ask them to read aloud the related sentence from the chalkboard, making sure they stress the underlined words. Have students note that the subjects of the related sentences are the same and that the verbs are different. Ask students to explain why the verbs are different. [*The subjects are indefinite pronouns whose antecedents are not the same number.*]

Meeting INDIVIDUAL NEEDS

MODALITIES

Auditory Learners. Before students begin **Exercise 4**, ask them to identify the subject and the verb in each sentence. Then, ask students to read aloud each sentence, encouraging them to emphasize the subject and the verb.

As they revise the sentences from **Exercise 4**, ask students to underline the subjects and the verbs. After they have completed their revisions, you may want students to read aloud the new sentences, emphasizing the underlined words.

Oral Practice 1 — Using Verbs That Agree with Indefinite Pronouns

Read the following sentences aloud, stressing the italicized words.

1. *One* of those cups *is* broken.
2. Choose a bicycle; *either is* ready to go.
3. A *few* of the girls *are* experienced riders.
4. *Each* of the mariachi bands *has* performed one number.
5. *Some* of your mice *were* eating the cheese.
6. *Most* of the milk that I bought *is* gone.
7. *Neither* of these cars *has* a radio.
8. Here are the apples. *None are* ripe.

Exercise 4 — Writing Sentences with Verbs That Agree with Their Subjects

Rewrite each of the following sentences according to the directions in parentheses. Then, change the number of the verb to agree with the new subject.

EXAMPLE 1. Each of these books was written by Margaret Atwood. (Change *Each* to *All*.)

1. All of these books were written by Margaret Atwood.

1. Most people/understand
2. Both/were
3. Have/both
4. crop/was
5. Has/wheat
6. Many of our neighbors/have
7. Several/are
8. All/need
9. pears/were
10. Some/are

1. Everyone easily understands the rules of this game. (Change *Everyone* to *Most people*.)
2. Neither of the actresses was nominated. (Change *Neither* to *Both*.)
3. Has each of your cousins had a turn? (Change *each* to *both*.)
4. Some of the trees were destroyed. (Change *trees* to *crop*.)
5. Have any of the apples been harvested? (Change *apples* to *wheat*.)
6. Nobody has visited that "haunted" house. (Change *Nobody* to *Many of our neighbors*.)
7. Each is well trained. (Change *Each* to *Several*.)
8. One of the tires needs air. (Change *One* to *All*.)
9. All of the fruit was eaten. (Change *fruit* to *pears*.)
10. One of the puzzle pieces is missing. (Change *One* to *Some*.)

Exercise 5 — Correcting Errors in Subject-Verb Agreement

The subjects and verbs in some of the sentences on the next page do not agree. If a sentence is incorrect, write the correct form of the verb. If the sentence is already correct, write *C*.

EXAMPLE   1. Most of the world's diamonds comes from mines in Africa.
          1. come

1. Several of the forwards on the team was commended by the captain. 1. were
2. Neither of the coaches were happy with the decision. 2. was
3. Each of us are going to make a large poster for the upcoming election. 3. is
4. Some of the frozen yogurt have started to melt. 4. has
5. Does both of those games require special gear? 5. Do
6. Either of Mr. Catalano's assistants have approval and can go. 6. has
7. None of the buildings were damaged by the hail. 7. C
8. None of the food have been frozen. 8. has
9. Neither of the book reports were finished on time. 9. was
10. Does anyone want to help me make gefilte fish for the Passover feast? 10. C

Review B Selecting Verbs That Agree with Their Subjects

For each of the following sentences, choose the verb in parentheses that agrees with the subject.

EXAMPLE   1. How (*does, do*) astronauts on a space shuttle prepare their meals?
          1. do

1. (*Has, Have*) any of you ever wondered how meals are served to space-shuttle astronauts?
2. Each of the items for the day's menu (*comes, come*) sealed in its own container.
3. To help reduce weight on the spacecraft, many of the foods (*is, are*) dehydrated.
4. At mealtime, someone in the crew (*adds, add*) water to the scrambled eggs, vegetables, and puddings.
5. All of the water mixed with these foods (*is, are*) a byproduct of the fuel cells that provide the spacecraft's electricity.
6. Of course, because there is no gravity, not one of the beverages (*is, are*) pourable.
7. If a container is accidentally jolted, any uncovered liquid (*bounces, bounce*) into the air like a ball, as you can see.

Critical Thinking
Evaluation. Have students look carefully at the sentences in **Exercises 4** and **5** and **Review B** to identify any phrases that come between the subject and verb and to evaluate which of the phrases are helpful for determining subject-verb agreement.

8. Some of the food (*is*, *are*) covered in sauce so that surface tension will help to keep the food in dishes.
9. Amazingly, most of the foods (*tastes*, *taste*) delicious.
10. The menu for the astronauts even (*includes*, *include*) steaks and strawberries.

Compound Subjects

A *compound subject* consists of two or more subjects that are joined by a conjunction and that have the same verb.

16c. Subjects joined by *and* generally take a plural verb.

EXAMPLES   **Ramón** and **she like** hiking.

Her **brother,** her **uncle,** and her **cousin are** teachers.

Both the **scout** and the **counselor were** helpful guides.

NOTE   Subjects joined by *and* that name only one person, place, thing, or idea take singular verbs. Singular compound nouns containing *and* also take singular verbs.

EXAMPLE   The club's **secretary and treasurer was** Eduardo. [one person]

Country and western has become our favorite kind of music. [one kind of music]

The **bed and breakfast** down the street **is** always reserved weeks in advance. [one place to stay]

STYLE TIP

You can usually avoid awkward constructions like those shown under Rule 16e by rewording your sentence so that each subject has its own verb.

EXAMPLES
Either **Harry is planning** the activities for the beach party, or his **aunts are.**

The **potatoes are** not done, and neither **is** the **roast.**

16d. Singular subjects joined by *or* or *nor* take a singular verb. Plural subjects joined by *or* or *nor* take a plural verb.

EXAMPLES   **Marcelo** or **Donya knows** the address.

Neither our **phone** nor our **doorbell was working.**

Do the **Wilsons** or the **Campbells live** there?

Neither **cardinals** nor **finches come** to the birdfeeder.

16e. When a singular subject and a plural subject are joined by *or* or *nor,* the verb agrees with the subject nearer the verb.

EXAMPLES   Either **Harry** or his **aunts are planning** the activities for the beach party.

Neither the **potatoes** nor the **roast is** done.

Crossing the Curriculum

Math. Point out to students that the word *compound,* as in *compound subject* in language arts, is paired with many other words to form terms that relate to other courses of study. For example, in mathematics and economics, *compound* is paired with *number,* with *fraction,* and with *interest.* Have students consult a dictionary to find the meanings of *compound number, compound fraction,* and *compound interest.*

In addition, ask students to find in the dictionary other terms that include the word *compound* and to identify the courses of study to which the terms relate. You may want to have students write the meaning of each term to reinforce their understanding of the word *compound.* [*Terms and courses of study include* compound animal, compound eye, compound leaf, *and* compound microscope (*science*); compound meter *and* compound time (*music*); compound fracture (*health*); *and* compound engine (*mechanical engineering*).]

Oral Practice 2: Using Verbs That Agree with Compound Subjects

Read the following sentences aloud, stressing the italicized words.

1. *Both* Steve *and* Edie *want* to be first chair violin.
2. You *and* I *are* in the same Spanish class.
3. *Neither* Gretchen *nor* Colleen *knows* the answer.
4. *Neither* Sam *nor* Miguel *likes* sports.
5. *Either* Judy *or* Bob *washes* the dishes tonight.
6. Roger *and* Carla *play* basketball every Saturday.
7. *Are* cats *or* dogs popular pets in the United States?
8. *Both* Marilyn *and* Marge *have* summer jobs.

Exercise 6: Choosing Verbs That Agree with Their Subjects

For each of the following sentences, choose the verb in parentheses that agrees with the subject of the sentence.

EXAMPLE
1. The *pipa* and the *cheng* (is, are) the main instruments used in Chinese music.
   1. are

1. Neither my older brother Alexander nor my sister Elizabeth (has, have) a car.
2. Marlon and she (is, are) the dance champions.
3. Our relatives and yours (is, are) having a barbecue together next Saturday afternoon.
4. Both Michael Chang and Zina Garrison Jackson (plays, play) a good game of tennis.
5. Either the director or the actors (is, are) going to have to compromise.
6. Neither the grapes nor the cantaloupe (was, were) ripe enough for us to eat.
7. Both Hakeem Olajuwon and Reggie Miller (is, are) popular with fans.
8. Our class or theirs (is, are) going to sponsor the spring festival and dance.
9. Either the faucet or the shower head (leaks, leak).
10. Either a transistor or a capacitor (has, have) burned out in this receiver.

Special Problems in Subject-Verb Agreement

16f. Collective nouns may be either singular or plural, depending on their meaning in a sentence.

A *collective noun* is a noun whose singular form names a group.

Commonly Used Collective Nouns			
army	club	group	school
assembly	committee	herd	squad
audience	crowd	jury	staff
band	faculty	majority	swarm
choir	family	number	team
class	flock	public	troop

Reference Note
For more about **nouns,** see page 405.

A collective noun is
- singular when it refers to the group as a unit
- plural when it refers to the individual members or parts of the group

SINGULAR The **class has met** its substitute teacher. [the class as a unit]
PLURAL The **class were disagreeing** with one another about the answers. [the class as individuals]

SINGULAR The **team is** on the field. [the team as a unit]
PLURAL The **team are working** together. [the team as individuals]

Exercise 7 Writing Sentences with Singular and Plural Collective Nouns

For each of the following collective nouns, write one sentence using the singular and one sentence using the plural.

EXAMPLE 1. cast

1. singular—The cast is having a wrap party.

   plural—After the play, the cast are joining their friends and family for a wrap party.

1. squad
2. choir
3. flock
4. jury
5. group
6. band
7. troop
8. committee
9. crowd
10. family

Exercise 7 Writing Sentences with Singular and Plural Collective Nouns

POSSIBLE ANSWERS

1. singular—The squad is meeting in the operations room.
   plural—After the meeting, the squad are going out on individual missions.

2. singular—The choir is singing the oratorio.
   plural—The choir are singing different parts.

3. singular—That flock has been in the field all morning.
   plural—The flock are scattering to different parts of the field.

4. singular—That jury was unanimous.
   plural—The jury were divided in their opinions.

5. singular—The group has voted to disband.
   plural—The group have handed in their resignations.

6. singular—Our band is marching in the parade.
   plural—The band are not playing well together.

7. singular—Andrew's Boy Scout troop is going to the state park tomorrow.
   plural—The troop have enough abilities and interests for all kinds of projects to be possible.

8. singular—The committee is adjourning for lunch.
   plural—The committee are submitting their recommendations.

9. singular—At the stadium, the crowd is tense.
   plural—The crowd are singing, clapping, and eating popcorn.

10. singular—Our family is going to Germany.
    plural—The family are arguing with one another again.

Review C: Writing Sentences with Verbs That Agree with Their Subjects

Rewrite the following sentences according to the instructions in parentheses. Change the number of the verb if necessary.

EXAMPLE 1. The faculty are discussing their class schedules with the guidance counselors. (Change *discussing their class schedules* to *in a meeting*.)
1. *The faculty is in a meeting with the guidance counselors.*

1. Both of the records are in the Top Forty. (Change *Both* to *Neither*.)
2. The choir has been rehearsing with the conductor. (Change *with the conductor* to *in small groups*.)
3. Everybody in the chorus is trying out for the school play. (Change *Everybody* to *No one*.)
4. Neither Carrie nor Jana is in the Pep Club this semester. (Change *Neither . . . nor* to *Both . . . and*.)
5. Gabriel García Márquez and Octavio Paz have won prizes in literature. (Change *and* to *or*.)
6. All of your papers were graded. (Change *All* to *Each*.)
7. Some of the wood burns. (Change *wood* to *logs*.)
8. The delighted team was waving and running around the stadium. (Change *waving and running around the stadium* to *assembling to accept their medals*.)
9. Either my cousins or Adrienne is bringing the pizza. (Reverse the order of the subjects.)
10. Macaroni and cheese always tastes good. (Change *and* to *or*.)
11. The archaeologist and the geologist are lecturing tomorrow. (Change *and* to *or*.)
12. They exercise regularly. (Change *They* to *She*.)
13. Either a banana or grapes are my favorite dessert. (Reverse the order of the subjects.)
14. Each of the flowers was beautiful. (Change *Each* to *All*.)
15. Tamisha and Heather's favorite pastime is jumping rope. (Change *Tamisha and Heather's* to *Tamisha's*.)
16. Neither of the flights is full. (Change *Neither* to *Both*.)
17. Most of the beans were gone. (Change *beans* to *bread*.)
18. The family was in the living room. (Change *in the living room* to *reading their favorite books*.)
19. The man or the woman is going to win. (Change *or* to *and*.)
20. All of us are happy. (Change *All* to *Not one*.)

1. Neither/is
2. have/in small groups
3. No one
4. Both/and/are
5. or/has
6. Each/was
7. logs/burn
8. were/assembling to accept their medals
9. Adrienne/my cousins/are
10. or
11. or/is
12. She/exercises
13. grapes/a banana/is
14. All/were
15. Tamisha's
16. Both/are
17. bread/was
18. were/reading their favorite books
19. and/are
20. Not one/is

STYLE TIP

When a construction like the ones under Rule 16g seems awkward to you, revise the sentence to avoid using a predicate nominative.

EXAMPLE
I use tomatoes as the main ingredient in salsa.

STYLE TIP

Many people consider contractions informal. Therefore, in formal speech and writing, it is generally best to avoid using contractions.

16g. A verb agrees with its subject but not necessarily with a predicate nominative.

EXAMPLES
    S   PN
The main **ingredient** in salsa **is tomatoes.**

    S   PN
Tomatoes are the main **ingredient** in salsa.

16h. When the subject follows the verb, find the subject and make sure that the verb agrees with it.

In sentences beginning with *here* or *there* and in questions, the subject generally follows the verb or part of the verb.

EXAMPLES   Here **is** a **set** of keys.
                Here **are** the **keys.**

                Do they know the price?
                Does he know the price?

NOTE A contraction such as *here's, how's, there's, what's,* or *where's* includes the singular verb *is* or *has.* Use such a contraction only when a singular subject follows it.

INCORRECT   In an article in this magazine, there's several photos of the construction of the memorial to Chief Crazy Horse.

CORRECT   In an article in this magazine, there **are** several **photos** of the construction of the memorial to Chief Crazy Horse.

CORRECT   In this magazine, there**'s** an **article** with several photos of the construction of the memorial to Chief Crazy Horse.

Exercise 8   Proofreading for Subject-Verb Agreement

For each of the following sentences, if the subject and verb do not agree, write the correct form of the verb. If the verb already agrees with the subject, write *C.*

EXAMPLE   1. Sore muscles is a symptom of the flu.
                 1. *are*

1. When's your finals?
2. One requirement for becoming a pilot are quick reflexes.
3. Where's the nearest movie theater?
4. The highlight of the evening were the performances by the dance troupes.
5. Do the club meet Tuesday, Wednesday, and Thursday?

Answers:
1. When are
2. is
3. C
4. was
5. Does

6. Methods for conserving energy is what the panel will discuss. **6.** are
7. The most important component in this watch are the batteries. **7.** is
8. Here's the books you reserved. **8.** Here are
9. Maria Theresa's favorite part of the movie was the scenes in New England. **9.** C
10. There's the keys that you misplaced. **10.** There are

Review D — Identifying Sentences with Subject-Verb Agreement

For each of the following sentences, if the subject and verb do not agree, write the correct form of the verb. Be ready to explain your correction. If the verb already agrees with the subject, write *C*.

EXAMPLE
1. What's the typical ingredients of the soup called gazpacho?
1. are

1. Steven and Maria is the first team to finish. **1.** are
2. There's the boats I told you about. **2.** There are
3. Both my father and sister wants to see the Dodgers game. **3.** want
4. Either the twins or Jamie are playing a practical joke. **4.** is
5. How was the swimming and sailing at the beach? **5.** were
6. Each of these old photos show your Uncle Ahmad wearing a colorful, flowing dashiki. **6.** shows
7. Neither the windows nor the door is locked. **7.** C
8. Contemporary rock-and-roll are rooted in ancient rhythms. **8.** is
9. There's several football games on television on Sunday. **9.** There are
10. Where's my socks? **10.** Where are

16i. An expression of an amount (a measurement, a percentage, or a fraction, for example) may be singular or plural, depending on how it is used.

An expression of an amount is
- singular when the amount is thought of as a unit
- plural when the amount is thought of as separate parts

SINGULAR **Two years is** a long time. [one time]
PLURAL Two **years** (1995 and 1998) **were** especially rainy. [separate years]

SINGULAR **Fifteen dollars was** the price. [one price]
PLURAL Fifteen **dollars were** torn. [separate dollar bills]

HELP

In the example for Review D, the verb is changed to agree with the plural subject, *ingredients*.

Meeting INDIVIDUAL NEEDS

ADVANCED LEARNERS
After students have completed **Review D**, ask them to revise the sentences in the exercise by following these directions:

Revise each sentence whose subject and verb do not agree by changing the subject, not the verb form.

Encourage students to make minimal changes. To illustrate, point out that in the example for **Review D**, *the typical ingredients* could be changed to *a typical ingredient*. Revisions will vary. Here are some possibilities:

1. C
2. the boat
3. Neither my father nor my sister
4. Either Jamie or the twins
5. the swimming or sailing
6. All
7. C
8. rock-and-roll songs
9. a football game
10. other sock

A fraction or a percentage is

- singular when it refers to a singular word
- plural when it refers to a plural word

SINGULAR **Nine tenths** [*or* **Ninety percent**] of the student body **is** present today. [The fraction, or the percentage, refers to the singular noun *student body*.]

PLURAL **Nine tenths** [*or* **Ninety percent**] of the students **are** present today. [The fraction, or the percentage, refers to the plural word *students*.]

Generally, a measurement (such as length, weight, capacity, or area) is singular.

EXAMPLES **Nine square feet equals** one square yard.

Six hundred kilometers is the distance we traveled today.

Three cups of flour is what the recipe requires.

NOTE In the expression *the number of*, *number* takes a singular verb. In the expression *a number of*, *number* takes a plural verb.

EXAMPLES **The** number of female athletes **is growing.**

A number of girls **like** strenuous sports.

16j. When the relative pronoun *that*, *which*, or *who* is the subject in an adjective clause, the verb in the clause agrees with the word to which the relative pronoun refers.

EXAMPLE A *corps de ballet* is a group of ballet dancers **that perform** together. [*That* refers to the plural noun *dancers* and therefore requires the plural verb *perform*.]

The Dutch painter Piet Mondrian, **who was** part of an art movement known as *de Stijl,* was fond of the colors red, yellow, and blue. [*Who* refers to the singular noun *Piet Mondrian* and therefore requires the singular verb *was*.]

NOTE When preceded by *one of* + a plural word, the relative pronoun takes a plural verb. When preceded by *the only one of* + a plural word, the relative pronoun takes a singular verb.

PLURAL Melba is **one of those players who** always **try** their best.
SINGULAR Melba is **the only one of those players who** always **tries** her best.

16k. A subject preceded by *every* or *many a(n)* takes a singular verb.

EXAMPLE **Every** parent and grandparent **is looking** on proudly.

Many a hopeful performer **has gone** to Broadway in search of fame.

Exercise 9 Proofreading for Subject-Verb Agreement

For each of the following sentences, if the subject and verb do not agree, write the correct form of the verb. If the verb already agrees with the subject, write *C*.

EXAMPLES
1. Twenty-four dollars was scattered on the counter.
1. were

2. Every one of them have left.
2. has

1. Many a sophomore and junior are participating.
2. Every takeoff and landing are cleared with the control tower.
3. Two thirds of my research paper have been typed.
4. Emilio has cousins who raise tropical fish.
5. Eight pounds were the baby's weight at birth.
6. Forty-eight percent of the seniors is planning to go to college.
7. Fifteen dollars is all we have raised so far.
8. Egypt is one of the nations that borders the Red Sea.
9. Silvia knows some people who owns a Christmas-tree farm.
10. Pluto is the only one of the planets that cross the orbit of another planet in our solar system.

1. is
2. is
3. has
4. C
5. was
6. are
7. C
8. border
9. own
10. crosses

16l. The contractions *don't* and *doesn't* should agree with their subjects.

Use *don't* (the contraction of *do not*) with the subjects *I* and *you* and with all plural subjects.

EXAMPLES **I don't** have any paper.

You don't need special permission.

The **players don't** seem nervous.

Reference Note

For more information about **contractions**, see page 763.

Agreement of Subject and Verb

TEACHING TIP

Exercise 10 Using *don't* with third-person singular subjects is a common error. To help students avoid this error, suggest that they check each of their answers by using *do not* or *does not* in place of the contraction they have chosen.

Use *doesn't* (the contraction of *does not*) with all singular subjects except *I* and *you*.

EXAMPLES **Doesn't it** show up in this picture?

The **tire doesn't** have enough air.

Exercise 10 Using *Don't* and *Doesn't* Correctly in Sentences

Choose the correct form (*don't* or *doesn't*) for each of the following sentences.

EXAMPLES
1. _____ Lea speak several languages?
1. *Doesn't*

2. The birds _____ seem bothered by the wind.
2. *don't*

1. The calf _____ look very strong. **1. doesn't**
2. It _____ look good with that jacket. **2. doesn't**
3. We _____ play racquetball. **3. don't**
4. _____ these piñatas look colorful? **4. Don't**
5. I _____ mind helping out. **5. don't**
6. You _____ have to watch the program. **6. don't**
7. Loretta _____ enjoy cleaning house. **7. doesn't**
8. A few of the contests _____ award cash prizes. **8. don't**
9. _____ it arrive tomorrow? **9. Doesn't**
10. _____ they tinker with cars? **10. Don't**

16m. **Some nouns that are plural in form take singular verbs.**

The following nouns take singular verbs.

civics	gymnastics	molasses
economics	linguistics	mumps
electronics	mathematics	news
genetics	measles	physics

EXAMPLES **Linguistics is** the science of language.

News of the concert's cancellation **was** disappointing to the band members.

Has mathematics always **been** your best subject?

NOTE Many nouns ending in *–ics,* such as *acoustics, athletics, ethics, politics, statistics,* and *tactics,* may be singular or plural, depending on how they are used. Generally, such a noun takes a singular verb when the noun names a science, system, or skill. The noun takes a plural verb when the noun names qualities, activities, or individual items.

EXAMPLES **Acoustics deals** with the transmission of sound.

The **acoustics** in the new auditorium **are** excellent.

Some nouns that are plural in form but that refer to single items take plural verbs.

binoculars	pants	shears
eyeglasses	pliers	shorts
Olympics	scissors	slacks

EXAMPLES **Are** the **scissors** sharp enough?

The **pliers seem** to be missing.

Your gray **slacks are** in the laundry.

HELP

If you do not know whether a noun that is plural in form is singular or plural in meaning, look up the word in a dictionary.

COMPUTER TIP

Some word-processing programs can find problems in subject-verb agreement. You can use such a program to search for errors when you proofread your writing. If you are not sure that a usage that the program identifies as an error is truly an error, check this textbook.

16n. Even when plural in form, the title of a creative work (such as a book, song, movie, or painting) generally takes a singular verb.

EXAMPLES **Majors and Minors is** a collection of Paul Laurence Dunbar's poetry. [one book]

The Gleaners is a famous painting by Jean-François Millet. [one work of art]

Four Saints in Three Acts, with music by Virgil Thomson and words by Gertrude Stein, **was** first **produced** in 1934, with an African American cast. [one musical work]

16o. Even when plural in form, the name of a country, a city, or an organization generally takes a singular verb.

EXAMPLES The **Solomon Islands has** a population of 350,000.

Is Grand Rapids smaller than Detroit?

Carrier Computers is having a sale on laptops.

TEACHING TIP

Mnemonic. To help students remember that the nouns in the chart on this page take plural verbs, point out that, except for *Olympics,* each noun can be preceded by the word group *a pair of,* which suggests more than one.

Exercise 11 Proofreading for Subject-Verb Agreement

For each of the following sentences, if the subject and verb do not agree, write the correct form of the verb. If the verb already agrees with the subject, write *C*.

EXAMPLE 1. Mumps are a contagious disease.
   1. is

1. is
2. has
3. is
4. comprises
5. is
6. generates
7. is
8. C
9. was
10. C

1. Des Moines are the capital of Iowa.
2. The United Nations have its headquarters in New York City.
3. "Tales from the Vienna Woods" are one of Johann Strauss's most popular waltzes.
4. The Philippines comprise more than seven thousand islands.
5. Statistics are the collection of mathematical data.
6. The United Arab Emirates generate most of its revenue from the sale of oil.
7. Civics are definitely Alejandra's best subject.
8. When he is making alterations, the tailor's scissors usually hang around his neck on a leather band.
9. *Vermilion Lotuses* were among the paintings by Chinese artist Chang Dai-chien exhibited at the Smithsonian Institution.
10. Are the Olympics on television this afternoon?

Review E Choosing Verbs That Agree with Their Subjects

Choose the correct form of the verb given in parentheses in each of the following sentences.

EXAMPLE 1. (*Doesn't, Don't*) the French phrase *joie de vivre* mean "joy of living"?
   1. Doesn't

1. Nguyen, along with her family, (*has, have*) invited me to the Vietnamese National Day celebration in the park.
2. They (*wasn't, weren't*) interested in learning how to play the accordion.
3. Carlos, not Martha or Jan, (*was, were*) answering all the letters.
4. Many of them (*has, have*) already read the novel.
5. *The Birds* (*was, were*) one of Alfred Hitchcock's great movies.
6. (*Doesn't, Don't*) Chuck intend to join the Air Force when he graduates?

7. Caroline, like most of her classmates, (*wishes*, *wish*) vacation could last forever.
8. There (*is*, *are*) some good programs on educational television.
9. Neither of those books by Naguib Mahfouz (*is*, *are*) on our reading list.
10. The shears (*doesn't*, *don't*) need sharpening.

Review F **Choosing Verbs That Agree with Their Subjects**

For each of the following sentences, choose the correct form of the verb in parentheses.

EXAMPLE   1. The quills of a porcupine (*was*, *were*) used to make this pair of moccasins.
          1. were

1. (*Doesn't*, *Don't*) these quilled moccasins look as if they are beaded?
2. Quillwork, one of the traditional Plains Indians handicrafts, (*is*, *are*) an ancient and sophisticated art form.
3. The number of quills that grow on one porcupine (*is*, *are*) greater than you might think—about thirty thousand!
4. Five inches (*is*, *are*) the maximum length of these tubular spines.
5. Before being used in quillwork, every porcupine quill (*is*, *are*) dyed a bright color, softened in water, and flattened in an unusual way.
6. The quillworker, usually a woman, (*squeeze*, *squeezes*) each quill flat by pulling it between her teeth.
7. Among the Sioux, worn teeth were considered a badge of great honor because items decorated with the colorful quillwork (*was*, *were*) so important in tribal life.
8. Working the quills into complex geometric patterns (*require*, *requires*) great skill and coordination.
9. In quill weaving, each of the ribbonlike quills (*is*, *are*) passed tightly over and under threads of fiber or leather.
10. The finished quillwork (*is*, *are*) sewn onto clothing, saddlebags, or cradleboards as a decoration.

Agreement of Pronoun and Antecedent

Rules 16p–v (pp. 532–542)

OBJECTIVES

- To complete sentences by writing pronouns that agree with their antecedents
- To identify correct subject-verb and pronoun-antecedent agreement

---

Review G — Making Verbs Agree with Their Subjects

For each of the following sentences, if the verb and the subject do not agree, supply the correct form of the verb. If the verb and subject already agree, write *C*.

EXAMPLE
1. *Sleeping Musicians* were painted by Rufino Tamayo.
   1. was painted

1. helps — Gymnastics help keep me limber.
2. were — Few objections, besides the one about chartering the bus, was raised.
3. C — *Six Characters in Search of an Author* is a modern play that raises many interesting questions about art and reality.
4. C — Some of this land is far too hilly to farm.
5. there are — In Maine, there's many miles of rocky coastline.
6. was — Four minutes were his time in that race.
7. doesn't — Performing in front of a thousand people don't seem to bother the cellist Yo-Yo Ma.
8. C — Two thirds of a cup of milk is needed for this recipe.
9. has — Every three years my family have a reunion in Sierra Leone, the land from which our ancestors came.
10. is — Every student, teacher, and administrator are contributing to the fund-raising drive.

Agreement of Pronoun and Antecedent

The noun or pronoun that a pronoun refers to is called its *antecedent*.

16p. A pronoun should agree in both number and gender with its antecedent.

(1) Use singular pronouns to refer to singular antecedents. Use plural pronouns to refer to plural antecedents.

SINGULAR **Richard Strauss** composed many operas. *Der Rosenkavalier* is perhaps **his** most famous.

PLURAL The mountain **climbers** believe that **they** will reach the summit by Friday.

(2) Some singular pronouns indicate *gender*—masculine, feminine,* or *neuter* (neither masculine nor feminine).

RESOURCES

Agreement of Pronoun and Antecedent

Practice
- *Grammar, Usage, and Mechanics,* pp. 124, 125, 126, 127, 128, 129
- *Language Workshop CD-ROM,* Lesson 8

Masculine	he	him	his	himself
Feminine	she	her	hers	herself
Neuter	it	it	its	itself

EXAMPLES   Does **Margaret** like **her** dance class?

Arturo is doing **his** homework.

Because the **car** wouldn't start, **it** had to be towed.

Indefinite Pronouns

16q. Indefinite pronouns agree with their antecedents according to the following rules.

(1) The indefinite pronouns *anybody, anyone, anything, each, either, everybody, everyone, everything, neither, nobody, no one, nothing, one, somebody, someone,* **and** *something* **are singular.**

Notice that the use of a phrase or a clause after the antecedent does not change the number of the antecedent.

EXAMPLES   **Each** of the teams had **its** mascot at the game.

One of the boys left **his** pen behind.

Everybody in the girls' league has paid **her** dues.

When you do not know the gender of the antecedent, use both the masculine and the feminine pronoun forms, connected by *or*.

EXAMPLES   **Someone** left **his or her** pen behind.

Everybody in the club has paid **his or her** dues.

> **NOTE** When the meaning of *everyone* or *everybody* is clearly plural, it is common in informal speech and writing to use a plural pronoun to refer to it. In formal speech and writing, you should revise the sentence to eliminate the confusion rather than use the wrong pronoun form.
>
> CONFUSING   When everyone arrives, explain the situation to him or her.
> INFORMAL   When everyone arrives, explain the situation to them.
> FORMAL   When **all** the people arrive, explain the situation to **them.**

STYLE TIP

Some of the words listed in Rule 16q (1) can also be used as adjectives and as parts of correlative conjunctions.

ADJECTIVE
Each flea hops.

CORRELATIVE CONJUNCTION
Either Fido **or** the flea hops.

Reference Note

For more about **adjectives,** see page 412. For more about **correlative conjunctions,** see page 428.

Relating to Vocabulary Skills

Ask students to find the word *antecedent* in a dictionary and to read its etymology [< L *ante,* before + *cedens* < L *cedere,* to go]. Ask students how the etymology of the word can help them remember the meaning of the word as it applies to pronoun-antecedent agreement. [*An antecedent generally goes before the pronoun that refers to it.*]

STYLE TIP

You can often avoid the awkward *his or her* construction by substituting an article (*a*, *an*, or *the*) for the construction or by revising the sentence and using the plural forms of both the pronoun and its antecedent.

AWKWARD Someone left his or her pen behind.

BETTER Someone left **a** pen behind.

AWKWARD Each of the club members has paid his or her dues.

BETTER **All** of the club members have paid **their** dues.

(2) The indefinite pronouns *both*, *few*, *many*, and *several* are plural.

EXAMPLES **Both** of the candidates clearly stated **their** positions on the issue.

Many of the actors already know **their** lines.

(3) The indefinite pronouns *all*, *any*, *more*, *most*, *none*, and *some* may be singular or plural, depending on how they are used in a sentence.

Each of these pronouns is singular when it refers to a singular word and is plural when it refers to a plural word.

SINGULAR **Most** of this money belongs to Ms. Hayek. Would you take **it** to her, please? [*It* is used because *Most* refers to the singular noun *money*.]

PLURAL **Most** of these coins are rare, but I don't know what **they** are worth. [*They* is used because *Most* refers to the plural noun *coins*.]

Exercise 12 Choosing Pronouns That Agree with Their Antecedents

For the blanks in the following sentences, choose pronouns that agree with their antecedents.

EXAMPLE 1. Everyone on the boys' wrestling team did ____ best at practice today.

1. his

1. Some of the nations successfully defended ____ borders.
2. Neither of the sisters wanted to recite ____ lines.
3. Did any of the visitors forget ____ personal belongings?
4. One of the exhibits had ____ date changed from A.D. 1200 to A.D. 1350.
5. Each of the candidates bought ____ own TV air time.
6. Someone left ____ books behind.
7. Everyone who will need extra time should raise ____ hand.
8. Many of these blossoms were smaller than we had expected ____ to be.
9. If you find a few of the pieces, Sara said she could use ____.
10. Each of the dolphins displays ____ particular characteristics.

1. their
2. her
3. their
4. its
5. his or her
6. his or her
7. his or her
8. them
9. them
10. its

534   Chapter 16   Agreement

Exercise 12

ALTERNATIVE LESSON

Explain to students that the present tense form of a verb expresses an action or a state of being that occurs now or habitually. Write on the chalkboard the following examples:

1. One of my pen pals <u>lives</u> in Alaska.
2. Each of these puppies <u>is</u> two weeks old.
3. Both of my brothers <u>work</u> part time.

Remind students that present tense forms of verbs must agree in number with their subjects. Have students identify the number of the subject and verb in each of the sentences on the chalkboard [sentence 1—singular; sentence 2—singular; sentence 3—plural].

Then, for each of the following sentences from **Exercise 12**, ask students to replace the verb with the present tense form that agrees with its subject.

  sentence 1 [*defend*]

  sentence 2 [*wants*]

  sentence 5 [*buys*]

  sentence 8 [*are*]

Compound Antecedents

16r. Pronouns agree with compound antecedents according to the following rules.

(1) Use a plural pronoun to refer to two or more antecedents joined by *and*.

EXAMPLE   The **guide** and the **ranger** wrapped **their** rain ponchos in **their** saddle rolls.

> **NOTE** Antecedents joined by *and* that name only one person, place, thing, or idea take singular pronouns.
>
> EXAMPLE   For dinner, I'm preparing **liver and onions**. I think you'll enjoy **it**.

(2) Use a singular pronoun to refer to two or more singular antecedents joined by *or* or *nor*.

EXAMPLE   Neither Heidi nor Beth took **her** umbrella with **her**.

Using a pronoun to refer to antecedents of different number may create an unclear or awkward sentence.

UNCLEAR   Neither the parrots nor the macaw has eaten its fruit. [*Its* agrees with the nearest antecedent, *macaw*, but the sentence is unclear. Does it mean that none of the birds have eaten their own fruit, that the parrots have not eaten the macaw's fruit, or that the macaw has not eaten its own fruit?]

Neither the macaw nor the parrots have eaten their fruit. [*Their* agrees with the nearest antecedent, *parrots*, but the sentence is unclear. Does it mean that none of the birds have eaten their own fruit, that the parrots have not eaten their own fruit, or that the macaw has not eaten the parrots' fruit?]

AWKWARD   Neither the macaw nor the parrots has eaten its or their fruit.

It is best to revise sentences to avoid unclear and awkward constructions like the ones above.

REVISED   Neither the macaw nor the parrots has eaten **the** fruit.
None of the birds have eaten **their** fruit.

STYLE TIP

Sentences with singular antecedents joined by *or* or *nor* can be misleading or may sound awkward when the antecedents are of different genders. Avoid using such sentences in your writing.

MISLEADING
Neither Karen nor Brian took his camera along. [Did Karen not take along Brian's camera, either?]

AWKWARD
Neither Karen nor Brian took her or his camera along. [Did Karen and Brian intend to take only one camera along—either hers or his?]

IMPROVED
Neither Karen nor Brian took **a** camera along. [The article *a* replaces the confusing pronoun.]

IMPROVED
Karen and Brian did not take **their** cameras along. [Antecedents joined by *and* require a plural pronoun, which does not indicate gender.]

TEACHING TIP

Rules 16s and 16t. During your presentation of the examples for **Rules 16s** and **16t**, which relate to pronoun-antecedent agreement, reinforce students' understanding of subject-verb agreement by calling on volunteers to point out each form of the verb *be* in the examples and to identify its number. Guide students to infer from the examples that a verb and any pronoun referring to the subject must agree with the subject in number. Tell students that keeping in mind such consistency in number may help them avoid many errors in agreement.

USAGE

Special Problems in Pronoun-Antecedent Agreement

Reference Note
For a list of commonly used **collective nouns,** see page 522.

16s. A collective noun is singular when the noun refers to the group as a unit and plural when the noun refers to the individual members or parts of the group.

SINGULAR   The **orchestra** was looking forward to performing **its** rendition of Beethoven's *Pastoral Symphony*. [*Its* is used because the orchestra would perform the rendition as a unit.]

PLURAL   The **orchestra** were tuning **their** instruments when the conductor arrived. [*Their* is used because the members of the orchestra were tuning separate instruments.]

16t. An expression of an amount (a measurement, a percentage, or a fraction, for example) may take a singular or plural pronoun, depending on how it is used.

An expression of an amount is

- singular when the amount is thought of as a unit
- plural when the amount is thought of as separate parts

SINGULAR   **Two days** is a long time. **It** could seem like forever. [one time]
PLURAL   **Two days** (Monday and Friday) were especially cold and rainy. **They** were so wet that baseball practice was canceled. [two separate days]

SINGULAR   **Five dollars** was the price. I had **it** in my pocket. [one price]
PLURAL   **Five dollars** were torn. The vending machine would not accept **them**. [separate dollars]

A fraction or a percentage is

- singular when it refers to a singular word
- plural when it refers to a plural word

SINGULAR   **Nine tenths** [or **Ninety percent**] of the colony has returned to **its** usual routine. [The fraction, or the percentage, refers to the singular noun *colony*.]

PLURAL   **Three tenths** [or **Thirty percent**] of the ants have returned to **their** usual routines. [The fraction, or the percentage, refers to the plural word *ants*.]

Generally, a measurement (such as a length, weight, capacity, or area) is singular.

EXAMPLES **Nine square feet** equals one square yard. **This** is how much material you will need.

Six hundred kilometers is the distance we traveled today. How far is **that** in miles?

Reference Note
For information on when **to spell out numbers** and **when to use numerals,** see page 791.

16u. Some nouns that are plural in form take singular pronouns.

(1) The following nouns take singular pronouns.

civics	genetics	mathematics	mumps
economics	gymnastics	measles	news
electronics	linguistics	molasses	physics

EXAMPLE I have good **news.** Would you like to hear **it**?

NOTE Many nouns ending in –ics, such as *acoustics, athletics, ethics, politics, statistics,* and *tactics,* may take singular or plural pronouns, depending on how they are used. Generally, when such a noun names a science, system, or skill, the noun takes a singular pronoun. When the noun names qualities, activities, or individual items, the noun takes a plural pronoun.

SINGULAR The colonel explained **tactics** and how **it** differs from strategy.

PLURAL The colonel outlined the **tactics,** and the general approved **them.**

HELP
Check a dictionary if you are not sure whether to use a singular or plural pronoun to refer to an antecedent ending in –ics.

Some nouns that are plural in form but that refer to single items take plural pronouns.

binoculars	shears	pants
Olympics	slacks	scissors
pliers	eyeglasses	shorts

EXAMPLE Marissa is looking for the **scissors.** Do you know where **they** are?

(2) Even when plural in form, the title of a creative work (such as a book, song, movie, or painting) or the name of a country, a city, or an organization generally takes a singular pronoun.

EXAMPLES Have you read ***Thousand Cranes***? **It** was written by Yasunari Kawabata.

Agreement of Pronoun and Antecedent 537

Learning for Life

Continued on pp. 538–539

To show that language usage skills, such as those that pertain to agreement, are relevant to students' lives outside the classroom, explain that people looking for jobs must often write letters of application.

Explain that such a letter tells why the applicant is interested in the position and how his or her skills and experience are relevant to the job.

My all-time favorite film is **Dances with Wolves.** One of **its** principal characters is played by the Canadian actor Graham Greene.

When we visited the **Philippines,** we spent most of our time on **its** chief island, Luzon.

I grew up near **Hot Springs,** Arkansas. **Its** claim to fame is **its** popular health resort.

Have you gone to **Sir Books–A–Lot**? **It** may have a copy of the book you need.

NOTE The names of some teams, though plural in form, may take singular or plural pronouns. When the name refers to the organization as a unit, use a singular pronoun. When the name refers to the members of the organization, use a plural pronoun.

SINGULAR   The **St. Louis Cardinals** won **its** first World Series title in 1926. [*Its* is used because the St. Louis Cardinals won as a unit.]

PLURAL   Signing autographs, the **St. Louis Cardinals** thanked **their** fans for supporting **them** throughout the season. [*Their* and *them* are used because the individual players signed autographs and thanked the fans.]

16v. The number of a relative pronoun (such as *that, which,* **or** *who***) is determined by the number of its antecedent.**

SINGULAR   Jessica, **who** always takes pride in **her** work, has been appointed editor of the school yearbook. [*Who* is singular because it refers to the singular noun *Jessica. Her* is used to agree with *who*.]

PLURAL   All **who** want to volunteer for the yearbook staff should raise **their** hands. [*Who* is plural because it refers to the plural pronoun *All. Their* is used to agree with *who*.]

Exercise 13 Choosing Pronouns That Agree with Their Antecedents

For the blanks in the following sentences, choose pronouns that agree with their antecedents.

EXAMPLE   1. I just read *Franny and Zooey;* have you read _____?
            1. *it*

1. them   **1.** If I don't pack the binoculars now, I'll forget _____.

Learning for Life

Have students imagine they are searching for summer jobs. To get ideas for the kinds of jobs they might like, students could look through classified ads in newspapers or on the Internet or through job listings from the school's guidance office. To find out the responsibilities of various jobs, students could interview people who have such positions. Then, ask each student to select a job and to write a letter of application. For more information about the content and form of a letter of application, refer stu-

2. I'm looking for someone on the boys' swimming team who has parked _____ car in my space.
3. They have twelve dollars; is _____ enough?
4. Did the team scrimmage with _____ arch-rival?
5. Two thirds of the crew members have already had _____ turns standing watch.
6. The Millers and the Doyles had _____ windows broken by the hail last night.
7. All of the art class buy _____ own paper.
8. I could buy a bag of peanuts for sixty cents if I had _____ in correct change.
9. Either Stu or Mike will lend me _____ fishing gear.
10. The eyeglasses broke when _____ were dropped.

2. his
3. it [or that]
4. its
5. their
6. their
7. their
8. it
9. his
10. they

Review H — Making Pronouns Agree with Their Antecedents

Most of the following sentences contain pronouns that do not agree with their antecedents. If any pronoun does not agree with its antecedent, supply the correct pronoun or pronouns. If all of the pronouns in a sentence agree with their antecedents, write C.

EXAMPLE 1. Each of the girls is enjoying themselves.
         1. *herself*

1. All of these students at the Royal School of Dance in College Park, Florida, are learning traditional dances that come from her African heritage.   1. their
2. Some of the African and Caribbean dances have its roots in African folk tales.   2. their
3. At performances the members of the audience are often seen clapping its hands and swaying along with the music.   3. their
4. Before the last dance recital, I noticed either Carla or Shana practicing their steps.   4. her
5. Carla is one of those students who always know their steps ahead of time.   5. C
6. Angelique and Pamela moved her arms gracefully during the first dance.   6. their
7. Every authentic costume adds their color and movement to the dramatic spectacle.   7. its
8. Each of the girls brings their own personal style to the dances.   8. her

Agreement of Pronoun and Antecedent   539

9. Many contemporary dancers and singers give a great deal of credit to the traditional sources of their art forms. **9. C**
10. Both their hip-hop dancing and their clothing style have its origins in ancient African culture. **10. their**

Review I — Identifying Subject-Verb Agreement and Pronoun-Antecedent Agreement

Some of the following sentences contain an ~~error in agreement~~. If a verb or pronoun is wrong, correct it. If the sentence is already correct, write *C*.

EXAMPLE 1. The gorilla, as well as many other mammals, are in danger of becoming extinct.
1. *is*

1. **C** — Both Sid and Nikki like their new neighborhood and their new apartment.
2. **Is** — Are either of you a member of the African American Cultural Society?
3. **This is** — The computer camp lasts for five weeks. These are two weeks more than the tennis camp.
4. **his or her** — One of the police officers turned in their badge today.
5. **his** — Neither Fernando nor Bruce has brought all of their camping gear.
6. **is** — *All Dogs Go to Heaven* are my young nephews' favorite animated feature.
7. **was** — Which pair of these Navajo earrings were made by Narciso?
8. **C** — Where is the Athletics Department?
9. **his** — Just before the parade started, each of the eight men inside the gigantic dragon costume got their final instructions from Mr. Yee.
10. **were** — A few in the crowd was murmuring impatiently.
11. **Are** — Is any of those peanuts left?
12. **C** — Either Tiger Woods or Se Ri Pak is Melinda's golf hero.
13. **is** — Every one of those stray cattle are going to have to be rounded up.
14. **is** — An additional feature of these models are the built-in stereo speakers.
15. **his or her** — Somebody has gone off and left their car running.
16. **him or her** — If anybody calls, tell them I'll be back by six o'clock this evening.
17. **C** — Each team has its own colors and symbol.
18. **was** — One of the goats were nibbling on a discarded popcorn box.
19. **Is** — Are there no end to these questions?
20. **C** — Here's a pair of gloves for you.

TEACHING TIP

Review I You may want to use the first ten items in **Review I** as guided practice. Then, have students complete the exercise as independent practice.

Review J — Choosing Verbs That Agree with Their Subjects and Pronouns That Agree with Their Antecedents

For each of the following sentences, choose the correct verb or pronoun given in parentheses.

EXAMPLE
1. Not every one of the world's deserts (*is, are*) hot and sandy.

1. *is*

1. Neither the manager nor the two salespeople (*was, were*) prepared for the number of customers.
2. Neither of the sets of barbells (*was, were*) easy to lift.
3. Where (*is, are*) the box of nails that came with this bookshelf kit?
4. The class have had (*it's, their*) individual portraits made.
5. The Harlem Globetrotters (*is, are*) surely one of the best-loved basketball teams in the world.
6. There (*is, are*) leftover macaroni and cheese in the refrigerator.
7. If anybody likes a spectacle, (*he or she, they*) will love seeing a drum corps competition.
8. Several members of the audience (*was, were*) waving wildly, hoping that Martin Yan would wave back.
9. Where (*has, have*) the sports section of today's newspaper gone?
10. Anyone who wants to get (*his or her, their*) program autographed by Jimmy Smits had better hurry.

Review K — Using Subject-Verb Agreement and Pronoun-Antecedent Agreement Correctly

Revise each of the following sentences according to the directions given in parentheses. Be sure to change other words, especially verbs and pronouns, as necessary.

EXAMPLE
1. Both of the boys desperately want to go to the circus. (Change *Both* to *Each*.)

1. Each of the boys desperately wants to go to the circus.

1. Both of their parents have agreed to the idea. (Change *Both* to *One*.)
2. To pay for the tickets, Jorge has to empty his piggy bank or his secret hiding place of all its money. (Change *his piggy bank or* to *both his piggy bank and*.)
3. Because of the excitement, none of the boys will eat much of their dinner tonight. (Change *none* to *neither*.)

1. One/has
2. both/and/their
3. neither/his

Agreement of Pronoun and Antecedent 541

4. One/wants/his

5. All/have

6. All/have/their

7. Not one/wants

8. Not every family/has

9. Only/has

10. Many of the donations/they

4. Both of the boys want to bring their cameras. (Change *Both* to *One*.)

5. Each of them has earned an enjoyable evening of watching clowns, tigers, and elephants. (Change *Each* to *All*.)

6. Every one of the clowns has his or her own special tricks and stunts. (Change *Every one* to *All*.)

7. None of the people from town want to miss tonight's performance. (Change *None* to *Not one*.)

8. Not all of the families in town have money for tickets. (Change *Not all of the families* to *Not every family*.)

9. All but one of the free tickets to the circus have been picked up. (Change *All but* to *Only*.)

10. Much of the money the circus takes in will be given to the Children's Hospital; it will help pay for a new X-ray machine. (Change *Much of the money* to *Many of the donations*.)

CHAPTER 16 Chapter Review

A. Identifying Subject-Verb and Pronoun-Antecedent Agreement

For each sentence, write the verb in parentheses that agrees with its subject.

1. Either the dog or the cat (*get, gets*) the party leftovers.
2. There (*is, are*) four herbs that almost any gardener can grow: basil, thyme, marjoram, and oregano.
3. All of these old letters (*was, were*) tied with ribbon and stored in a trunk in the attic.
4. Each of them (*is, are*) penned in bold, flowing handwriting.
5. Both Alicia and Isabel (*thinks, think*) that the former owner of the house put the letters in the attic.
6. Neither potatoes nor peanuts (*is, are*) grown on this farm anymore.
7. Two thirds of the electorate (*was, were*) at the polls in the last election.
8. Is it true that *Troilus and Cressida* (*is, are*) by Shakespeare?
9. Here (*is, are*) the latest scores of today's basketball games.
10. Most of the children on the island (*was, were*) not able to read very well.
11. Don't you think that five miles (*is, are*) too far to walk tonight?
12. A cool spring near the cottages (*supply, supplies*) them with water.
13. Politics (*is, are*) a popular topic of conversation during an election year.
14. Every man, woman, and child (*was, were*) frightened by the earthquake.
15. Neither of them (*knows, know*) for sure who wrote that message.
16. The jury (*has, have*) returned a verdict.
17. On the supervisors (*rest, rests*) the responsibility for implementing safe procedures.
18. The two songs we played at the Independence Day concert (*was, were*) written by Carly Simon.
19. There (*has, have*) been many visitors on the fairground today.
20. Everybody in the theater (*was, were*) thrilled by the rescue scene.

Using the Chapter Review

To assess student progress, you may want to compare the types of items missed on the **Diagnostic Preview** with those missed on the **Chapter Review.** You may want to work out specific goals with individual students who are still having difficulty mastering information.

B. Choosing Pronouns That Agree with Their Antecedents

Provide personal pronouns to complete the following sentences correctly.

21. her — 21. Either my sister Lavinia or my friend Millicent will let me borrow _____ camping equipment.
22. them — 22. I looked in the cupboard for the scissors, but I couldn't find _____.
23. their — 23. Three of the cars had _____ windows broken by thieves last night.
24. it — 24. Not long ago, I saw *Romeo and Juliet;* have you seen _____ ?
25. them — 25. I'm looking for Stan and Joel; do you know _____ ?
26. its — 26. We visited Honduras and spent three days in _____ capital, Tegucigalpa.
27. its — 27. Mothers Against Drunk Driving has _____ meeting in the conference room tonight.
28. their — 28. Three quarters of the city's voters cast _____ ballots.
29. it — 29. I need fifty cents; could you lend _____ to me?
30. their — 30. The sunglasses had stains on _____ lenses.

C. Identifying Subject-Verb Agreement and Pronoun-Antecedent Agreement

In most of the following sentences, either a verb does not agree with its subject or a pronoun does not agree with its antecedent. Revise each incorrect sentence to correct the error. If a sentence is already correct, write *C*.

31. his or her — 31. The meeting got out of hand when the discussion period began because everyone tried to express their opinion at the same time.
32. is — 32. There on the corner of your desk are the package of books that I returned and that you claimed you never received.
33. are — 33. Two students from each class is going to the state capital to attend a special conference on education.
34. is — 34. Each of them are expected to bring back a report on the conference so that classmates can get firsthand information.
35. is — 35. Since they will be on vacation next month, neither Miguel nor his sister are going to enter the mixed-doubles tennis tournament.
36. its [*or* C] — 36. The audience expressed their admiration for the dancer's grace and skill by applauding wildly.

544 Chapter 16 Agreement

RESOURCES

Agreement
Review
- *Grammar, Usage, and Mechanics,* pp. 130, 131, 132, 133, 134

Assessment
- *Assessment Package*
  —*Chapter Tests,* Ch. 16
  —*Chapter Tests in Standardized Test Formats,* Ch. 16
- *Test Generator (One-Stop Planner CD-ROM)*

37. After the senator had read the proposed amendment, anyone who disagreed with the ruling was allowed to state ~~their~~ reason.
38. This collection of old Italian folk tales ~~demonstrate~~ the wisdom, humor, and creativity of my ancestors.
39. She is one of those competitive people who perform best under pressure.
40. Since neither of you ~~have~~ ever tasted fried plantains, my mother has invited you to eat a Cuban meal at our house tonight.

Writing Application
Using Agreement in a Letter

Pronoun Antecedent Agreement Your best friend moved away two months ago. You have just received a postcard from him or her, asking what's been happening recently in the old neighborhood. You answer the postcard by writing a short letter that brings your friend up to date. In your letter, include at least five pronouns that agree with their antecedents.

Prewriting Make a list of several interesting things to tell your friend. You may write about your real neighborhood or about one you have made up. Decide on the order in which you will tell about the items on your list. You may want to use time order (telling when things happened) or spatial order (telling where things happened).

Writing As you write, think about how to make your letter interesting to your friend. Use details that will help him or her picture the neighborhood and its people.

Revising Ask a classmate to read your letter. Are the events you describe interesting? Is it absolutely clear who did what and what belongs to whom? Use your reader's suggestions to revise your letter so that nothing in the letter is confusing.

Publishing Proofread your letter for any errors in grammar, usage, and mechanics. Be sure that all pronouns agree with their antecedents. The class may wish to post the completed letters on a class bulletin board or Web page.

Chapter Review 545

RESOURCES
Writing Application
Extension
- *Grammar, Usage, and Mechanics,* p. 137
- *Language Workshop CD-ROM,* Lessons 5–8

PREVIEWING THE CHAPTER

- This chapter identifies pronouns according to their uses within sentences and focuses on special problems in pronoun usage and pronouns in incomplete constructions. Students may want to return to this chapter throughout the year as they concentrate on correct pronoun usage in their writing.

- The chapter concludes with a **Chapter Review** featuring a **Writing Application** that asks students to write a letter including ten pronouns with clear antecedents.

- For help in integrating this chapter with composition chapters, use the **Teaching Strands** chart on pp. T401A–T401B.

USING THE DIAGNOSTIC PREVIEW

- By tenth grade, many students will be able to use pronouns correctly as subjects and objects if the subjects and objects are not in compound constructions. Compile data on your class's common mistakes on the preview to use as a guide for instruction.

- Students who make few errors on the preview may still make errors in written work. You might have these students focus on **Special Problems in Pronoun Usage** and have them keep a chart to record pronoun errors they find as they proofread their writing assignments.

17 Using Pronouns Correctly
Nominative, Objective, and Possessive Case; Clear Reference

Diagnostic Preview

A. Proofreading Sentences for Correct Pronoun Forms

Most of the following sentences contain an incorrect pronoun form. Revise each sentence by supplying the correct pronoun form. If a sentence is already correct, write *C*.

EXAMPLE 1. She and myself have different tai chi instructors.
    1. *She and I have different tai chi instructors.*

1. Del is as good at math as her. **1.** she
2. He's the sportscaster who irritates me with his pretentious talk. **2.** C
3. Do you remember to who the letter was addressed? **3.** whom
4. Steve showed the negatives to Cecilia and I. **4.** me
5. It can't be them; that's not their car. **5.** they
6. Ben and you can come with they and me. **6.** them
7. Leontyne Price's accomplishments were familiar to everyone in the class except him and I. **7.** me
8. Us band members have to be at school early to practice marching. **8.** We
9. There was some misunderstanding between he and his brother. **9.** him
10. In front of the school stood two children, Charlene and he. **10.** C

546 Chapter 17 Using Pronouns Correctly

CHAPTER RESOURCES

Planning
- One-Stop Planner CD-ROM

Practice and Extension
- *Grammar, Usage, and Mechanics*, p. 138
- Language Workshop CD-ROM

Internet
- go.hrw.com (keyword: EOLang)

Evaluation and Assessment
- Assessment Package
  —*Chapter Tests*, Ch. 17
  —*Chapter Tests in Standardized Test Formats*, Ch. 17
- Test Generator (One-Stop Planner CD-ROM)

B. Proofreading Sentences for Correct Forms and Uses

Most of the following sentences contain at least one incorrect pronoun form or an unclear pronoun reference. Revise each sentence either by supplying the correct pronoun form(s) or by correcting the faulty pronoun reference. If a sentence is already correct, write C. Answers will vary.

EXAMPLES
1. Dad and me went to the all-star basketball game.
1. Dad and I went to the all-star basketball game.

2. Many people outside the arena wanted to buy our tickets, which didn't surprise us.
2. That many people outside the arena wanted to buy our tickets didn't surprise us.

11. There's nothing like an action-packed all-star basketball game to give Dad and I a thrill! **11. me**
12. Our team was only two points behind when Barkley's shot bounced off the rim, and Pippen and Robinson rushed for it. **12. the ball**
13. As gravity pulled him and Robinson toward the floor, Pippen managed to tip the ball to Miller. **13. C**
14. Miller saw Stockton coming, dribbled behind his own back, and eluded he and Malone. **14. him**
15. When Stockton and Malone collided, nobody was more surprised than them. **15. they**
16. If they made this, the score would be tied. **16. this basket**
17. Miller looked for Hill and realized that the blur streaking up the court on the left was him. **17. he**
18. He had to pass to whomever was open, and Hill was the one. **18. whoever**
19. Hill took a shot and missed; four players struggled for the ball, which went in, which meant that Hill and his teammates won. **19. so**
20. In the whirlwind action during the last couple of seconds, the frantic referee couldn't see whom had fouled who. **20. who/whom**

Case Forms of Personal Pronouns

Case is the form that a noun or pronoun takes to show its relationship to other words in a sentence. In English, there are three cases: *nominative*, *objective*, and *possessive*. Nouns have the same form in both the nominative and the objective cases. Nouns usually add an apostrophe and an *s* to form the possessive case.

Case Forms of Personal Pronouns **547**

RESOURCES
Case Forms of Personal Pronouns
Practice
- *Grammar, Usage, and Mechanics*, p. 139
- *Language Workshop CD-ROM*, Lesson 13

Case Forms of Personal Pronouns
(pp. 547–549)

OBJECTIVE
- To identify personal pronouns and their person, number, case, and gender

Using Pronouns Correctly, pp. 546–570
Alignments
TEKS 3B, 3D
TAAS W3, W6
English II End-of-Course 5, 6

Texas Resources
- *TAAS Tool Kit*
- *Preparation for TAAS*
- *One-Stop Planner CD-ROM*

Personal pronouns have different forms for the different cases.

Case Forms of Personal Pronouns		
Nominative Case		
	Singular	Plural
First Person	I	we
Second Person	you	you
Third Person	he, she, it	they
Objective Case		
	Singular	Plural
First Person	me	us
Second Person	you	you
Third Person	him, her, it	them
Possessive Case		
	Singular	Plural
First Person	my, mine	our, ours
Second Person	your, yours	your, yours
Third Person	his, her, hers, its	their, theirs

STYLE TIP

Use the neuter pronoun *it* when referring to an animal unless the gender of the animal is made clear by another word in the sentence.

EXAMPLES
The sparrow was gathering twigs and taking them to **its** nest.

That bull was known for **his** bad temper. [The word *bull* indicates that the animal is male.]

Eric gave his poodle, Fifi, **her** squeaky toy. [The name *Fifi* indicates that the animal is female.]

Reference Note

For information on **forming the possessives of nouns,** see page 758.

NOTE Notice that *you* and *it* have the same form in the nominative and objective cases. All other personal pronouns have different forms for each. Notice also that only third-person singular pronouns indicate gender (masculine, feminine, or neuter).

Exercise 1 **Identifying Personal Pronouns in a Paragraph**

Each sentence in the following paragraph contains at least one pronoun. Identify each personal pronoun. Then, give its person, number, case, and, if applicable, its gender.

EXAMPLE 1. Jeffrey and I were chatting in front of his locker before the Art Club meeting.

1. I—first person, singular, nominative case; his—third person, singular, possessive case, masculine

1. Jeffrey mentioned your interest in African art and Francine's interest in modern art.

2. Did you and she know that African masks like the one below left influenced the development of the Modernist movement in art?
3. I've learned that African carvings inspired such twentieth-century artists as Pablo Picasso, who created this painting on the right.
4. The year 1905 was probably when he and his friends first saw African masks exhibited in Paris.
5. Amedeo Modigliani was especially affected by the stark masks, and he and Picasso created many works based on them.
6. Notice that the eyes in Modigliani's carving are very close together and that they and the lips look much like small knobs.
7. I used to think that Modigliani made his faces too long by mistake, but the error was mine.
8. Ms. Keller told me that he was copying the exaggerated shapes of Ivory Coast masks.
9. Picasso and Modigliani were only two of many European artists who got their inspiration from African art.
10. Obviously, we students weren't giving credit where credit was due!

The Nominative Case

Personal pronouns in the nominative case—*I, you, he, she, it, we,* and *they*—are used as subjects of verbs and as predicate nominatives.

17a. A subject of a verb should be in the nominative case.

A *subject of a verb* tells whom or what a sentence or a clause is about.

EXAMPLES **I** solved the problem. [*I* is the subject of *solved.*]

They know that **we** are going. [*They* is the subject of *know,* and *we* is the subject of *are going.*]

Al and **she** cleaned the house. [*Al and she* is the compound subject of *cleaned.*]

HELP

Personal pronouns in the nominative case may also be used as **appositives.**

Reference Note

For information on **appositives,** see page 483.

Case Forms of Personal Pronouns **549**

RESOURCES

The Nominative Case
Practice
- *Grammar, Usage, and Mechanics,* pp. 140–141
- *Language Workshop CD-ROM,* Lesson 13

Exercise 1 Identifying Personal Pronouns in a Paragraph

ANSWERS

1. your—second person, singular or plural, possessive case
2. you—second person, singular or plural, nominative case; she—third person, singular, nominative case, feminine
3. I—first person, singular, nominative case
4. he—third person, singular, nominative case, masculine; his—third person, singular, possessive case, masculine
5. he—third person, singular, nominative case, masculine; them—third person, plural, objective case
6. they—third person, plural, nominative case
7. I—first person, singular, nominative case; his—third person, singular, possessive case, masculine; mine—first person, singular, possessive case
8. me—first person, singular, objective case; he—third person, singular, nominative case, masculine
9. their—third person, plural, possessive case
10. we—first person, plural, nominative case

The Nominative Case

Rules 17a, b *(pp. 549–552)*

OBJECTIVES

- To read aloud sentences containing pronouns used as subjects
- To supply personal pronouns as subjects and predicate nominatives

TEACHING TIP

To give students an understanding of the importance of personal pronouns, have groups of four or five students orally create a brief story in round-robin fashion without using personal pronouns. You could help students get started by giving them the following beginning. You may wish to tape-record the students as they create their stories.

> Kevin told Kevin's father that Kevin wanted to stay out past Kevin's curfew to see one of Kevin's favorite bands.

After each student in the group has had a turn adding to the story, have the groups discuss what they think about their stories without personal pronouns. Then, have each group tell a new story or revise the one they have taped, this time using personal pronouns.

Exercise 3 Writing Sentences with Pronouns in the Nominative Case

POSSIBLE ANSWERS

1. We teenagers go through many changes.
2. The other shoppers and I missed the sale.
3. He and his friends never have much money.
4. Liz, Michelle, and she are the best dancers.

TIPS & TRICKS

To help you determine which pronoun form(s) to use for a compound subject, try each form as the simple subject of the verb.

EXAMPLE
(*He, Him*) and (*I, me*) both studied for the test.

CHOICES
He studied or *Him* studied?

I studied or *me* studied?

ANSWER
He and *I* both studied for the test.

Reference Note
For information on **subjects of verbs,** see page 439.

Oral Practice 1 Using Pronouns as Subjects

Read each of the following sentences aloud, stressing the italicized words.

1. *She* and *I* gave the dog a bath.
2. Terry and *he* plan to try out for the soccer team.
3. *We* sophomores organized the recycling campaign.
4. James Earl Jones and *she* are excellent role models for young actors.
5. Are *you* and *he* doing the report?
6. Either *we* or *they* may go to the championship finals.
7. The drill team and *we* took the bus.
8. The twins said that *they* go everywhere together.

Exercise 2 Using Personal Pronouns in the Nominative Case to Complete Sentences

Supply a personal pronoun for each blank in the following sentences. Vary your pronouns, but do not use *you* or *it*. Pronouns will vary.

EXAMPLE 1. What part in the play does ___ have?
  1. she

1. The judge and ___ studied the evidence. **1. she**
2. Ted and ___ took the wrong train. **2. he**
3. Linda and ___ are planning a party. **3. they**
4. ___ are having a science fair. **4. We**
5. Either Julius or ___ will give you a ride. **5. she**
6. ___ and ___ have been rivals for years. **6. We/they**
7. I'm sure ___ knew about the meeting. **7. he**
8. Soon ___ and ___ will be graduating. **8. she/I**
9. Did you know that ___ and ___ saw Chita Rivera in a Broadway production of *West Side Story*? **9. he/I**
10. ___ and ___ love the Asian dumplings served at restaurants. **10. She/they**

Exercise 3 Writing Sentences with Pronouns in the Nominative Case

Use the following subjects in sentences of your own.

EXAMPLE 1. we and they
  1. *We and they are meeting after dinner.*

1. we teenagers
2. the other shoppers and I
3. he and his friends
4. Liz, Michelle, and she

5. they and their classmates
6. she and her mother
7. you and he
8. the children and I
9. we boys
10. they and their dogs

17b. A predicate nominative should be in the nominative case.

A *predicate nominative* completes the meaning of a linking verb and identifies or refers to the subject of the verb. A personal pronoun used as a predicate nominative generally completes the meaning of a form of the verb *be: am, is, are, was, were, be, been,* or *being*.

EXAMPLES It was **I** who took the message.

The winner might be **he**.

Could the caller have been **she**?

Exercise 4 Using Pronouns as Predicate Nominatives

Complete each of the following sentences by supplying the personal pronoun called for in parentheses.

EXAMPLE 1. It was _____ who was the first emperor of China's Yuan dynasty (*third person, singular, masculine*)
1. he

1. Do you think it was _____? (*third person, singular, feminine*) **1. she**
2. It must have been _____. (*third person, singular, masculine*) **2. he**
3. Good friends are _____. (*third person, plural*) **3. they**
4. The pranksters were _____. (*first person, plural*) **4. we**
5. It was _____ at the door. (*third person, plural*) **5. they**
6. It is _____. (*first person singular*) **6. I**
7. It may have been _____ on the phone. (*third person, singular, feminine*) **7. she**
8. The winners should be _____. (*third person, plural*) **8. they**
9. The best cook here is _____. (*third person, singular, masculine*) **9. he**
10. The volunteers were _____. (*first person, plural*) **10. we**

Review A Using Pronouns in the Nominative Case Correctly in Sentences

Supply a personal pronoun for the blank in each of the following sentences. Use a variety of different pronouns, but do not use *you* or *it*. Be ready to explain the reasons for your choices. **Pronouns will vary.**

EXAMPLE 1. Are you and _____ going to the Fourth of July celebration?
1. he

TIPS & TRICKS

To help you determine which pronoun form to use as a predicate nominative, try each form as the simple subject of the verb.

EXAMPLE
The two teams in the final round were (*they, them*).

CHOICES
they were or *them were*?

ANSWER
The two teams in the final round were **they**.

Reference Note
For information on **predicate nominatives,** see page 453.

STYLE TIP

Expressions such as *It's me, This is her,* and *It was them* are examples of informal usage. Though common in everyday situations, such expressions should be avoided in formal speaking and writing. (The formal versions of the italicized expressions above are *It is I, This is she,* and *It was they.*)

HELP

In the example for Review A, the nominative-case pronoun *he* is correct because the pronoun is used as a subject.

Case Forms of Personal Pronouns **551**

Exercise 3 Writing Sentences with Pronouns in the Nominative Case

POSSIBLE ANSWERS continued

5. They and their classmates have part-time jobs.
6. She and her mother took up rock climbing.
7. I believe that you and he are the finalists.
8. The children and I will be picking blackberries at this time tomorrow.
9. Tomorrow, we boys will be competing for the basketball championship.
10. They and their dogs were at the swimming hole.

Relating to Writing

Emphasize to students that some constructions of standard English may sound awkward. Review with the class the examples on this page. Tell students that if the standard form sounds awkward and hampers the flow of their writing, they can usually find a way to revise the sentence. Ask students to revise sentences 3 and 4 in **Exercise 4**.

[3. *They are good friends.*]
[4. *We were the pranksters.*]

Relating to Literature

Have students read William Stafford's poem "Fifteen," and ask them to pay special attention to Stafford's use of nominative case pronouns. Ask the students why the narrator switches from *I* to *we* in the third stanza. [*This switch indicates that the boy and the motorcycle have become one in the boy's fantasy.*] Point out that writers convey point of view largely through pronoun choices. Then, ask students why they think Stafford uses first-person pronouns instead of third-person pronouns or a name. [*The use of first-person pronouns creates first-person point of view and a closer relationship between the narrator and the audience.*] Explain to students that this poem is an example of how the use of pronouns can relay meaning beyond that of the words themselves.

HELP
Personal pronouns in the objective case may also be used as **appositives**.

Reference Note
For information on **appositives**, see page 483. For more about **direct objects**, see page 456. For information on **transitive verbs**, see page 421. For more about **indirect objects**, see page 457.

HELP
Although more than one answer is possible for some items in Review B, you need to give only one response for each.

1. Everyone applauded when Patty and ____ took a bow. **1.** he
2. When I saw Dame Kiri Te Kanawa in front of Lincoln Center, I couldn't believe it was ____. **2.** she
3. Where did Barry and ____ go after school? **3.** they
4. Jimmy and ____ caught the runaway piglets. **4.** I
5. The one that you need to see is ____. **5.** she
6. Skip argued that Lana and ____ made the error. **6.** they
7. Was it Teresa or ____ who hit the home run? **7.** he
8. Either David or ____ might be able to do it. **8.** I
9. My sister and ____ love the South African musical group Ladysmith Black Mambazo. **9.** I
10. I believe that the Masked Marvel has to be ____. **10.** she

Review B   Using Pronouns in the Nominative Case

For each blank in the following paragraph, supply an appropriate personal pronoun. Do not use *you* or *it*.   Pronouns will vary.

EXAMPLE   [1] ____ have learned from Mrs. Soto the value of recycling.
   1. We

[1] **1. We** who are in Mrs. Soto's class are determined to win this year's "Save the Earth" trophy at our school. The two most enthusiastic people in our class are probably Pilar and [2] **2. I**. I guess that's why Mrs. Soto asked whether [3] **3. she** and [4] **4. I** would organize the paper drive. Pilar explained to the class that if Americans recycled only their Sunday newspapers, half a million trees would be saved every Sunday! To illustrate her point, [5] **5. we** showed this photo. That is [6] **6. she** standing next to 580 pounds of paper—the amount the average American uses in one year. [7] **7. We** have gathered some other facts to inspire our classmates to recycle. Our friend Ben said that [8] **8. he** and his mother heard on the radio that the average American uses 1,500 aluminum drink cans every year. [9] **9. We** were amazed to learn that the energy saved from recycling just one aluminum can could keep a TV set running for three hours! No matter who wins the trophy, it will definitely be [10] **10. we** who share the prize of a cleaner, healthier planet.

The Objective Case

Personal pronouns in the objective case—*me, you, him, her, it, us,* and *them*—are used as direct objects, indirect objects, and objects of prepositions.

17c. A direct object should be in the objective case.

A *direct object* tells who or what either receives the action of a transitive verb or shows the result of the action.

EXAMPLES   Coach Johnson has been training **us**.

The coach has turned **them** into the best team in the state.

17d. An indirect object should be in the objective case.

An *indirect object* often appears in sentences containing direct objects. An indirect object tells *to whom* or *to what,* or *for whom* or *for what,* the action of a transitive verb is done.

EXAMPLES   Serena paid **him** a compliment.

Carlos saved **me** a seat in the first row.

NOTE Indirect objects do not follow prepositions. A pronoun preceded by a preposition is the object of a preposition.

Exercise 5 Using Pronouns in the Objective Case to Complete Sentences

Supply a personal pronoun for the blank in each of the following sentences. Use a variety of pronouns, but do not use *you* or *it*.

EXAMPLE   1. Donya sent Celie and ____ a postcard from Mexico City.
          1. him   Pronouns will vary.

1. The old sailor warned ____ about the danger.   **1. us**
2. The city awarded ____ its highest honor for their bravery.   **2. them**
3. You could ask Deborah or ____.   **3. him**
4. The crowd cheered ____ heartily.   **4. us**
5. Make sure that you ask ____ what her telephone number is.   **5. her**
6. The shark in that movie didn't scare ____ at all.   **6. me**
7. How can I recognize ____?   **7. him**
8. We saw Norman and ____ in their horse costume at the party.   **8. her**
9. Did you give Paula and ____ their assignments?   **9. them**
10. I bought my father and ____ identical birthday presents this year.   **10. her**

TIPS & TRICKS

To help you determine which pronoun form(s) to use in compound direct and indirect objects, try each form with the verb.

EXAMPLE
The news surprised both (*they, them*) and (*we, us*).

CHOICES
surprised *they* or surprised *them*?

surprised *we* or surprised *us*?

ANSWER
The news surprised both **them** and **us**.

HELP
Although more than one answer is possible for some items in Exercise 5, you need to give only one response for each.

The Objective Case
Rules 17c–e (pp. 553–556)

OBJECTIVES

- To use pronouns in the objective case as direct objects, indirect objects, and objects of prepositions
- To read aloud sentences, stressing the pronouns used as objects of prepositions
- To identify the correct pronoun form for objects of prepositions
- To write sentences using the correct pronoun form for objects of prepositions

Meeting INDIVIDUAL NEEDS

ENGLISH-LANGUAGE LEARNERS
General Strategies. Not all languages follow the subject-verb-object pattern, so you may want to give additional review in identifying objects if you suspect doing so is a problem for students.

RESOURCES

The Objective Case
Practice
- *Grammar, Usage, and Mechanics,* pp. 142–143, 144
- *Language Workshop CD-ROM,* Lesson 13

TEACHING TIP

Review C Direct students' attention to the second example in **Review C**. Explain that because the two numbers are joined by an italicized *and*, they should be treated together as one unit. Therefore, the replacement is the plural pronoun *we* rather than *she and I*.

Critical Thinking

Metacognition. After students have completed **Review C**, have them ask the following questions to analyze the process they used.

1. Did you make any notes on an extra piece of paper about the names and genders associated with the numbers?
2. Did you refer to the picture for each sentence?
3. Did you do the sentences in order?
4. What did you like about this review? What didn't you like?
5. Do you think your strategies for working this review were effective and efficient?
6. Upon reflection, is there anything you would like to change about your strategy?

HELP
In Review C, the expression *Number 1* indicates a first-person singular pronoun.

Review C — Using Pronouns in the Nominative and Objective Cases

The cheerleading squad is learning a new pyramid routine. To help organize the cheerleaders, the coach has assigned each one a number. In the following sentences, use a correct personal pronoun in place of each italicized expression.

EXAMPLES
1. Coach Welber tells Cara and *Number 5* where to position themselves.
1. her

2. I asked whether *Number 8 and Number 1* can be in the pyramid next time.
2. we

1. The three people forming the base of the pyramid are Harley, Michael, and *Number 5*. **1. she**
2. Kimiko is the smallest, so it is *Number 6* who is at the top first. **2. she**
3. *Number 8 and Number 1* give *Number 6* a boost. **3. We/her**
4. After *Number 4* and Emilio have been in the middle row awhile, Rosie and *Number 1* ask for a turn. **4. she/I**
5. Please show Luisa and *Number 6 and Number 3* their new positions. **5. them**
6. Give Rosie or *Number 1* a signal when you are ready to jump down, Kimiko. **6. me**
7. Next time, the ones in the middle row will be Harley and *Number 8*. **7. she**
8. If anyone can support the person on top well, it's *Number 3*. **8. he**
9. The winners of the next cheerleading meet will surely be *Numbers 1 through 8*. **9. we**
10. Come here, and I'll tell you and *Number 4* about the next new formation. **10. her**

554 Chapter 17 Using Pronouns Correctly

17e. **An object of a preposition should be in the objective case.**

A noun or pronoun that follows a preposition is called an *object of the preposition.* Together, a preposition, its object, and any modifiers of that object make up a *prepositional phrase.*

EXAMPLES   to **them**   with **him**   for both **her** and **us**

from **me**   next to **us**   between **you** and **me**

Reference Note

For lists of **commonly used prepositions,** see page 426. For more about **prepositional phrases,** see page 467.

Oral Practice 2 — Using Pronouns as Objects of Prepositions

Read each of the following sentences aloud, stressing the italicized words.

1. There were calls for Walker and *us.*
2. This message is from Dolores and *her.*
3. With Arnie and *them* were the Malone twins.
4. Margo looked toward Francine and *me.*
5. They gave copies to *him* and *me.*
6. This drawing is by either Hector or *him.*
7. Don't hold this against Cho and *her.*
8. Between Vince and *him* sat an iguana.

TIPS & TRICKS

To help you determine which pronoun form(s) to use in a compound object of a preposition, try each form with the preposition.

EXAMPLE
Gwen wrote to (*she, her*) and (*I, me*).

CHOICES
to *she* or to *her*?

to *I* or to *me*?

ANSWER
Gwen wrote to **her** and **me.**

Exercise 6 — Selecting Pronoun Forms for Objects of Prepositions

Choose the correct pronoun forms in parentheses in the following sentences.

EXAMPLE   1. Have you spoken to (*he, him*) or (*she, her*) recently?
   1. him, her

1. The referee called fouls on (*them, they*) and (*I, me*).
2. Fishing with Grandpa and (*he, him*) was fun.
3. We didn't want to leave without you and (*she, her*).
4. They assigned the same lab equipment to (*them, they*) and (*we, us*).
5. The duke directed a haughty sneer at the jester and (*he, him*).
6. After Carmen rolled the corn husks around the tamales, she handed them to Arturo and (*me, I*).
7. Everyone but Kevin and (*she, her*) thinks Ed Bradley is the best news commentator on television.
8. Between you and (*me, I*), I'd rather not.
9. The wary skunk circled around (*she, her*) and (*me, I*).
10. Uncle Vic will get the details from you and (*we, us*).

Exercise 7 Writing Sentences Using Pronouns as Objects of Prepositions

POSSIBLE ANSWERS

1. He competed against John and her in the golf tournament.
2. Jana handed the paper across me and Tim.
3. Mom bought new clothes for him and me.
4. No one lived in that house before Harold and them.
5. Will all the family except us and Raoul attend the party?
6. Please take the seat between Colleen and him.
7. Without him and Lawanda, we may have trouble winning the debate.
8. Do you live near her and Selina?
9. The game was won by Max and me.
10. We enjoyed the picnic even though rain clouds hung over us and our boat.

The Possessive Case
Rules 17f–h *(pp. 556–558)*

STYLE TIP

As a matter of courtesy, first-person pronouns are placed at the end of compound constructions.

NOMINATIVE CASE
Dad and **I** went shopping.

OBJECTIVE CASE
Mom met Dad and **me** for lunch.

POSSESSIVE CASE
I surprised them by paying for both their lunches and **mine**.

Exercise 7 Writing Sentences Using Pronouns as Objects of Prepositions

Write sentences of your own, using each of the following prepositions with a compound object. Use a personal pronoun for at least one of the objects in each sentence.

EXAMPLE   1. toward
           1. *The whooping crane stalked toward Mike and me.*

1. against   3. for   5. except   7. without   9. by
2. across   4. before   6. between   8. near   10. over

Review D Selecting Correct Forms of Pronouns

For the numbered sentences, in the following paragraph, choose the correct pronoun forms in parentheses.

EXAMPLE   [1] Tina, Susan, and (*I, me*) are best friends.
           1. *I*

[1] Last fall, Tina talked Susan and (*I, me*) into going on a canoe trip with the Wilderness Club. [2] She warned (*we, us*) that we might get a good dunking before we were through. [3] When we set out, Susan and (*I, me*) could barely steer our canoe. [4] We watched another canoeist and saw how (*she, her*) and her partner maneuvered their craft. [5] Both they and (*we, us*) did well until we hit the rapids or, rather, until the rapids hit (*we, us*). [6] Susan grabbed our sleeping bags, and (*she, her*) and (*I, me*) both scrambled for our ice chest. [7] All of (*we, us*) were drenched, but no quitters were (*we, us*). [8] Tina's warning haunted all of (*we, us*) as (*we, us*) contemplated waterlogged sandwiches, soggy salads, and banana muffins with tadpoles in them. [9] Later, Susan and (*I, me*) discovered that our bedrolls had become portable water beds. [10] After a cold, squishy night, (*I, me*) concluded that wise are (*they, them*) who heed the voice of experience.

The Possessive Case

The personal pronouns in the possessive case—*my, mine, your, yours, his, her, hers, its, our, ours, their* and *theirs*—are used to show ownership or possession.

17f. The possessive pronouns *mine, yours, his, hers, its, ours,* and *theirs* can be used in the same way that the personal pronouns in the nominative and objective cases are used.

RESOURCES

The Possessive Case
Practice
- *Grammar, Usage, and Mechanics,* pp. 145, 146–147
- *Language Workshop CD-ROM,* Lesson 39

SUBJECT	**Mine** has a flat tire.
PREDICATE NOMINATIVE	This key is **yours**.
DIRECT OBJECT	Mrs. Fong takes **hers** for a walk twice a day.
INDIRECT OBJECT	Most teachers are not assigning **theirs** any homework for the holidays.
OBJECT OF PREPOSITION	Their coach spoke to **ours** about a possible rematch.

17g. The possessive pronouns *my, your, his, her, its, our,* and *their* are used to modify nouns and pronouns.

EXAMPLES **My** bicycle has a flat tire. [*My* modifies *bicycle*.]

This is **your** key. [*Your* modifies *key*.]

Mrs. Fong takes **her** dogs for a walk twice a day. [*Her* modifies *dogs*.]

Most teachers are not assigning **their** students any homework for the holidays. [*Their* modifies *students*.]

Their coach spoke to **our** coach about a possible rematch. [*Their* and *our* each modify *coach*.]

NOTE Some authorities prefer to call the possessive pronouns *my, your, his, her, its, our,* and *their* adjectives. Follow your teacher's instructions regarding these possessive forms.

17h. A noun or pronoun preceding a gerund generally should be in the possessive case.

A **gerund** is a verb form that ends in *–ing* and functions as a noun. Since a gerund serves as a noun, the noun or pronoun that precedes it should be in the possessive case in order to modify the gerund.

EXAMPLE They approved of the **students'** [or **their**] organizing a cleanup campaign.

Do not confuse a gerund with a **present participle,** which is also a verb form that ends in *–ing*. A gerund acts as a noun, whereas a present participle serves as an adjective or as part of a verb phrase. The noun or pronoun preceding a present participle should generally not be in the possessive case.

EXAMPLE Every day after school, the principal saw the **students** [or **them**] working diligently.

Reference Note
For more on **gerunds** and **present participles,** see pages 476 and 472.

Meeting INDIVIDUAL NEEDS

ENGLISH-LANGUAGE LEARNERS
Spanish. In Spanish, the possessive adjective *su* can mean *your, his, her, its,* or *their,* and *suyo* can mean *yours, his, hers, its,* or *theirs*. These possessive pronouns, *su* and *suyo,* agree—*su* in number, *suyo* in number and gender—with the thing possessed, not with the possessor. Therefore, Spanish speakers may be tempted to say "her class" and "hers classes." To help your students avoid such errors and see that possessive pronouns like *her* are used to modify nouns and those like *hers* are used only as pronouns, use template sentences such as the following ones.

This is ____ apartment.
This apartment is ____.

USAGE

Case Forms of Personal Pronouns

Special Problems in Pronoun Usage

Rules 17i, j *(pp. 558–565)*

OBJECTIVES

- To use *who* and *whom* correctly in sentences
- To identify subordinate clauses and to tell how *who* or *whom* is used in each clause
- To use and identify reflexive and intensive pronouns in sentences

Meeting INDIVIDUAL NEEDS

ENGLISH-LANGUAGE LEARNERS

General Strategies. Most languages do not have an equivalent of the *who/whom* distinction. Thus, students may not have a first-language context to which they can relate this concept. You may want to provide some additional examples. Encourage students to use the examples for oral practice.

STYLE TIP

In informal English, the use of *whom* is becoming less common. However, in formal speech and writing, it is still important to distinguish between *who* and *whom*.

Reference Note

For information on **subordinate clauses,** see page 493.

NOTE Often the form of a noun or pronoun before an *–ing* word depends on the meaning you want to express. If you want to emphasize the *–ing* word, use the possessive form. If you want to emphasize the noun or pronoun preceding the *–ing* word, do not use the possessive form. Notice the difference in emphasis in the following sentences.

EXAMPLES I can't imagine cousin **Liam's** [or **his**] driving. [emphasis on the gerund *driving*]

I can't imagine cousin **Liam** [or **him**] driving. [emphasis on the noun or pronoun preceding the present participle *driving*]

Special Problems in Pronoun Usage

The Relative Pronouns *Who* and *Whom*

17i. The use of *who* or *whom* in a subordinate clause depends on how the pronoun functions in the clause.

Nominative Case	who, whoever
Objective Case	whom, whomever

Follow these steps to decide whether to use *who* or *whom* in a subordinate clause.

STEP 1 Find the subordinate clause.

STEP 2 Decide how the pronoun is used in the clause—as subject, predicate nominative, direct object, indirect object, or object of a preposition.

STEP 3 Determine the case of the pronoun according to the rules of standard, formal English.

STEP 4 Select the correct form of the pronoun.

EXAMPLE Roscoe is the only student (*who, whom*) earned a perfect score.

STEP 1 The subordinate clause is (*who, whom*) *earned a perfect score*.

STEP 2 In this clause the pronoun is the subject of the verb *earned*.

STEP 3 As a subject the pronoun should be in the nominative case.

STEP 4 The nominative form is *who*.

ANSWER Roscoe is the only student **who** earned a perfect score.

RESOURCES

Special Problems in Pronoun Usage
Practice

- *Grammar, Usage, and Mechanics,* pp. 148, 149, 150
- *Language Workshop CD-ROM,* Lesson 14

EXAMPLE	Did they say (*who, whom*) the winner is?
STEP 1	The subordinate clause is (*who, whom*) *the winner is.*
STEP 2	In this clause the pronoun is the predicate nominative: *the winner is (who, whom).*
STEP 3	As a predicate nominative, the pronoun should be in the nominative case.
STEP 4	The nominative form is *who.*
ANSWER	Did they say **who** the winner is?

EXAMPLE	I saw Sabrina, (*who, whom*) I know from school.
STEP 1	The subordinate clause is (*who, whom*) *I know from school.*
STEP 2	In this clause the pronoun is the direct object of the verb *know: I know (who, whom).*
STEP 3	As a direct object, the pronoun should be in the objective case.
STEP 4	The objective form is *whom.*
ANSWER	I saw Sabrina, **whom** I know from school.

Remember that no words outside the subordinate clause affect the case of a pronoun in the clause. In the second example above, the whole clause *who the winner is* is the direct object of the verb *did say* in the independent clause. In the subordinate clause, though, *who* is used as a predicate nominative, which takes the nominative case.

NOTE The relative pronoun *whom* is often left out of a subordinate adjective clause but is nevertheless understood.

EXAMPLE The man [whom] we saw on the elevator looked familiar.
[*Whom* is understood to be the direct object of *saw.*]

Exercise 8 Selecting *Who* or *Whom* to Complete Sentences Correctly

For each of the following sentences, choose the correct form, *who* or *whom*, in parentheses.

EXAMPLE 1. (*Who, Whom*) did you speak to yesterday?
1. Whom

1. The student (*who, whom*) saw the eclipse is here.
2. (*Who, Whom*) did you vote for in the election?
3. Are the you the person to (*who, whom*) I give my essay?

COMPUTER TIP
If you use a computer, you can use the search feature of a word-processing program to find each use of *who* or *whom* in a document. Then you can check to make sure that you have used the correct form of the pronoun in each instance.

Special Problems in Pronoun Usage   559

TEACHING TIP

Activity. Point out to students that if they have trouble determining whether to use *who* or *whom* in a subordinate clause, they could do a simple diagram of the clause alone to identify the function of the relative pronoun. Write the following sentence and diagram on the chalkboard.

Malik is the baby sitter (*who, whom*) saved the child's life.

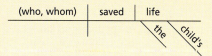

Explain to students that the diagram shows graphically that the relative pronoun functions here as the subject of the clause and should be in the nominative case. Therefore, *who* is the correct choice. Then, erase *whom* in the diagram.

Write the following sentence on the chalkboard, and ask students to diagram the subordinate clause, determine the function and case of the relative pronoun, and choose the correct relative pronoun.

I voted for Quay, (*who, whom*) I know from the soccer team. [*direct object, objective case, whom*]

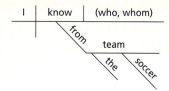

Meeting INDIVIDUAL NEEDS

LEARNERS HAVING DIFFICULTY
The process of determining whether to use *who* or *whom* often requires more knowledge of English grammar than many students possess. Tell students that one quick test of case is to substitute *he* for *who* and *him* for *whom* in the sentence. [Who lost the book? He lost the book. On whom do you depend? You depend on him.]

ADVANCED LEARNERS
You may wish to challenge students to write sentences of their own containing *who* and *whom* in subordinate clauses, using **Exercise 9** as a model. After students have composed their sentences, they could exchange papers and identify the usage of the relative pronouns, as in **Exercise 9**.

MODALITIES
Auditory Learners. Students might benefit from hearing the sentences in **Exercise 9** read aloud. Organize students into groups of four or five, and have them take turns reading the sentences aloud. Remind students that while the use of *who* in situations requiring the objective case is acceptable in informal speech, in formal speech and in writing they will need to employ formal usage of *who* and *whom*.

USAGE

PEANUTS reprinted by permission of United Feature Syndicate, Inc.

4. I don't know (who, whom) has my notebook.
5. (Who, Whom) is on the telephone?
6. To (who, whom) are you speaking?
7. They are the people about (who, whom) I was talking.
8. He is not (who, whom) won the award.
9. Jonathan saw (who, whom) you greeted.
10. I feel sometimes that I don't know (who, whom) you are anymore.

Exercise 9 Determining the Use of *Who* and *Whom* in Subordinate Clauses

Identify the subordinate clause containing *who* or *whom* in each of the following sentences. Then, tell how *who* or *whom* is used in the clause—as *subject*, *predicate nominative*, *direct object*, or *object of a preposition*.

EXAMPLES
1. She is someone whom we all admire.
1. whom we all admire—direct object

2. He is the person about whom I wrote my report.
2. about whom I wrote my report—object of a preposition

1. The people who are born in Puerto Rico live in a commonwealth, with its own Senate, Supreme Court, and Cabinet. **1. s.**
2. In 1969, the governor needed a secretary of labor on whom he could depend. **2. o.p.**
3. The person whom he appointed would occupy the most difficult and sensitive position in the Cabinet. **3. d.o.**
4. Do you know who the choice was? **4. p.n.**
5. The choice fell to Mrs. Julia Rivera De Vincenti, who became the first woman to occupy a Cabinet post in Puerto Rico. **5. s.**
6. De Vincenti, who had completed the requirements for a Ph.D. degree in management and collective bargaining at Cornell University, was a good choice. **6. s.**
7. De Vincenti, who was later appointed to the U.S. Mission to the United Nations, was the first Puerto Rican to serve in that capacity. **7. s.**
8. She addressed the General Assembly and showed that she was a person on whom they could rely. **8. o.p.**
9. She praised her compatriots, from whom new advances in agriculture had recently come. **9. o.p.**
10. I'm sure her compatriots appreciated her praise, for De Vincenti was someone who herself was worthy of praise. **10. s.**

Appositives

17j. A pronoun used as an appositive should be in the same case as the word to which it refers.

An *appositive* appears next to another noun or pronoun to identify or describe that noun or pronoun.

EXAMPLES   The late arrivals—**she, he,** and **I**—missed the first act. [The pronouns are in the nominative case because they refer to the subject *arrivals*.]

The co-captains should be the best bowlers, **he** and **she**. [The pronouns are in the nominative case because they refer to the predicate nominative *bowlers*.]

The article you're reading mentions the winners, **her** and **me**. [The pronouns are in the objective case because they refer to the direct object *winners*.]

Ms. Lee gave the debaters, **them** and **us,** name tags. [The pronouns are in the objective case because they refer to the indirect object *debaters*.]

The contestants were narrowed to two finalists, **him** and **her**. [The pronouns are in the objective case because they refer to *finalists*, the object of the preposition *to*.]

The pronoun *we* or *us* is sometimes followed by a noun appositive.

EXAMPLES   **We** sophomores raised the most money for charity. [The pronoun is in the nominative case because it is the subject of the verb *raised*. The appositive *sophomores* identifies *We*.]

The judges awarded **us** members of the marching band a superior rating. [The pronoun is in the objective case because it is the indirect object of the verb *awarded*. The appositive *members* identifies *us*.]

TIPS & TRICKS

To help you determine which pronoun form(s) to use as an appositive or with an appositive, read the sentence with only the pronoun.

AS AN APPOSITIVE
The coach congratulated the two starting forwards, Angela and (*I, me*).

CHOICES
The coach congratulated *I* or The coach congratulated *me*?

ANSWER
The coach congratulated the two starting forwards, Angela and **me**.

BEFORE A NOUN APPOSITIVE
(*We, Us*) girls made the playoffs!

CHOICES
We made the playoffs or *Us made the playoffs*?

ANSWER
We girls made the playoffs!

Reference Note
For information on **appositives,** see page 483.

Looking at Language

Word Origins. To help students fix in their minds the function of appositives, ask them to consult a dictionary to find the etymology and meaning of the word *appositive*. *Appositive* comes from Latin *apponere*, "to put near to." Discuss with students how an appositive is placed near to the word it identifies or explains. Ask students to think of other words that might be related to *appositive* and to check their etymologies and meanings. [*Some possibilities are* oppose, position, pose, posit, disposition.]

LEARNERS HAVING DIFFICULTY
As you assign **Review E,** you may wish to modify the instructions for some students. You could have students work in groups of four or five and go through the ten sentences together to determine the correct responses. Allow them to omit the analysis of how the pronouns are used in the sentences.

Review E — Selecting Pronouns to Complete Sentences Correctly

Choose the correct pronoun form in parentheses in each of the following sentences. Then, tell whether the pronoun is used as a *subject*, a *predicate nominative*, a *direct object*, an *indirect object*, an *object of a preposition*, or an *appositive*.

EXAMPLE   1. Andre is giving Jena and (*I, me*) marimba lessons.
1. me—indirect object

Special Problems in Pronoun Usage   **561**

Continued on p. 562

Punctuating Appositives. Remind students that appositives and appositive phrases are set off by commas unless the appositive is essential to the basic meaning of the sentence. Write the following sentences on the chalkboard.

1. Have you ever read the book *Jane Eyre*?
2. The winners, Mary and I, received gift certificates.

Explain to the class that in the first sentence, *Jane Eyre* is an essential appositive.

TEACHING TIP

Activity. To help students with the review exercises, have them watch a favorite family sitcom and write down phrases and sentences in which characters use personal pronouns.

Have students share their findings and categorize their examples of pronoun usage as appropriate for informal dialogue or appropriate for formal writing.

Review F Proofreading for Correct Pronoun Forms

ANSWERS

1. Us—We; me—I
2. me—I
3. who—whom
4. C
5. her—she
6. him and her—he and she
7. I—me
8. whomever—whoever
9. we—us
10. I—me

---

1. The two winners, Sean and (*she*, *her*), received huge green ribbons decorated with shamrocks.   **1.** a.
2. Will Meg and (*she*, *her*) run the concession stand?   **2.** s.
3. The coach asked you and (*I*, *me*) for help with the equipment.   **3.** d.o.
4. Becky and (*she*, *her*) rode their bikes to the meeting.   **4.** s.
5. The lighting crew for the play was Manuel and (*I*, *me*).   **5.** p.n.
6. They treat very well (*whoever*, *whomever*) they hire.   **6.** d.o.
7. I think that Denzel Washington and (*he*, *him*) starred in *Much Ado About Nothing*.   **7.** s.
8. They met my cousins—Jennie and (*she*, *her*)—at the airport.   **8.** a.
9. Joe Leaphorn and Jim Chee are the Navajo detectives (*who*, *whom*) Tony Hillerman writes about in his crime stories.   **9.** o.p.
10. The people who were costumed as pirates are (*they*, *them*).   **10.** p.n.

Review F Proofreading for Correct Pronoun Forms

Most of the sentences in the following paragraph contain at least one pronoun that is used incorrectly. Identify each incorrect pronoun, and write the correct form. If the sentence is already correct, write *C*.

EXAMPLE [1] Two of my cousins and me tried to determine how everyone else at the family reunion was related to we cousins.

1. me—I; we—us

[1] Us cousins were getting so confused at the family reunion that Rochelle, Darla, and me made the Family Relationship Chart shown at left. [2] Before long, the busiest people at the picnic were they and me! [3] Aunts and uncles consulted us to find out who they were related to and just how they were related. [4] It all started when Jules wanted to know the connection between him and Vicky. [5] We figured out that Vicky is the great-granddaughter of Jules's grandmother's brother, so her and Jules are second cousins once removed. [6] Looking at our chart, we could see that Vicky and Jules are in different generations, even though him and her are the same age. [7] All afternoon, curious relatives besieged Rochelle, Darla, and I with many questions. [8] We helped whomever asked us. [9] Grandmother said she was very proud of we girls. [10] Everyone learned something new about our family ties that day and gave the two other girls and I a big round of applause.

MINI-LESSON

Without the appositive, the basic meaning of the sentence would not be the same. Therefore, no comma is needed. In the second sentence, because the appositive *Mary and I* is not essential to the basic meaning of the sentence, it is set off by commas. For more information on appositives, refer students to **Chapter 14: The Phrase** and **Chapter 22: Punctuation**.

Review G — Determining Correct Pronoun Forms

Write the correct form of each incorrect pronoun in the following sentences. Write *C* if all of the pronouns in a sentence are in the correct case.

EXAMPLE   1. Nelson Mandela, whom shared the Nobel Peace Prize in 1993, was elected president of South Africa in 1994.
   1. who

1. Be careful who you tell.   **1.** whom
2. May Marie and I cut a few pictures out of this old copy of *Ebony*?   **2.** C
3. My family goes to the dentist who Ms. Calhoun recommended.   **3.** whom
4. Coretta said there would be other flag bearers in addition to Hugh and I.   **4.** me
5. At the head of the parade were us Girl Scouts.   **5.** we
6. The treaty gave them and the Ojibwa people the right to harvest wild rice there.   **6.** C
7. Nobody except Josh and him finished the marathon.   **7.** C
8. Joanne and us found a great beach.   **8.** we
9. Did your father and them reach an agreement about the boundary dispute?   **9.** they
10. We wish we had neighbors that were more like Sylvia and he.   **10.** him

Review H — Selecting Pronouns to Complete Sentences

For each of the following sentences, choose the correct pronoun in parentheses. Be prepared to give a reason for your answer.

EXAMPLE   1. Jason and (I, me) attended the Golden Spurs horse show.
   1. *I*

1. Heather and (*he*, *him*) live on a blueberry farm.
2. Did the teacher give that assignment to (*whoever*, *whomever*) was absent yesterday?
3. We wondered (*who*, *whom*) started the rumor.
4. Do you intercept passes as well as Robin and (*she*, *her*) do?
5. The supporting players were Dina, Janelle, and (*she*, *her*).
6. I was standing in line behind Dave and (*he*, *him*).
7. You and (*I*, *me*) could write our biographical sketches on General Colin L. Powell, who was chairman of the Joint Chiefs of Staff under President George Bush.
8. The skit was written by Cy and (*he*, *him*).

HELP
In the example for Review H, the nominative-case pronoun *I* is correct because the pronoun is used as a subject.

TEACHING TIP

Reviews To assess students' use of pronoun forms, you may wish to use **Review G** as guided practice. Then, have students complete **Review H** as independent practice.

9. The electrician warned (*he, him*) and (*I, me*) about the frayed wires.
10. Amy Tan, (*who, whom*) the critics had praised, autographed a copy of her novel for me.

Reflexive and Intensive Pronouns

Reflexive and intensive pronouns (sometimes called *compound personal pronouns*) have the same forms.

Reflexive and Intensive Pronouns		
	Singular	**Plural**
First Person	myself	ourselves
Second Person	yourself	yourselves
Third Person	himself, herself, itself	themselves

A *reflexive pronoun* refers to the subject of a verb and may serve as a direct object, an indirect object, a predicate nominative, or an object of a preposition.

DIRECT OBJECT	Diners at this restaurant serve **themselves.**
INDIRECT OBJECT	I made **myself** a gyro sandwich.
PREDICATE NOMINATIVE	Dale is just not **himself** today.
OBJECT OF PREPOSITION	He suddenly remembered the promise he had made to **himself.**

An *intensive pronoun* has only one function: to emphasize its antecedent.

EXAMPLES   Don't you think we can install the computer program **ourselves**?

Only you **yourself** can make that decision.

NOTE   A pronoun ending in *–self* or *–selves* should not be used in place of a personal pronoun.

NONSTANDARD	Sonia and myself sang a duet in the talent show.
STANDARD	Sonia and **I** sang a duet in the talent show.
NONSTANDARD	Chad bought tickets for himself and myself.
STANDARD	Chad bought tickets for himself and **me.**

STYLE TIP

The words *hisself, theirself,* and *theirselves* are non-standard English. Always use *himself* and *themselves* instead.

TIPS & TRICKS

To help you decide whether a pronoun ending in *–self* or *–selves* is reflexive or intensive, use this test: Omit the pronoun from the sentence. You can omit an intensive pronoun, but not a reflexive pronoun, from a sentence without significantly changing the meaning of the sentence.

INTENSIVE
Did you change the oil in the car **yourself**?
[*Yourself* can be omitted: *Did you change the oil in the car?*]

REFLEXIVE
Did you hurt **yourself**?
[*Yourself* is the direct object of *Did hurt* and cannot be omitted without changing the meaning of the sentence.]

564 Chapter 17   Using Pronouns Correctly

Exercise 10 Using Reflexive and Intensive Pronouns

For each blank in the following sentences, supply a pronoun ending in *–self* or *–selves* that correctly completes the sentence. Then, identify the pronoun as *reflexive* or *intensive*. If neither a reflexive nor an intensive pronoun would be correct, give a personal pronoun.

EXAMPLE   1. Did Jamal make this delicious stew _____ ?
1. *himself—intensive*

1. Working quickly and efficiently, we volunteers decorated the auditorium all by _____ .
2. Mona's cat cleans _____ right after it eats.
3. Did Julio and _____ have a good time at the concert?
4. Having gotten my braces off, I finally feel like _____ again.
5. The judges _____ could not reach a consensus.
6. How are Eric and _____ supposed to react in this scene?
7. Only time _____ will prove one of us right.
8. Give _____ a big pat on the back.
9. Where do you think they have hidden _____ ?
10. With her fever gone, Carla is _____ today.

HELP
Some sentences in Exercise 10 have more than one possible correct answer, but you need to give only one answer for each.

Pronouns in Incomplete Constructions

17k. A pronoun following *than* or *as* in an incomplete construction should be in the same case as it would be if the construction were completed.

EXAMPLES   I know Mac better than **he** [knows Mac].
I know Mac better than [I know] **him.**

Do you visit Aunt Bessie as often as **we** [visit Aunt Bessie]?
Do you visit Aunt Bessie as often as [you visit] **us**?

Exercise 11 Selecting Pronouns for Incomplete Constructions

For each of the sentences on the next page, choose the correct form of the pronoun in parentheses. Also, supply in parentheses the missing part of the incomplete construction. Then, give the use of the pronoun in its clause. If the construction may be completed in two different ways, provide both completions. Then, tell how the pronoun in each completion is used in the sentence.

Special Problems in Pronoun Usage   565

RESOURCES

Pronouns in Incomplete Constructions
Practice
- *Grammar, Usage, and Mechanics,* p. 151
- *Language Workshop CD-ROM,* Lesson 14

Exercise 11 Selecting Pronouns for Incomplete Constructions

POSSIBLE ANSWERS

1. they (played defense)—subject
2. I (was pleased)—subject
3. she (tried)—subject
4. he (is)—subject
5. she (knows her)—subject (I know) her—direct object
6. I (did)—subject
7. we (bought)—subject
8. we (live)—subject
9. I (visited Lisa)—subject (she visited) me—direct object
10. he (plays classical guitar)—subject

Clear Pronoun Reference

Rule 17l *(pp. 566–568)*

OBJECTIVE

- To revise sentences to correct unclear pronoun references

USAGE

HELP

Not all sentences in Exercise 11 can be completed in more than one way.

Reference Note
For information on **pronoun-antecedent agreement,** see page 532.

EXAMPLE
1. I like Jay Leno better than (*she, her*).
   1. she (likes Jay Leno)—subject; (I like) her—direct object

1. We played defense better than (*they, them*).
2. When Pete Sampras won the men's singles title at the French Open, nobody was as pleased as (*I, me*).
3. Nobody tried harder than (*she, her*).
4. You are a month younger than (*he, him*).
5. I know Millie better than (*she, her*).
6. Did you walk as far in the walkathon as (*I, me*)?
7. Richard bought more tickets than (*we, us*).
8. Bianca lives farther away than (*we, us*).
9. She visited Lisa more often than (*I, me*).
10. Carlos plays classical guitar in the style of Andrés Segovia but, of course, not as well as (*he, him*).

Clear Pronoun Reference

Generally, a pronoun has no definite meaning by itself. Its meaning is clear only when the word or word group it stands for is known. This word or word group is called the *antecedent* of the pronoun.

17l. A pronoun should refer clearly to its antecedent.

(1) Avoid an *ambiguous reference*, which occurs when any one of two or more words can be a pronoun's antecedent.

AMBIGUOUS	Marissa called Yolanda while she was at the library last weekend. [Who was at the library, Marissa or Yolanda?]
CLEAR	While Marissa was at the library last weekend, **she** called Yolanda.
	or
CLEAR	While Yolanda was at the library last weekend, Marissa called **her.**

AMBIGUOUS	After viewing Roy's paintings and Elton's sculpture, the judges awarded his work the blue ribbon. [Whose work was awarded the blue ribbon?]
CLEAR	The judges awarded Elton the blue ribbon after viewing **his** sculpture and Roy's paintings.
	or
CLEAR	The judges awarded Roy the blue ribbon after viewing **his** paintings and Elton's sculpture.

566 Chapter 17 Using Pronouns Correctly

RESOURCES

Clear Pronoun Reference
Practice
- *Grammar, Usage, and Mechanics,* pp. 152, 153, 154–155
- *Language Workshop CD-ROM,* Lesson 15

(2) Avoid a *general reference,* which is the use of a pronoun that refers to a general idea rather than to a specific antecedent.

Most general reference errors are caused by the misuse of the pronouns *it, this, that, which,* and *such.*

GENERAL Paul has a job interview after school today. That explains why he is wearing a suit. [*That* has no specific antecedent.]

CLEAR Paul is wearing a suit because he has a job interview after school today.

or

CLEAR The reason Paul is wearing a suit is that he has a job interview after school today.

GENERAL My biology class is going to the coast this week, which should be fun. [*Which* has no specific antecedent.]

CLEAR My biology class is going to the coast this week. The trip should be fun.

or

CLEAR Going to the coast with my biology class this week should be fun.

(3) Avoid a *weak reference,* which occurs when a pronoun refers to an antecedent that has been suggested but not expressed.

WEAK Ryan is multilingual. One of those that he speaks fluently is Mandarin. [The antecedent *languages* is suggested by the use of the pronoun *those* but is not expressed.]

CLEAR Ryan speaks several languages. One of those that he speaks fluently is Mandarin.

or

CLEAR Ryan is multilingual. One of the languages that he speaks fluently is Mandarin.

WEAK Royale writes stories, and she hopes to make it her career. [The antecedent *writing* is suggested by the use of the pronoun *it* but is not expressed.]

CLEAR Royale writes stories, and she hopes to make writing her career.

(4) Avoid an *indefinite reference,* which is the use of a pronoun that refers to no specific antecedent and that is unnecessary to the meaning of the sentence.

Most indefinite reference errors are caused by the misuse of the pronouns *it, they,* and *you.*

Relating to Literature

If Anne Sexton's "Courage" is available in students' literature books, have them read the poem and answer the following questions about Sexton's use of pronouns.

1. What is the antecedent for the pronoun *it* in the first line of the poem? [*While the antecedent for the pronoun* it *is not explicitly identified in the line, the meaning is revealed by the title—"Courage."*]

2. How many times does *it* appear in the poem? [*thirteen*]

3. Does the word *it* always have the same antecedent? [*No; there are many different antecedents.*]

4. What comprehension problem can the use of pronouns cause? [*If the pronouns are separated from their antecedents by many words, readers may misidentify the antecedents. To prevent this, writers must supply readers with enough clues to identify each antecedent clearly.*]

Clear Pronoun Reference

Learning for Life

Continued on p. 568

Tell students that they will practice answering questions for an entrance interview for a camp, college, or trade school or for a job. Have students work in small groups to list qualities that interviewers would be looking for and to write a prompt for each quality. For example, for the quality of persistence, the prompt could be *Describe an experience to demonstrate your persistence in seeking a goal.*

Have each student choose a prompt and prepare an answer to it, paying particular

Exercise 12 Revising Unclear Pronoun References

POSSIBLE ANSWERS

1. The newest twist in recycling is *precycling*—cutting waste off at its source.
2. Last month, after reading the EPA's brochure, my family decided to put the brochure's ideas into practice.
3. We now choose products that have less packaging; we carry groceries home in reusable cloth bags instead of paper or plastic ones; and we buy containers that can be refilled easily.
4. Sara asked Mom to write to the Mail Preference Service, Direct Marketing Association and ask that our names not be sold to mailing-list companies.
5. Writing that letter greatly reduced the amount of junk mail we get.
6. When we do have waste products, inventing new ways to use them becomes a challenge in creative thinking; one idea was mine.
7. Now we pack fragile objects in bits of plastic foam and other non-recyclable materials so that the fragile objects don't get broken in shipping.
8. We use plastic produce bags as sandwich wrappers or as liners for small trash cans, and the bags work just fine.
9. We also convert cottage cheese cartons and margarine tubs into food-storage containers, and we plan to make a habit of reusing items.
10. In just a few short weeks, we've learned that by remembering the three *r*'s—*r*educe, *r*euse, and *r*ecycle—people can help to protect our precious environment.

STYLE TIP

Familiar expressions such as *it is raining, it's early,* and *it seems* are standard and acceptable, although they do not refer to definite antecedents.

COMPUTER TIP

If you use a computer, you can use the search feature to locate all occurrences of the pronoun *it* in a piece of your writing. Every time the pronoun appears, check its reference carefully. Is the reference clear?

If necessary, use the replace function to substitute a better word for the pronoun, or rewrite the sentence so that the pronoun clearly refers to a specific antecedent. Use the same procedure to check your uses of the pronouns *you, they, this, that, which,* and *such.*

INDEFINITE	In the newspaper, it reported that the robbers had been caught. [The pronoun *it* is not necessary to the meaning of the sentence.]
CLEAR	The newspaper reported that the robbers had been caught.
INDEFINITE	During the Middle Ages in Europe, you very likely would not live past the age of thirty. [The pronoun *you* does not truly refer to the reader and does not have any specific antecedent.]
CLEAR	During the Middle Ages in Europe, a person very likely would not live past the age of thirty.

Exercise 12 Revising Unclear Pronoun References

Most of the following sentences contain unclear pronoun references. Revise each faulty sentence. If a sentence is already clear, write *C*.

EXAMPLE
1. In a brochure recently published by the Environmental Protection Agency (EPA), it promotes precycling to reduce waste.

1. A brochure recently published by the Environmental Protection Agency (EPA) promotes precycling to reduce waste.

1. The newest twist in recycling is *precycling*—cutting it off at its source.
2. Last month, after reading the EPA's brochure, my family decided to put its ideas into practice.
3. We now choose products that have less packaging; we carry groceries home in reusable cloth bags instead of paper or plastic ones; and we buy containers that can be refilled, which is easy.
4. Sara asked Mom if she could write to the Mail Preference Service, Direct Marketing Association and ask that our names not be sold to mailing-list companies.
5. That greatly reduced the amount of junk mail we get.
6. When we do have waste products, inventing new ways to use them becomes a challenge in creative thinking; one of them was mine.
7. Now we pack fragile objects in bits of plastic foam and other non-recyclable materials so that they don't get broken in shipping.
8. We use plastic produce bags as sandwich wrappers or as liners for small trash cans, and it works just fine.
9. We also convert cottage cheese cartons and margarine tubs into food-storage containers, and we plan to make a habit of it.
10. In just a few short weeks, we've learned that by remembering the three *r*'s—*r*educe, *r*euse, and *r*ecycle—you can help to protect our precious environment.

Learning for Life

attention to his or her use of pronouns. Students could conduct interviews within their groups, taking turns acting as interviewers and applicants. You could videotape the interviews and allow groups or the entire class to view the tapes, giving feedback on attention to the prompt and the use of pronouns.

CHAPTER

Chapter Review

A. Using Pronouns Correctly in Sentences

For each sentence, choose the correct word in parentheses.

1. Francis said that in a few years he would give his stamp collection to his brother and (I, *me*).
2. Everyone was waiting impatiently to find out (*who*, whom) the new cheerleader would be.
3. My little sister is a much better basketball player than (I, *me*).
4. After the accident, the police questioned (he, *him*).
5. We found that (*she*, her) was the one who called twice last night.
6. At the self-service gas station, drivers must pump gasoline (theirselves, *themselves*).
7. Speaking of Ken Griffey, Jr., (*he*, him) and his dad are the first father and son ever to play professional baseball together on the same team.
8. Seeing a car with an out-of-state license plate in my driveway, I ran inside to see (*who*, whom) was there.
9. That trailer with the silver stripe is (our, *ours*).
10. Do you mind (me, *my*) eating while we walk?

B. Selecting Pronouns to Complete Sentences Correctly

Choose the correct pronoun form in parentheses. Then, tell whether the pronoun is used as a subject, a predicate nominative, a direct object, an indirect object, an object of a preposition, or an appositive.

11. The two Italian drivers, Dario and (*he*, him), came in first and second. **11.** a.
12. The entire cast in the first scene of the second act consisted of Beth and (I, *me*). **12.** o.p.
13. They met Stuart and (he, *him*) at the railroad station. **13.** d.o.
14. I thought the best soloists in the band were (*they*, them). **14.** p.n.
15. Teddy and (*she*, her) arrived with minutes to spare. **15.** s.
16. (*Whoever*, Whomever) wants to learn about good manners should listen to my Aunt Rita. **16.** s.

Using the Chapter Review

To assess student progress, you may want to compare the types of items missed on the **Diagnostic Preview** to those missed on the **Chapter Review.** If students have not made significant progress, you may want to refer them to **Chapter 27: Correcting Common Errors, Exercises 10–12,** for additional practice.

17. The stars of that movie were Robert Duval and (*he, him*). **17.** p.n.
18. Edmond Dantès was the wronged prisoner about (*who, whom*) Alexandre Dumas wrote in *The Count of Monte Cristo*. **18.** o.p.
19. Will Colin and (*he, him*) help us with the painting? **19.** s.
20. Ms. Oliveira asked you and (*I, me*) about staying and helping with the decorations. **20.** d.o.
21. I asked my mother (*who, whom*) called last night. **21.** s.
22. The pair of ballad singers, Tommy and (*she, her*), left the stage to great applause. **22.** a.
23. The person (*who, whom*) you spoke about will be the next leader of the expedition. **23.** o.p.
24. We gave Louis and (*he, him*) a ride to school. **24.** i.o.
25. She is a better swimmer than (*I, me*), but the coach said he needed both of us on the team. **25.** s.
26. I will support (*whoever, whomever*) is selected for president. **26.** s.
27. It is not fair to give (*they, them*) extra responsibilities just because they are more responsible. **27.** i.o.
28. (*Who, Whom*) is supervising the drama festival this year? **28.** s
29. To go on the field trip, you need written permission from your parents and (*I, me*). **29.** o.p.
30. Everyone else finished the test earlier than (*they, them*). **30.** s.

C. Proofreading Sentences for Correct Pronoun Usage

Most of the following sentences contain errors in pronoun usage. Write the correct pronoun form for each error. If a sentence is already correct, write *C*.

31. Us athletes have little time to spend watching television. **31.** We
32. The one who organized the new filing system was she. **32.** C
33. Ask Lorna and he about the outcome of the race. **33.** him
34. Ramona had not decided who she would vote for in the election. **34.** whom
35. Between you and I, that painting is worth much more. **35.** me
36. We are willing to help whoever is in need. **36.** C
37. Edna said that you speak Spanish better than her. **37.** she
38. We can only guess whom it was. **38.** who

RESOURCES

Using Pronouns Correctly
Review
- *Grammar, Usage, and Mechanics*, pp. 156, 157, 158–159, 160

Assessment
- *Assessment Package*
  —Chapter Tests, Ch. 17
  —Chapter Tests in Standardized Test Formats, Ch. 17
- *Test Generator (One-Stop Planner CD-ROM)*

39. The package was sent to Rob and I.   **39.** me
40. The drama coaches are Mr. Rolando and she.   **40.** C

Writing Application
Using Pronouns Correctly in a Letter

Case Forms of Pronouns   Your favorite musical group isn't happy with the director of their latest video. As a result, they are sponsoring a "Be a Music Video Director" contest. To enter, you have to write a letter explaining your idea for a different video of the same song. Tell which singers, dancers, and musicians you would cast in your video. Include at least ten pronouns in your sentences. Be sure that no pronoun has an unclear antecedent.

Prewriting   Start by choosing the song for which you want to make a video. Then, list some ideas for three or four scenes in your video. Next to each scene idea, list the performers you would use in that scene and describe the action. In addition to actual people, you may want to have cartoon characters or other animated figures in your video.

Writing   As you write sentences about your music video, make the sequence of events clear. Make the spatial relationships clear, too, telling where the cast members are in relation to each other.

Revising   Check the rough draft of your letter to be sure that your explanation is clear. If you have included too many performers or too many details, eliminate the least interesting ones now.

Publishing   Read your letter, looking for inexact uses of the pronouns *it*, *this*, *that*, and *which*. If your sentences contain inexact pronoun references, revise those sentences. Proofread your letter to correct errors in grammar, punctuation, and spelling. Your class may wish to vote on the best music video idea in each of several categories, such as rock, country, and rap.

Reference Note
For information on **writing letters,** see "Writing" in the Quick Reference Handbook.

Chapter Review   571

RESOURCES
Writing Application
Extension
- *Grammar, Usage, and Mechanics,* p. 163
- *Language Workshop CD-ROM,* Lessons 13–15

CHAPTER 18

Using Verbs Correctly
Principal Parts, Tense, Voice, Mood

PREVIEWING THE CHAPTER

- The material in this chapter will clarify for students the sometimes confusing nature of verbs. The chapter discusses the four principal parts of regular and irregular verbs, including the troublesome verbs *lie* and *lay, sit* and *set,* and *rise* and *raise.* In addition, the chapter explores the uses of the six verb tenses, ten modals, the active and passive voices, and the three kinds of mood.

- You may want to refer to this chapter throughout the year, especially as students work on revising and proofreading the compositions assigned in **Chapters 1–8.** For help in integrating this chapter with writing chapters, see the **Teaching Strands** chart on pp. T401A–T401B.

- The chapter concludes with a **Chapter Review,** which includes a **Writing Application** feature that asks students to write a short essay using at least five different verb tenses.

USING THE DIAGNOSTIC PREVIEW

- The **Diagnostic Preview** can be used in conjunction with an assessment of students' writing to pinpoint areas in which students need more instruction and practice. Test results may also be used to determine grouping for cooperative-learning activities, as it is often helpful to group together students with varying levels of proficiency.

Diagnostic Preview

A. Writing the Past and Past Participle Forms of Irregular Verbs

For each of the following sentences, write the correct form (past or past participle) of the italicized verb.

EXAMPLES 1. *know* I have _____ Zoe since we were in kindergarten together.
 1. known

 2. *swim* Has Samuel ever _____ out to the rocky island in the middle of the lake?
 2. swum

1. ridden 1. *ride* Jeffrey and Lee have _____ their bikes fifty miles today.
2. wrote 2. *write* I read the letters Grandpa _____ to Grandma in 1960.
3. taken 3. *take* Dad, I know that you've _____ us to two concerts this year, but please take us to just one more.
4. fell 4. *fall* All that winter day the snow _____, blanketing everything.
5. saw 5. *see* Rebecca soon _____ why the old house had sold so cheaply.
6. drunk 6. *drink* The gerbil has _____ most of its water.
7. began 7. *begin* As darkness fell and the children still had not returned, I _____ to worry.
8. brought 8. *bring* Margot has _____ popcorn and apples for the party.

572 Chapter 18 Using Verbs Correctly

CHAPTER RESOURCES

Planning
- *One-Stop Planner CD-ROM*

Practice and Extension
- *Grammar, Usage, and Mechanics,* p. 164
- *Language Workshop CD-ROM*

Internet
- go.hrw.com (keyword: EOLang)

Evaluation and Assessment
- *Assessment Package*
  —*Chapter Tests,* Ch. 18
  —*Chapter Tests in Standardized Test Formats,* Ch. 18
- *Test Generator (One-Stop Planner CD-ROM)*

9. *speak* At the assembly yesterday, Sergeant Lewis ____ about responsible driving.

10. *give* The Nez Perce had ____ the starving fur traders food and helped them repair their canoes.

9. spoke

10. given

B. Revising Sentences to Correct Problems in Verb Tense and Voice

Rewrite the following sentences, replacing verbs that are in the wrong tense or that are in an awkward voice. If a sentence is already correct, write C. Some answers may vary.

EXAMPLES [1] Genna gave her report on Captain James Cook and shows us some maps and pictures of the areas he had explored.

1. Genna gave her report on Captain James Cook and showed us some maps and pictures of the areas he had explored.

[2] We were surprised to learn how many places were explored by him.

2. We were surprised to learn how many places he had explored.

[11] Captain Cook, one of the greatest explorers of all time, sailed large areas of the Pacific Ocean and makes accurate maps of the region. [12] Cook joins the navy as a seaman in 1755, and many promotions were received by him before he became the master of a ship in 1757. [13] Because of his knowledge of geography, astronomy, and mathematics, he is selected to lead a scientific expedition to the Pacific. [14] The purpose of Cook's expedition is to observe the passage of Venus between Earth and the sun, a very rare occurrence.

[15] On the voyage, Cook wins a battle against scurvy, a serious disease caused by lack of vitamin C. [16] Raw cabbage, which contained vitamin C, was eaten by the sailors to prevent the disease. [17] By the time the voyage is over, the ship traveled around Cape Horn to Tahiti in the Pacific Ocean. [18] After he observes the passage of Venus, Cook sails off to explore the east coast of New Zealand, which was claimed by him for England. [19] The Hawaiian Islands were later explored by Cook on his final voyage to the Pacific and were named the Sandwich Islands by him. [20] In a dispute over a canoe, Cook was killed by island inhabitants, and in accordance with naval tradition, he was buried at sea in 1779.

11. made
12. joined/he received
13. was
14. was
15. won
16. The sailors ate/contains
17. was/had
18. had observed/sailed/he
19. Cook explored/them
20. C

Using Verbs Correctly, pp. 572–610
Alignments
TEKS 3B, 3D
TAAS W3, W6
English II End-of-Course 5, 6

Texas Resources
- TAAS Tool Kit
- Preparation for TAAS
- One-Stop Planner CD-ROM

C. Determining Correct Uses of *Lie* and *Lay*, *Sit* and *Set*, and *Rise* and *Raise*

If a verb form in one of the following sentences is incorrect, write the correct form. If a sentence is already correct, write *C*.

EXAMPLE 1. Has Maurizio already risen the flag?
1. raised

21. set
22. C
23. rose
24. lie
25. laid

21. You can sit the wastebasket in the corner.
22. Everyone rose when the judge entered the courtroom, and then everyone sat when she sat.
23. The mysterious shape suddenly raised from the shadows.
24. I like to lay out under the stars and just think.
25. The servant had lain out the emperor's robes of yellow, the color that only members of Chinese royalty were permitted to wear.

The Principal Parts of Verbs

Verbs have four basic forms called **principal parts.** All of a verb's other forms come from its principal parts.

18a. The four principal parts of a verb are the *base form,* the *present participle,* the *past,* and the *past participle.*

> **NOTE** Some authorities refer to the base form as the *infinitive.* Follow your teacher's instructions when labeling this verb form.

─HELP─

The words *is* and *have* are included in the chart to the right because helping verbs are used with the present participle and past participle to form some tenses.

Reference Note

For more about using **helping verbs with present participles and past participles,** see page 417.

Base Form	Present Participle	Past	Past Participle
believe	[is] believing	believed	[have] believed
walk	[is] walking	walked	[have] walked
teach	[is] teaching	taught	[have] taught
run	[is] running	ran	[have] run
do	[is] doing	did	[have] done
be	[is] being	was, were	[have] been
cost	[is] costing	cost	[have] cost

574   Chapter 18   Using Verbs Correctly

NOTE Sometimes a past participle is used with a form of *be,* as in *was chosen, are known, is being seen.* This use of the verb is called the **passive voice**.

EXAMPLES   A complete list of rules **is given** to all the contestants two weeks before the competition.

If a book is due on a Sunday, no fines **are charged** if the book **is returned** by the following Monday.

Reference Note
For more about **passive-voice verbs**, see page 601.

Regular Verbs

18b. A *regular verb* generally forms its past and past participle by adding *–d* or *–ed* to the base form.

Base Form	Present Participle	Past	Past Participle
receive	[is] receiving	received	[have] received
blame	[is] blaming	blamed	[have] blamed
work	[is] working	worked	[have] worked

One common error in the use of the past and the past participle forms of a regular verb is leaving off the *–d* or *–ed* ending.

NONSTANDARD   They use to live in Waco, Texas.
STANDARD   They **used** to live in Waco, Texas.

NONSTANDARD   Are you suppose to meet with them tomorrow?
STANDARD   Are you **supposed** to meet with them tomorrow?

NONSTANDARD   She ask me to go to the dance.
STANDARD   She **asked** me to go to the dance.

Reference Note
For a discussion of **standard** and **nonstandard usage**, see page 638.

NOTE Most regular verbs that end in *e* drop the *e* before adding *–ing.* Some regular verbs double the final consonant before adding *–ing* or *–ed.*

EXAMPLES   snore   snoring   snored
nap   napping   napped

Reference Note
For guidelines on spelling verbs when **adding *–d, –ed,* or *–ing,*** see page 782.

The Principal Parts of Verbs   **575**

RESOURCES

The Principal Parts of Verbs and Regular and Irregular Verbs

Practice
- *Grammar, Usage, and Mechanics,* pp. 165, 166, 167–171
- *Language Workshop CD-ROM,* Lesson 9

Meeting INDIVIDUAL NEEDS

ENGLISH-LANGUAGE LEARNERS
General Strategies. Many students may not realize that the past forms of some verbs they hear every day, such as *believed* or *missed,* end with the letter *d*. This confusion arises because native English speakers often either barely pronounce the *d* sound or pronounce it as a *t*.

Write the following sentences on the chalkboard. Have students read each sentence aloud as a group, pronouncing the sound at the end of the verb as a strong *d*. You may want to model the first sentence.

1. I walked home.
2. She missed the bus.
3. We worked in the yard.
4. He's supposed to give me a ride.
5. I packed my bag.

HELP

The regular verbs *deal* and *mean* always form the past and the past participle by adding *t*: dealt, (have) dealt; meant, (have) meant.

A few regular verbs have alternative past and past participle forms ending in *t*.

Base Form	Present Participle	Past	Past Participle
burn	[is] burning	burned or burnt	[have] burned or burnt
leap	[is] leaping	leaped or leapt	[have] leaped or leapt
dream	[is] dreaming	dreamed or dreamt	[have] dreamed or dreamt

Exercise 1 Using the Past Form of Regular Verbs

Give the correct past form of each verb in parentheses.

EXAMPLE
1. With a mighty heave, the elephant (*push*) the log out of the river.
   1. pushed

1. answered — 1. Charlene (*answer*) all the questions correctly.
2. kissed — 2. When Greg was in Ireland, he (*kiss*) the Blarney stone.
3. smiled — 3. As I walked by, they (*smile*).
4. pulled — 4. Melissa (*pull*) the wagon, which was full of rag dolls.
5. watched — 5. Denise (*watch*) the wildlife through her binoculars.
6. played — 6. Spence and James (*play*) the trombone and the clarinet at the concert last night.
7. helped — 7. Mother Teresa (*help*) many people.
8. laughed — 8. After receiving the postcard, Eduardo (*laugh*).
9. danced — 9. Last Saturday, my friends (*dance*) the polka at our school's international festival.
10. painted — 10. Tracy (*paint*) a powerful self-portrait that will appear in next month's exhibit.

Irregular Verbs

18c. An *irregular verb* forms its past and past participle in some way other than by adding –d or –ed to the base form.

An irregular verb forms its past and past participle in one of the following ways: (1) changing consonants, (2) changing vowels, (3) changing vowels *and* consonants, or (4) making no change.

MINI-LESSON

Pronunciation of Past Participles. Remind students that the past participle forms of some verbs can be used as adjectives and that such a verb form is a type of verbal called a *participle*. Explain that in some regional dialects and in certain literary uses, the *–ed* ending of the participle is pronounced as a separate syllable.

Write on the chalkboard the following words, and call on volunteers to pronounce

	Base Form	Past	Past Participle
Consonant Change	bend	bent	[have] bent
	send	sent	[have] sent
Vowel Change	sing	sang	[have] sung
Vowel and Consonant Change	catch	caught	[have] caught
	go	went	[have] gone
	fly	flew	[have] flown
No Change	set	set	[have] set

Principal Parts of Common Irregular Verbs

Base Form	Present Participle	Past	Past Participle
become	[is] becoming	became	[have] become
begin	[is] beginning	began	[have] begun
blow	[is] blowing	blew	[have] blown
break	[is] breaking	broke	[have] broken
bring	[is] bringing	brought	[have] brought
build	[is] building	built	[have] built
burn	[is] burning	burned or burnt	[have] burned or burnt
burst	[is] bursting	burst	[have] burst
buy	[is] buying	bought	[have] bought
catch	[is] catching	caught	[have] caught
choose	[is] choosing	chose	[have] chosen
come	[is] coming	came	[have] come
cost	[is] costing	cost	[have] cost
cut	[is] cutting	cut	[have] cut
dive	[is] diving	dove or dived	[have] dived
do	[is] doing	did	[have] done
draw	[is] drawing	drew	[have] drawn
drink	[is] drinking	drank	[have] drunk
drive	[is] driving	drove	[have] driven

(continued)

HELP — Since most English verbs are regular, people sometimes try to make irregular verbs follow the regular pattern. However, such verb forms as *throwed, knowed, shrinked,* and *choosed* are considered nonstandard.

If you are not sure whether a verb is regular or irregular, look it up in a dictionary. Entries for irregular verbs list the principal parts. If an entry for a verb does not list the principal parts, the verb is a regular verb.

Meeting INDIVIDUAL NEEDS

ENGLISH-LANGUAGE LEARNERS

General Strategies. Point out to students that when they have questions about the principal parts of irregular verbs, they can often find the answers in a dictionary. Tell them that the base forms of verbs are listed as entry words and that the past, past participle, and present participle forms of irregular verbs are usually given following the entry word. For example, if students look up *draw*, they will find *drew, drawn,* and *drawing*. For practice, ask each student to look up three irregular verbs in a dictionary and to find the principal parts of each verb.

INCLUSION

Students might be overwhelmed by the **Principal Parts of Common Irregular Verbs** chart. Ask each student to choose five of these verbs and to write autobiographical sentences that incorporate the past or past participle form of each of the five verbs. For example, a student might incorporate the past participle form of *dive* into the autobiographical sentence "I have dived off the highest diving board at the public pool." Because this activity allows students to work with a manageable number of verbs and to use the verbs in context, it may make the material more meaningful and less intimidating. Be sure students pick autobiographical subjects about which they are comfortable writing.

USAGE

---

the words: *learned, hallowed, blessed, winged, beloved, striped.* Discuss with the class any differences in pronunciation that are discovered, and ask students to suggest other examples of such participles. Then, have students consult a dictionary to check the pronunciation of each of the words.

Meeting INDIVIDUAL NEEDS

MODALITIES

Auditory and Kinesthetic Learners. To help students learn the principal parts of irregular verbs, divide the class into groups of three or four. Ask each group to prepare a simple rhythmic recitation of the base, past, and past participle forms of ten irregular verbs. You may want to suggest to groups some forms of rhythmic recitations (for example, rap and choral singing). Encourage groups to integrate into their recitations some physical movement, such as swaying, dancing, or clapping.

HELP

Some verbs have two correct past or past participle forms. However, these forms are not always interchangeable.

EXAMPLES

He **shone** the candle into the cellar. [*Shined* would also be correct.]

I **shined** my shoes. [*Shone* would be incorrect in this usage.]

If you are unsure about which past participle to use, check an up-to-date dictionary.

(continued)

Principal Parts of Common Irregular Verbs

Base Form	Present Participle	Past	Past Participle
eat	[is] eating	ate	[have] eaten
fall	[is] falling	fell	[have] fallen
feel	[is] feeling	felt	[have] felt
fight	[is] fighting	fought	[have] fought
find	[is] finding	found	[have] found
fly	[is] flying	flew	[have] flown
forgive	[is] forgiving	forgave	[have] forgiven
freeze	[is] freezing	froze	[have] frozen
get	[is] getting	got	[have] got or gotten
give	[is] giving	gave	[have] given
go	[is] going	went	[have] gone
grow	[is] growing	grew	[have] grown
have	[is] having	had	[have] had
hear	[is] hearing	heard	[have] heard
hide	[is] hiding	hid	[have] hidden or hid
hit	[is] hitting	hit	[have] hit
know	[is] knowing	knew	[have] known
lead	[is] leading	led	[have] led
leave	[is] leaving	left	[have] left
let	[is] letting	let	[have] let
light	[is] lighting	lighted or lit	[have] lighted or lit
lose	[is] losing	lost	[have] lost
make	[is] making	made	[have] made
pay	[is] paying	paid	[have] paid
put	[is] putting	put	[have] put
read	[is] reading	read	[have] read
ride	[is] riding	rode	[have] ridden
ring	[is] ringing	rang	[have] rung
run	[is] running	ran	[have] run
say	[is] saying	said	[have] said

Chapter 18 Using Verbs Correctly

 Continued on pp. 579–580

Spelling. To help students correctly form the principal parts of verbs, review with them the spelling rules that apply when adding suffixes.

1. Drop the final silent *e* before a suffix beginning with a vowel (*dine* + *ing* = *dining*).

2. Double the final consonant before a suffix that begins with a vowel if the verb ends

Principal Parts of Common Irregular Verbs

Base Form	Present Participle	Past	Past Participle
see	[is] seeing	saw	[have] seen
seek	[is] seeking	sought	[have] sought
sell	[is] selling	sold	[have] sold
send	[is] sending	sent	[have] sent
sing	[is] singing	sang	[have] sung
sink	[is] sinking	sank *or* sunk	[have] sunk
sleep	[is] sleeping	slept	[have] slept
speak	[is] speaking	spoke	[have] spoken
spend	[is] spending	spent	[have] spent
stand	[is] standing	stood	[have] stood
steal	[is] stealing	stole	[have] stolen
swim	[is] swimming	swam	[have] swum
take	[is] taking	took	[have] taken
teach	[is] teaching	taught	[have] taught
tear	[is] tearing	tore	[have] torn
tell	[is] telling	told	[have] told
think	[is] thinking	thought	[have] thought
throw	[is] throwing	threw	[have] thrown
wear	[is] wearing	wore	[have] worn
win	[is] winning	won	[have] won
write	[is] writing	wrote	[have] written

Oral Practice 1 Using Regular and Irregular Verbs

Read each sentence aloud, stressing each italicized verb.

1. Keisha *is braiding* Tiffany's hair in cornrows.
2. Bob *read* the want ads today, just as he *has read* them all week.
3. Mom, I *am bringing* you breakfast, but I *have eaten* your toast!
4. Warren *drew* the designs for the posters.
5. Paloma Picasso, the jewelry designer, *has chosen* an artistic career different from her famous father's.
6. Carrie *went* to Penn State; Hector *is going* to Boston College.
7. Someone *ate* the spaghetti, but nobody *has touched* the baked beans.
8. If you *have* never *seen* a meteor shower, *run* outside right now!

---

in a single consonant preceded by a single vowel and either has only one syllable (*drop + ed = dropped*) or else is accented on the last syllable (*refer + ed = referred*). Point out to students that they should not double the final consonant unless the verb satisfies both conditions (*droop + ed = drooped* [single consonant preceded by double vowel]; *differ + ing = differing* [accent on first syllable]).

Relating to Writing

Have students think of someone who taught them to do something special. Perhaps a girl's aunt taught her to fish or a boy's older sister taught him to ride a bike. You may want to discuss some of your own experiences to help students generate ideas. Then, ask students to write paragraphs describing their experiences. Have students include in their paragraphs the past or past participle forms of at least three irregular verbs.

TEACHING TIP

Exercises You may want to use **Exercise 2** as guided practice and have students complete **Exercises 3** and **4** as independent practice.

USAGE

Exercise 2 Using the Past and Past Participle Forms of Irregular Verbs

Give the correct form (past or past participle) of the verb given before each of the following sentences.

EXAMPLE 1. write   Diego has _____ a report on Pueblo culture.
        1. written

1. sung
2. begun
3. froze
4. flew
5. saw
6. taken
7. fallen
8. thrown
9. broken
10. spoke

1. *sing*   The rain fell after we had _____ the national anthem.
2. *begin* I had already _____ my homework.
3. *freeze* The subzero winds nearly _____ the Pawnee hunters as they tracked the herd of bison.
4. *fly*   Last summer we _____ in a lighter-than-air balloon.
5. *see*   During our visit to Hawaii, we _____ a group of performers do a traditional hula dance.
6. *take*   My sister has _____ that course.
7. *fall*   By the time Rolando finished carving the little figure, hundreds of tiny wood shavings had _____ to the floor.
8. *throw* The horse had _____ its shoe.
9. *break* We hoped we hadn't _____ the machine.
10. *speak* Harley's grandmother _____ to our class about her parents' lives as sharecroppers in the early 1900s.

Exercise 3 Using the Past and Past Participle Forms of Irregular Verbs

Give the correct form (past or past participle) of each italicized verb in the following paragraph.

EXAMPLE   Have you [1] (*see*) any of the artwork by Henry Ossawa Tanner?
        1. seen

1. saw
2. chosen
3. come
4. wrote
5. brought
6. taught
7. went
8. fell

We recently [1] (*see*) paintings by the African American artist Henry Ossawa Tanner. Tanner had [2] (*choose*) his lifelong career in art by the time he was thirteen years old. While walking in a park one day, he and his father had [3] (*come*) upon a landscape artist at work. Years later, Tanner [4] (*write*), "It was this simple event that . . . set me on fire." Young Henry [5] (*bring*) such eagerness to his work that, before long, he [6] (*teach*) himself to draw well enough to be admitted to one of the finest art schools in the country. His paintings were beautiful but did not sell well, so Tanner [7] (*go*) abroad. He [8] (*fall*) in love with the city of Paris and lived and worked there for the rest of his life,

580 Chapter 18 Using Verbs Correctly

MINI-LESSON

Write the following exercise on the chalkboard, and have students add suffixes as indicated.

1. propel + ed [*propelled*]
2. fire + ing [*firing*]
3. live + ed [*lived*]
4. leap + ing [*leaping*]

For more information on adding suffixes, refer students to **Chapter 26: Spelling.**

winning many important painting awards. Shown here is his best-known work, *The Banjo Lesson,* which he painted in Paris from sketches he had [9] (*draw*) years earlier in North Carolina. In 1969, long after Tanner's death, a touring exhibit finally [10] (*give*) Americans a look at the work of this gifted artist.

9. drawn
10. gave

Henry Ossawa Tanner, *The Banjo Lesson* (1893). Hampton University Museum, Hampton, VA.

Exercise 4 Choosing the Past and Past Participle Forms of Irregular Verbs

Choose the correct verb form in parentheses in each of the following sentences.

EXAMPLE 1. Frieda has (*gave, given*) much thought to pursuing a career in engineering.

1. given

1. We (*did, done*) everything we could to help him.
2. Who has (*drank, drunk*) all the orange juice?
3. Someone has already (*tore, torn*) out the coupon.
4. I wish you had (*spoke, spoken*) to me about it sooner.
5. I dived off the board and (*swam, swum*) the length of the pool.
6. You must have (*rung, rang*) the doorbell while I was outside.
7. Nancy had never (*ate, eaten*) a tamale before.
8. Lois (*blowed, blew*) up the balloon.
9. Suddenly the balloon (*burst, bursted*).
10. We (*drove, driven*) to the train station in a hurry.

The Principal Parts of Verbs

Six Troublesome Verbs

(pp. 582–590)

OBJECTIVES

- To read aloud sentences containing the correct forms of *lie* and *lay*, *sit* and *set*, and *rise* and *raise*
- To select the correct forms of *lie* and *lay* and *sit* and *set* in sentences
- To proofread and correct sentences containing *lie* and *lay*
- To complete sentences by supplying the correct forms of *sit* and *set* and *rise* and *raise*

Meeting INDIVIDUAL NEEDS

MULTIPLE INTELLIGENCES
Bodily-Kinesthetic. Divide the class into groups of five or six for an activity in which you ask students to pantomime sentences illustrating the uses of the troublesome verbs. For each group, write on strips of paper six sentences using the troublesome verbs—for example, "Set the groceries on the counter" or "Sit down in that chair." Place the sentence strips in a box or other container. Ask the members of each group to take turns drawing sentence strips and pantomiming the sentences, and have the other group members guess what the sentences are. Continue the activity until each student has had an opportunity to pantomime a sentence.

USAGE

STYLE TIP

The verb *lie* can also mean "to tell an untruth." Used in this way, *lie* still does not take an object. The past and past participle forms of this meaning of *lie* are *lied* and [*have*] *lied*.

Six Troublesome Verbs

Lie and Lay

The verb *lie* means "to rest," "to recline," or "to be in a place." *Lie* does not take a direct object. The verb *lay* means "to put (something) in place." *Lay* generally takes a direct object.

Principal Parts of *Lie* and *Lay*			
Base Form	Present Participle	Past	Past Participle
lie	[is] lying	lay	[have] lain
lay	[is] laying	laid	[have] laid

EXAMPLES
Please **lie** down. [no direct object]
The packages **are lying** here. [no direct object]
The key **lay** on the shelf. [no direct object]
The old papers **had lain** on the desk for months. [no direct object]

Please **lay** the tools down. [*Tools* is the direct object.]
I **am laying** your packages here. [*Packages* is the direct object.]
The boy **laid** the key on the shelf. [*Key* is the direct object.]
He **had laid** the old papers on the desk. [*Papers* is the direct object.]

Oral Practice 2 Using the Forms of *Lie* and *Lay* in Sentences

Read each of the following sentences aloud, stressing the italicized verb.

1. The mason *is laying* the tiles on the patio.
2. A light haze *lay* over the hills.
3. The cat *laid* its toy on the doorsill.
4. Someone's books *are lying* in the hall.
5. She *had lain* down for a nap.
6. Where *could* I *have laid* the recipe?
7. *Lay* the material on the counter.
8. You *could lie* down and relax.

582 Chapter 18 Using Verbs Correctly

RESOURCES

Six Troublesome Verbs
Practice
- *Grammar, Usage, and Mechanics*, pp. 172, 173, 174, 175
- *Language Workshop CD-ROM*, Lesson 11

Exercise 5 Choosing the Forms of *Lie* and *Lay*

Choose the correct verb form in parentheses in each of the following sentences.

EXAMPLE 1. The sheet music is (*lying*, *laying*) on the piano.
1. lying

1. Do not (*lay*, *lie*) the socks there.
2. Eduardo (*lay*, *laid*) in the sleeping bag and waited for sleep.
3. The pasture (*lies*, *lays*) in the valley.
4. A sheet (*lay*, *laid*) over the rug to catch paint spatters.
5. The clothing had (*lain*, *laid*) on the floor all week.
6. Kitty had (*lay*, *laid*) the book down.
7. Mrs. Nakamoto was (*lying*, *laying*) out everything necessary for the tea ceremony.
8. The theories developed by Albert Einstein have (*lay*, *laid*) the groundwork for many other scientific discoveries.
9. The cat has been (*lying*, *laying*) on my coat.
10. (*Lying*, *Laying*) the tip by my plate, I rose to leave the restaurant.

Exercise 6 Using the Forms of *Lie* and *Lay*

If a verb in the following sentences is incorrect, write the correct form. If the verb is already correct, write *C*.

EXAMPLES 1. On the bed laid the child's favorite kachina doll.
1. lay

2. Julia had lain rose petals along the stage.
2. laid

1. The towels laying in the corner all need to be washed.
2. Yesterday, all we did was lie around and play CDs.
3. The runner crossed the finish line and laid down in the grass.
4. The fox had laid in the thicket until the hunters had passed.
5. After I had tripped, I sat there feeling embarrassed, my groceries laying all around me.
6. He was lying under the car, tinkering with the muffler.
7. The workers had lain down their tools and gone to lunch.
8. My gym bag was laying right where I had left it.
9. In his speech, Cesar Chavez lay the responsibility for social change on the shoulders of all citizens.
10. She sighed and lay down the phone receiver.

TIPS & TRICKS

To decide whether to use *lie* or *lay*, ask yourself the following questions:

QUESTION 1
What do I mean? (Is the meaning "to be in a place," or is it "to put in a place"?)

QUESTION 2
What time does the verb express?

QUESTION 3
Which principal part shows this time?

EXAMPLE
Feeling very drowsy, I (*lay*, *laid*) on the couch.

QUESTION 1
Here the meaning is "to be in place." Therefore, the verb should be a form of *lie*.

QUESTION 2
The time is past.

QUESTION 3
The past form of *lie* is *lay*.

ANSWER
Feeling very drowsy, I **lay** on the couch.

Cooperative Learning

Have students work on a group project to practice standard usage of the verbs *lie* and *lay*, *set* and *sit*, and *rise* and *raise*. Divide the class into groups of four or five. Assign each group the task of writing a short skit that includes the six troublesome verbs. Have each group appoint a scribe to write the dialogue as the group develops it. Each person in the group should have a part to play in the skit. Give students ample time to rehearse; then, have each group perform its skit for the rest of the class.

Exercise 6 Using the Forms of *Lie* and *Lay*

ANSWERS
1. lying
2. C
3. lay
4. lain
5. lying
6. C
7. laid
8. lying
9. laid
10. laid

Exercise 7 **Proofreading for the Correct Forms of *Lie* and *Lay***

In each of the following sentences, a form of *lie* or *lay* is used. If the wrong form is used, write the correct form. If a sentence is already correct, write *C*.

EXAMPLES
1. Oscar rarely spends the weekends laying on the couch.
1. lying

2. He had planned to spend his Saturday lying new tile in the kitchen.
2. laying

1. lay — 1. Several boxes of fired-clay tiles laid on the floor of the garage.
2. laid — 2. Before he started, he lay out all his materials and carefully read the directions on the container of adhesive.
3. laid — 3. At first, he made good progress and had lain sixteen rows of tile by lunch time.
4. lay — 4. Then he ate a sandwich and laid down on the sofa for a few minutes.
5. lying — 5. When he returned to the kitchen, Oscar found that his dog, Stanley, was laying where the next row of tiles was supposed to go.
6. lie — 6. Oscar had forgotten that Stanley liked to lay in that particular place on the kitchen floor.
7. C — 7. In fact, Stanley had lain there for his morning nap ever since he was a puppy.
8. C — 8. Oscar got a juicy meat scrap out of the refrigerator and laid it on the floor just beyond Stanley's snoring nose.
9. lying — 9. The wily Stanley had been laying in wait and, in a flash, grabbed the meat.
10. lie — 10. To Oscar's dismay, Stanley resumed his nap with a satisfied sigh, and Oscar learned that the worker isn't the only one who can lay down on the job!

584 Chapter 18 Using Verbs Correctly

Transitive and Intransitive Verbs. Having students determine which of the troublesome verbs are transitive and which are intransitive may help them better understand the uses of the verbs. Remind students that transitive verbs take direct objects and that intransitive verbs do not take direct objects. Ask students to identify which of the six troublesome verbs are generally transitive or intransitive. [*transitive:*

Sit and *Set*

The verb *sit* means "to rest in a seated, upright position" or "to be in a place." *Sit* seldom takes a direct object. The verb *set* means "to put (something) in a place." *Set* generally takes a direct object. Notice that the past and the past participle of *set* are the same as the base form.

Principal Parts of *Sit* and *Set*			
Base Form	Present Participle	Past	Past Participle
sit	[is] sitting	sat	[have] sat
set	[is] setting	set	[have] set

STYLE TIP

You may know that the word *set* has more meanings than the one given here. Check in a dictionary to see if the meaning you intend requires an object.

EXAMPLE
    The sun **sets** in the West. [Here, *sets* does not take an object.]

EXAMPLES
You **may sit** here. [no direct object]
Where **are** Diana and Vince **sitting**? [no direct object]
The guest speaker **sat** between Eduardo and me. [no direct object]
His bicycle **has sat** in our driveway for a week. [no direct object]

You **may set** your books here. [*Books* is the direct object.]
Where **are** Diana and Vince **setting** the computer desk? [*Desk* is the direct object.]
The guest speaker **set** his briefcase between Eduardo and me. [*Briefcase* is the direct object.]
He **had set** his bicycle in our driveway last week. [*Bicycle* is the direct object.]

Oral Practice 3 Using the Correct Forms of *Sit* and *Set* in Sentences

Read each of the following sentences aloud, stressing the italicized verb.

1. *Set* the groceries on the counter.
2. The travelers *set* out early to avoid the midday heat.
3. Would you please *set* the chairs under the tree in the front yard?
4. The bird *sat* on the wire.
5. During Hanukkah, we always *set* the menorah in a place of honor.
6. We *had sat* in the lobby for an hour.
7. They *have been sitting* on the porch.
8. Rosa Parks made history when she chose to *sit* rather than to give up her seat to a white passenger.

Six Troublesome Verbs

---

set, lay, *and* raise; *intransitive:* sit, lie, *and* rise]. For more information on transitive and intransitive verbs, refer students to **Chapter 12: Parts of Speech Overview.**

Exercise 8 — Selecting the Correct Forms of *Sit* and *Set*

Choose the correct verb form in parentheses in each of the following sentences.

EXAMPLE 1. He (*sat*, *set*) on the park bench and read the newspaper.
1. sat

1. A few of us were (*sitting*, *setting*) at our desks.
2. He had (*sat*, *set*) in the rocker since dusk.
3. He (*sat*, *set*) the package on the doorstep.
4. Ida was (*sitting*, *setting*) out the chips and dip for the guests.
5. We had been (*sitting*, *setting*) on a freshly painted bench.
6. They (*sat*, *set*) the seedlings in the window boxes.
7. He had (*sit*, *set*) his retainer on his lunch tray.
8. (*Sit*, *Set*) this Pueblo pottery in the display case.
9. I could (*sit*, *set*) and watch the birds all day.
10. We patiently (*sat*, *set*) and waited for the travelers to arrive.

Exercise 9 — Writing the Forms of *Sit* and *Set*

For each numbered blank in the following paragraph, write the correct form of *sit* or *set*.

EXAMPLE Before [1] _____ down to rest, Meriwether Lewis and William Clark decided that the group should climb to the top of the bluff.
1. sitting

To gain a view of the surrounding land, Lewis and Clark's group climbed to an outcropping of gray rocks that [1] _____ atop the bluff. It was late afternoon, and the Shoshone guide Sacagawea [2] _____ her pack down beside the rocks and [3] _____ down in their shade to rest. Lewis saw her from where he was [4] _____ nearby and approached with a friendly "May I [5] _____ here with you?" Several other members of the expedition saw them [6] _____ together and wondered what they were discussing. In fact, Lewis was asking her in what direction she thought the party should [7] _____ out in the morning. Gazing westward from the bluff, Sacagawea saw that she was in familiar territory and soon [8] _____ her mind on heading down the mountainside toward the northwest. By the time the sun had [9] _____, Lewis agreed that the route she had chosen would be the easiest to follow. A wise leader, he realized that he had never [10] _____ foot in these lands, while she had passed this way before.

1. sat
2. set
3. sat
4. sitting
5. sit
6. sitting
7. set
8. set
9. set
10. set

Looking at Language

Idioms. Since Exercise 9 contains idiomatic uses of *set*, you may want to take this opportunity to teach the concept of idioms. Explain to the class that an idiom is an expression that has a meaning different from the literal meaning of the words, for example, *straight from the horse's mouth*, *fall in love*, or *lose your head*.

Lead the class in a discussion of the meanings of the idiomatic uses of *set* in **Exercise 9**—sentence 7, *set out*; sentence 8, *set her mind on*; and sentence 10, *set foot*. Then, ask students to keep track of all the idioms they notice in their own and others' speech or writing for one week and to display the list of idioms.

The Granger Collection, New York.

Review A **Choosing the Correct Forms of *Lie* and *Lay* and *Sit* and *Set***

Choose the correct verb form in parentheses in each of the following sentences.

EXAMPLE 1. She (*set*, *sat*) at the computer, reading her e-mail.
1. sat

1. (*Setting*, *Sitting*) on the table was a pair of scissors.
2. Please (*sit*, *set*) the carton down carefully.
3. Sakura folded her kimono and (*lay*, *laid*) down to sleep.
4. (*Sit*, *Set*) all the way back in your seat.
5. The dirty dishes had (*laid*, *lain*) in the sink for hours.
6. Yesterday, Tom (*lay*, *laid*) the blame for his lateness on his clock.
7. The cat always (*sits*, *sets*) on the couch.
8. If only we could have (*laid*, *lain*) our hands on the treasure!
9. The tickets to the Wynton Marsalis concert were (*lying*, *laying*) right where I had left them.
10. King Tut's tomb (*lay*, *laid*) undisturbed for centuries.
11. Have you ever (*sat*, *set*) around with nothing to do?
12. She (*sat*, *set*) down at her desk with her checkbook and calculator in front of her.
13. Santa Anna, (*setting*, *sitting*) on his horse, ordered his troops to attack the Alamo.
14. The beached rowboat (*lay*, *laid*) on its side.

Six Troublesome Verbs **587**

Meeting INDIVIDUAL NEEDS

MODALITIES

Visual Learners. Ask students to make collages of magazine pictures that illustrate the uses of the verbs *lie*, *lay*, *sit*, *set*, *rise*, and *raise*. Have students also look in magazines for forms of these verbs, cut out the verb forms, and include them as labels in their collages. You may want to display the collages in the classroom.

USAGE

Relating to Literature
As a means of emphasizing to students that incorrect use of these troublesome verbs will affect the meaning of what they write, have students read a poem in which a form of *lie, lay, sit, set, rise,* or *raise* is used correctly, such as "Miss Rosie" by Lucille Clifton. After students have read the poem, have them analyze how the poem would have been different if the poet had used the incorrect verb choice from the troublesome pair. Discuss these questions with the class: Would the meaning of the poem have been clear? Would the incorrect usage have been distracting? What might incorrect usage indicate about the speaker of the poem?

ADVANCED LEARNERS
You may want to have your advanced learners develop rules for using other verb pairs that frequently cause problems, such as *learn* and *teach* and *leave* and *let.* Ask students to write definitions and explanations of the verbs and to include sentences that illustrate the correct forms and usage. Then, have students present the material to the rest of the class.

STYLE TIP
You may know that the verb *raise* has more meanings than the ones given here.

EXAMPLE
The O'Malleys **raise** sheep. [*Raise* does not mean "lift" here, but it still takes an object.]

15. She (*sat, set*) looking toward the horizon.
16. Laura had just (*sat, set*) down when the phone rang.
17. Julie (*lay, laid*) her handbag on the counter.
18. Pieces of the jigsaw puzzle were (*lying, laying*) on the floor.
19. Jack was (*setting, sitting*) outside on the top step.
20. Were you (*lying, laying*) down for a while before dinner?

Rise and *Raise*

The verb *rise* means "to go up" or "to get up." *Rise* does not take a direct object. The verb *raise* means "to lift" or "to cause (something) to rise." *Raise* generally takes a direct object.

Principal Parts of *Rise* and *Raise*			
Base Form	**Present Participle**	**Past**	**Past Participle**
rise	[is] rising	rose	[have] risen
raise	[is] raising	raised	[have] raised

EXAMPLES I usually **rise** at 6:00 A.M. [no direct object]
She **is rising** uncertainly. [no direct object]
The banner **rose** in the gust of wind. [no direct object]
Has the price of gasoline **risen**? [no direct object]

I usually **raise** the blinds at 6:00 A.M. [*Blinds* is the direct object.]
She **is raising** her hand uncertainly. [*Hand* is the direct object.]
The gust of wind **raised** the banner. [*Banner* is the direct object.]
The gas station **has raised** the price of gasoline. [*Price* is the direct object.]

Oral Practice 4 Using the Forms of *Rise* and *Raise*

Read each of the following sentences aloud, stressing the italicized verb.

1. *Has* the moon *risen* yet?
2. The builders *raised* the roof of the new house at noon.
3. The temperature *rose* as the sun climbed higher.

4. Listening to "I Have a Dream," a speech by Dr. Martin Luther King, Jr., always *raises* my spirits.
5. Trails of mist *were rising* from the lake.
6. How much *did* the river *rise* during the flood?
7. The butterfly *rose* from the leaf and flitted away.
8. My baby sister *was raising* her head to look around.

Exercise 10 Using the Correct Forms of *Rise* and *Raise*

For the blank in each of the following sentences, write the correct form of *rise* or *raise*. Some answers may vary.

EXAMPLE 1. Does the orderly _____ the flag every morning?
1. raise

1. _____ the cards higher, please.
2. The gigantic Kodiak bear is _____ on its hind legs to look around.
3. The tide _____ and falls because of the moon.
4. Carlos and Pilar _____ the piñata above the heads of the children.
5. Up toward the clouds _____ the jet.
6. Many American Indian peoples have traditionally _____ corn as a staple food crop.
7. Prices have _____ in the last few years.
8. The traffic officer had _____ his hand to signal us.
9. My sister and I had _____ before the sun came up this morning.
10. Robert Kennedy _____ to fame in the 1960s.

1. Raise
2. rising
3. rises
4. raised
5. rose
6. raised
7. risen
8. raised
9. risen
10. rose

Review B Using the Correct Forms of *Lie* and *Lay*, *Sit* and *Set*, and *Rise* and *Raise*

If a verb in one of the following sentences is incorrect, write the correct form. If a sentence is already correct, write *C*.

EXAMPLE 1. The baby starlings were setting in the nest.
1. sitting

1. Set the eggs down carefully.
2. The frog was setting on the lily pad and croaking loudly.
3. The judge studied the papers and then lay them beside her gavel.
4. The cattle were lying in the shade by the stream.
5. Do you think the temperature will raise much higher?
6. Wanda sat out the equipment for the experiment.
7. Why don't you lie those things down?

1. C
2. sitting
3. laid
4. C
5. rise
6. set
7. lay

Tense

Rules 18d–g (pp. 590–601)

OBJECTIVES

- To identify tenses of verbs in pairs of sentences and to explain the difference in meaning between the sentences in each pair
- To change the tenses of verbs in sentences
- To proofread and revise a passage for consistency of tense

---

8. lying
9. rose
10. Sit

8. Instead of ~~laying~~ down, you should be getting some type of strenuous exercise.
9. The raccoon ~~raised~~ up on its hind legs.
10. ~~Set~~ down for a while and relax.

Tense

18d. The *tense* of a verb indicates the time of the action or the state of being expressed by the verb.

Verbs in English have six tenses: *present, past, future, present perfect, past perfect,* and *future perfect.* These tenses are formed from the four principal parts of verbs. The following time line shows how the six tenses are related to one another.

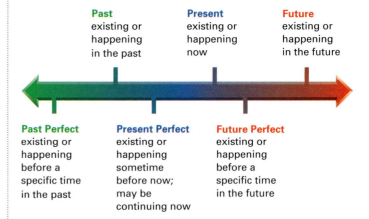

Past existing or happening in the past

Present existing or happening now

Future existing or happening in the future

Past Perfect existing or happening before a specific time in the past

Present Perfect existing or happening sometime before now; may be continuing now

Future Perfect existing or happening before a specific time in the future

Verb Conjugation

Listing all of the forms of a verb according to tense is called **conjugating** a verb. The following charts show all six tenses of a regular verb (*talk*) and of an irregular verb (*give*).

Principal Parts of the Regular Verb *Talk*			
Base Form	Present Participle	Past	Past Participle
talk	[is] talking	talked	[have] talked

590   Chapter 18   Using Verbs Correctly

RESOURCES

Tense and Modals

Practice

- *Grammar, Usage, and Mechanics,* pp. 176–177, 178, 179, 180, 181
- *Language Workshop CD-ROM,* Lesson 10

Conjugation of the Regular Verb *Talk*

Present Tense

Singular	Plural
I talk	we talk
you talk	you talk
he, she, *or* it talks	they talk

Past Tense

Singular	Plural
I talked	we talked
you talked	you talked
he, she, *or* it talked	they talked

Future Tense

Singular	Plural
I will (shall) talk	we will (shall) talk
you will (shall) talk	you will (shall) talk
he, she, *or* it will (shall) talk	they will (shall) talk

Present Perfect Tense

Singular	Plural
I have talked	we have talked
you have talked	you have talked
he, she, *or* it has talked	they have talked

Past Perfect Tense

Singular	Plural
I had talked	we had talked
you had talked	you had talked
he, she, *or* it had talked	they had talked

Future Perfect Tense

Singular	Plural
I will (shall) have talked	we will (shall) have talked
you will (shall) have talked	you will (shall) have talked
he, she, *or* it will (shall) have talked	they will (shall) have talked

STYLE TIP

Traditionally, the helping verbs *shall* and *will* were used differently. Now, however, *shall* can be used almost interchangeably with *will*.

Reference Note

For information on **using shall and will,** see page 599.

Meeting INDIVIDUAL NEEDS

ENGLISH-LANGUAGE LEARNERS

General Strategies. You may discover that some students neither write nor pronounce the *–(e)s* ending of present-tense, third-person singular verbs, as in "She miss the bus almost every day." Similarly, they might have a tendency to omit the *–(e)d* ending of verbs in the past tense, as in "She miss the bus yesterday." You may want to give students sentences containing such verb forms. Ask students to underline the *–(e)s* and *–(e)d* endings and to read the sentences aloud. Listen carefully and model standard pronunciation when necessary.

Each tense has another form, called the **progressive form,** which is used to express continuing action or state of being. The progressive form consists of the appropriate tense of the verb *be* and the present participle of a verb.

Present Progressive	am, are, is talking
Past Progressive	was, were talking
Future Progressive	will (shall) be talking
Present Perfect Progressive	has, have been talking
Past Perfect Progressive	had been talking
Future Perfect Progressive	will (shall) have been talking

Only the present and the past tenses have another form, called the **emphatic form,** which is used to show emphasis. In the present tense, the emphatic form consists of the helping verb *do* or *does* and the base form of the verb. In the past tense, the emphatic form consists of the verb *did* and the base form of a verb.

Present Emphatic	do, does talk
Past Emphatic	did talk

NOTE The emphatic form is also used in questions and negative statements. These uses do not place any special emphasis on the verbs.

QUESTION   Why **do** snakes **shed** their skins?

NEGATIVE STATEMENT   If Uncle Pedro **does**n't **arrive** soon, we should call Aunt Lu.

Principal Parts of the Irregular Verb *Give*			
Base Form	Present Participle	Past	Past Participle
give	[is] giving	gave	[have] given

Conjugation of the Irregular Verb *Give*	
Present Tense	
Singular	*Plural*
I give	we give
you give	you give
he, she, *or* it gives	they give
Present Progressive: *am, are, is giving*	
Present Emphatic: *do, does give*	

592   Chapter 18   Using Verbs Correctly

MINI-LESSON

Verbals. Point out to students that the present participle and past participle forms of verbs are sometimes used as adjectives—for example, "*Walking* through the park, we spotted a small bird with an *injured* wing." (*Walking* modifies the pronoun *we,* and *injured* modifies the noun *wing.*) Explain that another verb form ending in *–ing,* a gerund, can be used as a noun—for example, "*Training* my dog takes much of my spare time." (*Training* is the subject of the verb *takes.*)

Conjugation of the Irregular Verb *Give*

Past Tense

Singular	Plural
I gave	we gave
you gave	you gave
he, she, *or* it gave	they gave

Past Progressive: *was, were giving*
Past Emphatic: *did give*

Future Tense

Singular	Plural
I will (shall) give	we will (shall) give
you will (shall) give	you will (shall) give
he, she, *or* it will (shall) give	they will (shall) give

Future Progressive: *will (shall) be giving*

Present Perfect Tense

Singular	Plural
I have given	we have given
you have given	you have given
he, she, *or* it has given	they have given

Present Perfect Progressive: *has, have been giving*

Past Perfect Tense

Singular	Plural
I had given	we had given
you had given	you had given
he, she, *or* it had given	they had given

Past Perfect Progressive: *had been giving*

Future Perfect Tense

Singular	Plural
I will (shall) have given	we will (shall) have given
you will (shall) have given	you will (shall) have given
he, she, *or* it will (shall) have given	they will (shall) have given

Future Perfect Progressive: *will (shall) have been giving*

HELP

The conjugation of the verb *give* in the chart at left is in the active voice. Many verbs can be in either the active voice or the passive voice.

Reference Note

For a discussion of the uses of the **active voice** and the **passive voice**, see page 601. For the **conjugation of *give* in the passive voice**, see page 602.

Ask students to identify and classify the verbals in the following sentences.

1. Her winning the race surprised no one. [winning—*gerund*]
2. Fascinated, the children watched the tropical fish swimming in the aquarium. [Fascinated—*participle*; swimming—*participle*]

For more information about verbals, refer students to **Chapter 14: The Phrase.**

The Uses of the Tenses

18e. Each of the six tenses has its own uses.

(1) The *present tense* expresses an action or a state of being that is occurring now, at the present time.

EXAMPLES   Sonja **owns** a calculator. [present]

Larry **is** in the Chess Club. [present]

We **are rehearsing** the play. [present progressive]

I **do appreciate** your helping me. [present emphatic]

The present tense is also used

- to show customary or habitual action or state of being

EXAMPLE   He **runs** two miles a day.

- to state a general truth—something that is always true

EXAMPLE   The equator **divides** the earth's surface into the Northern and Southern Hemispheres.

- to summarize the plot or subject matter of a literary work (such use is called *literary present*)

EXAMPLE   In Act III of *The Tragedy of Julius Caesar*, the conspirators **assassinate** the Roman leader.

- to make a historical event seem current (such use is called *historical present*)

EXAMPLE   During the unstable years following the 1910 Mexican Revolution, Emiliano Zapata and his army **occupy** Mexico City three different times.

- to express future time

EXAMPLE   We **travel** abroad next month.

(2) The *past tense* expresses an action or a state of being that occurred in the past and did not continue into the present.

EXAMPLES   I **ran** toward the door. [past]

Tomás **was** the club's president last year. [past]

The boys **were playing** football. [past progressive]

We certainly **did enjoy** your performance. [past emphatic]

(3) The *future tense* expresses an action or a state of being that will occur. The future tense is usually formed with the helping verb *will* or *shall* and the base form of a verb.

EXAMPLES   I **will travel** this fall. [future]

               I **shall leave** soon. [future]

               Gia and I **will be** there at seven o'clock. [future]

               Will you **be waiting** for us? [future progressive]

A future action or state of being may also be expressed by using

- the present tense of *be* followed by *going to* and the base form of a verb

EXAMPLE   **Are** you **going to drive** her to the airport?

- the present tense of *be* followed by *about to* and the base form of the verb

EXAMPLE   They **are about to begin** the ceremony.

- the present tense of a verb with a word or word group that expresses future time

EXAMPLE   I **take** my driving test **next Friday**.

(4) The *present perfect tense* expresses an action or a state of being that occurred at an indefinite time in the past. The present perfect tense is usually formed with the helping verb *have* or *has* and the past participle of a verb.

EXAMPLES   She **has visited** Chicago. [present perfect]

               They **have been** to the office. [present perfect]

The present perfect tense may also be used to express an action or a state of being that began in the past and that continues into the present.

EXAMPLES   She **has worked** there several years. [present perfect]

               I **have been taking** guitar lessons for nearly six months. [present perfect progressive]

NOTE Use the past tense, not the present perfect tense, to express a specific time in the past.

EXAMPLE   We **saw** [*not* have seen] the movie last night.

Meeting INDIVIDUAL NEEDS

ADVANCED LEARNERS

After discussing with students the uses of the six tenses (pp. 594–596), point out that certain irregular verbs, such as *let* and *burst,* form their past and past participle by making no change. In other words, the base form, past, and past participle are all the same. Have students brainstorm a list of such verbs. [*let, burst, set, put, cost, cast, cut, hit, spread, thrust*]

Write the following sentences on the chalkboard. For each sentence, ask students to explain how they can tell the tense of the verb *let.*

1. My mother will let me go after I finish my chores. [*The helping verb* will *indicates future tense of* let.]

2. Yesterday I let Ramona use my bike. [*The adverb* Yesterday *indicates past tense of* let.]

3. By that time, Arnie had already let him have the skateboard. [*The phrase* By that time *and the helping verb* had *indicate past perfect tense of* let.]

Ask each student to choose a verb whose base form, past, and past participle are the same and to write sentences that illustrate the six tenses of the verb. You may want to call on volunteers to read their sentences aloud and to have listeners identify the tenses of the verbs.

(5) The ***past perfect tense*** expresses an action or a state of being that ended before another past action or state of being occurred. The past perfect tense is usually formed with the helping verb *had* and the past participle of the verb.

EXAMPLES After Mary Anne **had revised** her essay, she handed it in. [past perfect]

Mr. Hahn told us that he **had been** a Peace Corps volunteer in Somalia. [past perfect]

The frustrated chemist finally realized that she **had been overlooking** an important step in the experiment. [past perfect progressive]

(6) The ***future perfect tense*** expresses an action or a state of being that will end before another future action or state of being. The future tense is usually formed with the helping verbs *shall have* or *will have* and the past participle of a verb.

EXAMPLES By the time you receive this postcard, **I will have returned** home. [future perfect]

Before then, you and he **will have become** U.S. citizens by naturalization. [future perfect]

At the end of this year, **I will have been attending** school for ten years. [future perfect progressive]

---HELP---

In Exercise 11, the use of the past and present perfect verb tenses gives the example sentences different meanings.

My sister took piano lessons for two years. [The past tense *took* indicates that the piano lessons occurred in the past and did not continue into the present.]

My sister has been taking piano lessons for two years. [The progressive form of the present perfect tense *has been taking* indicates that the piano lessons began in the past and are continuing into the present.]

Exercise 11 Identifying the Tenses of Verbs

Identify the tenses of the verbs in each of the following pairs of sentences. Also tell whether the verbs are in progressive or emphatic form. Be prepared to explain the difference in meaning between the sentences in each pair.

EXAMPLE 1. My sister took piano lessons for two years.
My sister has been taking piano lessons for two years.

1. *took*—past; *has been taking*—present perfect progressive

1. I will start working this afternoon.
I will have started working by this afternoon.
2. What happened here?
What has been happening here?
3. She lived in Cleveland for four years.
She has lived in Cleveland for four years.

Exercise 11 Identifying the Tenses of Verbs

ANSWERS

1. The first sentence expresses an action that will occur in the future (future tense). The second sentence expresses an action that will be completed before some future action or event takes place (future perfect tense).

2. The first sentence expresses an action that occurred in the past and did not continue into the present (past tense). The second sentence expresses a continuing action that occurred in the past and continues into the present (present perfect progressive tense).

3. The first sentence expresses an action that occurred in the past and did not continue into the present (past tense). The second sentence expresses an action that occurred in the past and continues into the present (present perfect tense).

4. I do have an after-school job.
   I did have an after-school job.
5. Some students were practicing karate during their lunch break.
   Some students have been practicing karate during their lunch break.

Exercise 12 Using the Different Tenses of Verbs

Change the tense of the verb in each of the following sentences by following the directions given in the parentheses.

EXAMPLE 1. Have you done your homework? (Change to past emphatic.)

1. Did you do your homework?

1. Otto lived here for a year. (Change to future perfect.)
2. I leave for school at 7:00 A.M. (Change to future.)
3. Have you read Thomas Sowell's excellent how-to book *Choosing a College*? (Change to present perfect progressive.)
4. Will you go? (Change to past emphatic.)
5. Were they at the party? (Change to past perfect.)
6. Were you there? (Change to present perfect.)
7. The soloist sings well. (Change to present emphatic.)
8. The bus arrives on time. (Change to future.)
9. By then, Cammi had returned. (Change to future perfect.)
10. The klezmer band will play for an hour without a break. (Change to future perfect progressive.)

1. will have lived
2. will leave
3. been reading
4. Did
5. Had/been
6. Have/been
7. does sing
8. will arrive
9. will have returned
10. will have been playing

Consistency of Tense

18f. Do not change needlessly from one tense to another.

(1) When describing events that occur at the same time, use verbs in the same tense.

EXAMPLES Roy **looked** through his binoculars and **saw** a large bear as it **raced** back to the woods. [All of the verbs are in the past tense.]

Roy **looks** through his binoculars and **sees** a large bear as it **races** back to the woods. [All of the verbs are in the present tense.]

(2) When describing events that occur at different times, use verbs in different tenses to show the sequence of events.

Exercise 11 Identifying the Tenses of Verbs

ANSWERS continued

4. The first sentence expresses an action that is occurring now (present emphatic tense). The second sentence expresses an action that occurred in the past and did not continue into the present (past emphatic tense).

5. The first sentence expresses a continuing action that was occurring in the past and did not continue into the present (past progressive tense). The second sentence expresses a continuing action that was occurring in the past and continues into the present (present perfect progressive tense).

Relating to Literature

To reinforce students' understanding of **Rule 18f**, ask them to read a short story and to identify the various verb tenses it incorporates. If the Tom Godwin short story "The Cold Equations" is included in your literature textbook, have students analyze Godwin's use of verb tense. Then, ask why they think short stories often include so many different verb tenses. [In the narrative parts of his story, Godwin uses past and past perfect tenses. In dialogue, however, he uses all the tenses that would normally occur in conversation. A short story is a fictional narrative that relates a series of events. In order to show the sequence of events, a writer often must use more than one tense.]

EXAMPLES Yesterday, Donald **told** us that his brother **works** part time at the animal shelter. [The past tense *told* is correct because the action of telling occurred at a specific time in the past. The present tense *works* is correct because the action of working occurs now.]

Sela's family **lives** next door but **will be moving** to Salinas, California, next month. [The present tense *lives* is correct because the action of living occurs now. The future tense *will be moving* is correct because the action of moving will be occurring in the future.]

—HELP—

Some sentences in Exercise 13 contain more than one error.

Exercise 13 Proofreading for Consistency of Tense

Most of the sentences in the following passage contain at least one error in the use of tenses. Revise the incorrect sentences to correct each error. If a sentence is already correct, write *C*.

EXAMPLE [1] The American Revolution began in 1775 and ends in 1783.

1. The American Revolution began in 1775 and ended in 1783.

1. C
2. was

[1] The painting below depicts the outcome of one of the most important battles of the American Revolution, a battle that took place in September and October 1777 at Saratoga, New York. [2] The leader of the British troops, General John Burgoyne, had set up camp near Saratoga and is planning to march south to Albany. [3] Burgoyne's

Viewing the Art

The Surrender of Burgoyne. John Trumbull, born in 1756 in Lebanon, Connecticut, was left nearly blind in one eye by a boyhood injury. Nevertheless, Trumbull went on to become a colonel by the age of twenty-one, an amateur architect, an author, and a well-respected artist. Trumbull is best known for his paintings depicting momentous occasions in American history. In 1843, John Trumbull died and, according to his wishes, was buried under the Yale Art Gallery.

army has been weakened by a recent attack from an American militia, which had ambushed some of his troops at Bennington, Vermont. [4] Although the march to Albany is dangerous, Burgoyne decided to take the risk because he feels bound by orders from London.

[5] Meanwhile, also near Saratoga, the American troops under General Horatio Gates gather reinforcements and supplies. [6] The American forces outnumbered their British enemies by a margin of nearly two to one. [7] The Americans are much better equipped than the British, whose provisions are badly depleted.

[8] In spite of these disadvantages, the British launch an attack on the Americans on September 19, 1777. [9] After four hours of fierce fighting, the Americans, led by General Gates or General Benedict Arnold (who later became an infamous traitor to the American cause), withdraw. [10] The British, however, have suffered serious losses, including many officers. [11] Burgoyne urgently sends messages to the British command in New York and asked for new orders. [12] He never received a response, possibly because the messages are intercepted. [13] Burgoyne's tactics became desperate. [14] He boldly leads a fresh attack against the Americans on October 7. [15] This time, however, his troops endure even worse casualties, and the next day Burgoyne prepares to retreat.

[16] The Americans surround Burgoyne's army before it could leave Saratoga. [17] As the painting shows, Burgoyne had surrendered to Benedict Arnold. [18] The Convention of Saratoga, under which Burgoyne gave up his entire force of six thousand troops, is signed on October 17. [19] Saratoga becomes a turning point in the American Revolution. [20] Six years later, in 1783, the British signed a peace treaty with the Americans, and the American Revolution ended.

3. had
4. was/felt
5. had gathered [or were gathering or gathered]
6. C
7. were/were
8. launched
9. withdrew

10. had
11. sent
12. had been [or were]
13. C
14. led
15. endured/prepared
16. surrounded
17. surrendered
18. was

19. became
20. C

Modals

18g. A *modal* is a helping (or auxiliary) verb that is joined with a main verb or an infinitive to express an attitude toward the action or state of being of the main verb.

The helping verbs *can, could, may, might, must, ought, shall, should, will,* and *would* are used as modals.

(1) The modal *can* or *could* is used to express ability.

EXAMPLES **Can** you **speak** French?

I **could have gone**, but I was too tired.

Reference Note

For more about **helping (auxiliary) verbs** and **main verbs,** see page 417.

(2) The modal *may* is used to express permission or possibility.

EXAMPLES You **may leave** the table. [permission]

It seems that her truck's struts **may be** defective. [possibility]

(3) The modal *might*, like *may*, is used to express possibility. Often, the possibility expressed by *might* is less likely than the possibility expressed by *may*.

EXAMPLE Rumor has it that Mel Gibson **might be** there, but I doubt it.

(4) The modal *must* is used most often to express a requirement. Sometimes, *must* is used to express an explanation.

EXAMPLES The hippopotamus **must spend** most of its time in the water, or its skin will become dry. [requirement]

He **must have been caught** in traffic. [explanation]

(5) The modal *ought* is used to express an obligation or a likelihood.

EXAMPLES Does Ms. Garza think that she **ought to promote** Mr. Whitman? [obligation]

The tornado **ought to be gone** soon. [likelihood]

STYLE TIP

In the past, careful writers and speakers of English made a distinction between the modals *shall* and *will*. Nowadays, however, writers and speakers tend to use *will* in most cases. Only in certain situations do they typically use *shall*.

EXAMPLE
Shall we dance?

(6) The modal *will* or *shall* is used to express future time.

EXAMPLES When **will** (or **shall**) we **leave** for lunch?

Tim **will take** a look at your car.

(7) The modal *should* is used to express a recommendation, an obligation, or a possibility.

EXAMPLES Mom **should go** to the doctor for her sprain. [recommendation]

Students **should hand in** their homework on time. [obligation]

Should you **have** any complaints about the service, please do not hesitate to let us know. [possibility]

(8) The modal *would* is used to express the conditional form of a verb.

A conditional verb form usually appears in an independent clause that is joined with an "if" clause. The "if" clause explains *under what condition(s)* the action or state of being of the conditional verb takes place.

600 Chapter 18 Using Verbs Correctly

EXAMPLE If the economy had been better, the president **would have won** reelection. [conditional]

Would is also used to express future time in a subordinate clause when the main verb in the independent clause is in the past tense.

EXAMPLE They promised us that they **would bring** the music. [subordinate clause]

Additionally, *would* is used to express an action that was repeated in the past, an invitation or offer, or a polite request.

EXAMPLES Every day I **would get up** early and **go** for a walk. [repeated past action]

Would you **like** some of this pie? [offer]

Would you please **tell** me the time? [polite request]

Exercise 14 Writing Appropriate Modals

For each of the following sentences, supply an appropriate modal.

EXAMPLE 1. If we are all agreed, I ____ write the final document.
1. will

Answers will vary.
1. I ____ have forgotten to answer that question. **1. must**
2. No, Jeff, you ____ not let your hamster out of its cage. **2. may**
3. "I ____ try to finish by tomorrow," Maria said. **3. will**
4. The weather report said it ____ snow, or it ____ not. **4. may/may**
5. All participants ____ return the permission slips by Friday. **5. must**
6. Colleen ____ almost reach the light bulb. **6. can**
7. After reviewing the entries, the panel ____ announce its decision. **7. will**
8. Even with the manual, I simply ____ not figure out this program. **8. could**
9. Frank ____ be happy to help, if you ask him nicely. **9. would**
10. As soon as you finish your part of the report, Sharon ____ write the conclusion. **10. can**

Active Voice and Passive Voice

Voice is the form a transitive verb takes to indicate whether the subject of the verb performs or receives the action.

18h. When the subject of a verb performs the action, the verb is in the *active voice*. When the subject of a verb receives the action, the verb is in the *passive voice*.

---

18 h, i

Active Voice and Passive Voice

Rules 18h, i *(pp. 601–605)*

OBJECTIVES

- To identify whether verbs in sentences are in the active or the passive voice
- To rewrite sentences containing awkward passive-voice constructions

USAGE

RESOURCES
Active Voice and Passive Voice
Practice
- *Grammar, Usage, and Mechanics,* pp. 182, 183
- *Language Workshop CD-ROM,* Lesson 12

Reference Note

For further discussion of **transitive verbs,** see page 421. For more information about **direct objects,** see page 456.

STYLE TIP

Choosing between the active voice and the passive voice is a matter of style, not correctness. Be aware, however, that using the passive voice can sometimes produce an awkward or weak effect.

AWKWARD PASSIVE
The yardwork will be finished tomorrow by me.

ACTIVE
I **will finish** the yardwork tomorrow.

As the following examples show,

- a verb in the active voice has a direct object, which tells who or what receives the action; a verb in the passive voice does not have a direct object.
- a verb in the passive voice may or may not be followed by a prepositional phrase that begins with *by* and tells who or what performs the action.

	S V DO
ACTIVE VOICE	The blazing fire **destroyed** the outside walls. [The subject *fire* performs the action; the direct object *walls* receives the action.]
	S V
PASSIVE VOICE	The outside walls **were destroyed** by the blazing fire. [The subject *walls* receives the action; *fire*, the object of the preposition *by*, performs the action.]
	S V
PASSIVE VOICE	The outside walls **were destroyed.** [The subject *walls* receives the action; the performer of the action is not given.]
	S V DO
ACTIVE VOICE	She **grows** corn on her farm. [The subject *She* performs the action; the direct object *corn* receives the action.]
	S V
PASSIVE VOICE	Corn **is grown** on her farm. [The subject *corn* receives the action; the performer of the action is not given.]

As shown above, a verb in the passive voice is always a verb phrase that consists of a form of the verb *be* and the past participle of a verb. The following chart shows the conjugation of the verb *give* in the passive voice.

Reference Note

For the **conjugation** of the **verb** *give* **in the active voice,** see the chart on page 592.

Conjugation of the Irregular Verb *Give* in the Passive Voice	
Present Tense	
Singular	*Plural*
I am given	we are given
you are given	you are given
he, she, *or* it is given	they are given

602 Chapter 18 Using Verbs Correctly

Learning for Life

Continued on pp. 603–604

Writing a Résumé. Since many tenth-graders turn sixteen during the school year and become eligible for a wider range of jobs, they will probably be interested in learning to write a good résumé. Explain that using active voice verbs to describe duties performed rather than simply listing a descriptive job title creates a more dynamic résumé. For example, "Volunteer office worker, Boys and Girls Club: operated switchboard, entered membership data into database, and reorganized filing sys-

Conjugation of the Irregular Verb *Give* in the Passive Voice	
Past Tense	
Singular	*Plural*
I was given	we were given
you were given	you were given
he, she, *or* it was given	they were given
Future Tense	
Singular	*Plural*
I will (shall) be given	we will (shall) be given
you will (shall) be given	you will (shall) be given
he, she, *or* it will (shall) be given	they will (shall) be given
Present Perfect Tense	
Singular	*Plural*
I have been given	we have been given
you have been given	you have been given
he, she, *or* it has been given	they have been given
Past Perfect Tense	
Singular	*Plural*
I had been given	we had been given
you had been given	you had been given
he, she, *or* it had been given	they had been given
Future Perfect Tense	
Singular	*Plural*
I will (shall) have been given	we will (shall) have been given
you will (shall) have been given	you will (shall) have been given
he, she, *or* it will (shall) have been given	they will (shall) have been given

—HELP—

Because the use of *be* or *been* with *being* is awkward, in the passive voice the progressive form is generally used only in the present tense and past tense.

EXAMPLES
My favorite teacher **is being given** an award.
[present progressive, passive voice]

My favorite teacher **was being given** an award.
[past progressive, passive voice]

Meeting INDIVIDUAL NEEDS

ADVANCED LEARNERS
Tell students that although as a general rule they should use the passive voice sparingly in their writing, there are times when it is effective. For example, the passive voice can be used to create a sense of evasiveness or suspense. Have students look in their literature books or in newspapers or magazines for examples of the effective use of passive voice. You may want to ask students to share with one another the examples they find and to explain why the examples are effective.

Critical Thinking
Analysis. For one week, have students listen for and note the use of the passive voice in their own speech and in the speech of others. Ask students to analyze the effectiveness of the passive voice in each instance.

---

tem" is more dynamic and gives a prospective employer much more to go on than "Volunteer office worker, Boys and Girls Club."

Have students gather information they need to include in résumés—education, work experience, hobbies and interests, awards and honors, employment goals, and references. Provide the class with sample résumés from the school's library, business education department, or guidance counseling office. Guide students through

Exercise 15 Identifying Verbs in the Active and Passive Voices

POSSIBLE ANSWERS

1. passive—Artists around the world admire the art of Lucia Wilcox.
2. active
3. passive—Raoul Dufy, Fernand Léger, Robert Motherwell, and Jackson Pollock befriended and taught her.
4. passive—Gallery exhibits around the world have shown her paintings often.
5. active
6. passive—A tumor near the optic nerve caused her blindness.
7. active
8. passive—She described her vision and her mind as free of "static" and "distractions."
9. passive—Because of her blindness, she altered her style and subject matter from energetic silhouettes to larger canvases in lush colors.
10. passive—Many well-known artists imitated her style.

COMPUTER TIP

If you use a computer when you write, you may want to find out about the different kinds of style-checking programs that are available. Some programs check for use of verbs in passive voice. Remember, though, that the program can only highlight the passive-voice verbs; it cannot determine whether you have used them intentionally for a particular stylistic effect.

Using the Passive Voice

18i. The passive voice should be used sparingly.

Use the passive voice

- when you want to emphasize the receiver of the action

EXAMPLE   The mayor **was reelected** by a landslide.

- when you do not know, or do not want to reveal, the performer of the action

EXAMPLE   Vicious rumors **have been spread** about the politician.

Exercise 15 Identifying Verbs in the Active and Passive Voices

Identify the verb in each of the following sentences as *active* or *passive*. If the verb is in the passive voice, revise the sentence so that the verb is in the active voice.

EXAMPLE   1. We were shown by our art teacher some prints of Lucia Wilcox's artwork.

1. passive—Our art teacher showed us some prints of Lucia Wilcox's artwork.

1. The paintings of Lucia Wilcox are admired by many artists around the world.
2. Her blindness during her last years made her final works particularly interesting.
3. She was befriended and taught by Raoul Dufy, Fernand Léger, Robert Motherwell, and Jackson Pollock.
4. Her paintings have been shown often in gallery exhibits around the world.
5. She lost her eyesight suddenly, though not unexpectedly.
6. Her blindness was caused by a tumor near the optic nerve.
7. According to Wilcox, after losing her vision, she had better sight than anyone else.
8. Her vision and her mind were described by her as free of "static" and "distractions."
9. Because of her blindness, her style and subject matter were altered from energetic silhouettes to larger canvases in lush colors.
10. Her style was imitated by many well-known artists.

Learning for Life

revising any of the résumés that do not contain active voice verbs.

Then, have students write their own résumés, working in pairs to analyze each other's work so that the finished products will be dynamic, thorough, and ready to use. If possible, have students keep their résumés on computer disks so that revisions can be made easily. Word-processing programs make it possible to produce very professional-looking résumés, so encourage students to be creative.

Exercise 16 Using the Passive Voice

Rewrite any of the following sentences that contain awkward passive-voice constructions. If you think a sentence is best the way it is, write *C* and be prepared to explain your answer.

EXAMPLE   1. My car was serviced by Tom, my favorite mechanic.
              1. Tom, my favorite mechanic, serviced my car.

1. According to the editorial, the city's surplus money was wasted by inefficient politicians.
2. My home was damaged by a tornado recently.
3. The right-rear tire must have been punctured by a nail in the driveway.
4. The bridge was damaged by rushing water.
5. The classroom computer was stolen over the weekend.
6. While I was away visiting my cousins in Nebraska, my cat was fed by my neighbor.
7. My sleep was interrupted by loud, bass-heavy music from our neighbors' party.
8. The president's failure to be reelected was caused by sudden economic downturn.
9. The farmer's crops were destroyed by drought back in the 1980s.
10. The book was read by them.

Review C Choosing the Correct Forms of Verbs

Choose the correct verb form in parentheses in each of the following sentences.

EXAMPLE   1. Has the club (*risen, raised*) its membership dues?
              1. raised

1. Little Billy was (*lying, laying*) in wait for us.
2. He had accidentally (*thrown, throwed*) his homework away.
3. The spilled laundry (*laid, lay*) in a wet heap.
4. We ate until we almost (*burst, bursted*).
5. The kitten (*drank, drunk*) from the dog's bowl.
6. Haven't you ever (*swam, swum*) in a lake before?
7. When Chief Dan George walked to the podium, cheers (*rang, rung*) out.
8. Have you ever (*rode, ridden*) a roller coaster?
9. I knew I should have (*brought, brung*) my camera.
10. Uh-oh, I think this phone is (*broke, broken*).

HELP

In the example for Exercise 16, the performer of the action is known, and there is no reason to emphasize the receiver of the action. The passive voice is unnecessary and awkward.

Exercise 16 Using the Passive Voice

POSSIBLE ANSWERS

1. According to the editorial, inefficient politicians wasted the city's surplus money.
2. A tornado damaged my home recently.
3. A nail in the driveway must have punctured the right-rear tire.
4. Rushing water damaged the bridge.
5. C [*performer unknown*]
6. While I was away visiting my cousins in Nebraska, my neighbor fed my cat.
7. Loud, bass-heavy music from our neighbors' party interrupted my sleep.
8. Sudden economic downturn caused the president's failure to be reelected.
9. Drought destroyed the farmer's crops back in the late 1980s.
10. They read the book.

Relating to Writing

Ask students to write in the passive voice brief narratives about experiences they have had. Students should pick experiences they are comfortable sharing with classmates. Ask volunteers to read their papers aloud. The class should listen carefully to the readers, noting examples of passive voice. Then, have students change their narratives to the active voice; have volunteers read their revised narratives aloud. Discuss the differences that the use of the active voice makes.

Mood

Rule 18j *(pp. 606–607)*

OBJECTIVE

- To identify mood forms of verbs

Mood

18j. Mood is the form a verb takes to indicate the attitude of the person using the verb.

(1) The *indicative mood* is used to express a fact, an opinion, or a question.

EXAMPLES Jose Saramago **is** the Portuguese writer who **won** the Nobel Prize in literature in 1998. [fact]

They **think** we **are** next in line. [opinion]

Can you **name** the first three presidents of the United States? [question]

(2) The *imperative mood* is used to express a direct command or request.

EXAMPLES **Close** that window! [direct command]

Please **read** that paper aloud. [request]

(3) The *subjunctive mood* is used to express a suggestion, a necessity, a condition contrary to fact, or a wish.

EXAMPLES Her parents recommend that Alison **try** cooking as a career. [suggestion]

It is essential that we **be** at the airport on time. [necessity]

If I **were** you, I would call them immediately. [condition contrary to fact]

I wish you **were** here. [wish]

Exercise 17 Identifying Mood Forms of Verbs

Identify the mood of the italicized verb in each of the following sentences as *indicative*, *imperative*, or *subjunctive*.

EXAMPLE 1. It is necessary that we *review* the safety instructions.
1. subjunctive

1. ind.   1. What *is* Purnima's favorite book?
2. imp.   2. *Look* at my uncle's photos of Kenya.
3. sub.   3. It is required that we *take* a foreign language next year.
4. ind.   4. Mr. McEwan *toured* the Aran Islands last summer.
5. sub.   5. I suggest that you *put* on a life jacket before water-skiing.

RESOURCES

Mood

Practice

- *Grammar, Usage, and Mechanics*, p. 184

6. I *think* Rosalinda's stereo will be perfect for the party.
7. Soon-hee wishes the camping trip *were* next Saturday.
8. *Try* out for the leading role, Eric.
9. Sri Lanka *is* off the southern coast of India.
10. My friend David teases me as though he *were* my brother.

6. ind.
7. sub.
8. Imp.
9. ind.
10. sub.

Review D — Choosing the Correct Forms of Irregular Verbs

Supply the correct form of each italicized verb in the following paragraph.

EXAMPLE   I liked this picture as soon as I [1] (*see*) it.
    1. saw

Have you ever [1] (*see*) this fascinating picture of an impossible structure? It is called Waterfall, and it was [2] (*draw*) by the Dutch artist M. C. Escher. He [3] (*take*) the basic idea for this artwork from the optical illusion shown below. As you can see, a two-story waterfall has [4] (*set*) a miller's wheel in motion. Then, after the water has [5] (*leave*) the wheel, it zigzags through a channel until it [6] (*come*) to the top of the waterfall again. Wait, though—has the water [7] (*go*) uphill on its way back to the top of the waterfall? No, obviously the stream has [8] (*run*) away from the fall on the same level as the bottom of the fall. Then how can the water now be back at the top where it [9] (*begin*)? Escher never answered that question, but he once wrote that if the miller simply [10] (*throw*) in a bucket of water now and then to replace water that had evaporated, he would have a "perpetual motion" machine!

1. seen
2. drawn
3. took
4. set
5. left
6. comes
7. gone
8. run
9. began
10. threw

M. C. Escher, *Waterfall*. Copyright © 1999. Cordon Art-Baarn-Holland. All rights reserved.

© Roger Penrose

Mood   607

CHAPTER 18 Chapter Review

A. Writing the Past or Past Participle Form of Verbs

Write the correct past or past participle form of the italicized verb in parentheses in each of the following sentences.

1. Although Emily Dickinson (*write*) poetry most of her life, very little of her work was published until after her death.
2. When he saw that the animals had (*drink*) all the water, he gave them more.
3. Regarding weeds as unwanted intruders, she pulled them from the ground and (*throw*) them over the fence.
4. The water was cold and daylight was fading, so he (*swim*) only a short distance before turning back to shore.
5. The dew (*freeze*) during the night, covering each twig and blade of grass with a crisp, silvery coating.
6. After my brother had given his new puppy a bath, he (*seem*) to be wetter than the dog.
7. She (*speak*) in such a low, hushed voice that the people in the audience had to strain to hear her remarks.
8. Frightened by the traffic, the deer (*run*) back into the forest.
9. At the front of the parade was an officer who (*ride*) a prancing black horse.
10. When the church bell (*ring*) on Tuesday evening, the villagers became alarmed.

B. Revising Verb Tense or Voice

Revise the following paragraph, correcting verbs that are in the wrong tense or that use passive voice awkwardly. If a sentence is already correct, write *C*.

[11] Miguel de Cervantes was born in 1547 in Alcalá de Henares, near Madrid, Spain. [12] Unlike most other writers of his time, he does not attend a university. [13] Cervantes is acquiring a somewhat different form of education by serving as a soldier and being captured by pirates. [14] He is held captive by the pirates for five years until his

family ransoms him. **[15]** Little was written by him until he is in his late thirties. **[16]** In 1605, at the age of fifty-eight, Cervantes is publishing the first part of his masterwork, *Don Quixote;* then he wrote nothing significant for eight years. **[17]** In 1615, the second part of *Don Quixote* was published. **[18]** Cervantes' life has been continuing to have ups and downs, and a series of government jobs prevent him from writing full-time. **[19]** However, in the last three years of his life, many fine works were written by him. **[20]** Cervantes has lived a fascinating life, and world literature is richer because of it.

C. Determining Correct Use of *Lie* and *Lay, Sit* and *Set,* and *Rise* and *Raise* in Sentences

Most of the following sentences contain at least one error in the use of *lie* or *lay, sit* or *set,* or *rise* or *raise.* Identify each incorrect verb, and write the correct form. If a sentence is already correct, write *C.*

21. We left our lawn furniture setting on the patio.
22. Grandpa decided to sit the plates on the sideboard.
23. They lain the bricks next to where we set out the logs.
24. When the dough has raised for thirty minutes, turn it onto the floured board.
25. The sun has set and the moon is rising.
26. When we in America are rising from bed in the morning, people in China are laying down to sleep.
27. As the enemy patrol passed by, the parachutists laid quietly in the undergrowth.
28. Cadet Rojas rose the flag to the sound of reveille on the bugle.
29. I feel a little dizzy; I think I'll lay down for a while.
30. The architect raised to go find the blueprints.

21. sitting
22. set
23. laid
24. risen

25. C
26. lying

27. lay

28. raised

29. lie

30. rose

D. Using the Different Tenses of Verbs

Change the tense of the verb in each of the following sentences by following the directions given in parentheses.

31. Pamela sat at her desk for an hour. (Change to *future perfect.*)
32. The lead actor changes costumes quickly. (Change to *present emphatic.*)

31. will have sat
32. does change

Chapter Review
B. Revising Verb Tense or Voice

POSSIBLE ANSWERS continued
Revisions may vary.

15. He wrote little until he was in his late thirties.
16. In 1605, at the age of fifty-eight, Cervantes published the first part of his masterwork, *Don Quixote;* then he wrote nothing significant for eight years.
17. In 1615, he published the second part of *Don Quixote.*
18. Cervantes' life continued to have ups and downs, and a series of government jobs prevented him from writing full-time.
19. However, in the last three years of his life, he wrote many fine works.
20. Cervantes lived a fascinating life, and world literature is richer because of it.

33. been watching	33. Have you ~~watched~~ the TV miniseries on Thomas Jefferson? (Change to *present perfect progressive*.)
34. have been speaking	34. Sean will ~~speak~~ for half an hour. (Change to *future perfect progressive*.)
35. Had/been	35. ~~Were~~ you at the inauguration? (Change to *past perfect*.)
36. Have/been	36. ~~Were~~ we ever informed? (Change to *present perfect*.)
37. will leave	37. Dad ~~leaves~~ for the office at 7:30 A.M. (Change to *future*.)
38. will arrive	38. The plane ~~arrives~~ on time. (Change to *future*.)
39. will have	39. By then, the Holts ~~had~~ checked in at the hotel. (Change to *future perfect*.)
40. did talk	40. They ~~are talking~~ to the police. (Change to *past emphatic*.)

E. Choosing the Correct Forms of Verbs

Write the correct form of each italicized verb in the following sentences. In some instances you will need to add *have, has,* or *had*.

41. have lain	41. The bed is unmade; he must (*lie*) down for a while before he went out.
42. broke	42. During yesterday's storm, flying debris (*break*) most of the windows and littered the floors.
43. have taken	43. The car isn't in the garage; they must (*take*) it.
44. lay	44. I was feeling very tired when I got home, so I (*lie*) down right away.
45. drank	45. Hot and dusty from their long walk up the sloping road, the men seized the water jugs and (*drink*) every drop.
46. rose	46. Several people (*rise*) to protest, but the presiding officer silenced their complaints at once.
47. have shrunk	47. That sweater didn't fit when I tried it on this morning; it must (*shrink*) in the wash yesterday.
48. burst	48. After heavy rains had continued day after day, the water (*burst*) through the dam and flooded the fields.
49. has taken	49. So far, she (*take*) every opportunity to promote the plan.
50. had ridden	50. After they (*ride*) several miles in silence, the leader suddenly started singing.

RESOURCES

Using Verbs Correctly

Review
- *Grammar, Usage, and Mechanics,* pp. 185, 186, 187, 188, 189

Assessment
- *Assessment Package*
  —*Chapter Tests,* Ch. 18
  —*Chapter Tests in Standardized Test Formats,* Ch. 18
- *Test Generator (One-Stop Planner CD-ROM)*

Writing Application
Using Verb Tense in an Essay

Establishing Time of Action   It's Cultural Appreciation Week at your school. Your teacher has asked you to write a short essay about your own cultural or ethnic group. In your essay, you should explore several ways in which people of your heritage have enriched life in your community. Use correct verb tenses to describe some of the contributions these people have made in the past, some activities they are currently involved in, and what you think they might offer in the future. Use at least five different verb tenses in your essay.

Prewriting   Brainstorm a list of your ethnic or cultural group's outstanding leaders, scholars, athletes, and artists, as well as activities, events, clubs, and community service projects. Select three or four of the group's main contributions to mention in your essay. Many people can claim more than one ethnic or cultural heritage. If you can, you may want to write about the group you know the best or the one in which you are most interested.

Writing   While you are writing your first draft, try to add details that show the uniqueness of your cultural heritage. Consider how you can use verb tenses to make the sequence of events in your essay clear.

Revising   Read through your essay to be sure that you have included at least one contribution from each different time period: the past, the present, and (speculatively) the future. Check to see that you have used at least five different tenses.

Publishing   Make sure that you have formed all verbs correctly, paying special attention to irregular verbs. Proofread your essay for any errors in grammar, usage, and mechanics. You might create a bulletin board display of all the essays your classmates have written; or your class may wish to prepare a cultural-appreciation presentation for another class or for the whole school. If one is available, you may also want to post your essay on a class Web site.

Chapter Review   **611**

RESOURCES
Writing Application
Extension
- *Grammar, Usage, and Mechanics*, p. 192
- *Language Workshop CD-ROM*, Lessons 9–12

CHAPTER 19

Using Modifiers Correctly
Forms, Comparison, and Placement

Diagnostic Preview

A. Revising Sentences to Correct Errors in the Use and Placement of Modifiers

Most of the following sentences contain an error in the use or placement of modifiers. Revise each incorrect sentence to correct the faulty modifier. If a sentence is already correct, write *C*.

EXAMPLE   1. The planets that are most farthest from the sun are Neptune and Pluto.

           1. *The planets that are farthest from the sun are Neptune and Pluto.*

Answers may vary.

1. Manaba was/her
1. While building a fire in front of the hogan, Manaba's dog began to tug at the hem of her doeskin dress.
2. The greenhouse effect may be causing more higher temperatures worldwide.
3. else
3. Adrianne knows more about chemistry than anybody in her class.
4. hastily
4. Hank worked rather hasty so he could catch up with Nina.

PREVIEWING THE CHAPTER

- This chapter begins with a discussion of one-word, phrase, and clause modifiers. Eight troublesome modifiers are discussed. The chapter ends with lessons on comparison of modifiers and dangling and misplaced modifiers.

- For help in integrating the chapter with writing chapters, use the **Teaching Strands** chart on pp. T401A–T401B.

- The chapter concludes with a **Chapter Review**, which includes a **Writing Application** feature that asks students to write a comparison and contrast essay using modifiers correctly.

USING THE DIAGNOSTIC PREVIEW

- You may want to use the results of the **Diagnostic Preview** to help you create individual lesson plans for students having difficulty with specific rules.

Diagnostic Preview: Part A
Revising Sentences to Correct Errors in the Use and Placement of Modifiers

POSSIBLE ANSWERS

1. While Manaba was building a fire in front of the hogan, her dog. . .
2. . . . causing higher temperatures. . . .
3. . . . than anybody else in her class.
4. . . . rather hastily so. . . .

---

612   Chapter 19   Using Modifiers Correctly

CHAPTER RESOURCES

Planning
- *One-Stop Planner CD-ROM*

Practice and Extension
- *Grammar, Usage, and Mechanics,* p. 193
- *Language Workshop CD-ROM*

Internet
- go.hrw.com (keyword: EOLang)

Evaluation and Assessment
- *Assessment Package*
  —*Chapter Tests,* Ch. 19
  —*Chapter Tests in Standardized Test Formats,* Ch. 19
- *Test Generator (One-Stop Planner CD-ROM)*

5. Marian felt bad, but she knew things could be ~~worser~~.
6. Millie can sing as well as Scott, but of the two, he's the ~~best~~ dancer.
7. By playing carefully, the game ~~was won~~.
8. ~~Steady and confident,~~ a keen sense of balance enables Mohawk ironworkers to help build tall bridges and buildings.
9. Although Helen would be better in the leading role, Wenona will probably get the part because she is more reliable.
10. Because one carton of chemicals smelled ~~badly~~, it was examined before being used in the laboratory.

5. worse
6. better
7. the team won
8. ,steady and confident,
9. C
10. bad

B. Revising a Paragraph to Correct Errors in the Use and Placement of Modifiers

Most of the sentences in the following paragraph contain an error in the use or placement of modifiers. Revise each incorrect sentence. You may need to add or rearrange words for clarity. If a sentence is already correct, write C.

EXAMPLE [1] My aunt Penny had enclosed a ticket in my birthday card for Bobby McFerrin's concert.

1. My aunt Penny had enclosed in my birthday card a ticket for Bobby McFerrin's concert.

[11] Hailed by many critics as one of today's greatest male vocalists, my aunt Penny took me to see Bobby McFerrin. [12] Waiting for the concert to start, the auditorium was filled with eager fans. [13] Wondering where the band was, I kept my eyes on the empty stage. [14] When it was time for the show to start, a slender, barefoot man walked out from the wings, carrying a cordless microphone dressed only in blue jeans. [15] Assuming he was a stagehand, he began to sing, and then I realized that this was Bobby McFerrin! [16] Instantly, the complex rhythm of the music fascinated the audience that he made up as he went along. [17] I suddenly understood why one of his popularest albums is called *Spontaneous Inventions*! [18] Alone in the spotlight with only his voice and no band at all, two thousand people sat spellbound until he took his final bow. [19] All his life, Bobby McFerrin has enjoyed listening to and performing jazz, pop, rock, soul, African, and classical music. [20] Bobby's parents are both classical musicians, and he thanks them for giving him a rich musical environment on the back of every album he makes.

Diagnostic Preview: Part A
Revising Sentences to Correct Errors in the Use and Placement of Modifiers

POSSIBLE ANSWERS continued

5. . . . be worse.
6. . . . the better dancer.
7. . . . the team won the game.
8. A keen sense of balance enables steady and confident Mohawk . . .
9. C
10. Because one carton of chemicals smelled bad . . .

Diagnostic Preview: Part B
Revising a Paragraph to Correct Errors in the Use and Placement of Modifiers

POSSIBLE ANSWERS

11. My aunt Penny took me to see Bobby McFerrin, who is hailed by many critics as one of today's greatest male vocalists.
12. The auditorium was filled with eager fans waiting for the concert to start.
13. C
14. . . . man, dressed only in blue jeans and carrying a cordless microphone, walked out from the wings.
15. I assumed he was a stagehand until he began to sing . . . .
16. Instantly the audience was fascinated by the complex rhythm of the music that he made up as he went along.
17. . . . his most popular albums . . .
18. . . . at all, he kept two thousand people spellbound until . . .
19. C
20. . . . musicians, and on the back of every album he makes, he thanks them for giving him a rich musical environment.

Using Modifiers Correctly, pp. 612–634
Alignments
TEKS 3B, 3D
TAAS W3, W6
English II End-of-Course 5, 6

Texas Resources
- *TAAS Tool Kit*
- *Preparation for TAAS*
- *One-Stop Planner CD-ROM*

What Is a Modifier?

Rules 19a–c (pp. 614–620)

OBJECTIVES

- To identify adjectives and adverbs and the words they modify in a paragraph
- To select adjective and adverb forms to complete sentences
- To identify and correct errors in the use of adjectives and adverbs in sentences

Meeting INDIVIDUAL NEEDS

ENGLISH-LANGUAGE LEARNERS

Spanish. Because one-word adjectives in Spanish generally follow the nouns they modify, encourage students to pay special attention to the placement of one-word adjectives in English. As students complete the relevant exercises, you may want to have them identify the position of each adjective in relation to the word it modifies. Guide students to infer that adjectives in English may come before or after the words they modify.

Reference Note
For more information on **adjectives,** see page 412.

Reference Note
For information on **adverbs,** see page 422.

Reference Note
For information on **subjects and predicates,** see page 439. For information on **predicate adjectives,** see page 454.

What Is a Modifier?

A *modifier* is a word or word group that makes the meaning of another word or word group more specific. The two kinds of modifiers are *adjectives* and *adverbs*.

One-Word Modifiers

Adjectives make the meanings of nouns and pronouns more specific.

ADJECTIVES   Etta has a **mischievous** smile. [The adjective *mischievous* makes the meaning of the noun *smile* more specific.]

Only he answered the letter. [The adjective *Only* makes the meaning of the pronoun *he* more specific.]

Isn't his dog **well-trained**? [The compound adjective *well-trained* makes the meaning of the noun *dog* more specific.]

Adverbs make the meanings of verbs, adjectives, and other adverbs more specific.

ADVERBS   Etta smiled **mischievously.** [The adverb *mischievously* makes the meaning of the verb *smiled* more specific.]

The tree is **quite** healthy. [The adverb *quite* makes the meaning of the adjective *healthy* more specific.]

The car went **surprisingly** fast. [The adverb *surprisingly* makes the meaning of the adverb *fast* more specific.]

19a. If a word in the predicate modifies the subject of the verb, use the adjective form. If it modifies the verb, use the adverb form.

ADJECTIVE	The cantor's voice was **beautiful.** [*Beautiful* modifies *voice.*]
ADVERB	The cantor sang **beautifully.** [*Beautifully* modifies *sang.*]
ADJECTIVE	The corn grew **tall.** [*Tall* modifies *corn.*]
ADVERB	The corn grew **quickly.** [*Quickly* modifies *grew.*]

614   Chapter 19   Using Modifiers Correctly

RESOURCES

What Is a Modifier?
Practice
- *Grammar, Usage, and Mechanics,* pp. 194, 195, 196, 197, 198, 199, 200
- *Language Workshop CD-ROM,* Lesson 16

Adjective or Adverb?

While many adverbs end in –*ly,* others do not. Furthermore, not all words with the –*ly* ending are adverbs. Some adjectives also end in –*ly.* Therefore, you cannot tell whether a word is an adjective or an adverb simply by looking for the –*ly* ending.

Adverbs Not Ending in –*ly*	
call **soon**	remain **here**
not concerned	let **loose**
arrive **home**	**very** tall

Adjectives Ending in –*ly*	
elderly dachshund	**holy** place
curly lettuce	**silly** remark
only time	**timely** event

Some words can be used as both adjectives and adverbs. To decide whether a word is an adjective or an adverb, determine how the word is used in the sentence.

Adjectives	Adverbs
She is an **only** child.	She has **only** one brother.
That fighter is a **fast** plane.	The plane goes **fast**.
He caught the **last** boat.	They left **last**.

Exercise 1 — Identifying Adjectives and Adverbs and the Words They Modify

Identify the adjectives and adverbs in the paragraph on the following page, and give the words they modify.

EXAMPLE [1] First, get a craft knife and some stiff black paper.

1. *First—adverb—get; craft—adjective—knife; some— adjective—paper; stiff—adjective—paper; black— adjective—paper*

HELP — Include only one-word modifiers in Exercise 1. Also, do not include the articles *a, an,* and *the.*

 Continued on pp. 616–617

Participles Used as Adjectives. Remind students that the present participle and past participle forms of verbs can be used as adjectives because they modify nouns by telling *what kind* or *which one.* Write on the chalkboard the following examples:

1. the sound of shattering glass
2. a broken window
3. the partially restored building

Have students read the examples and

Exercise 1 Identifying Adjectives and Adverbs and the Words They Modify

ANSWERS

1. many—adjective—cultures; traditional—adjective—art
2. Mexican—adjective—artisans; small—adjective—knife; very—adverb—sharp; sharp—adjective—knife; colored—adjective—paper
3. oddly—adverb—shaped; shaped—adjective—scraps; away—adverb—fall; slowly—adverb—is revealed
4. each—adjective—part; somehow—adverb—must connect; another—adjective—part
5. these—adjective—designs; sometimes—adverb—leaves; background—adjective—pattern; main—adjective—subject
6. not—adverb—must be; even—adverb—slightly; slightly—adverb—dull; dull—adjective—knife; accidentally—adverb—might tear; tiny—adjective—bridges; paper—adjective—bridges
7. very—adverb—intricate; intricate—adjective—work
8. meticulous—adjective—Artisans
9. finished—adjective—product; actually—adverb—completing; necessary—adjective—skill
10. important—adjective—skill; too—adverb—is

Exercise 1

ALTERNATIVE LESSON

To reinforce students' understanding of predicate adjectives, ask students to identify those that appear in **Exercise 1** and to give reasons for their choices.

[*sentence 6*: dull—*completes the meaning of the verb* must be *and modifies the subject* knife; *sentence 7*: intricate—*completes the meaning of the verb* is *and modifies the subject* work; *sentence 8*: meticulous—*completes the meaning of the verb* must be *and modifies the subject* Artisans]

Reference Note
For information about **different kinds of phrases,** see page 467.

[1] In many cultures, cutting paper to make pictures is a traditional art. [2] For example, Mexican artisans use a small, very sharp knife to cut designs in pieces of colored paper. [3] As the oddly shaped scraps fall away, an image is slowly revealed. [4] Planning the work is a challenge because each part of the picture must connect somehow to the border or to another part of the design. [5] As you can see in these designs, the artist sometimes leaves a background pattern of stripes or lines to support the main subject. [6] The knife must not be even slightly dull, or the artist might accidentally tear one of the tiny paper bridges! [7] The work is very intricate. [8] Artisans must be meticulous. [9] Visualizing the finished product before actually completing it is a necessary skill. [10] Sharpening the knives that are used is an important skill, too.

Phrases Used as Modifiers

Like one-word modifiers, phrases can also be used as adjectives and adverbs.

EXAMPLES   It is time **for departure.** [The prepositional phrase *for departure* acts as an adjective that modifies the noun *time*.]

Bringing tears to our eyes, the comedian told some of her best jokes. [The participial phrase *Bringing tears to our eyes* acts as an adjective that modifies the noun *comedian*.]

Dr. Makowski is the one **to ask.** [The infinitive phrase *to ask* acts as an adjective that modifies the pronoun *one*.]

Tina is becoming fluent **in Italian.** [The prepositional phrase *in Italian* acts as an adverb that modifies the adjective *fluent*.]

Speak **with clarity in debates.** [The prepositional phrases *with clarity* and *in debates* act as adverbs that modify the verb *Speak*.]

The truck driver swerved just quickly enough **to avoid a collision.** [The infinitive phrase *to avoid a collision* acts as an adverb that modifies the adverb *enough*.]

MINI-LESSON

identify the parts of speech of the words *glass, window,* and *building* [nouns]. Then, ask students the following questions:

1. What kind of glass? [shattering]
2. What kind of window? [broken]
3. Which building? [restored]

Have students explain why these words should be classified as adjectives and not as verbs. [*They make the meanings of nouns more specific.*]

Next, point out that like most other

Clauses Used as Modifiers

Like words and phrases, clauses can also be used as adjectives and adverbs.

EXAMPLES   Raphael is the painter **that I like best.** [The adjective clause *that I like best* modifies the noun *painter.*]

Before my great-grandfather left Russia, he sat in his kitchen one last time. [The adverb clause *Before my great-grandfather left Russia* modifies the verb *sat.*]

> **Reference Note**
> For information on **clauses,** see page 492.

Eight Troublesome Modifiers

Bad and *Badly*

Bad is an adjective. In most uses, *badly* is an adverb.

ADJECTIVE   Fido was **bad.**
ADVERB   Fido behaved **badly.**

Remember that a word that modifies the subject of a verb should be in adjective form.

NONSTANDARD   The cheese smelled badly.
STANDARD   The cheese smelled **bad.** [*Bad* modifies *cheese.*]

NOTE   In informal situations, *bad* or *badly* is acceptable after *feel.*

INFORMAL   She feels **badly** about the mistake.
FORMAL   She feels **bad** about the mistake.

> **Reference Note**
> For information on **using standard English,** see page 638.

Good and *Well*

Good is an adjective. It should not be used to modify a verb.

NONSTANDARD   She sings good.
STANDARD   She sings **well.**
STANDARD   Her singing sounds **good.** [*Good* is an adjective that modifies the noun *singing.*]

Well may be used either as an adjective or as an adverb. As an adjective, *well* has two meanings: "in good health" and "satisfactory."

EXAMPLES   Trish is **well.** [Trish is in good health.]

All is **well.** [All is satisfactory.]

As an adverb, *well* means "capably."

EXAMPLE   Pedro did **well** in the music competition.

Slow and Slowly

In informal situations, *slow* is used as both an adjective and an adverb.

EXAMPLES   We took a **slow** boat to China. [*Slow* is an adjective modifying *boat*.]

Please go **slow**. [*Slow* is an adverb modifying *go*.]

Slowly is always an adverb. In formal uses, you should use *slowly* rather than *slow*.

EXAMPLES   The train **slowly** came to a stop.

Drive **slowly** on slippery roads.

Real and Really

Real is an adjective meaning "actual" or "genuine." *Really* is an adverb meaning "actually" or "truly."

EXAMPLES   Tom is a **real** mountain climber. [*Real* is an adjective modifying *climber*.]

The flood victims **really** need assistance. [*Really* is an adverb modifying *need*.]

Although in everyday situations *real* is commonly used as an adverb meaning "very," avoid using it as an adverb in formal speaking and writing.

INFORMAL   He kicked **real** well in the game.
FORMAL   He kicked **really** well in the game.

STYLE TIP

Really is overused in everyday speech. When possible, use another more descriptive adverb in place of *really*.

Exercise 2 Choosing Correct Adjective and Adverb Forms

In each of the following sentences, choose the modifier that is correct according to the rules of formal, standard English.

EXAMPLE   1. Each of the gymnasts performed (*real, really*) well.
              1. really

1. I can't hear you (*good, well*) when the water is running.
2. The opening paragraph is written (*good, well*).
3. The situation looks (*bad, badly*).

Chapter 19   Using Modifiers Correctly

4. Why does ketchup come out of the bottle so (*slow, slowly*)?
5. She certainly plays the marimba (*good, well*).
6. Can you dance (*real, really*) well?
7. These shoes don't fit (*bad, badly*) at all.
8. Our coach said that we should do the exercise (*slow, slowly*).
9. Did you do (*good, well*) on the last algebra test?
10. The chef at the corner cafe cooks (*real, really*) spicy food.

Exercise 3 Using Adjective and Adverb Forms Correctly

Each of the following sentences contains at least one italicized adjective or adverb. If the italicized word is incorrect according to the rules of formal, standard English, give the correct word. If the sentence is already correct, write *C*.

EXAMPLE 1. Soon after my brother Skipper opened his new shop, he grew *real* concerned about its future.

1. really

1. My brother opened Skipper's Skate City last April 1, and as the graph below shows, the shop did not do *well* at first.
2. Skipper wondered whether business had started *slow* because he wasn't advertising enough or because his display window wasn't drawing in people.
3. He'd see people walking *slow* past the shop and pointing at the gear on display, but hardly anyone stopped.

1. C

2. slowly

3. slowly

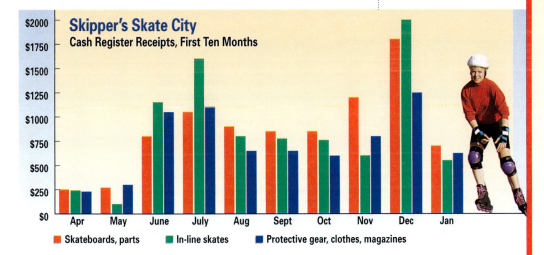

Eight Troublesome Modifiers

USAGE

Comparison of Modifiers

Rules 19d–h *(pp. 620–625)*

OBJECTIVES

- To write the comparative and superlative forms of modifiers
- To identify and correct errors in the use of modifiers in sentences

Meeting INDIVIDUAL NEEDS

ENGLISH-LANGUAGE LEARNERS

Spanish. Spanish speakers may need extra practice adding *–er* and *–est* to words to form comparatives and superlatives because suffixes are not used to form most comparatives or superlatives in Spanish. For example, the English words *fast, faster, fastest* are translated in Spanish as *rápido* (fast), *más rápido* (more fast), and *el más rápido* (the most fast).

---

4. badly
5. really
6. well
7. really
8. well
9. bad, well
10. good

4. By the end of May, Skipper thought about giving up because he was doing so *bad*.
5. He would have felt *real* bad about failing, especially because Dad had lent him money to open the shop.
6. Then school let out, and within days, business was going *good*.
7. In-line skates and skateboards started selling *real* well; in fact, by the end of summer, Skipper was able to pay Dad back.
8. When school started, skateboards kept selling *good*, but total sales fell somewhat.
9. Skipper's receipts looked rather *badly* during the fall, but thanks to Christmas and Hanukkah, all went *good* in December.
10. By then, Skipper was a veteran of seasonal business cycles; he wasn't fazed when January's receipts weren't as *well* as those of other months.

Comparison of Modifiers

Modifiers—adjectives and adverbs—may be used to make comparisons.

ADJECTIVES   Juan is nearly as **tall** as I.
Robert is **taller** than I.
Of all the players, Antoine is the **tallest**.

ADVERBS   No other land animal can run as **fast** as the cheetah.
The cheetah can run **faster** than any other land animal.
Of all land animals, the cheetah can run the **fastest**.

19b. Modifiers change form to show comparison.

The three degrees of comparison are *positive, comparative,* and *superlative*.

Positive	Comparative	Superlative
low	lower	lowest
fearful	more fearful	most fearful
good	better	best
promptly	more promptly	most promptly
badly	worse	worst

620 **Chapter 19** Using Modifiers Correctly

RESOURCES

Comparison of Modifiers

Practice

- *Grammar, Usage, and Mechanics,* pp. 201, 202, 203–204, 205–207
- *Language Workshop CD-ROM,* Lessons 16, 17

Regular Comparison

(1) Most one-syllable modifiers form the comparative degree by adding –er and the superlative degree by adding –est.

Positive	Comparative	Superlative
thin	thinn**er**	thinn**est**
safe	saf**er**	saf**est**
dry	dri**er**	dri**est**
fast	fast**er**	fast**est**
soon	soon**er**	soon**est**

(2) Two-syllable modifiers may form the comparative degree by adding –er and the superlative degree by adding –est, or they may form the comparative degree by using *more* and the superlative degree by using *most*.

Positive	Comparative	Superlative
lovely	lovel**ier**	lovel**iest**
tricky	trick**ier**	trick**iest**
awkward	**more** awkward	**most** awkward
firmly	**more** firmly	**most** firmly
rapid	**more** rapid	**most** rapid

(3) Modifiers that have three or more syllables form the comparative degree by using *more* and the superlative degree by using *most*.

Positive	Comparative	Superlative
enthusiastic	**more** enthusiastic	**most** enthusiastic
fortunate	**more** fortunate	**most** fortunate
predictably	**more** predictably	**most** predictably
effectively	**more** effectively	**most** effectively
significantly	**more** significantly	**most** significantly

Reference Note

For guidelines on how to spell **comparative and superlative forms** correctly, see page 623.

STYLE TIP

Many two-syllable modifiers may correctly form the comparative and superlative degrees by either adding –er and –est or using *more* and *most*.

If adding –er or –est makes a word sound awkward, use *more* or *most* instead.

AWKWARD
  specialer

BETTER
  more special

HELP

A dictionary will tell you when a word forms its comparative or superlative form in some way other than by adding –er or –est or *more* or *most*. Look in a dictionary if you are not sure whether a word has irregular comparative or superlative forms or whether you need to change the spelling of a word before adding –er or –est.

(4) To show a decrease in the qualities they express, modifiers form the comparative degree by using *less* and the superlative degree by using *least*.

Positive	Comparative	Superlative
calm	less calm	least calm
frequent	less frequent	least frequent
helpful	less helpful	least helpful
slowly	less slowly	least slowly
courageously	less courageously	least courageously

Irregular Comparison

The comparative and superlative degrees of some modifiers are irregular in form.

Positive	Comparative	Superlative
bad	worse	worst
badly	worse	worst
ill	worse	worst
good	better	best
well	better	best
little	less	least
many	more	most
much	more	most
far	farther *or* further	farthest *or* furthest

TIPS & TRICKS

The word *little* also has regular comparative and superlative forms: *littler, littlest*. These forms are used to describe physical size (the *littlest* toad). The forms *less* and *least* are used to describe an amount (*less* money).

NOTE Do not add *–er*, *–est* or *more*, *most* to irregularly compared forms. For example, use *worse*, not *worser* or *more worse*.

Exercise 4 Writing the Comparative and Superlative Forms of Modifiers

Write the comparative and superlative forms of each of the following modifiers.

EXAMPLE 1. skillful
1. more (less) skillful; most (least) skillful

622 Chapter 19 Using Modifiers Correctly

Learning for Life

Continued on pp. 623–624

Comparison Shopping. Ask students if they have heard an expression such as "That's a good value at that price." Explain to students that people use comparisons to make decisions every day. At a supermarket, for example, shoppers often compare prices of similar products to determine which product offers the best value. Write on the chalkboard the following scenario:

Jorge is shopping for a box of Shop Smart Wheat Puffs cereal. A 12-ounce box sells

1. loudly
2. bad
3. humid
4. efficiently
5. silly
6. good
7. likely
8. well
9. fundamental
10. clearly
11. dark
12. wild
13. deep
14. heavy
15. pretty
16. healthy
17. attractive
18. intelligent
19. eccentric
20. friendly

Use of Comparative and Superlative Forms

19c. Use the comparative degree when comparing two things. Use the superlative degree when comparing more than two.

COMPARATIVE Omaha is **larger** than Lincoln.
Roberto is a **better** typist than I am.
Which of these two shirts is **less expensive**?

SUPERLATIVE Omaha is the **largest** city in Nebraska.
Roberto is the **best** typist in the class.
Which of these four shirts is **least expensive**?

19d. Include the word *other* or *else* when comparing one member of a group with the rest of the group.

ILLOGICAL Rhode Island is smaller than any state in the Union. [Rhode Island is a state in the Union. Logically, Rhode Island cannot be smaller than itself.]
LOGICAL Rhode Island is smaller than any **other** state in the Union.

ILLOGICAL Stan is taller than anyone in his class. [Stan is a member of his class. Logically, Stan cannot be taller than himself.]
LOGICAL Stan is taller than anyone **else** in his class.

19e. Avoid using double comparisons.

A *double comparison* is incorrect because it contains both *–er* and *more* (*less*) or both *–est* and *most* (*least*).

STYLE TIP

In informal situations, the superlative degree is commonly used to compare two things.

EXAMPLES
May the best team [of two] win.
Put your best foot forward.

In formal speaking and writing, however, the comparative degree should be used when two things are being compared.

Exercise 4 Writing the Comparative and Superlative Forms of Modifiers

ANSWERS
The following answers indicate an *increase* in the qualities that the modifiers compare. Remind students that to show a *decrease* in the qualities, they would write *less* or *least* before the positive form of each modifier.

1. more loudly, most loudly
2. worse, worst
3. more humid, most humid
4. more efficiently, most efficiently
5. sillier, silliest *or* more silly, most silly
6. better, best
7. likelier, likeliest *or* more likely, most likely
8. better, best
9. more fundamental, most fundamental
10. more clearly, most clearly
11. darker, darkest
12. wilder, wildest
13. deeper, deepest
14. heavier, heaviest *or* more heavy, most heavy
15. prettier, prettiest *or* more pretty, most pretty
16. healthier, healthiest *or* more healthy, most healthy
17. more attractive, most attractive
18. more intelligent, most intelligent
19. more eccentric, most eccentric
20. friendlier, friendliest *or* more friendly, most friendly

---

for $1.99. A 16-ounce box sells for $2.35. Jorge is looking for the better value. Which box should Jorge purchase?

Ask students to help Jorge determine the better value. If students have difficulty, suggest the following steps:

1. Find the price per ounce for the 12-ounce box.
   [$1.99 ÷ 12 = $0.1658]
2. Find the price per ounce for the 16-ounce box.

Meeting INDIVIDUAL NEEDS

LEARNERS HAVING DIFFICULTY

To help students remember when to use comparative or superlative forms of modifiers, share this mnemonic device:

The two-letter suffix *–er* is added to a modifier to compare two items (for example, Sara is *younger* than Ben). The three-letter suffix *–est* is added to a modifier to compare three or more items (for example, Sara is the *youngest* of the three children).

USAGE

Reference Note

For a discussion of **standard** and **nonstandard English,** see page 634.

NONSTANDARD	The second movie was more funnier than the first one.
STANDARD	The second movie was **funnier** than the first one.
NONSTANDARD	What is the most deadliest snake?
STANDARD	What is the **deadliest** snake?
STANDARD	What is the **most deadly** snake?
NONSTANDARD	Pancho is the least dullest debater.
STANDARD	Pancho is the **least dull** debater.

19f. Be sure your comparisons are clear.

When making comparisons, indicate clearly what items are being compared.

UNCLEAR	The climate of Arizona is drier than South Carolina. [The sentence incorrectly compares a climate to a state.]
CLEAR	The climate of Arizona is drier than **the climate** of South Carolina.
CLEAR	The climate of Arizona is drier than **that** of South Carolina.
UNCLEAR	Fresh vegetables at a farmers' market are sometimes lower in price than a grocery. [The sentence incorrectly compares vegetables to a grocery.]
CLEAR	Fresh vegetables at a farmers' market are sometimes lower in price than **those at** a grocery.

State both parts of a comparison completely if there is any chance of misunderstanding.

Reference Note

For information on **irregular comparisons,** see page 622.

UNCLEAR	We know her better than Dena.
CLEAR	We know her better than **we know** Dena.
CLEAR	We know her better than Dena **does.**

Exercise 5 Using Modifiers Correctly

Most of the following sentences contain an error in the use of modifiers. Identify each error, and then write the correct form. If a sentence is already correct, write *C*.   Answers may vary.

EXAMPLE   1. Of the Ganges and Amazon rivers, which is more longer?
1. more longer—longer

1. Laurie is ~~more~~ friendlier than she used to be.
2. Which of the four seasons do you like ~~better~~?   2. best
3. I never saw a leader ~~more~~ stronger than Chief Billie of the Seminoles.

624 Chapter 19 Using Modifiers Correctly

Learning for Life

[$2.35 ÷ 16 = $0.1468]

3. Compare the results. [*According to the price per ounce, the 16-ounce box is the better value.*]

Remind students that the comparative form—*better*—is used in this scenario because Jorge is comparing the prices of *two* boxes of cereal.

4. Margaret Mead was one of the world's most famous anthropologists. **4. C**
5. Of the two colleges that I am considering, Spelman College in Atlanta looks more interesting. **5. C**
6. Anika arrived earlier than anyone in her family. **6. else**
7. Muscles in the leg are stronger than the arm. **7. those in**
8. Denver's elevation is higher than that of any major city in the United States. **8. other**
9. I wrote to Sally more often than Carlos. **9. I wrote to**
10. This year's drought was much worse than last year. **10. year's.**

Review A — Correcting Errors in the Use of Modifiers

Each of the sentences in the following paragraph contains at least one error in the use of adjectives and adverbs. Find each error, and supply the necessary correction. **Answers may vary.**

EXAMPLE   [1] Of the four pots shown on this page, which do you think is the more delicate one?

1. more delicate—most delicate

[1] Among ceramic artists of the Southwest, perhaps the most ~~famousest~~ are the four women who made these coiled pots, using techniques handed down for more than 2,000 years. **1. famous** [2] Lucy Lewis's Acoma pottery is more delicate than any Southwest pottery. **2. other** [3] Lewis used the ~~most~~ whitest clay. [4] Because this clay is scarce, the walls of her pots are the ~~thinner~~ of them all. **4. thinnest** [5] Maria Martinez's San Ildefonso pottery is ~~more~~ thicker and heavier than Lewis. **5. 's** [6] Of all the Southwest pottery styles, Martinez's black-on-black pottery may be the ~~most~~ best known. [7] No color is used, but the background areas of the black pot are burnished slowly with a small smooth stone until they become quite a bit ~~more~~ shinier than the main design. **8. heavier** [8] Many of Margaret Tafoya's Santa Clara pots are also solid black, but of these two kinds of black pottery, the Santa Clara pots are the heaviest. [9] The bold, colorful Hopi pots of Fannie Nampeyo may be the ~~more~~ impressive achievement of all, because Nampeyo's family had to re-create the technique by studying shards of ancient pots found in 1895. **9. most** [10] The pottery by these four women is ~~beautifuller~~ than many other artists. **10. more beautiful / that of**

Dangling Modifiers

Rule 19i (pp. 626–627)

OBJECTIVE

- To revise sentences by correcting dangling modifiers

USAGE

STYLE TIP

A dangling modifier may occur when a sentence is in the passive voice. Rewriting sentences in the active voice not only eliminates many dangling modifiers but also makes your writing more interesting and lively. If you frequently find dangling modifiers in your writing, concentrate on staying in the active voice.

PASSIVE VOICE
Reaching as high as I could, the ball was caught just before it reached the fence. [*Reaching as high as I could* is a dangling modifier.]

ACTIVE VOICE
Reaching as high as I could, I caught the ball just before it reached the fence. [*Reaching as high as I could* modifies *I*.]

Reference Note
For information on the **understood subject**, see page 447.

Dangling Modifiers

19g. Avoid using dangling modifiers.

A modifying word, phrase, or clause that does not clearly and sensibly modify a word or word group in a sentence is a ***dangling modifier.*** To correct a dangling modifier, add or replace words to make the meaning clear and logical.

DANGLING	Frustrated, all of the scientists' data were reexamined. [Were the scientists' data frustrated?]
CLEAR	Frustrated, the **scientists** reexamined all of their data.
DANGLING	Looking back over my shoulder, the team went into a huddle. [Was the team looking back over my shoulder?]
CLEAR	Looking back over my shoulder, **I** saw the team going into a huddle.
DANGLING	While riding to the store, my front bicycle tire went flat. [Was the bicycle tire riding to the store?]
CLEAR	While **I** was riding to the store, my front bicycle tire went flat.
DANGLING	To qualify for the Olympics, many trial heats must be won. [Do trial heats qualify for the Olympics?]
CLEAR	To qualify for the Olympics, a **runner** must win many trial heats.

or

Before a runner may qualify for the Olympics, **he or she** must win many trial heats.

When a modifying participial or infinitive phrase or a clause comes at the beginning of a sentence as in the examples above, the phrase is followed by a comma. Immediately after that comma should come the word or word group that the phrase modifies.

NOTE A sentence may appear to have a dangling modifier when *you* is the understood subject. In such cases, the modifier is not dangling; it is modifying the understood subject.

EXAMPLE   To assemble the bookcase, (you) read the instructions.

Exercise 6   Correcting Dangling Modifiers

The following sentences contain dangling modifiers. Revise each sentence so that its meaning is clear and correct.

Chapter 19   Using Modifiers Correctly

RESOURCES
Dangling Modifiers
Practice
- *Grammar, Usage, and Mechanics,* p. 208
- *Language Workshop CD-ROM,* Lesson 18

Using Modifiers Correctly

EXAMPLE 1. Running through the park, the lake looked cool and inviting.

1. Running through the park, I thought the lake looked cool and inviting.

or

As I ran through the park, I thought the lake looked cool and inviting.

1. Hurrying through the last fifty pages, the book was fascinating.
2. Being a novice basketball player, my dribbling needs work.
3. When leaving the train, the station is on the right.
4. Exhausted by the hard work, a long nap sounded good.
5. Driving through the Rockies, the landscape was magnificent.
6. Having overslept, my exam results were poor.
7. Although excited, sleep came easily.
8. As a new student, it was difficult at first to find my way around.
9. To repair an appliance, experience is helpful.
10. Looking at recent consumer surveys, more Americans are working at home.

Misplaced Modifiers

19h. Avoid using misplaced modifiers.

A word, phrase, or clause that seems to modify the wrong word or word group in a sentence is a *misplaced modifier.* Place modifying words, phrases, and clauses as near as possible to the words they modify.

Misplaced One-Word Modifiers

MISPLACED   Alone, thoughts of returning soon to earth comforted the astronaut living in the space station. [Were the thoughts alone?]

CLEAR   Thoughts of returning soon to earth comforted the astronaut living **alone** in the space station.

MISPLACED   Exhausted, a good night's rest was what the hikers needed. [Was a good night's rest exhausted?]

CLEAR   A good night's rest was what the **exhausted** hikers needed.

HELP

Although two revisions for the example in Exercise 6 are shown, you need to give only one for each item.

Reference Note

For more about **active voice** and **passive voice**, see page 601.

19j

Exercise 6 — Correcting Dangling Modifiers

POSSIBLE ANSWERS

1. Hurrying through the last fifty pages, Mary described the book as fascinating.
2. Being a novice basketball player, I need to work more on dribbling.
3. When you leave the train, the station is on your right.
4. Exhausted by the hard work, we thought a long nap sounded good.
5. While we were driving through the Rockies, the landscape was magnificent.
6. Because I had overslept, my exam results were poor.
7. Although excited, the children fell asleep easily.
8. When I was a new student, it was difficult at first to find my way around.
9. If someone is going to repair an appliance, experience is helpful.
10. Looking at recent consumer surveys, I discovered that more Americans are working at home.

Misplaced Modifiers

Rule 19j (pp. 627–632)

OBJECTIVES

- To revise sentences by correcting misplaced one-word and phrase modifiers
- To revise sentences by correcting misplaced clause modifiers

---

RESOURCES

Misplaced Modifiers
Practice
- *Grammar, Usage, and Mechanics,* pp. 209, 210–211
- *Language Workshop CD-ROM,* Lesson 18

TEACHING TIP

Activity. To show students the importance of the correct placement of modifiers, write on separate strips of paper the following word groups:

climbing a tree
containing three tiny eggs
Sandra discovered
a bird's nest

Then, tape to the chalkboard the strip showing *Sandra discovered.* Call on volunteers to tape the remaining strips wherever they think appropriate to form a complete sentence. Then, have students answer the following questions about the sentence:

1. Does the sentence clearly state who or what is climbing the tree?

2. Does the sentence clearly state who or what contains three tiny eggs?

If the answer to either question is no, call on other volunteers to rearrange the strips, and then repeat the questions above. Guide students to a sensible arrangement of the word groups (for example, *Climbing a tree, Sandra discovered a bird's nest containing three tiny eggs*).

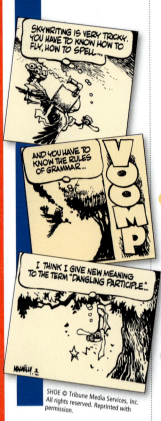

SHOE © Tribune Media Services, Inc. All rights reserved. Reprinted with permission.

Reference Note

For a discussion of the different kinds of **phrases,** see "Chapter 14: The Phrase." For information on **using commas to set off modifying phrases,** see page 704.

Be sure to place modifiers correctly to state clearly the meaning you intend.

EXAMPLES **Only** on Saturdays, my brother and I watch cartoons for an hour. [My brother and I watch on Saturdays, not on any other days.]

On Saturdays, my **only** brother and I watch cartoons for an hour. [I have no other brothers.]

On Saturdays, my brother and I watch **only** cartoons for an hour. [My brother and I watch nothing but cartoons.]

On Saturdays, my brother and I watch cartoons for **only** an hour. [My brother and I watch for no more than an hour.]

NOTE One-word modifiers such as *almost, even, hardly, just, merely, nearly, not,* and *only* generally should be placed directly before the words they modify.

MISPLACED According to the club's minutes, all of the members were not at the meeting on Friday.

CLEAR According to the club's minutes, **not** all of the members were at the meeting on Friday.

MISPLACED Before 6:00 P.M. a movie ticket only costs $3.50.
CLEAR Before 6:00 P.M. a movie ticket costs **only** $3.50.

Misplaced Phrase Modifiers

Adjective phrases, adverb phrases, and verbal phrases should be placed near the words they modify.

MISPLACED I'm lucky because I feel that I can always talk about my problems with my dad. [Does *with my dad* modify *talk* or *problems*?]

CLEAR I'm lucky because I feel that I can always talk **with my dad** about my problems.

MISPLACED Early Spanish explorers encountered a hostile environment searching for gold in the Americas. [Does *searching for gold in the Americas* modify *explorers* or *environment*?]

CLEAR **Searching for gold in the Americas,** early Spanish explorers encountered a hostile environment.

MISPLACED   You will need a crescent wrench to assemble the bookshelf.
             [Does *to assemble the bookshelf* modify *You* or *wrench*?]

CLEAR   **To assemble the bookshelf,** you will need a crescent wrench.

Exercise 7 Revising Sentences by Correcting Misplaced One-Word and Phrase Modifiers

The following sentences contain misplaced one-word and phrase modifiers. Revise each sentence so that its meaning is clear and correct.

EXAMPLE   1. Our cat was waiting on the front porch for us to come home patiently.
           1. *Our cat was waiting patiently on the front porch for us to come home.*

1. Rosa Parks calmly refused to move to the back of the bus with quiet dignity.
2. I found a huge boulder taking a shortcut through the woods.
3. On one of his fruit trees, Mr. Tate noticed some caterpillars.
4. Our ancestors hunted deer, bison, and other large animals with weapons made of wood and stone.
5. Flying over the bridge, Missie spotted a blue heron.
6. We noticed several signs advertising the new theme park riding down the highway.
7. We could see corn growing from our car window.
8. Barking wildly and straining at the chain, the letter carrier was forced to retreat from the dog.
9. The softball team almost practices every afternoon.
10. He recounted an incident about a nuclear chain reaction during his chemistry lecture.
11. Pierre saw a Great Dane cycling through the park.
12. Tired from their hiking, we offered shelter to the backpackers.
13. Stress has almost caused all of his hair to turn gray.
14. She had a raincoat over her arm with a blue lining.
15. The two women hurried before the bus's departure to get a snack from the vending machine.
16. I have nearly read all of his books.
17. The boy ate all the yogurt with red sneakers.
18. Jan watched a deer sitting in a chair on the porch.
19. They listened to the symphony standing in the mezzanine of the auditorium.
20. Running, the course seemed very long to the athlete.

Misplaced Modifiers   629

Exercise 7 Revising Sentences by Correcting Misplaced One-Word and Phrase Modifiers

POSSIBLE ANSWERS

1. With quiet dignity, Rosa Parks calmly refused to move to the back of the bus.
2. Taking a shortcut through the woods, I found a huge boulder.
3. Mr. Tate noticed some caterpillars on one of his fruit trees.
4. With weapons made of wood and stone, our ancestors hunted deer, bison, and other large animals.
5. Missie spotted a blue heron flying over the bridge.
6. Riding down the highway, we noticed several signs advertising the new theme park.
7. From our car window we could see corn growing.
8. Barking wildly and straining at the chain, the dog forced the letter carrier to retreat.
9. The softball team practices almost every afternoon.
10. During his chemistry lecture he recounted an incident about a nuclear chain reaction.
11. Cycling through the park, Pierre saw a Great Dane.
12. We offered shelter to the backpackers, who were tired from their hiking.
13. Stress has caused almost all of his hair to turn gray.
14. Over her arm she had a raincoat with a blue lining.
15. The two women hurried to get a snack from the vending machine before the bus's departure.
16. I have read nearly all of his books.
17. The boy with red sneakers ate all the yogurt.
18. Sitting in a chair on the porch, Jan watched a deer.
19. Standing in the mezzanine of the auditorium, they listened to the symphony.
20. The course seemed very long to the running athlete.

USAGE

Misplaced Modifiers   629

Misplaced Clause Modifiers

Adjective and adverb clauses should be placed near the words they modify.

MISPLACED	Each player on the team will receive a trophy that wins the tournament.
CLEAR	Each player on the team **that wins the tournament** will receive a trophy.
MISPLACED	The bowl slipped off the table, which was full of gravy, and broke.
CLEAR	The bowl, **which was full of gravy,** slipped off the table and broke.
MISPLACED	The spelunkers saw many bats hanging upside down from their roosts while they were exploring the cave.
CLEAR	**While they were exploring the cave,** the spelunkers saw many bats hanging upside down from their roosts.
MISPLACED	Kirstie couldn't attend the farewell party for her nephew who was moving to El Paso because she was ill.
CLEAR	Because she was ill, Kirstie couldn't attend the farewell party for her nephew **who was moving to El Paso.**

Exercise 8 Revising Sentences by Correcting Misplaced Clause Modifiers

The following sentences contain misplaced clause modifiers. Revise each sentence so that its meaning is clear and correct.

Answers may vary.

EXAMPLE 1. Because he has allergies, Dr. Crane gives our pet beagle a shot once a month.

1. Because our pet beagle has allergies, Dr. Crane gives him a shot once a month.

1. I gave some of the baseball cards ~~to my cousin~~ that I had acquired over the years. **1. my cousin**
2. The plane landed safely on the runway ~~that had the engine trouble~~. **2. that had the engine trouble**
3. That picture was hanging on the wall ~~which we bought in Canada~~. **3. , which we bought in Canada,**
4. They took the backpack to the manager's office ~~which appeared to be lost~~. **4. , which appeared to be lost,**
5. Jan showed the rooms to her visitors ~~that she had painted~~. **5. that she had painted**
6. That is a good plan for meeting the deadline next Friday ~~that you have proposed~~. **6. that you have proposed**

Reference Note
For a discussion of the different kinds of **clauses,** see Chapter 15. For information on **using commas to set off modifying clauses,** see page 704.

COMPUTER TIP
A spell-checker can easily find nonstandard forms such as *baddest, expensiver,* and *mostest.* However, you will need to examine placement of modifiers yourself.

MINI-LESSON

Comma Usage. You may want to familiarize students with the following rules governing the use of commas with modifying phrases and clauses.

1. Use a comma after an introductory modifying phrase or clause (except for short prepositional phrases).

   Example: **Filled with a sense of pride,** Miguel unveiled his work of art.

7. She sang a song titled "On the Shore" at the talent show, which she had written herself. 7. , which she had written herself,
8. I adopted a kitten at the animal shelter that needed a home.
9. I served dinner to a friend that I cooked myself.
10. The plate fell on the floor that was full of baked beans.

8. At the animal shelter
9. that I cooked myself
10. that was full of baked beans

Review B — Correcting Dangling and Misplaced Modifiers

The following sentences contain dangling and misplaced modifiers. Revise each sentence so that its meaning is clear and correct.

EXAMPLE 1. Hurrying, my books slipped out of my hands and fell down the stairs.
1. As I was hurrying, my books slipped out of my hands and fell down the stairs.

1. Caught in the net, escape was impossible.
2. Looking through the telescope, the moon seemed enormous.
3. While out running, his mouth got dry.
4. The ocean came into view going around the bend.
5. Doing a few tap-dance steps, the wooden floor got scratched.
6. Built on a steep hillside overlooking the sea, we found the ocean view breathtaking.
7. I mentioned the book to my sister Roseanne that I recently read.
8. After finishing the housework, the room almost sparkled.
9. To make manicotti, pasta is stuffed with ricotta cheese.
10. Glenda sang a song about finding true love in a high, clear voice.
11. Looking at her passport, there was no visa stamp.
12. Running up and down the bungalow walls, she saw dozens of mice.
13. While standing in front of the fun-house mirror, her reflection was tall and thin.
14. Painted, we thought the house looked much better.
15. Singing in the shower, the hot water ran out.
16. Reaching for the telephone, the books toppled and fell to the floor.
17. Lauren told the interviewer about the time she performed for the president when she was interviewed.
18. While driving to work, the radio broke.
19. Songbirds have been coming to the birdfeeders, which migrate this time of year.
20. Sitting in the freezer, she saw two kinds of frozen yogurt.

Review B — Correcting Dangling and Misplaced Modifiers
POSSIBLE ANSWERS
1. For the fish caught in the net, escape was impossible.
2. Seen through the telescope, the moon seemed enormous.
3. His mouth got dry while he was out running.
4. As we went around the bend, the ocean came into view.
5. The wooden floor got scratched when we did a few tap-dance steps.
6. From the house, built on a steep hillside overlooking the sea, we found the ocean view breathtaking.
7. I mentioned to my sister Roseanne the book that I recently read.
8. After they finished the housework, the room almost sparkled.
9. To make manicotti, cooks stuff pasta with ricotta cheese.
10. In a high, clear voice, Glenda sang a song about finding true love.
11. Looking at her passport, she saw that there was no visa stamp.
12. She saw dozens of mice running up and down the bungalow walls.
13. Her reflection in the fun-house mirror was tall and thin.
14. We thought the house looked much better painted.
15. The hot water ran out while I was singing in the shower.
16. As she reached for the telephone, the books toppled and fell to the floor.
17. When she was interviewed, Lauren told the interviewer about the time she performed for the president.
18. The radio broke while I was driving to work.
19. Songbirds, which migrate this time of year, have been coming to the birdfeeders.
20. She saw two kinds of frozen yogurt sitting in the freezer.

---

2. Use commas to set off a modifying phrase or clause that provides nonessential information.

Example: My sister Eileen, **who is a vegetarian,** makes delicious dishes with tofu.

To reinforce students' understanding of these rules, you may want to use the first five items in **Exercise 8** as guided practice. For additional information, refer students to **Chapter 15: The Clause** and **Chapter 22: Punctuation.**

Review C — Correcting Errors in the Use of Modifiers

POSSIBLE ANSWERS

1. Before the 1800s, much about life in ancient Egypt was unknown because nobody could read Egyptian hieroglyphics.
2. Then, this black stone found in the Nile Delta gave Egyptology more publicity than it had ever had before.
3. Archaeologists called the slab, found in 1799 near a village called Rosetta, the Rosetta Stone.
4. The slab was inscribed across its polished surface with three bands of writing, each in a different language: hieroglyphics on the top, another unknown language in the middle, and Greek on the bottom.
5. C
6. Full of excitement, the archaeologists hoped that they could use the Greek part to decipher the hieroglyphics.
7. Progress in translating the individual hieroglyphics, however, went very slowly.
8. Until this time, it had been thought that each of the symbols stood for a whole word.
9. However, Jean François Champollion, a French scholar working on the Rosetta Stone, wondered why it took more hieroglyphic symbols than Greek words to write the same message.
10. He correctly guessed that certain symbols stand for parts of words, and after working hard for twenty years, he proved that many of the signs stand for sounds.

HELP—
In Review C, you may need to rearrange or add words to make the meaning clear.

Review C — Correcting Errors in the Use of Modifiers

Most of the sentences in the following paragraph contain at least one error in the use of modifiers. Revise each sentence according to the rules of standard, formal English. If a sentence is already correct, write *C*.

EXAMPLE [1] Egyptian priests inscribed a decree on a black stone honoring Ptolemy V, a king of Egypt (203–181 B.C.).
1. *Egyptian priests inscribed on a black stone a decree honoring Ptolemy V, a king of Egypt (203–181 B.C.).*

[1] Much about life in ancient Egypt before the 1800s was unknown because nobody could read Egyptian hieroglyphics. [2] Then, this black stone found in the Nile Delta gave Egyptology the most publicity than it had ever had before. [3] Found in 1799 near a village called Rosetta, archaeologists called the slab the Rosetta Stone. [4] The slab was inscribed with three bands across its polished surface of writing, each in a different language: hieroglyphics on the top, another unknown language in the middle, and Greek on the bottom. [5] Scholars could read the Greek writing, which stated that each of the three bands contained the same decree in honor of Ptolemy V. [6] Full of excitement, it was hoped by archaeologists that they could use the Greek part to decipher the hieroglyphics. [7] Progress in translating the individual hieroglyphics, however, went real slowly. [8] It had been thought that each of the symbols stood for a whole word until this time. [9] However, a French scholar working on the Rosetta Stone named Jean François Champollion wondered why it took more hieroglyphic symbols than Greek words to write the same message. [10] He correctly guessed that certain symbols stand for parts of words, and after working hard for twenty years, many of the signs were proved to stand for sounds.

CHAPTER 19

Chapter Review

A. Correcting Errors in the Use of the Comparative and Superlative Forms

Each of the following sentences contains an error in the use of modifiers. Identify each error, and then write the correct form.

Answers may vary.

1. I was ~~more~~ hungrier than I thought, so I ate three plums.
2. He was the ~~more~~ able and intelligent of the three job applicants. — **2. most**
3. Was Hitler ~~notoriouser~~ than Stalin? — **3. more notorious**
4. John, Richard's twin brother, was ~~the oldest~~ by three minutes. — **4. older**
5. After Diego had started lifting weights, he bragged that he was stronger than anyone in town. — **5. else**
6. People who live along this road complain because it is the ~~worse~~ road in the entire township. — **6. worst**
7. Both Floyd and his brother are landscape designers who are in demand throughout the state, but Floyd is ~~best~~ known in this area. — **7. better**
8. After the band practiced, it sounded ~~more~~ better.
9. When I had a choice of strawberry or vanilla, I took vanilla because I liked it ~~best~~. — **9. better**
10. Looking across the water at sunset, you can see the ~~beautifullest~~ view you can imagine. — **10. most beautiful**

B. Revising Sentences by Correcting Dangling and Misplaced Modifiers

HELP

In Part B of the Chapter Review, you may have to add or delete some words. Be sure to use commas where they are needed to set off the introductory and interrupting modifiers.

Each of the following sentences contains a dangling or misplaced modifier. Write each sentence, arranging the words so that the meaning is logical and clear. *Answers may vary.*

11. Yipping and running in circles, they saw that the dogs could herd the sheep into the pen.
12. The winners marched off the platform carrying trophies.
13. A police officer warned students who drive too fast about accidents during the defensive-driving class.
14. After escaping from slavery, the importance of education was often stressed by Frederick Douglass.
15. We went to visit my grandmother, who used to be a history teacher at my school yesterday.

Chapter Review
B. Revising Sentences by Correcting Dangling and Misplaced Modifiers

ANSWERS continued

16. While he was climbing the stairs, his glasses fell off.
17. Using a telephoto lens, Maria took a close-up photograph of a lion.
18. I see a small bird nesting in a tree outside my window.
19. A young woman wearing a suit and hat knocked on the door.
20. As we walked in the sunshine, it felt warm to us.

Chapter Review
C. Revising Sentences by Correcting Unclear Comparison and Incorrect, Misplaced, and Dangling Modifiers

POSSIBLE ANSWERS

21. Seeing that no damage had been done, onlookers drove away in opposite directions.
22. Working long hours and taking few vacations, he achieved the longed-for success after many years.
23. The temperature in Houston is higher than the temperature in Chicago.
24. Looking through a telescope, we saw the Cliffs of Dover.
25. The branches of the tree that we planted hung over the fence.
26. Walking very carefully over the uneven cobblestones, the elderly woman made her way from one end of the lane to the other.
27. The gift was more costly than I had expected it to be.
28. The glass, which was full of cranberry juice, fell onto the floor.
29. I quickly grew frustrated with the balking mule.
30. Michael hoped that his time on the sprint was faster than Patrick's.

---

16. Climbing the stairs, his glasses fell off.
17. Maria took a close-up photograph of a lion with a telephoto lens.
18. Nesting in a tree outside my window, I see a small bird.
19. A young woman knocked on the door wearing a suit and hat.
20. Walking in the sunshine, it felt warm to us.

C. Revising Sentences by Correcting Unclear Comparisons and Incorrect, Misplaced, and Dangling Modifiers

Most of the following sentences contain an unclear comparison, an incorrect form of a modifier, a misplaced modifier, or a dangling modifier. Write each sentence, correcting the error. If a sentence is already correct, write C. *Answers may vary.*

21. the onlookers/their cars
22. the director achieved/for
23. the temperature in
24. As we looked
26. ly
27. costly
29. balking
30. 's time

21. Seeing that no damage had been done, ~~their cars~~ drove away in opposite directions.
22. Working long hours and taking few vacations, the success that he had longed for ~~came to him after~~ many years.
23. The temperature in Houston is higher than Chicago.
24. ~~Looking~~ through a telescope, the Cliffs of Dover came into view.
25. The branches of the tree hung over the fence that we planted.
26. Walking very careful over the uneven cobblestones, the elderly woman made her way from one end of the lane to the other.
27. The gift was more ~~costlier~~ than I had expected it to be.
28. The glass fell onto the floor, which was full of cranberry juice.
29. ~~Balking~~, I quickly grew frustrated with the mule.
30. Michael hoped that his time on the sprint was faster than Patrick.

RESOURCES

Using Modifiers Correctly

Review
- *Grammar, Usage, and Mechanics,* pp. 212, 213, 214, 215, 216

Assessment
- *Assessment Package*
  —*Chapter Tests,* Ch. 19
  —*Chapter Tests in Standardized Test Formats,* Ch. 19
- *Test Generator (One-Stop Planner CD-ROM)*

Writing Application
Using Comparison in a Consumer Guide

Comparative and Superlative Degrees   You and your sister Charlotte plan to buy a piece of audio equipment together. You have found a magazine article comparing several brands and showing the information in a big table. However, because Charlotte is visually impaired, the table can't help her decide. She asks you to narrow the choices to four brands, and then to write and record on audiotape a short comparison of their prices and features.

Prewriting   Find a magazine article that contains a table comparing different kinds of audio equipment. Study the table, and list the features that you think would be most important. Then, choose four products that seem acceptable, and jot down some comparisons.

Writing   As you write your first draft, carefully select comparative and superlative modifiers so that your explanation is not confusing. Tell why you would eliminate certain models from consideration. Include each of the degrees of comparison: positive, comparative, and superlative.

Revising   Ask a classmate to evaluate the clarity of your comparison. Add or revise details of the comparison to eliminate confusion.

Publishing   Using your textbook, check to be sure that you have used adjectives and adverbs correctly. Proofread your comparison for any errors in grammar, usage, and punctuation. Post the completed paragraphs on the class bulletin board or Web page, or you may want to collect them and bind them in a booklet titled *An Audio Equipment Consumer Guide*.

Chapter Review   **635**

Writing Application
(p. 635)

OBJECTIVE
- To write and record on audiotape a comparison-contrast study, using positive, comparative, and superlative degrees of modifiers

Writing Application
Tip. Before students begin the writing stage of this activity, you may want to discuss with them the two methods for organizing comparison-contrast paragraphs: the block method and the point-by-point method. For examples of each method, refer students to **Chapter 2: Exploring Comparisons and Contrasts.**

Scoring Rubric.   While you will want to pay particular attention to students' use of modifiers, you will also want to evaluate overall writing performance. You may want to give a split score to indicate development and clarity of the composition as well as usage skills.

Critical Thinking
Analysis.   In the prewriting stage of this activity, before students examine the tables from the consumer magazines, have the class brainstorm features of a piece of audio equipment that would be particularly important to Charlotte, who is visually impaired.

USAGE

RESOURCES
Writing Application
Extension
- *Grammar, Usage, and Mechanics*, p. 219
- *Language Workshop CD-ROM*, Lessons 16–18

Writing Application
Alignments
TEKS 1A, 2A, 2E, 3B, 3D, 13B
TAAS W1, W3, W6
English II End-of-Course 4, 5, 6

Texas Resources
- *One-Stop Planner CD-ROM*

Chapter Review   **635**

CHAPTER 20

A Glossary of Usage
Common Usage Problems

PREVIEWING THE CHAPTER

- This chapter includes a glossary that shows how to identify and correct many common errors in English usage, a section that focuses on the double negative, and discussion of the importance of using nonsexist language.

- The chapter concludes with a **Chapter Review,** which includes a **Writing Application** feature that asks students to create a descriptive flier using correct, standard English.

- For help in integrating this chapter with composition chapters, use the **Teaching Strands** chart on pp. T401A–T401B.

USING THE DIAGNOSTIC PREVIEW

- To help you determine whether students make usage errors in their writing, you may want to supplement the **Diagnostic Preview** with a short writing activity. Using the results of the preview and of the writing assignment, you can design group activities for students who are at different levels of proficiency.

Diagnostic Preview

A. Revising Errors in Usage   Some revisions may vary.

In each of the following sets of word groups, one word group contains an error in the use of standard, formal English. <u>Identify the word group that contains an error</u>, and then write the word group correctly.

EXAMPLE   1. a. Her speech implies that a change is needed.
              b. Leave me have some oranges, too.
              c. This house is somewhat larger than our old one.

         1. b. Let me have some oranges, too.

1. a. wasn't ~~no~~ reason   **1.** any [*or* was no]
   b. words had no effect
   c. can hardly wait

2. a. families that ~~emigrated~~ to New Zealand   **2.** immigrated
   b. sail as far as the channel marker
   c. made allusions to classical literature

3. a. ~~being that~~ he was alone   **3.** because [*or* since]
   b. when the people accepted new ways
   c. the woman who was elected

4. a. what kind of frog
   b. overtime besides the regular work
   c. ~~an~~ hypnotic speaker   **4.** a

---

636   Chapter 20   A Glossary of Usage

CHAPTER RESOURCES

Planning
- One-Stop Planner CD-ROM

Practice and Extension
- *Grammar, Usage, and Mechanics,* p. 220
- *Language Workshop CD-ROM*

Internet
- go.hrw.com (keyword: EOLang)

Evaluation and Assessment
- Assessment Package
  —*Chapter Tests,* Ch. 20
  —*Chapter Tests in Standardized Test Formats,* Ch. 20
- Test Generator (One-Stop Planner CD-ROM)

5. a. saw on TV that our team had won
   b. Lee Haney proudly ~~excepted~~ his Mr. Olympia trophy. 5. accepted
   c. the house beside the highway

6. a. that he is doing ~~alright~~ 6. all right
   b. Let him have his own way.
   c. Leave the door open when you go.

7. a. Teach your dog this trick.
   b. I'm feeling ~~kind of~~ ill. 7. rather [or somewhat]
   c. might have been too late

8. a. Simira is taller than her sister.
   b. Dough will rise in a warm place.
   c. We read ~~where~~ the damage was extensive. 8. that

9. a. Try to be on time.
   b. They walked a long way.
   c. ~~Them~~ stairs are dangerous and need repairs. 9. Those

10. a. The bag burst, spilling the rice.
    b. The Polynesian alphabet has ~~less~~ characters than the English alphabet does. 10. fewer
    c. Take those books off that shelf.

B. Proofreading Paragraphs to Correct Usage Errors

Revise each of the sentences in the following paragraphs to correct the error in the use of standard, formal English. **Some revisions may vary.**

EXAMPLE   [1] The last time I visited my aunt and uncle in Florida, they told me about a interesting town.

1. The last time I visited my aunt and uncle in Florida, they told me about an interesting town.

[11] After the Civil War ended, Joseph E. Clarke decided that African Americans ~~had~~ ought to start a town of their own. [12] He wanted to build such a town, but no one would sell or donate land for this kind of ~~an~~ endeavor. [13] However, Joseph Clarke was a man who had great determination, and he wasn't ~~hardly~~ going to give up hope. [14] Finally, in 1877, with money ~~what~~ was donated by a New York philanthropist and with land offered by a Floridian named Josiah Eaton, Clarke obtained the first twelve acres of what would become Eatonville, Florida.

[15] Eatonville, located just beside Orlando, is recognized as the oldest incorporated African American town ~~anywheres~~ in the United

13. [or was hardly]
14. that

15. anywhere

Diagnostic Preview   637

A Glossary of Usage, pp. 636–664
Alignments
TEKS 3B, 3D
TAAS W3, W6
English II End-of-Course 5, 6

Texas Resources
- TAAS Tool Kit
- Preparation for TAAS
- One-Stop Planner CD-ROM

Crossing the Curriculum

All Disciplines. To reinforce what students know about a glossary's purpose, ask them to check for glossaries in textbooks from their other courses. Ask students to describe what the glossaries contain and how they make use of the glossaries. [*Generally, a glossary defines and illustrates difficult or technical terms used elsewhere in the textbook.*] Lead students to understand that they should use this glossary of usage as a resource to check difficult or questionable word usage for all of their school courses.

A, An–But, Only

(pp. 638–644)

OBJECTIVES

- To identify standard usage in sentences
- To proofread sentences for errors in usage

17. who [*or* that]

18. any [*or* lost no time]

19. effects

20. as

Reference Note

For a list of **words often confused,** see page 793. Use the **index** at the back of the book to find information about other usage problems.

Reference Note

For more information about **articles,** see page 412.

RESOURCES

A, An–But, Only
Practice
- *Grammar, Usage, and Mechanics,* p. 221
- *Language Workshop CD-ROM,* Lesson 50

States. [16] This ~~here~~ community has always been populated and governed entirely by black people. [17] The African Americans ~~which~~ flocked to Eatonville built homes, churches, and schools, and they cultivated gardens and orange groves. [18] The residents didn't lose ~~no~~ time in establishing a library, a post office, and a newspaper. [19] Today, after more than a hundred years of self-government, the citizens of Eatonville continue to feel the affects of Joseph Clarke's courage and vision. [20] With its light industry, new businesses, and booming real estate development, Eatonville enjoys economic growth, just ~~like~~ the rest of central Florida does.

About the Glossary

This chapter provides a compact glossary of common problems in English usage. A *glossary* is an alphabetical list of special terms or expressions with definitions, explanations, and examples. You will notice that some examples in this glossary are labeled *nonstandard, standard, formal,* or *informal.*

The label *nonstandard* identifies usage that is suitable only in the most casual speaking situations and in writing that attempts to re-create casual speech. *Standard* English is language that is grammatically correct and appropriate in formal and informal situations. *Formal* identifies standard usage that is appropriate in serious speaking and writing situations (such as in speeches and in compositions for school). The label *informal* indicates standard usage common in conversation and in everyday writing such as personal letters. In doing the exercises in this chapter, be sure to use only standard English.

Formal	Informal
angry	steamed
unpleasant	yucky
agreeable	cool
very impressive	totally awesome
accelerate	step on it

a, an Each of these words, called an **indefinite article,** refers to a member of a general group. Use *a* before words beginning with a consonant sound; use *an* before words beginning with a vowel sound.

EXAMPLES In ancient Greece and Rome, **a** person would go to see **an** oracle to consult the gods.

Did Jimmy Lee have to buy **a** uniform for his new job? [*A* is used before *uniform* because *uniform* begins with a consonant sound.]

Several of the tourists searched for **a** hotel for more than **an** hour. [*A* is used before *hotel* because *hotel* begins with a consonant sound. *An* is used before *hour* because *hour* begins with a vowel sound.]

accept, except *Accept* is a verb that means "to receive." *Except* may be either a verb or a preposition. As a verb, *except* means "to leave out." As a preposition, *except* means "excluding."

EXAMPLES Gary did not **accept** the bribe.

Students who were absent last week will be **excepted** from the group of students taking today's test.

Everybody **except** me knew the answer.

affect, effect *Affect* is generally used as a verb meaning "to influence." *Effect* used as a verb means "to accomplish" or "to bring about." Used as a noun, *effect* means "the result of some action."

EXAMPLES Working part time did not seem to **affect** his study habits.

Did the medicine **effect** a cure?

Coach Cortez said that the weather had little **effect** on the teams' performances.

ain't *Ain't* is nonstandard. Avoid using *ain't* in formal speaking and in all writing other than dialogue.

EXAMPLES These **aren't** [not *ain't*] my shoes.

Chris **isn't** [not *ain't*] going to the concert.

all ready, already See page 793.

all right *All right* means "satisfactory"; "unhurt, safe"; "correct"; or, when used in reply to a question or to introduce a remark, "yes." Although the spelling *alright* is sometimes used, it has not become accepted as standard usage.

EXAMPLES The storm is over, and everyone is **all right**.

All right, I'll call you later.

Reference Note
For more about **verbs**, see page 417. For more about **prepositions**, see page 426.

TEACHING TIP

Activity. To help students understand the importance of matching language to the situation and the audience, ask students to listen while you read aloud the following newscast.

> Just minutes ago, the city council busted a week-long deadlock and voted to build a new recycling plant. This here new plant will serve the city and outlying regions real good. The council they ain't sure about a completion date, but there isn't no reason to think construction will be delayed. We'll try and keep you updated on this new development.

Ask students to comment on the language used in the newscast. [*It is too informal for a newscast. Some of the usage is nonstandard.*] Explain to students that while nonstandard English is suitable for the most casual speech and for writing that intentionally re-creates such casual speech, it is unacceptable in formal speech and writing.

Meeting INDIVIDUAL NEEDS

MODALITIES

Auditory. Have students work in pairs to read aloud the glossary entries. Suggest that for the entries showing examples of standard and nonstandard usage, students read aloud several times, for emphasis, each example of standard usage. In addition, for word pairs that are similar in spelling and sound, such as *accept* and *except* and *affect* and *effect,* have students emphatically pronounce the syllables that distinguish the paired words.

USAGE

all the farther, all the faster   These expressions are used informally in some parts of the United States. In formal situations, use *as far as* and *as fast as*.

INFORMAL   This is all the farther we can go.
FORMAL   This is **as far as** we can go.

allusion, illusion   An *allusion* is an indirect reference to something. An *illusion* is a mistaken idea or a misleading appearance.

EXAMPLES   The poem's title is an **allusion** to a Hopi folk tale.

The documentary shattered viewers' **illusions** about migrant workers.

The magician was a master of **illusion.**

The expression *a lot* is overused. Try replacing *a lot* with a more descriptive, specific word or phrase.

EXAMPLES
mountains of homework
four subjects' worth of homework

a lot   Write the expression *a lot* as two words. *A lot* is often used informally as a noun meaning "a large number or amount" or as an adverb meaning "a great deal" or "very much."

INFORMAL   A lot of critics have praised the film.
FORMAL   **A large number** of critics have praised the film.

INFORMAL   Our guests arrived a lot earlier than we had expected.
FORMAL   Our guests arrived **much** earlier than we had expected.

among   See **between, among.**

and etc.   *Etc.* is the abbreviation of the Latin words *et cetera,* meaning "and others" or "and so forth." Therefore, *and* should not be used before *etc.*

EXAMPLE   I earn money by baby-sitting, running errands, mowing lawns, **etc.** [not *and etc.*]

Like other abbreviations, *etc.* is rarely appropriate in formal writing and speaking.

anyways, anywheres, everywheres, nowheres, somewheres   Use these words without an *s* at the end.

EXAMPLE   **Anywhere** [not *Anywheres*] you travel, you see the same hotel chains.

as   See **like, as.**

as if, as though   See **like, as if, as though.**

at   Do not use *at* after *where*.

NONSTANDARD   Where did you see them at?
STANDARD   Where did you see them?

640   Chapter 20   A Glossary of Usage

Continued on pp. 641–643

Parts of Speech. Reviewing the eight parts of speech may help students better understand many of the glossary entries. You may want to display in the classroom the following information so that students can refer to it as they work through the chapter.

- A **noun** names a person, a place, a thing, or an idea: The <u>colors</u> in the <u>painting</u> symbolize <u>patriotism</u>.

a while, awhile The noun *while*, often preceded by the article *a*, means "a period of time." *Awhile* is an adverb meaning "for a short period of time."

EXAMPLES I haven't heard from my pen pal for **a while.**

I usually read **awhile** before going to bed.

bad, badly See page 617.

barely See **The Double Negative** (page 656).

because In formal situations, do not use the construction *reason . . . because*. Instead use *reason . . . that*.

INFORMAL The reason we are holding the fund-raiser is because we want to buy new band uniforms.

FORMAL The **reason** we are holding the fund-raiser is **that** we want to buy new band uniforms.

The sentence may also be revised without the use of *the reason*.

FORMAL We are holding the fund-raiser because we want to buy new band uniforms.

being as, being that Use *because* or *since* instead of these expressions.

NONSTANDARD Being as her grades were so good, she got a scholarship.
STANDARD **Because** her grades were so good, she got a scholarship.

NONSTANDARD Being that he was late, he had to stand.
STANDARD **Since** he was late, he had to stand.

beside, besides *Beside* is a preposition meaning "by the side of." *Besides* as a preposition means "in addition to." As an adverb, *besides* means "moreover."

EXAMPLES He glanced at the person **beside** him.

Did anybody **besides** you see what happened?

I liked the sweater; **besides,** I needed a new one.

between, among Use *between* when referring to two things at a time, even if they are part of a larger group.

EXAMPLES A strong bond exists **between** the twins.

I paused **between** chapters. [Although there are more than two chapters, I paused only between any two of them.]

Reference Note
For more about **nouns**, see page 405. For more about **adverbs**, see page 422.

COMPUTER TIP

The spellchecker on a computer will catch misspelled words such as *anywheres* and *nowheres*. The grammar checker may catch errors such as double negatives. However, in the case of words often confused, such as *than* and *then* and *between* and *among*, you will need to check your work yourself for correct usage.

Use *among* when referring to all members of a group rather than to separate individuals in the group.

EXAMPLES   We distributed the pamphlets **among** the crowd.

There was some disagreement **among** the editorial staff.

borrow, lend, loan   The verb *borrow* means "to take [something] temporarily." The verb *lend* means "to give [something] temporarily."

EXAMPLES   May I **borrow** your binoculars?

I'll be glad to **lend** you my binoculars.

Loan, a noun in formal English, is sometimes used in place of the verb *lend* in informal situations.

INFORMAL   Will you **loan** me your umbrella?
FORMAL   Will you **lend** me your umbrella?

bring, take   *Bring* means "to come carrying something." *Take* means "to go away carrying something." Think of *bring* as related to *come* and *take* as related to *go*.

EXAMPLES   **Bring** your radio when you come over tomorrow.

Don't forget to **take** your coat when you go.

bust, busted   Avoid using these words as verbs. Instead, use a form of *break* or *burst* or *catch* or *arrest*.

EXAMPLES   I **broke** [not *busted*] the switch on the stereo.

The water main **burst** [not *busted*].

Did the police **arrest** [not *bust*] the suspects?

but, only   See **The Double Negative** (page 656).

Exercise 1   Identifying Standard Usage

For each of the following sentences, choose the correct word from the pair given in parentheses.

EXAMPLE   1. They stood there for (*a while, awhile*), gazing at the clear night sky.

    1. a while

1. The tasks were divided evenly (*among, between*) the two scouts.
2. The audience was deeply (*affected, effected*) by Simon Estes's powerful baritone voice.

642   Chapter 20   A Glossary of Usage

Exercise 1

ALTERNATIVE LESSON

To reinforce students' understanding of the parts of speech, ask them to identify the part of speech of each correct choice in **Exercise 1**.
[1. preposition; 2. verb; 3. verb; 4. preposition; 5. verb; 6. noun; 7. adverb; 8. noun; 9. preposition; 10. noun]

MINI-LESSON

- A **preposition** shows the relationship of a noun or a pronoun to some other word in the sentence: Our flight <u>from</u> Atlanta <u>to</u> Tampa was delayed <u>because of</u> bad weather.

- A **conjunction** joins words or groups of words: <u>Although</u> the presentation ran long, <u>both</u> the teachers <u>and</u> the students enjoyed it.

3. We were afraid the bull had (*busted, broken*) loose.
4. No one (*accept, except*) the sophomores will attend.
5. Please (*bring, take*) these papers when you leave.
6. Penicillin has had a profound (*affect, effect*) on modern medicine.
7. I couldn't find the cat (*anywhere, anywheres*).
8. Uncle Joe said that the crosslike rays radiating from the moon were an (*allusion, illusion*) caused by the screen door.
9. (*Beside, Besides*) Julie and Zack, who else has signed up for Saturday's 10K walk?
10. In his remarks about Dr. King, the speaker last night made an (*allusion, illusion*) to Gandhi, whose nonviolent protests paved the way for the civil rights movement in the United States.

Exercise 2 — Proofreading to Correct Usage Errors

Revise each of the following sentences by correcting the error or errors in usage. If a sentence is already correct, write *C*.

EXAMPLE
1. Where was Frank Matsura's photography studio at?
1. Where was Frank Matsura's photography studio?

1. In 1903, this young Japanese artist, Frank Matsura, arrived somewhere in the backwoods settlement of Conconully, Washington.
2. This was all the farther he would go, for he lived in or near this rough frontier settlement for the remaining ten years of his life.
3. When he came to town, Matsura was wearing a elegant formal suit and was carrying bulky camera equipment he had taken with him.
4. Back in Seattle, Matsura had excepted a job in Conconully as a helper and laundryman at the Elliott Hotel.
5. Soon he was living in a tiny room behind the kitchen and performing his menial job with alot of energy and cheer.
6. When he was off duty, he carried his camera everywheres he went, photographing the area's people, scenery, events, and etc.
7. After a while, he settled in nearby Okanogan and opened a small studio.
8. Being as Matsura was a warm, extroverted person, he made many friends between settlers and American Indians alike.

A Glossary of Usage 643

Exercise 2 Proofreading to Correct Usage Errors

ANSWERS continued

9. Oddly, though, he never told anyone about his past, even after he had lived there awhile.
10. To this day, nobody knows who he really was, where he was born, or why he chose to live and die so far from his home.

Can, May–It's, Its

(pp. 644–647)

OBJECTIVES

- To identify standard usage in sentences
- To proofread sentences for errors in usage

---

9. Oddly, though, he never told anyone about his past, even after he had lived there a while.
10. To this day, nobody knows who he really was, where he was born at, or why he chose to live and die so far from his home.

can, may Use *can* to express ability. Use *may* to express possibility.

EXAMPLES Do you think you **can** repair this camera?

Ethan has said that he **may** run for class president.

To express permission in formal situations, use *may*, not *can*.

INFORMAL Can I sit here?
FORMAL **May** I sit here?

can't hardly, can't scarcely See **The Double Negative** (page 656).

could of Do not use *of* in place of *have* after verbs such as *could, should, would, might, must,* and *ought.*

EXAMPLE Muriel **could have** [not *could of*] gone with us.

discover, invent *Discover* means "to find, see, or learn about something that already exists." *Invent* means "to be the first to make or do something."

EXAMPLES Luis W. Alvarez **discovered** many subatomic particles.

Sarah Boone **invented** the ironing board.

Reference Note
For more information about **contractions**, see page 763.

don't, doesn't *Don't* is the contraction of *do not*. *Doesn't* is the contraction of *does not*. Use *doesn't*, not *don't*, with singular subjects except *I* and *you*.

EXAMPLES It **doesn't** [not *don't*] matter to me.

The poem **doesn't** [not *don't*] rhyme.

effect See **affect, effect**.

emigrate, immigrate *Emigrate* means "to leave a country to settle elsewhere." *Immigrate* means "to come into a country to settle there."

EXAMPLES My great-grandfather **emigrated** from Mexico.

Much of Australia's population is composed of people who **immigrated** there in recent centuries.

644 Chapter 20 A Glossary of Usage

RESOURCES

Can, May–It's, Its
Practice
- Grammar, Usage, and Mechanics, pp. 222, 223
- Language Workshop CD-ROM, Lesson 50

everywheres   See **anywheres**, etc.

except   See **accept, except**.

fewer, less   *Fewer* is used with plural nouns. It tells "how many." *Less* is used with singular nouns. It tells "how much."

EXAMPLES   There are **fewer** whales than there once were.

We should have bought **less** meat and more vegetables.

good, well   See page 617.

had of   Do not use *had of* for *had*.

EXAMPLE   If I **had** [not *had of*] known that you wanted to read Forrest Carter's *The Education of Little Tree*, I would have lent you my copy.

had ought, hadn't ought   Do not use *had* or *hadn't* with *ought*.

NONSTANDARD   You hadn't ought to say such things.
STANDARD   You **ought** not to say such things.
STANDARD   You **shouldn't** say such things.

NONSTANDARD   They had ought to have left earlier.
STANDARD   They **ought** to have left earlier.
STANDARD   They **should** have left earlier.

hardly   See **The Double Negative** (page 656).

he, she, it, they   Do not use a pronoun along with its antecedent as the subject of a verb. Such an error is called the **double subject**.

NONSTANDARD   My father he works downtown.
STANDARD   My **father works** downtown.

hisself, theirself, theirselves   These words are nonstandard. Use *himself* instead of *hisself*, and use *themselves* instead of *theirself* or *theirselves*.

EXAMPLES   My uncle considers **himself** [not *hisself*] an average golfer.

The members of the Ecology Club should be very proud of **themselves** [not *theirself* or *theirselves*].

hopefully   *Hopefully* is an adverb meaning "in a hopeful manner." In formal situations, avoid using *hopefully* for an expression such as *I hope* or *it is hoped*.

Reference Note

For more information about **pronouns**, see page 408.

Meeting INDIVIDUAL NEEDS

MULTIPLE INTELLIGENCES

Linguistic Intelligence. Because linguistic learners enjoy playing with language, ask them to use some of the paired boldface words from the glossary to create mnemonics, rhymes, tongue twisters, or word games. You may want to provide students with the following example of a mnemonic:

To distinguish between *emigrate* and *immigrate*, remember that *immigrate* and *into* both start with *i*: *Immigrate* means "to come into a country to settle." Similarly, *emigrate* and *exit* both start with *e*: *Emigrate* means "to exit a country."

Encourage students to share their creations with the rest of the class.

A Glossary of Usage

INFORMAL	Hopefully, Gloria Estefan's next concert tour will include a performance in our city.
FORMAL	**I hope** Gloria Estefan's next concert tour will include a performance in our city.
FORMAL	We listened **hopefully** as the disc jockey gave the details of Gloria Estefan's next concert tour.

illusion See **allusion, illusion.**

immigrate See **emigrate, immigrate.**

imply, infer *Imply* means "to suggest." *Infer* means "to interpret" or "to draw as a conclusion."

EXAMPLES In her speech, the candidate **implied** that she is for tax reform.

From the candidate's speech, I **inferred** that she is for tax reform.

invent See **discover, invent.**

it's, its See page 796.

Exercise 3 Identifying Standard Usage

For each of the following sentences, choose the correct word from the pair given in parentheses.

EXAMPLE 1. (*Gary Soto, Gary Soto he*) is my favorite writer.
  1. Gary Soto

1. Did he say that he had painted the mural (*himself, hisself*)?
2. From his letter, I (*implied, inferred*) he would be away all summer.
3. He (*don't, doesn't*) always say what he means.
4. (*Emigration, Immigration*) to Alaska was spurred by the gold rush.
5. The heat has affected the growing season; we'll harvest (*fewer, less*) olives this year.
6. You could (*have, of*) borrowed some paper and a pencil from me.
7. As beasts of burden, dogs served the Comanches (*good, well*), often pulling a travois laden with more than forty pounds of baggage.
8. Mary Beth Stearns (*discovered, invented*) a technique for studying electrons.
9. Many French Canadians (*emigrated, immigrated*) from Quebec to work in the industries of New England.
10. Audrey must (*have, of*) taken my jacket by mistake.

Chapter 20 A Glossary of Usage

Exercise 4 **Proofreading to Correct Usage Errors**

Revise the following sentences to correct each error in the use of standard, formal English. If a sentence is already correct, write *C*.

EXAMPLE   1. Hopefully, the ambigrams shown here will motivate you to create similar designs.
     1. *I hope the ambigrams shown here will motivate you to create similar designs.*

1. A scientist, philosopher, and writer, Douglas R. Hofstadter ~~he~~ enjoys creating symmetrical designs from written words.
2. He and a friend ~~discovered~~ a new pastime; the resulting designs are called ambigrams. — **2. invented**
3. Not every word lends itself to this method, but you might be surprised at how many words can be made into ambigrams. — **3. C**
4. As you might ~~of~~ known already, a *palindrome* is a word or expression that has the same letters in the same sequence both forward and backward—for example, *toot* or *Madam, I'm Adam*. — **4. have**
5. I don't mean to ~~infer,~~ though, that an ambigram has to be a palindrome—an ambigram simply has to look symmetrical. — **5. imply**
6. Usually, ambigrams ~~they~~ can't be formed unless you tinker with the letter shapes and connect them in new ways.
7. You ~~had~~ ought to start with a word that has six letters or fewer.
8. For some good ideas, you may want to look below at the ambigrams for the words *Jamal, Steve, Chris, Felix, Wendy, Mexico,* and *dance*. — **8. C**
9. Don't forget that you can mix cursive, printed, capital, and lowercase letters to create ~~affects~~ like the ones in these ambigrams. — **9. effects**
10. If you become stumped, you might find that you could ~~of~~ succeeded by adding some decorative flourishes. — **10. have**

A Glossary of Usage

Kind of, Sort of–Ought to of
(pp. 648–651)

OBJECTIVES
- To identify standard usage in sentences
- To proofread sentences for errors in usage

Critical Thinking
Metacognition. Ask students to think about the strategies they use to avoid repeating usage errors. Do they look in this glossary for the entry relating to the usage? Do they read aloud the example sentences from the glossary entry? Do they create their own example sentences? What other steps do they follow?

You may want to show students the following sequence chain demonstrating the steps one student followed. Suggest that students use similar graphics to sequence the steps they use. Encourage students to evaluate the effectiveness of their strategies and to consider more effective alternatives as needed.

Read the glossary entry several times.
↓
Read aloud all examples.
↓
Create other examples.
↓
Practice the usage five times daily for several days, noting in my writing portfolio each instance of the usage.
↓
Ask a friend to quiz me.

Reference Note
For more information about **subordinate clauses,** see Chapter 15. For more about **conjunctions,** see page 428.

---

kind of, sort of   In formal situations, avoid using either of these expressions for the adverb *rather* or *somewhat*.

INFORMAL   The waves were sort of rough.
FORMAL   The waves were **rather** [or *somewhat*] rough.

kind of a(n), sort of a(n)   In formal situations, omit the *a* or *an*.

EXAMPLE   This bolt takes a special **kind of** [not *kind of a*] nut.

kinds, sorts, types   With the singular form of each of these words, use *this* or *that*. With the plural form, use *these* or *those*.

EXAMPLE   I know more about **that kind** of music than about any of **those** other **kinds.**

learn, teach   *Learn* means "to gain knowledge." *Teach* means "to provide with knowledge."

EXAMPLES   She **learned** how to saddle a horse.
The stable owner **taught** her how.

leave, let   *Leave* means "to go away." *Let* means "to allow" or "to permit." Avoid using *leave* for *let*.

EXAMPLES   We had to **leave** early to catch the plane.
Let [not *Leave*] them go first.
We **let** [not *left*] the trapped bird go free.

less   See **fewer, less.**

lie, lay   See page 582.

like, as, as if, as though   In formal situations, do not use the preposition *like* for the conjunction *as, as if,* or *as though* to introduce a subordinate clause.

INFORMAL   This animal sheds its skin like a snake does.
FORMAL   This animal sheds its skin **as** a snake does.

INFORMAL   This looks like it might be the right place.
FORMAL   This looks **as if** [or *as though*] it might be the right place.

might of, must of   See **could of.**

neither, never, no, nobody, no one, not (–n't), nothing, nowhere   See **The Double Negative** (page 656).

RESOURCES
Kind of, Sort of–Ought to of
Practice
- *Grammar, Usage, and Mechanics,* p. 224
- *Language Workshop CD-ROM,* Lesson 51

nowheres See **anywheres,** etc.

a number of, the number of *A number of* is generally plural and *the number of* is generally singular. Make sure that the verb agrees with the subject.

EXAMPLES   **A number of** job positions **are** open.
           The number of job positions **is** limited.

of See **could of.**

of Do not use the preposition *of* after other prepositions such as *inside, off,* and *outside.*

EXAMPLES   The diver jumped **off** [not *off of*] the board.
           Outside [not *Outside of*] the building was a patio.

off, off of Do not use *off* or *off of* in place of *from.*

NONSTANDARD   Here's the money I borrowed off of you.
STANDARD   Here's the money I borrowed **from** you.

only See The Double Negative (page 656).

ought to of See **could of.**

Exercise 5 Identifying Standard Usage

For each of the following sentences, choose from the choices given in parentheses the word or expression that is correct according to the rules of standard, formal English.

EXAMPLE   1. Who (*learned, taught*) you how to play mah-jongg?
          1. taught

1. The total length of the Great Wall of China is about 4,000 miles, if branches (*off, off of*) the main wall are included.
2. Carlos was (*outside, outside of*) the house.
3. We went to the hardware store for a special (*kind of, kind of a*) wrench.
4. Rachel Carson's books (*learned, taught*) me to care about ecology.
5. (*Leave, Let*) us listen without any interruptions.
6. How many pamphlets did you get (*from, off of*) the sales representative?
7. Why did she feel (*like, as if*) she'd said something wrong?
8. T. J. said the number of unclaimed prizes (*was, were*) surprising.

Exercise 5

ALTERNATIVE LESSON
To reinforce students' understanding of prepositional phrases, have them identify in **Exercise 5** each sentence in which the correct choice is a preposition. Then, ask students to classify the prepositional phrase as adjective or adverb and to identify the word or word group the phrase modifies. [*sentence 1:* off the main wall—*adjective*—branches; *sentence 2:* outside the house—*adverb*—was; *sentence 6:* from the sales representative—*adverb*—did get]

9. Why didn't the U.S. government (*leave, let*) the Cherokee people stay in their Southeast homelands?
10. They didn't want to take the boat out because the waves looked (*kind of, rather*) choppy.

HELP
Some sentences in Exercise 6 contain more than one error.

Exercise 6 Proofreading to Correct Usage Errors

Revise each of the following sentences by correcting the error or errors in the use of formal, standard English. If a sentence is already correct, write *C*.

EXAMPLE
1. My mother once tried to learn me how to do fancy needlework.
1. My mother once tried to teach me how to do fancy needlework.

1. C
2. rather [*or* somewhat] / teach

1. Until recent times, most young girls learned to do fancy needlework.
2. Beginning when a girl was kind of young, her mother or another woman would learn her many embroidery stitches.
3. Then, at the age of nine or ten, the girl would be given the task of making a sampler like the one shown here, using every kind of a stitch she knew.

4. let
5. as if

4. Usually, the girl's parents wouldn't leave her be idle.
5. She had to work on the sampler every day like her life depended on it!
6. When the sampler was finished, it didn't lie inside of a drawer.

7. Instead, it was left on display to show that the girl was industrious and well educated in homemaking skills.
8. Many people think ~~these~~ sort of sampler must have been popular in America and nowhere else.
9. However, a number of countries in Europe, Asia, and Africa have prized this kind of ~~a~~ needlework exercise for centuries.
10. Today, American girls aren't judged by their stitchery ~~like~~ they once were, and some never learn anything about needlework.

7. C

8. this

10. as

reason . . . because   See **because**.

rise, raise   See page 588.

scarcely   See **The Double Negative** (page 656).

she   See **he, she, it, they**.

should of   See **could of**.

sit, set   See page 585.

some, somewhat   In formal situations, avoid using *some* as an adverb meaning "to some extent." Use *somewhat*.

INFORMAL   This medicine should help your cough some.
 FORMAL   This medicine should help your cough **somewhat**.

somewheres   See **anywheres**, etc.

sort of   See **kind of, sort of**.

sort of a   See **kind of a(n), sort of a(n)**.

sorts   See **kinds, sorts, types**.

suppose to, supposed to   To express an intention or plan, use the verb form *supposed* before an infinitive.

EXAMPLE   We were **supposed to** [not *suppose to*] meet Wendy at eight o'clock.

take, bring   See **bring, take**.

teach   See **learn, teach**.

than, then   *Than* is a subordinating conjunction used in comparisons. *Then* is an adverb meaning "at that time" or "next."

EXAMPLES   She is younger **than** you are.

I swept the floor; **then** I emptied the trash.

Reference Note

For more information about **infinitives**, see page 479.

Reference Note

For more information about **subordinating conjunctions**, see page 498.

A Glossary of Usage   **651**

Reason . . . Because–Your, You're
(pp. 651–656)

OBJECTIVE

- To revise sentences to correct errors in usage

**ENGLISH-LANGUAGE LEARNERS
General Strategies.** Some of the usage guidelines in this glossary depend on context; others do not. For example, choosing between *than* and *then* depends on understanding the relationship between ideas in the sentence. However, the use of *anywhere* rather than *anywheres* is always correct, regardless of context. You may want to have students select from the glossary the entries that cover preferred usage regardless of context.

RESOURCES

Reason...Because–Your, You're
Practice
- *Grammar, Usage, and Mechanics*, p. 225
- *Language Workshop CD-ROM*, Lesson 51

Meeting INDIVIDUAL NEEDS

ADVANCED LEARNERS
Some students will benefit from exposure to usage rules not covered in this chapter. Have students review manuals of style such as Strunk and White's *The Elements of Style*. Encourage students to identify additional usage rules that might help them in formal writing and speaking situations. Have students create examples that illustrate correct usage. After assessing their work, you may want to display it prominently in the classroom.

Reference Note
For more information about **adjective clauses,** see page 495.

---

that See **who, which, that.**

their, there, they're See page 799.

theirself, theirselves See **hisself, theirself, theirselves.**

them Do not use *them* as an adjective. Use *those* instead.

EXAMPLE   It's one of **those** [not *them*] fancy show dogs.

they See **he, she, it, they.**

this here, that there Avoid using *here* or *there* after *this* or *that*.

EXAMPLE   Let's rent **this** [not *this here*] movie instead of **that** [not *that there*] one.

try and, try to Use *try to*, not *try and*.

EXAMPLE   When you're at bat, you must **try to** [not *try and*] relax.

types See **kinds, sorts, types.**

unless See **without, unless.**

use to, used to Do not leave off the *d* when you write *used to*.

EXAMPLE   Alicia **used to** [not *use to*] take tae kwon do lessons.

way, ways Use *way*, not *ways*, when referring to a distance.

EXAMPLE   She lives quite a **way** [not *ways*] from here.

well See page 617.

what Do not use *what* in place of *that* to introduce an adjective clause.

EXAMPLE   This is the book **that** [not *what*] I told you about.

when, where Do not use *when* or *where* incorrectly to begin a definition.

NONSTANDARD	*SRO* is when tickets for all the seats have been sold, leaving standing room only.
STANDARD	*SRO* means that tickets for all the seats have been sold, leaving standing room only.
STANDARD	*SRO* is the abbreviation for *standing room only;* it means that tickets for all the seats have been sold.

where Do not use *where* for *that*.

EXAMPLE   I read **that** [not *where*] the word *bayou* comes from the Choctaw word *bayuk*, meaning "small stream."

652   Chapter 20   A Glossary of Usage

Continued on pp. 653–654

Subordinate Clauses. Correct usage of some glossary entries, such as *like, as, as if,* and *as though,* depends upon an understanding of subordinate clauses. Write on the chalkboard the following definitions and examples (without underlining the clauses):

- A **clause** is a group of words with a subject and a verb that is used as a sentence or part of a sentence.
- An **independent clause** expresses a complete thought and can stand alone as a sentence.

where . . . at   See **at**.

who, which, that   *Who* refers to people only. *Which* refers to things only. *That* refers to either people or things.

EXAMPLES   Carlotta, **who** is a sophomore, won the gold medal.
Her medal, **which** is actually gold plated, is quite heavy.
Carlotta is the runner **that** [or *who*] won the gold medal.
This medal is not the first one **that** she has won.

who, whom   See page 558.

who's, whose   See page 800.

without, unless   Do not use the preposition *without* in place of the conjunction *unless* to introduce a subordinate clause.

EXAMPLE   I can't use the car **unless** [not *without*] I ask Mom.

would of   See **could of**.

your, you're   See page 800.

Exercise 7   Revising Errors in Usage

Revise each of the following sentences to correct the error in usage.

Answers may vary

EXAMPLE   1. I am use to the noise.
   1. I am used to the noise.

1. A solar eclipse is when the moon comes between the earth and the sun and blocks the light.
2. The workers which put up that new office building certainly finished it quickly.
3. Ronald E. McNair was aboard the space shuttle what exploded in January 1986.
4. Was the senator suppose to arrive this morning?
5. A run-on sentence is where two sentences are erroneously joined as a single sentence.
6. As soon as the rain lets up some, we'll leave.
7. Them mosquitoes can drive a person nearly crazy.
8. Antonio Freeman carried the ball a long ways down the field before he was tackled.
9. I think I read in the paper where Amy Tan has a new novel coming out next month.
10. I'm tired of trying to cut the grass with this here old lawn mower, which should be in an antique exhibit.

1. occurs
2. who [or that]
3. that
4. supposed
5. that
6. somewhat
7. Those
8. way
9. that

TEACHING TIP

Activity. You may want to have students work in groups of three to review standard usage. First, give each group a stack of note cards, and ask students to write on a separate card each glossary entry that is not followed by a cross-reference. Students may want to use their cards from the **Meeting Individual Needs** activity on p. 641.

Then, with the cards face down, have group members take turns drawing a card and illustrating the standard usage pertaining to the entry. Students can draw, act out, or otherwise illustrate the entry. Encourage groups to make notes on the cards to help them with troublesome entries.

- A **subordinate clause** does not express a complete thought and cannot stand alone as a sentence.
1. <u>As a polite guest should</u>, I smiled graciously.
2. My friends reacted to my news <u>as though they had already heard it</u>.
3. He responded to the question <u>as if he had not been paying attention</u>.

Relating to Speaking and Writing

To reinforce the concept that a speaker's or writer's audience will influence the choice of usage, have students compile a class list of polite slang expressions they commonly use. Discuss with the class occasions when formal language would be appropriate and occasions when it would be required. Then, have students generate a directory of formal expressions that they can use in place of the slang expressions.

Review B

ALTERNATIVE LESSON

To review with students the three kinds of subordinate clauses, have them identify in **Review B** each sentence in which the correct choice begins a subordinate clause. Then, ask students to write the subordinate clause and to classify it as *noun, adjective,* or *adverb.*

[sentence 1: *as if he's ever going to stop*—adverb; sentence 16: *who used to wear running clothes*—adjective; sentence 20: *that the space shuttle someday may be going to the moon*—noun]

Review A Identifying Standard Usage

For each of the following sentences, choose the correct word or word group from the choices given in parentheses.

EXAMPLE 1. If it (*don't, doesn't*) rain tonight, we'll start harvesting the crop tomorrow.
 1. *doesn't*

1. Thanks to modern medicine, there are (*fewer, less*) cases of tetanus and diphtheria nowadays.
2. I tried to (*learn, teach*) my dog to do tricks, but he just sat and stared at me.
3. I see (*where, that*) pandas are an endangered species.
4. Cape Porpoise is (*somewhere, somewheres*) near Portsmouth.
5. Priscilla wrote a longer paper (*than, then*) Tammy did.
6. To make American Indian fry bread, you need flour, baking powder, salt, (*and etc., etc.*).
7. We (*hadn't ought, ought not*) to decide until we are certain of all the facts.
8. Amy couldn't see the screen (*without, unless*) I took off my hat.
9. Someone must (*of, have*) left the door unlocked.
10. Lewis Latimer (*discovered, invented*) an improved filament for the earliest electric light bulbs.

Review B Identifying Standard Usage

For each of the following sentences, choose from the choices given in parentheses the word or word group that is correct according to the rules of formal, standard English.

EXAMPLE 1. The rear-view mirror fell (*off, off of*) Ted's bike.
 1. *off*

1. Stevie Wonder has written a number of hit songs since the 1960s, and he (*don't, doesn't*) look (*as if, like*) he's ever going to stop.
2. (*Inside, Inside of*) the box was (*a, an*) heap of glittering gems.
3. May I (*imply, infer*) from your yawns that you are bored?
4. My great-grandmother (*emigrated, immigrated*) from Italy when she was a young woman.
5. (*Beside, Besides*) speaking Spanish, Vera can speak a little Portuguese.
6. Linda (*doesn't, don't*) enjoy doing (*them, those, that*) sort of exercise.
7. Ahead of us on the desert, a lake seemed to sparkle, but it was only an (*allusion, illusion*).

MINI-LESSON

Then, ask students to identify the subordinate clause [underlined] in each sentence. Next, ask students to point out the subject and the verb in each subordinate clause. [*guest, should; they, had heard; he, had been paying*]. Finally, review with students why *like* cannot be used in place of *as, as though,* or *as if* in each example. For additional information and practice, refer students to **Chapter 15: The Clause.**

8. This prolonged water shortage will (*affect, effect*) the whole state (*accept, except*) for two counties.
9. I don't think my parents will (*leave, let*) me borrow the car in this kind of weather.
10. Because of the indiscriminate slaughter, each year there were (*fewer, less*) bison.
11. When Wilmer is very tired, he (*don't, doesn't*) talk much.
12. The disagreement (*between, among*) the two friends caused a number of problems.
13. When he goes to the next potluck dinner, he will (*bring, take*) potato salad.
14. We saw several puffins, eight sea lions, a humpback whale, and (*a, an*) eagle while we were on a daylong Alaskan cruise.
15. I felt as if I (*could have, could of*) run forever.
16. The mayor (*which, who*) used to wear running clothes has been reelected.
17. (*Them, Those*) Asian currencies are rising rapidly in value.
18. Rick wanted to (*try and, try to*) complete a painting each week.
19. The weary explorers traveled quite a (*way, ways*) during their three-week journey.
20. Did you read (*where, that*) the space shuttle someday may be going to the moon?

Review C — Proofreading a Paragraph to Correct Usage Errors

Revise each of the sentences in the following paragraph by correcting the error or errors in the use of formal, standard English. If a sentence is already correct, write *C*.

EXAMPLE [1] Sequoyah was the person which devised the Cherokee alphabet.

1. Sequoyah was the person who devised the Cherokee alphabet.

[1] Imagine single-handedly discovering a system for writing a language that had never before been written! [2] In about 1809, the Cherokee scholar Sequoyah became aware of "talking leaves," the written pages that were used by white people to communicate with one another. [3] Being that Sequoyah he felt that the ability to write had greatly helped white people, he decided he had ought to create a similar system for his people. [4] Instead of making up an alphabet like the one used in English, he chose to create this here syllabary. [5] Each

Review C Proofreading a Paragraph to Correct Usage Errors

ANSWERS continued

5. Each character in Sequoyah's syllabary stands for one of the eighty-five syllables that are used in speaking Cherokee.
6. Sequoyah copied some letters from an English book, but in his system they have different meanings.
7. During the twelve years that it took Sequoyah to complete his writing system, he was ridiculed by many Cherokees who thought his efforts were rather [*or* somewhat] foolish.
8. However, after the syllabary was finished and accepted by most Cherokees, they realized they should not have scoffed.
9. C
10. Sequoyah was honored by his people for teaching them to read and write, and his writing method is still used today.

The Double Negative
(pp. 656–658)

OBJECTIVE
- To revise sentences that contain double negatives

ENGLISH-LANGUAGE LEARNERS
Spanish. Because the use of double negatives is acceptable in Spanish, some students may transfer this usage to English. If students have difficulty, you could have them periodically read correct sentences aloud.

USAGE

The Granger Collection, New York

character in Sequoyah's syllabary stands for one of the eighty-five syllables what are used in speaking Cherokee. [6] Sequoyah copied some letters from a English book, but in his system they have different meanings. [7] During the twelve years that it took Sequoyah to complete his writing system, he was ridiculed by many Cherokees who thought his efforts were kind of foolish. [8] However, after the syllabary was finished and accepted by most Cherokees, they realized they should not of scoffed. [9] After a while, thousands learned how to read and write, and soon books and newspapers were being printed in Cherokee. [10] Sequoyah was honored by his people for learning them to read and write, and his writing method is still used today.

The Double Negative

A *double negative* is the use of two or more negative words to express a single negative idea. Before the 1700s, two or more negatives were often used in the same sentence for emphasis. In English, this usage is no longer considered correct, and a double negative is regarded as nonstandard. Avoid using double negatives in your writing and speaking.

Common Negative Words			
barely	neither	none	nowhere
but (meaning "only")	never	no one	only
	no	not (–n't)	scarcely
hardly	nobody	nothing	

NONSTANDARD   Jade wasn't but a child then.
STANDARD   Jade **was but** a child then.

NONSTANDARD   We hadn't scarcely enough time to finish the test.
STANDARD   We **had scarcely** enough time to finish the test.

NONSTANDARD   There isn't no reason to be nervous.
STANDARD   There **is no** reason to be nervous.
STANDARD   There **isn't any** reason to be nervous.

656   Chapter 20   A Glossary of Usage

RESOURCES
The Double Negative
Practice
- *Grammar, Usage, and Mechanics*, p. 226
- *Language Workshop CD-ROM*, Lesson 51

NONSTANDARD	We searched for clues but didn't find none.
STANDARD	We searched for clues but **found none.**
STANDARD	We searched for clues but **didn't find any.**

NONSTANDARD	I didn't hear nothing.
STANDARD	I **heard nothing.**
STANDARD	I **didn't hear anything.**

Exercise 8 Revising Sentences That Contain Double Negatives

Each of the following sentences contains too many negative words. Revise each sentence. Be careful not to change the intended meaning.

EXAMPLE
1. Theo wanted some ancient Greek coins, but the coin dealer didn't have none.

1. *Theo wanted some ancient Greek coins, but the coin dealer had none.*

   or

   Theo wanted some ancient Greek coins, but the coin dealer didn't have any.

1. The boy hadn't never been in an airplane.
2. After a lazy summer, Pat can't hardly jog a mile.
3. She was sleeping so soundly she didn't hear nothing.
4. Angela looked for Easter eggs but she didn't see none.
5. Lee Ann has not never been to the Grand Canyon.
6. Char did not want no part of the childish plan.
7. Isn't there no milk left at the store?
8. The stranded motorist doesn't have no spare tire.
9. No one has never walked on the planet Mars.
10. There isn't scarcely any hope for that team to win.

—HELP—

The sentences in Exercise 8 may be correctly revised in more than one way. You need to give only one revision for each.

The Double Negative   657

Review D **Revising Errors in Usage**

Revise each of the following sentences, correcting the error or errors in the use of formal, standard English. Practice saying aloud the corrected sentences. Revisions may vary.

EXAMPLE
1. Now a museum, the Imperial Palace (also called the Forbidden City) use to be the home of China's royal family.

1. Now a museum, the Imperial Palace (also called the Forbidden City) used to be the home of China's royal family.

1. rather
2.
3. have
4. can / between
5. have
6. Those
7. that
8. Shouldn't / to
9. who / as
10. those
11. any
12. have / have / a
13. occurs
14. fewer
15. rather
16. any
17. that

1. They don't have hardly any chance to score before the buzzer sounds; the situation looks sort of hopeless to me.
2. You ought to have seen how beautiful Santa Fe was at Christmas, with nearly every house surrounded by flickering *farolitos*—paper-bag lanterns that have candles inside of them.
3. I might of gone to the concert if I had of heard about it earlier.
4. Pam and her sister Stacey look so much alike that you can't hardly see the differences among them.
5. My cousins didn't hardly know how to swim, but they wouldn't of missed going to the lake.
6. Them reference books in the library are kept in some kind of a special section.
7. This here is the car what I told you about.
8. Hadn't you ought to try and help them?
9. Many of the American Indian leaders which visited Washington, D.C., in the late 1800s proudly wore their traditional clothing rather than dress like their white hosts did.
10. I wonder where them fishing poles are at.
11. We don't live in that there neighborhood no more.
12. We might of gone on the tour, but we wouldn't of had no camera to take pictures.
13. A foot fault in tennis is when the server steps over the base line before hitting the ball.
14. Since there wasn't scarcely any rainfall last spring, there are less mosquitoes this summer.
15. When the play was over, the audience seemed sort of subdued.
16. Shing searched for rice noodles in the grocery store but didn't find none.
17. I saw on the news where many manufacturers will install an improved security system in their new cars.

18. Miss Kim ~~she~~ likes to give those kind_ of surprise quizzes.
19. Let's try ~~and~~ finish early so we can relax ~~some~~.
20. In the early 1500s, Ponce de León searched for the Fountain of Youth ~~somewheres~~ on the island of Bimini.

18. kinds
19. to / somewhat
20. somewhere

Nonsexist Language

Nonsexist language is language that applies to people in general, both male and female. For example, the nonsexist terms *humanity, human beings,* and *people* can substitute for the gender-specific term *mankind*.

In the past, many skills and occupations were generally closed to either men or women. Words like *seamstress, stewardess,* and *mailman* reflect those limitations. Since most jobs can now be held by both men and women, language is adjusting to reflect this change.

When you are referring generally to people, use nonsexist expressions rather than gender-specific ones. Following are some widely used nonsexist terms that you can use to replace gender-specific ones.

Gender-Specific	Nonsexist
businessman	executive, businessperson
chairman	chairperson, chair
common man	ordinary person
congressman	representative
deliveryman	delivery person
fireman	firefighter
foreman	supervisor
housewife	homemaker
mailman	mail carrier
male nurse	nurse
man-made	synthetic, manufactured
mankind	humanity
manpower	workers, human resources
May the best man win!	May the best person win!
policeman	police officer
salesman	salesperson, salesclerk
seamstress	needleworker
steward, stewardess	flight attendant
weatherman	meteorologist

Nonsexist Language
(pp. 659–660)

OBJECTIVE

- To avoid gender-specific terms and awkward expressions by rewriting sentences

USAGE

RESOURCES
Nonsexist Language
Practice
- *Grammar, Usage, and Mechanics,* p. 227

If the antecedent of a pronoun may be either masculine or feminine, use both masculine and feminine pronouns to refer to it.

EXAMPLES   **Anyone** who wants to be considered should present **his or her** application to the office.

Any applicant may bring a résumé with **him or her** to the office.

STYLE TIP

Avoid using the awkward expressions *s/he* and *wo/man*.

Often, you can often avoid the awkward *his or her* construction (or the alternative *his/her*) by substituting an article (*a*, *an*, or *the*) for the construction. Another solution is to reword the sentence, using the plural forms of both the pronoun and its antecedent.

EXAMPLES   Any interested **applicant** may submit **a** proposal.

All interested **applicants** may submit **their** proposals.

Exercise 9 Using Nonsexist Language

Rewrite each of the following sentences to avoid using gender-specific terms and awkward expressions.   Revisions may vary.

EXAMPLE   1. The factory is advertising for a night watchman.
           1. *The factory is advertising for a security guard.*

1. meteorologists
2. chairperson
3. author

5. U.S. representative
6. mail carrier
7. humanity

8. ordinary person

9. firefighter
10. flight attendants

1. The weathermen predict sunny skies for the rest of the week.
2. The new chairman is in the office.
3. She was a published authoress and an admired public figure.
4. The male nurse in Grandma's ward was helpful and kind.
5. One of Suzi's ambitions is to become a congressman.
6. We wanted to find the address, so we looked for a mailman.
7. The research done aboard the space shuttle will benefit all mankind.
8. Senator Dupont's political platform was full of references to the common man.
9. The career of fireman is a noble one.
10. Aboard that airline, the stewardesses wear red.

PEANUTS reprinted by permission of United Feature Syndicate, Inc.

Chapter 20   A Glossary of Usage

CHAPTER 20

Chapter Review

A. Revising Expressions by Correcting Errors in Usage

In each of the following sets of word groups, one word group contains an error in usage. Rewrite this word group correctly, using standard, formal usage.

1. a. anywheres you travel **1. anywhere**
   b. as fast as sound travels
   c. to learn Greek cooking from him

2. a. affect the outcome
   b. the candidate implied in his speech
   c. among his two opponents **2. between**

3. a. made illusions to the Bible **3. allusions**
   b. fewer participants in the contest
   c. asked what kind of car that is

4. a. family that emigrated from Germany
   b. should of gone yesterday **4. have**
   c. discovered another planet

5. a. to try and win the game **5. to**
   b. feeling all right
   c. that kind of car

6. a. letting the dog out
   b. an effect of cold weather
   c. books, pencils, papers, and etc.

7. a. ate everything accept the peas and dessert **7. except**
   b. older than you
   c. bringing your records when you come over

8. a. I heard nothing.
   b. Lisa can hardly tell the difference.
   c. That cat ain't Samantha, is it? **8. isn't**

9. a. picture that fell off the wall
   b. that kind of a dog
   c. larger than he is

Using the Chapter Review

To assess student progress, you may want to compare the types of items missed on the **Diagnostic Preview** to those missed on the **Chapter Review**. Then, you could work out specific goals with individual students who are still having difficulty mastering essential information. If students need additional practice, refer them to **Exercises 21–23** in **Chapter 27: Correcting Common Errors.**

10. a. sitting beside the tree
    b. going a little ~~ways~~   **10.** way
    c. not reality but illusion

11. a. whose coat doesn't fit well
    b. that fewer people learned to read back then
    c. inside ~~of~~ the cabinet

12. a. car looking ~~like~~ it had been wrecked   **12.** as if
    b. chair that was blue
    c. water jug that burst

13. a. She effected an improvement.
    b. This is a problem that must be resolved.
    c. ~~Less~~ students joined the club this year.   **13.** Fewer

14. a. Take the package to the mail room.
    b. Apples fell off ~~of~~ the tree.
    c. That will scarcely be enough food for all of them.

15. a. invented a better safety device
    b. if no one ~~beside~~ my aunt knows   **15.** besides
    c. if you're feeling all right

16. a. Funds were allotted among six counties.
    b. Where is my hammer ~~at~~?
    c. This is as far as the fence extends.

17. a. We are going nowhere, Mary Sue.
    b. Doesn't he know the way?
    c. He knows more ~~then~~ he reveals.   **17.** than

18. a. We were gone for ~~a~~ hour.   **18.** an
    b. Try to learn this poem.
    c. Leave the green grapes on the vine.

19. a. I have saved ~~alot~~ of money.   **19.** a lot
    b. Please stay awhile, John.
    c. One of the glasses broke.

20. a. It was an illusion caused by light on the surface.
    b. Their report implies a need for funds.
    c. That dog ~~he~~ limps.

21. a. no exception to this rule
    b. ~~being that~~ she is the oldest   **21.** because [*or* since]
    c. taking a torque wrench to Robin's garage

662   Chapter 20   A Glossary of Usage

22. a. The reason he left is that he's upset.
    b. The crust looked ~~like~~ it had been burned.   22. as if
    c. They ought to study before the test.

23. a. when the ice ~~busted~~ a pipe   23. burst
    b. so he can lend me a dollar
    c. emigrate from their birthplace

24. a. and ~~leave~~ me have my turn   24. let
    b. the mechanic who worked on our car
    c. somewhat cold for swimming

25. a. ~~haven't~~ only three days of vacation   25. have
    b. the effects of smoking
    c. learned that the winner had been announced

26. a. Davenport, Iowa, was as far as we could go on a tank of gas.
    b. Name the borders between the three countries.
    c. Davy will ~~learn~~ the children good manners.   26. teach

27. a. should have taken more time
    b. ~~everywheres~~ you go   27. everywhere
    c. Uncle Mark and Aunt Zita taught themselves how to repair a computer.

28. a. A number of different kinds of birds nest there.
    b. I'm reporting on the invention of the internal-combustion engine.   28. implies
    c. By calling me by my last name, the teacher ~~infers~~ disapproval.

29. a. outside ~~of~~ the assembly hall
    b. as if he had seen a ghost
    c. asking how much he borrowed from you

30. a. In the morning we let the raccoon go.
    b. Engine knock ~~is~~ when a car engine makes a pinging sound because of low-octane fuel.   30. occurs
    c. Kathryn is supposed to work late.

B. Proofreading a Paragraph to Correct Usage Errors

Revise the paragraph on the following page by rewriting each sentence to correct the error or errors in the use of formal, standard English. If a sentence is already correct, write *C*.   Revisions may vary.

Chapter Review   **663**

USAGE

31. can
32. any
33. C
34. implies
35. allusions
36. accepted
37. have
38. between
39. C
40. any

[31] I ~~can't~~ hardly believe what this book says about King Arthur. [32] It says that there wasn't ~~no~~ real King Arthur who ruled England during the Middle Ages. [33] Arthur was actually a powerful chieftain around A.D. 500, at the outset of the so-called Dark Ages. [34] The book ~~infers~~ that the legend of a noble king who introduced chivalry into England is the work of storytellers. [35] Most of the ~~illusions~~ to the Round Table are based on a fifteenth-century work called *Le Morte Darthur* by Sir Thomas Malory. [36] Some of the legends say that Arthur ~~excepted~~ more than a thousand knights for membership at the Round Table. [37] Although there might ~~of~~ been some truth to these legends, Malory's version says there were two hundred fifty knights who earned the right to sit at the Round Table; others say twelve. [38] Some of the most famous contests were ~~among~~ Modred, a wicked man, and Sir Lancelot, a brave defender of honor. [39] When Arthur lay dying, he was taken away to the magical isle of Avalon. [40] The story doesn't go ~~no~~ further, but it implies that Arthur will return someday to inspire noble deeds.

C. Identifying Standard Usage

For each of the following sentences, choose from the choices given in parentheses the word or word group that is correct according to the rules of standard, formal English.

41. With a little effort you (*could have, could of*) written a better report.
42. Shane's answer to my question was (*kind of, rather*) vague.
43. For the band trip I must remember to take my uniform, music, instrument, (*etc., and etc.*)
44. We wanted to go (*everywhere, everywheres*) on our one-week vacation.
45. It looked (*like, as if*) the fire had started in the hayloft.
46. Our team (*had ought, ought*) to win the championship.
47. (*This, This here*) store is having sales in all of its departments.
48. (*Whose, Who's*) briefcase is that?
49. Where should we (*meet, meet at*)?
50. I heard (*where, that*) the mayor would not run for reelection.

RESOURCES

A Glossary of Usage
Review
- *Grammar, Usage, and Mechanics,* pp. 228, 229, 230, 231

Assessment
- *Assessment Package*
  —Chapter Tests, Ch. 20
  —Chapter Tests in Standardized Test Formats, Ch. 20
- *Test Generator (One-Stop Planner CD-ROM)*

Writing Application
Creating a Flier

Using Formal, Standard English Create a flier for an organization that will soon be providing a public service in your community. The organization you choose might provide health, recreation, or housing services, or it might do something else. In a one-page flier, describe the organization's goals and achievements and explain some of the services it offers. Include at least five examples of standard usage covered in this chapter, and underline each example.

Prewriting Begin by listing services that your community needs, and note what kinds of organizations supply these services. You may write about a real service group, such as the American Heart Association, or you may wish to write about a fictitious group. Also, list some of the positive effects the group will likely have on your community. Organize your notes so that you can present your information in several coherent paragraphs.

Writing As you write your first draft, you may think of points you would like to add or changes you would like to make in the presentation of your information. If so, look back over your prewriting notes and determine where your additions and changes will best fit.

Revising Give your flier to a classmate to read, and use your partner's comments on the clarity of your writing to help you make any necessary revisions.

Publishing Check your flier for errors in grammar, spelling, and usage. With your teacher's permission, you could post your flier on the class bulletin board or Web page.

CHAPTER 21 Capitalization
Standard Uses of Capitalization

PREVIEWING THE CHAPTER

- This chapter presents seven main capitalization rules, some of which include numerous parts. As students study the examples for each rule, you may wish to have them suggest other examples that are relevant to their lives.

- The chapter closes with a **Chapter Review** for checking students' capitalization and a **Writing Application** offering students an opportunity to apply the rules of capitalization to writing a visitors' guide.

- Encourage students to refer to this chapter when they proofread their writing assignments.

- For help in integrating the chapter with writing chapters, use the **Teaching Strands** chart on pp. T401A–T401B.

USING THE DIAGNOSTIC PREVIEW

- You may want to use the **Diagnostic Preview** to gauge students' general knowledge of basic capitalization rules. Some students may profit by reading the rules and examples in problem areas and working the exercises at the end of each set. Other students may use this chapter as a reference tool.

Diagnostic Preview

A. Capitalizing Sentences Correctly

For each of the following sentences, correctly write the words that should be capitalized.

EXAMPLE   1. Renée searched everywhere in freeport, maine, until she found a gift at l. l. bean for her grandparents.

1. Freeport; Maine; L. L. Bean

1. Our september trip to ireland included a stay in kilkee, a coastal village.
2. At the end of class, ms. kwan said that friday's geology II exam will include questions about the appalachian mountains.
3. We should change our dollars to pesos before we board the flight to santiago, chile.
4. The thanksgiving day parade travelled from martin luther king, jr., boulevard to fifty-first street.
5. During their trip to colorado, the barreras hiked up pikes peak.
6. The title of her new television special is *one in a million*.
7. Both ernest hemingway and walt disney once worked for the *kansas city star*.
8. Every easter sunday, grandma penny sings "we praise thee, o god, our redeemer, creator," which was translated from german.
9. One of the cities of the incas, machu picchu, lay hidden among the andes mountains in southern peru and was never discovered by spanish conquerors.

666   Chapter 21   Capitalization

CHAPTER RESOURCES

Planning
- *One-Stop Planner CD-ROM*

Practice and Extension
- *Grammar, Usage, and Mechanics*, p. 235
- *Language Workshop CD-ROM*

Internet
- go.hrw.com (keyword: EOLang)

Evaluation and Assessment
- *Assessment Package*
  —*Chapter Tests*, Ch. 21
  —*Chapter Tests in Standardized Test Formats*, Ch. 21
- *Test Generator (One-Stop Planner CD-ROM)*

10. In 1982, the colombian writer gabriel garcía márquez was awarded the nobel prize in literature.
11. The winner of the first kentucky derby, the annual race at churchill downs in louisville, was a horse named aristides.
12. In 1983, sally ride became the first american woman in space when the space shuttle *challenger* was launched from cape canaveral.
13. Frederick douglass was the first african american member of the department of justice's u.s. marshals service.
14. If Beth improves her grades in english and history II, her parents will let her apply for a job at the walgreens drugstore on forty-third street.
15. Our debate team argued in favor of pro-american economic policies as the best way to foster democracy in the developing countries of africa, asia, and south america.

B. Capitalizing a Paragraph Correctly

For each sentence in the following paragraph, correctly write the words that should be capitalized.

EXAMPLE [1] Last summer we visited my uncle carlos, who lives in new york city.

1. Carlos; New York City

[16] One of new york city's most popular tourist attractions is the empire state building. [17] The building, at fifth avenue and thirty-fourth street, attracts 2,500,000 visitors a year. [18] Among them are troops of boy scouts and girl scouts, who camp out on the eighty-sixth floor. [19] The building was financed by john jakob raskob, the founder of general motors. [20] It opened in 1931, during the great depression. [21] At the time, it was the tallest building on earth (1,250 feet), but it's since been overshadowed by the world trade center (1,350 feet) and by chicago's sears tower (1,450 feet). [22] The observatory on the one hundred and second floor accounts for much of the empire state building's continuing appeal; when the weather is clear, the observatory provides a view of five states: new york, new jersey, connecticut, pennsylvania, and massachusetts. [23] On may 1, 1991, publicists threw a party to mark the building's sixtieth birthday. [24] One of those who attended was the actress fay wray, who starred in the 1933 movie *king kong*, in which the building was featured. [25] Another attendee was jack brod, one of the original tenants, who proclaimed of the building, "it's got history woven into it."

Timesaver

To save time, you might want to establish a way to check at a glance students' progress in mastering capitalization rules. After you have evaluated the **Diagnostic Preview,** have each student make a chart of capitalization rules by letter and number, with columns for recording results of the Diagnostic Preview (DP) and subsequent exercises (EX). Have students place an **M** next to the rules they have mastered or an **L** next to those they are still learning. Students should record the numbers of the exercises they have completed and mark an **M** or an **L** to show whether they have mastered each exercise. Students may wish to use the chart below as a guide.

RULE	DP	EX.	
a	M		
c	L	1.	M
d (1)	L	2.	L

Capitalization, pp. 666–690
Alignments
TEKS 3A, 3D
TAAS W3, W7
English II End-of-Course 5, 6

Texas Resources
- *TAAS Tool Kit*
- *Preparation for TAAS*
- *One-Stop Planner CD-ROM*

Using Capital Letters Correctly

Rules 21a–g (pp. 668–688)

OBJECTIVES

- To correct errors in capitalization in paragraphs
- To correct errors in capitalization in phrases
- To correct errors in capitalization in sentences

TEACHING TIP

To demonstrate to students that the use of capitalization is important for effective communication, write the following pair of sentences on the chalkboard. Then, discuss with students how the use of capitalization affects the meaning of each sentence.

1. You can reach the old pioneer settlement by crossing the little Yellow River and turning right at the sandy road exit. [In this example, *old* and *pioneer* modify *settlement, little* modifies *Yellow River,* and *sandy* and *road* modify *exit.*]

2. You can reach the Old Pioneer Settlement by crossing the Little Yellow River and turning right at the Sandy Road exit. [In this example, *Old Pioneer Settlement, Little Yellow River,* and *Sandy Road* are all compound proper nouns.]

HELP

In your reading, you will notice variation in the use of capitalization. Most writers, however, follow the rules presented in this chapter. In your own writing, following these rules will help you communicate clearly with the widest possible audience.

Reference Note

For more about using **capital letters in quotations,** see page 743.

STYLE TIP

Some poets do not capitalize lines of poetry. When you quote from a writer's work, use capital letters as the writer uses them.

Using Capital Letters Correctly

21a. Capitalize the first word in every sentence.

EXAMPLES **T**he Second Seminole War lasted nearly eight years.

After the war many Seminoles remained in the Everglades and never officially made peace with the U.S. government.

The first word of a quoted sentence should begin with a capital letter, whether or not the quotation begins your sentence.

EXAMPLE In *Walden,* Henry David Thoreau writes, "**I**f you have built castles in the air, your work need not be lost; that is where they should be."

When quoting only part of a sentence, capitalize the first word of the quotation if (1) the person you are quoting capitalized it or (2) it is the first word of your sentence.

EXAMPLES What is suggested by the metaphor "**c**astles in the air"?

"**C**astles in the air" is a metaphor that suggests one's dreams, goals, or ambitions.

NOTE Capitalize the first word of a sentence fragment used in dialogue.

EXAMPLE When he was asked whether he had read *Walden,* Mario answered, "**O**nly part of it."

Traditionally, the first word in a line of poetry is capitalized.

EXAMPLES **S**torm, blow me from here
With your fiercest wind
Let me float across the sky
'Till I can rest again.

Maya Angelou, "Woman Work"

21b. Capitalize the pronoun *I* and the interjection *O.*

The interjection *O,* usually used only for invocations, is followed by the name of the person or thing being addressed. Do not confuse *O* with the common interjection *oh,* which is capitalized only when it begins a sentence or is part of a title.

EXAMPLES The first line **I** read in the poem was "Hear us, **O** Zeus."

I finished the race, but **oh,** was **I** exhausted.

668 Chapter 21 Capitalization

RESOURCES

Using Capital Letters Correctly
Practice

- *Grammar, Usage, and Mechanics,* pp. 236, 237, 238, 239, 240, 241, 242, 243, 244, 245, 246, 247, 248, 249, 250
- *Language Workshop CD-ROM,* Lessons 45, 46

NOTE *Oh,* unlike *O,* is followed by a mark of punctuation, usually a comma or an exclamation point.

21c. Capitalize the first word in both the salutation and the closing of a letter.

EXAMPLES   **D**ear Mr. Velazquez: **M**y dear Jennifer,

Sincerely yours,   **Y**ours truly,

Reference Note
For information on **commas and colons in salutations,** see pages 716 and 730.

21d. Capitalize proper nouns and proper adjectives.

A *common noun* names one of a group of persons, places, things, or ideas. A *proper noun* names a particular person, place, thing, or idea. A *proper adjective* is formed from a proper noun.

A common noun is capitalized when it

- begins a sentence
    or
- begins a direct quotation
    or
- is part of a title

Common Nouns	Proper Nouns	Proper Adjectives
a **w**riter	**D**ickens	**D**ickensian character
a **r**eligion	**B**uddhism	**B**uddhist monk
a **c**ountry	**F**rance	**F**rench bread
a **q**ueen	**V**ictoria	**V**ictorian era
a **p**lanet	**V**enus	**V**enusian terrain
a **r**egion	the **M**idwest	**M**idwestern values

In a compound proper noun, articles, coordinating conjunctions, and short prepositions (those with fewer than five letters) are not capitalized.

Reference Note
For more information about **common nouns** and **proper nouns,** see page 406. For more about **proper adjectives,** see page 415.

EXAMPLES   Prince **o**f Wales

National Association **f**or **t**he Advancement **o**f Colored People

Girl Scouts **o**f **t**he United States **o**f America

ENGLISH-LANGUAGE LEARNERS
Spanish. Many Spanish rules for capitalization differ from the English rules. For example, Spanish speakers do not capitalize the first-person singular pronoun; the words for "street," "highway," "avenue," "lane," and so forth; or the names of days of the week and of months of the year. As the class progresses through the chapter, invite English-language learners to share with the rest of the class how other capitalization rules in their native languages differ from those in English.

MULTIPLE INTELLIGENCES
Intrapersonal Intelligence. Because intrapersonal learners are independent and self-motivated, you may want to give them individual folders containing the objectives, lesson plans, and assignments for several days. Allow students to work at their own pace, rejoining the rest of the class at a designated time.

Looking at Language

Word Origins. As mentioned in the Note at the top of this page, proper nouns and proper adjectives may lose their capitals after long use. There are interesting stories behind many of the common nouns derived from proper nouns. For example, *sandwich* comes from the title of John Montagu (1718–1792), the fourth Earl of Sandwich. He was an avid games player. Supposedly, on one occasion, unwilling to leave the gaming table for food, he asked for some cold roast beef between two slices of bread—the first sandwich.

Ask students to explore the origins of other common nouns derived from proper nouns, such as *graham cracker, cologne, teddy bear, maverick,* and *cardigan.* Explain that while most dictionaries will provide brief etymologies, encyclopedias of word origins will offer more extensive explanations. Refer students to such books as *The Facts on File Encyclopedia of Word and Phrase Origins* by Robert Hendrickson or *Panati's Extraordinary Origins of Everyday Things* by Charles Panati.

COMPUTER TIP
The range of correct spellings of personal names can foil even the best spell-checking software. One way to avoid this problem is to customize your spell-checker. If your software allows, add to it frequently used names that you have difficulty spelling or capitalizing correctly.

Reference Note
For information about **capitalizing abbreviations** such as *Dr.* and *Jr.,* see page 686.

NOTE Proper nouns and proper adjectives may lose their capitals after long use.

EXAMPLES   **d**iesel   **b**ologna   **b**raille   **w**att

When you are not sure whether to capitalize a word, check a dictionary to see in which uses (if any) it is capitalized.

(1) Capitalize the names of persons and animals.

Persons	**N**olan **R**yan	**L**atrice **K**antor	**H**. **H**. **M**unro
	William the **C**onqueror	**D**r. **E**ileen **C**ruz	**J**erome **W**ilson, **J**r.
		Bill **G**ates	
Animals	**L**assie	**S**ocks	**W**hite **F**ang
	Babe	**R**over	**F**luff

NOTE Some names contain more than one capital letter. Usage varies in the capitalization of *van, von, du, de la,* and other parts of multiword names. When possible, verify the spelling of a name with the person with that name, or check in a reference source.

EXAMPLES   **D**e **L**a **C**ruz   **M**c**E**nroe   **R**ed **C**loud   **V**an **D**ongen
de la **M**are   **O**'**S**hea   **W**ells-**B**arnett   **v**an **G**ogh

(2) Capitalize initials in names and abbreviations that come before or after names.

EXAMPLES   **J**. **D**. **R**ockefeller   **L**ouis **J**. **H**alle   **D**r. **S**uzi **C**ohen
Tom **T**aliaferro, **M.D.**   **S**r. **G**arcia   **M**s. **B**radford

Exercise 1   Proofreading Paragraphs for Correct Capitalization

Most of the sentences in the following paragraphs contain errors in capitalization. Write the correct form of each incorrect word. If the capitalization of a sentence is already correct, write *C*.

Words that should be capitalized or lowercased are underscored.
EXAMPLE   [1] These pictures capture only a few of the many sides of Gordon parks, renowned Photographer, film director, writer, and composer.

1. Parks; photographer

[1] A self-taught photographer, gordon Parks grew up in Fort Scott, Kansas. [2] after winning a rosenwald Fellowship for a series of pictures about life in Chicago's Slums, He got his first full-time photography job with the Farm Security Administration in Washington, D.C. [3] In 1949, he joined the staff of *Life* magazine. [4] During his nearly twenty years with *Life*, Parks covered assignments ranging from Junior High School science conventions to Paris Fashion Shows. [5] He also wrote many of the essays that accompanied his photographs, as well as two Volumes of autobiography, *A Choice of Weapons* and *Voices in the Mirror.*

[6] turning to a career in the movie industry in 1968, Parks moved to Hollywood, where his son Gordon Parks, jr., took this photograph of him preparing to direct a scene from the film version of *The Learning Tree*. [7] Parks also wrote the film's screenplay and, working at the grand piano in his Hollywood apartment, its musical score. [8] His success with the film led to other writing and directing projects, including *Leadbelly*, the story of the blues musician Huddie ledbetter.

[9] In September 1997, an exhibition of his photography opened at the Corcoran Gallery in Washington, D.C. [10] Some of his best-known projects have included *Voices in the Mirror* and the words and music for *Martin*, a classical Ballet honoring the late dr. martin luther king, jr.

Crossing the Curriculum

Social Science. In various social science courses, such as world history and world geography, students will be exposed to many geographical names. Direct students' attention to the charts on pp. 672–673, and ask students to provide examples that are relevant to their current work in their social science courses. Ask volunteers to write the examples on the chalkboard, paying particular attention to capitalization.

Have students repeat this activity when they study other charts in the chapter. You may want to extend the activity by calling on volunteers to explain the historical or social significance of some of the examples.

MECHANICS

---

(3) Capitalize geographical names.

Type of Name	Examples	
Countries	the **N**etherlands **G**hana	**A**rgentina **S**witzerland
Towns, Cities	**C**hicago **S**tratford-on-**A**von **S**an **D**iego	**L**aredo **B**erlin **St.** **P**etersburg
Counties, Townships, Parishes, Provinces	**O**range **C**ounty **F**ranklin **T**ownship **E**ast **B**aton **R**ouge **P**arish	**C**addo **P**arish **Y**orkshire **C**ape of **G**ood **H**ope **P**rovince
States	**O**regon **N**ew **Y**ork	**T**exas **S**outh **C**arolina
Regions	the **M**iddle **E**ast the **W**est the **N**ortheast	**G**reat **P**lains **Y**ukon **S**un **B**elt

> **NOTE** Words such as *south, east,* and *northwest* are not capitalized when they indicate direction.
>
> **EXAMPLES** **w**est of the bridge   heading **n**orth

Type of Name	Examples	
Continents	**S**outh **A**merica **A**sia	**E**urope **A**frica
Islands	**G**alveston **I**sland the **L**esser **A**ntilles	the **I**sle of **W**ight **K**ey **W**est
Mountains	**A**llegheny **M**ountains **S**ierra **M**adre	**M**ount **St.** **H**elens **P**ikes **P**eak
Other Geographical Names	**S**henandoah **V**alley **B**ryce **C**anyon **C**ape **H**atteras	**K**alihari **D**esert **T**impanogos **C**ave **S**inai **P**eninsula

672   **Chapter 21**   Capitalization

MINI-LESSON

Using Commas with Geographical Names. You may want to review with students the following rules for punctuation.

1. In an address for a letter, use a comma to separate the names of the city and the state. Do not use a comma between the house number and the street name or between the two-letter state code and the ZIP Code, for example,

   1909 Weston Point
   Austin, TX 72746

Type of Name	Examples	
Bodies of Water	**A**tlantic **O**cean	**S**uwanee **R**iver
	Red **S**ea	**R**io **G**rande
	Persian **G**ulf	**L**ake of the **O**zarks
Parks, Forests	**R**edwood **S**tate **P**ark	**B**ernheim **F**orest
	North **T**ongass **N**ational **F**orest	**S**tone **M**ountain **M**emorial **P**ark
Roads, Highways, Streets	**R**oute 41	**C**entral **A**venue
	Interstate 10	**S**outh **F**iftieth **S**treet
	Sunshine **S**tate **P**arkway	**P**leasant **H**ill **R**oad

NOTE The second word in a hyphenated street number begins with a lowercase letter.

EXAMPLE   Fifty-third Street

A word such as *city, island, river,* or *street* is generally not capitalized unless it is part of a proper noun.

Proper Nouns	Common Nouns
traffic in **M**exico **C**ity	traffic in a large city
visiting **C**aptiva **I**sland	visiting a barrier island
bridging the **O**hio **R**iver	bridging the river
across **D**elancey **S**treet	across a congested street

Exercise 2 Using Correct Capitalization

If one or more words in each of the following word groups should be capitalized, write the entire word group correctly. If a word group is already correct, write *C*.

EXAMPLE   1. atop granite peak
          1. atop Granite Peak

1. zion national park
2. gulf of tonkin
3. explored Mount ararat
4. hiking trails in a state park   **4. C**
5. at moon lake
6. a house on starve island
7. beside the ohio river
8. in lancaster county

STYLE TIP

Since *rio* is Spanish for "river," *Rio Grande River* is redundant. Use only *Rio Grande*.

Other terms to watch for are

- *sierra*, Spanish for "mountain range" [Use only *Sierra Nevada*, not *Sierra Nevada Mountains*.]
- *yama*, Japanese for "mountain" [Use only *Fuji-yama* or *Mount Fuji*, not *Mount Fuji-yama*.]
- *sahara*, Arabic for "desert" [Use only *Sahara*, not *Sahara Desert*.]
- *gobi*, Mongolian for "desert" [Use only *Gobi*, not *Gobi Desert*.]

Cooperative Learning

To give students additional practice in the capitalization of geographical names, have students of mixed abilities work in small groups to write a set of directions to a location. Either assign a starting point and a destination, or allow each group to determine its own. Ask students to include references to at least five types of geographical names as well as to the points of direction suggested by the **Note** on p. 672. Have groups check each other's directions for clarity and for correct use of capitalization.

Critical Thinking

Metacognition. After students have completed the **Cooperative Learning** activity above, ask them to think about the ways they interacted within their groups. Did they generally take the initiative to lead the group? Did they readily follow the lead of another and perform tasks assigned? Did they feel confident contributing to the group, or were they reluctant to suggest ideas? Help students see that an awareness of the roles they play within groups can assist them in better understanding how they think and learn.

9. mekong delta
10. across baffin bay
11. ventura boulevard
12. the tides in the bay   **12. C**
13. new york skyline
14. forty-fifth street
15. near the isle of wight
16. the west side of the river   **16. C**
17. population of the north
18. near dundee mountain
19. coffee from brazil
20. coast of australia

Exercise 3 Proofreading a Paragraph for Correct Capitalization

Capitalize the words that should begin with a capital letter in the following paragraph. Do not include the words already capitalized. If a sentence is already correct, write C.

EXAMPLE [1] Until last year I'd never been farther from lawrenceburg, tennessee, than pulaski, which is only seventeen miles east.

1. Lawrenceburg; Tennessee; Pulaski

[1] Naturally, I was excited when our choir decided to have an international arts and crafts fair to raise money for a trip to washington, d.c. [2] Colleen O'Roark suggested that the fair feature crafts and food from countries in europe, africa, and asia. [3] Juana Santiago, whose family is from venezuela, pointed out that we should also include items from central america and south america. [4] Julian   **4. C** Moore, who recently returned from visiting relatives in Monrovia, said he'd bring a display of Liberian baskets. [5] Karen Cohen offered items from quebec, one of our neighbors to the north. [6] Maxine Hirano, who was born in tokyo, japan, promised to demonstrate paper folding. [7] Some of us met later at Paula Bowen's house, on the northeast corner of columbus street and hickory lane, to choose items to represent the united states. [8] We selected American Indian artifacts from the southwest, country crafts from the appalachian mountains, and shell gifts from the states along the gulf of mexico. [9] Erin McCall, whose family moved to lexington avenue from phoenix, arizona, volunteered to bring rocks that she had bought at a gift shop in petrified forest national park. [10] When the fair was over, we had raised enough money to include on our trip to the nation's capital a tour of mammoth cave national park in kentucky.

(4) Capitalize the names of organizations, teams, institutions, and government bodies.

Type of Name	Examples
Organizations	American Medical Association National Honor Society League of Women Voters Organization of American States
Teams	Eastside Jets Harlem Globetrotters New York Rangers Portsmouth Chess Masters
Institutions	Good Samaritan Hospital Ridgemont High School Stanford University
Government Bodies	Department of the Interior Tampa City Council the Nuclear Regulatory Commission

NOTE Do not capitalize words such as *democratic, republican,* and *socialist* when they refer to principles or forms of government. Capitalize these words only when they refer to specific political parties.

EXAMPLES Voting is part of the democratic process.

Was George W. Bush the Republican nominee?

(5) Capitalize the names of businesses and brand names of business products.

Type of Name	Examples	
Businesses	Thrifty Dry Cleaners Sears, Roebuck and Co.	First National Bank Fields Department Store
Business Products	Schwinn Mesa GMC Jimmy	Callaway Big Bertha Apple Macintosh

STYLE TIP

The word *party* in the name of a political party may be capitalized or not; either way is correct.

EXAMPLE
Republican Party
or
Republican party

Within a piece of writing, be consistent about using a capital or lowercase letter to begin the word *party*.

Using Capital Letters Correctly   675

NOTE A common noun that follows a brand name and identifies the type of product is not capitalized.

EXAMPLES Schwinn **b**icycle, Callaway **g**olf **c**lub, Apple **c**omputer

HELP
Do not capitalize words like *hotel, theater, college,* or *high school* unless they are part of a proper name.

EXAMPLES
a local **h**igh **s**chool

Jackson **H**igh **S**chool

(6) Capitalize the names of buildings and other structures.

Type of Name	Examples	
Buildings and Other Structures	**D**etroit **W**estin **H**otel	**M**osque of **O**mar
	Fox **T**heater	**B**uckingham **P**alace
	Colosseum	**S**an **R**oque **D**am
	Washington **M**utual **T**ower	**Q**ueens-**M**idtown **T**unnel
	Natchez **T**race **P**arkway **B**ridge	**M**etropolitan **M**useum

(7) Capitalize the names of monuments, memorials, and awards.

Type of Name	Examples
Monuments, Memorials, and Awards	**D**inosaur **N**ational **M**onument
	Korean **W**ar **V**eterans **M**emorial
	Effigy **M**ounds **N**ational **M**onument
	Nobel **P**rize
	Perry's **V**ictory and **I**nternational **P**eace **M**emorial
	Heisman **T**rophy

Do not capitalize a word such as *building, monument,* or *award* unless it is part of a proper noun.

(8) Capitalize the names of historical events and periods, special events, and holidays and other calendar items.

Type of Name	Examples	
Historical Events and Periods	the **B**attle of **G**ettysburg	the **D**ark **A**ges
	the **Y**alta **C**onference	**G**reat **D**epression
	Children's **C**rusade	the **S**tone **A**ge

676 Chapter 21 Capitalization

Type of Name	Examples	
Special Events	the **B**oston **M**arathon the **N**ational **M**inority **J**ob **E**xpo	the **A**ll-**S**tar **G**ame the **I**owa **S**tate **F**air **S**pecial **O**lympics
Holidays and Other Calendar Items	**V**alentine's **D**ay **E**arth **D**ay **C**inco de **M**ayo	**F**riday **M**arch **K**wanzaa

NOTE Do not capitalize the name of a season unless the season is being personified or is part of a proper name.

EXAMPLES We looked forward to **s**pring after the long **w**inter.

Autumn in her russet garb followed green **S**ummer.

Are you going to the **W**inter Wonderland Dance?

Exercise 4 Identifying and Correcting Errors in Capitalization

Correct the capitalization errors in each of the following sentences by capitalizing letters as needed.

EXAMPLE 1. Some Norse folk tales originated in the Dark ages.

1. Ages

1. Dr. Bourgeois applied to his local branch of the American medical association.
2. Gary works in the afternoons at Ridgeway discount appliance mart.
3. The house of Representatives passed the bills, but they died in the senate.
4. One of Lena's ancestors was at the battle of the Argonne.
5. Did you say you were planning to run in the Boston marathon?
6. Thanksgiving day always falls on the fourth Thursday in november.
7. When it was completed in 1973, the Sears tower in Chicago was the tallest building in the world.
8. Aaron couldn't decide whether to cheer for his hometown team, the Wisconsin badgers, or his new favorite, the Texas longhorns.
9. Her ambition is to win a pulitzer Prize someday.
10. The library's new Apple macintosh is scheduled to be delivered next week.

Exercise 4

ALTERNATIVE LESSON
After students have studied **Rule 21g,** pp. 686–687, ask them to return to **Exercise 4** and to rewrite the following sentences, using acceptable abbreviations, as if they were writing informal notes.

1. Sentence 1 [*Dr. Bourgeois applied to his local branch of the American Medical Assn. (or AMA)*]

2. Sentence 6 [*Thanksgiving Day always falls on the fourth Thurs. in Nov.*]

Meeting INDIVIDUAL NEEDS

MULTIPLE INTELLIGENCES
Linguistic Intelligence. Provide small groups of students different issues of magazines and newspapers. Ask each group to look for advertisements that do not follow the accepted rules of capitalization, such as "Littering is unlAWFUL," or "Reading is FUNdamental." Have groups share specific examples and suggest reasons for the unconventional capitalization. [Students may suggest that the capitalization was used to instill an attitude in the reader's mind, to create humor, or to draw attention to a serious issue.]

MECHANICS

STYLE TIP
The words *black* and *white* may or may not be capitalized when they refer to races. Either way is correct. Within a piece of writing, be consistent in using capital or lowercase letters to begin those words.

STYLE TIP
Some writers capitalize all pronouns that refer to a specific deity. Other writers capitalize such pronouns only to prevent confusion.

EXAMPLE
Job wondered why the Lord allowed **H**is servant to suffer. [Capitalizing *His* makes it clear that the pronoun refers to *the Lord* and not to *Job*.]

Reference Note
For information on using italics with **names of ships, trains, aircraft, and spacecraft,** see page 741.

---

(9) Capitalize the names of nationalities, races, and peoples.

Type of Name	Examples		
Nationalities, Races, and Peoples	**I**talian	**C**anadian	**C**aucasian
	African	**J**ewish	**H**ispanic
	Navajo	**M**icronesian	**I**ndo-**I**ranian

(10) Capitalize the names of religions and their followers, holy days and celebrations, sacred writings, and specific deities.

Type of Name	Examples	
Religions and Followers	**J**udaism	**M**uslim
	Buddhism	**C**onfucian
	Christianity	**M**ormon
Holy Days and Celebrations	**A**sh **W**ednesday	**H**anukkah
	Ramadan	**C**hristmas **E**ve
	Yom **K**ippur	**P**entecost
Holy Writings	the **B**ible	**R**ig-**V**eda
	the **T**almud	**E**xodus
	the **K**oran	**D**ead **S**ea **S**crolls
Specific Deities	**A**llah	**V**ishnu
	God	the **H**oly **S**pirit

NOTE The words *god* and *goddess* are not capitalized when they refer to the deities of ancient mythology. The names of specific mythological deities are capitalized, however.

EXAMPLE The Roman **g**oddess of grain was **C**eres.

(11) Capitalize the names of ships, trains, aircraft, and spacecraft.

Type of Name	Examples	
Ships, Trains, Aircraft, and Spacecraft	*Queen **M**ary*	*Spirit of **S**t. **L**ouis*
	*R.M.S. **T**itanic*	*Orient **E**xpress*
	*Lake **S**hore **L**imited*	*Enterprise*
	Electra	*Atlantis*

678 Chapter 21 Capitalization

NOTE The names of the make and model of a vehicle also are capitalized.

EXAMPLES   **M**itsubishi **E**clipse [car]

Kris **K**raft [boat]

(12) Capitalize the names of planets, stars, constellations, and other heavenly bodies.

EXAMPLES   **P**luto [planet]   **P**ollux [star]

Andromeda **G**alaxy [galaxy]   **U**rsa **M**ajor [constellation]

Great **N**ebula [nebula]   **T**itan [moon]

NOTE The word *earth* is not capitalized unless it is used along with the name of another heavenly body that is capitalized. The words *sun* and *moon* are generally not capitalized.

EXAMPLES   Unlike **E**arth, neither **M**ercury nor **V**enus has a **m**oon.

The **s**un is a star.

The **m**oon is the **e**arth's only natural satellite.

21e. Do not capitalize the names of school subjects, except course names followed by a number and the names of language classes.

Type of Name	Examples		
School Subjects	**a**lgebra	**c**hemistry	**m**usic
	Algebra II	**C**hemistry I	**M**usic 101
	Latin	**G**erman	**M**andarin
	English	**S**panish	**D**utch

NOTE Do not capitalize the class name *freshman, sophomore, junior,* or *senior* unless it is part of a proper noun.

EXAMPLES   A number of **s**ophomores attended this spring's **J**unior **P**rom.

The **S**ophomore **S**ingers performed for the **f**reshmen.

TIPS & TRICKS

Generally, a singular noun identified by a number or letter is capitalized.

EXAMPLES
Room 13   **F**igure C
Chapter 21   **E**xample D
Channel 32   **S**uite 4A

However, the word *page* is usually not capitalized, nor is a plural noun followed by two or more numbers or letters.

EXAMPLE
Look at **c**harts A and B on **p**age 273.

Using Capital Letters Correctly   679

TEACHING TIP

Reviews You may want to use **Review A** as guided practice and have students complete **Review B** as independent practice. To give students additional help with the exercises, you may want to tell them how many capital letters they must add to each sentence.

Review A:
1. 6   2. 11   3. 6   4. 6
5. 4   6. 7   7. 6   8. 4
9. 3   10. 3

Review B:
1. 3   2. 4   3. 6   4. 5
5. 4   6. 9   7. 9   8. 13
9. 3   10. 6

Review A Correcting Capitalization Errors

Identify the words that should be capitalized in each of the following sentences. Do not include words that are already capitalized.

EXAMPLE
1. The spanish explorer juan ponce de león landed in florida in 1513.
1. *Spanish; Juan Ponce de León; Florida*

1. The area now known as florida was originally inhabited by native american peoples, including the apalachees, the creeks, and the seminoles.
2. The state is bounded on the north by alabama and georgia, on the east by the atlantic ocean, on the south by the straits of florida and the gulf of mexico, and on the west by alabama and the gulf of mexico.
3. The spanish founded st. augustine, the state's first permanent european settlement, in 1565, making it the oldest colonial city in the united states.
4. When spain ceded florida to the united states in 1821, the u.s. government demanded that the native peoples move west.
5. The strength and dignity of the seminole leader osceola, who led his people in the fight to retain their lands, are evident in this 1838 painting by george catlin.
6. Most of the seminoles eventually moved to present-day oklahoma, but a few hundred fled to the everglades, a huge wilderness area in southern florida that now includes everglades national park.
7. Founded in 1886, eatonville, florida, is the oldest incorporated african american town in the united states.
8. After the cuban revolution in the late 1950s, and again in the early 1980s, many cubans fled to miami.
9. Miami has also served as a major point of entry for haitian refugees who have braved the atlantic ocean in search of a better life.
10. Among the asians who have settled in the state are refugees from vietnam, many of whom make their living fishing along the northern coast of florida.

Osceola by George Catlin. Courtesy of the Department of Library Services. American Museum of National History.

680   Chapter 21   Capitalization

Review B Proofreading Paragraphs for Correct Capitalization

Identify the words that should be capitalized in each sentence in the following paragraphs. Do not include words that are already capitalized.

EXAMPLES
[1] Trivia games test your knowledge of subjects as diverse as american inventors, the korean war, and popular music.

1. American, Korean War

[2] my parents have played trivia games against my brother and me since we moved to cleveland four years ago.

2. My, Cleveland

[1] Last saturday, may 18, my brother Ted and i finally won our first trivia match against our parents. [2] Some of the courses Ted is taking this semester are history, political science, and french; mine include world literature I and geography II. [3] We surged into the lead when our parents couldn't remember that the first united states satellite, *explorer I*, followed the soviet union's *sputnik I* into space. [4] From my geography class, I remembered that mount McKinley is the highest point and death valley is the lowest point on the north american continent.

[5] Our parents rallied for the lead by knowing that the boy on the cracker jack box is named jack and that his dog's name is bingo. [6] Then Ted came up with the fact that the steel framework of the statue of liberty was designed by the frenchman alexandre gustave eiffel, who also designed the eiffel tower in paris. [7] None of us knew that john wilkes booth was only twenty-six years old when he shot abraham lincoln at ford's theater on good friday in 1865. [8] Mom, who has always been a loyal democrat, knew that *engine 1401*—the southern railways locomotive that carried franklin d. roosevelt's body from warm springs, georgia, to washington, D.C.—can now be seen in the smithsonian institution.

[9] Ted and I lost several points because I didn't know that kleenex tissues were first used as gas-mask filters during world war I. [10] However, Ted won the game for us by remembering that the white house was called the executive mansion before it was burned by the british during the war of 1812.

Meeting INDIVIDUAL NEEDS

ENGLISH-LANGUAGE LEARNERS

Spanish. When discussing with students the rules pertaining to capitalization of titles, keep in mind that the rules in English differ from those in Spanish. Invite students whose native language is Spanish to use some of the examples for **Rule 21f (1), (2),** and **(3), pp. 682–683,** to point out those differences. [*In Spanish, the titles of persons are not capitalized before a name unless the title is abbreviated:* el doctor Vigil; Dr. Vigil.]

MECHANICS

Reference Note

For more information about **capitalizing and punctuating abbreviations,** see page 686.

STYLE TIP

For special emphasis or clarity, writers sometimes capitalize a title used alone or following a person's name.

EXAMPLES
The **G**overnor firmly stated her opinion on the issue.

Her predecessor called the new **P**rincipal **C**hief "the best person for the job."

HELP

Some titles are traditionally always capitalized. If you are unsure whether to capitalize a title, look it up in a dictionary.

21f. Capitalize titles.

(1) Capitalize a person's title when the title comes before the person's name.

Type of Name	Examples	
Titles	**G**eneral Powell	**D**r. Sakamoto
	President Kennedy	**M**arshal Foch
	Queen Margrethe	**A**rchbishop Tutu

Generally, a title used alone or following a person's name is not capitalized, especially if the title is preceded by *a* or *the*.

EXAMPLES   In 1991, Boris Yeltsin became the first freely elected **p**resident of the Russian Federation.

Who was the U.S. **p**resident during World War II?

Christine Todd Whitman served as **g**overnor of New Jersey in the 1990s.

A title used alone in direct address is generally capitalized.

EXAMPLES   Well, **M**ayor, will you please test the microphone?

Do you intend to visit the disaster area, **G**overnor?

Please be seated, **S**ir [*or* sir].

(2) Capitalize a word showing family relationship when the word is used before or in place of a person's name, unless the word follows a possessive noun or pronoun.

EXAMPLES	**A**unt Edith	**U**ncle Fred	**G**randmother Bechtel
	my **a**unt Edith	your **u**ncle Fred	Maria's **g**randmother

(3) Capitalize the first and last words and all other important words in titles and subtitles.

Unimportant words in a title include

- articles: *a, an, the*
- coordinating conjunctions: *and, but, for, nor, or, so,* and *yet*
- short prepositions (fewer than five letters): *of, to, in, for, from, with*

682   Chapter 21   Capitalization

NOTE Capitalize an article (*a*, *an*, or *the*) at the beginning of a title or subtitle only if it is the first word of the official title or subtitle.

EXAMPLES Last summer, Joan read *The Outsiders* and *Harriet Beecher Stowe: A Life*.

Joan reads both *The Atlantic Monthly* and *the Rocky Mountain News*.

Type of Title	Examples
Books	**S**ongs of the **T**ewa **S**ilent **D**ancing: **A P**artial **R**emembrance of **P**uerto **R**ican **C**hildhood
Chapters and Other Parts of Books	"**T**he **P**hilippines: **I**ts **L**and and **R**esources" "**I**ndex of **L**iterary **S**kills: **A W**riter's **G**uide"
Periodicals	**U.S. N**ews & **W**orld **R**eport **C**hicago **S**un **T**imes
Poems	"**L**ove **W**ithout **L**ove" "**I L**ike to **S**ee **I**t **L**ap the **M**iles"
Short Stories	"**T**he **M**an to **S**end **R**ain **C**louds" "**T**he **W**oman **W**ho **H**ad **N**o **E**ye for **S**mall **D**etails"
Plays	**A R**aisin in the **S**un **S**unday in the **P**ark with **G**eorge
Historical Documents	**T**reaty of **V**ersailles **A**rticles of **C**onfederation
Movies	**A**ntz **E**ver **A**fter **T**he **P**arent **T**rap **T**he **P**rince of **E**gypt
Radio and TV Programs	**W**ar of the **W**orlds **F**ace the **N**ation **H**ercules: **T**he **L**egendary **J**ourneys
Works of Art	**C**rossing the **B**rook **T**wo **M**exican **W**omen and **C**hild

(continued)

HELP
The official title of a book is found on its title page. The official title of a newspaper or other periodical is found on its masthead, which usually appears on the editorial page or the table of contents.

Reference Note
For information about which **titles** should be **italicized** and which should be in **quotation marks**, see pages 740 and 747.

Relating to Literature
If poems by Emily Dickinson and E. E. Cummings are available in students' literature textbooks, ask students to read these poems and to note the poets' unconventional use of capitalization. Ask students to suggest reasons for each poet's style. [*Dickinson often capitalizes common nouns, perhaps to personify objects, to exalt ideas, or to make abstract ideas concrete. Cummings often lowercases proper nouns, perhaps to heighten humor or whimsy or to support one of his main themes—the need for poets to have a distinctive voice and style.*]

Using Capital Letters Correctly   **683**

Continued on pp. 684–685

Punctuating Titles. Along with capitalizing titles, you may want to review the relevant punctuation rules. Write on the chalkboard the following rules and incomplete sentences. Then, ask students to complete the sentences, exchange papers, and check each other's work for accuracy.

- Use italics (underlining) for titles and subtitles of books; plays; periodicals; movies; radio and TV programs; videos and video games; audiotapes, CDs, and other long musical works; and works of art.

Using Capital Letters Correctly   **683**

(continued)

Type of Title	Examples	
Musical Works	"Blue Moon" Amahl and the Night Visitors	
Audiotapes and CDs	Echoes of Time and the River In Memory of a Summer Day	
Videos and Video Games	Pocahontas II: Journey to a New World Fast Break	
Comic Strips	Calvin and Hobbes Cathy	Dilbert Jump Start

Review C **Correcting Capitalization Errors**

Most of the following sentences contain errors in capitalization. Write the correct form of each word that contains an error. If the capitalization of a sentence is already correct, write C.

EXAMPLE
1. In 1995, a. leon higgenbotham, the jurist and civil rights advocate, was awarded the presidential medal of freedom.

1. A. Leon Higgenbotham, Presidential Medal, Freedom

1. At the hirshhorn museum in washington, d.c., Millicent and James saw one of georgia o'keeffe's finest paintings, cow's skull: red, white and blue.
2. In people magazine, Kim read about bill cosby's earlier television series the cosby show.
3. When I visited grandma Sánchez at white sparrow Hospital, I read to her from jimmy santiago baca's martín & meditations on the south valley.
4. In 1908, mary baker eddy founded the christian science monitor.
5. My cousin Judy's favorite statue is indian hunter by paul manship.
6. I enjoyed reading annie dillard's pilgrim at tinker creek, particularly the chapter "the horns of the altar."
7. The prize-winning journalist carl t. rowan was the first african american to serve on the National Security council.
8. The president addressed the american people in a television news broadcast after he had met with the president of France.
8. [or President . . . President]

MINI-LESSON

Use quotation marks to enclose titles of short stories, essays, poems, songs; episodes of TV and radio programs; chapters and other parts of books; and articles and other parts of periodicals.

1. Is _____ your favorite song on the CD _____?
2. Our class just read the short story _____.

TEACHING TIP

Reviews You may wish to have students do **Review C** as guided practice and complete **Review D** as independent practice.

9. Well, Governor, will Mayor Johnson and the county commissioners attend the groundbreaking ceremony for the new hospital?
10. Jane White, the president of the latin club, showed us a videotape of julius caesar.

9. C [*or* County Commissioners]
10. [*or* President]

Review D Proofreading Paragraphs for Correct Capitalization

The sentences in the following paragraphs contain errors in capitalization. Write the correct form of each incorrect word.

Words that should be capitalized or lowercased are underscored.

EXAMPLE   [1] The energetic personality of montana's former state senator from the Fiftieth District is obvious in the Painting by Christopher Magadini below.

1. Montana's, painting

[1] Bill Yellowtail, jr., the first member of the crow people to serve in the Montana State Senate, represented an area hit hard by drought and a decline in the demand for beef. [2] Yellowtail, a democrat, ran for office to help save the Area's remaining small family farms and ranches. [3] A Rancher himself, he raises cattle in the Lodge Grass valley in Southeastern Montana with his Mother, his brother, and his sister.

[4] Yellowtail supplements his income from ranching by outfitting fly-fishing trips on the Bighorn river. [5] In addition, he works as a Tour Guide on the Crow reservation and at the Custer battlefield national monument. [6] He has also served as a consultant for the Montana-wyoming Agriculture-Tourist Project, which is helping ranchers develop tourism as an industry; as a member of the Board of Directors of the Nature Conservancy; and as the director of the Environmental protection agency.

[7] After graduating from Lodge Grass high school at the head of his class, Yellowtail attended dartmouth College in hanover, New Hampshire. [8] Although Dartmouth was founded to educate american Indians, Yellowtail was the first american indian to enroll there in twenty years. [9] At first he was unprepared academically, but by the time he Graduated in 1971, he was on the dean's list. [10] Regarding his major subject, Geography, Yellowtail said, "the relationship between humanity and the environment is little understood; it's a Discipline we very much need today."

MECHANICS

Using Capital Letters Correctly   685

---

3. The film _____ has finally been released on video.
4. Have you read the book _____?
5. My favorite television show is _____.

For additional information and practice, refer students to **Chapter 24: Punctuation.**

Using Capital Letters Correctly   685

Critical Thinking

Analysis. You may want to have students review the capitalization errors in their writing and in the exercises in this chapter to determine which rules they should focus on for improvement. Ask students whether they recognize any particular error patterns. For example, students might erroneously capitalize the noun that follows a brand name, or they might neglect to capitalize the word *park, river,* or *street* as part of a proper noun. Ask students to record in their writing portfolios any error patterns.

Perhaps, as a result of their analyses, students will realize that they truly understand the rules of capitalization and that their errors are a result of carelessness. Proofreading can help them avoid such errors.

Metacognition. If students discover particular patterns in capitalization errors, ask them to think about the process they will use to try to break the patterns. Will they read the relevant rules aloud and note the examples in the textbook? Will they rewrite their incorrect sentences correctly? Will they write new sentences to practice using the rules? Will they ask a classmate to quiz them? Encourage students to evaluate the effectiveness of their strategies and to consider more effective alternatives as needed.

Reference Note

For information on **punctuating abbreviations** that come before or after names in sentences, see page 696.

STYLE TIP

Only a few abbreviations are appropriate in the regular text of a formal paper written for a general audience. In tables, notes, and bibliographies, abbreviations are used more freely in order to save space.

Abbreviations

21g. Generally, abbreviations are capitalized if the words that they stand for are capitalized.

An *abbreviation* is a shortened form of a word or word group.

EXAMPLE The **G**en. Science I [General Science I] classes will be going to the planetarium on **F**ri. [Friday], **D**ec. [December] 15.

Abbreviations of most proper nouns and of titles used along with proper nouns are capitalized.

(1) Capitalize abbreviations that come before or after names of persons, such as *Mr., Mrs., Ms., Dr., Gen., Ph.D., Jr.,* **and** *Sr.*

EXAMPLES **M**s. Christina O'Reilly   **G**en. Marcus Whitman

John H. Glenn, **J**r.   Sharon Roberts, **Ph.D**.

(2) Capitalize abbreviations of geographical names.

EXAMPLES **M**t. **S**t. **H**elens   Madera **C**o.   **T**ex.

Ozark **M**ts.   Bahama **I**s.   **F**la.

 NOTE A two-letter state code without periods is used when the abbreviation is followed by a ZIP Code. Each letter of the abbreviation is capitalized.

EXAMPLE Atlanta, **GA** 30328-1647

(3) In addresses, capitalize abbreviations such as *St., Ave., Dr., Rd., P.O., Rm.,* **and** *Apt*.

EXAMPLES 531 Guadalupe **A**ve.   **P.O.** Box 1628

2414 Grand **S**t.   33 Hillside **D**r., **A**pt. 17A

Witte Hall, **R**m. 1018   658 Culver **C**t.

(4) Capitalize abbreviations of the names of organizations, government bodies, and businesses.

EXAMPLES American Dental **A**ssn.   **U.S. D**ept. of Transportation

Motorola, **I**nc.   Digital Equipment **C**orp.

686 Chapter 21 Capitalization

 Learning for Life

Applications. As students approach the end of their high school years, their need to plan for the future becomes more pressing. You may want to collect different kinds of application forms, such as applications for jobs, for college admissions, and for school loans or grants. Ask students to practice filling out these applications and evaluating the completed forms for correct capitalization. Students could use the following questions as a self-evaluation guide:

Some proper nouns are often abbreviated to a series of capital letters without periods.

National Aeronautics and Space Administration	NASA
Federal Communications Commission	FCC
General Motors	GM
Brigham Young University	BYU
Public Broadcasting Service	PBS

Some common nouns, too, are abbreviated to a series of capital letters without periods.

personal computer	PC	television	TV
chief executive officer	CEO	vice president	VP
central processing unit	CPU	deoxyribonucleic acid	DNA
frequency modulation	FM	videocassette recorder	VCR

STYLE TIP

As you can see in the examples to the left, many common abbreviations are capitalized though the spelled-out words are not.

However, the abbreviations of most common nouns, with or without periods, are not capitalized.

pages	pp.	pound	lb
lines	ll	tablespoon	tbsp
transitive verb	vt.	centimeter	cm
abbreviation	abbr.	kilogram	kg
inch(es)	in.	miles per hour	mph

NOTE The abbreviations of most units of measurement do not include periods. To prevent confusion with the word *in,* however, writers should include a period in the abbreviation of *inch* or *inches* (*in.*).

Exercise 5 Correctly Capitalizing Abbreviations

For the following word groups, correct any errors in the capitalization of abbreviations. If a word group is already correct, write *C*.
Letters that should be capitalized or lowercased are underscored.

EXAMPLE 1. to get his teeth cleaned by dr. Larson
   1. Dr.

1. 330 Farley rd.
2. two sources written by Herbert Hunter, ph.d.
3. 2904 Spring st., apt. 1501
4. that Widgets, inc., is hiring summer help

HELP

If you are not sure how to capitalize or punctuate an abbreviation, look it up in a dictionary.

Did I capitalize correctly

- the names and titles of persons?
- the geographical names and abbreviations in addresses?
- the names of organizations and teams?
- the names of business firms and of institutions?
- the names of school subjects?

5. because ms. Lynch will be the interim ceo
6. visiting Tulsa, okla.; Wichita, kans.; and Omaha, neb.
7. the guest speaker maj. Felicia Payne
8. writing your research paper on a PC   8. C
9. ability to lift 50 lbs   9. C
10. sending entries to p.o. box 1770, San Antonio, Tx 78297-1770
11. the educational tape from Nasa that is stuck in the vcr
12. said mr. Wills wrote a book about st. Augustine
13. to contact dr. Tuomala by writing to rm. 302, 1403 Washtenaw ave., Ann Arbor, mi 48014-3177
14. reaching a speed of 250 MPH   14. mph
15. the CPU in your new computer   15. C
16. a convention in ft. Worth, Texas
17. 1 Tbsp of oregano   17. tbsp
18. Brian Donovan, Jr.   18. C
19. the film school at ucla
20. the u.s. dept. of the Treasury

CHAPTER 21

Chapter Review

A. Using Capitalization Correctly

For each of the following sentences, identify the word or words containing an error in capitalization and correct each error. If a sentence is already correct, write *C*.

1. This year my easiest classes are geometry, spanish, and American history.
2. Mexico city is built on the site of tenochtitlán, the aztec capital.
3. We rent videotapes from the Grand Video company.
4. Colorado is located West of the Great Plains.
5. Lansing, Michigan, is in Ingham county.
6. She lives at 321 Maple boulevard, which is south of here.
7. My RCA Stereo is ten years old and still works well.
8. Maggie entered her poodle in the San Marcos Dog club's show.
9. They live half a block north of Twenty-first Street.   **9. C**
10. Our neighbors are alumni of Howard university in Washington, d.c.
11. Last Spring my stepsister Lisa joined the National Audubon society.
12. While we were in San Juan, puerto rico, we toured El Morro Castle.
13. The club members celebrated Bastille Day by having dinner at a French restaurant.   **13. C**
14. Has Ms. Davis written to the U.S. department of Agriculture for information on soybean cultivation in the Midwest?
15. Mars was the Roman God of war.
16. We're holding a car wash next Saturday to raise money for the Habans high school fall festival.
17. The Islands that make up the west indies separate the Atlantic ocean from the gulf of mexico and the Caribbean sea.
18. Would you like to be the first student to ride in a Spaceship to another planet?
19. The post–Civil war period known as reconstruction officially ended in 1877.
20. Erica wants to be secretary of the Shutterbug Club.
   20. C [or Secretary]

Chapter Review   **689**

Using the Chapter Review

To assess student progress, you may want to compare the types of items missed on the **Diagnostic Preview** with those missed on the **Chapter Review**. If students have not made significant progress, you may want to refer them to **Chapter 27: Correcting Common Errors, Exercises 24–25** for additional practice.

B. Capitalizing Words in a Paragraph Correctly

For each sentence in the following paragraph, write correctly the words that should be capitalized or made lowercase. If a sentence is already correct, write C.

[21] Cartoons and Caricatures have been popular since at least the Eighteenth Century. [22] George cruikshank and William hogarth were two of the most famous cartoonists in england in the 1700s and 1800s. [23] In the early 1840s, the famous British satirical magazine *punch* was established. [24] *punch*, a weekly, ran a feature called "*punch's* cartoons," which became very popular. [25] However, the person who is sometimes considered the originator of modern cartooning was the french artist Honoré Daumier (1808–1879), who was once briefly imprisoned for creating a vicious caricature of king Louis-Philippe. [26] In the United States, Thomas nast gained Fame in 1874 by introducing the elephant into his cartoons as the symbol of the Republican party. [27] Nast also made the Donkey the symbol of the democratic party. [28] In the early twentieth century, other well-known american cartoonists included Charles Addams, peter arno, and James thurber. [29] More recently, Gary Larson, Scott Adams, and Garry Trudeau have been among the best-known U.S. cartoonists. [30] The next time you pick up the Comics page in your favorite paper, spare a thought for all the History behind those cartoons!

26. [or Party]
27. [or Party]
29. C

C. Using Capitalization Correctly

For each of the following items, write the entire word group, correcting the words that should be capitalized or made lowercase. If a word group is already correct, write C.

31. Forty-Second Street
32. cars from germany
33. interstate 35
34. hernandez high school
35. the Metropolitan museum of modern art
36. Thomas Jefferson State Park   36. C
37. african american artist
38. the *titanic*
39. andromeda galaxy
40. American History 101   40. C

690 Chapter 21 Capitalization

RESOURCES

Capitalization

Review
- *Grammar, Usage, and Mechanics,* pp. 251, 252, 253, 254

Assessment
- *Assessment Package*
  —Chapter Tests, Ch. 21
  —Chapter Tests in Standardized Test Formats, Ch. 21
- Test Generator (One-Stop Planner CD-ROM)

D. Correcting Sentences by Capitalizing Words

Most of the following sentences contain errors in capitalization. Write the correct form of each word that contains an error. If the capitalization of a sentence is already correct, write *C*.

41. Mom and dad subscribe to *Newsweek* and *U.S. news and world report*.
42. Lotte enjoyed reading Mark Twain's *The Innocents Abroad* and has been asking for other Twain titles. 42. C
43. The speed of 100 MPH is roughly equivalent to 160 KPH (kilometers per hour).
44. Ramon is registered to take english, math II, and German.
45. Everyone was happy that Monday, columbus day, was a Holiday.

Words that should be capitalized are underscored; those that should be lowercased are struck through.

Writing Application
Writing a Guidebook

Using Capital Letters You have been asked to write a guidebook for a group of visitors from your town's sister city in Japan. Write an informative booklet that helps your visitors take a brief walking or driving tour through your town. Be sure to capitalize the proper nouns you use.

Prewriting List the sights you will include in your guidebook. (If you live in a large city, you may need to limit the tour to only one part of the city or to the city's main sights.) For information on the town's history, you may want to check the local library.

Writing As you write your first draft, keep in mind that this is your guests' first visit. Try to anticipate their questions without overwhelming them with details. You may want to make a map of your tour with the various sights labeled.

Revising Have you included enough information about each sight, and is the information correct? Add, delete, change, or rearrange details as necessary to make your guidebook clearer and more interesting.

Publishing Proofread your work carefully for errors in grammar, usage, and mechanics. Pay special attention to the correct use of capital letters. After sharing your guidebook with your classmates, you and they may want to compile a larger guidebook to give to new students.

Chapter Review **691**

Writing Application
Extension
- *Grammar, Usage, and Mechanics,* p. 257
- *Language Workshop CD-ROM,* Lessons 45, 46

CHAPTER 22 Punctuation
End Marks and Commas

PREVIEWING THE CHAPTER

- The chapter begins with a discussion of end marks—period, question mark, and exclamation point—which are used to indicate the purpose of sentences. The chapter also discusses the use of the period in forming abbreviations. The remainder of the chapter explains how commas are used to separate or set off sentence elements.

- For help in integrating the chapter with writing chapters, use the **Teaching Strands** chart on pp. T401A–T401B.

- The chapter concludes with a **Chapter Review,** which includes a **Writing Application** feature that asks students to apply their understanding of end marks and commas to the creation of instructions for a board game or computer game.

USING THE DIAGNOSTIC PREVIEW

- The results of the **Diagnostic Preview** can be used in conjunction with an assessment of students' writing to identify the strengths and weaknesses in students' understanding of end marks and commas. Such an assessment can be helpful in determining the kind of instruction or practice—guided, independent, or cooperative—that will be most beneficial to students as they study the chapter.

Diagnostic Preview

A. Correcting Sentences by Adding Periods, Question Marks, Exclamation Points, and Commas

Rewrite the following sentences, adding periods, question marks, exclamation points, and commas where they are needed.

EXAMPLE   1. When is the bus coming or has it already left
         1. When is the bus coming, or has it already left?
Optional commas are underlined.

1. On June 1, 2000, I wrote to the Wisconsin Department of Development at 123 Washington Ave., Madison, WI 53702-0645.
2. Federico Peña, the mayor of Denver, Colorado, from 1983 to 1991, was born in Laredo, Texas, in 1947.
3. Wow, Bill, what a great save you made on the last play of last night's game!   [or Wow! Bill, or Wow, Bill!]
4. Water transports nutrients throughout the body, aids in digestion, and helps regulate body temperature.
5. I.M. Pei, who was born in China, has designed many buildings in the United States, for example, City Hall in Dallas, Texas, and the Government Center in Boston, Massachusetts.
6. The chief crops grown in Trinidad, an island in the Caribbean, are sugar, coffee, cocoa, citrus fruits, and bananas.

692   Chapter 22   Punctuation

CHAPTER RESOURCES

Planning
- One-Stop Planner CD-ROM

Practice and Extension
- *Grammar, Usage, and Mechanics,* p. 258
- *Language Workshop CD-ROM*

Internet
- go.hrw.com (keyword: EOLang)

Evaluation and Assessment
- *Assessment Package*
  —*Chapter Tests,* Ch. 22
  —*Chapter Tests in Standardized Test Formats,* Ch. 22
- *Test Generator (One-Stop Planner CD-ROM)*

7. Did you know that Diné College, located in Tsaile, Arizona, was founded in 1968?
8. If I finish my report, if I do the laundry, and if I promise to be home by eleven, may I go to the concert?
9. After I stayed up very late, I was exhausted, of course, yet I couldn't fall asleep right away.
10. Along with the letters and magazines in our mailbox last Wednesday, we found a large, heavy package addressed to Phyllis M. Saunders, M.D.

B. Correcting Paragraphs by Adding Periods, Question Marks, Exclamation Points, and Commas

Rewrite each sentence in the following paragraphs, adding periods, question marks, exclamation points, and commas where they are needed.

EXAMPLE   [1] As soon as I got home I called my best friend Stephanie to tell her about my vacation

1. As soon as I got home, I called my best friend, Stephanie, to tell her about my vacation.

Optional commas are underlined.

[11] Stephanie, have you ever visited Cody, Wyoming? [12] Well, if you do visit, be sure to stop by the Buffalo Bill Historical Center. [13] Opened in 1927 in memory of William "Buffalo Bill" Cody, an army scout who later had his own Wild West show, the center is actually four museums in one. [14] The Buffalo Bill Museum, the Whitney Gallery of Western Art, the Cody Firearms Museum, and the Plains Indian Museum are all under one roof.

[15] All of the museums are interesting, but the best one, I believe, is the Plains Indian Museum, which has artifacts from American Indian cowhands, settlers, and roving artists. [16] Of all the treasures in the museum's collections, the highlight is an exhibit on Tatanka Iyotake, better known as Sitting Bull, the mighty Sioux warrior, holy man, chief, and statesman. [17] The exhibit includes a dozen drawings that Sitting Bull, who was born about 1831 and died in 1890, made while he was a prisoner at Fort Randall, an army post in the Dakota Territory. [18] Depicting some of his many battlefield conquests, the drawings reveal his talent for design and composition.

[19] Other displays show weapons, clothing, and accessories of the Cheyenne, Shoshone, Crow, Arapaho, Blackfoot, and Gros Ventre peoples. [20] What a journey back through time the museum offers!

STYLE TIP

As you speak, the tone and pitch of your voice, the pauses in your speech, and the gestures and expressions you use all help make your meaning clear. In writing, marks of punctuation, such as end marks and commas, show readers where various nonverbal cues occur.

Punctuation alone will not clarify the meaning of a confusing sentence, however. If you have trouble punctuating a sentence, check to see whether revising it would help express your meaning more clearly.

End Marks

Rules 22a–d (pp. 694–696)

OBJECTIVE

- To correct sentences by adding, deleting, or replacing end marks

Meeting INDIVIDUAL NEEDS

ENGLISH-LANGUAGE LEARNERS
General Strategies. Punctuation marks differ from language to language. Encourage students to discuss the differences in punctuation between their native languages and English. For example, a period in English is equivalent to a vertical line in Hindi and to a circle in Japanese. In languages such as Greek, Korean, Persian, and Arabic, the period is slightly raised. The Greek question mark looks like an English semicolon. Point out also that an interrogative or exclamatory sentence in Spanish has a question mark or exclamation point at both its beginning and its end (the mark at the beginning is inverted).

Discussing such variations among languages will increase students' awareness of these differences and at the same time may help students remember many of the English punctuation rules.

Reference Note
For more information on **classifying sentences according to purpose,** see page 459.

In dialogue, a declarative or an interrogative sentence that expresses strong emotion may be followed by an exclamation point instead of a period or a question mark.

EXAMPLES
There you are!
Why are you always late!

End Marks

An *end mark*—a period, a question mark, or an exclamation point—is used to indicate the purpose of a sentence. A period is also used at the end of many abbreviations.

22a. A statement (a declarative sentence) is followed by a period.

EXAMPLES Barb needed a ride home.

Margaret Walker's poems celebrate the trials and triumphs of African Americans.

22b. A direct question (an interrogative sentence) is followed by a question mark.

EXAMPLES What score did you get on the road test?

Weren't you nervous?

A direct question should be followed by a question mark even if the word order is like that of a declarative sentence.

EXAMPLES You got what score on the road test?

You weren't nervous?

NOTE Be sure to distinguish between a declarative sentence that contains an indirect question and an interrogative sentence, which asks a direct question.

INDIRECT QUESTION She asked me who nominated him for class president. [declarative sentence]
DIRECT QUESTION Who nominated him for class president? [interrogative sentence]

22c. An exclamation (an exclamatory sentence or a strong interjection) is followed by an exclamation point.

EXAMPLES What an exciting game that was! [exclamatory sentence]

Oh, no! Not again! [strong interjection]

A mild interjection is generally followed by a comma.

EXAMPLES Well, what do you think I should do?

Oh, I suppose that would be acceptable.

694 Chapter 22 Punctuation

RESOURCES

End Marks

Practice
- Grammar, Usage, and Mechanics, p. 259
- Language Workshop CD-ROM, Lesson 38

NOTE Instead of an exclamation point or a comma, another mark of punctuation—a period, a question mark, or a dash, for example—may be used after an interjection, depending on the meaning of the sentence.

EXAMPLES "Hmm. That's a difficult question," responded Alina.

"Well? What's the answer?" Roberto inquired.

"Oh—no, that's not right," Salvador said, changing his mind.

22d. A request or command (an imperative sentence) is followed by either a period or an exclamation point.

Generally, a request or a mild command is followed by a period; a strong command is followed by an exclamation point.

EXAMPLES Open the door, please. [request]
Open the door. [mild command]
Open the door right now! [strong command]

Exercise 1   Using End Marks

Rewrite the following sentences, adding or replacing end marks as needed. If a sentence is already correct, write *C*.

EXAMPLE   1. Ouch Please be more careful, Sarah
1. *Ouch! Please be more careful, Sarah.*

1. Did you know that Teresa is moving to Hammond   1. ?
2. Yikes A rattlesnake   2. ! / !
3. Alexander the Great was born more than two thousand years ago.   3. C
4. I read an article about chuckwallas?   4. .
5. "Wow Great shot?"   5. ! / !
6. Can you tell me the way to the Prater Park!   6. ?
7. Generally, the green chile is spicier than the red   7. .
8. St. Stephen's Cathedral is certainly a beautiful sight?   8. . or !
9. Did you know that Paul McCartney is actually Sir Paul   9. ?
10. Gloria wakes up early every day to go for a walk   10. .
11. Irene asked whether the student named most likely to succeed was Phil Assad?   11. .
12. Will you be able to meet us at the Bristol Hotel!   12. ?
13. The master of ceremonies was Joel Bourgeois   13. .
14. The author Laura Ingalls Wilder was born in Wisconsin   14. .
15. When did the Harts move to San Marcos   15. ?

Reference Note
For more information about **dashes**, see page 770. For more about **interjections**, see page 429.

STYLE TIP
In dialogue, sometimes a command or request is expressed as if it were a question. The meaning, however, may be imperative, in which case a period or exclamation point is used.

EXAMPLES
May I have your full attention, please.
Will you pay attention!

STYLE TIP
Sometimes (most often in dialogue), a writer will use more than one end mark to express (1) intense emotion or (2) a combination of emotions.

EXAMPLES
"I will never—and I mean never—ride a roller coaster again!!" Barbara exclaimed. [intense emotion]

"You said what?!" Alejandro shouted. [combination of curiosity and surprise]

Although acceptable in informal or creative writing, the use of double end punctuation should be avoided in formal writing.

End Marks   **695**

Relating to Literature

You may want to have students examine the use of end marks in various poems. Refer students to "Miss Rosie" by Lucille Clifton, "Hanging Fire" by Audre Lorde, and "A Voice" by Pat Mora if the selections are available in the students' literature textbooks. Ask students to comment on the effect each poet achieves by either using or not using end marks. [The presence of end marks conveys definitive breaks between thoughts; as a result, each thought receives special emphasis. The absence of end marks creates a steady flow of thoughts, thereby simulating the actual thinking process, in which thoughts are often jumbled, fragmented, or run together.]

Abbreviations
Rule 22e (pp. 696–700)

OBJECTIVE
- To correct errors in the use of abbreviations in sentences

---

22 e

16. Have you ever heard the music of Theseus Flatow. **16. ?**
17. Ask Tonya whether Kennedy is one of her favorite presidents. **17. C**
18. How exciting the first moonwalk must have been. **18. !**
19. Did you know that some of the world's most venomous snakes are found in Australia! **19. ?**
20. Boy I'd love to be a veterinarian. **20. , / . [or ! / !]**

Abbreviations

An *abbreviation* is a shortened form of a word or phrase.

22e. Many abbreviations are followed by a period.

Personal Names

Abbreviate given names only if the person is most commonly known by the abbreviated form of the name.

| EXAMPLES | Louis **J.** Halle | **J. F.** Kennedy | **W.E.B.** DuBois |
| | Ida **B.** Wells | **M.F.K.** Fisher | **M. C.** Escher |

HELP
Leave a space between two initials, but not between three or more.
EXAMPLES
P. D. James
J.R.R. Tolkien

Titles

You may abbreviate social titles whether used before the full name or before the last name alone.

| EXAMPLES | **Mr.** Xavier Jackson | **Mrs.** Laval |
| | **Dr.** Beth Higgins | **Sr.** (Señor) Guzman |

You may abbreviate civil and military titles used before full names or before initials and last names. Spell them out before last names alone.

| EXAMPLES | **Sen.** John Glenn | **Senator** Glenn |
| | **Gen.** Colin Powell | **General** Powell |

Abbreviate titles and academic degrees that follow proper names.

EXAMPLES   Harry Connick, **Jr.**   John H. Watson, **M.D.**

If a statement ends with an abbreviation, do not use an additional period as an end mark. However, do use a question mark or an exclamation point if one is needed.

EXAMPLES   This is Patrick Lewis, Jr.
Do you know Patrick Lewis, Jr.?

696   Chapter 22   Punctuation

RESOURCES
Abbreviations
Practice
- *Grammar, Usage, and Mechanics*, pp. 260, 261, 262, 263
- *Language Workshop CD-ROM*, Lesson 43

NOTE Do not include the titles *Mr., Mrs., Ms.,* or *Dr.* when you use a professional title or degree after a name.

EXAMPLE **Dr.** Peter Neibergall *or* Peter Neibergall, **M.D.** [not *Dr. Peter Neibergall, M.D.*]

Agencies and Organizations

An *acronym* is a word formed from the first (or first few) letters of a series of words. Acronyms are written without periods. The abbreviations for many agencies and organizations are written as acronyms.

AMA, American Medical Association	USN, United States Navy
CIA, Central Intelligence Agency	UN, United Nations

After spelling out the first use of the names or agencies and organizations, abbreviate these names and other things commonly known by their acronyms.

EXAMPLE After the fall of the Berlin Wall in 1989, most Eastern European nations applied to join the **North Atlantic Treaty Organization,** their former enemy. Poland, Hungary, and the Czech Republic subsequently joined **NATO** in 1999.

Geographical Terms

In regular text, spell out names of states and other political units whether they stand alone or follow other geographical terms. Abbreviate them in tables, notes, and bibliographies.

TEXT Frank McCourt spent his early years in Brooklyn, New York, and Limerick, Ireland.

On our vacation to Canada, we visited Québec City, the capital of the Province of Québec.

TABLE

London, U.K.	Dublin, Ire.
Québec City, P.Q.	Oxnard, Calif.

FOOTNOTE ³The Public Library in New Castle, Del., has an entire collection of early Thomaston manuscripts.

BIBLIOGRAPHY ENTRY *The Great Law of Peace and the Constitution of the United States of America.* Akwesasne, **NY**: Tree of Peace, 1988.

STYLE TIP

Only a few abbreviations are appropriate in the regular text of a formal paper written for a general audience. In tables, notes, and bibliographies, abbreviations are used more freely in order to save space.

HELP

Look up an abbreviation in a dictionary if you are unsure whether it requires periods.

STYLE TIP

A few acronyms, such as *radar, laser,* and *sonar,* are now considered common nouns. They do not need to be spelled out on first use and are no longer capitalized. When you are unsure whether an acronym should be capitalized, look it up in an up-to-date dictionary.

STYLE TIP

Include the traditional abbreviation for the District of Columbia, *D.C.,* with the city name, *Washington,* to distinguish it from the state of Washington.

In regular text, spell out every word in an address. Some words should be abbreviated in envelope addresses and may be abbreviated in tables and notes.

NOTE Two-letter state abbreviations without periods are used only when the ZIP Code is included.

EXAMPLE   Stilwell, **KS** 66085-8808

Time

Abbreviate the two most frequently used era designations, A.D. and B.C. The abbreviation A.D. stands for the Latin phrase *anno Domini*, which means "in the year of the Lord." It is used with dates in the Christian era. When used with a specific year number, A.D. precedes the number. When used with the name of a century, it follows the name. The abbreviation B.C., which stands for "before Christ," is used for dates before the Christian era. It follows either a specific year number or the name of a century.

EXAMPLES   In **A.D.** 1452, the Ottoman Turks invaded Constantinople.

By the end of the first century **A.D.**, the Romans had conquered much of Europe.

Cleopatra was a Greek-speaking queen of Egypt in the first century **B.C.**

In regular text, spell out the names of months and days whether they appear alone or in dates. Both types of names may be abbreviated in tables, notes, and bibliographies.

TEXT   Our next meeting will take place on the last **Tuesday** in **October.**

TABLE   Tues. afternoon
        Oct. 13, 2002

FOOTNOTE   ¹¹These authors first met on **Jan.** 16, 1887.

BIBLIOGRAPHY   Ibata, David. "Information Highway to the Future,"
ENTRY   *Chicago Tribune*, 17 **Nov.** 1992, final **ed.**, **sec.** 1:8.

Abbreviate the designations for the two halves of the day measured by clock time. The abbreviation A.M. stands for the Latin phrase *ante meridiem*, meaning "before noon." The abbreviation P.M. stands for

COMPUTER TIP

Publishers usually print time abbreviations as small capitals, like this: A.M. Your word processor may offer small capitals as a style option. If it does not, or if you are writing by hand, you may use either uppercase or lowercase letters for time abbreviations, as long as you are consistent in each piece of writing.

STYLE TIP

In your reading, you may come across the abbreviations *C.E.* and *B.C.E.* These abbreviations stand for *Common Era* and *Before Common Era*. They are used instead of *A.D.* and *B.C.*, respectively, and are used after the date.

EXAMPLES
752 **C.E.**
3000 **B.C.E.**

post meridiem, meaning "after noon." Both abbreviations follow the numerals designating the specific time.

EXAMPLES   Andrew works five days a week from 8:00 **A.M.** until 5:00 **P.M.**

Units of Measurement

In regular text, spell out the names of units of measurement, whether they stand alone or follow a spelled-out number or a numeral. Such names may be abbreviated in tables and notes when they follow a numeral. Most such abbreviations are written without periods. However, do use a period after the abbreviation for *inch* (*in.*) to prevent confusion with the word *in*.

TEXT   The speed limit here is sixty **miles per hour** [not *mph*].
The dorm room measured twenty **feet** [not *ft*] by fourteen.

TABLE
1 **tbsp** vinegar	75°**F**
6 **ft** 6 **in.**	5 **oz** cumin

Exercise 2   Using Abbreviations

Rewrite the following sentences, correcting errors in the use of abbreviations in formal writing.

EXAMPLE   1. I was born in Miami, FL.
              1. I was born in Miami, Florida.

1. A. Lincoln was president of the United States from 1861 to 1865 and led the Union during the Civil War.
2. The flight for Santiago departs today at 4:30 P.M. ~~in the afternoon.~~
3. Charlemagne ruled as Emperor of the Romans until 814 A.D.
4. Duluth, MN, and Superior, WI, are two principal United States ports on Lake Superior.
5. The parcel was addressed to Mrs. Clare on Newcome Street in Ashburton Falls, MA.
6. Alexander the Great was born in Macedonia in B.C. 356.
7. The final speaker of the evening was Lt. Holden.
8. Please chew with your mouth closed, J. R.
9. Did that happen in 47 B.C?
10. The dogs were tired, as they had been playing since 6:00 A.M. ~~in the morning.~~

STYLE TIP

Do not use *A.M.* or *P.M.* with numbers spelled out as words or as substitutes for the words *morning, afternoon,* or *evening*.

EXAMPLE
The festival will begin at **8:00 P.M.** (or **eight o'clock in the evening**) Saturday [not *eight P.M. Saturday*].

Also, do not use the words *morning, afternoon,* or *evening* with numerals followed by *A.M.* or *P.M.*

EXAMPLE
The next train for Greenwich leaves at **1:30 P.M.** (or **one-thirty in the afternoon**) [not *1:30 P.M. in the afternoon*].

1. Abraham

2. *or* four-thirty in the afternoon

4. Minnesota / Wisconsin

5. Massachusetts

7. Lieutenant

9. .

10. *or* six in the morning.

22 f–m

Review A Using Periods, Question Marks, and Exclamation Points

Insert periods, question marks, and exclamation points correctly in the following sentences. Use each type of end mark—period, question mark, and exclamation point—at least once. **Answers may vary.**

EXAMPLE
1. Oh boy, it was a good thing we were friends?
1. *Oh boy, it was a good thing we were friends!*

1. Hey, Jo, my cousin Liz and I went hiking near Denver, Colorado!
2. We carried our backpacks and slept in tents along the way.
3. Each afternoon, we would make a cup of cocoa.
4. Halfway through our trip, I wondered where the other box of instant cocoa was.
5. Liz appeared puzzled.
6. Which of us was responsible for packing all the food items?
7. She thought I was, and I thought she was.
8. Luckily, we have always gotten along well.
9. At the end of the trip, Liz reached into her pack to get a jacket.
10. Instead of a jacket, there was the other box of cocoa!

Commas

Rules 22f–m *(pp. 700–718)*

OBJECTIVES

- To proofread sentences, adding commas to separate items in a series and to separate two or more adjectives preceding a noun
- To proofread sentences, adding commas to separate independent clauses joined by coordinating conjunctions
- To proofread sentences, adding commas to set off nonessential phrases and clauses
- To proofread sentences, adding commas after introductory elements
- To proofread sentences, adding commas to set off nonessential appositives and appositive phrases
- To proofread sentences, adding commas in conventional situations

Commas

Items in a Series

22f. Use commas to separate items in a series.

EXAMPLES The camp counselor distributed baseballs, bats, volleyballs, tennis rackets, and bandages. [words in a series]

We have a government of the people, by the people, and for the people. [phrases in a series]

I know I will pass the test if I take good notes, if I study hard, and if I get a good night's sleep. [clauses in a series]

When the last two items in a series are joined by *and, or,* or *nor,* the comma before the conjunction is sometimes omitted when the comma is not needed to make the meaning of the sentence clear.

CLEAR WITHOUT COMMA   The entertainers sang, danced and juggled.

RESOURCES

Commas

Practice

- *Grammar, Usage, and Mechanics,* pp. 264, 265, 266, 267, 268, 269, 270, 271
- *Language Workshop CD-ROM,* Lesson 34–37, 43

NOT CLEAR	John, Sue and Marian went fishing.
WITHOUT COMMA	[Did John go fishing, or is he being addressed?]
CLEAR WITH COMMA	John, Sue, and Marian went fishing.

NOTE Words customarily used in pairs—such as *macaroni and cheese* and *law and order*—are set off as one item in a series.

EXAMPLE   We could order a sandwich, macaroni and cheese, or soup.

If all the items in a series are joined by *and*, *or*, or *nor*, do not use commas to separate them.

EXAMPLES   We ran **and** walked **and** even limped to the finish line.

He said that neither poverty **nor** discrimination **nor** discouragement prevented Derek Walcott from becoming an accomplished writer.

Independent clauses in a series are generally separated by semicolons. Short independent clauses, however, may be separated by commas.

EXAMPLES   We swam laps in the cool, refreshing pool; after that, we jogged around the lake; and we exercised with free weights, stationary bicycles, and rowing machines.

We swam, we jogged, and we exercised.

22g. Use commas to separate two or more adjectives preceding a noun.

EXAMPLE   I've had a long, hectic, tiring day.

When the last adjective in a series is thought of as part of the noun, the comma before the adjective is omitted.

EXAMPLES   I mailed the package at the main post office. [Together, *post* and *office* name a place.]

For lunch we had smooth, creamy broccoli soup. [Together, *broccoli* and *soup* name a thing.]

You can use two tests to determine whether an adjective and a noun form a unit.

TEST 1:   Insert the word *and* between the adjectives preceding the noun. If *and* fits sensibly between them, use a comma. In the first example above, *and* cannot be logically inserted: *main and post office*. In the second example, *and* sounds sensible between the first two adjectives (*smooth and creamy*) but not between the second and third adjectives (*creamy and broccoli*).

STYLE TIP

For clarity, some writers prefer always to use the comma before the conjunction in a series. Follow your teacher's instructions on this point.

Reference Note

For more about using **semicolons,** see page 724.

Reference Note

A word such as *post office* is called a **compound noun.** For more about **compound nouns,** see page 406.

Commas 701

TEACHING TIP

Activity. To show students the importance of using commas correctly, write the following sentences on the chalkboard:

1. Lee Ann and Kim are my best friends.
2. No, cameras will be allowed at the concert.

Call on volunteers to change the meanings of the sentences by adding, moving, or deleting commas. Have students discuss the changes in meaning. [*In sentence 1, the writer has two friends—Lee Ann and Kim. Adding a comma after* Lee *would indicate that the writer is speaking directly to Lee, saying that Ann and Kim are friends. Adding a comma after* Lee *and after* Ann *would indicate that the writer has three friends. In sentence 2, cameras are allowed. Deleting the comma would indicate that cameras are not allowed.*]

MODALITIES

Auditory Learners. You may want to read aloud the example sentences on pp. 700–701 so that students can hear the pauses where the commas have been placed. Suggest that students read aloud the sentences in the exercises if they have difficulty deciding where commas should be placed.

MECHANICS

Continued on pp. 702–703

Parallel Structure. Direct students' attention to **Rule 22f** on p. 700. Explain to students that the items in a series are of equal importance and therefore should be expressed in the same grammatical form.

Direct students' attention to the example sentences at the bottom of p. 700 and the top of this page. Ask students to identify the

TEST 2: Change the order of the adjectives. If the order of the adjectives can be reversed sensibly, use a comma. *Creamy, smooth broccoli soup* makes sense, but *broccoli creamy soup* and *post main office* do not.

NOTE If a word modifies one of the adjectives preceding the noun, the word is an adverb, not an adjective, and therefore should not be followed by a comma.

EXAMPLE Which of these neckties looks best with this **light** green shirt? [*Light* modifies the adjective *green,* not the noun *shirt*.]

Exercise 3 Correcting Sentences by Adding Commas

For each of the following sentences, write each word that should be followed by a comma, and then add the comma. If a sentence is already correct, write C.   Optional commas are underlined.

EXAMPLE 1. The king wore a thick warm luxurious robe.
   1. thick, warm,

1. One terrible summer when we were little, I had mumps, you had measles, and he had chickenpox.
2. The river overflowed again and filled our basement and drenched our neighbor's carpet.   **2. C**
3. Coriander, cumin, and saffron are three spices that are widely used in traditional Mexican cooking.
4. I took a flashlight, a sleeping bag, extra tennis shoes, a rod and reel, and a parka on our camping trip.
5. Magic Johnson, Michael Jordan, Larry Bird, and Julius Erving have each received a Most Valuable Player award at least once for their achievements on the basketball court.
6. At the gymnastics meet, Les performed on the parallel bars, the rings, and the high bar.
7. With a quick, powerful leap, the stunt double bounded over the burning balcony.
8. We looked in the sink, on the floor, and on Kim's clothing for her missing contact lens.
9. Have you read any of the novels by Jane Austen or the Brontë sisters or Virginia Woolf?   **9. C**
10. A little blond child in faded bluejeans emerged from the shrubbery to stare at the mail carrier.

MINI-LESSON

grammatical form of the items in each of the example series. [*first example—nouns; second example—prepositional phrases; third example—adverb clauses*] Then, write the following sentence on the chalkboard and discuss with students how to revise it to create parallel structure.

The newspaper article praised the quar-

Independent Clauses

22h. Use a comma before *and, but, for, nor, or, so,* or *yet* when the conjunction joins independent clauses.

EXAMPLES Patrick brought the sandwiches**,** **and** Cindy brought the potato salad.

We got there on time**,** **but** Jeff and María were late.

NOTE Always use a comma before *yet, so,* or *for* joining independent clauses. The comma is sometimes left out before *and, but, or,* or *nor* if the independent clauses are very short and the sentence will not be misunderstood without it.

EXAMPLES He was apprehensive**,** **yet** he was also excited.

The bears failed to catch any salmon**,** **so** they went away.

I applied for the job **and** I got it.

Do not confuse a compound sentence with a simple sentence that has a compound verb. Generally, a comma does not precede the conjunction joining the parts of a compound verb.

COMPOUND SENTENCE Han brought charcoal and lighter fluid**,** **but** she forgot matches. [two independent clauses]

SIMPLE SENTENCE Han brought charcoal and lighter fluid **but** forgot matches. [one independent clause with a compound verb]

Reference Note
For more about **simple sentences and compound sentences,** see page 504. For more about **compound subjects and compound verbs,** see page 447.

If the independent clauses contain commas, a semicolon may be required to separate them.

EXAMPLE One of the cats had brown**,** black**,** and yellow spots**;** and the other**,** younger one was pure black.

Reference Note
For more about **semicolons,** see page 724.

Exercise 4 Correcting Sentences by Adding Commas

For each of the following sentences, write the word that should be followed by a comma, and add the comma after it. If a sentence is already correct, write C.

EXAMPLE 1. Uncle Phil carefully steered the boat through the narrow channel and Lynn began baiting the hooks.
1. channel,

1. All students must arrive on time**,** for no one will be admitted late.

Exercise 4

ALTERNATIVE LESSON
To reinforce students' understanding of subjects and verbs, ask them to identify the simple subject(s) and the verb(s) in each independent clause in sentences 1, 4, and 8 from **Exercise 4**. [1. *students—must arrive; no one—will be admitted;* 4. *actors—do speak; they—pantomime;* 8. *groups—disagreed; they—settled; losers—moved, founded*]

Critical Thinking
Metacognition. Ask students to think about the strategies they use to determine whether commas are needed in the sentences in **Exercise 4**. Do students first search for coordinating conjunctions? Do they read the sentences carefully to understand the meanings? Do they locate the verbs and then find the subjects? Do they try to determine what sounds right? Encourage students to evaluate the effectiveness of their strategies and to consider more effective alternatives as needed.

TIPS & TRICKS
Generally, a subordinate clause or a participial phrase that modifies a proper noun is nonessential.

---

2. The movie review complimented all the performers, but the leading actress received the strongest praise.
3. A few rowdy spectators tried to grab the star, so the bodyguards formed a ring around him.
4. The Japanese actors in Kabuki plays do not speak, but they pantomime lines chanted by narrators on the stage.
5. Some people today work fewer hours than their grandparents did, yet for many there never seem to be enough hours in a day.
6. The cost of living is rising, for consumers pay higher prices than they did last year for gasoline and other products.

7. C [*or* led, and]
7. Our guide led and we followed closely.
8. Two groups of Hopi disagreed about how to run the town of Oraibi; they settled the matter with a tug of war, and the losers moved away and founded the town of Hotevilla.
9. She did not like the story in the science fiction magazine, nor did she enjoy the illustrations.

10. C
10. High school graduates may go on to college or may begin working immediately.

Nonessential Clauses and Phrases

22i. Use commas to set off nonessential subordinate clauses and nonessential participial phrases.

A *nonessential* (or *nonrestrictive*) subordinate clause or participial phrase contains information that is not necessary to the basic meaning of the sentence.

NONESSENTIAL CLAUSES	Emilia Ortiz, **who lives across the street from me,** won a scholarship to Stanford University.
	The capital of Massachusetts is Boston, **which is sometimes called the Athens of America.**
NONESSENTIAL PHRASES	Kelly, **waiting outside the stage door,** got the band leader's autograph.
	Born in Detroit, Robert Hayden was educated at the University of Michigan and later became a distinguished professor there.

The nonessential clause or phrase in each of the preceding examples can be left out without changing the main idea of the sentence.

704   Chapter 22   Punctuation

MINI-LESSON

Independent and Subordinate Clauses. Review with students the following terms:

- A **clause** is a group of words that contains a verb and its subject and is used as a sentence or as a part of a sentence.

- An **independent** (or **main**) **clause** expresses a complete thought and can stand alone as a sentence.
- A **subordinate** (or **dependent**) **clause** does not express a complete thought and cannot stand alone as a sentence.

EXAMPLES   Emilia Ortiz won a scholarship to Stanford University.

The capital of Massachusetts is Boston.

Kelly got the band leader's autograph.

Robert Hayden was educated at the University of Michigan and later became a distinguished professor there.

An *essential* (or *restrictive*) *subordinate clause* or *participial phrase* is not set off by commas because it contains information that is necessary to the meaning of the sentence.

ESSENTIAL CLAUSES   The sophomores **who made the Honor Roll** were listed in the school newspaper.

Library books **that are lost or damaged** must be replaced.

ESSENTIAL PHRASES   Students **planning to try out for a role in the play** should sign up no later than Friday afternoon.

Two poems **written by Lorna Dee Cervantes** are included in our literature book.

Notice how leaving out the essential clause or phrase affects the main idea of each of the examples above.

EXAMPLES   The sophomores were listed in the school newspaper. [Which sophomores?]

Library books must be replaced. [Which library books?]

Students should sign up no later than Friday afternoon. [Which students?]

Two poems are included in our literature book. [Which two poems?]

Some subordinate clauses and participial phrases may be either essential or nonessential. The presence or absence of commas tells the reader how the clause or phrase relates to the main idea of the sentence.

NONESSENTIAL CLAUSE   Marla's sister, **who attends Stanford University,** sent her a sweatshirt. [Marla has only one sister. That sister sent the sweatshirt.]

ESSENTIAL CLAUSE   Marla's sister **who attends Stanford University** sent her a sweatshirt. [Marla has more than one sister. The one attending Stanford University sent the sweatshirt.]

TIPS & TRICKS

Generally, a subordinate clause or a participial phrase that tells *which one(s)* of two or more is essential. Also, a subordinate clause beginning with *that* and modifying a noun or pronoun is generally essential.

Reference Note

For more about **subordinate clauses,** see page 493. For more about **participial phrases,** see page 473.

Write the following sentences on the chalkboard and classify each of the clauses as independent (I) or subordinate (S).
1. That carnival ride looks exciting [*I*], but Al seems frightened [*I*].
2. Rudy [*part of I clause*], who is the editor of the school newspaper [*S*], plans to major in journalism [*rest of I clause*].
3. Before you arrived [*S*], I was reading a fascinating novel [*I*].

For additional information and practice, refer students to **Chapter 15: The Clause.**

Meeting NEEDS

MODALITIES

Kinesthetic Learners. If students are having difficulty deciding whether a clause or phrase is essential or nonessential, suggest that they try the following strategy:

1. Copy the sentence onto a slip of paper.
2. With scissors, cut out the clause or phrase in question.
3. Place the remaining parts of the sentence together. If the resulting sentence retains the meaning of the original sentence, the clause or phrase is nonessential and should be set off by commas.

Visual or Auditory Learners. The activity above can be adapted for other learning styles. Visual learners could write a sentence and then mark out the clause or phrase in question. Auditory learners could read a sentence aloud, omitting the clause or phrase. In either instance, if the sentence without the clause or phrase retains the meaning of the original sentence, the clause or phrase is nonessential and should be set off by commas.

MECHANICS

NONESSENTIAL PHRASE	My former lab partner**,** **now living in Chicago,** visited me last week. [I have only one former lab partner. That person visited me last week.]
ESSENTIAL PHRASE	My former lab partner **now living in Chicago** visited me last week. [I have more than one former lab partner. The one living in Chicago visited me last week.]

Exercise 5 Correcting Sentences by Adding Commas

For each of the following sentences, write each word that should be followed by a comma and add the comma after it. If a sentence is already correct, write *C*.

EXAMPLE
1. Gigantic supermarkets which offer a stunning variety of goods and services developed from much smaller stores that first opened in the nineteenth century.

   1. supermarkets, services,

1. The stores that became the world's first self-serve supermarkets were designed by Clarence Saunders**,** who was an innovative entrepreneur.
2. Saunders**,** who lived in Memphis, Tennessee**,** named his stores Piggly Wiggly.
3. Some say that he got the idea for the name when he saw a fat pig wiggling under a fence.   **3. C**

706 Chapter 22 Punctuation

MINI-LESSON *Continued on pp. 707–708*

Participial Phrases. To help students better understand **Rules 22i** and **22j(2),** you may want to review the following terms:

- A **phrase** is a group of related words that is used as a single part of speech and does not contain both a verb and its subject.
- A **participle** is a verb form that can be used as an adjective, such as "*smiling* faces" or "*chipped* tooth."

706 Punctuation

4. The first Piggly Wiggly store, which opened in 1916, had only one long aisle.
5. Customers shopping there saw all the products before they came to the exit.   5. C
6. Noticing that people often had difficulty finding products, Albert Gerrard opened his own grocery store.
7. All of the items that were for sale were arranged alphabetically.   7. C
8. The name that Gerrard selected for his store was Alpha-Beta.   8. C
9. George Hartford, who founded the Great Atlantic & Pacific Tea Company in 1859, nicknamed his stores A&P.
10. Developed by Michael Cullen, the model for today's huge supermarkets opened in an abandoned garage in New York in 1930.

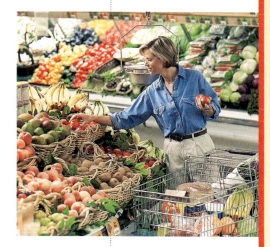

Introductory Elements

22j. Use a comma after certain introductory elements.

(1) Use a comma to set off a mild exclamation such as *well, oh,* or *why* at the beginning of a sentence. Other introductory words such as *yes* and *no* are also set off by commas.

EXAMPLES   **Sure,** I'll go with you.

Oh, look at that car!

No, I haven't taken the exam yet.

(2) Use a comma after an introductory participle or participial phrase.

EXAMPLES   **Shivering,** the couple hurried into the warm lobby of the movie theater.

Calling for a timeout, the referee blew his whistle and signaled.

Exhausted after a three-mile swim, Diana emerged from the water.

- A **participial phrase** consists of a participle and its complements or modifiers, such as "born in Chicago in 1986" or "leaving the game early." The entire participial phrase serves as an adjective.

Then, write the following sentences on the chalkboard, leaving out the underlining, and have students identify the participial phrases.

1. The lunch prepared by Mother was delicious.

Relating to Writing

Explain to students that varying the correct placement of modifying phrases and clauses can make their writing more effective. To demonstrate, write on the chalkboard the following sentences. Ask students to notice particularly the use of commas in the sentences.

1. At night in the desert, the temperature falls rapidly.
2. In the desert the temperature falls rapidly at night.
3. At night the temperature in the desert falls rapidly.
4. The temperature falls rapidly at night in the desert.

Then, ask each student to choose a piece of writing from his or her writing portfolio and to revise the writing so that the sentence structures vary. To ensure that students do not create misplaced modifiers, remind them that they should place each modifying phrase or clause as close as possible to the word or words it modifies. You may want to have students exchange papers to assess each other's revisions.

Reference Note
For more information about correcting **misplaced and dangling modifiers,** see page 626.

NOTE When writing an introductory participial phrase, make sure that it modifies the subject in the sentence; otherwise, the phrase is a misplaced or dangling modifier.

MISPLACED	Swimming in the huge aquarium, visitors of all ages were fascinated by the rare species of tropical fish. [Were visitors swimming in the aquarium?]
REVISED	Swimming in the huge aquarium, the rare species of tropical fish fascinated visitors of all ages.
REVISED	Visitors of all ages were fascinated by the rare species of tropical fish swimming in the huge aquarium.
DANGLING	Looking through the magazine, a recipe for *fattoush,* a delicious Syrian bread salad, caught Chris's attention. [Was a recipe looking through the magazine?]
REVISED	Looking through the magazine, Chris spotted a recipe for *fattoush,* a delicious Syrian bread salad.

Reference Note
For more information about **prepositional phrases,** see page 467.

(3) Use a comma after an introductory prepositional phrase if the phrase is long or if two or more phrases appear together.

EXAMPLES **During the long bus ride home,** we sang songs and told stories to amuse ourselves.

By the light of the harvest moon in September, we went on an old-fashioned hayride.

A single, short introductory prepositional phrase is not followed by a comma unless the sentence is awkward to read without one or unless the phrase is parenthetical.

Reference Note
For more information about **parenthetical expressions,** see page 770.

EXAMPLES In the book the writer develops a clever plot. [The sentence is clear without the comma.]

In the book, review pages 236–290. [Without the comma, *book review* could be read as a compound noun.]

In the book review, the critic praised the writer's clever plot. [Without the comma, *review* could be read as a verb.]

By the way, do you have a copy of the book? [The phrase is parenthetical.]

(4) Use a comma after an introductory adverb clause.

An introductory adverb clause may appear at the beginning of a sentence or before any independent clause in the sentence.

708 Chapter 22 Punctuation

MINI-LESSON

2. Looking around carefully, Sue stepped outside.
3. Only farmers growing organic produce attended the conference.
4. The new album, released just last week, is a success.

Ask students to explain why commas are included in sentences 2 and 4. [2. introductory participial phrase; 4. nonessential participial phrase]

For more information and practice, refer students to **Chapter 14: The Phrase.**

EXAMPLES   When you've gone to this school for a while, you'll know your way around, too.

The first game of the season is Friday; after we claim our first victory, we'll celebrate at Darcy's Deli.

Reference Note
For more about **adverb clauses,** see page 498.

NOTE Generally, an adverb clause that comes at the end of a sentence is not preceded by a comma.

EXAMPLE   Wolfgang Amadeus Mozart composed his first opera **when he was twelve years old.**

Exercise 6 Correcting Sentences with Introductory Elements by Adding Commas

For each of the following sentences, write the word that should be followed by a comma and add the comma after it. If a sentence is already correct, write C.

EXAMPLE   1. Trying to reduce the amount of fat in their diets many Americans are eating less meat.
   1. *diets,*

1. Yes, for many people around the world, meat is not a daily food staple.
2. Serving as a main source of nutrition, whole grains such as corn, oats, wheat, and rice feed millions.
3. C
3. In Mexico a favorite nutritious dish is a corn tortilla with beans.
4. Because the soybean is high in protein, it has been a principal crop in Asian countries for more than five thousand years.
5. If you'd like more variety in your diet, you may want to substitute unrefined whole grains for meat occasionally.
6. Offering healthful alternatives to meat, whole grains contain nutrients such as vitamins, proteins, amino acids, and starches.
7. In the process of making spoilage-resistant products, some food manufacturers refine whole grains.
8. Refined for commercial use, the grains lose most of their food value because the nutritious outer hulls are stripped away.
9. If you take time in the supermarket, you should be able to find whole grains.
10. Since many cookbooks now include recipes for grain dishes, you can learn to use grains in many tasty snacks and meals.

Review B Using Commas in a Paragraph

For the following sentences, write each word that should be followed by a comma. Then, add a comma after each word.

EXAMPLES [1] Throughout the ages around the world people have used weapons for hunting for fighting, and for defending themselves from wild animals.

1. world, hunting,

[2] According to archaeologists weapons were among the earliest tools.

2. archaeologists,   Optional commas are underlined.

[1] Many weapons that were produced in early times were similar in appearance function and design. [2] The English word *weapon* is related to the Old English *wæpen* the Dutch *wapen* the German *Waffe* and an earlier common root. [3] Sticks stones and natural poisons such as the toxic sweat of these Central and South American frogs were probably the first weapons. [4] Among those varieties of weapons the stick thrown by hand became one of the most heavily specialized. [5] As you can see the dart the arrow the spear the lance and the javelin were all developed from the stick thrown by hand. [6] Another kind of weapon, the sling, was used all over the world for it was easy to make and not too difficult to master. [7] According to the Biblical account, when the Hebrew king David was just a boy he killed the Philistine giant Goliath with a simple hand-made sling. [8] An unusual weapon similar to the sling is the bola which is a cord with heavy weights of stone or wood or metal at the ends. [9] In some parts of South America gauchos still use bolas which can entangle cattle without inflicting pain injury or death. [10] Over the centuries these simple weapons have been developed into highly sophisticated and deadly artillery such as the missiles that were used in Operation Desert Storm.

Interrupters

22k. Use commas to set off an expression that interrupts a sentence.

(1) Use commas to set off nonessential appositives and nonessential appositive phrases.

An *appositive* is a noun or pronoun placed beside another noun or pronoun to identify or describe it. An *appositive phrase* consists of an appositive and its modifiers.

EXAMPLES   A senator from Kansas, **Nancy Landon Kassebaum,** was the principal speaker. [appositive]

Do you know him, **the boy wearing the blue shirt**? [appositive phrase]

A *nonessential* (or *nonrestrictive*) *appositive* or *appositive phrase* adds information that is unnecessary to the basic meaning of the sentence. In other words, the meaning of the sentence is clear and complete with or without the appositive or appositive phrase.

EXAMPLES   Have you read *At Home in India*, **a book by Cynthia Bowles**?

On July 20, 1969, Neil Armstrong, **one of the three astronauts on the Apollo 11 mission,** became the first person to walk on the moon.

Notice that the meaning of each of the examples above remains clear and complete without the appositive phrase.

EXAMPLES   Have you read *At Home in India*?

On July 20, 1969, Neil Armstrong became the first person to walk on the moon.

An *essential* (or *restrictive*) *appositive* or *appositive phrase* is not set off by commas because it adds information that makes the noun or pronoun it identifies or explains more specific. In other words, if you were to omit an essential appositive or appositive phrase, you would leave out key information or would change the intended meaning of the sentence.

EXAMPLES   My friend **James** helped me.

Speaking of movies, have you seen the animated film ***The Prince of Egypt***?

TIPS & TRICKS
Generally, an appositive or appositive phrase that tells *which one(s)* of two or more is essential.

Reference Note

For more information about **appositives** and **appositive phrases,** see page 711.

Notice how omitting the appositive from each of the preceding examples changes the meaning of the sentence.

EXAMPLES   My friend helped me. [Which friend?]

Speaking of movies, have you seen the animated film? [Which animated film?]

Exercise 7   Correcting Sentences with Appositives and Appositive Phrases by Adding Commas

Correctly punctuate the appositives and appositive phrases in the following sentences. If a sentence is already correct, write *C*.

EXAMPLE   1. Leonardo da Vinci an Italian Renaissance artist is perhaps best remembered for painting *Mona Lisa.*

1. *Leonardo da Vinci, an Italian Renaissance artist, is perhaps best remembered for painting* Mona Lisa.

1. Between 1500 and 1506, Leonardo da Vinci a brilliant man created several major works.
2. My favorite painting *Mona Lisa* was painted then.
3. Leonardo's painting *Mona Lisa* is a prized possession of the Louvre in Paris.   3. C
4. The painting a portrait of a young Florentine woman is slightly cracked as a result of temperature changes.
5. The *Mona Lisa* an ideal type of portrait revolutionized portrait painting.
6. Leonardo's work influenced the young painter Raphael.   6. C
7. Raphael's painting *The Grand Duke's Madonna* was done in the style of *Mona Lisa.*   7. C
8. In 1911 an Italian house painter Vincenzo Perugia stole the *Mona Lisa* from its frame.
9. For two years members of the Paris police some of the world's cleverest detectives were baffled by the crime.
10. Since its recovery, the painting one of the most valuable portraits in the world has been closely guarded.

Mona Lisa by Leonardo da Vinci.

(2) Use commas to set off words used in direct address.

EXAMPLES   **David,** please close the door.

Did you call me, **Mother**?

Yes, **Mr. Ramos,** I turned in my paper.

Reference Note

For information on **words of direct address,** see page 447.

(3) Use commas to set off parenthetical expressions.

A *parenthetical expression* is a side remark that adds information or shows a relationship between ideas.

Common Parenthetical Expressions		
after all	however	nevertheless
at any rate	I believe	of course
consequently	in fact	on the contrary
for example	in the first place	on the other hand
for instance	meanwhile	that is
generally speaking	moreover	therefore

EXAMPLES **In fact,** Emily Dickinson is my favorite poet.

You are**, I hope,** planning to arrive on time.

Sometimes such expressions are not used parenthetically and are not set off by commas.

PARENTHETICAL Long-distance calls are a bargain**,** at any rate.
[meaning "in any case"]

NOT PARENTHETICAL Long-distance calls are a bargain at any rate.
[meaning "at any cost"]

NOTE A contrasting expression introduced by *not* is parenthetical and should be set off by commas.

EXAMPLE Emily Brontë**, not her sister Charlotte,** wrote *Wuthering Heights*.

Review C — Correcting Paragraphs by Adding Commas

For the following paragraphs, write each word that should be followed by a comma and add the comma after it. Optional commas are circled.

EXAMPLE [1] The artist Faith Ringgold painstakingly hand-letters her beautiful unique story quilts.

1. beautiful,

[1] Continuing the ancient tradition of quilting, Ringgold combines printed, dyed, and pieced fabric with acrylic paintings or photo etchings. [2] By placing the tradition in a new context, the artist gives it new meaning.

Reference Note

Parentheses and **dashes** are sometimes used to set off parenthetical expressions. See page 770.

COMPUTER TIP

If you use a computer, you may want to create a file of the parenthetical expressions listed on this page. Refer to this file as you proofread your writing, and be sure that you have punctuated these expressions correctly. If your word-processing software has a search function, use the function to speed up your proofreading. The computer will search for and highlight each occurrence of whatever expression you select.

Meeting INDIVIDUAL NEEDS

ENGLISH-LANGUAGE LEARNERS

General Strategies. The chart **Common Parenthetical Expressions** can help students expand their vocabularies. Have students look up the meanings of the single-word expressions (*consequently, however, meanwhile, moreover, nevertheless,* and *therefore*) in a bilingual dictionary and in an English dictionary. To help students understand the more idiomatic expressions, such as *at any rate, in the first place,* and *on the other hand,* pair English-language learners with classmates who can explain the expressions to them.

Viewing the Art

About the Artist. Faith Ringgold's art is boldly political, focusing on the discrimination and repression facing African Americans and women in American society. Born in Harlem in 1930, she attended City College of New York and received her bachelor of science degree in 1955 and her master of fine arts degree in 1959.

Ringgold later helped to found the Women Students and Artists for Black Liberation, an organization that helped to ensure that exhibitions of black artists' works gave equal space to art by both men and women. Later, she donated to the Women's House of Detention in Manhattan a large mural that depicts the roles of women in American society.

Relating to Writing

Point out to students that the sub-rules of **Rule 22l** are very important when preparing job applications and résumés. To help students recognize the importance of understanding the comma usage discussed in the section on conventional situations, have students write cover letters for jobs that appeal to them. Students might need to refer to "Writing" in the **Quick Reference Handbook** for the correct form of a business letter. Finally, have students exchange letters and assess each other's use of correct punctuation.

Faith Ringgold, *Double Dutch on the Golden Gate Bridge* (1988). Acrylic, canvas, painted, dyed, pieced fabric (68½" × 68"). © 1988 Faith Ringgold Inc. Private Collection.

Reference Note

For more information about **punctuating addresses,** see page 715.

[3] Ringgold whose earlier works include landscapes murals masks and soft sculptures began making story quilts in 1980. [4] Titled *Echoes of Harlem* the first one was a collaboration between the artist and her mother the dress designer Willi Posey who learned quilting from her own grandmother who had learned it from her own mother a slave.

[5] Most of Ringgold's story quilts are designed to be viewed as parts of a series not as separate pieces and many include portions of a narrative linking the works in the series. [6] The work pictured here *Double Dutch on the Golden Gate Bridge* has no accompanying text and is from the *Woman on a Bridge* series which includes five works.

[7] Capturing the excitement of a childhood game it depicts a pastime cherished by generations of African Americans. [8] The work speaks however to more than a single culture and appeals to all people who recognize in it joyful moments from their childhoods.

[9] Ringgold still lives and works in Harlem the section of New York City where she was born. [10] Did you know Amy that one of her story quilts sold for $40,000 and is in the permanent collection of the city's Guggenheim Museum a major gallery of modern art?

Conventional Uses of Commas

22l. Use commas in certain conventional situations.

(1) Use commas to separate items in dates and addresses.

EXAMPLES   On Saturday, June 21, 1999, Robert moved to Miami Beach, Florida, with his parents.

His new address is 814 Georgia Avenue, Miami Beach, FL 33139-0814.

Notice that a comma generally separates the last item in a date or an address from the words that follow it.

Do not use commas to set off the following items.

- the month from the day

EXAMPLE My brother's birthday is **October 22**.

- the month from the year when the day is given before the month

EXAMPLE Was the date of your graduation **20 May 2000**?

- the month from the year when no day is given

EXAMPLE The hottest month on record here is **August 1996**.

- a house number from a street number

EXAMPLE Ms. Lee lives at **531 Winchester Street**.

- a state abbreviation from a ZIP Code

EXAMPLE Is the last part of your new address Richmond, **VA 23235-4766**?

- items preceded by prepositions

EXAMPLE The McCaslins moved to 419 Cedar Avenue **in** Chicago **on** September 10 **of** 1998.

(2) Use a comma after the salutation of a personal letter and after the closing of any letter.

EXAMPLES Dear Marcus,   Dear Aunt Meg,

Affectionately yours,   Sincerely yours,

NOTE Use a colon after the salutation of a business letter.

EXAMPLES Dear Dr. Cho:

To whom it may concern:

(3) Use a comma to set off an abbreviation, such as *Jr., Sr.,* or *M.D.,* that follows a person's name.

Notice that when words follow a person's title, a comma appears both before and after the title.

EXAMPLES Elena Moreno, **M.D.**

Russell E. Davis, **Jr.,** has been elected mayor.

Reference Note

For more about **colons,** see page 729. For more about writing **letters,** see "Writing" in the Quick Reference Handbook.

Crossing the Curriculum

Math. To demonstrate that commas and periods are used in disciplines other than language arts, write the following number on the chalkboard:

10,305,230.7

Call on volunteers to read the number and to explain the purposes of the commas and the period. [*Ten million, three hundred five thousand, two hundred thirty and seven tenths. The commas help to identify place values and make reading the number easier. The period indicates a decimal.*]

TEACHING TIP

Activity. To help students eliminate unnecessary commas from their writing, ask each student to review a piece of writing from his or her writing portfolio and to highlight every comma. Then, have students find in the chapter the rule that applies to the use of each comma. If students have used an excessive number of unnecessary commas, help them determine whether their errors follow certain patterns.

Unnecessary Commas

22m. **Do not use unnecessary commas.**

Too many commas can be as confusing as too few. Do not use a comma unless a rule requires one or unless the meaning would be unclear without it.

CONFUSING On Friday, after school, my friend, Rita, and I played badminton at her house until her dog, Ruffles, a frisky, golden retriever, joined us and ran off with the shuttlecock, clenched in its teeth.

CLEAR On Friday after school, my friend Rita and I played badminton at her house until her dog Ruffles, a frisky golden retriever, joined us and ran off with the shuttlecock clenched in its teeth.

Exercise 8 Correcting Sentences by Adding Commas

For the following sentences, write each word that should be followed by a comma and add the comma after it.

EXAMPLE
1. On our way to Birmingham Alabama we stayed overnight in Chattanooga Tennessee.

1. Birmingham, Alabama, Chattanooga,

1. On August 1 1999 we moved from Eureka California to 220 Tuxford Place Thousand Oaks California.
2. We left Tampa Florida on Monday June 15 and arrived in Albuquerque New Mexico on June 17.
3. The hotel on Gulfport Road was destroyed by fire on Tuesday March 13 1984.
4. My brother received a letter that began, "Dear John There's something I've been meaning to tell you."
5. We interviewed Franklin R. Thomas M.D. at his emergency clinic on Wilson Road.
6. On July 11 2001 Christa and Jerry will join hundreds of other cyclists and ride from Minneapolis Minnesota to Chicago Illinois.
7. The party will take place October 9 at 2480 Hastings Road in Birmingham Alabama.
8. Raphael X. Gideon Sr. is our new police chief.
9. Marcia traveled to Tyler Texas and Orlando Florida last month.
10. Dr. Martin Luther King Jr. was born on January 15 1929.

716 Chapter 22 Punctuation

Learning for Life

Thank-you Letters. Most students have had or will have the opportunity to write thank-you letters. Explain to students that one common life experience that leads to writing a thank-you letter is the job interview.

Ask students to imagine that they have just interviewed for a part-time job. Have each student write a thank-you letter to the interviewer. For an example of the content and the form of a thank-you letter, you

Review D: Proofreading a Letter for Correct Comma Usage

Proofread the following letter, adding or deleting commas as needed.

EXAMPLE [1] Uncle Victor lives in a small white house.

1. small,   Optional commas are underlined.

[1] August 26, 2001

[2] Dear Amy,
   [3] I received your letter <u>,</u> and wanted to send a quick reply answering your questions. [4] Uncle Victor does, in fact, have a new address; he and Aunt Margo moved to a faraway, beautiful land of sunshine. [5] Their new address is 1300 Fairwood Drive, San Diego, CA 99069. [6] They moved last month, and Uncle Victor started his new job last Wednesday <u>,</u> morning. [7] I plan to be back in town to tie up loose ends by selling their house, picking up their dogs, and visiting with friends on Friday, September 4. [8] I will have a few friends over for dinner that night <u>,</u> and hope you can come. [9] I will, by the way, be cooking my famous Greek dinner.

[10] Affectionately yours,

Roy

Review E: Revising Paragraphs by Adding Commas

For the sentences in the following paragraphs, write each word that should be followed by a comma and add the comma after it. If a sentence is already correct, write C.   Optional commas are underlined.

EXAMPLE [1] In their study of the culture of the ancient Greeks the drama students read about the three playwrights Aeschylus Sophocles, and Aristophanes.

1. Greeks, Aeschylus,

[1] As early as the sixth century B.C. plays were performed in Athens, Greece in the amphitheater pictured on the next page, the

HELP
Some of the sentences in Review E need more than one comma.

MULTIPLE INTELLIGENCES
Interpersonal Intelligence. To give students additional practice with correct comma usage, divide the class into groups of four or five. Prepare for each group a sheet of paper with the following instructions:

1. Write a sentence that includes a series of phrases.
2. Write a sentence that consists of a series of short independent clauses.
3. Write a sentence with two or more adjectives preceding a noun.
4. Write a compound sentence in which the two clauses are joined by *or*.
5. Write a sentence with a nonessential clause.
6. Write a sentence with an introductory participial phrase.
7. Write a sentence with an introductory adverb clause.
8. Write a sentence with a nonessential appositive phrase.
9. Write a sentence that includes a word used in direct address.
10. Write a sentence that includes a parenthetical expression.

Encourage each group to brainstorm topics for the ten sentences. Instruct the members of each group to take turns writing, editing, and proofreading the sentences. Then, have groups check each other's work, paying particular attention to comma usage. Encourage students to refer to the rules in the chapter when evaluating each other's work.

---

may want to refer students to "Writing" in the **Quick Reference Handbook.**
  In the postwriting stage, remind students to pay close attention to their use of end marks and commas. You may want to have students exchange thank-you letters and check for correct punctuation usage. Encourage students to add their thank-you letters to their writing portfolios for future reference.

Cooperative Learning

Divide the class into groups of four, and ask each group to create a quiz, along with an answer key, that covers all of the rules in this chapter.

Then, ask groups to exchange the quizzes they have created. Encourage members of each group to work cooperatively to complete the quiz. Then, ask each group to return the quiz to the group that created it. Have groups use their answer keys to assess the completed quizzes. Tell students to write beside each incorrect answer the rule number that applies. Finally, have each group return the quiz to the group that completed it so that group members can examine and correct their errors.

3. C

Theater of Dionysus. [2] The Theater of Dionysus is located on the south slope of the Acropolis, an elevated, fortified section of Athens. [3] The plays presented in ancient Greece marked the beginning of drama in the Western world. [4] In fact, the English word *theater* comes from the Greek word *theatron*, which means "a place for seeing."

[5] Wearing masks to show which characters they were portraying, the actors in ancient dramas often played several different roles. [6] In addition, all roles, including those of female characters, were performed by men.

[7] Although records show that Greek playwrights wrote hundreds of tragedies, fewer than thirty-five of these plays survive. [8] The earliest Greek dramatist, Aeschylus, wrote the *Oresteia*, a powerful story of murder, revenge, and divine mercy. [9] Sophocles, often regarded as the greatest dramatist of all time, is credited with writing more than one hundred plays. [10] Among the surviving works of Aristophanes, whom the ancient Greeks considered the greatest comic playwright, are the three satires *The Clouds*, *The Wasps*, and *The Frogs*.

CHAPTER 22

Chapter Review

A. Using End Marks

Add or replace end marks in the following sentences, as needed.

1. Have you heard of the Bengali writer Rabindranath Tagore?
2. Wow! Look at that sunset! 2. [or sunset.]
3. Last week I saw the cartoon version of *Alice in Wonderland*. 3. .
4. The first speaker was the Reverend James Elliot.
5. Will you be in town next Friday? 5. ?
6. Will you turn the radio down a little? 6. ?
7. When was the impressive Swedish golfer Eric Estlund born? 7. ?
8. "Oh darn it," exclaimed Paul in exasperation. 8. !
9. Musical backup was provided by the J. L. Bourgeois Trio.
10. What an absolutely marvelous exercise! 10. !

B. Correcting Sentences by Adding Punctuation

Add periods, question marks, exclamation points, and commas where they are needed in the following sentences. If a sentence is already punctuated correctly, write C.   Optional commas are underlined.

11. Although scholars aren't certain about who was the first European printer to use movable type, Johann Gutenberg is usually credited.
12. The students who have signed up for the field trip may leave at noon, but all the others must attend classes.
13. Gloria, did you notice where I left my bowling ball?
14. Miriam Colón, who was born in Puerto Rico, founded the Puerto Rican Traveling Theatre.
15. Was the Great Pyramid in Egypt built sometime between 2600 and 2500 B.C.? 15. C
16. Vendors sold T-shirts, buttons, caps, and pennants to the sports fans outside the stadium.
17. Listening to the orchestra play "The Star-Spangled Banner," I realized that I'm proud to be American.
18. The hikers munched on sunflower seeds and quenched their thirst with ice-cold, refreshing spring water.
19. Isn't their address 1042 Cleveland Ave., Enid, OK 73703?

Using the Chapter Review

To assess student progress, you may want to compare the types of items missed on the **Diagnostic Preview** with those missed on the **Chapter Review**. If students have not made significant progress, you may want to refer them for additional practice to **Exercises 26–27** in **Chapter 27: Correcting Common Errors**.

Meeting INDIVIDUAL NEEDS

ADVANCED LEARNERS

To promote creative thinking, initiate a discussion about reading literature aloud. Ask students why some stories hold a listener's interest while others do not. Have students consider subject matter, the choice and arrangement of words, sentence structure, and punctuation.

Then, have students work in pairs to analyze various kinds of literature, such as short stories, children's books, poems, and essays. Ask each pair to find two examples—one that has exceptional read-aloud quality and one that does not. If students have difficulty finding selections with excellent read-aloud quality, you may want to suggest these books by Jim Trelease: *Read All About It!: Great Read-Aloud Stories, Poems, and Newspaper Pieces for Preteens and Teens* and *The Read-Aloud Handbook*. Ask students to analyze their selections to determine why they made their choices. Encourage students to pay particular attention to the role that punctuation plays.

Then, have students share the results of their analyses to determine the characteristics that are common to selections with excellent read-aloud quality. Finally, call on volunteers to read aloud excerpts from selections that exhibit those qualities.

MECHANICS

20. Marian Anderson, a contralto, was the first African American to become a permanent member of the Metropolitan Opera Company.
21. Wow! That's amazing!
22. We rushed to the airport, stood in line, bought our tickets, and then heard that the flight had been delayed for three hours.
23. Norm has had quite a run of bad luck, yet he still says tomorrow will be a better day, for he prides himself on being an optimist.
24. That Ming vase, wrapped in cotton and packed in a crate, was delivered to the museum earlier today.
25. If we're late for practice again, however, Ms. Stubbs will drop us from the team.
26. How lucky I was!
27. At the beginning of the eighteenth century, Chikamatsu Monzaemon wrote the first Japanese tragedies to focus on the lives of common, ordinary people.
28. Nowadays the Sioux, generally speaking, make their living as farmers and ranchers.
29. Jan Matzeliger, an inventor in Lynn, Massachusetts, revolutionized the shoe industry in 1883 with his machine that joined the top of a shoe to its sole.
30. These four students should report to the auditorium after lunch: Jeff Malone, Mary Holt, Kathryn Rogers, and Hartmut Boylan Barthzwinger, Jr.

C. Correcting Paragraphs by Adding Punctuation

For each sentence in the following paragraph, add periods, question marks, exclamation points, and commas where they are needed. If a sentence is already correct, write *C*.   Optional commas are underlined.

[31] Going to visit Uncle Ricky is one of my greatest pleasures, for he owns and operates a semitrailer. [32] His big rig, an eighteen-wheeler affectionately named "Pug," is used to haul produce from coast to coast. [33] One of Uncle Ricky's craziest experiences was the time he left Boston and drove to 2842 Beltline Drive, Logan, Virginia, to deliver a load of oranges, grapefruit, and lemons. [34] When he arrived at the address, he was dumbfounded. [35] As a matter of fact,

---

RESOURCES

Punctuation

Review
- *Grammar, Usage, and Mechanics*, pp. 272, 273, 274, 275

Assessment
- Assessment Package
  —*Chapter Tests*, Ch. 22
  —*Chapter Tests in Standardized Test Formats*, Ch. 22
- *Test Generator* (One-Stop Planner CD-ROM)

the address turned out to be that of a citrus orchard. [36] Obviously, the orchard had been producing Logan's finest fruit for years. [37] Climbing back on board "Pug," Uncle Ricky checked his shipping order. [38] He realized with dismay that he should have delivered the shipment to Logan, Vermont, instead of Logan, Virginia. [39] Fortunately, it was a clear run up a couple of interstates for "Pug," and Uncle Ricky delivered his fruit only half a day late. [40] Now he chuckles about it and says wryly, "Well, I did wonder how I had managed to arrive a whole day early."

Writing Application
Using Commas in Instructions

Using Commas Correctly Create an educational board game or computer game, and write instructions explaining how to play it. Include information from at least one of your school subjects, such as math, science, or history. Use commas to make your instructions as clear as possible.

Prewriting Choose a subject area that interests you. Then, decide what the object of the game will be. Jot down notes about the number of players, the kinds of supplies or equipment needed, and other rules of the game. Give your game a catchy title, and then arrange the instructions in an order that will be easy for players to follow.

Writing Keep in mind that your instructions will be the players' only source of information. Try to anticipate their questions, and aim for a conversational tone, as if you were explaining the game in person.

Revising Ask some of your friends to play the game. As you watch, note any problems they have with understanding the instructions. Then, add, delete, replace, or rearrange information to make the instructions easier to understand.

Publishing Proofread your instructions, paying special attention to your use of end marks and commas. Use a computer to make a clean printout, or photocopy a neatly handwritten copy. You might offer copies of your game to your school's media center or to one of the organizations that serve your community.

Chapter Review 721

RESOURCES
Writing Application
Extension
- *Grammar, Usage, and Mechanics*, p. 278
- *Language Workshop CD-ROM*, Lesson 34–38, 43

CHAPTER 23 Punctuation
Semicolons and Colons

Diagnostic Preview

Correcting Sentences by Adding Semicolons and Colons

For each of the following sentences, write the word or numeral that precedes each punctuation error. Then, add the semicolon or colon needed. If a sentence is already correct, write *C*.

HELP—
Some sentences in the Diagnostic Preview contain more than one punctuation error.

EXAMPLE 1. Please bring the following items books, pencils, and newspapers.
 1. items:

1. My aunt Pam loves to play backgammon and chess, however, she rarely has time because she works at two jobs.
2. In 1904, Mary McLeod Bethune founded a school for girls in Daytona Beach, Florida, that school is now Bethune-Cookman College.
3. Psalm 23:1–6 is one of the best-known passages in the Bible.
4. According to one book that I have read, *The Real McCoy, The Life of an African-American Inventor,* an oil can used in railroad maintenance gave rise to the popular expression "the real McCoy."
5. If I had a million dollars, I would visit London, England, Cairo, Egypt, Buenos Aires, Argentina, and Tokyo, Japan.
6. We have to write reports for gym class on one of the following athletes, Jesse Owens, Sonja Henie, Jim Thorpe, Althea Gibson, or Babe Didrikson Zaharias.

7. Our neighbor's cocker spaniel barked all night long; as a result, I did not sleep well.
8. Candace will have to take Sandra's place in tonight's performance; unfortunately, Sandra sprained her ankle and cannot walk.
9. I have ridden bicycles, horses, and motorcycles; and I have traveled in trains, buses, and planes.
10. Asia has both the highest and the lowest points on the earth's surface: Mount Everest, the highest, soars 29,028 feet; the Dead Sea, a salt lake, lies 1,300 feet below sea level.
11. Instructed to be prompt, we arrived at school at 7:15 A.M., but the doors were locked; consequently, we had to wait until 7:30 A.M. to enter the building.
12. Indira Gandhi, who served for many years as the prime minister of India, grew up in the world of civic life, politics, and government, for her father, Jawaharlal Nehru, was the first prime minister of India, from 1947 to 1964.
13. My friends Ruth and Cindy disagree about the role of fate in life: Ruth believes that people can control their own destiny, but Cindy insists that people are simply pawns of fate.
14. I don't like to prepare outlines; nevertheless, the highest grade I ever received was for a report that I wrote from an outline.
15. Mr. Kowalski has always regretted that he did not learn to speak Polish when he was a child; now he is taking a conversational Polish class at the college.
16. The computer software business is an enormous, growing industry; in fact, people can buy software that does everything from balancing budgets to plotting biorhythm charts.
17. Every morning Lonnie rises at 5:00, jogs until 5:30, showers, eats breakfast by 6:15, and catches the 6:35 bus.
18. Red Cloud, a leader of the Oglala Sioux, was a military genius; he successfully defended Sioux lands against settlers who wanted to build a trail from Laramie, Wyoming, to Virginia City, Montana.
19. Gates of the Arctic National Park, which is located in northern Alaska, is known for its large populations of certain animals: caribou, grizzly bears, moose, and wolves.
20. If you want to send fragile items through the mail, the post office recommends that you do the following: pack them in fiberboard containers; use foam, plastic, or padding to cushion them; and then seal the package carefully, reinforcing it with filament tape.

Punctuation, pp. 722–736
Alignments
TEKS 3A, 3D
TAAS W3, W7
English II End-of-Course 5, 6

Texas Resources
- *TAAS Tool Kit*
- *Preparation for TAAS*
- *One-Stop Planner CD-ROM*

Semicolons

Rules 23a–d (pp. 724–728)

OBJECTIVE

- To correct sentences by adding semicolons and commas

TEACHING TIP

Activity. Before introducing **Rules 23a** and **23b** and the examples for each rule, write on the chalkboard the following sentences:

1. Everyone else in my family excels in a particular sport, so I seem to be the only exception.
2. The river is rising rapidly, and it is expected to crest by noon.
3. Leonor is planning to become an engineer, but she is also interested in graphic design.
4. Only two people registered for the pottery lessons, so the class was canceled.

Call on volunteers to read aloud **Rules 23a** and **23b** and the examples for each rule. Then, ask other volunteers to explain how each sentence on the chalkboard differs from the corresponding example in the textbook. As students respond, underline each comma and coordinating conjunction in the chalkboard examples. [*Each sentence on the chalkboard has a comma and a coordinating conjunction, whereas the corresponding example in the textbook has only a semicolon or has a semicolon, a conjunctive adverb or transitional expression, and a comma.*]

Reference Note
For information on using a **comma** to **separate independent clauses that are joined by a coordinating conjunction,** see page 703.

Reference Note
For information about **conjunctive adverbs** see page 492.

STYLE TIP

Use a semicolon to join independent clauses only if the ideas in the clauses are closely related.

INCORRECT
Greg likes Italian food; Marla prefers going to the beach.

CORRECT
Greg likes Italian food; Marla prefers Chinese food.

Semicolons

23a. Use a semicolon between independent clauses that are closely related in thought and that are not joined by *and, but, for, nor, or, so,* or *yet.*

EXAMPLES   Everyone else in my family excels in a particular sport; I seem to be the only exception.

The river is rising rapidly; it is expected to crest by noon.

23b. Use a semicolon between independent clauses joined by a conjunctive adverb or a transitional expression.

EXAMPLES   Leonor is planning to become an engineer; **however,** she is also interested in graphic design.

Only two people registered for the pottery lessons; **as a result,** the class was canceled.

Notice in the examples above that the conjunctive adverb and the transitional expression are each followed by a comma.

Commonly Used Conjunctive Adverbs			
accordingly	however	moreover	besides
also	nevertheless	consequently	instead
indeed	next	still	then
otherwise	furthermore	meanwhile	therefore

Commonly Used Transitional Expressions			
as a result	for example	for instance	in fact
in spite of	in conclusion	in other words	that is

 NOTE   When a conjunctive adverb or a transitional expression appears within one of the clauses instead of between the clauses, it is usually set off by commas. The two clauses may still be separated by a semicolon.

EXAMPLES   Ralph Ellison is best known for his 1952 novel, *Invisible Man;* he also, **however,** wrote short stories and essays.

Not all birds migrate south for the winter; cardinals, **for instance,** can stay in northern climates year round.

724   Chapter 23   Punctuation

RESOURCES

Semicolons

Practice

- *Grammar, Usage, and Mechanics,* pp. 280, 281, 282
- *Language Workshop CD-ROM,* Lessons 35, 37, 43

Using conjunctive adverbs and transitional expressions can help you clearly show relationships between ideas. Notice in the examples below how these expressions clarify the relationship between the ideas expressed in the clauses.

EXAMPLES The class has finished the nonfiction unit**;** **therefore,** we will begin the poetry unit on Monday. [Two ideas have a cause-and-effect relationship.]

The poems will be discussed in class**;** **meanwhile,** we will be working on our research papers on our own time. [Two ideas have a time relationship.]

Most students are studying poets from the distant past**;** **I, however,** am researching the poetic devices of a modern songwriter. [Two ideas have a contradictory relationship.]

Exercise 1 Correcting Sentences by Adding Commas and Semicolons

For the following sentences, write each word that should be followed by a semicolon or a comma. Add the needed punctuation mark after the word.

EXAMPLE 1. The clever carving shown here was handmade in Mexico today carvings like this are sold all over the world.

1. Mexico;

1. The carvings come from the Oaxaca (pronounced wä•hä´•kä) Valley in fact 90 percent of the two hundred families who make them live in just three villages.
2. Carving has been a tradition among Oaxacans for hundreds of years only recently however have the artists sold their works outside the valley.
3. In many families, the fathers and older sons do the actual carving meanwhile the other family members sand and paint the figures.
4. The artists find inspiration for their creations in everyday life for example religion and nature are rich sources of ideas.
5. Even those carvers whose works have won worldwide acclaim have chosen to continue living in the valley their ties to their families and communities are very strong.

Meeting INDIVIDUAL NEEDS

ENGLISH-LANGUAGE LEARNERS
General Strategies. Before students can be expected to use conjunctive adverbs and transitional expressions effectively in their writing, they must first understand the meanings of these connectors. Have students find in a bilingual dictionary the meaning in their native languages of each connector listed in the charts on p. 724. Ask students to record the meanings in their writing portfolios. You may want to point out that some of these connectors have similar meanings and therefore can often be used almost interchangeably—for example, *consequently/as a result/therefore; furthermore/moreover; for example/for instance;* and *however/nevertheless.*

Cooperative Learning

To determine where to place semicolons between the independent clauses in each sentence from **Exercise 1,** students must be able to recognize where one complete thought stops and another begins. To help them determine each complete thought, have students work in pairs to locate the main subject(s) and verb(s) in each independent clause. Point out that in two of the sentences (1 and 5), a subordinate clause appears within an independent clause. Remind students that subordinate clauses can appear before, after, or within an independent clause.

Exercise 1

ALTERNATIVE LESSON

Point out to students that **Exercise 1** contains eight compound sentences and two compound-complex sentences. Ask students to identify the compound-complex sentences and to write the subordinate clause that appears in each one. [1. *who make them;* 5. *whose works have won worldwide acclaim*]

Relating to Writing

Because students might be reluctant to use semicolons in their writing, you may want to use the following activity to help students acquire confidence. Ask students to select from their own writing three compound sentences whose independent clauses are joined by a comma and a coordinating conjunction. Have students use semicolons in their selected sentences to join the independent clauses.

Then, call on volunteers to read aloud the original sentences and the revised versions. Discuss with students whether the revisions are more effective than the original sentences. Finally, ask students whether adding conjunctive adverbs or transitional expressions would make the relationships between the ideas in the independent clauses clearer.

STYLE TIP

Use a semicolon between clauses joined by a coordinating conjunction only when a semicolon is needed to prevent misreading, as in the examples of confusing sentences given to the right. If a sentence is clear without a semicolon, don't add one just because the clauses contain commas.

EXAMPLE
Lana, you are the best musician I know, and you're a great dancer, too. [clear without a semicolon]

---

6. Art in Mexico is varied and distinctive, and it exhibits a strong Spanish influence.
7. The Zapotec and Mixtec peoples of Puebla and Oaxaca have a long history of artistic craftsmanship; the Mixtec were considered master goldsmiths.
8. The Mixtec built a tremendous pyramid in Cholula; it was the largest pyramid of the ancient world.
9. During the thirteenth century, stone was a favorite medium of these peoples; they also used bone, gold, jade, and wood.
10. Much of the art from southern Central America was destroyed during the years of the Spanish conquest, but several historical manuscripts survive today.

23c. You may need to use a semicolon (rather than a comma) before a coordinating conjunction to join independent clauses that contain commas.

CONFUSING	June sat with Tony, Pat, and me, and Josh sat with Flora, Zack, and Geraldo.
CLEAR	June sat with Tony, Pat, and me; and Josh sat with Flora, Zack, and Geraldo.
CONFUSING	Searching for the house key, I found a dime, a nickel, and a penny, and John, my brother, found his lost watch.
CLEAR	Searching for the house key, I found a dime, a nickel, and a penny; and John, my brother, found his lost watch.

23d. Use a semicolon between items in a series if the items contain commas.

EXAMPLES In 1990, the three largest cities in the United States were New York, New York; Los Angeles, California; and Chicago, Illinois.

You may turn in your book reports on Thursday, September 14; Friday, September 15; Monday, September 18; or Tuesday, September 19.

Exercise 2 Correcting Sentences by Adding Semicolons

For the following sentences, write each word that should be followed by a semicolon. Add the needed punctuation mark after the word. If a sentence is already correct, write *C*.

MINI-LESSON Continued on pp. 727–728

Punctuating Compound-Complex Sentences. Point out that all of the example sentences on pp. 724–725 are compound. Explain that **Rules 23a** and **23b** also apply to compound-complex sentences. Remind students that a compound-complex sentence consists of two or more independent clauses and at least one subordinate clause. To give students practice with semicolons in compound-complex sentences, write the following formulae on the chalkboard:

EXAMPLE
1. The winners of the regional science fair were Anya Garcia, who came in first, Jeff Ford, who came in second, and Alberto Robinson, who came in third.
    1. first; second;

1. The president of the student council has appointed the following members to chair committees: Anna Maria Chen, fundraising; Ben Cohen, volunteer services; and Donna Massad, event planning.
2. Fortunately, Candace remembered the address, or we would have been quite late, Roseanne.   2. C
3. Eli went to the matinee with Jae, Kerry, and Sung; but Josh, Taylor, and I preferred to go hiking.   3. C
4. After his concert in New York, my Uncle Vittorio will come to visit on Thursday, March 25; Friday, March 26; or Saturday, March 27.
5. Would you prefer to live in Boston, Massachusetts; San Francisco, California; or Seattle, Washington?
6. Performers in the show were Tony Fernandez, trumpet and trombone; Donna Lee Bryant, clarinet and saxophone; and Danica Ward, drums and steel guitar.
7. I bought my sister several gifts, including a book, a skirt, and a tennis racquet; but, unfortunately, I couldn't find a present for my mother, who wants an antique desk.
8. We admired the atrium's flowering vines, rock formations, and fountains; and then we stepped out into the courtyard, followed the flagstone path, and crossed the bridge over the goldfish pond.
9. To prepare for the performance we must set the stage, check the lights, and test the sound system; then, the dancers will take their places, the audience will be seated, and the curtain will rise.   9. C
10. On our backpacking trip to Eastern Europe, we hope to visit Prague, Czech Republic; Budapest, Hungary; Bucharest, Romania; and Krakow, Poland.

Review A Correcting Sentences by Adding Commas and Semicolons

For the following sentences, write each word that should be followed by a semicolon or a comma. Add the needed punctuation mark after each word. If a sentence is already correct, write *C*.

EXAMPLE
1. The diagram on the next page shows the typical seating plan of a symphony orchestra a conductor occupies the podium.
    1. orchestra;

HELP
Some sentences in Review A may need more than one punctuation mark.

Semicolons   727

Exercise 2

ALTERNATIVE LESSON
Ask students to write the definition of *simple sentence* [*a sentence that consists of only one independent clause and no subordinate clauses*]. Then, have them identify the five simple sentences in **Exercise 2**. [*1, 4, 5, 6, 10*]

Relating to Literature
If the Tom Godwin story "The Cold Equations" is available in students' literature textbooks, have them read the first three paragraphs. Ask students to suggest reasons why the author chose to join the independent clauses with semicolons. [*The ideas flow quickly to maintain the suspense. Periods would signal longer pauses between the clauses. In addition, the clauses joined by semicolons are closely related in thought.*]

You may want to extend the activity by having students explore the use of semicolons in other professional writing, such as magazine or newspaper articles.

---

1. independent clause + independent clause + subordinate clause = compound-complex sentence
2. independent clause + subordinate clause + independent clause = compound-complex sentence
3. independent clause + conjunctive adverb + subordinate clause + independent clause = compound-complex sentence

Ask each student to write and punctuate a sentence that represents each word equation. Remind students to make sure the

Semicolons   727

TEACHING TIP

Review A To reinforce students' understanding of the rules governing the use of semicolons, ask students to provide the rule number that applies to each semicolon they add to the sentences in **Review A.** Answers are as follows:

1. Rule 23a
2. no semicolon
3. Rule 23a
4. Rule 23c
5. Rule 23c
6. Rules 23b and 23c
7. Rule 23b
8. Rule 23b
9. Rule 23a
10. Rule 23d

Meeting INDIVIDUAL NEEDS

MODALITIES
Visual Learners. To help visual learners determine where to add each semicolon or comma in the sentences from **Review A,** have them underline each subject once and each verb twice, circle each independent clause, and draw a rectangle around each conjunctive adverb or transitional expression. Remind students that a clause may contain more than one subject or verb and that a subordinate clause may appear within an independent clause.

---

1. All of the instruments in a symphony orchestra are divided into classes based on how they produce sound; many musicians can play several instruments within a class.
2. **C** The four classes are strings, woodwinds, brass, and percussion.
3. Some of the stringed instruments are played with a bow; some are plucked with the fingers or with a pick; still others are operated by means of a keyboard.
4. Woodwinds, which were once made mainly of wood, include the flute, the clarinet, and the saxophone; but other materials, such as metal or plastic, are often used nowadays.
5. Most brass instruments, such as the trumpet, tuba, and cornet, have valves that regulate the pitch; but the trombone, my favorite instrument, has a sliding section for this purpose.
6. Kettledrums, or timpani, are percussion instruments that can be tuned to a specific pitch; most other kinds of drums, the cymbals, and the triangle, however, cannot be tuned.
7. A conductor's job is to coordinate the sounds produced by these different instruments; however, this task is only one of a conductor's responsibilities.
8. Conductors must study the theory of music for years; furthermore, they must be skilled at playing at least one instrument.
9. Many people think a conductor just establishes the tempo of the music; they do not realize that he or she also selects the music, interprets the composer's meaning, and brings out the best performance in each musician.
10. The goal of many conductors is to lead a major orchestra such as one of those in London, England; Mexico City, Mexico; Boston, Massachusetts; or Chicago, Illinois.

Chapter 23 Punctuation

MINI-LESSON

clauses they join are closely related in meaning.

Have students exchange papers and assess each other's sentences by using the following criteria:

1. Are the clauses closely related in meaning?
2. Are semicolons and commas correct?

Then, ask students to revise any sentence that does not meet the criteria.

Colons

23e. Use a colon to mean "note what follows."

(1) Use a colon before a list of items, especially after expressions such as *the following* and *as follows*.

EXAMPLES In Washington, D.C., we visited four important national sites: the White House, the Washington Monument, the Vietnam Veterans Memorial, and the Lincoln Memorial.

The only articles allowed in the examination area are **as follows:** pencils, compasses, rulers, and protractors.

During summer vacation, Juanita read biographies of **the following** people: John Ross and Annie Wauneka.

> NOTE Do not use a colon between a verb and its complements or between a preposition and its objects.

INCORRECT At the new amusement park we rode: the roller coaster, the Ferris wheel, the bumper cars, and the water slide.
CORRECT At the amusement park we rode the roller coaster, the Ferris wheel, the bumper cars, and the water slide.
[The list serves as the direct object of the verb *rode*.]

INCORRECT Our family has lived in: California, Arizona, and Texas.
CORRECT Our family has lived in California, Arizona, and Texas.
[The list serves as the object of the preposition *in*.]

(2) Use a colon before a long, formal statement or quotation.

EXAMPLE Thomas Paine's first pamphlet in the series *The American Crisis* starts with these famous words:

> These are the times that try men's souls. The summer soldier and the sunshine patriot will, in this crisis, shrink from the service of their country; but he that stands it *now* deserves the love and thanks of man and woman.

23f. Use a colon before a statement that explains or clarifies a preceding statement.

EXAMPLES He deserves a raise: He completed the project on schedule and under budget.

Preston slapped his forehead: He had forgotten to put oregano in the sauce.

HELP

When a list of words, phrases, or subordinate clauses follows a colon, the first word of the list is generally lowercase.

EXAMPLE
When you walk into class, you need to have the following with you: **y**our textbook, a pen and a pencil, writing paper, and a good attitude.

Reference Note

For information on **complements**, see page 450. For information on **objects of prepositions**, see page 467.

Reference Note

For information on using **long quotations**, see page 747.

HELP

When an independent clause follows a colon, the first word of the clause begins with a capital letter.

EXAMPLE
The current debate is still best summed up by Mark Twain: "**I**t is better to support schools than jails."

Colons **729**

RESOURCES

Colons
Practice
- *Grammar, Usage, and Mechanics,* pp. 283, 284, 285
- *Language Workshop CD-ROM,* Lessons 35, 37, 43

23g. Use a colon in certain conventional situations.

(1) Use a colon between the hour and the minute.

EXAMPLES   6:15 P.M.   9:55 tomorrow morning

(2) Use a colon between chapter and verse in Biblical references.

EXAMPLES   Psalms 8:9   I Corinthians 13:1–13

(3) Use a colon between a title and a subtitle.

EXAMPLES   *I like Jazz:* The Essence of Billy Holiday [recording]

Tilting Knights: King Richard and Saladin [painting]

(4) Use a colon after the salutation of a business letter.

EXAMPLES   Dear Ms. Weinberg: Dear Sir or Madam:

HELP
Use a comma after the salutation of a personal letter.

EXAMPLE
Dear Suzanne,

Reference Note
For more about writing **business letters** and **personal letters**, see "Writing" in the Quick Reference Handbook.

HELP
Some sentences in Exercise 3 may need more than one colon added.

Exercise 3 Correcting Sentences by Adding Colons

For the following sentences, write each word or numeral that should be followed by a colon, and add the colon. If a sentence is already correct, write *C*.

EXAMPLE   1. I began my acceptance speech as follows "Fellow students, thank you for your votes!"

1. follows:

1. My little sister's favorite book is *The Great Kapok Tree A Tale of the Amazon Rain Forest* by Lynn Cherry.
2. Sometimes the paper comes at 7 15 A.M., but other times it doesn't hit the driveway until 8 00.
3. My niece has several items embossed with that logo a poster, a nightgown, a notebook, and a clock.
4. In William Shakespeare's play *Julius Caesar,* Caesar has this to say of courage "Cowards die many times before their deaths, /The valiant taste of death but once."
5. Sherry's favorite artists are Jacob Lawrence, Romare Bearden, and Margaret Burroughs.
6. I think the story of Moses and Pharaoh's daughter is told in Exodus 2 5–10.
7. The directions were as follows Cover with plastic wrap, place in microwave oven, and cook for at least ten minutes.
8. I prefer my bicycle to a car for three reasons I don't have to pay for gasoline, I don't need insurance, and I don't waste time looking for a place to park.

Learning for Life

Continued on pp. 731–732

Taking Standardized Tests. You may want to use this opportunity to discuss the meanings of colons used in analogy items. Point out that a typical analogy item requires a person to determine the relationship between two words and then supply two other words that have the same relationship. To illustrate, write on the chalkboard the following analogy item: write : author :: _____ : _____

1. snake : slither   2. poem : book

9. In Cuba, which is a Spanish-speaking country, most of the people are of Spanish, African, or Spanish-African descent. 9. C
10. We should buy a house; Our taxes would be lower, and we'd have more space.

Review B — Proofreading Sentences for Correct Use of Semicolons and Colons

Most of the following sentences contain at least one error in the use of semicolons or colons. For each error, write the word or numeral that precedes the missing or incorrect punctuation and add the correct punctuation.

EXAMPLE
1. The electricity was out for three days, the phones were not working for a week.
1. days;

1. I made a list so that I would remember everything we needed: toothpaste, milk, wax paper, and cat food.
2. The entrance exam was finished; however, I would remain nervous until the results came back.
3. The carpet was green, black, and brown; so red, orange, and pink have been ruled out for the wall color.
4. The awards went to John, who read from *Evangeline*; Ann, who read from *The Bridge*; and Garrett, who read from *The Waste Land*.
5. The vacuum hose was brittle and cracked; therefore, taping it was not going to be enough.
6. The bus to the game will be leaving at precisely 3:45.
7. Lupe was going to title her essay "Mary Had a Little Lamb: The Social and Personal Benefits of Pet Ownership."
8. The three-person teams will be as follows: Takara, Lani, and Nick; Jessica, Vince, and Tyrone; and Peter, Dolores, and Ruben.
9. Jeremy had this Mark Twain quote taped to his folder: "Man is the only animal that blushes. Or needs to."
10. Sue Ann thought she had all the homework she could handle; on the other hand, she still had two more classes in the afternoon.

Review C — Correcting a Business Letter by Adding Semicolons and Colons

For the numbered word groups in the letter on the following page, write each word that should be followed by a semicolon or a colon. Place the needed punctuation mark after each word.

COMPUTER TIP
Some software programs can evaluate your writing for common errors in the use of semicolons and colons. Such programs can help you as you proofread your drafts. Remember, however, that software cannot find every error. You will still need to proofread your writing carefully.

TECHNOLOGY TIP

You may want to discuss with students the use of emoticons—combinations of punctuation marks, symbols, numbers, and letters that are used to express emotions in e-mail messages. Write the following examples on the chalkboard, and encourage students to add acceptable emoticons to the list.

:-)   User is smiling.
;-)   User is winking.
:-O   User is shocked.
:-(User is unhappy.
:-D   User is laughing.

MECHANICS

HELP
Some word groups in Review C need more than one punctuation mark.

EXAMPLE [1] Hampton University was founded in 1868 it was originally named Hampton Normal and Agricultural Institute.

1. 1868;

[1] Dear Sir or Madam

   [2] The media coordinator at Central High School suggested that I write to you she explained that Hampton has an extensive collection of materials on African American history. [3] For my history class I am preparing an oral report on the March on Washington of August 28, 1963 and if possible, I would like to display pictures of the march.

   [4] I am particularly interested in pictures of the following speakers Floyd McKissick, John Lewis, Roy Wilkins, and Dr. Martin Luther King, Jr. [5] I would also like pictures showing the size and diversity of the crowd for example, a shot of the marchers filling the area around the Reflecting Pool between the Lincoln Memorial and the Washington Monument would be especially effective. [6] Either prints or slides will be useful however, I would prefer slides if they are available.

   [7] My grandfather, who took part in the march, vividly remembers these words of Dr. King "Let us not seek to satisfy our thirst for freedom by drinking from the cup of bitterness and hatred." [8] Grandfather took several rolls of film himself that day unfortunately, the pictures were lost in a fire a few years ago.

   [9] Please send me information on ordering copies of suitable pictures a stamped, self-addressed envelope is enclosed. [10] Thank you for your help I appreciate your attention to my request.

Sincerely,

Jesse Fletcher

732   Chapter 23   Punctuation

Learning for Life

of the paired words given as choices [1. *performer* to *action*; 2. *part* to *whole*; 3. *whole* to *part*; 4. *action* to *performer*]. Finally, ask students to choose the paired words that have the same relationship as *write* and *author* [*draw* and *illustrator*].

732   Punctuation

Chapter 23 Chapter Review

A. Correcting Sentences by Using Semicolons and Colons

Most of the following sentences have a comma or no punctuation mark where a semicolon or a colon should be used. Write the word or numeral preceding each error; then, add the needed punctuation mark. If a sentence is already correct, write *C*.

1. American Indians inhabited North America long before any Europeans; however, many Native Americans weren't recognized as citizens of the United States until 1924.
2. The planning committee meeting is scheduled for 3:15 this afternoon; please don't be late.
3. The following committees will report at that time: budget, membership, awards, and programs.
4. Every morning after I get up, I read a Bible verse; this morning I read John 14:27.
5. We left some food out for the stray dog; it looked so forlorn huddled in the doorway.
6. Our modern literature class has read these poems: "Incident," by Countee Cullen; "The Love Song of J. Alfred Prufrock," by T. S. Eliot; and "Ars Poetica," by Archibald MacLeish.
7. When she transferred to Barton Academy, Millie joined several clubs, helped in planning the Spring Carnival, and worked at a food bank for the needy; nevertheless, it took her months to make some new friends.
8. While campaigning to become mayor of San Antonio, Maria Antonieta Berriozabal summed up her point of view in these words. "Our greatest resource is our people. We have to deal with business interests and human needs simultaneously."   8. C
9. Conrad Aiken was a correspondent for *The New Yorker* and also wrote essays and short stories; he is best known, however, for his narrative and philosophical poetry.
10. The Bering Strait links the Arctic Ocean with the Bering Sea; both the strait and the sea are named for Vitus Bering, a Danish explorer of the eighteenth century.

Using the Chapter Review

To assess student progress, you may want to compare the types of items missed on the **Diagnostic Preview** with those missed on the **Chapter Review.** If students have not made significant progress, you may want to refer them to **Exercise 28** in **Chapter 27: Correcting Common Errors** for additional practice.

11. The late S. I. Hayakawa once made this statement▲"It is not true that we have only one life to live; if we can read, we can live as many more lives and as many kinds of lives as we wish."
12. The winners in the Douglas Fun Run last Saturday morning were Otis Williams, a sophomore▲ Janice Hicks, a senior▲ and Rodrigo Campas, a junior.
13. They opposed every motion that came before the council meeting▲ in addition, they said they would circulate petitions if any of the proposals passed.
14. At first the children were afraid, believing that they were lost▲ only after their teacher reassured them that she knew the way did they settle down.
15. This design will be applied to the following types of machines▲ commercial, manufacturing, military, and agricultural.
16. Uncle Ed became manager of Zaharias Cars and Trucks, Inc.▲ he is a former Formula One racing driver.
17. In addition to her coming-of-age short stories, Doris Lessing, who grew up in Rhodesia (now Zimbabwe), has written several novels, one of which is *African Laughter*▲*Four Visits to Zimbabwe*.
18. In the past twelve years, Justin has lived in Tucson, Arizona▲ Dallas, Texas▲ Shreveport, Louisiana▲ and Tulsa, Oklahoma.
19. For the golf tournament, seasoned players were paired with players new to the game▲ consequently, the experienced players were frustrated and the novices were confused.
20. When Hernando Cortes invaded Mexico in 1519, he burned his ships▲ as a result, his troops were unable to desert, and there was little point in mutiny.

B. Correcting Sentences by Adding Colons

Correct the following sentences by writing each word or numeral that should be followed by a colon and then adding the colon. If a sentence is already correct, write *C*.

21. For the first time he could remember, the 6▲52 train to Grand Central was late.
22. At his retirement dinner, Mr. Gonzalo had this to say▲"It was a long and rewarding career, but I'm glad it's over."
23. Dr. Duran's favorite dishes are spiced pork, Spanish rice, fried zucchini, and julienned King Edward potatoes.   **23. C**

RESOURCES

Punctuation
Review
- *Grammar, Usage, and Mechanics,* pp. 286, 287, 288, 289

Assessment
- *Assessment Package*
  —Chapter Tests, Ch. 23
  —Chapter Tests in Standardized Test Formats, Ch. 23
- *Test Generator (One-Stop Planner CD-ROM)*

24. In his office, Mr. McMurdo has various mementos of the war: a German helmet, a recruiting poster, a bullet casing, a model of a tank, and a signed photograph of General Bradley.
25. In Rome, they visited three famous attractions: St. Peter's Church, the Colosseum, and the Spanish Steps.
26. On the car ferry, signs were posted with the following directions: Roll Up Your Windows, Turn Off Your Engine, No Smoking, and Stay in Your Car.
27. I live in the mountains for two reasons: The air is clean, and there aren't too many people.
28. Exodus 20:3 contains the following famous quote: "Thou shalt have no other gods before me."
29. There are three countries I'd like to visit above all: France, Japan, and Greece.
30. Ms. Lozano assigned us to write an essay on one of the following American leaders: Franklin D. Roosevelt, Abraham Lincoln, or Susan B. Anthony.

C. Correcting Sentences by Adding Semicolons and Colons

For each of the following sentences, write the word or numeral preceding each punctuation error; then, write the missing semicolon or colon. If a sentence is already correct, write *C*.

HELP
Some items in Part C contain more than one punctuation error.

31. The Bible reading began with John 14:27 and ended with Psalms 39:1–6.
32. Mr. Jackson's plane arrived twenty minutes late because of the dense fog; consequently, he missed the flight to Denver.
33. I have finally narrowed my choices for a housewarming gift: a self-cleaning iron, a blender, some place mats and napkins, or casserole dishes.
34. You should start saving your money: Open a savings account, invest in stocks or bonds, or buy a certificate of deposit.   **34. C**
35. The following clubs will have their yearbook pictures taken at 2:15: the Pep Club, the Photography Club, and the Modern Dance Club.
36. At the airfield we saw two signs: To the North Pole and To the South Pole.
37. Aunt Patty and my cousin Josh will be leaving with us; fortunately, Mom and Dad should be able to join us later, after all.

38. Sandra, Dan, Gottlieb, and Pete nominated Latrice and Kris; Bertha and the Hobbs twins chose Jerry.
39. You need to get the following supplies at the store: orange juice, laundry detergent, bread, and dog food.
40. The hideous painting had been taken down. In its place someone had put up a poster.
41. Maria says she wants to go to a college in the Northeast; however, she still has two years to decide.
42. Mrs. Patel's favorite colors are green, beige, and turquoise. **42. C**
43. I quote from the introduction: "The main purpose of this book is to educate, not to entertain."
44. She had two main objections to the film. It was too long, and she could hardly understand a word the actors said.
45. Three days a week Mom is up by 6:30, but on the other days she sleeps until 7:15 or so.
46. Marquand's survey included the three most critical locations: Mount Jefferson, Gurney Point, and Fort Rollerton.
47. Dr. Burkhardt loudly requested sesame oil, flour, vinegar, and caraway seeds. **47. C**
48. Mario had forgotten his clarinet; he was, therefore, prevented from practicing with the others.
49. Mr. Cahill assumed that everyone in the room had read his book; he referred to it several times during his talk.
50. The membership of the international committee was as follows: Japan, two; Italy, five; Mexico, three; France, five; Germany, four; United States, five.

Writing Application
Punctuating a Business Letter

Using Semicolons and Colons You have just won the grand prize in Blue Star Airlines' Fly-by-Night Sweepstakes. For one week, you can travel free to anywhere Blue Star flies in the United States—just so long as your flights depart between 8:00 P.M. and 4:00 A.M. You can remain in one location for the whole week, or you can travel to as many places as you like. To use your prize, you must give Blue Star Airlines a detailed itinerary of your trip before you plan to take it. Write a letter, giving the information needed. Use semicolons and colons to make your information easy to understand.

Prewriting First, decide where you would most like to go. (If you plan to include more than one destination, remember that the trip is to last only one week from start to finish.) Then, arrange the information in a clearly understandable order.

Writing As you write your first draft, remember that the accuracy and completeness of your letter will affect how well the trip is planned and, therefore, how much you enjoy your trip.

Revising Put yourself in the ticket agent's place as you evaluate the letter. Have you included all the necessary information? Have you arranged the details in a clearly understandable order?

Publishing Make sure that you use the correct form for a business letter. Proofread your letter carefully, paying special attention to your use of semicolons and colons. Also, be sure that you correctly spell the names of your destinations. You might want to ask a classmate to play the part of the ticket agent. Ask him or her to read the letter. With your teacher's permission, post the completed letter on a class bulletin board or Web page.

Reference Note
For more about **writing a business letter,** see "Writing" in the Quick Reference Handbook.

Chapter Review   737

CHAPTER 24 Punctuation
Italics, Quotation Marks, and Ellipsis Points

Diagnostic Preview

Correcting Sentences by Adding Italics (Underlining), Quotation Marks, and Ellipsis Points

Add or correct italics (underlining), quotation marks, and ellipsis points where they are needed in the following sentences. If a sentence is already correct, write *C*.

EXAMPLE 1. Have you read the Mayan folk tale The Hummingbird King? asked Soledad.

1. "Have you read the Mayan folk tale 'The Hummingbird King'?" asked Soledad.

1. Why did you buy another sleeping bag? she asked.
2. In his speech, Chief Joseph of the Nez Perce said that he would never fight again. 2. C
3. The dance company is performing Swan Lake, a ballet composed by Tchaikovsky.
4. Anita asked, Why did he say, I won't go to the game?
5. The Boston Cooking School Cookbook, now known as The Fannie Farmer Cookbook, was first published in 1891.
6. The first word my baby brother said was bird.
7. There's an article in this issue of Newsweek that I'd like you to read, said Joan.
8. Orson Welles wrote and directed the movie Citizen Kane.
9. Her street address has four 4's in it, said Rose. Did you know that?

CHAPTER RESOURCES

Planning
- One-Stop Planner CD-ROM

Practice and Extension
- Grammar, Usage, and Mechanics, p. 293
- Language Workshop CD-ROM

Internet
- go.hrw.com (keyword: EOLang)

Evaluation and Assessment
- Assessment Package
  —Chapter Tests, Ch. 24
  —Chapter Tests in Standardized Test Formats, Ch. 24
- Test Generator (One-Stop Planner CD-ROM)

10. "Susan drove one hundred miles," he replied, "to see you and your family on your birthday."
11. My art teacher subscribes to *Godzilla*, a periodical about Asian artists working in New York City.
12. "Please write to me," Joyce requested. "I want to keep in touch with you during your travels."
13. In my report on Dee Brown's book *Bury My Heart at Wounded Knee*, I almost forgot to cite the *New Republic* magazine as the source of one of the quotations I used.
14. As we ran down the street, Charles shouted, "Faster! Faster!"
15. Sally said, "John just whispered, 'I'll be at the game tonight.'"
16. Mrs. Rivera said that our next history assignment is Chapter 14, "Great Ideals in the Constitution."
17. Did you read the article "The Costs of College Today?"
18. My aunt asked, "What did your friend mean when he said that you look 'rad' in your new glasses?"
19. "The Novelist" is in a collection of W. H. Auden's shorter poems.
20. "You often use the French expression *au revoir*," said Hannah.
21. The editorial concluded with the statement, "The end result . . . will be a total breakdown of communications."
22. "I'll bring a cooler for the sandwiches," Jason said. **22. C**
23. Isn't the song "One Headlight" on The Wallflowers' second album, *Bringing Down the Horse*?
24. Jaime said, "We need to get that finished before . . well, at least before the shop closes."
25. Maria is reading *The Hobbit* again; this will be the third time she's read the book.

Italics

Italics are printed letters that lean to the right, *like this*. When you are writing or typing, indicate italics by underlining. If your composition were printed, the typesetter would set the underlined words in italics. For instance, if you were to type

```
All sophomores in our school read The Good
Earth by Pearl Buck.
```

the sentence would be printed like this:

All sophomores in our school read *The Good Earth* by Pearl Buck.

COMPUTER TIP

If you use a computer, you can probably set words in italics yourself. Most word-processing software and printers are capable of producing italic type.

Italics   **739**

Italics
Rules 24a–c *(pp. 739–742)*

OBJECTIVE

- To correct sentences by adding italics (underlining)

RESOURCES

Italics

Practice

- *Grammar, Usage, and Mechanics,* pp. 294, 295, 296
- *Language Workshop CD-ROM,* Lessons 41, 43

Punctuation, pp. 738–754
Alignments
TEKS 3A, 3D
TAAS W3, W7
English II End-of-Course 5, 6

Texas Resources
- *TAAS Tool Kit*
- *Preparation for TAAS*
- *One-Stop Planner CD-ROM*

Italics

TEACHING TIP

Activity. After discussing with students **Rule 24a** and its chart of italicized titles, you may want to direct students' attention to **Rule 24g** and its chart of titles enclosed in quotation marks. Point out to students that titles in quotation marks generally refer to works that are parts of larger works, the titles of which are italicized.

You may want to create and then display in the classroom a large poster that juxtaposes the related types and examples of titles from the charts on pp. 740 and 747. Then, organize students into small groups, and have them create their own posters, using the one displayed as a model. Encourage students to include titles of their favorite books, movies, songs, and so on.

Before students begin creating their posters, you may want to teach the **Mini-Lesson** on pp. 740–742.

Reference Note
For information about **capitalizing titles**, see page 682.

TIPS & TRICKS

Generally, the title of an entire work (book, magazine, TV series) is italicized, and the title of a part (chapter, article, episode) is enclosed in quotation marks.

Reference Note
For examples of **titles that are not italicized but are enclosed in quotation marks**, see page 747.

HELP
Long musical works include operas, symphonies, ballets, oratorios, and concertos.

24a. Use italics (underlining) for titles and subtitles of books, plays, long poems, periodicals, works of art, movies, TV series, and long musical works and recordings.

Type of Title	Examples	
Books	The Bean Trees	Summer Sisters
Plays	Hedda Gabler	Twelfth Night
Long Poems	Sundiata: An Epic of Old Mali	Evangeline
Periodicals	Kansas City Times	Sports Illustrated
Works of Art	Three Musicians	Hercules and Antaeus
Movies	The Return of Jafar	Jaws
TV Series	Touched by an Angel	Nova
Long Musical Works and Recordings	The Maid of Orleans / The Magic Flute	The Nutcracker / The Four Seasons

NOTE A long poem is one that is long enough to be published as a separate volume. Such poems are usually divided into titled or numbered sections, such as cantos, parts, or books. The titles of these sections should be enclosed in quotation marks.

EXAMPLE Alejandro's report is on "What the Thunder Said," the fifth stanza of T. S. Eliot's poem **The Waste Land.**

The articles *a*, *an*, and *the* written before a title are italicized (and capitalized) only when they are part of the official title. If you are not sure whether to include an article in a title, you can check the title page of a book or the masthead or table of contents of a periodical for the official title.

EXAMPLES Charles Dickens's book **A** Christmas Carol is a holiday favorite.

The article in **The** Wall Street Journal mentioned that among his other accomplishments, Frederick Douglass founded **the** North Star, a newspaper he published for seventeen years.

MINI-LESSON Continued on pp. 741–742

Capitalizing Titles. You may want to remind students to capitalize the first and last words and all other important words of titles and subtitles. Words considered unimportant in a title or subtitle are the following items.

- articles: *a, an, the*
- short prepositions (fewer than five letters): *for, from, of, in, to, with*
- coordinating conjunctions: *and, but, for, nor, or, so, yet*

Then, write the following sentences on

24b. Use italics (underlining) for the names of ships, trains, aircraft, and spacecraft.

Type of Name	Examples
Ships	*Lusitania*
Trains	*Orient-Express*
Aircraft	*Air Force One*
Spacecraft	*Pioneer 11*

24c. Use italics (underlining) for words, letters, symbols, and numerals referred to as such and for foreign words that have not been adopted into English.

EXAMPLES   The first **o** in **zoology** is pronounced with a long **o** sound.

In math, what does the **%** mean?

Sometimes his **3**'s look just like his **8**'s.

Montana's state motto is **Oro y Plata,** the Spanish phrase for "gold and silver."

NOTE English has borrowed many words and expressions from other languages. Some of these words and expressions have become part of the English vocabulary and are no longer italicized.

EXAMPLES   hors d'oeuvre (French)   quesadilla (Spanish)

moccasin (Algonquian)   tae kwon do (Korean)

If you are not sure whether to italicize a word of foreign origin, look it up in a recent dictionary.

Exercise 1   Correcting Sentences by Adding Italics (Underlining)

Identify all the words and word groups that should be italicized in the following sentences.

EXAMPLE   1. In 1988, Toni Morrison won the Pulitzer Prize for her novel Beloved.

1. *Beloved*

1. Does the Vietnamese word chiao mean the same thing as the Italian word ciao?

STYLE TIP

Generally, do not use italics for the title of your own paper. However, if your title contains a title that belongs in italics, you will need to use italics for that part of the title.

EXAMPLES
The Universal Appeal of the Works of Barbara Kingsolver [contains no title that belongs in italics]

The Allusions to Nature in **The Education of Little Tree** [contains a book title, which belongs in italics]

Be creative when giving your paper a title. Avoid using the title of another work as the complete title of your own work.

Looking at Language

Loanwords. The **Note** below **Rule 24c** on this page shows examples of foreign words that have become part of English. Explain to students that such words are called *loanwords*. Have students brainstorm other foreign words that have become loanwords in English. You may want to begin the brainstorming by listing on the chalkboard the following words and their origins:

kindergarten [*German*]
gumbo [*Bantu*]
canyon [*Spanish*]
chauffeur [*French*]
gyro [*Greek*]
troika [*Russian*]

After the brainstorming, call on volunteers to look in a dictionary to see whether any words in their list belong in italics. Remind students that after a foreign word has been accepted into common usage in the English language, the word is no longer italicized.

Italics   741

---

the chalkboard. Ask students to revise the sentences by capitalizing and punctuating titles correctly.
1. Have you read Sandra Cisneros' book The house on mango street? [The House on Mango Street]

2. The complete title of our astronomy club's magazine is The Stargazer: a travelogue about space. [The Stargazer: A Travelogue About Space]
3. We have tickets to see the play a raisin in the sun. [A Raisin in the Sun]

Relating to Literature

If your literature book contains the Tom Godwin short story "The Cold Equations," ask students to read the story and to find examples of the use of italics. In a discussion, have the class explore why the author used italics. [*Italics set off the name of the spacecraft, place emphasis on words in dialogue, and separate a character's spoken words from his or her thoughts.*]

Crossing the Curriculum

Mathematics. To help students see that the use of italics is not specific to language arts, have students examine the use of italics in their math textbooks. [*Math textbooks use italics for the names of points, lines, and angles in geometric designs; for the variables in algebraic equations; and for the symbols in formulas used to determine such measurements as area, perimeter, circumference, and volume.*]

You may want to extend the activity by asking students to examine the use of italics in textbooks from their other courses of study.

MECHANICS

STYLE TIP

Writers sometimes use italics (underlining) for emphasis, especially in written dialogue. The italic type shows how the sentence is supposed to be spoken. Read the following sentences aloud. Notice that by italicizing different words, the writer can change the meaning of a sentence.

EXAMPLES

"Are you going to buy the *green* shirt?" asked Ellen. [Will you buy the green shirt, not the blue one?]

"Are you going to buy the green *shirt*?" asked Ellen. [Will you buy the green shirt, not the green pants?]

"Are *you* going to buy the green shirt?" asked Ellen. [Will you, not your brother, buy it?]

Italicizing (underlining) words for emphasis is a handy technique that should not be overused. It can quickly lose its impact.

---

2. The first full-length animated film, Snow White and the Seven Dwarfs, used two million drawings.
3. Among the items that the Pilgrims brought with them on the Mayflower were apple seeds.
4. James Earle Fraser, best known for his painting End of the Trail, designed the U.S. buffalo nickel.
5. In the eighteenth century, Edward Gibbon wrote the influential book History of the Decline and Fall of the Roman Empire.
6. In Voyage to the Bottom of the Sea, an old TV series, the submarine Seaview was commanded by Admiral Nelson.
7. Daktari is Swahili for the English word doctor.
8. The first U.S. space shuttle was named Columbia.
9. Richard Sears met Alvah Roebuck through an ad in the Chicago Daily News.
10. The three M's referred to in the company name 3M stand for Minnesota Mining and Manufacturing.

Exercise 2 Correcting Sentences by Adding Italics (Underlining)

Identify all the words and word groups that should be italicized in the following sentences.

EXAMPLE 1. Have you read The Wonderful Adventures of Nils by Selma Lagerlöf?
1. *The Wonderful Adventures of Nils*

1. I just finished reading Ellen Gilchrist's book The Courts of Love.
2. Kay enjoyed the movie Antz.
3. Occasionally, my cousins like to watch reruns of The Brady Bunch on television.
4. Antigone is a play by Sophocles.
5. Every morning while eating a bagel, she reads The New York Times.
6. My oldest brother's favorite painting is The Potato Eaters by Vincent van Gogh.
7. Europe's first transcontinental express train was the Orient-Express.
8. Charles Lindbergh flew across the Atlantic Ocean in the airplane Spirit of Saint Louis.
9. A poster of Salvador Dali's painting The Persistence of Memory hangs in our school library.
10. I subscribe to several magazines, including Escape and Entertainment Weekly.

MINI-LESSON

4. One of my favorite paintings, books on a table, is by John Frederick Peto. [Books on a Table]
5. The television show called you can't do that on television is entertaining. [You Can't Do That on Television]

If you have introduced **Rule 24g** along with **Rule 24a,** you may want to add to this activity sentences containing titles that belong in quotation marks.

Quotation Marks

24d. Use quotation marks to enclose a *direct quotation*—a person's exact words.

DIRECT QUOTATION Joan said, "My legs are sore from jogging."

Remember to place quotation marks at both the beginning and the end of a direct quotation.

INCORRECT "I'm taking the road test tomorrow, said Reed.
CORRECT "I'm taking the road test tomorrow," said Reed.

Do not use quotation marks to enclose an *indirect quotation*—a rewording of a person's exact words.

INDIRECT QUOTATION Joan said that her legs were sore from jogging. [a rewording of Joan's exact words]

(1) A directly quoted sentence begins with a capital letter.

EXAMPLE Bianca asked, "When do we get our uniforms?"

Capitalize a directly quoted remark, even if the remark is not a complete sentence.

EXAMPLE Mr. Lozano answered, "On Friday, of course."

NOTE If a direct quotation is obviously a fragment of the original quotation, it may begin with a lowercase letter.

EXAMPLE Christine promised to be here "as soon as possible."

(2) When an interrupting expression divides a quoted sentence into two parts, the second part begins with a lowercase letter.

EXAMPLES "I hope," said Diego, "that it doesn't rain during the fiesta."

"I'm not sure," remarked Annette, "whether I'll be able to attend the meeting."

If the second part of a quotation is a complete sentence, a period (not a comma) follows the interrupting expression, and the second part begins with a capital letter.

EXAMPLE "The date has been set," said Greg. "We can't change it."

—HELP—
An expression identifying the speaker is not part of a direct quotation and should not appear inside the quotation marks.

INCORRECT
"Where, I inquired, have I seen you before?"

CORRECT
"Where," I inquired, "have I seen you before?"

Quotation Marks 743

Quotation Marks
Rules 24d–i (pp. 743–749)

OBJECTIVE
- To correct sentences by adding quotation marks

TEACHING TIP

Activity. Before the class begins its study of the rules for using quotation marks, ask each student to create a one-page conversation in which three speakers participate. Encourage students to use all of the kinds of sentences: declarative, interrogative, exclamatory, and imperative. Point out to students that as they write their dialogues, they must make sure that their readers will at all times be aware of who is speaking.

Collect students' dialogues. After students have studied **Rule 24d** and its four subrules on pp. 743–745, return the dialogues to the students. Ask them to check their own work to see whether they have followed the rules for using quotation marks to enclose direct quotations. Have them circle and then revise any errors. You may want to hold a class discussion to determine the most common errors.

RESOURCES
Quotation Marks
Practice
- *Grammar, Usage, and Mechanics,* pp. 297, 298–299, 300, 301
- *Language Workshop CD-ROM,* Lessons 41, 42, 43

Meeting INDIVIDUAL NEEDS

ENGLISH-LANGUAGE LEARNERS

Spanish. Quotation marks in Spanish look like this: << >>. However, it is far more common in Spanish to use dashes to introduce direct quotations.

Examples:
   No —he said— I don't believe you.
   —Why not? —she asked.

You may want to monitor students' progress as they make the transition from using dashes to using quotation marks.

When a direct quotation of two or more sentences by the same speaker is not divided, only one set of quotation marks is used.

INCORRECT	Tamisha suggested, "Let's donate the profits from the car wash to Project Day Care." "It provides help for many low-income working parents in this area."
CORRECT	Tamisha suggested, "Let's donate the profits from the car wash to Project Day Care. It provides help for many low-income working parents in this area."

(3) A direct quotation can be set off from the rest of the sentence by a comma, a question mark, or an exclamation point, but not by a period.

EXAMPLES   "Remember that your research reports are due Monday," Mrs. Castañeda announced.

"On what date does the Ides of March fall?" Elwyn asked.

"That's easy! It's March 15!" Dot exclaimed.

(4) When used with quotation marks, other marks of punctuation are placed according to the following rules:

- Commas and periods are placed inside the closing quotation marks.

EXAMPLE   "The concert tickets are sold out," Mary said, "and I had really hoped to go."

- Colons and semicolons are placed outside the closing quotation marks.

EXAMPLES   The following students have been named "most likely to succeed": Corey Brown and Sally Ling.

Paka quoted a Cameroonian proverb, "By trying often, the monkey learns to jump from the tree"; it reminded me of the expression "If at first you don't succeed, try, try again."

- A question mark or an exclamation point is placed inside the closing quotation marks if the quotation itself is a question or an exclamation. Otherwise, a question mark or exclamation point is placed outside the closing quotation marks.

EXAMPLES   "What time is the game tomorrow?" Maria asked.

Why did you shout, "It doesn't matter"?

744   Chapter 24   Punctuation

While I was at bat, Vicky kept shouting, "Hit it over the fence!"

Don't say "I'd rather not"!

NOTE When both the sentence and the quotation at the end of the sentence are questions (or exclamations), only one question mark (or exclamation point) is used. It is placed inside the closing quotation marks.

EXAMPLE   Who asked "What time is it?"

Exercise 3 Writing Sentences with Direct and Indirect Quotations

Add quotation marks where they are needed in the following sentences. If a sentence is already correct, write C.

EXAMPLE   1. When I saw this ad in the paper, I said to Grandmother Hsu, T'ai chi is Chinese, isn't it?

1. When I saw this ad in the paper, I said to Grandmother Hsu, "T'ai chi is Chinese, isn't it?"

1. She seemed pleased that I'd asked and replied, "Yes, it's short for t'ai chi ch'uan."
2. She explained that t'ai chi ch'uan was developed in ancient China as a system of self-defense and as an aid to meditation. **2. C**
3. The ad says that it's for health and relaxation, I said.
4. Yes, she agreed, it's that, too; it improves coordination and flexibility. In fact, in China people of all ages practice it.
5. You see, she went on, its postures and movements are all based on those of animals such as monkeys, birds, and snakes.
6. Snakes! I exclaimed.
7. Why do you twist your face so? Grandmother asked. If you observe a snake closely, you'll see how gracefully it moves.
8. That's true, I admitted.
9. Maybe, I said, thinking aloud, I'll check out this grand opening.
10. Imagine my surprise when Grandmother replied with a wide smile, I'll see you there. I'm one of the instructors.

ANNOUNCING
The Grand Opening of
Pathway T'ai Chi Studio
for health and relaxation
604 49th St.
Sunday, November 10
1:00 P.M.–5:00 P.M.
Complimentary refreshments will be served.
All Ages Welcome

Exercise 3

ALTERNATIVE LESSON
Ask students to identify in **Exercise 3** the direct quotations that can be classified as follows:

1. a sentence fragment [*"Snakes!"*—item 6]
2. an interrogative sentence [*"Why do you twist your face so?"*—item 7]
3. a compound sentence [*"Yes, it's that too; it improves coordination and flexibility."*—item 4]

Critical Thinking

Metacognition. Ask students to think about the processes they used to complete **Exercise 3**. Did students first read the entire sentence to establish meaning, or did they look only for interrupting expressions? Did they use capitalization and existing punctuation as clues? After adding quotation marks, did students read aloud the direct quotations to see whether they made sense? Did they check the rules in the textbook to determine placement of other punctuation marks in relation to the quotation marks? Encourage students to evaluate their personal strategies and to consider more-effective alternatives as needed.

Relating to Writing

When revising dialogue, students can add interest and variety by shifting the position and wording of interrupting expressions. Write the following sentences on the chalkboard to demonstrate the shifting of interrupting expressions.

1. "The swimming party has been canceled," announced Beth.
2. "The swimming party," announced Beth, "has been canceled."
3. Beth announced, "The swimming party has been canceled."

Next, to help students avoid overusing the verbs *said* and *asked* in interrupting expressions, have students brainstorm verbs that they can use in place of those two commonly used verbs. Possibilities include *announced, replied, wondered, answered, inquired, demanded, questioned, explained,* and *warned.*

To give students practice varying the position of interrupting expressions and using a variety of verbs, ask students to cut comic strips from newspapers and to write dialogues based on the comic strips. Emphasize the importance of following **Rule 24e** for this activity.

Check students' dialogues for variety of placement and wording of interrupting expressions, as well as for correct punctuation and format. Then, if necessary, have students revise their dialogues. You may want to have students display their comic strips and dialogues in the classroom.

MECHANICS

STYLE TIP

In dialogue, a paragraph may be only one line long and may consist of one or more sentence fragments.

24e. When you write dialogue (a conversation), begin a new paragraph every time the speaker changes, and enclose each speaker's words in quotation marks.

EXAMPLE   A man of Merv, well known as the home of complicated thinkers, ran shouting one night through the city's streets. "Thief, Thief!" he cried.

The people surrounded him, and when he was a little calmer, asked: "Where was the thief?"

"In my house."

"Did you see him?"

"No."

"Was anything missing?"

"No."

"How do you know there was a thief then?"

"I was lying in bed when I remembered that thieves break into houses without a sound, and move very quietly. I could hear nothing, so I knew that there was a thief in the house, you fool!"

Niamat Khan, "The Thief"

NOTE   A long passage quoted from a book or another printed source is usually set off from the rest of the text. The entire passage is usually indented and double-spaced. When a quoted passage has been set off in one of these ways, no quotation marks are necessary unless the passage contains dialogue.

EXAMPLE
```
In his speech after his last battle
against the whites, the Sauk chief
Black Hawk displayed pride and honor
in the face of defeat:

    The bullets flew like birds in
    the air, and whizzed by our
    ears like the wind through the
    trees in winter. My warriors
    fell around me; it began to
    look dismal. I saw my evil day
    at hand. The sun rose dim on
    us in the morning, and at
    night it sank in a dark cloud,
    and looked like a ball of fire.
    That was the last sun that
    shone on Black Hawk.
```

746   Chapter 24   Punctuation

Learning for Life

False Advertisements. Every day, consumers are bombarded with a variety of advertisements, some of which include claims, promises, or guarantees that consumers should view with suspicion.

Continued on pp. 747–748

Encourage students to imagine (or recall) a situation in which they have been misled by a false advertisement. Then, have each student write a complaint letter, either to the business responsible for the advertise-

24f. When a quoted passage consists of more than one paragraph, put quotation marks at the beginning of each paragraph and at the end of the entire passage. Do not put quotation marks after any paragraph but the last.

EXAMPLE
"Now, this car is one of our hottest sellers. It has bucket seats, a CD player, and alloy wheels.

"It's also one of the safest cars on the road because of its heavy suspension and antilock brake system. It gets good gas mileage, too.

"All in all, I think this would be the perfect car for you."

24g. Use quotation marks to enclose titles (including subtitles) of short works such as short stories, poems, essays, articles, songs, episodes of TV series, and chapters and other parts of books and periodicals.

Type of Title	Examples
Short Stories	"The Unicorn in the Garden" "The Gift of the Magi"
Poems	"Fire and Ice" "I Am of the Earth"
Essays	"Choice: A Tribute to Dr. Martin Luther King, Jr." "Marco Polo: Journey to China"
Articles	"The Ghost Dance" "Searching for Freedom"
Songs	"What's Going On" "I Will Remember You"
Episodes of TV Series	"Jerry's High School Reunion"
Chapters and Other Parts of Books, Periodicals	"Twentieth-Century Playwrights" "In Search of a New Frontier"

24h. Use single quotation marks to enclose a quotation or title within a quotation.

EXAMPLES Ron said, "Dad yelled, 'No way!'"

Val asked, "Did you like my rendition of 'America the Beautiful'?"

Reference Note
For examples of **titles that are italicized, not enclosed in quotation marks,** see page 740.

HELP
The titles of long poems are italicized.

STYLE TIP

Generally, do not use quotation marks for the title of your own paper. However, if your title contains a title that belongs in quotation marks, you will need to use quotation marks for that part of your title.

EXAMPLES
Aesop: A Master Storyteller [contains no title that belongs in quotation marks]

Cassie in "Song of the Trees": A Character Analysis [contains a short-story title, which belongs in quotation marks]

Quotation Marks 747

TEACHING TIP

Reviews You may want to use **Review A** as guided practice and then have students complete **Review B** as independent practice.

STYLE TIP

Avoid using slang words in formal writing and speaking. When using technical terms, be sure to explain their meanings. If you are using a technical term throughout a piece of writing, you will need to enclose in quotation marks only your first use of the term.

If you are not sure whether a word is appropriate or its meaning is clear, consult a recent dictionary.

24i. Use quotation marks to enclose slang words, technical terms, and unusual uses of words.

EXAMPLES My oldest brother said my new shoes look very "fly."

Is there now a computer that can perform more than fifteen "gigaflops" (that is, fifteen billion operations) a second?

Fire burns oxygen quickly; my chemistry teacher says flame is a "gas-guzzler."

Review A Correcting Sentences by Adding Italics (Underlining) or Quotation Marks

For each of the following sentences, correctly write all the words that should be italicized (underlined) or enclosed in quotation marks.

EXAMPLE 1. He read aloud The Tell-Tale Heart from The Collected Stories of Edgar Allan Poe.

1. "The Tell-Tale Heart"; The Collected Stories of Edgar Allan Poe

1. Mr. Croce used the word denouement when he was discussing Rudolfo Anaya's novel Bless Me, Ultima.
2. By next Thursday I have to read the following works: The Medicine Bag, a short story by Virginia Driving Hawk Sneve; Crown of Shadows, a play by Rodolfo Usigli; and Daisy Bates: First Lady of Little Rock, an article by Lerone Bennett, Jr.
3. Have you read the newspaper article El Niño, Global Weather Disaster? asked Ewan.
4. While we were working on our essays, Karen asked me how many m's are in the word accommodate.
5. Oswald Rivera's novel Fire and Rain is about the Vietnam War.
6. Kim said her report, titled The Wit of Oscar Wilde, includes quotes from the short story titled The Happy Prince as well as the play The Importance of Being Earnest.
7. We had risotto alla milanese for dinner.
8. Mr. Guerra explained that the short story Luke Baldwin's Vow deals with conflicts in values.
9. Wouldn't Words to Live By be an excellent title for our song? Tomás asked.
10. She crossed the t with such a flourish that she obscured the letters above it.

748 Chapter 24 Punctuation

Learning for Life

Times stated, "You can return any purchase, along with your sales receipt, within thirty days and receive your money back." However, when I attempted to return a purchase, I was told by the manager that I could receive only store credit.

After they have completed the writing activity, ask students to check each other's letters for correct punctuation of direct and indirect quotations.

Review B **Correcting Sentences by Adding Italics (Underlining) and Quotation Marks**

Rewrite the following dialogue, and add italics (underlining), quotation marks, and paragraph breaks and indentations where they are needed in the following sentences.

EXAMPLE [1] Look at this intriguing painting, said Marshall.
    1. "Look at this intriguing painting," said Marshall.

[1] He told us that he'd found the painting in Mexican American Artists, a book by Jacinto Quirate; the painting is in the chapter called The Third Decade.
[2] The painting is by the man in the photograph below, Emilio Aguirre, he explained, who titled it Alpha 1.
[3] What do you see when you look at it? he asked.
[4] You can't miss the Y on the left and the T on the right, he said.
[5] He went on, Can you make out the profile of a person sitting on the ground to the left of the T?
[6] Laura said, Yes, the head is an O; but I objected, saying that it looked more like a Q to me.
[7] I guess you're right, she said. Anyway, the G outlines the front of the body.
[8] Ben asked, Is the little b on the big O supposed to be the person's glasses? Also, he added, isn't that an M in the background, behind the T?
[9] Look at this! exclaimed Marlene. If you turn the painting ninety degrees to the left, the body looks like a question mark.
[10] Can you see why we all agreed when she said, Intriguing really is the word for Alpha 1?

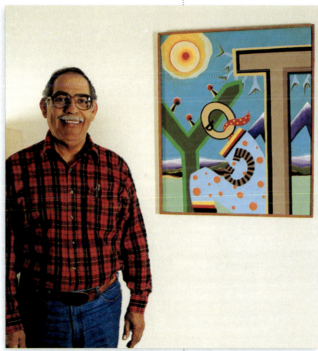

Ellipsis Points

Rules 24j, k (pp. 750–752)

OBJECTIVE

- To use ellipsis points and end marks to punctuate passages from which words or sentences have been omitted

TEACHING TIP

Rule 24j. After introducing **Rule 24j** and its four subrules, emphasize to students that (1) omitting part of a passage should not change the meaning of the original passage and (2) the remaining part of the passage should express a complete thought. Use the examples for the subrules to reinforce students' understanding of these two points.

HELP

Notice that in the example under Rule 24j(2) the word *next* is capitalized, even though it was not capitalized in the original. *Next* is capitalized in the example because it is being used as the first word of the sentence. The capital *N* is in brackets to show that the capital was added by the person quoting the material—that *next* was lowercased in the original.

Ellipsis Points

24j. Use ellipsis points (. . .) to mark omissions from quoted material.

ORIGINAL   The room overlooking the square had an ornate stone balcony with a view of the chateau. That building was an early-Renaissance confection of towers and turrets, partly encircled by the old city walls. I remember that next to the chateau was the town hall, a handsome, square Second Empire structure. A stand of plane trees and a parking lot full of cars adjoined the main gate. Beyond the city walls lay the yellow mustard fields rolling into the hazy distance.

(1) When you omit words from the middle of a sentence, use three spaced ellipsis points.

EXAMPLE   "The room overlooking the square had . . . a view of the chateau."

NOTE   Be sure to include a space before the first ellipsis point and after the last one.

(2) When you omit words from the beginning of a sentence within a quoted passage, keep the previous sentence's end punctuation and follow it with the points of ellipsis.

EXAMPLE   "That building was an early-Renaissance confection of towers and turrets, partly encircled by the old city walls. . . . [N]ext to the chateau was the town hall, a handsome, square Second Empire structure."

(3) When you omit words at the end of a sentence within a quoted passage, keep the sentence's end punctuation and follow it with the points of ellipsis.

EXAMPLE   "That building was an early-Renaissance confection of towers and turrets. . . . I remember that next to the chateau was the town hall, a handsome, square Second Empire structure."

(4) When you omit one or more complete sentences from within a quoted passage, keep the previous sentence's end punctuation and follow it with the points of ellipsis.

RESOURCES

Ellipsis Points

Practice

- *Grammar, Usage, and Mechanics,* pp. 302, 303–304

EXAMPLE "That building was an early-Renaissance confection of towers and turrets, partly encircled by the old city walls. . . . Beyond the city walls lay the yellow mustard fields rolling into the hazy distance."

To show that one or more lines of poetry have been omitted, use an entire line of spaced periods.

COMPLETE POEM
Loveliest of trees, the cherry now
Is hung with bloom along the bough,
And stands about the woodland ride
Wearing white for Eastertide.

Now, of my threescore years and ten,
Twenty will not come again,
And take from seventy springs a score,
It only leaves me fifty more.

And since to look at things in bloom
Fifty springs are little room,
About the woodlands I will go
To see the cherry hung with snow.

A. E. Housman, "Loveliest of Trees"

POEM WITH OMISSION
Loveliest of trees, the cherry now
Is hung with bloom along the bough,
And stands about the woodland ride
Wearing white for Eastertide.

. . . .

And since to look at things in bloom
Fifty springs are little room,
About the woodlands I will go
To see the cherry hung with snow.

Notice that the line of periods here marks the omission of four lines of poetry. Also, notice that the line of ellipses is as long as the preceding line of poetry.

24k. Use three ellipsis points (. . .) to indicate a pause in written dialogue.

EXAMPLE "Yes, but . . . oh well, all right," she said.

─HELP─

Do not begin a quoted passage with points of ellipsis.

INCORRECT
". . . That building was an early-Renaissance confection of towers and turrets, partly encircled by the old city walls."

CORRECT
"That building was an early-Renaissance confection of towers and turrets, partly encircled by the old city walls."

Meeting INDIVIDUAL NEEDS

MULTIPLE INTELLIGENCES
Interpersonal Intelligence. Organize students into groups of four. Have members of each group choose from a short story or an essay in their literature textbooks a paragraph that consists of at least four sentences. Ask group members to read their paragraphs carefully and then to choose a sentence from which they can omit words to illustrate the first subrule of **Rule 24j** on p. 750. Have students write the sentence, using ellipsis points to mark the omission. Then, have groups repeat the activity to illustrate each of the other subrules.

After groups have finished, have them check each other's work according to the following criteria:

1. Are the ellipsis points and end marks placed correctly?
2. Do the parts that show omissions express complete thoughts?
3. Do the omissions cause no change in the meanings of the original passages?

Encourage groups to work together to correct any errors.

Exercise 4 Using Ellipsis Points Correctly

ANSWERS

1. Santa Fe is one of the most popular vacation destinations in the United States. . . . The climate is superb, the cuisine is outstanding, and the combination of cultures is unique.
2. Senator McRory . . . has decided to run for governor in the next election.
3. According to the newspaper article, "Master Gardener Yamamoto won the top award in the international bonsai competition. . . . He plans to use the money to build an addition to his nursery."
4. A mature bull elephant . . . charged toward the water hole and scared the lions away.
5. The path curves onward and up
. . . .
Guiding us to higher things.
6. Ambition and duty are the twin motives of the character of Teng in this movie. . . .
7. The new airport . . . will open next May.
8. "This novel . . . is quite unsatisfactory as a thriller. Its young author . . . has much to learn before he can master the subtleties of plot and atmosphere," the book review said.
9. Mr. Sánchez . . . promised he would show us his slides as soon as he had fully recovered the use of his voice.
10. "Was it true? Was it even possible? . . . her decision seems to contradict everything I know about her character," May thought aloud.

Exercise 4 Using Ellipsis Points Correctly

Omit the underscored parts of the following passages. Use ellipsis points and end marks to punctuate each omission correctly.

EXAMPLE
1. The old twin-gabled house, which my aunt had intended to sell, was struck by lightning.
   1. The old twin-gabled house . . . was struck by lightning.

1. Santa Fe is one of the most popular vacation destinations in the United States. Why is a small city in the mountains of northern New Mexico, more than an hour's drive from the nearest airport, such a top tourist draw? The climate is superb, the cuisine is outstanding, and the combination of cultures is unique.
2. Senator McRory, a key figure in state politics for most of his fifty-four years, has decided to run for governor in the next election.
3. According to the newspaper article, "Master Gardener Yamamoto won the top award in the international bonsai competition, the first such event of the season. He plans to use the money to build an addition to his nursery."
4. A mature bull elephant, huge yet graceful, charged toward the water hole and scared the lions away.
5. The path curves onward and up,
Shining like a scimitar's blade
In the early morning rain,
Guiding us to higher things.
6. Ambition and duty are the twin motives of the character of Teng in this movie, as they frequently are in the lives of real people.
7. The new airport, which will greatly increase the city's commercial and cultural ties to the outside world, will open next May.
8. "This novel is well-written but is quite unsatisfactory as a thriller. Its young author is known and deservedly respected for his realistic short stories set along the coast of Oregon and northern California, but he has much to learn before he can master the subtleties of plot and atmosphere," the book review said.
9. Mr. Sánchez arrived early from his long journey and promised he would show us his slides as soon as he had fully recovered the use of his voice.
10. "Was it true? Was it even possible? A complete reversal, her decision seems to contradict everything I know about her character," May thought aloud.

CHAPTER 24

Chapter Review

A. Correcting Sentences by Adding Italics (Underlining) and Quotation Marks

Write each letter, word, title, or word group that should be italicized (underlined) or in quotation marks. Then, supply the needed underlining or quotation marks.

1. Carlos Chavez, a Mexican composer and conductor, wrote the *Sinfonía de Antígona* in 1933.
2. We have subscribed to the *Orlando Sentinel* for two years.
3. "Are you going to help me," he asked, "or shall I look for someone else?"
4. Michael Crichton wrote the book *Jurassic Park*, which was made into a movie by Steven Spielberg.
5. Grandma's favorite expression is "Mind your p's and q's!"
6. Carla served a delicious Mediterranean appetizer called *pulpo*; when I asked her what it was, she told me it was octopus.
7. For our homework assignment we have to define *ionization*, *electrolyte*, *quark*, and *neutrino*.
8. During the Civil War, the *Merrimack*, on the Confederate side, and the *Monitor*, on the Union side, fought to a draw in the first battle between ironclad ships.
9. "I never should have agreed to be on that committee," wailed Ellie. "When I asked Mary to help, she said, 'Not on your life!' Now I'm stuck doing all the work!"
10. "Where have you been, Ron?" asked Leroy. "The bus is leaving."
11. "These students are Elwood High's finest scholars," the principal said, announcing the following scholarship winners: Daphne Johnson, Michael Lewis, Ruben Perez, and Winnie Chung.
12. One of my favorite TV shows, *Disaster Chronicles*, ran an episode called "Volcanoes in Italy."
13. Sam, who's from Boston, drops the r's from the ends of words.
14. Politicians still quote Abraham Lincoln's expression "government of the people, by the people, for the people."
15. We discussed Ann Bank's magazine article "Rafting with Kids."
16. "Indians Today, the Real and the Unreal" is the opening chapter in Vine Deloria's book *Custer Died for Your Sins*.

Using the Chapter Review

To assess student progress, you may want to compare the types of items missed on the **Diagnostic Preview** with those missed on the **Chapter Review**. If students have not made significant progress, you may want to refer them to **Exercises 29–30** in **Chapter 27: Correcting Common Errors** for additional practice.

17. My mother has never liked the term baby boomer.
18. Many articles about Emily Dickinson's poems contain the term paradox.
19. When the players came onto the field, the fans shouted, "Go for it!"
20. Have you seen Louise Nevelson's sculpture Young Shadows?

B. Correcting Sentences by Adding Italics (Underlining)

Write all the words and word groups that should be italicized in the following sentences.

21. Have you seen the movie A Bug's Life?
22. One of Claude Monet's first paintings was called Impression: Sunrise.
23. One of Bernard Shaw's best-known plays is Pygmalion, on which the musical My Fair Lady was based.
24. My cousins Suzi and Désirée, happy to be on vacation, took the train California Zephyr to Los Angeles last summer.
25. One of Dad's favorite TV programs is The X-Files.
26. I read an article in Sports Illustrated while I waited.
27. One of the fastest locomotives of its time was the Flying Scotsman, built in Britain in 1923.
28. Was Enola Gay the plane that dropped the atomic bomb on Hiroshima?
29. A Clergyman's Daughter is a novel by George Orwell.
30. Last night we all watched Star Trek: The Next Generation; one of my favorite episodes was showing.

C. Using Ellipsis Points Correctly

Omit the underscored parts of the following passages. Use ellipsis points and end marks to punctuate each omission correctly.

31. Our cousin Carlos, one of his college's star baseball players, is going to training camp in Arizona this spring.
32. The man was tall, in his mid-thirties, with a full mustache and short brown hair. His hair was combed straight back. He spoke with what I thought was a slight Midwestern accent.

33. Here, take my hand and follow me
    Thou eager one, dreamer of dreams,
    Singer of life's oldest song,
    And together we will find the golden crown.
34. Dr. Bustamante, a widely-admired personality in the Chilean emigrant community, is almost certain to be chosen as deputy mayor.
35. The film is atmospheric and well acted but it is too long by at least half an hour.

Writing Application
Writing an Interior Dialogue

Using Punctuation You are scheduled to give an oral report on a short story of your own choosing. Write an interior dialogue recording your thoughts as you decide which of two stories to use. Use the marks of punctuation covered in this chapter in your interior dialogue.

Prewriting List the titles of several short stories you have read. Then, choose the two about which you feel most strongly. Next, determine how you will distinguish between your different points of view as you decide which story to choose. For example, you could use your first name for one side, your middle name for another, and other names for as many different points of view as you have.

Writing Write down your thoughts as you consider the pros and cons of using the two stories, presenting each thought in a correctly punctuated dialogue spoken from each point of view. Keep writing until you reach a decision. Try to keep track of where you are in the decision-making process.

Revising Read over your dialogue and check whether your diction (word choice) and sentence structure sound authentic to you. Can you tell at all times to which story you're referring? Is it clear which one you decided to report on, and why?

Publishing Check your dialogue for errors in grammar, spelling, and punctuation. Then, photocopy your dialogue, or post it on a class bulletin board or Web page. You and your classmates could record your dialogues on audiotape or act them out for one another in person or on film.

Chapter Review 755

RESOURCES
Writing Application
Extension
- *Grammar, Usage, and Mechanics,* p. 311
- *Language Workshop CD-ROM,* Lessons 41–43

Writing Application
Alignments
TEKS 1A, 2A, 2C, 2E, 3A, 3D
TAAS W1, W3, W7
English II End-of-Course 4, 5, 6
Texas Resources
- *One-Stop Planner CD-ROM*

CHAPTER 25

Punctuation
Apostrophes, Hyphens, Dashes, Parentheses, Brackets

PREVIEWING THE CHAPTER

- This chapter explores the uses of apostrophes, hyphens, dashes, parentheses, and brackets. As you discuss with students the uses of each punctuation mark, you may want to review with them the relevant information in other chapters (**Chapter 17: Using Pronouns Correctly,** apostrophes, uses of the possessive case; **Chapter 22: Punctuation,** parentheses, comma usage; **Chapter 23: Punctuation,** dashes, colon usage; **Chapter 24: Punctuation,** brackets, uses of quotation marks).

- The chapter concludes with a **Chapter Review,** which includes a **Writing Application** feature that asks students to write a poem using at least four dashes.

- For help in integrating the chapter with writing chapters, use the **Teaching Strands** chart on pp. T401A–T401B.

USING THE DIAGNOSTIC PREVIEW

- The results of the **Diagnostic Preview** will suggest which of the rules and exercises in the chapter will be most troublesome to students. To help students master the application of those rules, you may want to organize the class into small groups so that students can work together to complete the relevant exercises. Students who demonstrate mastery on the **Diagnostic Preview** could serve as group leaders to help you monitor the groups' progress.

Diagnostic Preview

A. Correcting Sentences by Using Apostrophes and Hyphens

For each of the following sentences, write the word or words that should have an apostrophe or a hyphen, and add the appropriate punctuation mark. If a sentence is already correct, write *C*.

EXAMPLE   1. Michaels stamp collection contains thirty two rare stamps.

  1. *Michael's*
     thirty-two   Hyphens are indicated by the ‸ symbol.

1. Because of the sudden blizzard, the armies supplies were cut off.
2. Its frustrating when the car wont start because its battery is dead.
3. After hours of discussion, we decided that we need a two thirds majority to pass new rules in the student council.
4. Even though Li moved here from Korea just last year and is still learning English, shes making As in most of her classes.
5. If you go to the game on Saturday, whos going to watch the children at home?
6. Miranda had the flu this past week, and now she has five days worth of homework to do this weekend.
7. Rodney interviewed the treasurer elect of the honor society for the "Personality Profile" column in the school newspaper.

CHAPTER RESOURCES

Planning
- One-Stop Planner CD-ROM

Practice and Extension
- Grammar, Usage, and Mechanics, p. 312
- Language Workshop CD-ROM

Internet
- go.hrw.com (keyword: EOLang)

Evaluation and Assessment
- Assessment Package
  —Chapter Tests, Ch. 25
  —Chapter Tests in Standardized Test Formats, Ch. 25
- Test Generator (One-Stop Planner CD-ROM)

8. James Berry, who was born in Jamaica, wrote the well-received collection of short stories *A Thief in the Village and Other Stories*.
9. You should know that my aunt's favorite expression is "Never let the sun set on your anger."
10. My brother-in-law Murray has worked at a resort in New York's Catskill Mountains for twenty-one years.
11. The store clerk said she would refund our deposit if we return the tape recorder by five o'clock.
12. The alarm clock hasn't worked since the morning I knocked it off the shelf.
13. Last week at the trial in New York City, the senator presented as evidence the anti-American pamphlets distributed by the terrorist group.
14. You have such a wonderful singing voice that I'm sure you'll get a part in the children's summer theater production.
15. Don't be alarmed, Brian; the red +'s on your history paper indicate correct answers.

B. Correcting Sentences by Using Dashes, Parentheses, and Brackets

Rewrite the following sentences, adding dashes, parentheses, and brackets where they are needed. **Answers may vary. Carets indicate placement of dashes.**

EXAMPLE 1. The books on that table they are all nonfiction are on sale today.

1. The books on that table—they are all nonfiction—are on sale today.

16. The discovery of gold at Sutter's Mill brought floods of people settlers, miners, prospectors, and merchants to California in their covered wagons.
17. The old white house on Tenth Street (it was once a governor's mansion) is a landmark in our town.
18. Answer the ten questions on this English quiz (be careful, they're tricky!) and then write a couplet or a limerick for extra credit.
19. John Steinbeck (1902–1968) won the Nobel Prize in literature in 1962.
20. According to O'Neal, Satchmo (the great jazz musician Louis Armstrong [1900–1971]) profoundly influenced American music.

—HELP—

Although some of the sentences in Part B of the Diagnostic Preview may be correctly revised in more than one way, you need to give only one revision for each sentence.

Punctuation, pp. 756–776

Alignments
TEKS 3A, 3D
TAAS W3, W7
English II End-of-Course 5, 6

Texas Resources
- TAAS Tool Kit
- Preparation for TAAS
- One-Stop Planner CD-ROM

Apostrophes

Rules 25a–h (pp. 758–766)

OBJECTIVES

- To write the singular, singular possessive, plural, and plural possessive forms of nouns
- To correct phrases by adding necessary apostrophes
- To complete sentences by supplying appropriate contractions
- To recognize the correct uses of contractions and possessives

MECHANICS

Apostrophes

Possessive Case

The possessive case of a noun or a pronoun shows ownership or possession.

EXAMPLES **Jorge's** calculator has a solar battery.

Where did you buy **yours**?

Pam's aunt is a plumber.

The birds had fed **their** young.

Nouns in the Possessive Case

25a. To form the possessive of most singular nouns, add an apostrophe and an *s*.

EXAMPLES Barbara's house   one boy's uniform

a week's salary   that stereo's speakers

When forming the possessive of a singular noun ending in an *s* or a *z* sound, add only an apostrophe if

- the noun has more than one syllable

    and

- the addition of *s* would make the noun awkward to pronounce

EXAMPLES Odysseus' adventures   for goodness' sake

Buenos Aires' citizens   the species' characteristics

Xerxes' army   each of that TV series' characters

If a singular noun ending in an *s* or a *z* sound does not satisfy both of these conditions, add an apostrophe and an *s*.

EXAMPLES Carlos's bicycle   a bus's tires

Charles Dickens's novels   my boss's orders

25b. To form the possessive case of a plural noun ending in *s*, add only the apostrophe.

EXAMPLES cats' owners   cities' problems

coaches' records   princesses' duties

758   Chapter 25   Punctuation

RESOURCES

Apostrophes

Practice

- *Grammar, Usage, and Mechanics,* pp. 313, 314, 315, 316, 317, 318, 319–320
- *Language Workshop CD-ROM,* Lessons 39, 40

The few plural nouns that do not end in *s* form the possessive case by adding an apostrophe and an *s*.

EXAMPLES geese's migration   children's stories

NOTE In most cases, you should not use an apostrophe to form the plural of a noun.

INCORRECT   The four horse's pulled the wagon.
CORRECT   The four **horses** pulled the wagon.

Reference Note
For more examples of **plural nouns that do not end in s**, see page 787.

Reference Note
For information on using an apostrophe and an *s* to form the **plurals of letters, numerals, symbols, and words referred to as words**, see page 789.

HELP
If you do not know how to spell a plural form, look up the word in a dictionary.

Exercise 1 — Writing the Possessive Forms of Nouns

Make four columns headed *Singular*, *Singular Possessive*, *Plural*, and *Plural Possessive*. Write those forms of each of the following nouns.

EXAMPLE

	Singular	Singular Possessive	Plural	Plural Possessive
1.	temple	temple's	temples	temples'

1. governor
2. secretary
3. bird
4. spacecraft
5. woman
6. picture
7. pencil
8. class
9. chief
10. mouse
11. stereo
12. president
13. bear
14. photograph
15. grandmother
16. jacket
17. dress
18. novel
19. cup
20. lapse

Pronouns in the Possessive Case

25c. Do not use an apostrophe with possessive personal pronouns or with the possessive pronoun *whose*.

Possessive Personal Pronouns	
Singular	**Plural**
my, mine	our, ours
your, yours	your, yours
his, her, hers, its	their, theirs

Apostrophes 759

Exercise 1 — Writing the Possessive Forms of Nouns

ANSWERS

1. governor, governor's, governors, governors'
2. secretary, secretary's, secretaries, secretaries'
3. bird, bird's, birds, birds'
4. spacecraft, spacecraft's, spacecraft, spacecraft's
5. woman, woman's, women, women's
6. picture, picture's, pictures, pictures'
7. pencil, pencil's, pencils, pencils'
8. class, class's, classes, classes'
9. chief, chief's, chiefs, chiefs'
10. mouse, mouse's, mice, mice's
11. stereo, stereo's, stereos, stereos'
12. president, president's, presidents, presidents'
13. bear, bear's, bears, bears'
14. photograph, photograph's, photographs, photographs'
15. grandmother, grandmother's, grandmothers, grandmothers'
16. jacket, jacket's, jackets, jackets'
17. dress, dress's, dresses, dresses'
18. novel, novel's, novels, novels'
19. cup, cup's, cups, cups'
20. lapse, lapse's, lapses, lapses'

MECHANICS

Meeting INDIVIDUAL NEEDS

MODALITIES

Visual Learners. Organizational charts often help make instructional material more accessible to visual learners. The following chart represents **Rules 25a–d**.

Apostrophe and *s*	Apostrophe only	No Apostrophe
Most singular nouns (25a)	Singular nouns ending in *s* or *z* that have more than one syllable and would sound awkward if *s* were added (25a)	Possessive personal pronouns and *whose* (25c)
boss's desk	*Hercules*' labors	a book of *hers*
Plural nouns not ending in *s* (25b)	Plural nouns ending in *s* (25b)	
women's fashions	*horses*' saddles	
Indefinite pronouns (25d)		
everyone's opinion		

Display the chart in the classroom, and call on volunteers to add at least two other examples below each chart entry.

Reference Note
Do not confuse the possessive personal pronouns *your, their, theirs, its* and *whose* with the contractions *you're, they're, there's, it's,* and *who's.* See page 763.

Reference Note
See page 535 for a list of **indefinite pronouns.**

My, your, his, her, its, our, and *their* are generally used before nouns. *Mine, yours, his, hers, ours,* and *theirs* are used as subjects, complements, or objects of prepositions. Note that *his* may be used either way.

EXAMPLES   This is **my** desk.   This desk is **mine**.

I borrowed **your** pencil.   I borrowed a pencil of **yours**.

His work is excellent.   **His** is the best work.

25d. To form the possessive of an indefinite pronoun, add an apostrophe and an *s*.

EXAMPLES   anyone**'s** choice   either**'s** idea

NOTE The correct possessive forms of *someone else* and *each other* are *someone else's* and *each other's*.

Compounds in the Possessive Case

25e. Form the possessive of only the last word in a compound noun, such as the name of an organization or a business, and in a word group showing joint possession.

Compound Nouns	Urban League**'s** office Acosta and Rivera**'s** law firm sister-in-law**'s** office
Joint Possession	Bob and Jim**'s** canoe my aunt and uncle**'s** photograph

When a possessive pronoun is part of a word group showing joint possession, each noun in the word group is also possessive in form.

EXAMPLE   Sean**'s** and **her** conversation

Reference Note
For more about **acronyms** and **initialisms**, see page 688.

NOTE The possessive of an **acronym** (a word formed from the first—or first few—letters of a series of words) or of an **initialism** (an abbreviation pronounced letter by letter) is formed by adding an apostrophe and an *s*.

ACRONYM   NATO**'s** member nations

INITIALISM NBC**'s** new television program

25f. Form the possessive of each noun in a word group that expresses individual possession of similar items.

EXAMPLES Michael's and Lila's wallets

Denise's and Mark's books

Exercise 2 Using Apostrophes Correctly

Rewrite the following word groups, adding and deleting apostrophes where needed. If a word group is already correct, write *C*.

EXAMPLE 1. the cameras lens
1. *the camera's lens*

1. one of your's
2. Anns and my project
3. their tennis shoes   3. C.
4. my father-in-laws boat
5. each others books
6. Joe and Roys room
7. Lynns and Mikes shoes
8. someones art
9. whose feats   9. C.
10. PBSs fundraiser
11. a Jazz Festivals end
12. anyone elses pizza
13. Jims and Debs parents
14. the UNs general assembly
15. my loaves of bread   15. C.
16. Sallys and his horses
17. any of their's
18. neithers hope
19. Jeremiahs and Josephs toys
20. Ross and Reeds team

Review A Correcting Paragraphs by Adding Apostrophes

For the sentences in the following paragraphs, write each word that should be in the possessive case, and add the missing apostrophe.

EXAMPLE [1] Last week I followed my parents suggestion and enrolled in an amateur photography class offered by our citys art center.
1. *parents'; city's*

[1] I shared my mom and dads exasperation when, once again, I spent a whole weeks allowance on disappointing pictures. [2] I had borrowed Uncle Freds expensive camera, but even with the cameras extra features, my photographs looked like childrens smudged finger paintings.

[3] My pictures of Bob and Ruths wedding reception, our familys social event of the year, were destroyed when I fell into the pool with

---

STYLE TIP

To avoid forming a possessive that sounds awkward, use a phrase beginning with *of* or *for* instead.

AWKWARD the Samuel H. Scripps American Dance Festival Award's winner

IMPROVED the winner **of** the Samuel H. Scripps American Dance Festival Award

---

Meeting INDIVIDUAL NEEDS

MULTIPLE INTELLIGENCES

Interpersonal Intelligence. To provide students with additional practice forming possessives, organize the class into small groups. Ask each group to prepare a list of twenty nouns and pronouns and to write next to each one a thing that the noun or pronoun can possess. To illustrate, write on the chalkboard this partial list.

1. dog   collar
2. Mr. Smith   sports car
3. it   location
4. anyone   help
5. Eli and Sam   project

As groups are preparing their lists, encourage them to include examples representative of **Rules 25a–f**.

Have groups exchange lists, and instruct each group to write the possessive form of each noun or pronoun shown in the first column of the list. Then, ask each group to create a humorous paragraph using the possessive forms with the things listed in the other column. After they have finished writing, ask groups to check each other's work for correct possessive forms. You may want to ask each group to share its humorous paragraph with the rest of the class.

Meeting INDIVIDUAL NEEDS

MULTIPLE INTELLIGENCES
Linguistic Intelligence. Because students with strong linguistic intelligence generally have good vocabularies and enjoy playing with language, suggest that they write sentences, poems, or dialogues that contain pairs of rhyming words. Tell students that one of the words in each pair should be in the possessive case. Ask students to underline each possessive they have formed and to note the rule number they have applied. For example,

"The <u>king's</u> rings are for sale," they say, **(Rule 25a)**

But the <u>store's</u> doors are closed today. **(Rule 25a)**

Review B Proofreading for Errors in Possessive Forms

ANSWERS
1. country's
2. yo-yo's
3. mother's
4. C
5. Tina
6. Philippines'
7. Kim's
8. anyone's

---

my camera. [4] Last summer I also took pictures during our week-long visit to <u>Arizonas</u> famous Painted Desert. [5] Unfortunately, I did not understand enough about the <u>suns</u> strong light at midday; consequently, most of my photographs had a washed-out look.

[6] My <u>lifes</u> most embarrassing moment occurred when I took a picture of my class for the <u>schools</u> yearbook and then discovered that I had forgotten to put film in the camera. [7] Another time, I took my camera to <u>Toms</u> party but could not get <u>anyones</u> attention long enough to set up the shots that I wanted. [8] As a result, I gave up on people and tried to take my two <u>pets</u> pictures; however, a <u>parakeets</u> wings and a <u>dogs</u> will are hard to control. [9] After all these bad experiences, I knew that I needed a <u>professionals</u> advice. [10] I'm pleased to report that during the first meeting of the photography class, the instructor raised all the <u>students</u> confidence, including mine.

Review B Proofreading for Errors in Possessive Forms

Most of the following sentences contain an ~~incorrect possessive form~~. For each error, give the correct form of the word. If a sentence is already correct, write *C*.

EXAMPLE
1. The island nation of the Philippines shows signs of both Spains and the United States occupations.

1. Spain's; United States'

1. The ~~countrys~~ national languages are Pilipino and English, but its people also speak Spanish and various regional languages.
2. Did you know that the ~~yo-yos~~ earliest use was as a weapon in the Philippine jungles?
3. My ~~mothers~~ boss was visiting the Philippines when Joseph Estrada became president in 1998.
4. President Estrada's previous career was that of film actor. **4. C**
5. ~~Tina's~~ and Phil's plan to visit the Philippines was postponed when their baby was born.
6. The ~~Philippines~~ capital and largest city is Manila, which is on the big island of Luzon.
7. Both Kim and Marta's lunches came with delicious Filipino custard.
8. It's ~~anyones~~ guess how many islands actually make up the Philippines, though there are certainly more than seven thousand islands.

9. The Spanish monarch who's soldiers named the Philippines was King Philip II.
10. Childrens pastimes in the Philippines include kite flying and swimming.

Contractions

25g. Use an apostrophe to show where letters, words, or numerals have been omitted in a contraction.

A *contraction* is a shortened form of a word, a group of words, or a numeral. The apostrophes in contractions show where letters, words, or numerals have been left out.

Common Contractions	
who is .... who's	she will ..... she'll
there is ...... there's	I am .... I'm
could have .... could've	you are ..... you're
1999 .... '99	we had ...... we'd
of the clock ... o'clock	she has ..... she's
let us .... let's	Lisa is ...... Lisa's
I would .... I'd	they are ..... they're

Generally, the adverb *not* can be shortened to *n't* and added to a verb without any change in the spelling of the verb.

EXAMPLES	is not .... isn't	were not .... weren't
	are not .... aren't	has not .... hasn't
	does not .... doesn't	have not .... haven't
	do not .... don't	had not .... hadn't
	did not .... didn't	would not ..... wouldn't
	was not .... wasn't	should not .... shouldn't
EXCEPTIONS	cannot .... can't	will not .... won't

STYLE TIP

Many people consider contractions informal. Therefore, it is generally best to avoid using them in formal writing and speech.

Apostrophes 763

Review B Proofreading for Errors in Possessive Forms

ANSWERS continued
9. whose
10. Children's

Review B

ALTERNATIVE LESSON
To reinforce students' understanding of direct quotations, have them change each of the following sentences from **Review B** into a divided direct quotation by adding quotation marks and using the speaker tag given.

1. sentence 1—explained the teacher ["The country's national languages are Pilipino and English," explained the teacher, "but its people also speak Spanish and various regional languages."]

2. sentence 2—asked the teacher ["Did you know," asked the teacher, "that the yo-yo's earliest use was as a weapon in the Philippine jungles?" or tag could go between *use* and *was*.]

3. sentence 10—the teacher pointed out ["Children's pastimes in the Philippines," the teacher pointed out, "include kite flying and swimming."]

Apostrophes 763

Looking at Language

Homonyms. Direct students' attention to the chart on this page. Explain to students that words such as *who's* and *whose* are called homonyms—words that sound the same but have different meanings and, usually, different spellings. Have students scan the chart to identify the homonyms. Call on volunteers to pronounce the words aloud, point out the differences in spelling, and read aloud the definitions of the words.

Do not confuse contractions with possessive pronouns.

Contractions	Possessive Pronouns
Who's [Who is] next? **Who's** [Who has] helped you?	**Whose** turn is next?
It's [It is] purring. **It's** [It has] been asleep.	Listen to **its** purr.
You're [You are] late.	**Your** report is late.
There's [There is] a mule. **They're** [They are] healthy pets.	That mule is **theirs**. **Their** pets are healthy.

Exercise 3 Using Contractions

Provide appropriate contractions that correctly complete the following sentences. *Answers may vary. Possible responses are given.*

EXAMPLE 1. We tried to call Beth and Jennifer, but they ____ answer their phone.
   1. didn't

1. Isn't
2. aren't
3. they're
4. She'll
5. Let's
6. there's
7. isn't
8. don't
9. shouldn't
10. haven't

1. ____ he going to the awards ceremony?
2. I fed the fish, but they ____ eating.
3. Marla has two cats, and ____ beautiful.
4. ____ bring me her notes tonight so I can study them.
5. ____ go to a movie.
6. Mom said ____ one apple in the basket.
7. He is sick, so he ____ coming with us.
8. I ____ believe the summer is already over.
9. You ____ read a scary book when you're home alone.
10. I ____ gotten the mail yet.

Exercise 4 Recognizing the Correct Uses of Contractions and Possessives

Choose the correct word in parentheses in each of the following sentences.

EXAMPLE 1. (*It's, Its*) never too late to learn something new.
   1. It's

1. (*You're*, *Your*) sure that (*you're*, *your*) allowed to bring (*you're*, *your*) book to the exam?

764 Chapter 25 Punctuation

 Continued on pp. 765–766

Avoiding Double Negatives. Explain to students that when the adverb *not* is shortened to *n't* and added to a verb to form a contraction, such as *isn't, don't,* and *can't,* the contraction is considered a negative word. Emphasize to students that the use of two negative words to express a single negative idea is called a **double negative** and is regarded as nonstandard.

2. (*Whose*, *Who's*) idea was it to visit the National Civil Rights Museum in Memphis during (*you're*, *your*) trip?
3. (*They're*, *Their*) trying to sell (*they're*, *their*) house.
4. (*It's*, *Its*) the best one of (*it's*, *its*) kind.
5. Do you know (*who's*, *whose*) responsible for (*they're*, *their*) confusion?
6. I hope the dog can find (*it's*, *its*) way (*they're*, *there*).
7. (*It's*, *Its*) Philip (*who's*, *whose*) always late.
8. Although (*it's*, *its*) been snowing all day, they're still planning to go.
9. (*Who's*, *Whose*) the designer of (*they're*, *their*) float in Galveston's Mardi Gras parade?
10. I know (*you're*, *your*) upset with the plan, but (*it's*, *its*) the only way to solve the problem.

Review C — Correcting Sentences by Adding Apostrophes

Identify each word that needs an apostrophe in the following sentences. Then, correctly write the word.

EXAMPLE 1. Werent you the one who said you didnt like eggplant?
1. Weren't; didn't

1. Whos going to be at Leon and Joshs party?
2. Lets hide and see whether theyll look for us.
3. I cant find the calamata olives and the feta cheese for the Greek salad.
4. Is the doctors appointment at nine oclock?
5. Cleve doesnt have time to mow both David's and Rays lawns.
6. The parents faces brightened as their children crossed the stage.
7. Were lucky that that dogs howls didn't awaken them.
8. Im trying to follow Pauls map to Jeans house.
9. Its extremely cold; therefore, I dont think you should go skiing.
10. Elise couldnt remember the characteristics of the tiger in the Chinese zodiac.
11. After track practice, hes going to record his best times.
12. It doesnt matter to me, but shes adamant about making her point.
13. We dont know whos batting next.
14. Im going to the dance with my best friend.
15. The Salvation Armys office is organizing the benefit concert.
16. Nothings going to stop them from playing volleyball after school.
17. You must stir the ingredients until theyre well blended.
18. After spending two weeks in Italy, Mary didnt want to come home.
19. Mom, please hang Teds jacket next to yours.
20. Youre responsible for counting the money.

Apostrophes 765

Write the following sentences on the chalkboard. Ask students to find the double negative in each sentence and then to revise the sentence to omit one of the negative words.

1. Won't nobody [*Won't anybody* or *Will nobody*] help me carry this?
2. I can't [*can*] hardly read the words.
3. We don't have no [*don't have any* or *we have no*] laundry detergent.

Meeting INDIVIDUAL NEEDS

ENGLISH-LANGUAGE LEARNERS

Spanish. In many Spanish dialects, a word's final *s* is often not pronounced. As a result, students may have difficulty understanding the importance of the final *s* of plural forms in English, even when the *s* is spoken clearly. To give students practice hearing the final *s,* as well as practice applying **Rule 25h,** dictate to students several sentences that contain plural forms of numerals, symbols, letters, or words referred to as words. Have students write the sentences as you dictate. Then, check students' work for the inclusion of the final *s* and the correct use of apostrophes.

Review D

ALTERNATIVE LESSON

To reinforce students' understanding of the uses of italics, ask them to give the reason for the use of italics in each of the following sentences from **Review D.**

1. sentence 2 [*the letter a referred to as a letter;* the word *aardvark* referred to as a word]
2. sentence 4 [*titles of novel*]
3. sentence 9 [*the word very referred to as a word*]

Reference Note

For more on forming the **plurals of numerals, symbols, letters, and words referred to as words,** see page 789.

STYLE TIP

Many writers add only an *s* to some of the kinds of plurals listed in Rule 25h. However, using both an apostrophe and *s* is not wrong and may be necessary to make your meaning clear. Therefore, it is a good idea always to include the apostrophe.

Be sure to use apostrophes consistently.

EXAMPLE
 Are those *I*'**s** or *L*'**s**?
 [Without an apostrophe, the plural of *I* would spell the word *Is*. Since an apostrophe and *s* are used to form the plural of one letter, an apostrophe and *s* are used with the other letter for consistency.]

Plurals

25h. Use an apostrophe and an *s* to form the plurals of numerals, symbols, all lowercase letters, some uppercase letters, and some words referred to as words.

EXAMPLES
 Most of your cursive *u*'**s** and *U*'**s** are the same size.

 Mr. Carr suggested that I replace some of the *so*'**s** in my paper with other words.

 These *2*'**s** look like *7*'**s**.

 It appears that the author has confused *@*'**s** and *&*'**s**.

Note that in the first example, the plurals of *u* and *U* could be misread as *us* and *Us* if the apostrophes were omitted. In the second example, the plural of *so* could be misread as the acronym *sos* if the apostrophe were omitted.

Review D — Correcting Sentences by Adding Apostrophes

For each of the following sentences, write all the items needing apostrophes, and add the apostrophes.

EXAMPLE
 1. You may agree with the school boards decision, but I dont.
 1. school board's; don't

1. Are these &s or 8s?
2. You forgot that there are two *a*s at the beginning of *aardvark*.
3. My stepsister graduated from high school in 97 and graduated from college in 01.
4. Lewis Carrolls novel *Alices Adventures in Wonderland* was originally called *Alices Adventures Underground*.
5. Whos going to change the babies diapers?
6. After school were going to visit his sister; shes in St. Marys Hospital.
7. Did you write *o*s or *O*s in the margin?
8. Its been six weeks since I checked the cars oil and its tires.
9. Your story would be better if youd remove about ten *very*s.
10. She learned the Hawaiian alphabets twelve letters, but Max didnt.

766 Chapter 25 Punctuation

MINI-LESSON

4. I've never seen nothing [*never seen anything* or *I've seen nothing*] like this!
5. There weren't no [*weren't any* or *were no*] spoons in the drawer.

For additional information about double negatives, refer students to **Chapter 20: A Glossary of Usage.**

Hyphens

Word Division

25i. Use a hyphen to divide a word at the end of a line.

EXAMPLE How long had the new museum been under construction before it was opened?

When dividing a word at the end of a line, keep in mind the following rules:

(1) Do not divide a one-syllable word.

INCORRECT After a long journey the Spanish explorers reached their destination.
CORRECT After a long journey the Spanish explorers reached
their destination.
CORRECT After a long journey the Spanish explorers
reached their destination.

(2) Divide a word only between syllables.

INCORRECT The fans stood and cheered while the band was playing the victory song.
CORRECT The fans stood and cheered while the band was playing the victory song.

(3) Divide an already hyphenated word only at the hyphen.

INCORRECT My stepsister Melissa plans to take a course in self-defense.
CORRECT My stepsister Melissa plans to take a course in self-
defense.
INCORRECT Ms. Malamud always seems to have such a hap-
py-go-lucky attitude.
CORRECT Ms. Malamud always seems to have such a happy-
go-lucky attitude.
CORRECT Ms. Malamud always seems to have such a happy-go-
lucky attitude.

(4) Do not divide a word so that one letter stands alone.

INCORRECT In the gloomy twilight, we had caught a momentar-
y glimpse of them.
CORRECT In the gloomy twilight, we had caught a momen-
tary glimpse of them.

HELP

If you are not entirely sure about the **syllabication** of a word—that is, the division of a word into syllables—look up the word in a dictionary.

TIPS & TRICKS

Generally, a word containing double consonants may be divided between the double consonants.

EXAMPLES
cor-rect   begin-ning

Generally, a word with a prefix or suffix made up of more than one letter may be divided between the prefix and the base word (or root) or between the base word and the suffix.

EXAMPLES
semi-circle   pro-mote
peace-ful   sign-ing

Hyphens   767

Hyphens
Rules 25i–l (pp. 767–769)

OBJECTIVES

- To use hyphens to divide words at the ends of lines
- To identify and hyphenate compound words that should be hyphenated

Meeting INDIVIDUAL NEEDS

ENGLISH-LANGUAGE LEARNERS
General Strategies. To be sure that students are familiar with dividing words into syllables, you may want to review the concept. Explain that a *syllable* is a word or part of a word pronounced as a single, uninterrupted sound.

Write the following divided words on the chalkboard. Read them aloud, emphasizing the syllables.

en•cy•clo•pe•di•a
re•al•is•tic
de•pend•a•ble

Conclude by showing students how syllabication is indicated in a dictionary.

MECHANICS

RESOURCES

Hyphens
Practice
- *Grammar, Usage, and Mechanics,* pp. 321, 322, 323
- *Language Workshop CD-ROM,* Lesson 44

> **TEACHING TIP**
>
> **Exercise 5** You may want to use the first five items in **Exercise 5** as guided practice and then have students complete the exercise as independent practice.
>
> ### Relating to Literature
> William Shakespeare used many compound adjectives in his plays and poems. In *The Tragedy of Julius Caesar,* for example, Cicero uses the term, "strange-disposéd" (Act I, Scene 3, Line 33). Ask students to suggest reasons for Shakespeare's use of the compound adjective *strange-disposéd* [to conform to a metrical pattern; to avoid using a lengthy or convoluted phrase or clause; to convey more vividly the eerie mood of the scene]. If they have access to the play, students could look for more compound adjectives and discuss their meanings. Some examples of other compound adjectives can be found in the play in Act 1, Scenes 1, 2, and 3.

Word breaks are based on *Webster's New World College Dictionary, Fourth Edition.*

5. no hyphen   10. no hyphen

18. no hyphen

6. no hyphen

> **STYLE TIP**
>
> The prefix *half* often requires a hyphen, as in *half-life, half-moon,* and *half-truth.* However, sometimes *half* is used without a hyphen, either as part of a single word (*halftone, halfway, halfback*) or as a separate word (*half shell, half pint, half note*). If you are not sure how to spell a compound containing *half,* look up the word in a dictionary.

Exercise 5 Using Hyphens to Divide Words at the Ends of Lines

Write each of the following words, adding hyphens in each place where you could divide the word at the end of a line. If a word should not be divided, write *no hyphen.* If you are unsure where to divide a word, look in a dictionary. Carets indicate possible word division.

EXAMPLE   1. harmonious
          1. har-mo-ni-ous

1. Olympic
2. algebra
3. toast
4. pemmican
5. drummer
6. alert
7. someone
8. Honduras
9. reservation
10. ditch
11. circle
12. traveling
13. kudzu
14. satisfaction
15. donation
16. mansion
17. topography
18. greet
19. self-esteem
20. Johnny-come-lately

Compound Words

Some compound words are written as one word (*blueberry*); some are hyphenated (*blue-collar*); and some are written as two or more words (*blue jay, Blue Ridge Mountains*).

Whenever you are not sure about the spelling of a compound word, look up the word in an up-to-date dictionary.

25j. Use a hyphen with compound numbers from *twenty-one* to *ninety-nine* and with fractions used as modifiers.

EXAMPLES   **twenty-seven** students

a **two-thirds** majority [but *two thirds of the class*]

25k. Use a hyphen with the prefixes *all–, ex–, great–,* and *self–;* with the suffixes *–elect* and *–free;* and with all prefixes before a proper noun or proper adjective.

EXAMPLES   **all-**purpose   detergent-**free**

ex-president   **anti-**Stalinist

great-grandmother   **mid-**December

self-control   **non-**Francophile

secretary-**elect**   **pro-**American

Chapter 25 Punctuation

25l. Hyphenate a compound adjective when it precedes the noun it modifies.

EXAMPLES a **well-organized** trip [but *a trip that was well organized*]

an **after-school** job

Do not use a hyphen if one of the modifiers is an adverb ending in *ly*.

EXAMPLE a **perfectly good** answer

NOTE Some compound adjectives are always hyphenated, whether they precede or follow the nouns they modify.

EXAMPLES a **down-to-earth** person

a person who is **down-to-earth**

If you have any doubt about whether a compound adjective is hyphenated, look up the word in an up-to-date dictionary.

Exercise 6 Hyphenating Words Correctly

For each of the following sentences, write and hyphenate the compound words that should be hyphenated. Hyphens are indicated by the ˰ symbol.

EXAMPLE 1. The host of that late night show interviewed an expert on Italy's pre Renaissance years.

1. late-night; pre-Renaissance

1. Ex˰students were not allowed at the festively decorated prom party.
2. His self˰confidence faded when he forgot his well˰planned speech.
3. Twenty˰five students said they had never heard of the well˰traveled Overland Trail to California.
4. Three fourths of the class voted, and the proposal was defeated by a seven˰tenths majority.
5. Our governor˰elect was once an all˰American football player.
6. In our debate on the United Nations, the pro˰UN side defeated the anti˰UN side.
7. General Colin Powell, who is a former resident of the Bronx, spoke quite eloquently about the importance of self˰determination.
8. Christopher's test scores ranked in the eighty˰eighth percentile.
9. You must turn in your reports by mid˰November.
10. My uncle's recipe for halftime nachos calls for fat˰free cheese and spicy salsa.

STYLE TIP

Although you may see a variety of spellings for some words with prefixes (*reelect, re-elect*), the preferred style today is to use no hyphen between most prefixes (except those indicated in Rule 25k) and the base word.

EXAMPLES
bimonthly reexamine
antihero nonessential

Be sure to include the hyphen, however, when one is necessary to prevent confusion or awkwardness.

EXAMPLES
re-creation [to prevent confusion with *recreation*]

pro-offshore drilling [to prevent awkwardness of *prooffshore*]

Relating to Writing

As suggested in the **Relating to Literature** activity on p. 768, the use of vivid compound adjectives helps writers make their work more expressive and more concise. Student writers, like professional writers, can create colorful descriptions by inventing compound adjectives.

Write the following expressions on the chalkboard, and ask students to use words from each expression to form a word group that contains a compound adjective.

1. a bee flitting from flower to flower
   [*a flower-flitting bee*]
2. a child throwing a tantrum
   [*a tantrum-throwing child*]
3. a stove that burns coal
   [*a coal-burning stove*]
4. a shirt stained with strawberries
   [*a strawberry-stained shirt*]
5. a face streaked with tears
   [*a tear-streaked face*]

Then, ask students to choose samples from their writing portfolios and to experiment with adding compound adjectives. Have paired students read and assess each other's changes.

Dashes, Parentheses, and Brackets

Rules 25m–p *(pp. 770–774)*

OBJECTIVE

- To correct sentences by adding dashes, parentheses, and brackets where needed

Cooperative Learning

To help students practice applying the two rules for using dashes, have students work in pairs to develop a dialogue between two characters. Explain that the first character (in the example below, Max) is indecisive and abruptly jumps from one thought to another and that the second character (in the example below, Mabel) always wants to add explanations to clarify her own words. The following example may help students begin:

> Max said, "Mabel, let's have lunch—or is it still time for breakfast?"
>
> Mabel answered quickly, "Brunch—a combination of breakfast and lunch—would be lovely. The restaurant Chez Nous—even the wait staff speaks French—serves delicious food."
>
> "French food—have I ever even eaten it?—sounds good to me," said Max.

You may want to call on volunteers to read their dialogues to the rest of the class.

COMPUTER TIP

When you use a word processor, you can indicate a dash with two hyphens. Do not leave a space before, between, or after the hyphens. When you write by hand, use an unbroken line about as long as two hyphens.

STYLE TIP

Dates in parentheses after a person's name indicate the years of that person's birth and death. If the person is still alive, put the closing parenthesis immediately after the dash.

EXAMPLE
George Lucas (1944–) was born in Modesto, California.

Dashes

Sometimes a word, phrase, or sentence is used parenthetically; that is, it breaks into the main thought of a sentence. Most parenthetical elements are set off by commas or by parentheses.

EXAMPLES Felipe**,** **however,** had a better idea.

Her suggestion **(that we serve fruit and cheese instead of junk food)** was approved unanimously.

Sometimes, though, such elements call for a sharper separation from the rest of the sentence. In such cases, dashes are used.

25m. Use a dash to indicate the beginning and the end of an abrupt break in thought or speech or to indicate an unfinished thought.

EXAMPLES The party—I'm sorry I forgot to tell you—was not changed to next week.

"What I meant was—" Vonda began as the doorbell rang.

25n. Use a dash to mean *namely, that is,* or *in other words,* or to otherwise introduce an explanation. Also, use a dash after the explanation if the sentence continues.

EXAMPLES Our family owns two vehicles—a station wagon and a pickup truck. [*namely*]

The weather was unseasonably warm—in the low eighties—for February. [*that is*]

 NOTE Either a dash or colon is acceptable in the first example for 25n.

Parentheses

25o. Use parentheses to enclose informative or explanatory material of minor importance.

EXAMPLES The Temple of the Magician **(**I never thought I'd actually see it**)** rose majestically against the purple sky of Uxmal, in the Mexican Yucatán.

Eleanor Roosevelt **(**1884–1962**)** helped draft the Universal Declaration of Human Rights.

RESOURCES

Dashes, Parentheses, and Brackets
Practice
- *Grammar, Usage, and Mechanics,* pp. 324, 325, 326, 327
- *Language Workshop CD-ROM,* Lesson 36

Be sure that the material enclosed in parentheses can be omitted without affecting the intended meaning or basic structure of the sentence.

INCORRECT	When my six-year-old cousin said ("It's the first inning"), the rest of us watching the football game started laughing.
CORRECT	When my six-year-old cousin said, **"It's the first inning,"** the rest of us watching the football game started laughing.
INCORRECT	I sent the package on October 12 (that was ten days ago via express mail.)
CORRECT	I sent the package on October 12 **(that was ten days ago)** via express mail.

A sentence enclosed in parentheses may fall within another sentence or may stand by itself.

(1) A parenthetical sentence that falls within another sentence

- does not begin with a capital letter unless it begins with a word that should be capitalized
- does not end with a period but may end with a question mark or exclamation point

EXAMPLES   When we reached Shaker Heights **(it's just outside of Cleveland),** we met our cousins for dinner.

The John Hancock Tower **(isn't it in Boston?)** was designed by I. M. Pei.

NOTE Generally, when parenthetical material falls within a sentence, punctuation does not precede the opening parenthesis but may follow the closing parenthesis.

INCORRECT	Reading the novel by Samuel Clemens, (better known as Mark Twain) I learned much about American society in the nineteenth century.
CORRECT	Reading the novel by Samuel Clemens (better known as Mark Twain)**,** I learned much about American society in the nineteenth century. [The comma following the closing parenthesis is used to set off the introductory participial phrase.]

(2) A parenthetical sentence that stands by itself

- begins with a capital letter
- ends with a period, a question mark, or an exclamation point

---

STYLE TIP

Too many parenthetical expressions in a piece of writing can distract the reader from the main idea. Keep your meaning clear by limiting the number of parenthetical expressions you use.

Crossing the Curriculum

Math. Parentheses play an important part in mathematical equations by indicating which operation should be performed first. For example, when solving the following equation, one should subtract ten from sixty before dividing by five.

$y = (60 - 10) \div 5$
$y = 50 \div 5$
$y = 10$

To extend the discussion, write the following equation on the chalkboard, and ask a volunteer to insert parentheses so that y is equal to thirty-two.

$y = 30 + 4 \div 2$
$[y = 30 + (4 \div 2)]$

Relating to Literature
To illustrate the use of parentheses in plays, write the following dialogue on the chalkboard:

Miranda (*uneasy*) I have a job interview tomorrow.

Mother (*leans over and kisses her*) You'll do fine, dear. You're surely qualified—

Miranda (*interrupting her mother*) But Mother, I'm really nervous!

Ask students to explain the purpose of the playwright's use of parentheses. [*The information in parentheses tells the actors how to behave or what to do when they say their lines.*] Finally, have students scan a play in their literature textbooks and note the use of parentheses.

COMPUTER TIP
With the search-and-replace function of a word-processing program, you can check your writing for the incorrect or inappropriate uses of apostrophes, hyphens, dashes, and parentheses. Take full advantage of such a program when you are proofreading your work.

EXAMPLES   On the scoring sheet, mark your answers with a lead pencil. **(Do not use ink.)**

In 1996 he won another gold medal for the high dive. **(That was his ninth!)**

Follow these guidelines for determining when to use commas, dashes, and parentheses to enclose parenthetical material:

1. Remember that only material that can be omitted without changing the basic meaning or structure of the sentence is considered parenthetical.
2. Use commas to set off parenthetical material that is closely related to the rest of the sentence.

EXAMPLE   We rehearsed for the show, a wonderful musical comedy.

3. Use a dash to indicate the beginning and the end of an abrupt change in thought or to indicate an unfinished thought.

EXAMPLE   We rehearsed for the show—which many called the musical event of the year!

4. Use parentheses to indicate that the parenthetical material is of minor importance.

EXAMPLE   We rehearsed for the show **(**at least those of us who could remember our lines did**)**.

5. Don't overuse parenthetical material, or you may confuse your readers.

Brackets

25p. Use brackets to enclose an explanation or added information within quoted or parenthetical material.

EXAMPLES   The secretary of state, in her speech, said: "Diplomatic efforts seek to establish talks between the two nations **[**North and South Korea**]**." [The words are enclosed in brackets to show that they have been inserted into the quotation and are not the speaker's words.]

The faltering performance of the Russian economy in recent years has caused fluctuations in the world's financial markets. (See page 15 **[**Graph 1A**]** for a chronology.)

Learning for Life

Making Decisions. Point out that when making decisions, people often engage in internal conversations, identifying and weighing all options. If they were to transcribe their flow of thoughts, they would probably use dashes, parentheses, and brackets to indicate abrupt changes in thought or to set off relevant but less important information.

Encourage students to think of a decision they have been weighing (such as what to wear to an upcoming event or how to save

Exercise 7 Correcting Sentences by Using Dashes, Parentheses, and Brackets

Rewrite the following sentences, adding dashes, parentheses, and brackets where they are needed. If a sentence is already correct, write C.

EXAMPLE 1. Garth Brooks and Shania Twain I have every one of their albums have won many awards.

1. Garth Brooks and Shania Twain (I have every one of their albums) have won many awards.

Answers may vary. Carets indicate placement of dashes.

1. "Yankee Doodle"(it was the unofficial United States anthem at the time)was played after the signing of the Treaty of Ghent.
2. While standing at the top of Pikes Peak, Katherine Lee Bates wrote the words to the song "America the Beautiful." **2. C**
3. Lauryn Hill(I love her songs!)gave a concert here, and it sold out.
4. There were three original members of the Sons of the Pioneers ^Roy Rogers(his real name was Leonard Slye)^ Bob Nolan, and Tim Spencer.
5. Linda Ronstadt has recorded many kinds of music, including rock, songs from the 1930's and 1940's, and Mexican tunes. **5. C**
6. The Beatles used several names^Foreverly Brothers, the Cavemen, the Moondogs, and the Quarrymen^before they became the Beatles.
7. Last night's concert was about average^the songs were good, but the singers were uninspired.
8. Cathy said, "I will listen to one of your CDs^Mozart's *Requiem*, perhaps^if you will listen to one of Lenny Kravitz's CDs."
9. Bob Dylan ([1941–]born Robert Allen Zimmerman) wrote "Blowin' in the Wind."
10. Whitney Houston's version of "The Star-Spangled Banner"(have you heard it? wouldn't Francis Scott Key be pleased?)was a hit.

HELP
Some sentences in Exercise 7 have more than one possible answer. You need to give only one answer for each sentence.

Review E Proofreading for Errors in Punctuation

Each of the following sentences contains at least one error in punctuation. Correct the errors by adding apostrophes, hyphens, dashes, parentheses, and brackets where they are needed.

EXAMPLE 1. Dont you ever wonder I frequently do about who invented different kinds of machines and tools?

1. Don't you ever wonder—I frequently do—about who invented different kinds of machines and tools?

or

Don't you ever wonder (I frequently do) about who invented different kinds of machines and tools?

HELP
Although two possible answers are given for the example in Review E, you need to give only one answer for each sentence.

Brackets 773

Answers may vary. The - symbol indicates placement of hyphens; carets indicate placement of dashes.

1. Both Trish's and Robert's reports—the ones required for social studies—were about the shoe industry.
2. Trish said that she chose the subject because at least seventy-five percent of the world's students wear shoes.
3. I thought the other report—the one Robert gave on the invention of the lasting machine—was more interesting, though.
4. Robert wrote, "The lasting machine (its parts are numbered in the patent drawing provided [see the picture below]) changed its [the shoe industry's] future."
5. The machine's inventor, the distinguished-looking young man pictured below, was Jan Matzeliger.
6. He came to the United States from Dutch Guiana (now Suriname) before 1880 and found work as a shoemaker's apprentice.
7. Matzeliger wasn't happy with how much of the workers' time was spent putting shoes together.
8. Within ten years' time he perfected a machine that shaped leather for the upper shoe and attached it to the sole.
9. Matzeliger's patent for this much-needed machine was granted in 1883.
10. The United Shoe Manufacturing Company's decision to buy the machine ultimately gave that company control of the United States' shoe market.

CHAPTER 25

Chapter Review

A. Using Apostrophes and Hyphens Correctly

Add or delete apostrophes and hyphens as necessary in the following sentences. *Hyphens are indicated by the - symbol.*

1. The town's record on supporting youth projects has been good.
2. The wet, muddy boots were lined up outside the door to the house. *2. house*
3. Only fifty-three people went to our ballet recital, and thirty of them were our relatives.
4. Everyone's favorite performer was certainly the man in the turtleneck.
5. Christopher's writing is hard to read because his *a*'s look like *o*'s.
6. The women's basketball team, which is coached by an ex-Laker, has run up quite an impressive string of victories.
7. Sampson and Smith's French Bakery, which displays its pastries in the window, is around the corner from my house.
8. Mr. Miller's watercolors don't appeal to me, but they were given the jury's highest award.
9. Approximately twenty out of twenty-five students agree that self-esteem is among the most important personal qualities.
10. To verify safety standards, we have compared twenty-seven sport utility vehicles. *10. twenty-seven*
11. There's someone at the door, and we're already late for school!
12. He's used too many *therefore*'s in his sentences to get an A on his composition.
13. There are three 5's and four 8's missing from your answer's. *13. answers*
14. My sister-in-law's job is selling children's sportswear.
15. The Jameses' address contains four 7's. *15. Jameses*

B. Using Dashes, Brackets, and Parentheses Correctly

Answers may vary. Carets indicate placement of dashes.

Add dashes, brackets, and parentheses where they are needed in each of the following sentences. Do not add commas or colons.

16. My cousins like many of Charley Pride's songs — his "Crystal Chandeliers" is their favorite.

HELP
Some sentences in the Chapter Review contain more than one error.

Using the Chapter Review

To assess student progress, you may want to compare the types of items missed on the **Diagnostic Preview** with those missed on the **Chapter Review.** If students have not made significant progress, you may want to refer them to **Exercise 31** of **Chapter 27: Correcting Common Errors** for additional practice.

17. This report contains information about agriculture in those three South American countries(Brazil, Argentina, and Colombia [see Graph 3A on pp. 24–25.

17. 24–25])

18. I read the wrong chapter for my homework a disastrous mistake!
19. Mary Ellen Jefferson, a former district attorney, will speak at Thursday's assembly I'll have to miss gym class and will address the topic of student rights.
20. Bessie Coleman(I read an article about her)was the first licensed African American pilot.

C. Writing the Possessive Forms of Nouns

Write the singular possessive and plural possessive form of each of the following nouns.

21. house
22. computer
23. uncle
24. coach
25. cow
26. president
27. trellis
28. goose
29. wife
30. theory

D. Proofreading a Paragraph for Errors in Punctuation

Each sentence in the following paragraph contains at least one error in punctuation. Correct the errors by adding or deleting apostrophes, hyphens, dashes, and parentheses. *Answers may vary. Hyphens are indicated by the - symbol; carets indicate placement of dashes.*

[31] The kangaroo, possibly Australias most famous indigenous animal, is a marsupial, a kind of mammal. [32] Marsupial's offspring are born extremely undeveloped. [33] A newborn joey(a baby kangaroo) measures only about one inch long. [34] A kangaroos pouch the pocket-like opening in the mother's belly where the joey completes its development is one of the animal kingdoms' most unusual features. [35] With their huge hind feet, long tails, and small, deer-like heads, kangaroos are among the worlds' most distinctive creatures. [36] Kangaroos and wallabies(their smaller cousins)both belong to an animal family called macropods the name means "big foot" in Latin which includes other animals such as the so-called hare wallaby, the bettong, and the potoroo. [37] Kangaroo's life spans vary from six to eight years, on average. [38] They have few enemies and are protected by Australias no-poaching laws. [39] Theyre fast, too; large specimens top speed is as

---

Chapter Review
C. Writing the Possessive Forms of Nouns

ANSWERS

21. house's / houses'
22. computer's / computers'
23. uncle's / uncles'
24. coach's / coaches'
25. cow's / cows'
26. president's / presidents'
27. trellis's / trellises'
28. goose's / geese's
29. wife's / wives'
30. theory's / theories'

32. Marsupials'
34. Kingdom's
35. world's
37. Kangaroos'

RESOURCES

Punctuation
Review
- *Grammar, Usage, and Mechanics,* pp. 328, 329, 330, 331

Assessment
- Assessment Package
  —*Chapter Tests,* Ch. 25
  —*Chapter Tests in Standardized Test Formats,* Ch. 25
- Test Generator (One-Stop Planner CD-ROM)

high as 30 mph. [40] So closely are they bound up with Australias identity that the symbol of Qantas, the national airline, is yes, you guessed it a leaping "roo."

Writing Application
Punctuating a Poem

Using Dashes You have decided to enter a local poetry contest for high school students. All the poems must reflect students' ideas about current events. For the contest, write a poem that uses at least four dashes.

Prewriting Start by making a list of subjects that interest you. Then, choose a subject from your list, and freewrite about it. List as many sensory details as you can to describe your subject. Then, start grouping the details to create a loose structure for your poem.

Writing Use your freewriting notes to write your first draft. As you form your ideas into lines of poetry, choose words and punctuation carefully, paying attention to both the images and the rhythms they create.

Revising Read your poem silently to be sure that it says what you want it to say. Add, cut, or rearrange details to express your ideas more effectively. Then, read your poem aloud and listen to the rhythm of the words you have used. Make any changes that you feel will improve the rhythm, keeping in mind that you must include at least four dashes in the poem.

Publishing Be sure to check the spelling and punctuation in your poem. If you have typed your poem or are using a word processor, check to see that the spacing around hyphens and dashes is correct. If your class has a Web page, you may want to collect your poems and publish them on the Internet.

Chapter Review 777

Writing Application
Extension
- *Grammar, Usage, and Mechanics,* p. 334
- *Language Workshop CD-ROM,* Lessons 36, 39–40, 44

CHAPTER 26

PREVIEWING THE CHAPTER

- This chapter discusses good spelling habits, specific spelling rules, and distinctions between words that are often confused. At the end of the chapter are alphabetical lists titled **100 Commonly Misspelled Words** and **300 Spelling Words**, which can serve as a handy reference for students, especially during the revising stage of a writing activity.

- The chapter concludes with a **Chapter Review**, which includes a **Writing Application** feature that asks students to write a letter of application, using ten words from the spelling lists at the end of the chapter.

- For help in integrating the chapter with writing chapters, use the **Teaching Strands** chart on pp. T401A–T401B.

USING THE DIAGNOSTIC PREVIEW

- The **Diagnostic Preview** requires students to proofread sentences for errors in spelling and word usage. You may want to use the results of the preview in conjunction with an assessment of students' writing assignments to determine the amount of time you should spend reteaching each rule and term in the chapter. If your evaluation suggests that some students would benefit from guided practice throughout the chapter, you may want to ask students who demonstrate sound spelling skills to assist less-proficient learners as they complete the exercises.

CHAPTER 26 Spelling
Improving Your Spelling

Diagnostic Preview

Correcting Misspelled and Misused Words and Numerals

Proofread the following sentences, and correctly write any misspelled or misused words or numerals.

EXAMPLE 1. Our parents will be dineing out tonight.
           1. dining

1. calves
2. whether/deity
3. first/second
4. potatoes
5. principal's
6. carefully
7. misspell
8. forfeit
9. a thousand
10. deceived
11. effects/ completely
12. courageous
13. 217
14. exceed

1. When I went to the barn, the cows and calfs were eating hay.
2. Do you know weather Mars was a Roman diety?
3. I don't know whether the relay team won 1st or 2nd place.
4. Our Thanksgiving meal consists of turkey, stuffing, beans, cranberries, and potatos.
5. The principle's name is Mr. Goodson.
6. The child carried the turtle carefuly across the road.
7. Jill didn't mispell any words on the test.
8. The basketball team missed the bus, so they had to forfiet the game.
9. If I've told you once, I've told you 1,000 times: Don't exaggerate!
10. We decieved Janice so that she would not know we were throwing a surprise birthday party for her.
11. The affects of this weather system were completly unexpected.
12. I felt that the emergency team was quite couragous.
13. The director said two hundred seventeen people applied for the job.
14. If you excede the speed limit, you might get a ticket.

778 Chapter 26 Spelling

CHAPTER RESOURCES

Planning
- One-Stop Planner CD-ROM

Practice and Extension
- Grammar, Usage, and Mechanics, p. 335
- Language Workshop CD-ROM

Reinforcement
- Spelling

Evaluation and Assessment
- Assessment Package
  —Chapter Tests, Ch. 26
  —Chapter Tests in Standardized Test Formats, Ch. 26
- Test Generator (One-Stop Planner CD-ROM)

15. I was grateful to be ~~offerred~~ the lead in the play.
16. My parents' dog, an enormous Great Dane, is ~~scarred~~ of thunder and lightning.
17. ~~Arguement~~ is useless in this situation.
18. A Japanese animated cartoon will ~~preceed~~ the action movie.
19. Ed wants to write ~~playes~~ for a living.
20. Lauren ate 6 pieces of kiwi fruit.

15. offered
16. scared
17. Argument
18. precede
19. plays
20. six

Good Spelling Habits

26a. To learn the spelling of a word, pronounce it, study it, and write it.

(1) Pronounce words carefully.

EXAMPLES   a**thl**etic [not *athaletic*]

e**sc**ape [not *excape*]

heigh**t** [not *heighth*]

(2) Spell by syllables.

A *syllable* is a word part that can be pronounced as one uninterrupted sound.

EXAMPLES   pul • sate [two syllables]

bul • le • tin [three syllables]

en • vi • ron • ment [four syllables]

(3) Use a dictionary.

Do not guess about correct spelling. Look up any words you do not know how to spell. In the dictionary, you can often find other, related words that may help you remember the correct spelling. For example, you may find *denomination* easier to spell after you see its kinship with the words *nominate* and *denominator*.

(4) Proofread for careless spelling errors.

Always proofread what you have written so that you can eliminate careless spelling errors, such as typos (*thier* for *their*), missing letters (*temperture* for *temperature*), and the misuse of words that sound similar (*principal* for *principle*).

HELP

If you are not sure about the correct pronunciation of a word, look it up in a current dictionary. The pronunciation of the word will usually be given in parentheses after the main entry. Use the pronunciation key in the dictionary to help you pronounce the word correctly.

COMPUTER TIP

Spellcheckers can help you proofread your writing. Even the best spellcheckers are not foolproof, however. Some accept British spellings, obsolete words, archaic spellings, and words that are spelled correctly but are used incorrectly (such as *affect* for *effect*). Always double-check your writing to make sure that your spelling is error-free.

Spelling, pp. 778–805
Alignments
TEKS 3A, 3D
TAAS W3, W7
English II End-of-Course 5, 6
Texas Resources
• *TAAS Tool Kit*
• *Preparation for TAAS*
• *One-Stop Planner CD-ROM*

Internet
■ go.hrw.com (keyword: EOLang)

TEACHING TIP

Activity. To show students that miscommunication results from misspelling, slowly pronounce the word *pharmaceutical,* and ask each student to write how he or she thinks the word should be spelled. Then, call on volunteers to write their spellings on the chalkboard. Add the absurd spellings *farmesuiticle* and *pharmusootakel* to the list. Lead students to understand that misspellings occur because some sounds can be spelled in various ways.

Have students work in small groups to make charts of the various spellings of sounds. To help students begin, display the following partial chart:

Sound	Examples
ā	**ai**d, w**eigh**, h**ey**, p**ay**, m**a**de
ē	w**e**, s**ee**, **ea**sy, l**ei**sure
ĕ	s**e**t, w**ea**ther
f	**f**ar, o**ff**, **ph**armacy, rou**gh**

Have students suggest other consonant and vowel sounds that can be spelled in various ways. Require students to give original examples if they use a pronunciation key from a dictionary to help develop the charts.

Have groups compare their charts and compile the information to create a large classroom poster, to which they can refer anytime they need to locate the spelling of a word in a dictionary.

Crossing the Curriculum

Multidisciplinary. Encourage students to use their spelling notebooks in all courses, not just in language arts. Suggest to students that when they misspell words in other courses or encounter difficult words in their reading, they add the words to their notebooks and note the rule that applies to the spelling of each word, if applicable.

MECHANICS

26 b–p

TEACHING TIP

Mnemonics. Here are some additional spelling strategies that you could suggest to students:

1. Generate mnemonic devices. For example, students might use the sentence *An island is land surrounded by water* to help them remember how to spell *island.*

2. Write troublesome spelling words on index cards, and post them in prominent places.

3. Periodically review spelling notebooks for duplicate entries, which might suggest that particular spelling rules should be studied.

Spelling Rules
Rules 26b–p *(pp. 780–793)*

OBJECTIVES

- To proofread sentences to correct spelling errors
- To add prefixes or suffixes to words
- To spell the plural forms of nouns

---

(5) Keep a spelling notebook.

Divide each page into four columns:

COLUMN 1 Correctly write any word you find troublesome.

COLUMN 2 Write the word again, dividing it into syllables and marking the stressed syllable(s). (You may need to use a dictionary.)

COLUMN 3 Write the word again, circling the difficult part(s).

COLUMN 4 Write down any comments that might help you remember the correct spelling.

Spelling Rules

ie and *ei*

26b. Write *ie* when the sound is long *e*, except after *c*.

EXAMPLES ch**ie**f, bel**ie**ve, n**ie**ce, ach**ie**ve, perc**ei**ve, rec**ei**pt

EXCEPTIONS **ei**ther, l**ei**sure, n**ei**ther, prot**ei**n

26c. Write *ei* when the sound is not long *e*.

EXAMPLES forf**ei**t, fr**ei**ght, h**ei**ght, n**ei**ghbor, v**ei**l, w**ei**gh

EXCEPTIONS anc**ie**nt, misch**ie**f, pat**ie**nce

–*cede*, –*ceed*, and –*sede*

26d. The only English word ending in –*sede* is *supersede*. The only words ending in –*ceed* are *exceed*, *proceed*, and *succeed*. Most other words with this sound end in –*cede*.

EXAMPLES con**cede**, pre**cede**, re**cede**, ac**cede**

TIPS & TRICKS

Remember this rhyme:
i before *e*
except after *c*
or when sounded like *a*
as in *neighbor* and *weigh.*

HELP

Rules 26b and 26c apply only when the *i* and the *e* are in the same syllable.

EXAMPLES
sci • ence   de • i • ty

---

780   Chapter 26   Spelling

RESOURCES

Spelling Rules
Practice
- *Grammar, Usage, and Mechanics,* pp. 336–353
- *Language Workshop CD-ROM,* Lessons 47, 48

Exercise 1 — Proofreading Sentences to Correct Spelling Errors

Proofread each of the following sentences, and correctly write the misspelled word or words.

EXAMPLE
1. Niether my neice nor I have tried bungee jumping.
1. Neither, niece

1. During the 1920s, one craze superceded another, each one weirder than the one that preceeded it.
2. Pictured at right is fifteen-year-old Avon Foreman, who acheived fame in Baltimore for his bizarre liesure-time activity.
3. In 1929, he spent ten days, ten hours, ten minutes, and ten seconds perched atop a hickory sapling, at a hieght of eighteen feet.
4. Freinds and neighbors crowded around to give encouragement.
5. He even succeded in attracting the attention of the mayor, William F. Broening, who wrote to him that his "grit and stamina . . . show that the old pioneer spirit of early America is being kept alive by the youth of today."
6. The mayor beleived that Avon was indeed someone to look up to, evidently.
7. People continue to participate in and succede at a number of curious endeavors.
8. There are attempts to cross Antarctica using only dog sleds, leaps from great hieghts, and contests to see how many people will fit into a small car.
9. It seems that humans will always try to acheive unusual goals.
10. Undoubtedly, many people have recieved great entertainment from these occasionally ridiculous activities.

Adding Prefixes

A *prefix* is one or more letters or syllables added to the beginning of a word to create a new word that has a different meaning.

26e. When adding a prefix, do not change the spelling of the original word.

EXAMPLES
mis + spell = mis**spell**   dis + advantage = dis**advantage**
un + likely = un**likely**   il + legible = il**legible**

—HELP—
None of the proper nouns in Exercise 1 are misspelled.

Reference Note
For a list of **prefixes**, see page 892.

Spelling Rules 781

Relating to Vocabulary Skills

Emphasize that adding a prefix to a word creates a new word whose meaning differs from that of the original word. To help students build vocabulary, share with them the following chart, which groups prefixes according to meaning.

Prefixes that show quantity:
semi–	"half"	semicircle
uni–	"one"	unicycle

Prefixes that show negation:
un–	"not"	unhappy
dis–	"lack of"	disrespect
anti–	"against"	antiwar

Prefixes that show time:
fore–	"before"	forecast
pre–	"before"	predate
post–	"after"	postwar
re–	"again"	review

Prefixes that show direction or position:
super–	"above, over"	supervision
trans–	"across, over"	trans-continental
co–	"together"	coexist

You may want to have students add to the chart other words that include these prefixes.

Exercise 2 — Spelling Words with Prefixes and Suffixes

ANSWERS

1. heaviness
2. dissatisfied
3. illegal
4. unnerve
5. sincerely
6. wholly
7. misunderstood
8. readiness
9. unlikely
10. happily
11. ordinarily
12. immature
13. suddenness
14. specially
15. overrate
16. illogical
17. unflattering
18. disillusion
19. stubbornness
20. shyness

MECHANICS

Reference Note
For a list of **suffixes**, see page 893.

Adding Suffixes

A *suffix* is one or more letters or syllables added to the end of a word to create a new word with a different meaning.

26f. When adding the suffix *–ly* or *–ness,* do not change the spelling of the original word.

EXAMPLES nice + ly = **nice**ly   mean + ness = **mean**ness

usual + ly = **usual**ly   same + ness = **same**ness

Words ending in *y* usually change the *y* to *i* before *–ness* and *–ly*:

EXAMPLES empty—empt**i**ness; easy—eas**i**ly

However, most one-syllable adjectives ending in *y* follow Rule 26f:

EXAMPLES shy—**shy**ly; dry—**dry**ness

True, due, and *whole* drop the final *e* before *–ly*:

EXAMPLES true—**tru**ly; due—**du**ly; whole—**whol**ly

Exercise 2 — Spelling Words with Prefixes and Suffixes

Write each of the following words, adding the prefix or suffix given.

EXAMPLE 1. il + legible
1. illegible

1. heavy + ness
2. dis + satisfied
3. il + legal
4. un + nerve
5. sincere + ly
6. whole + ly
7. mis + understood
8. ready + ness
9. un + likely
10. happy + ly
11. ordinary + ly
12. im + mature
13. sudden + ness
14. special + ly
15. over + rate
16. il + logical
17. un + flattering
18. dis + illusion
19. stubborn + ness
20. shy + ness

26g. Drop the final silent *e* before adding a suffix beginning with a vowel.

EXAMPLES dine + ing = **din**ing   safe + er = **saf**er

use + able = **us**able   nice + est = **nic**est

782 Chapter 26 Spelling

MINI-LESSON

Suffixes and Parts of Speech. Point out to students that adding a suffix to a word will often create a new word whose part of speech differs from that of the original word. Using some of the suffixes and examples from pp. 782–783, write on the chalkboard the following information:

1. nice (adj.) + –ly = nicely (adv.)
2. kind (adj. *or* n.) + –ness = kindness (n.)

EXCEPTIONS   Keep the final silent *e*

- in a word ending in *ce* or *ge* before a suffix beginning with *a* or *o*

    service + able = **service**able

    advantage + ous = **advantage**ous

- in *dye* and in *singe* before *–ing*: **dye**ing and **singe**ing [to avoid confusion with *dying* and *singing*]

- in *mile* before *–age*: **mile**age

26h. Keep the final silent e before adding a suffix beginning with a consonant.

EXAMPLES   use + ful = **use**ful   care + less = **care**less

            pave + ment = **pave**ment   live + ly = **live**ly

            hope + ful = **hope**ful   large + ly = **large**ly

EXCEPTIONS true + ly = **tru**ly   nine + th = **nin**th

            argue + ment = **argu**ment   awe + ful = **aw**ful

Exercise 3 Spelling Words with Suffixes

Write each of the following words, adding the suffix given.

EXAMPLES   1. amuse + ing
           1. amusing

           2. care + ful
           2. careful

1. courage + ous
2. nine + ty
3. advance + ing
4. hope + less
5. approve + al
6. note + able
7. ride + ing
8. outrage + ous
9. dye + ing
10. true + ly

26i. For words ending in y preceded by a consonant, change the y to i before adding any suffix that does not begin with i.

EXAMPLES   lively + ness = **liveli**ness   rely + ed = **reli**ed

            bury + al = **buri**al   funny + er = **funni**er

            hasty + est = **hasti**est   study + ing = **study**ing

HELP
Some one-syllable words do not follow Rule 26i.

EXAMPLES
dry—**dry**ness
shy—**shy**ly

Exercise 3 Spelling Words with Suffixes

ANSWERS
1. courageous
2. ninety
3. advancing
4. hopeless
5. approval
6. notable
7. riding
8. outrageous
9. dyeing
10. truly

---

3. sense (n.) + –ible = sensible (adj.)
4. use (v. *or* n.) + –ful = useful (adj.)
5. argue (v.) + –ment = argument (n.)

Call on volunteers to create sentences using the words written on the chalkboard. Conclude by explaining that a familiarity with the meanings of suffixes can help students improve their vocabularies.

26j. For words ending in *y* preceded by a vowel, keep the *y* when adding a suffix.

EXAMPLES   enjoy + able = **enjoy**able   play + ful = **play**ful

survey + or = **survey**or   delay + ing = **delay**ing

EXCEPTIONS   lay—**lai**d   pay—**pai**d   say—**sai**d   day—**dai**ly

Exercise 4   Spelling Words with Suffixes

Write each of the following words, adding the suffix given.

EXAMPLES
1. ready + ly
1. *readily*

2. relay + ing
2. *relaying*

1. happy + est **1.** *happiest*   6. spy + ing **6.** *spying*
2. marry + ing **2.** *marrying*   7. employ + ing **7.** *employing*
3. relay + ed **3.** *relayed*   8. try + ed **8.** *tried*
4. shiny + er **4.** *shinier*   9. day + ly **9.** *daily*
5. obey + ed **5.** *obeyed*   10. busy + ly **10.** *busily*

26k. Double the final consonant before adding a suffix that begins with a vowel if the word (1) has only one syllable or has the accent on the final syllable and (2) ends in a single consonant preceded by a single vowel.

EXAMPLES   drop + ed = dro**pped**   run + er = ru**nner**

begin + ing = begi**nning**   regret + able = regre**ttable**

EXCEPTIONS   For words ending in *w* or *x,* do not double the final consonant.

few + er = **few**er   throw + ing = **throw**ing

fax + es = **fax**es   perplex + ed = **perplex**ed

When a word satisfies both conditions but the addition of the suffix causes the accent to shift, do not double the final consonant.

EXAMPLES   confer + ence = **confer**ence

prefer + able = **prefer**able

EXCEPTIONS   excel—exce**llent**, exce**llence**, exce**llency**

MECHANICS

Exercise 4

ALTERNATIVE LESSON

Ask students to identify the part of speech of each of the following words from **Exercise 4**. Then, have students identify the part of speech of each word they formed when they added the given suffix to the word.

1. happy [*adjective; happiest—adjective*]

9. day [*noun; daily—adjective or adverb*]

10. busy [*adjective; busily—adverb*]

HELP

The final consonant of some words may or may not be doubled. Either spelling is acceptable.

EXAMPLES
travel + ed = trave**led**
or trave**lled**

cancel + ing = cance**ling**
or cance**lling**

784   Chapter 26   Spelling

Exercise 5 — Spelling Words with Suffixes

Write each of the following words, adding the suffix given.

EXAMPLE 1. slip + ed
1. slipped

1. sad + er
2. propel + er
3. shovel + ing
4. refer + al
5. repel + ent
6. confer + ed
7. suffer + ance
8. hop + ing
9. shop + ed
10. remit + ance
11. excel + ence
12. run + ing
13. wax + ed
14. droop + ed
15. drop + ing
16. accept + ance
17. refer + ence
18. beep + ing
19. endow + ing
20. mow + er

Review A — Proofreading a Paragraph to Correct Spelling Errors

Proofread the following paragraph, correcting each misspelled word.

EXAMPLE [1] In what battle were the Shawnee cheif Tecumseh, his brother, and thier followers defeatted by William Henry Harrison?
1. chief; their; defeated

HELP—
No proper nouns in Review A are misspelled.

Review A — Proofreading a Paragraph to Correct Spelling Errors

ANSWERS

1. commited–committed
2. siezing–seizing
3. forfiet–forfeit
4. succeded–succeeded
5. liveing–living
6. thier–their
7. easly–easily
8. consede–concede
9. Overun–Overrun
10. planed–planned

George Catline, *The Open Door, Known as the Prophet, Brother of Tecumseh.* National Museum of American Art, Washington, DC/Art Resource, New York.

[1] The Shawnee war chief Tecumseh was commited to the goal of uniting American Indians. [2] He believed that unification was the only way to prevent white settlers from siezing the land on which his people lived. [3] Opposed to treaties that forced Native Americans to forfiet their land, Tecumseh believed that the land was owned by no one. [4] After much hard work, he succeded in convincing some midwestern American Indian peoples to join together. [5] With his brother, known as the Shawnee Prophet, Tecumseh urged his people to preserve their traditional ways of liveing and not to surrender the land. [6] Tecumseh and the Shawnee Prophet at left led thier followers in building Prophetstown at the location indicated on the map of Indiana below. [7] In 1811, while Tecumseh was delivering a speech in a neighboring village, the governor of the Indiana Territory, William Henry Harrison, and his forces easly attacked Prophetstown. [8] Against Tecumseh's wishes, the Shawnee Prophet and his followers proceeded to counterattack and finally had to consede defeat in the Battle of Tippecanoe. [9] Overun by Harrison, Tecumseh's people scattered, leaving the town in ruins and bringing to an end twenty years of Tecumseh's work. [10] Tecumseh had planed to start over, but his death in 1813 at the Battle of the Thames ended all hopes of uniting the various Native American nations.

Forming Plurals of Nouns

26l. The singular form of a noun names one person, place, thing, or idea. The plural form names more than one. Remembering the following rules will help you spell the plural forms of nouns.

(1) For most nouns, add *s*.

SINGULAR	dog	kite	pencil	video	club	McGregor
PLURAL	dog**s**	kite**s**	pencil**s**	video**s**	club**s**	McGregor**s**

(2) For nouns ending in *s, x, z, ch,* or *sh*, add *es*.

SINGULAR	glass	suffix	waltz	trench	bush	Gomez
PLURAL	glass**es**	suffix**es**	waltz**es**	trench**es**	bush**es**	Gomez**es**

(3) For nouns ending in *y* preceded by a vowel, add *s*.

SINGULAR	alloy	turkey	essay	attorney	decoy	Sunday
PLURAL	alloy**s**	turkey**s**	essay**s**	attorney**s**	decoy**s**	Sunday**s**

(4) For nouns ending in *y* preceded by a consonant, change the *y* to *i* and add *es*.

SINGULAR	city	enemy	spy	penny	country
PLURAL	cit**ies**	enem**ies**	sp**ies**	penn**ies**	countr**ies**

NOTE For most proper nouns ending in *y* preceded by a consonant, add *s*.

EXAMPLES Murphy—Murphy**s**
Brody—Brody**s**

(5) For some nouns ending in *f* or *fe*, add *s*. For others, change the *f* or *fe* to *v* and add *es*.

SINGULAR	belief	roof	fife	wolf	knife	leaf
PLURAL	belief**s**	roof**s**	fife**s**	wol**ves**	kni**ves**	lea**ves**

(6) For nouns ending in *o* preceded by a vowel, add *s*.

SINGULAR	patio	rodeo	ratio	barrio	kangaroo	Valerio
PLURAL	patio**s**	rodeo**s**	ratio**s**	barrio**s**	kangaroo**s**	Valerio**s**

(7) For most nouns ending in *o* preceded by a consonant, add *es*.

SINGULAR	tomato	potato	hero	echo	torpedo
PLURAL	tomato**es**	potato**es**	hero**es**	echo**es**	torpedo**es**

HELP

Some one-syllable words ending in *z* double the final consonant when forming plurals.

EXAMPLES
quiz   fez
quiz**zes**   fez**zes**

HELP

For most proper nouns ending in *f* or *fe*, add *s*.

EXAMPLES
van Cleef—van Cleef**s**
Radcliffe—Radcliffe**s**

TIPS & TRICKS

Noticing how the plural is pronounced will help you remember whether to change the *f* or *fe* to *v*.

Meeting INDIVIDUAL NEEDS

ENGLISH-LANGUAGE LEARNERS

General Strategies. Not all languages form plurals by adding suffixes, as in English. For example, in Swahili, a language of East Africa, plurals are formed by changing prefixes. If you have students who speak other languages, encourage them to show how they form plurals in their native languages.

Meeting INDIVIDUAL NEEDS

MULTIPLE INTELLIGENCES

Interpersonal Intelligence. To help students learn to form plurals of nouns, divide the class into small groups. Begin the activity by reading **Rule 26l (2)** aloud. (You may want to write the rule on the chalkboard.) Set a timer for one minute. Challenge groups to think of as many singular-plural pairs as possible in that time that illustrate the subrule. Have one student in each group be the secretary and write down the words. When the timer sounds, read **Rule 26l(3),** and have students repeat the activity with a new secretary. Continue until students have illustrated all the remaining subrules of **Rule 26l**, except for **Rule 26l(1).**

Then, have groups exchange lists and check for correct spellings of plurals. When they have completed their assessments, encourage group members to identify and discuss the subrules they found most troublesome to apply.

For some common nouns ending in *o* preceded by a consonant (especially those referring to music) and for proper nouns, add *s*.

SINGULAR	taco	dojo	soprano	allegro	Sato
PLURAL	taco**s**	dojo**s**	soprano**s**	allegro**s**	Sato**s**

NOTE For some nouns ending in *o* preceded by a consonant, you may add either *s* or *es*.

SINGULAR	cargo	mosquito	motto	zero
PLURAL	cargo**s**	mosquito**s**	motto**s**	zero**s**
	or	or	or	or
	cargo**es**	mosquito**es**	motto**es**	zero**es**

(8) The plurals of a few nouns are formed irregularly.

SINGULAR	child	ox	woman	tooth	mouse	foot
PLURAL	child**ren**	ox**en**	wom**en**	t**ee**th	m**ice**	f**ee**t

(9) For a few nouns, the singular and the plural forms are the same.

SINGULAR AND PLURAL	Chinese	scissors	salmon
	sheep	aricraft	binoculars

Compound Nouns

(10) For most compound nouns, form the plural of only the last word of the compound.

SINGULAR	bookkeeper	stepchild	two-year-old	grand jury
PLURAL	bookkeeper**s**	stepchild**ren**	two-year-old**s**	grand juri**es**

(11) For compound nouns in which one of the words is modified by the other word or words, form the plural of the word modified.

SINGULAR	editor in chief	son-in-law	chief of staff	runner-up
PLURAL	editor**s** in chief	son**s**-in-law	chief**s** of staff	runner**s**-up

NOTE Some compound nouns have two acceptable plural forms.

SINGULAR	surgeon general	court-martial
PLURAL	surgeon**s** general	court**s**-martial
	or	or
	surgeon general**s**	court-martial**s**

Words Borrowed from Other Languages

(12) For some nouns borrowed from other languages, plurals are formed as in the original languages.

Singular	Plural
alumn**us** [male]	alumn**i** [male]
alumn**a** [female]	alumn**ae** [female]
phenomen**on**	phenomen**a**
parenthes**is**	parenthes**es**
dat**um**	dat**a**

NOTE A few nouns borrowed from other languages have two acceptable plural forms. For each of the following nouns, the plural form preferred in English is given first.

SINGULAR	formula	index	cactus	seraph
PLURAL	formul**as**	ind**exes**	cactus**es**	seraph**s**
	or	or	or	or
	formul**ae**	ind**ices**	cact**i**	seraph**im**

If you are ever in doubt about which spelling to use, remember that a dictionary generally lists the preferred spelling first.

Numerals, Letters, Symbols, and Words Used as Words

(13) To form the plurals of numerals, most capital letters, symbols, and most words referred to as words, add an *s* or both an apostrophe and an *s*.

SINGULAR	8	1700	T	&	and
PLURAL	8**s**	1700**s**	T**s**	&**s**	and**s**
	or	or	or	or	or
	8**'s**	1700**'s**	T**'s**	&**'s**	and**'s**

EXAMPLES His 7**s** [or 7**'s**] look like T**s** [or T**'s**].

Do not write &**s** [or &**'s**] for and**s** [or and**'s**].

Phillis Wheatley wrote during the 1700**s** [or 1700**'s**].

Looking at Language

Borrowed Nouns. Have students find in a dictionary the etymologies of the words *alumnus, alumna, phenomenon, parenthesis,* and *datum.* [*Alumnus, alumna,* and *datum* are ultimately derived from Latin. *Phenomenon* and *parenthesis* ultimately come from Greek.] Then, direct students' attention to the **Note** on p. 789. You may want to challenge students to find in a dictionary other borrowed nouns that have two acceptable plural forms in English.

HELP
Whenever you are unsure how to form the plural of a word, look up the word in a dictionary.

Exercise 6 Spelling the Plurals of Nouns

ANSWERS

1. girls
2. valleys
3. skies
4. coaches
5. Japanese
6. sisters-in-law
7. solos
8. selves
9. notebooks
10. stereos
11. cafeterias
12. dormitories
13. geese
14. parentheses
15. diaries
16. blizzards
17. patios
18. deer *or* deers
19. abolitionists
20. 1900s *or* 1900's

Review B Applying Spelling Rules

ANSWERS

1. *crises:* Some nouns borrowed from other languages form their plurals as they do in the original languages. **Rule 26l(12)**
2. *deceive:* Write *ie* when the sound is long *e*, except after *c*. **Rule 26b**
3. *proceed:* The only English words ending in *–ceed* are *exceed*, *proceed*, and *succeed*. **Rule 26d**
4. *placement:* Keep the final silent *e* before adding a suffix beginning with a consonant. **Rule 26h**
5. *sopranos:* Some common nouns ending in *o* preceded by a consonant, especially those referring to music, form the plural by adding only *s*. **Exception to Rule 26l(7)**
6. *misstep:* When adding a prefix, do not change the spelling of the original word. **Rule 26e**
7. *meanness:* When adding the suffix *–ly* or *–ness* do not change the spelling of the original word. **Rule 26f**
8. *noticeable:* Keep the final silent *e* in a word ending in *ce* or *ge* before a suffix beginning with *a* or *o*. **Exception to Rule 26g**

STYLE TIP

When forming the plurals of numerals, letters, symbols, and words used as words, using both an apostrophe and an *s* is never wrong. Therefore, if you have any doubt about whether or not to use the apostrophe, it is usually best to use it.

To prevent confusion, add both an apostrophe and an *s* to form the plurals of all lowercase letters, certain capital letters, and some words referred to as words.

EXAMPLES The word *accommodate* has two *a*'s, two *c*'s, two *o*'s, and two *m*'s.

His essay is filled with *I*'s. [Without an apostrophe, the plural of the pronoun *I* could be confused with the word *Is*.]

Make sure that each one of your *her*'s has a clear antecedent. [Without an apostrophe, the plural of the word *her* could be confused with the possessive pronoun *hers*.]

Exercise 6 Spelling the Plurals of Nouns

Write the plural form of each of the following nouns.

EXAMPLES
1. piano
1. *pianos*
2. curriculum
2. *curricula*

1. girl
2. valley
3. sky
4. coach
5. Japanese
6. sister-in-law
7. solo
8. self
9. notebook
10. stereo
11. cafeteria
12. dormitory
13. goose
14. parenthesis
15. diary
16. blizzard
17. patio
18. deer
19. abolitionist
20. 1900

Review B Applying Spelling Rules

Use Rules 26b–26l to explain the spellings of the following words.

EXAMPLE
1. boxes
1. Add *es* to form the plural of a noun ending in *x*.

1. crises
2. deceive
3. proceed
4. placement
5. sopranos
6. misstep
7. meanness
8. noticeable
9. referred
10. countries

Writing Numbers

26m. Spell out a number that begins a sentence.

EXAMPLE **Two thousand** students attend Shawnee High School, I believe.

If a number appears awkward when spelled out, revise the sentence so that it does not begin with the number.

EXAMPLE I believe the number of students who attend Shawnee High School is **2,103**.

26n. Spell out a *cardinal number*—a number that states how many—that can be expressed in one or two words. Otherwise, use numerals.

EXAMPLES
| **fourteen** dogs | **thirty-one** days | **one thousand** votes |
| **514** dogs | **331** days | **2,670** votes |

Generally, do not spell out some numbers and use numerals for others in the same context. If numerals are required for any of the numbers, be consistent by using numerals for all of the numbers.

INCONSISTENT In the election, Lou Ann received ninety votes, and Darla received 103.

CONSISTENT In the election, Lou Ann received **90** votes, and Darla received **103**.

However, to distinguish between numbers that appear beside each other but that count different things, spell out one number and use numerals for the other.

EXAMPLE They bought **two 25**-pound bags of dog food.

26o. Spell out an *ordinal number*—a number that expresses order.

EXAMPLE My brother placed **third** [not *3rd*] in the **first** [not *1st*] race.

26p. Use numerals to express numbers in conventional situations.

Conventional situations include

- identification numbers

EXAMPLES
| Room **16** | pages **359–407** | Chapter **3** |
| Channel **32** | Interstate **10** | Rule **26k** |

STYLE TIP

For large round numbers, you may use words only, numerals only, or a combination of words and numerals.

EXAMPLES
eight million dollars
or
$8 million

32,800,000,000
or
32.8 billion

Reference Note

Compound cardinal numbers from twenty-one to ninety-nine are hyphenated. For more about **hyphenated numbers**, see page 768.

HELP

Compound ordinal numbers from twenty-first to ninety-ninth are hyphenated.

ANSWERS continued

9. *referred:* Double the final consonant before adding a suffix that begins with a vowel if the word (1) has the accent on the final syllable and (2) ends in a single consonant preceded by a single vowel. **Rule 26k**

10. *countries:* If the noun ends in *y* preceded by a consonant, change the *y* to *i* and add *es*. **Rule 26l(4)**

Meeting INDIVIDUAL NEEDS

LEARNERS HAVING DIFFICULTY
To help students review the rules and examples in this chapter, give each student a stack of index cards. Ask students to make a flashcard for each spelling rule—with the rule and any exceptions on one side of the card and with original examples on the other side. Then, organize students into pairs. Encourage students to take turns displaying their examples and asking their partners to state the rules that apply.

Review C — Proofreading a Paragraph to Correct Spelling Errors

ANSWERS
1. fortyeth–fortieth
2. learrner's–learner's
3. wifes–wives
4. hopeing–hoping
5. heavyly–heavily
6. 85–eighty-five
7. unecessary–unnecessary
8. truely–truly
9. chiped–chipped
10. planing–planning, fiftieth

STYLE TIP

In sentences, spell out the names of units of measurement (such as *pounds* and *feet*) whether they stand alone or follow numerals or spelled-out numbers. In charts and tables, however, you may use the abbreviations for units of measurement (such as *lb* and *ft*) when they follow numerals.

Similarly, spell out the words for symbols (such as *degrees* for ° and *percent* for %). In charts and tables, however, you may use the symbols when they follow numerals.

STYLE TIP

Do not use *A.M.* or *P.M.* with a spelled-out number or as a substitute for the words *morning, afternoon,* and *evening*.

INCORRECT
The concert begins at eight P.M.

CORRECT
The concert begins at **8:00 P.M.** (or **eight o'clock in the evening**).

- measurements/statistics

EXAMPLES 68 degrees   4½ feet   14.5 pounds
20 percent   16 years old   score of 32 to 18

- addresses

EXAMPLES 18 Kresge Way   Charlotte, NC 28243-0018

- dates

EXAMPLES May 5, 2000   44 B.C.   A.D. 893

- times of day

EXAMPLES 6:30 A.M.   11:15 P.M.

NOTE Spell out a number used with *o'clock*.

EXAMPLE **five o'clock** in the morning

Review C — Proofreading a Paragraph to Correct Spelling Errors

Proofread the following paragraph, correcting the misspelled or misused words or expressions.

EXAMPLE [1] 5 days ago, all of the members of my family except one joined my grandparentes in a lovly celebration of their wedding anniversary.

1. Five; grandparents; lovely

[1] Last Saturday my mom's parents, Grandma and Grandpa Reyes, celebrated their fortyeth anniversary by repeating their wedding vows in a beautiful ceremony at St. Teresa's Church. [2] Since I have my learrner's permit now and it was light out when we went to the church, Mom let me drive. [3] My aunts and uncles on Mom's side of the family were there with their husbands and wifes. [4] In addition, all of my cousins except Ernesto, whom I had been especially hopeing to see, attended the ceremony. [5] Unfortunately, the flights from Denver, where Ernesto goes to college, had been canceled because it had snowed heavyly there the night before. [6] Although I missed Ernesto, I enjoyed visiting with many of the 85 friends and family members who had come to the celebration. [7] Grandma and Grandpa had insisted that anniversary gifts were unecessary, but this time they were overruled. [8] You could tell that they were truely stunned when they

opened the gift from their children. [9] Mom and her sisters and brothers had chiped in to buy them plane tickets to Mexico City, where they were born. [10] Everyone had such a good time that we have already started planing for Grandma and Grandpa's 50th anniversary.

Words Often Confused

You can prevent many spelling errors by learning the difference between the words grouped together in this section. Some of them are confusing because they are **homonyms**—that is, they are pronounced alike. Others are confusing because they are spelled the same or nearly the same.

Reference Note
In the Glossary of Usage, Chapter 20, you can find many other words that are often confused or misused. You can also look the words up in a dictionary.

affect	[verb] to influence
	How did that sad movie *affect* you?
effect	[verb] to accomplish, to bring about; [noun] a consequence; a result
	Head Start centers can *effect* an improvement in the lives of many children.
	What *effect* did the rain have on the crops?
all ready	[adjective] all prepared
	We were *all ready* to leave.
already	[adverb] previously
	We had *already* painted the sets.
all right	[adjective] satisfactory; [adverb] satisfactorily
	The match was difficult, but your playing was *all right*. I think I did *all right*, too. [This is the only acceptable spelling. Although the spelling *alright* is in some dictionaries, it has not become standard usage.]
all together	[adjective] in the same place; [adverb] at the same time
	The players were *all together* in the gym.
	Sing *all together*, now.
altogether	[adverb] entirely
	I am not *altogether* convinced.
altar	[noun] a table or stand at which religious rites are performed
	When you reach the *altar*, you must kneel.
alter	[verb] to change
	When did you *alter* the schedule?

(continued)

RESOURCES

Words Often Confused
Practice
- *Grammar, Usage, and Mechanics,* pp. 354, 355, 356, 357, 358

- *Language Workshop CD-ROM,* Lesson 49

TEACHING TIP

Mnemonics. Direct students' attention to the information in **Tips & Tricks** on pp. 794, 797, 798, and 799. Explain to students that such memory devices, or mnemonics, may help them master the spellings and uses of other troublesome words. Share the following mnemonics with students, and then call on volunteers to add to the list.

1. all right—Alright is all wrong.
2. dessert—When dessert is served, some often want two (two s's).
3. hear—We hear with our ears.

TIPS & TRICKS

Here is an easy way to remember the difference between *capital* and *capitol*. There is a d**o**me on the capit**o**l building.

TIPS & TRICKS

Here is an easy way to remember the difference between *complement* and *compliment*. A compl**e**ment is something that compl**e**tes.

(continued)

brake	[verb] to *slow down or to stop;* [noun] *a device used to slow down or to stop* She tried to *brake* the bicycle with the hand *brake.*
break	[verb] *to cause to come apart, to fracture;* [noun] *a fracture* I did not *break* my wrist; I sprained it. The doctor said it is not a *break,* but a sprain.
capital	[noun] *center of government; money or property used in business;* [adjective] *punishable by death; of major importance; excellent; uppercase* What is the *capital* of Zimbabwe? You need *capital* to start a business. Do you support *capital* punishment? Begin every sentence with a *capital* letter.
capitol	[noun] *a building where a legislature meets* We could see the *capitol* from our hotel.
choose	[verb, rhymes with *shoes*] *to select* We *choose* partners today.
chose	[verb, past form of *choose*, rhymes with *nose*] *selected* Each of us *chose* a partner yesterday.
coarse	[adjective] *rough, crude* Burlap is a *coarse* fabric.
course	[noun] *a part of a meal; a series of studies; a playing field; a path of action;* [also used after *of* to mean *naturally* or *certainly*] She skipped the first *course* at dinner. The speech *course* helped my diction. A new golf *course* opened last week. What *course* will resolve the conflict? Of *course,* you are always welcome.
complement	[noun] *that which makes whole or complete;* [verb] *to make whole or complete* Without a *complement,* the sentence is incomplete. That scarf *complements* your outfit nicely.
compliment	[noun] *praise, a courteous act or statement;* [verb] *to express praise or respect* He received many *compliments* on his cooking. I *complimented* her on her success.

794 Chapter 26 Spelling

MINI-LESSON

Pronunciation and Meaning. As shown on p. 795, *des´ert* (n.) and *de•sert´* (v.) are spelled the same but are different parts of speech and are stressed differently. You may want to introduce students to other such pairs of words.

1. *con´flict* (n.) an opposition
   con•flict´ (v.) to be in opposition
2. *per´mit* (n.) a document granting permission
   per•mit´ (v.) to allow

consul	[noun] *a person appointed by a government to serve its citizens in a foreign country* The United States *consul* in Tokyo met with a group of tourists.
council	[noun] *a group called together to accomplish a job* Members of the *council* voted on the resolution.
counsel	[noun] *advice;* [verb] *to advise* Sue followed her aunt's *counsel*. Sue's aunt *counseled* her to take judo lessons.
councilor	[noun] *a member of a council* The majority of the *councilors* voted for the resolution.
counselor	[noun] *an advisor* Ask your guidance *counselor*.
desert	[noun, pronounced des′•ert] *a dry region* The caravan crossed the *desert* at night.
desert	[verb, pronounced de•sert′] *to leave or abandon* They did not *desert* the sinking ship.
dessert	[noun, pronounced des•sert′] *the final, sweet course of a meal* For *dessert* we had fresh fruit.

Exercise 7 Distinguishing Between Words Often Confused

From the choices in parentheses, select the correct word or word group for each of the following sentences.

EXAMPLE 1. Is the Kalahari (*Desert, Dessert*) in Africa?
  1. Desert

1. They were (*all together, altogether*) in favor of the party.
2. The illness has had a strange (*affect, effect*) on everyone.
3. My cousin knows the (*capitol, capital*) city of every state.
4. Have you had your car's (*brakes, breaks*) inspected?
5. The British (*council, consul*) (*counciled, counseled*) the reporter to leave the country.
6. After all his worry, everything turned out (*all right, alright*).
7. Christopher said that the two new players for the guard position will (*compliment, complement*) our basketball team.
8. The actors were (*all ready, already*) for the audition.
9. My uncle will serve either flan or sopapillas for (*desert, dessert*).
10. Did you (*choose, chose*) that topic for your essay?

Cooperative Learning

Some of the often-confused words are **homonyms**—words that sound alike but have different spellings and meanings. Have students work in pairs to generate a list of at least five additional homonyms, along with their parts of speech and definitions. You could offer the following examples to help students begin:

1. **aisle** (n.) a path
   I'll the contraction for *I will*
   isle (n.) an island
2. **beat** (v.) to pound
        (n.) a pulse
   beet (n.) a vegetable
3. **crews** (n.) groups of workers
   cruise (v.) to sail
          (n.) a water voyage
   cruse (n.) a small container for liquid

Have students share their lists with one another, perhaps by asking them to create and display posters in the classroom.

MECHANICS

---

3. *pres´ent* (adj.) in attendance
   pres´ent (n.) now
   pre•sent´ (v.) to give
4. *pro´duce* (n.) something made
   pro•duce´ (v.) to make

Ask students to use the words in sentences, paying particular attention to pronunciation and meaning.

MECHANICS

Relating to Literature

Have students read an excerpt from a work of fiction in which nonstandard English is used; Mark Twain's *The Adventures of Huckleberry Finn* is a good choice. Then, ask students to identify the words spelled phonetically rather than according to the rules of standard, formal English. Ask students what the author's purpose might have been in using phonetic spellings. [*Representing colloquial speech phonetically can help make characters believable.*]

RUBES by Leigh Rubin. By permission of Leigh Rubin and Creators Syndicate.

Miner surgery.

formally	[adverb] *in a proper or dignified manner, according to strict rules* Do you plan to dress *formally* for the party?
formerly	[adverb] *previously, in the past* This lake was *formerly* a valley.
hear	[verb] *to receive sounds through the ears* Please speak up; I can't *hear* you.
here	[adverb] *at this place* Let's sit *here*.
its	[possessive form of *it*] *belonging to it* The town has not raised *its* tax rate in years.
it's	[contraction of *it is* or *it has*] *It's* cold, and *it's* started to snow.
lead	[verb, rhymes with *need*] *to go first; to guide* Who will *lead* the Juneteenth parade?
led	[verb, past form of *lead*] He *led* us five miles out of the way.
lead	[noun, rhymes with *red*] *graphite in a pencil; a heavy metal* A pencil *lead* is not made of the metal *lead*.
loose	[adjective, rhymes with *goose*] *free; not close together; not firmly fastened* I forgot to lock the gate, and now the pigs are *loose*. Put all your *loose* papers in a folder. My little brother has two *loose* teeth.
lose	[verb, rhymes with *snooze*] *to suffer loss of* Don't *lose* your tickets.
miner	[noun] *a worker in a mine* The trapped *miners* were finally rescued.
minor	[noun] *a person under legal age;* [adjective] *less important* The curfew applies only to *minors*. He suffered *minor* injuries in the accident.
moral	[adjective] *good, virtuous;* [noun] *a lesson of conduct* We admire a *moral* person. The story's *moral* is "Look before you leap."
morale	[noun] *mental condition, spirit* After three defeats, the team's *morale* was low.

Chapter 26 Spelling

passed	[verb, past form of *pass*] went by, beyond, over, or through The tortoise *passed* the hare and won the race.
past	[noun] time gone by; [adjective] of a former time; [preposition] beyond Sitting Bull told many stories about the *past*. Adele read the minutes of the *past* meeting. The dog walked right *past* the cat.
peace	[noun] calmness (as opposed to strife or war) All hoped that the treaty would bring *peace*.
piece	[noun] a part of something We found the missing *piece* of the puzzle.

TIPS & TRICKS

Here is a way to remember the difference between *peace* and *piece*. You eat a p**ie**ce of p**ie**.

Exercise 8 Distinguishing Between Words Often Confused

From the choices in parentheses, select the correct word for each of the following sentences.

EXAMPLE 1. Marcy would like a (*peace, piece*) of pumpkin bread.
          1. piece

1. Where did you (*here, hear*) that Kiowa legend?
2. If you (*lose, loose*) the directions, we will never get there.
3. The mail from home improved the troops' (*moral, morale*).
4. The estate is being held in trust until the heir is no longer a (*minor, miner*).
5. My horse (*lead, led*) the parade.
6. In only a few minutes, the guest speaker will be (*hear, here*).
7. After he went on a diet, his clothes were too (*lose, loose*).
8. (*Formerly, Formally*), Lauryn Hill performed with the Fugees.
9. (*It's, Its*) not every day that her parents let her use the car.
10. On the tour, we (*past, passed*) the homes of many celebrities.

Review D Proofreading an Article for Errors in the Use of Words Often Confused

Proofread the article on the next page, correcting each incorrectly used word. If all words in a sentence are already used correctly, write *C*.

EXAMPLE [1] The state legislature was not in session when the NHS members toured the capital.
        1. capitol

HELP

Some sentences in Review D contain more than one error.

MECHANICS

1. capital

2. capitol
3. led

4. formerly
5. all ready
6. C

7. minors/hear

8. it's

9. counselor/past

10. C

TIPS & TRICKS

Here is an easy way to remember the difference between *principal* and *principle*. The princi**pal** is your **pal**.

NHS MEMBERS MEET GOVERNOR
by Cornelia Charnes, Staff Writer

[1] One of the advantages of living in the state ~~capitol~~ is having the opportunity to see state government up close. [2] Last Friday, twenty-seven members of our school's National Honor Society chapter toured the nearby ~~capital~~ building. [3] Tour guide Floyd Welty, who ~~lead~~ the group, outlined the workings of the government's three branches and pointed out many of the building's architectural features. [4] The students ate lunch in the underground cafeteria and even got to meet Governor (~~formally~~ State Senator) Iola Jones.

[5] The group met Governor Jones just as they were ~~already~~ to leave the building. [6] Said student Botan Park, "Governor Jones shook hands with each of us and complimented us on being honor students. [7] Even though we're still ~~miners~~, she told us, 'I want to ~~here~~ from you whenever you have a concern with my administration's policies.'"

[8] "Of course," added student Elena Cruz, "~~its~~ her first term as governor, and we will be eligible to vote when she comes up for reelection."

[9] The group's sponsor, guidance ~~councilor~~ Diego Vargas, said, "I have been taking groups there for the ~~passed~~ ten years, but I have never met a governor before. [10] Meeting Governor Jones had a big effect on the students and on me."

personal	[adjective] individual, private
	The store manager gave us her *personal* attention.
personnel	[noun] a group of people employed in the same work or service
	The management added *personnel* to handle the increased workload.
principal	[noun] the head of a school; [adjective] main or most important
	The *principal* of our school is Mr. Osaka.
	The *principal* export of Brazil is coffee.
principle	[noun] a rule of conduct; a fact or a general truth
	Her *principles* are very high.
	Dr. Martin Luther King, Jr., supported the *principle* of nonviolence.
quiet	[adjective] silent, still
	The library is a *quiet* place to study.
quite	[adverb] completely, rather, very
	Are you *quite* sure this is the right path?

shone	[verb, past form of *shine*] gave off light The stars *shone* brightly last night.
shown	[verb, past participle tense of *show*] put or brought into view The slides were *shown* after dinner.
stationary	[adjective] in a fixed position Are these desks movable or *stationary*?
stationery	[noun] writing paper Colored *stationery* is not appropriate for business letters.
than	[conjunction, used for comparisons] She arrived earlier *than* I did.
then	[adverb] at that time; next I didn't know you *then*. We swam for an hour; *then* we ate.
their	[possessive of *they*] belonging to them *Their* apartment has a view of the river.
there	[adverb] at that place; [also used as an expletive to begin a sentence] I have not been *there* in a long time. *There* is too much pepper in my soup.
they're	[contraction of *they are*] *They're* reading a book by Virginia Driving Hawk Sneve.

Here is an easy way to remember the difference between *stationary* and *stationery*. You write a lett**er** on station**er**y.

Reference Note

For information on **possessive pronouns,** see page 556. For information on **adverbs,** see page 422. For information on **forming contractions,** see page 763.

Exercise 9 Distinguishing Between Words Often Confused

From the choices in parentheses, select the correct word for each of the following sentences.

EXAMPLE 1. We stayed in San Juan longer (*than, then*) we had planned.
    1. than

1. I am learning some of the (*principals, principles*) of physics.
2. The gold ring (*shone, shown*) with a warm glow.
3. He acts much older (*than, then*) he is.
4. The bookstore is having a big sale on (*stationery, stationary*).
5. You ask too many (*personnel, personal*) questions.
6. Soon after the strange uproar, all became (*quite, quiet*) again.
7. The *pad thai* they serve here is (*quite, quiet*) good.

8. Several Pueblo artists are displaying (*there*, *their*, *they're*) work.
9. If you see the (*principle*, *principal*) in the hall, tell her she's wanted in the main office.
10. (*Their*, *They're*, *There*) parents may not let them go.

to	[preposition; also part of the infinitive form of a verb] Please return these books *to* the library. He began *to* whistle.
too	[adverb] *also; more than enough* Rubén Blades is a musician and an attorney, *too*. You are *too* young to drive.
two	[adjective] *the sum of one + one*; [noun] *the number between one and three* I will graduate in *two* years. *Two* of my friends and I have great tickets for the Yo-Yo Ma concert.
waist	[noun] *the midsection of the body* At the Japanese restaurant, the server wore an obi around her *waist*.
waste	[noun] *a needless expense; unused material;* [verb] *to use foolishly* Waiting in line was a *waste* of time. *Waste* not; want not.
weather	[noun] *conditions outdoors* As the meteorologist predicted, the *weather* has been perfect all week.
whether	[conjunction; indicates alternative or doubt] They don't know *whether* or not they will go to the concert next weekend.
who's	[contraction of *who is* or *who has*] *Who's* there? *Who's* been coaching them?
whose	[possessive form of *who*] *belonging to whom* *Whose* book is this?
your	[possessive form of *you*] *belonging to you* *Your* coat is in the closet.
you're	[contraction of *you are*] *You're* always on time.

800   Chapter 26   Spelling

Learning for Life

Continued on pp. 801–802

The Importance of Proofreading. Discuss with students the importance of proofreading, especially for errors in spelling. Explain that writing that contains misspellings may give the reader the impression that the writer is careless, lazy, or irresponsible. Furthermore, the misspellings may be so distracting that the reader is unable to focus on the meaning of the writing.

Some students may mention that computer spellcheckers help to eliminate

Exercise 10 — Distinguishing Between Words Often Confused

From the choices in parentheses, select the correct word for each of the following sentences.

EXAMPLE 1. Are you planning (*to, too, two*) go (*to, too, two*) the dance, (*to, too, two*)?

1. to; to; too

1. Around his (*waste, waist*) he wore a handmade leather belt.
2. (*You're, Your*) mother made a delicious Korean dinner of *bulgogi*.
3. There was (*too, to, two*) much traffic on the interstate for us (*too, to, two*) enjoy the ride.
4. (*Whose, Who's*) going to use that ticket now?
5. It really doesn't matter (*whose, who's*) fault it is this time.
6. You, (*to, two, too*), can be a better speller if you try.
7. (*Weather, Whether*) or not it rains, we will be there.
8. Don't you agree that this is fine (*whether, weather*) for a softball game, Ivory?
9. (*Your, You're*) sure Ms. Thompson wanted to see me?
10. I don't know (*whose, who's*) taller, Hakeem Olajuwon or Reggie Miller.

Exercise 11 — Proofreading a Paragraph to Correct Errors in the Use of Words Often Confused

Proofread the following paragraph, correcting errors in the use of words often confused.

EXAMPLE [1] Who's face is on this postage stamp?

1. Whose

[1] The face on the postage stamp on the next page is that of Benjamin Banneker, considered too be the first African American man of science. [2] First issued on February 15, 1980, this stamp honors a man who's contributions in the areas of mathematics and astronomy are impressive. [3] Banneker grew up on a farm in Maryland in the 1700s, a time when life was particularly difficult for African American people weather they were slaves or not. [4] Although free, Banneker, to, faced prejudice and discrimination. [5] However, a neighbor who was interested in science gave some astronomy equipment too Banneker.

Exercise 11 Proofreading a Paragraph to Correct Errors in the Use of Words Often Confused

ANSWERS

1. too–to
2. who's–whose
3. weather–whether
4. to–too
5. too–to

Exercise 11 Proofreading a Paragraph to Correct Errors in the Use of Words Often Confused

ANSWERS continued
6. waisted–wasted
7. whether–weather
8. to–two
9. waisted–wasted
10. your–you're

Relating to Speaking

Mispronunciations sometimes cause misspellings. To demonstrate the difference between the misspoken word and the correctly spelled word, write the following chart on the chalkboard. Read aloud each word or word group, pronouncing clearly the underlined parts. Call on volunteers to add other examples.

Misspoken	Correctly Spelled
r<u>ow</u> model	r<u>ole</u> model
c<u>or</u>poration	c<u>oo</u>peration
mirr<u>ow</u>	mirr<u>or</u>
ped<u>al stool</u>	ped<u>es</u>tal
jew<u>lery</u>	jew<u>elry</u>

Review E Proofreading an Essay to Correct Errors in Spelling and in the Use of Words Often Confused

ANSWERS
1. occured–occurred, too–to
2. their–there
3. tryed–tried
4. shakeing–shaking, noticably–noticeably
5. C
6. coarse–course, peice–piece, ilegal–illegal
7. proceded–proceeded, steadyly–steadily, overeact–overreact
8. C
9. alright–all right, accidentaly–accidentally, slamed–slammed, breaks–brakes
10. niether–neither, sustainned–sustained, injurys–injuries, mistakeing–mistaking

---

[6] Banneker waisted no time in using it to determine when the sun and moon rose and set, when the brightest stars set, and when eclipses occurred. [7] All of this information was very helpful to a variety of people, including sailors who needed to chart courses and farmers who needed to know the whether. [8] Banneker compiled his data into an almanac, and after to or three attempts, he succeeded in getting his almanacs published each year for several years. [9] These popular books received widespread attention, and Benjamin Banneker became a symbol of what African Americans could do when their lives were not waisted in slavery. [10] If your someone who collects commemorative postage stamps, you will likely want this one, which celebrates the achievements of this gifted scientist.

Review E Proofreading an Essay to Correct Errors in Spelling and in the Use of Words Often Confused

HELP — Some sentences in Review E contain more than one error.

Proofread the following paragraphs, correcting errors in spelling and in the use of words often confused. If all the words in a sentence are correct, write *C*.

EXAMPLE [1] When you take the road test for your driver's license, I hope that you're expereince will be better then mine was.

1. your; experience; than

[1] One of my most embarrassing moments occured the day I took the road test too get my driver's license. [2] Since one of the branches of the Motor Vehicle Department is near my dad's office, I met Dad their after school. [3] He tryed to calm me down by telling me that the world would not end if I did not pass the first time. [4] Still, my hands were shakeing noticably when I got behind the wheel.

[5] The examiner, Mrs. Ferro, was very patient. [6] She assured me that the coarse was "a peice of cake" and that she would not ask me to do anything ilegal to try to trick me. [7] She said I would be fine if I just proceded steadyly and did not overeact to her instructions.

[8] Everything went surprisingly well until we reached the end of the course and Mrs. Ferro told me to stop the car and turn off the ignition. [9] I stopped, alright; I accidentaly slamed on the breaks so hard that we both went lurching forward against our seat belts. [10] Luckily, niether of us sustainned any injurys, and I succeeded in passing the test, despite mistakeing the end of the course for a cliff.

802 Chapter 26 Spelling

Learning for Life

drafts backward to focus on individual words and to avoid being distracted by other words in the sentence. Ask students to circle any questionable spellings. Then, have students exchange papers and repeat the procedure. Finally, ask the readers of each rough draft to work together to confirm and correct any misspellings. If students are in doubt about any of their corrections, encourage them to refer to the rules and examples in this chapter or to use a dictionary.

CHAPTER 26

Chapter Review

A. Proofreading Sentences to Correct Spelling Errors

Proofread the following sentences, and correctly write the misspelled words. If a sentence is already correct, write *C*.

HELP—
None of the proper nouns in the Chapter Review are misspelled. Some sentences in the Chapter Review contain more than one error.

1. The new model with two sliding doors will ~~supercede~~ the old model with only one. **1.** supersede
2. We had to wait for a long time at the level crossing for the ~~frieght~~ train to pass. **2.** freight
3. The restaurants of New Orleans are known for their atmosphere and fine ~~dineing~~. **3.** dining
4. On the long drive through the Australian outback, we saw several kangaroos ~~hoping~~ alongside the road. **4.** hopping
5. When nations are ~~enemys~~, they send ~~spys~~ to gather information about one another. **5.** enemies/spies
6. Last Saturday we felt tired, so we decided to stay home and rent a couple of ~~videoes~~. **6.** videos
7. Timothy Grant is actually one of my ~~brother-in laws~~; the other is Sammy Dunn. **7.** brothers-in-law
8. Dot your *i*'s and cross your *t*'s, as my aunt Edna always used to say. **8.** C
9. Do we put those figures inside brackets, or should we use ~~parenthesises~~? **9.** parentheses
10. ~~245~~ people signed the petition. **10.** Two hundred forty-five
11. The great French writer Voltaire lived during the 1700s. **11.** C [*or* 1700's]
12. The best-looking horses at the ranch were a pair of ~~three-years-old~~. **12.** three-year-olds
13. Is this word ~~mispelled~~? **13.** misspelled
14. People should be considerate of each other and not display ~~meaness~~ or hostility. **14.** meanness
15. The first impression of the cathedral interior was one of great, echoing ~~emptyness~~. **15.** emptiness
16. As Mr. Spock would say, their decision was ~~ilogical~~. **16.** illogical
17. Dad impulsively sent away for a set of Japanese steak ~~knifes~~. **17.** knives
18. On the sewing table there were a sewing kit, a bolt of cloth, and Mom's and Grandma's ~~scissorses~~. **18.** scissors

Using the Chapter Review

To assess student progress, you may want to compare the types of items missed on the **Diagnostic Preview** with those missed on the **Chapter Review.** If students have not made significant progress, you may want to refer them to **Exercises 33** and **34** in **Chapter 27: Correcting Common Errors** for additional practice.

MECHANICS

Chapter Review 803

19. When he writes, his eights look like threes. **19. C**
20. My brother Walter wieghs one hundred and forty pounds and stands six feet tall. **20. weighs**

B. Proofreading a Paragraph to Correct Spelling Errors

Proofread the following paragraph, and correctly write the misspelled words. If a sentence is already correct, write *C*.

21. choose
22. course/extremely/patient
23. C
24. Normally
25. C

26. teeth
27. they're
28. propellers
29. their/especially
30. Whether/beautiful

[21] If I had to chose my favorite animal, it might be the Florida manatee, or sea cow. [22] Of coarse, I like dogs, cats, and elephants, but I have heard that manatees are extremly gentle and pateint. [23] I also read somewhere that manatees are more closely related to elephants than to seals or whales. [24] Normaly, manatees live near the shore in swamps or near the banks of canals. [25] A hungry sea cow can eat two hundred pounds of grass. [26] Unlike many other animals, manatees never run out of teath. [27] Manatees are very useful in clearing vegetation from the canals, so there often protected by law. [28] However, boat propelers often injure the animals. [29] Also, manatees and there cousins the dugongs have been hunted, especialy as sources of meat and oil. [30] Weather these beautyful creatures manage to survive as a species depends largely on us humans.

C. Distinguishing Between Words Often Confused

For each of the following sentences, write the correct word or words in parentheses.

31. That organization is growing; it is (*there, they're, their*) belief that society should devote more resources to the poor.
32. The sky is (*quite, quiet*) clear this evening, so we should be able to see the constellations.
33. The tiger slowly made (*its, it's*) way through the underbrush and then disappeared from view.
34. The gardener gave me a (*personal, personnel*) tour of the center's famous rose garden.
35. "Don't (*waste, waist*) your money on that CD; the songs are terrible," Luis warned us.
36. The mayor welcomed the new Swedish (*council, consul, counsel*) and her staff at a special reception.

RESOURCES

Spelling
Review
- *Grammar, Usage, and Mechanics,* pp. 359, 360, 361, 362, 363

Assessment
- *Assessment Package*
  —*Chapter Tests,* Ch. 26
  —*Chapter Tests in Standardized Test Formats,* Ch. 26
- *Test Generator (One-Stop Planner CD-ROM)*

37. I'm not sure what is meant by a (*capitol*, *capital*) offense.
38. The stock market crash in 1929 (*affected*, *effected*) the economy.
39. Do you know if the movie will be (*shone*, *shown*) at the children's film series?
40. Working conditions for coal (*minors*, *miners*) in the United States improved significantly during the twentieth century.
41. (*Your*, *You're*) coat is lying on the sofa.
42. We went out after dinner, but there were (*two*, *to*, *too*) many people in the street, so we came home.
43. What is the (*capitol*, *capital*) of Portugal?
44. Put on the emergency (*brake*, *break*) when you park on a hill.
45. Sometimes it's hard to know the (*moral*, *morale*) thing to do, but we must try.
46. She was so considerate that we (*complimented*, *complemented*) her on her kindness.
47. Striding off into the fields, Archie (*led*, *lead*) his troupe toward the mountains.
48. It was remarkable to watch the space shuttle land at great speed and for it to be completely (*stationery*, *stationary*) minutes later.
49. Uncle Ruben never eats junk food; he worries about his (*waste*, *waist*).
50. When you apply for a job, your application is forwarded to the (*personal*, *personnel*) department.

Writing Application
Using Correct Spelling in an Application Letter

Spelling Words   Imagine the best job you could have. Then, write the letter of application that will get you that job. The letter should be short—no longer than two paragraphs—and should be as clear as possible. In your letter use ten words from the spelling list on the following pages.

Prewriting   Start by making a list of five jobs that might interest you. Do some research in specialist publications or on the Internet to find the major requirements of your dream job so that you can use professional terms authoritatively in your letter. Once you have drawn up a list of dream jobs, choose one job and freewrite about it. Write down as many details as you can to describe the job, its responsibilities, and where you see the job taking you in the future.

Writing Use your freewriting notes to help you write the first draft of your letter. You may want to begin your letter by stating how you learned of the job opening. Then, go on to explain how your training and experience make you suited for this particular job.

Revising Ask a classmate to play the part of a personnel officer, and read your letter to him or her. Rearrange or cut details to make the letter more effective.

Publishing Proofread your letter for any errors in grammar, usage, and mechanics. Be sure that all words are spelled correctly. With your teacher's approval, you might suggest a contest among your classmates to determine which students get their dream jobs. Post the completed letters on the class bulletin board or Web page, and follow up with the announcement of the successful applicants.

100 Commonly Misspelled Words

ache	could	happiness	raise	tonight
again	country	having	read	too
always	dear	hear	ready	trouble
among	doctor	here	said	truly
answered	does	hoarse	says	Tuesday
any	don't	hour	scene	two
been	done	instead	seems	very
beginning	early	knew	separate	wear
believe	easy	know	shoes	Wednesday
break	enemy	laid	similar	week
built	enough	loose	since	where
business	every	lose	straight	whether
busy	existence	making	sugar	which
buy	February	meant	sure	whole
can't	finally	minute	tear	women
chief	forty	none	their	won't
choose	friend	often	there	would
color	grammar	once	though	write
coming	guess	piece	through	writing
cough	half	probably	tired	wrote

300 Spelling Words

absence	agriculture	athlete	civilization
absorption	amateur		cocoon
abundant	ambassador	bankruptcy	commencement
acceptable	analysis	basically	commissioner
accidentally	analyze	beneficial	committed
accommodation	angel	benefited	comparative
accompaniment	annual	bicycle	comparison
accurate	apparatus	breathe	competition
accustomed	appearance	brilliant	conceivable
achievement	application	bulletin	confidential
acquaintance	appropriate		confirmation
actuality	approximately	calendar	conscientious
adequately	arousing	category	consciousness
administration	arrangement	changeable	consequently
adolescent	ascend	characteristic	considerable
aggressive	association	chemistry	consistency
		circumstance	

Spelling Words **807**

Meeting INDIVIDUAL NEEDS

ADVANCED LEARNERS
Some students will not have any difficulty spelling the words in the **100 Commonly Misspelled Words** list. Allow such students to work as a group to compile a list of words that they have encountered in their reading and have difficulty spelling. Students can then study words from the list they have compiled instead of spending time studying words they already know how to spell.

Cooperative Learning
Organize students into small groups. Assign the groups the same number of different words from the list of **300 Spelling Words**. Challenge group members to examine each word for the part they think generally causes the misspelling of the word. Have them circle the troublesome part.

You may want to have the groups create and display in the classroom posters showing their analyses of the words. Suggest using white poster board and blue and red markers (red for the troublesome parts of the words).

MECHANICS

continuous
controlled
controversial
cordially
corps
correspondence
criticize
curiosity
curriculum

definition
delegate
denied
develop
difference
disastrous
disciple
dissatisfied
distinction
distinguished
dividend
dominant
dormitory

earnest
easily
ecstasy
eighth
eliminate
embroidery
endeavor
enormous
equipment
especially
essential
estimation
etiquette
exaggeration
examination
exceedingly
exceptional
excitable
executive
exercise
exhaustion

exhibition
expense
experience
extension
extraordinary

fallacy
fantasies
favorably
fiery
financial
foreigner
forfeit
fragile
fulfill
fundamentally

gasoline
gentleman
grammatically
grateful
guidance
gymnasium

handkerchief
heroic
hindrance
humorist
hygiene
hypocrisy

illustrate
imitation
immense
inability
incidentally
indispensable
influential
innocence
inquiry
institute
intellect
interference
interpretation
interruption
interval

irrelevant
irresistible
island

jealousy
journal

laborious
liability
lightning
likelihood
liveliest
locally
luxury
magnificence
maintenance
maneuver
mansion
martyr
maturity
medical
merchandise
merit
miniature
mischievous
missile
misspelled
monotony
mortgage
municipal

narrative
naturally
neighbor
noticeable
nuisance

obstacle
occasionally
occupy
odor
offensive
omitted
opinion
opposition
optimism

ordinary
organization
ornament

pageant
pamphlet
parachute
parallel
pastime
peaceable
peasant
peril
permanent
persistent
perspiration
pertain
phase
picnic
pigeon
playwright
pleasant
poison
politician
positively
possibility
practically
practice
precede
precisely
predominant
preferred
prejudice
preliminary
preparation
primitive
priority
prisoner
procedure
proceedings
procession
prominent
proposition
prosperous
prove

psychology
publicity
purposes

qualities
quantities
questionnaire

readily
reference
referring
regard
register
rehearsal
religious
remembrance
representative
requirement
resistance

resolution
responsibility
restaurant
ridiculous

satisfactorily
security
senator
sensibility
sheer
sheriff
significance
simile
situated
solution
sophomore
souvenir
specific
specimen

spiritual
strenuous
stretch
substantial
subtle
successful
sufficient
summarize
superintendent
suppress
surgeon
suspense
syllable
symbol
symphony

technique
temperature
tendency

tournament
traffic
twelfth
tying
tyranny

unanimous
undoubtedly
unforgettable
unpleasant
unusually

vacancies
varies
vengeance
villain

MECHANICS

CHAPTER 27

PREVIEWING THE CHAPTER

- This chapter provides application and review of the concepts of grammar, usage, and mechanics that students generally find most troublesome. Consequently, you could use the exercises and tests in this chapter in a variety of ways: as diagnostic tests to determine which concepts require reteaching and additional practice; as resources for reteaching and providing extra practice; as reviews of key concepts to help students prepare for standardized tests of language skills mastery; or in any combination of these ways.

CHAPTER 27 Correcting Common Errors

Key Language Skills Review

This chapter reviews key skills and concepts that pose special problems for writers.

- Sentence Fragments and Run-on Sentences
- Subject-Verb and Pronoun-Antecedent Agreement
- Pronoun Usage
- Verb Forms
- Comparison of Modifiers
- Misplaced and Dangling Modifiers
- Standard Usage
- Capitalization
- Punctuation
- Spelling

Most of the exercises in this chapter follow the same format as the exercises found throughout the grammar, usage, and mechanics sections of this book. You will notice, however, that two sets of review exercises are presented in standardized test formats. These exercises are designed to provide you with practice not only in solving usage and mechanics problems but also in dealing with these kinds of problems on standardized tests.

HELP
Remember that all of the exercises in Chapter 27 are testing your knowledge of the rules of standard, formal English. These are the rules you should use in your schoolwork.

Reference Note
For more about **standard** and **nonstandard English** and **formal** and **informal English,** see page 638.

810   Chapter 27   Correcting Common Errors

CHAPTER RESOURCES

Planning
- *One-Stop Planner CD-ROM*

Practice and Extension
- *Grammar, Usage, and Mechanics,* pp. 367–402

Internet
- go.hrw.com (keyword: EOLang)

Evaluation and Assessment
- *Assessment Package*
  —*Chapter Tests,* Ch. 27
  —*Chapter Tests in Standardized Test Formats,* Ch. 27
- *Test Generator (One-Stop Planner CD-ROM)*

Exercise 1 Identifying Sentences and Sentence Fragments

Identify each of the following word groups as either a *sentence fragment* or a *sentence*.

EXAMPLE   1. Running along the bank of the shallow creek.
          1. sentence fragment

1. Science Technology Associates creating multimedia science products.
2. Claudia needs a new ink cartridge for her printer.
3. A new art exhibit from January 1 until March 15.
4. When he went to the new restaurant, Marchel ordered chicken satay.
5. A line of cars miles long.
6. The tadpoles under the log when the rain began.
7. We played checkers first; then we played chess.
8. Because there is an expiration date.
9. The rocks on the beach were very smooth.
10. Otters swimming and playing in the river.

Reference Note
For information about **sentence fragments,** see page 437.

1. s.f.
2. s.
3. s.f.
4. s.
5. s.f.
6. s.f.
7. s.
8. s.f.
9. s.
10. s.f.

Exercise 2 Identifying Sentences and Run-on Sentences

Identify each of the following word groups as either a *run-on sentence* or a *sentence*.

EXAMPLE   1. On Saturday I went to the park to walk my dog and play soccer with my friends, they were visiting from out of town for the weekend.
          1. run-on sentence

1. All of my friends went to the concert last Saturday, I couldn't go.
2. The triathletes swam, biked, and ran, I bet they slept well that night.
3. The villagers work together when it is time to harvest the crops.
4. After the storm, the porch was covered with leaves and sticks.
5. It was a hot summer day, Joshua played in the pool.
6. The telephone repairman rang the doorbell our dog barked.
7. If we don't hurry, we'll be late for the play, we won't be allowed to enter until the first intermission.
8. Vincent van Gogh, who is famous for paintings such as *Starry Night,* was born in the Netherlands.
9. Tom realized he had no pen he asked Bob if he could borrow one.
10. After falling asleep on the sofa, the children were carried to bed by their parents.

Reference Note
For information about **run-on sentences,** see page 347.

1. r.o.s.
2. r.o.s.
3. s.
4. s.
5. r.o.s.
6. r.o.s.
7. r.o.s.
8. s.
9. r.o.s.
10. s.

Exercise 1
OBJECTIVE
- To identify word groups as sentences or sentence fragments

TEACHING TIP

Exercises Remind students before they do **Exercises 1, 3,** and **5** that a sentence fragment is a word group that is capitalized and punctuated as a sentence but that does not contain both a subject and a verb or does not express a complete thought as a sentence does.

Exercise 2
OBJECTIVE
- To identify word groups as sentences or run-on sentences

TEACHING TIP

Exercises Remind students before they do **Exercises 2, 4,** and **5** that a run-on sentence is two or more complete sentences that are written as one sentence. Point out that a run-on sentence may also be called a *fused sentence* (when there is no punctuation between the sentences) or a *comma splice* (when there is only a comma between the sentences).

Correcting Common Errors, pp. 810–843
Alignments
TEKS 3A, 3B, 3D
TAAS W3, W6, W7
English II End-of-Course 5, 6

Texas Resources
- *TAAS Tool Kit*
- *Preparation for TAAS*
- *One-Stop Planner CD-ROM*

Exercise 3
OBJECTIVE
- To identify word groups as sentences or sentence fragments and to correct sentence fragments

Exercise 3 Identifying Sentences and Correcting Sentence Fragments

POSSIBLE ANSWERS

1. Lisa fixed the smoke detector in the hall.
2. Did Tony have a new picture taken for his passport?
3. Sara was born in Cleveland, Ohio, in the autumn of 1991.
4. S
5. Trina is in the park, playing basketball with friends from the neighborhood.
6. S
7. I would like to attend Lakeside High because that high school has a new athletic program for students with disabilities.
8. We saw the new movie about dinosaurs on Tuesday.
9. S
10. Is he a good role model?

Exercise 4
OBJECTIVE
- To correct run-on sentences

COMMON ERRORS

Reference Note
For information about **sentence fragments**, see page 437.

Reference Note
For information about **run-on sentences**, see page 347.

HELP
Although sentences in Exercise 4 can be connected in more than one way, you need to give only one revision for each sentence.

Exercise 3 Identifying Sentences and Correcting Sentence Fragments

Most of the following word groups are sentence fragments. If a word group is a sentence fragment, write it correctly, making it a complete sentence. You may need to change the punctuation and capitalization. If the word group is already a complete sentence, write *S*.

EXAMPLE 1. When we left the soccer field.
1. *It was still morning when we left the soccer field.*

1. Fixed the smoke detector in the hall.
2. A new picture taken for his passport.
3. Born in Cleveland, Ohio, in the autumn of 1991.
4. Ruth tried out her new in-line skates today.
5. Playing basketball with friends from the neighborhood.
6. Wasn't that an exciting and pleasant surprise?
7. Because that high school has a new athletic program for students with disabilities.
8. The new movie about dinosaurs on Tuesday.
9. By the time the clowns arrived, the party was almost over.
10. Is a good role model?

Exercise 4 Correcting Run-on Sentences

Correctly write each of the following run-on sentences.

EXAMPLE 1. Thunder roared and rumbled lightning flashed across the dark skies.
1. *Thunder roared and rumbled, and lightning flashed across the dark skies.*
   or
   Thunder roared and rumbled; lightning flashed across the dark skies.

Answers may vary.
1. David Diaz has captured many honors for his artwork he won the 1995 Caldecott Medal for the picture book *Smoky Night*.
2. Jeremy wants to ask Iris to the dance, he doesn't know if she already has a date.
3. Rabindranath Tagore wrote the national anthems of two countries, India and Bangladesh, I wonder if anyone else has written two national anthems. 3. ;
4. The math problems in the homework assignment were easy there were too many of them. 4. but

Chapter 27 Correcting Common Errors

5. Five golfers from Madison High School were chosen for the tournament, this will be the first tournament for three of them.   5. ;
6. Radio waves travel at the speed of light they can go through many solid objects, including the walls of most buildings.
7. My mother supports the incumbent candidate for treasurer my father will vote for the challenger.
8. Socrates was not afraid to die, he faced his own death sentence with bravery and self-assurance.   8. ;
9. The largest province in Canada is Quebec, the capital of the province is Quebec City.   9. and
10. Lena wanted to learn how to stencil, she enrolled in a stenciling course at the library.   10. so

Exercise 5   Correcting Sentence Fragments and Run-on Sentences

Each of the following word groups is a sentence fragment, a run-on sentence, or a complete sentence. First, identify each by writing *F* for a sentence fragment, *R* for a run-on sentence, or *S* for a complete sentence. Then, correct each sentence fragment or run-on sentence.

EXAMPLE 1. Nearly all cultures having traditional folk dances.
    1. F—Nearly all cultures have traditional folk dances.

1. Most folk dances start as celebrations or religious rituals, such dances are often passed down from generation to generation.   1. R
2. Certain dances to bring good fortune to the dancers.   2. F
3. Some communities developed dances that they believed cured diseases, for instance, the tarantella developed in Italy as a ritual antidote for the bite of the tarantula.   3. R
4. Other dances celebrating birth, marriage, harvests, success in battle, and even death.   4. F
5. Over time, most folk dances change.   5. S
6. That some dances originally having religious or ritual significance have come to be danced purely for recreation.   6. F
7. Anyone who knows the origins of "Ring-Around-the-Rosy"?   7. F
8. In the United States, the square dance may be the most popular kind of folk dance clogging is common, too.   8. R
9. The do-si-do is a movement in square dancing in which two dancers start out facing one another, circle each other back-to-back, and then return to a facing position.   9. S
10. The term *do-si-do* from *dos à dos,* which, I believe, is French for "back-to-back."   10. F

Reference Note
For information about **sentence fragments,** see page 437. For information on **run-on sentences,** see page 347.

Grammar and Usage   813

Exercise 6

OBJECTIVE

- To identify verbs that agree in number with their subjects

TEACHING TIP

Exercises To help students find the subjects in **Exercises 6** and **7** so that they can identify the correct verb forms, you may want to encourage students to write down the sentences and to strike through all of the prepositional phrases and subordinate clauses. In addition, you may want to remind students that a subject may appear before or after its verb.

Exercise 7

OBJECTIVE

- To proofread sentences for correct subject-verb agreement

Reference Note

For information about **subject-verb agreement**, see page 512.

Reference Note

For information about **subject-verb agreement**, see page 512.

1. drops
2. has

Exercise 6 Identifying Verbs That Agree with Their Subjects

For each of the following sentences, choose the form of the verb in parentheses that agrees with the subject.

EXAMPLE 1. The cultural heritage of New Mexico's cities (*is, are*) reflected in their architecture, food, and customs.

1. is

1. Many of the people who visit New Mexico (*spend, spends*) time in Albuquerque.
2. The architecture of the buildings (*represent, represents*) various periods in the city's history.
3. (*Has, Have*) anyone here ever read about or seen Albuquerque's Old Town?
4. One of the books Ana read (*identify, identifies*) Old Town as the site of the city's original settlement, founded by Spanish settlers in 1706.
5. Arts, crafts, and food now (*fill, fills*) the shops around the Old Town Plaza.
6. Amy's family (*has, have*) its annual reunion in Albuquerque.
7. Near Albuquerque (*is, are*) a number of American Indian reservations.
8. The pictures we took of the Rio Grande gorge (*give, gives*) you an idea of what the landscape is like in central New Mexico.
9. Neither Juan nor his parents (*was, were*) aware that near Albuquerque are mountains that often have snow on them.
10. Just to the east of the city (*is, are*) the Sandia Mountains.

Exercise 7 Proofreading Sentences for Correct Subject-Verb Agreement

Most of the following sentences contain errors in subject-verb agreement. If a verb does not agree with its subject, write that subject and the correct form of the verb. If a sentence is already correct, write C.

EXAMPLE 1. Each of them repeat the chorus after the soloist finishes.

1. Each repeats

1. Someone I know drop in every time I try to finish my work.
2. News of his accomplishments have spread in recent years.

814 Chapter 27 Correcting Common Errors

3. ~~Here's~~ the articles about Buck Ramsey that Han said she would lend you.
4. Has everybody signed up for a service project?
5. The picture of Nanci, Lyle, and Michelle ~~are~~ on the bulletin board.
6. St. Elmo's fire, which has been seen around the masts of ships, the propellers and wingtips of planes, and even the horns of cattle, is an odd glow that sometimes accompanies a steady electric discharge.
7. Under some rocks in the woods ~~were~~ a small box.
8. Tornadoes that occur in the Northern Hemisphere ~~whirls~~ in a counterclockwise direction.
9. The herd of cattle ~~belong~~ to Ms. Tallerud.
10. Singing and playing the guitar ~~is~~ also among Jan's talents.

3. Here are
4. C
5. is
6. C

7. was
8. whirl

9. belongs
10. are

Exercise 8 Selecting Pronouns That Agree with Their Antecedents

For each blank in the following sentences, select a pronoun that agrees with its antecedent.

EXAMPLE   1. One of the boys left _____ report card in the gym today.
          1. his

1. Each member of the women's soccer team had played _____ best during the game.
2. All of the students in my biology class have planted _____ seeds along the school's front entrance.
3. Nicholas or Benjamin will demonstrate _____ favorite drawing technique in class today.
4. Mr. Williams told us that anyone who wants to go on the field trip should turn in _____ permission slip on Monday.
5. Each of the novels has _____ own significance in the trilogy.
6. If someone wants to use the computer in the library, _____ should do so this afternoon.
7. Neither Karen nor Susan has finished researching _____ topic.
8. Any one of the passengers could have left _____ jacket on the train.
9. If Ricky and Joe are ready at 7:45 A.M., _____ will be able to ride the bus to school.
10. If we're going to go hiking, everyone should bring _____ own lunch and wear a comfortable pair of shoes.

Reference Note
For information about **pronoun-antecedent agreement,** see page 532.

1. her
2. their
3. his
4. his or her
5. its
6. he or she
7. her
8. his or her
9. they
10. his or her

Grammar and Usage   815

Exercise 9

OBJECTIVE

- To proofread sentences for correct pronoun-antecedent agreement

Reference Note

For information about **pronoun-antecedent agreement,** see page 532.

CALVIN & HOBBES © 1989 Watterson. Distributed by Universal Press Syndicate. Reprinted with permission. All rights reserved.

Exercise 9 Proofreading Sentences for Correct Pronoun-Antecedent Agreement

Most of the following sentences contain pronouns that do not agree with their antecedents. If a sentence contains an error, rewrite the sentence to correct the error. If a sentence is already correct, write *C*.

EXAMPLE
1. Almost everybody I know has their favorite comic strips.
1. *Almost everybody I know has his or her favorite comic strips.*

1. Sara, one of my friends in the fourth-period art class, raised their hand and asked Mrs. Seymour about the history of comic strips.   **1. her**
2. Mrs. Seymour asked everyone to bring a sketchpad, their drawing pencils, and the Sunday comics to class the following day so that we could begin designing a class comic strip.   **2. his or her**
3. I can't remember whether it was Sara or Gillian who showed me a copy of the *Calvin and Hobbes* collection titled *Scientific Progress Goes "Boink,"* which they had bought at the mall.   **3. she**
4. The vivid colors and elaborate artistry of a comic strip like *Prince Valiant* or *Calvin and Hobbes* often help make them a popular Sunday strip.   **4. it**
5. Today, about 100 million people in the United States spend some of his or her time each day reading comics.   **5. their**
6. Juan and Robert offered to show the class their collections of adventure comics from the 1940s; each of them will give his presentation on Thursday.   **6. C**
7. Are you familiar with Linus and Lucy Van Pelt and his or her friends Charlie Brown and Snoopy?   **7. their**
8. In 1894, Joseph Pulitzer, one of the most famous newspaper publishers in the United States, introduced the first newspaper comic strip in their paper, *New York World*.   **8. his**
9. The magazine-style comic book first appeared in the 1930s; they usually feature serialized stories about the same group of characters.   **9. it/features**
10. If anyone wants to learn more about the history of comics, they could research the topic at a library.   **10. he or she**

816   Chapter 27   Correcting Common Errors

Exercise 10 — Identifying Correct Forms of Pronouns

Choose the correct pronoun in parentheses in each of the following sentences.

EXAMPLE   1. Jesse and (*I, me*) will compete at the track meet.
   1. I

1. The police officer gave (*them, they*) tickets for speeding in a school zone.
2. The state's best hockey coach is (*he, him*).
3. The soloists in tonight's choir concert will be accompanied on piano by (*she, her*) and Paul.
4. Mr. Fishburn wondered (*who, whom*) had left a gift on his front doorstep.
5. The next president of the debate team will likely be (*she, her*).
6. Yes, the university has offered (*us, we*) scholarships.
7. Three volunteers, Hester, Kim, and (*I, me*), will help paint the mural in the gym.
8. Mrs. Murphy paid my sister and (*I, me*) ten dollars to shovel snow from her driveway.
9. "Are you going with Christy and (*him, he*) to tomorrow's soccer game?" Janet asked.
10. Carl Lewis and Michael Johnson are the two athletes (*who, whom*) I watched most closely during the 1996 Olympics.

Exercise 11 — Proofreading Sentences for Correct Forms of Pronouns

Identify each incorrect pronoun in the following sentences, and write the correct form. If a sentence is already correct, write *C*.

EXAMPLE   1. The new neighbors thought that we and them should have a picnic.
   1. them—they

1. Are you going to ride with him or I?   1. me
2. Us girls are tutoring students this summer.   2. We
3. The new exchange students are here; do you know them?   3. C
4. The most talented artist in our class is her.   4. she
5. When I was raising money for charity, the executives who I contacted were very generous.   5. whom
6. My father and me plan to drive to New York this summer.   6. I

Exercise 12

OBJECTIVE

- To revise sentences to correct inexact pronoun references

Exercise 12 Rewriting Sentences to Correct Inexact Pronoun References

POSSIBLE ANSWERS

1. The catalog tells about Tomás Rivera's novel, which is titled . . . *y no se lo tragó la tierra.*
2. Rivera may have written so vividly about migrant workers in his book because he himself worked as a migrant field hand when he was a boy.
3. Rivera's working long hours in the fields interrupted his formal education.
4. The novel focuses on a Mexican American family of migrant workers.
5. Because the family follows crops and the work they provide, the family has to move often.
6. Rivera's inspiring novel is about the migrant workers' search for justice.
7. After reading a novel by Tomás Rivera and short stories by Reuben Sánchez, I decided to read more of their works.
8. After Mandy had read Rivera's novel, she talked to Adrianne about the conflicts in it.
9. The biography of Rivera states that in his later life, he became the first Mexican American chancellor in the University of California system.
10. After Rajiv said that the film *And the Earth Did Not Swallow Him* was based on Rivera's novel, Todd went with Rajiv to the library to check out the video.

---

7. Did the teacher give them an assignment different from the one she gave us?   **7. C**
8. The boy thanked she and Paula for buying some of his lemonade.   **8. her**
9. It would be nice if they would bring our friends and we a pitcher of water.   **9. us**
10. He is the author who everyone adores.   **10. whom**

Reference Note

For information about **inexact pronoun reference,** see page 566.

Link to Literature

Exercise 12 Rewriting Sentences to Correct Inexact Pronoun References

Rewrite each of the following sentences to correct the inexact pronoun reference.

EXAMPLE   1. Domingo first read about Tomás Rivera when he was in the school library.

1. *When Domingo was in the school library, he read about Tomás Rivera for the first time.*

1. In the catalog, they tell about Tomás Rivera's novel, which is titled . . . *y no se lo tragó la tierra.*
2. As a boy, Rivera worked as a migrant field hand. That may partly explain why he wrote so vividly about migrant workers in his book.
3. Rivera worked long hours in the fields, and it interrupted his formal education.
4. In the novel, it focuses on a Mexican American family of migrant workers.
5. The family follows crops and the work they provide; it means that they have to move often.
6. Rivera's novel is about the migrant workers' search for justice, and it is inspiring.
7. After reading a novel by Tomás Rivera and short stories by Reuben Sánchez, I decided to read more of his works.
8. Mandy talked to Adrianne about the conflicts in Rivera's novel after she had read it.
9. In the biography of Rivera, it states that in his later life he became the first Mexican American chancellor in the University of California system.
10. After he said that the film *And the Earth Did Not Swallow Him* was based on Rivera's novel, Todd went with Rajiv to the library to check out the video.

Exercise 13 Writing the Forms of Irregular Verbs

For each of the following sentences, provide the correct past or past participle form of the verb in italics.

EXAMPLE 1. *write*   Joyce Carol Thomas ____ *Brown Honey in Broomwheat Tea.*

1. wrote

1. *become* During the Cenozoic era, South America and North America ____ linked by a land bridge.
2. *speak* I had ____ to Jim before he left.
3. *bring* Geraldine has ____ me her new copy of *A Gathering of Flowers: Stories About Being Young in America.*
4. *give* Yesterday, Teresa ____ flowers to her grandmother.
5. *know* We ____ that the first czar of Russia was known as Ivan the Terrible.
6. *hear* Jonas had ____ that the picnic was postponed.
7. *choose* I wonder what subject Celeste ____ for her world history presentation last week.
8. *drive* My aunt Judy has ____ me to my ballet lessons every week this year.
9. *teach* Who ____ Jorge to play the clarinet?
10. *ride* I once ____ a bus across Oklahoma.
11. *break* Two hundred million years ago, the land mass known as Pangaea ____ apart.
12. *forget* Danny ____ to leave the front door unlocked so that I could get in.
13. *sing* Sandra ____ a ballad, which she dedicated to her mother and grandmother.
14. *fall* When I stepped on the patch of ice, I almost ____.
15. *leave* They ____ hours ago.
16. *begin* The Paleozoic era ____ 540 million years ago.
17. *think* Conrad ____ he had money in his checking account, but he didn't.
18. *do* How many times ____ you have to work that math problem before you got it right?
19. *freeze* When Chris and Michael were hiking in Colorado, their water ____ overnight.
20. *go* Last year, her family ____ to Asia.

Reference Note
For information about **using verbs correctly,** see page 572.

1. became
2. spoken
3. brought
4. gave
5. knew
6. heard
7. chose
8. driven
9. taught
10. rode
11. broke
12. forgot
13. sang
14. fell
15. left
16. began
17. thought
18. did
19. froze
20. went

Exercise 13

OBJECTIVE

- To complete sentences by supplying the correct forms of irregular verbs

TEACHING TIP

Exercises Before students begin **Exercises 13** and **14,** you may want to remind them that an irregular verb forms its past and past participle in some other way than by adding –d or –ed to the base form. You may also want to refer students to the charts of irregular verbs on pp. 577–579 and to call on a volunteer to explain the significance of including the helping verb *have* before the past participle forms.

COMMON ERRORS

Exercise 14

OBJECTIVE

- To proofread sentences for correct verb forms

Reference Note

For information about **verb forms,** see page 592.

Exercise 14 Proofreading Sentences for Correct Verb Forms

Identify each incorrect verb form in the following sentences, and write the correct form. If a sentence is already correct, write *C*.

EXAMPLE 1. From the 1920s through the 1940s, people in the United States listened to radio programs and gone to the movies more than they do now.

    1. *gone—went*

1. The popularity of TV programs brung about the end of many radio shows.   **1. brought**
2. It has not took very long for television to become one of the most popular forms of entertainment in the United States.   **2. taken**
3. I use to think television had always been around, but the first regular TV broadcasts in the United States weren't until 1939.   **3. used**
4. Demonstrations of televisions drawed big crowds at the New York World's Fair in 1939.   **4. drew**
5. In 1941, when the United States begun fighting in World War II, television broadcasting was suspended, but it resumed in 1945.   **5. began**
6. The sales of television sets soared after World War II, and by 1951 telecasts reached viewers from coast to coast.   **6. C**
7. Color programs weren't showed until 1953.   **7. shown**
8. Of course, I've seen old black-and-white TV programs.   **8. C**
9. I also have heared some of the old radio shows from before the days of television.   **9. heard**
10. Have you ever thought about how television has changed the way people in the United States spend their leisure time?   **10. C**

Exercise 15

OBJECTIVE

- To revise sentences by changing the tenses of verbs

Reference Note

For information on **verb tenses,** see page 590.

1. will have graduated
2. had purchased

Exercise 15 Using the Different Tenses of Verbs in Sentences

Change the tense of the verb in each of the following sentences according to the directions given after the sentence.

EXAMPLE 1. Ingrid studied French for two years. (Change *studied* to a present perfect form.)

    1. *Ingrid has studied French for two years.*

1. Will's brother will graduate from college in the spring. (Change *will graduate* to a future perfect form.)
2. Adrian purchased new glasses before he went on vacation. (Change *purchased* to a past perfect form.)

820   Chapter 27   Correcting Common Errors

COMMON ERRORS

3. Have you read any of Naomi Shihab Nye's poems? (Change *Have read* to a present perfect progressive form.)
4. The twins will play the same kind of instrument at the talent show. (Change *will play* to a past emphatic form.)
5. The acrobats are performing this evening. (Change *are performing* to a present perfect form.)
6. Will you work in your uncle's blacksmith shop this summer? (Change *will work* to a past progressive form.)
7. Bianca and Charles asked whether the building has an emergency evacuation plan. (Change *asked* to a future form.)
8. The new amusement park gives discounts to groups every day of the week. (Change *gives* to a past perfect form.)
9. Scott had hoped to take the driving test on Tuesday. (Change *had hoped* to a present emphatic form.)
10. The jugglers demonstrated their talent all afternoon. (Change *demonstrated* to a future form.)

3. been reading
4. did play
5. have performed
6. Were/working
7. will ask
8. had given
9. does hope
10. will demonstrate

Exercise 16 **Revising a Paragraph to Make the Tenses of the Verbs Consistent**

Read the following paragraph, and decide whether to rewrite it in the present or past tense. Then, rewrite it, changing the verb forms to correct any unnecessary changes in tense.

EXAMPLE   [1] The children were eager to hear a story, so I begin to tell them the Navajo legend of Eagle Boy.

1. The children are eager to hear a story, so I begin to tell them the Navajo legend of Eagle Boy.

or

The children were eager to hear a story, so I began to tell them the Navajo legend of Eagle Boy.

[1] A young Navajo boy who lives with his parents often dreamed of eagles flying overhead. [2] One day, Father Eagle flew down to the boy, caught hold of his shirt, and carries him to a nest high on a cliff. [3] Father and Mother Eagle feed the boy cornmeal and then took him to the eagle people at the top of the sky. [4] Eventually, the boy goes to the home of Eagle Chief, who told him to remain there. [5] After Eagle Chief leaves, the boy became curious about an animal that he sees outside. [6] When the boy opens the door slightly to look more closely, Big Wind blew it completely open, pulling the boy outside, where the trickster Coyote is waiting. [7] The boy was soon tricked into touching Coyote's fur and turns into a coyote himself. [8] When Eagle Chief

Reference Note
For information about **consistent verb tense**, see page 597.

HELP
Although the example in Exercise 16 gives two possible revisions, you need to give only one revision for each sentence.

Exercise 16

OBJECTIVE
- To revise a paragraph to achieve consistency in verb tense

TEACHING TIP

Exercise 16 You may want to ask students to underline each verb as they revise the paragraph in Exercise 16. Then, encourage them to proofread the verbs carefully to make sure that every verb is either in the present tense or in the past tense.

Exercise 16 **Revising a Paragraph to Make the Tenses of the Verbs Consistent**

ANSWERS
Answers will vary depending upon whether students rewrite the paragraph in the present tense or past tense.

1. lives, dreams (lived, dreamed or dreamt)
2. flies, catches, carries (flew, caught, carried)
3. feed, take (fed, took)
4. goes, tells (went, told)
5. leaves, becomes, sees (left, became, saw)
6. opens, blows, is waiting (opened, blew, was waiting)
7. is tricked, turns (was tricked, turned)

COMMON ERRORS

Grammar and Usage 821

Exercise 16 Revising a Paragraph to Make the Tenses of the Verbs Consistent

ANSWERS continued

8. returns, restores (returned, restored)
9. names, gives (named, gave)
10. returns, becomes (returned, became)

Exercise 17

OBJECTIVE

- To proofread sentences for correct comparative and superlative forms of modifiers

TEACHING TIP

Exercise 17 To reinforce students' understanding of the distinction between comparative and superlative forms of modifiers, you may want to ask them to identify the items being compared in each of the sentences in **Exercise 17** before they write the correct form of the modifier.

Exercise 18

OBJECTIVE

- To revise sentences to correct errors in the use of modifiers

---

returns, he restored the boy. [9] Afterward, Eagle Chief names him Eagle Boy and gave him an eagle feather. [10] Eagle Boy then returns home to his parents, and he eventually became a great medicine man.

Exercise 17 Proofreading for Correct Comparative and Superlative Forms

Most of the following sentences contain errors in the use of comparative and superlative forms of modifiers. If a modifier is incorrect, give the correct form. If a sentence is already correct, write *C*.

EXAMPLE 1. The second time I made lasagna, I prepared it most quickly.
1. more quickly

Reference Note
For information about **using modifiers correctly**, see page 612.

1. better
2. most
3. taller
4. least
5. most
6. more
7.
8. most colorful
9. C
10. most

1. I planted lantana and petunias next to each other; the lantana grew best because it could withstand heat and drought.
2. The more exciting field trip of any this year is scheduled for this fall.
3. I wonder which of the two mountain peaks is tallest.
4. Of the club's many members, he is less likely to run for president because he is so shy.
5. The more suspenseful chapter in the novel told of a violent storm that damaged the sails of the pirate ship and drove the ship off course.
6. Which is most fun for you, painting with watercolors or sketching?
7. Watching the two dogs dig in the ground, Carl laughed as the more younger one retrieved a small toy.
8. The colorfulest sunset I ever saw in Montana was near Billings.
9. Outside the theater, we all agreed that the movie was the least satisfying sequel that we had ever seen.
10. Of all the mailboxes in the neighborhood, ours is the more unusual.

Exercise 18 Proofreading Sentences for Correct Use of Modifiers and Comparisons

Revise the following sentences to correct each error in the use of modifiers and comparisons.

EXAMPLE 1. In most areas, daisies are more easier to grow than orchids.
1. *In most areas, daisies are easier to grow than orchids.*

Reference Note
For information about **using modifiers correctly**, see page 612.

1. likely
2. other

1. Termites work in the dark and are less likelier to be seen than many other insects.
2. Raphael types faster than any student in his class.

822 Chapter 27 Correcting Common Errors

3. Fortunately, no one was injured bad when the boats collided.
4. Although elephants are the largest land mammals, blue whales are the most largest mammals of all.
5. My friend Tim is more creative than anyone in his school.
6. The lion is more bigger than the lioness.
7. Aunt Gloria is more resilient than anyone I know.
8. I don't see good without my glasses.
9. The trekkers walked careful up the hill.
10. Kilimanjaro is the more magnificent mountain of any in Africa.

3. badly

5. else

7. else
8. well
9. carefully
10. most

Exercise 19 Correcting Misplaced Modifiers

Each of the following sentences contains a misplaced modifier. Rewrite each sentence to correct the placement of the modifier.

EXAMPLE
1. Flying in close formation, the crowd watched the squadron of small biplanes overhead.
1. *The crowd watched the squadron of small biplanes flying in close formation overhead.*

1. Gathered into a heap, Nathan looked at the stalks of sugar cane.
2. I have always enjoyed listening to stories about my mother's childhood with my sister.
3. We watched the sun rise from our front porch.
4. Frank listened to music climbing the mountain.
5. We watched a film about how comets are formed in science class.
6. I saw a deer going to check the mail.
7. About six inches long, the *Tyrannosaurus rex* had sharp teeth.
8. They noticed a turtle on a log wading across the river.
9. We learned that the bridge had once collapsed as we rode over it.
10. Mr. Spinoza saw many earthworms planting his garden.

Reference Note
For information about **misplaced modifiers,** see page 627.

Exercise 20 Correcting Dangling Modifiers

Each of the following sentences contains a dangling modifier. Rewrite each sentence so that the modifier clearly and sensibly modifies a word in the sentence.

EXAMPLE
1. Looking through the binoculars, the bird was brightly colored.
1. *Looking through the binoculars, I saw that the bird was brightly colored.*

1. While practicing the piano, the music fell off the music rack.

Reference Note
For information about **dangling modifiers,** see page 626.

Grammar and Usage   823

Exercise 19
OBJECTIVE
- To revise sentences to correct misplaced modifiers

Exercise 19 Correcting Misplaced Modifiers
POSSIBLE ANSWERS

1. Nathan looked at the stalks of sugar cane gathered into a heap.
2. I have always enjoyed listening with my sister to stories about my mother's childhood.
3. From our front porch we watched the sun rise.
4. Frank listened to music while he was climbing the mountain.
5. In science class we watched a film about how comets are formed.
6. Going to check the mail, I saw a deer.
7. The *Tyrannosaurus rex* had sharp teeth about six inches long.
8. Wading across the river, they noticed a turtle on a log.
9. As we rode over the bridge, we learned that it had once collapsed.
10. While planting his garden, Mr. Spinoza saw many earthworms.

Exercise 20
OBJECTIVE
- To revise sentences to correct dangling modifiers

COMMON ERRORS

Exercise 20 Correcting Dangling Modifiers

POSSIBLE ANSWERS

1. While I was practicing the piano, the music fell off the music rack.
2. Peering down from the top of the Empire State Building, I thought the people below looked like ants.
3. Unable to complete the assignment on time, Bob had to turn in his report late.
4. Perched on a high stool by the kitchen counter, I easily peeled the potatoes.
5. After stretching to warm up, I tightly laced my running shoes on my feet.
6. Right after I had walked in the front door, my telephone rang.
7. The marathon seemed endless to Anjana, who was determined to reach the finish line.
8. Because their lawn was looking overgrown and scraggly, the McKinneys decided to spend the weekend doing yardwork.
9. The geologist studying fossil oysters found in Kansas hypothesized that a shallow sea once covered at least part of that state.
10. All alone, the boy found the dark woods mysterious and silent.

Exercise 21

OBJECTIVE

- To revise sentences to correct double negatives and other errors in formal, standard usage

---

2. The people below looked like ants, peering down from the top of the Empire State Building.
3. Unable to complete the assignment on time, Bob's report had to be turned in late.
4. Perched on a high stool by the kitchen counter, the potatoes were easy to peel.
5. After stretching to warm up, the running shoes were tightly laced on my feet.
6. My telephone rang right after walking in the front door.
7. Determined to reach the finish line, the marathon seemed endless.
8. Looking overgrown and scraggly, the McKinneys decided to spend the weekend doing yardwork.
9. Studying fossil oysters found in Kansas, it was hypothesized that a shallow sea once covered at least part of that state.
10. All alone, the dark woods were mysterious and silent.

Exercise 21 Correcting Double Negatives and Other Errors in Usage

Eliminate the double negatives and other errors in formal, standard usage in the following sentences.

EXAMPLE
1. Karen should of brought her delicious chow mein to the potluck dinner yesterday.
1. Karen should have brought her delicious chow mein to the potluck dinner yesterday.

Answers may vary. Possible responses are given.

1. I went to the beach yesterday to look for driftwood and shells but couldn't find none. **1. any**
2. Just try and imagine a city without vehicles of any sort! **2. to**
3. I would rather go to the county park on this beautiful afternoon then stay indoors. **3. than**
4. Our track team practiced until we weren't able to run no more. **4. anymore**
5. The engine sounds like it is ready to fall out of the old truck. **5. as if**
6. We didn't want to see neither of the movies that were showing at the theater. **6. either**
7. At breakfast this morning, my little brother found a small toy inside of that box of cereal. **8. way**
8. Joel drove a long ways across town just to trade one football card.
9. Unfortunately, my science experiment didn't work as good as I thought it would. **9. well**
10. This long stretch of highway has hardly no curves in it. **10. any**

HELP—
Although the sentences in Exercise 21 can be corrected in more than one way, you need to give only one revision for each sentence.

Reference Note
For information about **double negatives,** see page 656. For information about **common usage errors,** see page 636.

Exercise 22 Correcting Errors in Usage

Identify and correct each error in the use of formal, standard English in the following sentences.

EXAMPLE 1. Young people with inventive minds had ought to be encouraged!

1. had ought—ought

1. People from five to nineteen years old have ~~discovered~~ some new and important products and processes.   **1. invented**
2. As a teenager, young Jerrald Spencer ~~use~~ to take apart electronic appliances just to see how they worked.   **2. used**
3. In 1977, at the age of fifteen, Spencer created his first marketed invention, a kind of ~~an~~ electronic toy.
4. That ~~there~~ toy led to a whole series of specialty toys sold in major department stores.
5. In 1895, the teenager Cathy Evans invented ~~an~~ unique process known as "tufting" for decorating bedspreads.   **5. a   6. effect**
6. Her invention had a tremendous ~~affect~~ on the carpet industry; in fact, most carpet made today involves the process she developed.
7. In 1922, eighteen-year-old Ralph Samuelson decided to try ~~and~~ use snow skis to ski on water.   **7. to**
8. He didn't think that skiing on water would be much harder ~~then~~ skiing on snow.   **8. than**
9. ~~Like~~ he thought, after many tries his skis worked!   **9. As**
10. If you want to be an inventor, you won't succeed ~~without~~ you try.   **10. unless**

Exercise 23 Proofreading Sentences to Correct Errors in Usage

Each of the following sentences contains an error in the use of formal, standard English. Identify each error. Then, write the correct usage.

EXAMPLE 1. The tour guide last summer learned us much about the Lincoln Memorial.

1. learned—taught

1. This memorial, ~~who~~ was dedicated in 1922, is a popular attraction in Washington, D.C.
2. No ~~less~~ than 150 million people have visited the monument.
3. I was ~~kind of~~ amazed to hear that the memorial was built on what used to be marshland.
4. The architect Henry Bacon ~~he~~ designed the memorial.

Reference Note

For information about **common usage errors,** see page 632.

Reference Note

For information about **common usage errors,** see page 636.

1. which

2. fewer

3. rather

Exercise 22

OBJECTIVE

- To proofread sentences to identify and correct errors in usage

Exercise 23

OBJECTIVE

- To proofread sentences to identify and correct errors in usage

5. inferred
6. illusion
7. effect
8. that
9. emigrated

5. I ~~implied~~ ^inferred from our guide's talk that the Parthenon in Greece inspired Bacon's design.
6. It is not an ~~allusion~~ ^illusion that the massive columns of both the Parthenon and the Lincoln Memorial tilt slightly inward.
7. The architects designed the columns this way because rows of truly straight columns give buildings the ~~affect~~ ^effect of bulging at the top.
8. I read ~~where~~ ^that Daniel Chester French interviewed Lincoln's son Robert before sculpting the memorial's statue of Lincoln.
9. The spectacular 175-ton statue was carved in sections by the Piccirilli brothers, whose family had ~~immigrated~~ ^emigrated from Italy and settled in the United States.
10. The Gettysburg Address is inscribed on a wall inside ~~of~~ the memorial's hall.

Grammar and Usage Test: Section 1

DIRECTIONS In the following sentences, either part or all of each sentence is underlined. Using the rules of formal, standard English, choose the answer that most clearly expresses the meaning of the sentence. If there is no error, choose A. Indicate your response by shading in the appropriate oval on your answer sheet.

EXAMPLE
1. Has everyone chosen a topic for their essay?
   - (A) chosen a topic for their
   - (B) chose a topic for their
   - (C) choosed a topic for their
   - (D) chosen a topic for his or her
   - (E) chosen a topic for his and her

ANSWER 1. (A) (B) (C) ●D (E)

1. In the 1936 Olympic Games, I read that Jesse Owens won four gold medals.
   - (A) In the 1936 Olympic Games, I read that Jesse Owens won four gold medals.
   - (B) In the 1936 Olympic Games, I read that four gold medals were won by Jesse Owens.
   - (C) I read where Jesse Owens won four gold medals in the 1936 Olympic Games.
   - (D) I read in the 1936 Olympic Games that Jesse Owens won four gold medals.
   - (E) I read that Jesse Owens won four gold medals in the 1936 Olympic Games.

2. In some sports, a "goose egg" is when a player has a score of zero.
   - (A) when a player has a score of zero
   - (B) where a player has a score of zero
   - (C) a score of zero
   - (D) scoring a zero
   - (E) that a player has a score of zero

3. I can't hardly remember a time when the temperature was lower than it is today.
   - (A) I can't hardly remember a time when the temperature was lower than it is today.
   - (B) I can't hardly remember a time when the temperature was lower then it is today.
   - (C) I can hardly remember a time when the temperature was more lower than it is today.
   - (D) I can hardly remember a time when the temperature was lower then it is today.
   - (E) I can hardly remember a time when the temperature was lower than it is today.

4. This evening less people will be driving cars to the parade because there is less space available for parking.
   - (A) less people will be driving
   - (B) fewer people will be driving
   - (C) less people will have been driving
   - (D) fewer people will have been driving
   - (E) fewer people driven

5. The first tennis match was between she and I.
   - (A) between she and I
   - (B) between her and I
   - (C) between her and me
   - (D) between she and me
   - (E) among her and me

6. While running to the bus stop this morning, some books fell out of my backpack.
   - (A) While running to the bus stop this morning, some books fell out of my backpack.
   - (B) While running this morning, some books fell out of my backpack at the bus stop.
   - (C) While I was running to the bus stop this morning, some books fell out of my backpack.
   - (D) Some books fell out of my backpack while running to the bus stop this morning.
   - (E) I was running to the bus stop this morning while some of my books fell out of my backpack.

7. Raymond knows how to repair lawn mowers, and he plans to make it his summer job.
   - (A) and he plans to make it his summer job
   - (B) and he plans to make that his summer job
   - (C) and that is his plan for a summer job
   - (D) and he plans to make repairing lawn mowers his summer job
   - (E) which is his plan for a summer job

8. Creole dishes, the origins of which can be traced to Spanish, African, and Caribbean cooking.
   (A) Creole dishes, the origins of which can be traced to Spanish, African, and Caribbean cooking.
   (B) The origins of Creole dishes, which can be traced to Spanish, African, and Caribbean cooking.
   (C) Tracing the origins of Creole dishes to Spanish, African, and Caribbean cooking.
   (D) Spanish, African, and Caribbean cooking, which are the origins of Creole dishes.
   (E) The origins of Creole dishes can be traced to Spanish, African, and Caribbean cooking.

9. The coach doesn't think that him and I have practiced free throws enough today.
   (A) doesn't think that him and I
   (B) don't think that him and me
   (C) doesn't think that he and I
   (D) don't think that he and me
   (E) doesn't think that him and me

10. Some of the people who are standing in line have all ready bought their tickets.
    (A) who are standing in line have all ready
    (B) who are standing in line have already
    (C) whom are standing in line have all ready
    (D) whom are standing in line have already
    (E) which are standing in line have already

Grammar and Usage Test: Section 2

DIRECTIONS Read the paragraph below. For each numbered blank, select the word or group of words on the next page that best completes the sentence. Indicate your response by shading in the appropriate oval on your answer sheet.

EXAMPLE   **(1)** you ever heard of sick building syndrome?

1. (A) Has
   (B) Have
   (C) Did
   (D) Were
   (E) Hasn't

ANSWER   1.   Ⓐ   ●B   Ⓒ   Ⓓ   Ⓔ

In the early 1980s, a number of health problems suffered by office workers __(1)__ for the first time as symptoms of a single ailment called sick building syndrome. In addition to fatigue and eye irritation, __(2)__ symptoms included headaches, sore throats, colds, and flu. Studies indicate that sick building syndrome, __(3)__ has been responsible for a 30 percent rise in absenteeism in some businesses, can cause as much as a 40 percent drop in productivity. The problems resulting from this syndrome __(4)__ are caused by such indoor pollutants as formaldehyde, benzene, and trichloroethylene. These substances, which are found in furniture, insulation, and paint, __(5)__ trapped in climate-controlled buildings. Even though these pollutants are so widespread, the situation __(6)__ hopeless. Research originally conducted to help astronauts __(7)__ to a simple, effective solution—houseplants. Microorganisms in the roots of a potted plant __(8)__ with the plant to remove harmful substances from the air. The __(9)__ plants include chrysanthemums, which remove benzene, and spider plants, which remove formaldehyde. In addition, both peace lilies and English ivy __(10)__ trichloroethylene.

---

830   Chapter 27   Correcting Common Errors

1. (A) identified
   (B) was identified
   (C) were identified
   (D) being identified
   (E) was being identified

2. (A) these
   (B) them
   (C) these here
   (D) these kind of
   (E) them kind of

3. (A) they
   (B) which
   (C) who
   (D) what
   (E) it

4. (A) more likely
   (B) more likelier
   (C) likelier
   (D) most likely
   (E) most likeliest

5. (A) becomes
   (B) becomed
   (C) becoming
   (D) become
   (E) is becoming

6. (A) is in no way
   (B) is not in no way
   (C) aren't in no way
   (D) it isn't hardly
   (E) isn't hardly

7. (A) have led
   (B) has led
   (C) has lead
   (D) leads
   (E) have lead

8. (A) they interact
   (B) it interacts
   (C) interact
   (D) interacts
   (E) is interacting

9. (A) most useful
   (B) usefullest
   (C) most usefullest
   (D) more usefuller
   (E) usefuller

10. (A) removes
    (B) they remove
    (C) removed
    (D) were removing
    (E) remove

Grammar and Usage   831

COMMON ERRORS

Exercise 24
OBJECTIVE
- To correct errors in capitalization

Reference Note
For information about **capitalization,** see page 666.

Exercise 24 Correcting Errors in Capitalization

Each of the following word groups contains at least one error in capitalization. Correct the errors either by changing capital letters to lowercase letters or by changing lowercase letters to capital letters. Some capital letters are already correctly used.

EXAMPLE
1. Robert Burns's poem "a red, red rose"
1. Robert Burns's poem "A Red, Red Rose"

1. my aunt elizabeth
2. growing up in the midwest
3. *the middle passage* by V. S. Naipaul
4. kansas city royals
5. west of sixty-fifth street
6. winter in denver
7. grandma's brother
8. senator Ann Greene
9. latin, art, and geometry II
10. a buddhist temple
11. the battle Of vicksburg
12. dr. l. f. livingstone
13. the book *a room with a view*
14. American indian pictographs
15. french-Speaking countries
16. a xerox® photocopier
17. Father's day
18. A vietnamese festival
19. orbiting mars or earth
20. Grand teton national park
21. the archaeology of greece and the aegean
22. a jewish synagogue
23. toni Morrison's book *jazz*
24. 7926 broadway boulevard
25. William Shakespeare's play *twelfth night*

Exercise 25
OBJECTIVE
- To revise sentences to correct errors in capitalization

Reference Note
For information about **capitalization,** see page 660.

Exercise 25 Correcting Errors in Capitalization

Each of the following sentences contains errors in capitalization. Correct the errors either by changing capital letters to lowercase letters or by changing lowercase letters to capital letters. Some capital letters are already used correctly.

EXAMPLE 1. oren lyons's formal title is faith keeper of the turtle clan.
1. Oren Lyons's formal title is Faith Keeper of the Turtle Clan.

1. i recently read about oren lyons, an Influential onondaga chief.
2. he is an american indian leader featured in *The Encyclopedia Of Native America*, which is a reference we use in our American History class.
3. the onondaga are an iroquois people.
4. before assuming this important position, mr. lyons was a successful commercial artist in new york city.
5. the iroquois tradition of having faith keepers dates back to hundreds of years before the pilgrims landed at plymouth rock.
6. mr. lyons edits a publication called *daybreak*, which is dedicated to the seventh generation to come.
7. as faith keeper, mr. lyons is responsible for making decisions that will ensure that the earth is habitable for another seven generations.
8. He also has many other responsibilities, including speaking before the united nations.
9. mr. lyons, other members of the iroquois league, and a group of lakota sioux addressed the united nations in geneva, switzerland.
10. Faith keepers work to uphold the traditions of their people as well as the principles of Democracy, community, and reverence for the Natural World.

Exercise 26 Proofreading Sentences for the Correct Use of Commas

Each of the following sentences needs at least one comma. Write the word or numeral that comes before each missing comma, and add the comma. Optional commas are underscored.

EXAMPLE 1. The Green Club collects aluminum clear glass colored glass and paper for recycling.
1. aluminum, glass, glass,

1. Orb weavers are spiders that create beautiful complicated round webs.
2. We had planned to climb the mountain but the trail was closed because mountain lions had been sighted in the area.
3. Cheeky the neighbor's dog that chewed up my athletic shoes is now kept in his own yard.
4. Oh when will I stop worrying about things that will never happen?

Reference Note
For information about **using commas,** see page 692.

Exercise 26

OBJECTIVE
- To add commas as needed in sentences

COMMON ERRORS

5. Italy, in my opinion, is the most beautiful country in the world.
6. On July 20, 1969, the Apollo 11 lunar module landed on the moon.
7. I wasn't chosen for the track team, but I am trying out for soccer next week.
8. The American painter Charles Russell, who is famous for his scenes of life in the West, is my favorite artist.
9. The Perseid meteor shower, which occurs annually, appears to originate in the constellation Perseus.
10. Tired of waiting for the movie to start, the audience began to murmur and fidget.

Exercise 27 Using Commas Correctly

Each of the following sentences needs at least one comma. Write the word or numeral that comes before each missing comma, and add the comma. Optional commas are underscored.

EXAMPLE 1. Tony have you ever heard of Dr. Percy L. Julian?
1. Tony,

1. Julian, born in Montgomery, Alabama, in 1899, grew up to become a renowned scientist.
2. After studying at DePauw University, he graduated with highest honors; in fact, he received a Phi Beta Kappa key and delivered the valedictory address.
3. Julian went on to Harvard, where he earned a master's degree, and then traveled to Austria to earn a Ph.D. at the University of Vienna.
4. As Ahmed says, Dr. Julian must have been a brilliant man.
5. Dr. Julian taught at Howard University and West Virginia University, but his fame began after he went to work as a research chemist for Glidden, a paint company in Chicago, Illinois.
6. During World War II, Dr. Julian created a firefighting foam which, by the way, was made from soybean protein.
7. He received the 1947 Spingarn Medal, which is the NAACP's highest award.
8. Interested in finding other uses for soybeans, Dr. Julian established Julian Laboratories and its subsidiaries.
9. Over the course of his lifetime, he developed an inexpensive cortisone for arthritis sufferers, drugs to relieve glaucoma, drugs to help victims of rheumatic fever, and many other helpful medicines.
10. Dr. Julian died in 1975, but his impressive achievements live on.

Exercise 27

OBJECTIVE

- To add commas as needed in sentences

Reference Note
For information about **using commas,** see page 692.

Exercise 28 Using Semicolons and Colons Correctly

The following sentences need semicolons and colons. Write the word or numeral preceding and the word or numeral following the needed punctuation, and add the proper punctuation. In some instances you will need to replace commas with either semicolons or colons.

EXAMPLE
1. My brother likes to read adventure novels I prefer autobiographies of sports figures.

1. novels; I

1. We both signed up for field hockey, however, the heavy snow has prevented practice all month.
2. In art class Juanna, Elaine, and Jim used acrylics, and Todd, Tonya, and Jasper used oils.
3. We missed the 4:15 bus and had to wait for the 5:30 one.
4. The movie she recommended was *Geronimo An American Legend*.
5. From this airport there are direct flights to Frankfurt, Germany, Rome, Italy, London, England, and Paris, France.
6. Our choir is singing a song based on Psalm 19:14.
7. Our neighborhood has fiestas for various holidays, for example, we have a piñata party on Cinco de Mayo each year.
8. I walk to school each day with Darla, Gene, and Greg, and Sven, Petra, and Arnold join us on the walk home.
9. I have several postcards that my stepsister sent me from towns with unusual names, for instance, here are ones from Cut and Shoot, Texas, and Truth or Consequences, New Mexico.
10. The Ecology Club has adopted the following projects this semester: setting out recycling bins, planting trees in the schoolyard, and adopting two miles of highway to keep clean.

Exercise 29 Punctuating Dialogue

Add paragraph indentions and insert quotation marks and other punctuation where needed in the dialogue on the following page.

EXAMPLES

[1] Hey, Sarah, I hear you've become a vegetarian Colin said. Won't you get tired of eating just vegetables?

1. *"Hey, Sarah, I hear you've become a vegetarian," Colin said. "Won't you get tired of eating just vegetables?"*

[2] You've got some things to learn about vegetarians! Sarah said.

2. *"You've got some things to learn about vegetarians!" Sarah said.*

Mechanics 835

Exercise 29 Punctuating Dialogue

ANSWERS continued

4. ¶Colin replied, "Okay, what else do vegetarians eat?"
5. ¶"Well," Sarah answered, "I eat whatever I want that isn't meat, and I try to eat healthful foods. I eat vegetables, of course, but also grains, breads, pastas, beans, nuts, soups, cereals, and fruit."
6. ¶"Do you eat eggs and dairy products?"
7. ¶"Yes," Sarah replied, "I do, but some vegetarians don't. For instance, I sometimes eat quiche, cheese and vegetable enchiladas, and bowls of cereal with milk." [*or* "Yes," Sarah replied. "I do. . . ."]
8. ¶Colin said, "I guess you aren't having any trouble finding things to eat. I'm wondering, though, why you decided to become a vegetarian."
9. ¶"I just wanted to feel better. Studies show that being a vegetarian is very healthful," Sarah said.
10. ¶Colin said, "I remember learning that a diet without any animal products is cholesterol-free. You'll have to tell me about other health benefits of vegetarianism."

Exercise 30

OBJECTIVE

- To revise sentences by adding quotation marks, other punctuation, and capitalization

TEACHING TIP

Exercise 30 You may want to point out to students that some of the sentences in **Exercise 30** require the use of single quotation marks.

COMMON ERRORS

---

[1] Well, teach me Colin said. What is a vegetarian?
[2] You know that a vegetarian is a person who doesn't eat meat Sarah said but you don't know what a vegetarian does eat.
[3] Your mistake is one that many people make. They think that a vegetarian eats only vegetables, but vegetarians eat quite a variety of foods.
[4] Colin replied Okay, what else do vegetarians eat?
[5] Well, Sarah answered I eat whatever I want that isn't meat, and I try to eat healthful foods. I eat vegetables, of course, but also grains, breads, pastas, beans, nuts, soups, cereals, and fruit.
[6] Do you eat eggs and dairy products?
[7] Yes, Sarah replied I do, but some vegetarians don't. For instance, I sometimes eat quiche, cheese and vegetable enchiladas, and bowls of cereal with milk.
[8] Colin said, I guess you aren't having any trouble finding things to eat. I'm wondering, though, why you decided to become a vegetarian.
[9] I just wanted to feel better. Studies show that being a vegetarian is very healthful Sarah said.
[10] Colin said I remember learning that a diet without any animal products is cholesterol-free. You'll have to tell me about other health benefits of vegetarianism.

Reference Note

For information about **punctuating quotations and titles,** see page 743.

Exercise 30 Punctuating and Capitalizing Quotations and Titles

For each of the following sentences, insert quotation marks and other marks of punctuation where needed, and change lowercase letters to capital letters as necessary.

EXAMPLE
1. Should the U.S. flag be flown at the same level as or higher than a state flag asked Earl

1. "Should the U.S. flag be flown at the same level as or higher than a state flag?" asked Earl.

1. Megan's note says, "The electrician at the repair shop said that our VCR would be ready by 5:00 P.M."
2. "Physical therapy," Karen said, "is really strengthening my brother's legs."
3. "Leiningen Versus the Ants," by Carl Stephenson, is a frightening short story," Bob said.
4. "That's right, Victoria," he replied, "you will want to plant the azaleas in partial sunlight."

5. Sean asked why did Paul yell Get off the porch! at the dog?
6. The following graduates have been named "most likely to succeed: Alexandra, Michael, and Jim.
7. When she hit her finger with the hammer while repairing the roof, Hannah yelled that does it!
8. What I asked the doctor is the patella?
9. The song Long Distance Call was one of the hits of the Chicago blues singer Muddy Waters.
10. No! Paula exclaimed I didn't say to use the green paint!

Exercise 31 Using Apostrophes Correctly

Revise the following word groups, adding apostrophes where they are needed. If a word group is already correct, write C.

EXAMPLE   1. giving to United Ways fund
           1. giving to United Way's fund

1. somebodys hat
2. Are these Kims poems?
3. Judys and his show
4. ten oclock
5. both planes engines
6. The box was theirs.
7. How many as are in *aardvark*?
8. womens sizes
9. Anya and Tonis team
10. hadnt finished
11. that canoes hull
12. no one elses parents
13. Its memory capacity is huge.
14. that clubs newsletter
15. Mr. Harriss Irish setter
16. neithers fault.
17. Howards and Marilyns tests
18. because Im sleepy
19. whose ring
20. Its going to rain.

Reference Note
For information about **apostrophes,** see page 758.

Exercise 32 Using Punctuation Correctly

The following sentences contain errors in the use of end marks, commas, semicolons, colons, quotation marks, apostrophes, and hyphens. Rewrite each sentence correctly.

EXAMPLE   1. When Mr Andrews finished painting the hall we asked him to paint the front porch
           1. When Mr. Andrews finished painting the hall, we asked him to paint the front porch.

1. While she was in Hades Persephone ate the seed's of a pomegranate, in Greek mythology this fruit symbolizes marriage.
2. Someones father works on Royal Street but I cant remember whose.

Mechanics   837

Exercise 32 Using Punctuation Correctly

ANSWERS continued

3. The cities that I have most enjoyed visiting are the following: New Orleans, Louisiana; Seattle, Washington; and Philadelphia, Pennsylvania.
4. "Yes, I have been to Guadalajara," said Liza, "but not recently; however, I would like to go there again soon."
5. "Twenty-nine crows are cackling in the front yard, and the noise is driving me crazy!" exclaimed Cathy.
6. Weren't you nervous when the lizards, snakes, and scorpions started crawling around the two actors' legs?
7. David's and Mary's houses are both near the new shopping center, which was completed in mid-February.
8. You can give those posters to Margaret, Zack, and Greta; and Phillip, Craig, and Matthew will give theirs to me.
9. "Bobby yelled, 'The dog's dish is gone!'" said Suzu.
10. That beautiful, well-known song is "Over the Rainbow"; it's my sister-in-law's favorite song.

Exercise 33

OBJECTIVE

- To correct spelling errors in sentences

TEACHING TIP

Exercise 33 To help students proofread for spelling errors in **Exercise 33,** you may want to tell them that the exercise contains twenty misspellings or that each sentence contains two misspellings.

---

3. The cities that I have most enjoyed visiting are the following New Orleans Louisiana Seattle Washington and Philadelphia Pennsylvania
4. Yes I have been to Guadalajara said Liza but not recently however I would like to go there again soon.
5. Twenty nine crows are cackling in the front yard and the noise is driving me crazy exclaimed Cathy.
6. Werent you nervous when the lizards snakes and scorpions started crawling around the two actors legs
7. Davids and Marys houses are both near the new shopping center which was completed in mid February.
8. You can give those posters to Margaret, Zack, and Greta and Phillip, Craig, and Matthew will give theirs to me.
9. Bobby yelled The dogs dish is gone said Suzu
10. That beautiful well known song is Over the Rainbow its my sister-in-laws favorite song.

FRANK & ERNEST reprinted by permission of Newspaper Enterprise Association, Inc.

Reference Note

For information about **spelling rules,** see page 778.

Exercise 33 Correcting Spelling Errors

Each of the following sentences contains spelling errors. Correctly write each misspelled word.

EXAMPLE 1. We forfieted the free vacation and enjoied our leisure time at home.
  1. *forfeited, enjoyed*

1. weird/staring
2. pitiful/wailing
3. mapped/proceeded
4. conceded/third
5. weighed/gratified

1. The dog reacted in a wierd way, stareing straight ahead.
2. The pityful wailling of the kitten helped us find it.
3. We traveled on the route maped out for us and proceded at a steady pace.
4. They finally conceeded that the new system would cost a 3rd less to run than the old one did.
5. When the paper we collected for recycling was wieghed, we were gratifyed to learn that the amount exceeded one ton.

6. ~~Cleanlyness~~ of the work space is ~~especialy~~ important when food is being handled.
7. ~~40~~ people signed up for the dance classes to learn ~~waltzs~~, polkas, and line dances.
8. All the ~~puppys~~ at the animal shelter were cute, but the ~~1st~~ one they showed us was the one we adopted.
9. My cousin drives ~~30~~ miles each way to her job at a wildlife park, where she takes care of the lions, tigers, and ~~wolfs~~.
10. Both of the ~~monkies~~ are likely to throw ~~tomatos~~.

6. Cleanliness/especially
7. Forty/waltzes
8. puppies/first
9. thirty/wolves
10. monkeys/tomatoes

Exercise 34 Choosing Between Words Often Confused

From each pair of words in parentheses, choose the word or word group that correctly completes the sentence.

EXAMPLE   1. (*You're, Your*) endangering the pedestrians by skating too fast.

1. You're

1. When I applied for work at the restaurant, I spoke with the (*personal, personnel*) manager.
2. It is important to check the (*breaks, brakes*) on any vehicle before you start driving.
3. We had (*already, all ready*) opened the windows in the art room before Ms. Wong asked us.
4. What theme should we (*choose, chose*) for the prom?
5. Eleanor and Lupita said we could use (*they're, their*) binoculars when we go on the Audubon Society field trip.
6. What (*effect, affect*) will all the rain have on the mown hay?
7. The elephant returned to (*its, it's*) enclosure at feeding time.
8. What did the members of the (*counsel, council*) decide?
9. The (*lose, loose*) wing nut created a rattle in the trunk.
10. Use very fine, not (*course, coarse*), sandpaper for the finishing work on wood furniture or toys.

Reference Note

For information about **words often confused,** see page 793.

> **TEACHING TIP**
>
> **Using the Mechanics Tests.** A **Correcting Common Errors Standardized Test Answer Sheet** that students may use for this **Mechanics Test** is provided in *Chapter Tests in Standardized Test Formats.*

Mechanics Test: Section 1

DIRECTIONS Each of the following sentences contains an underlined word or word group. Choose the answer that shows the correct capitalization, punctuation, and spelling of the underlined part. If there is no error, choose answer E (Correct as is). Indicate your response by shading in the appropriate oval on your answer sheet.

EXAMPLE

1. Please post these announcements for <u>the Columbus winter Carnival</u>.

   (A) the Columbus Winter Carnival
   (B) the columbus winter carnival
   (C) The Columbus Winter carnival
   (D) the Columbus Winter carnival
   (E) Correct as is

ANSWER 1.

1. "Can you tell us the <u>moral of the fable, Josh</u>"? asked Ms. Chen.

   (A) moral of the fable, Josh?"
   (B) morale of the fable, Josh?
   (C) moral of the fable," Josh?
   (D) moral of the fable, Josh?,"
   (E) Correct as is

2. <u>We'll need streamers balloons</u> and confetti to decorate for the baby shower.

   (A) Well, need streamers, balloons,
   (B) We'll need streamers, balloons,
   (C) We'll need: streamers, balloons,
   (D) We'll need streamers balloons,
   (E) Correct as is

3. The words of <u>Dr. Martin Luther King, Jr.,</u> are engraved on the Civil Rights Memorial.

   (A) Dr Martin Luther King, Jr.,
   (B) Dr. Martin Luther King Jr.,
   (C) Dr. Martin Luther King, Jr,
   (D) Dr. Martin Luther King, jr.,
   (E) Correct as is

4. "Did Coach really say, 'Run another <u>mile?'"</u> gasped Carla.

   (A) mile?"
   (B) mile,"
   (C) mile'?"
   (D) mile,'"
   (E) Correct as is

840　Chapter 27　Correcting Common Errors

5. Choose a free subscription to one of these magazines Time, Newsweek, Scientific American, or Harper's.
   - (A) magazines Time
   - (B) magazines; Time,
   - (C) magazines: "Time,"
   - (D) magazines: Time,
   - (E) Correct as is

6. The men's and womens shoe departments and the housewares department are having sales now.
   - (A) mens and women's
   - (B) men's and women's
   - (C) mens' and womens'
   - (D) mens and womens
   - (E) Correct as is

7. The bus driver said "that we should be quiet."
   - (A) said, "That we should be quiet."
   - (B) said "That we should be quiet."
   - (C) said, that we should be quiet.
   - (D) said that we should be quiet.
   - (E) Correct as is

8. I've visited three state capitals: Boise, Idaho, Tallahassee, Florida; and Montpelier, Vermont.
   - (A) capitals: Boise, Idaho, Tallahassee, Florida,
   - (B) capitols: Boise, Idaho; Tallahassee, Florida;
   - (C) capitols: Boise; Idaho; Tallahassee; Florida;
   - (D) capitals: Boise, Idaho; Tallahassee, Florida;
   - (E) Correct as is

9. The weather will not effect their plans for this weekend.
   - (A) The weather will not affect their plans
   - (B) The whether will not affect their plans
   - (C) The weather will not affect they're plans
   - (D) The weather will not effect they're plans
   - (E) Correct as is

10. Its not John whose left his papers in the library.
    - (A) Its not John who's
    - (B) It's not John whose
    - (C) Its' not John who's
    - (D) It's not John who's
    - (E) Correct as is

Mechanics 841

Mechanics Test: Section 2

DIRECTIONS Each numbered item below contains an underlined word group. Choose the answer that shows the correct capitalization, punctuation, and spelling of the underlined part. If there is no error, choose answer E (Correct as is). Indicate your response by shading in the appropriate oval on your answer sheet.

EXAMPLE   [1] February 9 2001

(A) Febuary 9 2001

(B) Febuary 9, 2001

(C) February 9th 2001

(D) February 9, 2001

(E) Correct as is

ANSWER 1.

---

327 Hickory Lane
[1] Ankeny Iowa 50021
February 9, 2001

[2] Susan Washington DVM
49-A Johnson Circle
Des Moines, IA 51219

[3] Dear Dr. Washington:

Thank you for [4] agreeing to lead the discussion at our club's next meeting. We members of [5] Future Farmers of America know how important the practice of veterinary medicine is to agriculture. [6] 39 students have already signed up to attend. As I mentioned on the phone last [7] week, our meeting will take place in Healy Lecture hall. We will begin at [8] 3:00 P.M, and if things go as planned, I will introduce you soon thereafter. We look forward to hearing [9] your views on veterinary medicine, and hope that you will stay for refreshments after the meeting.

[10] yours sincerely,

Michael Yoder

Michael Yoder
President, FFA
Ankeny High School

---

842   Chapter 27   Correcting Common Errors

1. (A) Ankeny, Ia. 50021
   (B) Ankeny, IA 50021
   (C) Ankeny IA, 50021
   (D) Ankeny I.A., 50021
   (E) Correct as is

2. (A) Susan Washington DVM.
   (B) Susan Washington; DVM
   (C) Susan Washington, DVM
   (D) Susan Washington: DVM
   (E) Correct as is

3. (A) Dear Dr Washington:
   (B) Dear Dr. Washington,
   (C) Dear dr. Washington,
   (D) Dear Dr. Washington;
   (E) Correct as is

4. (A) agreing to led
   (B) agreeing, to lead
   (C) agreeing to lead
   (D) agreeing too lead
   (E) Correct as is

5. (A) Future Farmers Of America
   (B) future farmers of america
   (C) future farmers of America
   (D) future Farmers of America
   (E) Correct as is

6. (A) Thirty nine students
   (B) Thirty-nine students
   (C) Thirty nine student's
   (D) Thirty-nine students'
   (E) Correct as is

7. (A) week: our meeting will take place in Healy lecture hall
   (B) week: our meeting will take place in Healy Lecture Hall
   (C) week, our meeting will take place in Healy lecture hall
   (D) week, our meeting will take place in Healy Lecture Hall
   (E) Correct as is

8. (A) 3:00 P M and if things go as planned,
   (B) 3:00 P M., and if things go as planed,
   (C) 3:00 P.M. and if things go as planned,
   (D) 3:00 P.M., and if things go as planned,
   (E) Correct as is

9. (A) your'e views on veterinary medicine, and
   (B) you're views on veterinary medicine; and
   (C) your views on veterinary medicine and
   (D) your views on veterinary medicine: and
   (E) Correct as is

10. (A) Yours sincerely,
    (B) Yours Sincerely
    (C) Your's sincerely,
    (D) Yours sincerely:
    (E) Correct as is

Mechanics 843

RESOURCES

Correcting Common Errors
Review
- *Grammar, Usage, and Mechanics,* pp. 403, 404, 405, 406

Assessment
- *Assessment Package*
  —*Chapter Tests,* Ch. 27
  —*Chapter Tests in Standardized Test Formats,* Ch. 27
- *Test Generator (One-Stop Planner CD-ROM)*

Mechanics 843

PART 4
Quick Reference Handbook

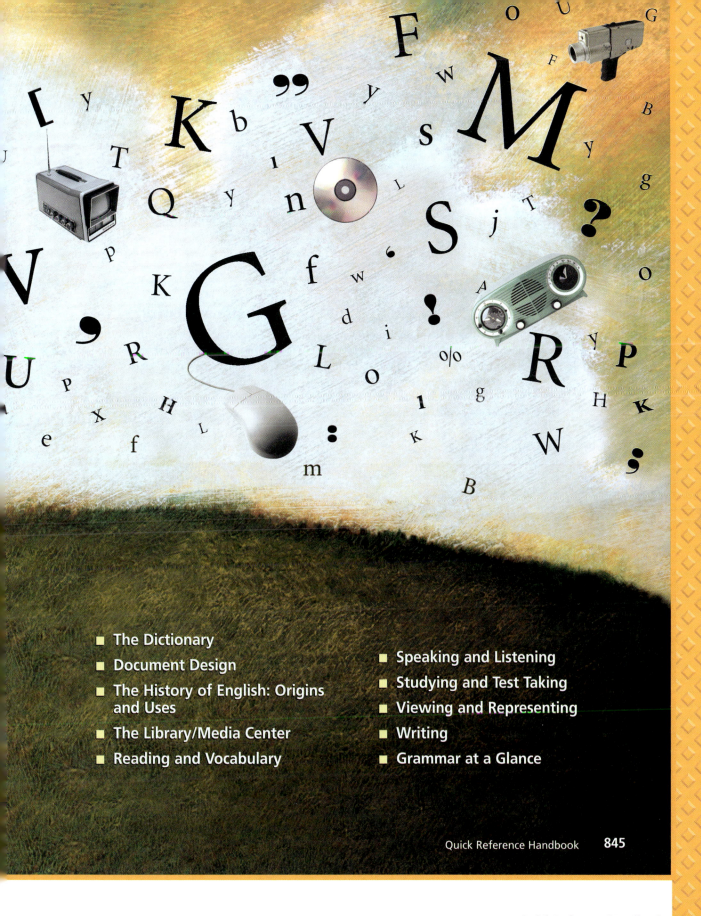

- The Dictionary
- Document Design
- The History of English: Origins and Uses
- The Library/Media Center
- Reading and Vocabulary
- Speaking and Listening
- Studying and Test Taking
- Viewing and Representing
- Writing
- Grammar at a Glance

The Dictionary

Information about Words

Dictionaries record how words are used in language. A dictionary of the English language shows how most English speakers say or spell a word and what the word means in different contexts. In a dictionary, you will also find information such as word histories and the various forms in which a word may appear.

Dictionary Entry

A dictionary entry gives the word and information about it. Each part of the following entry from an abridged dictionary is labeled and explained below.

1. **Entry word.** The boldface entry word shows how the word is spelled and divides it into

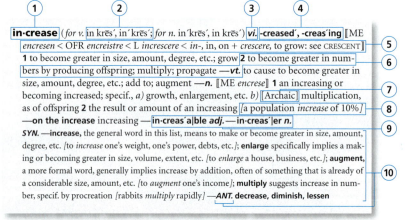

From *Webster's New World Dictionary, Fourth College Edition.* 1999 by Webster's New World Dictionaries, A division of Simon and Schuster, New York. Reprinted by permission of the publisher.

syllables. The entry word may also show capitalization and alternate spellings.

2. **Pronunciation.** The pronunciation is shown by the use of accent marks and either phonetic spellings or *diacritical marks*, the marks added to letters to indicate a change in their sound. A pronunciation key explains the meaning of diacritical marks or phonetic symbols.

3. **Part-of-speech labels.** The part-of-speech labels, which are generally abbreviated, indicate how the entry word should be used in a sentence. In cases where a word can be used as more than one part of speech, a part-of-speech label is given in front of each numbered or lettered series of definitions.

4. **Other forms.** To clarify spelling and usage, a dictionary may list plural forms of nouns, tenses of verbs, or the comparative forms of adjectives and adverbs.

5. **Etymology.** The etymology is the origin and history of a word. It shows how a word or part of a word passed into English from another language.

6. **Definitions.** Definitions are numbered or lettered when a word has more than one meaning.

7. **Special usage labels.** These labels identify words that have special meanings or are used in special ways in certain situations.

8. **Examples.** A simple phrase or sentence using the entry word may be included to clarify how the word is used.

9. **Related word forms.** These are various forms of the entry word, usually created by adding suffixes or prefixes.

10. **Synonyms and antonyms.** A list of synonyms and antonyms may appear at the end of some word entries. Sometimes synonyms, printed in capital letters, may also be included within the list of definitions.

Other Parts of a Dictionary

In addition to entry words, most dictionaries also include the following parts that provide additional information.

Abbreviations
Many dictionaries include a chart of common *abbreviations*. The chart may include abbreviations for weights, measurements, governmental agencies, and the names of states or geographical regions.

Biographical and Geographical Entries
Many dictionaries include a section that identifies famous historical figures, including important writers, musicians, politicians, scientists, inventors, and explorers. The entries identify each person's profession and provide the dates of his or her birth and death. The geographical section lists most of the populated places in the world, the pronunciation of their place names, and the size of their populations.

Colleges and Universities
The names of all the colleges and universities in the United States and Canada appear in many dictionaries, particularly school or college editions. The entries provide the school's location, the date of its establishment, and the number of students attending at the time of the dictionary's publication.

Copyright
The *copyright* indicates when a dictionary was published. When looking up the meaning of a word, use the latest edition of a dictionary to make sure that new words and new meanings of old words are included.

Guide to the Dictionary
Most dictionaries have a few pages near the beginning that give helpful hints about using the dictionary. The

Information about Words **847**

The Dictionary, pp. 846–848
Alignments
TEKS 6E, 6D

guide usually explains how the material is organized and what the abbreviations and fonts mean.

Index Some dictionaries have an *index* that indicates where to find various dictionary features, including the pronunciation key, the section with word entries, and the biographical and geographical entries.

Pronunciation Key A *pronunciation key* appears at the front of any dictionary and at the bottom of each page or pair of pages.

Scholarly Essays The *scholarly essays* are written by language experts and provide information about subjects such as the history and growth of the English language, the way a new edition of the dictionary is different from a previous one, and how the dictionary was researched and prepared.

Types of Dictionaries

Different types of dictionaries provide different types and amounts of information. The dictionary you choose should be determined by the kind of information that you need.

Abridged An *abridged* dictionary is the most common type of dictionary. It contains most of the words the average person uses or encounters in writing or reading. One advantage of abridged dictionaries is that they are frequently updated, so they can provide the most up-to-date information on meanings and uses of words. Abridged dictionaries are arranged in alphabetical order and include basic information, such as the spelling, definition, pronunciation, part of speech, and source of a word. They also include tables of commonly used abbreviations, selected biographical entries, and tables of signs and symbols.

Online *Online dictionaries* are accessible on the Internet and may be abridged, unabridged, or specialized. You can often search for a word in this type of dictionary by entering not only the word itself, but also the word's part of speech or etymology. Some online dictionaries have audio features that allow you to hear a word's pronunciation. You can usually find online dictionaries under the reference section of a search engine's subject catalog. (See also **World Wide Web, Searching** on page 873.)

Specialized *Specialized dictionaries* contain entries that relate to a specific subject or field. For example, there are specialized dictionaries for terms used in art, music, sports, gardening, mythology, as well as other subjects. Specialized dictionaries will include information that an abridged dictionary might not have. (See also the **Reference Sources** chart on page 870.)

Unabridged An *unabridged dictionary* contains nearly all the words in use in a language. For example, the present twenty-volume edition of the *Oxford English Dictionary* contains over 500,000 entries. Each entry in the *OED* gives detailed descriptions of a word's source, its first appearance in the language, its various forms, and the way its meaning has changed over the last millennium. Each word's meanings and usage are illustrated with quotations from historical and literary sources that date back as far as the year 1150.

Document Design

Manuscript Style

The following chart provides guidelines for preparing handwritten or typed papers. (See also **Writing** on page 000.)

Guidelines for Submitting Papers

1. Use only one side of a sheet of paper.
2. Write in blue or black ink, or type your paper.
3. If you write by hand, do not skip lines, unless your teacher directs you otherwise. If you type, double-space the lines.
4. Leave one-inch margins at the top, sides, and bottom of each page.
5. Indent the first line of each paragraph (about five letter spaces).
6. Number all the pages except the first page. Place the number in the upper right-hand corner of the page.
7. Keep all pages neat and clean. You may make a few corrections with correction fluid. If you have several errors on a page and the page is difficult to read, write out or type the page again.
8. Follow your teacher's instructions for placing your name, the date, your class, and the title of your paper on a cover sheet or on the first page of your paper.

Desktop Publishing

Desktop publishing is the production of professional-looking documents, such as reports or newsletters, on a personal computer. Desktop publishers set words (text) on a page with images and graphics in a way that communicates a message and attracts readers' attention.

Page Design or Layout

Before computers changed the printing industry, documents were designed by hand. Page designers worked page by page, cutting up, arranging, and pasting strips of text, illustrations, headings, and captions. Now anyone with a computer can design an entire document. This section explains key concepts for designing pages that contain text. (Remember that the principles of effective page design also apply to pages that you write and lay out by hand.)

Alignment *Alignment* refers to how lines of text are arranged on a page. Text can be aligned in several ways.

- **Left aligned** Text that is *left aligned* is set so each line forms a neat edge against the

**Document Design,
pp. 849–860
Alignments**
TEKS 2E, 3A, 3D, 4D
TAAS W3, W7
English II End-of-Course 5, 6

left margin. Most printed documents are set left aligned to facilitate reading from left to right.

EXAMPLE
This text is left aligned.
The lines form a straight
edge along the left margin.

- **Right aligned** Text that is *right aligned,* such as pull-quotes and poetry, has lines that end against the right margin. Use right-aligned text sparingly because it is not easy to read. (See also **Pull-quote** on page 852.)

EXAMPLE
This text is right-aligned.
Notice how it forms a straight
edge along the right margin.

- **Center aligned** Text that is *center aligned,* or *centered,* is set in the middle of the page. Center-aligned text usually appears in invitations, posters, or advertisements.

EXAMPLE
This text is center-aligned.
Each line is evenly spaced
on both sides of an invisible, vertical line
in the center of this column.

- **Justified alignment** With *justified alignment,* both ends of each line of text form a straight edge. Extra spaces added between words ensure that the lines are even.

EXAMPLE
This sample text is justified. The
lines of text form neat edges
along the right and left margins.

- **Ragged alignment** *Ragged alignment* means that the lines of text do not create a straight edge on both sides. Usually the right-hand side of the text is ragged in alignment.

EXAMPLE
This sample text is left-aligned and also ragged. Notice how the lines form a neat edge on the left but not on the right.

Bullet A *bullet* (•) is a symbol used to make information in a text stand out. Bullets are often used to separate information into lists. They attract attention and help readers remember the information included in the lists.
1. **Always indent a bulleted list** from the body of the text.
2. **Use plain bullets in formal documents.** Other, decorative symbols (such as ¶, $, or +) may be used as bullets in less formal forms of writing, such as journal entries and advertisements.
3. **Make sure that the items in your list are parallel in construction.** For example, use all nouns or all imperative sentences.

Call out A *call out* is a line or phrase of text that describes some aspect of a graphic image. Usually the call-out text is connected to the graphic by an arrow or line. Notice in the following diagram how the call outs identify the various parts of the illustration.

EXAMPLE

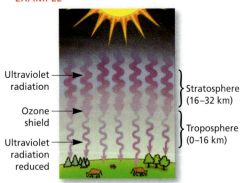

Columns and Blocks of Text Text is easier to read when it is contained in rectangular shaped areas, such as in *columns* or *blocks*. The width of a column or block of text varies, depending on the size of the text and the format of the document. The text in posters, advertisements, and fliers, for example, is usually set in blocks so that it may be read quickly. Text in textbooks, reference books, and newspapers, which contain large quantities of information, usually appears in columns. (See also **Line Length** on page 852.)

Contrast *Contrast* refers to the balance of light and dark areas on a page. Dark areas are those that contain blocks of text or graphics. Light areas have little type. A page with high contrast, or roughly balanced light and dark areas, is easier to read than a page with low contrast, such as one that is mostly light or one that is filled with text and images. (See also **Contrast** on page 854 and on page 856.)

Emphasis *Emphasis* is how a page designer indicates to a reader which information on a page is most important. For example, the front page of a newspaper uses photographs and bold or large headlines to place emphasis on a particular story. Because readers' eyes are drawn naturally to color, large and bold print, and graphics, these elements are commonly used to create emphasis.

Graphic A *graphic* is a picture, chart, illustration, or piece of artwork that is used to convey information visually. Short sections of text, such as headings, subheadings, titles, headers, and footers, may also be considered graphics because they serve a visual function. (See also **Graphics** on page 855 and **Headings and subheadings** on this page.)

Gray Page A *gray page* contains text almost exclusively. It has few or no graphics to indicate visually the organization or structure of the material on the page. As a result, reading and understanding the information on a gray page may be more difficult and time-consuming than reading information on a page that uses some graphics.

Grid Lines *Grid lines* are vertical and horizontal intersecting lines that provide structure to a page by dividing it into neat sections. Grid lines are often used to plan the design or layout of a page but do not appear in the final printed document.

Gutter A *gutter* is the crevice or margin of space between two pages in a bound book. For example, there is a gutter between this page and page 850.

Headers and Footers *Headers* and *footers* provide information about a printed document. A header appears in the top margin of a page, and a footer appears in the bottom margin. Headers and footers may include

- the name of the author
- the name of the publication
- the date of the publication
- chapter or section titles
- page numbers

Headings and Subheadings *Headings* and *subheadings* (also called *heads* and *subheads*) are used to give readers clues about the content and organization of a document.

- **Headings** Headings give readers a general idea what a section of text, such as a chapter, will be about. Headings appear at the beginning of a section of text and are often set in larger or heavier letters or in a different style of letters from the rest of the text.

- **Subheadings** Subheadings are more descriptive than headings and are used to indicate a new section or idea in the text. Several subheadings often appear under one heading. Like headings, subheadings are often set in larger or heavier letters or in a different style of letters from the rest of the text.

EXAMPLE

Goats Used in Park Beautification — heading

Goats take on weeds the old-fashioned way; they eat them — subheading

In a move to combat the invasion of nonnative weeds to Denver's city parks, the city has arranged for a herd of one hundred cashmere goats to graze in the city parks. — text

Indentation An *indentation* is the space skipped over from the left margin to indicate the beginning of a new paragraph in a text. An indentation should be about one-half inch. If you are preparing text on a computer or typewriter, one-half inch is equivalent to about five letter spaces.

Line Length *Line length* is the number of characters (letters, spaces between words, and punctuation marks) a line contains. (Remember, a line is not a sentence; it is a single line of text that may or may not form a complete thought.) The best line length for a document depends on the size of the type and the format of the document. In general, limit line length to nine or ten words, or sixty-five characters. This makes the text easier to read.

Margins *Margins* are the space that surrounds the text on a page. Most word-processing programs automatically set the side margins at 1.25 inches and the top and bottom margins at one inch. Margins are flexible, however. If your teacher recommends a different set of measurements for the margins of your papers, use them instead. (See also **White space** on page 853.)

Pull-quote A *pull-quote* is a quotation from a text, such as a magazine article or story, that has been turned into an eye-catching graphic. Pull-quotes should be short and concise; often they are excerpts of a longer thought from the text. The purpose of the pull-quote is to catch the reader's interest.

EXAMPLE

There were once three brothers who had fallen deeper and deeper into poverty, and at last their need was so great that they had to endure hunger, and had nothing to eat or drink. Then said they: "It cannot go on like this, we had better go into the world and seek our fortune." They therefore set out.

"We had better go seek our fortune."

Rule Lines *Rule lines* are lines used to create visual effects on a page. Rule lines may be thick or thin, vertical or horizontal, and they may set text off from a headline or caption, separate columns, or draw your eye to something on the page.

Title and Subtitle A *title* is the name of an entire document. *Subtitles* are longer and more descriptive than titles. Often subtitles are attached to a title by a colon and appear in smaller letters.

In books, titles (and sometimes also subtitles) appear alone on a separate page, called the title page, at the very beginning of the book.

EXAMPLE

The Timetables of Women's History
A Chronology of the Most Important People and Events in Women's History

Visuals   *Visuals,* like *graphics,* are pictures, charts, illustrations, or artwork that convey information. (See also **Graphics** on page 855.)

White Space   *White space* is any area on a page where there is little or no text or graphics. White space provides a contrast to the dark ink on a page and makes the print more readable. Usually, white space is limited to the margins, the gutter, and the spaces between words, lines, and columns. (See also **Contrast** on page 851.)

Type

Type refers to the letters and markings used in printing and publishing. When Johannes Gutenberg introduced his printing press over 500 years ago, each letter of type was cut out of wood. Today, computers make printing considerably easier. The following section provides basic information about type and how to use it effectively. (See also **Font** on page 854.)

Capital Letters   *Capital* (or *uppercase*) *letters* help readers identify the beginning of a new sentence or idea. Capital letters command readers' attention and may be used in the following ways to create emphasis in a document.

- **Dropped cap**   A *dropped cap* is an artistic use of a capital letter in the first word of a first paragraph of a text or section of a text. Dropped caps imitate medieval illuminated manuscripts in which the first letter of a section or chapter was enlarged and transformed into a colorful drawing.

EXAMPLE

nce upon a time there lived a young boy named Oliver.

- **Headings or titles**   When headings or titles appear in the same typeface as the text, setting them in all capital letters helps them stand out from the rest of the document.

EXAMPLES

LOCAL RUNNER WINS NEW YORK CITY MARATHON

KEEPING AN EYE ON STUDENTS' NUTRITION

- **Small caps**   *Small caps* are uppercase letters that are reduced in size. Usually they appear in abbreviations of time, such as 9:00 A.M. and A.D. 1500, or in the names of organizations, such as in NASA or NATO. Small caps may also be combined with true capital letters for an artful effect.

NOTE   Long sections of capital letters can be difficult to read. Use capital letters for contrast or emphasis, not for large bodies of text.

Captions   *Captions* are lines of text that appear under photographs or illustrations. They explain the meaning or importance of the graphic and connect it to the text. Because readers tend to look first at the graphics on a page, captions are often the first text they read. Therefore, captions should be concise, accurate, and interesting. Captions may appear in a smaller size type (usually two point sizes smaller) than the text, or they may appear in the same type size but italicized. (See also **Font** and **Font size** on page 854.)

Contrast   In terms of type, *contrast* refers to the visual effect of using different fonts in a document. As a general rule, use only two different fonts in a single document—one for the body of your text and captions and one for the headings and subheadings.

Font   A *font* is one complete set of characters (such as letters, numbers, and punctuation marks) of a given size and design. (The terms *font* and *typeface* are often used interchangeably, although those in the printing industry make a distinction between the two.) Thanks to computer technology, there are now more than ten thousand fonts available.

Font, Categories of   Thousands of fonts are available, each with its own name and unique appearance. In general, though, all fonts belong to one of the three following categories.

- **Decorative, or script**   Decorative fonts are elaborately designed characters that convey a distinct mood or feeling. Script fonts, in which the letters touch each other, simulate handwriting. Because decorative fonts are too difficult to read as regular text, they should be used in small amounts for an artistic effect. They are most commonly used in wedding invitations or graduation announcements.

    EXAMPLES
    This is an example of the Zapf Chancery font.
    This is an example of the Linoscript font.
    This is an example of the Fresh Script font.

- **Sans-serif**   The characters in *sans-serif* fonts are formed by neat straight lines, with no small strokes at the ends of the letters. (*Sans serif* means "without serifs, or strokes.") Sans serif typefaces work well as headings and subheadings, pull-quotes, and captions because they have clean edges and are easy to read.

    EXAMPLES
    Helvetica is a sans serif font.
    Franklin Gothic is a sans serif font.
    Futura is a sans serif font.

- **Serif**   The characters in *serif* fonts have little strokes (serifs) attached at each end. The serifs are modeled on the connectors between letters in handwriting. As in handwriting, the little strokes help guide the reader's eyes from letter to letter and word to word. Serif type is commonly used to set large bodies of type because of its readable quality. (See also **Readability** on page 855.)

    EXAMPLES
    Palatino is a serif font.
    New Century Schoolbook is a serif font.
    Times is a serif font.

    NOTE   Mixing types of fonts on a page creates high contrast; however, you should not use more than one font from each category. Too many fonts on a page confuses readers.

Font Size or Point Size   The size of the type in any document is called the *font size* or *point size*. Word-processing software provides many options for sizing text. In general, newspapers and textbooks use type measured at 12 points. Type for headings and headlines may range anywhere from 18 to 48 points. Captions usually appear in 9- to 11-point type.

Fonts, Styles of   In addition to the three categories of fonts, there are also several different *font styles*. Most text is set in *roman* font (in this case, "roman" means "not slanted"). *Italic* font has special uses, as for captions or book titles. Desktop publishing software has made available more elaborate font styles. Look at the following examples of eye-catching fonts. (See also **Font, Categories of** on page 854.)

EXAMPLES

roman boldface	*italic boldface*
<u>roman underscored</u>	r o m a n e x p a n d e d
roman condensed	ROMAN CAPITALS
italic lowercase	*ITALIC CAPITALS*

NOTE Select your font styles carefully, and avoid using too many font styles in one document. Be consistent, as your reader may be confused if you change styles in the middle of your text.

Knockout Type
Knockout, or *reversed type,* is light type set against a contrasting, dark background.

EXAMPLES
Here is dark type set against a light background.
Here is knockout, or reversed, type.

Leading or Line Spacing
Leading (rhymes with *sledding*), or **line spacing,** is the distance between lines of text. Most word processors and typewriters allow you to adjust the amount of line spacing to single-, double-, or even triple-space measurements. For formal documents, use double-spacing.

Lowercase
Lowercase type is the set of letters that are not capital letters. Lowercase letters are characterized by **ascenders** (rising strokes, as in the letters *b* and *h*) and **descenders** (dropping strokes, as in the letters *g* and *y*). Most text is set in lowercase type because it is easy to read.

Readability
Readability refers to how easy a text is to read. Text with high readability is set in simple fonts and appropriate font sizes and has high contrast. (See also **Font size** and **Font, Styles of** on page 854.)

Graphics

Graphics organize and communicate information visually. They may be used to

- display data or information
- explain a process
- illustrate how something looks, works, or is organized
- show trends or relationships over time

Whether you use a computer to generate your graphics or prepare them by hand, you should select and design your graphics carefully. They must always convey information clearly and support the text that appears on the page. Text and graphics should fit together like the pieces of a jigsaw puzzle, so that readers will understand the overall goal and design of your document.

Arrangement and Design
The challenge of designing a document that contains text and graphics is to arrange all the components in a balanced and organized way. Consider the following elements when you design a document with graphics.

Accessibility *Accessibility* refers to the ease with which readers can find information in a document. Increase a document's accessibility by using bulleted lists, headers, headings, footers, and subheadings.

Accuracy All graphics or visuals must contain true information. Never manipulate or change images or the data shown in charts, graphs, or tables. Readers must be able to trust the information in the graphics you use in your document.

Color *Color* naturally attracts a reader's eye, especially when it contrasts with the black and white of text and white space. Color may be used to attract the reader's attention, highlight a piece of information, indicate that certain items on a page belong together, or show the organization of the parts of a document or page.

- **Choosing color** When choosing colors for graphics, remember the following guidelines.
    1. **Colors are for emphasis, not for text.** Text may look nicer in color, but readers will find it more difficult to read and won't remember it as well.
    2. **Colors should be used in pairs or schemes.** Color schemes provide contrast. A single color in a document will simply look out of place.
    3. **Choose colors that complement each other.** The colors that appear opposite one another on the color wheel on this page are always complements.
    4. **Use warm colors, such as red and orange, sparingly.** These colors appear to expand or "jump off" the page.
    5. **Use cool colors, such as blue and green, as background.** Because of their calming effect, blue and green will not compete with your text for the reader's attention.

- **Color Wheel** The *color wheel* shows the relationships colors have to one another. The primary colors are yellow, red, and blue; all other colors are the result of combining these colors or mixing them with white or black. Colors that complement each other appear opposite each other on the wheel.

Contrast *Contrast* is the effect of a striking difference between two things. Create contrast within graphics by using different visual cues for different kinds of information. For example, set important terms in boldface type or in bulleted lists and set chart labels in boldface or capital letters. Use color in your charts, graphs, and tables to make it easy to distinguish columns or bits of information. Contrast makes it easier for your reader to visualize your text and remember its content.

Emphasis *Emphasis* refers to the use of visual cues such as color, capital letters, boldface or italic fonts, and large type size to draw attention to what you want readers to see. Graphics provide emphasis because they usually attract readers' attention first.

Focus *Focus* refers to the most important part of an illustration or photograph—what the reader looks at first. Usually, photographs and illustrations depict a subject as seen through the photographer's or artist's eyes. When you design or select an image to include in your document, ask yourself the following questions about its focus.

- **Is the subject of the graphic clear?** Choose a graphic whose subject is immediately recognizable. Be sure that important parts of the subject are not covered or hidden from view.
- **Is the subject shown at the angle that you intend?** If you wish to emphasize a subject's height, show it from a low angle; if you want to show how small a subject is, show it from above. Always ask, "Will this graphic give readers a clear sense of what the text describes?"
- **Does the graphic include any distracting details?** Cut or trim the graphic so that its focus is clear.
- **Will you need to add labels to the graphic so readers will understand?** If the meaning of the graphic is unclear, add labels or captions. Remember, however, that too many labels make a graphic hard to understand. If the graphic becomes too cluttered, group labels into larger categories or find a simpler graphic.

Integration *Integration* refers to the way the content of graphics and text fit together on the page. Place graphics and text that are related or cover the same material close together on the page. In addition, the text should direct the reader's attention to the visual and explain its content.

Labels or Captions To help readers understand them, many graphics need *labels* or *captions*. Labels identify the content of charts, tables, and diagrams. Usually labels appear within the body of the graphic or visual, but sometimes they are attached to the visual or graphic by thin rule lines. Captions are usually full sentences that describe a photograph or illustration. They appear directly under, beside, or above the graphic. (See also **Captions** on page 853.)

Organization *Organization,* or arrangement, refers to the placement or grouping of the text and graphics on a page. All the text and graphics that deal with a similar subject should be grouped together. Use visual cues such as headings and subheadings, similar fonts, color, and rule lines to show that certain elements are related. (See also **Integration** on this page.)

Voice *Voice* refers to the unique sound and rhythm of a writer's language. Because the text and the graphics support one another, they should have a similar voice. For example, if a text is about a serious topic, then the graphics that accompany it should be serious and straightforward.

Types of Graphics

Graphics can add to the effectiveness and appeal of a document. Designing or selecting the right kind of graphic to support your text can be a challenge. However, the following list will help you decide from among some of the most common and helpful types.

Chart A *chart* shows relationships among ideas or data. Two types of charts you are likely to use are *flow charts* and *pie charts*.

- **Flowcharts** *Flowcharts* use geometric shapes linked by arrows to show a sequence of events in a process. Notice how the following boxes on page 858 are set so that you read them from left to right and from top to bottom. In flow charts, all text is contained inside the shapes, and direction arrows indicate the direction of movement between boxes.

How to Make Lasagna

- Preheat the oven to 375°. → Spread a thick layer of tomato sauce on the bottom of a 9" x 13" pan.
- Cover with a layer of lasagna noodles. → Spoon ricotta or cottage cheese on the noodles.
- Add tomato sauce to cheese. → Spread grated mozzarella cheese on the top.
- Repeat the layers until ingredients are gone. → Sprinkle with Parmesan cheese and bake for forty-five minutes.

■ **Pie charts** *Pie charts* are circles that are divided into wedges like slices of a pie. Each wedge represents a certain amount of the total, depending on its size.

Where Old Tires Go
What happens to the 242 million scrap tires that are disposed of each year?

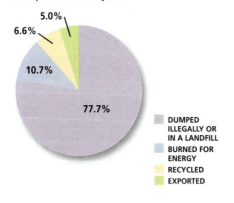

- DUMPED ILLEGALLY OR IN A LANDFILL
- BURNED FOR ENERGY
- RECYCLED
- EXPORTED

Diagram *Diagrams* use symbols or pictures to compare abstract ideas, show a process, or provide instruction. Diagrams may be hand drawn, computer generated, or photographed. They tend to be simple, showing only the important details of their subjects. The diagram below illustrates the circular movement of water in an ocean swell.

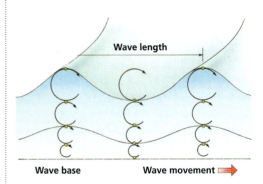

Graph A *graph* can either show a comparison of quantities or display changes or trends over time. Notice in the following examples that the horizontal axis in a line or bar graph indicates points in time or categories of things, while the vertical axis shows quantities.

Line Graph

U.S. Resident Vacation Travel, 1993–97

858 Quick Reference Handbook Document Design

Bar Graph

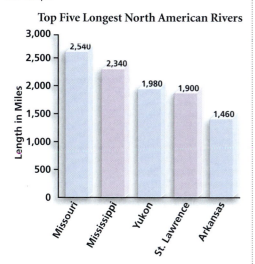

Illustration *Illustrations,* such as drawings, photographs, and other artwork, may be used to show readers something new, unfamiliar, or indescribable; what something or someone looks like; or how something works. Illustrations differ from diagrams in that illustrations usually have more detail and are often in color. (See also **Diagram** on page 858.)

Storyboard *Storyboards* illustrate the course of an event or the scenes of a story. Storyboards may be used to plan a video or to map out the events in a story. The boxes in a storyboard contain drawings as well as text; text may also appear outside or under the boxes.

A boy finds a bottle on the beach. He sees a slip of paper inside the bottle.

He pulls out the slip of paper and reads what is written on it.

Table *Tables* provide detailed information arranged, using rows and columns, in an accessible, organized way. In the following example, notice that the information is logically organized and clearly labeled.

EXAMPLES

Two-Column Table

Top Five Travel Destinations, 1997	
Country	Number of Visitors (in millions)
France	66.8
United States	48.9
Spain	43.4
Italy	34.0
United Kingdom	26.0

Graphics 859

Three-Column Table

Spending by International Visitors to the U.S. in 1996		
Country	Number of Visitors (in thousands)	Amount of Money Spent (in millions)
Canada	15,301	$ 6,763.00
Mexico	8,530	$ 3,001.00
Japan	5,047	$13,163.00
United Kingdom	3,105	$ 7,306.00
Germany	1,973	$ 4,573.00
France	990	$ 2,255.00

Time Line Time lines identify events that have occurred over a given period of time. Usually, events are identified or described above the time line, and the time demarcations can be indicated above or below it. Some time lines are illustrated.

Timeline of Discoveries in Chemistry

The History of English: Origins and Uses

The History of English

The oldest English-language documents still in existence were first written about 1,300 years ago, but the English language was spoken long before that. Over the centuries, English has evolved into the very different but equally rich and expressive language that it is today. The history of this development is a story of people, places, and times.

similarities of many words. The word *north* is an example.

EXAMPLE
ENGLISH: *north*
FRENCH: *nord*
GERMAN: *norden*
ITALIAN: *nord*
SPANISH: *norte*

Beginnings of English

Many of the world's languages come from an ancient language called **Proto-Indo-European.** There are no records of this parent language, but it was probably spoken by peoples who lived in southeast Europe or Asia Minor six or seven thousand years ago. Tribes of these people slowly migrated throughout Europe and as far east as India. As they wandered in different directions, each tribe developed its own **dialect,** or distinct version of the language. The dialects eventually developed into separate languages. English, French, German, Italian, and Spanish are just a few of the languages that eventually developed through many stages from Proto-Indo-European. The kinship is obvious in the

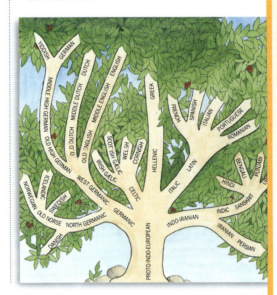

The History of English

The History of English, pp. 861–865
Alignments
TEKS 6D, 16B

Old English

Around A.D. 450, three Germanic tribes from northern Europe—the Angles, Saxons, and Jutes—began to invade, conquer, and settle parts of Britain. They took over land that had been settled centuries earlier by the Celts and later conquered, settled, then abandoned by the Romans. The separate dialects of the Germanic language the Angles, Saxons, and Jutes spoke eventually blended into one language, which was called *Englisc*. Today this language is referred to as **Old English.** Many Old English words have come down to us only slightly altered. Here are some examples:

EXAMPLES

Old English	Modern English
etan	eat
drincan	drink
daeg	day
niht	night

The structure of Old English, however, was very different from English today. Old English relied on word endings, or **inflections,** to indicate a word's gender, number, case, and person. For example, the noun *hund* ("hound" or "dog") was written *hund, hundes, hunde, hundas, hunda,* or *hundum,* depending on its use in a sentence. In contrast, Modern English relies on a word's position in a sentence to show the word's role in that sentence.

As Old English speakers came into contact with speakers of other languages, particularly Latin-speaking missionaries and Norse invaders, new words, or **loanwords,** entered the language. As English speakers learned Latin, they borrowed words such as *school, altar, candle,* and *paper* and made them part of English. Similarly, as Nordic Vikings settled in Britain, Norse words such as *skalpr (scalp), skrap (scrap), skith (ski),* and *sky* became part of the English language. In fact, most English words that begin with *sc* or *sk* are of Norse origin.

Middle English

In 1066, the Normans from France seized control of England. For the next 150–200 years, French was used for almost all written communication. It was the language of government, business, law, and literature in England. The common people of England, however, still spoke English—a form gradually changing into the language now called **Middle English.**

Why did the English language not die out under French rule? Several factors weighed in favor of English. For one thing, the English-speaking people—the common people, such as farmers, herders, servants, and craftspeople—outnumbered their French-speaking rulers. For another, the French rulers in England gradually lost contact with their French culture and language. As a result, three hundred years after the French invasion, English was once again the language of government, business, literature, and law in England. By this time, however, its grammar was becoming simpler as many of the complicated word endings disappeared. Both the grammar and structure were more like the English spoken today, as you can see from the following passage by the fourteenth-century poet Geoffrey Chaucer.

> Bifel that in that sesoun on a day
> In Southwerk at the Tabard, as I lay
> Redy to wenden on my pilgrymage
> To Caunterbury with ful devout corage,

Modern English

By 1500, almost everyone in England spoke English. However, because speakers and writers in different parts of England used different versions of the language, they often had trouble understanding each other. Gradually, the version spoken in London—the center of English culture, business, and trade—became the most widely used. When William Caxton brought the first printing press to London in 1476, he printed books in the London dialect. As printed books began to spread across England, spelling and grammar began to be "fixed" in print, and London English became the standard throughout England. The availability of cheap books meant that more people were reading and using the new standardized language. Handbooks of proper English usage, spelling, and pronunciation were soon published, along with the first dictionaries.

Although it had been standardized, the English language did not stop growing. As the Renaissance revived interest in classical languages, thousands of Greek and Latin words entered English. At the same time, English expanded into an international language. From the sixteenth century to the nineteenth century, English merchants, explorers, and settlers spread English to other parts of the globe. They also learned new words from other languages, enriching English with imports such as the following:

EXAMPLES

AFRICAN: marimba
DUTCH: cruise
HINDI: jungle
SPANISH: fiesta
TURKISH: yogurt

American English

Immigration to the American colonies in the late seventeenth and early eighteenth centuries brought about a new version of the language—*American English.* Over time, English colonists in America invented new words and changed the pronunciations and uses of some old words. They also borrowed words, such as *squash,* from American Indian languages. By 1776, the version of English spoken in America was distinct enough from that spoken in England to be called American English.

Like the United States itself, American English represents a variety of cultures and peoples. American Indians, Africans, and immigrants from countries around the world have enriched the language with words from their native tongues. Here are some examples:

EXAMPLES

AFRICAN: gumbo, okra
AMERICAN INDIAN: coyote, toboggan
CHINESE: yen, chop suey
GERMAN: kindergarten, frankfurter
SPANISH: canyon, patio

English in the Twenty-First Century

English has become the most widely used language in the world. It is an official language in more than eighty-seven nations and territories. About one-third of the world's population speaks English. Diplomats frequently use it to communicate, and it is the world language of science, technology, aviation, and international trade. As people around the world contribute to the language, the word count continues to grow; the last count was over 600,000 words.

Varieties of American English

American English is a rich and flexible language that offers many choices. To speak and write effectively—at home, at school, and on the job—you need to know what the varieties of American English are and how to choose among them.

Dialects of American English

Like all languages, American English has many distinct versions, called *dialects*. Each has unique features of grammar, vocabulary, and pronunciation.

Ethnic Dialects   An *ethnic dialect* is often used by people who share the same cultural heritage. Because Americans come from many different cultures, American English includes many different ethnic dialects. These dialects include, among others, Irish English, Yiddish English, and the Hispanic English of people from Puerto Rico, Cuba, Mexico, and Latin America. Black English, one of the largest ethnic dialects, has elements of African languages and the dialect of the American South.

Regional Dialects   The United States has four major regional dialects: the *Northern,* the *Midland,* the *Southern,* and the *Western.* The pronunciations of words often vary from one dialect to another. For example, some Southerners pronounce the words *ten* and *tin* the same way—as "tin." Some Midlanders and Southerners add an *r* sound to words, so that *wash* sounds like "warsh."

Similarly, regional dialects differ in vocabulary and grammar. For example, someone from New England might call a soft drink *tonic,* while people in other parts of the country might call it *soda* or *pop.* Someone from the South might say "sick *at* my stomach," while someone from the North might say "sick *to* my stomach."

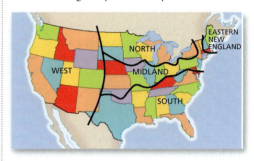

Standard American English

No variety of English is better or more correct than another. However, **standard American English** is the variety of English that is more widely used and accepted than any other in the United States. Because it is commonly understood, it allows people from different regions and cultures to communicate with one another clearly. It is the variety of English you read and hear most often in books and magazines and on radio, television, and the Internet. People are expected to use standard English in most school and business situations. This textbook presents rules and guidelines for using standard American English. To distinguish between standard American English and other varieties, this book uses the labels *standard* and *nonstandard*. Nonstandard language is not "wrong" language—it is language that is inappropriate in situations where standard English is expected.

Standard English—Formal to Informal

Your use of standard English can be formal, informal or anywhere in between. Which type you choose for communication will depend on many factors, including the occasion and purpose for which you are writing or speaking and your intended audience. The following chart shows some of the appropriate uses of formal and informal standard English.

Uses of Formal and Informal Standard English

Formal

Speaking formal classroom presentations, banquets, dedication ceremonies, and interviews

Writing serious papers and reports, tests, business letters, and job or college applications

Informal

Speaking everyday conversations, group discussions, informal speeches and telephone conversations

Writing personal letters, many types of classroom writing, and many newspaper and magazine articles

Standard English gives you the freedom to say the same things in many different ways. For example, in a formal setting you might say, "I'm pleased to meet you." On a less formal occasion you might choose to say, "Hi, how are you?" or "How's it going?" The differences between formal and informal English are mainly in sentence structure, word choice, and tone.

Features of Formal and Informal Standard English

Formal

Sentence Structure longer and more complex

Word Choice more precise and refined, sometimes technical or scientific

Tone serious and dignified

Informal

Sentence Structure shorter and simpler

Word Choice simple and ordinary, often includes contractions, colloquialisms, and slang

Tone conversational

Colloquialisms The word *colloquial* comes from a Latin word that means "conversation." *Colloquialisms* are the informal words and phrases of conversational language. They bring flavor and color to everyday speech and a friendly tone to writing. Many colloquialisms are figures of speech.

EXAMPLES She told me to quit **making such a racket.**

Since quitting her high-paying job, Pat has been **living hand-to-mouth.**

Slang *Slang* is highly informal English consisting of made-up words or old words used in new ways. It is often used by specific groups of people, such as students, musicians, or military personnel.

EXAMPLES **bad:** good, excellent
make like: imitate
scarf down: eat greedily

Although some slang words become accepted parts of the language, most have a relatively short life span.

Varieties of American English

The Library/Media Center

Using Print and Electronic Sources

The library/media center in your school or community provides a range of print and electronic sources you may consult to find information for classroom assignments and your personal interests. **Print sources** include books, periodicals (magazines, newspapers, and journals), and specialized forms (such as microforms or vertical files). **Electronic sources** include CD-ROMs, the Internet, DVDs, and online databases.

Call Number A *call number* is a unique number or letter code assigned to a library book. The call number indicates how a book is classified and where it can be found in the library. Librarians use two systems of classification to assign call numbers: the Dewey decimal system and the Library of Congress system. (See also **Card Catalog** on this page.)

- **Dewey decimal system** Many school libraries use the *Dewey decimal system*. This classification system assigns numbers to nonfiction books according to ten general subject categories. Each area is assigned a range of numbers, and within each range, subgroups of numbers identify more specific categories. Novels and short stories are grouped together under the category *Fiction* and are arranged by the author's last name. Biographies and autobiographies are arranged alphabetically by the subject's last name.

- **Library of Congress System** The *Library of Congress system* uses code letters to identify subject categories. The first code letter of a book's call number identifies its general category (such as history), and the second letter identifies the subcategory (such as American). The string of numbers beside each pair of letters identifies a specific book within a category.

Card Catalog A traditional card catalog is a collection of index cards that contains important information about the books in a library. For each book, there are at least two cards, a *title card* and an *author card.* Nonfiction books also have a third card, a *subject card.* Occasionally you will also see *cross-reference cards,* which contain the words *see* or *see also* and advise you where to look for additional information.

Catalog cards are arranged in alphabetical order in a cabinet of drawers, and each card contains the following information:

- the **call number** assigned to a book by the Dewey decimal or Library of Congress classification system
- the **author's full name,** last name first
- the full **title** and **subtitle** of a book
- the place and date of **publication**
- the general **subject** of a book (a subject card may show specific headings)
- a **description** of the book, such as its size and number of pages, and whether it is illustrated
- **cross-references** to other headings or related topics under which a book is listed

Many libraries have replaced or supplemented traditional card catalogs in drawers with electronic or online card catalogs. (See also **Online Card Catalog** on page 000.)

CD-ROMs A *CD-ROM* (*C*ompact *D*isc-*R*ead *O*nly *M*emory) is a digitally-encoded compact disc that is designed to hold visual as well as audio information. A single CD-ROM may contain the equivalent of 250,000 pages of printed text. Many reference tools, such as encyclopedias, dictionaries, and indexes, are now available on CD-ROMs. CD-ROMs contain the same text as the printed versions but have the added attractions of searching capabilities, interactive graphics, and audio. The data can be accessed only by a computer with a CD-ROM drive, and the information can be printed out or downloaded directly to a disk. (See also the **Reference Sources** chart on page 870.)

Internet The *Internet* is a global network of computers that enables a computer user to access information from other computers or networks anywhere in the world. Created in the late 1960s, the Internet was originally used by research scientists to share data electronically, but today the Internet has grown far beyond its beginnings and contains information on thousands of topics, scientific and nonscientific. Almost anyone who has a computer equipped with a modem can use the Internet, and there are many ways to view Internet material, including FTP (File Transfer Protocol), Gopher, Telnet, and ***World Wide Web browsers,*** which provide access to files and documents, news and discussion groups, bulletin boards, e-mail, and the ***World Wide Web*** (see page 871). The World Wide Web is the place on the Internet you are most likely to go for your research.

Microforms *Microforms* are photographically-reduced articles from newspapers and magazines. The two most common kinds of microforms are *microfilm* (a roll or reel of film) and *microfiche* (a small sheet of film). Special machines are needed in order to enlarge microfilm and microfiche images and project them onto a screen for viewing or reading. Libraries with documents on microfilm or microfiche typically provide these machines.

Online Card Catalog An *online card catalog* is an electronic or computerized version of the card catalog. Instead of searching through individual cards, you may find a book by typing in a book's ***title, author,*** or ***subject,*** or you can use the ***key words*** command to find all the books that contain a certain word or words in their titles or descriptions. The computer quickly retrieves information based on your request and provides you with a screen similar to the one on the next page.

The Library/Media Center, pp. 866–875
Alignments
TEKS 8B, 13B

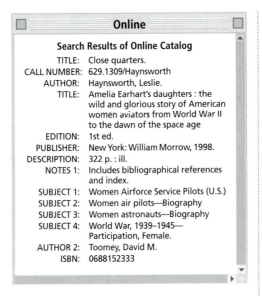

One advantage of using an online catalog is that the computer can tell you the *status* of a book—whether it is checked out, on loan to another library, or available at another library. Some online card catalogs even tell when a book that has been checked out is due back at your library.

Online Databases An *online database* is a contained system of electronic information that may be accessed only by computer. In most cases, organizations such as universities, libraries, or businesses create or subscribe to databases that are of specific interest to the people in those organizations. LEXIS–NEXIS is an example of a subscription-only database. Users must have an identification number that allows them to read the information. Other databases are public and may be accessed through the World Wide Web.

Online Sources Information that is *online* is information that may be located and accessed by using computers. Computers that are online are able to communicate with each other over telecommunication lines, such as telephone lines and fiber-optic cables, and via satellite. When computers are linked, they form a *network*. Computer networks are what make the Internet and the World Wide Web possible.

Radio, Television, and Film A large portion of the programming on *radio* and *television* is made up of newscasts, newsmagazines, and documentaries, which are all important sources of information. Documentaries and educational materials are also produced on *film* or *video*. Descriptive listings of radio and television programs appear in newspapers and, in some cases, on the Internet. Indexes of educational films and videos, such as *The Video Source Book* (Gale, 1998), are available at libraries and book stores. Be sure to check the ratings provided for the films and videos before viewing them.

Readers' Guide to Periodical Literature The *Readers' Guide to Periodical Literature* is an index of articles, poems, and stories from more than two hundred magazines and journals (periodicals). The articles are listed alphabetically by author and by subject, but not by title, and the headings are set in boldface type. A key located in the front of the *Readers' Guide* explains the meanings of the abbreviations used in the entries.

In addition to maintaining an updated bound set of the *Readers' Guide,* some libraries subscribe to an online version. To use this version, enter a search word or phrase into the computer and choose the records that interest you from the search results.

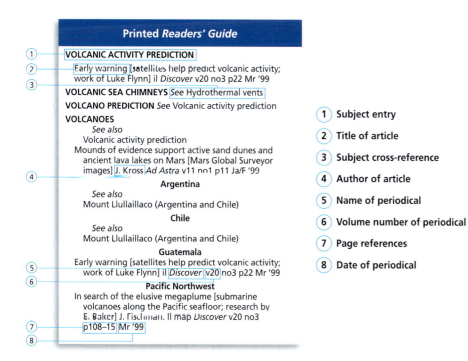

1	Subject entry
2	Title of article
3	Subject cross-reference
4	Author of article
5	Name of periodical
6	Volume number of periodical
7	Page references
8	Date of periodical

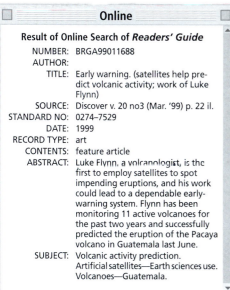

Reference Books Reference books are books of specialized information that are set aside in a separate section of any library. Reference books contain facts and information organized in a logical way, such as by alphabetical or chronological order or by category. Examples of reference books include encyclopedias, dictionaries, thesauruses, indexes, books of quotations, atlases, and almanacs. (See also the **Reference Sources** chart on page 870.)

Reference Sources There are many different kinds of reference sources that you can use to find specific kinds of information. The chart on the next page identifies and describes common reference sources and provides examples of print and electronic reference sources.

Reference Sources

Types of Reference Sources	Description	Examples
ALMANACS	Up-to-date information about current events, facts, statistics, and dates	• *Information Please Almanac* • *TIME Almanac- The Reference Edition* CD-ROM
ATLASES	Maps and geographical information	• *Hammond Atlas of the World* • *Microsoft Encarta World Atlas* CD-ROM
BIOGRAPHICAL REFERENCES (GENERAL)	Information about birth, nationality, and major accomplishments of prominent people, past and present	• *Biography Index* • *The International Who's Who* • *Biography Index* CD-ROM • *Dictionary of American Biography* on CD-ROM
BIOGRAPHICAL REFERENCES (SPECIALIZED)	Information about people noted for accomplishments in a specific field or for membership in a specific group	• *American Men and Women of Science 1998–9* (Bowker) • *Who's Who Among African Americans* • *The Multimedia Encyclopedia of the American Indian* CD-ROM
BOOKS OF QUOTATIONS	Famous quotations indexed or grouped together by subject	• *American Heritage Dictionary of American Quotations* • *The Oxford Dictionary of Quotations*
BOOKS OF SYNONYMS	Lists of exact or more interesting words to express ideas	• *Roget's International Thesaurus* • *Oxford Thesaurus on CD-ROM*
ENCYCLOPEDIAS	Articles of general information arranged alphabetically by subject in a single volume or in several volumes	• *The Columbia Encyclopedia* • *New Encyclopaedia Britannica* • The *World Book Encyclopedia* • *The Columbia Encyclopedia on CD-ROM*
INDEXES	Information in list form of articles found in periodicals or other information sources	• *Biography Index* • *New York Times Index* • *Art Index* CD-ROM • *Book Review Index* on CD-ROM
LITERARY REFERENCES	Information about where to locate various works of literature; information about authors and about individual literary works	• *Columbia Granger's Index to Poetry* • *Contemporary Authors* series • *Columbia Granger's World of Poetry* on CD-ROM • *Masterplots Nonfiction, Drama, Poetry* CD-ROM

Reference Sources

Types of Reference Sources	Description	Examples
SPECIAL REFERENCE SOURCES FOR SPECIFIC SUBJECTS	Information related to specific subjects or topics of interest to researchers in specific fields	• *Encyclopedia of North American Sports History* (Facts on File) • *The Lives of the Artists* • *History of Music* CD-ROMs • *The Dictionary of Science and Technology* CD-ROM
STYLE AND WRITING MANUALS	Information about proper writing style and preparation of research papers	• *The Chicago Manual of Style* • *MLA Style Manual and Guide to Scholarly Publishing,* Second Edition • *Harbrace College Handbook* CD-ROM

Vertical File A *vertical file* is a set of file drawers containing materials that are not likely to be cataloged anywhere else, such as pamphlets, newspaper clippings, and photographs. As the use of electronic or online resources increases, vertical files are less likely to be maintained by libraries.

World Wide Web (*WWW* or the *Web*) Perhaps the best-known part of the Internet, the *World Wide Web* is an enormous system of linked, or connected, documents that contain text, graphics, sounds, and even video. The Web can be navigated only by computer users who have *browser* software installed on their computers. Documents (*Web sites* or *Web pages*) on the World Wide Web are connected by *hyperlinks,* which are specially coded parts of each document. When you click on a hyperlink, the computer accesses a new site and makes it appear on-screen so it can be viewed, printed, or downloaded.

World Wide Web, Key Terms The following terms will help you understand the workings of the World Wide Web.

- **Browser** A *browser* is a software application that allows you to access, save, and download documents, images, sounds, and videos from the Web. Searching the Web in this way is called *browsing* (See also **World Wide Web** on this page and **Web Site** on page 000.)

- **Domain** A *domain* is the name of a computer or server on the Internet from which you may access information. Every Web address specifies a domain, or particular computer.

- **Home page** A *home page* is the first screen or page of a Web site, and it usually functions as a guide to the rest of the site. Usually, the home page identifies the person or organization that sponsored or created the site and provides an index or table of contents for the site. Often a home page includes hyperlinks to related sites on the Web. (See also **Web Site** on page 872.)

- **Hyperlink** A *hyperlink,* or *link,* is a "button" or code word that allows a user to move from one place or page on the World Wide Web to another. On screen, hyperlinks usually appear in a contrasting color and are underlined. (See also **Hypertext Markup Language** on this page.)

- **Hypertext**   A *hypertext* program allows a user to find and open related files and documents on the Web without having to quit or close the original file. It allows a user to move to and from one document to another via hyperlinks.

- **Hypertext Markup Language**   *Hypertext Markup Language (HTML)* is the language used to create documents on the World Wide Web.

- **Hypertext Transfer Protocol**   *Hypertext Transfer Protocol (HTTP)* is the language used by browser software to connect to different sites or documents on the World Wide Web.

- **Search engine**   A search engine is a tool for finding specific information on the Web. (See also **World Wide Web, Searching** on page 873.)

- **URL** (*U*niform *R*esource *L*ocator)   A *URL* is the address of a specific document on the Web. A typical URL includes words, abbreviations, numbers, and punctuation. The URL shown below would connect you to newspapers from around the world, organized by country and region, that can be read online through the Internet Public Library. The parts of the address are explained below.

  http://www.ipl.org/reading/news

  1. The **protocol,** or how the site is formatted
  2. The **domain name.** Domain names have at least two parts. The part on the left is the name of the company, institution, or other organization. The part on the right is a general domain. Here are the abbreviations of the most common general domains. (see also **Domain** on page 871.)

Common Domains on the World Wide Web	
com	commercial
edu	educational
gov	governmental
net	administrative
org	nonprofit organization

  3. The **subdirectory name** that shows where the specific piece of information you want is stored. (Each word following a slash requests a narrower search into the site.) Not all addresses will have this part.

- **Web Site** (or **Web Page**)   A *Web site* or *Web page* is a document or location on the Web that is linked to other locations on the Web. A site may contain several Web pages. The screen on page 873 shows the most important parts of a browser and a typical Web site.

World Wide Web, Plagiarism   To take another person's idea or work and present it as your own is called *plagiarism*. Because the World Wide Web is such a vast source of information and because it is easy to download or copy information, plagiarism of electronic material has become a serious concern. Treat any information you find on the World Wide Web as if it were from a printed or published source. Avoid plagiarism by **paraphrasing** information you find on the Web, and **be sure to cite the sources of your information.** (See also page 237.)

TEACHING TIP

- **URL** (*Uniform Resource Locator*)
The most common general domains listed in the chart on this page are only for the United States. Countries other than the United States often have other domain names.

1. **Toolbar** The buttons on the toolbar allow you to complete different functions such as moving to different pages, printing out information, searching, and seeing or hiding images.
2. **Location Window** This box shows you the URL, or address, of the site you are viewing.
3. **Content area** The area of the screen where the text, images, hyperlinks, and other parts of a Web page appear.
4. **Hyperlinks** Clicking on internal hyperlinks takes you to other parts of the same Web site. External hyperlinks take you to other Web sites.
5. **Scroll bar** Clicking along the horizontal or vertical scroll bar (or on the arrows at either end) allows you to move left to right or up and down in the image area.

World Wide Web, Searching Computer users can locate information on the World Wide Web by using three different search methods: *direct address, search engines,* and *subject catalogs*. A combination of all three types of searches usually works best. Most search services on the Web allow you to use all three.

- **Direct address** The easiest way to find a Web site is to enter its address, or URL, in the location box. Type the address exactly, since the Internet will only identify it if the case and punctuation are correct. Of course, this search method does not work unless you have an exact address for the site you want to find.
- **Search engines** Search engines allow you to search *databases* that contain information about the millions of sites available on the Web. These databases are compiled automatically by computer programs called *robots*. (See also **World Wide Web, Using Search Engines** on page 874.)
- **Subject catalogs** A *subject catalog* provides an extensively organized table of contents of the World Wide Web. Unlike search engines, subject catalogs are organized by humans, not by machines. Information from Web sites is organized in broad categories, such as *Education* and *Entertainment,* which contain many specific subcategories. These subcategories in turn break down into even more specific sub-subcategories. To research a topic using a subject catalog, users identify a broad category and keep narrowing their focus through the subcategories and

sub-subcategories until they find the specific information they need.

World Wide Web, Using Search Engines

Unlike subject catalogs, *search engines* allow you to search for Web sites that contain key words or phrases. These search tools also allow you to refine your searches.

- **Key word search**   A *key word search* helps you locate sites that contain specific words or phrases. It works best when you have selected a very clear topic to research. To begin a search, type key words in the space provided on the search engine screen and press the return key or the search or find button. The search engine checks the key words against the Web sites indexed in its database, noting the frequency and importance of the words you requested. When the comparison is completed, the results appear in the form of a list. The sites that contain all your key words should appear at the top of the list, and sites that contain fewer appear later, in descending

Refining a Key Word Search	
Tip	**How It Works**
Replace general terms with more specific ones.	A key word that is common or used in ways you do not expect can result in irrelevant matches. EXAMPLE If you are interested in classical dance, enter *ballet* instead of *dance*.
Use quotation marks.	By placing your key words or phrases in quotation marks, the search engine will find sites that use the words exactly as you have typed them. EXAMPLE Enter *Irish dance* to find sites specific to traditional Irish dancing rather than sites about Irish culture or ballet.
Use *and* and *not*.	Narrow your search by putting the word *and* between your key words. The search engine will find only Web sites that contain all words connected by *and*. EXAMPLE For sites that mention either form of entertainment, enter *Irish dance and Irish music*. Use *not* between key words to make sure that the search engine does not pull up sites that deal with topics that are similar but unrelated. EXAMPLE Enter *Celtic not Boston* to find information about Irish history and culture and avoid sites about the basketball team.
Use *or*.	To broaden your search, use *or* to let the search engine know that you would accept sites that contain any of your key words. EXAMPLE If you want sites that discuss either Irish dance or Irish music, enter *Irish dance or Irish music*.

order of relevant matches. Most search engines assign the items on the list a percentage or rank number to indicate how well the site matched your request.

- **Refining a Key Word Search** Because search engines may identify hundreds or thousands of Web sites—or none at all—that contain your key words, you may find it useful to refine or focus your search to get good results. The chart on page 874 suggests some strategies that may help you. Keep in mind, however, that different search engines may require slightly different commands than those listed here. The Help section of your search engine should tell you the specific commands that limit searches on engine.

World Wide Web, Web Site Evaluation

The content of the World Wide Web is not monitored for accuracy in the way most newspapers, books, or magazines are. Consequently, you must think critically about the information you find there to make sure it is authoritative and reliable. Here are questions to help you to *evaluate* a Web site's value as a source of information.

Evaluating Web Sites	
Questions to Ask	**Why You Should Ask**
Who created or sponsored the Web site?	The information on a Web site is selected by the site's creator or sponsor, which the Web site's home page should identify. To make sure the information you get from the Web is reliable, use only Web sites that are affiliated with reputable organizations, such as government agencies, universities, and museums. The Web sites for these organizations will usually belong in the *edu, gov,* or *org* domains.
When was the page first posted and is it frequently updated?	This information usually appears at the end of a home page. Most often, it includes a copyright notice, the date of the most recent update, and a link to the creator's e-mail address. Since you want your information to be up-to-date, only use sites that have been updated recently.
What other Web pages is the site linked to?	Looking at the links provided in a Web site can help you determine how legitimate it is. If a site is a source of accurate information, it will have links to other reputable Web sites.
Does the Web site present information objectively?	Look for signs of bias, such as strong language or statements of opinion. An objective site will present ideas from both sides of an issue or debate clearly and fairly.
Is the Web site well designed?	A well-designed Web site has legible type, clear graphics, and working links and is easily searched or navigated. The written content of the site should be well organized and use proper spelling, punctuation, and grammar.

Quick Reference Handbook

Reading and Vocabulary

Reading

Skills and Strategies

You can use the following skills and strategies to become a more effective reader.

Author's Purpose and Point of View, Determining
An author has a reason or *purpose* for writing a selection—to inform, to persuade, to entertain, or to express feelings. In addition, authors have *points of view;* that is, they express their opinions or attitudes about their subjects. To better understand a text, read carefully to determine an author's purpose and point of view.

EXAMPLE   In a matter of minutes you can learn a lifesaving technique. Using the Heimlich maneuver, you can dislodge an object from the throat of a choking victim. First, stand behind the victim and place your closed fist just below the victim's rib cage. Then pull your fist upward in a short thrust. In two quick steps you may have saved a life.

Author's purpose: To inform about the steps of the Heimlich maneuver

Author's point of view: The Heimlich maneuver can save lives and is therefore a good thing to know.

Cause-and-Effect Relationships, Analyzing
A *cause* is the reason something happens. An *effect* is the result of that cause. By asking the questions "Why did this happen?" and "What are the effects?" as you read, you are analyzing cause-and-effect relationships in a text.

EXAMPLE   We find fossils—the remains, preserved in rock, of plant and animal organisms—because of the conditions in which the organism died. If an organism died in a soft, wet place, such as a riverbed, its soft tissue soon dissolved or was eaten and its plant remains or its skeleton was covered by sediment. Minerals in the watery sediment then reacted with the plant remains or with the animal's shell and hardened it. More sediment covered the remains or the hardened shell, thus preserving it in stone.

Analysis: Fossilization is caused by an organism that died and decomposed in a watery environment. The effects of the moist climate were that the moisture and sediment preserved the dead organism's remains.

Clue Words				
Cause-Effect	Chronological Order	Comparison-Contrast	Listing	Problem-Solution
as a result	after	although	also	as a result
because	as	as well as	for example	nevertheless
consequently	before	but	in fact	therefore
if . . . then	finally	either . . . or	most important	this led to
nevertheless	first	however	to begin with	thus
since	not long after	not only . . . but also	such as	consequently
so that	now	on the other hand	finally	otherwise
therefore	second	similarly		
this led to	then	unless		
thus	when	yet		

Clue Words, Using Writers use certain *clue words* to connect their ideas or to show relationships between ideas. Readers can use these clue words to identify the text's structure or organizational pattern. Common clue words are listed in the chart above. (See also **Text Structures** on page 885.)

Conclusions, Drawing When you *draw conclusions,* you combine the information in a text with information you already know. As you read, you interpret and evaluate the information from a text, connect it to your experiences, and then draw conclusions that are logical yet specific to the text. (See also page 172.)

EXAMPLE I must admit that writing is not an easy job nor is it one that lets you socialize much. Often I have spent my vacations and weekends in the library or at the computer trying to finish an article or a paper before a deadline. Still, when you finally see your name in print, the effort seems worth it.

Conclusion: The writer is a professional writer.

Fact and Opinion, Distinguishing A *fact* is information that can be proven true or false. An *opinion* expresses a belief or point of view. You cannot prove that an opinion is true or false. Facts, however, are statements which can be checked in other reference works for accuracy. Facts are often used to support opinions. A reader who can distinguish between a fact and an opinion will not be easily misled. (See also page 255.)

EXAMPLE

Fact: Wolfgang Amadeus Mozart was a composer who lived from 1756–1791. [Reference works support this as a true statement.]

Opinion: Mozart was the greatest composer who ever lived. [This statement cannot be proved true or false; it represents what one writer believes about Mozart.]

Generalizations, Forming A reader forms a *generalization* by combining information in a text with personal experience to make a judgment that applies to the world beyond the text. (See also page 132.)

Reading and Vocabulary, pp. 876–895
Alignments
TEKS 6B, 6C, 6D, 6F, 6G, 7A, 7B, 7D, 7E, 7F, 7G, 7H, 12C
TAAS R1, R2, R3, R4, R5, R6
English II End-of-Course 1, 2, 3

EXAMPLE The Antarctic continent, the southernmost landmass, is buried under more than a mile of ice and surrounded by oceans and seas that are partly frozen and filled with icebergs. In summer, the temperatures rarely climb above freezing. On land, there are very few plants or animals that can withstand the cold, especially the deep cold (as low as –112°F) of winter.

Generalization: The Antarctic continent is not a place many creatures can or would want to live because it is so cold.

Graphics, Interpreting

Graphics convey information by using pictures or symbols. Writers use them to provide supporting evidence for their ideas. The most common forms of graphics used in informational writing are **charts, diagrams, graphs, tables,** and **time lines.** Graphics illustrate complex information in a simple, visual format. Most often, they provide a clear comparison of different but related points of information. As a reader, your job is to interpret the information presented in a graphic and to draw your own conclusions. You will most likely encounter the following types of graphics in your reading.

- **Charts** show the relationships of the parts of a whole to each other. Some charts are rectangular, but a pie chart is circular. The point of a pie chart is usually to show the proportions of the sections, not to show the specific amounts of each section or the value of the whole pie. The following pie chart shows the percentage of people in each class of Malory High School that regularly wear athletic shoes. Notice how the segments of the pie chart are identified as percentages.

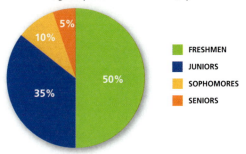

- **Diagrams** use pictures or symbols, such as circles or arrows, to illustrate a process, to compare abstract ideas, or to provide instruction. Diagrams should not be used to present numerical data because the shapes and forms used in diagrams do not accurately represent amounts. Look, for example, at the following diagram illustrating one octave (eight notes) of the C-major scale. These notes would correspond to the white keys on a piano keyboard.

A **Venn Diagram** uses intersecting circles to show how two ideas or things compare. The section of the diagram where the circles overlap contains the elements shared by the two things being compared. The remaining area in each circle contains the elements that are unique to each thing being compared. The Venn diagram on the next page illustrates the similarities and differences between the games of tennis and squash.

Venn Diagram

Tennis — **Similarities** — **Squash**

- **Tennis**
  - Outdoor court; court surface may be clay or grass
  - Ball hit over a net between opposing players
  - Sets of games comprise matches; men play up to five sets; women play up to three

- **Similarities**
  - Equipment includes a racket and small, rubberized ball
  - Ball must be hit by opponent before it bounces twice on the floor or ground

- **Squash**
  - Indoor, enclosed court; walls are part of the playing court
  - Ball hit onto any of the walls by players alternating shots
  - Games played to nine points; best of three or five games comprises match

- **Line and Bar Graphs** show changes or trends over time. Usually the horizontal axis in a line or bar graph indicates points in time, and the vertical axis shows quantities. The line and bar graphs below illustrate the sales trends of two brands of athletic shoes.

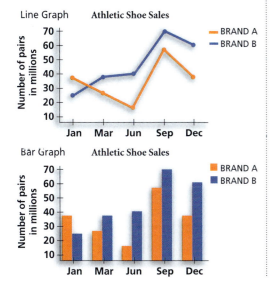

Notice that the vertical axes on both graphs begin at zero. Beginning a vertical axis with zero ensures that the data will be plotted accurately. Check for this when reading line or bar graphs. Also, be wary of any graph that switches the vertical and horizontal axes. If the vertical axis indicates the passing of time, the resulting peaks and valleys shown on the graph may be misleading. In the line graph below, the vertical axis indicates time. Notice how difficult it is to draw any conclusions from the graph.

Reading 879

Sales of Three Brands of Athletic Shoes in Units of Millions					
Athletic Shoes	January	March	June	September	December
Brand A	40	33	20	57	41
Brand B	27	40	39	71	60
Brand C	11	15	19	21	25

- **Tables, like the one above,** provide information in an easy-to-read format. Tables do not show trends and patterns in data. Readers must draw their own conclusions about any relationships among the data.

- **Time lines** identify events that take place over the course of time. A time line is basically the horizontal axis of a graph. Usually, events are identified or described above the time line and the time demarcations are indicated below it. The time line below outlines important literary events in early Persian and Arabic literature.

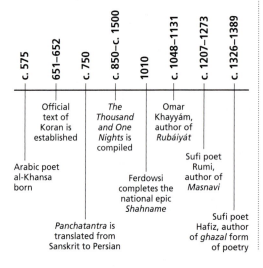

Effective graphics contain the following elements:

- a **body** that presents information in the form of a chart, diagram, graph, table, or time line; the body is specific to the type of information or data that is presented
- **labels** that identify and give meaning to the information shown in the graphic
- a **legend** that identifies special symbols, color coding, scale, or other features you need to understand the graphic; the legend appears as a small box placed near the body
- a **source** that tells where the information contained in the graphic was found; knowing the source helps you evaluate the accuracy of the graphic
- a **title** that identifies the subject or main idea of the graphic

As a reader, you should always read graphics carefully and with a critical eye. Keep in mind the following tips.

1. **Always read the title, labels, and legend** of any graphic before analyzing its data.
2. **Draw your own conclusions** and compare them to those of the writer.
3. **Think about what information is *not* included in the graphic.** Important information is sometimes left out because it does not support the author's conclusions.

4. **Watch out for optical illusions in graphs.** For example, bar graphs and pie charts that are shown in three dimensions are easily misread because some sections look more dense than others. Also, pie charts are often "exploded," with one segment pulled away from the others. Your eye naturally will be drawn to the exploded piece, but you should still pay attention to the whole picture.

5. **Look for manipulated data** by making sure that the horizontal axis of any graph indicates time, not amount. Also, make sure that the axes of a graph or sections of a pie chart are clearly labeled and consistently marked.

Implied Main Idea, Identifying
Some writers do not directly state the main idea of their writing; instead, they choose to *imply*, or suggest, it. In this case, as a reader, you must analyze the meaning of the details you are given and decide what overall meaning these details combine to express. (See also **Stated Main Idea** on page 884.)

EXAMPLE Every Thursday Lila Martinez spends a few hours at the senior citizens' center. Her activities vary from week to week. Sometimes she reads aloud; other times she plays checkers; but mostly she listens to stories the older people tell. Occasionally, she hears a story more than once, but she does not mind because listening to the older folks reminds Lila of her own grandmother.

Implied main idea: Lila Martinez's Thursday sessions at the senior citizens' center are important to her because the residents remind her of her own grandmother.

Inferences, Making
An *inference* is a conclusion that a reader reaches based on information in a text and on the reader's prior knowledge and experience. As you read, you analyze the text to interpret what writers do not state directly and come to a decision. (See also **Conclusions, Drawing** on page 877.)

EXAMPLE Garrett Morgan, an African American inventor, received a patent in 1914 for his invention of the Safety Hood. The hood, which was like a helmet connected by tubing to a clean air source, allowed its wearer, including firefighters and miners, to enter poisoned atmospheres and breathe safely. The Safety Hood was updated during World War I, becoming the modern gas mask.

Inference: Fires, mines, and battlefields are all dangerous situations in which a person might benefit from wearing a Safety Hood.

Memorizing
Memorizing is the ability to read material and learn the exact words or the general concepts by heart. To develop your memorization skills, follow the tips in the chart below.

How to Memorize

1. Condense the information, if possible. Information can often be summarized or condensed in your notes.

2. Rehearse the material in several different ways. Using different senses often helps you to commit the material to memory. For example, write your notes, and then silently read them, remembering what they look like. Next, read the notes aloud into a tape recorder. Finally, listen to the recording. After some practice, you will learn which way or combination of ways helps you remember best.

3. Use memory tricks. Use the first letter of each word in a series to form a new word. Make a rhyme to help you remember facts. Associate information with a mental image.

4. Repeat the material. Review the material frequently in short, focused sessions. Try reading the material aloud, over and over again.

Paraphrasing A *paraphrase* is a type of summary in which you restate an author's ideas in your own words. Paraphrasing is a good way to check your understanding of the original text. To develop your paraphrasing skills, follow the tips in the chart below. Then, look at the example and paraphrase that follows the chart.

How to Paraphrase

1. **Read the entire selection.** Get the overall meaning before you begin writing your paraphrase.

2. **Identify the main idea of the selection.** Keep it in mind while you write your paraphrase.

3. **Identify the speaker in fictional material.** Is it the poet or author who is speaking or is a character speaking?

4. **Write your paraphrase in your own words.** Use complete sentences and standard paragraph form.

5. **Review the selection.** Be sure that your paraphrase expresses the same ideas as the original.

EXAMPLE   A camera is actually a simple mechanism. Images are made on film by aiming a camera at an object. Light reflected off the object travels toward the camera. Pushing the camera's shutter-release button opens and closes a tiny window in front of the camera, allowing the light to pass through a curved lens and reach the film. The shutter speed may be adjusted to allow for more or less light to shine through onto the film, varying the film exposure.

Paraphrase: A camera is a simple mechanism that works by aiming at an object. The reflection of the object enters the camera when you push the shutter button, which opens a tiny window in the front of the camera and lets the light reach the film. The speed of the shutter can be changed to allow more or less light into the camera, varying the film exposure.

Persuasive Techniques, Analyzing An author uses *persuasive techniques* to convince readers to think or act in a certain way. As you read persuasive writing, look for logical reasoning and facts; don't be misled by an overemphasis on emotional appeals or faulty reasoning. (See also page 257.)

EXAMPLE   Nick Moseley is the best choice for the tenth grade student council representative. Nick is an honors student, plays trumpet in the school band, serves as the goalie on the soccer team, and is active in his church. He knows how to be a team member and wants the tenth grade class to have fun and to make a difference in the community this year. Do the right thing and vote for Nick on Thursday.

Analysis: The first sentence is the opinion, which is supported by evidence in the second and third sentences. The last sentence, however, appeals to emotions.

Predicting   *Predicting* is making an educated guess about what will happen next in a narrative or about the main idea of an expository or persuasive composition. To make predictions, use information from the text— including headlines, subheadings, and illustrations or graphics—plus your own knowledge and experience.

EXAMPLE   In the past, family gatherings always turned into tense showdowns between us kids and Great-uncle Leo, the oldest member of the family. At the end of the meal, he would lean back in his chair and work his way down the table, telling each of us how we had disappointed him. This year, however, Leo was weakened from illness. His fierce blue eyes seemed faded, and he ate little.

Prediction: The younger members of the family may not get a lecture from Great-uncle Leo because he has been ill.

Problem-Solution Relationships, Analyzing When you read about a *problem,* you are dealing with an unanswered question. A *solution* is an attempt to answer the question. Writers will usually discuss a problem and then offer one or more solutions. Think about the problem as you read by asking questions such as "What is the problem?", "Who has the problem?" and "Why is it a problem?" Consider the offered solutions by asking "What is the outcome of each proposed solution?" and "What is the final result of the solution?" (See also page 134.)

EXAMPLE The only way for most students at Langley High to get to school is to take the bus. There is only one bus, however, and if students miss it, they miss the day. The student council proposed adding another bus to the route or asking students old enough to drive to form a car pool for the stragglers. The principal explained that the solutions were expensive or unfair to other students and suggested instead that students call each other to make sure they got to the bus. Now there is less absenteeism due to missing the bus.

Analysis: *What is the problem?* Students who miss the bus have no way to get to school. *Who has the problem?* Students who miss the bus. *Why is it a problem?* Students who miss the bus miss school. *What is the outcome of each proposed solution?* The student council proposals were too expensive or unfair to students who could drive. The principal's idea seemed easy and effective. *What is the final result?* Students call each other and get to school on time.

Reading Log, Using a A *reading log* is simply a place where you write about reading. As you read, write down your honest reactions to the text: Ask questions, make associations, and note especially important passages. You can also use a reading log to record any prereading predictions or postreading reflections. Because readers have different experiences, interests, beliefs, and opinions, no two reading logs will be alike.

Reading Rate, Adjusting Your *reading rate* is the speed at which you read a text. How quickly or how slowly you read depends upon why you are reading—your purpose. Your reading rate also depends on your background and experience with the material and the text's difficulty. Adjusting your reading rate to suit your purpose helps you to read more efficiently.

Reading Rates According to Purpose

Reading Rate	Purpose	Example
Scanning	Reading for specific details	Hunting for the scenes with the main character in them
Skimming	Reading for main points	Reviewing a textbook's chapter headings, subheadings, and illustrations in preparation for a test
Reading for mastery	Reading to understand and remember	Taking notes and outlining a section in a textbook before beginning an assignment
Reading for enjoyment	Reading at the speed you find most comfortable	Reading a magazine article about an interest or hobby

SQ3R *SQ3R* is a popular reading and study strategy. SQ3R stands for the five steps in the reading process:

S *Survey* the entire text. Look briefly at each page—the headings, titles, illustrations, charts, and the material in boldface and italics.

Q *Question* yourself as you do your survey. What should you know after completing your reading? Make a list of questions to be answered.

R *Read* the entire selection. Think of answers to your questions as you read.

R *Recite* in your own words answers to each question.

R *Review* the material by re-reading quickly, looking over the questions, and recalling the answers.

Stated Main Idea and Supporting Details, Identifying

A *main idea* is the focus or key idea in a piece of writing. Main ideas often appear as topic sentences of paragraphs or in an introductory or concluding paragraph of a longer work. *Supporting details* support or explain the main idea.

> **NOTE** A stated main idea is also called an **explicit main idea.** (See also **Implied Main Idea, Identifying** on page 881.)

EXAMPLE Professional journalism as a career for women began as early as 1828, when Sarah Hale, a noted advocate of women's rights, published the first magazine created by and for women. Women writers often reported on fashion and domestic issues. However, some women reporters went beyond those topics and wrote headline stories, went undercover for assignments, corresponded from abroad, or set up their own newspapers and magazines.

Main idea: Professional journalism as a career for women began in the early nineteenth century.

Supporting details: Sarah Hale published the first magazine for women. Some women reporters moved beyond fashion and domestic issues to cover national and international news or to set up their own newspapers.

Summarizing

A *summary* is a short restatement of the main points of a selection. When you summarize, you try to present a complete picture using as few words as possible. To practice your summarizing skills, follow the tips in the chart below. Then, look at the following example and its summary.

How to Summarize

1. **Review the material carefully.** Identify the main ideas and supporting details.

2. **Condense the material.** Focus only on key ideas, removing unnecessary details, examples, or repetitions. Write a sentence in your own words about each main idea.

3. **Use your list of sentences to write your summary in paragraph form.** Add transitional words to show how the ideas are related, if necessary.

4. **Revise your summary.** Be sure that it covers the most important points, that the information is expressed clearly, and that your words remain faithful to the author's intent.

EXAMPLE A sonnet is a fourteen-line poem, usually written in iambic pentameter. The Petrarchan sonnet has two parts: an octave (the first eight lines) and a sestet (the remaining six lines). Often the octave raises a question that is answered by the sestet. The Shakespearean sonnet has three quatrains (groups of four lines) and a concluding couplet (two lines). Both forms also have traditional rhyme schemes.

Summary: A sonnet is a fourteen-line poem set in iambic pentameter. The type of sonnet depends on how the lines are arranged. The Petrarchan sonnet has an octave and a sestet, while the Shakespearean sonnet has three quatrains and a couplet. Both forms have their own rhyme schemes.

Text Structures, Analyzing A *text structure* is the pattern a writer uses to organize ideas or events. Writers commonly use five major patterns of organization: *cause-effect*, *chronological order*, *comparison-contrast*, *listing*, and *problem-solution*. Being able to recognize the way people, things, events, and ideas are related will help you to better understand a text. Use the following guidelines in your analysis.

1. **Search the text for the main idea.** Look for clue words that signal a specific pattern of organization (See also **Clue Words, Using** on page 877).

2. **Study the text for other important ideas.** Think about how the ideas connect, and look for an obvious pattern.

3. **Remember that a writer might use one organizational pattern throughout an entire text or might combine patterns.**

4. **Use a graphic organizer to map the relationships among the ideas.** The four common text structures, or organizational patterns, are illustrated below.
   - **Cause-effect pattern** shows the relationship between results and the ideas or events that made the results happen. (See also page 95.) The example in the next column shows the effects of low body temperature during surgery.

- **Chronological order** shows events or ideas happening in sequence. The following example shows the sequence for making a decoupage project.

- **Comparison-Contrast pattern** points out similarities and differences in two or more topics. (See also page 62.) The following example compares two eighteenth-century African American women writers, Phillis Wheatley and Jarena Lee.

Phillis Wheatley — Similarities — **Jarena Lee**

(1753?–1784)
- Born into slavery
- Pursued vocation as poet
- Published poetry

Similarities:
- First African American women writers to publish in United States
- Avid readers of the Bible

(1783–?)
- Born a free woman
- Pursued vocation as preacher
- Published autobiography

- *Listing pattern* presents material according to certain criteria such as size or importance. The following example lists the levels of a food chain.

List

1. Producers (Green plants that make food from sunlight)
2. Primary consumers (Plant eaters)
3. Secondary consumers (Carnivores that eat plant eaters and other carnivores)
4. Decomposers (Bacteria and fungi that decompose dead organisms)

- *Problem-Solution pattern* presents a problem and explains attempted solutions, their outcomes, and the final or end result. (See also **Problem-Solution Relationships, Analyzing** on page 883.) The following example illustrates the problem of stage fright for an inexperienced performer and lists solutions. The chart shows the questions asked about the problem, the analysis of the proposed solutions and their outcomes, and the final result.

Problem

What is the problem? A performer experiences extreme nervousness, or stage fright, before going on stage.

Who has the problem? Inexperienced performers suffer from stage fright before a performance.

Why is it a problem? The thought of performing in front of people seriously frightens the performer.

Proposed Solutions

- Deep breathing
- Stretching tense neck muscles
- Making positive statements

Outcomes

- Deep breathing can help the performer.
- Stretching tense neck muscles can relax the performer.
- Making positive statements, such as *I am calm* or *I am prepared,* can boost the performer's confidence.

Results

The combined solutions of deep breathing, muscle relaxation, and positive statements can help combat stage fright.

Transitional Words and Phrases, Using

Transitions are used by writers to connect ideas and create coherence. Recognizing transitions will help you to understand how the ideas in a selection fit together. (See also **Clue Words** on page 877.)

Vocabulary

Context Clues Frequently, you may be able to figure out the meaning of an unfamiliar word by examining its *context,* or the group of words or sentences surrounding the unfamiliar word. Determining the meaning of new words in this way is called using *context clues.* The following chart shows examples of some of the common types of context clues. (See also pages 64, 136, and 304.)

How to Use Context Clues

Antonyms: Look for clues indicating that an unfamiliar word is opposite in meaning to a familiar word or phrase.

*After the **erratic** results of the first test, a second test was ordered in which the patient's heartbeat appeared to be regular and normal.*

Cause and Effect: Look for clues indicating that an unfamiliar word is related to the cause or is the result of an action, feeling, or idea.

*Because of Lara's **affinity** for animals, she will make an excellent veterinarian.*

Comparisons: Sometimes an unknown word may be compared with a more familiar word.

*The expression "Just say 'No'" is so overused that it has become a **cliché**.*

Contrasts: An unfamiliar word may sometimes be contrasted with a more familiar word.

*The team's uniforms were **immaculate** before the game, but by the end of the first inning, they were filthy.*

Definition and Restatements: Look for words that define the term or restate it in other words.

*The **rift**, or break, between the two sisters had upset the entire family.*

Examples: Look for examples used in context that reveal the meaning of an unfamiliar word.

*The scientist was accused of several acts of **espionage**, including photographing secret documents and taping private conversations.*

Synonyms: Look for familiar words that may be synonyms for unfamiliar words.

*The club's **coffers** were so low that the members had to raise new funds in order to buy new uniforms.*

Word Bank One method of increasing your vocabulary is to make a habit of collecting words in a *word bank,* a list of words gathered from your reading, listening, and viewing. Consult your dictionary for the definition of each new word. You may want to compile your personal word bank in a notebook or on a computer file.

Word Formations Many English words are made up of word parts that come from other languages or that have been inherited from earlier forms of English. A complete word, one that can stand independently, is called a *base word,* or *root.* Word parts, such as prefixes and suffixes, may be added to base words to form new words. Look at the examples in the chart on the next page. They show how word parts can be combined with base words to create new words. (See also **Word Parts** on page 891.)

Word Formations

Prefix	Base Word	Suffix	New Word
dis–	continue	–ous	discontinuous
in–	compare	–able	incomparable
mis–	judge	–ment	misjudgment

Word Meanings   Words have many layers of meanings. Their meanings can change depending on the time, the place, and the situation in which they are used. Whether you are speaking or writing, it is very important that the words you choose match your purpose. Most words in the English language have a number of different meanings. Use the following definitions and examples to help you choose words that say what you want them to say.

- **Analogies**   *Analogies* provide a special type of context in which you are asked to analyze the relationship between two words and then identify another pair of words with that same relationship. Analogy questions usually appear on standardized tests in multiple-choice form because they measure your knowledge of vocabulary as well as your ability to identify relationships and patterns among words.

  EXAMPLE
  1. SOUR : VINEGAR : __B__
  A. sugar : sweet   C. loyal : faithful
  B. hot : fire   D. chef : cooking

- **Clichés**   A *cliché* is a tired expression whose overuse has made its message weak and boring. Some clichés began as vivid expressions or figurative language, but then became trite and lifeless.

  EXAMPLES   blanket of snow, easier said than done, butterflies in my stomach, fit for a king, the long arm of the law, the dog ate my homework

- **Colloquialisms**   *Colloquialisms* are words and phrases characteristic of conversational language. In fact, *colloquial* derives from a Latin word meaning "conversation." Used appropriately and sparingly, colloquialisms can give your informal writing and speaking a lively, personal tone. Avoid colloquialisms in formal writing and speaking.

  Informal: What's going on?
  Formal: How are you today?

- **Denotation and connotation**   The *denotation* of a word is its literal meaning, or the definition given in a dictionary. The *connotation* includes the emotional ideas and feelings that people may connect to the word. Because connotations often stir people's feelings, they can have powerful effects on the listener or reader.

  EXAMPLE   The words *persistence* and *stubbornness* have similar denotations, "the quality of not relenting, or continuing even in the face of opposition." Their connotations suggest different ideas, however. *Persistence* has a positive connotation of following a task through to the very end. *Stubbornness* has a negative connotation of being unreasonable or unwilling to listen to others.

- **Euphemisms**   A *euphemism* is an indirect, agreeable term that is substituted for a more direct, less appealing one. Some euphemisms are used as a courtesy to avoid offending people; others, however, are used to mislead people—to hide unpleasant truths or misrepresent the facts.

Euphemism	More Direct Term
memorial park	cemetery
facilities	restrooms
previously owned	used
passed on	died

- **Figurative language** *Figurative language* goes beyond the literal meaning of the words to create a special effect or feeling. The following chart shows the most common types of figurative language.

Type of Figurative Language	Example
A **metaphor** says that something *is* something else.	The sun is a giant glowing ball.
Personification gives human characteristics to nonhuman things.	The cold drink of water offered in friendship spoke volumes to the tired, thirsty traveler.
A **simile** compares two basically unlike things, using the words *like* or *as*.	Her mouth snapped shut like a purse.

- **Idioms** *Idioms* are conversational phrases that mean something different from the literal meanings of the words they contain. Idioms often cannot be explained grammatically, and they make no sense if translated word-for-word into another language.

  EXAMPLES
  I did not want to go to the museum, but Shelly *talked me into it.*
  Nora will be late because she couldn't *get out of* choir practice.
  I asked her, *"What's up with that?"*

- **Jargon** *Jargon* is a special language used by people in a particular profession, occupation, hobby, or field of study. Jargon is effective only if the reader or listener is familiar with its special meaning. Note in the following example how the single word *set* can mean different things to different groups.

  EXAMPLE *Set*
  Theater and film—the scenery of a production
  Library—a complete series of a book or periodical
  Mathematics—a collection of distinct elements, such as negative integers
  Surfing—a group of waves (usually three)

- **Loaded words** Words that have very strong connotations, either positive or negative, are said to be **loaded words**. Loaded words appeal to our emotions. They may influence us positively or negatively because of the feelings they arouse.

  EXAMPLES
  The diner serves *cheap, greasy food.*
  The diner serves *inexpensive, home-style* food.
  The *mob* of protesters *shouted their demands.*
  The *group* of protesters *made their opinions heard.*

- **Multiple meanings** Many English words have more than one meaning and may function as more than one part of speech. When using a dictionary to find a word's meaning, look at all the definitions given. Keep in mind the context in which you read or heard the word. Then, try the various definitions in that context until you find the one that fits.

  EXAMPLE
  When I asked Melba about her plans, she replied with a *blank* stare. [The third definition below best fits the meaning of *blank* in this context.]
  blank (blank) *adj.* **1.** not covered by writing, print, or other markings **2.** not filled in **3.** expressionless **4.** lacking or unproductive

- **Nonsexist language** *Nonsexist language* is language that applies to people in general, both male and female. For many years it was acceptable practice to use English gender-specific terms, such as *man* or *mankind*, to describe groups that included both men and women. In recent years, writers have begun to use nonsexist terms instead, using, for example, *humanity* and *humankind* in place of the gender-specific *mankind*. In addition, many occupations that once were limited only to men or only to women are now open to both. As a result, many job titles have been adjusted to reflect the change. Below are some widely used nonsexist terms that you may use to replace older, gender-specific ones.

Gender-specific Terms	Nonsexist Terms
chairman	chairperson (or chair)
deliveryman	delivery person
fireman	firefighter
mailman	mail carrier
man-made	synthetic
policeman	police officer
salesman	sales representative
steward, stewardess	flight attendant
watchman	security guard

- **Slang** *Slang* is highly informal language. It consists of made-up words or of old words used in new ways. Slang is usually lively and colorful, and it can make the user seem up-to-date. Slang words are often a special vocabulary for close-knit groups such as students, musicians, and surfers. For example, in the 1980s the word *tubular* was surfer's slang for "pleasing, fine." Like *tubular*, most slang words have a short life.

- **Synonyms** *Synonyms* are words that have the same or nearly the same meaning. However, synonyms often have subtly different meanings. Use a dictionary or thesaurus to make sure that you understand the exact differences in meaning between synonyms. Often the difference between two synonyms is a matter of connotation. In the following sentences, it is clear that *stared* and *gazed* are synonyms for *looked*, but while *looked* is a general verb, *stared* and *gazed* describe specific ways of looking. (See also **Denotation and connotation** on page 888.)

   EXAMPLES
   The child on the bus *looked* at the bus driver.
   The child on the bus *stared* at the bus driver.
   [*Stared* suggests the child finds the bus driver's appearance startling or unusual.]
   The child on the bus *gazed* at the bus driver.
   [*Gazed* suggests the child finds the bus driver's appearance appealing or interesting.]

- **Tired words** A *tired word* is a word that once was clear and forceful but has now become vague and weak. The word has been used so often and so carelessly that it has become worn-out and almost meaningless.

   EXAMPLES nice, fine, pretty, wonderful, terrific, great

Word Origins The *origin* of a word is the way it came into existence in a language. The origin and history of a word—its etymology—often appear in brackets along with its dictionary definition. The following etymology indicates that the origin of the word *eleven* is Middle English (ME) from Old English (OE).

EXAMPLE eleven [ME *elleven* < OE *endleofan*]

Word Parts English words are made up of units called *word parts*. The three types of word parts are *roots*, *prefixes*, and *suffixes*. Knowing the meanings of roots, prefixes, and suffixes can help you determine the meanings of many unfamiliar words.

- **Roots** The main part of a word is called the *root*, or *base word*. The root carries the word's basic meaning. Other word parts can be added to a root to create many different words. For example, the root –*port*– means "to carry." This root can be combined with other word parts to make new words, such as *portable, transportation,* or *import.* This root and many others come from Latin and ancient Greek.

Commonly Used Roots

Root	Meaning	Example
Greek		
–anthrop–	human	anthropology, misanthrope
–chrono–	time	chronology, chronometer
–cycl–	circle	cyclone, bicycle
–dem–	people	democracy, demography
–graph–	write, writing	autograph, biography
–hydr–	water	hydrant, hydrate
–log–, –logy–	study, word	biology, monologue
–morph–	form	metamorphosis, polymorph
–phon–	sound	phonograph, symphony
Latin		
–cis–	cut	decision, concise
–cred–	believe	incredible, discredit
–dic–, –dict–	say, speak	dictate, predict
–fac–, –fact–, –fec–, –fic–	do, make	deface, manufacture, defective, efficient
–fid–	belief, faith	confident, fidelity
–frag–, –fract–	break	fragment, fracture
–ject–	throw	eject, trajectory
–junct–	join	conjunction, juncture
–magn–	large, grand	magnate, magnificent
–mal–	bad	malice, dismal
–mit–, –miss–	send	missionary, transmit
–ped–	foot	biped, pedestrian
–pend–, –pens–	hang, weigh	pendant, pensive
–pon–, –pos–	place, put	exponent, position

(continued)

(continued)

Commonly Used Roots		
Root	**Meaning**	**Example**
–scrib–, –script–	write	inscribe, postscript
–solv–	loosen, accomplish	solvent, resolve
–ven–, –vent–	come	convention, prevent
–vers–, –vert–	turn	reverse, convertible
–voc–, –vok–	call	vocal, provoke
–volv–	roll, turn around	revolve, evolve

- **Prefixes** A *prefix* is a word part that is added before a root or base word. The word that is created from a prefix and a root combines the meanings of both its parts. Prefixes come from other languages and other forms of English.

Commonly Used Prefixes		
Prefixes	**Meanings**	**Examples**
Greek		
anti–	against, opposing	antimissile, antisocial
hyper–	over, above, excessive	hyperactive, hyperventilate
mon–, mono–	one	monarch, monologue
para–	beside, beyond	parallel, paralegal
psych–, psycho–	mind	psychiatry, psychology,
Latin and French		
contra–	against	contradict, contravene
de–	away, from, off, down	deflect, defrost
dif–, dis–	away, not, opposing	differ, disappoint
e–, ef–, ex–	away from, out	emigrate, efface, extract
il–, im–, in–, ir–	not in	illogical, impolite, incite, irrational
post–	after, following	postpaid, postwar
pre–	before	prejudge, preview
pro–	forward, favoring	proceed, pro-American
re–	back, backward, again	return, reflect, reforest
Old English		
be–	around, about	beset, behind
mis–	badly, not, wrongly	misbehave, misfire, mispronounce
un–	not, reverse of	unhappy, unlock

■ **Suffixes** A *suffix* is a word part that is added at the end of a base or root word. Often, adding a suffix changes both a word's part of speech and its meaning. The following suffixes are primarily those that change a root word's part of speech and meaning.

Commonly Used Suffixes		
Suffixes	**Meanings**	**Examples**
Greek, Latin, and French		
Nouns		
–ance, –ence	act, condition	forbearance, excellence
–cy	state, condition	accuracy, normalcy
–er, –or	doer, actor	singer, conductor
–ion	action, result, state	union, fusion, confusion
–ism	act, doctrine, manner	baptism, patriotism, barbarism
–tude	quality, state	fortitude, magnitude
–ty, –y	quality, state, action	novelty, enmity, jealousy
Adjectives		
–able, –ible	able, likely	washable, divisible
–ate	having, characteristic of	desolate, collegiate
–ive	tending to, given to	reflective, pensive
–ous	marked by, full of	glorious, nervous
–ulent	full of, characterized by	turbulent, fraudulent
Adjectives or Nouns		
–al	doer, pertaining to	rival, autumnal
–ary	belonging to, one connected with	primary, adversary, auxiliary
–ent	doing, actor	confident, adherent
–ic	dealing with, caused by, person or thing showing	classic, choleric, workaholic
–ite	native, product, formed	Hittite, vulcanite, favorite
Verbs		
–ate	become, cause	animate, sublimate
–esce	become, grow, continue	convalesce, acquiesce
–ize	cause to be, subject to	jeopardize, oxidize
Old English		
Nouns		
–dom	state, rank, condition	kingdom, wisdom
–hood	state, condition	statehood, falsehood
–ness	quality, state	kindness, tenderness

(continued)

(continued)

Commonly Used Suffixes		
Suffixes	Meanings	Examples
Adjectives or Adverbs		
–ly	like, characteristic of	yearly, positively
–ward	in the direction of	downward, outward
Verbs		
–en	cause to be	blacken, weaken

Words to Learn The three hundred words in the list below may be used as the basis of your vocabulary study this year. Make it a habit to study unfamiliar words from this list regularly.

abdicate
abound
acquittal
admirably
aesthetic
affidavit
affiliate
amiable
amnesty
analogy
annihilate
antiquity
apex
appease
apprehensive
aptitude
arbiter
archaic
assert
astute
atrocious
aura
autonomy
axiom
balmy
bayou
bedlam
beguile
besiege

bestride
bias
botch
bourgeois
breach
buffet
callous
canine
cant
carp
casement
caustic
censure
charisma
clangor
clemency
cliché
clientele
closure
coffer
coincidental
colloquial
commence
commendable
compassion
compatible
compliance
composure
conceive

concession
condescend
condole
conducive
consolidate
constituent
contemptuous
contend
convene
crony
curtail

daunt
debase
debut
decimate
decrepit
defunct
delectable
demure
destitute
deteriorate
detonate
devastation
diminutive
discern
disconcerting
dissent
diversion
documentary

edifice
edify
effervescent
eject

electorate
elite
emancipate
emphatically
encompass
encumber
enjoin
ensue
episode
equilibrium
erratic
espionage
ethical
evade
evolve
exalted
excerpt
expedient
explicate
exultant

fabricate
facilitate
facsimile
farce
flagrant
fluctuate
fortitude

gloat
grimace

heresy
hieroglyphic
hors d'oeuvre

894 **Quick Reference Handbook** Reading and Vocabulary

immaculate
impartial
impediment
implacable
imposition
inaccessible
inadvertent
inalienable
inanimate
inarticulate
incendiary
incentive
inclement
inconsistent
indestructible
indict
indifferent
indignant
indomitable
ineffectual
infallible
influx
inhibition
innate
innovation
insipid
insolence
intermittent
intuition
invariably
invincible
irksome
irrational
irrelevant
itinerary

jargon
jostle
judicious
juncture

lament
lapse
latitude
legacy
lexicon
livid

loathe

malignant
malleable
mandatory
mannerism
martial
meager
mediocre
melancholy
melodramatic
mentor
meticulous
militant
moderation
momentum
mortify
mosque
mull
mutable
mystic

naive
negligible
notoriety

obligatory
obliterate
oblivious
odious
opportune
ornate
ossify

pacifist
painstaking
palatable
pallid
paradox
paraphrase
parody
pastoral
patent
paternal
patriarch
pauper
perceive
perception

perseverance
personification
pertinent
pivotal
plausible
pompous
portly
posthumous
postulate
precarious
prelude
pretext
prevalent
prolific
prone
prophetic
protocol
protrude
proximity
purge

qualm
quantitative
quibble

rankle
ravage
reactionary
rebuke
recipient
recourse
rectify
recur
redundant
rejuvenate
reminiscent
rendezvous
repress
reprieve
requiem
requisite
resonant
retainer
retribution
rift
rivulet

sardonic
scenario
sequel
simulate
sordid
sporadic
stamina
steppe
stimulant
stipulate
stratagem
stringent
submission
subsidiary
subsidize
substantially
succulent
succumb
synopsis
synthesis

tawny
theoretical
throng
timorous
transcend
transition
transitory
translucent

ultimatum
unprecedented

vehement
verbatim
vibrant
vigilant
visage
vulnerable

wan
wane
wheedle
whimsical
wreak

zealous
zenith
zephyr

Speaking and Listening

Speaking

Casual conversations with family and friends account for most of your speaking. At times, however, you will be required to speak in situations that are not so casual. **Conventions of oral language** are those generally agreed upon rules and regulations covering the grammar, vocabulary, and style of oral communication, and based upon the audience, occasion, purpose, and task of the communication. For example, the word choice and style of speech used in informal conversations between peers would not be the same as that used for job interviews or formal speeches. No matter what the occasion, you can use certain strategies and techniques to become a better speaker.

Debate

In a formal *debate* two teams (or sides) engage in a systematic discussion of a *proposition,* the issue being debated. The team that argues against the proposition is the *negative* team. The team that argues for the proposition is the *affirmative* team.

Features of a Debate   All debate formats share certain features.

- **Debate Proposition**   The proposition, or issue of the debate, is stated as a resolution and limited to a specific idea. The proposition should be debatable; that is, it should give the affirmative and negative sides the opportunity to build a reasonable case. For example, a debatable proposition is "Resolved: That four years of a foreign language be required for graduation from public high schools."

- **Debate Etiquette**   Debaters are required to show proper etiquette and good manners, and avoid ridicule, sarcasm, and personal attacks. A debate should be won or lost only on the basis of a well-prepared case delivered convincingly. Referring to participants in a debate with polite terms such as "the first affirmative speaker," "my worthy opponent," or "my teammates," is customary.

- **Debate Officials**   Often a chairperson decides on questions of debate rules raised by either side. Usually three appointed judges determine the winner of a debate, but the winning team is sometimes decided by a vote of the audience.

Formats of Debate In the first part of most debates, both sides build their cases with constructive speeches. The affirmative side argues for the proposition and against anticipated arguments of the negative side. The negative side does just the opposite. The two sides take a break before making **rebuttal speeches,** in which they respond to the most effective arguments of the opposition. Debaters are given specific time limits for each speech. These time limits vary according to the debate format.

- **Traditional or Formal Debate** In this format, two teams of two speakers each debate. Each member of the affirmative and negative teams speaks twice. Each speech must be completed within a set time limit.
- **Cross-examination Debate** In this format, two members of each team can question their opponents. During cross-examination, speakers clarify issues and try to bring out the weaknesses in their opponents' case.
- **Lincoln-Douglas Debate** This type of debate commemorates the famous debates between Abraham Lincoln and Stephen A. Douglas, candidates for senator from Illinois in 1858. This format pits one affirmative speaker against one negative speaker.

Preparing for Debate Effective debaters prepare their cases carefully by researching their sides of the debate proposition thoroughly. To prepare for a debate, you first identify the **issues,** or main differences between your position and the position of the opposing team. Then, you organize support for your arguments by gathering examples, expert testimony, statistics, and logical reasons. Your arguments and supporting evidence are put into a **brief,** or outline of your team's position in the debate. Next, you prepare to **refute,** or disprove, the arguments of your opponents with logical reasons, facts, statistics, and the like. Last, you prepare for **rebuttal,** rebuilding your case by answering the points your opponents made in refuting your arguments; in addition, you anticipate weaknesses your opponents might find in your case.

Formal Speaking Occasions

Formal speaking is done at a specific time and for a specific reason. There are steps you can take to prepare for every formal speaking occasion.

Formal Speeches Formal speeches require thoughtful preparation. The process of preparing a formal speech is similar to the process of writing a paper. To prepare a formal speech, follow the steps explained below.

1. **Identify purpose and task** Your general purpose is the overall reason you have for giving the speech. The most common purposes of a speech are to inform and to persuade. Common purposes for giving speeches are described in the chart on page 898.
2. **Select a topic** If you may choose the topic of your speech, be sure to select one that you find interesting. It will be difficult to interest your audience in your topic if you are not interested in it yourself. As you select a topic, keep the following questions in mind.
    - *What is the occasion of your speech?* What task prompts you to speak? For example, have you been asked to speak on behalf of your friend's candidacy for class treasurer? Your topic should fit the occasion.
    - *How much time will you have to deliver your speech?* Limit the scope of your speech to fit the time you are given.

TEACHING TIP

16A, 16C, 16D, 17A, 17B, 17C, 17D, 17E, 17F

Formal Speeches
Have students use the instruction on formal speaking that starts on this page and continues through p. 901 to prepare and deliver a formal persuasive speech. Besides following the procedures explained in their texts, students should complete the following steps.

1. Present and advance a clear thesis or claim supported by valid proofs from reliable sources.
2. Include appropriate appeals, both logical and emotional, to support claims and arguments.
3. Ensure that the speech is informed, accurate, truthful, and ethical.
4. When delivering the speech, use effective pitch, tone of voice, posture, and eye contact.

Speaking and Listening, pp. 896–910
Alignments
TEKS 7H, 14A, 14B, 15A, 15C, 16A, 16B, 16C, 16D, 16E, 16F, 17D, 18A, 18B

General Types of Speeches

General Purpose for Speech	Purpose	Examples
Informative Speech	To present new information to an audience or to provide a new view of old information	- Lecture - News broadcast - Orientation - Instruction
Persuasive Speech	To change an attitude or belief or to move an audience to action	- Campaign speech - Advertisement - Debate
Special Occasion Speech	To entertain or amuse an audience or to acknowledge a special reason for the audience's presence	- After-dinner speech - Anecdote - Oral interpretation of a piece of literature - Campaign speech for student council - Speech honoring a retiring teacher

3. **Analyze the audience** After selecting a topic, consider how you can appeal to your audience's needs or interests. Use the following questions for adapting material to a particular audience.

   - *Are the people in your audience mostly younger or older than you?* For a younger audience, use simple language, age-specific examples, and clear explanations. For an older audience, adopt a respectful tone, avoid slang, and use general examples an adult audience will understand.
   - *What does the audience already know about the topic?* Provide enough background information for your audience to understand your speech. If you feel your audience will have some knowledge of your topic, provide an appropriate amount of background information. For the audience that knows a good deal, provide an advanced discussion that focuses on interesting issues or aspects of the topic.
   - *How interested will the audience be in your topic?* The degree of the audience's interest in your topic should influence the content of your speech. An uninterested audience needs to be convinced that the topic is worthwhile. An interested audience needs to hear information that will justify and maintain its interest.

4. **Gather material and organize content** The next step in preparing a speech is to research the topic you have selected. Your school or community library can be a valuable resource in conducting your research. (See also **Library/Media Center** on page 866 and the **How to Take Study Notes** chart on page 912.)

5. **Write the speech** The structure, language, and techniques you use to involve your audi-

ence in your topic are the three main factors to consider when you write your speech. The chart below gives guidelines for each of the basic features of a formal speech.

Features of a Formal Speech

Structure

The speech should be composed of three parts:
- an *introduction* with a thesis statement or main idea
- a *body*
- a *conclusion*

Language

The language you use should be appropriate for your audience. Keep in mind the following points.
- Use formal, standard English.
- Use technical terms sparingly and be sure to define them.
- Avoid slang, jargon, and euphemisms in your speech.

Audience Involvement

It is important to remember that written English sounds different when it is delivered orally. Make your speech more "listener-friendly" by doing the following.
- Use personal pronouns. For example, say "you may think" or "we believe" instead of "one may think" or "people believe."
- Ask rhetorical questions instead of making statements. For example, instead of telling the audience a fact or statistic, ask them "Did you know that . . . ?"

---

6. **Determine method of delivery** Now you need to decide how you will deliver your speech. There are several methods, each of which has advantages and disadvantages.

- The *manuscript speech* is read word-for-word from your written manuscript. This method allows little chance for omissions and mistakes, but it does not permit you to respond to audience feedback and often sounds dull and lifeless.
- The *memorized speech* is memorized word-for-word from your written manuscript. This method does give you the freedom to move around and to maintain eye contact with the audience, but it may sound stiff and unnatural. With this method, you also run the risk of forgetting parts of the speech.
- The *extemporaneous speech* is carefully outlined and rehearsed but not memorized. You can use notes to help you stay organized. This method sounds natural and allows you to respond to the audience, but requires much rehearsal time.

The extemporaneous speech is the most common type of speech. When you organize your materials for an extemporaneous speech, first write a complete outline. Then, prepare note cards to refer to as you present your speech.

Guidelines for Extemporaneous Speech Note Cards

1. Put only one key idea, possibly accompanied by a brief example or detail, on each card.

2. Make a special note card for material that you plan to read word-for-word, such as a quotation, a series of dates, or a list of statistics.

3. Make a special note card to indicate when you should pause to show a visual, such as a chart, diagram, graph, picture, or model.

4. Number your completed cards to keep them in order.

7. Rehearse the speech You will be a more effective speaker if you rehearse your speech beforehand, including your use of *nonverbal* and *verbal signals.* You use these signals whenever you speak, but they stand out very clearly when you are making a formal speech to a live audience.

- **Nonverbal Signals** You can communicate effectively with nonverbal signals like those described in the following chart.

Communicating with Nonverbal Signals	
Nonverbal Signals	**Tips and Effects**
Eye contact	• Look directly into the eyes of as many members of the audience as you can. Eye contact communicates honesty and sincerity. It makes the audience feel as if you are speaking *with* them rather than *to* them.
Facial expression	• Facial expressions—smiling, frowning, raising an eyebrow, and so on—can reveal your feelings and add to or even take the place of a verbal message.
Gesture	• Making relaxed and natural gestures with your head, hands, or arms as you speak emphasizes verbal messages. Nodding the head for "yes" or shaking it for "no" or pointing with the index finger can effectively punctuate your speech.
Posture	• Stand up straight and look alert to communicate an air of confidence to your audience.

- **Verbal Signals** The expressiveness of your voice is a major factor in the effectiveness of your speech. The following verbal signals will help you communicate your message to an audience.

Communicating with Verbal Signals	
Verbal Signals	**Tips**
Diction (the clarity of your pronunciation)	• Always speak clearly so that your listeners can understand you.
Emphasis (the stress put on a word or phrase)	• Emphasize key ideas or points in your speech by saying those words a little more loudly.
Pause (small silences in your speech)	• Use pauses to help listeners catch up or to suggest that what you have said or are about to say is important.
Pitch (how your voice sounds)	• When speakers are nervous, the pitch in their voices tends to become higher. Take a deep breath and relax before you speak to keep your voice's pitch at its most natural.
Rate (the speed with which you talk)	• Normal speed is about 120 to 160 words per minute. When delivering a speech, speak at a slower rate.
Volume (the level of sound you create)	• When giving a speech, speak more loudly than usual. Be sure to ask listeners if they can hear you before you begin your speech.

8. **Deliver the speech** No matter how much you have practiced your speech, you face a challenge when you stand in front of your audience. If you are like most people, you will be nervous. Here are some tips for overcoming your nerves and delivering an effective speech.
   - *Be prepared.* Avoid excessive nervousness by organizing and being familiar with your speech notes and any audiovisual devices you plan to use.
   - *Practice your speech.* Rehearse as if you are actually delivering your speech.
   - *Focus on your purpose for speaking.* Think about what you want your listeners to do, believe, or feel as a result of your speech.
   - *Pay attention to audience feedback.* Audiences send messages to speakers. Pay attention to them. Are people in the audience alert or are they yawning? Are they shaking their heads in disagreement or nodding in agreement? Depending upon the feedback you receive from the audience, you might need to adjust your pace, use more gestures, or speak more loudly.

9. **Use audiovisual devices (if appropriate).** You might want to use audiovisual devices to clarify or enhance your presentation by making it a multimedia presentation. Following are several types of audiovisual devices often used in multimedia presentations.
   - audio recordings (such as cassettes or compact discs)
   - images, audio files, and text stored and presented on a computer
   - videotapes or videodiscs
   - short films
   - slides or filmstrips
   - graphics such as charts, graphs, illustrations, diagrams

Use the following questions to determine if your presentation will benefit from the use of audiovisual devices.
   - *Will audiovisual devices help you clarify a point?* Some ideas are easily explained verbally, but others need a visual to help clarify them. In those cases, using a chart or a poster will save you time and keep the audience on track.
   - *Will the audiovisual devices help the audience remember a point?* Not every point in your speech is equally important. Decide which points will benefit from the emphasis given by an audiovisual.
   - *Will the audiovisuals or multimedia distract the audience while you are speaking?* Make sure that the audiovisual devices are essential to your talk and can be displayed without taking the audience's attention away from what you are saying.

NOTE Make certain your audience can see or hear the audiovisual device you have chosen. Audio materials should be cued up and ready to play. Visuals should be large and clear enough to be seen from the back of the audience. (See also **Graphics** on page 855.)

Group Discussion *Formal group discussions* take place when clubs, organizations, and other groups meet on a regular basis to discuss important issues. Formal groups often follow an established set of rules known as *parliamentary procedure.* The basic principles of parliamentary procedure, listed below, protect the rights of the individual members of the group while providing a system for dealing with issues that come before the group.
- The majority decides.
- The minority has the right to be heard.

TEACHING TIP 15C

Deliver the Speech
Have students evaluate a professional speech that is delivered on television. A good source of informative and persuasive speeches is C-SPAN cable television network, which broadcasts speeches by government officials and others. If students do not have access to these presentations, you could videotape one or more speeches and show them in class so that students can practice evaluating a speech. Students can use the following chart to help them as they evaluate a speech.

Criteria	Comment
Purpose is clear.	
Main ideas are easily identifiable.	
Speaker considers audience, task, occasion, and purpose.	
Key points or claims are understandable and believable.	
Language is precise.	
Tone and pitch are appropriate for the audience and the occasion.	
Speaker's articulation, enunciation, and pronunciation are correct.	
Speaker keeps eye contact and uses other nonverbal signals to connect with the audience.	
Speaker uses verbal signals such as diction, emphasis, and pauses to communicate the message.	

- Decisions are made by voting.
- Only one issue is decided at a time.
- Everyone is assured of the chance to be heard and has the right to vote.
- All votes are counted as equal.
- All sides of an issue are debated in open discussion.

A good source for information about parliamentary procedure is *Robert's Rules of Order, Newly Revised*, by Henry Robert. According to *Robert's Rules*, formal meetings should follow the procedure set forth in the following chart.

Order of Business

A formal meeting usually follows the standard order of business suggested in *Robert's Rules of Order:*

1. Call to order: The chairperson says, "The meeting will come to order."

2. Reading and approval of the minutes: The chairperson says, "The secretary (or recorder) will read the minutes from our previous meeting." The secretary reads the minutes, and the chairperson inquires, "Are there any additions or corrections to the minutes?" The minutes are then approved, or they are corrected and then approved.

3. Officers' reports: The chairperson calls for a report from other officers who need to report by saying, for example, "Will the treasurer please give us a report?"

4. Committee reports: The chairperson may ask the presiding officer of standing committees to make reports to the group.

5. Old business: Any issues that have not been fully resolved at the last meeting may now be discussed. The chairperson may ask the group, "Is there any old business to be discussed?"

6. New business: Any new issues that have not been previously discussed may now be addressed.

7. Announcements: The chairperson may ask the members, "Are there any announcements?"

8. Adjournment: The chairperson ends the meeting by saying, "The meeting is now adjourned."

Interviewing

Interviews are communication situations in which one person, the *interviewer*, gathers ideas or information from another person, the *interviewee*. You may need to be an interviewer when you want to obtain firsthand information from people for a research project or report. When a potential employer questions you about your personal habits and work skills, you become the interviewee.

- **Conducting an Interview** Successful interviews require careful planning. The following chart provides useful suggestions for planning and conducting an interview.

Conducting an Interview

Preparing for the Interview
- Identify the person you want to interview. Select a reliable source—someone who is knowledgeable about your subject and who can be depended upon to give accurate information.
- Make arrangements well in advance. Set up a time that is convenient for the other person to meet with you.
- Gather background information about your subject, and about the person you will be interviewing. Then, make a list of questions to ask. Make sure the questions are arranged in a logical order and require more than yes or no answers.

Participating in the Interview
- Arrive on time, and be polite and patient.
- Ask the other person's permission to take notes or use a tape recorder.

Conducting an Interview

- Avoid argument. Be tactful and courteous. Remember the interview was granted at your request.
- Be aware of your nonverbal communication—your facial expressions and your gestures. Keep good eye contact and nod to show understanding.
- Listen carefully, and ask follow-up questions if you do not understand an answer or if you think you need more information.

Following up on the Interview
- Review your notes to refresh your memory, and then make a summary of the material you have gathered.
- Send a note expressing your appreciation for the interview.

■ **Interviewing for a Job** Most people approach a job interview with a certain amount of nervousness. Such nervousness is understandable because most people do not often practice their interviewing skills before they need them. Being thoroughly prepared to be interviewed, however, can help relieve some of the anxiety. The suggestions in the following chart can help you prepare to be a successful interviewee.

NOTE The more you know about the company or job before you interview, the more confident you will feel. Your knowledge will also impress the interviewer with your interest, initiative, and responsibility. Do research in the library as part of your preparation for the interview.

How to Interview for a Position

1. Arrange an appointment. Write a business letter of application in which you request an interview for the job. If you are granted an interview, be prompt for your appointment.

2. Bring a résumé. If you have not already submitted a résumé, take one to the interview and give it to the interviewer. (See also **Résumé** on page 957.)

3. Be neat and well-groomed. It is important to look your best when you are interviewing to apply for any type of job.

4. Answer questions clearly and honestly. Answer the questions the interviewer asks, adding any additional information that might inform the employer that you are the right person for the job.

5. Ask questions. Questions that job applicants usually ask include requests for information about work hours, salary, or chances for advancement. By your questions, you show that you are interested in the company or business.

6. Be prepared to be tested. The employer may require you to take tests that demonstrate your skills, intelligence, or personality.

7. Follow up the interview. After the interview, write a short thank-you note. Tell the interviewer that you appreciated the opportunity for the interview and that you look forward to hearing from the company in the near future.

Informal Speaking Situations		
Situation	Purpose	Preparation and Presentation
Directions	To explain how to get to a particular place (Informational situation)	• Choose easiest route. • Divide the route into logical steps. • Use terms that are accurate or visual. If necessary, draw a map. • Repeat any steps if necessary.
Impromptu Speech	To speak for five minutes on a particular topic without any previous preparation (Informational situation)	• If you must choose the topic, think of one that is appropriate for your audience. • Think of a main idea, an attention-getting beginning, and some supporting ideas. • Speak clearly and in a confident voice. • Use a tone that is appropriate to the topic.
Instructions	To give information on how to do a particular task (Informational situation)	• Divide the information into clear, logical steps. • Give the steps in order. • Make sure your listener understands your instructions.

Introductions	To introduce yourself or another person to a person or group (Social situation)	• Take the initiative and introduce yourself if no one else does.
		• When introducing another person, identify the person by name.
		• When introducing another person, it is customary to address first
		  • a person of higher status
		  • an older person before a younger one
		  • the person you know better

Telephone Conversations	To communicate via telephone (Social situation)	• Call people at appropriate times of day. • Identify yourself and state the reason for your call. • Be polite and patient. • Keep your call to an appropriate length.

Informal Speaking Occasions

Informal speaking occasions are more personal and casual than formal occasions. Informal speaking situations tend to be either informative or social in nature. The chart above describes some common informal speaking situations.

Informal Group Discussion *Informal group discussions* usually involve a small number of people discussing items of interest to the group as a whole. The following section explains two elements of group discussion.

■ **Identifying a Purpose** Most group discussions have an announced specific purpose or goal. The following are typical purposes for group discussion.

> **Purposes for Discussion**
> - to brainstorm ideas
> - to learn cooperatively
> - to make a decision, evaluation, or recommendation
> - to make plans
> - to negotiate agreements
> - to resolve conflicts
> - to solve a problem

- **Participating in Discussion** Every member of a group involved in a discussion has certain responsibilities.

> **All group members:** All members of a group discussion are responsible for paying attention to the discussion, respecting all group members' opinions, and offering thoughtful comments.
>
> **Chairperson:** If a group has chosen a discussion leader or chairperson, he or she is responsible for introducing, guiding, moderating, and closing the discussion. The chairperson helps resolve any conflicts between members and makes sure that the group stays focused on its purpose or goal.
>
> **Group secretary or recorder:** One person from the group is usually asked to take notes on important points or decisions made during a discussion. The group secretary or recorder is responsible for these notes and for reading them aloud at the beginning of the next group discussion.

Oral Interpretation

In *oral interpretation* you read a work of literature aloud, using acting as well as speaking skills—vocal techniques, facial expressions, body language, and gestures—to express your interpretation of the work. Following are the steps for preparing an oral interpretation.

1. **Find and cut material.** You usually have a specific purpose and audience in mind before you select and prepare material for an oral interpretation. You can, therefore, select material interesting to and appropriate for your audience. Consider, also, how much time you have for your presentation. For your oral interpretation, you will need to make an abbreviated version or *cutting* of a work of fiction, nonfiction, poetry, or drama. Use the following guidelines:
   - Follow the story line of the literary work in time order.
   - Delete tag lines such as "he said slowly." Instead, use these clues to tell you how to interpret the character's words as you express them.
   - Delete passages that do not contribute to the overall effect or impression you intend to create with your oral interpretation.

2. **Prepare the reading script.** You can type (double-spaced) and mark your reading script to help you in your interpretive reading. Underline words you want to give special emphasis, or use a slash mark (/) to indicate where you would like a dramatic pause.

3. **Rehearse your interpretation.** Rehearse different readings of your script until you find the one that expresses your interpretation. Use your voice in a manner that suits your presentation, and pronounce words carefully. Practice using your body and your voice to portray different characters.

4. **Deliver your presentation.** Begin your presentation by introducing the work of literature you are interpreting. Introduce the author, set the scene, and provide the necessary background for your audience to understand your interpretation. Then, deliver your interpretation.

Cooperative Learning

14A, 14B, 15C

Listening Pairs. Have students work in pairs to practice critical listening by analyzing, evaluating, and critiquing an informative radio broadcast. Students should use the questions below to complete their evaluations. Remind them that besides evaluating what they hear, they need to focus their attention, interpret, and respond to the broadcast. When students have completed their evaluations, have them discuss their findings with the class.

Critical-Listening Questions

- Does the speaker's information or advice seem believable? Why or why not?
- Who is the target audience for this program?
- Does the speaker have a particular viewpoint? What is it? Why do you think so?
- What is the speaker's main point? How does the speaker support the main point?
- Does the speaker use any propaganda techniques such as biased opinions, exaggerations, loaded words, or hasty generalizations? If so, give examples.

Listening

Good listening takes more than good hearing. Listening is an active process. When you listen actively, you receive verbal and nonverbal messages, construct meanings for those messages, and respond to those meanings.

Basics of the Listening Process

Listening is as important to the communication process as speaking. The stages in the listening process are explained in the following chart.

The Three Stages of the Listening Process	
Before you listen	• **Be physically and mentally prepared to listen.** To be an effective listener, you should be physically comfortable and free of mental distractions that will interfere with your ability to focus. • **Determine your reason for listening.** Are you listening to be entertained? To be informed? To provide support or understanding? To receive instructions or directions? Identifying a reason for listening sets you up as an active listener. • **Decide what you already know about the speaker and the subject.** Bringing your prior knowledge of a subject or of a speaker to the surface can make your listening experience more productive. • **Add to your prior knowledge of the speaker and the subject.** Brainstorming with others or doing individual research to increase your knowledge of speaker and subject will improve your ability to understand and evaluate both. • **Keep an open mind.** Set aside any biases, prejudices, or preconceived notions you might have concerning the speaker or the topic of the speech. Make your judgments after listening to what the speaker has to say.
As you listen	• **Make connections to prior knowledge and experience.** Try to relate what the speaker is saying to what you know from any source—experience, books and magazines, television, school, and so on. • **Think of questions you would like to ask the speaker.** You may not have an opportunity to ask the speaker to clarify a point or expand upon an idea, but thinking of questions helps you to focus on the speaker's meaning. • **Make educated guesses about what a speaker will say next.** If you are wrong, try to determine what misled you. • **Find meaning behind what the speaker says directly.** Make inferences about a speaker's attitudes or opinions by paying attention to what he or she does not say.
After you listen	• **Discuss the speaker and the message with others.** Get together with others to exchange ideas, agree or disagree with the speaker's opinions, and relate what the speaker has said to what you have experienced, seen, and read. • **Write a summary and evaluation of the speaker and the presentation.** Writing about a presentation while it is fresh in your mind can help you clarify and solidify your thoughts and opinions.

Evaluating Yourself as a Listener

In order for oral communication to be effective, the listener must take as much of the responsibility for clear communication as the speaker. Therefore, it is important for you to be able to evaluate yourself as a listener. The following chart suggests points you should consider.

Evaluating Yourself as a Listener

A good listener should

- be mentally and physically prepared to listen
- be able to ignore distracting behavior by the speaker and members of the audience
- focus on the speaker throughout the presentation
- follow the organization of the speaker's presentation
- distinguish between facts and opinions
- think of questions to ask the speaker
- determine the speaker's main idea and primary supporting details
- withhold judgment until the presentation is over
- listen for and detect bias or prejudice on the speaker's part
- reflect upon the presentation after it is over
- discuss the presentation with others
- ask questions of the speaker if given the opportunity
- write a summary or evaluation of the presentation

Four Types of Listening

There are four basic types of listening and a number of purposes or reasons for listening associated with each type.

Appreciative (or Aesthetic) Listening

When you listen for pleasure, such as hearing someone read a story or a poem, for example, you are engaged in appreciative listening. Certain strategies can make this type of listening experience more rewarding.

- **Before Listening** Before you listen, ask (and use your prior knowledge to answer) as many questions as you can about the material you are going to hear. What is it about? What is the title of the piece? What kind of literature is it? Who is the author? **Make predictions based on your questions and answers.** You might predict, for example, that a poem entitled "Dawn" will involve a sunrise. **Based on the type of literature you will hear—poetry, fiction, drama—recall or research some of its basic elements.** If you are to listen to a poetry reading, for example, you might recall the kinds of figurative language or the importance of imagery.

- **While Listening** As you listen, visualize what you are hearing. Jot down notes on any reactions, questions, or ideas you have while listening. Does the presentation remind you of a personal experience or something you have read? **Make personal connections** to the literature.

- **After Listening** After you listen, confirm or correct the predictions you made before listening. Were your predictions correct, or did they require adjusting as you listened? Why did your predictions need to change? **Evaluate your response to the literature.** What did you like or learn or feel while listening? **Identify and discuss any artistic or literary elements that appeared in the literature, such as rhyme scheme, rhythm, imagery, theme, and so on.** What or how did these elements add to your listening experience? **Write a short evaluation of the presentation.**

TEACHING TIP
14B, 15A, 15D, 18C

Appreciative Listening
Arrange students in small groups to practice presenting interpretations and listening for pleasure. Have each student select a piece of his or her own writing or a work by a favorite author—a poem or an excerpt from a short story. Group members can take turns presenting their intepretations. The listeners should take notes on their predictions, impressions, questions, and ideas about the piece. After the presentation, group members should confirm their predictions and then evaluate the presentation in a two- or three-sentence conclusion. Members can share their personal connections with the group before the next person presents.

TEACHING TIP

Critical Listening

Allow students to practice their critical-listening skills by playing a videotape or an audiotape of a speech in class. Before you play the tape, have students copy the steps in the **How to Listen Critically** chart to make a checklist. As students are listening to the speech, they should note each element on their lists. After playing the tape, discuss each item with students. Finally, you might ask volunteers to name real-life situations in which listening critically is important.

Critical Listening When you listen to understand, analyze, and evaluate a speaker's message, you engage in critical listening—the type of listening you should apply to messages you hear in school, in the workplace, or in the media. You can use the strategies in the following chart to analyze and evaluate media presentations as well as live presentations.

How to Listen Critically	
What to do	**What to listen for**
Identify the speaker's purpose.	• Does the speaker make clear why he or she is giving the speech?
Distinguish between facts and opinions.	• Does the speaker make statements with which you agree or disagree? Ask yourself why you disagree. (Such statements are opinions. An *opinion* is a belief or a judgment about something that cannot be proved. A *fact* is a statement that can be proved true.)
Identify main ideas.	• What are the most important points? (Listen for clue words or phrases, such as *major, main,* and *most important.*)
Identify significant or supporting details.	• What dates, names, or facts does the speaker use to support the main points of the speech? What kinds of examples or explanations are used to support the main ideas?
Identify the order of organization.	• What kind of order does the speaker use to present the information—time sequence, spatial order, order of importance?
Listen to detect bias.	• Is the speaker biased, or prejudiced, toward one point of view? Does the speaker use extreme or all-inclusive words such as *never* or *always*? Does the speaker acknowledge other points of view?
Evaluate the speaker's credibility.	• Does the speaker refer to sources of information? Are the sources respectable or credible, such as newspaper and journal articles or reference materials?
Note comparisons and contrasts.	• Are some details compared or contrasted with others?
Predict outcomes and draw conclusions.	• What can you reasonably conclude from the facts and evidence presented in the speech?
Look for logic.	• Does the speaker build arguments in a logical way? Does the speaker use false logic, such as hasty generalization, false cause and effect, or circular reasoning?
Look for emotional appeals.	• Does the speaker use the bandwagon appeal? The glittering generality? Snob appeal? Plain folks appeal? The veiled threat?
Understand cause and effect.	• Do some events described by the speaker relate to or affect others? Does the speaker make the logical connections between cause and effect?

Comprehensive Listening This type of listening is sometimes called *informational listening* because you listen for the content of a message. Much of the listening you do in school, for example, is comprehensive listening. There are several instances in which you use comprehensive listening:

- **Listening for Information** You are often in situations where you listen to acquire information. When a veterinarian explains the required treatment of a problem your pet is having, for example, he or she is delivering information you need to understand, not attempting to persuade or entertain you. The following strategies are helpful in these situations.

  1. **The LQ2R Method** helps you when you listen for information from a speaker. The steps are described below.

     L Listen carefully to material as it is being presented.

     Q Question yourself as you listen. Mentally, or in your notes, make a list of questions as they occur to you.

     R Recite in your own words the information as it is being presented. Summarize the material in your mind.

     R Review the whole presentation. You should restate or reemphasize major points.

  2. **Note Taking** One method of keeping track of a speaker's ideas is to take notes. Because you cannot write down every word a speaker says, you need to develop an effective way to jot down a speaker's main points and supporting details as well as your own thoughts, questions, or comments. You could use split-page notes: Divide your paper so that forty percent of the page lies to the left and sixty percent lies to the right. Take brief notes on the left-hand side only, leaving the right-hand side for reorganizing and expanding your notes after listening. (See also the **How to Take Study Notes** chart on page 912.)

- **Listening to Instructions** Because instructions are usually made up of a series of steps, you can easily misunderstand them. The following steps can help you make sense of instructions.

  1. **Listen for the order of the steps.** Listen for words such as *first, second, next, then,* and *last* to tell you when one step ends and the next one begins.
  2. **Identify the number of steps in the process.** Take notes if the instructions are long or complicated. Do not hesitate to ask for clarification or for the speaker to slow down as you take notes.
  3. **Visualize each step.** Imagine yourself actually performing each step. Try to get a mental image of what you should be doing at every step in the process.
  4. **Review the steps.** When the speaker is finished, be sure you understand the process from beginning to end. Ask questions if you are unsure.

NOTE When you take a message on the telephone, you are listening for information that answers the basic *5W-How?* questions—*Who? What? When? Where? Why?* and *How?* For example, you should take down details that answer questions such as *Who* is calling? *What* is the message or purpose for the call? *Where* can the caller be reached? *When* can the caller be reached? and *How* may you help the caller?

Empathic (or Reflective) Listening

When you want to help a friend understand a

Cooperative Learning

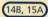

Reflective Groups. To allow students to practice their reflective-listening skills, read aloud an excerpt from a published personal narrative—a portion of Anne Frank's diary is a good selection. Before you read the selection, have students review the listening strategies on this page. After the reading, have students working in groups discuss appropriate responses to the emotions expressed in the narrative. You might ask students to demonstrate facial expressions and body language that would show empathy.

---

difficult problem or when you want to show someone your understanding and acceptance, you engage in empathic listening. You indicate your empathy through your facial expressions and body language and through your responses to the speaker. Here are some strategies to use.

- Do much more listening than talking.
- Show genuine warmth and concern.
- Paraphrase what the speaker says to show your understanding.
- Respond to the speaker's feelings rather than analyzing the facts.
- Keep your opinions to yourself.

Special Listening Situations

Group discussions and *interviews* are situations that require that you participate not only as a careful listener, but also as a speaker.

Listening in a Group Discussion
Being a member of a group discussion is a little different from being a member of a large audience. The following tips should help you participate effectively in a group discussion.

- Maintain nonverbal communication by sitting up, looking at each speaker, and nodding to show agreement or understanding.
- Demonstrate respect for the other group members by paying attention and not making comments while they are speaking or listening.
- Take notes on each speaker's points and list your questions or comments.
- When you are ready to speak, raise your hand and be recognized.
- Concentrate on what the speaker is saying, not on what you intend to say when it is your turn to speak.

Listening in an Interview
An interview is a unique listening situation that takes place between two people: the interviewer and the interviewee. Here are some listening techniques you can use to make the most of an interview. (See also **Conducting an Interview** on page 902 and **Interviewing for a Job** on page 903.)

- **As interviewer**
  1. **When you ask a question, listen to the complete answer.** Be courteous and patient as your interviewee answers. Think of follow-up questions as he or she responds.
  2. **Respect the interviewee's opinions, even if you do not agree with him or her.** You may state your disagreement politely only if your comment will prompt the interviewee to clarify, expand, or provide support for a statement or claim. Do not express your disagreement if it is likely to upset your interviewee and disrupt the interview.
  3. **Monitor your nonverbal communication.** Make sure that your nonverbal reactions, such as your facial expressions and your gestures, reflect a respectful tone. Maintain good eye contact, nod to show understanding, and smile to indicate your interest.
  4. **Always thank the interviewee at the end of your interview.**

- **As interviewee**
  1. **Listen to the interviewer's complete question before answering.** If you start answering the question before the interviewer finishes asking it, you might answer the wrong question.
  2. **Listen to the interviewer's complete response to a question before asking another one.** It is impolite to interrupt the interviewer, whose complete response might answer your next question anyway.

Quick Reference Handbook

Studying and Test Taking

Study Skills and Strategies

To be successful in your high school studies, you need to develop skills and strategies for efficient studying. The methods on the following pages will help you get better grades and give you practical ways to approach the task of studying so you can understand and remember information you may need later.

Making a Study Plan

The following suggestions may help you make effective use of your study time.

1. **Know your assignments.** Keep an assignment calendar or planner for recording your assignments and their due dates. Make sure that you understand all the instructions for each assignment.
2. **Create a study plan.** Break your large assignments into small steps. Schedule deadlines for completing each step.
3. **Focus your attention.** Set aside a specific time and place for studying. Find out what study environment works best for you. Avoid distractions.

Organizing and Remembering Information

The strategies listed below can help you organize and remember information as you study.

Classifying *Classification* is organizing information by arranging items into categories. You use classification when you make an outline, deciding which supporting ideas fit together under a major heading. In order to group things, you need to identify relationships among them.

EXAMPLE	What do the following people have in common?
	Steven Spielberg, James Cameron, John Ford, Frank Capra
ANSWER	They are all Academy Award-winning film directors.

You can also use classification to identify patterns in data. For example, look at the following chart.

Studying and Test Taking 911

Studying and Test Taking, pp. 911–927
Alignments
TEKS 2A, 4B, 4F, 7D, 7H, 13C
TAAS W4

Study Skills and Strategies 911

What would be the heights of columns 6 and 7?

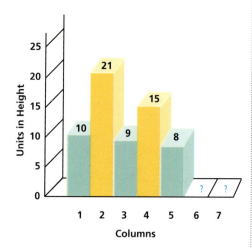

ANSWER The height of column 4 is six units less than the height of the preceding even-numbered column (column 2). Based on this pattern, column 6 would be nine units high. The heights of columns 3 and 5 are each one unit less than the height of the preceding odd-numbered columns (columns 1 and 3). Based on this pattern, column 7 would be seven units high.

Graphic Organizers Using maps, diagrams, charts, and other graphic organizers can help you visually arrange information and understand it more easily. (See also **Types of Graphics** on page 857.)

Memorization Frequent, short, focused sessions of practice are best when you are trying to memorize and retain material. Cramming for a test is not very efficient since you will not retain the information well.

Notes on Reading or Lectures When reading or listening to a lecture, take notes that will help you organize and remember information later when you are studying or writing. The following steps explain how to take notes.

How to Take Notes

1. Recognize and record main points.

In a lecture, listen for clues such as **key words** and **phrases** used by the speaker. Repeated or stressed words and phrases such as *most importantly* or *pay close attention* usually indicate points that you should remember.

In a textbook, look for clues such as chapter headings or subheadings, lists, or graphic organizers like charts, time lines, and illustrations.

2. Make summaries of information you read or hear. Instead of recording every detail, put the ideas into your own words. Abbreviate and condense information about key ideas. Distinguish supporting points from the main points by indenting them in your notes.

3. Pay close attention to examples. The main points of lectures or lessons are often illustrated through examples. Sketching a simple diagram of the example in your notes—for instance, a diagram of a human nerve cell—may later help to jog your memory.

In the following notes, important details are arranged in groups. Each group is then given a heading that indicates the key idea that unifies the details in each group.

Rosa Parks

<u>Biography</u>
- African American, born Feb. 4, 1913—Tuskegee, Ala.
- grew up in Montgomery, Ala.
- despised injustice in treatment of blacks
- incident in Dec. 1955 started bus boycott
- fired from her tailoring job because of boycott
- sat in the front of a city bus on Dec. 21, 1956 after a Supreme Court ruling
- hired by congressman in Michigan—worked for him for more than 20 years
- 1987—founded Rosa and Raymond Parks Inst. for Self-Development

<u>Examples of Inequality in Treatment</u>
- had to sit at back of shoe stores
- had to sit at back of buses
- had to stand if white person wanted seat on bus

<u>Details of Montgomery Bus Boycott</u>
- Ms. Parks refused to give up seat to white man
- Ms. Parks said, "My only concern was to get home after a hard day's work."
- Ms. Parks arrested for her refusal
- Ms. Parks stopped using the bus
- Ms. Parks helped form the Montgomery Improvement Association with Dr. Martin Luther King, Jr.
- thousands joined her boycott of bus system
- many risked jobs
- many employers gave rides instead of losing workers
- boycott lasted 382 days
- sparked American civil rights movement

Outlines An *outline* organizes the most important ideas and information from a passage. To create an outline, group ideas and information in an organized pattern that identifies their order and relationship to one another. To sort and group items, ask yourself, *Which details belong together? What do they have in common?* Also think of a heading—a word or a phrase—that identifies what the details do have in common. For example, the words *bicycle helmet, water bottle,* and *tire repair kit* may all be grouped under the heading *Safety Items*.

To define the order of your organizational pattern, first decide upon the relationship between the groups. Sometimes the topic itself suggests a clear order. One type of order is **chronological (time),** or a step-by-step process. Another type is **spatial order,** which describes the layout of something. A third type of order is **order of importance,** which arranges ideas from the least important to the most important, or vice versa. (See also **Outlines** on page 950.)

Paraphrasing When you *paraphrase,* you restate someone else's words in your own words. When you restate an idea in your own words, you are not just switching around words, but actually concentrating on the idea expressed in those words. Paraphrasing is a good way to check your understanding of what you read, especially if the original is written in poetic or elaborate language. A written paraphrase is usually approximately the same length as the original, so the technique of paraphrasing is generally not used for long pieces of writing. (See also **Paraphrasing** on page 882.)

SQ3R *SQ3R* is a strategy designed to help you study from a book or textbook. The letters stand for:

<u>**S**urvey</u> the chapter.
<u>**Q**uestion</u> while you are surveying.
<u>**R**ead</u> actively.
<u>**R**ecite</u> after you have read a section.
<u>**R**eview</u> what you have studied.

(See also **SQ3R** on page 884.)

Summarizing A *summary* restates the main points from a lecture, book, or notes in a condensed way. A summary helps you identify and remember the most important points of the material you are studying. When you write a summary, you analyze the material, determining the most important points of the passage and deciding what information should be included or omitted in the summary. Making these decisions helps you remember the information in a passage. (See also **Summarizing** on page 884.)

Writing to Learn Writing is useful as a study tool with which you may focus your thoughts, respond to ideas, record your observations, plan your work, and restate ideas in your own words. Writing about what you have read or heard helps you see relationships among ideas and to comprehend the text. Use the following different forms of writing as you study.

Type of Writing	Purpose	Example
Diary	helps you recall your impressions and express your feelings for class.	Write about your reactions to a play you have seen or an article you read
Freewriting	helps you focus your thoughts on an assignment or after listening to a lecture to focus on the most important points.	Write for three minutes after reading
Journal	helps you record your observations, descriptions, solutions, and questions	Write about problems or successes you had in solving word problems in math.
Learning Log	helps you present a problem, analyze it, and propose a solution	Write about the way you will incorporate a source or piece of information into a research paper for your social studies class.

Test-Taking Skills and Strategies

There are two types of tests you are likely to encounter in school: *classroom tests* and *standardized tests*. You will need to learn new skills and consider different strategies for approaching the different kinds of questions you will be asked on each of these different types of tests.

Classroom Tests

The typical *classroom test* measures your ability to use key academic skills or to demonstrate your knowledge of specific academic subjects. In your student career, you have probably seen several types of test questions—essay questions, matching questions, multiple-choice questions, and true/false questions—used in various combinations through the years. The best way to prepare for classroom tests is by familiarizing yourself with the material on which you will be tested or by practicing the skill or skills you will be asked to demonstrate at the time of testing. Also, make sure that you are prepared for each kind of question that can appear on a classroom test by reading the following descriptions, tips, and examples.

Essay Tests ask you to demonstrate two things:

- that you can think critically about material you have learned
- that you are able to express your understanding in one or more well-written and organized paragraphs.

Essay questions provide different challenges than the other kinds of test questions since an essay question may ask you to consider several ideas in your answer. Also, an essay question requires you to do more than just know details such as dates and definitions; often you must know how these details relate to one another. To study for an essay test, follow these steps:

1. **Read your textbook, class notes, or other study materials carefully.**
2. **Make an outline** that identifies the main points and important details from material being covered.
3. **Create a set of possible questions and practice writing out answers.**
4. **Evaluate and revise your practice answers.** Check your notes and textbook for accuracy.

How to Answer Essay Questions

1. **Scan the questions on the test.** Make sure you know how many answers you are expected to write. If you have a choice of several items, decide which ones you think you can answer best. Then, plan how much time to spend on preparing and writing each answer.

2. **Read the questions carefully.** Highlight or circle the key terms in the question to be sure you have covered all the parts of the question. Familiarize yourself with the key verbs that commonly appear on essay tests. (See also the **Key Verbs That Appear in Essay Questions** chart on page 916.)

3. **Use prewriting techniques to plan your answer.** Make notes or create an outline to help you decide what you want to say. (See also **Prewriting Techniques** on page 952.)

4. **Evaluate and revise your answer as you write.** You probably won't have time to redraft your entire essay. Instead, leave yourself a little time to re-read your answer and correct any spelling, punctuation, or grammar errors.

Essay questions usually ask you to perform specific tasks that are expressed with action verbs. You can prepare to complete each task by familiarizing yourself with the key verbs and the kinds of information they request.

Key Verbs That Appear in Essay Questions		
Key Verb	**Task**	**Sample Question**
Analyze	Look carefully at the parts of a situation or issue to see how each part works.	**Analyze** the U.S. government's role in Operation Desert Storm.
Argue	Take a stand on an issue and give reasons to support your viewpoint or opinion.	**Argue** whether your school should require all students to participate in extracurricular activities.
Compare or Contrast	Point out similarities between things, people, or ideas.	**Compare** the lives and inventions of George Washington Carver and Thomas Edison.
Define	Give specific details that make something or some idea unique.	**Define** the term *imperialism* as it applies to early U.S. history.
Demonstrate	Provide examples to support a point.	**Demonstrate** that a line intersecting parallel lines produces equivalent angles.
Describe	Give a picture in words, presenting explicit details.	**Describe** your childhood home.
Discuss	Examine in detail.	**Discuss** the term *Manifest Destiny*.
Explain	Give reasons or make the meaning clear.	**Explain** why the United States entered World War II.
Identify	Point out specific persons, places, things, or characteristics.	**Identify** the leaders of the Confederacy and their importance in the Civil War.
Interpret	Explain the meaning or significance of an event, idea, or quotation.	**Interpret** the role of Cesar Chavez in organizing the farm labor movement.
List	Give the steps in order or provide certain details about a subject.	**List** the events leading up to the Montgomery bus boycott.
Summarize	Give a brief overview of the main points.	**Summarize** the effects of ozone depletion in the atmosphere.

Although there are a wide variety of essay questions, nearly all good answers contain the same qualities.
- The essay is well organized.
- The essay clearly presents main ideas and supporting points.
- The sentences are complete and well written.
- There are no errors in spelling, punctuation, or grammar.

Matching Questions In matching questions, you must match each item on one list to a logically related item on another list.

EXAMPLE

Directions: Match each term in the first column to a description in the second column.

_D_	1. Shakespearean sonnet	A.	group of eight rhymed lines
_C_	2. couplet	B.	Italian sonnet
_A_	3. octave	C.	group of two rhymed lines
_B_	4. Petrarchan sonnet	D.	English sonnet
_E_	5. sestet	E.	group of six lines

> **How to Answer Matching Questions**
>
> **1. Carefully read all directions.** Be sure you know whether answers can be used only once or more than once.
>
> **2. Match the items that you are sure of first.** This will narrow the possible choices for the items of which you are less sure.
>
> **3. Guess intelligently on any remaining items.** In the previous example, if the items remaining to be matched were 1 and 4, and B and D, you might guess that 1 matches D—because Shakespeare was English—leaving you with 4 matching B.

Multiple-Choice Questions A multiple-choice question asks you to choose a correct answer from a given number of possible answers.

EXAMPLE

1. After she was arrested for refusing to yield her seat on a bus, Rosa Parks
   - (A.) decided to stop using the bus system.
   - B. was elected to Congress.
   - C. moved to Tuskegee, Alabama.
   - D. avoided the American civil rights movement.

> **How to Answer Multiple-Choice Questions**
>
> **1. Read the initial statement carefully.** Make sure you understand the statement completely before looking at your choices. Look for qualifiers, such as *not*, *always*, or *never*, because these words limit or affect the answer. In the example, you must choose the answer that best completes the sentence.
>
> **2. Read all the answers before making a choice.** Sometimes the answer includes two or more choices, such as "Both A and B" or "All of the above."
>
> **3. Narrow your choices by eliminating the incorrect answers.** Some answers are clearly wrong, such as D, while others may be only somewhat related to the correct answer. Looking at the example, you know that Rosa Parks was not elected to Congress, so you can rule out B.
>
> **4. From the remaining choices, select the answer that makes the most sense.** The answer is A.

Short-Answer Questions *Short-answer questions* ask you to show your knowledge about a subject in a brief, written reply. In general, short-answer questions require a specific answer of one or two sentences. Some short-answer questions, such as a map, diagram, or fill-in-the-blank questions, can be answered with one or a few words. Usually, short-answer questions have only one correct answer; however, you are not given possible answers from which to choose.

EXAMPLE
1. What famous reason did explorer George Mallory give in 1924 for climbing Mt. Everest?
1. "Because it is there."

True/False Questions *True/False questions* ask you to determine whether a given statement is correct.

EXAMPLE
1. T (F) The percentage of school-age children in the United States increased over the course of the twentieth century.

How to Answer True/False Questions

1. **Read the statement carefully.**
2. **Check for qualifiers.** Words such as *always* or *never* qualify or limit a statement's meaning.
3. **Choose the correct answer based on the following principles:**
   - If any part of the statement is false, the entire statement is false.
   - A statement is true only if it is entirely and always true.

Standardized Tests

Standardized tests evaluate your score according to a "standard" compiled from the scores of many other students who have taken the same test. The best-known tests of this type, such as the Scholastic Aptitude Test (SAT) and the American College Testing Program (ACT), are given to students across the entire United States; however, other standardized tests may be developed by states or school districts. The two basic types of standardized tests are **aptitude** tests (intended to evaluate basic skills or reasoning abilities needed in various *general* areas of study) and **achievement** tests (intended to measure knowledge of *specific* subjects such as history, literature, sciences, mathematics, or foreign languages.) To prepare for both kinds of standardized tests, keep in mind the three tips in the following chart.

How to Prepare for Standardized Tests

1. **Learn what skills will be tested.** Your school may provide information booklets that tell you about the types of questions and how the test is scored. Practice with these or with published study guides available through bookstores and libraries.

2. **Know what materials you need for the test.** You may need to bring specific materials, such as your official test registration card, number-two pencils, or lined paper for writing an essay.

3. **Determine how the test is evaluated.** If there is no penalty for wrong answers, make your best educated guess on all questions possible. If wrong answers are penalized, however, make guesses only if you are fairly sure of your answers.

Finally, you should familiarize yourself with the different kinds of questions that standardized tests ask as well as the writing prompts that they include.

Analogy Questions *Analogy questions* ask you to analyze the relationship between one pair of words and to identify or supply a second pair of words that has the same relationship.

Analogy questions usually appear on standardized tests in multiple-choice form.

EXAMPLE

1. Directions: Select the appropriate pair of words to complete the analogy.
   SHIRT: CLOTHING :: __C__
   A. wheel : car
   B. page : read
   C. bicycle : vehicle
   D. globe : round

Sometimes, however, analogies are written as fill-in-the-blank questions, and you will need to fill in the missing item.

EXAMPLE

2. Complete the following analogy.
   DRIZZLE : DOWNPOUR:: dime : __fortune__

How to Answer Analogy Questions

1. Identify the relationship between the first pair of words. In Example 1, a *shirt* is a type of *clothing*; the relationship is one of classification. (See also the **Types of Analogies** chart on page 920.)

2. Express the analogy in sentence or question form. Example 1 could be expressed as, "A *shirt* is a kind of *clothing*, just as a _____ is a kind of _____." Fill the blanks with each of the possible answers and see which makes sense. For example, "Is a *wheel* a kind of *car*?" It is not, so A is not the answer.

3. Find the best available choice to complete the analogy. If multiple-choice answers are provided, select the pair of words that shares the same relationship as the pair of words in the question. If you must fill in a word, select a word that has the same relationship to the word to the right of the double colons (::) as the two words in the question to the left of the colons. Example 2 shows a relationship of degree—a *drizzle* is a small amount of rain, and a *downpour* is a lot of rain. A *dime* is a small amount of money, and a *fortune* is a lot of money.

In addition to the three guidelines above, remember the following helpful tips.

- **Know the meanings of the symbols used in analogy questions.** The symbol : means "related to," while :: means "equals" or "is equivalent to."

- **Consider the parts of speech.** Some words may be used as more than one part of speech. Thinking about a word as a noun, a verb, or an adjective might help unlock the relationship in the analogy. If you cannot decipher the relationship between the words in the analogy, it may help to determine if one of the words can be another part of speech.

- **Become familiar with the types of analogy relationships.** Familiarize yourself with types of analogies typically found on standardized tests. Using the **Types of Analogies** chart on page 920, practice designing test questions of each type. Exchange with a peer and work through each other's questions.

- **Remember that it is the relationship between the words that is important, not the meanings of the individual words.** Look at Example 2. A *drizzle* and a *dime* have very little in common; but the relationship a *drizzle* has to a *downpour* is the same as the relationship a *dime* has to a *fortune:* degree. A downpour is more than a drizzle and a fortune is more than a dime.

Although there are many different relationships that can be represented in analogies, a smaller number of specific relationships are fairly common in standardized tests. Examples of these common types are shown in the chart on the following page.

Types of Analogies		
Type	**Example**	**Solution**
Action to Performer or **Performer to Action**	TEACHING : PROFESSOR : : cleaning : housekeeper	*Teaching* is performed by a *professor,* just as *cleaning* is performed by a *housekeeper.*
Antonyms	PATRIOT : TRAITOR : : loyal : unfaithful	A *patriot* is the opposite of a *traitor,* just as *loyal* behavior is the opposite of *unfaithful* behavior.
Cause	GERM : SICKNESS : : water : dampness	A *germ* causes *sickness,* just as *water* causes *dampness.*
Characteristic	MAMMALS : FUR : : fish : scales	*Mammals* always have *fur,* just as *fish* always have *scales.*
Classification	BAGELS : BREAD : : pork : meat	A *bagel* is type of *bread,* just as *pork* is a type of *meat.*
Degree	COLOSSAL : LARGE : : microscopic : small	*Colossal* means very *large,* just as *microscopic* means very *small.*
Effect	TEARS : SORROW : : smiles : joy	*Tears* are the effect of *sorrow,* just as *smiles* are the effect of *joy.*
Measure	BAROMETER : AIR PRESSURE : : scale : weight	A *barometer* measures *air pressure,* just as a *scale* measures *weight.*
Part to Whole or **Whole to Part**	WATER : OCEAN : : sand : desert	*Water* makes up the *ocean,* just as *sand* makes up a *desert.*
Place	SPACE NEEDLE : SEATTLE : : Lincoln Memorial : Washington, D.C.	The *Space Needle* is located in *Seattle,* just as the *Lincoln Memorial* is located in *Washington, D.C.*
Synonyms	ROUND : CIRCULAR : : strong : muscular	*Round* is similar in meaning to *circular,* just as *strong* is similar in meaning to *muscular.*
Use	DESK : STUDY : : bed : sleep	A *desk* is used to *study,* just as a *bed* is used to *sleep.*

Critical-Reading Questions Standardized tests may include questions that require you to look critically at a reading passage and to find its organizational pattern, meaning, and purpose. These *critical-reading questions* (sometimes called *on-demand reading questions*) measure your ability to analyze and interpret a reading passage. In addition, these questions may ask you to decide if the passage effectively communicates the writer's intended meaning. Critical-reading test questions focus either on a particular approach to the passage or on one topic within the passage. The following chart shows types of critical-reading test questions and the actions you must take to answer them. For more information and practice with any of the bulleted elements indicated, see the pages referred to in parentheses following each item.

Critical-Reading Test Questions

Rhetorical-strategy questions, or **evaluation questions,** ask you to judge the effectiveness of techniques used in a passage. These questions often ask you to identify and analyze

- the author's intended audience (page 264)
- the author's opinions (page 255)
- the author's purpose (page 84)
- the author's tone or point of view (page 88)

Inference questions, or **interpretation questions,** ask you to draw conclusions or make inferences about the meaning of information presented in a passage. These test items often ask you to identify

- ambiguities in information
- conclusions or inferences based on given material (page 27)

- specific conclusions or inferences that can be drawn about the author or the topic of a passage (page 172)

(See also page 27.)

Organization questions, or **main idea** or **detail questions,** ask you to identify the organizational techniques that the writer of a passage uses. You should be able to identify

- the main idea of a passage (page 65)
- arrangement of supporting details (page 60)
- the author's use of particular writing strategies (page 177)
- techniques used to conclude the passage
- transitional devices that make the passage coherent (page 886)

Style questions, or **tone questions,** ask you to evaluate the author's use of style in a passage. These test questions often ask you to identify

- the author's intended audience (page 264)
- the author's style
- the author's voice and tone (page 959)

Synthesis questions test your knowledge of how parts of a passage fit together to form a whole. These questions ask you to interpret

- the cumulative meaning of details in a passage (page 24)
- techniques used to unify details

Vocabulary-in-context questions ask you to infer the meaning of an unfamiliar word by looking at its context. These test items ask you to determine the meaning of an unfamiliar word using context clues (page 217). (See also page 216.)

NOTE To help you make the best use of the time allotted, first scan the entire reading passage and the critical-reading questions that follow. Write notes in your test booklet as you are pre-reading both the passage and the questions. Then, read more slowly through the passage. Refer to your jotted notes as you answer the questions.

Here is a typical **reading passage** followed by sample test questions based on this passage.

> With the rise of capitalism, a new middle class emerged who wanted their children to speak the dialect of the "upper" classes. This desire led to the publication of many prescriptive grammars. In 1762 an influential grammar, *A Short Introduction to English Grammar with Critical Notes,* was written by Bishop Robert Lowth. Lowth, influenced by Latin grammar and by personal preference, prescribed a number of new rules for English. Before the publication of his grammar, practically everyone—upper-class, middle-class, and lower-class speakers of English—said *I don't have none, You was wrong about that,* and *Mathilda is fatter than me.* Lowth, however, decided that "two negatives make a positive" and therefore one should say *I don't have any;* that even when *you* is singular it should be followed by the plural *were;* and that *I* not *me, he* not *him, they* not *them,* and so forth should follow *than* in comparative constructions. Many of these "rules" were based on Latin grammar, which had already given way to different rules in languages that developed from Latin. Because Lowth was influential and because the rising new class wanted to speak "properly," many of these new rules were legislated into English grammar, at least for the "prestige" dialect.

Sample Critical-Reading Questions

1. According to the passage, in which order (from earliest to latest) did the following events occur?
   I. "Two negatives make a positive" became a rule of English grammar.
   II. New rules developed in languages that developed from Latin.
   III. Lowth wrote *A Short Introduction to English Grammar.*
   IV. A new middle class emerged.

   A. I, IV, III, II
   B. II, IV, III, I
   C. IV, III, II, I
   D. II, I, IV, III

   [This is an organizational question; it requires you to identify the time sequence of these events and to arrange them in the correct historical time order.]

2. The word *prescribed* in the fourth sentence may be defined as
   A. claimed a right or title through long use
   B. advised as a medicine or treatment
   C. arose from long-standing usage or custom
   D. set down or imposed rules

   [This is a vocabulary-in-context question; it requires you to determine the appropriate definition by examining the word's context in the passage.]

3. After reading the passage, one of your classmates wrote the following paragraph.

   > Lowth's *A Short Introduction to English Grammar* did not help the English language as much as it caused a setback of hundreds upon hundreds of years. The book severely stunted the growth of a vibrant and living language. Grammar should be descriptive

922   Quick Reference Handbook   Studying and Test Taking

rather than prescriptive. That is to say, it should attempt to describe linguistic knowledge rather than tell you how you should speak.

From this paragraph, you could assume that your classmate is critical of the idea that

A. grammar should describe language
(B.) grammar rules save our language from deteriorating
C. language changes with time
D. there is a no "correct" way to speak

[This is a rhetorical-strategy question; it requires you to identify the main points of the original passage and to recognize which of these points your classmate disputed.]

4. The new middle class wanted their children to speak "properly" so that

A. they could read and write better
(B.) they could be associated with the upper rather than the lower class
C. their language more closely followed its Latin roots
D. they could do better in the world of commerce

[This is an inference question; you are asked to draw a conclusion based on the material given in the passage.]

5. It can be inferred from the passage that Bishop Lowth was

A. a man who represented the eighteenth century
B. a pious man who strictly followed the rules of Latin grammar
(C.) a man who changed the English language significantly
D. a capitalist concerned with the welfare of his class

[This is a synthesis question; it requires you to read, in the passage as a whole, about the new rules applied to the English language. Then, adding up all the details, you might infer that Lowth and his book,

described as influential, prescribed rules that you know are still followed today.]

6. Readers of the reading passage are likely to describe it as

A. informal
(B.) historical
C. inspirational
D. biographical

[This is a question of style; it requires you to analyze the way the passage is written to determine the category or type of writing it represents.]

NOTE At times it will help you to compare the vocabulary and details in the prompt to those in the reading passage. If no vocabulary or details from the prompt appear in the reading passage, you must draw your own conclusions or come up with your own examples. For example, question 2 in the chart cites a word (*prescribed*) that is clearly present in the fourth sentence of the reading passage. Question 6, however, does not lead you to a specific section or detail in the passage. Instead you must draw your own conclusion about the passage as a whole.

Multiple-Choice Questions When you take a standardized test, you will probably find *multiple-choice questions* similar to those found on classroom tests. However, on standardized tests the multiple-choice questions will generally be easier at the beginning and become increasingly more difficult as you progress through the test. To tackle these questions, begin by answering all the easily answered questions first, then attempting the more difficult ones. Since each question, whether easy or difficult, is worth the same amount, this will help you make sure that all of the "guaranteed" points will already be in your pocket before you attempt the challenging ones. Do not spend too much time on any single question, though. Also, don't let time limits pressure you. Instead, stay calm and avoid making careless mistakes. (See also **Multiple-Choice Questions** on page 917.)

On-Demand Writing Questions   Like essay questions, *on-demand writing questions* ask you to express yourself in one or more well-written and organized paragraphs in a limited amount of time. On-demand writing questions are different from essay questions, however, because you do not know the topic about which the prompt will require you to write. Usually these questions ask you to write a persuasive, informative, or descriptive essay in answer to a prompt that is broad but related to your general knowledge or experience. Because the ability to write on demand is such an important skill both in school and in the workplace, you will find that many states include on-demand writing questions as the core of their standardized testing.

EXAMPLES

    Many high schools are now requiring students to participate in volunteer programs in order to graduate. Students receive credit for hours spent working for volunteer organizations in their communities. Write a persuasive essay in which you argue whether requiring students to volunteer is a good idea.

    Most people have a favorite holiday, a time of the year or an occasion they like better than any other. Choose your favorite holiday and explain why you made that choice.

You may encounter a variation of the on-demand writing prompt in placement tests. The essays you write in response to placement test prompts will ask you to demonstrate your knowledge of a specific subject area. While the exact topic will not be known to you, you will still be able to supply details for an answer from your educational background. For example, a prompt for an English-literature placement test may require you to know literary elements and pull details from certain plays, novels, or poems that you have studied in the past. Here is one example:

    Define the term *poetic justice* and show how it applies to a major character in a literary work of your choice. Make sure that your essay is well organized and does not rely heavily on plot summary. Do not base your essay on an adaptation of a work, such as a movie or television program.

> **How to Answer an On-Demand Writing Question**
>
> **1. Determine what the question is asking.** By reading the passage carefully, you should be able to spot key verbs that indicate whether your answer should be persuasive, informative, or descriptive. (See also the **Key Verbs that Appear in Essay Questions** chart on page 916.)
>
> **2. Use prewriting techniques to plan your answer.** On scratch paper or the inside cover of your test booklet, get your ideas flowing and begin determining how your answer will be organized. Freewriting, brainstorming, and clustering are some ways to get started. (See also **Prewriting Techniques** on page 952.)
>
> **3. Evaluate and revise your answer as you write.** Make sure that your answer has a topic sentence, supporting details, transitions between ideas, and a clear conclusion.

    Although you cannot study for the content of an on-demand writing test, you can still prepare yourself by following the steps below.

- Become familiar with the kinds of writing that on-demand writing questions often

require. Read and learn to recognize the key qualities of persuasive, informative, and descriptive essays.

- **Practice writing answers to on-demand writing questions.** If possible, practice with questions that have appeared on state tests administered at your school in the past. Use a timer and the prewriting techniques to formulate answers. (See also **Prewriting Techniques** on page 952.)
- **Revise and proofread your answers.** If possible, share your answers with classmates. Have a discussion about which aspects of your answer are persuasive, informative, or descriptive.

Reasoning or Logic Questions

Some questions test your reasoning abilities rather than your knowledge of a specific subject. *Reasoning or logic questions* may ask you to

- identify the relationship between two or more items, such as words, pictures, or numbers
- identify a pattern in a sequence of numbers
- predict the next item in a series of images

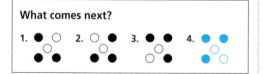

What comes next?

> **How to Answer Reasoning or Logic Questions**
>
> **1. Be sure that you understand the instructions.** Reasoning or logic questions are usually multiple choice. However, sometimes you may need to write a word, phrase, or number or draw a picture for your answer. To answer the previous example, you will need to draw a pattern of shaded and unshaded circles.

2. Analyze the relationship implied in the question. Look carefully at the question to gather information about the relationship shared by the items. The two unshaded circles in the example are pointed outwards and moving in a counterclockwise direction.

3. Draw reasonable conclusions. Evaluate the relationship of the items to decide your answer. In the fourth frame of the example, the white dots should point toward the bottom right.

Verbal-Expression Questions

Verbal-expression questions assess how well you understand the meaning of written passages and grammatical correctness or clarity of written expression. The chart on page 927 shows the four standard types of verbal-expression questions. (For more information and practice with any of the **grammar, usage, and mechanics elements** indicated in the right-hand column, see the pages referred to in parentheses behind each item.)

Multiple-choice verbal-expression questions are not often asked in isolation. Instead, you find them within the context of a reading passage. Within a sample passage, usually a long paragraph, you will be given several words and phrases that are underlined and numbered. You are then asked to choose the answer that best expresses the meaning, is grammatically correct, or is consistent with the style and tone of the passage. Here is a typical verbal-expression test passage followed by sample questions:

> The young Williams sisters share a dream$_{(1)}$ of being ranked number one and number two in women's tennis. Their father, Richard Williams$_{(2)}$ has coached Venus and Serena since they were four and five years old. The girls began their professional careers as teens and soon caught people's attention. Venus played the U.S. Open in 1997.

She was the first African American woman to reach the U. S. Open finals in nearly forty years. About her <u>attitude that is sometimes overly confident</u>$_{(3)}$,

Venus has said "You have to believe in yourself when no one else does—that makes you a winner right there."

Sample Verbal-Expression Questions

1. **(A.)** NO CHANGE
   B. shared
   C. has shared
   D. are sharing

[This is a question about grammar; it requires you to know the correct subject-verb agreement.]

2. A. NO CHANGE
   B. father (Richard Williams)
   (C.) father, Richard Williams,
   D. father Richard Williams,

[This is a question about punctuation; it requires you to know which mark of punctuation is appropriate here.]

3. Which is the best revision of this portion of the passage?
   A. NO CHANGE
   B. attitude, sometimes overly-confident
   C. sometimes over confident attitude
   (D.) sometimes overly-confident attitude

[This is a revision-in-context question; it requires you to use revision skills to best express the ideas in the passage.]

4. How should sentences four and five be combined?
   A. Since Venus played the U.S. Open in 1997; she was the first African-American woman to reach the U. S. Open finals in nearly forty years.
   B. Venus played the U.S. Open in 1997 and she was the first African-American woman to reach the U. S. Open finals in nearly forty years.
   (C.) When Venus played the U.S. Open in 1997, she was the first African-American woman to reach the finals in nearly forty years.
   D. Venus was the first African-American woman to reach the U. S. Open finals in nearly forty years in 1997.

[This is a question about sentence structure; it requires you to know how to combine sentences effectively.]

Most current, best-known national tests contain only two basic types of test items used to test verbal expression. You should learn to recognize them as follows:

Most Common Types of Verbal-Expression Test Items

"NO CHANGE" Items
- give a list of suggested revisions of under-lined, numbered portions of passage
- always contain one "NO CHANGE" choice (these words are often printed in capital letters) to be selected if the indicated part is correct as is

Critical Thinking Items
- ask you to analyze and evaluate the passage as a whole
- ask you to make inferences about portions of a passage as related to the whole

Studying and Test Taking

Verbal Expression Questions	
Type of Question	**What You Do**
Grammar Questions	Identify the correct answer, using standard grammar and usage rules. These test items often cover use of - principal parts of verbs (page 574) - pronouns (page 532) - subject-verb agreement (page 512)
Punctuation Questions	Identify use of correct punctuation. These test items often cover correct use of - apostrophes and hyphens (pages 758 and 767) - end marks and commas (pages 694 and 700) - parentheses and quotation marks (pages 770 and 743) - semicolons, colons, and dashes (pages 724, 729, and 770)
Sentence-Structure Questions	Demonstrate knowledge of what is (and what is not) a complete sentence. These test items often cover - combining sentences (page 352) - fragments and run-ons (pages 340 and 347) - parallel structure (page 362) - transitional words (page 959) - verb usage (page 572)
Revision-in-Context Questions	Show appropriate revision to a part of or to an entire composition. These test items often cover correct use of - arranging ideas - composition structure (page 943) - tone (page 959) - unity and coherence (page 391)

Viewing and Representing

TEACHING TIP

Media Terms

Point out to students that these media terms may be applied to any of the mass media they experience from day to day. Because we are only now beginning to analyze these different forms—some of which, such as the Internet, are recent developments—the terms in the lists are constantly evolving. You may want to discuss with students other terms they think should be included. For definitions of more media terms, please refer to the ancillary *Media Literacy and Communication Skills: A How-to Handbook for High School Students.*

Media Terms

Because media messages, such as advertisements, television programs, music videos, and movies, are a constant part of life, it is important to be able to understand, interpret, analyze, evaluate, and create media messages. The terms defined below refer to many different areas of media communication, including television and film production, advertising, and journalism. The terms are grouped into three lists: **electronic media terms** (below), **general media terms** (page 932), and **print media terms** (page 936). (Terms relating to the Internet and the World Wide Web can be found in the **Library/Media Center** section on page 866; terms relating to use of type and graphics can be found in **Document Design** on page 849.)

Electronic Media Terms

Advertising (See **Advertising** on page 936.)

Affiliate An *affiliate* is a privately owned, local television or radio station that presents the programming of a national network. (See also **Network** on page 931.)

Animation *Animation* is the film art of making drawings appear to move. An animated film may combine drawing, painting, sculpture, or other visual arts. Animators take film or video pictures of a scene at a rate of twenty-four frames per second, making small changes as they go. When viewed, the frames create the illusion of movement. Animation is used in many different types of media messages, including advertising and cartoons. (See also **Advertising** on page 936.)

Broadcasting *Broadcasting* means using airwaves to send television or radio content over a wide area of potential viewers or listeners. **Commercial broadcasting** is for profit. Advertisers pay broadcasters for airtime in which to persuade the audience to buy their products or services. **Public broadcasting** is not-for-profit. In the United States, the Public Broadcasting Service (PBS) has more than three hundred affiliates, or member stations. The service is funded mostly by the federal government, corporations, and individual viewers and listeners. (See also **Affiliate** on this page.)

Byline (See **Byline** on page 936.)

Cable Television   *Cable television* is a method of distributing TV signals using cables and wiring instead of airwaves to bring messages into people's homes. There are two principal types of cable TV companies. Some companies *create* original programming in the form of channels or networks, such as all-news networks or all-music channels. Other companies *distribute* packages, or groups, of many different channels into homes. (See also **Channel** on this page and **Network** on page 931.)

Camera Angle   The *camera angle* refers to the angle at which a camera is set when it is pointed at its subject. The angle may be low, high, or tilted. The effect of a low angle is to make the subject look tall and powerful. The high angle makes the subject look small. The tilted angle suggests that the subject is not balanced.

Camera Shots   A *camera shot* is what the viewer sees in a movie or video. Just as a written story needs many words, a film or video needs many shots in order to create a scene or story. Below are the most common shots used in film production.

- **Close-up shot**   A *close-up shot* is a shot of only the subject, usually a person's face.
- **Extreme close-up shot**   An *extreme close-up shot* is a very close shot, usually of only part of a person's face or part of the subject.
- **Medium shot**   A *medium shot* is a shot that shows the subject, usually a person from the waist up, and perhaps some of the background.
- **Long shot**   A *long shot* is a shot that shows a scene from far away, usually to show a place or setting of a scene.
- **Reverse angle shot**   A *reverse angle shot* is a view of the opposite side of a subject or of another person in the scene.

Channel   In general communication, a *channel* is the means by which a message is communicated. For example, if you are communicating verbally (such as by talking or singing), the channel is sound waves. If you communicate nonverbally (for instance, in pantomime), the channel is waves of light, because you see the facial expressions and exaggerated gestures of the pantomimist. In television and radio, the word *channel* means a fixed band of frequencies used for the transmitting of television or radio broadcasts. (See also **Medium** and **Message** on page 937.)

Copy   (See **Copy** on page 936.)

Credits   *Credits* refer to the list of names of people who worked to produce a program. This list usually appears at the end of a television program, film, or video or on the back of a compact disc case.

Demographics   (See **Demographics** on page 936.)

Digital Editing   (See **Digital Editing** on page 936.)

Docudrama   *Docudrama* is a type of documentary that blends elements of both documentary and drama to explore an actual historical, political, or social event. For example, docudramas may use actors, scripted dialogue, and special locations to re-create important events such as the signing of the Declaration of Independence.

Documentary   *Documentary* is a genre of film and television programming which uses language, sounds, and imagery to provide an interpretation of real-life events. Although

Media Terms   929

Viewing and Representing, pp. 928–938
Alignments
TEKS 19B, 19C, 20A, 20E

documentaries attempt to relate factual information, they may only show one producer's perceptions or point of view. Documentaries often have informative, persuasive, and artistic purposes.

Drama   *Drama* is an art form that tells a story through the speech and actions of the characters in the story. Most dramas use actors who impersonate the characters. Some dramas are performed in a theater, while others are presented on film.

Editor   (See **Editor** on page 936.)

Electronic Media   The term *electronic media* refers to the forms of mass media products that are available to consumers through some type of electronic technology such as a computer or a television. Electronic media products can be found on the Internet, on the radio, and on television.

Feature News   (See **Feature News** on page 936.)

Hard News   (See **Hard News** on page 936.)

In-Camera Editing   *In-camera editing* refers to any editing that is performed through the operation of a video or film camera and not by the cutting and shaping of an editor. The sequence of shots and scenes remains exactly as they were gathered by the camera operator. In-camera editing is an effective method of creating video when editing is time-consuming or equipment is unavailable. To create an effective work using in-camera editing, a great deal of pre-production planning is required, including a complete shot list and storyboards. In most cameras, sound can be added after the images have been shot.

Internet   The *Internet* is a global network of computers. With the Internet and a computer equipped with a modem, a computer user may access information from another computer or a network of computers anywhere in the world.

Lead   (See **Lead** on page 937.)

Marketing   (See **Marketing** on page 937.)

Medium   (See **Medium** on page 937.)

Message   (See **Message** on page 937.)

Multimedia Presentation   A *multimedia presentation* is any presentation that involves two or more forms of media. For example, when you give an oral presentation and include a videotaped production or posters you have made, you are giving a multimedia presentation. One medium is your speaking voice, and the other medium is the videotape or the posters you use to support your presentation. A multimedia presentation that involves the use of presentation software or Web sites is sometimes called a **technology presentation.**

Nielsen Rating   *Nielsen rating* refers to the ratings system invented by the A. C. Nielsen Company, one of the largest marketing research companies in the United States. Nielsen ratings gather information about household television viewing choices from a sample of five thousand households selected to represent the population as a whole. Using a device called a peoplemeter, the firm gathers and distributes information including the program watched, the people watching it, and the amount of time each viewer spent watching. Nielsen ratings are used to measure a program's popularity and to pinpoint target audiences for shows. Advertisers make decisions about buying airtime for their commercials during specific shows based in part on Nielsen ratings.

Network A *network* is a company that obtains and distributes programming to affiliated local stations or cable systems. Networks are not TV stations, but nearly 85 percent of all TV stations are affiliated with a network. Examples of networks include CBS, ABC, NBC, FOX, and WB. Each local station is responsible for its own programming, but a station that is affiliated with a network receives morning news programs, talk shows, soap operas, national news programs, sports programming, situation comedies, dramas, and late-night programming. The networks provide the programs free to stations in exchange for the right to sell advertising. (See also **Affiliate** on page 928.)

News (See **News** on page 937.)

Newsmagazine (See **Newsmagazine** on page 937.)

Photography (See **Photography** on page 937.)

Political Advertising (See **Political Advertising** on page 938.)

Producer A *producer* is the person responsible for overseeing the creation of a movie or television or radio program. He or she is responsible for the following tasks:
- developing the overall message
- finding appropriate materials
- organizing a crew or staff
- finding and budgeting funding
- keeping the production on a timetable

Public Access *Public access* refers to the channels on a cable television system set aside specifically for the public's use to create a variety of programs. These channels are often controlled by education officials or government leaders.

Ratings *Ratings* are the system of categorizing films, TV programs, or video games by considering whether the content is appropriate for people of different ages. Ratings help adults and children evaluate the content of a message before viewing. (See also **Nielsen rating** on page 930.)

Reality TV *Reality television* is the presentation of actual video footage taken by amateurs with police monitors and by surveillance cameras. Usually the footage is highly edited, but because reality TV is presented as an eyewitness account, people tend to find it believable.

Reporter (See **Reporter** on page 938.)

Script A *script* is the text or words of a film, play, or television or radio show. The format for film and TV scripts often includes information about the images to be shown. The script for news broadcasts is called *copy*. (See also **Copy** on page 936.)

Sequencing *Sequencing* is the order in which scenes or images appear in a narrative. In television, film, and video, the editing process enhances sequencing by splicing together scenes, usually filmed separately and in different locations, to create a sense of flow or sequence.

Situation Comedy A *situation comedy* is a television format that involves stories about a set of characters. The characters appear regularly each week in either a home, school, or work setting. Situation comedies involve humor and focus on life's ordinary problems and solutions. (See also **Genre** on page 934.)

Soft News   (See **Soft News** on page 938.)

Source   (See **Source** on page 938.)

Sponsorship   A *sponsorship* takes place when a business gives money to support a particular TV or radio program in return for commercial air time. Sponsorship is different from advertising because in sponsorship, a company's name is acknowledged but usually the product is not promoted. For example, public broadcasting may include sponsors' names and slogans. (See also **Broadcasting** on page 928.)

Storyboard   A *storyboard* is a visual script, or series of drawings, that indicates the appearance and order of shots and scenes in a script as well as audio and visual cues. (For an example of a **storyboard**, see page 50.)

Target Audience   (See **Target Audience** on page 938.)

Text   (See **Text** on page 938.)

General Media Terms

Audience   An *audience* is a group of receivers of a media message. Audiences may receive a message by listening, reading, or viewing. In the economics of the mass media business, advertisers pay to reach specific audiences when they place ads in newspapers, magazines, radio, television, or the Internet. Audiences are often identified by specific characteristics, or demographics. (See also **Demographics** on page 936.)

Authority   *Authority* refers to a quality of a message. A message that seems believable because it comes from a trustworthy and knowledgeable individual has authority. For example, a message about new regulations for teenage drivers would have more authority coming from a traffic safety instructor than from an outdated driver's handbook. (See also **Credibility** on this page and **Source** on page 938.)

Bias   A *bias* is a negative connotation or point of view. An editorial writer with a bias may present only one side of an issue or ignore information that does not support his or her position. (See also **Point of View** on page 935.)

Communicator   A *communicator* is a person involved in the act of communicating or sending messages to another person or persons (the audience). The receiver takes on the role of communicator when he or she returns the message.

Credibility   *Credibility* is the willingness to believe in or to trust what a person says and does. Credibility is not a characteristic of a speaker but a perception that exists in the minds of a listener or viewer. (See also **Authority** on this page.)

Critical Viewing   *Critical viewing* is the ability to use critical thinking skills to view, question, analyze, and understand issues presented in visual media, including photography, film, television, and other mass media. Critical viewers use **media literacy** concepts to access, analyze, evaluate, and communicate media messages. On page 933 are five key concepts of media literacy and some questions to help you evaluate media messages.

932   Quick Reference Handbook   Viewing and Representing

Media Concepts	Evaluation Questions
1. All messages are made by someone. Every media message is written, edited, selected, illustrated, or composed by one or more individuals. Writers, photographers, artists, illustrators, and TV and radio producers all decide which elements (words, images, sounds) to include in a media message, which ones to leave out, and how to arrange and sequence the chosen elements. Knowing how media messages are constructed will help you better interpret the meaning of a message.	Ask yourself: "What words, images, or sounds are used to create the message?" and "What words, images, or sounds may have been left out of the message?"
2. Media messages are not reality. Media messages are *representations* of reality that in turn shape people's ideas of the world. Fictional stories in the media can seem realistic if characters act in ways that seem authentic, but, of course, the stories are not real. An eyewitness news account of a natural disaster can seem real, but it usually reflects only one person's point of view, filtered through a TV camera and carefully edited down to a few images and words. Media messages can never match the complexity of the real world. Every media message also affects the way you think about the world. It is important that you judge the accuracy of media messages and whether or not you think the messages reflect reality.	Ask yourself: "What is the point of view or experience of the message maker?" and "How does this message affect the way I think about a particular topic or idea?"
3. Each person interprets media messages differently. Your interpretation of a media message is based on your knowledge and experience. You can use your prior knowledge and experience to examine the many different stylistic features of a message and to evaluate the message within its context.	Ask yourself: "How does the message make me feel?" or "What does the message make me think of?"
4. People have a wide range of purposes for creating media messages. People create and share messages for many reasons; in modern culture making money is one of the most important. When people have political purposes, they use messages to gain power or authority over others. Understanding how messages operate in terms of their economic, political, social, and aesthetic purposes will help you better understand the context of a work.	Ask yourself: "Who created the message and why?" or "Is the producer's purpose to inform, to influence, to present ideas, to make money, to gain power, or to express ideas?"
5. Each mass medium—from TV to the newspaper to the Internet—has unique characteristics. Media messages come in different forms. A media producer makes choices about which kinds of media are most appropriate to convey a particular message. For example, TV news favors messages that are immediate and visual, while news photographs favor messages that have an emotional component. Knowing how the medium shapes the message will help you understand why its creator used certain elements and why the message makes you feel the way it does.	Ask yourself: "Through what medium is the message delivered?" and "How does the form affect the message?"

Media Terms

Cooperative Learning

(19B, 19C, 20A, 20B)

Evaluation Pairs. Have students work in pairs to evaluate a television news program of their choice. Students should use the following questions to guide their evaluations.

- What words, images, or sounds are used to create the message? What words, images, or sounds have been left out of the message?

- What is the point of view of the maker of the message? How does this message affect the way I think about this particular topic in the news?

- How does the message make me feel? Why? Of what does the message make me think?

- Who created the messages in the news and why? What is the producer's purpose in presenting the news—to inform, to influence, to present ideas, to make money, to gain power, to express ideas?

- Through what medium is the news delivered—visuals, text, or a combination?

TEACHING TIP

Media Law
Discuss with students how laws that control the delivery and the use of media impact their lives. Students may be interested to know, for example, that the Supreme Court in *Hazelwood v. Kuhlmeier* upheld the right of school officials to regulate the contents of student newspapers. You may want to have students research other stories pertaining to copyright law or censorship. Direct students to summarize their findings and document their sources.

Decoding *Decoding* is the making of meaning from verbal and nonverbal signals. For example, audiences decode symbols, such as words and pictures, when they watch TV or read a newspaper.

Deconstruction *Deconstruction* is the process of analyzing, or taking apart, the pieces of a media message to understand its meaning. The process of deconstruction involves looking at both what is stated, such as the words printed on a newspaper page, and what is not directly stated, including elements of the historical, economic, and political context in which the newspaper was created.

Feedback *Feedback* is a response from an audience to the sender of a message. It can be immediate or delayed. Applause, booing, and asking questions are typical forms of **immediate feedback** from an audience. Writing a letter to the editor to respond to a newspaper editorial and filling out a questionnaire on a Web page are forms of **delayed feedback.**

Formula A *formula* is an established model or approach. In television and film, it refers to a typical combination of characters or presentation of material. In dramas which feature aliens from space, for example, the non-human characters are usually portrayed in grotesque make-up with physical features that produce terror and awe. The conventions of make-up for the alien characters is part of the formula.

Genre A *genre* is a category of artistic forms or media products that share **conventions,** or commonly accepted ways of presenting messages. For example, before the opening commercials, prime-time TV news programs usually begin with a short, attention-grabbing segment that announces the day's headline events. Each genre has a particular audience and conventions. Some examples of genres within television are documentaries, dramas, and talk shows.

Interpretation *Interpretation* is the process of creating meaning from exposure to a message through reading, viewing, or listening. People's interpretations of messages differ, depending on their life experiences, backgrounds, and points of view.

Media Law Various government structures, laws, and policies regulate access, content, delivery, and use of the mass media. For example, the *First Amendment* to the Constitution forbids Congress to set up or in any way pass laws limiting speech or the press. *Copyright law* protects the rights of authors and other media owners against the unauthorized publishing, reproducing, and selling of their works. *Censorship* is any governmental attempt to suppress or control people's access to media messages. Some censorship, however, may be used to protect citizens against damage to their reputations (libel) or against invasions of their privacy.

News Values *News values* are the set of criteria journalists use to determine whether information is newsworthy. News values include

- **timeliness** events or issues that are happening now
- **conflict** unresolved events or issues that are interesting to the public
- **novelty** stories that contain unique, interesting elements
- **relevance** stories that are of interest to local audiences
- **human interest** stories that touch people's emotions

- **prominence** stories about celebrities, politicians, or other noteworthy people
- **impact** stories that make a difference in people's lives

If a news event has these features, it is more likely to be covered by the news media.

Newsworthiness *Newsworthiness* is the quality of an event that is worthy of being reported in a newspaper or news broadcast. An event must be of interest or importance to the public in order to be considered newsworthy. (See also **News Values** on page 934.)

Omission An *omission* is what is left out of a media message. All messages are selective and incomplete. For example, some films of historical events omit information or ignore historical figures in the events. Some news stories present only one side of a controversial issue, omitting information contrary to the slant of the story. Noticing what is not included in a message helps to identify the author's point of view. (See also **Point of View** below.)

Point of View *Point of view* can refer to the position or view of the person reporting a story or telling a tale in the mass media. Point of view is also a literary concept which can be used to interpret mass media texts ranging from docudramas to feature news stories. In the electronic media, point of view can be indicated by the type of narration used or by the type of camera shot used.

Propaganda *Propaganda* is any form of communication that uses persuasive techniques to reach a mass audience. Propaganda was originally defined as the spreading of biased ideas and opinions through lies and deception. This definition gave the concept of propaganda a negative connotation. However, as scholars began to study the topic in the 1940s, they came to realize that propaganda was everywhere. Over time, the concept of propaganda has lost some of its negative connotation. Propaganda is now thought of as the communication of a point of view with the goal of having audience members come to voluntarily accept this position as one of their beliefs. Advertising is one of the major forms of propaganda. (See also **Advertising** on page 936.)

Purpose The *purpose* of a media message is what its sender or creator intends to achieve. Usually, the purpose of a message is to inform, to educate, to persuade, to entertain, to express oneself, or to make money. A message may have both a primary and a secondary purpose.

Sensationalism *Sensationalism* is the media's use or portrayal of material that is intended to generate curiosity, fear, or other strong responses. The material can be exaggerated or shocking in content. Content that refers to romance, death, children, or animals is often sensational. (See also **Reality TV** on page 931 and **Tabloid** on page 938.)

Stereotypes *Stereotypes* are generalized beliefs based on misinformation or insufficient evidence about an entire group of individuals. A stereotype about teenagers, for example, would be that all teenagers are reckless drivers.

Visual Literacy *Visual literacy* is a person's awareness of how meaning is communicated through visual media, including the use of color, line, shape, and texture.

Print Media Terms

Advertising *Advertising* is the use of images or text to promote or sell a product, service, image, or idea to a wide audience. Advertising is a marketing technique that is designed to persuade an audience. Typical advertising formats include print advertisements in newspapers and magazines, billboards, radio and television commercials, and electronic billboards on the World Wide Web. (See also **Marketing** on page 937 and **Sponsorship** on page 932.)

Byline A *byline* is the name of the reporter or writer of a report published in a newspaper or magazine or presented on television or radio.

Circulation *Circulation* is a measurement of the size of the audience for print media. It includes the total number of copies of a publication, such as a newspaper, that is delivered to subscribers, newsstands, and vendors.

Copy *Copy* is the text in a media message.

Demographics *Demographics* are the characteristics that define a particular audience. They include gender, age, educational background, cultural heritage, and income. Advertisers use demographics to target certain audiences. For example, advertisers know that many teenagers watch music videos, so in the commercial breaks they advertise items—such as special brands of clothing or food products—that they believe will especially appeal to teens.

Digital Editing *Digital editing* is the use of computer technology to alter or change an image before it is presented to an audience. Photo editors often edit out distracting elements—such as telephone wires or shadows—from photo illustrations. However, large-scale digital editing of hard-news photographs is thought to be an unethical practice.

Editor An *editor* supervises reporters. Editors decide what news stories will appear in print media or in broadcasting. They also check facts for accuracy and correct errors. (See also **News Values** on page 934.)

Elements of Design *Elements of Design* are the parts of an idea's visual representation—such as *color, line, shape,* and *texture*—that give meaning to the visual representation. The following list explains how each element communicates meaning. (See also **Document Design** on page 849.)

- **Color** creates mood and adds realism with its eye appeal. Color designates areas of space by separating and emphasizing parts of a visual. Viewers also associate certain items with particular colors. For example, usually oranges and tangerines are associated with the color orange. (See also **Color** on page 856.)

- **Line** determines the direction and speed of the viewer's eye movement. For example, straight lines suggest decisiveness, while curvy lines indicate gracefulness. Lines also communicate factual information in graphic organizers. (See also **Types of Graphics** on page 857.)

- **Shape** emphasizes elements in the visual and adds interest. Often, shapes evoke emotional responses. For example, a square represents solidity, while a circle indicates completeness.

- **Texture** is the manner in which the visual representation appeals to a viewer's sense of touch. Sometimes superficial texture in a visual may be created by cross-hatching, diagonal lines, or stippling.

Feature News *Feature news,* also called soft news, refers to news stories whose primary purpose is to entertain. Feature stories usually are not timely. Stories about celebrities and ordinary people, places, animals, events, and products are considered feature news because they generate sympathy, curiosity, or amazement in viewers, readers, or listeners. An example of feature news would be a profile of a high school principal who had shown effective leadership in a high risk, large, urban school district. (See also **Hard News** below and **Soft News** on page 938.)

Font A *font* is a style of lettering used for printing text. (For more on **Fonts,** see page 854.)

Hard News *Hard news* refers to fact-based reporting of breaking news stories. Hard news answers the basic *5W-How?* questions about timely subjects, such as national and international politics, economics, social issues, the environment, and scientific discoveries. An example of hard news would be a story reporting the results of a devastating natural disaster. (See also **Feature News** above and **Soft News** on page 938.)

Headline A *headline* is the title of a newspaper or magazine article, usually set in large or bold type. It has two purposes: to inform the reader of the content of the article and to get the reader's attention.

Lead A *lead* is the introduction to a newspaper article or a broadcast report. It ranges from one sentence to several paragraphs in length and contains information that motivates a reader or viewer to continue with the story. A lead usually contains the major facts of a story and may also describe a curious or unusual situation to attract reader or viewer attention.

EXAMPLE

LONDON, August 20—The largest audience in history for a solar eclipse gathered Tuesday along a narrow arc of land running from the Isles of Scilly off England to eastern India, waiting for a celestial show that would last just a couple of minutes.

Marketing *Marketing* is the process of moving goods or services from the producer to the consumer. It includes identifying consumer wants or needs; designing, packaging, and pricing the product; and arranging for locations where the product will be sold. Marketing also includes promoting the product to a target audience through advertising or other means. (See also **Advertising** on page 936.)

Medium The *medium* of a message is the form in which it is presented or distributed, including film, video, radio, television, the Internet, and print.

Message A *message* is a combination of symbols that is communicated to one or more people. Messages are created by people who use symbols, including language, gesture, images, sounds, and electronic forms. Media messages are communicated through various mass media. (See also **Medium** above.)

News *News* is the presentation of current and interesting information that will interest or affect an audience. Local news is produced by local newspapers and radio and TV stations, which use their own equipment, reporters, and resources. The focus of local news is information that affects a small audience with regional interests. National news is produced by large newspapers and radio and TV stations. Because their resources are greater, national news organizations may cover more national and world issues or events.

Newsmagazine   A *newsmagazine* is a weekly, biweekly, monthly, or bimonthly printed journal that focuses on news issues. On TV, a newsmagazine is a news program divided into several news segments or stories.

Photography   *Photography* is a process of making pictures by using cameras to record patterns of light and images on film or on computer disks. Photography is both an art form and a major component of the mass media; it is used in making still photographs and motion pictures. People sometimes think that "a photograph never lies," but a photograph, like all media messages, is selective and incomplete. Photographers use a wide range of techniques to communicate their points of view, including the framing and composition of an image, the use of filters or digital editing, and the selection of what to include in the frame. (See also **Digital Editing** on page 936 and **Point of View** on page 935.)

Political Advertising   *Political advertising* is the use of the mass media to persuade listeners and viewers about a political candidate's ideas or opinions. Political candidates who use advertising must use techniques similar to those used to sell products. Their messages must be simple and attention-getting. (See also **Advertising** on page 936.)

Print Media   *Print media* refers to the hard copies of mass media products that are printed on paper to be read or looked at by consumers. Examples of print media are newspapers, magazines, pamphlets, and flyers.

Reporter   A *reporter* is a journalist who is responsible for information gathering. Reporters gather information and work with editors to create TV and print news. (See also **Editor** on page 936.)

Soft News   *Soft news,* or feature news, is the presentation of general interest material, such as unusual pet stories, in a news format. Soft news is designed to entertain readers or viewers. (See also **Feature News** and **Hard News** on page 936.)

Source   A *source* is the person who first supplies information or ideas that are then shared with others. Journalists rely on sources for the information they report and select individuals that they believe are credible and have authority. (See also **Authority** on page 932.)

Tabloid   A *tabloid* is a publication with a newspaper format that provides sensational news items and photographs. Tabloids are highly dependent on stories and photographs of media celebrities. Tabloid producers often admit that the stories they report are either false or exaggerations of the truth.

Target Audience   A *target audience* is a segment of the population for which a product or presentation is designed. (See also **Demographics** on page 936.)

Text   *Text* refers to the symbols used to create a message, such as the language found in a book or the images and sound in a TV show.

Writing

Skills, Structures, and Techniques

You can use the following ideas and information to become a more effective writer.

Business Letters A *business letter* is a formal way to share written information. Business letters may be used to request information, apply for a job, voice a complaint or express appreciation. Use the following guidelines to create professional-looking business letters.

- **Parts of a business letter** There are six parts of a business letter. They are usually arranged on the page in one of two styles. In *block form,* all six parts begin at the left margin, and paragraphs are not indented. In *modified block form,* the heading, the closing, and your signature begin to the right of the center of the page. All the other parts begin at the left margin, and all paragraphs are indented.

Business Letters

- Use white, unlined 8 1/2" x 11" paper.
- Type your letter or prepare your letter on a computer, using single-spacing and an extra line between paragraphs. If you write by hand, neatly write the letter, using black or blue ink. Check for typing errors and misspellings.
- Center your letter with equal margins on the sides and at the top and bottom.
- Use only one side of the paper. If your letter won't fit on one page, leave a one-inch margin at the bottom of the first page and carry over at least two lines onto the second page.
- Avoid mark-outs, erasures, or other careless marks.
- Use a polite, respectful, professional tone.
- Use formal, standard English. Avoid slang, contractions, and most abbreviations.
- Include all necessary information, but get to the point quickly. Be sure that your reader knows why you wrote and what you are asking.

Writing, pp. 939–959
Alignments
TEKS 1A, 1B, 1C, 2A, 2C, 2E, 3D, 4B, 4D
TAAS W1, W2, W3, W4, W7
English II End-of-Course 4, 5, 6

Block Style

Modified Block Style

1. The *heading* usually has three lines:
   - your street address (or post office box number)
   - your city, state, and ZIP Code
   - the date the letter was written
2. The *inside address* gives the name and address of the person to whom you are writing. Use a courtesy title (such as *Mr.*, *Mrs.*, *Ms.*, or *Miss*) or a professional title (such as *Dr.* or *Professor*) in front of the person's name. Include the person's business title (such as *Director* or *Editor*) after the name. Finally, follow the name with the name of the company or organization and its address. If you do not know the name of the person who will read your letter—for example if you are writing to the service department of a mail order company from which you bought an item that was damaged in shipping—put the position title in the place of the name.
3. The *salutation* is your greeting. If you are writing to a specific person, begin with *Dear*, followed by the courtesy title or professional title, and the person's last name. End with a colon. If you don't have the name of a specific person, use a general salutation such as *Dear Sir or Madam:*. You can also use a department or a position title, with or without the word *Dear*.
4. The *body*, or main part of your letter, contains the message. If the body of the message requires more than one paragraph, leave a blank line between paragraphs.
5. The *closing* is your ending. Appropriate closings are *Yours truly*, *Sincerely*, or *Respectfully yours*. End the closing with a comma. Capitalize only the first word of the closing.
6. Your *signature* should be handwritten in ink, directly below the closing and above your typed or printed name. Always sign your full name with no titles.

NOTE If you are including more in your envelope than just your letter, for example, a résumé, brochure, or writing sample, leave two lines blank after the signature, then type "encl." (for *enclosure*) plus the type of item or items you are enclosing.

- **Types of business letters** There are four types of business letters.
  1. **Appreciation or commendation letters** An *appreciation* or *commendation letter* is written to express appreciation or encouragement to a person, a group, or an organization. When you write an appreciation or commendation letter, it is important

to tell the person or organization exactly why you are pleased. Following is the body of a sample appreciation letter.

> I am writing to congratulate all of you at WQBK on your change in format from top 40 to alternative music. Although I enjoy listening to popular music, I am more interested in hearing what musicians outside the mainstream are recording. All my friends and I are really tired of hearing nothing but the same twenty or so top songs every day on the radio.
>
> I hope that you succeed with your new format. I know that my friends listen to your station, and sometimes even my parents listen to you, too. Good luck!

2. **Complaint or adjustment letters** The purpose of a *complaint* or *adjustment letter* is to express your dissatisfaction with a service or product. In the letter, you should identify what is wrong and suggest a solution. Here is the body of a sample adjustment letter.

> I have noticed that there are only two trash cans in Edgemont Park. I think that the litter situation would improve if the Parks Department would put more trash cans in the park. I think these cans should be placed so they are more convenient to the field, the picnic area, and the creek. More people would pick up their trash if there were containers close to where they are needed.
>
> Please give your attention to this suggestion. I think Edgemont Park is a wonderful neighborhood resource that should be kept clean for everyone in our community to enjoy.

When you write a complaint or adjustment letter, remember to register your complaint as soon as possible after noticing the problem and explain exactly what is wrong. Include information such as

- what product or service you ordered or expected
- why you are not satisfied (for example, the item was sized incorrectly)
- how you were affected (for example, you lost time or money)
- how you think the problem may be solved

Keep the tone of your letter calm and courteous. Despite your frustration, your letter will be more effective if you are coolheaded and communicate the problem clearly.

3. **Letters of Application** *Letters of application* provide a selection committee or a possible employer with information about you. The information helps your readers determine whether you are a good choice for a position or award such as a job or scholarship. When writing a complaint or adjustment letter, you should follow the guidelines below.

Guidelines for Letters of Application

1. Identify the position for which you are applying. Tell how you heard about it.

2. Depending on the position for which you are applying, you might mention
- your grade-point average
- your experience, or your activities, awards, and honors
- personal qualities or characteristics that make you a good choice for the position
- the date or times you are available to begin the position

3. Always offer to provide references. Your references should be responsible adults (usually not relatives) who have agreed to recommend you. Be prepared to supply their addresses and telephone numbers.

Skills, Structures, and Techniques

TEACHING TIP

Request Letters 1A, 2A, 3A, 5B
Have students write a request letter to either a real or fictional addressee. Students can brainstorm for topics by thinking of products or services in which they are interested. Before students begin writing, have them check the spelling of the person's or company's name and the address to which they will be sending the letter. Students can begin writing by composing a sentence expressing what they are writing to request. Finally, have them exchange their letters with partners to review and proofread.

Below is an example of an application letter.

```
                    1437 Windy Ridge Road
                    Milwaukee, WI 53224
                    January 20, 2001

Mrs. Elaine Fong, Director
Spanish Student Exchange Program
P.O. Box 3001
New York, NY 10002

Dear Mrs. Fong:
   I am writing to apply for the
summer exchange program to Barcelona,
Spain, as advertised in the January 13,
2001 edition of Student Voices.
   I am a sophomore at Vince
Lombardi High School in Milwaukee,
Wisconsin. My grade-point average
is 3.3, and I have studied Spanish
for three years. Last semester I
won an award for my work in this
class.
   I would be proud to be selected
for this program. I am aware of
the responsibility it involves.
I would feel privileged to gain a
new understanding of the Spanish
language and culture, and, on my
return, to share this information
with others in my school and
community.
   I will gladly furnish references
who can tell you more about my
qualifications. My parents, too,
are supportive of my interest.
   Please let me know if there is
any other information I need to
give you before you may consider
me as a candidate for this
program.

Sincerely,
Taneesha Collins
Taneesha Collins
```

4. Request or order letters In a *request letter,* you are asking for something, such as information about a product or someone's time or services. In an *order letter,* you are asking for something specific. You might write an order letter to purchase a product by mail or request a brochure. In request or order letters, it is important to say clearly what you want.

Here is a sample request letter.

```
                    Shackelton High School
                    19 Brookside Drive
                    Latham, NY 12110
                    September 3, 2001

Mr. Stuart Reinhardt, Manager
Rollerama
2008 Route 9
Latham, NY 12110

Dear Mr. Reinhardt:
   Shackelton High School's
sophomore class has voted to hold
a class party at Rollerama. As
class secretary, I am writing to
ask if we could plan this event
for Saturday, November 12, from
7:30 P.M. to 10:30 P.M. We expect
about 85 students.
   Could we rent the rink on the
same terms as you gave the senior
class last spring? The sophomore
class can guarantee a minimum
attendance of 75 students.
Students will pay an admission
price of $5.00. Skate rental will
be an additional $2.50 charge.
   Our class is looking forward
to an enjoyable evening at
Rollerama.

Yours truly,
Lindsey O'Donnell
Lindsey O'Donnell,
Class Secretary
Class of 2003
```

When you are writing a request or order letter, remember the following points.
- State your request clearly.
- If you are asking someone to send you information, enclose a self-addressed, stamped envelope.
- If you are asking someone to do something for you, make your request well in advance.
- If you are ordering something, include all important information, such as the size, color, brand name, or any other specific information. If there are costs involved, add the amount correctly.

Compositions A composition is a longer piece of writing that usually has three main parts: *introduction, body,* and *conclusion*. Each has a specific function, yet they all work together to communicate a main idea. The main idea is usually stated in the *thesis*. The three sections of a composition follow.

- **Introduction** Your composition's *introduction* should do three things:
  1. **Catch the reader's attention.** The introduction may be the most important paragraph in your composition. If the introduction is not written well, your readers might not bother to read the rest of your paper.
  2. **Set the tone.** The words you choose and what you say about your topic set your composition's **tone**. The tone of a composition may be serious, humorous, formal, informal, critical, or even outraged.
  3. **Present the thesis.** A *thesis statement* is a sentence or two that identifies your topic and explains your main idea about it. A

Strategy	Example
1. Review the facts and details in your prewriting notes. Identify the main or unifying idea and begin thinking about how your supporting ideas fit together.	You notice that in your notes about homelessness in your city, there is little discussion about the problem. Your thesis might read: *The problem of homeless teens in our city needs more attention.*
2. Check your thesis statement by asking both of the following questions: What is my topic? What am I trying to say about my topic?	Topic: *teen homelessness* Main Idea: *People should be better informed about teen homelessness in the city.*
3. Be clear and specific.	You might make the thesis more specific by adding more information. Your thesis might read: *In our city alone, there are about a hundred kids without regular homes. The problem of teen homelessness is one that city leaders need to address.*
4. Evaluate your thesis with your audience in mind. Will the reader care about what you are saying about your topic? About your arguments?	You might think to yourself "My classmates are the audience. They may not know much about the issue. They will probably be interested in it."

Skills, Structures, and Techniques

thesis statement works in a composition like a topic sentence works in a paragraph. Here are some strategies for writing a thesis statement. Often, but not always, the thesis statement comes at the end of the introduction. When this is the case, the introduction moves from a general discussion of the topic to a narrower, more specific focus, as shown in the following graphic.

Introduction

General

Specific (Thesis)

To write an effective introduction, try beginning with one of the techniques in the chart below. The examples show how

Techniques for Beginning Introductions	
Technique	**Example**
Begin with an anecdote or example.	Suppose almost every morning you woke up in an unfamiliar place. Then suppose that you had to be able to pack everything you own into a suitcase or shopping bag. How would you feel in these situations? This is the experience of many teenagers who happen to be homeless.
Begin with a startling factor by adopting an unusual position.	Mayor Ronnie Meyers attributes her career in politics to one thing —the six months that she, her two sisters, and her mother were homeless. Although she was only twelve at the time, she knew that the experience had changed her life. She decided that she would work to make sure other teens did not have to go through what she did.
Use an appropriate quotation.	"Being a teenager is hard enough without the added stress of being without a place to live," says Mario Ferrars, a social worker. "Too many kids are without a steady place to go to after school. It's a problem that is not recognized enough."
Start with background information.	In our city alone, there are more than two hundred people who are officially homeless. Half of these are under age of fifteen. Only twenty percent of these young people are going to school five days a week. It is important to get all these students to school every day. The question is, how do we do that?
Begin with a simple statement of your thesis.	The homelessness situation is becoming an obvious problem in even the smallest cities and towns. What is less obvious is the way the problem is affecting teenagers.
Begin with a question or a challenge to the reader.	When you walk downtown, do you find yourself trying not to notice the people sleeping on the sidewalks or in stairwells? Or are you the kind of person who carries loose change so that you can donate it to people who really need it? Either way, have you noticed how young some of these homeless people are? You cannot deny that homelessness, especially of young people, is a problem in many cities.

you might introduce a composition about homelessness.

> **NOTE** Often you will have an occasion for writing, too. That means that you are writing because some recent event in the news or in your community prompted you to think about your topic. In other words, your problem has a context in the outer world. If possible, mention this occasion in your writing—it will make your paper relevant to your readers, too.

- **Body** The *body* states and develops the composition's main points. Together, all the paragraphs in the body support one main idea—the thesis statement. When writing the body of your composition, keep in mind the following guidelines.
  1. **Arrange your information** in a way that makes sense to your readers and is appropriate to your topic. This gives your composition *coherence*. The table below indicates four common ways to arrange ideas in a composition.
  2. **Eliminate any details that do not support your thesis.** This gives your paper *unity*.
  3. **Show how your ideas are connected** by using *direct references* and *transitional expressions*. (See also pages 375–376.)

- **Conclusion** As the final part of your paper, the *conclusion* should do four things:
  1. **Provide readers with a sense of completion.** Your readers have invested in your ideas by reading your entire composition. Be fair to readers by bringing together all the ideas you mentioned earlier.
  2. **Restate your thesis.** Remember, your thesis statement was intended to show readers the direction your writing would take. Restating the thesis confirms that you have arrived at the place you wanted to be. Often a conclusion begins with a specific statement, such as a restatement of the thesis, and moves to general information. The following graphic may help you to visualize the organization.

Conclusion

Specific (Thesis)

General

Arranging Ideas		
Type of Order	**Definition**	**Example**
Chronological	order that presents events as they happen in time	explanation of a process; personal narrative; story
Spatial	order that describes objects according to their location	descriptions (near to far, left to right, top to bottom, and so on)
Importance	order that gives details from least to most importance or the reverse	descriptions, evaluative writing; explanations (main idea and supporting details); persuasive writing
Logical	order that relates groups and items	comparison-contrast; explanations of cause and effect or problem-solution; definitions

3. **Summarize your major points.** By summarizing the main points of your composition, you allow your readers to review all that they have learned from you. Summarizing helps your readers remember what they read.

4. **Offer a solution or make a recommendation.** If you have taken a stand on an issue in your composition, you should stress your point in the conclusion by offering a solution or recommending an action to take. Including a stand or recommendation in the conclusion makes it more likely that the reader will remember and act on your opinion or idea.

To write an effective conclusion, try one of the following techniques:

Technique	Example
Restate your main idea.	The problem of teenagers who are without homes is growing and will not resolve itself without more involvement of people in the community.
Summarize your major points.	Homelessness affects every part of a teenager's life—school work, social life, and involvement in sports, hobbies, and the community. Teens who might otherwise be active members of the community are too busy trying to hold their lives together. With more focused awareness on the part of the community, teen homelessness could be reduced, allowing teens to focus on the things that are important.
Close with a final idea or example.	The Spare Room program started by adults and teens in a neighboring city has reduced the number of homeless teens there by twenty percent in the last two years. The results speak for themselves—teen homelessness is a problem that can be solved in part by caring people with good ideas.
End with a comment on the topic (a thoughtful observation, a personal reaction, or a look to the future).	Look around your room and decide what you would put in a suitcase and carry with you. If it is not an easy choice, think of what it would be like to have no choice.
Call on your readers to take action.	If you and your family were to offer a homeless classmate a place to stay even one night a week, you would reduce the problem of teen homelessness in this city by a small but significant amount. Imagine how good it would feel to be able to say that you have done your part.
Refer to your introduction.	You don't have to have experienced homelessness, as Mayor Ronnie Meyers did, in order to get involved in the fight against homelessness.

E-Mail Guidelines

- Always be polite in your messages—even if you know the person to whom you are writing. Being rude to someone in an e-mail is called *flaming*. Flaming often backfires because there is always the chance that your angry message could be forwarded and read by someone you didn't intend to see it.

- Avoid using capital letters in your messages. CAPITAL LETTERS CONVEY SHOUTING. No one wants to be shouted at in cyberspace. (If you want to show emphasis, place asterisks (*) on either side of the important word or term. For example, "What do you think about the *metaphor* in chapter 2?")

- Use emoticons sparingly and never use them in formal e-mails. *Emoticons* are combinations of symbols that, when you tilt your head to the left, look like faces and suggest feelings that words alone cannot convey. For example, the emoticon :-) suggests laughter or "I'm just kidding." Use them in informal e-mails only.

- Always pay attention to the addresses entered in your address line. Make sure that you are sending appropriate messages to the right people.

- Always fill in the subject line before you send a message. Providing a subject will help your readers prioritize your message, which could be only one of many they receive.

- Avoid forwarding an e-mail without asking the permission of the original sender. Private e-mails are usually intended for your eyes only.

- Keep your message concise and to the point. If possible, limit yourself to one full screen or less of text. Scrolling through long e-mail messages can be tedious.

- Use bulleted lists and indentation to make the document easy for your readers to read on-screen. Bulleted lists are especially helpful if you are raising more than one question or point.

- Always use standard English and make sure that your spelling, grammar, and punctuation are correct.

- Include salutations, such as "Dear Mr. Tate," if you are writing for the first time to someone you do not know. Also, ending with "Sincerely" or "Thank you" followed by your full name is always considered polite.

E-mail Electronic mail, or *e-mail,* is correspondence sent by the computer rather than through your local post office. You can use e-mail to write personal, informal letters or to send formal, business messages. Because e-mail is so easy to use, many people ignore the guidelines associated with writing letters when they are composing e-mail messages. Informal content and format are often acceptable when you write to someone you know well or send comments to a newsgroup or chat group where the discussions are clearly relaxed. However, if you are writing to someone you do not know well for business or research purposes, you should follow the guidelines listed above. Online etiquette, or "Netiquette," stresses that good manners and common sense are as important in cyberspace as they are in the real world.

Envelopes If you want a letter to arrive promptly at its destination, you must address its envelope correctly. Place the return address in the top left-hand corner of the envelope. In the center of the envelope, write the name and

Skills, Structures, and Techniques

address of the person to whom you are writing. For a business letter, the addressee's name and address should exactly match the inside address. Use the proper two-letter state code rather than writing out the state name.

Forms Printed forms vary, but the following techniques will help you fill out any form accurately and completely.
- Read all of the instructions carefully.
- Type or write neatly. Unless a pencil is specified, type or print your information in either blue or black ballpoint pen.
- Proofread your completed form and correct errors neatly.

Graphic Organizers A *graphic organizer* is a visual device that helps you "see" what you are thinking. You can use graphic organizers to find a subject to write about, to gather information, and to organize your information. Following are some widely-used types of graphic organizers.

- **Charts** *Charts* are a practical, graphic way to arrange information. They help you see "blocks" of information, and their relationships, clearly. In the following chart, a writer has organized information about two minerals and their effects on health into three categories.

Mineral	Sources of Mineral	Uses by the Body	Deficiency Symptoms
Calcium	milk, cheese, whole grains, leafy vegetables, peas, and other legumes	bone and teeth development, muscular and nervous system functioning, blood clotting	soft bones, poor teeth, failure of blood to clot
Iron	liver, red meat, egg yolk, whole grains, prunes, nuts	healthy red blood cells	anemia

- **Clustering** (See **Clustering** on page 953.)

- **Mapping** (See **Mapping** on page 955.)
- **Sequence chain** A *sequence chain* is a diagram that helps you see how one event leads to another. It works well when you are narrating or explaining a process. In the following example, the writer uses a sequence chain to show the steps of the water cycle.

> Water in the oceans evaporates.
> ↓
> Airborne water, heated by the sun, evaporates into the atmosphere.
> ↓
> In the atmosphere, the water cools, condenses, and forms clouds.
> ↓
> Clouds release the water in the form of rain.
> ↓
> As rain, the water falls back to the surface of the earth and is absorbed.
> ↓
> Water that is not absorbed is caught up in rivers, streams, and creeks.
> ↓
> Water is transported back to the ocean.

- **Time line** A *time line* organizes information chronologically on a horizontal line, with the first or earliest events on the left end and the most recent or latest events on the right end of the line.

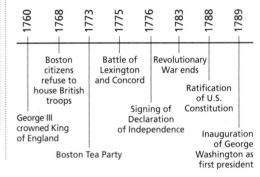

Venn Diagram

DIFFERENCES	SIMILARITIES	DIFFERENCES
Comets		**Asteroids**
• do not strike Earth
• may have periodic orbit around the sun
• develop million-mile long tails when orbiting close to sun
• formed by snow and dust	• space debris
• in orbit around the sun
• orbits may be affected by the gravitational force of planet Jupiter	• can strike Earth
• most exist in a wide belt between planets Mars and Jupiter
• vary widely in size, from a foot in diameter to hundreds of miles
• formed by hunks of rock

- **Venn diagram** A *Venn diagram* uses intersecting circles to show the similarities and differences between two subjects. The area of overlap between the two circles shows how the two subjects are similar; the remaining areas show how they are different. In the Venn diagram above, a writer compares and contrasts comets and asteroids.

Informal or Personal Letters A *personal letter* is less formal than a business letter in content and appearance. Personal letters are usually handwritten rather than typed. Use the *modified block form* for a personal letter, but do not include an inside address. There are three common types of informal or personal letters. (See also **Business Letters** on page 939.)

- **Invitations** Send an *invitation* to invite someone to an event. An informal invitation should contain specific information about the occasion, the time and place, and any other details your guest might need to know.

- **Letters of regret** Send a *letter of regret* if you have been invited somewhere and are unable to go. A written reply is especially appropriate if you were sent a written invitation with the letters *R.S.V.P.* (in French, an abbreviation for "please reply").

- **Thank-you letters** A *thank-you letter* tells someone that you appreciate his or her putting forth time, effort, or expense on your behalf.

Manuscript Form When you formally share with others a composition you have written, its appearance is important. Above all, the paper should be neat and legible. (For guidelines on improving the appearance of your paper, see **Manuscript Style** on page 849.)

Memos A memorandum, or *memo*, is a written message for conducting business within an organization. Most memos are for announcing meetings, sharing summaries of meetings, or requesting action or information. They are concise messages, generally covering only one topic.

Electronic mail (e-mail) is used in many businesses for memos because of its speed and the ease of record keeping.

```
                    MEMO
DATE:      May 2, 2000
TO:        All Falcon Quill Staff
FROM:      Doba Abeyto, Editor
cc:        Mr. Begay, Newspaper
           Sponsor
SUBJECT:   Schedule for June
           production

There will be a meeting Friday,
from 9:00 to 10:00 A.M., in the
journalism room to develop the
schedule for the June issue.
```

Memo Guidelines

Use the words *DATE, TO, FROM,* and *SUBJECT* at the top of your memo to quickly give your reader the most essential information.

State your information clearly and briefly.

If you are asking for action or information, include a deadline.

Send a copy of the memo to people who also need to know the information but are not directly involved with it. Use the abbreviation *cc,* which stands for "carbon copy." It refers to a once-common method of making copies by placing carbon paper between sheets of typing paper in a typewriter.

Messages Taking a *message* requires listening to information, usually by telephone, and then communicating that information to someone else. Think of the five "W" questions when writing a message.

Who is the message from and to **whom** is it directed?

What is the message?

When was the message written (date and time)?

Where can the sender be reached, if necessary?

Why is the message important?

Outlines An *outline* is a way of organizing information that shows the relationships among ideas. An outline can guide writers to present ideas clearly and can help readers understand the organization of information.

■ **Informal outlines or early plans** An *informal outline,* also known as an *early plan,* does not have a set form. You simply sort your ideas or facts into groups and arrange the groups in order. First, ask yourself: *Which items belong together? What do they have in common? Which items don't fit anywhere?* Then, give each group a heading that shows how the items in it are related. Next, arrange your information in a way that will make sense to your readers: chronological order, spatial order, logical order, order of importance, or another order that works. (See also **Compositions** on page 943.) Some papers will combine more than one type of order. Here is an informal outline about bicycle touring.

```
            Bicycle Touring
Preparing your bike
    —condition
    —equipment
Preparing yourself
    —exercise
Preparing clothing
    —weather-appropriate
    —safety gear
Preparing a route
    —miles per day
    —terrain
```

- **Formal outlines** A *formal outline* is a highly structured, clearly labeled writing plan. It has a set pattern, using letters and numbers to label main headings, subheadings and details. An outline can use either topics (words and phrases) or complete sentences for each item. Here is a portion of a formal outline about bicycle touring.

```
Title: Bicycle Touring

Thesis statement: If you are
interested in bicycle touring,
you need to make some specific
preparations involving your bike,
yourself, your clothing, and your
route.

  I. Your bike
     A. Type of bike
     B. Condition of the bike
     C. Equipment
        1. Map
        2. Light
        3. Kits
           a. Bicycle-repair kit
           b. First-aid kit
        4. Saddlebags
        5. Water container
 II. Your physical condition
     A. Exercise program
        1. Muscles
        2. Endurance
     B. Goal: 10-15 miles
```

Paragraphs A paragraph is a group of sentences that presents and supports a main idea; it is also the primary building block in a composition. Although most of the paragraphs in a single composition are often of one major type, many compositions contain more than one type of paragraph. The four types of paragraphs vary by purpose.

- **Descriptive paragraphs** A *descriptive paragraph* lets your readers visualize your subject, whether it is a person, an object, or a scene. Descriptive paragraphs are often organized according to spatial order and usually contain sensory details.

> **Sensory detail 1** The train pulled in, steaming and gasping, just as the sun came up. It had come from Dalian, 600 miles away, and it stopped everywhere. So it was sensationally **Sensory detail 2** littered with garbage—peanut shells, apple cores, chewed chicken bones, orange peels and greasy paper. It was very dirty **Sensory detail 3** and it was so cold inside the spit had frozen on the floor into misshapen yellow-green medallions of ice. The covering between coaches was a snow tunnel, the **Sensory detail 4** frost on the windows was an inch thick, the doors had no locks and so they banged and thumped as a freezing draft rushed through the carriages.
>
> Paul Theroux,
> *Riding the Iron Rooster*

- **Expository paragraphs** Writers use *expository paragraphs* to explain and inform. Expository paragraphs are usually organized according to logical order and contain factual and statistical information. The facts and statistics in the following expository paragraph support and prove the main idea that the enormous amount of trash United States residents throw away today is a big problem.

> Every year, the typical U.S. family throws out 2,460 pounds of paper, 540 pounds of metals, 480 pounds of glass, and 480 pounds of food scraps. All told, each of us throws away more than 1,200 pounds of trash per year, far more than people in most other countries. About 80 percent of that garbage ends up in landfills—dumps, as they are more commonly known. (Of the remaining 20 percent, about half is recycled and half is incinerated.) One big problem is that we are running out of landfill space—more than half of the nation's landfills will be full within ten years.
>
> John Elkington, Julia Hailes, Douglas Hill, and Joel Makower, *Going Green*

- **Narrative paragraphs**   A *narrative paragraph* is used to tell a story or to illustrate an event or series of events, usually in chronological order.

> In the radio room, Harold Bride was exhausted. The two operators were expected to keep the radio working twenty-four hours a day, and Bride lay down to take a much-needed nap. Phillips was so busy with the passenger messages that he actually brushed off the final ice warning of the night. It was from the *Californian*. Trapped in a field of ice, she had stopped for the night about nineteen miles north of the *Titanic*. She was so close that the message literally blasted in Phillips' ears. Annoyed by the loud interruption, he cut off the *Californian's* radio operator with the words "Shut up, shut up. I'm busy."
>
> Robert D. Ballard, *Exploring the Titanic*

- **Persuasive paragraphs**   A writer uses a *persuasive paragraph* to express his or her opinion about a particular subject, for the purpose of convincing others to share the opinion or to take action. Writers of persuasive paragraphs usually use order of importance or logical order to organize their ideas.

> Art history opens the child's imagination to other eras and cultures. If students of the next century are to work and live productively side by side with others from different cultures, they must respect and appreciate cultural differences and, at the same time, discern what they share in common with other peoples. The arts are one of the best ways of achieving this practical goal. Learning how to critique and judge art sharpens critical faculties by obliging the student to think independently, creatively, and to make reasoned judgments based on his or her knowledge and trained observations. Finally, consideration of aesthetic issues teaches them to be able to deal with the nature and meaning of art in their own lives.
>
> Harold M. Williams, "Don't Ignore the Arts," *USA Today* magazine

Prewriting Techniques   The following techniques can help you find a subject about which to write and gather information about that subject. Although the prewriting techniques are presented separately, you may often use more than one technique at a time. You may also find that you prefer to use some techniques more than others.

- **Asking the *5W-How?* questions**   Ask yourself the reporter's questions—*Who?*

What? When? Where? Why? and *How?*—to find ideas for your writing.

EXAMPLE

> **Who** are some famous Creek leaders or chiefs?
> **What** was a Creek community like when Europeans first settled in North America?
> **When** did the Creeks first encounter Europeans?
> **Where** did they live at the time?
> **Why** are they called "Creeks"—an English word?
> **How** did Creeks react to the European settlers?

- **Asking *what if?* questions** To stimulate your creative thinking, ask a variety of *What if?* questions about a subject. Imagine different everyday situations and see where these ideas take you.

> **What if** I could change one thing in the past?
> **What if** a familiar thing no longer existed?
> **What if** I could create something completely new?
> **What if** I could travel to another time?
> **What if** our society didn't use money?

- **Brainstorming** Write down a subject, and then list all your ideas about that subject as quickly as you can. Resist the urge to evaluate your ideas; remember that you are trying to come up with as many ideas as possible. Keep going until you run out of ideas, and then evaluate the ideas as possible topics for writing. Brainstorming is also a good group activity.

EXAMPLE

> **Weather**
> rain   heat   snow
> windchill   tornadoes   fog
> cloud formations hurricanes drought

- **Chaining** This technique uses questions and answers to help you make connections between ideas. It is a way to build new ideas from existing ones and often helps you to see subjects in a totally new light. Here are the steps for chaining.
  1. The first link in the chain is a question.
  2. The answer to that question becomes the next link.
  3. The third link is a question prompted by the answer in step 2. This process continues until you get the ideas you want.

EXAMPLE

Question: How will computers change our everyday world in the future?
Answer: It's possible that many people will work from their homes instead of in an office building.
Question: Won't this cause problems for the economy?
Answer: Possibly, but it could also open up the possibilities for new services and businesses.
Question: What kinds of new services would be needed?
Answer: Home offices, computer services for homes, and probably other businesses tied to home business needs.

- **Clustering** Like brainstorming, *clustering* (also called *webbing* or *making connections*) is useful for generating creative ideas. First, write a subject in the middle of your paper. Circle the subject. Then, in the space around the subject, write whatever related ideas occur

Skills, Structures, and Techniques   953

to you. Circle the new ideas and draw lines to connect the new ideas with the original subject. As you continue to think about the subject, write down your ideas and draw circles and lines to show connections among the ideas.

EXAMPLE

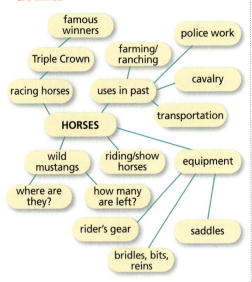

- **Cubing** Investigate a subject by imagining a cube that has one of the following directions on each of its six sides: *Describe it. Compare it. Associate it. Analyze it. Apply it. Argue for or against it.* Write for three minutes about each side of the cube.

Electric Guitar

EXAMPLE

Describe it. The electric guitar has a solid body, usually of wood, that is a sort of figure-eight shape. Six metal strings are connected at the base of the body and at the top of the long straight neck. At the top of the neck are the machine heads that let you tune the strings by making them tighter or looser. A magnetic plate under the strings on the body translates the vibrations of the strings into electric signals that are turned back into sound by the amplifier. The tremolo arm is slender and silver and works by stretching and loosening the strings a little to make the sound bend.

- **Freewriting** When you *freewrite,* you write whatever pops into your head. Think of a topic that interests you, and write about it for three to five minutes. Don't worry about using complete sentences or proper punctuation. Just write as much as you can, and stay focused on your topic. If you cannot think of anything new to write, copy the same word or phrase until something comes to mind.

EXAMPLE

RECYCLING: Using stuff again. Plastics, paper, glass, aluminum—in new products. Garbage landfills filling. Disposable diapers. Controversy. What's the right thing to do? And what's the use? Saving the Earth. OK, how? How can one person make a difference? Containers for collecting are great, and so is the fact that fast-food chains are using recycled sources. But still, there is so much stuff! Where will it all go in the end?

- **Listening with a focus** Printed words are not your only source of information. You can also listen—to radio and television programs, to videotapes and audiotapes, and to experts during personal or telephone interviews. Before you listen, follow the steps below.

1. Write down your topic, and then brainstorm or cluster what you already know.
2. Make a list of the information you need. Jot down questions that you would like to have answered as you listen. This list of questions should help guide and focus your listening.
3. Listen carefully with your questions in front of you. Take careful notes and pay close attention. Get the main points and supporting details by writing in phrases and using abbreviations.

- **Looping** Looping will help you to generate ideas that can be developed into an essay.
  1. In this prewriting activity, you start with a subject and freewrite about the subject for a set period of time.
  2. Include anything that comes into your mind on the subject. Even if you can't think of anything to say, continue writing for the specified period of time, even if all you write is "I can't think of anything to say." The important thing is to keep your pen or pencil moving.
  3. After the time limit is up, read what you have written and pick out what seems to be most important or weighty in the loop. This is the center of gravity for that loop. You may have stated this center of gravity, or you may have to figure it out.
  4. Finally, write your center of gravity sentence and begin the process again for two more loops.

- **Mapping** *Mapping* resembles clustering in form but is used to organize ideas rather than for generating ideas. It is a helpful visual way to determine whether you have enough support for each main idea. Notice how the following map groups main ideas and supporting details.

EXAMPLE

- **Pentad** A *pentad* is a star with five points, each of its points representing one of the following questions: *What is happening? Who is causing it to happen? How is it being done? Where and when is it being done? Why is it happening?* Think about your topic, and write an answer to each question. Then, read what you have written and determine a focus: Which points did you write the most about? Is there an interaction between those points? This focus will probably be your thesis statement. A pentad is a good prewriting technique to use when you are writing about literature.

Skills, Structures, and Techniques

EXAMPLE

What is happening? Members of a family sit on their front porch to worry as they wait to hear from a bank about a loan that will let them keep their house.

Why is it happening? The family needs a bank loan extension in order to keep the house and the family is not sure that it will receive it.

Who is causing it to happen? The women in the family are waiting while the father is at the bank.

Short story: "Home" by Gwendolyn Brooks

When and where is it being done? It is late afternoon on the front porch of the house.

How is it being done? The women are sitting and talking, pretending that having to move will be a good thing.

- **Reading with a focus** You can get ideas for writing by reading books, newspapers, or magazines. When you read to find information, don't read everything. If there is an index or table of contents, use it to narrow your search. Skim the material, searching only for information about your topic. When you find relevant information, read carefully and take notes.

- **Track Switching** This technique takes advantage of the fact that people often think in a familiar track about subjects. You start by freewriting along the familiar track and then purposefully switch to another track. This technique often leads to fresh ideas. The steps for track switching are as follows.

  1. Start by creating a statement about your subject, and freewrite about that statement for five minutes.
  2. Create another statement about your subject that switches tracks—that is as different as possible from the first statement you made.
  3. Write on this track for five minutes.
  4. Repeat this process for five tracks. Remember that there are no rules about what you write for each track; just let the words flow along the track.

- **Using your five senses** Gather information about your topic through the use of all five senses: sight, hearing, smell, taste, and touch. If you stop to focus on all the sensory details around you, you will have a nearly endless supply of specific details for your writing.

EXAMPLE

Night football game

sight: dark green grass; funny yellowish lights and dark sky; players in maroon, orange-gold, muddy uniforms; referees in crisp black and white; fans a sea of every color, with red jumping out—blankets, gloves, coats

sound: chants of cheerleaders and fans; deep roar and shrieks of fans; bands—sounds fading in and out as they turn in formation on the field; airplanes faint overhead

smell: hot dogs and mustard; popcorn; newly cut grass

taste: cherry lip balm; stale, too-salty popcorn; tangy mustard

touch: cold air; sharp gusts of wind; hard bleacher seats; scratchy wool scarf against cheek

- **Visualizing** *Visualizing* means forming a mental image of something. Picture your subject in your "mind's eye." As you do so, use your imagination to write down details for each of the five senses.

EXAMPLE

> The theater seems dark as you come in from the bright street. It is an old theater with a lobby carpeted in red. The walls have mirrors and old movie posters. The air smells of fresh popcorn that you know will taste like cardboard. We like to sit in the balcony, so we climb the curving staircase up two flights and find seats near the ceiling. The air is warmer than downstairs, and humid. Looking up, you can see the ceiling decorated with gold and with old-fashioned paintings. The seats are covered in red velour and feel squishy and uncomfortable and there is no place to put your bucket of popcorn.

- **Writer's notebook or journal** Use a special notebook or file folder to record your experiences and observations, feelings and questions. You can also collect print material that has special meaning to you, such as poems, songs, and newspaper articles. Try to write in your notebook daily, and date your entries. Soon your journal will be a sourcebook full of ideas about which you can write.

Résumé A *résumé* is a summary of your background and experience. For many job positions, you are required to submit a résumé along with a letter of application. There are many ways to arrange the information on a résumé. Whatever style you select, be sure that your résumé looks neat and businesslike. (See also **Letters of Application** on page 941.)

```
              TANEESHA COLLINS
              1437 Windy Ridge Road
              Milwaukee, WI 53224
              Telephone: (414) 555-7023
              E-mail: taneesh@milwaukee.net

OBJECTIVE:
Year abroad in Barcelona, Spain, as
part of Spanish Student Exchange
Program

WORK EXPERIENCE:
June 1998          Recorder of read-
to present         ings for blind in
                   English and in
                   Spanish
September 2000     Organized Spanish
                   Club book and bake
                   sale
January 2001       Helped design Spanish
                   Club Web page

EDUCATION:
Sophomore, Vince Lombardi High
 School
Grade-point average: 3.3

EXTRACURRICULAR ACTIVITIES:
Spanish Club
Chorale

ACHIEVEMENTS:
Excellence in Spanish Award,
 December 2000

REFERENCES:
Available on request
```

Revising and Proofreading Symbols

To some people, *editing* is simply making corrections, while to others, it includes both revising and proofreading. When you are revising or proofreading your own or a peer's work, use the following symbols to indicate any changes that should be made.

Skills, Structures, and Techniques 957

Symbols for Revising and Proofreading

Symbol	Example	Meaning of Symbol
≡	Maple High school	Capitalize a lowercase letter.
/	the First person	Lowercase a capital letter.
∧	on the fourth ⌃of May	Insert a missing word, letter, or punctuation mark.
∧	sep⌃arate	Change a letter.
——	in the East (West)	Replace a word.
ℯ	tell me the the plan	Leave out a word, letter, or punctuation mark.
⌒	an unusual idea	Leave out and close up.
⌒	a water fall	Close up space.
∽	recieve	Change the order of letters.
tr	the last Saturday of September (in the month)	Transpose the circled words. (Write tr in nearby margin.)
¶	¶ "Help!" someone cried.	Begin a new paragraph.
⊙	Please don't go⊙	Add a period.
∧	Well, what's the news?	Add a comma.
#	record#keeping	Add a space.
:	the following ideas:	Add a colon.
;	Houston, Texas; St. Louis, Missouri; and Albany, New York	Add a semicolon.
=	typed in single=space	Add a hyphen.
∨	Sally's new job	Add an apostrophe.
stet	an extremely urgent message	Keep the crossed-out material. (Write stet in nearby margin.)

Tone *Tone* refers to the feelings you convey through your writing. Your tone lets your readers know how you feel about them as well as how you feel about the subject of your writing. Tone is conveyed in three ways: by your choice of details, by the length and structure of your sentences, and by your choice of words.

■ **Choice of details** The *choice of details* in your writing lets your reader know what is important to you as a writer. For example, providing readers with lists of facts or statistics sets the tone as serious and objective, while writing about a childhood memories of a place conveys a more intimate tone.

- **Sentence length and structure** The *length and structure* of the sentences in your writing also informs your tone. If your writing is full of long, convoluted sentences, then it is clear to readers that you are serious—perhaps even too serious—about the subject. Short, snappy sentences suggest a sense of playfulness.
- **Word choice** Your *word choice* lets your readers know how seriously you care about the subject. For example, the choice of formal language conveys a more serious, concerned tone than informal language. Conversely, the use of informal language, such as contractions and colloquialisms, suggests a more friendly, personal tone. The connotations of the words you use will also greatly inform your tone. For example, "that guy" is informal or casual, while "the gentleman" is polite and respectful.

Keep in mind that the *occasion* for which you are writing always affects your tone. The occasion is the reason for writing. Often the occasion is to fulfill an assignment for school, but it might also be to communicate with a friend or family member or to instruct someone younger than yourself. In thinking about occasion, ask yourself these three questions:
1. Why am I writing—for school? for fun? to brainstorm ideas?
2. Who will read my writing—a teacher, a friend, a stranger, or only me?
3. When or where will the reader read my writing—in front of the class, alone at home, somewhere else?

Transitions *Transitions,* or *transitional expressions,* are words and phrases that show readers how ideas and details fit together. (See also the **Transitional Expressions** chart on page 376.)

To connect your ideas within paragraphs and between paragraphs, learn to use transitional expressions such as the following ones.

time	at last, meanwhile, then, now, later, at first, by this time
place	here, there, beyond, farther, to the left, next, over, between
addition	and, besides, for example, furthermore
contrast	but, still, although, however, nevertheless
conclusion	thus, consequently, in conclusion, looking back, in review, finally

Voice The way a piece of writing "sounds," or its *voice,* is determined by sentence structure, word choice, and tone. Although audience and purpose influence your writing voice, always try to sound honest and natural.

Writing to Learn You can use writing for more than just an extension of a lesson (such as an essay). Writing can help you to understand the relationships of ideas in the texts that you read; for example, you can use mapping to see relationships between main ideas and details. Writing can also be a way of knowing. For example, if you freewrite about information from one of your classes, it will help you to see what you know.

Grammar at a Glance

A

HELP

Grammar at a Glance is an alphabetical list of special terms and expressions with examples and references to further information. When you encounter a grammar or usage problem in the revising or proofreading stage of your writing, look for help in this section first. You may find all you need to know right here. If you need more information, **Grammar at a Glance** will show you where in the book to turn for a more complete explanation. If you do not find what you are looking for in **Grammar at a Glance,** turn to the index on page 1000.

abbreviation An abbreviation is a shortened form of a word or a phrase.

- **capitalization of** (See page 686.)

TITLES USED WITH NAMES	**M**r.	**R**ev.	**J**r.	**E**sq.
KINDS OF ORGANIZATIONS	**C**o.	**I**nc.	**A**dmin.	**C**orp.
PARTS OF ADDRESSES	**B**lvd.	**R**d.	**P**kwy.	**P.O. B**ox
NAMES OF STATES	[without ZIP Codes]		**K**y. **C**alif.	**O**kla. **S.C.**
	[with ZIP Codes]		KY CA	OK SC
TIMES	**A.M.**	**P.M.**	**B.C.**	**A.D.**

- **punctuation of** (See page 696.)

WITH PERIODS	(See preceding examples.)
WITHOUT PERIODS	RN IOU EPA UNICEF
	DC (D.C. without ZIP Code)
	mg oz yd mph km
	[Exception: in.]

action verb An action verb expresses physical or mental activity. (See page 418.)

EXAMPLE   David **drove** from Vicksburg to Austin.

active voice Active voice is the voice a verb is in when it expresses an action done by its subject. (See page 601. See also **voice.**)

EXAMPLE   Ann **nailed** the planks together.

adjective An adjective modifies a noun or a pronoun. (See page 412.)

EXAMPLE   **An old** oak cast its **huge** shadow across **the front** yard.

adjective clause An adjective clause is a subordinate clause that modifies a noun or a pronoun. (See page 495.)

EXAMPLE   The poetry **that my aunt wrote** remains unpublished.

adjective phrase A prepositional phrase that modifies a noun or a pronoun is called an adjective phrase. (See page 468.)

EXAMPLE   Most **of the school** will be taking part in the fair.

adverb An adverb modifies a verb, an adjective, or another adverb. (See page 422.)

EXAMPLE   Is there **really** enough time for the play?

adverb clause An adverb clause is a subordinate clause that modifies a verb, an adjective, or an adverb. (See page 498.)

EXAMPLE   **Before I went home,** I thanked my hosts.

adverb phrase A prepositional phrase that modifies a verb, an adjective, or an adverb is called an adverb phrase. (See page 469.)

EXAMPLE   Sean and Henry stayed **after school** to help Ms. Gallogly **with the decorations.**

agreement Agreement is the correspondence, or match, between grammatical forms. Grammatical forms agree when they have the same number and gender.

- **of pronouns and antecedents** (See page 532.)

SINGULAR	The teacher asked **Daniel** to name **his** favorite books, songs, and movies.
PLURAL	The teacher asked the **students** to name **their** favorite books, songs, and movies.
SINGULAR	I think Geraldo can name **each** of the countries and **its** capital city.
PLURAL	I think Geraldo can name **all** of the countries and **their** capital cities.
SINGULAR	Neither **Sue** nor **Christie** has **her** driver's license.
PLURAL	Both **Sue** and **Christie** have **their** driver's licenses.

Grammar at a Glance   **961**

Grammar at a Glance, pp. 960–985
Alignments
TEKS 3A, 3B, 3C, 3D
TAAS W3, W5, W6, W7
English II End-of-Course 5, 6

- **of subjects and verbs** (See page 512.)

SINGULAR	The **choreographer wants** to change some of the movements of the ballet.
SINGULAR	The **choreographer,** as well as the dancers, **wants** to change some of the movements of the ballet.
PLURAL	The **dancers want** to change some of the movements of the ballet.
PLURAL	The **dancers,** as well as the choreographer, **want** to change some of the movements of the ballet.
SINGULAR	**Each** of these beagle puppies **is** four weeks old.
PLURAL	**All** of these beagle puppies **are** four weeks old.
SINGULAR	**Either Paul or Sonia** usually **goes** fishing with me.
PLURAL	**Both Paul and Sonia** usually **go** fishing with me.
SINGULAR	Here **is** the **list** of sources I used to write my essay on the origins of jazz.
PLURAL	Here **are** the **sources** I used to write my essay on the origins of jazz.
SINGULAR	**Six days is** the length of time the astronauts will spend in space.
PLURAL	**Six days** of the school year **are reserved** for parent-teacher conferences.
SINGULAR	*The Adventures of Tom Sawyer* **includes** a hilarious scene in which Tom pretends to be sick.
PLURAL	Tom's **adventures include** some wild times.
SINGULAR	The principal **ingredient** in the Russian soup borscht **is** beets.
PLURAL	**Beets are** the principal ingredient in the Russian soup borscht.
SINGULAR	"For My People" is one poem **that was written** by Margaret Walker.
PLURAL	"For My People" is one of the poems **that were written** by Margaret Walker.
SINGULAR	"For My People" is the only one of the poems **that was written** by Margaret Walker.

ambiguous reference Ambiguous reference occurs when a pronoun incorrectly refers to either of two antecedents. (See page 566.)

AMBIGUOUS	One of the chief differences between the Seismosaurus and the Tyrannosaurus rex is that it did not eat meat. [Which dinosaur did not eat meat?]
CLEAR	One of the chief differences between the Seismosaurus and the Tyrannosaurus rex is that the Seismosaurus did not eat meat.

antecedent An antecedent is the word or words that a pronoun stands for. (See page 532.)

EXAMPLE	**Jim** and **Mimi** spent **their** summer traveling through New Mexico. [*Jim* and *Mimi* are the antecedents of *their*.]

apostrophe

- **to form contractions** (See page 763. See also **contraction**.)
EXAMPLES	aren't	we'll	o'clock	'02

- **to form plurals of letters, numerals, symbols, and words used as words** (See page 766.)
EXAMPLES	*v*'s and *w*'s	*A*'s, *I*'s, and *U*'s
	1700's	PC's
	$'s and ¢'s	replacing *so*'s with *therefore*'s

- **to show possession** (See page 758.)
EXAMPLES	the student's test score
	the students' test scores
	children's tickets
	somebody's gloves
	Mother's and Aunt Shashona's story quilts
	Philip and Nguyen's duet
	one week's [*or* seven days'] vacation

appositive An appositive is a noun or a pronoun placed beside another noun or pronoun to identify or describe it. (See page 483.)

EXAMPLE	The Oscar-winning actor **Tom Hanks** was featured on that program.

appositive phrase An appositive phrase consists of an appositive and its modifiers. (See page 483.)

EXAMPLE Mr. Trevelyan, **our new English teacher,** is from Maine.

article The articles, *a*, *an*, and *the*, are the most frequently used adjectives. (See page 412.)

EXAMPLE **A** new car dealership rejuvenated **an** abandoned shopping center in **the** suburbs.

B

bad, badly (See page 617.)

NONSTANDARD   This salad dressing smells badly.
STANDARD   This salad dressing smells **bad.**

base form The base form, or infinitive, is one of the four principal parts of a verb. (See page 574.)

EXAMPLE Dad is helping Stephanie **ride** her bike.

brackets (See page 772.)

EXAMPLES The Ashanti proverb "What is bad luck for one man is good luck for another" reminds me of an expression I've often heard at rummage sales: "One man's trash **[**bad luck**]** is another man's treasure **[**good luck**]**."

The *Iliad* and the *Odyssey* (both attributed to Homer **[**some historians question this authorship**]**) are epic poems about events before, during, and after the Trojan War.

C

capitalization

- **of abbreviations and acronyms** (See page 686. See also **abbreviation.**)
- **of first words** (See page 668.)

  EXAMPLES **S**mall wooden dolls called kachinas represent spirits and ancestors revered by the Hopi.

  Mr. Anaka told us, "**T**he publication of Rachel Carson's book *Silent Spring* in 1962 helped to launch our nation's environmental movement."

  Dear Dr. Yamaguchi:

  Best regards,

- **of proper nouns and proper adjectives** (See page 669.)

964   **Quick Reference Handbook**   Grammar at a Glance

Proper Noun	Common Noun
Dr. **M**artin **L**uther **K**ing, **J**r.	minister
Prince **H**enry the **N**avigator	explorer
Antarctica	continent
Sierra **L**eone	country
Los **A**lamos **C**ounty	county
New **B**runswick **P**rovince	province
Marquesas **I**slands	islands
Lake **T**anganyika	body of water
Mount **R**ainier	mountain
Pacific **R**im **N**ational **P**ark	park
Shoshone **N**ational **F**orest	forest
Ajanta **C**aves	cave
Great **S**alt **L**ake **D**esert	desert
Northeast	region
Fifty-**s**ixth **S**treet	street
Republican **P**arty (or **p**arty)	political party
Battle of **S**even **P**ines	historical event
Dark **A**ges	historical period
Cinco de **M**ayo	holiday
January, **A**pril, **A**ugust, **N**ovember	calendar items
Kiowa **A**pache	people
Christianity	religion
Muslim	religious follower
God (*but* the **g**od **P**oseidon)	deity
Sukkot, or **F**east of **T**abernacles	holy days
Upanishads	sacred writing
Great **S**and **D**unes **N**ational **M**onument	monument
Wells **F**argo **C**enter	building
National **B**ook **C**ritics **C**ircle **A**ward	award
Saturn	planet
Polaris, or the **N**orth **S**tar	star
Leo **M**inor, or the **L**esser **L**ion	constellation
Empress of Ireland	ship
Challenger	spacecraft
Punjabi	language

- **of titles** (See page 682.)

    EXAMPLES **G**overnor Robert La Follette [preceding a name]

    Robert La Follette, the former **g**overnor of Wisconsin [following a name]

    Welcome, **G**overnor. [direct address]

    Uncle Benjamin [*but* my **u**ncle Benjamin]

    The **P**eople **C**ould **F**ly: **A**merican **B**lack **F**olktales [book]

    Waterlilies in a **P**ond [work of art]

    "**M**any **R**ivers to **C**ross" [song]

    "**A V**isit to **G**randmother" [short story]

    "**T**he **S**ky **I**s **J**ust **B**eyond the **R**oof" [poem]

    Organic **G**ardening [magazine]

    Shoe [comic strip]

case of pronouns Case is the form a pronoun takes to show how it is used in a sentence. (See page 547.)

NOMINATIVE   My friend Justin and **I** are organizing a pet-sitting service.

The only sophomores on the school's debate team are Tyrone and **she**.

In my opinion, both gymnasts, Lori and **she**, deserved the first-place medal.

We student-council officers met with the principal to discuss the schedule of activities for Career Night.

Khufu was the Egyptian king **who** built the Great Pyramid at Giza.

Have you already heard **who** the winner is?

Do you think we should pay you more than **they**? [The pronoun is the subject of the incomplete adverb clause "more than they pay you."]

OBJECTIVE   The friendly park attendant directed **us** to the manatee aquarium.

Uncle Theo sent **me** his recipe for moussaka.

The chess match between Lucia and **him** was exciting.

A technical foul has been charged against both basketball players, Melinda and **her**.

Our art teacher showed **us** students some of the origami figures she had made.

Their supervisor wants **them** to learn to use different word-processing programs.

Michael Jordan, **whom** many consider the greatest basketball player of all time, retired from the sport in 1999.

"To **whom** do you wish to speak?" asked the secretary.

Do you think we should pay you as much as **them**? [The pronoun is the direct object of the verb *pay* in the incomplete adverb clause "as much as we pay them."]

POSSESSIVE **Your** stereo sounds better than **mine** does.

My parents don't approve of **my** watching television.

clause A clause is a group of words that contains a verb and its subject and that is used as part of a sentence. (See page 492.)

EXAMPLE While I sliced the onions [subordinate clause], Marcia peeled the avocado [independent clause].

colon (See page 729.)

- **before lists**

EXAMPLES In a heptathlon, athletes compete in the following events: the 100-meter hurdles, the shot put, the high jump, the 200-meter dash, the long jump, the javelin throw, and the 800-meter run.

The United States government is divided into three branches: executive, judicial, and legislative.

- **in conventional situations**

EXAMPLES 3:30 P.M.

Genesis 22:1–18

Lincoln at Gettysburg: The Words That Remade America

Dear Mrs. Wu:

comma (See page 700.)

- **in a series**

EXAMPLE The principal ingredients of the traditional Navajo dish called *posole* are meat, hominy, and chili.

- **in compound sentences**

EXAMPLE In our production of *Julius Caesar,* Saul portrayed the title character, and I played Brutus.

- **with nonessential phrases and clauses**

  EXAMPLES The roving vehicle *Sojourner*, deployed during the Mars Pathfinder mission in 1997, provided scientists valuable data about the planet Mars. [nonessential phrase]

  Scott Joplin, who helped make ragtime music popular in the early 1900s, composed the ragtime opera *Treemonisha*. [nonessential clause]

- **with introductory elements**

  EXAMPLES On his way to school this morning, Harold stopped at the post office to mail the invitations to his bar mitzvah.

  After we had read the poems by Gwendolyn Brooks, our teacher asked us to find examples of simile, metaphor, and personification.

- **with interrupters**

  EXAMPLES That, in my opinion, is a most amusing comic strip.

  Citrus fruits, such as oranges and lemons, are good sources of vitamin C.

- **in conventional situations**

  EXAMPLES On Tuesday, April 10, 2001, Mavis and I flew to Seattle, Washington, to attend a week-long computer seminar.

  She sent the job application to 345 Chestnut Street, Oshkosh, WI 54901-0345, on 15 May 2001.

comma splice A comma splice is a run-on sentence in which sentences have been joined with only a comma between them. (See page 347.) (See also **fused sentence, run-on sentence**.)

COMMA SPLICE	Usually the earth's moon is full only once each month, however, about every thirty-two months the moon is full twice in the same month, the second full moon is called a blue moon.
REVISED	Usually the earth's moon is full only once each month. **H**owever, about every thirty-two months the moon is full twice in the same month**;** the second full moon is called a blue moon.
REVISED	Usually the earth's moon is full only once each month. **H**owever, about every thirty-two months the moon is full twice in the same month. **T**he second full moon is called a blue moon.

comparison of modifiers (See page 620.)

- comparison of adjectives and adverbs

Positive	Comparative	Superlative
young	young**er**	young**est**
tasty	tast**ier**	tast**iest**
persuasive	**more** persuasive	**most** persuasive
gracefully	**less** gracefully	**least** gracefully
good/well	**better**	**best**

- comparing two

EXAMPLES   Of the giant sequoia and the bristlecone pine, which species is **older**?

Which of these two computer models processes data **more quickly**?

I read that the diamond is **harder** than **any other** natural substance known.

- comparing more than two

EXAMPLES   Extending 6,529 feet (1,990 meters), the Akashi Kaikyo Bridge in Japan is one of the **longest** suspension bridges in the world.

Of all of us in the room, Jorge reacted **most calmly** to the news.

complement A complement is a word or word group that completes the meaning of a verb. (See page 450. See also **direct object**, **indirect object**, **predicate adjective**, and **predicate nominative**.)

EXAMPLES   Have you given **Dale** that **book**?

This book is a **favorite**, but that one is even **better**.

complex sentence A complex sentence has one independent clause and at least one subordinate clause. (See page 505.)

EXAMPLES   My neighbor Ms. Tanaka, who is a freelance photojournalist, is planning a trip to the Australian outback.

As Ms. Tanaka and I talked about her plans for her trip to the outback, she showed me photographs of her South American trip, which included a visit to the Galápagos Islands.

compound-complex sentence A compound-complex sentence has two or more independent clauses and at least one subordinate clause. (See page 505.)

EXAMPLES Hattie Caraway was the wife of the United States senator Thaddeus Caraway, and when he died in 1931, she was asked to serve out his term.

After she had completed her husband's term, Hattie Caraway ran for the Senate seat in the election of 1932 and won; as a result, she became the first woman elected to the United States Senate.

compound sentence A compound sentence has two or more independent clauses but no subordinate clauses. (See page 504.)

EXAMPLES In his spare time, Joshua enjoys painting; he especially likes to paint with watercolors.

The bat has wings and can fly, but it is not a bird; it is a mammal.

conjunction A conjunction joins words or groups of words. (See page 428.)

EXAMPLE **Both** Andrea **and** Walter were hoping to win **or** at least qualify for the contest, **but** they soon withdrew their names **because** so many people were ahead of them **and** it was late in the year.

contraction A contraction is a shortened form of a word, a numeral, or a group of words. Apostrophes in contractions indicate where letters or numerals have been omitted. (See page 763. See also **apostrophe**.)

EXAMPLES

I've [I have]	here's [here is or here has]
who's [who is or who has]	they're [they are]
couldn't [could not]	it's [it is or it has]
can't [cannot]	don't [do not]
'50–'51 school year [1950–1951]	o'clock [of the clock]

dangling modifier A dangling modifier is a modifying word, phrase, or clause that does not clearly and sensibly modify a word or word group in a sentence. (See page 626.)

970 Quick Reference Handbook Grammar at a Glance

DANGLING   Leading us through the art museum, interesting anecdotes about the artists' lives were told. [Who is leading us through the art museum?]

REVISED   Leading us through the art museum, **the tour guide** told interesting anecdotes about the artists' lives.

dash (See page 770.)

EXAMPLE   Thousands of fans—23,764, to be exact—attended the championship game.

declarative sentence   A declarative sentence makes a statement and is followed by a period. (See page 459.)

EXAMPLE   Ben Nevis is the highest mountain in Scotland and is higher than any other peak in Great Britain.

direct object   A direct object is a word or word group that receives the action of the verb or shows the result of the action. A direct object answers the question *Whom?* or *What?* after a transitive verb. (See page 456.)

EXAMPLE   Tom painted the **mural** on the school wall.

double comparison   A double comparison is the nonstandard use of two comparative forms (usually *more* and *–er*) or two superlative forms (usually *most* and *–est*) to express comparison. In standard usage, the single comparative form is correct. (See page 623.)

NONSTANDARD   Of Neptune's eight moons, the most largest is Triton.
STANDARD   Of Neptune's eight moons, the **largest** is Triton.

double negative   A double negative is the nonstandard use of two or more negative words to express a single negative idea. (See page 656.)

NONSTANDARD   Despite the inclement weather, the pilot didn't have no difficulty landing the plane.
STANDARD   Despite the inclement weather, the pilot **didn't have any** difficulty landing the plane.
STANDARD   Despite the inclement weather, the pilot **had no** difficulty landing the plane.

double subject   A double subject occurs when an unnecessary pronoun is used after the subject of a sentence. (See page 645.)

Grammar at a Glance

| NONSTANDARD | Most of the businesses in town they close by 6:00 P.M. |
| STANDARD | Most of the businesses in town close by 6:00 P.M. |

end marks (See page 694.)

- **with sentences**

EXAMPLES For dessert, Grandmother served warm sopaipillas with honey. [declarative sentence]

Is the cedar waxwing, or cedarbird, indigenous to this area? [interrogative sentence]

Wow! [interjection] What a clever trick that was! [exclamatory sentence]

Please help your brother with his homework. [imperative sentence]

- **with abbreviations** (See **abbreviation**.)

EXAMPLES During spring break, we went to Washington, D.C.

When did you go to Washington, D.C.?

essential clause/essential phrase An essential, or restrictive, clause or phrase is necessary to the meaning of a sentence and is not set off by commas. (See page 705.)

EXAMPLES The woman **who helped us** is standing there. [clause]

The woman **standing there** helped us. [phrase]

exclamation point (See **end marks**.)

exclamatory sentence An exclamatory sentence expresses strong feeling and is followed by an exclamation point. (See page 459.)

EXAMPLE What a magnificent sight that is!

fragment (See **sentence fragment**.)

fused sentence A fused sentence is a run-on sentence in which sentences have been joined together with no punctuation between them. (See page 347.) (See also **comma splice, run-on sentence**.)

FUSED A tanka is a five-line poem that consists of thirty-one syllables the first and third lines contain five syllables each the other lines have seven each.

REVISED   A tanka is a five-line poem that consists of thirty-one syllables**;** the first and third lines contain five syllables each**,** **and** the other lines have seven each.

general reference A general reference is the incorrect use of a pronoun to refer to a general idea rather than to a specific noun. (See page 567.)

GENERAL   Misuko revised and proofread her rough draft on the French Revolution. That took her about three hours. [To what does *That* refer?]

REVISED   Revising and proofreading her rough draft on the French Revolution took Misuko about three hours.

gerund A gerund is a verb form ending in *–ing* that is used as a noun. (See page 476.)

EXAMPLES   **Painting** landscapes is Uncle Arthur's favorite hobby.

Some people say the best exercise is **swimming**.

gerund phrase A gerund phrase consists of a gerund and its modifiers and complements. (See page 478.)

EXAMPLE   By **leaving early,** Erica hoped to arrive before the others.

good, well (See page 617.)

EXAMPLES   Even a **good** bowler will occasionally roll a gutter ball.

I wish I could bowl as **well** [not *good*] as you.

hyphen (See page 767.)

- **for division of words**

  EXAMPLE   The words *hiss, sizzle, buzz,* and *roar* are good examples of the poetic device called onomatopoeia.

- **in compound numbers**

  EXAMPLE   The ratification of the Twenty-sixth Amendment in 1971 lowered the voting age from twenty-one to eighteen.

- **with prefixes and suffixes**

  EXAMPLES   In mid-December, the citizens of Mexico celebrate the Nine Days of Posada.

  The guest speaker will be ex-Mayor Franklin Jackson.

Grammar at a Glance

imperative sentence An imperative sentence gives a command or makes a request and is followed by either a period or an exclamation point. (See page 459.)

EXAMPLES   Please dry the dishes, Juan. [request]

                Sit down! [command]

incomplete construction An incomplete construction is a clause from which words have been omitted. (See page 565.)

EXAMPLE   The study shows that we performed better **than they** [did].

indefinite reference An indefinite reference is the incorrect use of the pronoun *you*, *it*, or *they* to refer to no particular person or thing. (See page 567.)

INDEFINITE   In the newspaper, it says that the governor is planning to run for president.

REVISED   The newspaper says that the governor is planning to run for president.

independent clause An independent clause (also called a *main clause*) expresses a complete thought and can stand by itself as a sentence. (See page 492.)

EXAMPLE   After we had finished class, **Mr. Smith took us to the park.**

indirect object An indirect object is a noun, pronoun, or word group that often appears in sentences containing direct objects. An indirect object tells *to whom* or *to what* (or *for whom* or *for what*) the action of a transitive verb is done. Indirect objects generally precede direct objects. (See page 457.)

EXAMPLE   Pedro gave the **twins** a snack, and now they're ready to play all day.

infinitive An infinitive is a verb form, usually preceded by *to*, that is used as a noun, an adjective, or an adverb. (See page 479.)

EXAMPLE   Her dearest wish was **to participate** in the rafting trip.

infinitive phrase An infinitive phrase consists of an infinitive and its modifiers and complements. (See page 480.)

EXAMPLE **To welcome our new neighbors,** we formed the committee called Feel at Home.

interjection An interjection expresses emotion and has no grammatical relation to the rest of the sentence. (See page 429.)

EXAMPLE **Well,** how long do we have to wait?

interrogative sentence An interrogative sentence asks a question and is followed by a question mark. (See page 459.)

EXAMPLE Would you like to come to Dr. Seymour's farewell dinner**?**

intransitive verb An intransitive verb is a verb that does not take an object. (See page 421.)

EXAMPLE The Shadwells **are sleeping.**

irregular verb An irregular verb is a verb that forms its past and past participle in some way other than by adding *d* or *ed* to the base form. (See page 576. See also **regular verb.**)

Base Form	Present Participle	Past	Past Participle
be	[is] being	was, were	[have] been
cast	[is] casting	cast	[have] cast
fall	[is] falling	fell	[have] fallen
find	[is] finding	found	[have] found
hit	[is] hitting	hit	[have] hit
make	[is] making	made	[have] made
ring	[is] ringing	rang	[have] rung
shake	[is] shaking	shook	[have] shaken
speak	[is] speaking	spoke	[have] spoken
think	[is] thinking	thought	[have] thought

italics (See page 739.)

- **for titles** *The Once and Future King* [book]

    Yahoo! Internet Life [periodical]

    Gamera: The Guardian of the Universe [movie]

Perseus with the Head of Medusa [work of art]

Tales from the Vienna Woods [long musical composition]

- **for words, letters, and symbols used as such and for foreign words**

  EXAMPLES Using the spellchecker, I discovered that I had transposed the letters **e** and **a** every time I had typed the word **research.**

  The story ends with **Requiescat in pace,** the Latin phrase that means "Rest in peace."

its, it's (See page 796.)

EXAMPLES **Its** [Mexico's] highest point is the volcanic mountain Citlaltépetl.

It's [It is] more than 18,000 feet high.

It's [It has] been a long time since the volcano has erupted.

lie, lay (See page 582.)

EXAMPLES Weary from their hike, the scouts **lay** down and rested awhile. [past tense of *lie*]

Weary from their hike, the scouts **laid** their backpacks down and rested awhile. [past tense of *lay*]

linking verb A linking verb connects the subject with a word that identifies or describes the subject. (See page 418.)

EXAMPLE Italy **became** a republic in 1946.

misplaced modifier A misplaced modifier is a word, phrase, or clause that seems to modify the wrong word or words in a sentence. (See page 627.)

MISPLACED The 4-H clubs throughout the United States, supported by the Department of Agriculture, strive to improve the head, heart, hands, and health of each of their members. [Is the United States supported by the Department of Agriculture?]

REVISED **Supported by the Department of Agriculture,** the 4-H clubs throughout the United States strive to improve the head, heart, hands, and health of each of their members.

976 Quick Reference Handbook Grammar at a Glance

modifier A modifier is a word or word group that makes the meaning of another word or word group more specific. (See page 614.)

EXAMPLE   Gustav Mahler, **a major Austrian** composer **of the early twentieth century, often** used **the** idioms **of popular music in his compositions.**

nonessential clause/nonessential phrase A nonessential, or nonrestrictive, clause or phrase, adds information not necessary to the main idea in the sentence and is generally set off by commas. (See page 704.)

EXAMPLES   The church on the corner, **in which the Reverend de Santis once preached,** is being renovated. [nonessential clause]

The top, **spinning wildly,** bounced down the steps. [nonessential phrase]

noun A noun names a person, place, thing, or idea. (See page 405.)

EXAMPLES   **Billie Holiday** sang beautifully.

We are vacationing in **Vermont.**

Please hand me the **scissors.**

Intelligence is difficult to measure.

noun clause A noun clause is a subordinate clause used as a noun. (See page 501.)

EXAMPLE   Tell me **what you did during the summer.**

number Number is the form a word takes to indicate whether the word is singular or plural. (See page 512.)

SINGULAR	tree	she	child	man
PLURAL	trees	they	children	men

object of a preposition An object of a preposition is the noun or pronoun that completes a prepositional phrase. (See page 426.)

EXAMPLE   One of the old **trees** was struck by **lightning.** [Of the old trees and by lightning are prepositional phrases.]

parallel structure Parallel structure is the use of the same grammatical forms or structures to balance related ideas in a sentence. (See page 362.)

NONPARALLEL　The main duties of the receptionist are to greet callers, to take messages, and providing information.

PARALLEL　The main duties of the receptionist are **to greet** callers, **to take** messages, and **to provide** information.

PARALLEL　The main duties of the receptionist are **greeting** callers, **taking** messages, and **providing** information.

parentheses (See page 770.)

EXAMPLES　The route traveled by the pony express riders **(**see the map on page 152**)** was dangerous.

The route traveled by the pony express riders was dangerous. **(**See the map on page 152.**)**

participial phrase A participial phrase consists of a participle and any complements and modifiers it has. (See page 473.)

EXAMPLE　**Considered famous for its resorts,** the Yucatàn is also a center of Mayan culture.

participle A participle is a verb form that can be used as an adjective. (See page 472.)

EXAMPLE　I prefer to live in the South, where there are no **freezing** winters.

passive voice The passive voice is the voice a verb is in when it expresses an action done to its subject. (See page 601. See also **voice**.)

EXAMPLE　Mr. Boylan's novel **has been translated** into German.

period (See **end marks**.)

phrase A phrase is a group of related words that does not contain a verb and its subject and that is used as a single part of speech. (See page 467.)

EXAMPLE　Stacy, **Aunt Maeve's golden retriever,** probably **will place** first **in the sporting-dog category.** [*Aunt Maeve's golden retriever* is an appositive phrase. *Will place* is a verb phrase. *In the sporting-dog category* is a prepositional phrase.]

predicate The predicate is the part of a sentence that says something about the subject. (See page 441.)

EXAMPLE   She **wants to be a commercial airline pilot.**

predicate adjective A predicate adjective is an adjective that completes the meaning of a linking verb and that modifies the subject of the verb. (See page 454.)

EXAMPLE   Despite the heat, Bob and Beth appeared **fresh** and **alert.**

predicate nominative A predicate nominative is a noun or pronoun that completes the meaning of a linking verb and identifies or refers to the subject of the verb. (See page 453.)

EXAMPLE   The president of the company is **Francis McGuire, Ph.D.**

prefix A prefix is a word part that is added before a base word or root. (See page 781.)

EXAMPLES
un + fair = **un**fair   re + usable = **re**usable

mis + pronounce = **mis**pronounce   dis + qualified = **dis**qualified

mid + February = **mid**-February   ex + judge = **ex**-judge

preposition A preposition shows the relationship of a noun or a pronoun to some other word in a sentence. (See page 426.)

EXAMPLE   That novel **by** Joseph Conrad is **about** spies **in** nineteenth-century Geneva.

prepositional phrase A prepositional phrase includes a preposition, a noun, or pronoun called the object of the preposition, and any modifiers of that object. (See page 426.)

EXAMPLE   **Before breakfast,** I like to watch the sun rise **over the rooftops.**

pronoun A pronoun is used in place of one or more nouns or pronouns. (See page 408.)

EXAMPLES   Paul and **I** wrote to Abigail and expressed **our** pleasure at **her** engagement.

All of the team members prepared **themselves** for the relay.

Who gave **you** this?

question mark (See **end marks**.)

quotation marks (See page 743.)

- **for direct quotations**

  EXAMPLE "In class tomorrow," said Mr. McDermott, "we will begin studying the decline of the Mayan civilization."

- **with other marks of punctuation** (See also preceding example.)

  EXAMPLES "In what country will the Summer Olympics of 2008 be held?" asked Katrina.

  Which poem by Dorothy Parker begins with the line "A single flow'r he sent me, since we met"?

  The teacher asked, "Who are the protagonist and the antagonist of Larry Woiwode's short story 'The Beginning of Grief'?"

- **for titles**

  EXAMPLES "Tuesday Siesta" [short story]

  "My Mother Pieced Quilts" [short poem]

  "Wind Beneath My Wings" [song]

regular verb A regular verb is a verb that forms its past and past participle by adding *d* or *ed* to the base form. (See page 575. See also **irregular verb**.)

Base Form	Present Participle	Past	Past Participle
ask	[is] asking	asked	[have] asked
deceive	[is] deceiving	deceived	[have] deceived
drown	[is] drowning	drowned	[have] drowned
risk	[is] risking	risked	[have] risked
suppose	[is] supposing	supposed	[have] supposed
use	[is] using	used	[have] used

rise, raise (See page 588.)

EXAMPLES Huge billows of smoke **rose** from the top of the mountain. [past tense of *rise*]

They **raised** the window blinds to let in the light and warmth of the sun. [past tense of *raise*]

run-on sentence A run-on sentence is two or more complete sentences run together as one. (See page 347. See also **comma splice** and **fused sentence**.)

RUN-ON Troy Menzies is a guitar player my father knew back in the 1960s and 1970s, they went to high school together.

REVISED Troy Menzies is a guitar player my father knew back in the 1960s and 1970s. They went to high school together.

REVISED Troy Menzies is a guitar player my father knew back in the 1960s and 1970s; they went to high school together.

semicolon (See page 724.)

- **in compound sentences with no conjunctions**

    EXAMPLE Norman Rockwell was a prolific artist; he is perhaps best remembered for his cover illustrations for the *Saturday Evening Post*.

- **in compound sentences with conjunctive adverbs or transitional expressions**

    EXAMPLE Many animals, such as frogs and alligators, are amphibious; **that is,** they can live both on land and in water.

- **between a series of items containing commas**

    EXAMPLE In the famous Hindu epic *Ramayana,* the main characters are Prince Rama; Sita, his loyal wife; Lakshmana, his devoted brother; and Ravan, the ruler of the demons.

sentence A sentence is a group of words that contains a subject and a verb and expresses a complete thought. (See page 437.)

EXAMPLE The swans glided low over the water before landing.

sentence fragment A sentence fragment is a group of words that is punctuated as if it were a complete sentence but that does not contain both a subject and a verb or that does not express a complete thought. (See pages 340 and 437.)

FRAGMENT	The samisen, a stringed instrument used in Japanese music.
SENTENCE	The samisen, a stringed instrument used in Japanese music, resembles a guitar.
FRAGMENT	Saying goodbye to our cousins.
SENTENCE	Outside, Mother was saying goodbye to our cousins.

simple sentence A simple sentence has one independent clause and no subordinate clauses. (See page 504.)

EXAMPLES Chief Ta-sunko-witko (Crazy Horse) led the Sioux and Cheyenne forces to victory at the Battle of the Little Bighorn.

Did Mike and Dana go with you to the Cherry Blossom Festival?

sit, set (See page 585.)

EXAMPLES **Sitting** in his favorite chair, Grandfather told us a story about a talking camel named Yak-yak.

Setting a bowl of popcorn in front of us, Grandfather began telling a story about a talking camel named Yak-yak.

slow, slowly (See page 618.)

EXAMPLES The traffic was so **slow** on the highway that we decided to take a back road.

The traffic moved so **slowly** on the highway that we decided to take a back road.

stringy sentence A stringy sentence is a sentence that has too many independent clauses. Usually, the clauses are strung together with coordinating conjunctions like *and* or *but*. (See page 363.)

STRINGY	The Greek hero Perseus went in search of the monster Medusa, and guiding the hero on his quest were the goddess Athena and the god Hermes, and in an effort to protect Perseus, Athena provided him with a mirrored shield.
REVISED	The Greek hero Perseus went in search of the monster Medusa. Guiding the hero on his quest were the goddess Athena and the god Hermes. In an effort to protect Perseus, Athena provided him with a mirrored shield.

subject The subject tells whom or what a sentence is about. (See page 439.)

EXAMPLES   **Doves** have always nested under the eaves of that old house.

Where have **Harry and Lucas** gone?

subject complement A subject complement is a word or word group that completes the meaning of a linking verb and identifies or modifies the subject. (See page 453. See also **predicate adjective** and **predicate nominative**.)

EXAMPLES   Yellow is my least favorite **color**.

Purple seems **richer**.

subjunctive mood The subjunctive mood is used to express a suggestion, a necessity, a condition contrary to fact, or a wish. (See page 606.)

EXAMPLES   Some of us recommended that Amy **be asked** to serve as the spokesperson for our group.

If I **were** you, I would deposit the money in a savings account.

subordinate clause A subordinate clause (also called a *dependent clause*) does not express a complete thought and cannot stand alone as a sentence. (See page 493. See also **adjective clause, adverb clause,** and **noun clause**.)

EXAMPLES   The one **that I like** is on order.

As soon as we get there, we will call you.

Do you know **what you want?**

suffix A suffix is a word part that is added after a base word or root. (See page 782.)

EXAMPLES   usual + ly = usual**ly**   heavy + ly = heavi**ly**

gentle + ness = gentle**ness**   employ + er = employ**er**

admire + able = admir**able**   replace + able = replace**able**

trap + ing = trapp**ing**   farm + ing = farm**ing**

tense of verbs The tense of verbs indicates the time of the action or state of being expressed by the verb. (See page 590.)

EXAMPLES   He and I **ride** the same bus to school. [present]

She **rode** a horse for the first time last weekend. [past]

Judy **will ride** with the Washingtons to next week's game. [future]

David **has ridden** in the parade for the last three years. [present perfect]

Kelley **had** always **ridden** to school with Dawn, but Dawn moved to another city. [past perfect]

By the time the carnival ends, I **will have ridden** on every ride. [future perfect]

transitive verb A transitive verb is an action verb that takes an object. (See page 421.)

EXAMPLE   Finally, Roderick **took** the step and **bought** the car.

underlining (See **Italics**)

verb A verb expresses an action or a state of being. (See page 417.)

EXAMPLES   He **carved** the figurine and **put** it on the windowsill.

They **are** very funny.

verbal A verbal is a form of a verb used as an adjective, an adverb, or a noun. (See page 472. See also **participle, gerund,** and **infinitive.**)

EXAMPLES   **Thrilled,** I said yes immediately. [participle]

I enjoy **playing** volleyball. [gerund]

The host asked us **to sit.** [infinitive]

verbal phrase A verbal phrase consists of a verbal and any modifiers and complements it has. (See page 472. See also **participial phrase, gerund phrase,** and **infinitive phrase.**)

EXAMPLE   Several large chicken hawks, **wheeling high in the sky,** were no threat to us.

verb phrase A verb phrase consists of a main verb and at least one helping verb. (See page 441.)

EXAMPLES   **Had** he **met** her before?

                Tony and Suzanne **are gardening.**

voice Voice is the form a transitive verb takes to indicate whether the subject of the verb performs or receives the action. (See page 601.)

ACTIVE VOICE   Laotzu **founded** the Chinese philosophy of Taoism in the sixth century B.C.

PASSIVE VOICE   The Chinese philosophy Taoism **was founded** by Laotzu in the sixth century B.C.

weak reference A weak reference is the incorrect use of a pronoun to refer to an antecedent that has not been expressed. (See page 567.)

WEAK   Joan of Arc was a fearless soldier, and it inspired the French troops whom she led into battle. [To what does *it* refer?]

REVISED   Joan of Arc was a fearless soldier, and **her courage** inspired the French troops whom she led into battle.

well (See *good, well*.)

who, whom (See page 558.)

EXAMPLES   Ms. Guitterez, **who** teaches courses in accounting and computer science, has been voted Teacher of the Year.

                Ms. Guitterez, **whom** the student body has voted Teacher of the Year, teaches courses in accounting and computer science.

wordiness Wordiness is the use of more words than necessary or the use of fancy words where simple ones will do. (See page 365.)

WORDY   Sandra Cisneros, who is the author who wrote the book titled *The House on Mango Street*, which is a collection of short stories, was born in the city of Chicago in Illinois in the year 1954.

REVISED   Sandra Cisneros, the author of the short-story collection *The House on Mango Street*, was born in Chicago, Illinois, in 1954.

Grammar at a Glance   985

Diagramming Appendix

Diagramming Sentences

A *sentence diagram* is a picture of how the parts of a sentence fit together and how the words in a sentence are related.

Reference Note
For more information about **subjects** and **verbs,** see page 439.

Subjects and Verbs

Every sentence diagram begins with a horizontal line intersected by a short vertical line, which divides the subject from the verb.

EXAMPLE **Alice Walker wrote** *The Color Purple.*

```
   Alice Walker  |  wrote
```

Reference Note
For more information about **understood subjects,** see page 447.

Understood Subjects

EXAMPLE Answer the phone, please.

```
     (you)      |  Answer
```

Reference Note
For more information about **nouns of direct address,** see page 447.

Nouns of Direct Address

EXAMPLE Pass me the picante sauce, **Gina.**

```
           Gina

     (you)     |  Pass
```

986   Diagramming Appendix

Compound Subjects

EXAMPLE **Arturo** and **Patsy** are dancing the conga.

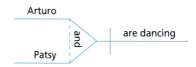

Reference Note

For more information about **compound subjects,** see page 447.

Compound Verbs

EXAMPLE Roger **swims** and **dives.**

Reference Note

For more information about **compound verbs,** see page 448.

Compound Subjects and Compound Verbs

EXAMPLE **Kittens** and **puppies can play** together and **become** friends.

When the parts of a compound subject or a compound predicate are joined by a correlative conjunction, diagram the sentence this way:

EXAMPLE **Both** Norma **and** Lisa will **not only** perform **but also** teach.

Reference Note

For more information about **correlative conjunctions,** see page 428.

Diagramming Sentences 987

Modifiers

Adjectives and Adverbs

Adjectives and adverbs are written on slanting lines beneath the words they modify.

Reference Note
For more information about **adjectives,** see page 412. For more about **adverbs,** see page 422.

EXAMPLE **The blue** car **quickly** swerved **left.**

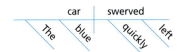

An adverb that modifies an adjective or an adverb is placed on a line connected to the word it modifies.

EXAMPLE The Neville Brothers performed **exceptionally** well.

Here, There, and Where as Modifiers

Reference Note
For more about questions and sentences beginning with **here** and **there,** see page 446.

EXAMPLES **Here** come the astronauts!

There goes the new Mohawk leader.

Where will the balloonists land?

NOTE Sometimes *there* begins a sentence but does not modify the verb. When used in this way, *there* is called an *expletive*. It is diagrammed on a line by itself.

EXAMPLE   **There** are seven stars in the Pleiades.

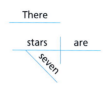

Subject Complements

A subject complement is placed after the verb on the same horizontal line as the simple subject and the verb. A line *slanting toward the subject* separates the subject complement from the verb.

Reference Note
For more information about **subject complements,** see page 453.

Predicate Nominatives

EXAMPLE   Some dogs are good **companions.**

Predicate Adjectives

EXAMPLE   That cockatiel is **friendly.**

Compound Subject Complements

EXAMPLE   Martin Yan is both a **chef** and a **comedian.**

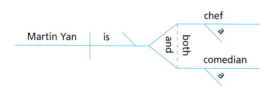

Objects

Direct Objects

> **Reference Note**
> For more information about **direct objects**, see page 456.

A direct object is placed after the verb on the same horizontal line as the simple subject and the verb. A *vertical* line separates the direct object from the verb.

EXAMPLE   Cathy led the **band.**

Compound Direct Objects

EXAMPLE   We heard **cheers** and **whistles.**

Indirect Objects

> **Reference Note**
> For more information about **indirect objects**, see page 457.

The indirect object is diagrammed on a horizontal line beneath the verb.

EXAMPLE   They gave **her** a present.

Compound Indirect Objects

EXAMPLE   Mr. Stephens lent **Karen** and **Shanna** *The Fire Next Time.*

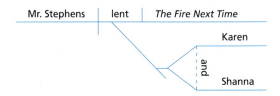

990   Diagramming Appendix

Phrases

Prepositional Phrases

The preposition is placed on a slanting line leading down from the word that the phrase modifies. The object of the preposition is placed on a horizontal line connected to the slanting line.

Reference Note

For more information about **prepositional phrases**, see page 467.

EXAMPLES The steep slopes **of the mountains** are covered **with forests.** [adjective phrase modifying the subject; adverb phrase modifying the verb]

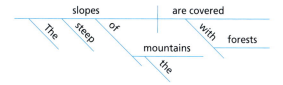

They sailed late **in the fall.** [adverb phrase modifying an adverb]

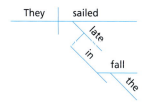

Nina read this Chinese folk tale to **Aaron** and **Joey.** [compound object of preposition]

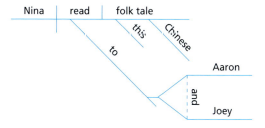

Down the valley and **across the plain** wanders the river. [two phrases modifying the same word]

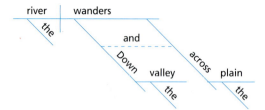

The princess lived **in a castle on the mountain.** [phrase modifying the object of another preposition]

Participles and Participial Phrases

Participles and participial phrases are diagrammed as follows.

EXAMPLES   I heard them **laughing.**

Waving her hat, Sara flagged the train **speeding down the track.**

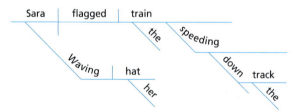

Notice above that the participle *Waving* has a direct object (*hat*), which is diagrammed in the same way that a direct object of a main verb is.

Reference Note

For more information about **participles** and **participial phrases,** see page 472.

Gerunds and Gerund Phrases

Gerunds and gerund phrases are diagrammed as follows.

EXAMPLES   **Waiting** is not easy. [gerund used as subject]

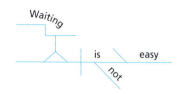

Waiting patiently for hours is often a sure means of **observing wild animals.** [gerund phrases used as subject and as object of a preposition]

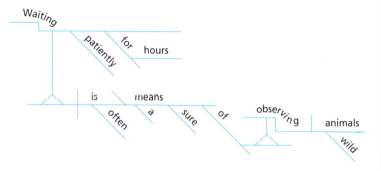

Notice above that the gerund *observing* has a direct object (*animals*).

Infinitives and Infinitive Phrases

Infinitives and infinitive phrases used as modifiers are diagrammed in the same way as prepositional phrases.

EXAMPLE   He plays **to win.** [infinitive used as adverb]

> **Reference Note**
> For more information about **gerunds** and **gerund phrases,** see page 476.

> **Reference Note**
> For more information about **infinitives** and **infinitive phrases,** see page 479.

Diagramming Sentences   **993**

Infinitives and infinitive phrases used as nouns are diagrammed as follows.

EXAMPLES **To choose the right career** takes careful consideration. [infinitive phrase used as subject]

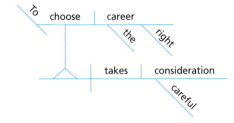

She is hoping **to visit Morocco soon.** [infinitive phrase used as direct object]

My brother watched **me prune the tree.** [infinitive clause with subject, *me,* and with *to* omitted]

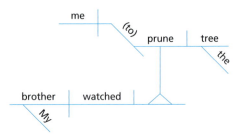

Appositives and Appositive Phrases

Place the appositive in parentheses after the word it identifies or describes.

Reference Note

For more information about **appositives** and **appositive phrases,** see page 483.

994 Diagramming Appendix

EXAMPLES   My cousin **Bryan** is a carpenter.

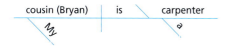

Mohammed Tahir comes from Yemen, **a country near Saudi Arabia.**

Subordinate Clauses

Adjective Clauses

An adjective clause is joined to the word it modifies by a broken line leading from the modified word to the relative pronoun.

Reference Note
For more information about **adjective clauses,** see page 495.

EXAMPLES   The coat **that I wanted** was too expensive.

The box, **which contained the treasure,** was missing.

Diagramming Sentences   995

She is the woman **from whom we bought the used car.**

Adverb Clauses

Place the subordinating conjunction that introduces the adverb clause on a broken line leading from the verb in the adverb clause to the word the clause modifies.

EXAMPLE   **Before a hurricane strikes,** ample warning is given.

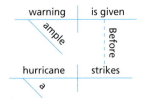

Noun Clauses

Noun clauses often begin with the word *that*, *what*, *who*, or *which*. These words may have a function within the subordinate clause or may simply connect the clause to the rest of the sentence. How a noun clause is diagrammed depends on how it is used in the sentence and whether or not the introductory word has a grammatical function in the noun clause.

EXAMPLES   **What she said** convinced me. [The noun clause is used as the subject of the independent clause. *What* functions as the direct object in the noun clause.]

Reference Note
For more information about **adverb clauses,** see page 478.

Reference Note
For more information about **noun clauses,** see page 501.

We know **that you won the prize.** [The noun clause is the direct object of the independent clause. *That* has no grammatical function in the noun clause.]

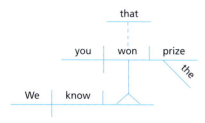

If the introductory word were omitted from the preceding sentence, the diagram would look like this.

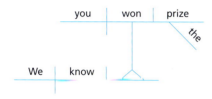

Sentences Classified According to Structure

Simple Sentences

EXAMPLES   The Hudson is a historic waterway. [one independent clause]

Denise hit a home run. [one independent clause]

Reference Note

For more information about **simple sentences,** see page 504.

Compound Sentences

Reference Note
For more information about **compound sentences,** see page 504.

EXAMPLE   A strange dog chased us, but the owner came to our rescue.
[two independent clauses]

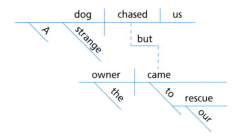

If the compound sentence has a semicolon and no conjunction, a straight broken line joins the two verbs.

EXAMPLE   Phillis Wheatley wrote poetry in the 1700s; she was the first published African American poet.

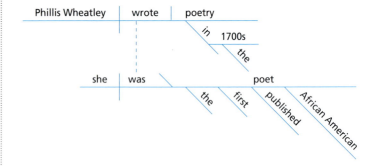

Notice above that the compound adjective *African American* is written on one slanted line.

If the clauses of a compound sentence are joined by a semicolon and a conjunctive adverb (such as *consequently, therefore, nevertheless, however, moreover,* or *otherwise*), place the conjunctive adverb on a slanting line below the verb it modifies.

Reference Note
For more information about **conjunctive adverbs,** see page 428.

EXAMPLE   Dylan works part time after school; **consequently,** he can afford to buy a new bike.

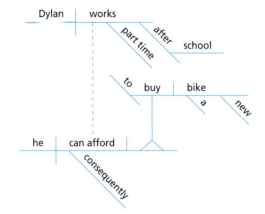

Complex Sentences

EXAMPLE   As night fell, the storm grew worse. [one independent clause and one subordinate clause]

Reference Note
For more information about **complex sentences,** see page 505.

Compound-Complex Sentences

EXAMPLE   The room that Carrie painted had been white, but she changed the color. [two independent clauses and one subordinate clause]

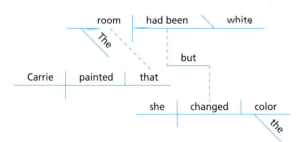

Reference Note
For more information about **compound-complex sentences,** see page 505.

INDEX

A, an, 412, 638–39
A lot, 640
A number of, the number of, 649
A while, awhile, 641
Abbreviations
    of addresses, 698
    capitalization of, 670, 686–87, 697–98, 960
    in dictionaries, 847
    of geographical terms, 697–98
    of organizations, 698
    of personal names, 696
    punctuation of, 696–99, 715, 960
    of states, 697–98
    of time of day, 698–99
    of titles used with names, 696–97
    of units of measure, 699
Abridged dictionaries, 848
Abstract nouns, 407
Accept, except, 639
"Access Denied" (Grassman), 389
Acronyms, 760
Action verbs
    definition of, 418, 960
Active listening, 161
Active voice
    definition of, 601, 960
    writing in, 277–78
Addresses
    abbreviations and, 698
    commas and, 714–15
    envelope addressing, 947
    hyphenated street numbers in, 673
Adjective(s)
    articles, 412–13
    commas separating series of, 701–702
    comparison of, 620–24
    compound adjectives, 769
    definition of, 412, 614, 960–61
    demonstrative adjectives, 414
    diagramming and, 988
    nouns used as, 415
    placement of, 412
    possessive pronouns as, 409, 557
    predicate adjectives, 454
    pronouns distinguished from, 414
    proper adjectives, 415, 669–70
    punctuation of, 701–702
Adjective clauses, 495–97
    beginning with *that,* 705
    combining sentences and, 359
    definition of, 189, 495, 961
    diagramming and, 995–96
    as essential or nonessential clauses, 496
    placement of, 495
    punctuation of, 359
    relative adverbs and, 497
    relative pronouns and, 496–97
Adjective phrases
    definition of, 468, 961
    placement of, 468
Adjusting reading rate, 7, 883
"Adopt-A-Bison," 297–99
Adverb(s)
    comparison of, 620–24
    conjunctive adverbs, 724–25
    definition of, 422, 614, 961
    diagramming and, 988
    modifying adjectives, 423
    modifying other adverbs, 424
    modifying verbs, 422
    overuse of, 79–80
    prepositions distinguished from, 427
    relative adverbs, 497
Adverb clauses
    combining sentences and, 345, 359–60
    definition of, 498, 961
    diagramming and, 996
    introductory adverb clauses, 359–60, 498, 708–709
    placement of, 345
    punctuation of, 359–60
    subordinating conjunctions and, 359–60, 498–99
Adverb phrases
    definition of, 469, 961
    placement of, 469–70
Advertising. *See also* headings beginning with Persuasive; Media; News; Television.
    compare/contrast persuasive elements of advertisements in oral presentation, 337
    creating documentary on print advertising, 329–36
    creating print advertisement about imaginary world, 337
    definition of, 936
    evaluating reasoning in advertising, 315
    oral presentation on advertising career, 337
    persuasive brochure, 306–26
    political advertising, 938
    write brochure about historical movement, 337
Affect, effect, 639, 793
Affiliate, definition of, 928
Affixes. *See* Prefixes; Suffixes.
Agenda, for group discussions, 120
Agreement (pronoun-antecedent), 532–38
    collective nouns and, 536
    compound antecedents, 535
    definition of, 961

  with expressions of amount and measurement, 536–37
  gender, 532–33
  indefinite pronouns and, 533–34
  names of teams and, 538
  nouns ending in *–ics*, 537
  number and, 532–33, 538
  personal pronouns and, 532–33
  plural nouns taking singular pronouns, 537
  special problems with, 536–38
  titles of creative works and, 537–38

Agreement (subject-verb), 512–29
  collective nouns and, 522
  combining sentences and, 357
  compound prepositions and, 514
  compound subjects and, 520
  contractions and, 524, 527–28
  definition of, 962
  every or *many a,* 527
  expressions of amount or measurement and, 525–26
  geographic location and, 529
  gerund phrases and, 513
  indefinite pronouns and, 516–17
  infinitive phrases and, 513
  intervening words and phrases and, 46, 513
  nouns plural in form with singular meaning, 528
  number and, 512–14, 525–26
  plural subjects and, 512–13
  predicate nominative and, 524
  singular subjects joined by *or* or *nor* taking singular verb, 520
  subject following verb, 524
  titles of work of art, music, literature, 529
  verb agreeing with subject nearer verb, 520
  verb with *I* or *you,* 512, 513

Ain't, 639
Alignment, of text, 849–50
All, any, more, most, none, some, 534
All the farther, all the faster, 640
All ready, already, 793
All right, 639, 793
All together, altogether, 793
Allusion, illusion, 640
Almanacs, 870
Altar, alter, 793
Ambiguous reference, 566, 962–63
American English *See also* English language.
  development of, 863.
  dialects of, 863–64
  standard American English, 863
Among, between, 641
An, a, 638–39
An American Childhood (Dillard), 19–20
Analogies
  analogy questions on tests, 918–20
  in editorial cartoons, 285, 287
  meanings of words and, 888
  types of analogies, 920

Analyzing
  analysis questions for foreshadowing, 180
  analyzing and writing about character's motivations, 125
  audience, 140
  comparative analysis, 123
  definition of, 138, 167
  editorial cartoons, 284–87
  effects of television, 122–24
  listing patterns, 886
  news genres, 162–64
  persuasive techniques, 327–28, 882
  persuasive visual elements, 303
  point of view analysis questions, 180
  problem analysis, 128–56, 141–43, 150–53
  problems of literary characters, 157
  reviews of movies or software programs, 205
  short story analysis, 167–94
  writing paragraphs about using analysis skills in career, 205
  writing prompts, 282

And etc., 640
Anecdotes, 143, 258, 259
Angelou, Maya, 668
Animation, definition of, 928
Announcements, as speaking situation, 902
Antecedent-pronoun agreement. *See* Agreement (pronoun-antecedent).
Antecedents
  agreement with pronoun, 532–38
  clear pronoun reference and, 566
  definition of, 408, 532, 963
  of relative pronouns, 496
Antigone (Sophocles), 157
Antonyms
  analogies and, 920
  context clues, 304, 887
  in dictionaries, 847
Anyways, 640
Anywheres, 640
Apostrophe
  with contractions, 763–64, 963
  indefinite pronouns and, 760
  plurals and, 766, 789–90, 963
  possessive case and, 758–61, 963
Appearance, persuasive speaking and, 290
Application letter, 941–42
Appositive(s)
  definition of, 343, 483, 561, 711, 963
  diagramming and, 994–95
  essential appositives, 711–12
  nonessential appositives, 711
  pronouns as, 561
  punctuation of, 355–56, 484, 711–12
Appositive phrases, 483–84

combining sentences and, 355–56
definition of, 343, 483, 711, 963
diagramming and, 994–95
placement of, 355–56, 483–84
punctuation of, 484, 711–12
as sentence fragment, 343
Appreciative listening, 907
to an oral interpretation, 204
to a professional story reading, 205
Argument. See opinion statements under Persuasive techniques.
Art activities
converting position papers into editorial cartoons, 293
drawing Rube Goldberg machine and explaining its causal chain, 125
writing paragraphs about art forms after researching them on World Wide Web, 249
"Art of Money, The" (Standish), 209–12
Articles, 412–13, 638–39, 964
Artistic oral performances, 205, 293, 357
Arts and Ideas (Fleming), 379
As follows, colon with, 729
As if, like, 648
As, like, 648
As though, like, 648
Assertion, definition of, 315
At, 640
Atlases, 870
Attacking the person, definition of, 315
Attention getters, 87–88
Audience
analyzing audience, 140
cause-and-effect explanation, 105–106
comparison/contrast and, 68
formal speeches, 897–98
identifying audience, 10
level of language, 400
literary analysis, 179
as media term, 932
persuasive brochure, 307–308
position paper, 264–65
problem-analysis essay, 139–40
research paper, 220
specific audience for personal reflection essay, 30
Audio reflection, of current event, 53
Audiovisual devices, for enhancing formal speeches, 901
Authority, as media term, 932
Auxiliary verbs. See Helping verbs.

Babbitt, Bruce, 93–94
Back panel, 312

Background information, writing process and, 11
Bad, badly, 617, 964
Bandwagon, 300
Bar graphs, 859, 879, 914
Base form, as principal part of verbs, 574, 964
Base words, 891
Be, forms of, 417, 419
as helping verb, 417
as linking verb, 419
passive voice and, 602
principal parts of, 574
progressive forms and, 592
Because, 641
Become, principal parts of, 577
Begin, principal parts of, 577
Being as, being that, 641
Believe, principal parts of, 574
Bend, principal parts of, 577
Berdichevsky, Norman, 57–59
Beside, besides, 641
Between, among, 641
Bias, definition of, 932
Bibliographical references. See Works Cited.
Biographical references, 847, 870
Blame, principal parts of, 575
Block method of comparison/contrast structure
definition of, 56, 62–63
organization diagram, 72
Block quotations, 192
Blow, principal parts of, 577
Body, coherence and, 391–92
of compositions, 391–92
elaboration and, 392
unity and, 391
Borrow, lend, loan, 642
Borrowed words. See Loanwords.
Both, few, many, several, 534
Brackets, 772, 964
Brainstorming
with a computer, 34
about brochures, 295
about research and investigation, 207
as prewriting technique, 953
Brake, break, 794
Break, principal parts of, 577
Bring, principal parts of, 577
Bring, take, 642
Broad generalizations, valid opinions and, 264
Broadcasting, definition of, 928
Brochures. See also Persuasive brochures.
definition of, 295
format of, 312–13
page layout, 313–14
panel design, 312–13
"Bug Zappers Miss Their Mark" (Nadis), 372
Build, principal parts of, 577
Bullets, definition and uses of, 850

Burn, **principal parts of,** 576, 577
Burst, **principal parts of,** 577
Business letters
    capitalization in, 669
    closing, 715
    complaint letters, 941
    letters of application, 941–42
    parts of, 939–40
    punctuation of, 715
    types of, 940–43
Business text
    e-mail, 947
    memos, 949–50
Bust, busted, 642
Buy, **principal parts of,** 577
Byline, definition of, 936

C

Cable television, 929
Caldwell, John, 785
Call numbers, 866
Callouts, 850
Camera techniques, in film, 200, 929
Can, could, 599
Can, may, 644
Capital, capitol, 794
Capitalization
    of abbreviations, 670, 686–87, 697–98, 964
    of building names, 676
    of business names, 675
    of businesses and brand names of business products, 675–76
    of comic strips, 684
    common nouns and, 669, 965
    of compass directions, 672
    correct usage, 668–87
    of dialogue, 668
    direct quotations and, 743
    of first words, 668, 964
    of geographical names, 672–73
    of historical events and periods, 676–77
    of holidays and other calendar items, 676–77
    of hyphenated numbers, 673
    of interjection *O,* 668–69
    of memorials, monuments, awards, 676
    of musical works, 684
    of names consisting of more than one word, 670
    of nationalities, races, and peoples, 678
    of organizations, teams, etc., 675
    of planets and celestial bodies, 679
    in poetry, 668
    of political parties, 675
    of pronoun *I,* 668
    of proper adjectives, 669–70, 964
    of proper nouns, 669–70, 964–65
    in quotations, 668
    of religions and their followers, holy days, sacred writings, 678
    of salutation and closing of business letters, 669
    of school subjects, 679
    of seasons of year, 677
    of ships, trains, aircraft, spacecraft, 678
    of special events, 676–77
    of specific deities, 678
    of titles of persons, 682
    of titles and subtitles, 682–84, 966
    of words showing family relationship, 682
Capitol, capital, 794
Captions
    document design and, 853
    in editorial cartoons, 285
    graphics and, 857
Card catalogs, 222, 866–67, 867–68
Card-stacking, definition of, 315
Career development activities
    creating posters highlighting pros and cons of career choice, 125
    interviewing health professional and presenting oral report, 165
    interviewing professional and writing about persuasive strategies and skills, 293
    making relevant features chart of careers, 89
    note-taking on research about particular careers, 249
    oral presentation on advertising career, 337
    oral response to interview question about personal failure, 53
    research and write informational essay about certain career, 15
    writing paragraphs about using analysis skills in career, 205
Cartoons. *See* Editorial cartoons.
Case forms of pronouns
    definition of, 547
    nominative case, 548, 549–51, 966
    objective case, 548, 553–55, 966–67
    possessive case, 548, 556–58, 967
Catch, **principal parts of,** 577
Causal chains
    definition of, 92
    diagram of, 99
    drawing Rube Goldberg machine and explaining its causal chain, 125
Causative verbs, 96
Cause-and-effect article (reading)
    cause-and-effect structure, 92, 97–100
    inferring causes and effects, 92, 95–96
    reading selection, 93–94
Cause-and-effect article (writing)
    prewriting, 104–109
    publishing (and proofreading), 118–19

revising, 114–15
writing, 110
Cause-and-effect relationships
    causal analysis, 91
    causal chains, 92, 99
    causative verbs, 96
    cause-and-effect order of ideas, 145
    clue words, 95, 877
    composite patterns for, 97, 100
    context clues, 887
    determining probable cause and probable effect, 22
    false cause and effect, 108
    implied cause-and-effect relationships, 95
    inferring causes and effects, 92, 95–96
    organizational patterns for, 97–100
    oversimplification of, 108
    patterns emphasizing causes, 97–98
    patterns emphasizing effects, 97, 98–99
    patterns tracing causal chains, 97–99
    structure of, 92, 97–100, 101, 876, 885
Causes
    definition of, 95
    diagram of organizational pattern, 98
    focus on causes, 97–98
    inferring causes, 103
    initial causes, 99
    intermediate causes, 99
–cede, –ceed, –sede, spelling rule for, 780
Chaining, definition of, 953
Channel, definition of, 929
Characters
    analysis questions for, 180
    conflicts of characters in literary works, 157
    definition of, 174
    development of, 195
    direct characterization, 199
    in film, 199
    freewriting about, 195
    representation of television characters, 122–23
    writing analysis of character's motivations, 125
Charts
    flowcharts, 857–58
    interpreting charts, 913
    organizing information, 948
    pie charts, 858, 878
Children's books, writing and illustrating children's books, 205
***Choose,* principal parts of,** 577
Choose, chose, 794
Choppy sentences, 352
Chronological order
    analyzing structure of, 885
    in cause-and-effect essay, 109
    clue words for, 877
    coherence and, 375
    definition of, 944

in personal reflection essay, 35–36
in problem-analysis essay, 145
Circular reasoning, definition of, 315
Circulation, as media term, 936
Clarity, color used for, 153–54
Classification, as study skill, 91–112
Clauses. *See also* Independent clauses; Subordinate clauses.
    adjective clauses, 189, 359, 495–97, 705, 961, 995–96
    adverb clauses, 345, 359–60, 498, 708–709, 961, 996
    definition of, 344, 492, 967
    essential (restrictive) clauses, 496, 705–706, 977
    infinitive clauses, 481
    as modifiers, 617
    nonessential (nonrestrictive) clauses, 496, 704–706, 977
    noun clauses, 360, 501–502, 977, 996–97
    placement of, 630
    punctuation of, 496
Clear reference, pronouns, 566–68
Clichés
    definition of, 37
    eliminating clichés in compositions, 322–23
    meanings of words and, 888
Clincher sentences, 371
Close-up, 331, 929
Clue words
    for cause-and-effect relationships, 877
    for chronological order, 877
    for comparison/contrast structure, 877
    for implied cause-and-effect relationships, 95
    for problem-solution structure, 877
Clustering, definition of, 953–54
Coarse, course, 794
Coherence. *See also* Order of ideas.
    connections between ideas and, 374–76
    definition of, 391
    direct references and, 375
    order of ideas and, 375
    transitional expressions, 376
Collaborative reading, sharing steps of reading process with partner, 15
Collaborative writing. *See* Peer review.
Collective nouns
    definition of, 407
    list of, 407
    pronoun-antecedent agreement and, 536
    subject-verb agreement and, 522
Colleges and universities, in dictionaries, 847
Colloquialisms
    definition of, 865
    meanings of words and, 888
Colons
    after salutation in business letter, 730
    before list of items, 729, 967

before long, formal statement or quotation, 729
between titles and subtitles, 730
in Biblical references, 730
in conventional situations, 730, 967
not before verb and complement or preposition and its object, 729
quotation marks and, 744

Colors
graphics design and, 153–54, 856
persuasive techniques and, 303

Combining sentences
with adjective clauses, 359
with adverb clauses, 345, 359–60
choppy sentences and, 352–53
with compound subject and compound verb, 357
inserting phrases and, 355–56
inserting words and, 353
into complex sentences, 359–60
with noun clauses, 360
subject-verb agreement and, 357

***Come,* principal parts of,** 577

Comma(s)
abbreviations set off with, 715
adjective clauses and, 359
adjectives preceding noun and, 701–702
adverb clauses and, 359–60, 498
appositive phrases and, 355–56, 711–12
compound nouns and, 701
compound sentences and, 358, 701, 968
conjunctive adverbs and, 724–25
conventional uses of, 714–15, 968
direct address and, 712
interjections and, 430
interrupters and, 711–13, 968
introductory elements and, 707–709, 968
items in series and, 700–702, 967
letter salutations and closings and, 715
nonessential clauses and phrases and, 704–706, 968
parenthetical expressions and, 713, 772
quotation marks and, 744
transitional expressions and, 724–25
unnecessary use of, 716

Comma splices, 347, 348, 968

Common nouns
capitalization and, 669
definition of, 406, 669

Communicator, definition of, 932
Comparative analysis, 123
Comparative degree of comparison, 82, 620–24, 969

Comparing
comparing reading passages from several sources, 15
as comparison/contrast, 67
context clues, 887

Comparison of modifiers
comparative degree, 620–24, 969
comparing two or more, 969
double comparison, 623–24, 971
irregular comparison, 622
positive degree, 620–22, 969
regular comparison, 621–22
superlative degree, 620–24, 969

Comparison/contrast article (reading)
comparison/contrast structure, 56
main idea and supporting details, 56
reading selection, 57–59

Comparison/contrast article (writing)
prewriting, 66–73
publishing (and proofreading), 82–83
revising, 78–81
writing first draft, 74

Comparison/contrast structure
analyzing comparison-contrast structure, 62–63, 885–86
block method, 56, 62–63
clue words for, 877
implied ideas and, 61
for persuasion, 67
point-by-point method, 56, 62–63
similarities and differences, 55
written explanation of comparison/contrast of two chemical compounds, 89

Complement, compliment, 794

Complements
compound complements, 450
definition of, 450, 969
direct objects as, 456–57
independent clauses and, 451
indirect objects as, 457–58
never in prepositional phrase, 451
predicate adjectives as, 454
predicate nominative as, 453–54
subject complements, 453–54
subordinate clauses and, 451, 494

Complete predicate, 439
Complete subject, 439

Complex sentences
combining sentences into, 189–90, 359–60
compound verbs and, 448
definition of, 505, 969
diagramming and, 999

Complexity, 87

Compositions. *See also* Writing process.
avoid beginning sentences with conjunctions in formal writing, 389
body of, 391–92, 945
conclusions of, 393–96
definition of, 382
framework for, 397
function of paragraphs in, 382
introductions in, 382–89, 943–44
writer's model, 398–99

Compound adjectives, 769

Compound-complex sentences
  definition of, 970
Compound direct objects, 456, 552, 990
Compound indirect objects, 458, 552, 990
Compound nouns, 406, 415, 441, 701
  definition of, 406
Compound numbers, hyphen with, 768
Compound prepositions, 427, 514
Compound sentences
  combining sentences and, 358
  compound verbs and, 448
  conjunctive adverbs and, 349, 358
  coordinating conjunctions and, 348, 358
  definition of, 348–49, 358, 504–505, 970
  diagramming and, 998–99
  punctuation of, 348–49, 358
  run-on sentence revision of, 348–49
  simple sentences with compound elements distinguished from, 703
Compound subjects
  combining sentences and, 357
  definition of, 447, 520
  diagramming and, 987
Compound verbs
  combining sentences and, 357
  compound sentences and, 448
  definition of, 448
  diagramming and, 987
  helping verbs and, 448
Compound words, 760, 768–69
Compound-complex sentences
  definition of, 505
  diagramming and, 999
Comprehensive listening, 909
Computers. *See also* Internet; World Wide Web.
  cut and paste commands and writing, 369, 383
  dimming the screen to brainstorm, 34
  grammar checking program, 341
  limitations of grammar checking programs, 80
  saving alternate versions of documents, 243, 400
  undo command, 115
  using FIND command to determine passive-voice construction, 279
Conclusions. *See also* Drawing conclusions.
  structure of, 396
  techniques for writing effective conclusions, 393–96
  typical length of, 396
  in writing process, 11, 393–96
Concrete nouns
  definition of, 407
  list of, 407
Conflicts
  of characters in literary works, 157
  external conflicts, 195
  internal conflicts, 195

Conjunctions
  avoid beginning sentences with conjunctions in formal writing, 389
  coordinating conjunctions, 348, 357, 358, 428, 492
  correlative conjunctions, 428
  definition of, 428, 970
  subordinating conjunctions, 359–60, 498–99
Conjunctive adverbs
  compound sentences and, 349, 358
  independent clauses and, 492–93
  list of, 493, 724
  punctuation of, 724–25
Connections between ideas. *See* Direct references; Transitional expressions.
Connections to life
  analyzing persuasion in media, 327–28
  distinguishing purposes of media forms, 84–85
  participating in group discussions, 120–21
  research in media, 246
  writing letters of application, 283
Connections to literature
  analyzing problems of literary characters, 157
  writing free-verse poetry, 48–49
  writing short stories, 195–97
Connotations
  meanings of words and, 888
  overuse of, 269
  in persuasive writing, 259, 269
  understanding connotations, 261
Consistency of tense, 597–98
Consul, council, councilor, counsel, counselor, 795
Context clues
  antonyms and, 304, 887
  comparison/contrast, 64
  definitions and restatements, 136, 887
  synonyms and, 304, 887
  using context clues, 136
Contractions
  of adverb *not,* 763
  agreement of subject and verb and, 524
  definition of, 763, 970
  list of, 763, 970
  possessive forms of pronouns distinguished from, 760, 764
  subject-verb agreement and, 524, 527–28
Contrast
  context clues, 887
  in graphics, 856
  in page layout, 851
  type and, 854
Controversy, 87
Conventions of oral language. *See* Speaking.
Conventions of written language. *See* Compositions.
Conversation. *See* Dialogue.
Coordinate ideas, in essay writing, 144
Coordinating conjunctions
  compound sentences and, 348, 358

compound subjects or verbs and, 357
definition of, 428
independent clauses and, 492
Copyright, of dictionaries, 847
Correlative conjunctions, 428
Cost, **principal parts of,** 574, 577
Could, can, 599
Could of, 644
Council, councilor, counsel, counselor, consul, 795
Course, coarse, 794
Cover shot, 331
Credibility, definition of, 932
Credits, definition of, 929
Critical listening, 908
to a debate, 165
to an informative speech, 161
to a persuasive speech, 291
Critical reading questions on tests, 921–23
Critical thinking
coordinating and subordinating ideas, 144
evaluating reasoning, 270
evaluating reasoning in advertising, 315
evaluating sources, 226
oversimplification and false cause and effect, 108
synthesizing information into a thesis, 71
Critical viewing, definition of, 932
Critiquing, critiquing films, 198–202
Cubing, definition of, 954
Cut, **principal parts of,** 577

D

"Danger Beneath the Dash" (Levingston), 129–31
Dangling modifiers, 118, 626, 970
Dashes
abrupt breaks in thought or speech and, 770
example of usage, 971
parenthetical elements and, 770
to mean *namely, that is, in other words,* 770
unfinished statements or questions and, 770
Databases, 867
Debate
analyze the debate process, 165
features of, 896
formats of, 896–97
preparing for, 897
Declarative sentences
definition of, 459, 971
punctuation of, 459–60, 694
Decoding, definition of, 934
Deconstruction, definition of, 934
Defining moments, definition of, 28
Definite articles, 413
Definition and restatement, context clues, 136, 887
Demographics, definition of, 936

Demonstrative adjectives, 414
Demonstrative pronouns
definition of, 410
Denotation, 261, 888
Dependent clauses. *See* Subordinate clauses.
Descriptive details
definition of, 18, 24
factual details as, 24
figurative details as, 24–25
sensory details as, 24
Desert, dessert, 795
Designing your writing. *See* Document design.
Desktop publishing. *See also* Document design.
page layout, 849–55
type, 853–55
Details. *See also* Descriptive details; Factual details; Figurative details; Narrative details; Sensory details; Support.
arranging details, 72–73
chart for details, 33–34
as expressing tone in writing, 106
organizing details, 35–36
supporting details, 56, 60–62
Diagramming sentences, 986–99
Diagrams, 858, 878, 913, 949
Dialects
definition of, 861
ethnic dialects, 863
regional dialects, 863–64
Dialogue
capitalization in, 668
dialogue bubbles in editorial cartoons, 285
fitting the speaker, 32
as narrative detail, 24
quotation marks and, 746
Diction, 900
Dictionaries
antonyms in, 847
definitions in, 847
determining verbs as transitive and intransitive and, 421
dictionary entries, 846–48
entry words, 846–47
etymology, 847
examples in, 847
guide to, 847–48
part-of-speech labels in, 847
pronunciation and, 847
related word forms in, 847
synonyms in, 847
types of, 848
usage labels, 847
Differences, comparison/contrast and, 68
Digital editing, definition of, 936
Dillard, Annie, 19–20
Direct address
nouns of, 447, 986

Index 1007

punctuation of, 712
Direct objects
    compound direct objects, 456
    definition of, 456, 553, 971
    diagramming and, 990
    never in prepositional phrase, 457
    pronouns in objective case and, 553
Direct quotations. *See also* Quotations.
    integrating direct quotations, 239
    paraphrasing and, 213
    punctuation of, 193, 743–45, 980
    summarizing and, 213
Direct references
    connecting ideas in writing, 375, 391–92
    examples of, 379
    and transitions, 375–76
Directions, 672
Discover, invent, 644
Discussion. *See* Group discussions.
Dive, **principal parts of,** 577
Divided quotation, 743
Do, **principal parts of,** 574, 577
Docudrama, definition of, 929
Document design. *See also* Desktop publishing; Page layout.
    alignment, 849
    bullets and, 850
    callout, 850
    color used for emphasis and clarity, 153–54, 856
    color wheel, 856
    contrast and emphasis, 851
    designing Web pages, 45
    desktop publishing, 849–55
    fonts, 854
    formatting an essay, 191
    graphics, 858–60
    grid lines, 851
    guidelines for submitting papers, 849
    gutters, 851
    heading/subheading, 851
    labels, 857
    page layout, 849
    persuasive brochure, 312–13
    transforming information into Web site, 243
    typefaces and fonts, 324, 854
    using flowcharts, 117
    using graphs, charts, tables, 279
    using subheads, 81
Documentaries
    creating a documentary on print advertising, 329–36
    definition of, 929–30
    as news genre, 162–63
    postproduction, 336
    preproduction, 329–35
    production, 335
    script writing, 331–35

    terminology, 331
Don't, doesn't, 527–28, 644
Double comparisons, 623–24, 971
Double negatives, 280, 656–57, 971
Double subjects, 645, 971
Drama, definition of, 930
Draw, **principal parts of,** 577
Drawing conclusions. *See also* Conclusions.
    definition of, 8, 21, 168, 877
    example of, 877
    steps in, 172–73
Dream, **principal parts of,** 576
Drink, **principal parts of,** 577
Drive, **principal parts of,** 577

E

E-mail
    guidelines for, 947
    peer review by e-mail, 151
Eat, **principal parts of,** 578
Editing, first drafts, 12. *See also* Proofreading.
Editorial cartoons
    analogy in, 285, 287
    converting position paper into, 293
    exaggeration/caricature in, 284–87
    irony in, 285, 286
    symbolism in, 284, 285
Editorials, writing editorials, 293
Editors, definition of, 936
Effect, affect, 639, 793
Effect. *See* Cause-and-effect essay.
Effects
    definition of, 95
    diagram of organizational pattern, 98
    final effects, 99
    focus on, 98–99
    inferring effects, 103
    intermediate effects, 99
    long-term effects, 99
    short-term effects, 99
ei **and** ***ie,*** **spelling rule for,** 780
Either, neither, 516
Either-or reasoning, 270, 351
Elaboration
    in compositions, 42, 78, 114, 150, 188, 240, 276, 321, 376–78
    example of, 379
    on key points, 183
    on main point, 11, 376–78
Electronic media. *See also* Computers; Internet; Media; Television; World Wide Web.
    definition of, 930
Elements of design, 936

Ellipsis points
   never beginning quoted passages with, 751
   for pause in dialogue, 751
   for words omitted from quoted material, 750–51
Else, other, 623
Emigrate, immigrate, 644
Emotional appeals
   anecdotes and, 259, 269
   connotative words and, 259, 269
   as element of persuasion, 252, 257, 259, 301
   examples and, 269
   loaded language and, 259
Emotional impact
   news stories and, 87
   in persuasive writing, 269
Empathic listening, 31, 909–10. *See also* Reflective listening.
Emphasis
   color used for, 153–54
   in formal speeches, 900
   in graphics design, 856
   in page layout, 851
Emphatic form, verb tense, 592
Employment. *See* Jobs.
End marks, 694–95, 972
English language
   American English, 863–64
   clichés, 37, 322–23
   colloquialisms, 865
   connotations and, 259, 261, 269, 888
   denotation and, 261
   dialects, 861, 863–64
   formal, standard English, 865
   future of, 863
   history of, 861–63
   inflections, 861
   informal, standard English, 865
   jargon, 216
   loanwords, 741, 861
   Middle English, 862
   Modern English, 862
   nonsexist language, 659–60, 890
   nonstandard English, 638
   Old English, 861, 893
   slang, 748, 865
   standard English, 638
Enthusiasm, persuasive speaking and, 290
Enunciation, persuasive speaking and, 290
Envelopes, addressing, 947
–er, –est, 621
Essays
   comparing writing process to another activity, 15
   comparison/contrast essay, 66–83
   personal reflection essay, 28–47
   problem-analysis essay, 138–56
   research and write informational essay about certain career, 15

Essential clauses and phrases, 496, 705–706, 972
Ethnic dialects, 863
Etymology, 847
Euphemisms, 888–89
Evaluating
   cause-and-effect essay, 114
   comparison/contrast essay, 78
   criteria for, 199
   evaluating text, 8
   first drafts, 12
   personal reflection essay, 42–43
   persuasive speeches, 291
   problem-analysis essay, 150
   reasoning, 270, 315
   Web sites, 247–48
Events
   as narrative detail, 24
   sequence of, 597–98
Every, many a, 527
Everywheres, 640
Evidence. *See also* Reasons; Support.
   anecdotes, 268
   as element of persuasion, 252, 258
   expert opinions, 268
   facts, 268
   inadequate evidence, 270
   opinions, 268
   reasons why, 268
   statistics, 268
Exaggeration
   in editorial cartoons, 284–87
   persuasive speeches and, 289
Examples
   context clues for, 887
   in dictionaries, 847
   as support, 143, 258, 266
Except, accept, 639
Exclamation points
   exclamatory sentences and, 694–95
   interjections and, 430
   quotation marks and, 744–45
Exclamatory sentences
   definition of, 459, 694–95, 972
   punctuation of, 459–60
Expert testimony, 143, 258
Expletives, 446
Exposition. *See* Comparison/contrast essay; Informative writing; Research papers.
Expressive writing, 144. *See also* Personal narrative. Extemporaneous speech.
Extemporaneous speech
   definition of, 899
   guidelines for note cards, 899
Eye contact, during formal speeches, 900

F

Facial expressions
　formal speeches and, 900
　persuasive speaking and, 290
Facts
　fact-and-opinion questions in test taking, 262
　opinion distinguished from, 228, 252, 255–57, 877
　as reasons in persuasive writing, 258
　relevant facts, 255–56
Factual details
　definition of, 24
　describing people and places, 31
　statistics, 143
Fade-in, 331
Fade-out, 331
Fall, **principal parts of,** 578
False cause and effect, 108
Feature news, definition of, 936
Feedback
　audience feedback during speeches, 160
　definition of, 934
　in group discussions, 121
Feel, **principal parts of,** 578
Fewer, less, 645
Fiction
　character conflict in, 157
　characters, 195
　climax, 195
　conflict in, 195
　elements of plot, 157
　meaning in, 203
　mood in, 203
　oral interpretation of, 203–204
　point of view in, 196, 203
　setting in, 196
　writing short stories, 195–97
Fight, **principal parts of,** 578
Figurative details
　definition of, 24
　describing people and places, 31
　metaphors, 25
　personification, 25
　similes, 25
Figurative language
　definition of, 37
　metaphors, 25, 37, 889
　personification, 25, 37, 889
　plot, 199
　in poetry, 49
　similes, 25, 37, 889
　using figurative language, 37
Figures of speech. *See* Figurative language.
Film
　character, 199
　critiquing films, 198–202
　model critique of, 201–202
　point of view, 198
　setting, 198
　theme, 199
Find, **principal parts of,** 578
First-person point of view, 196
First-person pronouns, 409, 548
　case forms, 548
5W-How? **questions,** 141–42, 952–53
Fix-it strategies, for reading process, 7
Flier. See Brochure.
Flowcharts, 857–58
Fly, **principal parts of,** 577, 578
Focus, in graphics design, 856–57
Fonts, 854–55, 936
"Force-Fed Television" (Hochschild), 253–54
Foreshadowing, analysis questions for, 180
Forgive, **principal parts of,** 578
Formal English, definition of, 638
Formal logical arguments, definition of, 266
Formal outlines, 951
Formal research, 215
Formal speeches
　audiovisual devices and, 901
　avoiding contractions, 524
　avoiding slang, 748
　delivery, 899
　extemporaneous speech, 899
　features of, 899
　formal speeches, 897–901
　nonverbal signals, 900
　superlative degree and, 623
　topic selection, 897
　verbal signals, 900–901
　writing speeches, 898–99
Formal writing
　avoid beginning sentences with conjunctions, 389
　avoiding slang, 748
Formally, formerly, 796
Format
　of brochures, 312–13
　definition of, 312
Forms, completing, 948
Formula, as media term, 934
4R test for sources, 226
Fractions, hyphens and, 768
Fragments. *See* Sentence fragments.
Free-verse poem
　creating a, 48–49
　definition of, 48
　elements of, 48–49
　example of, 48
　literary devices in, 49
Freewriting, definition of, 954–55
Freeze, **principal parts of,** 578
French loanwords, 893

"From an Introduction to Charles Dickens's *A Christmas Carol*" (Irving), 169–71
Front panel, 312
Full shot, 331
Fused sentences, 347, 972
Future perfect progressive tense, 592
Future perfect tense, 596, 985
Future progressive tense, 592
Future tense, 595, 984

G

Gender, agreement (pronoun-antecedent), 532–33, 548
General reference, pronouns and, 566–67, 973
Generalizations
  broad generalizations, 264
  fallacies, 133
  forming generalizations, 877–78
  glittering generalities, 301
  hasty generalizations, 133, 270
  making generalizations, 8, 21, 128, 132–34
  steps in making valid generalizations, 133–34
Generating ideas. *See also* Brainstorming.
  writing process and, 10–11
Genre, television genres, 934
Geographical terms, abbreviation of, 697–98
Gerund(s)
  definition of, 476, 557, 973
  diagramming and, 993
  present participle distinguished from, 477
Gerund phrases
  definition of, 478, 973
  diagramming and, 993
Gesturing
  formal speeches and, 900
  persuasive speaking and, 290
***Get*, principal parts of,** 578
Give
  conjugation of, 592–93
  conjugation in passive voice, 602–603
  principal parts of, 578, 592
Glittering generalities, 301
Glossary, definition of, 638
***Go*, principal parts of,** 577, 578
Good, well, 617–18, 974
Grammar Links
  consistent verb tenses, 325
  correcting misplaced modifiers, 244
  dangling modifiers, 118
  double negatives, 280
  sentence fragments, 155
  subject-verb agreement, 46
  using comparative and superlative forms, 82
  using quotation marks, 193
Graphic organizers, 912, 948

Graphics. *See also* Illustrations; Photography; Visuals.
  arrangement and design of, 855–57
  charts, 857–58
  diagrams, 858
  document design and, 855–60
  graphs, 858–59
  illustrations, 859
  interpreting graphics, 878–81, 913–14
  in page layout, 851
  storyboards, 859
  tables, 859–60
  time lines, 860
  types of, 857–60
Graphs
  definition of, 858–59
  interpreting graphs, 913–14
Gray pages, in page layout, 851
Greek, loanwords, 893
Grid lines, in page layout, 851
Group discussions. *See also* Informal group discussions.
  feedback in, 121
  note taking and, 120
  order of business, 902
  parliamentary procedure and, 902
  participating in, 120–21
  purpose of, 901–902
  roles in, 120
  speaking in, 121
***Grow*, principal parts of,** 578
Gutters, in page layout, 851

H

Had of, 645
Had ought, hadn't ought, 645
Hard news, 937
Hardly, 656
Hasty generalizations, 133, 270
***Have*, principal parts of,** 578
He, she, it, they, **as double subject,** 645
Headers and footers, in page layout, 851
Headings and subheadings, in page layout, 851–52
Headlines, definition of, 87, 937
Hear, here, 578, 796
Helping verbs
  agreement with subjects, 512–13
  compound verbs and, 448
  list of, 417
  with participles, 574
  passive voice and, 602
Henderson, Amy, 239
Here, there, 446, 524, 988
***Hide*, principal parts of,** 578
His or her **construction,** 533, 534
Hisself, theirself, theirselves, 645

Historical present tense, 594
History activities, writing brochure about historical movement, 337
Hit, **principal parts of,** 578
Hochschild, Adam, 253–54
Homographs, 26
Homonyms, 793–800
Hopefully, 645
Human-interest stories, 162
Hyphens
    compound numbers and, 768, 973
    compound words and, 768–69
    fractions used as adjectives and, 768
    prefixes and, 768, 973
    suffixes and, 768, 973
    word division at end of line and, 767, 973

Ideas for writing. *See* Brainstorming; Topics.
Idioms, 889
ie **and** *ei,* **spelling rule for,** 780
Illusion, allusion, 640
Illustrations, 205, 296, 859. *See also* Audiovisual devices; Graphics; Photography; Visuals.
Immigrate, emigrate, 644
Imperative mood, 606
Imperative sentences
    definition of, 459, 974
    punctuation of, 459, 695
Implied main ideas
    identifying implied main idea, 881
    lack of topic sentence and, 371
Imply, infer, 646
In-camera editing, definition of, 52, 332, 930
Inadequate evidence, 270
Incomplete construction, 974
Indefinite articles, 412, 638–39
Indefinite pronouns
    agreement with verb, 516–17
    definition of, 516
    list of, 411, 516
Indefinite reference, 567–68, 974
Indentation, in page layout, 852
Independent clauses
    commas and, 701, 703
    complements and, 451
    conjunctive adverbs and, 492–93
    coordinating conjunctions and, 492
    definition of, 344, 492, 974
    object of verbs and, 456
    semicolon and, 492, 701, 724–26
Index, in dictionaries, 848
Indicative mood, 606

Indirect objects
    compound indirect objects, 458, 552
    definition of, 457, 553, 974
    diagramming and, 990
    never following preposition, 553
    prepositional phrase distinguished from, 457
    pronouns in objective case and, 553
Indirect quotation, 743
Infer, imply, 646
Inferences. *See also* Making inferences.
    definition of, 18, 881
    inference questions on tests, 27, 921
    inferring causes and effects, 92, 95–96, 103
Infinitive(s)
    definition of, 479, 974
    diagramming and, 993–94
    prepositional phrases distinguished from, 479
    with *to* omitted, 481
    varying sentence beginnings with, 115–16
    as verbal, 479
Infinitive clauses, 481
Infinitive phrases
    definition of, 480, 974
    diagramming and, 993–94
    varying sentence beginnings with, 115–16
Inflections, 861
Infomercial, 85
Informal English, definition of, 638
Informal group discussions. *See also* Group discussions.
    identifying purpose for, 904–905
    participating in, 905
Informal outlines, 950
Informal research, 215
Informal speaking
    giving/receiving directions and, 904
    giving/receiving instructions, 904
    impromptu speeches, 904
    making introductions, 904
    social situations and, 904
    superlative degree and, 623
    telephone conversations, 904
Information. *See also* Details; Facts; Support.
    background information, 11
    gathering information, 68–70
    relevant information, 69
    synthesizing information into a thesis, 71
Informative oral messages
    interview health professional and present oral report, 165
    oral presentation on advertising career, 337
    videotape news program on cause-and-effect relationship and give oral presentation, 125
Informative speeches
    delivery, 160
    preparation, 158–59
    presentation, 158–61

purpose, 898
question-and-answer session afterwards, 160–61
structure, 159
visuals for, 160

Informative writing. *See also* Analyzing.
cause-and-effect explanation, 104–19
literary analysis, 178–94
position paper, 263–81
problem-analysis essay, 138–56
research article, 218–45

Infotainment programs, 85
Inside, 649
Inside addresses, business letters and, 940
Inside spread, 313
Instructions, 721, 904, 909
Intensive pronouns, definition of, 410, 564
Interjections
definition of, 429, 975
punctuation of, 430, 695
Internet
definition of, 930
as reference source, 867
writing online book review, 53
Interpretation, as media term, 934
Interpreting meaning, steps for, 35
Interrogative pronouns, 410
Interrogative sentences
definition of, 459, 975
punctuation of, 459–60, 694
Intervening phrases
definition of, 46
subject-verb agreement and, 513
Interviewing
conducting an interview, 902–903
creating writing checklist from interviewing author about writing strategies, 205
interviewing health professional and presenting oral report, 165
people with shared experiences, 32
preparing for, 902
Intransitive verbs, 421, 975
Introductions
"but" introduction, 389
in compositions, 382–89, 943–44
as setting tone in a composition, 385
structure of, 388–89
techniques for writing, 383–85
varying length of, 382
Introductory elements, punctuation of, 707–709
Invent, discover, 644
Invitations, 949
Irony
analysis questions for, 180
definition of, 180
in editorial cartoons, 285
Irregular verbs, 576–79, 975–76
Irving, John, 169–71

Italics (underlining)
for foreign words, 741
for ships, trains, aircraft, etc., 741
of titles and subtitles, 740, 976
used for emphasis, 742
of words, letters, symbols, and numerals, 741, 976
Items in series
colons and, 729
commas and, 700–702, 967
semicolons and, 726
as sentence fragment, 346
Its, it's, 796, 976

Jargon, definition of, 216, 889
Jobs
application letters, 283
interviewing for jobs, 903
résumés and, 957
Journalism activities, writing editorials, 293
Judgment opinions, 258
Juxtaposition, 87

Key points
coordinate ideas as, 144
as most important points, 142
relating directly to thesis, 183
Key verbs in essay questions, 916
Khan, Niamat, 746
Kind of a(n), sort of a(n), 648
Kind of, sort of, 648
Kinds, sorts, types, 648
Knockout type, 855
Know, **principal parts of,** 578

Labels, in editorial cartoons, 285, 286
Language. *See also* English language.
nonsexist language, 659–60
technical language, 159
Language skills, review of, 810–43
Latin loanwords, 893
Lay, **principal parts of,** 582
Lay, lie, 582, 976–77
Lead, as media term, 937
Lead, **principal parts of,** 578

Lead, led, 796
Leader, in group discussions, 120
Leap, **principal parts of,** 576
Learn, teach, 648
Least, less, 622
Leave, let, 578, 648
Legibility, 194
Lend, borrow, loan, 642
Less, fewer, 645
Let, **principal parts of,** 578
Letters. *See also* Business letters.
  R.S.V.P. and, 949
Letters (correspondence)
  application letters, 283
  invitations, 949
  letters of regret, 949
  thank-you letters, 949
  writing letter after researching influences on writing of particular author, 249
Levingston, Steven, 129–31
Library of Congress classification system, 866
Library/media center
  call numbers, 866
  card catalogs, 222, 866–67
  Dewey decimal classification system and, 866
  Internet, 867
  microforms, 867
  online card catalog, 867–68
  Readers' Guide to Periodical Literature, 868–69
Lie, **principal parts of,** 582
Lie, lay, 582, 976–77
Light, **principal parts of,** 578
Lighting, film and, 200
Like, as, 648
Like, as if, as though, 648
Line graphs, 859, 879, 914
Line length, in page layout, 852
Linking verbs
  definition of, 419, 977
  as intransitive, 421
  list of, 419
  subject complements and, 453
Listening
  active listening, 161
  in an interview, 903, 910
  appreciative listening, 907
  comprehensive listening, 909
  critical listening, 908
  empathic listening, 909–10
  evaluating self as listener, 907
  with focus, 955
  in group discussions, 910
  for information, 909
  note taking and, 909
  process, 906
  special listening situations, 910
  stages of, 906
  to instructions, 909
  types of listening, 907–10
Listing patterns, analyzing listing patterns, 886
Literary analysis
  definition of, 167
  purpose of, 175
Literary analysis (reading)
  drawing conclusions, 168, 172–73
  literary elements, 168, 173–75
  reading selection, 169–71
Literary analysis (writing)
  prewriting, 178–83
  publishing (and proofreading), 193–94
  revising, 188–89
  writing first draft, 184
Literary present tense, 594
Literary texts
  children's book (illustrated), 205
  free verse poem, 48–49
  short story, 195
Literature. *See* Literature activities; Short story.
Literature activities
  analyzing problems of literary characters, 157
  charting comparison/contrast of movie and book, 89
  comparing reading passages from several sources, 15
  conflicts of characters in literary works, 157
  creating print advertisement about imaginary world, 337
  describing literary elements on tests, 177
  development in, 175
  effects in literary texts, 175
  elements of literary texts, 168, 173–75, 180
  function in literary texts, 175
  literary analysis, 168–94
  summarizing short stories based on problems, 165
  writing analysis of character's motivations, 125
  writing letter after researching influences on writing of particular author, 249
  writing online book review, 53
  writing persuasive poetry and lyrics, 293
Loaded words, 889
Loan, borrow, lend, 642
Loanwords, 741, 789, 861
Logical appeals
  evidence, 266
  formal logical arguments, 266
  in persuasive writing, 257, 258
  reasons, 266
Logical arguments. *See* Logical appeals.
Logical order, 375, 944
Logical progression, 145. *See also* Coherence; Order of ideas.
Looping, definition of, 955
Loose, lose, 796
Lose, **principal parts of,** 578

–ly
    beginning sentences with words ending in *–ly,* 354
    parts of speech of words ending in *–ly,* 422
–ly, –ness, 782

M

Main clauses. *See* Independent clauses.
Main ideas. *See also* Thesis statement; Topic sentences.
    definition of, 56
    diagram of, 61
    elaboration in paragraphs, 376–78
    identifying main ideas and details, 6–7, 22, 60–62, 372, 884
    implied main idea, 371
    as main idea of persuasive writing, 257–58
    test taking and, 65
    as thesis, 60
***Make*, principal parts of,** 578
Making connections, reading process and, 7
Making generalizations. *See also* Generalizations.
    definition of, 21, 128
    methods of, 132–33
    prior knowledge and, 132
    steps in making valid generalizations, 133–34
Making inferences. *See also* Drawing conclusions.
    definition of, 21, 881
    difficulties with, 22
    drawing conclusions and, 21
    inference questions on tests, 27, 921
    making generalizations and, 21
    making predictions and, 21–22
    reading process and, 18
    three-step process of, 22–23
Manuscript speeches, 899
Many a, every, 527
Mapping
    definition of, 955–56
    ideas, 231
Margins, 852
Marketing, definition of, 937
Matching questions, 917
May, 600
May, can, 644
Meaning, in fiction, 203
Meaning of a word
    analogies, 888
    clichés, 888
    colloquialisms, 888
    connotations of, 888
    denotation, 888
    dictionary definitions, 847
    euphemisms, 888–89
    figurative language, 889
    idioms, 889
    jargon, 889
    loaded words, 889
    multiple meanings, 889–90
    nonsexist language, 890
    slang, 890
    synonyms, 890
    tired words, 890
Media
    analyzing persuasion in media, 327–28
    analyzing reviews of movies or software programs, 205
    attention-getting elements, 87–88
    attention-getting techniques, 87
    comparison/contrast of media coverage, 86–88
    concepts, 933
    creating Web pages from position paper, 293
    docudramas, 85
    infomercials, 85
    infotainment programs, 85
    print media, 936–38
    purposes of media forms, 84–85
    research in, 246
    terminology, 51–52, 331, 928–38
    and the law, 937
    watch/listen to government procedure and make written profile of problem-solving techniques, 165
Medium, of media messages, 937
Memorandums. *See* Memos.
Memorized speeches, 899
Memorizing, steps in, 881
Memos, 949–50
Message, as media term, 937
Messages, taking messages, 950
Metaphors, definition of, 25, 37, 889
Microfilm/microfiche, 222, 867
Middle English, 862
Might, 600
Might of, 644
Miner, minor, 796
Mini-lesson (critical thinking)
    coordinating and subordinating ideas, 144
    evaluating reasoning, 270
    evaluating reasoning in advertising, 315
    evaluating sources, 226
    oversimplification and false cause and effect, 108
    synthesizing information into a thesis, 71
Mini-lesson (test taking)
    analyzing writing prompts, 282
    describing literary elements, 177
    fact-and-opinion questions, 262
    identifying main idea, 65
    inference questions on reading tests, 27
    inferring causes and effects, 103
    logic questions, 137
    recognizing persuasive devices, 305
    using context to understand specialized or technical terms, 217

Mini-lesson (vocabulary)
    comparison/contrast context clues, 64
    context clues: definitions and restatements, 136
    multiple-meaning words, 26
    specialized and technical terms, 216
    suffixes, 102
    synonym and antonym context clues, 304
    understanding connotations and denotations, 261
    using word roots, 176
Mini-lesson (writing)
    using figurative language, 37
    weaving quotations into essays, 192
Misplaced modifiers, 244, 627–30, 977
Modals
    definition of, 417, 599
    uses of, 599–601
Modern English, 862–63. *See also* English language.
Modifiers. *See also* Adjective(s); Adverb(s).
    bad, badly, 617
    clauses used as, 617
    comparative degree of, 82, 620–24, 969
    comparison of, 620–24, 969
    dangling modifiers, 118, 626, 970
    definition of, 244, 614, 977
    diagramming and, 988
    forms of, 614–17
    irregular comparison, 622
    misplaced modifiers, 244, 627–30, 977
    one-word modifiers, 613
    phrases used as, 616–17, 628–29
    placement of, 627–30
    positive degree, 620–22
    possessive pronouns as, 557
    real, really, 618
    regular comparison, 621–22
    slow, slowly, 618
    superlative degree, 620–24
    well, good, 617–18
"Monitoring and Controlling Debris in Space" (Johnson), 390
Mood
    creating mood, 203
    definition of, 203
Mood (grammar)
    imperative mood, 606
    indicative mood, 606
    subjunctive mood, 606
Moral, morale, 796
More, most, 621
Movie critique, 198–201
Movies. *See* Film.
Multimedia presentation
    definition of, 930
    formal speeches and, 901
Multipoint thesis, 387
Multiple-choice questions, 917–18, 923–24
Multiple-meaning words, 26, 889–90

Music, in documentaries, 333
Must, 600

Name-calling, persuasive techniques and, 301, 315
Narrative details
    definition of, 18
    people, things, places, dialogue, and events of narratives, 24
Negative construction, agreement of subject and verb and, 514
Neither, either, 516
–ness, –ly, 782
Networks, definition of, 931
News
    analyzing news genres, 162–64
    controversy and, 87
    definition of, 937
    feature news, 936
    hard news, 937
    headlines and, 87, 937
    identifying manipulative news stories, 163
    juxtaposition and, 87
    news values, 934–35
    newsworthiness, 935
    point of view and, 87, 88
    soft news, 938
    startling images and, 87
    suspense and, 87
    teasers and, 87–88
    variety of purposes of, 163
News genres
    feature news, 936
    hard news, 937
    soft news, 938
Newsmagazines, 162, 937
Nielsen ratings, 930
Nominative case, 549–51, 649, 651–53. *See also* Predicate nominative; Pronouns; Subjects of sentences.
Nonessential clauses and phrases, 496, 704–705, 977
Nonrestrictive clauses/phrases. *See* Nonessential clauses and phrases.
Nonsexist language, 659–60, 890
Nonstandard English, 638
Nonverbal behavior
    appearance, 290
    eye contact, 290
    facial expressions, 290
    gesturing, 290
    posture, 290
Nonverbal communication. *See* Nonverbal behavior.
Note cards, for speech preparation, 899

Note taking
- during speeches, 161
- in group discussions, 120
- listening skills, 909
- note taking on research about particular careers, 249
- paraphrasing, 228
- quoting, 228
- researching and, 227–29
- as study skill, 912–13
- summarizing, 228

Noun(s)
- abstract nouns, 407
- collective nouns, 407, 522
- common nouns, 406, 669
- compound nouns, 406, 701
- concrete nouns, 407
- definition of, 977
- of direct address, 447
- plural formation, 787–90
- in possessive case, 758–59
- proper nouns, 406, 669–70
- used as adjective, 415

Noun clauses
- combining sentences and, 360
- definition of, 501, 977
- diagramming and, 996–97
- introductory words, 501–502

Novella, definition of, 169
Nowheres, 640
Number (grammar). *See also* Plurals.
- agreement in number, 512–38, 532–38
- definition of, 512, 978
- placement of subject and, 513–14
- plural in number, 512
- singular in number, 512

Numbers (numerals)
- cardinal numbers, 791
- forming plurals of, 789
- hyphenating compound numbers, 768
- ordinal numbers, 791
- spelling out, 791–92

***O, oh,* punctuation of,** 669
Object of preposition
- compound objects, 468
- definition of, 426, 555, 978
- pronouns, objective case, 555

Object of verb, 534. *See also* Direct objects; Indirect objects.

Objective case
- for direct object of verb, 553
- for indirect object of verb, 553
- for object of preposition, 555
- of personal pronouns, 548, 553–55

Objective complements, 978

Occasion for writing
- definition of, 139, 944
- persuasive brochure, 309

Of, 649
Off, off of, 649
Old English, 861, 893. *See also* English language.
Omission, as media term, 935
Omniscient point of view, 203
On the Air (Henderson), 239
One-word modifiers, misplaced one-word modifiers, 627–28
Online card catalog, 867–68
Online database, 868
Online dictionaries, 848. *See also* World Wide Web.

Opinions
- disguised opinions, 255
- fact-and-opinion questions in test taking, 262
- facts distinguished from, 228, 252, 255–57, 877
- judgment opinions, 258
- as main idea of persuasive writing, 257–58
- opinion statements, 252, 264, 266
- prediction opinions, 258
- "should" opinions, 258
- valid opinions, 264
- "why" opinions, 258

Oral interpretation
- considerations for, 203–204, 905
- definition of, 905
- evaluation of, 204

Oral performances and presentations
- compare/contrast persuasive elements of advertisements in oral presentation, 337
- interview health professional and present oral report, 165
- oral interpretation of short stories, 203–204
- oral presentation on advertising career, 337
- two-minute oral response to interview question about personal failure, 53
- videotape news program on cause-and-effect relationship and give oral presentation, 125

Order of ideas. *See also* Organizing information.
- cause-and-effect order, 145
- chronological order, 35–36, 109, 145, 375, 944
- logical order, 145, 271, 375, 944
- multiple orders, 375
- order of importance, 109, 145, 375, 944
- paragraph coherence and, 375
- spatial order, 375, 944

Order of importance, 109, 146, 375, 944
Organizing information. *See also* Order of ideas.
- as depending upon topics, 11
- diagram for block method, 72
- diagram for point-by-point method, 73
- ordered events list, 36

organizational plan, 230
organizational questions on tests, 921
Other, else, 623
Ought, 600
Ought to of, 644
Outlining
definition of, 231, 950
formal outlines, 951
informal outlines, 950
Outside, 649
Oversimplification, of cause and effect, 108

Page layout. *See also* Document design.
alignment of text, 849–50
bullets, 850
callouts, 850
columns/blocks of text, 851
contrast, 851
emphasis, 851
graphics, 851, 948–49
gray pages, 851
grid lines, 851
gutters, 851
headers and footers, 851
headings and subheadings, 851–52
indentation, 852
line length, 852
margins, 852
persuasive brochure, 313–14
pull-quotes, 852
rule lines, 852
titles and subtitles, 852–53
visuals, 853
white space, 853
Paragraphs
clincher sentences of paragraphs, 371
coherence, 374–76
in compositions, 382
connecting ideas in, 375–76
descriptive paragraphs, 951
direct references and, 375
expository paragraphs, 951–52
implied main idea, 371, 881
main ideas, 371, 372
narrative paragraphs, 952
order of ideas, 374
paragraph main ideas, 60
parts of body of, 370–72
persuasive paragraphs, 952
supporting sentences, 371
topic sentences, 371
transitional expressions, 376
unity in, 374

Parallel structure, 362–63, 978
Paraphrasing
definition of, 213
direct quotations and, 213
for note taking, 228
steps in, 214, 882
Parentheses
examples of, 978
for material of minor importance, 770–71
for parenthetical elements, 772
punctuation within, 770–72
Parenthetical citations, 237
Parenthetical expressions
definition of, 713
list of, 713
punctuation of, 713, 770–72
Part-of-speech labels, 847
Participants, in group discussions, 120
Participial phrases
combining sentences and, 355
definition of, 355, 473, 978
diagramming and, 992
placement of, 355, 474
punctuation of, 474, 707–708
reducing sentences to, 44
Participles
definition of, 44, 355, 472, 979
diagramming and, 992
helping verbs and, 574
past participles, 472–73
present participles, 472
as principal part of verbs, 574–79
as verbals, 472–73
Parts of speech. *See also* Sentence parts.
adjectives, 412–15
adverbs, 422–24
conjunctions, 428
determined by use, 430–31
interjections, 429–30
labels in dictionaries, 847
nouns, 405–407
prepositions, 426–27
pronouns, 408–11
verbs, 417–21
Passed, past, 797
Passive voice
as awkward or weak, 601, 602
be and, 602
conjugation of verb *give,* 602–603
conjugation of verbs in, 602
definition of, 601, 979
helping verbs and, 602
past participles and, 602
uses of, 603
writing in, 277–78
Past participles
passive voice and, 602

    as principal part of verb, 574–79
    as verbal, 472–73
Past perfect progressive tense, 592
Past perfect tense, 596, 985
Past progressive tense, 592
Past tense, 594, 984
Pay, **principal parts of,** 578
Peace, piece, 797
Peer review (evaluation)
    by e-mail, 151
    cause-and-effect essay, 114, 115
    comparison/contrast essay, 78, 79
    literary analysis, 188, 189
    personal reflection essay, 42, 43
    persuasive brochures, 321, 322
    position paper, 276, 277
    problem-analysis essay, 150, 151
    research paper, 240, 241
Pentad, definition of, 956
People
    describing people, 31
    interviewing people with shared experiences, 32
    as narrative detail, 24
    as sources in documentaries, 333–34
Periods
    after abbreviations, 696–99
    at end of sentences, 694
    quotation marks and, 744
Personal, personnel, 798
Personal pronouns
    case forms of, 547–58
    list of, 409
    possessive, 759–60
Personal reflection, definition of, 17
Personal reflection (reading)
    descriptive details, 18
    making inferences, 18
    narrative details, 18
    reading selection, 19–20
Personal reflection (writing)
    prewriting, 28–36
    publishing (and proofreading), 46–47
    revising, 42–43
    writing first draft, 38
Personal texts
    literary analysis, 178–94
    personal reflection essay, 28–47
Personification, definition of, 25, 37
Persuasion. *See* headings beginning with Persuasive.
Persuasive brochures (reading)
    visual elements for, 296
    reading selection, 297–99
Persuasive brochure (writing)
    prewriting, 306–14
    publishing (and proofreading), 325–26
    revising, 321–24
    writing first draft, 316–18

Persuasive newspaper article (reading)
    distinguishing facts from opinions, 252, 255–57
    elements of persuasion, 252, 257–60
    reading selection, 253–54
Persuasive oral messages. *See* Persuasive speeches.
Persuasive speeches
    avoiding unjust attacks or exaggerations, 289
    evaluating persuasive speeches, 291
    nonverbal behavior, 290
    practice, 289–91
    purpose, 898
    support, 289
    thesis, 288–89
    topics, 288
    using visuals, 289
    verbal behavior, 290–91
Persuasive techniques
    analyzing persuasive techniques, 882
    analyzing persuasive visual elements, 303
    bandwagon, 300
    elements of, 252, 257–60
    emotional appeals, 252, 257, 259–60, 301
    evidence, 252, 258
    glittering generalities, 301
    identifying persuasive techniques, 300–302
    interview professional and write about persuasive strategies and skills, 293
    logical appeals, 257, 258
    Name-calling, 301
    opinion statements, 252, 257
    plain folks, 300
    reasons, 252, 258
    test taking questions about, 305
    transfer, 300–301
Persuasive texts. *See* Advertising; Persuasive brochure (writing).
Photography, 937–38
Phrases
    adjective phrases, 468, 961
    adverb phrases, 469–70, 961
    appositive phrases, 355, 483–84
    definition of, 342, 467, 979
    diagramming and, 991–95
    gerund phrases, 478, 973, 993
    infinitive phrases, 115–16, 480, 974, 993–94
    intervening phrases, 46, 513, 903
    as modifiers, 616–17
    participial phrases, 44, 355, 473–74, 707–708, 978, 992
    phrase fragments, 342–43
    placement of, 628
    prepositional phrases, 343, 355, 426–27, 443, 451, 457, 467–70, 468, 708, 980, 991–92
    variety in beginning sentences and, 366–67
    verb phrases, 417, 441
    verbal phrases, 118, 342–43, 472–81, 628, 985
Pie charts, 858, 878

Piece, peace, 797
Places
  describing places, 31
  as narrative detail, 24
Plagiarism, 872
Plain folks, 300
Planning, comparison/contrast essay, 73
Plot
  analysis questions for, 180
  definition of, 174
  elements of, 157
  in film, 199
Plurals
  of compound nouns, 788
  irregular plurals, 788
  of letters, numerals, symbols, words referred to as words, 766, 789–90
  of loanwords, 789
  regular plurals, 787–88
Poetry
  capitalization in, 668
  figurative language, 49
  sensory details, 49
  sound elements, 49
  writing free-verse poetry, 48–49
  writing persuasive poetry, 293
Point of view
  analysis questions for, 180
  author's point of view, 876
  definition of, 174, 876
  in fiction, 203
  first-person point of view, 196
  in media, 198, 935
  in news stories, 87, 88
  omniscient point of view, 203
  third-person point of view, 196
Point-by-point method of comparison/contrast structure
  definition of, 56, 62–63
  organization diagram, 73
Political advertising, 938
Position, definition of, 251
Position paper (writing)
  prewriting, 263–71
  publishing (and proofreading), 280–81
  revising, 276–79
  writing first draft, 272
Positive degree of comparison, 620–22
Possessive case
  of acronyms, 760
  apostrophes and, 758–61
  of compound words, 760
  compounds and, 760–61
  contractions distinguished from, 760, 764
  individual possession and, 761
  joint possession and, 760
  of nouns, 758–59
  of organizations, businesses, 760
  of personal pronouns, 548, 556–58
Posture
  formal speeches and, 900
  persuasive speaking and, 290
Predicate(s). See also Verb(s).
  complete predicates, 439
  compound predicates, 441
  definition of, 439, 979
  simple predicates, 441
Predicate adjectives, 454, 979, 989
  definition of, 454
  diagramming and, 989
Predicate nominative, 453–54
  definition of, 551, 979
  diagramming and, 989
  pronoun as, 551
  subject and verb agreement and, 524
Predicting
  definition of, 21–22, 882
  example of, 882
  prediction opinions, 258
  reading process and, 7
Prefixes
  definition of, 781, 979–80
  hyphens and, 768–69
  list of, 892
  spelling rule for, 781
  as word parts, 892
Preposition(s)
  adverbs distinguished from, 427
  compound prepositions, 427, 514
  definition of, 426, 980
  list of, 426–27
  objects of, 426, 467
Prepositional phrases
  as adjective phrases, 468
  as adverb phrases, 469–70
  combining sentences and, 355
  definition of, 343, 355, 426, 443, 467, 980
  diagramming and, 991–92
  indirect objects distinguished from, 457
  infinitives distinguished from, 467
  never contains complement, 451, 457
  never contains subject, 443
  objects of prepositions, 468
  punctuation of, 708
  as sentence fragment, 343
Preproduction, documentary, 329–35
Prereading, reading process and, 4–5
Prereading strategies, 4–5
Present participles
  as principal part of verb, 574–79
  progressive form and, 592
  as verbals, 472
Present perfect progressive tense, 592
Present perfect tense, 595, 985

Present progressive tense, 592
Present tense, 594, 984
Prewriting
- 5W-How? questions, 141–42, 952–53
- chaining, 953
- comparison/contrast essay, 66–73
- literary analysis, 178–83
- looping, 955
- personal reflection, 28–36
- persuasive brochures, 306–14
- position paper, 263–71
- problem-analysis essay, 138–45
- research paper, 218–31
- techniques for, 952–57
- track switching, 956
- *what if* questions, 953
- writing process and, 9, 10

Primary purpose, of media forms, 85
Primary sources, 208, 214–15, 222–23
"Prince Edward Island; A World Apart No More"
(Darragh), 373
Principal, principle, 798
Print ads. *See also* Advertising; Persuasive brochure.
- creating a print ad, 337

Print media
- definition of, 938
- terminology of, 936–38

Problem-analysis article (reading)
- making generalizations, 128
- problem-solution structure, 128
- reading selection, 129–31

Problem-analysis article (writing)
- prewriting, 138–45
- publishing (and proofreading), 155–56
- revising, 150–53
- topic, 138–39

Problem-solution structure
- analyzing problem-solution pattern, 883, 886
- clue words for, 877
- focus on problems, 135
- focus on solutions, 135
- framework of, 128
- as persuasive, 135

Problems
- analyzing problems, 141–43
- focus on, 135
- watch/listen to government procedure and make written profile of problem-solving techniques, 165

Process explanation. *See* Cause-and-effect article (writing).
Producers, definition of, 931
Progressive form of verbs, 592
Pronunciation, dictionaries and, 847
Pronoun-antecedent agreement. *See* Agreement (pronoun-antecedent).

Pronouns
- adjectives distinguished from, 414
- agreement with antecedent, 532–38
- as appositives, 561
- case forms of, 547–58
- definition of, 408, 980
- demonstrative pronouns, 410
- gender and, 532–33
- in incomplete constructions, 565
- indefinite pronouns, 411
- intensive pronouns, 410, 564
- interrogative pronouns, 410
- in nominative case, 548, 549–51
- number and, 532–33
- as object of preposition, 553, 555
- in objective case, 548, 553–55
- personal pronouns, 409
- in possessive case, 759–60
- possessive case confused with contractions, 760, 764
- in possessive case before gerunds, 557
- as predicate nominative, 551
- reference, 566–68
- reflexive pronouns, 409, 564
- relative pronouns, 410, 496–97, 526, 538
- special usage problems, 558–65
- third-person singular pronouns, 548
- unnecessary pronouns as double subject, 645
- using correctly, 547–68
- *who, whom,* 558–60

Pronunciation
- dictionaries and, 847
- as spelling aid, 779

Proofreading
- guidelines for, 13
- comparison/contrast essay, 82
- personal reflection essay, 46
- persuasive brochure, 325
- position paper, 280
- problem-analysis essay, 155
- research paper, 244
- short story, 193
- symbols for, 958
- writing process and, 13

Proofs. *See* Support and Evidence.
Propaganda, definition of, 935
Proper adjectives
- capitalization of, 669–70
- definition of, 669

Proper nouns
- capitalization of, 669–70
- definition of, 406, 669

Proto-Indo-European language, 861
Public access, definition of, 931
Publishing
- cause-and-effect essay, 118–19
- comparison/contrast essay, 82–83

literary analysis, 193–94
personal reflection essay, 46–47
persuasive brochure, 325–26
position paper, 280–81
problem-analysis essay, 155–56
research paper, 244–45
writing process and, 9, 13–14

Pull-quotes, 852

Punctuation
apostrophes, 758–66
brackets, 772
colons, 729–30
commas, 700–16
dashes, 770
ellipsis points, 750
end marks, 694–95
exclamation points, 694
hyphens, 767–69
italics (underlining), 739–41
parentheses, 770–72
periods, 694, 698–99, 744
question marks, 694, 744–45
quotation marks, 743–48
semicolons, 724–26

Purpose
author's purpose, 876
cause-and-effect explanation, 105
comparison/contrast essay, 67–68
identifying purpose, 10
literary analysis, 179
of media messages, 935
personal reflection essay, 29–30
persuasive brochure, 307
position paper, 264–65
problem-analysis essay, 139
research paper, 220

Put, **principal parts of,** 578

Question marks
punctuating direct questions, 694
quotation marks and, 744–45

Questions. *See also* Interrogative sentences; Test taking.
5W-How? questions, 141–42, 952–53
developing research questions, 221
emphatic form of verbs in, 592
indirect questions, 694
parts of speech in, 446
question-and-answer sessions, 160–61
reading process and, 7
subject-verb agreement and, 524
using *there* or *here,* 446

Quiet, quite, 798

Quotation marks
with colons, 744
with commas, 744
dialogue and, 746
direct quotation and, 193, 743–45, 980
enclosing titles of short stories, 193
with exclamation points, 744–45
interrupting expressions and, 743–44
with other marks of punctuation, 193, 744–45, 980
with periods, 744
with question marks, 744–45
with semicolons, 744
single quotation marks to enclose quotation within quotation, 193, 747
for slang words, technical terms, 748
for titles of short stories, poems, essays, songs, television series, etc., 747, 981

Quotations. *See also* Direct quotations.
block quotations, 192
capitalization of, 668
colons and, 729
direct quotations, 743–45
indirect quotations, 743
long quotations set off from text, 746
note taking and, 228
pull-quotes, 852
punctuation of, 193, 743–45, 980
weaving quotations into essays, 192
within quotations, 193, 747

Radio, watch/listen to government procedure and make written profile of problem-solving techniques, 165
***Raise,* principal parts of,** 588
Raise, rise, 588, 981
Ratings, definition of, 931
***Read,* principal parts of,** 578
Readers' Guide to Periodical Literature, 219, 222, 868–69
Reading aloud, to find run-on sentences, 242, 347
Reading logs, 883
Reading process. *See also* Reading skills and focuses.
adjusting reading rate, 7
determining writer's intent, 7
drawing conclusions, 8
fix-it strategies for, 7
identifying main ideas and details, 6–7
making connections, 7
predicting and, 7
prereading, 4–5
questioning and, 7
reading with focus, 956

reading-writing connection, 14
share steps of reading process with partner, 15
Reading rate, adjusting reading rate, 7, 883
Reading skills and focuses. *See also* Reading process.
author's purpose and point of view, 876
brochures, 296–303
cause-and-effect article, 91–100
cause-and-effect structure, 92, 97–100
comparison/contrast article, 56–63
comparison/contrast structure, 56, 62–63
descriptive details, 18
distinguishing facts from opinions, 255–57
drawing conclusions, 168, 172–73
elements of persuasion, 252, 257–60
visual elements, 296
inferring causes and effects, 92, 95–96
literary analysis, 168–75
literary elements, 168, 173–75
main idea and supporting details, 56, 60–62
making generalizations, 128
making inferences, 18
narrative details, 18
paraphrasing, 208, 213–14
personal reflection essay, 18–25
persuasive newspaper article, 252–60
problem-analysis article, 128–35
problem-solution structure, 128
research article, 208–15
Reading-writing connection, 14
Real, really, 618
Reality TV, definition of, 931
Reasoning
either-or reasoning, 270
evaluating reasoning, 270
Reasoning or logic questions, 925
Reasons. *See also* Evidence; Support.
anecdotes, 258
definition of, 266
as element of persuasion, 252, 258
examples, 258
expert opinions, 258
as facts, 258
logical appeals and, 266
statistics, 258
steps in finding reasons, 267
Receive, **principal parts of,** 575
Recorder, in group discussions, 120
Reference
ambiguous pronoun reference, 566
clear pronoun reference, 566–68
general pronoun reference, 566–67
indefinite pronoun reference, 567–68
weak pronoun reference, 567
Reference books, 222
Reference materials. *See also* Information; Library/media center; Sources.
almanacs, 970

atlases, 970
biographical references, 847, 870
database, 867
geographical references, 847
literature reference books, 222
microfilm/microfiche, 222, 867
Readers' Guide to Periodical Literature, 219, 222, 868–69
vertical file, 871
Refining style. *See* Revising.
Reflective listening, 909
Reflexive pronouns, definition of, 409, 564
Regional dialects, 863–64
Regular comparison of modifiers, 621–22
Regular verbs, 575–76, 981
Relative adverbs, adjective clauses and, 497
Relative pronouns
adjective clauses and, 189, 496–97
list of, 410, 496
number and, 526, 538
understood relative pronouns, 497
Relevant features
chart for relevant features, 70
definition of, 69
making relevant features chart for careers, 89
steps in discovering relevant features, 69
Reporters, definition of, 938
Reports, collaborate on compiling research questions and early plan for report writing, 249
Representation, of characters on television, 122–23
Request letters. *See* Invitations.
Research. *See also* Sources; World Wide Web.
collaborate on compiling research questions and early plan for report writing, 249
developing research questions, 221
formal research, 215
informal research, 215
in media, 216
note taking and, 227–29
note taking on research about particular careers, 249
for problem-analysis essay, 140–41
research paper, 218–45
writing letter after researching influences on writing of particular author, 249
writing paragraphs about art forms after researching them on World Wide Web, 249
Research article (reading)
paraphrasing, 208, 213–14
primary sources, 208, 214–15
reading selection, 209–12
secondary sources, 208, 214–15
Research paper (writing)
prewriting, 218–31
publishing (and proofreading), 244–45
revising, 240–43
writing, 232

Restrictive appositives, 711–12
Restrictive clauses, phrases. *See* Essential clauses, phrases.
Résumé, definition of, 957
"Review of *The Eat a Bug Cookbook*" (Hubbard), 390
Revising
    cause-and-effect essay, 114–15
    comparison/contrast essay, 78–79
    literary analysis, 188–89
    personal reflection essay, 42–43
    persuasive brochures, 321–24
    position paper, 276–79
    problem-analysis essay, 150–53
    research paper, 240–43
    symbols for, 958
    writing process and, 9, 12
Ride, **principal parts of,** 578
Ring, **principal parts of,** 578
Rise, **principal parts of,** 588
Rise, raise, 588, 981
Roots, 176, 891–92
R.S.V.P., please reply, 949
Rule lines, 852
Run, **principal parts of,** 574, 578
Run-on sentences
    comma splices and, 347, 348
    definition of, 347, 981
    fused sentences and, 347
    revision of, 347–49

Salutation, of business letters, 940
Say, **principal parts of,** 578
Scarcely, 656
Science activities, written explanation of
    comparison/contrast of two chemical compounds, 89
"Science Fiction" (Wheeler), 393
Scripts
    definition of, 931
    script outline, 331–35
Second-person pronouns, 409, 548
Secondary purpose, of media forms, 85
Secondary sources, 208, 214–15
    –sede, –cede, and *–ceed,* 780
See, **principal parts of,** 579
Seek, **principal parts of,** 579
Self– (prefix), 768
Sell, **principal parts of,** 579
Semicolons
    compound sentences and, 358, 982
    conjunctive adverbs and, 348–49, 724–25, 982
    independent clauses and, 492, 701, 724–26

    for items in series containing commas, 726, 982
    quotation marks and, 744
Send, **principal parts of,** 577, 579
Sensationalism, definition of, 935
Sensory details
    definition of, 24
    describing people and places, 31
    in poetry, 49
Sentence. *See also* Sentence fragments; Sentence parts.
Sentence(s)
    beginning with *there* or *here,* 446
    capitalization of first word, 668
    classified by purpose, 459–60
    classified by structure, 504–505
    clincher sentences, 371
    combining sentences, 43–44, 352–60
    complements and, 450–58
    complex sentences, 189–90, 359–60, 448, 505, 969, 999
    compound sentences, 348–49, 358, 448, 504–505, 703, 970, 998–99
    compound-complex sentences, 505, 970, 999
    declarative sentences, 459, 694, 971
    definition of, 437, 982
    diagramming sentences, 986–99
    exclamatory sentences, 459–60, 694–95, 972
    fused sentences, 347, 972
    imperative sentences, 459, 695, 974
    interrogative sentences, 459, 694, 975
    punctuation of, 694–95
    simple sentences, 504, 703, 982, 997
    stringy sentences, 363–64, 983
    supporting sentences, 371
    varying sentence beginnings, 115–16, 366–67
    varying sentence length, 241–42
    wordy sentences, 365, 986
Sentence fragments
    appositive phrases, 343
    definition of, 340, 437, 982
    identification of, 340
    phrase fragments, 342–44
    prepositional phrases, 343
    series of items as, 346
    subordinate clause fragment, 344–45
    test for identifying, 155
    used for effect, 341
    used as writing style, 341
    verbal phrases and, 342–43
Sentence parts.
    complements, 450–58
    predicates, 439–48
    subjects, 439–48
Sentence structure, as expressing tone in writing, 106
Sentence style. *See also* Style.
    improving sentence style, 362–69
Sequence chain, definition of, 948
Sequence of events, verb tense and, 597–98

Sequencing, definition of, 931
Series of items. *See* Items in series.
Set, principal parts of, 577, 585
Set, sit, 585, 982
Setting
    analysis questions for, 180
    definition of, 174
    in film, 198
    in short stories, 198
Shall, will, 600
She, it, they, he, 645
Shone, shown, 799
Short story
    characters, 195
    climax, 195
    conflict, 195
    example of structure of, 196–97
    meaning in, 203
    mood in, 203
    point of view, 196, 203
    setting, 196
    summarizing short stories based on problems, 165
    writing short stories, 195–97
Shot, 331
Should, 600
Should of, 644
"Should" opinions, 258
Shown, shone, 799
Signature, business letter and, 940
Similarities, comparison/contrast and, 67
Similes, definition of, 25, 37
Simple predicates, 548–49. *See also* Verb(s).
Simple sentences
    compound sentences distinguished from, 703
    definition of, 504, 982
    diagramming and, 997
Simple subjects, definition of, 440
Sing, principal parts of, 577, 579
Single quotation marks, 747
Single-word modifiers, varying sentences beginnings, 366–67
Sink, principal parts of, 579
Sit, principal parts of, 585
Sit, set, 585, 982
Situation comedy, definition of, 932
Slang, 748, 865, 890
Sleep, principal parts of, 579
Slogans
    definition of, 310
    teaser slogans, 310
Slow, slowly, 618, 983
"Snake Venom Strikes at Heart Attacks" (Eliot), 373
Social studies activities, audio reflection of current event, 53
Soft news, 938
Solutions, focus on, 135
Some, somewhat, 651

Somewheres, 640
Sophocles, 157
Sort of a(n), kind of a(n), 648
Sort of, kind of, 648
Sorts, types, kinds, 648
Sound effects, 331
Sound elements
    in film, 200
    in poetry, 49
Sources. *See also* Library/media center; World Wide Web.
    4R test for, 226
    card catalogs, 222, 866–67, 867–68
    compare reading passages from several sources, 15
    crediting sources, 237–38
    evaluating sources, 226
    general reference books, 222
    government sources, 223
    guidelines for giving credit within papers, 237
    guidelines for recording source information, 224–25
    in journalism, 938
    microfilm/microfiche, 222
    museums, 223
    newspapers, 223
    online catalogs, 222
    people as source in documentaries, 333–34
    primary sources, 208, 214–15, 222–23
    Readers' Guide to Periodical Literature, 219, 222
    recent sources, 226
    relevant sources, 226
    reliable sources, 226
    representative sources, 226
    schools, 223
    secondary sources, 208, 214–15, 222–23
    source cards, 223
    videotapes and audiotapes, 222
    works cited list, 215, 238
Spatial order, definition of, 375, 944
Speak, principal parts of, 579
Speaking
    analyze the debate process, 165
    debate, 896–97
    extemporaneous speeches, 899
    form writing checklist from interviewing author about writing strategies, 205
    formal speaking, 623, 748, 897–903
    in group discussions, 121, 901–902
    informative speeches, 158–61, 898
    manuscript speeches, 899
    memorized speeches, 899
    nonverbal behavior, 290, 900
    note cards for, 899
    persuasive speeches, 288–91, 898
    special occasion speeches, 898
    tape-record story retelling an event, 89
    verbal behavior, 290–91, 900–901

Special occasion speeches, 898
Specialized dictionaries, 848
Specialized terms
    jargon and, 216
    using context for understanding of, 217
Spelling
    –cede, –ceed, –sede, 780
    –ly, –ness, 782
    commonly misspelled words, 807
    ie and ei, 780
    of numbers, 791–92
    plurals of nouns, 787–90
    prefixes, 781
    pronunciation as aid to, 779
    proofreading for errors, 779
    rules for, 780–92
    spelling notebook, 780
    suffixes, 782–84
    techniques for, 779–80
    words often confused, 793–800
Spend, **principal parts of,** 579
Sponsorship, definition of, 932
SQ3R study method, 884
Stand, **principal parts of,** 579
Standard English, 638
Standardized tests, 918–27
Standish, David, 209–12
Startling images, 87
State-of-being verbs, 419
Stationary, stationery, 799
Statistics, 143, 258
Steal, **principal parts of,** 579
Stereotypes, definition of, 935–36
Stills, 331
Story. *See* Short story.
Storyboards
    definition of, 50, 932
    for documentaries, 335
    example of, 51
    as graphics, 859
Stringy sentences, 363–64, 983
Student's model
    cause-and-effect essay, 113
    comparison/contrast essay, 77
    literary analysis, 187
    personal reflection essay, 41
    persuasive brochure, 319–20
    position paper, 275
    problem-analysis essay, 149
    research paper, 236
Study skills, 984–99. *See also* Reading skills and focuses.
    classification and, 911–12
    graphic organizers, 912
    interpreting graphics, 913–14
    memorizing, 912
    note taking, 912–13
    organizing and remembering information, 911–14
    outlining, 231
    study plans, 911
Style. *See also* Sentence style.
    combining sentences, 43–44, 352–62
    eliminating clichés, 322–23
    eliminating word-wasters, 152–53
    overuse of adverbs, 79–80
    revising stringy sentences, 363–64
    revising wordy sentences, 365
    sentence variety, 44
    style questions on tests, 921
    using active and passive voice, 277–78
    using complex sentences, 189–90
    using consistent verb tense, 325
    using parallel structure, 362–63
    varying sentence beginnings, 366–68
    varying sentence beginning with infinitives, 115–16
    varying sentence length, 241–42
    varying sentence structure, 368–69
Subheadings, in page layout, 851–52
Subject complements
    definition of, 453, 983
    diagramming and, 989
    linking verbs and, 453
    placement of, 453–54
    predicate adjectives, 454
    predicate nominative, 454
Subject-verb agreement. *See* Agreement (subject-verb).
Subjects of sentences, 439–48
    complete subjects, 440
    compound subjects, 447–48, 520
    definition of, 439, 983
    double subjects, 645
    finding of, 442–43
    nominative case and, 549–51
    simple subjects, 440
    understood subjects, 438, 447, 986
Subjects of verbs
    definition of, 549
    in nominative case, 549
    pronoun form and, 550
Subjunctive mood, 606, 983
Subordinate clauses
    adjective clauses, 495–97
    adverb clauses, 498–99
    complements and, 451, 493
    definition of, 493, 984
    diagramming and, 995–96
    noun clauses, 501–502
    object of verbs and, 456
    placement of, 345
    as sentence fragment, 344–45
    uses of, 494–502
    variety of sentence beginnings and, 366–67
    who, whom and, 558–59
Subordinate ideas, in essay writing, 144

Subordinating conjunctions, 359–60, 369, 498–99
Suffixes
    definition of, 782, 984
    hyphens and, 768
    list of, 102, 893
    meaning of, 102
    spelling rules for, 782–84
    using suffixes, 102
    as word parts, 893
Summarizing
    definition of, 213
    direct quotations and, 213
    example of, 884–85
    how to summarize, 884
    for note taking, 228
    short stories based on problems, 165
    as study skill, 884
Superlative degree of comparison, 82, 620–24
Support. *See also* Details; Facts.
    arranging details, 72–73
    cause-and-effect essay, 109
    literary analysis, 183
    persuasive newspaper article, 252, 257–60
    persuasive brochure, 311
    problem-analysis essay, 142–43
    supporting details, 56, 60–62
Suppose to, supposed to, 651
Suspense, 87
Swim, **principal parts of,** 579
Syllable
    as aid to spelling, 779
    definition of, 779
    word division at end of line and, 767
Symbolism, in editorial cartoons, 284
Synonyms
    analogies and, 920
    context clues for, 304, 887
    dictionaries and, 847
    meaning of a word and, 890
    reference books and, 870
Syntax. *See* Clauses; Complements; Phrases; Predicate(s); Sentence(s); Subjects of sentences.

Tables, 859–60, 880
Tabloids, 938
Take, **principal parts of,** 579
Take, bring, 642
Taking messages, 950
Taking notes. *See* Note taking.
Talk
    conjugation of, 590–91
    principal parts of, 590

Target audience
    for advertisements, 327–28
    definition of, 938
    for documentary on print advertising, 329
    for news programs, 163
Target market, persuasive brochure, 307
Teach, **principal parts of,** 574, 579
Teach, learn, 648
Tear, **principal parts of,** 579
Teaser, 87–88
Teaser slogans, 310
Technical elements, of film, 200
Technical language
    in informative speeches, 159
    media terminology, 51–52, 331, 928–38
Technical terms, 748
    jargon and, 216
    using context for understanding of, 217
Technology (and writing). *See* Computers.
Technology, analyzing reviews of movies or software programs, 205
"Teenage Lincoln Sculpture" (Yari), 386
Telephone communications, taking messages, 950
Television
    analyzing effects of, 122–24
    cable television, 929
    purposes of nonfiction television, 163
    watch/listen to government procedure and make written profile of problem-solving techniques, 165
Tell, **principal parts of,** 579
Tense
    conjugation of verb *give,* 592–93
    conjugation of verb *talk,* 590–91
    consistency of, 597–98
    definition of, 590, 984–85
    emphatic form, 592
    progressive form, 592
    sequence of events and, 597–98
    uses of, 594–96
    using consistent verb tense, 325
    verb conjugation and, 590–93
Test taking
    analogy questions, 918–20
    classroom tests, 915–18
    critical reading questions, 921–23
    describing literary elements, 177
    essay tests, 915–17
    fact-and-opinion questions, 262
    identifying main idea, 65
    inference questions on tests, 27, 921
    inferring causes and effects, 103
    logic questions, 137, 925
    matching questions, 917
    multiple-choice questions, 917–18, 923–24
    on-demand writing questions, 924–25
    reasoning questions, 925

recognizing persuasive devices, 305
short-answer questions, 917
standardized tests, 918–27
true/false questions, 918
verbal expression questions, 925–27
Text, as media term, 938
Text structures, analyzing text structures, 885–86
Than, then, 651, 799
Thank-you letter, 949
That there, this here, 652
That, who, which, 653
The, 413
Their, there, they're, 799
Theirself, theirselves, hisself, 645
Them, 652
Theme
analysis questions for, 180
definition of literary theme, 174
in film, 199
Themes, universal themes, 203
There, here, 446, 524
Thesis, synthesizing information into a thesis, 71
Thesis statement. *See also* Main ideas; Topic sentences.
adjustment, 70
for causal analysis, 106–107
definition of, 10, 386
hints for writing a, 386–87
literary analysis, 181–82
placement of, 60
preliminary thesis, 387
problem-analysis essay, 143
research paper, 229–30
steps in developing, 181
writing thesis statements, 70, 386–87
They, she, it, he, 645
"Thief, The," (Khan), 746
Things, as narrative detail, 24
Think, principal parts of, 579
Third-person limited point of view, 196
Third-person point of view, 196
Third-person pronoun, 409, 548
This here, that there, 652
Thoughts and feelings, as narrative detail, 24, 32
Throw, conjugation of, 579
Time, abbreviation of elements of, 698–99
Time lines, 860, 880, 948
Time order. *See* Chronological order.
Tired words, 890
Titles
agreement of subject and verb in, 529
italics (underlining) and, 740
page layout and, 852–53
quotation marks and, 747
To, too, two, 800
Tone
cause-and-effect explanation, 106
choice of details and, 959
comparison/contrast and, 68
definition of, 30, 106, 179, 959
literary analysis, 179
personal reflection essay, 30
as personality of writing, 68
persuasive brochure, 308
position paper, 266
problem-analysis essay, 139
research paper, 221
sentence length and structure, 959
setting the tone in compositions, 385
word choices and, 959
Topic sentences. *See also* Main idea; Thesis statement.
main idea and, 371, 372
in a paragraph, 371, 372
Topics
cause-and-effect explanation, 104–105
choosing topics, 10
comparison/contrast essay, 66–67
evaluating topics, 220
formal speeches, 897
literary analysis, 178
personal reflection essay, 28–29
persuasive brochure, 306–307
position paper, 263–64
problem-analysis essay, 138–39
research paper, 218–20
Track switching, 956
Transfer, persuasive techniques and, 300–301
Transitional expressions
definition of, 392, 886, 959
list of, 392, 493, 724
paragraph coherence and, 376
punctuation of, 724–25
signaling passage of time, 36
Transitive verbs
definition of, 455, 985
object of, 421
object of verbs, 455–57
True/false questions, 918
Try and, try to, 652
Third-person point of view, 196
"Two Peoples Divided by Common Road Signs" (Berdichevsky), 57–59
Two, to, too, 800
Type
capital letters, 853
captions and, 853
contrast and, 854
fonts, 854–55
knockout type, 855
leading or line spacing, 855
lowercase type, 855
Types, kinds, sorts, 648
Type sizes and fonts
limit use of, 324
persuasive techniques and, 303

U

Unabridged dictionaries, 848
Underlining (italics). *See* Italics (underlining).
Understood subject
    definition of, 447
Unity
    in compositions, 391
    in paragraphs, 374
Unless, without, 653
Usage, 738–56. *See also* Agreement; English language; Modifiers; Pronouns; Verb(s).
Usage labels, in dictionaries, 847
Use to, used to, 652

Valid generalizations, 133–34
Valid opinions, 264
"Vanishing Prairie Dog, The" (Long), 374
Venn diagram, 878, 913, 949
Verb(s)
    action verbs, 418–19
    active voice and, 601–602, 960
    agreement with subject, 512–29
    causative verbs, 96
    compound verbs, 448
    conjugation, 590–93
    definition of, 417, 985
    emphatic form, 592
    helping verbs, 417, 448, 602
    intransitive verbs, 421, 975
    irregular verbs, 576–79, 975–76
    lie, lay, 582
    linking verbs, 418–19
    main verbs, 417
    objects of, 421
    passive voice and, 601–603
    principal parts of, 574–79
    progressive form, 592
    regular verbs, 575–76, 981
    rise, raise, 588
    simple predicates, 441
    sit, set, 585
    tenses, 325, 590–98
    transitive verbs, 421
    troublesome verbs, 582–88
    verb phrases, 417
Verb mood. *See* Mood.
Verb phrases, 417, 441, 986
Verb-subject agreement. *See* Agreement (subject-verb).
Verbal(s)
    definition of, 342, 472, 985
    gerunds, 476–77
    infinitives, 479
    participles, 472–73
Verbal behavior
    enthusiasm, 290
    enunciation, 290
    rate, 291
    vocalization, 291
    vocalized pauses, 290
Verbal-expression questions on tests, 926–27
Verbal irony. *See* Irony.
Verbal phrases
    commas and, 628
    dangling modifiers and, 118
    definition of, 342, 417, 472, 985
    gerund phrases, 478
    infinitive phases, 480–81
    participial phrases, 473–74
    placement of, 343
    as sentence fragments, 342–43
Vertical files, 871
Video reflection
    definition of, 50
    in-camera editing, 52
    planning, 50
    storyboard for, 50–51
    terminology for videotaping, 51
    videotaping, 52
Videotaping
    terminology for, 51–52
    video reflections, 50–52
    videotape news program and analyze cause-and-effect story for oral presentation, 125
Video techniques, 52
Viewing. *See* Listening.
Viewing and representing
    analyzing editorial cartoons, 284–87
    analyzing effects of television, 122–24
    comparison/contrast of media coverage (analysis), 86–88
    creating documentary on print advertising, 329–36
    critiquing films, 198–202
    genres, 937–38
    interpretation, 84, 122, 934
    making video reflections, 50–52
    media terminology, 928–38
    production, 50, 85, 329–36
    videotape news program and analyze cause-and-effect story for oral presentation, 125
    writing and illustrating children's books, 205
Visual literacy, definition of, 936
Visualizing, definition of, 957
Visuals. *See also* Document design; Graphics; Illustrations; Photography.
    definition of, 853
    in documentaries, 332
    persuasive brochure, 313–14

persuasive visual elements, 303
visual message for future archaeologists, 53
Vocabulary, 963–65. See also Word parts.
antonyms, 304, 847, 887, 920
connotation, 261, 269, 888
context clues, 64, 136, 304, 887
definitions and restatements of context clues, 136, 887
denotation, 261, 888
homographs, 26
homonyms, 793–800
jargon, 216, 889
loanwords, 741, 789, 861
media terminology, 928–38
multiple-meaning words, 26, 889–90
prefixes and, 781, 892, 979–80
specialized and technical terms, 216
suffixes and, 102, 782–84, 893, 984
synonyms, 304, 847, 870, 887
technical language, 159
understanding connotations and denotations, 261
vocabulary-in-context questions on tests, 921–22
word roots, 176, 891–92
Vocalization, persuasive speaking and, 291
Vocalized pauses, persuasive speaking and, 290
Voice
of graphics, 857
in position paper, 266
writing voice, 30, 959
Voice (grammar)
active voice, 277–78, 601
passive voice, 277–78, 601–603
of verbs, 601–603, 986
Voice-over
definition of, 52
as narrator of film, 198, 332

Waist, waste, 800
Walk, principal parts of, 574
Way, ways, 652
Weak reference pronouns and, 567, 986
Wear, principal parts of, 579
Weather, whether, 800
Web sites
creating Web sites from position paper, 293
evaluating Web sites, 247–48, 875
transforming information into Web site, 243
Well, good, 617–18, 974
What, 652
What if questions, 953
When, where, 652
Where, 652
Where...at, 640

Which, 497
Which, that, who, 653
White space, in page layout, 853
Who, whom, 497, 558–59, 986
Who's, whose, 759, 800
"Why" opinions, 258
Will, shall, 600
Win, principal parts of, 579
Without, unless, 653
"Woman Work," (Angelou), 668
Word bank, 887
Word division, rules of, 767
Word formations, 887–88
Word parts. See also Vocabulary.
base words, 891
prefixes, 892
roots, 891–92
suffixes, 893
Word-processing tools, in writing process, 985–86. See also Computers.
Words
changing form of, 353
compound words, 760, 768–69
dividing at end of line, 767
as expressing tone in writing, 106
foreign words, 741
hyphenated words, 768–69
information about, 846–48
multiple-meaning words, 26
in scripts, 332
spelling list, 807–809
technical words, 748
word roots, 176, 891–92
words often confused, 793–800
words to learn, 894–95
Wordy sentences, 365
Work, principal parts of, 575
Working outline, 231
Workplace skills. See Career development activities; Interviewing; Jobs; Listening.
Works Cited List, 215, 238
World Wide Web
common networks on, 872
key terms of, 871–72
plagiarism and, 872
as research source, 219, 247, 867, 871–75
searching on, 872–75
Web site evaluation, 875
writing paragraphs about art forms after researching them on World Wide Web, 249
Would, 600
Would of, 644
Write, principal parts of, 579
Writer's intent, determining writer's intent, 7
Writer's model
cause-and-effect essay, 111–12
comparison/contrast essay, 75–76

composition model, 398–99
literary analysis, 185–86
personal reflection essay, 39–40
persuasive brochure, 316–18
position paper, 273–74
problem-analysis essay, 147–48
research paper, 233–35

Writer's notebook, 957

Writing activities, compare writing process to another activity, 15

Writing Application
capitalization in a guidebook, 691
comparative and superlative degrees of comparison in a consumer guide, 635
punctuation of poetry, 777
semicolons and colons in a business letter, 737
using adjectives in poetry, 435
using agreement (pronoun-antecedent) in letters, 545
using commas in instructions, 721
using correct spelling in an application, 805–806
using formal, standard English in a flier, 665
using pronouns correctly in correspondence, 571
using subordinate clauses in a paragraph, 509
using varied sentences in a letter, 465
using verbal and appositive phrases in newspaper article, 489
using verb tense in an essay, 611
writing interior dialogue, 755

Writing a first draft
cause-and-effect essay, 110
comparison/contrast essay, 74
literary analysis, 184
position paper, 272
problem-analysis essay, 146
research paper, 232
writing process and, 9, 11

Writing process. *See also* **Audience; Compositions; Evaluating; Prewriting; Proofreading; Publishing; Revising; Writing a first draft**
background information and, 11
conclusion and, 11
editing, 12
elaboration, 11
evaluating drafts, 12
form writing checklist from interviewing author about writing strategies, 205
organization plan, 11
prewriting, 9, 10
proofreading guidelines, 13

publishing, 9, 13–14
reading-writing connection, 14
as recursive, 9
reflecting on, 14
revising drafts, 9, 12
weaving quotations into essays, 192
writing first draft, 9, 11

Writing to clarify and remember information, 959

Writing to learn. *See also* **Research paper,** 219, 221, 249
about character's motivations, 125
definition of, 959
watch/listen to government procedure and make written profile of problem-solving techniques, 165
writing paragraphs about using analysis skills in career, 205

Writing to reflect
on cause-and-effect essays, 194
on comparison/contrast essay, 83
on literary analysis, 194
personal reflection essay, 28–47
on persuasive brochure, 326
position paper, 281
problem-analysis essay, 156
research paper, 245
on writing experience, 14

Writing workshop
cause-and-effect explanation, 104–19
comparison/contrast essay, 66–83
literary analysis, 178–94
personal reflection essay, 28–47
persuasive brochure, 306–26
position paper, 263–81
problem-analysis essay, 138–56
research paper, 218–45

You, as understood subject, 447
Your, you're, 800

Zoom, 332

ACKNOWLEDGMENTS

For permission to reprint copyrighted material, grateful acknowledgment is made to the following sources:

Cape Cod Scriveners Company, c/o Eugene Theroux, Baker & McKenzie: From "The Slow Train to Langsiang: Number 295" from *Riding the Iron Rooster* by Paul Theroux. Copyright © 1988 by Cape Cod Scriveners Co.

Contemporary Review Co. Ltd.: From "Two Peoples Divided by Common Road Signs" by Norman Berdichevsky from *Contemporary Review*, vol. 267, no. 1557, October 1995. Copyright © 1995 by Contemporary Review Co. Ltd.

Discover Magazine: Review by Kim Hubbard of *The Eat a Bug Cookbook* by David George Gordon from *Discover*, August 1998. Copyright © 1998 by Kim Hubbard. From "Science Fiction" by Mark Wheeler from *Discover*, August 1998. Copyright © 1998 by Mark Wheeler.

HarperCollins Publishers, Inc.: From *An American Childhood* by Annie Dillard. Copyright © 1987 by Annie Dillard.

Steven Levingston: From "Danger Beneath the Dash" by Steven Levingston from *Reader's Digest*, November 1998. Copyright © 1998 by Reader's Digest.

Macmillan General Reference USA, a division of IDG Consumer Reference, part of IDG Books Worldwide, Inc.: Entry "relish" from *Webster's New World Dictionary of American English*, 3rd Edition by Editor-in-Chief: Victoria Neufeldt and Editor- Chief Emeritus: David B. Guralnik. Copyright © 1988 by Simon & Schuster, Inc.

Madison Press Books: From "The Fateful Night" from *Exploring the Titanic* by Robert D. Ballard, edited by Patrick Crean. Copyright © 1988 by Ballard & Family. A Madison Press Book.

National Geographic Society: From "Prince Edward Island: A World Apart No More" by Ian Darragh from *National Geographic*, vol. 193, no. 5, May 1998. Copyright © 1998 by National Geographic Society. From "Snake Venom Strikes at Heart Attacks" by John L. Eliot from *National Geographic*, vol. 193, no. 5, May 1998. Copyright © 1998 by National Geographic Society. From "The Vanishing Prairie Dog" by Michael Long from *National Geographic* vol. 193, no. 4, , May 1998. Copyright © 1998 by National Geographic Society.

The Nature Conservancy: From brochure *Adopt A Bison*. Copyright © by The Nature Conservancy.

The New York Times Company: "Taken Hostage at the Airport" (retitled "Force-Fed Television") by Adam Hochschild from *The New York Times*, OP-ED, October 26, 1996. Copyright © 1996 by the New York Times Company.

The Octagon Press Ltd.: From "The Thief" from *Caravan of Dreams* by Idries Shah. Copyright © 1968 by Idries Shah.

Omni: From "Bug Zappers Miss Their Mark" by Steve Nadis from *Omni Online*, 1996. Copyright © 1996 by Omni Publications International.

Random House, Inc.: From "Woman Work" from *And Still I Rise* by Maya Angelou. Copyright © 1978 by Maya Angelou.

Scientific American, Inc.: From "Access Denied" by Wendy M. Grossman from *Scientific American*, August 1998. Copyright © 1998 by Scientific American, Inc. From "Monitoring and Controlling Debris in Space" by Nicholas L. Johnson from *Scientific American*, August 1998. Copyright © 1998 by Scientific American, Inc.

David Standish: From "The Art of Money" by David Standish from *Smithsonian*, August 1998. Copyright © 1998 by David Standish.

The Turnbull Agency, as agent for Garp Enterprises Ltd.: From "An Introduction to Charles Dicken's *A Christmas Carol*" by John Irving. Copyright © 1994 by Garp Enterprises Ltd.

The University of Chicago Press: From *Young Men & Fire* by Norman Maclean. Copyright © 1992 by The University of Chicago Press.

Viking Penguin, a division of Penguin Putnam Inc.: From *Going Green: A Kid's Handbook to Saving the Planet* by John Elkington, Julia Hailes, Douglas Hill, and Joel Makower. Text copyright © 1990 by John Elkington, Julia Hailes, Douglas Hill, and Viking Penguin, a division of Penguin Books USA Inc. Copyright © 1990 by Tony Ross.

SOURCES CITED:

From "Early 20th-Century Styles, Part II" from *Arts and Ideas*, Ninth Edition by William Fleming. Published by Harcourt Brace College Publishers, Fort Worth, 1995.

From "What Is Language?" from *An Introduction to Language*, Fourth Edition, by Victoria Fromkin and Robert Rodman. Published by Holt, Rinehart and Winston, Fort Worth, TX, 1988.

From "Teenage Lincoln Sculptor" by Ethel Yari from *American History*, vol. XXXII, no. 3. Published by American History, Leesburg, VA, 1997.

PHOTO CREDITS

Abbreviations used: (tl)top left, (tc)top center, (tr)top right, (l)left, (lc)left center, (c)center, (rc)right center, (r)right, (bl)bottom left, (bc)bottom center, (br)bottom right.

COVER: Scott Van Osdol/HRW Photo.

TABLE OF CONTENTS: Page ii (br), John Langford/HRW Photo; iii, William Wegman, *Tame Animals*, 1987, Color Polaroid, 24 x 20 inches. Courtesy of William Wegman; iv, Richard Megna/Fundamental Photographs; v, Ron Colvin / The Stock Illustration Source; vii, John Still/Photonica; viii, National Fluid Milk Processor Promotion Board/Bozell Advertising Agency; ix, Victoria Smith/HRW Photo; x, © 1990 Robert A. Tyrrell; xi, A & L Sinibaldi/Tony Stone Images; xii, Photo Edit; xiii, Image Copyright ©2001 PhotoDisc, Inc.; xiv, Peabody Essex Museum; xv, Keren Su/Tony Stone Images; xvi, Courtesy of McAllen International Museum/HRW photo by Eric Beggs; xviii (tl), Clayton Fogie/Tony Stone Images; xviii (tc), Art Wolfe/Tony Stone Images; xix, Jerry Jacka Photography/ Courtesy of the Heard Museum, Phoenix, Arizona; xx, SuperStock; xxi, George Skene/ Orlando Sentinel; xxii, SuperStock.

PART OPENERS: Page xxiv, 1, 338, 339, 402, 403, 844, 845, Dave Cultler/The Stock Illustration Source, Inc.

CHAPTER 1: Page 16, John Langford/HRW Photo; 20 Robert Dunne/Photo Researchers, Inc.; 40, Randal Alhadeff/HRW Photo; 45, Randal Alhadeff/HRW Photo.

CHAPTER 2: Page 54, William Wegman, *Tame Animals*, 1987, Color Polaroid, 24 x 20 inches. Courtesy of William Wegman.

CHAPTER 3: Page 90, Richard Megna/Fundamental Photographs.

CHAPTER 4: Page 126, Ron Colvin/The Stock Illustration Source, Inc.; 129, Sam Dudgeon/HRW Photo; 131, Photo by Jeremy Martin.

CHAPTER 5: Page 171, Archive Photos; 186, Archive Photos.

CHAPTER 6: Page 206, John Still/Photonica.

CHAPTER 7: Page 250, National Fluid Milk Processor Promotion Board/Bozell Advertising Agency; 274 (c), R.L. Kaylin/Tony Stone Images; 274 (bc), Nick Gunderson/Tony Stone Images; 285 (tr), Kasbohm & Company's You Can Draw!

CHAPTER 8: Page 294, Victoria Smith/HRW Photo; 297 (l), Peter Arnold, Inc.; 297 (cl), Daryl Wilson/Tulsa World; 297 (bl), The Nature Conservancy; 298 (t), Michael Bisceglie/Animals Animals; 298 (cl), Ed Reschke/Peter Arnold, Inc.; 298 (bl), S.J. Krasemann/Peter Arnold, Inc.; 299 (tl), Renne Lynn/Photo Researchers, Inc.; 299 (cl), Jeff Lepore/Peter Arnold, Inc.; 299 (bl), Breck P. Kent/Animals Animals/Earth Scenes; 299 (tr) Robert P. Comport/Animals Animals/Earth Scenes; 299 (cr), Michael Bisceglie/Animals Animals/ Earth Scenes; 299 (br), The Nature Conservancy; 309, Culver Pictures, Inc.; 317 (br), 319, 320 (tl), Sam Dudgeon/HRW Photo; 320 (cr), © 1998 Alan Krosnick/FoodPix; 330 U.S. Navy/BBDO, New York.

CHAPTER 9: Page 343, Joel Bennett/Tony Stone Images; 344 (tl), Associated Press NASA TV; 344 (bl), Art Wolfe/Tony Stone Images; 345, Library of Congress; 348 (bl) (br), Randal Alhadeff/HRW Photo; 349, John Elk III/Stock Boston.

CHAPTER 10: Page 352, John Lamb/Tony Stone Images; 356, Bill Nation/Sygma; 358, Will and Dent McIntyre/Tony Stone Images; 361, Giraudon/Art Resource, NY; 363, SuperStock; 365, Phil Degginger/Tony Stone Images; 367, A & L Sinibaldi/Tony Stone Images.

CHAPTER 11: Page 372, Sam Dudgeon/HRW Photo; 379, Centre de Arte Reina Sofia, Madrid, Spain/Art Resource, NY; 381, Tom Bean/Tony Stone Images; 383 Wyatt McSpadden, Austin, TX; 384, Alabama Bureau of Tourism; 386 (tl), George Caleb Bingham portrait of Vinnie Ream. Courtesy of the State Historical Society of Missouri, Columbia; 386 (bl), Debbi Morello / Tom Keller & Associates; 387, © 1990 Robert A. Tyrrell; 394, FPG International; 395, Roadsideamerica.com; 399, Hanson Carroll/Peter Arnold, Inc.; 400, 401, Courtesy of the Crazy Horse Memorial.

CHAPTER 12: Page 408, Ulf Sjostedt/FPG International; 413, FPG International; 420, Jose Fusta Raga/The Stock Market; 423, SuperStock; 432, Nebraska State Historical Society.

CHAPTER 13: Page 438, Nebraska State Historical Society; 442, Keren Su/Tony Stone Images; 443, Image Copyright ©2001 PhotoDisc, Inc.; 444, Martin A. Levick; 449, Corbis Images; 455 (cl) (bl), EyeWire, Inc./Image Club Graphics ©1998 Adobe Systems, Inc.; 457, Image Copyright ©2001 PhotoDisc, Inc.; 461, Tibor Bognar/The Stock Market.

CHAPTER 14: Page 469, Scala/Art Resource, NY; 471, Image Copyright ©2001 PhotoDisc, Inc.; 476, SuperStock; 481, AP/Wide World Photos; 482, Mark Wagner/Tony Stone Images; 485, J. Greenberg/The Image Works.

CHAPTER 15: Page 494, Kennedy/TexaStock; 500 (bl), Alain DEJEAN/Sygma; 500 (br), Ron Behrmann.

CHAPTER 16: Page 519, NASA; 531, Peabody Essex Museum; 539, George Skene/ Orlando Sentinel.

CHAPTER 17: Page 549 (tr), Scala/Art Resource, NY; 549 (c), People's Republic of Congo, Northeast Region, Mahongwe Ethnic Group, Mask, Musee Barbier-Mueller, Geneva; 549 (cr) Tate Gallery, London/Art Resource, NY; 552 (bl), Park Street Photography.

CHAPTER 18: Page 584, Peter Van Steen/HRW Photo.

CHAPTER 19: Page 616 (tl) (c), Courtesy of McAllen International Museum/HRW photo by Eric Beggs; 619, Michelle Birdwell/HRW photo; 625 (cr), Jerry Jacka Photography/ Courtesy of the Heard Museum, Phoenix, Arizona; 625 (r), Jerry Jacka Photography/ Courtesy of the

Faust Gallery, Scottsdale, Arizona; 625 (br), Jerry Jacka Photography; 625 (bc), Jerry Jacka Photography/Courtesy of Kathleen L. and William G. Howard; 632 (br) (cl), British Museum, London/Art Resource, NY.

CHAPTER 20: Page 643, Okanogan County Historical Society; 650, Cooper-Hewitt, National Design Museum, Smithsonian Institution/Art Resource, NY. Photo: Scott Hyde.

CHAPTER 21: Page 671 (cr), Gordon Parks/Archive Photos; 671 (bl), John Dominis/LIFE Magazine © Time Inc.; 674 (bl), James Holland/Stock Boston; 674 (bc), Photo Edit; 685, Christopher Magadini/HRW photo by Eric Beggs.

CHAPTER 22: Page 706, Rex A. Butcher/Tony Stone Images; 707, Dave Rosenberg/Tony Stone Images; 709 (cr) (r) (br), Image Copyright ©2001 PhotoDisc, Inc.; 710 (tl), Clayton Fogie/Tony Stone Images; 710 (tc), Art Wolfe/Tony Stone Images; 712, Scala/Art Resource, NY; 718, Art Resource, NY.

CHAPTER 23: Page 725, Vicki Ragan.

CHAPTER 24: Page 749, Courtesy of Emilio Aguirre/HRW Photo by Eric Beggs.

CHAPTER 26: Page 781, UPI/Corbis-Bettmann; 786 (br), Library of Congress.

CHAPTER 27: Page 813, Image Copyright ©2001 PhotoDisc, Inc.; 814, Museum of the American Indian, New York/HRW Photo Research Library; 820, Classic PIO Partners; 825 ©1997 Radlund & Associates for Artville; 826, Alan Schein/The Stock Market; 836, Image Copyright ©2001 PhotoDisc, Inc.

ILLUSTRATION CREDITS

TABLE OF CONTENTS: Page ii (tl), HRW; vi (tl), Jim Chow.
INTRODUCTION: Page 2 (all), HRW.
CHAPTER 1: Page 45 (all), Leslie Kell; 51 (b), HRW.
CHAPTER 4: Page 154 (b), HRW.
CHAPTER 5: Page 166 (all), Jim Chow.
CHAPTER 6: Page 223 (b), 229 (t), Leslie Kell.
CHAPTER 8: Page 312 (c), Leslie Kell; 316 (all), 317 (bl), 318 (all), HRW; 334 (b), Leslie Kell.
CHAPTER 11: Page 373 (cr), Ortelius Design; 388 (bl), 396 (t), Leslie Kell.
CHAPTER 17: Page 554 (bl), Rondi Collette; 562 (bl), Leslie Kell.
CHAPTER 19: Page 619 (b), Leslie Kell.
CHAPTER 20: Page 647 (br), Jack Scott.
CHAPTER 22: Page 710 (br), Uhl Studios, Inc.
CHAPTER 23: Page 728 (br), Leslie Kell.
CHAPTER 24: Page 745 (br), HRW; 763 (tr), Ortelius Design.
CHAPTER 26: Page 780 (c), Leslie Kell.
QRH: Page 850 (bl), Barry Erikson; 859 (bl), Robert Margulies/Margulies Medical Art; 859 (tr), 861 (bl), HRW; 862 (br), Leslie Kell; 864 (tr), MapQuest.com, Inc.; 873 (tr), 878 (br), Leslie Kell; 954 (bl), HRW.

Grade 10 ATE, Acknowledgments

SOURCES CITED:
Quote by Ellen Goodman from "Sometimes I Think Ellen Goodman is Tapping My Phone" by Gary Provost from *Writer's Yearbook,* 1981. Published by Writer's Digest, Cincinnati, 1981.

Grade 10 Reading Selection Amendments

INTRODUCTION, PAGE 7
Excerpted to demonstrate note-taking as a part of the reading process

CHAPTER 1, PAGE 19
Excerpted to focus on short personal reflection

CHAPTER 2, PAGE 57
Excerpted, with some word changes and internal deletions, as an example of a comparison-contrast article

CHAPTER 3, PAGE 93
Excerpted, with some word and mechanics changes and internal deletions, as an example of a cause-and-effect article

CHAPTER 4, PAGE 129
Excerpted, with some word changes, as an example of a problem-analysis article

CHAPTER 5, PAGE 169
Excerpted, with some internal deletions, as an example of a short story analysis

CHAPTER 6, PAGE 209
Excerpted, with some word and mechanics changes and internal deletions, as an example of a research article

CHAPTER 8, PAGE 297
Excerpted, with some word and mechanics changes and internal deletions, as an example of a persuasive brochure

CHAPTER 11, PAGE 372
Excerpted to show how parts of a paragraph work together

CHAPTER 11, PAGE 373
Excerpted, as part of an exercise in identifying parts of a paragraph

CHAPTER 11, PAGE 373
Excerpted, as part of an exercise in identifying parts of a paragraph

CHAPTER 11, PAGE 373
Excerpted, with some word changes, as part of an exercise in identifying parts of a paragraph

CHAPTER 11, PAGE 379
Excerpted to focus on the qualities (unity, coherence, and elaboration) of paragraphs

CHAPTER 11, PAGE 386
Excerpted as an example of a good thesis statement

CHAPTER 11, PAGE 389
Excerpted as an example of a "but" introduction

CHAPTER 11, PAGE 390
Excerpted, as part of an exercise in analyzing introductions

CHAPTER 11, PAGE 390
Excerpted, as part of an exercise in analyzing introductions

CHAPTER 11, PAGE 392
Excerpted, with some word changes and internal deletions, as part of an exercise in analyzing body paragraphs

CHAPTER 21, PAGE 668
Excerpted to focus on concept of capitalization presented in this chapter

CHAPTER 24, PAGE 746
Excerpted to focus on concept of quotations presented in this chapter

CHAPTER 24, PAGE 751
Excerpted to focus on concept of ellipses points presented in this chapter